Illinois Blue Book
2001-2002

Edited by
JESSE WHITE
Secretary of State

A message from Illinois Secretary of State Jesse White

America has seen its share of dramatic events during the first years of the 21st century. From a new presidency and the months of controversy that followed to the terrorist attacks on our nation's soil, the year 2001 will take its place in history as a period of unrest, vulnerability and uncertainty. However, it also marked a renewed sense of unity among our fellow men and women and a rebirth of patriotism in our great country.

Here in Illinois, we are not immune to the effects of these national events. As we begin to heal and go on with our lives, I take pride in knowing that the people of this great state have united together in answering the call of duty to their nation and their fellow citizens. As Secretary of State, I want to dedicate this 50th edition of the *Illinois Blue Book* to the men and women who put their lives on the line each day to protect our great country and our citizens. From the soldiers who fight in our armed services to the police and firefighters who risk their lives each day without thinking twice about their own welfare — thank you.

This *2001-2002 Blue Book* not only includes valuable information about our national and state government leaders, but also serves as an historic document about Illinois — its places, its people and its government. New this year is a three-page color photo section about Illinois State Parks and Natural Areas, showcasing a few of the state's more popular, picturesque outdoor sites. Immediately following that feature is a two-page color photo account of the restoration of the Senate and House chamber ceilings. Another new feature is a four-page section on Illinois State Capitol Sculptures on the grounds of the Capitol Complex in Springfield. Additionally, a new State Soil — Drummer Silty Clay Loam — was added to the list of Official State Symbols of Illinois on page 573.

As we enter 2002 with a renewed sense of pride and patriotism, I want to ensure you of my ongoing commitment to serving the people of Illinois. Enjoy your *2001-2002 Illinois Blue Book*.

JESSE WHITE
Secretary of State

TABLE OF CONTENTS

ILLINOIS STATE PARKS AND NATURAL AREAS

The State of Illinois has some of the most diverse and unique landscapes in the country and boasts more than 400 state parks and natural areas.

Featured here are just a few of the more popular and often-visited Illinois state parks. From the rocky bluffs and lush valleys of Mississippi Palisades State Park in northwestern Illinois to the centuries-old rock formations at Giant City State Park in the southern region of the state, these preserved outdoor areas provide visitors a place to relax, camp, fish, hike and learn about the history of Illinois and its native plants and animals.

For more information on these and other Illinois state parks and natural areas, log on to the Illinois Department of Natural Resources' Web site at **www.dnr.state.il.us**, or contact your local library or chamber of commerce.

MISSISSIPPI PALISADES STATE PARK — Breathtaking overlooks and scenic trails characterize this picturesque park situated along the banks of the Mississippi River in northwestern Illinois. Erosion has carved out several unique rock formations on the bluffs. In the spring, a dazzling display of wildflowers colors the valleys, slopes and nature trails.

ILLINOIS BEACH STATE PARK — Known as the "Florida of Illinois," the sandy beaches and vast marshes of Illinois Beach stretch 6 1/2 miles along Lake Michigan in northeastern Illinois. Swimming, hiking, picnicking, biking, fishing and camping are just some of the recreational opportunities awaiting you at the beach.

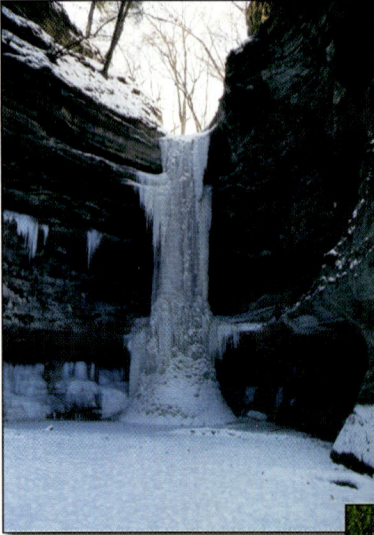

STARVED ROCK STATE PARK — Perhaps the most popular Illinois state park, Starved Rock, near Utica in north central Illinois, is an outdoor adventure any time of year. Enjoy the majestic waterfall at Wildcat Canyon in the spring and come back in the winter for ice climbing. Eighteen canyons formed by glacial meltwater and stream erosion welcome visitors along miles of well-groomed and boarded hiking trails, leading you to several scenic overlooks along the Illinois River.

WOLF CREEK STATE PARK — Saddle up for a horseback ride through wildflower fields and dense woods at this nature getaway in east central Illinois. Enjoy a day at the beach on Lake Shelbyville or a variety of other warm-weather activities, including boating, fishing, camping and hiking. Return in the winter for snowmobiling.

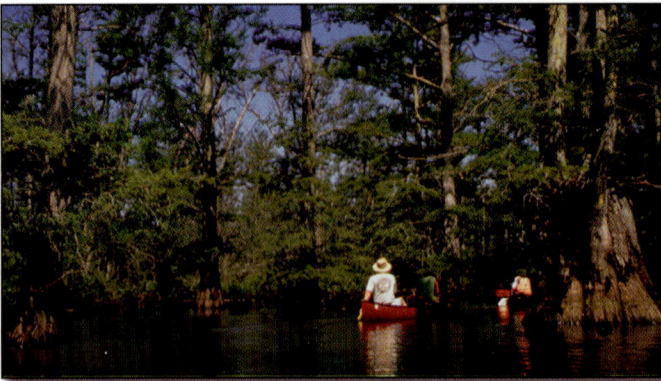

CACHE RIVER STATE NATURAL AREA — Thousand-year-old cypress trees rising from the swamps of this ancient river in southernmost Illinois mimic Louisiana swamps — without the alligators. Paddle a canoe down the murky, emerald river or enjoy a hike across the floating boardwalk in the swamps at Heron Pond.

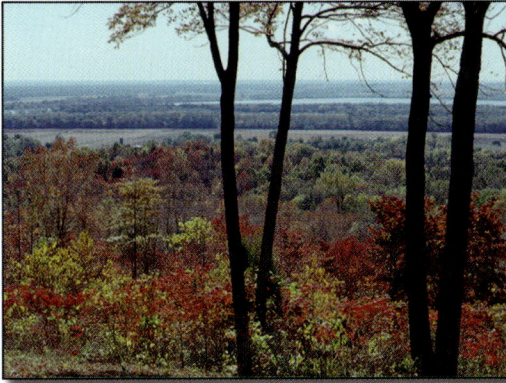

PERE MARQUETTE STATE PARK — Nestled along the scenic bluffs of the Mississippi River near Alton in west central Illinois, this 8,000-acre park is famous for its parade of colors in the fall and bald eagles in the winter. Twelve miles of scenic hiking trails and a 20-mile bike trail offer visitors an unforgettable outdoor experience.

GIANT CITY STATE PARK — Stoic rock formations, nature trails and the "Giant City Streets" are the features of this southern Illinois state park, situated in the Shawnee National Forest just south of Carbondale. Its unique landscape formed thousands of years ago by geological faulting is a haven for nature lovers, who come here to camp, hike, go horseback riding and rappel off the sandstone bluffs.

ARGYLE LAKE STATE PARK — Stocked full of fish, including bluegill, catfish, largemouth bass and rainbow trout, Argyle Lake is a fisherman's delight. Located in western Illinois near Macomb, outdoor opportunities await you year-round on the 93-acre lake and its surrounding foot trails and picnic areas.

Photos courtesy of the Illinois Department of Natural Resources.

RESTORING THE HOUSE AND SENATE CEILINGS

During the winter of 1999-2000, visible fractures and falling plaster from the ceilings of the Illinois Senate and House chambers in the State Capitol prompted Secretary of State Jesse White's office to install safety nets below the ceilings. Following adjournment of the spring 2000 legislative session, work began on restoring the ceilings to their original beauty and decoration.

Evergreen Painting Studios was selected to restore the ceilings. During an historic review of the ceilings' structure and design, it was discovered that

House of Representatives Chamber

A view of the House chamber following restoration work in fall 2000.

Inset: A close-up of the intricate painting and ornamentation of the newly-restored ceiling.

Inset: Cracks and falling plaster necessitated restoration of the supporting structures in the House chamber.

Decorative gold leaf painting was added to the pillars and frieze of the House chamber mezzanine.

Photos provided by House staff photographer Russ Nagel.

numerous layers of paint and plaster over the years had covered the original detail and decoration of the ceilings. Artists began recreating some of the original elements on canvas, and then decorative painters glazed, gilded and stenciled the ceilings to restore them to their original design.

Restoration work was completed in November 2000, and the General Assembly was back in session in their newly-renovated quarters.

The photographs on these two pages reveal the beauty of these historic chambers where our state legislators write, debate and pass laws and resolutions on behalf of the people of Illinois.

Senate Chamber

A view of the Senate chamber following restoration work in fall 2000.

Inset: Structural damage caused by water leakage and age made restoring the ceilings of the Senate chamber a priority.

Months of tedious restoration work culminated in a beautiful new ceiling in the Senate chamber.

Photos provided by Senate staff photographer Jay Barnard.

GEORGE W. BUSH
President of the United States

George W. Bush (Republican) was sworn in as the 43rd President of the United States on Jan. 20, 2001.

Formerly the 46th Governor of Texas, President Bush has earned a reputation as a compassionate conservative who shapes policy based on the principles of limited government, personal responsibility, strong families and local control.

President Bush is pursuing the same common-sense approach and bipartisan spirit that he used as Governor of Texas. He has proposed bold initiatives to ensure that America's prosperity has a purpose. He also has addressed improving our nation's public schools by strengthening local control and insisting on accountability; reducing taxes for all taxpayers, especially for those on the fringes of poverty; strengthening the military with better pay, better planning and better equipment; saving and strengthening Social Security and Medicare by providing seniors with more options, and ushering in the responsibility era in America.

In his first year as President, George W. Bush was forced to declare a "war on terrorism" following the Sept. 11, 2001, terrorist attacks on New York City's World Trade Center and the Pentagon in Washington, DC. In all, more than 6,000 Americans perished on that day, and Bush vowed to end terrorism by seeking out its perpetrators. In the months following the attacks, Bush summoned American allies, and U.S.-led forces launched the fight against terrorism in Afghanistan.

President Bush was born July 6, 1946, and grew up in Midland and Houston, TX. He received his bachelor's degree from Yale University and his MBA from Harvard Business School. He served as an F-102 pilot for the Texas Air National Guard before beginning his career in the oil and gas business in Midland in 1975, working in the energy industry until 1986.

After working on his father's successful 1988 presidential campaign, Bush assembled the group of partners that purchased the Texas Rangers baseball franchise in 1989. He served as managing general partner of the Texas Rangers until he was elected Governor on Nov. 8, 1994. In an historic re-election victory on Nov. 3, 1998, Bush became the first Texas Governor to be elected to consecutive four-year terms.

President Bush is married to Laura Welch Bush, a former teacher and librarian, and they have 19-year-old twin daughters, Barbara and Jenna.

Web site: www.whitehouse.gov

RICHARD B. CHENEY
Vice President of the United States

Vice President Richard B. Cheney has had a distinguished career as a businessman and public servant, serving three Presidents and as an elected official. Throughout his service, Cheney served with duty, honor and unwavering leadership, gaining him the respect of the American people during trying military times.

Cheney was born in Lincoln, NE, on Jan. 30, 1941, and grew up in Casper, WY. He earned his bachelor's and master's of arts degrees from the University of Wyoming. His career in public service began in 1969 when he joined the Nixon Administration, serving in a number of positions at the Cost of Living Council, at the Office of Economic Opportunity and within the White House.

When Gerald Ford assumed the Presidency in August 1974, Cheney served on the transition team and later as Deputy Assistant to the President. In November 1975, he was named Assistant to the President and White House Chief of Staff, a position he held throughout the remainder of the Ford Administration.

After he returned to his home state of Wyoming in 1977, Cheney was elected to serve as the state's sole Congressman in the U.S. House of Representatives. He was re-elected five times and elected by his colleagues to serve as Chairman of the Republican Policy Committee from 1981 to 1987. He was elected Chairman of the House Republican Conference in 1987 and elected House Minority Whip in 1988. During his tenure in the House, Cheney earned a reputation as a man of knowledge, character and accessibility.

Cheney also served a crucial role when America needed him most. As Secretary of Defense from March 1989 to January 1993, Cheney directed two of the largest military campaigns in recent history — Operation Just Cause in Panama and Operation Desert Storm in the Middle East. He was responsible for shaping the future of the U.S. military in an age of profound and rapid change as the Cold War ended. For his leadership in the Gulf War, Cheney was awarded the Presidential Medal of Freedom by President George H.W. Bush on July 3, 1991.

Cheney married his high school sweetheart, Lynne Ann Vincent, in 1964, and they have grown daughters, Elizabeth and Mary, and three granddaughters.

Web site: www.whitehouse.gov

RICHARD J. DURBIN
United States Senator

Dick Durbin, a Democrat from Springfield, is the 47th U.S. Senator from Illinois and the first Illinois Senator to serve on the powerful U.S. Senate Appropriations Committee in more than a quarter of a century. He is the state's senior senator and chairman of the bipartisan Illinois delegation.

Elected to the U.S. Senate on Nov. 5, 1996, Durbin filled the seat left vacant by the retirement of his long-time friend and mentor, U.S. Senator Paul Simon. In addition to the Appropriations Committee, Durbin serves on the Judiciary and Governmental Affairs committees and the Select Committee on Intelligence.

In the 107th Congress, U.S. Senate Democratic Leader Tom Daschle (D-SD) reappointed Durbin to his leadership team, where Durbin serves as Assistant Floor Leader.

The House author of landmark legislation to ban smoking on commercial airline flights, Durbin has taken to the Senate his fight to protect children from the harm caused by tobacco. For his work, he was awarded the Lifetime Achievement Award by the American Lung Association. Durbin also has worked successfully for increased federal funding to prevent childhood asthma, increase immunizations and expand medical research.

Continuing an effort spurred by a meeting with the mother of a Chicago six-year-old who died after eating contaminated hamburger, Durbin has led the effort to consolidate and modernize the fragmented federal food safety system under one agency.

Durbin has helped lead the fight for gun safety legislation to keep guns out of the hands of kids. He introduced bipartisan legislation to hold adults responsible if they fail to lock up their firearms and the weapons are subsequently taken by a child and used to kill or injure another person. He also teamed up with the Bureau of Alcohol, Tobacco and Firearms and local law enforcement agencies to launch an initiative to help Illinois become the first state to voluntarily trace every gun recovered from a crime scene.

Durbin has been a champion of Illinois farmers and has fought tirelessly to promote ethanol use. In 1998, he secured passage of a provision extending the ethanol tax incentive to 2007. In 2000, he worked with other members of the Illinois delegation for funding for the construction of an ethanol research pilot plant near the Southern Illinois University-Edwardsville campus, a project he has promoted since the early 1990s.

Durbin also continues to work for his legislation to provide a 100 percent deduction of health insurance premiums for the self-employed. When he took up the cause, only 25 percent of a farmer's health insurance costs could be deducted. In 2001, 60 percent can be deducted.

In addition to the self-employed health insurance tax deduction, Durbin's tax cut agenda includes tax credits for small businesses buying health insurance for their low-income workers, estate tax relief for family-owned small businesses and farms, tax incentives to promote charitable giving, and tax credits for long-term care insurance, child care and college tuition.

Durbin was born Nov. 21, 1944, in East St. Louis. He attended Georgetown University where he received his bachelor's degree in foreign service and economics in 1966 and his J.D. degree in 1969. He was first elected to Congress on Nov. 4, 1982, to represent the 20th Congressional District.

Durbin and his wife, Loretta Schaefer Durbin, reside in Springfield. They have three children and one grandchild.

E-mail: dick@durbin.senate.gov

PETER G. FITZGERALD
United States Senator

Peter G. Fitzgerald was elected to the U.S. Senate on Nov. 3, 1998. He was the first Republican in Illinois to win a Senate race in 20 years, and the only Republican challenger in the country to defeat an incumbent Democratic Senator in the 1998 election.

Born Oct. 20, 1960, Fitzgerald is the youngest member of the U.S. Senate. He serves on the Commerce, Science and Transportation Committee, the Agriculture, Nutrition and Forestry Committee, the Small Business Committee and the Aging Committee. He is also the ranking minority member on the Commerce Subcommittee on Consumer Affairs, Foreign Commerce and Tourism, and the Agriculture Subcommittee on Marketing, Inspection and Product Promotion.

Fitzgerald has quickly built a reputation as an independent voice for Illinois. He has backed his party in efforts to contain spending and reduce taxes, but has split from his caucus on issues such as health care and the environment. In 2000, a leading conservation group rated Fitzgerald among the most environmentally friendly Republican senators.

From his perch on the Commerce Committee, Fitzgerald has been active on aviation issues, with efforts to address the nation's air capacity shortage and promote greater competition in the airline industry. The senator has also focused on consumer safety issues. In 2000, Fitzgerald, the father of a young son, led a successful drive to modernize outdated federal testing and safety standards for child car seats and booster seats.

As the first Illinois senator since 1986 to serve on the Agriculture Committee, Fitzgerald has worked to improve international trading conditions for American agriculture, ensure that domestic markets remain open and competitive, promote renewable fuels, and provide tax relief for family farmers.

A strong taxpayer advocate, Fitzgerald has worked to ease the tax burden on working families and ensure taxpayer dollars are spent wisely and effectively. He has been a constant and vocal opponent of no-bid contracts and taxpayer giveaways. In 2000, he launched an effort to require federal competitive bidding guidelines for a major Springfield construction project, fearing that politically connected insiders could benefit at taxpayers' expense if stricter federal standards were not in place. For two days, in a filibuster the *Champaign News-Gazette* called "a wake-up call for Illinois taxpayers," Fitzgerald read into the Senate record a steady stream of newspaper accounts detailing chronic cronyism in Illinois State Government — cronyism the senator has attempted, in repeated instances, to reform.

Peter Fitzgerald grew up in Inverness, a suburb northwest of Chicago. He went to St. Theresa's Elementary School in Palatine and to Portsmouth Abbey, a secondary school in Portsmouth, RI. Fitzgerald attended Dartmouth College, where he majored in Latin and Greek. He graduated from Dartmouth cum laude and with "highest distinction." In 1982-83, Fitzgerald studied at the Aristotelian University in Salonica, Greece, as a Rotary Foundation International Graduate Scholar. He earned his J.D. degree from the University of Michigan School of Law. Fitzgerald practiced corporate law for 10 years in Chicago, first in private firms and later as general counsel for a multi-bank holding company. Before his election to the U.S. Senate, Fitzgerald served six years in the Illinois Senate.

In 1987, Peter married his wife, Nina. They have one son, Jake, born in May 1992.

E-mail: Senator_Fitzgerald@fitzgerald.senate.gov

19

GEORGE H. RYAN
Governor

George H. Ryan (Republican) was elected Governor on Nov. 3, 1998, winning 59 of the state's 102 counties. He has successfully initiated a forward-looking, efficient and effective administration that stresses progress in education, a high quality of life in Illinois and improvements to the state's human and physical infrastructure.

Ryan has kept his main campaign pledge and has earmarked 51 percent of each year's new state revenue to education and workforce training. This substantial allocation has increased state support for education to record levels — $12.7 billion in 2002. Governor Ryan also has allocated funds for the construction of 9,500 new classrooms to help relieve overcrowding and to modernize aging schools.

Another cornerstone of the Ryan Administration is the Illinois FIRST program, a five-year, $12 billion initiative that is rebuilding roads, bridges, highways, water and sewer systems, parks, trails, mass transit systems and local infrastructure. More than 7,000 projects have been funded through Illinois FIRST.

Governor Ryan's comprehensive economic development efforts have created or retained more than 78,000 jobs in Illinois and have led to more than $6.7 billion in new private investment.

Governor Ryan's commitment to strengthening the state's human infrastructure has led to funding increases of more than $1 billion for programs to help the state's neediest people.

Illinois crime rates continue to drop, thanks to Governor Ryan's commitment to tough crime laws, including a "15-20-LIFE" law that creates tougher penalties for using a gun during a criminal act. The Governor has become internationally known for imposing a moratorium on executions in Illinois due to the fact that 12 men have been executed in the state since 1977, while 13 originally sentenced to death have been exonerated.

To enhance Illinois' natural resources, Governor Ryan has bought more land for public use than any previous administration, mostly through a landmark $200 million Open Lands Trust. More than 28,500 new acres have been set aside for public use.

Together, the Governor and First Lady Lura Lynn Ryan have spearheaded the construction and establishment of the Abraham Lincoln Presidential Library and Museum in Springfield, a long-desired project that will enhance Illinois' reputation as an international center of Lincoln study.

On top of his extensive record of accomplishment, Governor Ryan has initiated $1.6 billion in tax relief. These efforts include tax breaks to help seniors deal with rising drug costs, to enhance school choice for families, and to provide income tax relief for poor families and a property tax rebate for 2.2 million homeowners.

Born in February 1934, Governor Ryan served as Secretary of State between 1991 and 1999 and as Lieutenant Governor from 1983 to 1991. He also had a distinguished 10-year legislative career, including a term as Illinois House Speaker.

A lifelong resident of Kankakee and pharmacist by profession, Governor Ryan served with the U.S. Army in Korea and, following his discharge, obtained a pharmacy degree from Ferris State College. George and Lura Lynn Ryan are the parents of a son and five daughters, including triplets. They have 15 grandchildren.

Web site: www.state.il.us/gov

CORINNE WOOD
Lieutenant Governor

Corinne Wood (Republican) made Illinois history with her election to state-wide office. On Jan. 11, 1999, she was inaugurated as the first female Lieutenant Governor of Illinois, pledging to be an active Lt. Governor for the people of Illinois. Wood has played an important role in leading administration efforts on health care, childcare, downtown economic development, rural affairs, senior citizen issues, public safety and the environment.

Lt. Governor Wood, the second highest-ranking state official, began a career in public service 20 years ago. Her experience includes service as a State Representative, attorney, local leader, community activist, wife and mother. She has also earned a reputation as a strong advocate for women, children and seniors. As a State Representative, Wood led efforts to reform education, strengthen drunk driving laws, protect children from drugs and crime, reform campaign finance laws and protect seniors from abuse. She earned distinction as one of "100 Women Making a Difference" in Illinois by *Today's Chicago Woman* magazine.

A breast cancer survivor, Wood is committed to women's health care as a top priority. As chair of Women's Health Illinois, the Lt. Governor coordinates more than 60 state programs that provide health services to women. The program has increased breast and cervical screening and treatment services, promoted the state's leading income tax check-off fund for breast cancer research, increased education and public awareness of women's health issues, and expanded community-based services for women and their families.

Lt. Governor Wood had led the state's efforts to preserve one of its most valuable natural resources, the Illinois River. As chair of the Illinois River Coordinating Council, Wood directs the state's strategy in protecting and restoring the Illinois River and its tributaries. The council was instrumental in developing Illinois Rivers 2020, a $2.5 billion federal/state blueprint to restore the Illinois River watershed. In 2000, Illinois Rivers 2020 received a $100 million authorization from Congress for its first three years. In 2001, the program received a $5.4 million state appropriation to begin implementation of the plan.

Lt. Governor Wood has worked to expand the Illinois Main Street program to preserve the state's history and enhance downtown revitalization efforts across the state. She has rebuilt the Governor's Rural Affairs Council and has developed a statewide plan to improve the quality of life for Illinois' rural residents. As chair of the Illinois Rural Bond Bank, Lt. Governor Wood has provided low-interest loans to rural communities in need of new water systems, fire protection equipment and school building repairs. In addition, she worked with lawmakers, firefighters, police officers and others to strengthen penalties for reckless drivers in emergency zones. Scott's Law, named after a fallen Chicago firefighter, was passed in 2001.

After graduating Phi Beta Kappa from the University of Illinois and Loyola University School of Law, Wood was named general counsel to the Illinois Commissioner of Banks and Trusts. She later joined the Chicago law firm of Hopkins and Sutter.

While Corinne and her husband, Paul, raised their three children, she served her community as an active member of charitable, political and governmental boards and commissions. Wood's community involvement spurred her election to the Illinois House of Representatives in November 1996.

Corinne and Paul, an investment banker, have been married for 23 years. They and their three children, Ashley, 16, Brandon, 15, and Courtney, 12, reside in Lake County.

Web site: www.state.il.us/ltgov

JIM RYAN
Attorney General

Jim Ryan (Republican) began his second term as Attorney General in January 1999 following his re-election by more than 2 million votes, making him only the second constitutional officer in Illinois history to top that plateau in an election. He was endorsed by every large newspaper in the state after winning acclaim for professionalizing Illinois' chief legal office and assuming statewide leadership in the war against crime.

Ryan was first elected Attorney General in 1994 after winning attention as one of the most successful prosecutors in Illinois while serving as DuPage County State's Attorney for 10 years. During his first term as Attorney General, Ryan developed anti-gang initiatives as chairman of the Governor's Commission on Gangs, fought for legislation to combat child abuse and domestic violence, beefed up protection for senior citizens and other consumers and accelerated litigation against large and small polluters alike.

Attorney General Ryan has made the fight against violent crime a high priority in the state's top legal office. He has emerged as the leader in mounting a statewide coordinated attack against crime, working with county prosecutors, sheriffs, local police officials and federal law enforcement authorities.

The Attorney General has greatly expanded use of the Statewide Grand Jury by hiring more prosecutors to bring cases there and successfully pushing for a new law setting up a second Grand Jury panel in Springfield to go along with the one earlier established in Chicago. This increased emphasis resulted in more than a 70 percent increase in the number of cases brought for multi-county drug, gang and gun violations.

Still in the crime area, Ryan established an Internet Crime Bureau that goes after criminals who commit crimes on the Internet, including those who stalk women and children. A skilled group of high-tech prosecutors has successfully prosecuted a number of cases stemming from computer crimes.

Ryan also led the effort to enact a new law, the Sexually Violent Persons Act, which keeps dangerous sex offenders institutionalized after their prison terms are completed if it can be demonstrated that they still pose a threat to society. To address the growing problem of violence in schools, Ryan chaired a summit of educators and law enforcement officials that produced a workable Safe to Learn Program aimed at making Illinois schools safer from guns and violence.

Ryan was elected DuPage County State's Attorney in March 1984 and was re-elected by overwhelming margins in 1988 and 1992. Prior to his election as State's Attorney, Ryan served that office as a prosecutor from 1971 to 1974. In 1974, he was named First Assistant State's Attorney, a position he held until 1976. From 1976 until 1984, Ryan was engaged in private practice.

Attorney General Ryan was born in Chicago on Feb. 21, 1946. He grew up in Villa Park and graduated from Illinois Benedictine College in 1968, where he received a Bachelor of Arts degree in political science. In 1971, he received his law degree from Chicago-Kent College of Law, Illinois Institute of Technology.

Ryan has served as President of the Illinois State's Attorneys' Association, and was presented with the 1994 Special Distinction Award by the Illinois Department of Public Aid in recognition of his outstanding management of the child support enforcement program in DuPage County.

Attorney General Ryan and his wife, Marie, live in Elmhurst. They have six children, John, Jim, Matt, Amy, Patrick and Anne Marie (deceased), and four grandchildren, Caitlyn, Joseph, Grace and Sarah.

Web site: www.ag.state.il.us

JESSE WHITE
Secretary of State

Jesse White (Democrat) is Illinois' 37th Secretary of State. He was elected on Nov. 3, 1998, by a margin of more than 450,000 votes. He is the first African-American to serve as Secretary of State.

During his first year in office, White launched the first Illinois license plate replating effort since 1983. New license plates began appearing on Illinois roads in July 2001, with all 8.5 million passenger plates due to be replated within one year. To meet this aggressive time line, White upgraded technology throughout his office to expedite license plate processing and enhance customer service. For the first time, license plate renewal is now available online, as well as by phone, by mail or at a Driver Services facility.

Traffic safety has been Secretary White's top priority. During the spring 2001 legislative session, the General Assembly approved several of White's legislative initiatives, including a DUI bill that increases penalties for drunk drivers with a blood-alcohol content of double the illegal limit of .08 and for those driving drunk with a child in the vehicle. The measure also requires repeat offenders to have a Breath Alcohol Ignition Interlock Device installed in their vehicles, which prevents them from starting the vehicles when they have been drinking. Another measure increases penalties for those caught driving on a suspended or revoked license. Legislative and administrative initiatives to reduce the fraudulent use of parking placards and license plates for persons with disabilities also were approved. Three new parking placards were created, and stricter eligibility requirements and procedural guidelines were put in place to ensure that parking privileges are reserved for those who truly need it.

In addition, White's initiative to increase investor protection against unscrupulous securities dealers became law, giving the Secretary of State the power to deny or revoke the registrations of securities dealers and brokers and raising penalties for violations of the Illinois Securities Act. Another law helps expedite corporate filings in White's Business Services Department.

Other initiatives during White's administration include his innovative "Project Next Generation" program. The first-ever, statewide mentoring program to be administered through Illinois libraries provides a mix of technology experiences and life skills to junior high-age students to set them on the path to success.

Secretary White's Highway Safety 2000 Program has resulted in tougher licensing requirements for commercial driver's licenses. In May 2001, several Chicago metro Driver Services facilities were equipped with electronic testing devices to reduce cheating on commercial driver's license exams. He also strengthened his Inspector General's office, giving it more investigative authority.

Prior to becoming Secretary of State, White served as Cook County Recorder of Deeds from 1992 to 1998. He also served in the Illinois House of Representatives from 1975 to 1992. In 1959, he founded the internationally known Jesse White Tumbling Team, and has spent the last 43 years working with the team to help keep at-risk youth in school and drug-free.

White earned his bachelor's degree in 1957 from Alabama State College (now Alabama State University). He served our country as a paratrooper in the U.S. Army's 101st Airborne Division and as a member of the Illinois National Guard. He played professional baseball with the Chicago Cubs organization, followed by a 33-year career as a teacher and administrator with Chicago Public Schools. Born in Alton in 1934, White now lives on Chicago's near-north side. He has two daughters and a grandson.

Web site: www.cyberdriveillinois.com

DANIEL W. HYNES
Comptroller

Daniel W. Hynes (Democrat) was elected State Comptroller on Nov. 3, 1998, at the youngest age of any constitutional officer since William Stratton was elected Treasurer in 1942. Hynes, 33, has committed his administration to increase accountability, efficiency and innovation in the areas of state and local government finance and fiscal policy, and in his office's administration of electronic commerce programs, debt collection and funeral home regulation.

As the state's chief fiscal officer, Hynes is the first Comptroller to successfully seek the establishment of a state "Rainy Day Fund." The General Assembly passed the measure in 2000 and the fund is currently slated to reach an estimated $200 million by July 2002. Comptroller Hynes may use the fund when the state sees a slowdown in revenues. The Rainy Day Fund is just one part of Hynes' plan to shore up the state's fiscal foundation. The Comptroller supports more disciplined spending on behalf of lawmakers, paying down the state's long-term debts and honoring a more accurate budget process.

Hynes believes the Comptroller should be a watchdog for taxpayers. He advocates for improved reporting in government — an effort he says will allow him to better inform taxpayers of how tax revenues are spent.

As Comptroller, Hynes' office also regulates private cemeteries and funeral homes. Hynes' long sought after reforms in the two industries received bipartisan support in the General Assembly in 2001. The legislation included input from hundreds of consumers who attended statewide hearings hosted by Hynes addressing the funeral and cemetery care industries. In an effort to promote better dialogue and respond to consumer problems with the funeral home and cemetery care industries, Hynes established a statewide, toll-free cemetery hotline (1-877-203-3401) and a special Web page (www.ioc.state.il.us/cemeterycare).

Hynes has also taken measures to re-energize the Local Government Division of his office. Under his administration, the division has seen a 40 percent increase in reporting compliance by the state's 7,200 units of local government that report to the Comptroller. The division regularly works with local governments and suggests better reporting and accounting practices.

During his tenure, Comptroller Hynes has expanded the office's commercial direct deposit program. The Comptroller encourages state vendors to receive their payments electronically — a method that saves paper as well as postage and increases efficiency. Under Hynes' leadership, state employee participation in the direct deposit program has grown to nearly 70 percent, a record number that the office intends to exceed.

Before taking office, Hynes was a health care attorney for a Chicago law firm, focusing on the negotiation, formation and operation of integrated health care delivery systems. As an attorney, he provided strategic and regulatory advice to physicians, hospitals and other health care providers as they prepared to compete in the managed care marketplace.

Hynes is active in various civic and charitable organizations, including membership in the Economic Club of Chicago, the James Jordan Boys and Girls Club, Pediatric AIDS Chicago and the Abraham Lincoln Association.

A native of Chicago, Hynes married Christina Kerger in June 1999. He graduated magna cum laude from the University of Notre Dame with a degree in economics and computer applications and earned a law degree with honors from Loyola University School of Law.

Web site: www.ioc.state.il.us

JUDY BAAR TOPINKA
Treasurer

Judy Baar Topinka (Republican) was elected to a second term as Treasurer on Nov. 3, 1998, making her the first woman to be re-elected to a constitutional office. Topinka's victory in the 1994 election made her the first woman Treasurer, and she was the first Republican to hold this office in more than three decades.

Topinka's political career began by representing the people of Chicago's western suburbs in 1981, when she was elected to the Illinois General Assembly as a State Representative. After two successful terms in the House, Topinka was elected to represent the 22nd District of the Illinois Senate in 1984, where she served for 10 years.

As State Treasurer, Topinka has taken a business-oriented approach to the office — streamlining banking, collection and investment processes, taking advantage of the latest technology, and racking up record investment earnings for the state. She is maximizing the state's resources and making the state's money work harder for its citizens. In fact, the local government investment pool has consistently earned an AAAm rating from Standard & Poor's — its highest rating.

Since taking over administration of the state's Unclaimed Property program two years ago, Topinka has returned a record amount of unclaimed property to its rightful owners and raised awareness of the program with owners and holders, such as businesses. The program helps reunite owners with their unclaimed property, such as bank accounts, proceeds from wills and estates, contents of abandoned safe deposit boxes and utility deposit checks.

Topinka's financial education efforts have expanded significantly over the past few years. Through her Financial Education Division, money management programs are now available for children, high school students, young adults, adults in transition and senior citizens. Under Topinka's leadership, the office's Bank At School program for grade school children has been expanded to serve more than 200,000 students statewide through a partnership with more than 700 schools and 400 financial institutions. Her latest initiative — Bright Start — is among the fastest growing college savings programs in the country.

Born in Riverside on Jan. 16, 1944, Topinka graduated from the Ferry Hall School in Lake Forest in 1962. She received her B.S. degree from Northwestern University's Medill School of Journalism in 1966. Upon graduation, she established herself as an accomplished journalist in the Cook County suburbs, including 11 years as a reporter and editor for several community newspapers. At the same time, she founded a public relations firm, served as a public affairs executive with the American Medical Association and was a public relations advisor for area political candidates and organizations.

Topinka's achievements have earned her awards from more than 250 civic, business, professional and social service organizations, including being named Legislator of the Year by the Illinois Bankers Association in 1992. The Illinois National Guard presented her with its Abraham Lincoln Legislator of the Year award in 1986 and 1993, and the Molly Pitcher award in 1994. The Reserve Officers Association awarded her the Silver Eagle award, and the Department of the Army presented her its Outstanding Civilian Service Medal. She belongs to more than 60 business and professional organizations.

Topinka continues to reside in Riverside. Her son, Joseph, is a graduate of Northern Illinois University Law School and is a Captain in the U.S. Army's JAG Corps.

Web site: www.state.il.us/treas

WILLIAM G. HOLLAND
Auditor General

William G. Holland was nominated by the 87th General Assembly as Illinois' second Auditor General. His term of office commenced on Aug. 1, 1992.

Holland began his government career as a legislative intern with the House Majority Staff in 1974. In 1976, he was appointed director of the House Majority Appropriations Committee staff.

In 1980, Holland was appointed the first director of the Illinois General Assembly's Washington Office. Under his leadership, a professional, bipartisan office was created to act as an advocate for the Illinois General Assembly in its dealings with Congress, executive agencies of the federal government, and national organizations such as the National Conference of State Legislatures.

From 1983 to 1992, Holland served as Chief of Staff for the President of the Illinois State Senate. In that position, his responsibilities included managing a staff of 90 committee and support personnel, guiding bills through the legislative process, representing the majority party on key issues, and responding to the concerns of legislators, state agencies, constituents and interest groups.

Holland is a member of the National Association of State Auditors, Comptrollers and Treasurers (NASACT) and the National State Auditors' Association (NSAA). As a member of NASACT, he serves on the Executive Committee and the Intergovernmental Financial Management Improvement Committee. He is the Secretary-Treasurer of NSAA and serves as a member of NSAA's Executive Committee.

In each of the past two years, the Auditor General's office has received the IMPACT Award from the National Legislative Program Evaluation Society for audits, titled "Management Audit of Pilsen-Little Village Community Mental Health Center, Inc." (2000) and "Management Audit of Tuition & Fee Waivers" (1999).

In 1991, Holland was given the honor of membership in the inaugural class of the Samuel K. Gove Illinois Legislative Internship Hall of Fame.

Holland graduated from Seattle University, Seattle, WA. He is active with Easter Seals and Habitat for Humanity. He has three children and resides in Springfield.

E-mail: auditor@mail.state.il.us
Web site: www.state.il.us/auditor/

ILLINOIS OFFICIALS' ADDRESSES

Governor George H. Ryan

207 State House
Springfield, IL 62706-1150
(217) 782-6830

100 W. Randolph, Ste. 16-100
Chicago, IL 60601-3220
(312) 814-2121

Lieutenant Governor Corinne Wood

214 State House
Springfield, IL 62706-1350
(217) 782-7884

100 W. Randolph, Ste. 15-200
Chicago, IL 60601-3220
(312) 814-5220

Attorney General Jim Ryan

500 S. Second St.
Springfield, IL 62706-1771
(217) 782-1090

100 W. Randolph, 12th Floor
Chicago, IL 60601-3218
(312) 814-3000

Secretary of State Jesse White

213 State House
Springfield, IL 62706-0001
(217) 782-2201

100 W. Randolph, Ste. 5-400
Chicago, IL 60601-3273
(312) 814-6165

Comptroller Daniel W. Hynes

201 State House
Springfield, IL 62706-1001
(217) 782-6000

100 W. Randolph, Ste. 15-500
Chicago, IL 60601-3252
(312) 814-2451

Treasurer Judy Baar Topinka

219 State House
Springfield, IL 62706-1000
(217) 782-2211

100 W. Randolph, Ste. 15-600
Chicago, IL 60601-3232
(312) 814-1700

U.S. Senator Richard J. Durbin

230 S. Dearborn St., Ste. 3892
Chicago, IL 60604
(312) 353-4952

332 Dirksen Senate Office Building
Washington, DC 20510
(202) 224-2152

U.S. Senator Peter G. Fitzgerald

230 S. Dearborn St., Ste. 3900
Chicago, IL 60604
(312) 886-3506

555 Dirksen Senate Office Building
Washington, DC 20510
(202) 224-2854

107th Illinois Congressional Delegation

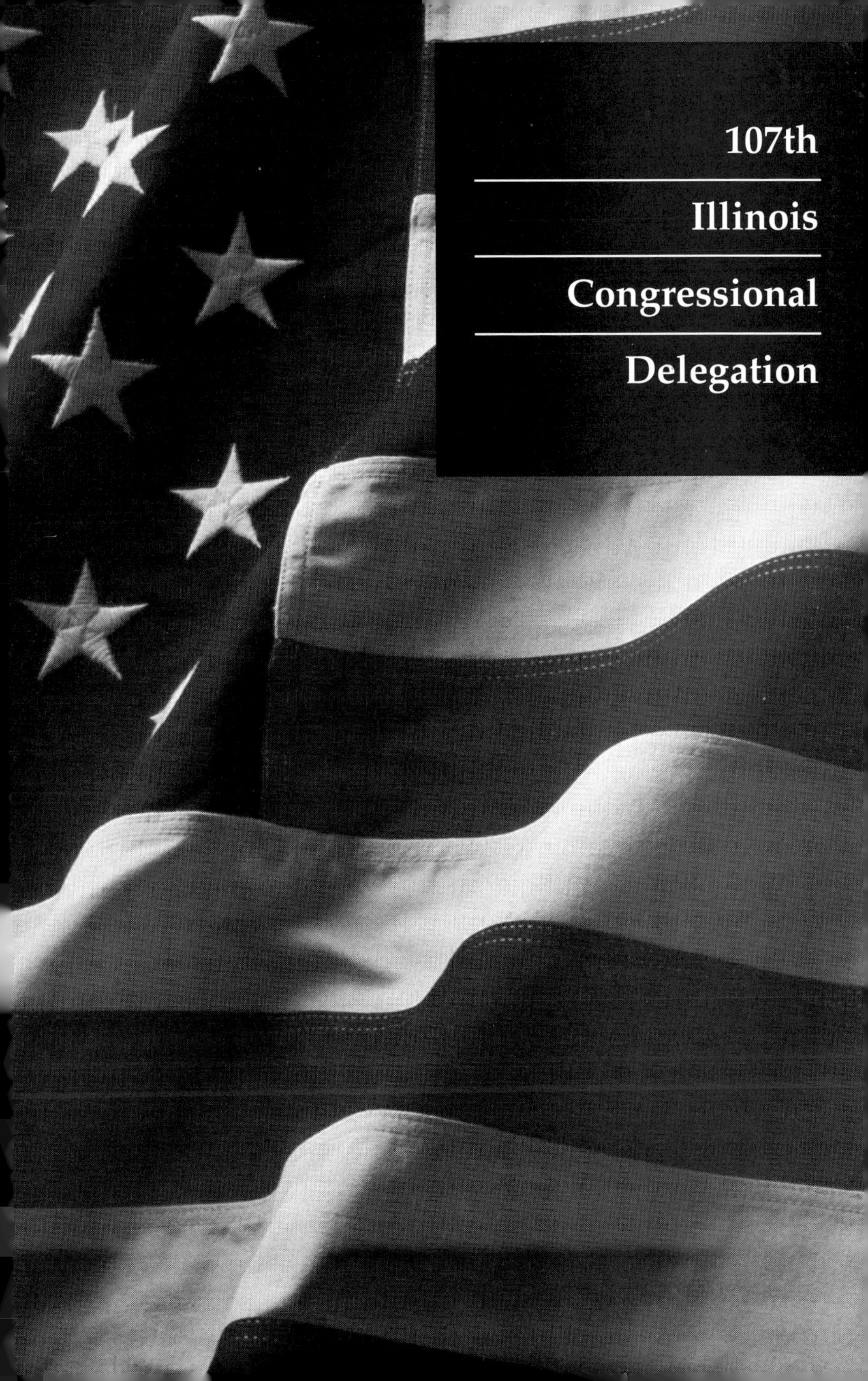

107TH CONGRESS

2001-2003

ILLINOIS MEMBERS

SENATORS *(term: six years)*

Richard J. Durbin (D)   Peter G. Fitzgerald (R)

REPRESENTATIVES *(term: two years)*

1. Bobby L. Rush (D)
2. Jesse L. Jackson, Jr. (D)
3. William O. Lipinski (D)
4. Luis V. Gutierrez (D)
5. Rod R. Blagojevich (D)
6. Henry Hyde (R)
7. Danny K. Davis (D)
8. Philip M. Crane (R)
9. Janice D. Schakowsky (D)
10. Mark Steven Kirk (R)
11. Jerry Weller (R)
12. Jerry F. Costello (D)
13. Judy Biggert (R)
14. J. Dennis Hastert (R)
15. Timothy V. Johnson (R)
16. Donald A. Manzullo (R)
17. Lane Evans (D)
18. Ray LaHood (R)
19. David D. Phelps (D)
20. John M. Shimkus (R)

As a result of the 2000 census, the State of Illinois was reapportioned into 19 Congressional districts with one representative elected from each. Illinois lost one of its Congressional seats, down from 20 seats in the 1990s, due to a shift in population from industrialized states such as Illinois to states in the western and southern regions of the country. That loss was similar to the 1991 reapportionment process when Illinois lost two of its Congressional seats and the 1981 reapportionment process when the state also lost two of its seats. Since 1970, Illinois has lost a total of five seats in the U. S. House of Representatives due to population shifts within the nation.

The 2001 reapportionment altered boundaries of every Congressional district in the state. The Hispanic-American majority district created in 1991 was preserved as were the three African-American districts. Each of these districts is located in Cook County, mainly in the City of Chicago.

To accommodate the loss of one seat, the Illinois General Assembly approved and Governor Ryan signed into law a Congressional map that eliminated the 19th Congressional District by merging it into the 12th, 15th, 17th, 18th and 20th districts.

The 2000 elections saw several changes in the makeup of the Illinois delegation. Tenth District Congressman John Porter and 15th District Congressman Tom Ewing both declared that they would not seek re-election. Their decisions led to competitive elections in both districts that were ultimately won by candidates Mark Kirk in the 10th and Tim Johnson in the 15th. Both seats remained in Republican hands and maintained the Congressional split between the parties of 10 Republican members and 10 Democrats.

In 2002, Senator Durbin will be up for his first re-election bid to his position in the U. S. Senate. All of the House members will be up for re-election with one already declaring his intention to run for a statewide office rather than re-election.

First District
Bobby L. Rush, Democrat
Washington Office: 2416 Rayburn Bldg., 20515

Bobby L. Rush was born Nov. 23, 1946, in Albany, GA. His family later moved to Chicago where he attended Marshall High School. Rush served in the U.S. Army from 1963 to 1968 and received an honorable discharge. He then earned a bachelor's degree with honors from Roosevelt University in 1973, a master's degree in political science from the University of Illinois at Chicago in 1994, and a master's degree in theological studies from McCormick Seminary in 1998. His first elected position was Alderman on the Chicago City Council, where he served for eight years. He was then elected to Congress in November 1992 and is now serving in his fifth term. Rush is a member of the House Committee on Energy and Commerce and Subcommittees on Telecommunications, Energy and Air Quality, Oversight and Investigations, and Commerce, Trade and Consumer Protection. Rush also is co-chairman of the Congressional Biotech Caucus, Secretary of the Congressional Black Caucus and serves on the U.S. delegation to the North Atlantic Assembly, an interparliamentary organization of NATO nations. Rush and his wife, Carolyn, have five children.

Second District
Jesse L. Jackson, Jr., Democrat
Washington Office: 313 Cannon Bldg., 20515

Jesse L. Jackson, Jr. was born March 11, 1965. He graduated magna cum laude from North Carolina A & T State University in Greensboro, NC, in 1987, where he earned a bachelor's degree in business management. Three years later, he earned a master's degree in theology from the Chicago Theological Seminary and, in 1993, received his J.D. degree from the University of Illinois College of Law. Jackson began service in the U.S. House of Representatives on Dec. 12, 1995, when he was sworn in as a member of the 104th Congress. He is the 91st African American ever elected to Congress. Jackson currently sits on the House Appropriations Committee and the Subcommittee on Labor, Health and Human Services, and Education. He also is on the Subcommittee on Foreign Operations, Export Financing and Related Programs. Prior to his congressional service, Jackson served as the National Field Director of the National Rainbow Coalition. He resides in Chicago with his wife, Sandi, and daughter, Jessica Donatella.

Third District
William O. Lipinski, Democrat
Washington Office: 2470 Rayburn Bldg., 20515

William O. Lipinski was born Dec. 22, 1937, in Chicago. He attended St. Patrick's High School in Chicago and Loras College in Dubuque, IA. He served as Alderman of the City of Chicago from 1975 to 1983 and has been Democratic Ward Committeeman from 1975 to the present. He was first elected to Congress in 1982. Lipinski is a member of the Transportation and Infrastructure Committee and the Subcommittee on Aviation (ranking minority member). He also sits on the Subcommittees on Highways and Transit, and Railroads. In addition, he is a member of the Democratic Steering Committee. He and his wife, Rose Marie, have one daughter and one son.

Fourth District
Luis V. Gutierrez, Democrat

Washington Office: 2452 Rayburn Bldg., 20515

Luis V. Gutierrez was born in Chicago on Dec. 10, 1953. He received his B.A. degree from Northeastern Illinois University in 1975. Gutierrez is a former public school teacher, social worker, community activist, assistant to Chicago Mayor Harold Washington and Alderman of the City of Chicago from 1986 to 1992. In the Chicago City Council, he led the fight for affordable housing, tougher ethics rules and a law to ban discrimination based on sexual orientation. Gutierrez was elected to the U.S. House in November 1992 and re-elected to a fifth term in November 2000. He is a member of the Committee on Financial Services and the Subcommittees on Oversight and Investigations (ranking minority member), Financial Institutions and Consumer Credit, and International Monetary Policy and Trade. He also sits on the Veterans' Affairs Committee and the Subcommittee on Health. Gutierrez and his wife, Soraida, have two daughters, Omaira and Jessica.

Fifth District
Rod R. Blagojevich, Democrat

Washington Office: 331 Cannon Bldg., 20515

Rod R. Blagojevich was born Dec. 10, 1956, in Chicago and attended Foreman High School. He received his bachelor's degree from Northwestern University and his J.D. degree from Pepperdine University in California. A former Assistant State's Attorney in Cook County, he served two terms in the Illinois House of Representatives. He currently is in his third term in the U.S. House of Representatives. He serves on the Armed Services Committee, Subcommittees on Military Research and Development, and Military Readiness, and the Government Reform Committee, Subcommittees on Criminal Justice Drug Policy and Human Resources and Energy Policy, Natural Resources and Regulatory Affairs. He and his wife, Patricia, have one daughter, Amy.

Sixth District
Henry Hyde, Republican

Washington Office: 2110 Rayburn Bldg., 20515

Henry Hyde was born April 18, 1924, in Chicago. He received his B.S. degree from Georgetown University in 1947 and his J.D. degree from Loyola University School of Law in 1949. He served in the U.S. Navy during World War II and retired from the active reserves with the rank of Commander in 1968. He was an Illinois State Representative from 1967 until his election to Congress in 1974. Hyde is a member of the House Judiciary Committee. He also serves on the House International Relations Committee. He married the late Jeanne Simpson, and he has four children and five grandchildren.

Seventh District
Danny K. Davis, Democrat

Washington Office: 1222 Longworth Bldg., 20515

Danny K. Davis was born in Parkdale, AR, on Sept. 6, 1941. He moved to the west side of Chicago in 1961 after receiving his B.A. degree from Arkansas A.M. & N. College. He subsequently received master's and Ph.D. degrees respectively from Chicago State University and the Union Institute in Cincinnati, OH. Before seeking public office, Davis was an educator, community organizer, health planner/administrator and civil rights advocate. He served 11 years as Alderman for the 29th Ward on the Chicago City Council and was on the Cook County Board of Commissioners from November 1990 until his election to Congress in November 1996. In the 107th Congress, Davis serves on the Government Reform Committee, Subcommittees on Civil Service (ranking minority member) and the Census. He also serves on the Small Business Committee, Subcommittees on Workforce, Empowerment and Government Programs, and Tax, Finance and Exports. Davis is a Regional Whip in the Democratic Caucus and is a member of the Black, Progressive, India, Steel and Hellenic Caucuses. He is married to Vera G. Davis and has two sons, Jonathan and Stacey.

Eighth District
Philip M. Crane, Republican

Washington Office: 233 Cannon Bldg., 20515

Philip M. Crane was born in Chicago on Nov. 3, 1930. He received his B.A. degree in psychology and history at Hillsdale College in Michigan and his M.A. and Ph.D. degrees in history at Indiana University. A U.S. Army veteran, he served in Europe from 1954 to 1956. Crane is an experienced farmer, teacher, historian and author, and he has been a member of Congress since 1969. He currently is vice chairman of the Ways and Means Committee and its Subcommittees on Trade (chair) and Health. He is a founding member and former chair of the Republican Study Committee and currently serves on two task forces for the Republican Policy and Research Committees. He also served on the Commission for the Bicentennial of the U.S. Constitution. Crane and his wife, Arlene, have eight children and six grandchildren.

Ninth District
Janice D. Schakowsky, Democrat

Washington Office: 515 Cannon Bldg., 20515

Janice D. Schakowsky was born in Chicago on May 26, 1944. She graduated from the University of Illinois in 1965 with a B.S. degree in elementary education. For 20 years, she fought for the public interest and rights of Illinois citizens. She was elected to the Illinois House of Representatives in 1990 where she served the 18th District for eight years. She was elected to the U.S. House of Representatives in 1998 and serves on the Financial Services and Government Reform Committee. She was appointed to a leadership whip position where she works to notify her colleagues about upcoming votes and issues, and is a member of the Health Care and Medicare Task Forces. Congresswoman Schakowsky resides in Evanston with her husband, Robert Creamer. She has three children, Ian, Mary and stepdaughter, Lauren Creamer, and granddaughters, Isabel and Eve.

Tenth District
Mark Steven Kirk, Republican

Washington Office: 1531 Longworth Bldg., 20515

Mark Steven Kirk was born Sept. 15, 1959, and is a native of the 10th Congressional District that he currently serves. He received a bachelor's degree in history from Cornell University in 1981, a master's degree from the London School of Economics and a law degree from Georgetown University. Congressman Kirk also studied at the Universidad Nacional Autonoma de Mexico in Mexico City, where he learned to speak Spanish. Kirk began his career in government in 1984 as an aide to U.S. Representative John Edward Porter, eventually serving as his Chief of Staff. In 1995, he joined the staff of the U.S. House International Relations Committee as counsel, conducting missions to 42 countries, including Bosnia, Kosovo and North Korea. A Naval Reserve officer, Congressman Kirk holds the rank of Lieutenant Commander and has served in Kosovo, Bosnia, Iraq and Panama. Kirk currently serves on the Budget, Armed Services, and Transportation and Infrastructure committees. He is married to Kimberly Vertolli of Alexandria, VA.

Eleventh District
Jerry Weller, Republican

Washington Office: 1210 Longworth Bldg., 20515

Jerry Weller was born July 7, 1957, in Streator, and was raised on his family's fifth-generation farm in Dwight. Weller received a B.S. degree in agriculture from the University of Illinois in 1979. He served as an aide to U.S. Representative Tom Corcoran (1980-81) and to U.S. Secretary of Agriculture John R. Block (1981-85). Weller was elected to the Illinois House of Representatives in 1988 and served six years. Elected to Congress in 1994, he currently is on the Ways and Means Committee, Subcommittees on Oversight and Select Revenue Measures. Weller also serves as chairman of the Policy Committee, Subcommittees on Bio-Technology, Telecommunications and Information Technology, and is an Assistant Majority Whip.

Twelfth District
Jerry F. Costello, Democrat

Washington Office: 2454 Rayburn Bldg., 20515

Jerry F. Costello was born Sept. 25, 1949, in East St. Louis. He received an A.D. degree from Belleville Area College in 1970 and a B.A. degree from Maryville College in 1972. He served as chair of the St. Clair County Board from 1980 until his election to Congress in 1988. His committee assignments include the Committee on Transportation and Infrastructure, Subcommittees on Economic Development, Public Buildings and Emergency Management (ranking minority member), Aviation and Highways and Transit, and the Committee on Science, Subcommittee on Energy. He is married, and he and his wife, Georgia, have three children and seven grandchildren.

Thirteenth District
Judy Biggert, Republican

Washington Office: 1213 Longworth Bldg., 20515

Judy Biggert was born Aug. 15, 1937, in Chicago. She received her B.A. degree in international relations from Stanford University in 1959 and earned her J.D. degree from Northwestern University School of Law in 1963. She has been an attorney specializing in real estate, estate planning and probate since 1975. She was elected to the Illinois House of Representatives in 1992 and served six years. Elected to Congress in 1998, she currently serves on the Committees on Education and the Workforce, Financial Services, Science and Standards of Official Conduct (Ethics). Biggert was elected Republican co-chair of the Congressional Caucus on Women's Issues. Congresswoman Biggert and her husband, Rody, have four children and four grandchildren.

Fourteenth District
J. Dennis Hastert, Republican

Washington Office: 2369 Rayburn Bldg., 20515

J. Dennis Hastert was born Jan. 2, 1942, in Aurora. He was educated at Wheaton College, from which he received a bachelor's degree in business and economics, and Northern Illinois University, from which he received a master's degree in philosophy. He is currently serving as Speaker of the House in his eighth term in Congress. Prior to his election to Congress, he served three terms in the Illinois House of Representatives. He is married to the former Jean Kahl, and they are the parents of two sons.

Fifteenth District
Timothy V. Johnson, Republican

Washington Office: 1541 Longworth Bldg., 20515

Timothy V. Johnson was born in July 1946 in Champaign. He attended Urbana public schools and graduated from Urbana High School. Johnson received his B.A. degree in history from the University of Illinois where he graduated with Phi Beta Kappa and Bronze Tablet honors. He graduated from the University of Illinois College of Law in 1972 with high honors, including induction into the Order of the Coif. In 1971, Johnson was elected to the Urbana City Council. He also founded the Urbana law firm, Johnson, Frank, Frederick and Walsh. In 1976, Johnson began his tenure in the Illinois General Assembly as a State Representative. In 1995, he was Deputy Majority Leader in the Illinois House. In November 2001, Johnson was elected to the U.S. Congress from Illinois' 15th District. He sits on the House Agriculture, Science and Transportation and Infrastructure committees. His Subcommittee assignments include General Farm Commodities and Aviation. He also is vice chairman of the Basic Research Subcommittee on Science. Johnson lives in Urbana and has nine children and nine grandchildren.

Sixteenth District
Donald A. Manzullo, Republican

Washington Office: 409 Cannon Bldg., 20515

Donald A. Manzullo was born in 1944 in Rockford. He received his B.A. degree from American University School of Government and Public Administration in Washington, DC, and his J.D. degree from Marquette University Law School in Milwaukee. Since 1970, Manzullo has practiced law before federal and state courts representing individuals impacted by state and federal agencies. He first ran for Congress in the 1990 Republican Primary, was elected to the U.S. House of Representatives in November 1992 and was re-elected in 1994, 1996, 1998 and 2000. Manzullo won the 1991 "George Washington Honor Medal for Excellence in Public Communications" from the Freedom Foundation, Valley Forge, PA. He currently serves as chairman of the House Small Business Committee. He also serves on the Financial Services Committee, Subcommittees on Financial Institutions and Consumer Credit, and International Monetary Policy and Trade. Manzullo and his wife, Freda, have three children.

Seventeenth District
Lane Evans, Democrat

Washington Office: 2211 Rayburn Bldg., 20515

Lane Evans was born in Rock Island on Aug. 4, 1951. He received a B.A. degree from Augustana College, graduating magna cum laude, and a J.D. degree from Georgetown University Law Center in Washington, DC. He served in the U.S. Marine Corps from 1969 to 1971. Prior to his election to the U.S. House of Representatives in 1982, he was a partner in the Community Legal Clinic in Rock Island and served as legal counsel for local chapters of the National Association for the Advancement of Colored People and the American Civil Liberties Union. Evans is the ranking minority member of the Veterans' Affairs Committee. He also serves on the National Security Committee and the Armed Services Committee, and is co-chair of the House Ethanol Caucus.

Eighteenth District
Ray LaHood, Republican

Washington Office: 1424 Longworth Bldg., 20515

Ray LaHood was born Dec. 6, 1945, in Peoria. He attended Spalding High School and Canton Junior College, and received his B.S. degree in education and sociology from Bradley University in 1971. LaHood taught junior high school students for six years. He served as chief planner of the Bi-State Metropolitan Planning Commission and director of the Rock Island County Youth Services Bureau, and was recruited to work for Congressman Tom Railsback in 1977. After serving in the Illinois House of Representatives in 1982, he was recruited by Congressman Bob Michel to head up his 18th District. LaHood served 12 years with Michel, the last four as chief of staff, and was elected to succeed him on Nov. 8, 1994. He was re-elected in 1996, 1998 and 2000. LaHood serves on the Appropriations, Budget and Intelligence committees. He and his wife, the former Kathleen Dunk, have four children, Darin, Amy, Sam and Sara.

42

Nineteenth District
David D. Phelps, Democrat

Washington Office: 1523 Longworth Bldg., 20515

David D. Phelps was born Oct. 26, 1947, in Eldorado. His deep roots in the Southern Illinois region led him to become involved in his local community through civic, church and school activities. Phelps received his B.S. degree in social studies from Southern Illinois University in 1967. He then became a public school teacher and assistant principal with the Harrisburg School District. Phelps also is lead singer for the Phelps Brothers Quartet, a gospel group that has achieved nationwide acclaim. In 1980, he was appointed to fill an unexpired term as Clerk and Recorder of Saline County, and was elected to a full term in 1982. Phelps was elected to the Illinois House of Representatives in 1984 and served until 1998 when he was elected to the U.S. Congress. He is a member of the Agriculture and Small Business committees. Congressman Phelps and his wife, Leslie, have four children and one grandchild.

Twentieth District
John M. Shimkus, Republican

Washington Office: 513 Cannon Bldg., 20515

John M. Shimkus was born Feb. 21, 1958. He received his B.S. degree in general engineering from the U. S. Military Academy at West Point, NY, in 1980, and his M.B.A. from Southern Illinois University at Edwardsville in 1997. Shimkus left the Army as a Captain in the Infantry. He still serves as a Lt. Colonel in the Army Reserves. Shimkus then taught government and history at Metro East Lutheran High School in Edwardsville. He was elected Madison County Treasurer in 1990 and served until his election to Congress in 1996. Shimkus is a member of the Energy and Commerce Committee and its Subcommittees on Commerce, Trade and Consumer Protection; Energy and Air Quality; Telecommunications and the Internet, and Environment and Hazardous Materials, of which he serves as vice chair. He is a U.S. delegate to the NATO Parliamentary Assembly, and serves as co-chair of the House Baltic Caucus. In addition, he was featured in a national PBS documentary, "Mr. Shimkus Goes to Washington." He and his wife, Karen, have three sons, David, Joshua and Daniel. They reside in Collinsville.

CONGRESSIONAL DIRECTORY

Name:	Washington, DC, Address/Phone:	District Address/Phone:
Bobby L. Rush *(D-1st District)*	2416 Rayburn Bldg. Washington, DC 20515 (202) 225-4372 bobby.rush@mail.house.gov	700-706 E. 79th St. Chicago, IL 60619 (773) 224-6500
Jesse L. Jackson, Jr. *(D-2nd District)*	313 Cannon Bldg. Washington, DC 20515 (202) 225-0773	17926 S. Halsted Homewood, IL 60430 (708) 798-6000
William O. Lipinski *(D-3rd District)*	2470 Rayburn Bldg. Washington, DC 20515 (202) 225-5701 www. house.gov/lipinski www.house.gov/writerep	5832 S. Archer Ave. Chicago, IL 60638 (312) 886-0481
Luis V. Gutierrez *(D-4th District)*	2452 Rayburn Bldg. Washington, DC 20515 (202) 225-8203	3181 N. Elston Ave. Chicago, IL 60618 (773) 509-0999 (773) 509-1536 (TDD)
Rod R. Blagojevich *(D-5th District)*	331 Cannon Bldg. Washington, DC 20515 (202) 225-4061 rod.blagojevich@mail.house.gov	4064 N. Lincoln Ave. Chicago, IL 60618 (773) 868-3240
Henry Hyde *(R-6th District)*	2110 Rayburn Bldg. Washington, DC 20515 (202) 225-4561	50 E. Oak St. Addison, IL 60101 (630) 832-5950
Danny K. Davis *(D-7th District)*	1222 Longworth Bldg. Washington, DC 20515 (202) 225-5006 www.house.gov/davis/	3333 W. Arthington, Ste. 130 Chicago, IL 60624 (773) 533-7520
Philip M. Crane *(R-8th District)*	233 Cannon Bldg. Washington, DC 20515-1308 (202) 225-3711	1100 W. Northwest Hwy. Palatine, IL 60067 (847) 358-9160
Janice D. Schakowsky *(D-9th District)*	515 Cannon Bldg. Washington, DC 20515 (202) 225-2111 jan.schakowsky@mail.house.gov	5533 N. Broadway Chicago, IL 60640 (773) 506-7100
Mark Steven Kirk *(R-10th District)*	1531 Longworth Bldg. Washington, DC 20515 (202) 225-4835 rep.kirk@mail.house.gov	102 Wilmot Rd., Ste. 200 Deerfield, IL 60015 (847) 940-0202
Jerry Weller *(R-11th District)*	1210 Longworth Bldg. Washington, DC 20515-1311 (202) 225-3635 www.house.gov/weller/	2701 Black Rd., Ste. 201 Joliet, IL 60435 (815) 740-2028
Jerry F. Costello *(D-12th District)*	2454 Rayburn Bldg. Washington, DC 20515 (202) 225-5661 www.house.gov/costello/	155 Lincoln Place Ct. Belleville, IL 62221 (618) 233-8026

CONGRESSIONAL DIRECTORY, concluded

Name:	Washington, DC, Address/Phone:	District Address/Phone:
Judy Biggert *(R-13th District)*	1213 Longworth Bldg. Washington, DC 20515 (202) 225-3515 www.house.gov/biggert/	115 W. 55th St., Ste. 100 Clarendon Hills, IL 60514 (630) 655-2052
J. Dennis Hastert *(R-14th District)*	2369 Rayburn Bldg. Washington, DC 20515 (202) 225-2976 dhastert@mail.house.gov	27 N. River St. Batavia, IL 60510 (630) 406-1114
Timothy V. Johnson *(R-15th District)*	1541 Longworth Bldg. Washington, DC 20515 (202) 225-2371 rep.johnson@mail.house.gov	2004 Fox Drive Champaign, IL 61820 (217) 403-4690
Donald A. Manzullo *(R-16th District)*	409 Cannon Bldg. Washington, DC 20515 (202) 225-5676 www.house.gov/manzullo/	415 S. Mulford Rd. Rockford, IL 61108 (815) 394-1231
Lane Evans *(D-17th District)*	2211 Rayburn Bldg. Washington, DC 20515 (202) 225-5905 lane.evans@mail.house.gov	1535 47th Ave., Ste. 5 Moline, IL 61265 (309) 793-5760
Ray LaHood *(R-18th District)*	1424 Longworth Bldg. Washington, DC 20515 (202) 225-6201 www.house.gov/lahood/	100 N.E. Monroe St., Rm. 100 Peoria, IL 61602 (309) 671-7027
David D. Phelps *(D-19th District)*	1523 Longworth Bldg. Washington, DC 20515 (202) 225-5201 david.phelps@mail.house.gov	901 State St., Ste. 1 & 3 Eldorado, IL 62930 (618) 273-8203
John M. Shimkus *(R-20th District)*	513 Cannon Bldg. Washington, DC 20515 (202) 225-5271 www.house.gov/writerep/ www.house.gov/shimkus/	3130 Chatham Rd., Ste. C Springfield, IL 62704 (217) 492-5090

CONGRESSIONAL DISTRICTS OF ILLINOIS
1991 Reapportionment

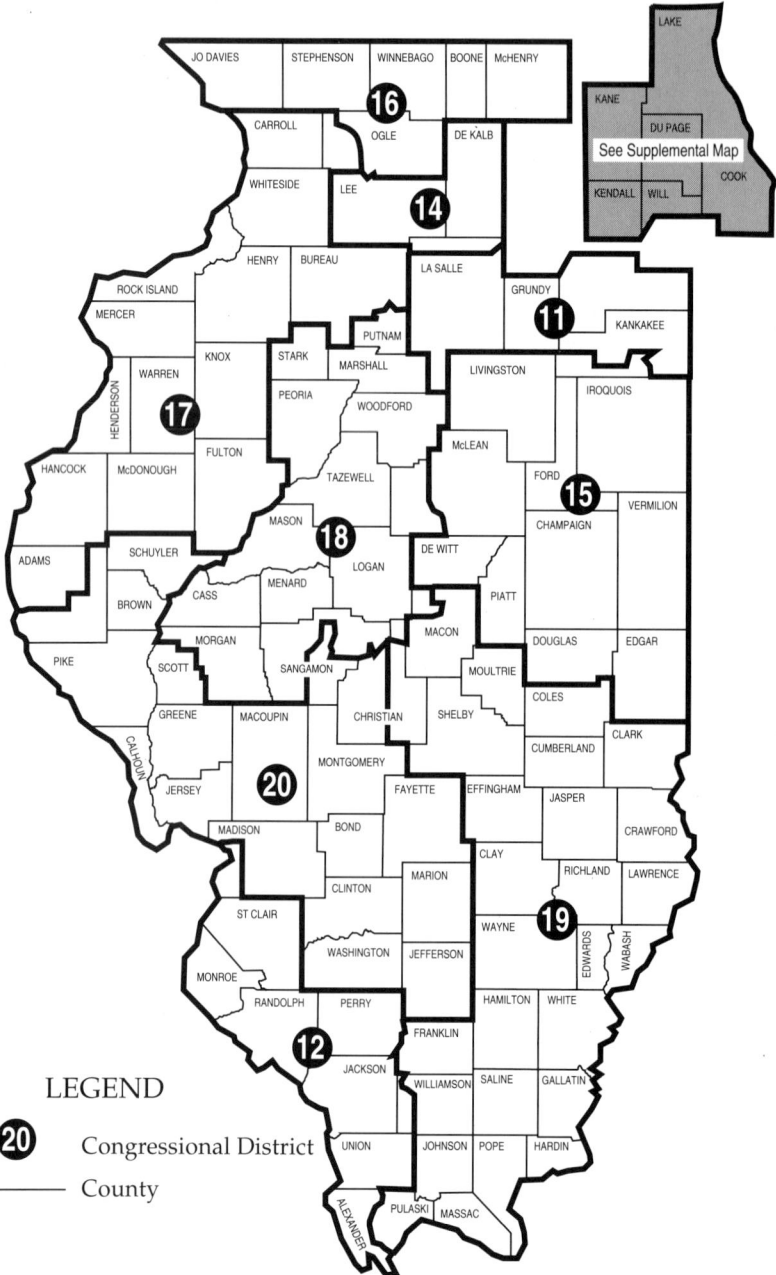

LEGEND

20 Congressional District

——— County

CONGRESSIONAL DISTRICTS OF
NORTHEASTERN ILLINOIS
1991 Reapportionment

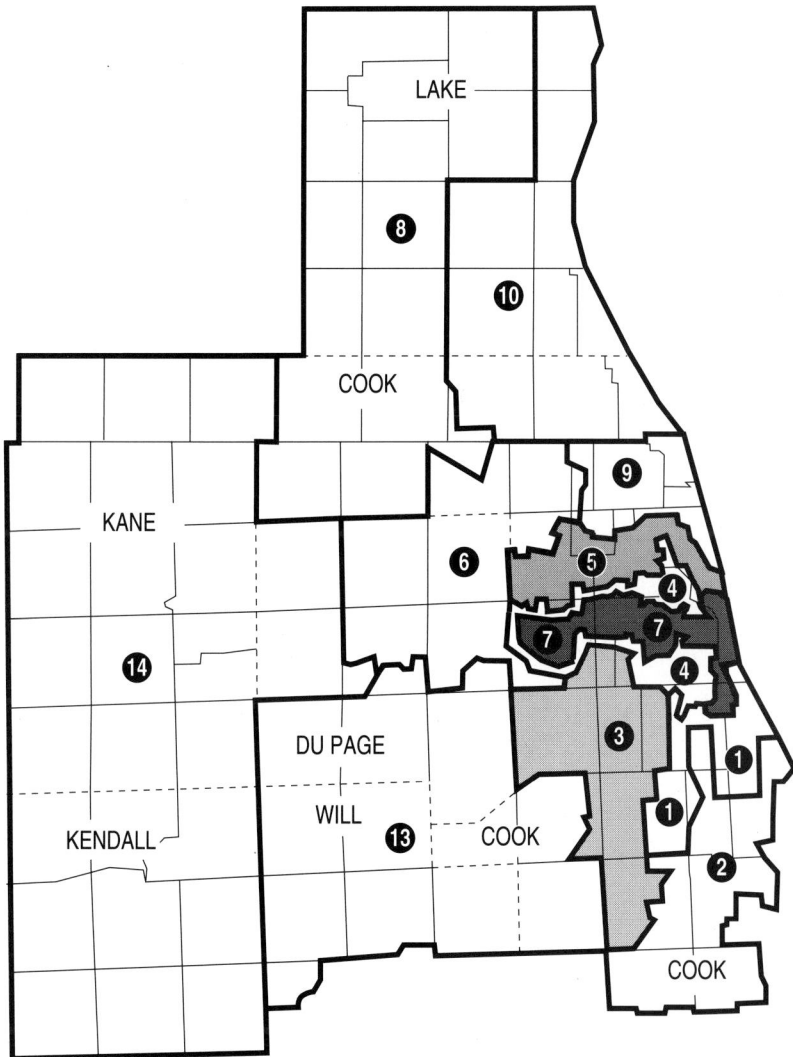

LEGEND

━━━━━━━━ Congressional District

------------ County

FEDERAL OFFICIALS

EXECUTIVE BRANCH

President of the United States: George W. Bush
Vice President of the United States: Dick Cheney

Members of the Cabinet

Secretary of Commerce: Don Evans
Secretary of Education: Rod Paige
Secretary of Agriculture: Ann Veneman
Secretary of Transportation: Norman Mineta
Secretary of Labor: Elaine Chao
Secretary of Health & Human Services: Tommy Thompson
Secretary of Energy: Spencer Abraham
Secretary of Housing & Urban Development: Mel Martinez
Secretary of the Treasury: Paul O'Neill
Secretary of State: Colin Powell
Attorney General: John Ashcroft
Secretary of the Interior: Gale Norton
Secretary of Defense: Donald Rumsfeld
Secretary of Veterans Affairs: Anthony Principi

Officers with Cabinet Rank

United States Trade Representative: Robert B. Zoellick
Director of the Central Intelligence Agency: George J. Tenet
United Nations Representative: John D. Negroponte
Office of Management & Budget Director: Mitchell E. Daniels, Jr.
Chief of Staff & Assistant to the President: Andrew H. Card, Jr.

LEGISLATIVE BRANCH

Senate Leadership

President of the Senate: Dick Cheney
President Pro Tempore of the Senate: Robert Byrd
Majority Leader: Tom Daschle
Minority Leader: Trent Lott

House Leadership

Speaker of the House: J. Dennis Hastert
Majority Leader: Richard K. Armey
Minority Leader: Richard Gephardt

JUDICIAL BRANCH

Supreme Court Justices

Chief Justice: William H. Rehnquist, AZ
Ruth Bader Ginsburg, NY
Anthony M. Kennedy, CA
Sandra Day O'Connor, AZ
Antonin Scalia, DC
David H. Souter, NH
John Paul Stevens, IL
Clarence Thomas, GA
Stephen G. Breyer, MA

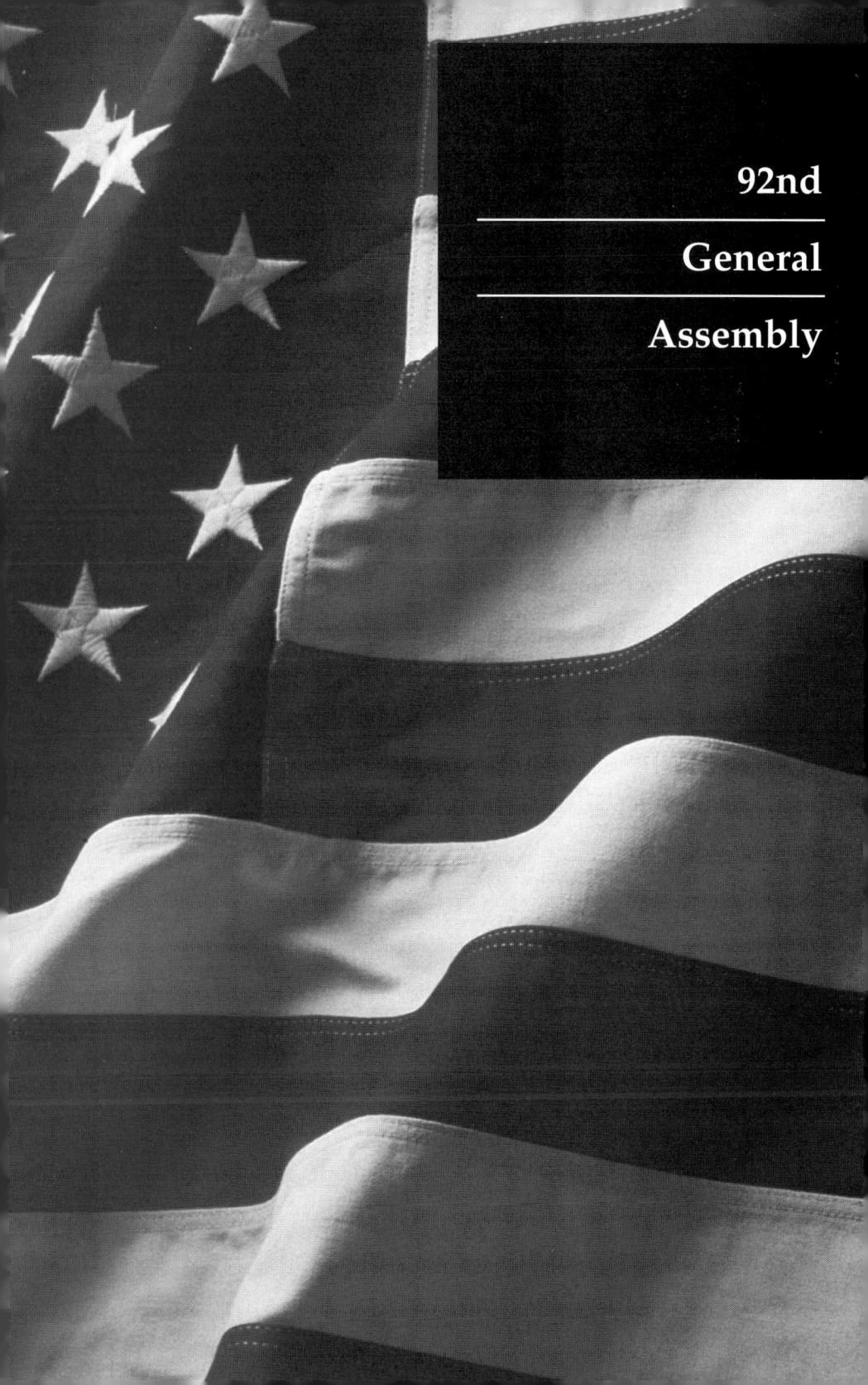

GENERAL ASSEMBLY

To be eligible to serve as a member of the General Assembly, a person must be a United States citizen, at least 21 years old and reside in the district being represented for at least two years prior to the election or appointment.

Functions and Powers

The legislative power of the State of Illinois is vested in the General Assembly, which is composed of a 59-member Senate and a 118-member House of Representatives. Its principal activities are enacting, amending or repealing laws, passing resolutions, adopting appropriation bills and conducting inquiries on proposed legislation. It also acts on amendments to the United States Constitution when they are submitted by Congress and proposes and submits amendments to the Illinois Constitution for consideration by voters.

In addition to legislative responsibilities, the Senate is constitutionally delegated the responsibility of advising and consenting to most gubernatorial appointments to state offices, boards and commissions.

The General Assembly may impeach and convict executive and judicial officeholders in the State of Illinois. The House of Representatives has the sole power of impeachment, while the Senate serves as adjudicator. If a majority of the members of the House vote to impeach, the case proceeds to the Senate for trial. No officeholder may be convicted and removed from office without a two-thirds guilty vote from the Senate. The Senate may not, however, impose any punishment on an impeached and convicted officeholder other than removal from office.

Organization and Composition

A 1980 ballot proposition reduced the size of the House of Representatives from 177 to 118 members and eliminated the system of electing three representatives from each district on the basis of cumulative voting. This provision marked the first constitutional reduction in the size of the Legislature since 1848. As of 1982, each legislative district is comprised of one senate district, which is divided into two representative districts. Every two years, one representative is elected from each representative district for a term of two years.

Members of the General Assembly are elected at the General Election in even-numbered years. Senate districts are divided into three groups, and one or two groups are elected every two years. Senators from one group are elected for terms of four years, four years and two years; another group serves for terms of four years, two years and four years; and the third group is elected for terms of two years, four years and four years.

In January of the odd-numbered year following the November General Election, the Secretary of State presides over the House until the members have elected a Speaker. In the Senate, the Governor presides until the senators have elected a President. Various other leaders and officers are selected by the Speaker and President as well as minority leaders in both the House and Senate to serve in leadership positions.

Bills may originate in either the House or the Senate and must be passed by a majority of all elected members before being sent to the Governor. Either chamber may amend or reject any bill. During recent sessions, about 5,000-6,000 bills have been introduced in each biennium. However, the total number of bills enacted is much smaller.

As the nature and number of proposed bills have increased, the Legislature has established numerous committees and commissions in an effort to concentrate on specific subject areas.

Legislative Cycle

The General Assembly convenes each year on the second Wednesday in January. The Governor's State of the State message to the Legislature is delivered early in the session. The legislative work schedule during the spring typically is laden with heavy committee schedules, extended plenary sessions, controversial budget issues and reconciling differences in substantive bills between the two chambers.

Constitutional provisions, formal rules and parliamentary procedures provide basic guidelines and relative stability to both chambers as the General Assembly acts on legislation. Any bill passed after May 31 cannot take effect until June 1 of the following year unless the bill passes both the House and Senate by a three-fifths vote. The assembly adjourns at the end of May and reconvenes in October or November for two weeks to consider the Governor's vetoes.

At other times, special sessions may be convened by the Governor or by a joint proclamation by the presiding officers of both chambers. This proclamation confines legislative deliberation to specific subjects, and no other matters except confirmations of appointments and impeachments may be considered by Assembly members.

Illinois House of Representatives

OFFICE OF THE SENATE PRESIDENT

The Senate President is the Presiding Officer of the State Senate, elected by and among the members of the Senate to serve a two-year term. The Illinois Constitution, statutes and rules define the functions and responsibilities of the office.

The President appoints Senate members to standing committees and permanent and interim study commissions, designating one member as chairman. The President also appoints the Majority Leader and Assistant Majority Leaders, who serve as officers of the Senate.

With the Speaker of the House, the President shares primary responsibility for legislative procedures and operations. By strategically directing the flow of legislation, the President ultimately can set the pace of work in the Senate. The President is required to approve all vouchers for the expenditure of funds appropriated for use by the Senate and to certify that all bills passed by the Senate are in accordance with Senate rules.

As chairman of the Senate Operations Commission, the President oversees a seven-member management committee responsible for deciding Senate policy, hiring Senate employees, purchasing supplies, renting equipment and maintaining the Senate chambers and office, among other sundry duties.

In addition to presiding over the Senate, the President is the leader of the majority party in the upper chamber. The President is also the chief spokesman of his/her political party.

Likewise, the Senate Minority Leader, selected by the minority party and formally elected by all Senate members, speaks on behalf of the minority party. Responsibilities of the Senate Minority Leader include appointing members to serve on certain boards, commissions and standing committees; selecting assistant leaders and staff; and serving as spokesman for constitutional officers from the minority party.

As spokesmen in the upper chamber, both the Senate President and Minority Leader can influence their respective party members and effectuate the passage or obstruction of legislation.

James "Pate" Philip
Senate President

Senator **James "Pate" Philip**, a Republican from Wood Dale, is the longest serving legislative leader — in either party — in Illinois history. He was elected Senate President on the first day of the 88th General Assembly, Jan. 13, 1993. Philip became the first Republican Senate President in 18 years. He was re-elected in January 1995, 1997, 1999 and 2001. Prior to that, he served as Senate Minority Leader for 12 years.

Senator Philip is widely recognized for his work to increase public access to the legislative process, improve our public school system schools, streamline government, hold the line on taxes and improve the state's jobs climate. His contributions to the state have earned him numerous awards and honors.

Senator Philip started his political career in 1965 as York Township Auditor. He was elected to the Illinois House in 1967 and served there until 1974 when he was elected to the Senate. He was appointed Assistant Senate Minority Leader in 1979 and was elected Minority Leader two years later. He also serves as DuPage County Republican Chairman, where he has helped build a strong political grassroots network.

In 1992, Senator Philip retired as District Sales Manager for Pepperidge Farms, Inc., where he worked for 38 years. He was born May 26, 1930, in Elmhurst. He is a lifelong resident of DuPage County, where he has been active in numerous civic and charitable organizations. Senator Philip is a U.S. Marine Corps veteran, serving from 1950 to 1953.

He and his wife, Nancy, have four children and five grandchildren.

Stanley B. Weaver
Senate Majority
Leader

Stanley B. Weaver (Republican) serves as Senate Majority Leader. As the second ranking Senate official, Weaver is a key adviser to the Senate President and the majority Caucus. He is chairman of the Senate Rules Committee, which reviews and assigns legislation to standing committees. He also is the Dean of the Illinois Senate, serving in the upper chamber since 1971.

Majority Leader Weaver has represented the 52nd District in the Senate since 1971, after serving one term in the House of Representatives. His priorities have always been those of the people he was elected to represent — quality education, agriculture and economic development. Many state and local organizations have honored his work.

Weaver attended Michigan State College and the University of Illinois and graduated from the Indiana College of Mortuary Science. He served in the Army Air Force during World War II in the Southwest Pacific Theater. He was Mayor of Urbana from May 1957 to January 1969, and is past president of the Illinois Municipal League. He is a member of the Veterans of Foreign Wars, American Legion; Masonic Lodge, Danville Consistory; Mohammed Temple and the International Chili Society.

Senator Weaver, a widower, has two children and two grandchildren.

Senate Minority Leader **Emil Jones, Jr.** (Democrat) has been a member of the Illinois General Assembly since 1973. He served in the Illinois House of Representatives for 10 years. During his tenure in the House, he served as Assistant Majority Leader. Jones was elected to the Illinois Senate in 1982 and was re-elected to the Senate to represent the newly-drawn 14th Senate District in 1992.

Emil Jones, Jr.
Senate Minority
Leader

In January 1993, Senator Jones was elected Minority Leader of the 88th General Assembly, and has been consistently re-elected. Prior to his election as Minority Leader, Jones served four two-year terms as chairman of the Senate Insurance, Pensions and Activities Committee. As chairman of the committee, he screened important legislation on liability insurance, horse racing reform, banning state investments in South Africa, and the licensure and regulation of medical professionals, including doctors, nurses and psychiatrists. Minority Leader Jones currently serves as a member of the Senate Executive Committee. He is known as a strong advocate for funding public education and social justice in Illinois, and his legislative and community endeavors have earned him numerous awards.

Senator Jones was born Oct. 18, 1935. He was educated at Chicago City Loop College and Roosevelt University School of Commerce. In 2001, he was awarded an honorary Doctor of Human Letters from Chicago State University.

He and his late wife, Patricia, are parents of four children.

OFFICE OF THE SPEAKER OF THE HOUSE

The Speaker of the House of Representatives derives responsibility and influence over legislative activities through statutes, Constitutional guidelines and House rules of procedure. Chosen from among members of the House, the Speaker invites participation from a wide range of philosophies from members of both parties in determining a legislative agenda.

The Speaker performs as the Presiding Officer of the House, determining when the House will meet and what type of business it will conduct. Serving as "manager of debate" on bills, resolutions and amendments, the Speaker is responsible for recognizing members, formally calling a vote, deciding parliamentary issues and maintaining decorum in the House chambers.

The comprehensive duties of the office include managing all House offices, facilities, professional and clerical staff, custodians and security personnel. Administratively, the Speaker signs and authenticates all acts, proceedings, orders, writs, warrants and subpoenas issued by the House.

In organizing a party "team" to help ensure smooth operation of House proceedings, the Speaker selects one Majority Leader, Assistant Majority Leaders and Whips. The House Majority Leader, in turn, serves as party spokesman and assists with the flow of legislation. In addition, the Speaker may appoint chairmen and majority members of standing committees, which are the public forums of proposed legislation.

Elected by members of the House, the Minority Leader is chief of his political party — responsible for delegating committee members and relating the will of the minority party.

Traditionally, the Office of the Speaker of the House has a profound bearing on the effectiveness of State Government and citizen representation in Illinois.

Michael J. Madigan
Speaker of the House

Michael J. Madigan (Democrat) was re-elected Speaker of the House in January 2001, a position he has held since 1983, with the exception of the 89th General Assembly. He also has served as House Democratic Leader and House Majority Leader.

As Speaker, Madigan has worked to build consensus and bring equitable treatment to all regions of the state. In recent sessions, he worked to reduce partisan fights. His efforts include the unprecedented act of naming Minority party members to chair House committees.

Madigan is a proponent of campaign and government ethics reforms and has fought to improve the quality of life for working families throughout his career. Independent surveys have named him an "outstanding" member of the Legislature.

Voters in the 22nd Representative District first elected Madigan as their delegate to the 1970 Constitutional Convention and then as a State Representative in November 1970.

A graduate of Loyola University Law School, Speaker Madigan practices law in Chicago. He was born April 19, 1942, in the southwest side district he now represents. A lifelong resident of Chicago, he was graduated from St. Ignatius High School and the University of Notre Dame.

In 1999, Speaker Madigan achieved the distinction of being one of the few lawmakers to serve alongside a child when his daughter, Lisa, was elected to the Illinois Senate from the 17th District. In 1998, Madigan was elected chairman of the Democratic Party of Illinois.

Madigan and his wife, Shirley, have two other daughters, Tiffany and Nicole, and a son, Andrew.

Barbara Flynn Currie (Democrat) in 1997 became the first woman Majority Leader in the history of the General Assembly. As the second ranking House official, Currie works closely with the Governor and with colleagues from both parties and all regions of the state to fashion solutions to the problems facing Illinois.

Majority Leader Currie is a 20-year veteran of the House. Her legislative accomplishments include sponsorship of the Illinois Freedom of Information Act and the state program that funds preschool education for disadvantaged youngsters. She successfully sponsored measures strengthening access to state contracts for businesses owned by women and members of minority groups.

Barbara Flynn Currie
Majority Leader

Currie graduated with honors from the University of Chicago, where she also earned a master's degree in political science. A past vice president of the Chicago League of Women Voters, she serves on the advisory board of the YWCA branch in the Woodlawn neighborhood and on the board of directors of the American Civil Liberties Union of Illinois. She also is a member of the Hyde Park Kiwanis Club, Women United for South Shore and the Sierra Club.

She is married to David P. Currie, professor of law at the University of Chicago. They have two children and four grandchildren.

Lee A. Daniels (Republican) is serving his ninth term as House Minority Leader. In 1995, he was elected House Speaker for the 89th General Assembly. As a 27-year veteran of the House, Daniels has been known as a tireless advocate for the developmentally disabled, school safety, lower taxes and welfare reform.

Minority Leader Daniels has authored hundreds of laws ranging from anti-stalking legislation to Chicago school reforms and tax cap legislation. He has been a leader on public education policy and was the force behind the first-in-the-nation trust fund to ensure adequate funding for long-term care. His work on behalf of people with disabilities has earned him numerous accolades and awards.

Lee A. Daniels
Minority Leader

Among Daniels' other initiatives are guarantees for the availability of health insurance and a law that requires early intervention services to address the growing problem of cocaine-addicted babies and infants. He has been one of the state's foremost leaders advocating quality and accountability in education. He also championed the state's renowned program that provides seniors in need with prescription drug assistance.

Minority Leader Daniels received the 1999 Leader of the Year award from the National Republican Leadership Association. He also was elected to the Elmhurst Hall of Fame and received an honorary doctorate degree from Elmhurst College. An attorney, Daniels was born April 15, 1942, and grew up in Elmhurst, a town he now represents. He earned his bachelor's degree from the University of Iowa and graduated from the John Marshall Law School. He is a partner in the law firm of Bell, Boyd and Lloyd and served as a York Township Trustee before his election to the House. He is a member of numerous civic and fraternal organizations.

Daniels and his wife, Pamela, live in Elmhurst and have five children.

Secretary of the Senate

Jim Harry (Republican) was born Dec. 30, 1939, in Quincy. Following graduation from Illinois College in Jacksonville, he worked as a reporter and anchorman for radio stations in Springfield and Chicago. He served as an assistant to the late Governor Richard B. Ogilvie, and from 1973 to 1987, he was press secretary for Senate Republican leaders William C. Harris, David Shapiro and James "Pate" Philip. He was elected Secretary of the Senate in January 1993 and was re-elected in 1995, 1997, 1999 and 2001. Prior to the change in party control at the beginning of the 88th General Assembly, he served three terms (1987-93) as Assistant Secretary of the Senate. He is past president of the American Society of Legislative Clerks and Secretaries. He and his wife, Leora, have three children and four grandchildren.

Assistant Secretary of the Senate

Linda Hawker (Democrat) was born May 13, 1949, in Springfield. She served as Secretary of the Senate for the 85th, 86th and 87th General Assemblies. In January 1993, she was elected Assistant Secretary of the Senate and was re-elected in 1995, 1997, 1999 and 2001. From 1971 to 1980, she worked for the Senate Democrat Leadership Staff and subsequently was employed as a Public Affairs Associate at Sangamon State University (now the University of Illinois at Springfield), where she received her degree. Prior to serving as Secretary of the Senate, she served as a special assistant to former Senate President Philip J. Rock. She serves on the Executive Committee of the American Society of Clerks and Secretaries and is active in numerous community organizations.

Clerk of the House

Anthony Devlin Rossi (Democrat) was born Jan. 31, 1962, in Jacksonville. Raised and educated in Virginia, he graduated from Virginia High School in 1980 before serving in the U.S. Navy from 1980 to 1983. He attended Southern Illinois University, graduating in 1987 with a degree in political science. Following graduation, he served as a Legislative Analyst on the Democratic Research/Appropriations Staff from 1987 to 1990, and as Staff Director from 1990 to 1993. He served as Chief Clerk of the House for the 88th General Assembly, Assistant Clerk for the 89th Assembly and was re-elected Chief Clerk for the 90th, 91st and 92nd Assemblies. He has four daughters, Rachel, Alexandra, Olivia and Natalie.

Assistant Clerk of the House

Bradley S. Bolin (Republican) was born April 15, 1964, in Anderson, IN. In 1986, he received a B.A. degree in political science from Purdue University. He then served as a Legislative Analyst on the House Republican Staff from 1986 to 1997. He was first elected Assistant Clerk of the House in January 1997. He is married to the former Brittan Ramey, and they have one daughter.

SENATE STANDING COMMITTEES

AGRICULTURE AND CONSERVATION — Sieben, chairperson; Noland, vice chairperson; Luechtefeld, Myers and Watson; O'Daniel, minority spokesperson; Bowles, L. Walsh and Woolard.

APPROPRIATIONS — Rauschenberger, chairperson; Donahue, vice chairperson; Burzynski, Karpiel, Lauzen, Radogno, Syverson and Weaver; Trotter, minority spokesperson; Clayborne, Halvorson, Madigan and del Valle.

COMMERCE AND INDUSTRY — Lauzen, chairperson; Radogno, vice chairperson; Cronin, Hawkinson and Parker; Halvorson, minority spokesperson; Clayborne, Hendon and Woolard.

EDUCATION — Cronin, chairperson; O'Malley, vice chairperson; Burzynski, Roskam, Sieben and Watson; Madigan, minority spokesperson; Demuzio, Lightford and Woolard.

ENVIRONMENT AND ENERGY — Mahar, chairperson; Sullivan, vice chairperson; Dillard, Donahue, Karpiel and Rauschenberger; Shaw, minority spokesperson; Jacobs, Ronen and Welch.

EXECUTIVE — Klemm, chairperson; Petka, vice chairperson; Dillard, Dudycz, Karpiel, Philip, Watson and Weaver; Molaro, minority spokesperson; Bowles, Demuzio, E. Jones and del Valle.

EXECUTIVE APPOINTMENTS — Petka, co-chairperson; DeLeo, co-chairperson; Myers, vice chairperson; Bomke, Burzynski, Peterson, Demuzio and Shadid.

FINANCIAL INSTITUTIONS — O'Malley, chairperson; W. Jones, vice chairperson; Geo-Karis, Mahar and T. Walsh; Lightford, minority spokesperson; Link, Munoz and Welch.

INSURANCE AND PENSIONS — T. Walsh, chairperson; Peterson, vice chairperson; O'Malley, Petka and Sieben; Jacobs, minority spokesperson; Cullerton, Hendon and Viverito.

JUDICIARY — Hawkinson, chairperson; Dillard, vice chairperson; Cronin, Geo-Karis, O'Malley, Petka and Roskam; Cullerton, minority spokesperson; Obama, Shadid and Silverstein.

LICENSED ACTIVITIES — Burzynski, chairperson; Noland, vice chairperson; Luechtefeld and Sullivan; Bowles, minority spokesperson; DeLeo, Shaw and Silverstein.

LOCAL GOVERNMENT — Dillard, chairperson; Bomke, vice chairperson; Dudycz, W. Jones, Klemm and Myers; L. Walsh, minority spokesperson; Halvorson, Link and Shaw.

PUBLIC HEALTH AND WELFARE — Syverson, chairperson; Parker, vice chairperson; Donahue, Mahar, Radogno, Rauschenberger and Sullivan; Obama, minority spokesperson; Munoz, Ronen and Smith.

REVENUE — Peterson, chairperson; Lauzen, vice chairperson; Burzynski, W. Jones, Radogno and Roskam; Clayborne, minority spokesperson; Jacobs, Obama and Trotter.

STATE GOVERNMENT OPERATIONS — Bomke, chairperson; Luechtefeld, vice chairperson; Noland, Sullivan and T. Walsh; Link, minority spokesperson; Hendon, O'Daniel and Silverstein.

TRANSPORTATION — Parker, chairperson; Syverson, vice chairperson; Bomke, Dudycz, Hawkinson and Klemm; Shadid, minority spokesperson; Molaro, Munoz and O'Daniel.

RULES — Weaver, chairperson; Dillard, vice chairperson; Dudycz; Demuzio, minority spokesperson; Cullerton.

OFFICERS OF THE SENATE

James "Pate" Philip	*President of the Senate*
Stanley B. Weaver	*Majority Leader*
Adeline J. Geo-Karis	*Assistant Majority Leader*
John W. Maitland, Jr.	*Assistant Majority Leader*
Laura Kent Donahue	*Assistant Majority Leader*
Frank C. Watson	*Assistant Majority Leader*
Walter W. Dudycz	*Assistant Majority Leader*
Doris C. Karpiel	*Majority Caucus Chair*
Ed Petka	*Majority Whip*
Emil Jones, Jr.	*Minority Leader*
Vince Demuzio	*Assistant Minority Leader*
Miguel del Valle	*Assistant Minority Leader*
Patrick D. Welch	*Assistant Minority Leader*
Louis Viverito	*Assistant Minority Leader*
Rickey R. Hendon	*Assistant Minority Leader*
Margaret Smith	*Minority Caucus Chair*
Evelyn M. Bowles	*Deputy Minority Caucus Chair*
Debbie Halvorson	*Minority Caucus Whip*
William Shaw	*Deputy Minority Caucus Whip*

Other officers: Jim Harry, *Secretary of the Senate*; Linda Hawker, *Assistant Secretary*; Tracey Sidles, *Sergeant-at-Arms*; Anita Robinson, *Assistant Sergeant-at-Arms*

HOUSE STANDING COMMITTEES

AGING — McGuire, chairperson; Franks, vice chairperson; Forby, Garrett, Giles, Jefferson, J. Lyons, Mendoza, Ryan, Soto, Coulson, spokesperson; Berns, Cowlishaw, Lawfer, J. Mitchell, Moffitt, Persico, Saviano, Wait.

AGRICULTURE — Smith, chairperson; Reitz, vice chairperson; Forby, Fowler, Hartke, Mautino, O'Brien, Lawfer, spokesperson; J. Jones, B. Mitchell, Myers, Poe.

APPROPRIATIONS-ELEMENTARY AND SECONDARY EDUCATION — Curry, chairperson; Giles, vice chairperson; Acevedo, Delgado, Mendoza, Murphy, Slone, Smith, Younge, J. Mitchell, spokesperson; Bellock, Coulson, Johnson, Lawfer, Meyer, B. Mitchell, Sommer.

APPROPRIATIONS-GENERAL SERVICES — Schoenberg, chairperson; Slone, vice chairperson; Burke, Fritchey, Garrett, Kenner, May, McKeon, Yarbrough, Biggins, spokesperson; J. Jones, Kosel, Mathias, Moffitt, Poe, Sommer, Tenhouse.

APPROPRIATIONS-HIGHER EDUCATION — Younge, chairperson; Erwin, vice chairperson; Crotty, S. Davis, Howard, S. Jones, Soto, Myers, spokesperson, Berns, Cowlishaw, Kosel, Poe, Wirsing.

APPROPRIATIONS-HUMAN SERVICES — M. Davis, chairperson; Osterman, vice chairperson; Feigenholtz, Giles, Hamos, Mautino, Mendoza, Miller, Ryan, Mulligan, spokesperson; Bassi, Bellock, Coulson, Kurtz, Leitch, B. Mitchell, J. Mitchell.

APPROPRIATIONS-PUBLIC SAFETY — Morrow, chairperson; Mautino, vice chairperson; Delgado, Franks, Hoffman, L. Jones, J. Lyons, McGuire, Stroger, Younge, Pankau, spokesperson; Brady, Johnson, McAuliffe, B. Mitchell, Saviano, Schmitz, Stephens, Wait.

AVIATION — Hamos, chairperson; Scully, vice chairperson; Erwin, Granberg, Jefferson, Turner, Wojcik, spokesperson; Beaubien, Osmond, Schmitz, Stephens.

CHILD SUPPORT ENFORCEMENT — McCarthy, chairperson; Crotty, vice chairperson; Curry, Hamos, O'Brien, Bassi, spokesperson; Black, E. Lyons, J. Mitchell.

CHILDREN AND YOUTH — Crotty, chairperson; Howard, vice chairperson; Flowers, May, Ryan, Klingler, spokesperson; Mulligan, Myers, Wirsing.

CITIES AND VILLAGES — Reitz, chairperson; McCarthy, vice chairperson; Forby, Mautino, May, Slone, Mathias, spokesperson; Berns, Durkin, Moore, Schmitz.

COMMERCE AND BUSINESS DEVELOPMENT — Scully, chairperson; Flowers, vice chaiperson; Collins, Forby, Miller, Ryan, Osmond, spokesperson; Hoeft, Lindner, Mulligan, Zickus.

COMPUTER TECHNOLOGY — Howard, chairperson; Hamos, vice chairperson; Hoffman, Lang, Stroger, Yarbrough, Righter, spokesperson; Klingler, Mathias, O'Connor, Parke.

CONSERVATION AND LAND USE — Slone, chairperson; Scully, vice chairperson; Acevedo, May, Osterman, Winters, spokesperson; Hassert, O'Connor, Parke.

CONSTITUTIONAL OFFICERS — S. Davis, chairperson; Crotty, vice chairperson; Brosnahan, Holbrook, McGuire, Kosel, spokesperson; Bassi, Bost, Mathias.

CONSUMER PROTECTION — Fritchey, chairperson; Garrett, vice chairperson; Delgado, Mendoza, Miller, Soto, Yarbrough, Brady, spokesperson; Berns, Kurtz, Pankau, Parke, Wirsing.

COUNTIES AND TOWNSHIPS — Fowler, chairperson; Delgado, vice-chairperson; Collins, Forby, Franks, Hartke, Moffitt, spokesperson; Durkin, J. Jones, Lawfer, McAuliffe.

ELECTIONS AND CAMPAIGN REFORM — Boland, chairperson; Garrett, vice chairperson; Curry, McCarthy, Osterman, Slone, E. Lyons, spokesperson; Cross, Hoeft, Lindner, Winkel.

ELEMENTARY AND SECONDARY EDUCATION — Giles, chairperson; M. Davis, vice chairperson; Collins, Crotty, Delgado, Fowler, Garrett, Miller, Murphy, Osterman, Smith, Cowlishaw, spokesperson; Bassi, Hoeft, Johnson, Kosel, Krause, J. Mitchell, Moffitt, Mulligan, Winkel.

ENVIRONMENT AND ENERGY — Novak, chairperson; S. Davis, vice chairperson; Bradley, Brunsvold, Hartke, Holbrook, S. Jones, Reitz, Soto, Hassert, spokesperson; Beaubien, Durkin, Hultgren, Lawfer, Moore, Parke, Persico.

EXECUTIVE — Burke, chairperson; Bugielski, vice chairperson; Acevedo, Bradley, Capparelli, L. Jones, McKeon, Poe, spokesperson; Beaubien, Biggins, Hassert, Pankau, Rutherford.

FINANCIAL INSTITUTIONS — Bugielski , chairperson; Burke, vice chairperson; Capparelli, M. Davis, Giles, S. Jones, J. Lyons, Morrow, Novak, Schoenberg, Meyer, spokesperson; Biggins, Durkin, Hassert, Hultgren, O'Connor, Persico, Righter, Saviano, Zickus.

HEALTH CARE AVAILABILITY AND ACCESS — Flowers, chairperson; Kenner, vice chairperson; May, Miller, Ryan, Soto, Krause, spokesperson; Coulson, Klingler, Mulligan, Ryder.

HIGHER EDUCATION — Erwin, chairperson; Fowler, vice chairperson; M. Davis, Giles, Howard, Mendoza, Wirsing, spokesperson; Berns, Bost, Myers, Righter, Winkel.

HUMAN SERVICES — Feigenholtz, chairperson; Schoenberg, vice chairperson; Flowers, Howard, Soto, Bellock, spokesperson; Myers, Winters, Wirsing.

INSURANCE — Mautino, chairperson; Bradley, Brunsvold, Bugielski, Kenner, Stroger, Yarbrough, Parke, spokesperson; Brady, Hultgren, Osmond, Pankau,Winters.

JUDICIARY I - CIVIL LAW — Dart, chairperson; Brosnahan, Hamos, Hoffman, Lang, Scully, Klingler, Meyer, Osmond, Righter, Wait.

JUDICIARY II - CRIMINAL LAW — O'Brien, chairperson; Brosnahan, vice chairperson; Bradley, Brunsvold, Delgado, L. Jones, Smith, Winkel, spokesperson; Brady, Johnson, Lindner, Wait.

LABOR — Stroger, chairperson; McKeon, vice chairperson; Acevedo, Curry, Dart, M. Davis, Hoffman, Howard, S. Jones, Slone, Beaubien, spokesperson; Bellock, Hassert, Hultgren, Johnson, Moore, Parke, Persico.

MENTAL HEALTH AND PATIENT ABUSE — Lang, chairperson; Crotty, vice chairperson; Collins, Jefferson, McCarthy, Schmitz, spokesperson; Bellock, Cowlishaw, E. Lyons.

PERSONNEL AND PENSIONS — Murphy, chairperson; Stroger, vice chairperson; S. Davis, Granberg, Reitz, Smith, Hoeft, spokesperson; Beaubien, Durkin, Poe, Zickus.

PROPERTY TAX REFORM AND SCHOOL FUNDING — McKeon, co-chairperson; Hultgren, co-chairperson; Curry, Feigenholtz, Fritchey, Giles, Mautino, Scully, Biggins, Kurtz, Rutherford, Winkel, Winters, Wojcik.

PUBLIC UTILITIES — S. Jones, chairperson; Morrow, vice chairperson; M. Davis, S. Davis, L. Jones, Bost, spokesperson; Cowlishaw, Krause, Moore.

REGISTRATION AND REGULATION — Saviano, chairperson; Fritchey, vice chairperson; Boland, Bradley, Brunsvold, Bugielski, Burke, Crotty, S. Davis, Novak, Reitz, Zickus, spokesperson; Coulson, Klingler, Kosel, E. Lyons, B. Mitchell, Osmond, Stephens, Winters, Wojcik.

REVENUE — J. Lyons, chairperson; Kenner, vice chairperson; Currie, Granberg, McGuire, Turner, Moore, spokesperson; Beaubien, Biggins, E. Lyons, Pankau.

STATE GOVERNMENT ADMINISTRATION — Kenner, chairperson; Collins, vice chairperson; Franks, Forby, Fowler, O'Connor, spokesperson; Pankau, Righter, Wirsing.

THE DISABLED COMMUNITY — Brosnahan, chairperson; Feigenholtz, vice chairperson; Flowers, McCarthy, O'Brien, Ryan, Yarbrough, Krause, spokesperson; Hoeft, Kurtz, Schmitz, Sommer, Winkel.

TOURISM — Holbrook, chairperson; Erwin, vice chairperson; Mautino, May, McGuire, J. Jones, spokesperson; Bassi, Lawfer, Moffitt.

TRANSPORTATION AND MOTOR VEHICLES — Hoffman, chairperson; O'Brien, vice chairperson; Brosnahan, Collins, Fowler, Garrett, Hamos, Hartke, J. Lyons, Osterman, Reitz, Wait, spokesperson; Bassi, Black, J. Jones, Kosel, Mathias, McAuliffe, O'Connor, Schmitz, Zickus.

URBAN REVITALIZATION — Schoenberg, vice chairperson; Dart, Jefferson, McCarthy, Scully, Berns, spokesperson; Kurtz, Leitch, Saviano.

VETERANS' AFFAIRS — McAuliffe, chairperson; Holbrook, vice chairperson; Acevedo, Fritchey, Mautino, Novak, Sommer, spokesperson; Bost, Brady, J. Jones, Meyer.

OFFICERS OF THE HOUSE

Michael J. Madigan .... *Speaker*
Barbara Flynn Currie .... *Majority Leader*
Ralph C. Capparelli .... *Deputy Majority Leader*
Arthur L. Turner .... *Deputy Majority Leader*
Kurt M. Granberg .... *Assistant Majority Leader*
Gary Hannig .... *Assistant Majority Leader*
Joel Brunsvold .... *Assistant Majority Leader*
Lovana "Lou" Jones .... *Assistant Majority Leader*
Louis I. Lang .... *Assistant Majority Leader*
Charles A. Hartke .... *Assistant Majority Leader*
Edward Acevedo .... *Majority Conference Chairman*
Lee A. Daniels .... *Minority Leader*
Tom Ryder .... *Deputy Minority Leader*
Art Tenhouse .... *Deputy Minority Leader*
William B. Black .... *Assistant Minority Leader*
Tom Cross .... *Assistant Minority Leader*
David R. Leitch .... *Assistant Minority Leader*
Dan Rutherford .... *Assistant Minority Leader*
Ron Stephens .... *Assistant Minority Leader*
Kathleen L. "Kay" Wojcik .... *Assistant Minority Leader*
Patricia Reid Lindner .... *Minority Conference Chairwoman*
Anthony Devlin Rossi .... *Clerk of the House*
Bradley S. Bolin .... *Assistant Clerk of the House*
Lee A. Crawford .... *Chief Doorkeeper*

62

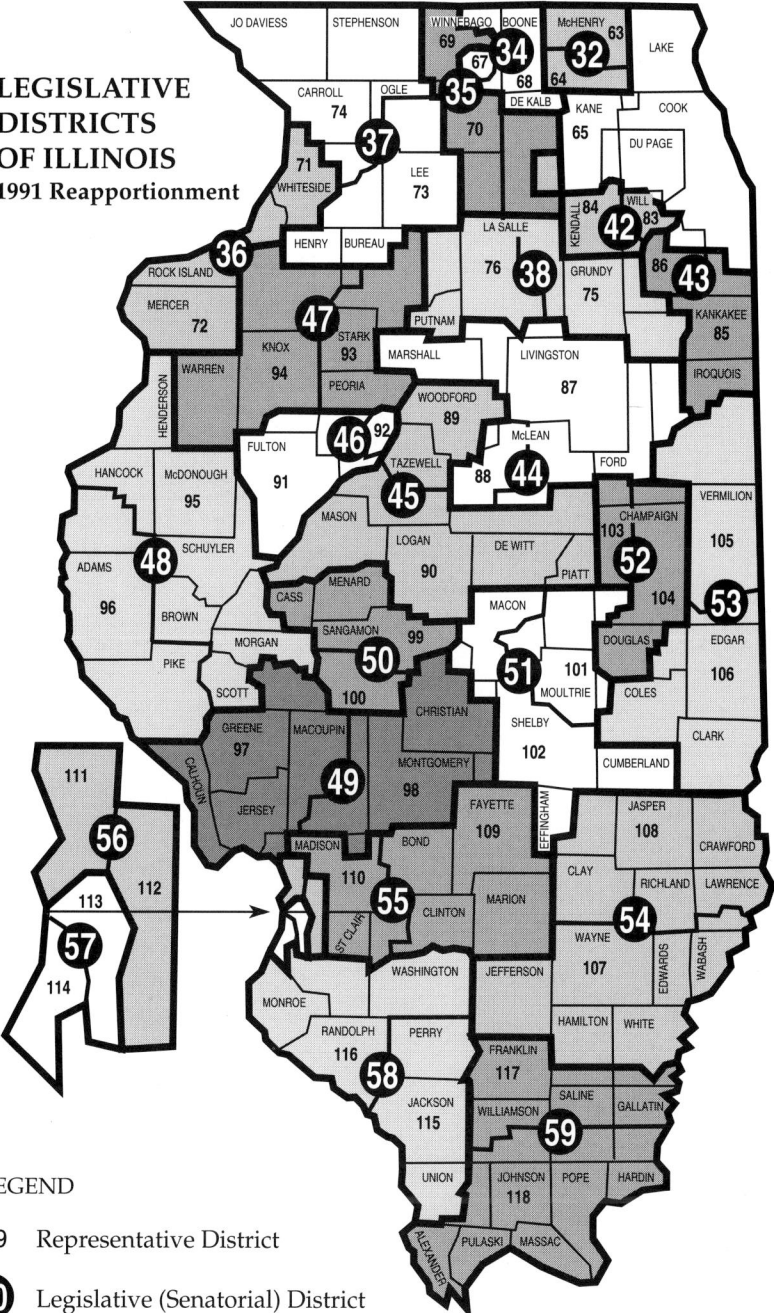

LEGISLATIVE DISTRICTS OF ILLINOIS
1991 Reapportionment

LEGEND

99 Representative District

50 Legislative (Senatorial) District

LEGISLATIVE DISTRICTS OF NORTHEASTERN ILLINOIS
1991 Reapportionment

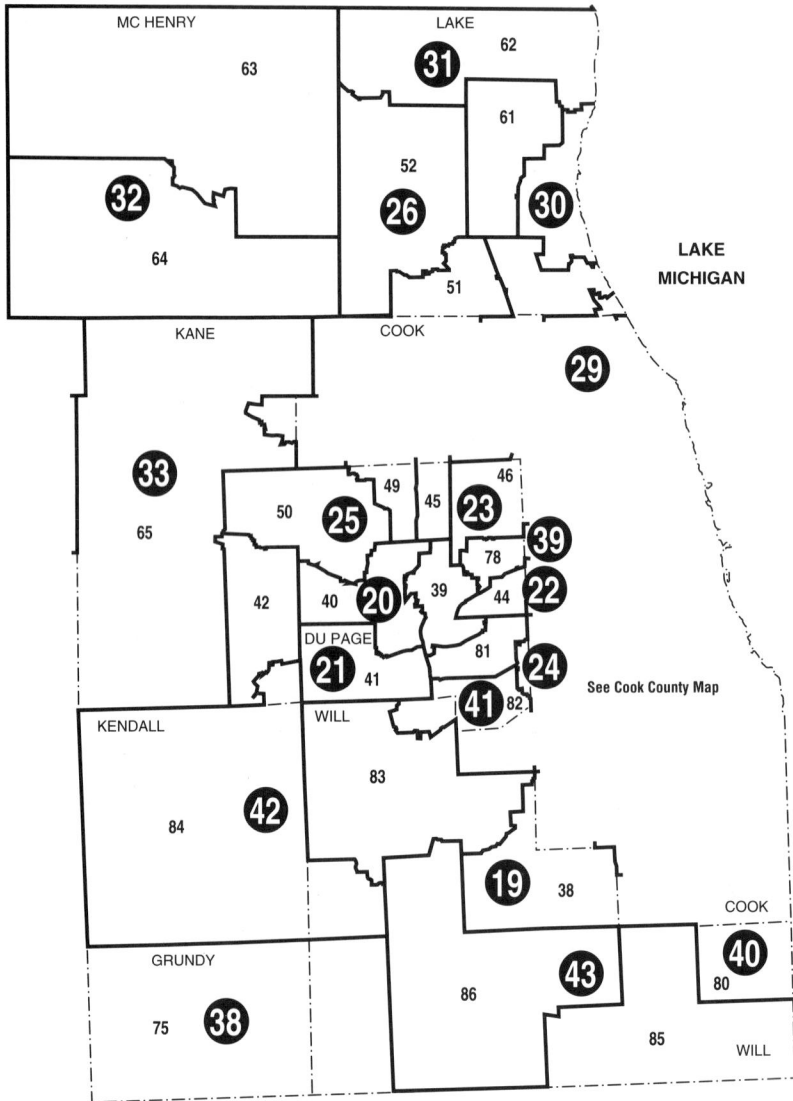

MC HENRY

63

LAKE

31 62

61

32

64

52

26

51

30

KANE

COOK

LAKE
MICHIGAN

29

33

65

50

49

25

45

23

46

78

39

42

40

20

39

44

22

DU PAGE

21 41

81

24

KENDALL

WILL

41 82

See Cook County Map

84

42

83

19 38

COOK

GRUNDY

43

40

80

75

38

86

85

WILL

LEGEND

--·-- County

86 Representative District

43 Legislative (Senatorial) District

64

LEGISLATIVE DISTRICTS OF COOK COUNTY
1991 Reapportionment

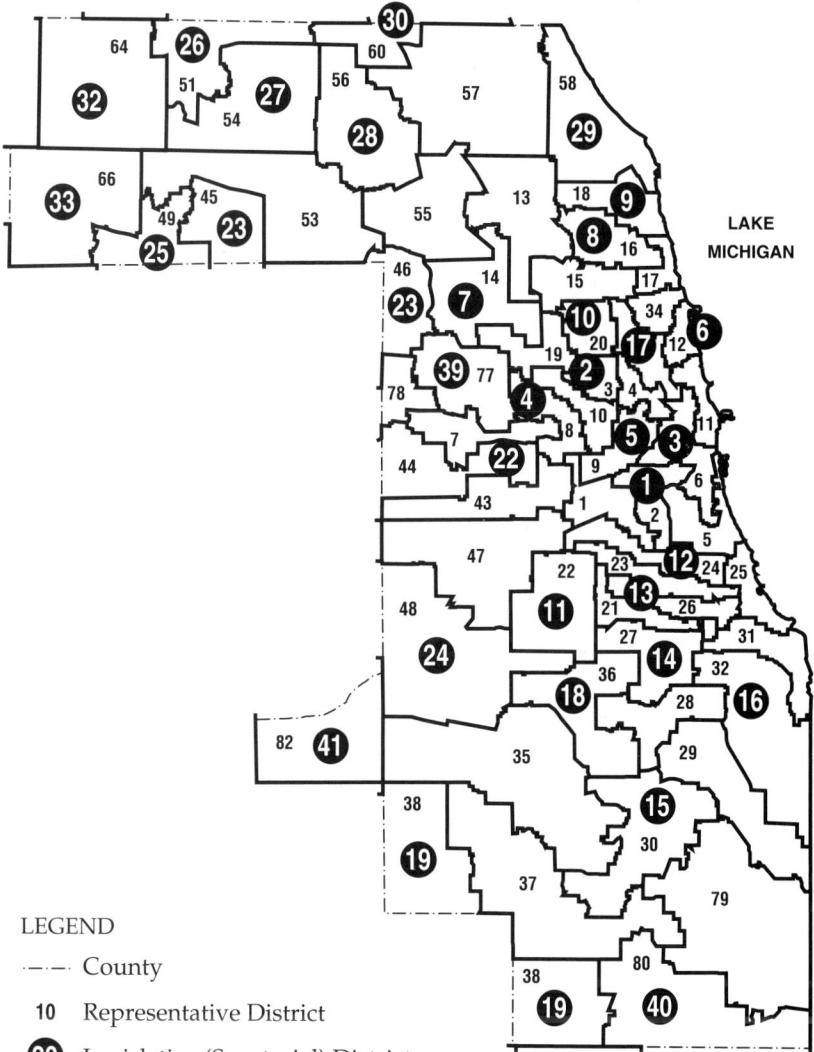

LAKE
MICHIGAN

LEGEND

—··— County

10   Representative District

20   Legislative (Senatorial) District

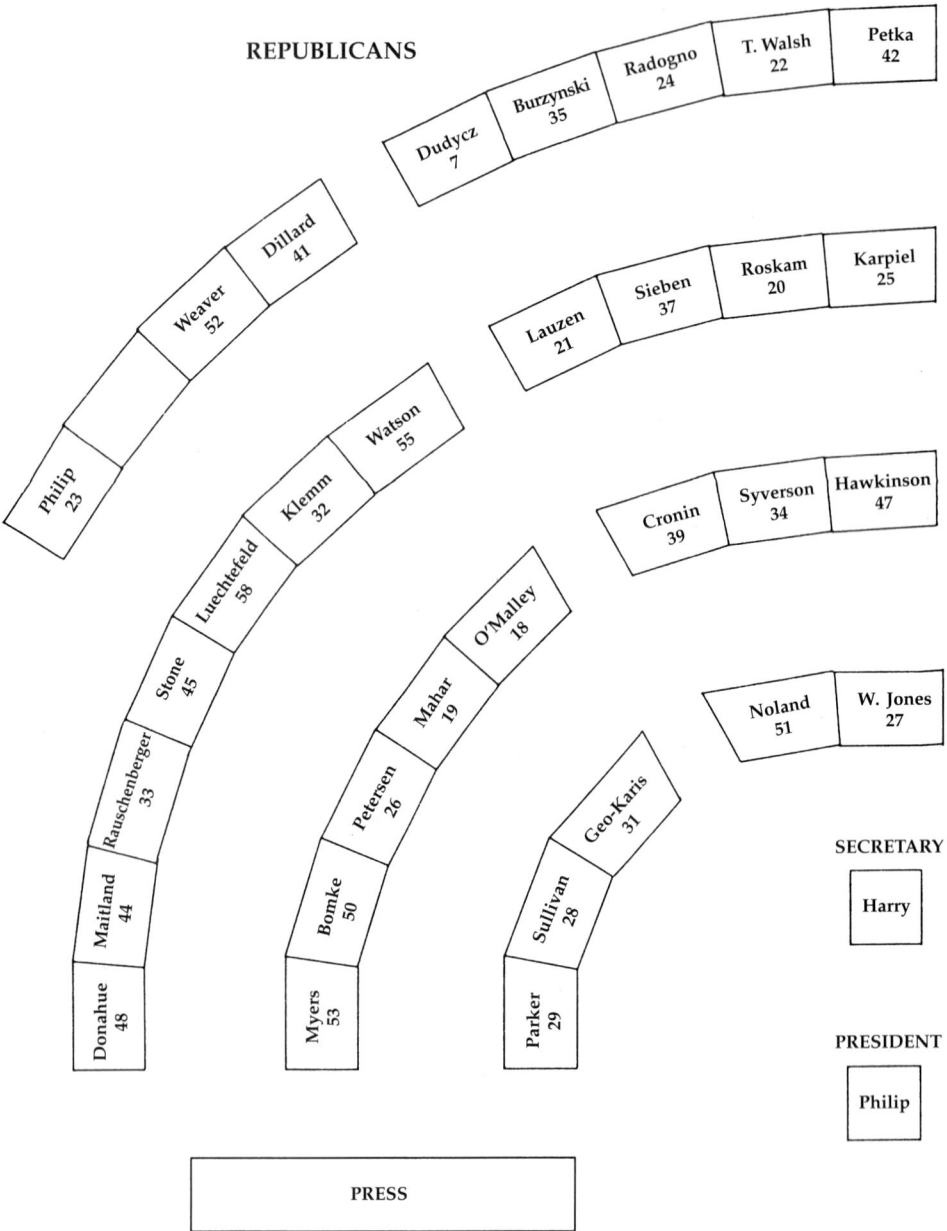

SENATE SEATING CHART

REPUBLICANS

Seat	Name	No.
	Petka	42
	T. Walsh	22
	Radogno	24
	Burzynski	35
	Dudycz	7

	Karpiel	25
	Roskam	20
	Sieben	37
	Lauzen	21

	Dillard	41
	Weaver	52
	Philip	23

	Hawkinson	47
	Syverson	34
	Cronin	39

	Watson	55
	Klemm	32
	Luechtefeld	58
	Stone	45
	Rauschenberger	33
	Maitland	44
	Donahue	48

	O'Malley	18
	Mahar	19
	Petersen	26
	Bomke	50
	Myers	53

	Geo-Karis	31
	Sullivan	28
	Parker	29

| | W. Jones | 27 |
| | Noland | 51 |

SECRETARY

Harry

PRESIDENT

Philip

PRESS

66

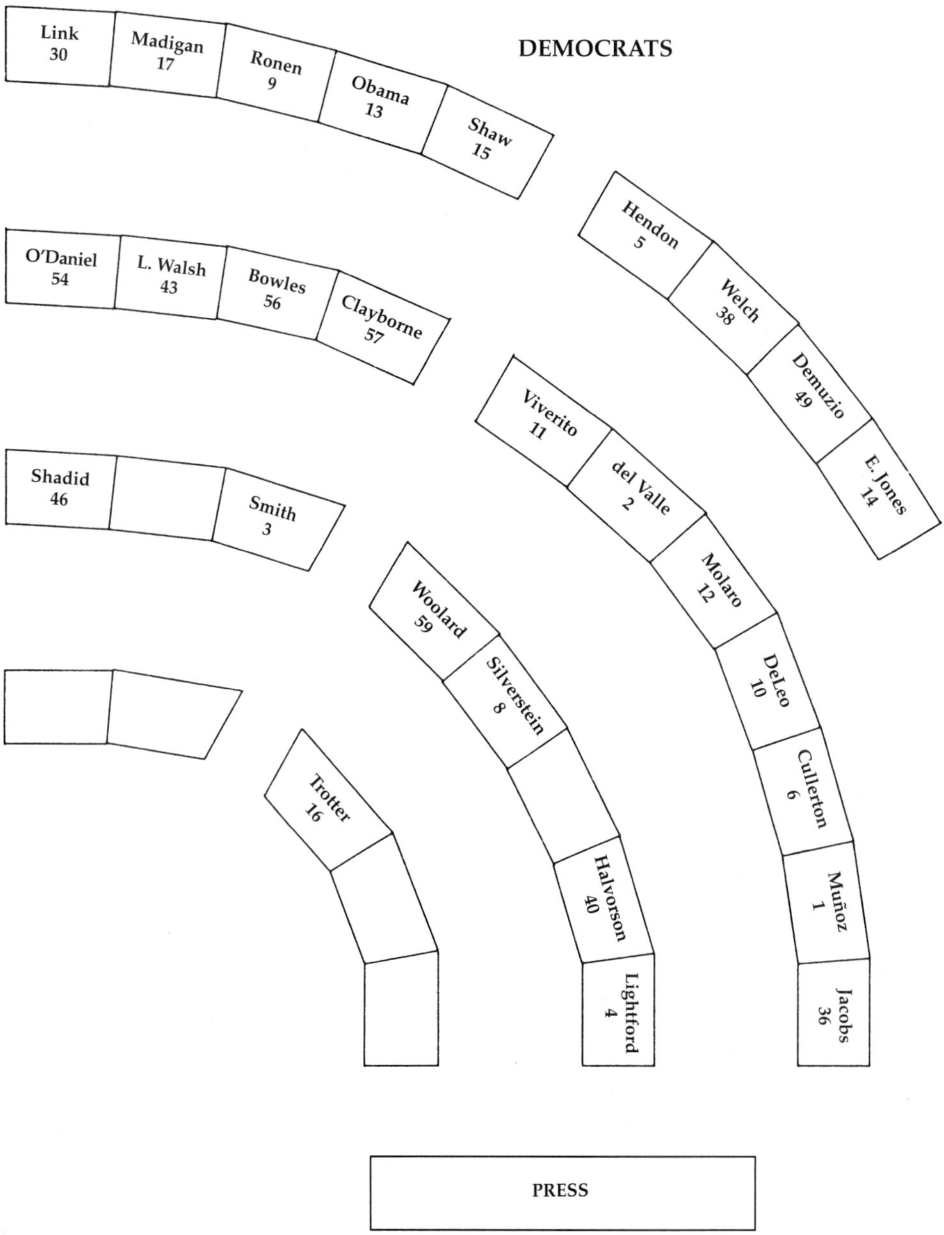

DEMOCRATS

Link
30

Madigan
17

Ronen
9

Obama
13

Shaw
15

Hendon
5

Welch
38

Demuzio
49

E. Jones
14

O'Daniel
54

L. Walsh
43

Bowles
56

Clayborne
57

Viverito
11

del Valle
2

Molaro
12

DeLeo
10

Shadid
46

Smith
3

Woolard
59

Silverstein
8

Culleton
6

Muñoz
1

Trotter
16

Halvorson
40

Lightford
4

Jacobs
36

PRESS

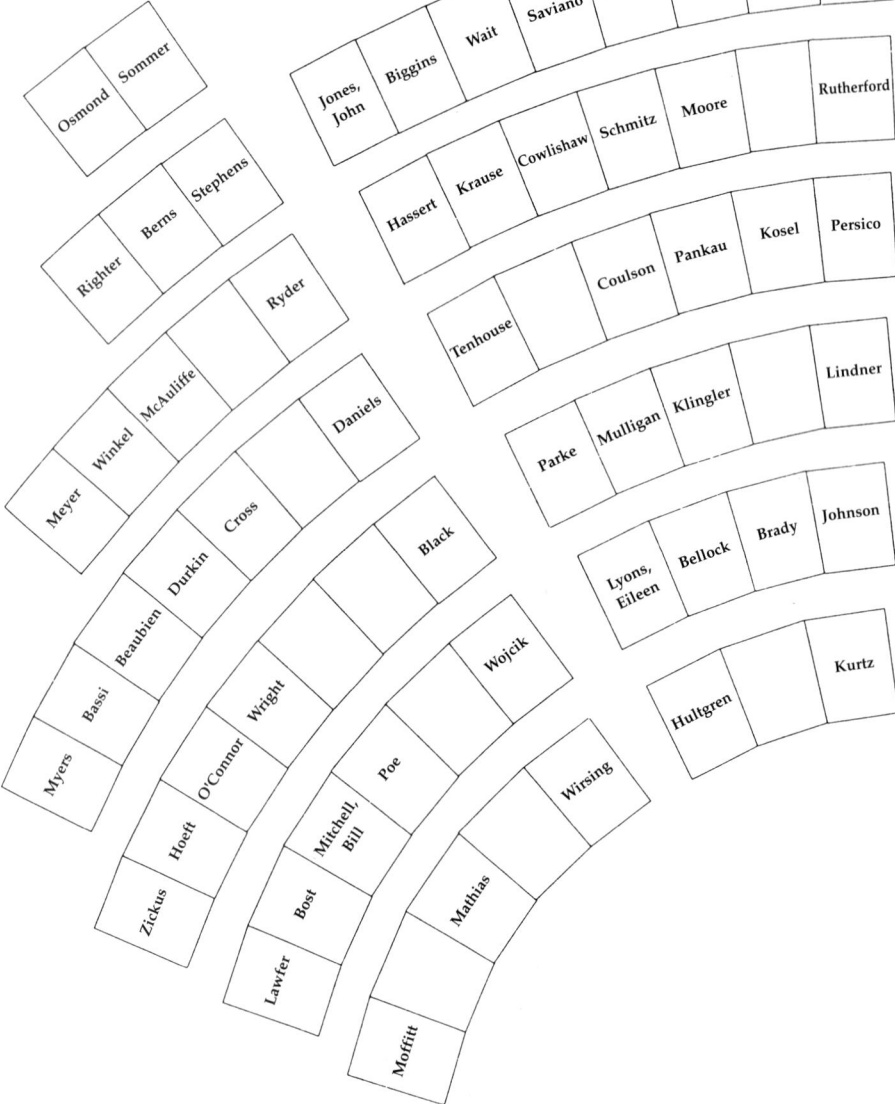

HOUSE SEATING CHART

Doorkeeper

REPUBLICANS

Osmond | Sommer

Righter | Berns | Stephens

Ryder

Meyer | Winkel | McAuliffe

Daniels

Bassi | Beaubien | Durkin | Cross

Black

Myers

Zickus | Hoeft | O'Connor | Wright

Lawfer | Bost | Mitchell, Bill | Poe

Moffitt

Mathias | Wirsing

Wojcik

Jones, John | Biggins | Wait | Saviano | Winters | Mitchell, Jerry | | Leitch

Hassert | Krause | Cowlishaw | Schmitz | Moore | | Rutherford

Tenhouse | Coulson | Pankau | Kosel | Persico

Parke | Mulligan | Klingler | | Lindner

Lyons, Eileen | Bellock | Brady | Johnson

Hultgren | Kurtz

PRESS

68

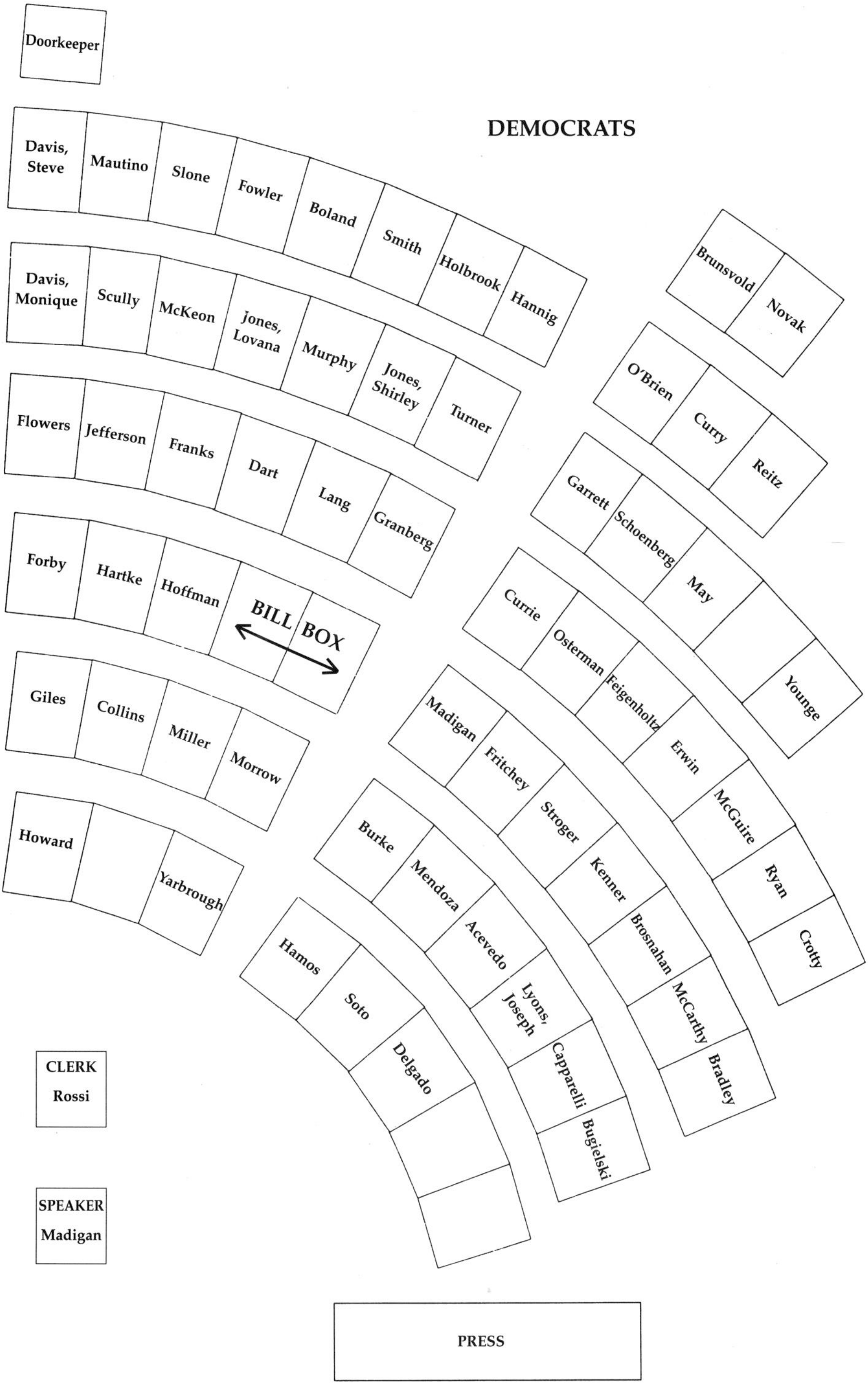

Doorkeeper

DEMOCRATS

Davis, Steve | Mautino | Slone | Fowler | Boland | Smith | Holbrook | Hannig

Brunsvold | Novak

Davis, Monique | Scully | McKeon | Jones, Lovana | Murphy | Jones, Shirley | Turner

O'Brien | Curry | Reitz

Flowers | Jefferson | Franks | Dart | Lang | Granberg

Garrett | Schoenberg | May

Forby | Hartke | Hoffman

BILL BOX

Currie | Osterman | Feigenholtz | Erwin

Younge

Giles | Collins | Miller | Morrow

Madigan | Fritchey | Stroger | Kenner | McGuire | Ryan | Crotty

Howard | Yarbrough

Burke | Mendoza | Acevedo | Lyons, Joseph | Brosnahan | McCarthy | Bradley

Hamos | Soto | Delgado | Capparelli | Bugielski

CLERK
Rossi

SPEAKER
Madigan

PRESS

69

NINETY-SECOND GENERAL ASSEMBLY

As a result of the 2000 General Election, the Senate is composed of 32 Republicans and 27 Democrats. The House includes 62 Democrats and 56 Republicans. Legislative rosters are provided as a quick reference to help you find your Senators and Representatives in the Blue Book. Legislators' photos, addresses, telephone numbers, legislative assignments and brief biographies are on the pages indicated.

Senators

Legislative Dist. Name and Page Number	Party	Legislative Dist. Name and Page Number	Party
50 Bomke, Larry K. (p. 121)	R	53 Myers, Judith A. (p. 124)	R
56 Bowles, Evelyn M. (p. 127)	D	51 Noland, N. Duane (p. 122)	R
35 Burzynski, J. Bradley (p. 106)`	R	13 Obama, Barack (p. 84)	D
57 Clayborne, James F., Jr. (p. 128)	D	54 O'Daniel, William L. (p. 125)	D
39 Cronin, Dan (p. 110)	R	18 O'Malley, Patrick J. (p. 89)	R
6 Cullerton, John J. (p. 77)	D	29 Parker, Kathleen K. (p. 100)	R
10 DeLeo, James A. (p. 81)	D	26 Peterson, William E. (p. 97)	R
2 del Valle, Miguel (p. 73)	D	42 Petka, Ed (p. 113)	R
49 Demuzio, Vince (p. 120)	D	23 Philip, James "Pate" (p. 94)	R
41 Dillard, Kirk W. (p. 112)	R	24 Radogno, Christine (p. 95)	R
48 Donahue, Laura Kent (p. 119)	R	33 Rauschenberger, Steven J. (p. 104)	R
7 Dudycz, Walter W. (p. 78)	R	9 Ronen, Carol (p. 80)	D
31 Geo-Karis, Adeline J. (p. 102)	R	20 Roskam, Peter J. (p. 91)	R
40 Halvorson, Debbie (p. 111)	D	46 Shadid, George P. (p. 117)	D
47 Hawkinson, Carl E. (p. 118)	R	15 Shaw, William "Bill" (p. 86)	D
5 Hendon, Rickey R. (p. 76)	D	37 Sieben, Todd (p. 108)	R
36 Jacobs, Denny (p. 107)	D	8 Silverstein, Ira I. (p. 79)	D
14 Jones, Emil, Jr. (p. 85)	D	3 Smith, Margaret (p. 74)	D
27 Jones, Wendell E. (p. 98)	R	45 Stone, Claude U., Jr. (p. 116)	D
25 Karpiel, Doris C. (p. 96)	R	28 Sullivan, Dave (p. 99)	R
32 Klemm, Dick (p. 103)	R	34 Syverson, Dave (p. 105)	R
21 Lauzen, Chris (p. 92)	R	16 Trotter, Donne E. (p. 87)	D
4 Lightford, Kimberly A. (p. 75)	D	11 Viverito, Louis S. (p. 82)	D
30 Link, Terry (p. 101)	D	43 Walsh, Lawrence M. "Larry" (p. 114)	D
58 Luechtefeld, David (p. 129)	R	22 Walsh, Thomas J. (p. 93)	R
17 Madigan, Lisa (p. 88)	D	55 Watson, Frank C. (p. 126)	R
19 Mahar, William F. (p. 90)	R	52 Weaver, Stanley B. (p. 123)	R
44 Maitland, John W., Jr. (p. 115)	R	38 Welch, Patrick D. (p. 109)	D
12 Molaro, Robert S. (p. 83)	D	59 Woolard, Larry D. (p. 130)	D
1 Munoz, Antonio "Tony" (p. 72)	D		

Representatives

Representative Dist. Name and Page Number	Party	Representative Dist. Name and Page Number	Party
2 Acevedo, Edward (p. 72)	D	57 Coulson, Elizabeth (p. 100)	R
54 Bassi, Suzanne "Suzie" (p. 98)	R	41 Cowlishaw, Mary Lou (p. 92)	R
52 Beaubien, Mark (p. 97)	R	84 Cross, Tom (p. 113)	R
81 Bellock, Patricia "Patti" (p. 112)	R	35 Crotty, Maggie (p. 89)	D
104 Berns, Thomas B. (p. 123)	R	25 Currie, Barbara Flynn (p. 84)	D
78 Biggins, Robert A. "Bob" (p. 110)	R	101 Curry, Julie A. (p. 122)	D
105 Black, William B. (p. 124)	R	46 Daniels, Lee A. (p. 94)	R
71 Boland, Mike (p. 107)	D	28 Dart, Thomas J. (p. 85)	D
115 Bost, Mike (p. 129)	R	27 Davis, Monique D. (p. 85)	D
20 Bradley, Richard T. (p. 81)	D	111 Davis, Steve (p. 127)	D
88 Brady, Dan (p. 115)	R	3 Delgado, William (p. 73)	D
36 Brosnahan, James D. (p. 89)	D	44 Durkin, James B. (p. 93)	R
72 Brunsvold, Joel (p. 107)	D	11 Erwin, Judy (p. 77)	D
19 Bugielski, Robert J. (p. 81)	D*	12 Feigenholtz, Sara (p. 77)	D
23 Burke, Daniel J. (p. 83)	D	21 Flowers, Mary E. (p. 82)	D
13 Capparelli, Ralph C. (p. 78)	D	117 Forby, Gary F. (p. 130)	D
10 Collins, Annazette R. (p. 76)	D	118 Fowler, James D. "Jim" (p. 130)	D

Representatives (Concluded)

Senator, 1st District
ANTONIO "TONY" MUÑOZ, D - Chicago
Springfield: M-103-E Capitol Bldg., 62706;
(217) 782-9415; Fax (217) 782-1631;
E-mail: munoz@senatedem.state.il.us
District: 2021 W. 35th St., Chicago 60609;
(773) 869-9050; Fax (773) 869-9046
Years served: 1999-present

Legislative assignments: Committees on Financial
Institutions; Public Health & Welfare; Transportation.

Biography: Chicago police officer; born Feb. 18, 1964, in
Chicago; married (wife, Pat), has three children.

Representative, 1st District
SUSANA MENDOZA, D - Chicago
Springfield: K-1 Stratton Bldg., 62706;
(217) 782-7752; Fax (217) 782-8917;
E-mail: repmendoza@aol.com
District: 2500 S. Millard, Chicago 60623;
(773) 277-7711; Fax (773) 277-6196
Years served: 2001-present

Legislative Assignments: Committees on Aging; Appropriations-Elementary & Secondary Education; Appropriations-Human Services; Consumer Protection; Higher
Education; Special Committee on Prosecutorial Misconduct.

Biography: Full-time state legislator; born in Chicago, raised in Bolingbrook; B.A., North-
east Missouri State University; served as coordinator of business outreach, Chicago Department of Planning & Development.

Representative, 2nd District
EDWARD ACEVEDO, D - Chicago
Majority Conference Chairman
Springfield: K-2 Stratton Bldg., 62706;
(217) 782-2855; Fax (217) 782-7762
District: 1939 S. Halsted, Chicago 60608; (312) 829-2555;
Fax (312) 850-2886
Years served: 1997-present

Legislative Assignments: Committees on Appropriations-
Elementary & Secondary Education; Conservation & Land
Use; Executive; Labor; Veterans' Affairs; Committee of the
Whole; Ex officio member of all House committees.

Biography: Chicago police officer; born July 23, 1963, in Chicago; educated Academy of
Cook County Sheriff's Department and Academy of Chicago Police Department; received
Award of Valor from the Sheriff's Department for saving the lives of residents trapped
in a fire; married (wife, Diana), has five children.

Senator, 2nd District
MIGUEL DEL VALLE, D - Chicago
Assistant Minority Leader

Springfield: 309-E Capitol Bldg., 62706;
(217) 782-5652; Fax (217) 782-3242;
E-mail: delvalle@senatedem.state.il.us
District: 4150 W. Armitage Ave., Chicago 60639;
(773) 292-0202; Fax (773) 292-1903
Years served: 1987-present

Legislative assignments: Committees on Appropriations;
Executive.

Biography: Full-time state legislator; born July 24, 1951,
in Puerto Rico; B.A., Spanish and M.A., guidance,
Northeastern Illinois University; married (wife, Lupe), has four children.

Representative, 3rd District
WILLIAM DELGADO, D - Chicago

Springfield: 2085-M Stratton Bldg., 62706;
(217) 782-0480; Fax (217) 557-9609
District: 4150 W. Armitage Ave., Chicago 60639;
(773) 292-0202; Fax (773) 292-1903
Years served: 1999-present

Legislative assignments: Committees on Counties &
Townships (vice chairperson); Appropriations-Elementary
& Secondary Education; Appropriations-Public Safety;
Consumer Protection; Elementary & Secondary
Education; Judiciary II-Criminal Law; Special Committee
on Prison Management Reform.

Biography: Full-time state legislator; born Oct. 31, 1956, in Newark, NJ; B.A., criminal
justice/sociology, Northeastern Illinois University; extensive history in community
involvement; served as statewide Hispanic liaison for former Attorney General Roland
Burris; was instrumental in "Gun Turn In Day" while at the Attorney General's office,
which led to the collection of 142 firearms in Chicago; served as Latino liaison for 1994
gubernatorial campaign of Dawn Clark Netsch; married (wife, Iris), has two children.

Representative, 4th District
CYNTHIA SOTO, D - Chicago

Springfield: 2084-M Stratton Bldg., 62706;
(217) 782-0480; Fax (217) 557-7210
District: 2615 W. Division St., Chicago 60622;
(773) 252-0402; Fax (773) 342-3860
Years served: 2001-present

Legislative assignments: Committees on Aging; Appropriations-Higher Education; Consumer Protection; Environment
& Energy; Health Care Availability & Access; Human Services; Special Committee on State Procurement.

Biography: Full-time state legislator; born July 8, 1962, in
San Antonio, TX; attended Harper College; paralegal; married (husband, David), has three children.

Senator, 3rd District
MARGARET SMITH, D - Chicago
Senate Minority Caucus Chair

Springfield: 103-B Capitol Bldg., 62706; (217) 782-5966;
E-mail: smith@senatedem.state.il.us
District: 2100 S. Indiana Ave., Ste. 306; Chicago 60616;
(312) 949-1908; Fax (312) 949-1958
Years served: 1981-83 (House); 1983-present (Senate)

Legislative assignments: Committees on Executive
Appointments; Public Health & Welfare; Legislative
Printing Unit; Legislative Space Needs Commission;
Intergovernmental Cooperation Commission.

Biography: Full-time state legislator; born in Chicago; educated at Tennessee State
University; member, board of trustees, Chicago Baptist Institute, where she received
honorary Doctor of Humanities degree; board member, Ada S. McKinley and Beatrice
Caffrey Youth Service Network; member, Sigma Gamma Rho Sorority, Inc.; Metropolitan
Business and Professional Women International.

Representative, 5th District
LOVANA "LOU" JONES, D - Chicago
Assistant Majority Leader

Springfield: 109 Capitol Bldg., 62706;
(217) 782-2023; Fax (217) 782-8569;
E-mail: lovanaj@aol.com
District: 435 E. 35th St., 1st Fl., Chicago 60616;
(773) 373-9400; Fax (773) 373-9787
Years served: 1987-present

Legislative assignments: Committees on Appropriations-
Public Safety; Executive; Judiciary II-Criminal Law; Public
Utilities; Special Committees on Prison Management
Reform; Prosecutorial Misconduct; Ex officio member of
all House committees; Legislative Space Needs Commission.

Biography: Full-time state legislator; born March 28, 1938, in Mansfield, OH; studies in
business administration, Ohio State University; has one child.

Representative, 6th District
SHIRLEY M. JONES, D - Chicago

Springfield: 2075-K Stratton Bldg., 62706;
(217) 782-5997
District: 47 W. Polk St., Ste. M-6, Chicago 60605;
(312) 786-1551; Fax (312) 786-2177
Years served: 1987-present

Legislative assignments: Committees on Public Utilities
(chairperson); Appropriations-Higher Education;
Environment & Energy; Financial Institutions; Labor &
Commerce; Special Committee on Electric Utility
Deregulation.

Biography: Full-time state legislator; attended George
Williams College; single, has two children.

Senator, 4th District
KIMBERLY A. LIGHTFORD, D - Maywood

Springfield: 311 Capitol Bldg., 62706;
(217) 782-8505; Fax (217) 782-3213;
E-mail: lightford@senatedem.state.il.us
District: 5943 W. Chicago Ave., Chicago 60651;
(773) 261-4400; Fax (773) 261-6844
Years served: Nov. 20, 1998-present

Legislative assignments: Committees on Financial Institutions (minority spokesperson); Education; Senate Black Caucus (chairperson); Commission on Intergovernmental Cooperation (co-chairperson).

Biography: Full-time state legislator & Village of Maywood Trustee; born May 10, 1968, in Chicago; B.A., public communications & human relations, Western Illinois University; master's in public administration, University of Illinois at Springfield.

Representative, 7th District
KAREN A. YARBROUGH, D - Maywood

Springfield: 2089-M Stratton Bldg., 62706;
(217) 782-8120; Fax (217) 782-1739;
E-mail: mikaylachg@aol.com
District: 1701 S. First Ave., Ste. 406, Maywood 60153;
(708) 615-1747; Fax (708) 615-1745
Years served: 2001-present

Legislative assignments: Committees on Appropriations-General Services; Computer Technology; Consumer Protection; Insurance; The Disabled Community.

Biography: Independent Agent, Owner/Operator, Real Estate Broker; born in Washington, DC; B.S., Chicago State University; M.A., Northeastern Illinois University; received Illinois Reaches Out award, Illinois State Chamber of Commerce; Unsung Heroine, Cook County Community Service award, Northeastern Illinois University; "I Care" award, United Way; married (husband, Henderson), has six children and five grandchildren.

Representative, 8th District
CALVIN L. GILES, D - Chicago

Springfield: 2090-M Stratton Bldg., 62706;
(217) 782-5962; Fax (217) 782-2779
District: 4909 W. Division St., Ste. LL12, Chicago 60651;
(773) 287-3804; Fax (773) 287-3805
Years served: 1993-present

Legislative Assignments: Committees on Elementary & Secondary Education (chairperson); Appropriations-Elementary & Secondary Education (vice chairperson); Aging; Appropriations-Human Services; Financial Institutions; Higher Education; Committee of the Whole; Special Committees on Property Tax Reform; Tobacco Settlement Proceeds.

Biography: Full-time state legislator; born July 10, 1962, in Chicago; B.A., management, Northeastern Illinois University; president, 37th Ward, Regular Democratic Organization; married.

Senator, 5th District
RICKEY R. HENDON, D - Chicago
Assistant Minority Leader

Springfield: 309-F Capitol Bldg., 62706; (217) 782-6252;
E-mail: hendon@senatedem.state.il.us
District: 3005 W. Madison, Chicago 60624;
(773) 265-8611; Fax (773) 265-8617
Years served: 1993-present

Legislative assignments: Committees on Commerce & Industry; Insurance & Pensions; State Government Operations; Economic & Fiscal Commission.

Biography: Full-time state legislator; born Dec. 8, 1953, in Cleveland, OH; 1st Class FCC License, Omega School of Communications (one-year trade school); past chair, Westside Black Elected Officials; married (wife, Dawn), has five children.

Representative, 9th District
ARTHUR L. TURNER, D - Chicago
Deputy Majority Leader

Springfield: 300 Capitol Bldg., 62706;
(217) 782-8116; Fax (217) 782-0888
District: 3849 W. Ogden Ave., Chicago 60623;
(773) 277-4700; Fax (773) 277-4703
Years served: 1981-present

Legislative assignments: Committees on Aviation; Revenue; Rules; Committee of the Whole; Special Committee on Conflicts of Interest; Ex officio member of all House committees.

Biography: Full-time state legislator; born Dec. 2, 1950, in Chicago; B.S., Illinois State University; M.S., Lewis University; married (wife, Rosalyn), has two children.

Representative, 10th District
ANNAZETTE R. COLLINS, D - Chicago

Springfield: 2102-N Stratton Bldg., 62706;
(217) 782-8077; Fax (217) 557-7643
District: 110 N. Pulaski Rd., Chicago 60624;
(773) 533-0010; Fax (773) 533-1971
Years served: Elected Nov. 7, 2000; Appointed Dec. 9, 2000

Legislative Assignments: Committees on State Government Administration (vice chairperson); Commerce & Business Development; Counties & Townships; Elementary & Secondary Education; Mental Health & Patient Abuse; Transportation & Motor Vehicles.

Biography: Full-time state legislator; born April 28, 1962, in Chicago; B.S., sociology, Chicago State University, 1984; M.S., criminal justice, Chicago State University, 1985; received National Association of Blacks in Criminal Justice 2001 Legislative award; HSI Youth Enhancement Services, Outstanding Service award; Academy of Scholastic Achievement Commitment to Education award; married (husband, Keith Langston), has one child.

Senator, 6th District
JOHN J. CULLERTON, D - Chicago

Springfield: 413 Capitol Bldg., 62706; (217) 782-7260;
  E-mail: statesencullerton@msn.com
District: 1051 W. Belmont Ave., Chicago 60657;
  (773) 883-0770; Fax (773) 296-0993
Years served: 1979-91 (House); 1991-present (Senate)

Legislative assignments: Committees on Judiciary
(minority spokesperson); Insurance & Pensions; Rules.

Biography: Attorney; born Oct. 28, 1948, in Chicago; B.A.,
political science, Loyola University; J.D., Loyola University
Law School; served in Illinois National Guard, 1970-76;
former Assistant Public Defender and instructor at
National Institute for Trial Advocacy; married (wife, Pamela Wilson), has five children.

Representative, 11th District
JUDY ERWIN, D - Chicago

Springfield: 2073-L Stratton Bldg., 62706;
  (217) 782-8404; Fax (217) 782-6592;
  E-mail: judy.erwin@nidus.com
District: 1520 N. Wells St., Chicago 60610;
  (312) 266-0340; Fax (312) 266-0699
Years served: 1992-present

Legislative assignments: Committees on Higher
Education (chairperson); Appropriations-Higher
Education (vice chairperson); Tourism (vice chairperson);
Aviation; Economic & Fiscal Commission.

Biography: Public relations executive; born March 7, 1950,
in Detroit, MI; B.S., education, University of Wisconsin-Whitewater; M.S., education,
National College of Education, Evanston; University of Illinois at Chicago, Ph.D., Public
Policy, currently enrolled.

Representative, 12th District
SARA FEIGENHOLTZ, D - Chicago

Springfield: 2107-N Stratton Bldg., 62706;
  (217) 782-8062; Fax (217) 557-7203;
  E-mail: staterep12@aol.com
District: 1051W. Belmont, Chicago 60657; (773) 296-4141;
  Fax (773) 296-0993
Years served: 1995-present

Legislative assignments: Committees on Human Services
(chairperson); Health Care Availability & Access (vice
chairperson); Appropriations-Human Services; State
Government Administration & Government Oversight;
Special Committee on Tobacco Settlement Proceeds (co-
chairperson); Legislative Research Unit (co-chair).

Biography: Full-time state legislator; born Dec. 11, 1956, in Chicago; B.A., political science,
speech and performing arts, Northeastern Illinois University; married (husband, Manny
Zelaya).

Senator, 7th District
WALTER W. DUDYCZ, R - Chicago
Assistant Majority Leader

Springfield: M-114 Capitol Bldg., 62706; (217) 782-3650;
E-mail: sen dudycz@aol.com
District: 6143 N. Northwest Hwy., Chicago 60631;
(773) 774-7717; Fax (773) 774-7877
Years served: 1985-present

Legislative assignments: Committees on Executive; Local
Government; Transportation; Rules; Legislative Space Needs
Commission.

Biography: Retired Chicago police detective; born March
11, 1950, in Chicago; served in U.S. Army, 1968-71; Vietnam
veteran; B.A., Northeastern Illinois University; married (wife, Oksana), has two
daughters, Valya and Nadya.

Representative, 13th District
RALPH C. CAPPARELLI, D - Chicago
Deputy Majority Leader

Springfield: 300 Capitol Bldg., 62706;
(217) 782-8198; Fax (217) 782-2906
District: 7452 N. Harlem Ave., Chicago 60631;
(773) 775-5775; Fax (773) 775-5773
Years served: 1971-present

Legislative assignments: Committee on Executive; Ex
officio member of all House committees.

Biography: Full-time state legislator; former school
teacher; B.A., education, Northern Illinois University;
served in U.S. Navy; has received numerous awards, including the Richard J. Daley
"Medal of Honor" and the "Golden Heart" award from Passionist Monastery; married
(wife, Cordelia); has two children and four grandchildren.

Representative, 14th District
MICHAEL P. McAULIFFE, R - Chicago

Springfield: 2115-N Stratton Bldg., 62706;
(217) 782-8182; Fax (217) 782-4553
District: 6650 N. Northwest Hwy., Chicago 60631;
(773) 792-0749; Fax (773) 792-1997
Years served: 1997-present

Legislative assignments: Committees on Veterans' Affairs
(chairperson); Appropriations-Public Safety; Counties &
Townships; Transportation & Motor Vehicles; Special Committees on Prison Management Reform; Prosecutorial Misconduct.

Biography: Full-time state legislator; born Dec. 7, 1963, in Chicago; single.

Senator, 8th District
IRA I. SILVERSTEIN, D - Chicago

Springfield: 105-D Capitol Bldg., 62706; (217) 782-5500;
E-mail: silverstein@senatedem.state.il.us
District: 6199 N. Lincoln Ave., Chicago 60659;
(773) 743-5015; Fax (773) 743-4750
Years served: 1999-present

Legislative assignments: Committees on Judiciary;
Licensed Activities; State Government Operations;
Legislative Reference Bureau.

Biography: Attorney; born Oct. 10, 1960, in Chicago; B.S.,
Loyola University; J.D., John Marshall Law School; past
president, Northtown Community Council; married (wife,
Debra), has four children.

Representative, 15th District
JOSEPH M. LYONS, D - Chicago

Springfield: 2035-J Stratton Bldg., 62706;
(217) 782-8400; Fax (217) 557-1934
District: 4404 W. Lawrence Ave., Chicago 60630;
(773) 286-1115; Fax (773) 736-2333
Years served: 1996-present

Legislative assignments: Committees on Revenue (chairperson); Aging; Appropriations-Public Safety; Financial
Institutions; Transportation & Motor Vehicles; Special Committee on Telecommunications Rewrite; Legislative Space
Needs Commission (co-chair).

Biography: Training/Education; born June 24, 1951, in
Chicago; bachelor's degree, political science/history, DePaul University, 1975; M.S.,
public administration, DePaul University, 1984; manager, Training and Education, Cook
County Department of Human Resources, 1983-present; married (wife, Kieran), has two
children, Ellie and Joey.

Representative, 16th District
LOUIS I. LANG, D - Skokie
Assistant Majority Leader

Springfield: 109 Capitol Bldg., 62706;
(217) 782-1252; Fax (217) 782-9903;
E-mail: reploulang@aol.com
District: 4350 W. Oakton, Skokie 60076; (847) 673-1131;
Fax (847) 982-0393
Years served: 1987-present

Legislative assignments: Committees on Mental Health
& Patient Abuse (chairperson); Computer Technology;
Judiciary I-Civil Law; Special Committee on Conflicts of
Interest (chairperson); Elder Abuse Task Force
(chairperson); Ex officio member of all House committees; House Democratic Floor
Leader.

Biography: Attorney; born Nov. 26, 1949, in Chicago; B.A., political science, University
of Illinois; J.D., DePaul University College of Law; married (wife, Teri), has five children.

Senator, 9th District
CAROL RONEN, D - Chicago

Springfield: 105-E Capitol Bldg., 62706; (217) 782-8492;
E-mail: carolronen@aol.com
District: 5533 N. Broadway, Chicago 60640;
(773) 769-1717; Fax (773) 769-6901
Years served: 1993-Jan. 2, 2000 (House); Appointed Jan.
2, 2000 (Senate); Elected Nov. 7, 2000 (Senate)

Legislative assignments: Committees on Environment &
Energy; Public Health & Welfare; Legislative Reference
Bureau; Legislative Research Unit.

Biography: Full-time state legislator; born March 28, 1945,
in Chicago; B.A., political science, Bradley University,
Peoria; M.A., public administration, Roosevelt University, Chicago; single.

Representative, 17th District
HARRY OSTERMAN, D - Chicago

Springfield: 2071-L Stratton Bldg., 62706;
(217) 782-8088; Fax (217) 782-6592;
E-mail: hjo17@aol.com
District: 5535 N. Broadway, Chicago 60640;
(773) 784-2002; Fax (773) 784-2060
Years served: Appointed Jan. 3, 2000; Elected Nov. 7,
2000

Legislative assignments: Committees on Appropriations-
Human Services (vice chairperson); Conservation & Land
Use; Election & Campaign Reform; Elementary &
Secondary Education; Transportation & Motor Vehicles;
Special Committee on Tobacco Settlement Proceeds.

Biography: Full-time state legislator; born April 14, 1967, in Chicago; attended Illinois
State University and Loyola University; single.

Representative, 18th District
JULIE HAMOS, D - Evanston

Springfield: 2098-M Stratton Bldg., 62706;
(217) 782-8052; Fax (217) 557-7204;
E-mail: julie@juliehamos.org
District: 1312 Chicago Ave., Evanston 60201;
(847) 424-9898; Fax (847) 424-9828
Years served: Dec. 31, 1998-present

Legislative assignments: Committees on Appropriations-
Human Services; Child Support Enforcement; Elections &
Campaign Reform; Judiciary I-Civil Law; Transportation
& Motor Vehicles; Special Committee on Tobacco
Settlement Proceeds; House Democratic Task Force on
Workforce Development (chair).

Biography: Attorney; born Jan. 29, 1949, in Budapest, Hungary; refugee during 1956
Hungarian Revolution; B.A., Washington University; J.D., George Washington University;
20 years experience in public policy advocacy; married to Judge Alan Greiman.

Senator, 10th District
JAMES A. DeLEO, D - Chicago

Springfield: 218 Capitol Bldg., 62706; (217) 782-1035;
E-mail: deleo@senatedem.state.il.us
District: 6839 W. Belmont, Chicago 60634;
(773) 237-2525; Fax (773) 237-7171
Years served: 1985-93 (House); 1993-present (Senate)

Legislative assignments: Committees on Executive
Appointments (co-chairperson); Licensed Activities.

Biography: Full-time state legislator; born Aug. 10, 1951,
in Chicago; attended Chicago Loop Junior College and
DePaul University; married (wife, Ann), has two children,
Jimmy and Alexa Marie.

Representative, 19th District
ROBERT J. BUGIELSKI, D - Chicago

Springfield: 2079-K Stratton Bldg., 62706; (217) 782-0017
District: 6839 W. Belmont Ave., Chicago 60634;
(773) 637-8770; Fax (773) 622-6250
Years served: 1987-present

Legislative assignments: Committees on Financial
Institutions (chairperson); Executive (vice chairperson);
Insurance; Registration & Regulation.

Biography: Systems analyst; born June 5, 1947, in Chicago;
B.S., business education, Chicago State University; former
high school administrator and teacher; received "Legislator
of the Year" award from American Legislative Exchange
Council (ALEC), 1991; married (wife, Dona).

Representative, 20th District
RICHARD T. BRADLEY, D - Chicago

Springfield: 2078-K Stratton Bldg., 62706;
(217) 782-8117; Fax (217) 558-6369
District: 3616 N. Pulaski, Chicago 60641; (773) 794-9444;
Fax (773) 794-9450
Years served: 1998-present

Legislative assignments: Committees on Environment &
Energy; Executive; Insurance; Judiciary II-Criminal Law;
Registration & Regulation; Committee of the Whole.

Biography: Assistant General Superintendent, City of
Chicago, Department of Streets & Sanitation; born May
18, 1955, in Chicago; B.A., political science, Concordia
Teachers College; member, Logan Square Lions Club, Pontage Park Chamber of
Commerce, Independence Park Library, Friends of the Library; married (wife, Cynthia),
has three children.

Senator, 11th District
LOUIS S. VIVERITO, D - Burbank
Assistant Minority Leader

Springfield: M-103-D Capitol Bldg., 62706;
(217) 782-0054;
E-mail: viverito@senatedem.state.il.us
District: 6215 W. 79th St., Ste. 1-A, Burbank 60459;
(708) 430-2510; Fax (708) 430-2610; 6500 S. Pulaski
Rd., Chicago 60629; (312) 581-8000
Years served: 1995-present

Legislative assignments: Committees on Executive Appointments; Insurance & Pensions; Legislative Information Service Commission.

Biography: Supervisor, Stickney Township; President, Stickney Township Public Health District; born in Chicago; Korean War Veteran; married (wife, Carolyn), has three children and five grandsons.

Representative, 21st District
MARY E. FLOWERS, D - Chicago

Springfield: 2048-J Stratton Bldg., 62706;
(217) 782-4207; Fax (217) 782-1130
District: 2539 W. 79th St., Chicago 60652; (773) 471-5200;
Fax (773) 471-1036
Years served: 1985-present

Legislative assignments: Committees on Health Care Availability & Access (chairperson); Children & Youth; Human Services; Special Committee on Tobacco Settlement Proceeds; Commission on Intergovernmental Cooperation.

Biography: Full-time state legislator; born July 31, 1951, in Inverness, MS; attended Kennedy King Community College; University of Illinois-Chicago Circle; received 1993 "Legislator of the Year" award from Illinois Alcoholism and Drug Dependence Association; married (husband, Daniel Coutee), has one daughter (Makeda).

Representative, 22nd District
MICHAEL J. MADIGAN, D - Chicago
Speaker of the House

Springfield: 300 Capitol Bldg., 62706;
(217) 782-5350; Fax (217) 524-1794
District: 6500 S. Pulaski Rd., Chicago 60629;
(773) 581-8000; Fax (773) 581-9414
Years served: 1971-present

Legislative assignments: Ex officio member of all House committees.

Biography: Attorney; born April 19, 1942, in Chicago; University of Notre Dame; Loyola University Law School; House Majority Leader, 80th and 81st General Assemblies; House Minority Leader, 82nd; Speaker of the House, 83rd, 84th, 85th, 86th, 87th and 88th; House Minority Leader, 89th; Speaker of the House, 90th, 91st and 92nd; married (wife, Shirley), has four children.

Senator, 12th District
ROBERT S. MOLARO, D - Chicago

Springfield: M-103-A Capitol Bldg., 62706;
(217) 782-5280; Fax (217) 782-1631;
E-mail: molaro@senatedem.state.il.us
District: 2650 W. 51st St., Chicago 60632;
(773) 436-1212; Fax (773) 767-1720
Years served: 1993-present

Legislative assignments: Committees on Executive
(minority spokesperson); Transportation; Pension Laws
Commission.

Biography: Attorney, born June 29, 1950, in Chicago;
graduated, St. Ignatius High School; B.S., business
administration, Loyola University; J.D., John Marshall Law School; married (wife,
Barbara), has five children.

Representative, 23rd District
DANIEL J. BURKE, D - Chicago

Springfield: 2034-J Stratton Bldg., 62706; (217) 782-1117;
E-mail: ilhouse@aol.com
District: 2650 W. 51st St., Chicago 60632; (773) 471-2299;
Fax (773) 471-1648
Years served: 1991-present

Legislative assignments: Committees on Executive (chairperson); Financial Institutions (vice chairperson);
Appropriations-General Services; Registration & Regulation; Legislative Reference Bureau.

Biography: Deputy City Clerk of Chicago; born Dec. 17,
1951, in Chicago; attended Loyola University and DePaul
University.

Representative, 24th District
HOWARD A. KENNER, D - Chicago

Springfield: 2101-N Stratton Bldg., 62706;
(217) 782-8197; Fax (217) 782-3220
District: 76 E. 61st St., Chicago 60637;
(773) 288-7144; Fax (773) 288-7150
Years served: 1995-present

Legislative Assignments: Committees on State Government Administration (chairperson); Health Care Availability & Access (vice chairperson); Revenue (vice chairperson);
Appropriations-General Services; Insurance.

Biography: CPA and state legislator; born Dec. 26, 1957,
in Chicago; B.S., accounting, University of Illinois, 1980;
CPA, Goodall, Kenner & Associates, Chicago; single.

Senator, 13th District
BARACK OBAMA, D - Chicago

Springfield: 105-B Capitol Bldg., 62706;
(217) 782-5338; Fax (217) 782-5340;
E-mail: senobama@aol.com
District: 1741 E. 71st St., Chicago 60649; (773) 363-1996;
Fax (773) 363-5099
Years served: 1997-present

Legislative assignments: Committees on Public Health & Welfare (minority spokesperson); Judiciary; Revenue; Joint Committee on Administrative Rules (co-chair).

Biography: Attorney; Senior Lecturer, University of Chicago Law School; born Aug. 4, 1961, in Hawaii; bachelor's degree, Columbia University, NY, 1983; graduate, Harvard Law School, Cambridge, MA, 1991; married (wife, Michelle), has two daughters, Malia Ann and Natasha.

Representative, 25th District
BARBARA FLYNN CURRIE, D - Chicago
House Majority Leader

Springfield: 300 Capitol Bldg., 62706;
217) 782-8121; Fax (217) 524-1794;
E-mail: repcurrie@earthlink.net
District: 1303 E. 53rd, Chicago 60615;
(773) 667-0550; Fax (773) 667-3010
Years served: 1979-present

Legislative assignments: Committees on Rules (chairperson); Revenue; Special Committee on Prosecutorial Misconduct; Ex officio member of all House committees.

Biography: Full-time state legislator; born May 3, 1940, in LaCrosse, WI; B.A., cum laude, University of Chicago; M.A., University of Chicago; married (husband, David), has two children and four grandchildren.

Representative, 26th District
CHARLES MORROW III, D - Chicago

Springfield: 2097-M Stratton Bldg., 62706;
(217) 782-1702; Fax (217) 782-9274;
E-mail: cmorrow26@aol.com
District: 68 E. 71st St., Chicago 60619;
(773) 224-1563; Fax (773) 224-3074
Years served: 1987-present

Legislative assignments: Committees on Appropriations-Public Safety (chairperson); Public Utilities (vice chairperson); Financial Institutions; Special Committees on Electric Utility Deregulation; State Procurement; Legislative Printing Unit (co-chair).

Biography: Full-time state legislator; born July 21, 1956, in Chicago, attended De LaSalle Institute; Illinois Institute of Technology; married (wife, Sherri), has three children.

84

Senator, 14th District
EMIL JONES, JR., D - Chicago
Senate Minority Leader

Springfield: 309-A Capitol Bldg., 62706;
   (217) 782-2728; Fax (217) 782-1967;
   E-mail: jones@senatedem.state.il.us
District: 507 W. 111th St., Chicago 60628;
   (773) 995-7748; Fax (773) 995-9061
Years served: 1973-83 (House); 1983-present (Senate)

Legislative assignments: Committee on Executive; Joint
Committee on Legislative Support Services.

Biography: Full-time state legislator; born Oct. 18, 1935,
in Chicago; A.A., Chicago Loop Junior College; attended Roosevelt University School
of Commerce; received honorary Doctor of Human Letters, Chicago State University;
strong advocate for funding public education and social justice in Illinois; he and his
late wife, Patricia, are parents of four children.

Representative, 27th District
MONIQUE D. DAVIS, D - Chicago

Springfield: 2040-J Stratton Bldg., 62706;
   (217) 782-0010; Fax (217) 782-1795
District: 1234 W. 95th St., Chicago 60643;
   (773) 445-9700; Fax (773) 445-5755
Years served: 1987-present

Legislative assignments: Committees on Appropriations-
Human Services (chairperson); Elementary & Secondary
Education (vice chairperson); Financial Institutions; Higher
Education; Labor & Commerce; Public Utilities; Special
Committee on Tobacco Settlement Proceeds.

   Biography: Educational administrator; born in Chicago;
B.S., elementary education; M.S., guidance and counseling; worked toward doctorate,
Roosevelt University; received "best legislator" award, 1998; listed in *Who's Who in African
American Biography,* 1988-93; has two children.

Representative, 28th District
THOMAS J. DART, D - Chicago

Springfield: 2068-L Stratton Bldg., 62706;
   (217) 782-8200; Fax (217) 525-1440
District: 3205 W. 111th St., Chicago 60655;
   (773) 881-3720; Fax (773) 881-9090
Years served: 1992-93 (Senate); 1993-present (House)

Legislative assignments: Committees on Judiciary I-Civil
Law (chairperson); Labor & Commerce; Urban
Revitalization; Special Committee on Prison Management
Reform (chairperson); Commission on Intergovernmental
Cooperation.

   Biography: Full-time state legislator; born May 22, 1962, in
Chicago; B.A., history and general social studies, Providence College, 1984; J.D., Loyola
University of Chicago School of Law, 1987; married (wife, Patricia).

Senator, 15th District
WILLIAM "BILL" SHAW, D - Chicago
Deputy Minority Caucus Whip

Springfield: 103-D Capitol Bldg., 62706;
 (217) 782-8066; Fax (217) 782-5252;
 E-mail: shaw@senatedem.state.il.us
District: 13 W. 144th St., Riverdale 60827;
 (708) 849-8800; Fax (708) 849-8811
Years served: 1983-93 (House); 1993-present (Senate)

Legislative assignments: Committees on Environment &
Energy; Licensed Activities; Local Government;
Legislative Reference Bureau (co-chair); Legislative
Research Unit.

Biography: Full-time state legislator; born July 31, 1937, in Fulton, AR; former assistant
to Alderman Ward and assistant director of Department of Support Services; married
(wife, Shirley), has three children.

Representative, 29th District
DAVID E. MILLER, D - Calumet City

Springfield: 2-M Stratton Bldg., 62706;
 (217) 782-8087; Fax (217) 558-6433;
 E-mail: repdavidmiller@aol.com
District: 1350 E. Sibley Blvd., Ste. 202, Dolton 60419;
 (708) 201-8000; Fax (708) 201-8200
Years served: 2001-present

Legislative assignments: Committees on Appropriations-
Human Services, Commerce & Business Development;
Consumer Protection; Elementary & Secondary Education;
Health Care Availability & Access.

Biography: Dentist; born Sept. 23, 1962, in Cleveland, OH;
B.S., biomedical engineering, Boston University, 1984; D.D.S., University of Illinois, 1988;
received BILLD (Bowhay Institute for Legislative Leadership Development) Fellowship,
2001; recipient of Illinois State Dental Society's William J. Greek Memorial Leadership
award, 1996; married (wife, Donna).

Representative, 30th District
HAROLD MURPHY, D - Markham

Springfield: 2046-J Stratton Bldg., 62706;
 (217) 782-5961; Fax (217) 557-2118
District: 2959 W. 159th St., P.O. Box 25, Markham 60426;
 (708) 339-8700; Fax (708) 339-8738
Years served: 1993-present

Legislative assignments: Committees on Personnel &
Pensions (chairperson); Appropriations-Elementary &
Secondary Education; Elementary & Secondary Education;
Environment & Energy; Public Utilities; Special
Committee on Prison Management Reform; Pension Laws
Commission (co-chair).

Biography: Full-time state legislator; born April 1, 1938, in Birmingham, AL; B.A.,
education, Northeastern Illinois University, Chicago; served in Army Reserves, eight
years; married (wife, Loretta), has three children.

Senator, 16th District
DONNE E. TROTTER, D - Chicago

Springfield: 417 Capitol Bldg., 62706; (217) 782-3201;
E-mail: trotter@senatedem.state.il.us
District: 8704 S. Constance, Ste. 324, Chicago 60617;
(773) 933-7715; Fax (773) 933-5498
Years served: 1988-93 (House); 1993-present (Senate)

Legislative assignments: Committees on Appropriations
(minority spokesperson); Revenue; Legislative Audit
Commission.

Biography: Public health administrator; born Jan. 30, 1950,
in Cairo, IL; B.A., Chicago State University; M.J., Loyola
University School of Law; married (wife, Rose), has four
children.

Representative, 31st District
TODD H. STROGER, D - Chicago

Springfield: 2093-M Stratton Bldg., 62706;
(217) 782-8272; Fax (217) 782-2404
District: 8539 S. Cottage Grove Ave., Chicago 60619;
(773) 783-8492; Fax (773) 783-8625
Years served: 1993-present

Legislative assignments: Committees on Labor
(chairperson); Appropriations-Public Safety; Computer
Technology; Insurance; Personnel & Pensions; Legislative
Reference Bureau.

Biography: Investment banker; born Jan. 14, 1963, in
Chicago; B.A., history, Xavier University, New Orleans,
LA; received Public Allies' "Certificate of Achievement for Outstanding Leadership"
award, 1993; married (wife, Jeanine), has one son.

Representative, 32nd District
CONSTANCE A. "CONNIE" HOWARD, D - Chicago

Springfield: 2094-M Stratton Bldg., 62706;
(217) 782-6476; Fax (217) 782-0952;
E-mail: choward32@worldnet.att.net/
District: 8949 S. Stony Island Ave., Chicago 60617;
(773) 356-6210; Fax (773) 356-6217
Years served: 1995-present

Legislative assignments: Committees on Computer
Technology (chairperson); Children & Youth (vice
chairperson); Appropriations-Higher Education; Higher
Education; Human Services; Labor; Special Committee
on Prosecutorial Misconduct; Legislative Research Unit.

Biography: Born Dec. 14, 1942, in Chicago; B.S. in liberal arts and M.S. in corrections
and criminal justice, Chicago State University; Democratic State Central
Committeewoman, First District, since 1984; alternate delegate, Democratic National
Convention, 1984 and 1988; married (husband, Phillip, Jr.), has one son and five
grandchildren.

Senator, 17th District
LISA MADIGAN, D - Chicago

Springfield: 105-C Capitol Bldg., 62706; (217) 782-8191;
Fax (217) 782-5340;
E-mail: lmadigan@senatedem.state.il.us
District: 2006 W. Addison, Chicago 60618;
(773) 477-1740; Fax (773) 477-2403;
E-mail: senatorlisa@ameritech.net
Years served: Dec. 10, 1998-present

Legislative assignments: Committees on Education
(minority spokesperson); Appropriations; Legislative
Information System.

Biography: Attorney; born July 30, 1966, in Chicago; B.A.,
government, Georgetown University; J.D., Loyola University, Chicago, School of Law;
former assistant dean, Adult/Continuing Education at Wright College; 1998 "Top 40
Under 40," *Crain's Chicago Business*; 1999 Fellow, Bowhay Institute for Legislative
Leadership Development; 1999 Fellow, Program for Emerging Political Leaders at the
Darden Graduate School of Business Administration, University of Virginia.

Representative, 33rd District
JOHN A. FRITCHEY, D - Chicago

Springfield: L-1 Stratton Bldg., 62706; (217) 782-2458;
Fax (217) 557-7214; E-mail: mystaterep@aol.com
District: 3649 N. Kedzie Ave., Chicago 60618;
(773) 583-3338; Fax (773) 478-8006
Years served: Dec. 30, 1996-present

Legislative assignments: Committees on Consumer Protection (chairperson); Registration & Regulation (vice chairperson); Appropriations-General Services; Property Tax
Reform & School Funding; Veterans' Affairs; Special Committee on Tobacco Settlement Proceeds (co-chairperson);
Legislative Printing Unit.

Biography: Attorney; born March 2, 1964, in Bossier City, LA; B.A., economics, University
of Michigan; J.D., Northwestern University; married, has one child.

Representative, 34th District
LARRY McKEON, D - Chicago

Springfield: 2076-K Stratton Bldg., 62706;
(217) 782-3835; Fax (217) 557-7650;
E-mail: lmckeon@larrymckeon.com
District: 1967 W. Montrose Ave., Chicago 60613;
(773) 348-3434; Fax (773) 348-3475
Years served: 1997-present

Legislative assignments: Committees on Property Tax Reform & School Funding (chairperson); Labor (vice chairperson); Appropriations-General Services; Executive;
Governor's Commission on Discrimination & Hate Crimes
(commissioner).

Biography: Full-time state legislator; born June 30, 1944, in Nampa, ID; B.A. and M.S.,
California State University at Los Angeles; Ph.D. coursework and exams, University of
Chicago; 1st Lieutenant, U.S. Army Infantry.

Senator, 18th District
PATRICK J. O'MALLEY, R - Palos Park
Springfield: 129 Capitol Bldg., 62706; (217) 782-5145
District: 12314 S. 86th Ave., Palos Park 60464;
(708) 923-1818; Fax (708) 671-1269
Years served: 1993-present

Legislative assignments: Committees on Financial Institutions (chairperson); Education (vice chairperson); Insurance & Pensions; Judiciary.

Biography: Attorney; born Oct. 22, 1950, in Evergreen Park; graduated, Marist High School; B.S., economics, and M.S., finance, Purdue University; J.D., The John Marshall Law School; member, Chicago, Illinois State and Southwest Bar Associations; Beta Gamma Sigma Honor Society; married (wife, Mary Judith), has two children.

Representative, 35th District
MAGGIE CROTTY, D - Oak Forest
Springfield: 2045-J Stratton Bldg., 62706;
(217) 782-9747; Fax (217) 782-6411
District: 16150 S. Cicero, Unit 11, Oak Forest 60452;
(708) 687-9696; Fax (708) 687-0308
Years served: 1997-present

Legislative assignments: Committees on Children & Youth (chairperson); Child Support Enforcement (vice chairperson); Constitutional Officers (vice chairperson); Appropriations-Higher Education; Elementary & Secondary Education; Registration & Regulation.

Biography: Full-time state legislator; born Oct. 16, 1948, in Chicago; graduated, Mercy High School; General Excellence Award, Illinois State Crime Commission, 2000; Legislator of the Year, Illinois Association of Park Districts, 2000; Friend of Taxpayers Award, National Taxpayers United of Illinois, 1999; Outstanding Freshman Legislator, Illinois Health Care Association, 1997; married (husband, Larry), has three children.

Representative, 36th District
JAMES D. BROSNAHAN,
D - Evergreen Park
Springfield: 2051-L Stratton Bldg., 62706; (217) 782-0515
District: 5311 W. 95th St., Oak Lawn 60453;
(708) 499-2810; Fax (708) 499-3991
Years served: 1997-present

Legislative assignments: Committees on The Disabled Community (chairperson); Judiciary II-Criminal Law (vice chairperson); Constitutional Officers; Judiciary I-Civil Law; Transportation & Motor Vehicles; Committee of the Whole.

Biography: Attorney; born July 5, 1963, in Evergreen Park; B.A., Loyola University of Chicago; J.D., Loyola University of Chicago Law School; member, Illinois State Bar Association; married (wife, Janet), has four children.

Senator, 19th District
WILLIAM F. MAHAR, R - Orland Park
Springfield: 121-A Capitol Bldg., 62706; (217) 782-9595;
  E-mail: williamfmahar@aol.com
District: 14700 Ravinia, Orland Park 60462;
  (708) 349-1400; Fax (708) 349-3818
Years served: 1985-present

Legislative assignments: Committees on Environment &
Energy (chairperson); Financial Institutions; Public Health &
Welfare; Legislative Research Unit.

Biography: Full-time state legislator; born Feb. 13, 1947, in
Chicago Heights; B.A., psychology, Southern Illinois University;
M.S., personnel services, Purdue University; served in U.S.
Army, 1970-72; trustee, Village of Homewood, 1979-85; married (wife, Elizabeth), has two sons.

Representative, 37th District
KEVIN A. McCARTHY, D - Orland Park
Springfield: 2032-J Stratton Bldg., 62706; (217) 782-3316;
  E-mail: kevmac37@att.net
District: 8951 W. 151st St., Orland Park 60462;
  (708) 226-1999; Fax (708) 226-9068
Years served: 1997-present

Legislative assignments: Committees on Child Support
Enforcement (chairperson); Cities & Villages (vice
chairperson); Elections & Campaign Reform; Mental
Health & Patient Abuse; The Disabled Community; Urban
Revitalization.

Biography: Senior Territory Manager; born Dec. 5, 1950, in
Chicago; B.A., Chicago State University, 1972; M.A., education administration & supervision,
DePaul University, 1976; U.S. Army Reserves, 1971-77; married (wife, Judy), has two children.

Representative, 38th District
RENÉE KOSEL, R - New Lenox
Springfield: 2139-O Stratton Bldg., 62706;
  (217) 782-0424; Fax (217) 557-7249
District: 19201 S. LaGrange Rd., Ste. 204-B, Mokena
  60448; (708) 479-4200; Fax (708) 479-7977
Years served: 1997-present

Legislative assignments: Committees on Constitutional
Officers (minority spokesperson); Appropriations-Higher
Education (vice spokesperson); Appropriations-General Ser-
vices; Elementary & Secondary Education; Registration &
Regulation; Transportation & Motor Vehicles.

Biography: Full-time state legislator; born April 3, 1943, in
Chicago; B.S., education, Western Illinois University, 1965; Lincoln-Way Foundation for
Educational Excellence, director, 1997-present; United Way Lincoln-Way Area Steering
Committee, 1997-present; New Lenox Rotary Club, 1998-present; New Lenox Lions Club, 1998-
present; Southstar Services, Inc., Advisory Council Member, 2000-present; Advocate Christ
Medical Center, Governing Council Member, 2000-present; American Legislative Exchange
Council, Education Task Force Member, 1999-present; Illinois Women in Government, 1998-
present; Women's Legislative Network, 1998-present; National Order of Women Legislators,
1998-present; Conference of Women Legislators, 1998-present; married (husband, Dr. Alfred),
has three adult children and one grandchild.

Senator, 20th District
PETER J. ROSKAM, R - Wheaton

Springfield: 121-B Capitol Bldg., 62706; (217) 782-8022;
   Fax (217) 782-9586;
   E-mail: peter@peterroskam.com
District: 500 Pennsylvania Ave., Glen Ellyn 60137;
   (630) 790-1709; Fax (630) 790-1726
Years served: 1993-1999 (House); 2000-present (Senate)

Legislative assignments: Committees on Education;
Judiciary; Revenue.

Biography: Attorney; born Sept. 13, 1961, in Hinsdale; B.A.,
University of Illinois, 1983; J.D., IIT Chicago-Kent College
of Law, 1989; Legislator of the Year award, Illinois State
Crime Commission; Leadership award, Illinois Family Institute; Humanitarian award,
Serenity House; married (wife, Elizabeth), has four children.

Representative, 39th District
VINCENT A. PERSICO, R - Glen Ellyn

Springfield: 2127-O Stratton Bldg., 62706;
   (217) 782-8037
District: 478 Pennsylvania Ave., Ste. 101, Glen Ellyn
   60137; (630) 858-0860; Fax (630) 858-0868
Years served: 1991-present

Legislative assignments: Committees on Aging; Environment & Energy; Financial Institutions; Labor; Special Committees on Electric Utility Deregulation (co-chairperson);
Telecommunications Rewrite.

Biography: Educator; born Dec. 9, 1948, in Oak Park; B.A.,
University of Illinois; M.A., Northern Illinois University;
has one child.

Representative, 40th District
RANDALL M. HULTGREN, R - Wheaton

Springfield: 2118-N Stratton Bldg., 62706;
   (217) 782-1653
District: 211 S. Wheaton Ave., Ste. 101, Wheaton 60187;
   (630) 221-0040; Fax (630) 221-9466
Years served: 1999-present

Legislative assignments: Committees on Property Tax Reform & School Funding (co-chairperson); Environment &
Energy; Financial Institutions; Insurance; Labor; Special
Committee on Telecommunications Rewrite (minority
spokesperson).

   Biography: Attorney; Law Offices of Randall Hultgren;
Vice President of Fortress Financial Management; born March 1, 1966, in Park Ridge;
B.A., Bethel College, St. Paul, MN (Magna Cum Laude); J.D., IIT Chicago-Kent College
of Law; married (wife, Christy), has two children, Karsten and Kylie.

Senator, 21st District
CHRIS LAUZEN, R - Aurora

Springfield: 613-B Capitol Bldg., 62706; (217) 782-0052;
Fax (217) 782-0116;
E-mail: admin@lauzen.com
District: 52 W. Downer Place, Ste. 201, Aurora 60506;
(630) 264-2334; Fax (630) 264-1566
Years served: 1993-present

Legislative assignments: Committees on Commerce &
Industry (chairperson); Revenue (vice chairperson);
Appropriations; Economic and Fiscal Commission;
Legislative Audit Commission.

Biography: Certified public accountant (CPA); owner,
Comprehensive Accounting Services, Geneva; B.S., cum laude, management science and
English, Duke University; MBA, Harvard Business School; elected delegate, 1996 White
House Conference on Small Business; member, Illinois Economic Development
Commission; married (wife, Sarah), has four children.

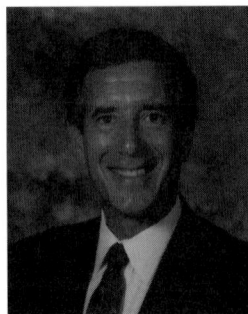

Representative, 41st District
MARY LOU COWLISHAW, R - Naperville

Springfield: 2016-H Stratton Bldg., 62706;
(217) 782-6507; Fax (217) 782-5257
District: 552 S. Washington St., Ste. 119, Naperville
60540; (630) 355-4113; Fax (630) 355-2847
Years served: 1983-present

Legislative assignments: Committees on Elementary &
Secondary Education (minority spokesperson); Aging;
Appropriations-Higher Education; Mental Health &
Patient Abuse; Public Utilities.

Biography: Full-time state legislator; born Feb. 20, 1932,
in Rockford; B.S., journalism, University of Illinois;
graduate studies, Northwestern University; numerous awards, including "Golden
Apple" award four times from Illinois Assn. of School Boards; namesake of Mary Lou
Cowlishaw Elementary School in Naperville; married (husband, Wayne), has three
children and eight grandchildren.

Representative, 42nd District
TIMOTHY L. SCHMITZ, R - Batavia

Springfield: 2109-N Stratton Bldg., 62706;
(217) 782-5457; E-mail: reptimschmitz@aol.com
District: 235 W. Wilson St., Batavia 60510;
(630) 879-6655; Fax (630) 879-3513
Years served: 1999-present

Legislative assignments: Committees on Mental Health
& Patient Abuse (minority spokesperson); Cities & Villages
(vice spokesperson); Appropriations-Public Safety;
Aviation; The Disabled Community; Transportation &
Motor Vehicles.

Biography: Paid, on-call firefighter with Batavia Fire
Department; born Sept. 26, 1965, in Geneva; B.A., public administration/political science,
Augustana College, 1988; married (wife, Julianne), has two sons, Alex and Ryan.

Senator, 22nd District
THOMAS J. WALSH, R - LaGrange Park

Springfield: 118 Capitol Bldg., 62706; (217) 782-2015;
Fax (217) 782-4079
District: 10544 W. Cermak Rd., Westchester 60154;
(708) 531-0390; Fax (708) 531-0467
Years served: 1993-94 (House); 1995-present (Senate)

Legislative assignments: Committees on Insurance & Pensions (chairperson); Financial Institutions; State Government Operations; Legislative Audit Commission (co-chairman).

Biography: Born July 4, 1960, in Chicago; B.A., business administration, Loras College, Dubuque, IA; former commissioner, Metropolitan Water Reclamation District of Greater Chicago, 1988-90.

Representative, 43rd District
WILLIAM A. O'CONNOR, R - Riverside

Springfield: 2136-O Stratton Bldg., 62706;
(217) 782-5821; Fax (217) 782-1275
District: 6825 W. Stanley Ave., Berwyn 60402;
(708) 442-0149; Fax (708) 442-0172
Years served: Appointed Aug. 9, 1998; Elected Nov. 3, 1998

Legislative assignments: Committees on State Government Administration (minority spokesperson); Computer Technology; Conservation & Land Use; Financial Institutions; Transportation & Motor Vehicles.

Biography: Attorney; born Nov. 17, 1949, in Chicago; A.B., English, Colgate University; J.D., IIT Chicago-Kent College of Law.

Representative, 44th District
JAMES B. DURKIN, R - Westchester

Springfield: 2003-G Stratton Bldg., 62706;
(217) 782-1061; Fax (217) 557-6394;
E-mail: durkinj@interaccess.com
District: 10544 W. Cermak Rd., Westchester 60154;
(708) 531-1444; Fax (708) 531-0467
Years served: 1995-present

Legislative assignments: Committees on Cities & Villages; Counties & Townships; Environment & Energy; Financial Institutions; Personnel & Pensions; Special Committee on Prosecutorial Misconduct (chairperson).

Biography: Attorney; born Jan. 28, 1961, in Chicago; B.S., criminal justice, Illinois State University; J.D., John Marshall Law School; former member, Triton Community College Board of Trustees; married (wife, Celeste).

Senator, 23rd District
JAMES "PATE" PHILIP, R - Wood Dale
President of the Senate

Springfield: 327 Capitol Bldg., 62706; (217) 782-3840
District: 50 E. Oak St., Ste. 250, Addison 60101;
(630) 941-0094; Fax (630) 832-2356
Years served: 1967-75 (House); 1975-present (Senate)

Legislative assignments: Committee on Executive.

Biography: Retired district sales manager, Pepperidge Farms, Inc.; born May 26, 1930, in Elmhurst; attended Kansas City Junior College; Kansas State College; chair, DuPage County Central Committee; former York Township Auditor; served in U.S. Marine Corps; "Statesman of the Year," International Union of Operating Engineers, Local 150, 1991; 33rd Degree Mason, Elmhurst Lodge 941, DuPage Shrine; B.P.O. Elks Lodge 1531; Loyal Order of Moose, Lodge 3; American Legion; married (wife, Nancy), has four children and five grandchildren.

Representative, 45th District
KATHLEEN L. "KAY" WOJCIK, R - Schaumburg
Assistant Minority Leader

Springfield: 628 Capitol Bldg., 62706; (217) 782-8192;
Fax (217) 782-1873; E-mail: kayw45@aol.com
District: 514 W. Wise Rd., Schaumburg 60193;
(847) 524-0461; Fax (847) 524-6938
Years served: 1983-present

Legislative assignments: Committees on Aviation (spokesperson); Property Tax Reform & School Funding; Registration & Regulation; Special Committee on Redistricting; Committee of the Whole; Ex officio member of all House committees; Commission on Intergovernmental Cooperation (co-chair).

Biography: Born in Chicago; educated, Chicago area; past director, Township Officials of Illinois; past president, Township Clerks of Illinois; member, Sarah's Grove Chapter DAR; owner/broker, Kay Nor Realty; married (husband, Norbert), has two children and five grandchildren.

Representative, 46th District
LEE A. DANIELS, R - Elmhurst
House Minority Leader

Springfield: 316 Capitol Bldg., 62706; (217) 782-4014;
Fax (217) 782-3234; E-mail: cyberelm@wwa.com
Web site: www.leedaniels.com
District: 611 N. York Rd., Elmhurst 60126;
(630) 530-2700; Fax (630) 279-8660
Years served: 1975-present

Legislative assignments: Ex officio member of all House committees; Legislative Information System.

Biography: Attorney; born April 15, 1942, in Lansing, MI; B.A., University of Iowa; J.D., John Marshall Law School; Majority Whip, 82nd General Assembly; Minority Leader, 83rd, 84th, 85th, 86th, 87th, 88th, 90th, 91st and 92nd; Speaker, 89th; former special assistant, Illinois Attorney General; married (wife, Pamela), has five children.

Senator, 24th District
CHRISTINE RADOGNO, R - LaGrange

Springfield: M-121 Capitol Bldg., 62706; (217) 782-9407;
Fax (217) 782-0650
District: 521 S. LaGrange Rd., Ste. 104, LaGrange 60525;
(708) 354-6700; Fax (708) 354-6730
Years served: 1997-present

Legislative assignments: Committees on Commerce & Industry (vice chairperson); Appropriations; Public Health & Welfare; Revenue; Legislative Reference Bureau.

Biography: Full-time state legislator; born Dec. 21, 1952, in Oak Park; B.A. and M.S.W. (master's in social work), Loyola University of Chicago; married (husband, Nunzio), has three children.

Representative, 47th District
EILEEN LYONS, R - Western Springs

Springfield: 2007-H Stratton Bldg., 62706;
(217) 782-0494; Fax (217) 557-7209;
E-mail: eileen@staterepeileenlyons.com
District: 1030 S. LaGrange Rd., Ste. 5, LaGrange 60525;
(708) 352-7700; Fax (708) 352-7702
Years served: 1995-present

Legislative assignments: Committees on Elections & Campaign Reform (minority spokesperson); Child Support Enforcement (vice spokesperson); Registration & Regulation (vice spokesperson); Mental Health & Patient Abuse; Revenue.

Biography: Full-time state legislator; born July 3, 1941, in New York City; B.A., English, Elmhurst College; married (husband, Arthur), has four children.

Representative, 48th District
ANNE ZICKUS, R - Palos Hills

Springfield: G-4 Stratton Bldg., 62706; (217) 782-8017;
Fax (217) 782-6053; E-mail: azickus48@aol.com
District: 10600 S. Roberts Rd., Palos Hills 60465;
(708) 974-8080; Fax (708) 974-8083
Years served: 1989-91; 1993-present

Legislative assignments: Committees on Registration & Regulation (minority spokesperson); Commerce & Business Development; Financial Institutions; Personnel & Pensions; Transportation & Motor Vehicles; Legislative Audit Commission; Long Term Care Funding Task Force.

Biography: Real Estate Broker; born April 6, 1939; Republican Committeeman, Palos Township; former alderman, City of Palos Hills; past president, South/Southwest Association of Realtors; executive board, Women in Government; director, Metropolitan Family Services Southwest; director, Helping Hand Rehabilitation Center, Countryside; numerous outstanding achievement awards; married (husband, Charles), has two children and three grandchildren.

Senator, 25th District
DORIS C. KARPIEL, R - Carol Stream
Majority Caucus Chair

Springfield: 123 Capitol Bldg., 62706; (217) 782-5572
District: 400 W. Lake St., Ste. 220, Roselle 60172;
(630) 894-2008; Fax (630) 894-2871
Years served: 1979-84 (House); 1984-present (Senate)

Legislative assignments: Committees on Appropriations;
Environment & Energy; Executive.

Biography: Full-time state legislator; B.A., political
science, Northern Illinois University; former township
supervisor of Bloomingdale Township, DuPage County;
Wayne Township Chairman; has four children and five
grandchildren.

Representative, 49th District
CAROLE PANKAU, R - Roselle

Springfield: 2122-O Stratton Bldg., 62706;
(217) 782-8158; Fax (217) 782-1336;
E-mail: carole@pankau.org
District: 1278-B W. Lake St., Roselle 60172;
(630) 582-0390; Fax (630) 582-0391
Years served: 1993-present

Legislative assignments: Committees on Appropriations-
Public Safety (minority spokesperson); Consumer Protection (vice spokesperson); State Government Administration
(vice spokesperson); Executive; Insurance; Revenue.

Biography: Full-time state legislator; born Aug. 13, 1947,
in Valparaiso, IN; B.S., accounting (honors graduate), University of Illinois; former
member, DuPage County Board, eight years; married (husband, John), has four children.

Representative, 50th District
THOMAS L. JOHNSON, R - West Chicago

Springfield: G-3 Stratton Bldg., 62706; (217) 782-1565;
Fax (217) 782-6053; E-mail: repjohnson@aol.com
District: 27 W. 031 North Ave., West Chicago 60185;
(630) 231-0340; Fax (630) 231-0464
Years served: 1993-present

Legislative assignments: Committees on Appropriations-
Elementary & Secondary Education; Appropriations-Public
Safety; Elementary & Secondary Education; Judiciary II-
Criminal Law; Labor; Special Committee on Prison
Management Reform (co-chairperson).

Biography: Attorney; born April 30, 1945, in Oakland, CA;
B.A., University of Michigan; J.D., DePaul University; U.S. Army (Vietnam); married
(wife, Virginia), has three children.

Senator, 26th District
WILLIAM E. PETERSON, R - Long Grove

Springfield: 307 Capitol Bldg., 62706; (217) 782-8010
District: 3050 N. Main St., Prairie View 60069;
(847) 634-6060; Fax (847) 634-1569
Years served: 1983-93 (House); 1993-present (Senate)

Legislative assignments: Committees on Revenue (chairperson); Executive Appointments; Insurance & Pensions; Commission on Intergovernmental Cooperation.

Biography: Full-time state legislator; born in Chicago; B.A., North Park College; M.S., education, Northern Illinois University; post-graduate studies, Loyola University; former school teacher and principal; served in U.S. Army; married (wife, Patricia Giuffre), has three grown children and five grandchildren.

Representative, 51st District
SIDNEY H. MATHIAS, R - Buffalo Grove

Springfield: 2124-O Stratton Bldg., 62706;
(217) 782-1664; Fax (217) 782-1275;
E-mail: sidneymath@email.msn.com
District: 4256 N. Arlington Heights Rd., Ste. 104,
Arlington Heights 60004; (847) 222-0061;
Fax (847) 222-0062
Years served: 1999-present

Legislative assignments: Committees on Cities & Villages (minority spokesperson); Computer Technology (vice spokesperson); Appropriations-General Services; Constitutional Officers; Transportation & Motor Vehicles; Special Committee on Prosecutorial Misconduct.

Biography: Practicing attorney, 30 years; offices in Arlington Heights; born Nov. 9, 1946; graduate, Roosevelt University and DePaul University College of Law; resident of Buffalo Grove since 1979; married (wife, Rita), has two sons, Elliot and Scott.

Representative, 52nd District
MARK BEAUBIEN, R - Barrington Hills

Springfield: 2001-G Stratton Bldg., 62706;
(217) 782-1517; Fax (217) 782-3189;
E-mail: strepmbeaubien@aol.com
District: 124-A E. Liberty St., Wauconda 60084;
(847) 487-5252; Fax (847) 487-0956
Years served: 1996-present

Legislative assignments: Committees on Labor (minority spokesperson); Aviation (vice spokesperson); Revenue (vice spokesperson); Environment & Energy; Executive; Personnel & Pensions.

Biography: Full-time state legislator; born Oct. 30, 1942, in Waukegan; B.A., Northwestern University, Evanston, 1964; J.D., Northwestern University, 1967; married (wife, Dee), has two sons, Mark and Bob.

Senator, 27th District
WENDELL E. JONES, R - Palatine

Springfield: 611-C Capitol Bldg., 62706; (217) 782-4471;
E-mail: senwjones@aol.com
District: 110 W. Northwest Hwy., Palatine 60067;
(847) 776-1490; Fax (847) 776-1494
Years served: Nov. 21, 1998-present

Legislative assignments: Committees on Financial
Institutions (vice chairperson); Local Government;
Revenue; Legislative Space Needs Commission.

Biography: President & owner of WENCO, Inc.,
advertising specialties, Palatine; born Nov. 4, 1937; B.S.,
speech & hearing therapy, and M.S., special education, Ball State University; 30 graduate
hours, education administration, Northern Illinois University; married (wife, Jane), has
three children and one grandchild.

Representative, 53rd District
TERRY R. PARKE, R - Hoffman Estates

Springfield: 2002-G Stratton Bldg., 62706;
(217) 782-0347; Fax (217) 782-3189;
E-mail: trparke@ameritech.net
District: 837 W. Higgins Rd., Schaumburg 60195;
(847) 882-0270; Fax (847) 884-6885
Years served: 1985-present

Legislative assignments: Committees on Insurance (minor-
ity spokesperson); Labor (vice spokesperson); Computer
Technology; Conservation & Land Use; Consumer Protec-
tion; Environment & Energy; Economic & Fiscal
Commission (co-chair); Employee Suggestion Award Board;
Secretary of State's Business Corporation Acts Committee.

Biography: Insurance agent; born Feb. 21, 1944, in Pittsfield; B.S., education, Southern Illinois
University; served in U.S. Army; President, Executive Committee, National Conference of
Insurance Legislators; married (wife, Joanne), has two children, Kelli and Tiffany.

Representative, 54th District
SUZANNE "SUZIE" BASSI, R - Palatine

Springfield: 2015-H Stratton Bldg., 62706;
(217) 782-8026; Fax (217) 782-4553;
E-mail: repbassi@aol.com
District 110 W. Northwest Hwy., Palatine 60067;
(847) 776-1880
Years served: 1999-present

Legislative assignments: Committees on Child Support
Enforcement (minority spokesperson); Appropriations-
Human Services; Constitutional Officers; Elementary &
Secondary Education; Tourism; Transportation & Motor
Vehicles; Committee of the Whole.

Biography: Full-time state legislator; B.A., Rosary College (now Dominican University),
River Forest; M.A.T., University of Illinois at Urbana-Champaign; former high school
teacher; former school board member; married (husband, Roger), has one daughter,
Carrie, and two sons, Steve and Greg.

Senator, 28th District
DAVE SULLIVAN, R - Mount Prospect

Springfield: M-108 Capitol Bldg., 62706; (217) 782-3875;
E-mail: senatordavesullivan@msn.com
District: 800 E. Northwest Hwy., Ste. 102, Mount
Prospect 60056; (847) 670-0280; Fax (847) 670-0291
Years served: Dec. 28, 1998-present

Legislative assignments: Committees on Environment &
Energy (vice chairperson); Public Health & Welfare; Licensed Activities; State Government Operations;
Subcommittee on Telecommunications Rewrite (chairperson); High Technology Task Force.

Biography: Business consultant; born Dec. 29, 1964, in
Hinsdale; B.A., political science, Marquette University, Milwaukee, WI; former Executive Assistant for Intergovernmental Affairs to Secretary of State George Ryan (1992-98);
member, Board of Directors, Lattof YMCA; member, Park Ridge Jaycees and Kiwanis;
married (wife, Dru), has two daughters and two sons.

Representative, 55th District
ROSEMARY MULLIGAN, R - Des Plaines

Springfield: 2133-O Stratton Bldg., 62706;
(217) 782-8007; E-mail: repmulligan@usa.net
District: 932 Lee St., Ste. 201, Des Plaines 60016;
(847) 297-6533; Fax (847) 297-2978
Years served: 1993-present

Legislative assignments: Committees on Appropriations-Human Services (minority spokesperson); Commerce & Business
Development; Elementary & Secondary Education; Health Care
Availability & Access; Legislative Research Unit.

Biography: Paralegal; born July 8, 1941, in Chicago; undergraduate studies, Illinois State University; A.A.S., legal technology, Harper College,
Palatine, 1982; Flemming Fellow Leadership Institute (Center for Policy Alternatives),
1995; received Illinois Community College Trustees Association's Distinguished Alumni
Award, 1993; single, has two children.

Representative, 56th District
CAROLYN H. KRAUSE, R - Mt. Prospect

Springfield: 2004-G Stratton Bldg., 62706;
(217) 782-3739; Fax (217) 557-7208;
E-mail: repkrause@aol.com
District: 111 E. Busse Ave., Ste. 605, Mount Prospect
60056; (847) 255-3100; Fax (847) 255-3184
Years served: 1993-present

Legislative assignments: Committees on Health Care Availability & Access (minority spokesperson); The Disabled
Community (minority spokesperson); Elementary & Secondary Education; Public Utilities; Special Committees on
Tobacco Settlement Proceeds; Telecommunications Rewrite.

Biography: Attorney; born Oct. 20, 1938, in Milwaukee, WI; B.A., University of Wisconsin,
Madison; J.D. with honors, IIT Chicago-Kent College of Law; former mayor, Village of
Mount Prospect, 1977-89; member, Chicago and Illinois State Bar Associations; married
(husband, David).

Senator, 29th District
KATHLEEN K. PARKER, R - Northbrook

Springfield: M-118 Capitol Bldg., 62706;
(217) 782-2119; Fax (217) 782-0650;
E-mail: senkathyparker@worldnet.att.net
District: 191 Waukegan Rd., Ste. 200, Northfield 60093;
(847) 441-0077; Fax (847) 441-0322
Years served: 1995-present

Legislative assignments: Committees on Transportation (chairperson); Public Health & Welfare (vice chairperson); Commerce & Industry; Mental Health Evaluation Task Force (chairperson); Legislative Printing Unit.

Biography: Full-time state legislator; born in Pittsburgh, PA; B.A., University of Miami, FL; married (husband, Keith), has two children.

Representative, 57th District
ELIZABETH COULSON, R - Glenview

Springfield: 2131-O Stratton Bldg., 62706;
(217) 782-4194; E-mail: coulson@earthlink.net
Web site: www.netpad.com/coulson/
District: 3801 W. Lake Ave., Glenview 60025;
(847) 724-3233; Fax (847) 724-8682
Years served: 1997-present

Legislative assignments: Committees on Aging (minority spokesperson); Appropriations-Human Services (vice spokesperson); Appropriations-Elementary & Secondary Education; Health Care Availability & Access; Registration & Regulation; Special Committee on Tobacco Settlement Proceeds; Commission on Intergovernmental Cooperation.

Biography: Licensed physical therapist; born Sept. 8, 1954, in Hastings, NE; B.S., education, Wellesley College and University of Kansas; M.B.A., Keller Graduate School of Management, 1985; P.T., Northwestern Medical School; Ph.D. candidate, health policy and administration, University of Illinois; associate professor, Chicago Medical School, 1981-96; chairman, Department of Physical Therapy, 1994-96; part-time faculty, 1997 to present; married (husband, William).

Representative, 58th District
JEFFREY M. SCHOENBERG, D - Evanston

Springfield: 2031-J Stratton Bldg., 62706; (217) 782-0490;
E-mail: jschoenberg@earthlink.net
Web site: www.jschoenberg.org
District: 1000 Skokie Blvd., Ste. 150, Wilmette 60091;
(847) 853-0130; Fax (847) 853-0135
Years served: 1991-present

Legislative assignments: Committees on Appropriations-General Services (chairperson); Human Services (vice chairperson); Urban Revitalization (vice chairperson); Financial Institutions; Special Committees on State Procurement (chairperson); Tobacco Settlement Proceeds; Economic & Fiscal Commission.

Biography: State legislator and private giving consultant; born July 28, 1959, in Chicago; attended Rutgers University and completed joint degree program (B.A.) at Jewish Theological Seminary and Columbia University; former Illinois director, Roosevelt Center for American Policy Studies; married (wife, Lynne Sered), has two children.

Senator, 30th District
TERRY LINK, D - Vernon Hills

Springfield: 105-A Capitol Bldg., 62706; (217) 782-8181;
Fax (217) 782-5340; E-mail: senator@link30.org
District: 425 Sheridan Rd., Highwood 60040;
(847) 266-1997; Fax (847) 266-1920
Years served: 1997-present

Legislative assignments: Committees on State Government Operations (minority spokesperson); Financial Institutions; Local Government; Legislative Space Needs Commission.

Biography: Past partner, Lake County industrial equipment business; born March 20, 1947, in Waukegan; attended Stout State University; married (wife, Susan McCall Link), has four children.

Representative, 59th District
SUSAN GARRETT, D - Lake Forest

Springfield: 2098-M Stratton Bldg., 62706;
(217) 782-6400; Fax (217) 557-7204;
E-mail: susan@garrett98.com
District: 100 N. Waukegan Rd., Ste. 108, Lake Bluff
60044; (847) 482-1999; Fax (847) 482-0674;
228 N. Genesee St., Waukegan 60085; (847) 782-9547
Years served: 1999-present

Legislative assignments: Committees on Elections & Campaign Reform (vice chairperson); Aging; Appropriations-General Services; Elementary & Secondary Education; Transportation & Motor Vehicles; Special Committee on Tobacco Settlement Proceeds.

Biography: Full-time state legislator; born Feb. 11, 1950, in Lake Forest; B.A., political science, Lake Forest College, 1992; founded Susan Garrett Marketing Associates in 1979, specializing in creative marketing campaigns for Chicago-area companies; married (husband, Scott), has two children, Brett and Elizabeth.

Representative, 60th District
KAREN MAY, D - Highland Park

Springfield: 2072-L Stratton Bldg., 62706;
(217) 782-0902; Fax (217) 782-6535;
E-mail: karenmay60@aol.com
District: 400 Lake Cook Rd., Ste. 110, Deerfield 60015;
(847) 948-0060; Fax (847) 948-0656
Years served: 2001-present

Legislative assignments: Committees on Appropriations-General Services; Children & Youth; Cities & Villages; Conservation & Land Use; Health Care Availability & Access; Tourism; Special Committee on Telecommunications Rewrite; chairperson, Smart Growth Task Force & Wetlands Task Force.

Biography: President, Karen May Communications; born Aug. 2, 1944, in Worden; B.S., communications, University of Illinois, Urbana; married (husband, Morton), has two children.

Senator, 31st District
ADELINE J. GEO-KARIS, R - Zion
Assistant Majority Leader

Springfield: 323 Capitol Bldg., 62706; (217) 782-7353;
Fax (217) 782-7818
District: 2610 Sheridan Rd., Ste. 213, P.O. Box 248,
Zion 60099; (847) 872-7500; Fax (847) 872-3131
Years served: 1973-79 (House); 1979-present (Senate)

Legislative assignments: Committees on Executive
Appointments; Financial Institutions; Judiciary; Senate
Operations Commission; NCSL Assembly on State Issues.

Biography: Attorney; born March 29, 1918, in Tegeas,
Greece; Northwestern University; LL.B., DePaul
University College of Law; Lt. Commander, U.S.N.R. (ret), with top secret clearance;
former justice of the peace and assistant state's attorney, Lake County; former Mayor of
Zion.

Representative, 61st District
ANDREA S. MOORE, R - Libertyville

Springfield: 2014-H Stratton Bldg., 62706;
(217) 782-3696; E-mail: andreamoore61st@aol.com
District: 131 E. Park Ave., Ste. B-1, Libertyville 60048;
(847) 549-1133; Fax (847) 549-0051
Years served: 1993-present

Legislative assignments: Committees on Revenue
(minority spokesperson); Cities & Villages; Environment
& Energy; Labor; Public Utilities; Special Committee on
Telecommunications Rewrite; Illinois Smart Growth Task
Force.

Biography: Full-time state legislator; born Sept. 2, 1944,
in Libertyville; attended Drake University, Des Moines, IA; has two children.

Representative, 62nd District
TIMOTHY H. OSMOND, R - Antioch

Springfield: 2129-O Stratton Bldg., 62706;
(217) 782-8151; Fax (217) 557-7207
District: 976 Hillside Ave., Antioch 60002;
(847) 838-6200; Fax (847) 395-9277
Years served: 1999-present

Legislative assignments: Committees on Commerce & Business Development (minority spokesperson); Aviation; Insurance; Judiciary I-Civil Law; Registration & Regulation;
Special Committee on Prosecutorial Misconduct (minority
spokesperson).

Biography: Owner, Osmond Insurance Service, Ltd.;
director, State Bank of the Lakes; born Jan. 12, 1949, in Sycamore; B.A., business, Western
Illinois University, 1971; certified insurance counselor, 1981; Antioch Township
Supervisor, 1997 to 1999; Antioch Township Trustee, 1989 to 1997; Community Service
award, Antioch Rotary Club, 1998; alternate delegate, Republican National Convention,
1992; married (wife, JoAnn), has two children, Colleen and Michael.

Senator, 32nd District
DICK KLEMM, R - Crystal Lake

Springfield: 124 Capitol Bldg., 62706; (217) 782-8000;
Fax (217) 782-4079
District: 3 W. Crystal Lake Ave., Crystal Lake 60014;
(815) 455-6330; Fax (815) 455-8284
Years served: 1981-93 (House); 1993-present (Senate)

Legislative assignments: Committees on Executive (chair-person); Local Government; Transportation; Legislative Printing Unit (co-chair).

Biography: President, Food Warming Equipment Company, Inc.; born in Chicago; bachelor's degree, engineering and industrial economics, Purdue University; served in U.S. Army and Air Force Reserves; former Township Official, School Board President and McHenry County Board chair; married (wife, Nancy), has seven children.

Representative, 63rd District
JACK D. FRANKS, D - Woodstock

Springfield: 2108-N Stratton Bldg., 62706;
(217) 782-1717; Fax (217) 557-7203; E-mail:
jack@jackfranks.org; Web site: www.jackfranks.org
District: 180 S. Eastwood Dr., Woodstock 60098;
(815) 334-0063; Fax (815) 334-9147; 3505 W. Elm,
McHenry 60050; (815) 344-6363; Fax (815) 344-5987
Years served: 1999-present

Legislative assignments: Committees on Aging (vice chair-person); Appropriations-Public Safety; State Government Administration; House Task Force on Higher Education.

Biography: Attorney, partner in law firm of Franks, Gerkin & McKenna; born Oct. 2, 1963, in Belvidere; B.A., international relations & political science, University of Wisconsin, 1985; law degree, American University, Washington College of Law, 1989; married (wife, Debby), has two sons, Sam, 6 and Henry, 4.

Representative, 64th District
ROSEMARY KURTZ, R - Crystal Lake

Springfield: 2112-N Stratton Bldg., 62706;
(217) 782-0432; Fax (217) 782-1275;
E-mail: rkurtz@mc.net
District: 460 Coventry Ln., Ste. 204,
Crystal Lake 60014-6201;
(815) 356-0064; Fax (815) 356-5013
Years served: 2001-present

Legislative assignments: Committees on State Procurement (minority spokesperson); Appropriations-Human Services; Consumer Protection; Property Tax Reform & School Funding; The Disabled Community; Urban Revitalization.

Biography: Full-time state legislator; born in Richmond, IN; B.A., University of Oklahoma; M.A., University of Kansas; completed course work toward Ph.D. at the University of Iowa; former educator (25 years), college and secondary levels; Treasurer, City of Crystal Lake (four years); board member, Crystal Lake Zoning Board of Appeals (20 years); board member, McHenry County Family Services and Mental Health Clinic; past president, Crystal Lake/Cary League of Women Voters; has received numerous awards; widow, has three children and three grandchildren.

Senator, 33rd District
STEVEN J. RAUSCHENBERGER, R - Elgin

Springfield: 615-A Capitol Bldg., 62706; (217) 782-7746
District: 1112 South St., Elgin 60123; (847) 622-1049;
  Fax (847) 622-0948
Years served: 1992-present

Legislative assignments: Committees on Appropriations
(chairperson); Environment & Energy; Revenue; Joint
Committee on Administrative Rules; Economic & Fiscal
Commission.

Biography: Born Aug. 29, 1956, in Elgin; B.B.A., College
of William and Mary; married (wife, Betty), has two
children.

Representative, 65th District
PATRICIA REID LINDNER, R - Aurora
Minority Conference Chairman

Springfield: 630 Capitol Bldg., 62706; (217) 782-1486;
  Fax (217) 782-1873
District: 32 Main St., Ste. A, Sugar Grove 60554;
  (630) 466-9791; Fax (630) 466-7124
Years served: 1993-present

Legislative assignments: Committees on Appropriations-
General Services; Children & Youth; Judiciary II-Criminal
Law; Mental Health & Patient Abuse; Ex officio member
of all House committees.

Biography: Family law attorney; born Nov. 29, 1939, in Aurora; B.S., Northwestern
University; M.S., University of Colorado; J.D., Northern Illinois University; law offices
of Patricia Reid Lindner, 1986-present; member, Kane County and Illinois State Bar
Associations; married (husband, George Philip), has four children.

Representative, 66th District
DOUGLAS L. HOEFT, R - Elgin

Springfield: 2136-O Stratton Bldg., 62706; (217) 782-8020;
  E-mail: danderson@dhoeft.com
District: 1112 South St., Elgin 60123; (847) 622-1048;
  Fax (847) 622-0948
Years served: 1993-present

Legislative assignments: Committees on Personnel & Pen-
sions (minority spokesperson); Elementary & Secondary
Education (vice spokesperson); Commerce & Business De-
velopment; Elections & Campaign Reform; The Disabled
Community; Special Committee on Prison Management
Reform.

Biography: Educator; born May 26, 1942, in Rochester, MN; B.A., Denison University,
Granville, OH; Ed.D., Northern Illinois University; former Kane County Regional
Superintendent of Schools, 1987-93; received "Those Who Excel" administrator award
from Illinois State Board of Education, 1985; married (wife, Libby), has two children.

Senator, 34th District
DAVE SYVERSON, R - Rockford

Springfield: M-113 Capitol Bldg., 62706; (217) 782-5413;
Fax (217) 782-0650; E-mail: senatedave@aol.com
District: E.J. "Zeke" Giorgi Center, 200 S. Wyman,
Ste. 302, Rockford 61101; (815) 987-7555;
Fax (815) 987-7563
Years served: 1993-present

Legislative assignments: Committees on Public Health &
Welfare (chairperson); Appropriations; Transportation;
Tollway Authority Advisory Committee; Legislative
Research Unit.

Biography: Born June 29, 1957, in Chicago; business major, Rock Valley College, Rockford;
partner, Market Insurance Group; involved in many local civic and social organizations;
married (wife, Shirley), has a daughter, Stephanie, and a son, J.D.

Representative, 67th District
CHUCK JEFFERSON, D - Rockford

Springfield: 2062-L Stratton Bldg., 62706;
(217) 782-3167
District: E. J. "Zeke" Giorgi Center, 200 S. Wyman,
Ste. 304, Rockford 61101; (815) 987-7433;
Fax (815) 987-7225
Years served: Appointed April 22, 2001

Legislative assignments: Committees on Aging; Aviation;
Mental Health & Patient Abuse; Urban Revitalization.

Biography: Full-time state legislator; former Winnebago
County Board Representative, 6th District; born March 31,
1945, in Waco, TX; graduated from A.J. Moore High School;
attended Paul Quinn College; served as military policeman in U.S. Army, six years;
widower, has three sons, Carl, Curtis and Charles, Jr., and two grandchildren.

Representative, 68th District
RONALD A. WAIT, R - Belvidere

Springfield: 2021-H Stratton Bldg., 62706;
(217) 782-0548; Fax (217) 782-1275;
E-mail: repwait@aol.com
District: 411 S. State St., Belvidere 61008;
(815) 547-7771; Fax (815) 547-7767
Years served: 1983-93; 1995-present

Legislative assignments: Committees on Transportation &
Motor Vehicles (minority spokesperson); Appropriations-
Public Safety (vice spokesperson); Aging; Judiciary I-Civil
Law; Judiciary II-Criminal Law; Special Committee on
Prison Management Reform.

Biography: Farmer & farm manager; born April 15, 1944, in Belvidere; J.D., Drake University
Law School; M.B.A., Northern Illinois University; M.S., special education, Northern Illinois
University; B.S., accounting, Drake University; has one son, Danny.

Senator, 35th District
J. BRADLEY BURZYNSKI, R - Sycamore

Springfield: 121-C Capitol Bldg., 62706; (217) 782-1977
District: 505 DeKalb Ave., P.O. Box 348, Sycamore
60178; (815) 895-6318; Fax (815) 895-2905; State of
Illinois Building, 200 S. Wyman, Ste. 301, Rockford
61101; (815) 987-7557; Fax (815) 987-7529
Years served: 1990-93 (House); 1993-present (Senate)

Legislative assignments: Committees on Licensed Activities (chairperson); Appropriations; Education; Revenue;
Joint Committee on Administrative Rules; Legislative Reference Bureau.

Biography: Full-time state legislator; born July 13, 1955,
in Christopher; B.M.E., Illinois Wesleyan University; married (wife, Judy), has two
children.

Representative, 69th District
DAVE WINTERS, R - Shirland

Springfield: 2119-N Stratton Bldg., 62706;
(217) 782-0455; Fax (217) 782-1139;
E-mail: repwinters@aol.com
District: 3444 N. Main St., Ste. 80, Rockford 61103;
(815) 282-0083; Fax (815) 282-0085
Years served: 1995-present

Legislative assignments: Committees on Conservation &
Land Use (minority spokesperson); Human Services; Insurance; Property Tax Reform & School Funding); Registration & Regulation.

Biography: Farmer; born June 30, 1952, in Springfield;
B.A., history, Dartmouth College; M.S., agricultural economics, University of Illinois;
member, Winnebago County Board, 1986-92; married (wife, Kathleen), has two children.

Representative, 70th District
DAVID A. WIRSING, R - Sycamore

Springfield: 2028-H Stratton Bldg., 62706;
(217) 782-0425
District: 2600 DeKalb Ave., Ste. C, Sycamore 60178;
(815) 748-3494; Fax (815) 748-4630
Years served: 1993-present

Legislative assignments: Committees on Higher Education (minority spokesperson); Appropriations-Higher
Education; Children & Youth; Consumer Protection; Human Services; State Government Administration;
Committee of the Whole.

Biography: Full-time state legislator; born Aug. 5, 1937,
in Sycamore; raised on family farm near Sycamore; has been grain and livestock producer 30 years; past president, Illinois Pork Producers Association and DeKalb County
Pork Producers Association, and has chaired the Illinois Pork PAC; married (wife, Nancy),
has four children and seven grandchildren.

Senator, 36th District
DENNY JACOBS, D - East Moline

Springfield: M-103-C Capitol Bldg., 62706;
(217) 782-5957; E-mail: jacobs@senatedem.state.il.us
District: 606 19th St., Moline 61265; (309) 797-0001;
Fax (309) 797-0003
Years served: 1986-present

Legislative assignments: Committees on Insurance & Pensions (minority spokesperson); Environment & Energy; Revenue; Legislative Space Needs Commission.

Biography: Full-time state legislator; born Nov. 8, 1937, in Rock Island County; B.A., business administration and political science, Augustana College; married (wife, Mary Ellen), has six children.

Representative, 71st District
MIKE BOLAND, D - East Moline

Springfield: 2041-J Stratton Bldg., 62706; (217) 782-3992
District: 4416 River Dr., Moline 61265;
(309) 736-3360; Fax (309) 736-3478
Years served: 1995-present

Legislative assignments: Committees on Elections & Campaign Reform (chairperson); Registration & Regulation; Special Committee on Tobacco Settlement Proceeds; Legislative Printing Unit.

Biography: Educator; born Aug. 20, 1942, in Davenport, IA; B.A., Upper Iowa University; M.S., education, Henderson State University; 48 semester hours, post master's degree, Western Illinois University and University of Iowa; married (wife, Mary), has two children.

Representative, 72nd District
JOEL BRUNSVOLD, D - Milan
Assistant Majority Leader

Springfield: 109 Capitol Bldg., 62706; (217) 782-5970;
Fax (217) 782-8569
District: 303 18th St., Rock Island 61201; (309) 793-4716;
Fax (309) 793-4764
Years served: 1983-present

Legislative assignments: Ex officio member of all House committees.

Biography: Born Feb. 26, 1942, in Mason City, IA; graduated, Rock Island High School; B.A., Augustana College, Rock Island; former Milan Mayor, 1977-83; Illinois Legislative Sportsmen's Caucus (chair); avid hunter and fisherman; married (wife, Barbara), has two children, Tim and Ted.

Senator, 37th District
TODD SIEBEN, R - Geneseo

Springfield: 307 Capitol Bldg., 62706; (217) 782-0180;
   E-mail: tsieben@geneseo.net
District: 137 S. State St., Geneseo 61254; (309) 944-5681;
   Toll Free (888) 874-3236; Fax (309) 944-3392;
   19 S. Chicago Ave., Freeport 61032; (815) 233-0037;
   Fax (815) 232-0777
Years served: 1987-93 (House); 1993-present (Senate)

Legislative assignments: Committees on Agriculture &
Conservation (chairperson); Education; Insurance &
Pensions.

Biography: Full-time state legislator; born July 11, 1945, in
Geneseo; B.S., business administration, Western Illinois University; lieutenant, U.S. Navy,
1968-72, Vietnam veteran; married (wife, Kay), has three children and two grandchildren.

Representative, 73rd District
JERRY MITCHELL, R - Sterling

Springfield: 2011-H Stratton Bldg., 62706;
   (217) 782-0535; Fax (217) 782-1275;
   E-mail: mitchl73@cin.net
District: 100 E. Fifth St., Rock Falls 61071;
   (815) 625-0820; Fax (815) 625-0839
Years served: 1995-present

Legislative assignments: Committees on Appropriations-
Elementary & Secondary Education (minority spokesperson);
Appropriations-Human Services; Aging; Child Support
Enforcement; Elementary & Secondary Education; Special
Committee on Prison Management Reform (vice spokes-
person).

Biography: Full-time state legislator; born June 18, 1942, in Jacksonville; U.S.M.C., 1960-
64; B.A., Eureka College, 1968; M.S., educational administration, Illinois State University,
1972; education specialist degree, Western Illinois University, 1992; retired public school
superintendent, Dixon Unit District #140; listed in "Who's Who in Colleges and Universities," 1964, and "Who's Who in Outstanding Americans," 1995-96; married (wife, Jan),
has three children and one grandchild.

Representative, 74th District
I. RONALD LAWFER, R - Stockton

Springfield: 2029-H Stratton Bldg., 62706; (217) 782-8186
District: 19 S. Chicago Ave., Freeport 61032;
   (815) 232-0774; Fax (815) 232-0777
Years served: 1993-present

Legislative assignments: Committees on Agriculture &
Conservation (minority spokesperson); Appropriations-
Elementary & Secondary Education (vice spokesperson);
Aging; Environment & Energy; Local Government;
Tourism.

Biography: Farmer; born May 15, 1934, in Stockton; B.S.,
agriculture, University of Illinois; served in U.S. Army, infantry officer in Korea; received
"Master Farmer" award from *Prairie Farmer* magazine, 1986; married (wife, Pat), has
five children.

Senator, 38th District
PATRICK D. WELCH, D - Peru
Assistant Minority Leader

Springfield: 218 Capitol Bldg., 62706; (217) 782-8287;
Web site: www.senatedem.state.il.us/welch
E-mail: welch@senatedem.state.il.us
District: 726 First St., LaSalle 61301; (815) 223-3747;
Fax (815) 223-8446
Years served: 1983-present

Legislative assignments: Committees on Environment & Energy; Financial Institutions; Economic & Fiscal Commission (co-chair).

Biography: Attorney; born Dec. 12, 1948, in Chicago; B.A., government, Southern Illinois University; J.D., IIT/ Chicago-Kent College of Law; received Statesman of the Year award and numerous environmental, labor, rehabilitation and agriculture awards; has one child.

Representative, 75th District
MARY K. O'BRIEN, D - Reddick

Springfield: 2052-L Stratton Bldg., 62706;
(217) 782-4535; Fax (217) 782-7631;
E-mail:mob6028389@aol.com
District: 760 E. Division, Coal City 60416;
(815) 634-3096; Fax (815) 634-3137
Years served: 1997-present

Legislative assignments: Committees on Judiciary II-Criminal Law (chairperson); Transportation & Motor Vehicles (vice chairperson); Agriculture; Child Support Enforcement; The Disabled Community.

Biography: Attorney, partner in the law firm O'Brien & Smith; born June 4, 1965, in Kankakee; Joliet Junior College; B.S., Western Illinois University, 1986; J.D., University of Illinois College of Law, 1994.

Representative, 76th District
FRANK J. MAUTINO, D - Spring Valley

Springfield: 2082-M Stratton Bldg., 62706;
(217) 782-0140; Fax (217) 557-7680;
E-mail: brandy@ivnet.com
District: 108 W. St. Paul St., Spring Valley 61362;
(815) 664-2717; Fax (815) 663-1629
Years served: 1991-present

Legislative assignments: Committees on Insurance (chairperson); Appropriations-Public Safety (vice chairperson); Agriculture; Appropriations-Human Services; Cities & Villages; Property Tax Reform & School Funding; Tourism; Veterans' Affairs; Special Committee on Prison Management Reform; Comprehensive Health Insurance Plan (CHIP) Board; Economic & Fiscal Commission; Legislative Audit Commission.

Biography: Full-time state legislator; born Aug. 7, 1962, in Spring Valley; B.S., marketing, Illinois State University, 1984; Corporate Brand Manager, Mautino Distributing Company, Inc., 1984-91; Bureau County Democratic Chair; received "Outstanding Legislator of the Year" award from Illinois Health Care Assn., 1998; married (wife, Lena), has three children, Pietro Joseph "Peter," Luciana Christina and James Michael.

Senator, 39th District
DAN CRONIN, R - Elmhurst

Springfield: 127 Capitol Bldg., 62706; (217) 782-8107;
  Fax (217) 782-4079; E-mail: senatorcronin@aol.com
District: 105 E. First St., Elmhurst 60126; (630) 941-0040;
  Fax (630) 941-1205
Years served: 1991-93 (House); 1993-present (Senate)

Legislative assignments: Committees on Education
(chairperson); Commerce & Industry; Judiciary; Legislative
Reference Bureau.

Biography: Lawyer, former prosecutor and current partner,
Power & Cronin, Ltd.; born Nov. 7, 1959, in Elmhurst; B.A.,
Dean's List, Northwestern University; J.D., captain,
National Trial Team, Loyola University School of Law; married (wife, Juliann), has three
children.

Representative, 77th District
ANGELO "SKIP" SAVIANO,
R - Elmwood Park

Springfield: 2112-N Stratton Bldg., 62706;
  (217) 782-3374; Fax (217) 782-0595
District: 8153 W. Grand Ave., River Grove 60171;
  (708) 453-7547; Fax (708) 453-7594
Years served: 1993-present

Legislative assignments: Committees on Registration &
Regulation (chairperson); Aging; Appropriations-Public
Safety; Financial Institutions; Urban Revitalization; Special
Committee on Prison Management Reform; Illinois
Council on Aging.

Biography: Full-time state legislator; born May 20, 1958, in Chicago; B.A., DePaul
University; married (wife, Julie), has two children.

Representative, 78th District
ROBERT A. "BOB" BIGGINS, R - Elmhurst

Springfield: 2010-H Stratton Bldg., 62706;
  (217) 782-6578; Fax (217) 782-5257;
  E-mail: bobbiggins@mediaone.net
District: 114 W. Park Ave., Elmhurst 60126;
  (630) 941-1278; Fax (630) 941-1285
Years served: 1993-present

Legislative assignments: Committees on Appropriations-
General Services (minority spokesperson); Property Tax
Reform & School Funding (vice spokesperson); Executive;
Financial Institutions; Revenue; Special Committee on
Electric Utility Deregulation; Legislative Audit Commis-
sion.

Biography: Real estate tax consultant; born Oct. 20, 1946; in Oak Park; B.A., education,
Northeastern Illinois University; Addison Township Assessor, 1973 to 1977; Board of
Directors, Suburban Bank of Elmhurst, 1975 to 1998 (chair, 1983 to 1984); co-founder,
Property Assessment Advisors, Inc., 1981; married (wife, Judy), has two children.

Senator, 40th District
DEBBIE HALVORSON, D - Crete
Minority Caucus Whip

Springfield: 417 Capitol Bldg., 62706;
(217) 782-7419; Fax (217) 782-5252;
E-mail: halvorson@senatedem.state.il.us
District: 241 W. Joe Orr Rd., Chicago Heights 60411;
(708) 756-0882; Fax (708) 756-0885
Years served: 1997-present

Legislative assignments: Committees on Commerce & Industry (minority spokesperson); Appropriations; Local Government; Legislative Information System; Legislative Research Unit.

Biography: Full-time state legislator; born March 1, 1958; B.A., Governors State University; received "Freshman Legislator of the Year" award from the Illinois Health Care Association, 1997; "Business Advocate of the Year" award from the Chicago Southland Chamber of Commerce; "Statesman of the Year" award from the International Union of Operating Engineers 150; "Outstanding Legislator of the Year" award from the Illinois Hospital & Health System, 1998; and the "Education Hero" award from the Illinois Education Association; has two children.

Representative, 79th District
ROBERT L. RYAN, JR., D - Lansing

Springfield: 2103-H Stratton Bldg., 62706;
(217) 782-5971; Fax (217) 558-6370
District: 3320 Ridge Rd., Lansing 60438;
(708) 474-2000; Fax (708) 474-1999
Years served: 2001-present

Legislative assignments: Committees on Aging; Appropriations-Human Services; Commerce & Business Development; Health Care Availability & Access; Labor; The Disabled Community; Special Committee on State Procurement.

Biography: Full-time state legislator; former bank examiner; born Sept. 12, 1959, in Chicago; North Central College; DePaul University; certified fraud examiner; single.

Representative, 80th District
GEORGE F. SCULLY, JR., D - Flossmoor

Springfield: 2036-J Stratton Bldg., 62706; (217) 782-1719
District: 344 Victory Dr., Park Forest 60466;
(708) 503-9350; Fax (708) 503-9611
Years served: 1997-present

Legislative assignments: Committees on Commerce & Business Development (chairperson); Aviation (vice chairperson); Conservation & Land Use (vice chairperson); Judiciary I-Civil Law; Property Tax Reform & School Funding; Urban Revitalization; Committee of the Whole.

Biography: Attorney; born Feb. 28, 1952, in Evergreen Park; B.S., Northern Illinois University; J.D., The John Marshall Law School; graduate studies, Oxford University; married (wife, Barbara), has three children.

Senator, 41st District
KIRK W. DILLARD, R - Hinsdale

Springfield: M-115 Capitol Bldg., 62706; (217) 782-8148;
  E-mail: senator@kdillard.com
District: 1 S. Cass Ave., Ste. 201, Westmont 60559;
  (630) 969-0990; Fax (630) 969-1007
Years served: 1993-present

Legislative assignments: Committees on Local
Government (chairperson); Judiciary (vice chairperson);
Rules (vice chairperson); Environment & Energy; Executive;
Commission on Intergovernmental Cooperation.

Biography: Attorney; born June 1, 1955, in Chicago; B.A.,
Western Illinois University; J.D., DePaul University College
of Law; former Chief of Staff for Governor Jim Edgar and Director of Legislative Affairs
for Governor James R. Thompson; former judge of the Illinois Court of Claims; member,
Illinois Issues Legislative Staff Hall of Fame; "Distinguished Alumni" award, Western
Illinois University, 1997; married (wife, Stephanie), has one daughter, Emma.

Representative, 81st District
PATRICIA "PATTI" BELLOCK, R - Hinsdale

Springfield: G-2 Stratton Bldg., 62706;
  (217) 782-1448; E-mail: pbellock@aol.com
District: 1 S. Cass Ave., Ste. 205, Westmont 60559;
  (630) 852-8633; Fax (630) 852-6530
Years served: 1999-present

Legislative assignments: Committees on Human Services
(minority spokesperson); Appropriations-Elementary &
Secondary Education; Appropriations-Human Services; La-
bor; Mental Health & Patient Abuse; Special Committee on
Tobacco Settlement Proceeds; Committee of the Whole;
Legislative Research Unit.

Biography: Teacher, business woman; born Oct. 14, 1946, in Chicago; B.A., history, St.
Norbert College, 1968; married (husband, Charles), has two children.

Representative, 82nd District
JAMES H. "JIM" MEYER, R - Bolingbrook

Springfield: 2018-H Stratton Bldg., 62706;
  (217) 782-8028; Fax (217) 557-7211;
  E-mail: jhmeyer@msn.com
District: 277 S. Schmidt Rd., Ste. 100, Bolingbrook 60440;
  (630) 759-3465; Fax (630) 759-3554
Years served: 1993-present

Legislative assignments: Committees on Financial Institutions (minority spokesperson); Appropriations-Elementary & Secondary Education; Judiciary I-Civil Law;
Veterans' Affairs; Special Committees on Electric Utility
Deregulation (minority spokesperson); Telecommunications Rewrite; Legislative Information System.

Biography: Born Oct. 28, 1943, in Sibley, IA; B.A., political science, Upper Iowa University,
Fayette, IA; served four years in U.S. Air Force, honorable discharge; served three terms
(10 years) as trustee for Village of Bolingbrook; married (wife, Bonnie), has one daughter,
a son-in-law and two grandsons.

112

Senator, 42nd District
ED PETKA, R - Plainfield
Majority Whip

Springfield: 122 Capitol Bldg., 62706; (217) 782-0422
District: 501 N. Division, P.O. Box 188, Plainfield 60544;
(815) 436-5577; Fax (815) 436-8065
Years served: 1987-93 (House); 1993-present (Senate)

Legislative assignments: Committees on Executive Appointments (chairperson); Executive (vice chairperson); Insurance & Pensions; Judiciary.

Biography: Attorney; born March 10, 1943, in Chicago; B.A., Southern Illinois University; J.D., John Marshall Law School; former president of Illinois State's Attorneys Association; appointed to Criminal Justice Committee, National Conference of State Legislatures; married (wife, Phyllis), has four children.

Representative, 83rd District
BRENT HASSERT, R - Romeoville

Springfield: 2135-O Stratton Bldg., 62706; (217) 782-4179;
E-mail: hassert83@aol.com
District: 1413 Sherman Rd., Ste. 60, Romeoville 60446;
(630) 739-7063; (815) 886-9300; Fax (630) 739-4055
Years served: 1993-present

Legislative assignments: Committees on Environment & Energy (minority spokesperson); Executive (vice spokesperson); Conservation & Land Use; Financial Institutions; Labor; Special Committee on Electric Utility Deregulation; Legislative Printing Unit.

Biography: Landscape contractor; born Oct. 29, 1952, in Joliet; horticulture, Joliet Junior College; former Commissioner and Executive Pro Tem, Will County Board, 1986-90; married (wife, Patricia), has two children.

Representative, 84th District
TOM CROSS, R - Oswego
Assistant Minority Leader

Springfield: O-2 Stratton Bldg., 62706; (217) 782-1331;
Fax (217) 782-6812
District: 520 Countryside Center, Yorkville 60560;
(630) 553-0000; Fax (630) 553-9999
Years served: 1993-present

Legislative assignments: Committees on Computer Technology; Revenue; Special Committees on Conflicts of Interest; Judicial Reapportionment; Ex officio member of all House committees.

Biography: Attorney; born July 31, 1958, in Nashville, TN; graduated, Yorkville High School, 1976; B.A., political science, Illinois Wesleyan University, 1980; J.D., Samford University, Cumberland School of Law, Birmingham, AL, 1983; married (wife, Genie), has one daughter, Reynolds, and one son, Hudson.

Senator, 43rd District
LAWRENCE M. "LARRY" WALSH,
D - Elwood

Springfield: 309-G Capitol Bldg., 62706;
(217) 782-8800; Fax (217) 558-6006;
E-mail: walsh@senatedem.state.il.us
District: 1100 Plainfield Rd., Joliet 60435; (815) 722-4200;
Fax (815) 722-4657; 750 Almar Pky., Ste. 201, P.O. Box
428; Bourbonnais 60914-0428; (815) 936-0043
Years served: 1997-present

Legislative assignments: Committees on Local
Government (minority spokesperson); Agriculture &
Conservation; Legislative Reference Bureau.

Biography: Farmer; born March 3, 1948, in Joliet; Joliet East High School, 1966; Associate
in Agriculture/Business, Joliet Junior College, 1968; married (wife, Irene), has six children
and four grandchildren.

Representative, 85th District
J. PHILIP NOVAK, D - Bradley

Springfield: 2064-L Stratton Bldg., 62706;
(217) 782-5981; Fax (217) 782-0945;
E-mail: jpnovak@keynet.net
District: 135 S. Schuyler Ave., Kankakee 60901;
(815) 939-1983; Fax (815) 939-0081
Years served: 1987-present

Legislative assignments: Committees on Environment &
Energy (chairperson); Financial Institutions; Registration &
Regulation; Veterans' Affairs; Special Committees on Electric
Utility Deregulation (co-chairperson); Tobacco Settlement
Proceeds; JCAR.

Biography: Full-time state legislator; born Feb. 15, 1946,
in Berwyn; B.S., education, M.A., political science, Eastern Illinois University; served in
U.S. Army, Panama Canal Zone, 1966-68; former Kankakee County Treasurer, 1982-87;
former Village Trustee, 1975-83; married (wife, Rebecca), has one son, Todd, a graduate
of ISU.

Representative, 86th District
JACK McGUIRE, D - Joliet

Springfield: 2037-J Stratton Bldg., 62706; (217) 782-8090;
E-mail: strep86@aol.com
District: 121 Springfield Ave., Joliet 60435;
(815) 730-8600; Fax (815) 730-8121
Years served: 1991-present

Legislative assignments: Committees on Aging
(chairperson); Appropriations-Public Safety; Constitutional
Officers; Revenue; Tourism; Legislative Information System.

Biography: Full-time state legislator; born May 12, 1933, in
Joliet; B.A., business education, Colorado State University;
former school teacher and coach; served overseas in U.S.
Army; former Joliet Township Supervisor; named "Legislator of the Year" by the American
Red Cross, 1991, and by Advocates United, 1997; received "Zeke Giorgi Labor" award, 1998,
and "Josephine Oblinger" senior citizens advocate award, 1999; widowed, father of four
children (one deceased), has nine grandchildren.

Senator, 44th District
JOHN W. MAITLAND, JR., R - Bloomington
Assistant Majority Leader

Springfield: 627 Capitol Bldg., 62706; (217) 782-6216;
Fax (217) 782-0116
District: 525 N. East St., Bloomington 61701;
(309) 828-7733; Fax (309) 828-4907
Years served: 1979-present

Legislative assignments: Committees on Environment &
Energy (vice chairperson); Appropriations; Executive;
Pension Laws Commission (co-chair); Economic & Fiscal
Commission; various state task forces.

Biography: Grain farmer; born July 29, 1936, in Normal; attended Illinois State University;
served in U.S. Marine Corps; married (wife, Joanne Sieg), has three children and seven
grandchildren.

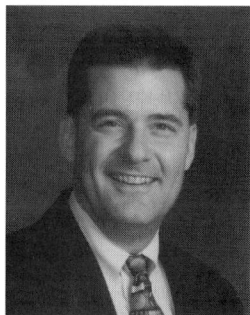

Representative, 87th District
DAN RUTHERFORD, R - Pontiac
Assistant Minority Leader

Springfield: H-1 Stratton Bldg., 62706; (217) 782-7776
District: 732 W. Madison St., Pontiac 61764;
(815) 842-3632; Fax (815) 842-2875
Years served: 1993-present

Legislative assignments: Committees on Constitutional
Officers; Executive; Special Committee on Conflicts of
Interest; Ex officio member of all House committees; Joint
Committee on Administrative Rules.

Biography: Vice President International, The Service
Master Co.; born May 26, 1955, in Pontiac; Pontiac Township High School; B.S., business
administration, Illinois State University (ISU); received "Outstanding Young Alumni"
award from ISU, 1993; single.

Representative, 88th District
DAN BRADY, R - Bloomington

Springfield: 2137-O Stratton Bldg., 62706;
(217) 782-1118; Fax (217) 558-6271;
E-mail: dan@repdanbrady.com
District: 514 E. Locust, Bloomington 61701;
(309) 827-8303; Fax (309) 827-8263
Years served: 2001-present

Legislative assignments: Committees on Consumer Protection (minority spokesperson); Appropriations-Public
Safety; Insurance; Judiciary II-Criminal Law; Veterans' Affairs; Special Committee on State Procurement.

Biography: Legislator/funeral director; born July 4, 1961,
in Bloomington; bachelor's degree, Ambrose University, Davenport, IA, 1983; associate's
degree in applied science, Southern Illinois University at Carbondale, 1982; received "He-
roes of the Highway" award, 1999; "Achievement" awards from the National Association
of Counties, 1995 and 1997; member, Corn Belt Chapter, Alzheimer's Foundation; Regional
Organ Bank of Illinois; American Red Cross; married (wife, Teri), has two children.

Senator, 45th District
CLAUDE U. STONE, JR., R - Morton

Springfield: 119 Capitol Bldg., 62706; (217) 782-6597
District: 618 N. Chicago St., Lincoln 62656;
(217) 732-1323; Fax (217) 735-4319; 106 S. Main,
P.O. Box 152, Eureka 61530; (309) 467-5464
Years served: Appointed July 12, 2001

Legislative assignments: Committees on Agriculture &
Conservation; Licensed Activities.

Biography: Full-time state legislator; retired from
management at Caterpillar; born April 30, 1926, in Peoria;
B.S., economics, Cornell University, Ithaca, NY, 1948; B.S.,
business marketing, Bradley University, Peoria, 1949;
MBA, Stanford University, CA, 1951; married (wife, Mary Louise), has three children
and six grandchildren.

Representative, 89th District
KEITH P. SOMMER, R - Mackinaw

Springfield: 2140-O Stratton Bldg., 62706; (217) 782-0221;
E-mail: sommer@mtco.com
District: 121 W. Jefferson, Morton 61550; (309) 263-9242;
Fax (309) 263-8187
Years served: 1999-present

Legislative assignments: Committees on Veterans' Affairs
(minority spokesperson); Appropriations-Elementary &
Secondary Education; Appropriations-General Services; The
Disabled Community; Special Committee on Prison Management Reform.

Biography: Real estate broker; born Sept. 6, 1946, in Morton;
B.A., government, University of Virginia; married (wife, Deb).

Representative, 90th District
JONATHAN WRIGHT, R - Hartsburg

Springfield: 2020-H Stratton Bldg., 62706;
(217) 782-0428; Fax (217) 782-5678
District: 407 Keokuk St., Lincoln 62656;
(217) 732-4011; Fax (217) 732-8791
Years served: Appointed June 21, 2001

Legislative assignments: Committees on Agriculture; Judiciary I-Civil Law; Judiciary II-Criminal Law; Labor;
Special Committees on Tobacco Settlement Proceeds (minority spokesperson); Prosecutorial Misconduct.

Biography: Full-time state legislator; born Oct. 11, 1966, in
Winfield; B.A., Monmouth College; J.D., IIT Chicago-Kent
College of Law; married (wife, Melanie), has three children.

Senator, 46th District
GEORGE P. SHADID, D - Edwards

Springfield: 309-H Capitol Bldg., 62706; (217) 782-8250;
Fax (217) 558-6006
District: 410 Court St., Pekin 61554; (309) 353-6276;
(309) 673-8404; Fax (309) 353-1819
Years served: 1993-present

Legislative assignments: Committees on Transportation
(minority spokesperson); Judiciary; Legislative Audit
Commission.

Biography: Full-time state legislator; born May 15, 1929,
in Clinton, IA; former Peoria County Sheriff, 1976-93;
received "Community Service" award from United Cerebral Palsy, 1992, and "Good
Government" award from Peoria Jaycees, 1992; married (wife, Lorraine), has two children.

Representative, 91st District
MICHAEL K. SMITH, D - Canton

Springfield: 2088-M Stratton Bldg., 62706;
(217) 782-8152; Fax (217) 557-4415
District: 45 East Side Square, Ste. 301, Canton 61520;
(309) 647-7479; Fax (309) 647-7482;
410 Court St., Pekin 61554; (309) 353-6276
Years served: 1995-present

Legislative assignments: Committees on Agriculture; Appropriations-Elementary & Secondary Education; Elementary
& Secondary Education; Judiciary II-Criminal Law; Personnel & Pensions; Pension Laws Commission.

Biography: Full-time state legislator; born May 23, 1966, in
Canton; B.A., political science, Bradley University; former township trustee; Fulton County
Democratic Party Chairman; Graham Hospital Trustee; past president, Canton Area Chamber of Commerce; former board member, Illinois Affiliate of the American Heart Association;
married (wife, Donna).

Representative, 92nd District
RICCA C. SLONE, D - Peoria Heights

Springfield: 2104-N Stratton Bldg., 62706;
(217) 782-3186; Fax (217) 558-6107
District: 456 Fulton St., Ste. 150, Twin Towers Mall,
Peoria 61602; (309) 673-0921; Fax (309) 673-0923;
E-mail: rslone@bwsys.net
Years served: 1997-present

Legislative assignments: Committees on Conservation &
Land Use (chairperson); Appropriations-General Services
(vice chairperson); Appropriations-Elementary & Secondary
Education; Cities & Villages; Elections & Campaign Reform;
Labor.

Biography: Attorney; B.A., Washington University, St. Louis; M.A., anthropology, Univer-
sity of California, Los Angeles; M.A., public administration, Ohio State University; J.D.,
University of Illinois College of Law, 1990; National Conference of State Legislatures, 2000-
2001; chair, NCSL Science, Energy & Environmental Resources Committee; member, NCSL
Federal Environment Committee; married (husband, Dr. William Berkman), has three sons,
Zachary, Sydney and Seth.

Senator, 47th District
CARL E. HAWKINSON, R - Galesburg

Springfield: 623 Capitol Bldg., 62706; (217) 782-1942;
Fax (217) 782-0116
District: 4 Weinberg Arcade, Galesburg 61401;
(309) 343-8176; Fax (309) 343-2683; 5415 N. University,
Ste. 105; Peoria 61614; (309) 693-4921;
Fax (309) 693-4923;
Years served: 1983-87 (House); 1987-present (Senate)

Legislative assignments: Committees on Judiciary
(chairperson); Commerce & Industry; Transportation.

Biography: Attorney; born Oct. 7, 1947, in Galesburg; B.A.,
history, North Park College; J.D., Harvard Law School;
former Knox County State's Attorney; married (wife, Karen Zeches), has three children.

Representative, 93rd District
DAVID R. LEITCH, R - Peoria
Assistant Minority Leader

Springfield: 220 Capitol Bldg., 62706; (217) 782-8108;
Fax (217) 557-3047
District: 3114 N. University, Peoria 61604;
(309) 685-3900; Fax (309) 685-3936
Years served: 1986-87 (Senate); 1989-present (House)

Legislative assignments: Committees on Appropriations-
Human Services; Public Utilities; Special Committee on
Electric Utility Deregulation; Ex officio member of all
House committees; Pension Laws Commission.

Biography: Vice President, National City Bank-Illinois; born Aug. 2, 1948, in Three Rivers,
MI; B.A., history, Kalamazoo College, Kalamazoo, MI; received the Dr. Nathan Davis
"Legislator of the Year" award, 1998; has received numerous other "Legislator of the
Year" awards; has three children.

Representative, 94th District
DONALD L. MOFFITT, R - Gilson

Springfield: 2025-H Stratton Bldg., 62706;
(217) 782-8032; Fax (217) 557-0179;
E-mail: moffitt@gallatinriver.net
District: 5 Weinberg Arcade, Galesburg 61401;
(309) 343-8000; Fax (309) 343-2683
Years served: 1993-present

Legislative assignments: Committees on Counties &
Townships (minority spokesperson); Aging; Appropriations-General Services; Elementary & Secondary
Education; Tourism; Special Committee on Prison Management Reform.

Biography: Full-time state legislator; born Feb. 18, 1947, in Galesburg; B.S., agricultural
education and economics, University of Illinois; former Knox County Treasurer, Knox
County Board member and chair, Knoxville City Council member, mayor of Oneida and
alderman in Oneida; married (wife, Carolyn), has three children.

Senator, 48th District
LAURA KENT DONAHUE, R - Quincy
Assistant Majority Leader

Springfield: 323 Capitol Bldg., 62706; (217) 782-2479
District: 640 Maine St., Quincy 62301; (217) 224-0644;
   Fax (217) 223-1565
Years served: 1981-present

Legislative assignments: Committees on Appropriations
(vice chairman); Environment & Energy; Public Health &
Welfare.

Biography: Full-time state legislator; born April 22, 1949,
in Quincy; B.S., Stephens College, Columbia, MO; Illinois
Federation of Republican Women; American Legislative
Exchange Council; Lincoln Club of Adams County; Daughters of the American
Revolution.

Representative, 95th District
RICHARD P. MYERS, R - Colchester

Springfield: H-2 Stratton Bldg., 62706; (217) 782-0416;
   Fax (217) 557-7211; E-mail: repmyers@legis.state.il.us
District: 331 N. Lafayette St., Macomb 61455;
   (309) 836-2707; Fax (309) 836-2231;
   E-mail: repmyers@macomb.com;
   224 W. State St., Jacksonville 62650; (217) 245-1981
Years served: 1995-present

Legislative assignments: Committees on Appropriations-
Higher Education (minority spokesperson); Agriculture;
Children & Youth; Higher Education; Human Services;
Special Committee on Tobacco Settlement Proceeds;
Economic & Fiscal Commission.

Biography: Full-time state legislator; born Dec. 27, 1947, in McDonough County;
graduated, Colchester High School, 1966; B.S., Western Illinois University, 1973; U.S.
Army Reserves, six years; married (wife, Christine), has one daughter, Alison.

Representative, 96th District
ART TENHOUSE, R - Liberty
Deputy Minority Leader

Springfield: 314 Capitol Bldg., 62706; (217) 782-8096;
   Fax (217) 782-7012
District: 640 Maine St., Quincy 62301; (217) 223-0833;
   Fax (217) 223-1565
Years served: 1989-present

Legislative assignments: Committees on Rules (minority
spokesperson); Appropriations-Elementary & Secondary
Education; Executive; Ex officio member of all House
committees; Legislative Space Needs Commission; past
chairman, House Republican Campaign Committee.

Biography: Legislator and farmer; born Dec. 27, 1950, in Quincy; B.S., agricultural
science/economics, M.B.A., finance accounting, University of Illinois; C.P.A.; partner,
Four-Ten-Farms; married (wife, Sharon), has three children.

Senator, 49th District
VINCE DEMUZIO, D - Carlinville
Assistant Minority Leader

Springfield: 309-D Capitol Bldg., 62706; (217) 782-8206;
E-mail: demuzio@senatedem.state.il.us
District: 140 Carlinville Plaza, Carlinville 62626;
(217) 854-4441; Fax (217) 854-5311;
E-mail: senator_demuzio@accunet.net
Years served: 1975-present

Legislative assignments: Committees on Rules (minority spokesperson); Education; Executive; Executive Appointments; Legislative Audit Commission.

Biography: Born May 7, 1941, in Gillespie; attended Southern Illinois University-Edwardsville; McKendree College; Lewis and Clark Community College; B.A., Sangamon State University; M.A., education and public policy, University of Illinois at Springfield, May 1996; honorary J.D., Lewis and Clark Community College; honorary Doctor of Laws degree, Blackburn College, Carlinville, May 2001; married (wife, Deanna Clemonds), has two children and four grandchildren.

Representative, 97th District
TOM RYDER, R - Jerseyville
Deputy Minority Leader

Springfield: 314 Capitol Bldg., 62706; (217) 782-1840;
Fax (217) 782-7012; E-mail: tryder@gtec.com
District: 100 S. State, P.O. Box 385, Jerseyville 62052;
(618) 498-4813; Fax (618) 498-3384; 224 W. State,
Jacksonville 62651; (217) 243-6221
Years served: 1983-present

Legislative assignments: Committees on Computer Technology; Health Care Availability & Access; Rules; Ex officio member of all House committees; Joint Committee on Administrative Rules (co-chair).

Biography: Attorney; born May 17, 1949, near Medora; B.A., Northern Illinois University; J.D., Washington and Lee University; served as first lieutenant JAG, Illinois National Guard; married (wife, Peggy), has two children, Joshua and Timothy.

Representative, 98th District
GARY HANNIG, D - Litchfield
Assistant Majority Leader

Springfield: 300 Capitol Bldg., 62706;
(217) 782-8071; Fax (217) 524-1794
District: 225 S. Macoupin St., Gillespie 62033;
(217) 839-2859; Fax (217) 839-4833
Years served: 1979-present

Legislative assignments: Committees on Agriculture & Conservation; Personnel & Pensions; Rules; Ex officio member of all House committees.

Biography: Full-time state legislator; born July 22, 1952, in Litchfield; 1970 graduate of Mount Olive High School; B.S. with honors, accounting, University of Illinois; C.P.A.; married (wife, Betsy).

Senator, 50th District
LARRY K. BOMKE, R - Springfield

Springfield: 111 Capitol Bldg., 62706; (217) 782-0228;
Fax (217) 782-4079;
E-mail: senator_bomke@yahoo.com
District: 111 Capitol Bldg., 62706; (217) 782-0228;
Fax (217) 782-4079
Years served: 1995-present

Legislative assignments: Committees on Local
Government (vice chairperson); Executive Appointments;
State Government Operations; Legislative Research Unit.

Biography: Partner, insurance agency; born June 6, 1950,
in Springfield; former chair, Sangamon County Board
(two years) and member (19 years); listed in Outstanding Young Men of America, 1983;
married (wife, Sally Jo), has two children.

Representative, 99th District
RAYMOND POE, R - Springfield

Springfield: E-1 Stratton Bldg., 62706; (217) 782-0044;
Fax (217) 782-0897;
E-mail: rpoe@housegopmail.state.il.us
District: E-1 Stratton Bldg., 62706; (217) 782-0044;
Fax (217) 782-0897
Years served: 1995-present

Legislative assignments: Committees on Executive (minority spokesperson); Appropriations-Higher Education
(vice spokesperson); Agriculture; Appropriations-General
Services; Personnel & Pensions; Legislative Space Needs
Commission.

Biography: Farmer; born March 26, 1944, in Lincoln; graduated, DeVry Institute of Technology, Chicago, 1963; married (wife, Carol), has three children and five grandchildren.

Representative, 100th District
GWENN KLINGLER, R - Springfield

Springfield: 1128-E Stratton Bldg., 62706;
(217) 782-0053; Fax (217) 782-0897;
E-mail: klingler@housegopmail.state.il.us
District: 1128-E Stratton Bldg., 62706; (217) 782-0053;
Fax (217) 782-0897
Years served: 1995-present

Legislative assignments: Committees on Children & Youth
(minority spokesperson); Computer Technology; Health
Care Availability & Access; Judiciary I-Civil Law; Mental
Health & Patient Abuse; Registration & Regulation; Special
Committees on Tobacco Settlement Proceeds; Gas Pricing;
Violent Crimes Advisory Commission; Legislative Reference Bureau; Legislative Space
Needs Commission.

Biography: Attorney; born May 28, 1944, in Toledo, OH; B.A., Ohio Wesleyan University; M.A., University of Michigan; J.D., George Washington University School of Law;
received Charlotte Danstrom "Woman of the Year" award in government; married (husband, W. Gerald), has two children.

Senator, 51st District
N. DUANE NOLAND, R - Blue Mound

Springfield: M-120 Capitol Bldg., 62706; (217) 782-8176;
E-mail: ndnoland@springnetl.com
District: 101 S. Main, Ste. LL2, 1, Decatur 62523; (217) 428-
4068; Fax (217) 428-4089; 315 E. Main St., Shelbyville
62565; (217) 774-5715; Fax (217) 774-5622; 210 N.
Hamilton, Monticello 61856; (217) 762-2994
Years served: 1990-99 (House); 1999-present (Senate)

Legislative assignments: Committees on Agriculture & Conservation (vice chairperson); Licensed Activities (vice
chairperson); State Government Operations.

Biography: Farmer (Vice President, Noland Farms, Inc.) and
state legislator; born Sept. 12, 1956, in Decatur; B.S., agriculture economics and education,
University of Illinois; DuPont "Young Leader" award; fellow, John J. McCloy European
Agriculture fellowship; private pilot; married (wife, Tina Beckett), has two sons and one
daughter.

Representative, 101st District
JULIE A. CURRY, D - Mt. Zion

Springfield: 2054-L Stratton Bldg., 62706; (217) 782-8398;
E-mail: jcurryrep@one-eleven.net
District: 101-A Ashland Ave., Mt. Zion 62549;
(217) 864-3746; 1-800-862-8388; Fax (217) 864-4576;
Sullivan (217) 728-4363; Monticello (217) 762-4712
Years served: 1995-present

Legislative assignments: Committees on Appropriations-
Elementary & Secondary Education (chairperson); Child
Support Enforcement; Elections & Campaign Reform; Labor;
Property Tax Reform & School Funding; Special Committee
on Telecommunications Rewrite; Legislative Audit Commis-
sion (co-chair); House Task Force on Child Support Enforcement.

Biography: Full-time state legislator; born June 7, 1962, in Granite City; B.A. and M.A. in
political science, Eastern Illinois University; Macon County Treasurer, 1990-94; has one child.

Representative, 102nd District
BILL MITCHELL, R - Forsyth

Springfield: 2117-N Stratton Bldg., 62706;
(217) 782-8163
District: 332 W. Marion, Ste. 12, Forsyth 62535;
(217) 876-1968; Fax (217) 876-1973; 315 1/2 Main St.,
Shelbyville 62565; (217) 774-4701; Fax (217) 774-4767
Years served: 1999-present

Legislative assignments: Committees on Aging; Agriculture;
Appropriations-Public Safety; Insurance; State Government
Administration; Special Committee on Tobacco Settlement
Proceeds (minority spokesperson); Legislative Space Needs
Commission.

Biography: Full-time state legislator; born March 29, 1960, in Decatur; B.A., political science,
Eastern Illinois University, 1982; Mayor of Decatur (Pro Tem), 1997-98; Decatur City Coun-
cilman, 1989-98, re-elected by one of largest margins ever; former Macon County Republican
Chairman, nine years; member, Farm Bureau.

Senator, 52nd District
STANLEY B. WEAVER, R - Urbana
Senate Majority Leader

Springfield: 329 Capitol Bldg., 62706; (217) 782-6904
District: 1717 Philo Rd., Ste. 17-B, Urbana 61802;
  (217) 367-0009
Years served: 1969-71 (House); 1971-present (Senate)

Legislative assignments: Committees on Rules (chairperson); Appropriations; Executive; Legislative Space Needs Commission; Senate Operations Commission; Legislative Ethics Commission.

Biography: Full-time state legislator; born May 23, 1925, in Harrisburg; attended Michigan State College and the University of Illinois; graduated, Indiana College of Mortuary Science; served in Army Air Force, Southwest Pacific Theater, WWII; has received numerous awards and honors; has two children and two grandchildren.

Representative, 103rd District
RICK WINKEL, R - Champaign

Springfield: 2005-G Stratton Bldg., 62706; (217) 782-2507;
  E-mail: rickwinkel@rickwinkel.com
District: One East A Huntington Towers,
  201 W. Springfield Ave., P.O. Box 1736, Champaign
  61824-1736; (217) 355-4994; Fax (217) 355-4996
Years served: 1995-present

Legislative assignments: Committees on Judiciary II-Criminal Law (minority spokesperson); Elections & Campaign Reform (vice spokesperson); The Disabled Community (vice spokesperson); Elementary & Secondary Education; Higher Education; Property Tax Reform & School Funding; Legislative Audit Commission.

Biography: Attorney; born Sept. 25, 1956, in Kankakee; B.A., economics, University of Illinois at Urbana-Champaign, 1979; J.D., DePaul University College of Law, Chicago, 1982; of counsel, Meyer, Capel, Hirschfeld, Muncy, Jahn & Aldeen, P.C., Champaign; member, Champaign County Board, 1992-94; married (wife, Debra), has two children, Meghan and David.

Representative, 104th District
THOMAS B. BERNS, R - Urbana

Springfield: 2008-H Stratton Bldg., 62706;
  (217) 782-8173; Fax (217) 557-7209;
  E-mail: bca@shout.net
District: 1717 Philo Rd., Ste. 27, P.O. Box 1047, Urbana
  61803-1047; (217) 384-5336; Fax (217) 384-5645
Years served: Elected Nov. 7, 2000; Appointed Nov. 13, 2000

Legislative assignments: Committees on Urban Revitalization (minority spokesperson); Aging; Appropriations-Higher Education; Cities & Villages; Consumer Protection; Higher Education.

Biography: Professional engineer & surveyor; born April 8, 1945, in Chicago; B.S., civil engineering, University of Illinois, 1968; Air Force ROTC; received "Distinguished Alumnus" award for 1996 from the Civil and Environmental Engineering Department of the University of Illinois Alumni Association; married (wife, Jeannie), has two children, Becky and Michael, and two grandchildren.

Senator, 53rd District
JUDITH A. MYERS, R - Danville

Springfield: M-106 Capitol Bldg., 62706; (217) 782-8899;
Fax (217) 782-0650
District: 809 Oak St., Danville 61832;
(217) 443-1997; Fax (217) 443-2725;
E-mail: jamyers@soltec.net; 1113 Lincoln Ave.,
Charleston 61920; (217) 348-1998; Fax (217) 348-1985;
115 E. Walnut, Watseka 60970; (815) 432-2293;
Fax (815) 432-2294
Years served: 1997-present

Legislative assignments: Committees on Executive Appointments (vice chairperson); Agriculture & Conservation; Local Government.

Biography: Full-time state legislator; born Oct. 29, 1939, in Winamac, IN; B.S., Purdue University; first recipient, Athena "Woman of the Year" award, 1992, Business and Professional Women, Chamber of Commerce and Oldsmobile; "Woman of Distinction" award, American Association of University Women; married (husband, Mel), has five children and three grandchildren.

Representative, 105th District
WILLIAM B. BLACK, R - Danville
Assistant Minority Leader

Springfield: 634 Capitol Bldg., 62706; (217) 782-4811;
Fax (217) 782-1873; E-mail: wbblack@soltec.net
District: 119 1/2 S. Gilbert, Danville 61832;
(217) 431-1986; Fax (217) 431-2088; 115 E. Walnut,
Watseka 60970; (815) 432-2293
Years served: 1986-present

Legislative assignments: Committee on Child Support Enforcement; Transportation & Motor Vehicles; Ex officio member of all House committees; Republican Floor Leader; Commission on Intergovernmental Cooperation.

Biography: Educator and community college administrator; born Nov. 11, 1941, in Danville; B.A., William Jewell College, Liberty, MO; M.A., University of Illinois; post-graduate studies, Eastern Illinois University and Illinois State University; has received many "Outstanding Legislator" awards from various associations; married (wife, Sharon), has two children and four grandchildren.

Representative, 106th District
DALE A. RIGHTER, R - Mattoon

Springfield: 2123-O Stratton Bldg., 62706; (217) 782-6674; E-mail: drighter@worthlink.net
District: 105 N. 10th St., Mattoon 61938; (217) 235-6033;
Fax (217) 235-6052
Years served: 1997-present

Legislative assignments: Committees on Computer Technology (minority spokesperson); Higher Education (vice spokesperson); Financial Institutions; Judiciary I-Civil Law; State Government Administration; Special Committee on State Procurement; Subcommittee on Department of Children & Family Services Reform.

Biography: Attorney, former prosecutor; born Aug. 23, 1966, in Mattoon; B.A., accounting, Eastern Illinois University; J.D., St. Louis University School of Law.

Senator, 54th District
WILLIAM L. O'DANIEL, D - Mt. Vernon

Springfield: 103-A Capitol Bldg., 62706; (217) 782-5304;
Fax (217) 782-5252;
E-mail: odaniel@senatedem.state.il.us
District: 2929 Broadway, Mt. Vernon 62864;
(618) 242-7388; Fax (618) 242-7393
Years served: 1974-77 (House); 1985-present (Senate)

Legislative assignments: Committees on Agriculture &
Conservation (minority spokesperson); State Government
Operations; Transportation; Joint Committee on
Administrative Rules; Agricultural Export Advisory
Committee; Forestry Development Council (Illinois); Rail
Passenger Advisory Council (Interagency); Board of State Fair Advisors; Swine Disease
Control Advisory Committee.

Biography: Farmer and businessman; born Dec. 4, 1923, in Union County, KY; Presidential
appointment as State Executive Director of the Agriculture Stabilization and Conservation
Service for the U.S. Department of Agriculture, 1977-81; paratrooper, Pacific theater,
WWII; married (wife, Norma), has five children.

Representative, 107th District
JOHN O. JONES, R - Mt. Vernon

Springfield: 2111-N Stratton Bldg., 62706;
(217) 782-0471; Fax (217) 782-1275;
E-mail: jojones@midwest.net
District: 2929 Broadway, Ste. 5, Mt. Vernon 62864;
(618) 242-9511; Fax (618) 242-9516
Years served: 1995-present

Legislative assignments: Committees on Tourism (minority
spokesperson); Appropriations-General Services (vice
spokesperson); Agriculture; Counties & Townships;
Transportation & Motor Vehicles; Veterans' Affairs.

Biography: Owner, Trucking Business; born Oct. 8, 1940, in
Broughton; graduated, Mt. Vernon Township High School; served four years in U.S. Air
Force; married (wife, Mimi), has two children, Natalie and Aaron.

Representative, 108th District
CHARLES A. HARTKE, D - Teutopolis
Assistant Majority Leader

Springfield: 2044-J Stratton Bldg., 62706; (217) 782-2087;
Fax (217) 524-0867; E-mail: leader@effingham.net
District: 110 E. Section, P.O. Box 1205, Effingham 62401;
(217) 342-2353; Fax (217) 347-3305
Years served: 1985-present

Legislative assignments: Committees on Agriculture; Cities
& Villages; Environment & Energy; Transportation & Motor
Vehicles; Special Committee on Prison Management Reform;
Ex officio member of all House committees.

Biography: Farmer; born May 7, 1944, in Effingham; served
in U.S. Army, Vietnam veteran; received "Public Service" award from Illinois Electric
Cooperative, 1992, and "Outstanding Efforts on Behalf of Education" award from Illinois
Association of Regional Superintendents of Schools, 1992; married (wife, Kathy), has two
children and five grandchildren.

Senator, 55th District
FRANK C. WATSON, R - Greenville
Assistant Majority Leader

Springfield: 321 Capitol Bldg., 62706; (217) 782-5755;
  Fax (217) 782-7818
District: 890 Franklin, Carlyle 62231; (618) 594-4553;
  Fax (618) 594-4918; Vandalia (618) 283-0955
Years served: 1979-83 (House); 1983-present (Senate)

Legislative assignments: Committees on Agriculture &
Conservation; Education; Executive; Southwest Illinois
Metropolitan & Regional Planning Commission; Special
Senate Committee on State Board of Education; Legisla-
tive Audit Commission; Legislative Printing Unit.

Biography: Pharmacist; born July 26, 1945, in St. Louis, MO; B.S., pharmacy, Purdue
University; former trustee and supervisor, Bond County Central Township; married (wife,
Susan Rasler), has two children.

Representative, 109th District
KURT M. GRANBERG, D - Carlyle
Assistant Majority Leader

Springfield: 300 Capitol Bldg., 62706; (217) 782-0066
District: 103 E. Broadway, P.O. Box 707, Centralia 62801;
  (618) 533-0296; Fax (618) 533-2153
Years served: 1987-present

Legislative assignments: Committees on Aviation;
Personnel & Pensions; Revenue; Special Committees on
Judicial Reapportionment (chairperson); Conflicts of
Interest; Prosecutorial Misconduct; Committee of the
Whole; Ex officio member of all House committees.

Biography: Attorney; born June 16, 1953, in Breese; B.A.,
political science and criminal justice, University of Illinois; J.D., IIT-Chicago-Kent College
of Law.

Representative, 110th District
RON STEPHENS, R - Troy
Assistant Minority Leader

Springfield: 220 Capitol Bldg., 62706; (217) 782-6401;
  Fax (217) 557-3047; E-mail: stephens@apci.net
District: 535 Edwardsville Rd., Ste. 110, Troy 62294;
  (618) 667-0110; Fax (618) 667-8669
Years served: 1985-91; 1993-present

Legislative assignments: Committees on Appropriations-
Public Safety; Aviation; Registration & Regulation; Special
Committee on State Procurement; Committee of the Whole;
Ex officio member of all House committees.

Biography: Self-employed pharmacist; born Feb. 19, 1948,
in East St. Louis; B.S., St. Louis College of Pharmacy, 1975; Vietnam veteran, awarded
Bronze Star and Purple Heart; married (wife, Karen), has five children and one grandchild.

Senator, 56th District
EVELYN M. BOWLES, D - Edwardsville
Deputy Minority Caucus Chair

Springfield: M-103-F Capitol Bldg., 62706;
(217) 782-5247; Fax (217) 782-1631;
E-mail: bowles@senatedem.state.il.us
District: #4 Club Centre, Ste. E, P.O. Box 248,
Edwardsville 62025; (618) 656-8422;
Fax (618) 656-2425
Years served: 1994-present

Legislative assignments: Committees on Licensed
Activities (minority spokesperson); Agriculture and
Conservation; Executive; Legislative Information System.

Biography: Full-time state legislator; born April 22, 1921, in Worden; attended Illinois
State University, Greenville College and Southern Illinois University; United States Coast
Guard Women's Reserve (SPARS) Intelligence Division, 1943-45; single.

Representative, 111th District
STEVE DAVIS, D - Bethalto

Springfield: 2057-L Stratton Bldg., 62706;
(217) 782-5996; Fax (217) 782-1333
District: 2 Terminal Drive, Ste. 18-B, East Alton 62024;
(618) 259-4934; Fax (618) 259-5043; Granite City
(618) 876-1565
Years served: 1995-present

Legislative assignments: Committees on Constitutional
Officers (chairperson); Environment & Energy (vice chairperson); Appropriations-Higher Education; Personnel &
Pensions; Public Utilities; Registration & Regulation; Special Committee on Telecommunications Rewrite; Joint Committee on Administrative Rules.

Biography: Full-time state legislator; born Sept. 22, 1949, in Alton; attended Southern
Illinois University-Edwardsville, majored in engineering; attended Lewis and Clark
Community College; served six years in the U. S. Army Reserves; married (wife, Carol),
has two children, Shane and Shelly.

Representative, 112th District
JAY C. HOFFMAN, D - Collinsville

Springfield: 2060-L Stratton Bldg., 62706;
(217) 782-8018; Fax (217) 557-2763
District: 126 Vandalia, Ste. 1, Collinsville 62234;
(618) 345-2176; Fax (618) 345-3338
Years served: 1991-present

Legislative assignments: Committees on Transportation
& Motor Vehicles (chairperson); Appropriations-Public
Safety; Computer Technology; Judiciary I-Civil Law; Labor.

Biography: Attorney; born Nov. 6, 1961, in Highland; B.S.,
finance, Illinois State University; J.D., St. Louis University
School of Law; married (wife, Laurie), has two children.

Senator, 57th District
JAMES F. CLAYBORNE, JR., D - Belleville

Springfield: 103-C Capitol Bldg., 62706;
(217) 782-5399; Fax (217) 782-5252;
E-mail: clayborne@senatedem.state.il.us
District: 327 Missouri Ave., Rm. 422, East St. Louis
62201; (618) 875-1212; Fax (618) 274-3010; 9200 W.
Main St., Ste. 2, Belleville 62223; (618) 397-2714
Years served: 1995-present

Legislative assignments: Committees on Revenue (minority spokesperson); Appropriations; Pension Laws Commission.

Biography: Attorney; born Dec. 29, 1963, in St. Louis, MO; B.S., political science, Tennessee State University; J.D., University of Miami; corporate counselor for City of East St. Louis; former St. Clair County Assistant State's Attorney; married (wife, Staci), has four children.

Representative, 113th District
THOMAS HOLBROOK, D - Belleville

Springfield: 2065-L Stratton Bldg., 62706;
(217) 782-0104; Fax (217) 782-1333
District: 9200 W. Main St., Ste. 4, Belleville 62223; (618)
394-2211; Fax (618) 394-2210; 1310 Niedringhaus,
Granite City 62040; (618) 451-0200
Years served: 1995-present

Legislative assignments: Committees on Tourism (chairperson); Constitutional Officers; Environment & Energy; Veterans' Affairs; Special Committee on Telecommunications Rewrite; Committee of the Whole; Legislative Space Needs Commission; Council on Aging; Advisory Board on Reuse of Military Bases.

Biography: Electrical/Instrumentation Maintenance; born Nov. 23, 1949, in St. Louis, MO; B.A., social science, government, Southern Illinois University at Edwardsville; member, St. Clair County Board, 1981-94; union member, 27 years; union official, 17 years; selected "Outstanding Young Man in America," 1984 and 1986; married (wife, Molly), has one daughter, Susan.

Representative, 114th District
WYVETTER H. YOUNGE, D - East St. Louis

Springfield: 2058-L Stratton Bldg., 62706;
(217) 782-5951; Fax (217) 782-8794
District: 1010 Martin Luther King Dr., East St. Louis
62201; (618) 875-1691; Fax (618) 875-6323
Years served: 1975-present

Legislative assignments: Committee on Appropriations-Higher Education (chairperson); Appropriations-Elementary & Secondary Education; Appropriations-Public Safety.

Biography: Attorney; B.S., Hampton Institute; J.D., St. Louis University School of Law; L.L.M., Washington University School of Law; former Assistant Circuit Attorney, City of St. Louis; received "Best Legislator" award from the UAW, 1993; married (husband, Richard G. Younge, attorney), has three children, Ruth, Torque and Margaret.

Senator, 58th District
DAVID LUECHTEFELD, R - Okawville

Springfield: M-122 Capitol Bldg., 62706; (217) 782-8137
District: 700 N. Front, Okawville 62271; (618) 243-9014;
  Fax (618) 243-5376; 508 N. Hickory, DuQuoin 62832;
  (618) 542-3363; Fax (618) 542-2947; 300 E. Main,
  Carbondale 62901; (618) 529-3866; Fax (618) 529-2788
Years served: 1995-present

Legislative assignments: Committees on State Government
Operations (vice chairperson); Agriculture & Conservation;
Licensed Activities.

Biography: Full-time state legislator; retired teacher,
basketball coach; born Nov. 8, 1940, in Lively Grove; graduate, Okawville High School (1958);
bachelor's degree, St. Louis University (1962); master's degree, Southern Illinois University
at Edwardsville (1970); former teacher, athletic director and baseball and basketball coach;
married (wife, Flo), has four children.

Representative, 115th District
MIKE BOST, R - Murphysboro

Springfield: 2023-H Stratton Bldg., 62706;
  (217) 782-0387; Fax (217) 557-7213
District: 300 E. Main, Carbondale 62901; (618) 457-5787;
  Fax (618) 457-2990; 158 E. Vienna St., Anna 62906;
  (618) 833-3247; Perry County Courthouse, 2nd Fl.,
  NE Corner, Pinckneyville 62274
Years served: 1995-present

Legislative assignments: Committees on Public Utilities
(minority spokesperson); Constitutional Officers (vice
spokesperson); Veterans' Affairs (vice spokesperson);
Higher Education; Special Committees on Telecommunications Rewrite; Tobacco Settlement Proceeds.

Biography: Full-time state legislator; born Dec. 30, 1960, in Murphysboro; graduated,
Murphysboro High School, 1979; Certified Firefighter II, University of Illinois; served in
U.S. Marine Corps (1979-82); married (wife, Tracy), has three children, Stephen, Kasey
and Kaitlin, and one grandson, Spencer.

Representative, 116th District
DAN REITZ, D - Steeleville

Springfield: 2062-L Stratton Bldg., 62706;
  (217) 782-1018; Fax (217) 782-0945;
  E-mail: repreitz@egyptian.net
District: 128-A W. Main, Sparta 62286; (618) 443-5757;
  Fax (618) 443-3800
Years served: 1997-present

Legislative assignments: Committees on Cities & Villages
(chairperson); Agriculture (vice chairperson); Environment
& Energy; Personnel & Pensions; Registration & Regulation; Transportation & Motor Vehicles; Special Committees
on Prison Management Reform; Telecommunications Rewrite.

Biography: Born March 16, 1954, in Red Bud; educated, Steeleville High School; former
Randolph County Commissioner, 1986-97; president, Illinois County Board Association, 1996;
married (wife, Joyce), has three children, Nathan, Nicholas and Natalie.

Senator, 59th District
LARRY D. WOOLARD, D - Carterville
Springfield: 311 Capitol Bldg., 62706;
(217) 782-5509; Fax (217) 782-3213;
E-mail: lwoolard@sendem.state.il.us
District: 308-B W. Plaza Dr., Carterville 62918;
(618) 985-5559; Fax (618) 985-2921;
E-mail: lwoolard@globaleyes.net
Years served: 1989-2001 (House); 2001-present (Senate)

Legislative assignments: Committees on Agriculture & Conservation; Commerce & Industry; Education; Intergovernmental Cooperation Commission.

Biography: Born Sept. 20, 1941, in Williamson County; graduated, Herrin High School, 1959; former business owner; elected Williamson County Commissioner and Chairman, two terms, 1984-88; elected to Carterville School Board, five terms, served as President; first President of Carterville Chamber of Commerce; honorable discharge from U.S. Army Reserves; married (wife, Mary Ann), has four children, Laurie, Scott, Michelle and Jason, and four grandchildren, Kyle, Matthew, Megan Ann and Courtney Marie.

Representative, 117th District
GARY F. FORBY, D - Benton
Springfield: 2086-M Stratton Bldg., 62706;
(217) 782-1051; Fax (217) 782-0882
District: P.O. Box 1000, Benton 62812;
(618) 439-2504; Fax (618) 438-3704
Years served: 2001-present

Legislative assignments: Committees on Aging; Agriculture; Cities & Villages; Commerce & Business Development; Counties & Townships; State Government Administration.

Biography: Full-time state legislator; born Jan. 4, 1945; former farmer; past owner, Forby Excavating, Inc., Benton; former member and chairman, Franklin County Board; former member, Franklin-Williamson Human Services Board; serves on Southern Illinois Workforce Man-Tra-Con Board; member, Operating Engineers and Laborers' International unions, 30 years; married (wife, Angie), has four children and one grandchild.

Representative, 118th District
JIM FOWLER, D - Harrisburg
Springfield: 2080-M Stratton Bldg., 62706;
(217) 782-5131; Fax (217) 557-7680
District: 617 E. Church St., Ste. 8, Harrisburg 62946;
(618) 253-4189; Fax (618) 253-3136; 106 W. 5th St.,
Metropolis 62960; (618) 524-8160
Years served: 1998-present

Legislative assignments: Committees on Counties & Townships (chairperson); Higher Education (vice chairperson); Agriculture; Elementary & Secondary Education; State Government Administration; Transportation & Motor Vehicles; Special Committee on Prison Management Reform.

Biography: Full-time state legislator; born June 11, 1934, in Galatia; served in U.S. Navy, four years; Illinois State Police, 28 years; Saline County Clerk, 13 1/2 years; married (wife, Mable), has two daughters and five grandchildren.

STATE CAPITOL BUILDING

Illinois has had six State Capitol buildings in three cities since becoming the 21st state on Dec. 3, 1818. The sixth and present Capitol was completed over a 20-year period in 1888 in Springfield. It was designed by architects John Cochrane, George Garnsey and Alfred Piquenard. The Capitol cost $4.5 million.

In addition to housing the executive officers and the legislators, the Capitol originally provided quarters for the Supreme Court, government agencies, regulatory boards and military leaders. There were also three museums, several libraries, a hall of flags and the state's archives. Many of those are now housed in separate buildings throughout the Capitol Complex.

The Capitol underwent major external restoration in 1983 and 1984, and the Capitol Dome was restored in 1986.

The Capitol Dome

The State Capitol Building

NINETY-SECOND GENERAL ASSEMBLY
Senate Republican Staff

Carter Hendren
Chief of Staff

Tom Taylor
Deputy Chief of Staff
Chicago Office

Patricia Schuh
Communications
Director

Phil Weber
Research Director

Tim Nuding
Appropriations
Director

MayeBeth Hadfield
Parliamentarian

Senate Democratic Staff

Courtney Nottage
Chief of Staff

David Gross
Deputy Chief of Staff

Lawren Tucker
Policy Director

Cindy Huebner
Director,
Communications
& Research

Elgie Sims
Appropriations
Director

NINETY-SECOND GENERAL ASSEMBLY
House Democratic Staff

Timothy D. Mapes
Chief of Staff

John Lowder
*Director, Research-
Appropriations Unit*

Eileen Mitchell
*Director, Issues
Development Unit*

Robert A. Uhe
*Counsel to the
Speaker*

Steve Brown
Press Secretary

House Republican Staff

Michael Tristano
Chief of Staff

Laura Anderson
Deputy Chief of Staff

Robert Churchill
General Counsel

Gregg Durham
Press Spokesman

Scott Reimers
Research Director

OFFICE OF THE AUDITOR GENERAL

One of the strengths of our government has been that no single person has been solely responsible for either operating or policing the system that maintains and accounts for public funds. In Illinois, until recent times, the policing of this system consisted almost exclusively of financial auditing, and then, almost solely as a pre-audit function of the Auditor of Public Accounts.

In 1957, the Legislature passed the Illinois Auditing Act and created the Department of Audits and the Legislative Audit Commission. The head of the Department of Audits was appointed by the Governor with the consent of the Senate and charged with the financial post-audit responsibility. The Legislative Audit Commission reviewed reports issued by the Department of Audits.

The Illinois Constitution of 1970 initiated a fundamental change by mandating the Office of the Auditor General as a legislative rather than executive branch agency, building on the doctrine of "separation of powers." This assures that the authority that grants the funds and sets the program goals ultimately will review the expenditures and the results. It also closes the loop on governmental activities and sets the cornerstone of accountability in the hands of the people through their elected representatives.

To implement the new Post-Audit Program, the General Assembly passed the Illinois State Auditing Act. The act established a comprehensive program that not only covers financial auditing but also compliance, management and program auditing. These constitutional and statutory provisions give maximum assurance that the Post-Audit Program will be carried out fairly and independently.

The Office of the Auditor General was established to provide useful, timely information to the Legislature for legislative oversight of the obligation, receipt, expenditure and use of public funds and the operations of State Government. This function is performed through comprehensive audit and evaluation of the operations and performance of state agencies and programs to determine their conformity with fiscal requirements, legislative intent, and statutory mandates and prohibitions. The Auditor General also determines the underlying causes of problems and deficiencies.

By law, every state agency is the subject of an audit at least once every two years for an accounting of its financial operations and its compliance with state statutes. This is accomplished in part by the use of outside certified public accountants who act as special assistant auditors under the direction and management of the Auditor General.

To support information requirements, the office has developed an information classification, storage and retrieval system to analyze, compare and synthesize information obtained through the audit process, and to determine trends, combined agency and program problems, and accumulated effects of agency conduct. This information is provided to the Legislature for its consideration in connection with legislative revisions for the improvement of State Government.

The Office of the Auditor General has its primary office in Springfield, with a Chicago office in the State of Illinois Building. All office expenditures are from funds appropriated by the General Assembly.

Administrative Personnel: William G. Holland, *Auditor General;* John W. Kunzeman, *Deputy Auditor General;* Charles "Chip" Woodward, *Deputy Auditor General;* Rebecca Patton, *Chief Legal Counsel;* Carol Clarke, *Assistant to the Auditor General.*

LEGISLATIVE SUPPORT SERVICES

The Joint Committee on Legislative Support Services provides for the general administration and policy oversight of the various legislative support agencies and commissions that assist the General Assembly: Joint Committee on Administrative Rules; Economic and Fiscal Commission; Intergovernmental Cooperation Commission; Legislative Audit Commission; Legislative Information System; Legislative Printing Unit; Legislative Reference Bureau; Legislative Research Unit; Legislative Space Needs Commission, and the Pension Laws Commission.

The bipartisan joint committee is composed of the four legislative leaders — Senators James "Pate" Philip and Emil Jones, Jr., and Representatives Michael J. Madigan and Lee A. Daniels. Chairmanship of the committee rotates among the legislative leaders on an annual basis.

JOINT COMMITTEE ON ADMINISTRATIVE RULES

Vicki Thomas
Executive Director

Springfield: 700 Stratton Building; 62706
(217) 785-2254

The Joint Committee on Administrative Rules is a bipartisan legislative oversight committee created by the General Assembly in 1977. Pursuant to the Illinois Administrative Procedure Act, the committee is authorized to conduct systematic reviews of administrative rules promulgated by state agencies. The committee conducts several integrated review programs, including a review program for proposed, emergency and peremptory rulemaking, a review of new public acts and a complaint review program.

The committee is composed of 12 legislators who are appointed by the legislative leadership, and the membership is apportioned equally between the two houses and the two political parties. Members serve two-year terms, and the committee is co-chaired by a member of each party and legislative house. Support services for the committee are provided by 20-25 staff members.

Two purposes of the committee are to ensure that the Legislature is adequately informed of how laws are implemented through agency rulemaking and to facilitate public understanding of rules and regulations. To that end, in addition to the review of new and existing rulemaking, the committee monitors legislation that affects rulemaking and conducts a public act review to alert agencies to the need for rulemaking. The committee also distributes a weekly report, the *Flinn Report,* to inform and educate Illinois citizens about current rulemaking activity, and maintains the state's database for the *Illinois Administrative Code* and the *Illinois Register.*

Members: Senators Barack Obama (*co-chair*), J. Bradley Burzynski, Doris Karpiel, Lisa Madigan, William L. O'Daniel and Steve Rauschenberger; and Representatives Tom Ryder (*co-chair*), Tom Cross, Steve Davis, Phil Novak, Dan Rutherford and Todd Stroger.

Staff: Vicki Thomas, *executive director;* Claire B. Eberle, *deputy director.*

ECONOMIC AND FISCAL COMMISSION

Springfield: 703 Stratton Building; 62706
(217) 782-5320

Dan R. Long
Executive Director

The Illinois Economic and Fiscal Commission was created in 1972 by the 77th General Assembly to provide the Legislature with research and information regarding state and national economies and the revenues and operations of State Government. In 1979, the commission was further charged by the 81st General Assembly with responsibility for monitoring the long-term debt position of Illinois. Later, the General Assembly made the commission responsible for contract monitoring and approval of the State Employee Group Insurance Plan.

In carrying out these duties, the commission prepares general studies and analyses, including periodic revenue estimates, economic updates and an annual capital plan analysis. Furthermore, the commission prepares specific revenue and debt impact notes on proposed legislation in those areas.

The commission consists of 12 members as mandated by the Legislative Commission Reorganization Act of 1984. The four legislative leaders each appoint members.

Members: Senators Patrick Welch (*co-chair*), Miguel del Valle, Rickey Hendon, Chris Lauzen, John W. Maitland, Jr. and Steven J. Rauschenberger; and Representatives Terry R. Parke (*co-chair*), Mark Beaubien, Judy Erwin, Frank J. Mautino, Richard Myers and Jeffrey Schoenberg.

Staff: Dan R. Long, *executive director;* Lisa Barutcu, Donna K. Belknap, Edward H. Boss, Jr., Trevor Clatfelter, Kristi Conrad, B. Louise Forney, Sonya Hedges, Mike Howard, Lynnae Kapp, Jim Muschinske, Eric Noggle and Linda Roberts.

COMMISSION ON INTERGOVERNMENTAL COOPERATION

Springfield: 707 Stratton Building; 62706
(217) 782-6924

Leroy Whiting
Executive Director

Established in 1937, the Illinois Commission on Intergovernmental Cooperation is a bipartisan legislative support agency that addresses public policy issues significant at the federal, state and local levels of government. As the information center for the General Assembly in the field of state/federal relations, the commission maintains up-to-date information on federal aid received by the state and analyzes federal programs. A federal aid tracking system was initiated in 1977, in cooperation with the Bureau of the Budget, to monitor federal grant applications, awards and receipts of state agencies. Quarterly reports of this information are provided to the General Assembly and other state officials.

With the federal shift in emphasis from categorical to block grants in the early 1980s, the commission's responsibilities were amended to include a 16-member advisory committee on block grants, which conducts meetings and hearings concerning the administration of block grants in Illinois. The commission also receives descriptions from state agencies of state and local programs funded by block grants, as well as detailed information on expenditures and recipients of block grant funds.

In the area of state/local relations, the commission examines topics such as the condition of the state's infrastructure and the effect of state mandates on local governments. Other projects concern cataloging technical and financial state assistance to local governments, in addition to tracking their receipt of federal aid by program.

The commission also participates in intergovernmental concerns by:
- Assisting members of the General Assembly and other state officials in maintaining communication with federal and local officials.
- Sponsoring conferences on major issues that bring together representatives of all levels of government.
- Representing Illinois in the Council of State Governments and the National Conference of State Legislatures.
- Facilitating the use of compacts and agreements, uniform or reciprocal statutes, and rules and regulations with other states.

As stated in the statute creating it, the commission enables Illinois to "do its part in forming a more perfect union among the various governments in the United States."

Members (of the commission and advisory committee on block grants): Senators Kimberly A. Lightford (*co-chair*), Kirk W. Dillard, William E. Peterson, Edward F. Petka, Margaret Smith and Larry D. Woolard; and Representatives Kathleen L. Wojcik (*co-chair*), William B. Black, Elizabeth Coulson, Thomas J. Dart and Mary E. Flowers.

Staff: Leroy Whiting, *executive director;* Sandy Roberts, *associate director;* Laura Davis, Robert Davis, Kathleen Hazelwood, Carol House, Betty Husky, Kevin Jones, Jamie Kanallakan, Gennea Logan, Courtney Lubrant and Carrie Serati.

LEGISLATIVE AUDIT COMMISSION

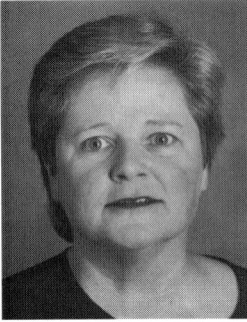

Springfield: 622 Stratton Building; 62706
(217) 782-7097

The Legislative Audit Commission is responsible for oversight of the State Audit Program, review of the stewardship of public funds, and the monitoring action to correct weaknesses disclosed by the audits of state agencies. The membership consists of 12 legislators appointed by the General Assembly leadership and is equally apportioned between the two houses and political parties.

The commission is empowered to direct the State Auditor General to undertake management, efficiency and program audits and special studies. During 2000, the commission took action on 178 compliance and financial audits and three management audits.

E. Jane Stricklin
Executive Director

The commission makes recommendations to the General Assembly for remedial legislation. It also recommends improvements to be implemented through administrative action by state agencies.

Members: Senators Thomas J. Walsh (*co-chair*), Vince Demuzio, Chris Lauzen, Donne E. Trotter, George P. Shadid and Frank Watson; and Representatives Julie A. Curry (*co-chair*), Robert Biggins, Frank J. Mautino, Mary K. O'Brien, Rick Winkel and Anne Zickus.

Staff: E. Jane Stricklin, *executive director.*

LEGISLATIVE INFORMATION SYSTEM

Springfield: 705 Stratton Building; 62706
(217) 782-3944

The Legislative Information System is the legislative support service agency responsible for providing the computer services and technical guidance required by the General Assembly and its committees, commissions and agencies.

Creation of the system can be traced to recommendations made in 1967 by the Illinois Commission on the Organization of the General Assembly. The commission identified areas where data processing could be applied to the operations of the General Assembly to improve the accuracy and timeliness of needed information and make it more readily available to legislators, their staffs and the public.

John T. Hatcher
Executive Director

The General Assembly and its agencies have rapidly expanded the applications and use of computerized data bases. These systems are used for drafting, processing, printing, filing and handling of bills, resolutions, journals, calendars, committee reports, research reports and other legislative documents. The use of these services and systems must be coordinated to ensure compatibility, facilitate the exchange of information and achieve operating economies.

The system is responsible for the operation of the legislative data center and associated equipment and software. Among the applications supported by this facility are the bill status, bill drafting and Illinois Revised Statutes data base. The system, in cooperation with the Secretary of State and the Joint Committee on Administrative Rules, also is responsible for the development and maintenance of the Illinois Administrative Code database.

Board Members: Senators Evelyn Bowles, Debbie Halvorson, Todd Sieben, David Sullivan and Louis Viverito; and Representatives Susan Garrett, Howard Kenner, Jack McGuire, James H. Meyer and Timothy H. Osmond.

Ex-officio Members: President of the Senate James "Pate" Philip, Senate Minority Leader Emil Jones, Jr., Speaker of the House Michael J. Madigan and House Minority Leader Lee A. Daniels.

Staff: John T. Hatcher, *executive director;* Tim Rice, *project manager;* Donna J. Burke, *administrative services;* Linda Lamberton, *support services;* Bernadette K. Emery, *application services,* and Daniel Winchester, *systems services.*

LEGISLATIVE PRINTING UNIT

John L. Rodems
Executive Director

Springfield: 105 Stratton Building; 62706
(217) 782-7312

The Legislative Printing Unit was established as a legislative support service agency by the Legislative Commission Reorganization Act of 1984. Prior to passage of this Act, the Printing Unit was part of the Legislative Council. The Act empowers the unit to provide printing services to members of the General Assembly, legislative committees and commissions and other legislative agencies in accordance with policies established by the Joint Committee on Legislative Support Services and with reasonable rules promulgated by the Legislative Printing Unit (par. 1009-2).

Among the services rendered is the designing and printing of stationery, envelopes, business cards, memo pads, postal cards, news release headings, legislative updates, legislative surveys and informational brochures. During the legislative session, the unit is responsible for the printing of calendars, bills, journals, amendments and conference committee reports. The *Legislative Synopsis and Digest*, which is published by the Legislative Reference Bureau, is prepared for print through the computer services of the Legislative Information System and printed by the Legislative Printing Unit.

The Printing Unit uses soybean inks manufactured in Illinois and uses 50 percent recycled content paper of various colors and weights for the requests of the members and Legislative Commissions.

The Legislative Printing Unit is headed by a bipartisan 12-member board, which oversees the unit's activities.

Members: Appointed by the Joint Committee on Legislative Support Services. Senators Dick Klemm *(co-chair)*, Kathleen K. Parker, Frank C. Watson, Patrick Welch, Margaret Smith and Antonio "Tony" Munoz; and Representatives Charles Morrow III *(co-chair)*, Mike Boland, John Fritchey, Brent Hassert, Michael P. McAuliffe and Raymond Poe.

Staff: John L. Rodems, *executive director;* Ron Rhone, *operations manager;* Sandra McDowell, *secretary;* Judy Gooding, *fiscal officer;* Wayne Lilly, *day shift supervisor;* Tom Kitchen, *assistant day shift supervisor;* Angelo Pescitelli, *night shift supervisor;* Roman Peter Dorr III, *assistant night shift supervisor.* **Typesetting:** Mike Powers, Mike Mohler, Robert McKinzie and Bruce Cody; **Printing:** Dale Cisco, Greg Keehner, Jermain Jefferson, Bobby Stoye, Bill Ryman, Gary Taylor, Marcus Laster and Ed Hopkins; **Bindery:** Mike Smith, Lynn Weber, Bill Hunt, Steve Yaris and Chris Patrinelis; **Delivery:** Audie Alexander.

LEGISLATIVE REFERENCE BUREAU

Richard C. Edwards
Executive Director

Springfield: 112 Capitol Building; 62706
(217) 782-6625

The Legislative Reference Bureau was created in 1913, the first of the modern legislative service agencies in Illinois. The bureau carries out a wide range of functions relating to the legal and technical operation of the General Assembly. The primary task of the bureau is the drafting and preparation of legislation, including bills, amendments, resolutions and conference committee reports. The vast majority of all legislation considered by the General Assembly is drafted by the bureau's staff, which in a typical biennium produces more than 25,000 documents. Attorneys employed by the bureau provide legal advice and drafting services to legislators of both parties and both houses, working on a nonpartisan basis in a confidential lawyer-client relationship. The bureau's drafting staff also includes paralegal professionals who draft resolutions and provide other drafting assistance.

For use in the drafting process, the bureau maintains a computer database of the current Illinois statutes, which it continually updates and edits as new laws are passed. While the statute database is primarily designed for internal use, it also is available on the Internet at www.legis.state.il.us/.

The Reference Bureau is responsible for recommending and preparing technical changes in the law. It prepares revisory bills that combine multiple enactments, correct technical errors, and revise, renumber and rearrange the law. The bureau also prepares bills to codify selected portions of the law and to implement executive branch reorganizations ordered by the Governor.

In 1989, the bureau began working on a plan for the reorganization of the Illinois statutes, and on Jan. 1, 1993, the new Illinois Compiled Statutes became effective. The bureau has a continuing duty to maintain the organization of the Illinois Compiled Statutes through periodic filings with the Secretary of State.

As an aid in tracking legislation, the bureau prepares and publishes the Legislative Synopsis and Digest. The digest contains a summary of legislative documents considered by the General Assembly, a record of all legislative actions on the documents and several indexes. The digest is made available electronically through the Legislative Information System. It also is published in book form during most weeks that the General Assembly is in session and is available to the public by subscription.

After the end of each spring legislative session, the bureau's legal staff reviews all reported decisions of the federal courts, the Illinois Supreme Court and the Illinois Appellate Court from the previous year. Cases that affect the interpretation of the Illinois constitution or statutes and cases that indicate a possible need for legislative action are identified and summarized in an annual case report, which is published by the bureau.

In addition, the bureau maintains a law library, which includes the current statutes of all 50 states, federal statutes and regulations, Illinois and federal case reports, an extensive collection of historical materials relating to Illinois statutes and legislative documents, and other materials relating to the development and interpretation of Illinois law. The bureau also coordinates the activities of the Illinois delegation to the National Conference of Commissioners on Uniform State Laws.

Subject to oversight by the Joint Committee on Legislative Support Services, the bureau has a 12-member board composed of three legislators appointed by each member of the Joint Committee.

Members: Senators William "Bill" Shaw (*co-chair*), Daniel J. Cronin, Patrick O'Malley, Christine Radogno, Carol Ronen and Ira Silverstein; and Representatives James B. Durkin (*co-chair*), Daniel J. Burke, Gwenn Klingler, Eileen Lyons, George F. Scully, Jr. and Todd H. Stroger.

Staff: Richard C. Edwards, *executive director;* E.F. "Fritz" Goebig, *deputy director;* Wayne Hedenschoug, *senior attorney;* Lori C. Bechtold, Robert L. Cohen, Andrea M. Creek, Lawrence R. Doll, David R. Heckleman, David R. Johnson, Jean A. McCay, Samuel J. Moore, James L. O'Brien, Amy R. Rosborough, John L. Shull and Nicole H. Truong, *staff attorneys;* Rebecca A. Hornbogen, *paralegal;* Bernadine Gretzer, *librarian;* Shirley Hatchett, *fiscal officer;* Kathleen Kenyon, *digest editor,* Debra Von Holten, *text supervisor*, and Sharon Eck, *administrative supervisor.*

Uniform Law Commissioners: Richard C. Edwards, Diane Ford, Steven G. Frost, Michael B. Getty, Harry D. Leinenweber, Jeremiah Marsh, Thomas J. McCracken, Jr., Randal C. Picker, Tom Ryder and Howard J. Swibel.

LEGISLATIVE RESEARCH UNIT

Patrick D. O'Grady
Executive Director

Springfield: 222 S. College,
Ste. 301; 62704
(217) 782-6851

The Legislative Research Unit (LRU) has served the research needs of the General Assembly for more than 60 years. Established in 1937 as the Illinois Legislative Council, the LRU is a bipartisan research agency for legislators, their staffs and the legislative leadership.

The LRU researches subjects such as: (1) *Law:* Illinois Constitution, laws and court decisions; laws of other states on an issue; federal laws, regulations and bills, and suggested or "model" laws. (2) *Science and health:* infectious and other diseases; health care; legal and illegal drugs; hazardous substances; environmental protection; water and energy resources, and public utilities. (3) *General:* business and economic development; insurance, tort and transportation laws; medical regulation and cost containment; taxation and revenue issues; campaign and election laws; local government and public school law and finance; public assistance programs and social services, and occupational licensing.

Major LRU publications include *First Reading,* a legislative newsletter; the *Directory of Illinois State Officials, Illinois Tax Handbook for Legislators* and *Visitors' Guide to the Illinois General Assembly* (annual); *Preface to Lawmaking* and State Government Organization Chart; *Constituent Services Guide, County Data Book* and Penalties for Crimes in Illinois chart (revised as needed), and *1970 Illinois Constitution Annotated for Legislators* (4th ed. 1996). Several LRU publications are available on the General Assembly Web site at www.legis.state.il.us/.

Other services of the LRU are a conference for newly elected legislators after each general election; the Legislative Staff Internship Program, in cooperation with the University of Illinois at Springfield, and the Legislative Information Booth on the third-floor rotunda of the State House.

Members: Senators William F. Mahar (*co-chair*), Larry Bomke, Debbie Halvorson, N. Duane Noland, Carol Ronen and William "Bill" Shaw; and Representatives Sara Feigenholtz (*co-chair*), Mark H. Beaubien, Jr., Patricia R. "Patti" Bellock, Constance A. "Connie" Howard, Susana Mendoza and Rosemary Mulligan.

Staff: Patrick D. O'Grady, *executive director;* David R. Miller, *deputy director of research;* Robert L. Bayless, *senior staff scientist;* George Rishel, *staff attorney;* Lillian Kinnel and Charles Minert, *senior research associates;* Neal Getz and Nicole Lisk Babcook, *research associates;* Taran Ley, *head librarian;* Susan K. Moseley, *fiscal officer;* Marilyn Flynn, *graphic artist,* and Sandy Bayless, *secretary to the director.*

142

LEGISLATIVE SPACE NEEDS COMMISSION

Mal Hildebrand
Executive Director

Springfield: 602 Stratton Building; 62706
(217) 782-7863

The Legislative Space Needs Commission provides facilities and meets space needs for the Illinois General Assembly and its supporting commissions and bureaus. The commission's goal is to provide a more functional facility with flexible and efficient space utilization resulting in effective processes and procedures.

The commission reviews and approves all contracts for the repair, rehabilitation, construction or alteration of all state buildings in the Springfield Capitol Complex, including tunnels, power and heating plants and surrounding grounds. In regard to areas of the Capitol and the William G. Stratton Building that are being rehabilitated, the commission correlates the House and Senate leadership's ideas with the needs and wants of the members and relays them to the architect. It also devised the Master Space Allocation Plan showing where all functions of the General Assembly, the supporting commissions and bureaus, and the executive offices in the Capitol Building will be located. The commission plans office layouts for General Assembly members, and also is responsible for purchasing for the State of Illinois, ground and buildings in the area of Springfield bounded by Third, Cook, Pasfield and Washington Streets.

Members: Senators Wendell Jones (*co-chair*), Walter W. Dudycz, Terry Link, Dennis J. Jacobs, Margaret Smith and Stanley Weaver; and Representatives Joseph M. Lyons (*co-chair*), Lovana "Lou" Jones, Thomas Holbrook, Gwenn Klingler, Raymond Poe and Thomas B. Berns.

Staff: Mal Hildebrand, *executive director;* Dean McGeath, *deputy director.*

PENSION LAWS COMMISSION

Springfield: 222 S. College,
Ste. 302; 62704
(217) 557-0688

The Pension Laws Commission performs a continuing study of the laws and practices relating to public pensions, retirement and disability benefits for persons in state or local government service and their survivors and dependents. Additionally, the commission evaluates existing laws and practices and makes recommendations on proposed changes to the Illinois Pension Code. The commission consists of 16 members, eight of whom are members of the General Assembly and eight members of the public, with knowledge and interest in public pension legislation.

Patricia A. Stevens
Executive Director

The commission prepares Pension Impact Notes that are filed with the General Assembly. The notes describe proposed legislative changes and estimate the impact on public pensions. The commission may make comments and recommendations to the General Assembly regarding the legislative proposals.

The commission performs studies and prepares reports on issues affecting public pensions, including the annual *Report on the Financial Condition of the State Retirement Systems*, which provides a periodic appraisal of the long-term financial status of the state-funded retirement systems.

Members: Senators Thomas Walsh *(co-chair)*, James Clayborne, Jr., Robert Molaro and Peter Roskam; and Representatives Harold Murphy *(co-chair)*, Doug Hoeft, David Leitch and Michael Smith; and public members Greg Bielawski, Christine Boardman, John J. Fennell, Jr., Stephen Kern, John L. Novak, Hank Scheff, Larry E. Sims and Sam Wolf.

Staff: Patricia A. Stevens, *executive director*; Timothy B. Blair, *senior pension analyst*.

ILLINOIS LEGISLATIVE
CORRESPONDENTS ASSOCIATION

Ben Kiningham
Illinois Radio Network
ILCA President

The Illinois Legislative Correspondents Association (ILCA) is an organization of newspapers, news services, television stations and radio stations whose representatives cover and report actions of the Illinois General Assembly and State Government.

Chicago and St. Louis newspapers, the Associated Press and various downstate newspapers maintain year-round bureaus at the Capitol.

Through these representatives, Illinois State Government is one of the most comprehensively reported in the nation.

The ILCA, as it is now constituted, dates back to February 1946. Led by the late Don E. Chamberlain, correspondents covering the Capitol at that time banded together to work with Governor Dwight H. Green, Secretary of State Edward J. Barrett and legislative leaders to set up modern press room facilities for the association.

Four rooms were given to the press in 1947, replacing the old system where reporters wrote their copy, elbow to elbow, in anterooms and under stairs. As the ILCA continued to grow and the television and broadcast media joined the ranks of those presenting detailed coverage of State Government, larger quarters were provided the association near the legislative halls.

Working with the officers of the ILCA in 1976, the Illinois Space Needs Commission designed an entirely new, modern press room on the mezzanine between the second and third floors of the State House. The most recent improvement, completed in 2000, was renovation of the television newsroom, where many of the formal press conferences are held.

Presidents of the ILCA, since the association was formalized in 1946, have included the late John Dreiske, political editor of the *Chicago Sun-Times;* the late Johnson Kanady, Jr., formerly with the *Chicago Tribune* and Illinois Power Co.; the late Robert P. Howard of the *Chicago Tribune;* the late Charles Whalen of the *Associated Press;* the late Marion "Hap" Lynes of the *St. Louis Globe-Democrat;* William J. O'Connell, Jr. of the *Peoria Journal-Star;* Burnell Heinecke, formerly of the *Chicago Sun-Times* and Heinecke News Service; Charles N. Wheeler III, formerly of the *Chicago Sun-Times;* Becky Enrietto, formerly of the Illinois News Network; Ray Serati, formerly of Copley News Service; Don Thompson, formerly of *The Daily Herald*, and current president Ben Kiningham of the Illinois Radio Network.

ASSOCIATION OFFICERS

Ben Kiningham, Illinois Radio Network .... *President*
Ray Long, *Chicago Tribune* .... *Vice-President*
Anthony Man, *Lee Enterprises* .... *Secretary*
Diane Ross, Statehouse News Service .... *Treasurer*
Dave McKinney, *Chicago Sun-Times* .... *Board Member*
Doug Finke, Copley Illinois Newspapers .... *Board Member*
Tom Massey .... *Press Secretary*

Rick Pearson
Chicago Tribune

Ray Long
Chicago Tribune

Christi Parsons
Chicago Tribune

Dave McKinney
Chicago Sun-Times

Kevin McDermott
St. Louis
Post-Dispatch

Chris Wills
Associated Press

John O'Connor
Associated Press

Seth Perlman
Associated Press

Kate Clements
Champaign
News-Gazette

Dan Vock
Chicago Daily
Law Bulletin

Dana Heupel
Copley Illinois
Newspapers

Doug Finke
Copley Illinois
Newspapers

Bernard Schoenburg
State
Journal-Register

Adriana Colindres
Copley Illinois
Newspapers

Dean Olsen
Copley Illinois
Newspapers

Diane Ross
Statehouse
News Service

Kurt Erickson
Bloomington
Pantagraph

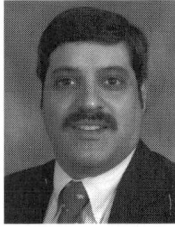

Anthony Man
Lee Enterprises

Rick Goldstein
Lee Enterprises

Nancy Chesley
Lee Enterprises

John Patterson
The Daily Herald

Madeleine Doubek
The Daily Herald

Chad Anderson
Rockford
Register Star

Aaron Chambers
Illinois Issues

Scott Reeder
Small Newspapers

Stephanie McClelland
Small Newspapers

Ben Kiningham
Illinois Radio
Network

Eva Goltermann
Illinois Radio
Network

Rich Denison
Metro Networks

Steve Grzanich
WBBM-Radio

Jim Leach
WMAY-Radio

Michelle Eccles
WTAX-Radio

Bill Wheelhouse
WUIS-IPR

Sean Crawford
WUIS-IPR

Rick Barrett
WAND-TV

Mike Flannery
WBBM-TV

Jolean Olson
WCIA-TV

Matt Purkes
WCIA-TV

Andy Shaw
WLS-TV

Dick Kay
WMAQ-TV

Rich Miller
Capitol Fax

Jim Broadway
Illinois School
News Service

Joe Harris
State Capital
Information Service

Luke Carey
State Capital
Information Service

Tom Massey
ILCA Press Secretary

Rick Millard
ILCA Assistant
Press Secretary

NEWS MEDIA IN ILLINOIS

CITY   NEWSPAPERS
Daily (D); Weekly .... PHONE
RADIO; TELEVISION; CABLE (C)

ADAMS

Augusta	Eagle	(217) 392-2715
Barry	Paper	(217) 335-2112
Camp Point	Journal	(217) 593-6515
Clayton	Enterprise	(217) 593-6515
Golden	New Era	(217) 593-6515
Liberty	Eliott Publishing	(217) 645-3033
	Liberty Bee Times	(217) 645-3033
Mendon	Dispatch	(217) 593-6515
Quincy	Herald-Whig (D)	(217) 223-5100
	WGCA-FM	(217) 224-9422
	WGEM-AM-FM-TV	(217) 228-6600
	WQUB-FM	(217) 228-5410
	WCOY-FM/WQCY-FM/WTAD-AM/ KGRC-FM/KZZK-FM/	
	....	(217) 224-4102
	WPWQ-FM	(217) 224-4653
	WTJR-TV	(217) 228-1616
	KHQA-TV	(217) 222-6200
	Insight Communications ..	(217) 224-1117

ALEXANDER

Cairo	Citizen	(618) 734-4242
	WKRO-AM	(618) 734-1490

BOND

Greenville	Advocate	(618) 664-3144
	WGEL-FM	(618) 664-3300
Sorento	News	(217) 532-3933

BOONE

Belvidere	Daily Republican	(815) 544-9811
	Boone County Journal	(815) 544-4430
	Cover Story	(815) 544-9811

BROWN

Mt. Sterling	Democrat Message	(217) 773-3371

BUREAU

Mendota	WGLC-FM	(815) 224-2100
Princeton	Bureau County Republican	(815) 875-4461
	WZOE-AM-FM/WRVY-FM	
	....	(815) 875-8014
Sheffield	Bulletin	(815) 454-2072
Spring Vally		
	WIVQ-FM	(815) 224-2100
Streator	WSPL-AM/WSTQ-FM	(815) 224-2100
Tiskilwa	Bureau Valley Chief	(815) 646-4731
Walnut	Leader	(815) 379-9290

CALHOUN

Hardin	Calhoun News	(618) 576-2244
	Calhoun Herald	(618) 576-2716
	Calhoun New-Herald	(618) 576-2345

CARROLL

Lanark	Prairie Advocate	(815) 493-2560
Mt. Carroll	Mirror-Democrat	(815) 244-2411
Savanna	Times-Journal	(815) 273-2277
	WCCI-FM	(815) 273-7757
Thomson	Carroll County Review	(815) 259-2131

CASS

Arenzville	Triopia Tribune	(217) 754-3369
Ashland	Sentinel	(217) 476-3332
Beardstown	Cass County Star-Gazette	(217) 323-1010
	WRMS-AM/FM	(217) 323-1790
Virginia	Gazette of Cass County ...	(217) 452-3513
	Cass Communications (C)	(217) 452-7725

CHAMPAIGN

Champaign	News-Gazette (D)	(217) 351-5252
	WBCP-AM	(217) 359-1580
	WBGL-FM	(217) 359-8232
	WDWS-AM/WHMS-FM .	(217) 351-5300

	WEFT-FM	(217) 359-9338
	WIXY-FM/WLRW-FM	(217) 355-2222
	WKIO-FM	(217) 352-1040
	WPCD-FM	(217) 351-2230
	WPGU-FM	(217) 244-3000
	WCIA-TV	(217) 356-8333
	WICD-TV	(217) 351-8500
Fisher	Reporter	(217) 897-1525
Mahomet	Citizen	(217) 586-2512
Ogden	Leader	(217) 582-2373
Philo	Southern Champaign County Today	(217) 832-4201
Rantoul	Press	(217) 892-9613
Tolono	County Star	(217) 485-4010
Urbana	WILL-AM/FM	(217) 333-0850
	WBNB-FM/WEBX-FM/WGKC-FM/	
	WQQB-FM	(217) 367-1195
	WCCU-TV	(217) 367-8827
	WILL-TV	(217) 333-1070
	Insight Communications .	(217) 384-2530

CHRISTIAN

Assumption		
	Golden Prairie News	(217) 226-3721
Edinburg	Herald-Star	(217) 623-5523
Morrisonville		
	Times	(217) 526-3323
Pana	News Palladium	(217) 562-2111
Taylorville	Breeze Courier (D)	(217) 824-2233
	WTIM-FM/WMKR-FM ...	(217) 824-3395
	Charter Communications	(217) 287-7991

CLARK

Casey	Reporter	(217) 932-5211
	Guardian	(217) 932-2093
	WKZI-AM	(217) 826-9673
Marshall	Advocate	(217) 826-3600
	Independent Choice	(217) 826-8661

CLAY

Flora	Daily Clay County Advocate Press	(618) 662-2108
	Hometown Journal	(618) 622-6622
	WNOI-FM-TV	(618) 662-8331
Louisville	Clay County Republican .	(618) 665-3135

CLINTON

Breese	Journal	(618) 526-7211
	Charter Communications .	(618) 526-4591
Carlyle	Union Banner	(618) 594-3131
	WCXO-FM	(618) 594-2490
New Baden	Clinton County News	(618) 588-7720
Trenton	Sun	(618) 224-9422

COLES

Charleston	Times Courier (D)	(217) 345-7085
	WEIC-AM	(217) 345-2148
	WEIU-FM	(217) 581-6116
	WEIU-TV	(217) 581-5956
	AT&T Broadband (C)	(217) 345-7071
Mattoon	Journal Gazette (D)	(217) 235-5656
	WHQQ-FM/WMCI-FM/WWGO-FM	
	....	(217) 235-5624
	WLKL-FM	(217) 234-5271
	WLBH-AM/FM	(217) 234-6464
Oakland	County Crossroads	(217) 346-2050

COOK

Alsip	Express	(708) 388-2425
	Star	(708) 802-8800
Arlington Heights		
	Daily Herald (D)	(847) 427-4300
	Journal	(847) 299-5511
	Post	(847) 797-5100
Barrington	Courier-Review	(847) 381-9200
Berkeley	WJJG-AM	(708) 493-1530
Berwyn	Berwyn Life	(708) 484-1234

149

COOK (cont'd)

Bridgeview	Independent	(708) 388-2425
Broadview	Suburban Life	(630) 368-1100
Brookfield	Suburban LIFE Citizen	(630) 368-1100
Buffalo Grove		
	Countryside	(847) 486-7300
	Journal & Topics	(847) 299-5511
Burbank	Burbank Stickney	
	Independent	(708) 388-2425
Calumet City		
	Star	(708) 802-8800
Chicago	Daily Defender (D)	(312) 225-2400
	Daily Herald	(847) 427-4300
	Daily Law Bulletin	(312) 644-7800
	Daily Southtown	(708) 633-6700
	El Manana Daily	(708) 652-5841
	Sun-Times (D)	(312) 321-3000
	Tribune (D)	(312) 222-3232
	Austin Weekly News	(773) 626-6332
	Back of the Yards Journal	(773) 927-7200
	Beverly News	(708) 388-2425
	Beverly Review	(773) 238-3366
	Booster	(847) 329-2000
	Bridgeport News	(312) 842-5883
	Brighton-McKinley Park Life	(773) 523-3663
	Calumet Herald	(773) 646-2800
	Chatham–Southeast Citizen	(773) 783-1251
	Crusader	(773) 752-2500
	Edgebrook-Sauganash Times Review	(847) 696-3133
	Edison-Norwood Times Review	(847) 696-3133
	Evergreen Gazette	(312) 472-2000
	Exito	(312) 654-3010
	EXTRA Community Newspapers	(773) 252-3534
	Harlem-Irving Times	(847) 329-2000
	Harlem-Foster/Norwood Park/Edison Park Times	(847) 329-2000
	Herald	(773) 643-8533
	Hollywood Park Journal	(773) 286-6100
	Hyde Park Citizen	(773) 783-1251
	Hyde Park Herald	(773) 643-8533
	Independent Bulletin	(773) 783-1040
	Inside Publications	(773) 878-7333
	Jefferson Park/Portage Park/Belmont Times	(847) 329-2000
	Jewish Star	(708) 674-7827
	Journal	(773) 286-6100
	Lerner Newspapers	(847) 329-2000
	Mt. Greenwood Express	(708) 388-2425
	Near North News	(312) 787-2677
	New City	(312) 243-8786
	New Metro News	(847) 791-0880
	News-Star	(847) 329-2000
	North Loop News	(773) 283-7900
	Northwest Leader	(773) 283-7900
	Northwestside Press	(773) 286-6100
	Pilsen/Little Village EXTRA	(773) 252-3534
	Post	(312) 463-5100
	Reader	(312) 828-0350
	Reporter	(773) 286-6100
	River North News	(312) 944-3300
	Scottsdale Ashburn Independent	(708) 388-2425
	Shoreland News	(312) 568-7091
	Skyline	(847) 329-2000
	Southend Citizen	(773) 783-1251
	South Shore Scene	(773) 363-0441
	South Suburban Citizen	(773) 783-1251

Southwest EXTRA	(773) 252-3534
Southwest News-Herald	(773) 476-4800
Spotlight Chicago	(773) 283-7900
Standard News	(708) 755-5021
Suburban Leader	(773) 283-7900
Suburban Post	(773) 283-7900
Weekend	(773) 783-2151
Wicker Park West Town EXTRA	(773) 252-3534
Associated Press	(312) 781-0500
Illinois Radio Network	(312) 943-6363
TLN TV Cable Network	(312) 433-3838
WBBM-AM	(312) 944-6000
WBBM-FM/TV	(312) 951-3497
WBEZ-FM	(312) 832-9150
WCEV-AM	(773) 282-6700
WCKG-FM/WYSY-FM	(312) 240-7900
WCRX-FM	(312) 344-8150
WEJM-AM/FM, WVAZ-FM	(312) 360-9000
WFMT-FM	(773) 279-2000
WGCI-AM/FM	(312) 986-6900
WGN-AM	(312) 222-4700
WHPK-FM	(773) 702-8289
WIIT	(312) 567-3087
WIND-AM	(312) 751-5560
WJJD-AM/WJMK-FM	(312) 977-1800
WKIE/WKIF/WDEK-FM	(312) 573-9400
WKKC-FM	(773) 602-5313
WKQX-FM	(312) 527-8348
WLIT-FM	(312) 329-9002
WLS-AM/FM	(312) 984-0890
WLUP-FM	(312) 440-5270
WLUW-FM	(312) 915-6558
WLXX-AM	(312) 867-2000
WMAQ-AM	(312) 670-6767
WMBI-AM/FM	(312) 329-4300
WMVP-AM	(312) 980-1000
WNDZ-AM/WZCH-FM/WRCA-FM	(773) 767-1000
WNIB-FM	(312) 633-9700
WNND-FM	(312) 297-5100
WNUA-FM	(312) 645-9550
WOJO-FM	(312) 649-0105
WRTE-FM	(312) 455-9455
WSBC-AM/WCFJ-AM	(773) 792-1121
WSCR-AM/WXRT-FM	(773) 777-1700
WSSD-FM	(773) 928-8800
WTAQ-AM	(773) 284-8184
WTMX-FM	(312) 946-1019
WUBT-FM	(312) 255-5100
WUSN-FM	(312) 649-0099
WVAZ-FM	(312) 360-9000
WVON-AM	(773) 247-6200
WWHN-AM	(773) 239-3100
WXCD-FM	(312) 984-9923
WXRT-FM	(773) 777-1700
WXXY/WYXX-FM	(312) 573-9400
WYLL-FM	(847) 956-5030
WZRD-FM	(773) 583-4050
WBBM-TV	(312) 944-6000
WCIU-TV/WFBT-TV	(312) 705-2600
WCPX-TV	(312) 410-9038
WFLD-TV	(312) 565-5532
WGBO-TV	(312) 670-1000
WGN-TV	(773) 528-2311
WLS-TV	(312) 750-7777
WMAQ-TV	(312) 836-5555
WPWR-TV	(773) 276-5050
WSNS-TV	(773) 929-1200
WTTW-TV	(773) 583-5000
WYCC-TV	(773) 838-7878

COOK (cont'd)

Chicago (cont'd)
AT&T Broadband (C) .... (773) 714-1900
RCN (C) .... (312) 955-2100
Chicago Heights
Chicago Standard Newspaper
.... (708) 755-5021
South Suburban Standard (708) 755-5021
Star .... (708) 802-8800
WCGO-AM .... (708) 755-5900
Chicago Ridge
Citizen .... (708) 388-2425
Star .... (708) 802-8800
Cicero   Cicero LIFE .... (708) 484-1234
Lawndale News .... (708) 656-6400
Country Club Hills
Star .... (708) 802-8800
Countryside
Press .... (708) 562-0900
Suburban LIFE Citizen ..... (630) 368-1100
Des Plaines Journal .... (847) 299-5511
Times .... (847) 696-3133
Edgebrook Times Review .... (847) 696-3133
Edison, Norwood
Times Review .... (847) 696-3133
Journal .... (847) 299-5511
Elk Grove Village
Journal .... (847) 299-5511
Times .... (847) 797-5100
WYLL-FM .... (847) 956-5030
Elmwood Park
Elm Leaves .... (708) 383-3200
Elmwood Park/River
Grove Times .... (847) 329-2000
Evanston   Clarion .... (847) 864-0488
Review .... (847) 866-6501
WNUR-FM .... (847) 491-7101
WONX-AM .... (847) 475-1590
Evergreen Park
Courier .... (708) 388-2425
Flossmoor   WHFH-FM .... (708) 798-9434
Forest Park Forest Leaves .... (708) 383-3200
Review .... (708) 366-0600
Forest View Berwyn Cicero Stickney
LIFE .... (708) 484-1234
Franklin Park
Herald Journal .... (708) 383-3200
Glencoe   News .... (847) 486-9200
Glenview   Announcements .... (847) 486-9200
Pioneer Press .... (847) 486-9200
Golf Mill   Journal .... (847) 299-5511
Golf Mill/ East Main Bugle
.... (847) 588-1900
Harvey   Star .... (708) 802-8800
WBEE-AM .... (708) 331-7840
Hickory Hills
Citizen .... (708) 388-2425
AT&T Broadband (C) .... (708) 430-4840
Hillside   Suburban LIFE Citizen ..... (630) 368-1100
West Proviso Herald .... (708) 383-3200
Hoffman Estates
Review .... (847) 797-5100
Homer Township
Star .... (708) 802-8800
Homewood Star .... (708) 802-8800
Indian Head Park
Suburban Life .... (630) 368-1100
LaGrange   Press .... (630) 368-1100
Suburban LIFE Citizen ..... (630) 368-1100
WLTL-FM .... (708) 482-9585
LaGrange Park
Press .... (630) 368-1100
Suburban LIFE Citizen ..... (630) 368-1100

Lansing   Star .... (708) 802-8800
The Times (D) .... (219) 933-3200
Lemont   Metropolitan .... (630) 257-5300
Reporter .... (630) 368-1100
Sun .... (815) 439-5300
Lincolnwood
Life .... (847) 329-2000
Review .... (847) 866-6501
Lyons   Suburban LIFE Citizen ..... (630) 368-1100
Matteson   Star .... (708) 802-8800
AT&T Broadband (C) .... (708) 748-8603
Maywood   Herald .... (708) 383-3200
Melrose Park
Herald .... (708) 383-3200
Midlothian   Bremen Messenger .... (708) 388-2425
Morton Grove
Bugle .... (847) 588-1900
Champion .... (847) 866-6501
Life .... (847) 329-2000
Mt. Prospect
Journal .... (847) 299-5511
Times .... (847) 696-3133
AT&T Broadband (C) .... (847) 813-7000
Niles   Bugle .... (847) 588-1900
Herald-Spectator .... (847) 696-3133
Journal .... (847) 299-5511
Life .... (847) 329-2000
Norridge   Norridge-Harwood
Heights News .... (847) 696-3133
Norridge-Harwood
Heights Times .... (847) 329-2000
North Riverside
Suburban LIFE Citizen ..... (630) 368-1100
Northbrook Star .... (847) 486-9200
WKTA-AM .... (847) 498-3350
Northlake   Herald-Journal .... (708) 383-3200
Oak Forest Star .... (708) 802-8800
Oak Lawn   Independent .... (708) 388-2425
Star .... (708) 802-8800
Multimedia Cablevision .. (708) 636-9571
Oak Park   Oak Leaves .... (708) 383-3200
Wednesday Journal of Oak Park
and River Forest .... (708) 524-8300
WPNA-AM .... (708) 848-8980
Villager .... (773) 233-3100
Orland Park Township Messenger .... (708) 388-2425
Star .... (708) 802-8800
Villager .... (773) 233-3100
AT&T Broadband (C) .... (708) 460-3900
Palatine   Countryside .... (847) 797-5100
Journal & Topics .... (847) 299-5511
Palos Heights
Regional News .... (708) 448-4000
Star .... (708) 802-8800
Palos Hills   Palos Citizen .... (708) 388-2425
Park Ridge Herald-Advocate .... (847) 696-3133
Journal .... (847) 299-5511
Voice .... (847) 329-2000
WMTH-FM .... (847) 692-8495
Prospect Heights
Journal .... (847) 299-5511
River Forest Forest Leaves .... (708) 383-3200
River Grove Messenger .... (708) 383-3200
WRRG-FM .... (708) 456-0300
Riverside   Suburban LIFE Citizen ..... (708) 368-1100
Rolling Meadows
Journal Topics .... (708) 299-5511
Review .... (847) 797-5100
Rosemont   Journal .... (847) 299-5511
Schaumburg
Review .... (847) 797-5100
AT&T Broadband (C) .... (847) 985-1736
Skokie   Life .... (847) 329-2000

COOK (cont'd)

Skokie (cont'd)
Review .... (847) 866-6501
Skokie/Lincolnwood Bugle
.... (847) 588-1900

South Holland
Star .... (708) 802-8800
AT&T Cable Services (C) .. (708) 339-2741

Stickney Berwyn Life .... (708) 484-1234
Cicero Life .... (708) 484-1234

Summit Des Plaines Valley
News .... (708) 594-9340
WARG-FM .... (708) 728-3222

Tinley Park Daily Southtown .... (708) 633-6700
Star .... (708) 802-8800
WJYS-TV .... (708) 633-0001

West Proviso
Herald .... (708) 383-3200

Westchester Suburban LIFE Citizen ..... (630) 368-1100
Herald .... (708) 383-3200
News .... (630) 368-1100

Western Springs
Suburban LIFE Citizen ..... (708) 368-1100
Doings .... (708) 887-0600
Jones Intercable .... (708) 460-3900

Wheeling Countryside .... (847) 797-5151
Journal & Topics .... (847) 299-5511

Willow Springs
Suburban LIFE Citizen ..... (708) 368-1100

Wilmette Life .... (847) 486-9200
Media One .... (708) 716-2000

Winnetka Talk .... (847) 486-9200
WNTH-FM .... (847) 446-7000

Worth Citizen .... (708) 388-2425
The Reporter .... (708) 448-6161

CRAWFORD
Mediacom .... (800) 443-1175

Oblong Gem .... (618) 592-3094
Palestine Pioneer .... (618) 945-9310
Robinson Daily News .... (618) 544-2101
Argus .... (618) 544-2174
Constitution .... (618) 544-2101
WTAY-AM/WTYE-FM .... (618) 544-2191

CUMBERLAND
Greenup Press .... (217) 923-3704
Mediacom .... (800) 824-6008
Neoga News .... (217) 895-2234
Toledo Democrat .... (217) 849-2000

DeKALB
DeKalb Daily Chronicle .... (815) 756-4841
Midweek .... (815) 758-0696
WDKB-FM .... (815) 758-0950
WLBK-AM/WDEK-FM ... (815) 758-8686
WNIJ-FM/WNIU-FM ..... (815) 753-9000
AT&T Broadband .... (815) 758-5134

Genoa, Kingston, Kirkland
News .... (815) 784-5138
Hinckley Country Courier .... (815) 286-7761
Sandwich Record .... (630) 553-7034
Sycamore News .... (815) 899-6397
WSQR-AM .... (815) 899-0000

DeWITT
Clinton Daily Journal .... (217) 935-3171
WHOW-AM/FM .... (217) 935-2161
DeWitt County Constitution .... (217) 935-0207
Farmer City Journal .... (309) 928-2193
WWHP-FM .... (309) 928-9876

DOUGLAS
Arcola Record Herald .... (217) 268-4959
Illini Cablevision, Inc. ...... (217) 253-2777
Arthur Graphic-Clarion .... (217) 543-2151

Atwood Herald .... (217) 578-3213
Newman Independent .... (217) 837-2414
Tuscola Regional .... (217) 253-2358
Review .... (217) 253-2358
Villa Grove News .... (217) 832-4201

DuPAGE

Addison Press .... (630) 368-1100
Metrovision of
DuPage County (C) ...... (708) 894-4949
Bartlett Examiner .... (630) 830-4145
Press .... (630) 368-1100
Bensenville Suburban Journal .... (847) 299-5511
Press .... (630) 368-1100
Bloomingdale
Examiner .... (708) 830-4145
Press .... (630) 368-1100
Time/Warner Cable .... (708) 894-4978
Burr Ridge Doings .... (630) 887-0600
Progress .... (630) 368-1100
Suburban LIFE Citizen ..... (630) 368-1100
Carol Stream
Examiner .... (630) 830-4145
Press .... (630) 368-1100
Clarendon Hills
Doings .... (630) 887-0600
Progress .... (630) 969-0188
Suburban LIFE .... (630) 368-1100
Darien Doings .... (630) 887-0600
Metropolitan .... (708) 257-5300
Progress .... (630) 969-0188
Suburban LIFE .... (630) 368-1100
Downers Grove
Reporter .... (630) 368-1100
Progress .... (630) 368-1100
WDGC-FM .... (630) 271-6414
Elmhurst Press .... (630) 368-1100
Suburban LIFE .... (630) 368-1100
WRSE-FM .... (630) 617-3729
WJJG-AM .... (708) 493-1530
AT&T Broadband (C) .... (630) 716-2250
Glen Ellyn News .... (630) 368-1100
Press .... (630) 834-0900
WDCB-FM .... (630) 942-4200
Glendale Heights
Press .... (630) 368-1100
Hinsdale Doings .... (630) 887-0600
Suburban LIFE Graphic ... (630) 368-1100
Progress .... (630) 368-1100
Itasca Press .... (630) 368-1100
Lisle Sun .... (630) 355-0063
Lisle/Naperville Reporter (630) 368-1100
AT&T Broadband (C) .... (630) 963-0107
Lombard Spectator .... (630) 368-1100
Lombardian .... (630) 627-7010
Suburban LIFE .... (630) 368-1100
Naperville Metropolitan .... (708) 257-5300
Sun .... (630) 355-0063
WAUR-AM .... (630) 428-1450
WONC-FM .... (630) 637-8989
AT&T Broadband (C) .... (630) 378-3808
Oak Brook Doings .... (630) 887-0600
Press .... (630) 834-0900
Chicagoland TV News (C) (630) 368-4000
Oak Brook Terrace
Doings .... (630) 887-0600
Press .... (630) 368-1100
Roselle Press .... (630) 368-1100
Villa Park Argus .... (630) 368-1100
Review .... (708) 627-7010
Suburban LIFE .... (630) 368-1100
AT&T Broadband (C) .... (630) 941-7925
Warrenville Digest .... (708) 393-1160

DuPAGE (cont'd)

Warrenville (cont'd)
Free Press .... (630) 469-0100
Post .... (630) 368-1100
Wayne Countryside Press .... (618) 842-2662
Examiner .... (603) 830-4145
West Chicago
Press .... (630) 368-1100
Westchester
News .... (630) 368-1100
Westmont Progress .... (630) 969-0188
Suburban LIFE .... (630) 368-1100
Wheaton Leader .... (630) 469-0100
Press .... (630) 368-1100
Sun .... (630) 355-0063
WETN-FM .... (630) 752-5074
AT&T Broadband (C) .... (630) 690-3500
Willowbrook
Doings .... (630) 887-0600
Progress .... (630) 368-1100
Winfield Estate .... (708) 668-7957
Press .... (630) 469-0100
Wood Dale Press .... (630) 368-1100
Woodridge Suburban LIFE Graphic ... (630) 368-1100
Progress .... (630) 368-1100

EDGAR
Chrisman Leader .... (217) 269-2811
Paris Beacon-News (D) .... (217) 465-6424
WPRS-AM/WACF-FM .... (217) 465-6336
Charter Communications. (217) 465-4128

EDWARDS
Albion Prairie Post .... (618) 445-2355
Grayville Navigator Journal Register
.... (618) 375-3300
West Salem Times Advocate .... (618) 456-8808

EFFINGHAM
Altamont Independent .... (618) 483-3333
News .... (618) 483-6176
Beecher City
Journal .... (618) 487-5634
Effingham Daily News .... (217) 347-7151
WCRA-AM/ WCRC-FM/WCBH-FM
.... (217) 342-4141
WXEF-FM/WKJT-FM ...... (217) 347-5518
Teutopolis Press .... (217) 857-3116

FAYETTE
Farina News .... (618) 245-6216
Ramsey News-Journal .... (618) 423-2411
WJLY-FM/WTRH-FM ...... (618) 423-2082
St. Elmo Banner .... (618) 829-3246
Vandalia Leader-Union .... (618) 283-3374
WPMB-AM/WKRV-FM .. (618) 283-2325
Charter Communications (618) 283-4021

FORD
Gibson City Courier .... (217) 784-4244
WGCY-FM .... (217) 784-8661
Mediacom (C) .... (800) 443-1175
Melvin Ford County Press .... (217) 388-7721
Paxton Daily Record .... (217) 379-2356
Weekly Record .... (217) 379-2356
WPXN-FM .... (217) 379-4333

FRANKLIN
Benton Evening News (D) .... (618) 438-5611
WQRL-FM .... (618) 435-8101
Christopher Progress .... (618) 724-9423
West Frankfort
Daily American .... (618) 932-2146
WFRX-AM/FM .... (618) 932-8121

FULTON
Astoria South Fulton Argus .... (309) 329-2151
Avon Sentinel .... (800) 500-1961

Canton Daily Ledger .... (309) 647-5100
WBYS-AM/FM .... (309) 647-1560
Farmington Bugle .... (309) 742-2521
Lewistown Fulton County Democrat . (309) 547-3055

GALLATIN
Ridgway News .... (618) 269-3147
Shawneetown
Gallatin Democrat .... (618) 269-3147
Ervin Cable TV .... (618) 269-4411

GREENE
Carrollton Gazette-Patriot .... (217) 942-3626
White Hall Green Prairie Press .... (217) 374-2871

GRUNDY
Coal City Courant .... (815) 476-7966
Gardner Chronicle .... (815) 584-1270
Morris Daily Herald .... (815) 942-3221
WCSJ-AM/WJDK-FM .... (815) 941-1000
AT&T Broadband (C) .... (815) 942-5589

HAMILTON
McLeansboro
Times-Leader .... (618) 643-2387
WMCL-AM .... (618) 643-2311

HANCOCK
Augusta Eagle-Scribe .... (217) 392-2715
Carthage Hancock County
Journal Pilot .... (217) 357-2149
WCAZ-AM .... (217) 357-3128
Mediacom (C) .... (800) 245-3861
Dallas City Enterprise .... (217) 852-3511
LaHarpe Hancock County Quill ..... (217) 659-3316
Nauvoo New Independent .... (217) 453-6771

HARDIN
Elizabethtown
Hardin County
Independent .... (618) 287-2361

HENDERSON
Oquawka Current .... (309) 867-2515
Stronghurst Henderson County Quill . (309) 924-1871

HENRY
Atkinson-Annawan
News .... (309) 936-7741
Cambridge Chronicle .... (309) 937-3303
Galva News .... (309) 932-2103
WHHK-FM/WGEN-AM
.... (309) 932-2288
Geneseo Republic .... (309) 944-2119
Mediacom (C) .... (309) 944-5685
Kewanee Star-Courier (D) .... (309) 852-2181
WKEI-AM/WJRE-FM ...... (309) 853-4471
Insight Communications . (309) 852-3316
Orion Gazette .... (309) 526-8085

IROQUOIS
Cissna Park Baier Publishing Co. .... (815) 457-2245
News .... (815) 457-2245
Clifton Advocate .... (815) 694-2122
Gilman Star .... (815) 265-7332
Loda Times .... (217) 379-4313
Milford Herald News .... (815) 889-4321
Sheldon Mediacom (C) .... (219) 944-5685
Watseka Iroquois County's
Times Republic (D) .... (815) 432-5227
WGFA-AM/FM .... (815) 432-4955
Mediacom (C) .... (815) 432-6166

JACKSON
Ava WXAN-FM .... (618) 426-3308
Carbondale Times .... (618) 549-2799
Southern Illinoisan (D) ..... (618) 529-5454
WCIL-AM-FM/WJPF-AM/WOOZ-FM/
WUEZ-FM/WXLT-FM ..... (618) 985-4843
WDBX-FM .... (618) 529-5900

153

JACKSON (cont'd)

Carbondale (cont'd)
WIBI-FM	(217) 854-4800
WSIU-FM/TV	(618) 453-4343
WTAO-FM	(618) 932-8121
WPSD-TV	(618) 457-6397
AT&T Broadband (C)	(618) 529-5749

Murphysboro
American	(618) 684-5833
WINI-AM	(618) 684-2128

JASPER

Newton
Press-Mentor	(618) 783-2324
WIKK-FM	(618) 783-8000

JEFFERSON

Mt. Vernon
Register News (D)	(618) 242-0113
WMIX-AM/FM	(618) 242-3500
Charter Communications	(618) 242-9512

JERSEY

Elsah	WTPC-FM	(618) 374-4934
Jerseyville	County Star	(618) 498-3377
	Telegraph County Edition	(618) 498-5551
	WJBM-AM	(618) 498-2185

JO DAVIESS

East Dubuque
Register	(815) 747-3171
Mediacom (C)	(319) 557-8020

Galena	Gazette	(815) 777-0019
	Mediacom (C)	(800) 747-8021

JOHNSON

Goreville	Gazette	(618) 995-9445
Vienna	Times	(618) 658-4321

KANE

Aurora	Beacon-News (D)	(630) 844-5844
	60504 Fox Valley Villages	(630) 355-0063
	North Aurora Republican	(630) 368-1100
	WBIG-AM	(630) 851-5200
	WKKD-AM/FM	(630) 898-1580
	WEHS-TV	(630) 585-6060
	Jones Intercable	(708) 897-2288
Batavia	Republican	(630) 368-1100
	AT&T Broadband (C)	(630) 879-9432

Carpentersville
AT&T Broadband (C)	(847) 428-6171

Elburn	Herald	(630) 365-6446
Elgin	Courier-News (D)	(847) 888-7800
	WEPS-FM	(847) 888-5000
	WRMN-AM/WJKL-FM	(847) 741-7700
Geneva	Kane County	
	Chronicle (D)	(630) 232-9222
	Republican	(630) 513-5050
Hampshire	Register	(847) 683-2627
St. Charles	Republican	(630) 513-5050

KANKAKEE

Bourbonnais
Herald	(815) 933-1131
WONU-FM	(815) 939-5330

Grant Park	Gazette	(708) 258-3473
Herscher	Courier-Press	(815) 584-1270
	Pilot	(815) 426-2132
Kankakee	Daily Journal	(815) 937-3300
	WVLI-FM	(815) 933-9287
	WKAN-AM	(815) 935-9555
	AT&T Broadband (C)	(815) 937-2700
Manteno	News	(815) 468-6397
Momence	Progress Reporter	(815) 472-2000
	Midwest Cablevision	(815) 472-4614
St. Anne	Record	(815) 427-6734

KENDALL

Oswego	Ledger- Sentinel	(630) 553-7034
	Sun	(630) 355-0063

Plano	Record	(630) 553-7034
	WSPY-FM	(630) 552-1000
	WFXV-TV	(630) 552-3030
Yorkville	Kendall County Record	(630) 553-7034

KNOX

Abingdon	Argus	(309) 462-5758
Galesburg	Register-Mail (D)	(309) 343-7181
	Post	(309) 343-5617
	Zephyr	(309) 342-2010
Knoxville	Journal	(309) 343-5617
	WAIK-AM	(309) 342-3161
	WGIL-AM/WAAG-FM/WLSR-FM/	
	WKAY-FM	(309) 342-5131
	WVKC-FM	(309) 341-7266
	Insight Communications (C)	
		(309) 342-2161
Williamsfield		
	Tri County News	(309) 742-2521
Yates City	Banner	(309) 742-2521

LAKE

Antioch	News	(847) 223-8161
Barrington	Courier-Review	(847) 381-9200
Deerfield	Review	(847) 680-6690
	AT&T Cable Services (C)	(708) 480-3335
Fox Lake	Press	(847) 223-8161
Grayslake	Review	(847) 680-6690
	Times	(847) 223-8161
Gurnee	Press	(847) 223-8161
	Review	(847) 680-6690
	Sun	(847) 623-2333
Highland Park		
	News	(847) 680-6690
	WEEF-AM	(847) 831-5440
	AT&T Broadband (C)	(847) 831-5900
Lake Forest	Lake Forester	(847) 680-6690
Lake Villa	Record	(847) 223-8161
Lake Villa, Lindenhurst		
	Review	(847) 680-6690
Lake Zurich	Courier	(847) 381-9200
	Enterprise	(708) 438-2395
	AT&T Broadband (C)	(847) 438-4246
Libertyville	Libertyville/Mundelein/Vernon Hills	
	Sun	(847) 623-2333
	News	(847) 223-8161
	Review	(847) 317-0500
	AT&T Broadband (C)	(847) 362-6124
Lindenhurst	News	(847) 223-8161
Long Grove	Northwest Journal	(847) 299-5511
Mundelein	News	(847) 223-8161
	Review	(847) 680-6690
Round Lake	News	(847) 223-8161
Vernon Hills		
	News	(847) 680-6690
	Review	(847) 680-6690
Wadsworth	News	
		(847) 223-8161
Warren, Newport		
	Press	(847) 223-8161
Wauconda	Leader	(847) 223-8161
Waukegan	News-Sun (D)	(847) 336-7000
	WKRS-AM/WXLC-FM	(847) 336-7900
	AT&T Broadband (C)	(847) 336-7200
Zion	Zion-Benton News	(847) 746-9000
	WNIZ-FM	(847) 746-1484

LaSALLE

Earlville	Leader	(815) 246-6911
Grand Ridge		
	Grand Ridge Cable	(815) 249-5517
LaSalle	News-Tribune (D)	(815) 223-3200
	Illinois Agri News	(815) 223-2558
	WALS-FM/WBZG-FM	(815) 224-2100
	WLPO-AM/WAJK-FM	(815) 223-3100

NEWS MEDIA IN ILLINOIS (Continued)

LaSALLE (cont'd)

Mendota	Reporter	(815) 539-9396
	WGLC-FM	(815) 539-6751
	Insight Communications (C)	(815) 538-6426
Ottawa	Daily Times	(815) 433-2000
	Thrift-T-Nickel/Town & Country	(815) 433-5595
	WCMY-AM/WRKX-FM ..	(815) 434-6050
	WKOT-FM	(815) 434-4000
	WWTO-TV	(815) 434-2700
	MediaCom	(309) 274-4500
Peru	WBZG-FM/WAIV-FM	(815) 224-2100
	Insight Communications (C)	(815) 223-1106
Seneca	Town & Country	(815) 433-5595
Streator	Times-Press (D)	(815) 673-3771
	WSPL-AM/WSTQ-FM	(217) 224-2100
Tonica	News	(815) 442-8419

LAWRENCE

Bridgeport	Leader-Times	(618) 945-9310
	Charter Communications (C)	(812) 882-8501
Lawrenceville		
	Daily Record	(618) 943-2331
	Lawrence County News ..	(618) 943-2331
	WAKO-AM/FM	(618) 943-3354
Sumner	Press	(618) 936-2212

LEE

Amboy	News	(815) 857-2311
Ashton	Gazette	(815) 453-2551
Dixon	Telegraph (D)	(815) 284-2222
	WIXN-AM/FM	(815) 288-3341
	WLLT-FM	(815) 284-1077
	Insight Communications (C)	(815) 284-2257

LIVINGSTON

Dwight	Star & Herald	(815) 584-3007
Fairbury	Blade	(815) 692-2366
Flanagan	Home Times	(815) 842-1153
Pontiac	Daily Leader	(815) 842-1153
	WJEZ-FM/WLDC-FM	(815) 844-6101

LOGAN

Lincoln	Courier (D)	(217) 732-2101
	WLNX-FM	(217) 735-3495
	WVAX-AM	(217) 735-2337
	Insight Communications (C)	(217) 735-3448
Mt. Pulaski	Weekly News	(217) 792-5557

MACON

Blue Mound	Leader	(217) 692-2323
Decatur	Herald & Review (D)	(217) 429-5151
	Tribune	(217) 422-9702
	Voice of the Black Community	(217) 423-2231
	WDZ-AM/WDZQ-FM	(217) 423-9744
	WEJT-FM	(217) 428-4487
	WJMU-FM	(217) 424-6377
	WSOY-AM/FM	(217) 877-5371
	WAND-TV	(217) 424-2500
	WBUI-TV	(217) 428-2323
	Insight Communications (C)	(217) 424-8455
Mt. Zion	Region News	(217) 864-4212
	WXFM-FM	(217) 864-4141
Niantic	County Line Observer	(217) 486-6496

MACOUPIN

Benld	Enterprise	(217) 835-4868
Brighton	Southwestern Journal News	(618) 372-8451

Bunker Hill	Gazette News	(618) 585-4411
Carlinville	Democrat	(217) 854-2561
	Macoupin County Enquirer	(217) 854-2534
	WCNL-FM	(217) 854-3131
	WIBI-FM	(217) 854-4800
	WSMI-AM/FM	(217) 324-5921
	WTSG-FM	(217) 854-4851
Gillespie	Area News	(217) 839-2130
Girard	Gazette	(217) 965-3355
Mt. Olive	Herald	(217) 999-3941
Palmyra	Northwestern News	(217) 965-3355
Staunton	Kwik Konnection	(618) 635-3172
	Star Times	(618) 635-2000
	Macoupin County Cablevision	(618) 635-5456
Virden	Recorder	(217) 965-3355

MADISON

Alton	Telegraph (D)	(618) 463-2500
	WBGZ-AM	(618) 465-3535
Collinsville	Herald/Journal	(618) 344-0264
East Alton	AT&T Broadband (C)	(618) 251-2660
Edwardsville		
	Intelligencer (D)	(618) 656-4700
	Journal	(618) 656-8000
	WRYT-AM	(314) 752-7000
	WSIE-FM	(618) 650-2228
Godfrey	WLCA-FM	(618) 466-3411
Granite City	Press Record/Journal	(618) 876-2000
	WGNU-AM	(618) 451-9950
Hamel	Madison County Chronicle	(618) 459-3655
	Madison/Macoupin Cable	(618) 633-2267
Highland	News Leader	(618) 654-2366
	WCBW-AM/WINU-AM .	(618) 654-7521
Maryville	Charter Communications (C)	(800) 231-2517
Troy	Times-Tribune	(618) 667-3111

MARION

Centralia	Sentinel (D)	(618) 532-5604
	WILY-AM/WRXX-FM	(618) 533-5700
Kinmundy	Express	(618) 547-3111
Salem	Times Commoner	(618) 548-3330
	WJBD-AM/FM	(618) 548-2000

MARSHALL

Henry	News Republican	(309) 364-3250
Lacon	Home Journal	(309) 246-2865
Wenona	Index	(309) 364-3250

MASON

Havana	Mason County Democrat	(309) 543-3311
	WDUK-FM	(309) 543-3331
Manito	Review	(309) 968-6705
Mason City	Banner Times	(309) 968-6705

MASSAC

Metropolis	Planet	(618) 524-2141
	WMOK-AM/WREZ-FM .	(618) 524-9209

McDONOUGH

Blandinsville	Star-Gazette	(309) 776-3700
Bushnell	McDonough Democrat	(309) 772-2129
Colchester	Chronicle	(309) 776-3700
Macomb	Journal (D)	(309) 833-2114
	Eagle	(309) 837-4428
	WIUM-FM	(309) 298-1873
	WIUS-FM	(309) 298-3217
	WJEQ-FM/WMQZ-FM ...	(309) 833-2121
	WKAI-FM/WLMD-FM/WLRB-AM	(309) 833-5561
	Insight Communications (C)	(309) 833-4539

155

NEWS MEDIA IN ILLINOIS (Continued)

McHENRY

Algonquin	Countryside	(847) 381-9200
Cary	Cary-Grove Countryside	(847) 381-9200
Crystal Lake		
	Northwest Herald (D)	(815) 459-4040
	WAIT-AM/WZSR-FM	(815) 459-7000
Harvard	WMCW-AM	(815) 943-7426
Huntley	Farmside	(847) 669-5621
Marengo	Union Press	(630) 368-1100
McHenry	AT&T Broadband (C)	(815) 344-3204
Wonder Lake		
	Star	(815) 385-2231
Woodstock	Independent	(815) 338-8040

McLEAN

Bloomington		
	Pantagraph (D)	(309) 829-9411
	WESN-FM	(309) 556-2634
	WJBC-AM/WBNQ-FM/WBWN-FM/	
		(309) 829-1221
	WYZZ-TV	(309) 662-4373
Carlock	Quill	(309) 454-5476
Chenoa	Town Crier	(815) 945-7388
Colfax	Ridge Review	(309) 723-2057
Gridley	Village Times	(309) 454-5476
	Gridley Cable	(309) 747-2324
Heyworth	Star	(309) 473-2414
LeRoy	Journal	(309) 962-4441
Lexington	Lexingtonian	(309) 365-8668
Normal	Normalite	(309) 454-5476
	WGLT-FM	(309) 438-2255
	WIHN-FM/WSNI-FM	(309) 888-4496
	TV-10 Illinois State	
	University	(309) 438-5484
	Insight Communications (C)	
		(309) 454-3350

MENARD

Greenview	Menard County Review	(217) 632-2236
Petersburg	Observer	(217) 632-2236
	WLUJ-FM	(217) 528-2300

MERCER

Aledo	Times Record	(309) 582-5112
	WRMJ-FM	(309) 582-5666

MONROE

Columbia	Herald	(618) 281-3333
	Monroe County	
	Clarion-Journal	(618) 281-7691
Waterloo	Republic-Times	(618) 939-3814

MONTGOMERY

Hillsboro	Journal	(217) 532-3933
	Montgomery County	
	News	(217) 532-3929
Litchfield	News Herald (D)	(217) 324-2121
	WAOX-FM	(618) 635-6000
	WSMI-AM/FM	(217) 324-5921
Nokomis	Free Press Progress	(217) 563-2115
Raymond	Panhandle Press	(217) 965-3355
	News	(217) 532-3933

MORGAN

Franklin	Times	(217) 675-2461
Jacksonville	Journal Courier (D)	(217) 245-6121
	WEAI-FM/WLDS-AM	(217) 245-7171
	WJIL-AM/WJVO-FM	(217) 245-5119
	Mediacom (C)	(217) 243-4621
Meredosia	Budget	(217) 754-3369
Murrayville	Gazette	(217) 675-2461
Waverly	Journal	(217) 435-9221

MOULTRIE

Lovington	Moultrie Telecommunications (C)	
		(217) 873-5215
Sullivan	News-Progress	(217) 728-7381
	WKJR-FM	(217) 728-2028

OGLE

Byron	Tempo	(815) 234-4821
Forreston	Journal	(815) 938-3320
Mt. Morris	Times	(815) 732-6166
Oregon	Ogle County Life	(815) 562-4171
	Republican Reporter	(815) 732-6166
Polo	Tri County Press	(815) 946-2364
Rochelle	News/Leader	(815) 562-4171
	WRHL-AM/FM	(815) 562-7001

PEORIA

Bartonville	Limestone Independent News	
		(309) 697-1851
Chillicothe	Independent	(309) 274-6800
	Times-Bulletin	(309) 274-2185
	Mediacom	(309) 274-4500
East Peoria	WEEK-TV	(309) 698-2525
Elmwood	Tri County News	(309) 742-2521
Glasford	Gazette	(309) 389-2811
Peoria	Journal Star	(309) 686-3035
	Labor Paper	(309) 647-3148
	Times-Observer	(309) 692-4910
	WCBU-FM	(309) 677-3690
	WGLO-FM/WFYR-FM/WIXO-FM/	
	WVEL-AM/WBDM-FM/WEEK-FM	
		(309) 673-9595
	WIRL-AM/WSWT-FM/WMBD-AM/	
	WPBG-FM	(309) 637-3700
	WOAM-AM/WXCL-FM	(309) 685-0977
	WPEO-AM	(309) 698-9736
	WTAZ-AM	(309) 693-0102
	WWCT-FM	(309) 686-9010
	WAOE-TV	(309) 674-5900
	WHOI-TV	(309) 698-1919
	WMBD-TV	(309) 699-3131
	WTVP-TV	(309) 677-4747
	Insight Communications (C)	
		(309) 686-2612
Peoria Heights		
	Herald	(309) 685-5421
Princeville	Tri-County News	(309) 742-2521

PERRY

DuQuoin	Evening Call	(618) 542-2133
	WDQN-AM/FM	(618) 542-3894
	Susquehanna Communications	
		(618) 542-5437
Pinckneyville		
	Democrat	(618) 357-2811

PIATT

Atwood	Herald	(217) 578-3213
Cerro Gordo		
	News Record	(217) 864-4212
Monticello	Piatt County Journal-	
	Republican	(217) 762-2511
	WCZQ-FM	(217) 762-2588

PIKE

Barry	Paper	(217) 335-2112
Pittsfield	Pike County Express	(217) 285-5415
	Pike Press	(217) 285-2345
	WBBA-AM/FM	(217) 285-2157
Pleasant Hill	Weekly Messenger	(217) 734-2345

POPE

Golconda	Herald-Enterprise	(618) 683-3531

PULASKI

Mounds	Pulaski Enterprise	(618) 745-6267
Ullin	Monday's Pub	(618) 833-2158

PUTNAM

Granville	Putnam County Record	(815) 339-2321

RANDOLPH

Chester	Randolph County Herald	
	Tribune	(618) 826-2385

156

RANDOLPH (cont'd)

Chester (cont'd)
KBDZ-FM .... (618) 826-2980
KSGM-AM .... (618) 826-2980
Percy County Journal .... (618) 497-8272
Red Bud North County News .... (618) 282-3803
Sparta News Plaindealer .... (618) 443-2145
WHCO-AM .... (618) 443-2121
Charter Communications (618) 443-3019
Steeleville Ledger .... (618) 965-3417

RICHLAND

Olney Daily Mail .... (618) 393-2931
WSEI-FM/WVLN-AM .... (618) 393-2156
Susquehanna Communications (C)
.... (618) 395-8663

ROCK ISLAND

Moline Dispatch (D) .... (309) 764-4344
WDLM-AM/WDLM-FM . (309) 234-5111
WQAD-TV .... (309) 764-9694
WQPT-TV .... (309) 796-2424
AT&T Broadband (C) .... (309) 797-2580
East Moline WDLM-AM/FM .... (309) 234-5111
Rock Island Argus (D) .... (309) 786-6441
WVIK-FM .... (309) 794-7500
WHBF-TV .... (309) 786-5441

SALINE

Carrier Mills
Galaxy Cablevision .... (573) 472-8200
Eldorado Daily Journal .... (618) 273-3379
Harrisburg Daily Register .... (618) 253-7147
WEBQ-AM/FM .... (618) 252-6307
WSIL-TV .... (618) 985-2333

SANGAMON

Auburn Citizen .... (217) 438-6155
Buffalo Tri-City Register .... (217) 629-9247
Chatham Clarion .... (217) 483-2614
Divernon News .... (217) 628-3332
Illiopolis Sentinel .... (217) 486-6496
New Berlin Bee .... (217) 626-1711
County Tribune .... (217) 488-3005
Pawnee Post .... (217) 625-7113
Pleasant Plains
Press .... (217) 626-1711
Riverton Register .... (217) 629-9247
Rochester Times .... (217) 438-6155
Springfield State Journal-Register (D) (217) 788-1300
Illinois Times .... (217) 753-2226
Illinois Radio Network ..... (217) 782-6290
WFMB-AM-FM/WCVS-FM
.... (217) 528-3033
WMAY-AM/WNNS-FM/WQLZ-FM
.... (217) 629-7077
WQNA-FM .... (217) 529-5431
WTAX-AM/WDBR-FM/WYXY-FM/
WQQL-FM/WVAX-AM/WYMG-FM
.... (217) 753-5400
WUIS-FM .... (217) 206-6516
WICS-TV .... (217) 753-5620
WRSP-TV .... (217) 523-8855
Insight Communications (C)
.... (217) 788-5898
Williamsville
Sun .... (217) 629-9247

SCHUYLER

Rushville Times .... (217) 322-3321
WKXQ-FM .... (217) 322-9200

SCOTT

Bluffs Times .... (217) 754-3369
Winchester Times .... (217) 742-3313

SHELBY

Shelbyville Daily Union .... (217) 774-2161

WEGY-FM/WRAN-FM ... (217) 774-3456
Windsor Shelby County News
Gazette .... (217) 459-2121

ST. CLAIR

Belleville News-Democrat (D) .... (618) 234-1000
Herald Scott Flier .... (618) 566-8282
Journal .... (618) 277-7000
AT&T Broadband Cable .. (618) 277-7820
Cahokia Cahokia/Dupo Journal .... (618) 277-7000
Herald .... (618) 337-7300
Charter Communications (C)
.... (618) 332-1060
East St. Louis
Monitor .... (618) 271-0468
News Journal .... (618) 281-7691
WESL-AM .... (618) 271-7687
Fairview Heights
Journal .... (618) 277-7000
Tribune .... (618) 566-8282
Freeburg Tribune .... (618) 539-3320
Lebanon Advertiser .... (618) 537-4498
Herald .... (618) 566-8282
Mascoutah Herald .... (618) 566-8282
County Journal .... (618) 277-7000
Millstadt Enterprise Journal .... (618) 281-7691
New Athens
Journal Messenger .... (618) 475-2166
O'Fallon City Recorder .... (618) 632-3643
Journal .... (618) 277-7000
Progress .... (618) 632-3643

STEPHENSON

Freeport Journal-Standard (D) .... (815) 232-1171
iNK .... (815) 297-0777
WFPS-FM .... (815) 235-7191
WFRL-AM/WFPS-FM ... (815) 235-7191
Insight Communications (C)
.... (815) 235-7183

TAZEWELL

Creve Coeur
WHOI-TV .... (309) 698-1919
Delavan Times .... (309) 244-7111
East Peoria Times-Courier .... (309) 263-2211
Minier Olympia Review .... (309) 392-2414
Morton Courier .... (309) 263-7414
Morton Times-News .... (309) 263-2211
Tazewell Times Extra .... (309) 263-2211
Media One .... (309) 263-2721
Pekin Daily Times .... (309) 346-1111
WCIC-FM .... (309) 353-9191
WVEL-AM/WGLO-FM/WFYR-FM/
WIXO-FM/WBZM-FM/WPPY-FM/
WRVP-FM .... (309) 673-9595
Insight Communications (C)
.... (309) 347-5866
Washington Courier .... (309) 444-3139
Times-Reporter .... (309) 444-2513

UNION

Anna Gazette-Democrat .... (618) 833-2158
Dongola Tri-County Record .... (618) 827-4353
WIBH-AM .... (618) 833-9424
Falcon Cable TV .... (314) 472-0244

VERMILION

Danville Commercial News (D) .... (217) 446-1000
WDAN-AM/WDNL-FM/WRHK-FM
.... (217) 442-1700
WIAI-FM .... (217) 443-5500
WITY-AM .... (217) 446-1312
Insight Communications . (217) 443-2941
Georgetown
Independent News .... (217) 662-2556
Hoopeston Chronicle .... (217) 283-5111
WHPO-FM .... (217) 283-7744

VERMILION (cont'd)

Hoopeston (cont'd)
Charter Communications (217) 283-5181
Rankin Independent .... (815) 457-2245
Sidell Reporter .... (217) 288-9365
Westville Charter Communications (C)
.... (217) 267-3194

WABASH

Mt. Carmel Daily Republican Register (618) 262-5144
Prairie Post .... (618) 445-2355
WVMC-AM/WSJD-FM ... (618) 262-4102
WVJC-FM .... (618) 262-8989
WCJT-TV .... (618) 262-4102

WARREN

Monmouth Daily Review Atlas .... (309) 734-3176
WRAM-AM/WMOI-FM . (309) 734-9452
Roseville Independent .... (800) 500-1961

WASHINGTON

Ashley News .... (618) 542-2133
Nashville News .... (618) 327-3411
WNSV-FM .... (618) 327-4444
Okawville Times .... (618) 243-5563

WAYNE

Fairfield Wayne County Press .... (618) 842-2662
WFIW-AM/FM .... (618) 842-2159
WOKZ-FM .... (618) 842-2159

WHITE

Carmi Times (D) .... (618) 382-4176
WROY-AM/WRUL-FM ... (618) 382-4161
Norris City Banner .... (618) 378-3014

WHITESIDE

Albany Mediacom (C) .... (319) 243-6350
Erie Review .... (309) 659-2761
Fulton Journal .... (815) 589-2424
Morrison Whiteside News Sentinel . (815) 772-7244
Prophetstown
Echo .... (815) 537-5107
Rock Falls Insight Communications (C)
.... (815) 625-5668
Sterling Daily Gazette .... (815) 625-3600
WSDR-AM/WZZT-FM/WSSQ-FM
.... (815) 625-3400

WILL

Beecher Russell Publications .... (708) 258-3473
Bolingbrook
Metropolitan .... (630) 969-0188
Bolingbrook/Romeoville Reporter
.... (630) 368-1100
Suburban LIFE Graphic ... (630) 368-1100
Sun .... (630) 355-0063
Braidwood Journal .... (815) 476-7966
Channahon Chanooka Weekly .... (815) 467-5991
Coal City Courant .... (815) 634-0315
Crete Record .... (708) 258-3473
Star .... (708) 802-8800
Dongola Tri-County Record .... (618) 827-4353
Frankfort Star .... (708) 755-6161
Grant Park Gazette .... (708) 258-3473
Joliet Herald-News (D) .... (815) 729-6161
Farmers Weekly Review .. (815) 727-4811
Times Weekly .... (815) 723-0325
WBVS-FM/WJOL-AM/WJTW-FM/
WLLI-FM .... (815) 556-0100
WCCQ-FM .... (815) 729-4400
WCSF-FM .... (815) 740-3425
WJCH-FM .... (815) 725-1331
WYKT-FM .... (815) 724-1055
Manhattan American .... (708) 258-3473
Manhattan Cable TV .... (815) 478-4444
Monee Monitor .... (708) 258-3473
New Lenox Community Reporter .... (708) 258-3473

Lincoln-Way Sun .... (815) 439-5300
Park Forest Star .... (708) 755-6161
AT&T Broadband (C) .... (708) 748-9300
Peotone Vedette .... (708) 258-3473
Plainfield Enterprise .... (815) 436-2431
Sun .... (815) 439-5300
Romeoville Metropolitan .... (708) 257-5300
Sun .... (630) 759-9169
WLRA-FM .... (815) 838-0500
AT&T Broadband (C) .... (630) 378-3890
Wilmington Free Press Advocate .... (815) 476-7966
Express .... (815) 476-7966

WILLIAMSON

Carterville WCIL-AM/WCIL-FM/WJPF-AM/
WXTL-FM .... (618) 985-4843
WSIL-TV .... (618) 985-2333
Herrin Spokesman .... (618) 942-5000
Marion Daily Republican .... (618) 993-2626
WDDD-AM-FM/WFRX-AM/WQUL-
FM/WTAO-FM/WVZA-FM
.... (618) 932-8121
WGGH-AM .... (618) 993-8102
WPSD-TV .... (618) 457-6397
WTCT-TV .... (618) 997-4700
AT&T Broadband (C) .... (618) 993-5216

WINNEBAGO

Durand Volunteer .... (815) 248-4407
Loves Park Journal .... (815) 877-4044
Machesney Park
Post Journal .... (815) 877-4044
Pecatonica Gazette .... (815) 239-1028
Rockford Register Star (D) .... (815) 987-1400
Vital Force .... (815) 963-7869
WLUV-AM .... (815) 877-9588
WNTA-AM/WKMQ-FM/WXRX-FM
.... (815) 874-7861
WQFL-FM/WGSL-FM .... (815) 654-1200
WROK-AM/WZOK-FM/WXXQ-FM/
WKMQ-FM .... (815) 399-2233
WIFR-TV .... (815) 987-5300
WQRF-TV .... (815) 987-3950
WREX-TV .... (815) 335-2710
WTVO-TV .... (815) 963-5413
Insight Communications (C)
.... (815) 962-4400
Rockton North Suburban Herald ... (815) 877-4044
WRWC-FM/WTJK-AM/WGFB-FM
.... (815) 624-2603
Cablevision of Greater Beloit
.... (800) 422-2588

WOODFORD

El Paso Times-Journal .... (309) 527-8595
Eureka Woodford County Journal (309) 467-3314
Woodford Courier .... (309) 444-3139
Metamora Herald .... (309) 367-2335
Minonk News-Dispatch .... (309) 432-2505
Roanoke Review .... (309) 923-5841
Washburn Leader .... (309) 367-2335

Sources: Newsclip's Illinois Media Directory (2001), Illinois Press Association's Illinois Newspaper Directory (2001), Illinois Broadcasters Association's Membership Directory (2000-2001) and Cable Television & Communications Association of Illinois' Membership Directory (2001).

158

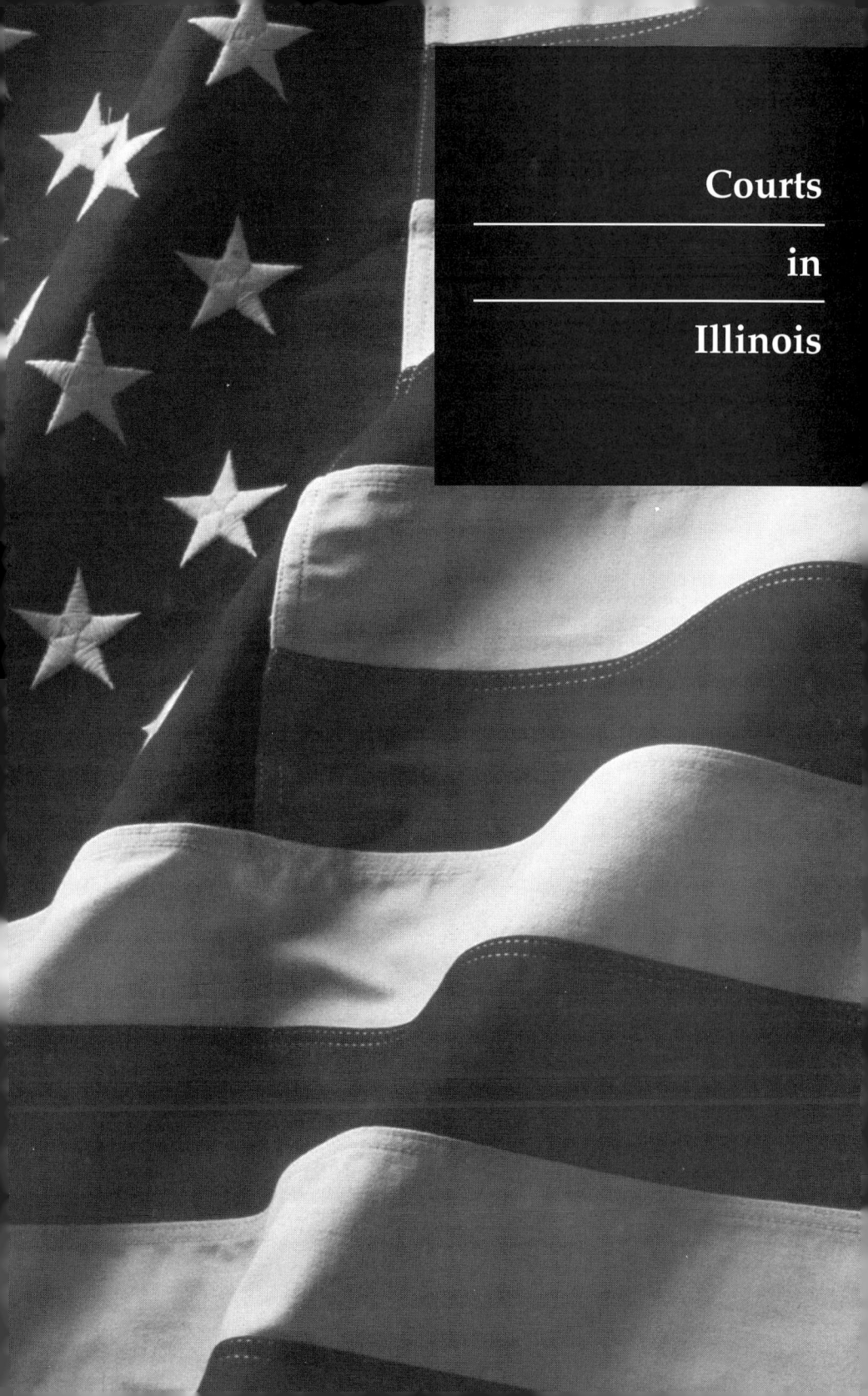

Courts

in

Illinois

COURTS IN ILLINOIS

The Supreme Court, highest tribunal in Illinois, has seven justices, elected from judicial districts for a term of 10 years. Three justices are elected from the First District (Cook County), and one from each of the other four districts. The Supreme Court has general administrative and supervisory authority over all courts in the state. This authority is exercised by the Chief Justice with the assistance of the Administrative Director and staff appointed by the Supreme Court. The Supreme Court hears appeals from lower courts and may exercise original jurisdiction in cases relating to revenue, mandamus, prohibition or habeas corpus.

The Appellate Court hears appeals from the Circuit Courts. There are five districts of the Appellate Court, and judges are elected for 10-year terms. Cook County, which comprises the First District, has 18 Appellate Judges. The remaining 101 counties are divided into four districts that elect six judges each. Additional judges are assigned by the Supreme Court to the Appellate Court, temporarily, on a showing of need. Elgin is the seat of the Second District; Ottawa, the Third District; Springfield, the Fourth District, and Mount Vernon, the Fifth District.

The Unified Trial Court in Illinois is the Circuit Court comprised of Circuit and Associate Judges. The state is divided into 22 judicial circuits, each having one Chief Judge elected by the Circuit Judges. The Chief Judge has general administrative authority in the circuit, subject to the overall administrative authority of the Supreme Court. Circuit Judges may hear any case assigned to them by the Chief Judge. Associate Judges may not preside over criminal cases in which the defendant is charged with an offense punishable by imprisonment for one year or more (felonies), unless approval is received from the Supreme Court. Circuit Judges are elected for a term of six years; Associate Judges are appointed by the Circuit Judges in accordance with Supreme Court rules for a four-year term.

When a Supreme, Appellate or Circuit Court Judgeship is vacant or newly created, candidates are nominated at Primary Elections and elected at the General Election. However, any judge previously elected may, at the expiration of his or her term, have his or her name submitted to the voters on a special judicial ballot without party designation and without an opposing candidate, on the sole question of whether he or she shall be retained in office for another term.

The Illinois Courts Commission, composed of one Supreme Court Justice, two Appellate Court Judges, two Circuit Judges and two citizens, has the authority after notice and public hearing (1) to remove from office, suspend without pay, censure or reprimand any member of the judiciary for willful misconduct in office, persistent failure to perform his or her duties or other conduct that is prejudicial to the administration of justice or that brings the judicial office into disrepute; or (2) to suspend, with or without pay, or retire any member of the judiciary who is physically or mentally unable to perform his or her duties.

A Judicial Inquiry Board created by the 1970 Illinois Constitution has the authority to conduct investigations, receive or initiate complaints concerning any member of the judiciary and file complaints with the Courts Commission.

Judges must devote full time to their judicial duties. They may not practice law, hold a position of profit, hold any other office under the United States, this state, unit of local government, or school district, or hold office in any political party.

ILLINOIS COURT OFFICIALS

Supreme Court

Moses W. Harrison II, Fairview Heights, *Chief Justice;* Charles E. Freeman, Chicago; Mary Ann G. McMorrow, Chicago; Thomas R. Fitzgerald, Chicago; Robert R. Thomas, Wheaton; Thomas L. Kilbride, Rock Island; Rita B. Garman, Danville, *Justices.*

Joseph A. Schillaci .... *Director, Administrative Office of the Illinois Courts*
Juleann Hornyak, Springfield .... *Clerk of the Supreme Court*
Carolyn D. Taitt, Springfield .... *Marshal of the Supreme Court*
Brian C. Ervin, Bloomington .... *Reporter of Decisions*
Brenda I. Larison, Springfield .... *Librarian of the Supreme Court*

Appellate Court Judges

First District (Court meets in Chicago)

Division 1 — Judith Cohen, William Cousins, Jr., Jill K. McNulty, John P. Tully.
Division 2 — Anne M. Burke, Robert Cahill, Joseph Gordon, Margaret S. McBride.
Division 3 — David Cerda, Shelvin Louise Marie Hall, Leslie E. South, Warren D. Wolfson.
Division 4 — Francis Barth, Allen Hartman, Thomas E. Hoffman, Mary Jane Theis.
Division 5 — Calvin C. Campbell, Alan J. Greiman, Patrick J. Quinn, Ellis E. Reid.
Division 6 — Robert Chapman Buckley, Margaret O'Mara Frossard, Michael J. Gallagher, Sheila M. O'Brien.
Clerk of the First District: Steven M. Ravid.

Second District (Court meets in Elgin)

John J. Bowman, Robert E. Byrne, Thomas E. Callum, Fred A. Geiger, R. Peter Grometer, Susan F. Hutchinson, Robert D. McLaren, Jack O'Malley, John W. Rapp, Jr.
Clerk of the Second District: Loren J. Strotz.

Third District (Court meets in Ottawa)

Peg Breslin, William E. Holdridge, Thomas J. Homer, Tom M. Lytton, Mary W. McDade, Kent F. Slater.
Clerk of the Third District: Gist Fleshman.

Fourth District (Court meets in Springfield)

Robert W. Cook, James A. Knecht, John T. McCullough, Sue E. Myerscough, Robert J. Steigmann, John W. Turner.
Clerk of the Fourth District: Darryl D. Pratscher.

Fifth District (Court meets in Mt. Vernon)

Melissa Ann Chapman, Richard P. Goldenhersh, Terrence J. Hopkins, Clyde L. Kuehn, Gordon E. Maag, Philip J. Rarick, Thomas M. Welch.
Clerk of the Fifth District: Louis E. Costa.

MOSES W. HARRISON II
Supreme Court Chief Justice
Fifth District

Moses W. Harrison II, Chief Justice of Illinois' highest court, was born in Collinsville on March 30, 1932, and educated in the Collinsville public school system. He received a B.A. degree from Colorado College in 1954 and a law degree from Washington University School of Law in St. Louis, MO, in 1958.

Chief Justice Harrison practiced law in East St. Louis and Collinsville and was senior partner in the law firm of Harrison, Rarick and Cadagin in Collinsville. While practicing law, he was elected to the Board of Governors of the Illinois State Bar Association and as president of the Madison County Bar Association.

In 1973, Chief Justice Harrison was appointed Circuit Judge by the Illinois Supreme Court and was elected to the bench in 1974. He served two terms as Chief Judge of the Third Judicial Circuit after having previously been assigned to the Felony Division and Major Civil Division of the Circuit Court of Madison County. In 1979, Chief Justice Harrison was appointed by the Illinois Supreme Court to the Illinois Appellate Court, Fifth District, in Mt. Vernon. He was elected as an Appellate Judge in 1980 and reelected in 1990. During his service on the Appellate Court, he served two terms as Presiding Judge of the Fifth District.

He was elected to the Illinois Supreme Court in 1992, and was appointed Chief Justice for a three-year term beginning Jan. 1, 2000.

Chief Justice Harrison is a member of the Illinois, Metropolitan, Tri-City, Madison County and American Bar Associations, the American Judicature Society, Justinian Society of Lawyers, and the Illinois Judges' Association. He has received numerous awards, including the Humanitarian Award from the NAACP and the Justinian Society Award of Excellence.

He and his wife, Sharon, have two sons and four grandchildren.

CHARLES E. FREEMAN
Supreme Court Justice
First District

Charles E. Freeman, the Illinois Supreme Court's senior member, is a resident of Chicago. He graduated from Virginia Union University in Richmond, VA, with a B.A. degree in liberal arts in June 1954. He received his J.D. degree from The John Marshall Law School in Chicago in February 1962.

Early in his career, Justice Freeman served as an Assistant Attorney General, Assistant State's Attorney and attorney for the Board of Election Commissioners. He was appointed as an arbitrator to the Illinois Industrial Commission in January 1965, where he served until September 1973. From September 1973 until December 1976, he served as a commissioner on the Illinois Commerce Commission.

Justice Freeman engaged in the general practice of law from 1962 to 1976, when he was elected to the Circuit Court. He served 10 years on the Cook County Circuit Court, winning two elections. While a Circuit Court Judge, Justice Freeman became the first African-American to swear in a Mayor of the City of Chicago, his good friend Harold Washington. He was elected to the Appellate Court in 1986.

Justice Freeman was elected to the Illinois Supreme Court in November 1990, as the first African-American to serve on the court. In May 1997, he was appointed Chief Justice and served until Jan. 1, 2000. He was retained for another 10-year term on the court in November 2000.

He is a member of the Cook County, Illinois State and DuPage County Bar Associations, the Illinois Judicial Council, the Illinois and American Judges' Associations and the American Judicature Society, and has received numerous awards throughout his career.

Justice Freeman and his wife, Marylee, have one son, Kevin.

MARY ANN G. McMORROW
Supreme Court Justice
First District

Mary Ann G. McMorrow received her law degree from Loyola University and was admitted to the practice of law in Illinois in 1953. She was employed by the law firm of Riordan & Linklater, engaging in the general practice of law. She was appointed Assistant State's Attorney of Cook County, assigned to the Criminal Division, and was the first woman to prosecute felony cases in Cook County. She was elected a judge of the Circuit Court of Cook County in 1976.

By order of the Supreme Court of Illinois, Justice McMorrow was assigned to the Appellate Court in 1985 and elected to that court in 1986. She was the first woman elected to serve as chairperson of the Executive Committee of the Appellate Court. She was elected to the Supreme Court of Illinois in 1992, the first woman to serve in its 173-year history.

Justice McMorrow is the 1991 recipient of the "Medal of Excellence" award from Loyola University School of Law Alumni Association. She is the 1996 recipient of "The Fellows of the Illinois Bar Foundation" award for Distinguished Service to Law and Society. She also has received three honorary degrees and numerous other awards.

Justice McMorrow is a member of the Illinois State and Chicago Bar Associations and past president of the Women's Bar Association of Illinois. She is a master bencher of the American Inns of Court and a member of the American Judicature Society, the National Association of Women Judges and a former member of the Board of Directors of the Illinois Judges' Association.

She is widowed and has one daughter.

THOMAS R. FITZGERALD
Supreme Court Justice
First District

A native of Chicago, Thomas R. Fitzgerald attended Loyola University before enlisting in the U.S. Navy. Following his tour of duty, he graduated with honors from The John Marshall Law School, where he was a founder of the school's *Law Review* and served as associate editor.

Justice Fitzgerald began his law career as a prosecutor in the Cook County State's Attorney's office. When elected to the bench in 1976, he was the youngest Cook County judge. In 1989, he was elevated to Presiding Judge of Cook County's Criminal Courts and appointed to serve as Presiding Judge of Illinois' first statewide Grand Jury. He was elected to the Illinois Supreme Court for the First District in November 2000.

As a law professor, Justice Fitzgerald has taught at The John Marshall Law School and Chicago-Kent College of Law, where he was assistant coordinator of the trial advocacy program from 1986 to 1996. He also has taught at the Einstein Institute for Science, Health and the Courts.

Justice Fitzgerald has served as President of the Illinois Judges' Association, chairman of the Illinois Supreme Court Special Committee on Capital Cases, chairman of several committees of the Illinois Judicial Conference and chairman of the Chicago Bar Association's Committees on Constitutional Law and Long-range Planning. He presently serves on the Supreme Court's Planning and Oversight Committee for Judicial Performance Review and Cook County's Judicial Advisory Council. He has received the Outstanding Judicial Performance Award from the Chicago Crime Commission, Celtic Man of the Year from the Celtic Legal Society and the Herman Kogan Media Award for Excellence in Broadcast Journalism.

He and his wife, Gayle, have five children and two grandchildren.

ROBERT R. THOMAS
Supreme Court Justice
Second District

Robert R. Thomas was born Aug. 7, 1952, in Rochester, NY. He received his B.A. degree in government from the University of Notre Dame in 1974 and was named an Academic All-American that year. He received his J.D. degree from Loyola University School of Law in 1981.

Justice Thomas was elected Circuit Court Judge in DuPage County in 1988, where he presided over civil jury trials and was Acting Chief Judge from 1989 to 1994. In 1994, he was elected to the Appellate Court, Second District.

In April 1996, he was inducted into the Academic All-American Hall of Fame, and in January 1999 he received the prestigious NCAA Silver Anniversary Award.

Justice Thomas was sworn in as an Illinois Supreme Court Justice for the Second District on Dec. 4, 2000. He is a member of the DuPage County Bar Association.

He and his wife, Maggie, have three children.

THOMAS L. KILBRIDE
Supreme Court Justice
Third District

Thomas L. Kilbride was born in LaSalle and received his B.A. degree magna cum laude from St. Mary's College in Winona, MN, in 1978. He received his law degree from Antioch School of Law in Washington, DC, in 1981.

Justice Kilbride practiced law for 20 years in Rock Island, engaging in the general practice of law, including appeals, environmental law, labor law, employment matters and other general civil and criminal matters. He was admitted to practice law in the U.S. District Court of Central Illinois and the U.S. Seventh Circuit Court of Appeals.

In November 2000, he was elected to the Illinois Supreme Court for the Third District.

Justice Kilbride is a past board member, past president and past vice president of the Illinois Township Attorneys Association, a past volunteer lawyer and charter member of the Illinois Pro Bono Center, and a member of the Illinois State Bar and Rock Island County Bar Associations. He has served as a volunteer legal advisor for the Community Caring Conference, charter chairman of the Quad Cities Interfaith Sponsoring Committee, volunteer legal advisor to Quad City Harvest, Inc., and past member of the Rock Island Human Relations Commission.

He and his wife, Mary, have three children.

RITA B. GARMAN
Supreme Court Justice
Fourth District

Rita B. Garman was born Nov. 19, 1943, in Aurora. She was valedictorian of Oswego High School in 1961. She received her B.S. degree in economics with highest honors (Bronze Tablet) from the University of Illinois in 1965, and earned her J.D. degree with distinction from the University of Iowa College of Law in 1968.

Justice Garman began the practice of law at the Vermilion County Legal Aid Society in 1968. She was Assistant State's Attorney in Vermilion County from 1969 to 1973, engaged in private practice with Sebat, Swanson, Banks, Lessen & Garman in 1973, and was an Associate Circuit Judge for 13 years. She was a Circuit Judge in the Fifth Judicial Circuit from 1986 to 1995 and served as Presiding Circuit Judge from 1987 to 1995.

Justice Garman was assigned to the Appellate Court for the Fourth District in July 1995, and was elected to the court in November 1996. She was appointed to the Illinois Supreme Court on Feb. 1, 2001.

In addition to her judicial duties, Justice Garman is a member of the Vermilion County, Illinois and Iowa State Bar Associations and the Illinois Judges' Association. She served as a member of the Illinois Judicial Conference and the Executive Committee from 1990 to 2001. She also was a member of the Judicial Education Committee during that time, serving as chairperson from 2000 to 2001. In 2001, Justice Garman received the Women's Bar Association of Illinois' Mary Heftel Hooton Award.

She and her husband, Gill, have two adult children, Sara Ellen and Andrew Gill, and one granddaughter, Kathleen Marie.

ADMINISTRATIVE OFFICE OF THE ILLINOIS COURTS

Joseph A. Schillaci

The Illinois Constitution empowers the Supreme Court to appoint an administrative director and staff to assist the chief justice in fulfilling administrative and supervisory duties. The office conducts in-service training for all judges, assigns judges between circuits, assists committees reviewing proposals for rule changes, collects and publishes statistical information on case loads and case flow in the unified court system, prepares the state judicial system budget, and organizes all payrolls for judicial personnel and court reporters. The administative director is secretary of the Illinois Courts Commission.

Joseph A. Schillaci was appointed Director of the Administrative Office of the Illinois Courts on May 12, 1997. Prior to being appointed director, he had served as deputy director since January 1995. Schillaci was born in Chicago in 1954 and is a graduate of Governors State University. He began his service to the Judicial Branch in 1986 as Administrator of the First District of the Illinois Appellate Court. He served as Executive Assistant to the Supreme Court from 1991 through 1994. Schillaci and his wife, Pamela, have two children.

OFFICE OF THE CLERK OF THE SUPREME COURT

The Clerk of the Supreme Court is appointed by the Supreme Court Justices according to constitutional prescription. In general, responsibilities include the receipt and processing of filings and maintenance of dockets, records, files and statistics on the activities of the Supreme Court. The clerk's office assists the court in the management of its case load by monitoring the flow of cases from initiation to the issuance of mandates and final orders. The clerk also maintains the roll of Illinois attorneys, processes the licensing of attorneys, registers and renews professional service corporations and associations and limited liability companies engaged in the practice of law, and serves as a public information office of the court.

Juleann Hornyak

Juleann Hornyak has served as Clerk of the Supreme Court since her appointment to this position in 1982. After receiving her B.A. and M.A.T. degrees from the University of Dayton and John Carroll University, respectively, she received a J.D. degree with high honors from the Illinois Institute of Technology/Chicago-Kent College of Law. Hornyak engaged in the practice of law, was Clerk of the Appellate Court, Fourth District, and served as Law Clerk for Appellate Court Judge Harold F. Trapp. Hornyak is married to J. Arthur Randles, and they reside in Springfield.

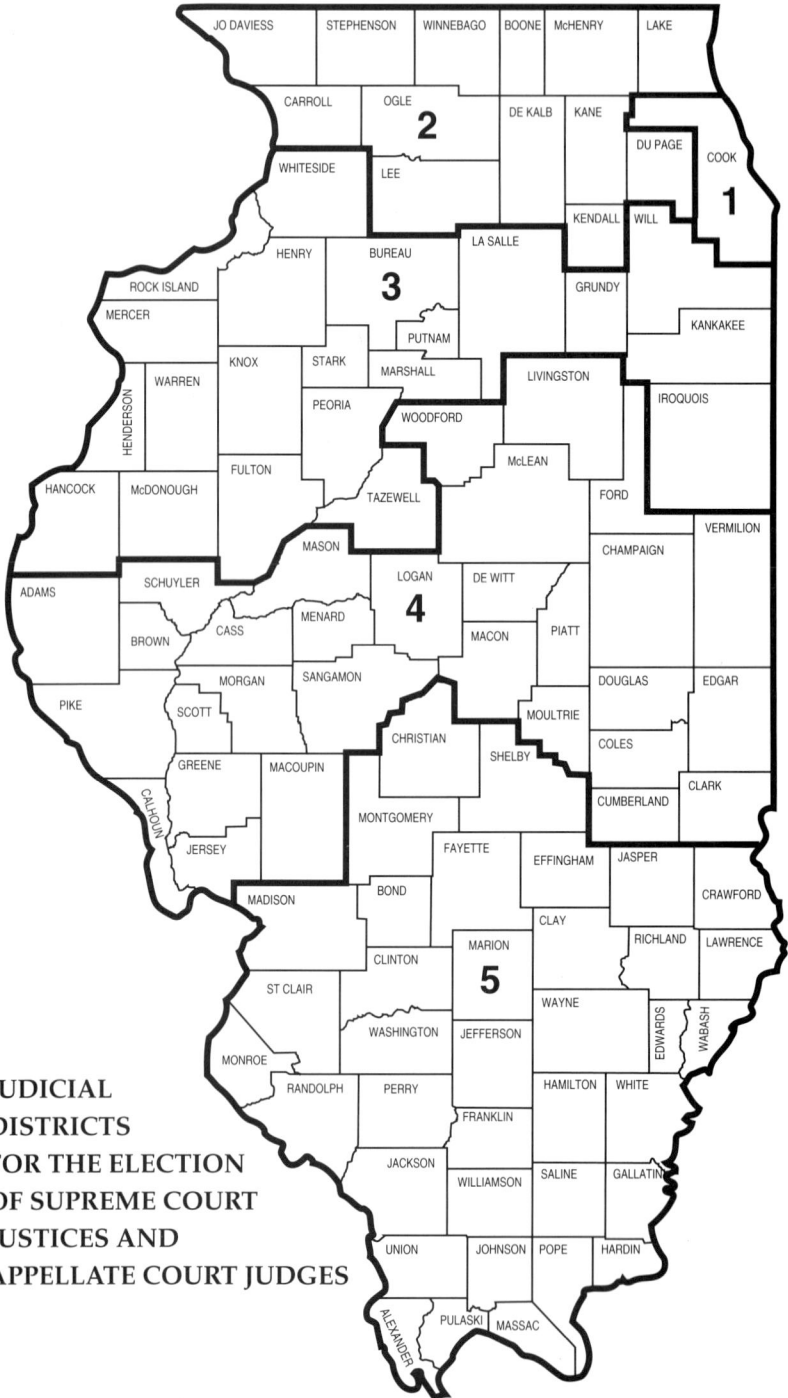

JUDICIAL
DISTRICTS
FOR THE ELECTION
OF SUPREME COURT
JUSTICES AND
APPELLATE COURT JUDGES

Appellate Judge

Judith Cohen
First District, 1st Division

A lifelong Chicagoan, Judith Cohen received her B.A. degree with highest honors from Northeastern Illinois University in 1975 and her J.D. degree from DePaul University College of Law in 1978. She had a litigation practice from 1978 to 1987, with an emphasis on medical malpractice, complex tort cases, contracts, extraordinary remedies and defamation. Judge Cohen was appointed an Associate Judge in 1987, appointed to the Circuit Court in 1996 and elected in December 1996. She was Presiding Judge of the Law Division from 1995 to July 2000, when she was appointed to the Appellate Court. Judge Cohen has served on the Illinois Judicial Conference, Circuit Court of Cook County Executive Committee, Cook County Children's Room Project and Human Genome Project. She also has served on the Board of Directors for Our Children in the Courts Foundation, the Chicago Bar Foundation and the Center for Conflict Resolution, and on the Board of Managers for the Chicago Bar Association. She received the 2000 American Board of Trial Advocates' "Judge of the Year" award.

Appellate Judge

William Cousins, Jr.
First District, 1st Division

William Cousins, Jr. was born Oct. 6, 1927, in Swiftown, MS. He was educated at the University of Illinois (B.A. with honors in political science, 1948) and Harvard Law School (LL.B., 1951). He was a Lieutenant and infantry platoon leader, U.S. Army in Korea (1952-53); an attorney with Chicago Title & Trust Company (1953-57); an Assistant State's Attorney of Cook County (1957-61); in private practice (1961-76); Alderman, 8th Ward, City of Chicago (1967-76); judge in the Circuit Court of Cook County (1976-92), and was elected as an Appellate Court Judge in 1992. He is a former chairperson and Executive Committee member of the Illinois Judicial Conference since 1983; board member of the National Center for State Courts and the National Judicial Council (chairperson, 1995-96); member and former chairperson of the Illinois Judicial Council, and a member and former board member of the Illinois Judges' Association. He is a member of the Cook County, National, Chicago, Illinois State and American Bar Associations. Judge Cousins was inducted into the Hall of Fame of the National Bar Association in 1994. He and his wife, Hiroko, have four children.

Appellate Judge

Jill K. McNulty
First District, 1st Division

Jill K. McNulty was born in Peoria and received her B.A. and J.D. degrees from Northwestern University. She served as a professor at IIT-Chicago Kent College of Law from 1972 to 1981, as an Associate Circuit Judge from 1979 to 1982, and as a Circuit Judge from 1982 to 1990. She is a member of the Illinois State, Chicago, Women's and Cook County Bar Associations, and the Illinois Judicial Council.

Appellate Judge

John P. Tully
First District, 1st Division

John P. Tully was born in Chicago. He received his Bachelor of Education degree from Chicago Teachers College and his J.D. degree from DePaul University Law School in 1970. Judge Tully practiced law for 14 years as a trial lawyer, dealing with a variety of trial work, including jury trials in the personal injury area and complex marital law. He served as a Circuit Court Judge in Cook County from 1984 to 1990, when he was elected an Appellate Judge in the First District Appellate Court. Judge Tully is the author of a book, *Divorce Without Tears*, published in 1982.

Appellate Judge

Anne M. Burke
First District, 2nd Division

Anne M. Burke was born Feb. 3, 1944, in Chicago. She received her B.A. degree in education from DePaul University in 1976 and her J.D. degree from IIT/Chicago-Kent College of Law in 1983. She was admitted to the Federal Court, Northern District of Illinois, in 1983, the U.S. Court of Appeals for the Seventh Circuit in 1985, and certified for the Trial Bar, Federal District Court, in 1987. That same year, Gov. James Thompson appointed her Judge to the Court of Claims and, in 1991, she was reappointed by Gov. Jim Edgar. In April 1994, Judge Burke was appointed special counsel to the Governor for Child Welfare Services, and in August 1995, she was appointed to the Appellate Court, First District. She was elected to the Appellate Court, First District, for a full term in 1996. She is married to Alderman Edward M. Burke, and they are parents of four children, Jennifer, Edward, Emmett and Sarah, and are legal guardians of a five-year-old child.

Appellate Judge

Robert Cahill
First District, 2nd Division

Robert Cahill was born in 1936 and educated at St. Louis University, Loyola University of Chicago and Loyola University School of Law, where he earned his J.D. degree in 1966. He began his legal career as a legislative draftsman in Springfield, then moved to the Illinois Senate where he served as legal counsel to the Education Committee and then chief of the Senate staff. From 1973 to 1980, he was an Assistant State's Attorney in Cook County and chief of special litigation in that office. In 1980, he joined the law firm of Rock, Fusco, Reynolds & Henaghan, where he practiced law until his appointment as an Associate Judge in 1983. His nine years as a trial judge included two years in the felony trial court and three years on civil jury cases in the Third Municipal District. He was found highly qualified for the Appellate Court by the Chicago Bar Association's Judicial Screening Committee in February 1992 and was elected to the court in November 1992.

Appellate Judge

Joseph Gordon
First District, 2nd Division

Joseph Gordon was born in Chicago on Dec. 4, 1932. He received his B.A. degree from Roosevelt University in 1954 and his J.D. degree from Northwestern University School of Law in 1960. He was a law clerk for Judge Julius Hoffman, Federal District Court for the Northern District of Illinois, from 1960 to 1961. From 1961 to 1964, he was a trial lawyer with the firm of Lord, Bissel and Brook. From 1964 to 1967, he was a trial lawyer with the firm now known as Sachnoff & Weaver, Ltd., and from 1969 until his election to the bench in 1976, he served as its senior litigation partner. Judge Gordon was a full-time professor of law at John Marshall Law School from 1967 to 1970 and again from 1983 to 1984, serving on its part-time faculty during various other years between 1964 and 1986. He served as judge of the Circuit Court of Cook County from 1976 to 1983 and from 1988 to 1989. Judge Gordon was appointed to the Illinois Appellate Court in 1989 and, subsequently, was elected to continue his service in 1990. He was retained for an additional term in 2000.

Appellate Judge

Margaret Stanton McBride
First District, 2nd Division

Margaret Stanton McBride was born in Evanston on Dec. 28, 1951. She received her B.A. degree from Newton College of the Sacred Heart in Newton, MA, and her J.D. degree from DePaul University College of Law. She served in private practice from 1976 to 1977 and then as a Cook County Assistant State's Attorney from 1977 to 1987. Judge McBride was appointed to the Circuit Court in 1987 and elected a Circuit Judge in 1990. She served in the First Municipal District, Criminal, Law and Chancery Divisions of the Circuit Court. When elected to the Appellate Court in November 1998, Judge McBride was the Presiding Judge of the Third Municipal District. She is married and has two children.

Appellate Judge

David Cerda
First District, 3rd Division

David Cerda was born in Chicago in 1927. He received B.S. degrees from the University of Illinois and the Universidad Nacional Autonoma de Mexico and a J.D. degree from DePaul University. He practiced law privately until his appointment as a magistrate in 1965. He became an Associate Judge in 1966 and a Circuit Court Judge in 1971, serving until his appointment to the Appellate Court in 1989. He was chairman of the Executive Committee of the First District Appellate Court in 1996. Judge Cerda was a co-founder and first President of both the Mexican American Lawyers' Association and the Midwest Council of the League of United Latin American Citizens, and has served on the Boards of Directors of SER Jobs for Progress, Inc. and the Mexican American Council on Education. He is a member of the Chicago Bar Association, the Illinois Judges' Association, the Illinois Judicial Council and the Hispanic Lawyers Association of Illinois.

Appellate Judge
Shelvin Louise Marie Hall
First District, 3rd Division

Shelvin Louise Marie Hall was born June 15, 1948. She is a graduate of Hampton University, Hampton, VA, and Boston University School of Law, Boston, MA. She then went into private practice for six years in Houston, TX. In 1980, she went to Washington, DC, as Legislative Director to the late U.S. Congressman Mickey Leland. In 1982, she served as senior attorney with the Illinois Department of Human Rights and subsequently became General Counsel in 1984. In January 1991, she was appointed as a Circuit Court Judge of Cook County, and was elected in November 1992. She serves on the Education and Executive Committees of the Supreme Court's Illinois Judicial Conference. In February 1999, she was assigned as an Appellate Court Judge. Judge Hall is chairperson of the Judicial Council of the National Bar Association, an organization for 1,500 African-American judges and former chair of the Illinois Judicial Council.

Appellate Judge
Leslie Elaine South
First District, 3rd Division

Leslie Elaine South is a product of the Chicago Public School System. She received her B.A. degree with honors from Loyola University of Chicago in 1976 and her J.D. degree from Northwestern University School of Law in 1978. She worked as an assistant prosecutor for the Cook County State's Attorney's office (1978-82) and as a staff attorney for the Chicago Transit Authority (1984-88). Judge South was appointed Associate Judge of the Circuit Court of Cook County in December 1988, and was assigned to the Sixth Municipal District in Markham. She was elected Circuit Judge of the Circuit Court of Cook County in November 1992, and to the Appellate Court, First District, in November 1996. Judge South is a former chairperson and current member of the Illinois Judicial Council and a member of the Cook County, Women's and South Suburban Bar Associations and the Illinois Judges' Association. She is married to Arthur Jackson and they have two sons, Wesley and Christopher.

Appellate Judge
Warren D. Wolfson
First District, 3rd Division

Warren D. Wolfson was born in Chicago on Feb. 14, 1933. He graduated from Gregory Grammar School and John Marshall High School. He received a B.S. degree in journalism from the University of Illinois at Chicago in 1955 and his bachelor of law degree from the University of Illinois at Urbana-Champaign in 1957. He was admitted to practice law before the Supreme Court of Illinois in 1957, the U.S. District Court, Northern District of Illinois, in 1963, the U.S. Court of Appeals for the Seventh Circuit in 1965 and the U.S. Supreme Court in 1970. He was appointed as a Judge of the Circuit Court of Cook County in 1975, elected to a full term in 1976 and retained in 1982, 1988, 1994 and 2000. Judge Wolfson was assigned to the Appellate Court, First District, in December 1994. He is married to Lauretta Wolfson.

174

Appellate Judge

Francis Barth
First District, 4th Division

Francis Barth was born in Chicago. He received his B.S. degree in management in 1959 and his J.D. degree in 1962, both from DePaul University in Chicago. He served as an Assistant Attorney General of Illinois from 1962 to 1969 and as an Assistant State's Attorney of Cook County from 1969 to 1971. In 1971, he served as Assistant to the President of the Cook County Board of Commissioners, a post he held until being appointed as Associate Judge in 1975. Judge Barth was elected a Circuit Judge in 1988, serving as Presiding Judge of the County Division from 1992 to 1999 and as Presiding Judge of the Chancery Division from 1999 until being assigned to the Appellate Court in 2000.

Appellate Judge

Allen Hartman
First District, 4th Division

Allen Hartman was born in Chicago. He was educated at Northwestern University where he received a B.S.L. degree in 1957 and an LL.B.-J.D. degree in 1959. He was admitted to the Illinois and Federal Bars in 1959. He served as law clerk to Appellate Judges Ulysses S. Schwartz and John T. Dempsey (1959-60) and was Assistant Corporation Counsel for the City of Chicago (1961-62), General Counsel to Corporation Counsel (1965-70) and First Assistant Corporation Counsel (1971-73). He was Executive Director of the Chicago Home Rule Commission in 1972. He was appointed Circuit Court Judge in 1973 and elected in 1974.
He was elected Appellate Court Judge in 1978, and was retained in 1988 and 1998. Judge Hartman has served as chairman of the First District Appellate Court Executive Committee and the Statewide Illinois Appellate Court, and is a member of the Illinois Supreme Court Rules Committee. He is an adjunct professor at the Loyola School of Law and is co-author of the *Illinois Lawyers Manual*.

Appellate Judge

Thomas E. Hoffman
First District, 4th Division

Thomas E. Hoffman was born Dec. 23, 1947, in Chicago. He was educated at Loyola University, where he earned his B.B.A. degree in 1969, and John Marshall Law School, earning his J.D. degree in 1971. He served as an Assistant Corporation Counsel for the City of Chicago from 1971 to 1976 before entering private practice. Judge Hoffman was appointed an Associate Judge of the Circuit Court of Cook County in 1984, elected a Circuit Judge of the Circuit Court of Cook County in 1988, assigned to service in the First Appellate District in 1993, and elected an Appellate Judge of the First Appellate District in 1994. He is a member of the Executive Committee of the Illinois Judicial Conference and serves as a trustee and chairman of the Judges' Retirement Board. He was president of John Marshall Law School's Alumni Association in 1996. Judge Hoffman is a member of the Chicago Bar Association, Justinian Society of Lawyers and the Chicago Inn of Court. He is married to Margarita T. Kulys, and they have four children.

Appellate Judge

Mary Jane Theis
First District, 4th Division

Mary Jane Theis was born Feb. 27, 1949, in Chicago. She received her B.A. degree from Loyola University of Chicago in 1971 and her J.D. degree from the University of San Francisco School of Law in 1974. She was an Assistant Cook County Public Defender from 1974 to 1983, an Associate Judge from 1983 to 1988, and Circuit Judge from 1988 to 1993. She was assigned to the Illinois Appellate Court, First District, in 1993, and was elected a Judge of the Illinois Appellate Court, First District, in 1994. Judge Theis is past president of the Illinois Judges' Association, a past member of the Board of Managers of the Chicago Bar Association, past member of the Board of Directors of the Appellate Lawyers' Association, a member the Illinois State Bar Association and the Women's Bar Association of Illinois. She is married to John T. Theis, and they have two children, John Kenneth and Claire.

Appellate Judge

Calvin C. Campbell
First District, 5th Division

Calvin C. Campbell was born and raised in Roanoke, VA. He received an A.B. degree from Howard University, Washington, DC, in 1948, a J.D. degree from the University of Chicago Law School in 1951, and was admitted to the Illinois Bar in 1951. He was admitted to practice before the U.S. Supreme Court in 1966. Judge Campbell was appointed to the Circuit Court by the Illinois Supreme Court in June 1977, then elected to the Illinois Appellate Court in November 1978. Prior to his election to the Appellate Court, he was an Assistant Attorney General from 1957 to 1977, serving as Chief of the Revenue Litigation Division. Judge Campbell is a member of the Illinois Judicial Council and the Cook County and Illinois Bar Associations. He served in the infantry during World War II, one of four sons serving in the Army at the same time. He was awarded a Bronze Star. Judge Campbell was retained for another term on the Appellate Court in November 1998. He has one daughter, Cathy.

Appellate Judge

Alan J. Greiman
First District, 5th Division

Alan J. Greiman was born in Chicago in 1931 and was educated at the University of Illinois, where he received his undergraduate and law degrees. He was admitted to the Illinois Bar in 1955 and practiced law until his appointment to the bench. He served in the Illinois General Assembly from 1974 to 1987, serving as chair of the House Democratic Conference and as Assistant Majority Leader. He was appointed to the Circuit Court of Cook County in 1987 and elected in 1988. After serving in the Law Jury and Law Motion Divisions of the Circuit Court, he was assigned to the Appellate Court in 1991. He was elected chairman of the Executive Committee of the First District Appellate Court in 1997 and re-elected each year thereafter. He is married to State Rep. Julie Hamos and has six daughters and seven grandchildren.

Appellate Judge

Patrick J. Quinn
First District, 5th Division

Patrick J. Quinn was born in Chicago on Oct. 1, 1953. He received his B.A. degree from the University of Illinois at Chicago in 1975 and his J.D. degree from John Marshall Law School in 1980. He served as an Assistant State's Attorney of Cook County from 1981 until his election to the Appellate Court in 1996. He was supervisor of the Sixth Municipal District from 1989 to 1991. Judge Quinn then headed the Public Integrity Unit and, subsequently, the Organized Crime Unit of the Cook County State's Attorney's Office. He and his wife, Susan, have three children.

Appellate Judge

Ellis E. Reid
First District, 5th Division

Ellis E. Reid was born in Chicago on May 19, 1934. He received his B.A. degree from the University of Illinois in 1956 and his J.D. degree from the University of Chicago Law School in 1959. He was admitted to the Illinois Bar in 1959 and admitted to practice before the U.S. District Court, Northern District of Illinois; the U.S. Court of Appeals for the Seventh Circuit; and the U.S. Supreme Court, where he has argued on three separate occasions. He was an associate attorney at McCoy, Ming & Leighton from 1959 to 1964 and partner of McCoy, Ming & Black until 1977, when he formed the firm of Ellis E. Reid & Associates, Ltd. In February 1985, he was appointed as a Circuit Judge, then elected to that position and retained twice. In November 2000, he was assigned to the Appellate Court, First District. Judge Reid is a member of the Illinois Supreme Court Rules Committee and a member of the Cook County and Illinois State Bar Associations, the Board of Directors of the Illinois Judges' Association and the Chicago Inn of Court. He and his wife, Sheila, have three children, Ellis IV, David and Noelle, and five grandchildren.

Appellate Judge

Robert Chapman Buckley
First District, 6th Division

Robert Chapman Buckley was born in Canton on Aug. 14, 1923. He attended Morton Junior College and DePaul University, where he received his A.B. degree, and Georgetown University Law Center, where he earned his J.D. degree. He is a retired Colonel in the U.S. Air Force and served in World War II and the Korean Conflict. From 1953 to 1966, he engaged in the private practice of law. He is a former Magistrate of the Village of Arlington Heights and was appointed Magistrate of the Circuit Court in 1966. Judge Buckley was appointed Circuit Court Judge in 1972, elected in 1974, assigned to the Appellate Court in 1978, and elected in 1982. He served as Presiding Judge of the First Division from 1983 to 1986 and again in 1990, He was on the First District Appellate Court Executive Committee in 1987, serving as chairman in 1989. He also was chairman of the Illinois Appellate Court Executive Committee in 1989. He is married to the former Patricia O'Callahan, and they have five children.

Appellate Judge

Margaret O'Mara Frossard
First District, 6th Division

Margaret O'Mara Frossard was born Nov. 23, 1951, in Chicago. She received her B.A. degree with honors in political science from Northwestern University in 1973 and her J.D. degree from IIT/Chicago-Kent College of Law in 1976, where she was a member of the Law Review and the National Moot Court Team. Judge Frossard was an Assistant State's Attorney in Cook County from 1976 to 1988, where she was Chief of the Felony Trial Division. Her judicial experience includes Associate Judge of the Circuit Court of Cook County from 1988 to 1994, Circuit Judge of the Circuit Court of Cook County from 1994 to 1997 and Judge of the Appellate Court, First District, since 1997. Judge Frossard is a member of the Illinois and American Judges' Associations, the Illinois State, Chicago, Women's and Northwestern Bar Associations, and is on the Board of Managers of the North Suburban Bar Association. She and her husband, Steve Yonover, have three children.

Appellate Judge

Michael J. Gallagher
First District, 6th Division

Michael J. Gallagher was born in Evergreen Park on Feb. 7, 1953. He was educated at the University of Illinois at Chicago, receiving his B.A. with honors in 1975, and at Chicago-Kent College of Law, where he served as editor of the *Law Review* and received his J.D. degree with honors in 1978. He was a staff attorney with the U.S. Securities and Exchange Commission from 1978 to 1979 and a law clerk to Justice William G. Clark of the Illinois Supreme Court from 1979 to 1981. From 1981 to 1988, Judge Gallagher was an associate and partner specializing in trial and appellate practice at Cassidy, Schade & Gloor. Appointed to the Circuit Court in 1988, he was elected in 1990 and retained in 1996. He was appointed to the Appellate Court in 1996 and elected in 1998. Judge Gallagher is a member of the Illinois Judges' Association and the Chicago Bar Association. He has published several articles in law journals.

Appellate Judge

Sheila M. O'Brien
First District, 6th Division

Sheila M. O'Brien was born Nov. 8, 1955. She graduated from the University of Notre Dame and its law school, was an Assistant Public Defender, engaged in a general trial law practice and taught at St. Louis University Law School. She was elected to the Appellate Court in 1994 after serving as an Associate Judge since 1985. Judge O'Brien has served as Vice Chair of the Executive Committee of the Appellate Court and as Presiding Judge of the First Division. In 1995, the University of Notre Dame awarded her its first "Women of Achievement" award and appointed her a member of its Law School Advisory Council. She also serves by gubernatorial appointment as a commissioner on the Illinois Juvenile Justice Commission. She is married and has three children.

Appellate Judge

John J. Bowman
Second District

John J. Bowman was born in Oak Park on Jan. 13, 1930. He received a B.A. degree in business administration from the University of Illinois and a J.D. degree from John Marshall Law School. He served in the Counter Intelligence Corps of the U.S. Army from 1952 to 1954. He was in the private practice of law from 1959 to 1973. Judge Bowman was a Deputy Public Defender from 1965 to 1973, State's Attorney of DuPage County from 1973 to 1976, and a judge in the 18th Judicial Circuit Court from 1976 to 1990. He was elected to the Second District Appellate Court in 1990 and retained in November 2000. Judge Bowman is a member of the Alpha Tau Omega Fraternity, DuPage County and Illinois Bar Associations and the Illinois Judges' Association. He is single and has five children.

Appellate Judge

Robert E. Byrne
Second District

Robert E. Byrne was born July 10, 1941, in Oak Park. He is a graduate of St. Ignatius High School and Loyola University of Chicago, where he received his J.D. degree in 1967. He was a litigation attorney in Cook, DuPage, Kane, Lake, McHenry and Will counties prior to his appointment as Associate Judge in the 18th Judicial Circuit in 1986. He was appointed a Circuit Judge in 1991 and elected in 1992, where he served as Presiding Judge of the Domestic Relations Division (1992-96) and the Chancery Division (1996-01). Judge Byrne is founder of the Arbitration Program in DuPage County and the Court Friends-Guardian Monitor Program for disabled adults. He served on the Judicial Conference Committee on ADR from 1990 to 2000, and as chair from 1997 to 2000. He has been a member of the Illinois Judicial Conference since 1997 and currently serves on the Court Automation Committee. Judge Byrne is a member of the Illinois State and DuPage County Bar Associations. He and his wife, Mame, reside in Glen Ellyn. They have two grown daughters.

Appellate Judge

Thomas E. Callum
Second District

Thomas E. Callum was born May 18, 1944, in Evergreen Park. He received his B.A. degree with honors in philosophy from St. Joseph's College in Rennselaer, IN, in 1966, and earned his J.D. degree with distinction from IIT-Chicago Kent College of Law in 1973. He served in the U.S. Marine Corps from 1967 to 1973, with a tour a duty in Vietnam from 1967 to 1969. Judge Callum was an Assistant State's Attorney in Cook County from 1973 to 1978, and was Deputy Chief of the Criminal Division of the DuPage County State's Attorney's Office from 1978 to 1980. From 1980-1986, he was engaged in the general practice of law with Callum, Anderson and Dietsch in Wheaton. He was appointed as an Associate Judge in 1986. In 1994, he was appointed as a Circuit Judge and was elected in 1996. Judge Callum served as Chief Judge of the 18th Judicial Circuit from February 1999 to February 2001, when he was appointed to the Appellate Court of Illinois. He and his wife, Mary Ann, have been married since 1972.

Appellate Judge

Fred A. Geiger
Second District

Fred A. Geiger was born in Waukegan on April 19, 1943. He received his B.A. degree from DePauw University in 1965 and his J.D. degree from the University of Illinois in 1968. He was an Assistant Public Defender in Lake County from 1969 to 1970, Assistant Corporation Counsel in Waukegan for more than five years and a partner in Finn, Geiger and Rafferty from 1970 to 1979. Judge Geiger was in private practice from 1979 to 1982, served as an Associate Judge from 1982 to 1984, and was elected Circuit Judge in 1984, where he served as Chief Judge in 1986. He was assigned to the Appellate Court in December 1989, where he served as Presiding Judge in 1997 and 1998. Judge Geiger is a member of the Illinois and Lake County Bar Associations, American Inns of Court, Jefferson Inn and the Illinois Judges' Association. He and his wife, Joan, have three sons.

Appellate Judge

R. Peter Grometer
Second District

R. Peter Grometer was born Feb. 19, 1946, in Aurora. He received his B.A. degree in economics and business from Michigan State University in 1968 and earned his J.D. degree from the University of Illinois in 1973. He served in the U.S. Army from 1969 to 1972, and practiced law in Aurora from 1973 to 1985. Judge Grometer served as an Associate Judge of the 16th Judicial Circuit from 1985 to 1992 and as a Circuit Judge from 1992 to 2001, serving as Chief Judge from 1996 to 1998. He was appointed to the Second District Appellate Court in 2001. He has served on the Illinois Judicial Conference, and was chairman of the Automation and Technology Committee from 1997 to 1999. Judge Grometer is a member of the Aurora Rotary Club, past president and director of Mental Health and Mental Rehabilitation, Inc., director of the Aurora Juvenile Protective Association, District Governor of the Boy Scouts of America and former member of the Board of Education, Dist. #129. He and his wife, Susan, have three children and one grandchild.

Appellate Judge

Susan F. Hutchinson
Second District

Susan F. Hutchinson was born April 1, 1950, in Monmouth. She received her B.A. degree in political science from Quincy University in 1971 and her J.D. degree from DePaul University School of Law in 1977. She served as an Assistant State's Attorney in McHenry County from 1977 to 1981 and a judge in the 19th Judicial Circuit from 1981 to 1994. In November 1994, she was elected to the Second District Appellate Court. Judge Hutchinson is a member of the Youth Service Bureau of McHenry County, the McHenry County and Illinois State Bar Associations, the Women's Bar Association of Illinois, the Illinois Judges' Association, the National Association of Women Judges and the Illinois Council of Juvenile and Family Judges. She and her husband, Steven McArdle, have one son.

180

Appellate Judge
Robert D. McLaren
Second District

Robert D. McLaren was born Oct. 1, 1944, in Oak Park and attended Oak Park and River Forest High School. He received his B.A. degree from Monmouth College in 1966 and his J.D. degree from Drake University Law School in 1969. Judge McLaren served as an Assistant and Special Assistant State's Attorney from 1970 to 1977 and was engaged in private practice from 1977 to 1981. He was appointed an Associate Judge of the 18th Circuit Court in 1981 and became a Circuit Judge in 1984. Judge McLaren was elected an Appellate Judge in 1988 and was retained in 1998. He is a member of the Illinois Judges' Association, the DuPage County Bar Association and the Appellate Lawyers' Association. He and his wife, the former Bonnie Janicek, have two children.

Appellate Judge
Jack O'Malley
Second District

Jack O'Malley was born in Chicago in 1951. He was educated at Loyola University of Chicago, graduating magna cum laude with a B.S. degree, at Cornell University Law School as a Charles Evans Hughes Scholar, and at the University of Chicago Law School as an Edwin F. Mandel Fellow. He worked as a police officer for the Chicago Police Department while attending college and law school. Judge O'Malley was first elected Cook County State's Attorney in 1990 and again in 1992. He began his law career as an Assistant Corporation Counsel for the City of Chicago and later was an associate and a partner at the Chicago office of Winston & Strawn. In 1996, he became vice president and general counsel of G.E. Marquette Medical Systems, a subsidiary of the General Electric Company. Judge O'Malley was elected to the Second District Appellate Court in November 2000. He and his wife, Terri, reside in McHenry County.

Appellate Judge
John W. Rapp, Jr.
Second District

John W. Rapp, Jr. was born in Oak Park on Dec. 12, 1940. He received his B.A. degree in philosophy in 1962 and his J.D. degree in 1965 from Loyola University of Chicago. Upon passing the Bar, he moved to Carroll County and practiced law for five years until being elected Associate Judge in 1970. He was elected Circuit Judge for the 15th Judicial Circuit in Carroll County in 1971, serving as Chief Judge from November 1982 through July 1998. Judge Rapp was elected by his fellow chief circuit judges to serve as chairman of the Conference of Chief Judges from 1987 to 1998. He was assigned to serve as an Appellate Judge for the Second District in August 1998. Judge Rapp is a member of the Judicial Inquiry Board. He and his wife, the former Mary K. Janco, have three adult sons, Mark, Matthew and Martin, and one grandchild, Sydney.

Appellate Judge

Peg Breslin
Third District

Peg Breslin was born in 1946 and raised on a farm near Ottawa. She earned her B.S. degree in political science from Loyola University of Chicago and a J.D. degree from Loyola Law School in 1970. She served as legal counsel to the State Board of Education for several years and was in private practice doing civil litigation. She served in the Illinois General Assembly from 1977 to 1990, including four terms as a member of Democratic House Leadership, first as Majority Whip and later as Assistant Majority Leader. After an unsuccessful bid for her party's nomination for State Treasurer, she retired from the House in 1990 to practice law in Ottawa. In 1992, she was elected to fill a vacancy on the Third District Appellate Court. Judge Breslin is the first woman elected to the Appellate Court outside Cook County in the history of the state. She and her husband, John, have two children.

Appellate Judge

William E. Holdridge
Third District

William E. Holdridge is a graduate of Farmington Community Schools. He received his B.S. degree in education from Illinois State University, his M.S. and Ph.D. degrees from the University of Illinois (U of I) and his J.D. degree from Southern Illinois University (SIU). Judge Holdridge has been a professor at the U of I and SIU and was engaged in the private practice of law in Peoria and Fulton counties. He has served as a Circuit Judge in the Ninth Judicial Circuit, Law Clerk for the Illinois Supreme Court and the Appellate Court, Third District, and as Director of the Administrative Office of the Illinois Courts. In November 1994, he was elected to the Appellate Court, Third District. Judge Holdridge has served on the Industrial Commission Division of the Illinois Appellate Court since 1995 and is a member of the Illinois and Missouri Bar Associations.

Appellate Judge

Thomas J. Homer
Third District

Thomas J. Homer was born in Canton on Jan. 12, 1947. He served as an officer in the U.S. Army Reserves from 1970 to 1976. He received his B.A. degree in political science from the University of Illinois in 1970 and his J.D. degree from Chicago-Kent in 1974, where he served on the *Law Review* and graduated with high honors. He was admitted to the Illinois Bar in 1974. From 1974 to 1975, he was an Assistant State's Attorney in Lake County. He served as the Fulton County State's Attorney from 1976 to 1982, and was a member of the Illinois House of Representatives from 1982 to 1994. From 1983 to 1996, he maintained a private law practice in Canton. Judge Homer has served on the Illinois Appellate Court since his election in 1996. He and his wife, Sandy, reside in Naperville with their three children.

Appellate Judge

Tom M. Lytton
Third District

Tom M. Lytton was born Oct. 6, 1943, in Raleigh, NC. He received his B.A. degree from Northwestern University in 1965, a certificate of graduation from the International School of Law, The Hague, Holland, in 1967, and a J.D. degree from Northwestern University Law School in 1968. Judge Lytton was an attorney with VISTA in Charleston, WV (1968-69), with Neighborhood Legal Services in Pittsburgh, PA (1969-73), a partner in the firm of Lytton, Lytton & Sutton (1973-92) and a special Assistant Attorney General (1981-92). He was elected to the Third District Appellate Court in 1992. He was admitted to the Illinois Bar in 1968, the California Bar in 1976 and the Arizona Bar in 1986. Judge Lytton is the author of an article, "Crossing State Lines to Practice Law," published in the *American University Law Review*, 1970. He and his wife, Mary Lind, have one child, Emilie.

Appellate Judge

Mary McDade
Third District

Mary McDade was born in Columbia, SC, in August 1939, and was raised in Ann Arbor, MI. She graduated with a B.A. in sociology from the University of Michigan in 1961. In 1963, she married Joe Billy McDade and for 18 years worked primarily at home as the mother of their four children. She was elected to the Peoria Board of Education, serving as president from 1972 to 1973, and was a member of the Peoria Public Library Board. She was a member of the Board of Trustees of Eureka College, serving as president in 1980 and 1982. In 1981, at the age of 41, she enrolled in the University of Illinois College of Law, earning her J.D. degree in 1984. She served as a law clerk for U.S. District Judge Michael Mihm from 1984 to 1986, and joined the law firm of Quinn, Johnston, Henderson & Pretorius in Peoria in 1986, becoming a partner in 1991. Judge McDade was named an Outstanding Alumnus of the University of Illinois College of Law in 2000. She is admitted to practice law in Illinois; U.S. District Courts, Central and Northern Districts of Illinois; U.S. Court of Appeals, Seventh Circuit, and the U.S. Supreme Court. Judge McDade is the first African-American woman elected to the Appellate Court outside Cook County.

Appellate Judge

Kent Slater
Third District

Kent Slater was born Nov. 25, 1945. He received his B.S. degree from the University of Illinois in 1968 and his J.D. degree from John Marshall Law School in 1975. He earned his L.L.M. degree from the University of Virginia Law School in 2001. Judge Slater served in Vietnam from 1970 to 1971 as an infantry officer in the U.S. Army. In 1984 and 1986, he was elected to the Illinois House of Representatives. He became a Circuit Judge in 1988 and an Appellate Judge in 1990. He is a member of the Illinois State Bar Association and the Illinois Judges' Association. Judge Slater resides in Macomb and has one daughter, Jaclyn.

Appellate Judge

Robert W. Cook
Fourth District

Robert W. Cook was born Nov. 6, 1943, in Springfield. He received his B.A. degree from the University of Illinois in 1965 and his J.D. degree from the University of Illinois College of Law in 1967, where he was a member of the *Law Review*. He was in the U.S. Marine Corps from 1967 to 1970, serving in Vietnam from 1969 to 1970. Judge Cook practiced law in Quincy from 1970 to 1983 and was a Circuit Judge in Adams County from 1983 to 1991. He was appointed to the Fourth District Appellate Court in 1991 and elected in 1994. Judge Cook has served on the faculty of judicial seminar programs for Domestic Relations, Children in the Law, Evidence, Judgments, and Enforcement of Orders. He is a member of the Illinois State and Adams County Bar Associations and the Illinois Judges' Association. Judge Cook and his wife, Fran, have three children.

Appellate Judge

James A. Knecht
Fourth District

James A. Knecht was born in Lincoln in 1944. He was educated at Illinois State University (ISU) and the University of Illinois College of Law, graduating with honors in 1973. He served as a law clerk to Illinois Supreme Court Justice Robert C. Underwood (1973-74), as an Associate Circuit Judge (1975-78) and as a Circuit Judge (1978-86) before being elected to the Appellate Court in 1986. He is secretary of the Appellate Lawyers Association of Illinois and a member of the Illinois State and McLean County Bar Associations, the American Judicature Society, the Illinois Judges' Association, and a fellow of the Illinois Bar Foundation. Judge Knecht is secretary of the ISU Foundation Board of Directors and serves on the Illinois Family Violence Coordinating Council and the National Board of Directors of the Corporate Alliance To End Partner Violence. He has been an adjunct professor at ISU since 1977 and is co-founder of the Robert C. Underwood Inn of Court. In 2000, he received the Distinguished Alumni Award from ISU. Judge Knecht and his wife, Ruth, reside in Normal. They have two children and two grandchildren.

Appellate Judge

John T. McCullough
Fourth District

John T. McCullough was born June 15, 1931, in Streator. He was educated at Lincoln College and the University of Illinois College of Law, where he earned his J.D. degree in 1955. He served in the U.S. Army from 1955 to 1957. He was elected as a county judge in 1962 and through transition became resident Circuit Judge. He was elected Chief Judge of the 11th Judicial Circuit in 1974 and elected chairman of the Chief Judges' Conference from January 1982 to December 1984. He was elected to the Fourth District Appellate Court in 1984. Judge McCullough has served as Presiding Judge of the Industrial Commission Division of the Appellate Court since 1991. He is a member of the Logan County Bar Association. Judge McCullough is married to B. Joann McCullough and has five daughters, two stepdaughters, a stepson and nine grandchildren.

Appellate Judge

Sue E. Myerscough
Fourth District

Sue E. Myerscough was born Oct. 22, 1951, in Springfield.
She received her B.A. with honors from Southern Illinois
University (SIU) in 1973 and her J.D. from SIU Law School
in 1980. She was an editor of the *Law Review*. She served as
a law clerk for Judge Harold A. Baker, U.S. District Court,
Danville, and was in private practice until her appointment
as associate judge in 1987. She served as an associate judge
until her election to the Circuit Court in 1990. In 1995, she
became Presiding Judge of Sangamon County, and in 1996
she became Chief Judge of the Illinois Seventh Judicial Circuit. Judge Myerscough was elected to the Fourth District
Appellate Court in 1998. She is a member of the Illinois Judges' Association, American
Bar Association, American Trial Lawyers Association and the Sangamon County Bar
Association. Judge Myerscough has been an adjunct professor at SIU School of Medicine since 1994. She and her husband, Bob, have two children.

Appellate Judge

Robert J. Steigmann
Fourth District

Robert J. Steigmann was born in December 1944. He received two degrees from the University of Illinois, a B.S. in
1965 and a J.D. in 1968. From 1968 to 1976, he was a staff
attorney with the Legislative Reference Bureau and an
Assistant State's Attorney in Sangamon and Champaign
counties. He was elected a judge of the Circuit Court in
1976 and assigned to the Appellate Court in July 1989. In
November 1994, he was elected to the Appellate Court.
Judge Steigmann is co-author of *Illinois Evidentiary Foundations* (2d ed., Michie 1997) and the author of the three-
volume treatise, *Illinois Evidence Manual* (3d ed., Lawyers
Co-op 1995). From 1997 through 1999, he served as a faculty member of the New York
University Law School Institute of Judicial Administration. He is an adjunct faculty member at the University of Illinois College of Law. Judge Steigmann, a resident of Urbana,
is married and has two children.

Appellate Judge

John W. Turner
Fourth District

John W. Turner was born March 23, 1956, in Lincoln. He
received his B.A. degree from the University of Illinois in
1978, with Phi Beta Kappa distinction. He earned his J.D.
degree from DePaul University College of Law in 1981.
Judge Turner was appointed as Logan County Public Defender in 1984, serving until 1987. In 1988, he was elected
as Logan County State's Attorney and was reelected in
1992. He was elected to the Illinois House of Representatives in 1994, where he served until June 2001, when he
was appointed to the Appellate Court, Fourth District. He
served as spokesman of the House Judiciary Civil Law
Committee from 1998 to 2001. Judge Turner is a member of the Illinois State and Logan
County Bar Associations and the Illinois Judges' Association. He and his wife, Kim,
have one child.

Appellate Judge

Melissa Ann Chapman
Fifth District

Melissa Ann Chapman was born in 1951 in Granite City. She received her B.A. degree in psychology in 1974 and her master's degree in education in 1975 from Southern Illinois University-Edwardsville. She worked as a mental health counselor from 1975 to 1980, counseling delinquent youths and emotionally disturbed children and their families. Judge Chapman earned her J.D. degree from St. Louis University Law School in 1983. She practiced general law and civil litigation for the next 18 years with Morris B. Chapman & Associates, where she was a partner, until her appointment to the Appellate Court in June 2001. She has served on the Attorney Registration and Disciplinary Commission Review Board and is a member of the Illinois Patterns Instruction Committee-Civil. Judge Chapman is a member of the American, Madison County and Tri-City Bar Associations, and the American and Illinois Trial Lawyers Associations. She also initiated and chaired the People's Court in Madison County to familiarize the public with the justice system. She and her husband, Phil Rheinecker, have two children, Chris and Julia.

Appellate Judge

Richard P. Goldenhersh
Fifth District

Richard P. Goldenhersh was born July 16, 1944, in East St. Louis. He attended Washington University, receiving his A.B. degree in 1966 and his J.D. degree in 1969. After seven years in private practice, Judge Goldenhersh was appointed an Associate Judge of the 20th Judicial Circuit in 1975 and became a Circuit Judge in 1982. He served as Circuit Judge until joining the Appellate Court in 1988. He is a member of the St. Clair County and Illinois State Bar Associations and former President of the Illinois Judges' Association. Judge Goldenhersh is a member of the Supreme Court Committee on Complex Litigation, the Administrative Committee of the Appellate Court, the ISBA Section Council on Civil Practice and Procedure, and former chairperson of the Associate Judge Coordinating Committee. He is married, and he and his wife, Barbara, have two children.

Appellate Judge

Terrence J. Hopkins
Fifth District

Terrence J. Hopkins was born March 6, 1948, in West Frankfort. He received his B.A. degree from Southern Illinois University at Carbondale in 1970 and his J.D. degree from St. Louis University in 1974. He was Franklin County State's Attorney from 1976 to 1983 and a Circuit Judge in the Second Judicial Circuit from 1983 to 1994. In November 1994, he was elected to the Appellate Court, Fifth District. Judge Hopkins is a member of the American Trial Lawyers' Association, the Franklin and Jefferson County Bar Associations, the Illinois Judicial Conference, and Elks and Moose Clubs. He previously belonged to the Illinois Appellate Service Commission of Illinois State's Attorneys from 1979 to 1983, and received "Best Actor" awards from the Pyramid Players in 1991 and 1992. Judge Hopkins and his wife, Jeri, have three children.

Appellate Judge

Clyde L. Kuehn
Fifth District

Clyde L. Kuehn was born in Belleville on Oct. 9, 1948. He received his B.A. degree from the University of Illinois and J.D. degree from the University of Kentucky. He served as a prosecutor for St. Clair, Monroe and Perry counties from 1973 to 1980 and was the St. Clair County State's Attorney from 1976 to 1980. He engaged in private law practice from 1980 to 1994, during which time he served as Public Defender for St. Clair County, attorney for the Metro East Transit District and attorney for the Village of Shiloh. He was appointed as Circuit Judge for the 20th Judicial Circuit in November 1994 and was assigned to the Fifth District, Appellate Court, in August 1995. Judge Kuehn is a past president of the St. Clair County Bar Association and a member of the Illinois State and American Bar Associations and the American Trial Lawyers' Association. He is married to Mary Jo Kuehn.

Appellate Judge

Gordon E. Maag
Fifth District

Gordon E. Maag was born Feb. 21, 1951, in East St. Louis. He received his B.A. degree from St. Louis University in 1973 and his J.D. degree from the University of Mississippi in 1979. He earned his LL.M. degree in 2001. Judge Maag served in the U.S. Army Infantry, 101st Airborne Division, from 1973 to 1977, and was discharged as a First Lieutenant. From 1979 to 1989, he was involved in a trial and litigation practice. In 1989, he was appointed associate judge and heard major civil and jury trials. He was appointed to the Fifth District Appellate Court in 1992 and elected in 1994. Judge Maag is a member of the American and Illinois State Bar Associations and the Illinois Trial Lawyers' Association. He and his wife, Stephanie, have two children.

Appellate Judge

Philip J. Rarick
Fifth District

Philip J. Rarick was born in Collinsville in 1940. He received his B.A. degree from Southern Illinois University and his law degree from St. Louis University. He practiced law in Collinsville from 1966 through 1975, serving as attorney for the City of Collinsville and the Townships of Collinsville and Jarvis, and as Assistant State's Attorney for Madison County. He assumed judicial office in 1975 and served as Presiding Judge of the Madison County Criminal Division from 1982 to 1985 and from 1987 to 1988. He was Chief Judge of the Third Judicial Circuit from 1985 to 1987. He was elected to the Fifth District Appellate Court in 1988. Judge Rarick is a member of the Illinois State Bar Association and the Illinois Judges' Association. He serves on the Executive Committee of the Illinois Judicial Conference and is chairman of the Complex Litigation Study Committee. He also serves as a member of the Industrial Commission Division of the Appellate Court and was a member of the Illinois Courts Commission from 1992 to 1999.

Appellate Judge

Thomas M. Welch
Fifth District

Thomas M. Welch was born Feb. 28, 1939, in St. Louis. He received his B.S. degree from the University of Illinois and his J.D. degree from the University of Missouri. He served as a Circuit Court Magistrate from 1965 to 1971, Madison County Assistant State's Attorney from 1971 to 1972 and attorney for the City of Collinsville. He practiced law as a partner with the firm of Welch, Welch and Welch from 1971 until his election to the Fifth District Appellate Court in 1980. He is a member of the Illinois, Madison County and Tri-City Bar Associations. Judge Welch and his wife, Cynthia, have three children.

APPELLATE COURT CLERKS

Steven M. Ravid
First District

Steven M. Ravid was born May 11, 1946, in Chicago. He was educated at the University of Wisconsin and Loyola University School of Law. He served in the Army Reserves, as a law clerk for Justice John J. Sullivan, and as an Assistant Attorney General, Revenue Litigation Division, for the State of Illinois. In 1980, he was appointed as Administrative Attorney for the Appellate Court, First District, and added the duties of Chief Deputy Clerk in 1986. He was appointed Clerk of the Court in April 2001. He is married to Mary R. Ravid.

Loren J. Strotz
Second District

Loren J. Strotz was born Feb. 22, 1927, in Aurora and was educated at the U.S. Merchant Marine Academy, John Marshall Law School and the University of Chicago. He was appointed Deputy Clerk to the Second District Appellate Court in 1964 and was appointed Clerk of the Court in 1972. He is a charter member of the National Conference of Appellate Clerks and has served on the Executive and Finance Committees.

Gist Fleshman
Third District

Gist Fleshman was born July 19, 1957, in St. Louis. He received degrees from Illinois State University (B.S., 1979) and DePaul University (J.D., 1985). Prior to law school, he worked two years in Washington, DC, as a Legislative Assistant to U.S. Representative Tom Corcoran. Following law school, he joined the Third District Appellate Court as a Staff Attorney and became a Law Clerk to Justice William Wombacher. In 1989, the court promoted him to Research Director, and in 1992, he became the Clerk of the Court. He and his wife, Christine, have four children.

Darryl Pratscher
Fourth District

Darryl Pratscher was born Nov. 10, 1951, in Chicago. He was educated at Illinois Wesleyan University (B.A.), the University of Minnesota (M.A.) and Southern Illinois University (J.D.). He served as Law Clerk and Research Director for the Fourth District Appellate Court and as a Staff Attorney for the State's Attorneys Appellate Service Commission before being appointed Clerk of the Fourth District Appellate Court in 1982.

Louis E. Costa
Fifth District

Louis E. Costa was born Dec. 17, 1952, in Detroit, MI. He was educated at the University of Iowa (B.A.) and the Southern Illinois University School of Law (J.D.). He served as Court Administrator and Law Clerk for the Fifth District Appellate Court before being appointed Clerk of the Court in 1988. He resides in Woodlawn with his wife, Sharon, and their three children.

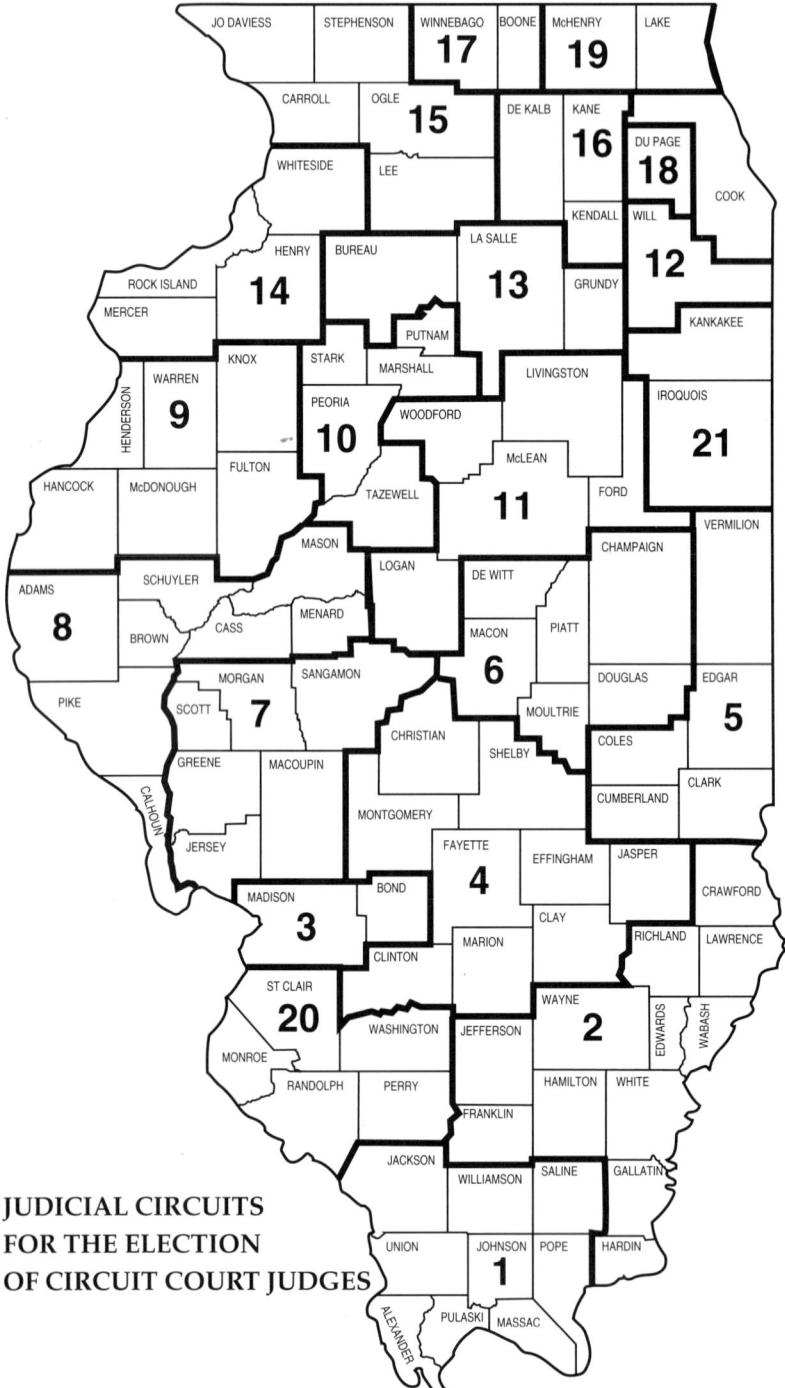

County	Circuit
JO DAVIESS	
STEPHENSON	
WINNEBAGO	17
BOONE	
McHENRY	19
LAKE	
CARROLL	
OGLE	15
DE KALB	
KANE	16
DU PAGE	18
COOK	
WHITESIDE	
LEE	
KENDALL	
WILL	12
HENRY	
BUREAU	
LA SALLE	
GRUNDY	
ROCK ISLAND	14
MERCER	
KANKAKEE	
PUTNAM	
KNOX	
STARK	
MARSHALL	13
LIVINGSTON	
WARREN	9
PEORIA	10
WOODFORD	
IROQUOIS	21
FULTON	
McLEAN	
HANCOCK	
McDONOUGH	
TAZEWELL	
FORD	
VERMILION	
MASON	
LOGAN	
DE WITT	
CHAMPAIGN	
ADAMS	8
SCHUYLER	
MENARD	
MACON	6
PIATT	
BROWN	
CASS	
DOUGLAS	
EDGAR	
MORGAN	
SANGAMON	
MOULTRIE	
PIKE	
SCOTT	7
CHRISTIAN	
COLES	5
SHELBY	
GREENE	
MACOUPIN	
CUMBERLAND	
CLARK	
CALHOUN	
JERSEY	
MONTGOMERY	
FAYETTE	
EFFINGHAM	
JASPER	
MADISON	3
BOND	
4	
CRAWFORD	
CLAY	
RICHLAND	
LAWRENCE	
CLINTON	
MARION	
ST CLAIR	20
WAYNE	
WASHINGTON	
JEFFERSON	
2	
EDWARDS	
WABASH	
MONROE	
RANDOLPH	
PERRY	
HAMILTON	
WHITE	
FRANKLIN	
JACKSON	
WILLIAMSON	
SALINE	
GALLATIN	
UNION	
JOHNSON	
POPE	
HARDIN	
1	
ALEXANDER	
PULASKI	
MASSAC	

JUDICIAL CIRCUITS
FOR THE ELECTION
OF CIRCUIT COURT JUDGES

CIRCUIT COURT AND ASSOCIATE JUDGES
(Outside of Cook County)

FIRST JUDICIAL CIRCUIT

The counties of Alexander, Jackson, Johnson, Massac, Pope, Pulaski, Saline, Union and Williamson.

Circuit Court Judges

Mark M. Boie (R) .... Jonesboro
Mark H. Clarke .... Cairo
Ronald R. Eckiss (R) .... Marion
Terry Foster (R) .... Metropolis
Michael J. Hensaw (R) ...... Harrisburg
Donald Lowery (R) .... Golconda
Paul S. Murphy .... Marion
George Oros (R) .... Mound City
Phillip G. Palmer, Sr. (R) .... Marion
William G. Schwartz (R)
.... Murphysboro
Stephen L. Spomer (R) .... Cairo
Bruce D. Stewart .... Harrisburg
David W. Watt, Jr. (R) .. Murphysboro
James R. Williamson (R) .... Vienna

Associate Judges

Rodney A. Clutts .... Jonesboro
Kimberly L. Dahlen ..... Murphysboro
Thomas H. Jones .... Murphysboro
E. D. Kimmel .... Murphysboro
Brocton D. Lockwood ...... Harrisburg
John Allen Speroni .... Marion
William Henry Wilson .... Marion

SECOND JUDICIAL CIRCUIT

The counties of Crawford, Edwards, Franklin, Gallatin, Hamilton, Hardin, Jefferson, Lawrence, Richland, Wabash, Wayne and White.

Circuit Court Judges

Larry O. Baker (R) .... Elizabethtown
David M. Correll (R) .... Robinson
Larry D. Dunn (R) .... Olney
Don A. Foster (R) .... Shawneetown
David K. Frankland (R) .... Albion
Terry H. Gamber (R) .... Mt. Vernon
Bennie Joe Harrison (R) .... Fairfield
Robert M. Hopkins (R) . Lawrenceville
Robert M. Keenan, Jr. (R)
.... Mt. Carmel
Loren P. Lewis (R) .... Benton

Thomas H. Sutton (R) .... Carmi
George W. Timberlake ...... Mt. Vernon
David L. Underwood (R)
.... McLeansboro
E. Kyle Vantrease .... Benton
James M. Wexstten .... Mt. Vernon

Associate Judges

Kathleen M. Alling .... Mt. Vernon
Leo T. Desmond .... Benton
James V. Hill .... Robinson
Robert W. Lewis .... Benton
Stephen G. Sawyer .... Mt. Carmel

THIRD JUDICIAL CIRCUIT

The counties of Bond and Madison.

Circuit Court Judges

Nicholas G. Byron (R) .. Edwardsville
Ann Callis (R) .... Edwardsville
Edward C. Ferguson ..... Edwardsville
Phillip J. Kardis (R) .... Granite City
John Knight (R) .... Greenville
A. Andreas Matoesian .. Edwardsville
George J. Moran .... Edwardsville
P. J. O'Neill .... Edwardsville
Charles V. Romani, Jr. ... Edwardsville

Associate Judges

Thomas William Chapman
.... Edwardsville
Barbara Crowder .... Edwardsville
Ellar Duff .... Edwardsville
James Hackett .... Edwardsville
Clarence W. Harrison II . Edwardsville
Robert P. Hennessey ..... Edwardsville
Lola Maddox .... Edwardsville
Lewis E. Mallott .... Edwardsville
Ralph J. Hennessey .... Edwardsville
Nelson F. Metz .... Edwardsville
Daniel J. Stack .... Edwardsville

FOURTH JUDICIAL CIRCUIT

The counties of Christian, Clay, Clinton, Effingham, Fayette, Jasper, Marion, Montgomery and Shelby.

Circuit Court Judges

John P. Coady .... Taylorville
Patrick L. Duke (R) .... Louisville

191

Patrick J. Hitpas (R) .... Carlyle
Dennis M. Huber (R) .... Hillsboro
Michael P. Kiley (R) .... Shelbyville
Kathleen P. Moran .... Carlyle
David Sauer (R) .... Centralia
S. Gene Schwarm (R) .... Vandalia
Steven P. Seymour (R) .... Effingham
Ronald D. Spears (R) .... Taylorville
Michael R. Weber (R) .... Hillsboro

Associate Judges

William J. Becker .... Breese
James R. Harvey .... Effingham
Mark M. Joy .... Hillsboro
John W. McGuire .... Salem
Dennis Middendorff .... Carlyle
Harold H. Pennock III .... Salem
David W. Slater .... Taylorville

FIFTH JUDICIAL CIRCUIT

The counties of Clark, Coles, Cumberland, Edgar and Vermilion.

Circuit Court Judges

Claudia J. Anderson .... Danville
H. Dean Andrews (R) .... Paris
Dale A. Cini .... Charleston
Michael D. Clary (R) .... Danville
Robert B. Cochonour (R) .... Casey
Craig H. DeArmond (R) .... Danville
Thomas J. Fahey (R) .... Danville
James R. Glenn .... Paris
Gary W. Jacobs (R) .... Charleston
Paul C. Komada .... Charleston
Tracy W. Resch (R) .... Marshall
Ashton C. Waller, Jr. (R) ... Charleston

Associate Judges

James K. Borbely .... Danville
Teresa Kessler Righter ...... Charleston
Joseph P. Skowronski, Jr. .... Danville
Gordon R. Stipp .... Danville

SIXTH JUDICIAL CIRCUIT

The counties of Champaign, DeWitt, Douglas, Macon, Moultrie and Piatt.

Circuit Court Judges

Arnold F. Blockman .... Urbana
Harry E. Clem .... Urbana
John R. DeLaMar (R) .... Urbana
Thomas J. Difanis .... Urbana
Dan L. Flannell (R) .... Sullivan
John K. Greanias (R) .... Decatur

Micheal Q. Jones (R) .... Urbana
Frank W. Lincoln (R) .... Tuscola
Katherine M. McCarthy .... Decatur
Theodore E. Paine .... Decatur
Stephen H. Peters (R) .... Clinton
John P. Shonkwiler (R) ...... Monticello

Associate Judges

Holly F. Clemons .... Urbana
James Coryell .... Decatur
Scott B. Diamond .... Decatur
Ann Adler Einhorn .... Urbana
Jeffrey B. Ford .... Urbana
Chris E. Freese .... Sullivan
John R. Kennedy .... Urbana
Heidi Ladd .... Urbana
Thomas E. Little .... Decatur
Timothy J. Steadman .... Decatur
Lisa Holder White .... Decatur

SEVENTH JUDICIAL CIRCUIT

The counties of Greene, Jersey, Macoupin, Morgan, Sangamon and Scott.

Circuit Court Judges

Thomas R. Appleton .... Springfield
J. David Bone (R) .... Jacksonville
Donald M. Cadagin (R) .... Springfield
Thomas P. Carmody .... Carlinville
James W. Day (R) .... Carrollton
Robert J. Eggers (R) .... Springfield
Leslie J. Graves .... Springfield
Patrick W. Kelley .... Springfield
Joseph P. Koval (R) .... Carlinville
Ronald F. Robinson (R) .... Winchester
Thomas G. Russell (R) .... Jerseyville
Leo J. Zappa, Jr. .... Springfield

Associate Judges

Diane L. Brunton .... Springfield
Charles J. Gramlich .... Springfield
Robert T. Hall .... Springfield
Roger W. Holmes .... Springfield
Theodis Lewis .... Springfield
John A. Mehlick .... Springfield
Steven H. Nardulli .... Springfield
Tim P. Olson .... Jacksonville
George H. Ray .... Springfield
Stuart H. Shiffman .... Springfield

EIGHTH JUDICIAL CIRCUIT

The counties of Adams, Brown, Calhoun, Cass, Mason, Menard, Pike and Schuyler.

Circuit Court Judges

Thomas L. Brownfield (R) ..... Havana
Dennis K. Cashman .... Quincy
Richard D. Greenlief (R) .... Hardin
Alesia A. McMillen (R) .... Rushville
M. Carol Pope (R) .... Petersburg
Michael R. Roseberry (R) ..... Pittsfield
Mark A. Schuering .... Quincy
David K. Slocum (R) .... Mt. Sterling
Scott H. Walden (R) .... Quincy
Robert L. Welch .... Quincy

Associate Judges

Mark A. Drummond .... Quincy
Diane M. Lagoski .... Mt. Sterling
Thomas J. Ortbal .... Quincy
Chet W. Vahle .... Quincy
John C. Wooleyhan .... Quincy

NINTH JUDICIAL CIRCUIT

The counties of Fulton, Hancock, Henderson, Knox, McDonough and Warren.

Circuit Court Judges

Harry C. Bulkeley (R) .... Galesburg
Stephen G. Evans (R) .... Oquawka
William D. Henderson (R) ... Macomb
David R. Hultgren .... Lewistown
Stephen C. Mathers .... Galesburg
James B. Stewart .... Galesburg
David F. Stoverink (R) .... Carthage
Chellis Eugene Taylor ...... Lewistown
Ronald C. Tenold (R) .... Monmouth

Associate Judges

Steven R. Bordner .... Lewistown
John R. Clerkin .... Macomb
Richard H. Gambrell .... Carthage
Larry W. Heiser .... Macomb
Gregory K. McClintock .... Monmouth
Patricia A. Walton .... Lewistown

TENTH JUDICIAL CIRCUIT

The counties of Marshall, Peoria, Putnam, Stark and Tazewell.

Circuit Court Judges

J. Peter Ault (R) .... Pekin
Robert A. Barnes (R) .... Peoria
John A. Barra .... Peoria
Bruce W. Black .... Peoria
Stuart P. Borden (R) .... Peoria

Michael E. Brandt (R) .... Peoria
Donald C. Courson .... Peoria
Richard E. Grawey (R) .... Peoria
Scott A. Shore (R) .... Pekin
Joe R. Vespa .... Peoria

Associate Judges

Erik I. Blanc .... Peoria
David J. Dubicki .... Peoria
Glenn H. Collier .... Peoria
Thomas G. Ebel .... Peoria
Chris L. Fredericksen .... Peoria
Kevin R. Galley .... Peoria
Jerelyn D. Maher .... Peoria
Richard McCoy .... Pekin
Brian M. Nemenoff .... Pekin
E. Michael O'Brien .... Peoria
Rebecca R. Steenrod .... Pekin

ELEVENTH JUDICIAL CIRCUIT

The counties of Ford, Livingston, Logan, McLean and Woodford.

Circuit Court Judges

Donald D. Bernardi .... Bloomington
David L. Coogan (R) .... Lincoln
Ronald C. Dozier (R) ..... Bloomington
John P. Freese .... Bloomington
Harold J. Frobish (R) .... Pontiac
John B. Huschen (R) .... Eureka
Stephen R. Pacey (R) .... Paxton
G. Michael Prall .... Bloomington
Elizabeth A. Robb .... Bloomington
W. Charles Witte (R) ...... Bloomington

Associate Judges

Donald A. Behle .... Lincoln
William D. DeCardy ...... Bloomington
Scott Drazewski .... Bloomington
Charles M. Feeney III .... Bloomington
Kevin Fitzgerald .... Bloomington
Charles H. Frank .... Pontiac
Joseph H. Kelley .... Bloomington
Robert L. Freitag .... Bloomington
James E. Souk .... Bloomington
Randolph R. Spires .... Pontiac

TWELFTH JUDICIAL CIRCUIT

The county of Will.

Circuit Court Judges

Amy M. Bertani-Tomczak (R) .... Joliet
Herman S. Haase .... Joliet

Gerald R. Kinney .... Joliet
Rodney B. Lechwar .... Joliet
Daniel J. Rozak .... Joliet
Stephen D. White (R) .... Joliet

Associate Judges

Barbara Jean Badger .... Joliet
Robert J. Baron .... Joliet
Cathy Block .... Joliet
Raymond Bolden .... Joliet
Vincent J. Cerri .... Joliet
Thomas A. Dunn .... Joliet
James E. Garrison .... Joliet
Edwin B. Grabiec .... Joliet
Lawrence C. Gray .... Joliet
Kathleen G. Kallan .... Joliet
Ludwig J. Kuhar, Jr. .... Joliet
Robert C. Lorz .... Joliet
William G. McMenamin .... Joliet
Gilbert L. Niznik .... Joliet
Richard C. Schoenstedt .... Joliet

THIRTEENTH JUDICIAL CIRCUIT

The counties of Bureau, Grundy and LaSalle.

Circuit Court Judges

Marc Bernabei (R) .... Princeton
Robert L. Carter (R) .... Ottawa
Eugene P. Daugherity .... Ottawa
James A. Lanuti (R) .... Ottawa
Cynthia M. Raccuglia .... Ottawa
Howard C. Ryan, Jr. .... Ottawa

Associate Judges

William P. Balestri .... Ottawa
William R. Banich .... Ottawa
James L. Brusatte .... Ottawa
A. Scott Madson .... Princeton
Robert C. Marsaglia .... Morris

FOURTEENTH JUDICIAL CIRCUIT

The counties of Henry, Mercer, Rock Island and Whiteside.

Circuit Court Judges

Joseph F. Beatty .... Rock Island
Martin E. Conway, Jr.(R) .... Aledo
Danny A. Dunagan (R) .... Morrison
Ted Hamer .... Cambridge
Lori R. Lefstein (R) .... Rock Island
Jeffrey W. O'Connor (R) .. Rock Island
Timothy J. Slavin (R) .... Morrison

Charles H. Stengel (R) ..... Rock Island
Ronald C. Taber .... Rock Island
James T. Teros (R) .... Rock Island
Larry S. Vandersnick .... Rock Island
Mark A. Van de Wiele ..... Rock Island

Associate Judges

John L. Bell .... Rock Island
Thomas C. Berglund .... Aldeo
Alan G. Blackwood .... Rock Island
Michael P. Brinn .... Rock Island
Dennis DePorter .... Rock Island
John L. Hauptman .... Morrison
John R. McClean, Jr. .... Rock Island
Dana R. McReynolds .... Kewanee
James J. Mesich .... Rock Island
Vicki Wright .... Morrison

FIFTEENTH JUDICIAL CIRCUIT

The counties of Carroll, JoDaviess, Lee, Ogle and Stephenson.

Circuit Court Judges

Barry Anderson (R) .... Freeport
David T. Fritts (R) .... Dixon
Charles R. Hartman .... Freeport
William A. Kelly (R) .... Galena
Tomas M. Magdich .... Dixon
Timothy Paul Nieman .... Oregon
Stephen C. Pemberton .... Oregon

Associate Judges

Charles T. Beckman .... Dixon
Richard E. DeMoss .... Mt. Carroll
David L. Jeffrey .... Freeport
Michael Mallon .... Oregon
John E. Payne .... Dixon
Victor V. Sprengelmeyer .... Galena
Theresa L. Urson .... Freeport

SIXTEENTH JUDICIAL CIRCUIT

The counties of DeKalb, Kane and Kendall.

Circuit Court Judges

F. Keith Brown .... St. Charles
Michael J. Colwell .... Geneva
Philip L. DiMarzio (R) .... St. Charles
Patrick J. Dixon (R) .... Geneva
James T. Doyle (R) .... St. Charles
Douglas R. Engel (R) .... Sycamore
Donald J. Fabian (R) .... St. Charles
Thomas E. Hogan .... Yorkville

Donald C. Hudson .... St. Charles
Pamela K. Jensen .... Geneva
Kurt Klein .... Sycamore
Gene Nottolini .... Geneva
Timothy Q. Sheldon .... Geneva
Grant S. Wegner (R) .... St. Charles
James M. Wilson (R) .... Yorkville

Associate Judges

Allen M. Anderson .... St. Charles
Judith M. Brawka .... St. Charles
Franklin D. Brewe .... St. Charles
James Donnelly .... Sycamore
Wiley W. Edmondson .... St. Charles
James R. Edwards .... St. Charles
Patricia P. Golden .... St. Charles
James C. Hallock .... St. Charles
Robert L. Janes .... St. Charles
Richard J. Larson .... Geneva
Thomas E. Mueller .... St. Charles
Mary Karen Simpson .... St. Charles
Robbin J. Stuckert .... St. Charles
Leonard J. Wojtecki .... St. Charles

SEVENTEENTH JUDICIAL CIRCUIT

The counties of Boone and Winnebago.

Circuit Court Judges

Timothy R. Gill .... Rockford
Gerald F. Grubb (R) .... Belvidere
Janet R. Holmgren (R) .... Rockford
Frederick J. Kapala .... Rockford
Michael R. Morrison .... Rockford
K. Craig Petersen .... Rockford
R. L. Pirrello (R) .... Rockford
Richard W. Vidal .... Rockford
Kathryn E. Zenoff .... Rockford

Associate Judges

Rosemary Collins .... Rockford
Patrick L. Heaslip .... Rockford
John Todd Kennedy .... Rockford
Angus S. More, Jr. .... Rockford
Stephen M. Nash .... Rockford
Steven L. Nordquist .... Rockford
J. Edward Prochaska .... Rockford
Gary Pumilia .... Rockford
R. Craig Sahlstrom .... Rockford
Brian Dean Shore .... Rockford
John R. Truitt .... Rockford
Steven G. Vecchio .... Rockford
Ronald J. White .... Rockford

EIGHTEENTH JUDICIAL CIRCUIT

The county of DuPage.

Circuit Court Judges

Robert J. Anderson (R) .... Wheaton
George J. Bakalis .... Wheaton
Kathryn E. Creswell .... Wheaton
Stephen J. Culliton .... Wheaton
Edward R. Duncan, Jr. .... Wheaton
John T. Elsner (R) .... Wheaton
Rodney W. Equi .... Wheaton
Ann B. Jorgensen .... Wheaton
Robert K. Kilander .... Wheaton
Ronald B. Mehling .... Wheaton
Kenneth Moy .... Wheaton
Perry R. Thompson .... Wheaton
Hollis L. Webster .... Wheaton
Bonnie M. Wheaton .... Wheaton

Associate Judges

Kenneth A. Abraham .... Wheaton
C. Stanley Austin .... Wheaton
Edmund P. Bart .... Wheaton
Joseph S. Bongiorno .... Wheaton
Michael J. Burke .... Wheaton
John W. Demling .... Wheaton
Peter J. Dockery .... Wheaton
Thomas C. Dudgeon .... Wheaton
Mark W. Dwyer .... Wheaton
William I. Ferguson .... Wheaton
Dorothy F. French .... Wheaton
Nicholas J. Galasso .... Wheaton
Donald J. Hennessy .... Wheaton
James W. Jerz .... Wheaton
James J. Konetski .... Wheaton
Patrick J. Leston .... Wheaton
Richard A. Lucas .... Wheaton
Brian R. McKillip .... Wheaton
Jane H. Mitton .... Wheaton
Cary B. Pierce .... Wheaton
Kenneth L. Popejoy .... Wheaton
Thomas J. Riggs .... Wheaton
Elizabeth W. Sexton .... Wheaton
Terence M. Sheen .... Wheaton
George J. Soltos .... Wheaton

NINETEENTH JUDICIAL CIRCUIT

The counties of Lake and McHenry.

Circuit Court Judges

Ward S. Arnold (R) .... Woodstock
James K. Booras (R) .... Waukegan
Barbara Gilleran Johnson . Waukegan

John R. Goshgarian (R) ..... Waukegan
David M. Hall .... Waukegan
Maureen P. McIntyre .... Woodstock
Raymond J. McKoski (R) .. Waukegan
Margaret J. Mullen (R) ...... Waukegan
Sharon Prather (R) .... Woodstock
Thomas A. Schermerhorn Woodstock
Mary S. Schostok .... Waukegan
Christopher C. Starck .... Waukegan
Michael J. Sullivan (R) ...... Woodstock
Henry C. Tonigan III (R) ... Waukegan
Jane D. Waller .... Waukegan
Stephen E. Walter (R) .... Waukegan

Associate Judges

Thomas F. Baker .... Woodstock
John D. Bolger .... Woodstock
Terrence J. Brady .... Waukegan
George Bridges .... Waukegan
Michael T. Caldwell .... Woodstock
Valerie Boettle Ceckowski . Waukegan
Joseph P. Condon .... Woodstock
Wallace B. Dunn .... Waukegan
Helen R. Franks .... Waukegan
Michael J. Fritz .... Waukegan
Donald H. Geiger .... Waukegan
Gordon E. Graham .... Woodstock
Mitchell L. Hoffman .... Waukegan
Brian P. Hughes .... Waukegan
E. Thomas Lang .... Waukegan
Patrick N. Lawler .... Waukegan
Sarah P. Lessman .... Waukegan
Victoria L. Martin .... Waukegan
Gary Neddenriep .... Waukegan
John T. Phillips .... Waukegan
John G. Radosevich .... Waukegan
Victoria A. Rossetti .... Waukegan
Emilio B. Santi .... Waukegan
Thomas R. Smoker .... Waukegan
Joseph R. Waldeck .... Waukegan
Charles P. Weech .... Woodstock
Diane E. Winter .... Waukegan
Gerald M. Zopp, Jr. .... Woodstock

TWENTIETH JUDICIAL CIRCUIT
The counties of Monroe, Perry, Randolph, St. Clair and Washington.

Circuit Court Judges

James W. Campanella (R)
.... Pinckneyville
Lloyd A. Cueto (R) .... Belleville

James K. Donovan .... Belleville
Jan V. Fiss .... Belleville
Jerry D. Flynn (R) .... Chester
Dennis J. Jacobsen (R) .... Waterloo
Lloyd A. Karmeier (R) .... Nashville
Stephen M. Kernan (R) .... Belleville
Robert P. LeChien (R) .... Belleville
Michael J. O'Malley .... Belleville
Milton S. Wharton .... Belleville

Associate Judges

Richard Aguirre .... Belleville
Walter C. Brandon, Jr. .... Belleville
Ellen A. Dauber .... Belleville
Annette A. Eckert .... Belleville
John M. Goodwin, Jr. .... Belleville
Dennis Hatch .... Belleville
Robert J. Hillebrand .... Belleville
Scott Mansfield .... Belleville
Alexis Otis-Lewis .... Belleville
James M. Radcliffe III .... Belleville
Stephen R. Rice .... Belleville
William A. Schuwerk, Jr. .... Chester
Patrick M. Young .... Belleville

TWENTY-FIRST JUDICIAL CIRCUIT
The counties of Iroquois and Kankakee.

Circuit Court Judges

Fred S. Carr, Jr. .... Kankakee
Kathy S. Elliott .... Kankakee
Clark E. Erickson .... Kankakee
J. Gregory Householter (R) . Kankakee
Michael J. Kick .... Kankakee
Gordon Lee Lustfeldt (R) ...... Watseka
Kendall O. Wenzelman (R) . Kankakee

Associate Judges

Duane J. O'Connor .... Kankakee
Sheldon W. Reagan .... Kankakee
Susan Sumner Tungate ...... Kankakee
David A. Youck .... Watseka

(R) denotes Resident Circuit Judge.

COOK COUNTY CIRCUIT JUDGES (Resident)

Peter Bakakos	Chicago	Daniel J. Lynch	Bridgeview
Robert V. Boharic	Chicago	William D. Maddux	Chicago
Henry A. Budzinski	Chicago	Susan J. McDunn	Chicago
Robert E. Cusack	Chicago	Paddy H. McNamara	Chicago
Loretta C. Douglas	Bridgeview	Judy I. Mitchell-Davis	Maywood
Jennifer Duncan-Brice	Chicago	W. P. O'Malley	Chicago
Glynn J. Elliott, Jr.	Chicago	Will P. Prendergast	Maywood
Leonard R. Grazian	Chicago	Robert J. Quinn	Chicago
Patrick S. Grossi	Bridgeview	Thomas P. Quinn	Chicago
Sophia H. Hall	Chicago	Irwin J. Solganick	Chicago
Curtis Heaston	Chicago	Daniel J. Sullivan	Rolling Meadows
Michael J. Hogan	Chicago	Fred G. Suria, Jr.	Chicago
Leo E. Holt	Chicago	Michael P. Toomin	Chicago
Michael J. Kelly	Chicago	Daniel S. Weber	Maywood
James W. Kennedy	Chicago	Alexander P. White	Chicago
David G. Lichtenstein	Chicago		

COOK COUNTY CIRCUIT JUDGES (At Large)

Nancy J. Arnold	Chicago	Vincent M. Gaughan	Chicago
Carole K. Bellows	Chicago	Francis W. Glowacki	Rolling Meadows
Richard B. Berland	Chicago	Albert Green	Chicago
Paul P. Beibel, Jr.	Chicago	Catherine M. Haberkorn	Chicago
Philip L. Bronstein	Chicago	Sheldon A. Harris	Chicago
Mary M. Brosnahan	Chicago	Marsha D. Hayes	Chicago
Edward R. Burr	Chicago	Michael T. Healy	Chicago
Diane Gordon Cannon	Chicago	Thomas L. Hogan	Chicago
Evelyn B. Clay	Chicago	Nathaniel R. Howse, Jr.	Chicago
Mary Ellen Coghlan	Chicago	Arnette R. Hubbard	Chicago
Mathew E. Coghlan	Chicago	Cheyrl D. Ingram	Maywood
Claudia Conlon	Markham	Aaron Jaffe	Chicago
Maureen E. Connors	Chicago	Daniel E. Jordan	Skokie
Kenneth J. Cortesi	Chicago	Michael S. Jordan	Skokie
Barbara J. Disko	Chicago	Aubrey F. Kaplan	Chicago
Frank J. Dolan	Chicago	Paul A. Karkula	Chicago
Deborah Mary Dooling	Chicago	Themis N. Karnezis	Maywood
Thomas P. Durkin	Chicago	Michael R. Keehan	Chicago
James D. Egan	Chicago	Daniel J. Kelley	Chicago
Lynn M. Egan	Chicago	Dorothy K. Kinnaird	Chicago
Richard J. Elrod	Chicago	John P. Kirby	Chicago
Kathy M. Flanagan	Chicago	Walter J. Kowalski	Chicago
Thomas E. Flanagan	Chicago	Diane Joan Larsen	Chicago
James P. Flannery, Jr.	Chicago	Leonard L. Levin	Chicago
Nicholas R. Ford	Chicago	Gay-Lloyd Lott	Chicago
Lester D. Foreman	Chicago	Michele F. Lowrance	Chicago
Allen A. Freeman	Chicago	Stuart F. Lubin	Chicago
Raymond Funderburk	Chicago		

COOK COUNTY CIRCUIT JUDGES (At Large)
(Concluded)

Daniel Joseph Lynch .... Chicago
Marcia Maras .... Chicago
Carol Pearce McCarthy .... Chicago
James P. McCarthy .... Chicago
Barbara A. McDonald .... Chicago
Kathleen M. McGury .... Maywood
Anthony S. Montelione ... Bridgeview
John J. Moran, Jr. .... Chicago
John E. Morrissey .... Chicago
Michael J. Murphy .... Chicago
Joyce M. Murphy Gorham ... Chicago
P. Scott Neville, Jr. .... Chicago
Benjamin E. Novoselsky .... Chicago
Julia M. Nowicki .... Chicago
Stuart A. Nudelman ....
.... Rolling Meadows
Donald J. O'Brien, Jr. .... Chicago
Joan M. O'Brienl .... Chicago
Donald P. O'Connell .... Chicago
Denise M. O'Malley .... Chicago
James P. O'Malley .... Bridgeview
Frank Orlando .... Chicago
Stuart E. Palmer .... Chicago

Sebastian T. Patti .... Chicago
Donna Phelps Felton
.... Rolling Meadows
James S. Quinlan, Jr. .... Chicago
Ronald C. Riley .... Chicago
Thomas D. Roti .... Chicago
Susan Ruscitti-Grussel .... Skokie
Nancy Sidote Salyers .... Skokie
Stephen A. Schiller .... Chicago
Colleen F. Sheehan .... Chicago
Kevin M. Sheehan .... Chicago
Henry R. Simmons, Jr. .... Chicago
Frank M. Siracusa .... Chicago
Victoria A. Stewart .... Chicago
Paul Stralka .... Chicago
Sharon M. Sullivan .... Skokie
Shelley Sutker-Dermer .... Skokie
Mary Maxwell Thomas .... Chicago
Charles M. Travis .... Chicago
Richard F. Walsh .... Chicago
John A. Ward .... Chicago
Willie M. Whiting .... Chicago

COOK COUNTY CIRCUIT JUDGES (Resident Subcircuit)

Judicial Subcircuit No. 1

Cynthia Y. Brim .... Bridgeview
Rodney Hughes Brooks .... Chicago
Sharon Johnson Coleman ..... Chicago
Wilbur E. Crooks .... Chicago
Vanessa A. Hopkins .... Chicago
Janice R. McGaughey .... Chicago
Elliott Muse, Jr. .... Markham
John O. Steele .... Chicago
Edna Turkington .... Chicago

Judicial Subcircuit No. 2

Bertina E. Lampkin .... Chicago
Marjorie C. Laws .... Chicago
William D. O'Neal .... Markham
James L. Rhodes .... Markham
Drella Savage .... Chicago
John D. Turner, Jr. .... Markham
Camille E. Willis .... Markham
E. Kenneth Wright, Jr. .... Chicago

Judicial Subcircuit No. 3

Thomas F. Carmody, Jr. ... Bridgeview
Daniel P. Darcy .... Chicago
Christopher J. Donnelly ..... Markham
David Donnersberger .... Chicago
Denise K. Filan .... Chicago
Peter A. Flynn .... Chicago
Patrick E. McGann .... Chicago
Colleen McSweeney Moore .. Chicago
Kenneth J. Wadas .... Chicago
Cyril J. Watson .... Chicago

Judicial Subcircuit No. 4

Richard J. Billik, Jr. .... Chicago
Thomas M. Davy .... Bridgeview
James J. Gavin .... Markham
Mary A. Mulhern .... Chicago
Daniel A. Riley .... Bridgeview
James G. Riley .... Chicago
Lon W. Schultz .... Chicago
James M. Varga .... Chicago

Judicial Subcircuit No. 5

Patricia Banks .... Chicago
Bernetta D. Bush .... Chicago
Jacqueline P. Cox .... Chicago
Loretta Eadie-Daniels .... Markham

Timothy C. Evans .... Chicago
Llwellyn L. Greene-Thapedi . Chicago
Rickey Jones .... Chicago
Jane L. Stuart .... Chicago
Shelli Williams Hayes .... Chicago
Llwellyn L. Greene-Thapedi . Chicago
Rickey Jones .... Chicago
Jane L. Stuart .... Chicago
Shelli Williams Hayes .... Chicago

Judicial Subcircuit No. 6

Richard William Austin .... Chicago
Robert Lopez Cepero .... Chicago
David Delgado .... Chicago
Raymond A. Figueroa .... Chicago
James J. Jorzak .... Chicago
Marya Nega .... Chicago
Kathleen M. Pantle .... Chicago
Edmund Ponce de Leon .... Chicago
Leida J. Gonzalez Santiago ... Chicago

Judicial Subcircuit No. 7

LaQuietta J. Hardy .... Chicago
Dorothy F. Jones .... Chicago
Patricia M. Martin Bishop .... Chicago
Cheryl A. Starks .... Chicago
Bill Taylor .... Chicago
Lawrence Terrell .... Maywood
Amanda S. Toney .... Chicago
Anthony L. Young .... Chicago

Judicial Subcircuit No. 8

Thomas R. Chiola .... Chicago
Candace J. Fabri .... Chicago
John J. Fleming .... Chicago
Sheldon Gardner .... Chicago
Robert E. Gordon .... Chicago
Maureen Durkin Roy .... Chicago
Nancy Drew Sheehan .... Chicago
Darryl B. Simko .... Chicago

Judicial Subcircuit No. 9

Gerald C. Bender .... Chicago
Andrew Berman .... Chicago
James R. Epstein .... Chicago
Allen S. Goldberg .... Chicago
Ronald A. Himel .... Chicago
Moshe Jacobius .... Chicago

RESIDENT SUBCIRCUIT JUDGES (Concluded)

Marvin P. Luckman .... Chicago
Sandra R. Otaka .... Chicago
Lee Preston .... Chicago

Judicial Subcircuit No. 10

Susan G. Fleming .... Chicago
Francis X. Golniewicz, Jr. ... Maywood
Garritt E. Howard .... Skokie
Robert J. Kowalski .. Rolling Meadows
Daniel M. Locallo .... Chicago
Dennis J. Morrissey .... Chicago
Gregory J. Wojkowski .... Chicago

Judicial Subcircuit No. 11

Ronald F. Bartkowicz .... Chicago
Carol A. Kelly .... Chicago
Kathleen G. Kennedy .... Chicago
James C. Murray, Jr. .... Chicago
Edward P. O'Brien .... Chicago
Barbara Riley .... Chicago
George J. W. Smith .... Chicago
Joseph J. Urso .... Rolling Meadows
Susan F. Zwick .... Chicago

Judicial Subcircuit No. 12

Donald M. Devlin .... Chicago
Edward R. Jordan .... Chicago
Joseph G. Kazmierski, Jr. ...... Chicago
John K. Madden .... Chicago
William O. Maki .... Chicago
Veronica B. Mathein .... Chicago
Richard A. Siebel .... Chicago
James Fitzgerald Smith .... Skokie

Judicial Subcircuit No. 13

Martin S. Agran .... Chicago
Janice L. Bierman .. Rolling Meadows
Clayton J. Crane .... Chicago
Thomas P. Fecarotta, Jr. .... Chicago
Anthony A. Iosco .... Chicago
Jeffrey Lawrence .... Chicago
Edward N. Pietrucha .... Chicago
James T. Ryan .... Chicago
Karen T. Tobin .... Rolling Meadows

Judicial Subcircuit No. 14

Robert W. Bertucci .... Chicago
Rodolfo Garcia .... Chicago
Adrienne M. Geary .... Chicago
James F. Henry .... Chicago
Raymond L. Jagielski .... Chicago
William G. Lacy .... Chicago
Lisa Ruble Murphy .... Chicago
Ralph Reyna .... Chicago
Maura Slattery Boyle .... Chicago

Judicial Subcircuit No. 15

Charles Burns .... Maywooe
Joanne L. Lanigan .... Chicago
Marcella C. Lipinski .... Chicago
Thomas E. Nowinski .... Bridgeview
Thomas P. Panichi .... Markham
William M. Phelan .... Bridgeview
David P. Sterba .... Bridgeview
Frank G. Zelezinski .... Markham

200

ASSOCIATE JUDGES — COOK COUNTY

Sam L. Amirante ... Rolling Meadows
Eward A. Antonietti .... Chicago
William J. Aukstik .... Bridgeview
Reginald H. Baker .... Markham
Mark J. Ballard .... Chicago
Robert P. Bastone .... Chicago
Consuelo E. Bedoya .... Skokie
Helaine L. Berger .... Chicago
John M. Berry .... Bridgeview
Samuel J. Betar III .... Chicago
Adam D. Bourgeois, Jr. .... Chicago
Preston L. Bowie, Jr. .... Chicago
William Stewart Boyd .... Chicago
Stephen Y. Brodhay .... Chicago
Michael Brown .... Chicago
Gary L. Brownfield .... Bridgeview
Dennis J. Burke .... Chicago
Joseph N. Casciato .... Chicago
Frank B. Castiglione .... Chicago
Donna L. Cervini .... Chicago
Timothy J. Chambers .... Skokie
Joseph M. Claps .... Chicago
Gloria G. Coco .... Chicago
George W. Cole .... Chicago
Susan M. Coleman .... Chicago
Thomas J. Condon .... Markham
Abishi C. Cunningham .... Chicago
Ronald S. Davis .... Chicago
Frank DeBoni .... Chicago
Dennis A. Dernbach .... Chicago
Grace G. Dickler .... Skokie
James G. Donegan .... Chicago
David A. Erickson .... Chicago
James P. Etchingham .... Maywood
Fe' Fernandez .... Chicago
Edward M. Fiala, Jr. .... Chicago
Howard L. Fink ..... Rolling Meadows
Lawrence E. Flood .... Chicago
Lawrence P. Fox .... Chicago
Nello P. Gamberdino .... Maywood
Sheldon C. Garber .... Chicago
Edwin A. Gausselin, Jr. ...... Markham
Marvin E. Gavin .... Markham
Francis A. Gembala .... Chicago
Daniel T. Gillespie .... Skokie
Susan Fox Gillis .... Chicago
Gregory R. Ginex .... Chicago
J.B. Grogan .... Chicago

Gilbert J. Grossi .... Chicago
R. Morgan Hamilton .... Chicago
Miriam E. Harrison .... Chicago
Earl B. Hoffenberg .... Chicago
Patricia B. Holmes .... Chicago
Ann Houser .... Chicago
Colleen A. Hyland .... Chicago
John J. Hynes .... Chicago
Marianne Jackson .... Chicago
Arthur L. Janura, Jr.
.... Rolling Meadows
Sandi G. Johnson-Speh ... Bridgeview
Jordan Kaplan .... Chicago
Pamela G. Karahalios
.... Rolling Meadows
Nancy J. Katz .... Chicago
Richard A. Kavitt .. Rolling Meadows
Lynne Kawamoto .... Chicago
Carol A. Kipperman .... Maywood
Randye A. Kogan .... Chicago
Thaddeus L. Kowalski .... Chicago
Lambros J. Kutrubis .... Chicago
Richard A. LaCien .... Bridgeview
John G. Laurie .... Chicago
Philip S. Lieb .... Maywood
Neil J. Linehan .... Chicago
James B. Linn .... Chicago
Mark J. Lopez .... Chicago
Patrick F. Lustig .... Chicago
Joseph M. Macellaio .... Markham
Thaddeus S. Machnik .... Chicago
Jeffrey A. Malak .... Chicago
John J. Mannion .... Bridgeview
Charles M. May .... Chicago
Brendan J. McCooey ... Rolling Meadows
Martin E. McDonough .... Markham
William F. McGlynn .... Chicago
Brigid Mary McGrath .... Chicago
Clifford L. Meacham .... Chicago
Frank W. Meekins .... Bridgeview
Daniel R. Miranda .... Maywood
George M. Morrissey .... Markham
J. Patrick Morse .... Skokie
James V. Murphy, II .... Maywood
Michael J. Murray .... Bridgeview
Raymond Myles .... Chicago
Paul J. Nealis .... Markham
Gregory M. O'Brien .... Chicago

Thomas J. O'Hara .... Markham
James M. Obbish .... Chicago
Jerome M. Orbach .... Skokie
Marcia B. Orr .... Skokie
Donald D. Panarese, Jr. .... Chicago
Luciano Panici .... Chicago
Alfred J. Paul .... Chicago
Arthur C. Perivolidis .... Chicago
William G. Pileggi .... Chicago
Nicholas T. Pomaro
.... Rolling Meadows
Michael J. Pope ...... Rolling Meadows
Charles E. Porcellino
.... Rolling Meadows
Dennis J. Porter .... Chicago
Joan M. Pucillo .... Maywood
Jesse G. Reyes .... Chicago
Wayne D. Rhine .... Chicago
Hyman Riebman .... Chicago
Elizabeth Loredo Rivera .... Chicago
Mary K. Rochford .... Skokie
Gerald T. Rohrer .... Skokie
James J. Ryan .... Bridgeview
Stanley J. Sacks .... Chicago
Marcus R. Salone .... Chicago

James M. Schreier .... Chicago
John J. Scotillo .... Rolling Meadows
Terrence V. Sharkey .... Chicago
Michael F. Sheehan, Jr. .... Chicago
Karen G. Shields .... Chicago
Michele M. Simmons .... Chicago
Robert M. Smierciak .... Bridgeview
Terence B. Smith .... Chicago
Oliver M. Spurlock .... Chicago
James F. Stack .... Bridgeview
Eddie A. Stephens .... Chicago
Richard A. Stevens .... Chicago
Michael W. Stuttley .... Markham
Thomas R. Sumner .... Chicago
John D. Tourtelot .... Chicago
Thomas M. Tucker .... Maywood
John A. Wasilewski .... Markham
Daniel G. Welter .... Bridgeview
LaBrenda E. White .... Bridgeview
Walter Williams .... Chicago
Gerald T. Winiecki .... Chicago
William S. Wood .... Chicago
Leon Wool .... Chicago
Willie B. Wright .... Chicago
Michael C. Zissman .... Chicago

COURT OF CLAIMS

The Court of Claims has exclusive jurisdiction to hear all claims regarding any contract with the State of Illinois; torts committed by agents of the state; time unjustly served by innocent persons in Illinois prisons; torts committed by escaped inmates of state-controlled institutions; and the recovery of funds deposited with the state pursuant to the Motor Vehicle Financial Responsibility Act.

The Court of Claims also administers assistance programs to compensate the families of law enforcement officers, firefighters and National Guard members killed in the line of duty, and has the authority to pay awards to innocent victims of violent crime as authorized by the Crime Victims Compensation Act.

CHIEF JUSTICE

Andrew M. Raucci was born in Oak Park on May 25, 1945. He graduated from DePaul University with a B.A. degree and received his J.D. degree from John Marshall Law School. A former Special Assistant State's Attorney for Cook, LaSalle and Kankakee counties, he served on the Court of Claims from 1984 to 1992. Judge Raucci returned to the court in 1994 and on Feb. 8, 1999, was appointed Chief Justice. He currently practices law with the firm, Kusper and Raucci Chartered, and is a registered lobbyist and frequent lecturer at legal and governmental seminars. He has two adult children, Lisa and Drew.

JUDGE

Robert G. Frederick was born Feb. 11, 1948, in Evanston. He graduated from Northern Illinois University with a B.S. degree and from the University of Illinois School of Law with a J.D. degree. He served as a Commissioner of the Court of Claims from 1983 until his appointment as a Judge in 1992. Judge Frederick is a partner in the law firm of Frederick, Hagle, Frank & Walsh in Urbana. He has three children, Robert, Christina and Julie.

JUDGE

Frederick J. Hess was born Sept. 22, 1941, in Highland. He received his B.A. degree from St. Louis University and his J.D. degree from Washburn University. He served as U.S. Attorney for the Eastern District and later the Southern District of Illinois. Judge Hess is past president of the National Association of Former United States Attorneys. He was appointed a Judge of the Court of Claims in 1997 and practices law with the firm of Lewis, Rice & Fingersh in Belleville. He and his wife, Mary, have two children.

JUDGE

Richard T. Mitchell was born Oct. 30, 1948, in Herrin. He graduated from Southern Illinois University-Carbondale with a B.A. degree and received his J.D. degree from John Marshall Law School. He was a member of the Illinois State Police Merit Board from 1989 until his appointment to the Court of Claims in 1993. Judge Mitchell is a partner in the law firm of Thomson, Mann, Mitchell & McNeely, P.C. in Jacksonville. He has two adult children.

JUDGE

Norma F. Jann was born in LaSalle on Jan. 2, 1954. She graduated from the University of Illinois-Champaign with a B.A. degree and from DePaul University College of Law with a J.D. degree. She served as a Commissioner of the Court of Claims from 1987 until her appointment as a Judge in 1991. Judge Jann is married to attorney Irwin G. Jann, and is counsel to Irwin G. Jann and Associates in Chicago.

JUDGE

David A. Epstein was born April 13, 1943, in Chicago. He graduated from the University of Chicago High School in 1960. He received his B.A. degree in chemistry from the University of Illinois in 1965 and his J.D. degree from the University of Illinois College of Law in 1968. He is admitted to the bars of Illinois; the U.S. District Court, Northern District of Illinois (trial bar); the U.S. Court of Appeals for the Seventh Circuit; and the U.S. Supreme Court. Judge Epstein first entered state service as a legislative staff intern from 1968 to 1969, served on the General Assembly staff from 1969 to 1981 and was Parliamentarian of the House of Representatives from 1975 to 1981. He is the principal of the law firm, David A. Epstein, Ltd. He is married to Susan K. Gordy and resides in the Lincoln Park area of Chicago.

JUDGE

Randy Patchett was born Sept. 10, 1949, in Christopher. He received both his B.S. and law degrees from Southern Illinois University-Carbondale. From 1978 to 1980, he was a Special Assistant Illinois Attorney General. Judge Patchett now operates Patchett Law Office in Marion. He is a retired major in the Illinois Air National Guard. He has five children.

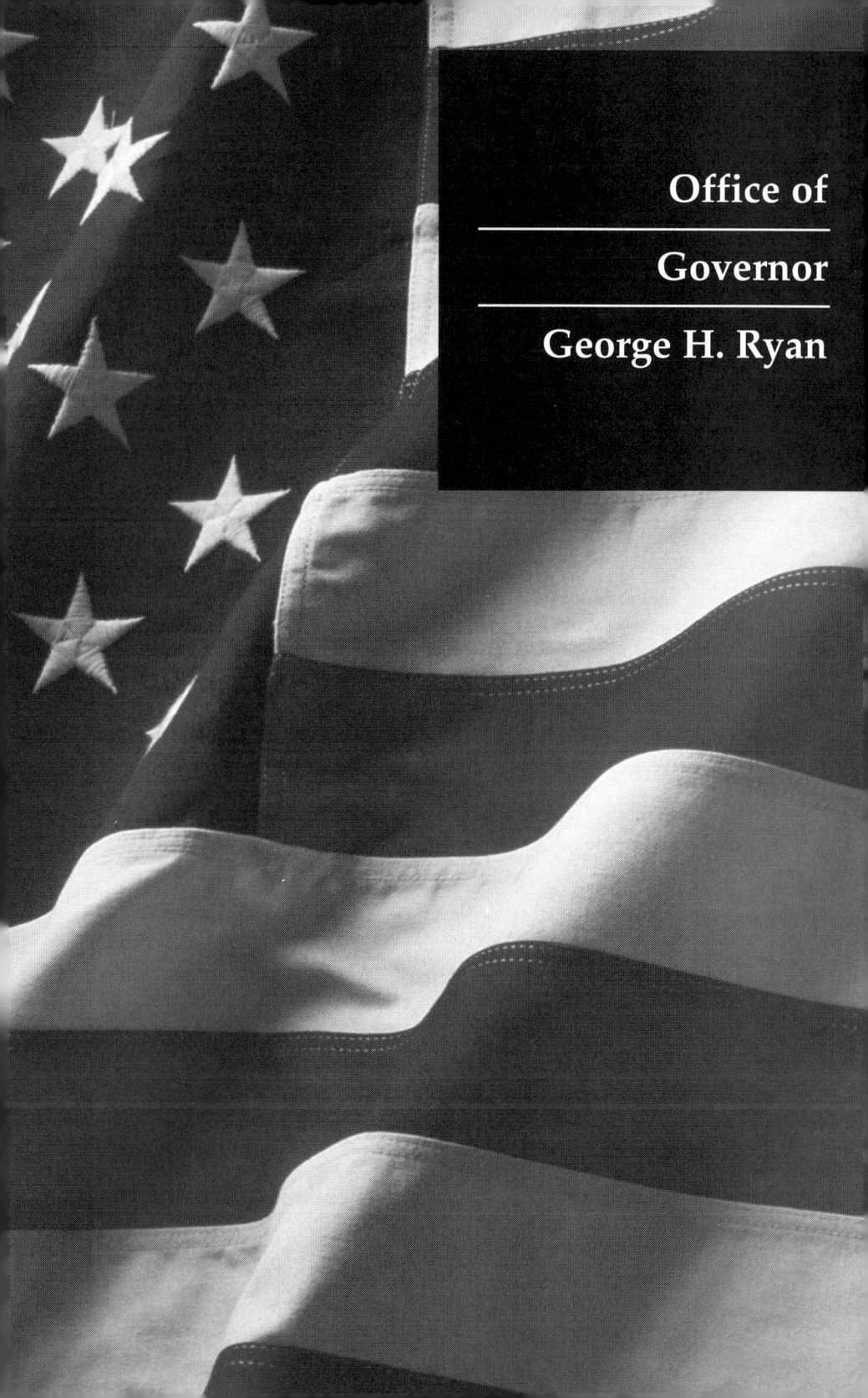

Office of
Governor
George H. Ryan

OFFICE OF THE GOVERNOR

"The Governor shall have the supreme executive power, and shall be responsible for the faithful execution of the laws."

— *Constitution of the State of Illinois*

The Governor of Illinois is the chief executive of the state and is responsible for the administration of most areas of the Executive Branch of Government.

The Governor appoints hundreds of key administrators, including department directors, subject to approval by the Illinois Senate. The Civil Administrative Code establishes clear lines of authority between the Governor and his code departments, giving him general administrative responsibility over a large number of semi-independent boards, commissions and agencies.

Each year the Governor appears before the General Assembly to propose a budget for State Government and to report on the condition of the state, set priorities and provide direction. The high public visibility of the office allows the Governor to call attention to problems or issues he believes require action.

The Governor's powers include granting pardons and reprieves, calling special legislative sessions, approving or vetoing thousands of bills, and approving state construction contracts. The Governor also serves as commander-in-chief of the state's military forces.

The Governor fills vacancies in the Offices of Secretary of State, Treasurer, Attorney General and Comptroller. Vacancies in the U.S. Senate are filled by the Governor until the next Congressional election. The Governor does not exercise direct administrative control over other elected state officers, but the constitution does empower him to require information on any subject relating to the condition, management or expenses of these offices.

To carry out his duties, the Governor is assisted by a staff that helps him develop policy, collect necessary information, offer legal advice, give direction to agencies and serve as liaisons to the General Assembly, the Federal Government and the news media.

The Governor's Office of Citizen's Assistance helps individuals find their way to the government services they need. His Bureau of the Budget offers the Governor the professional budgeting and fiscal analysis tools he needs to manage State Government. The bureau reviews agency requests for funds and develops the comprehensive annual budget for submission to the State Legislature.

Governor's Staff Members

Robert H. Newtson
Chief of Staff

Diane Ford
General Counsel

Kevin Wright
*Deputy Chief of Staff,
Springfield*

Raymond Marchiori
*Deputy Chief of Staff,
Chicago*

Robert C. Winchester
*Deputy Chief of Staff,
Marion*

Dr. Hazel Loucks
*Deputy Governor,
Education & Workforce*

Matthew Bettenhausen
*Deputy Governor,
Criminal Justice
& Public Safety*

Bridget L. Lamont
*Director,
Policy Development*

Dennis Culloton
Press Secretary

Michael P. Madigan
*Director,
Legislative Affairs*

Winifred Pizzano
*Director,
Washington, DC, Office*

Dave Urbanek
*Director,
Communications*

Susan Cavanaugh
*Director,
Office of the First Lady*

Thomas Herndon
*Director,
Office of
Strategic Planning*

Richard Larison
*Director,
Office of Performance
Review*

ADMINISTRATIVE PERSONNEL

Vicki Easley .... *Executive Assistant to the Governor*
Judith Garcia .... *Executive Secretary to the Governor*
Stephen B. Schnorf .... *Director, Bureau of the Budget*
Travis March ....*Director, Operations & Fiscal Management*
Mary Barber Reynolds ....*Director, Office of Technology*
Susan Rohrer ....*Director, Governor's Office of Citizens Assistance*
Helen H. Cashman ....*Executive Director, Chicago Office*
Penny Kendall .... *Director, International Relations/Chief of Protocol*
Lynn G. Raney .... *Director, Advance*
David Bourland .... *Curator of the Executive Mansion*
Deborah Williamson ....*Executive Assistant to the Chief of Staff*
Susan Nelson .... *Special Assistant for Scheduling*
Lucas Crater .... *Assistant to the Governor*
John Stevens ....*Deputy General Counsel*
Paul Thompson .... *Legal Counsel*
Rob Powers .... *Deputy General Counsel for Personnel*
Mark Warnsing ....*Deputy General Counsel for Public Safety*
Mike Colsch .... *Deputy Director, Bureau of the Budget*
George Hovanec .... *Deputy Director, Bureau of the Budget*
Wanda D. Taylor .... *Deputy Press Secretary*
Ray Serati ....*Deputy Press Secretary*
Matt Vanover .... *Assistant Press Secretary*
Karen Fincutter .... *Associate Press Secretary*
Katie Underwood .... *Associate Press Secretary*
Kraig Lounsberry .... *Assistant Director, Legislative Affairs*
Gordon Smith .... *Chief Liaison to the House of Representatives*
James Kaitschuk .... *Liaison to the House of Representatives*
Nita Crews .... *Assistant Director, Office of the First Lady*
Brent Crossland ....*Assistant Director, Office of Technology*
Eric Brenner ....*Senior Policy Advisor for Regulatory Affairs*
Lynne Padovan .... *Senior Policy Advisor for National Resources*
Thomas Jerkovitz .... *Senior Policy Advisor for Human Services*
Laurence Msall ....*Senior Policy Advisor for Economic Development*
Dr. Brenda Ferguson ....*Senior Policy Advisor for Education & Workforce*
Sarah Watson .... *Senior Policy Advisor for Literacy*
Phyllis Scott .... *Small Business Advocate*
Elizabeth Rim Gaffney .... *Assistant for Human Services*
Michelle Sterling .... *Assistant for Local Government*
Kimberly Beattie .... *Policy Advisor for Economic Development*
Justin Blandford .... *Policy Advisor for Policy Development*
Richard Guzman .... *Policy Advisor for Criminal Justice & Public Safety*
Cathy Leonis .... *Director, Futures for Kids*
Richard Kordesh .... *Director, Illinois Workforce Advantage*
Alice Smedstad .... *Executive Director, Commission on the Status of Women*
Pat Michalski ....*Special Assistant for Ethnic Affairs & Ethnic Media*
Joseph Muñoz .... *Assistant for Hispanic Affairs*
Jimmy Lee .... *Assistant for Asian-American Affairs*
Anthony Brady .... *Assistant for African-American Affairs*

ILLINOIS STATE BUDGET

APPROPRIATIONS

In Fiscal Year 2002, total state appropriations are estimated at $51.7 billion, including $23.4 billion in general revenue funds.

About 27 percent of the state budget is spent on education. More than $9.2 billion is appropriated for elementary and secondary education, while higher education appropriations total more than $4 billion.

With its medical assistance and child support enforcement programs, the Department of Public Aid has an appropriation of $8 billion. The Department of Transportation has an appropriation of $8.2 billion. The health and human services component of the state budget, which includes the Departments of Aging, Children and Family Services, Human Services and Public Health, totals $8.1 billion.

The remaining $14 billion supports all other governmental activities, including debt repayment, law enforcement, revenue collections, environmental programs, elected officials and the Legislative and Judicial Branches of State Government.

APPROPRIATIONS BY MAJOR PURPOSE - FY 2002 - Percent of Total

All Funds

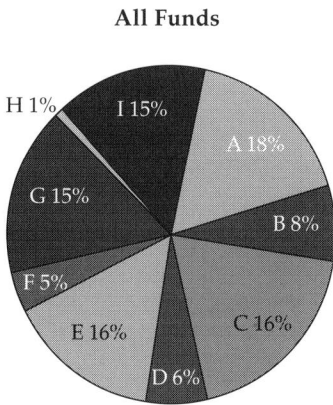

H 1%   I 15%
A 18%
G 15%
B 8%
F 5%
E 16%   C 16%
D 6%

$51.7 Billion Total

General Funds

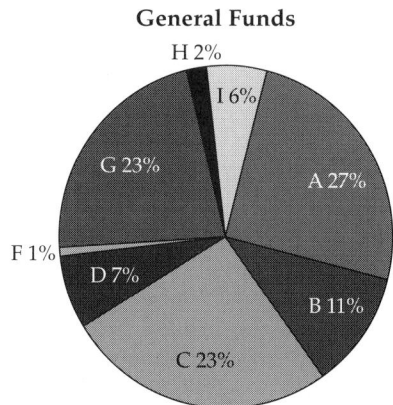

H 2%
I 6%
G 23%
A 27%
F 1%
D 7%
B 11%
C 23%

$23.4 Billion Total

A	Elementary and Secondary Education	E	Transportation
B	Higher Education	F	Environment and Natural Resources
C	Health and Human Services	G	Public Aid
D	Public Protection and Justice	H	Legislative and Judicial
		I	All Other

REVENUES BY SOURCE - FY 2002 - Percent of Total

All Appropriated Funds

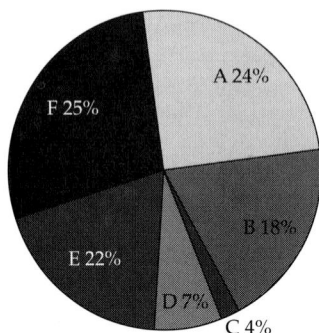

$39.5 Billion Total

General Funds

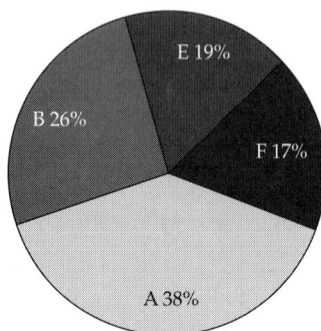

$25 Billion Total

A	Income Taxes
B	Sales Taxes
C	Bond Proceeds
D	Road Taxes and Fees
E	All Other Sources
F	Federal Aid

REVENUES

The State of Illinois will collect about $39.5 billion in total revenues from state and federal sources in Fiscal Year 2002. General fund receipts are expected to total $25 billion.

Income and sales taxes are the two major sources of state revenues. They account for 42 percent of the total receipts and 64 percent of the receipts into the general funds.

The next largest source of receipts is federal aid in the form of reimbursements for federally supported programs or in direct support of specific programs. About 50 percent of the federal receipts are related to public assistance expenditures.

Other major revenue sources are: public utility taxes, cigarette taxes, lottery receipts, insurance taxes and fees, intergovernmental payments and interest on investments.

Motor vehicle registration and driver's license fees, together with the motor fuel taxes, are the primary components of the Road Taxes and Fees Category.

BUDGET APPROPRIATIONS
($ millions)

ELECTED STATE OFFICES

Office	FY 2001	FY 2002
Governor	10.7	11.1
Lieutenant Governor	3.2	3.3
Attorney General	67.2	66.8
Secretary of State	376.6	372.5
Comptroller	55.7	57.7
Treasurer	991.0	949.8

MAJOR STATE DEPARTMENTS AND AGENCIES

Department/Agency	FY 2001	FY 2002
Aging	295.8	297.8
Agriculture	134.5	143.4
Central Management Services	2,339.6	2,588.7
Children and Family Services	1,412.0	1,418.4
Commerce and Community Affairs	1,894.1	2,137.1
Corrections	1,349.1	1,448.7
Emergency Management Agency	170.2	170.6
Employment Security	575.0	592.1
Environmental Protection Agency	1,026.4	1,206.2
Financial Institutions	9.6	10.2
Historic Preservation Agency	24.7	23.8
Human Rights	9.3	9.8
Human Services	4,793.3	5,003.7
Insurance	31.4	33.6
Labor	7.0	7.4
Military Affairs	31.0	31.9
Natural Resources	699.8	765.9
Nuclear Safety	32.5	31.2
Professional Regulation	25.2	30.5
Public Aid	7,735.0	8,017.3
Public Health	265.1	322.8
Revenue	1,145.0	979.5
State Lottery	357.3	357.3
State Police	373.3	385.8
Transportation	7,336.6	8,185.0
Veterans' Affairs	73.9	81.2

DEPARTMENT ON AGING

Margo E. Schreiber
Director

Springfield: 421 E. Capitol Ave.
#100; 62701-1789
(217) 785-3356

Chicago: 100 W. Randolph
Ste. 10-350; 60601
(312) 814-2630

Fiscal Year 2002 Appropriation: $297.8 million

The Illinois Department on Aging works to improve the quality of life for the state's nearly 2 million older citizens by coordinating programs and services that enable them to preserve their independence. Through a vast network of community-based nutrition, housekeeping, employment, training and transportation programs, to name a few, the department works to help maintain independence and prevent unnecessary institutionalization of senior citizens.

The department administers state and federal funds for senior citizen programs through 13 area agencies on aging, including 12 not-for-profit corporations and the City of Chicago. Funding to the 13 area agencies is based on the number of senior and minority citizens living in the geographic area, as well as the number living alone, in poverty and in rural areas.

Older American Services

More than 458,300 citizens age 60 and over receive social services provided through the Older Americans Act. These services, which enable many senior citizens to continue living in their own homes, include meal and transportation programs, employment programs, recreation, legal services, counseling, residential repair and renovation, health screening, housing assistance, education, information and assistance, outreach, in-home care and other services offered through senior centers or central access points.

Annually, the nutrition program in Illinois serves nearly 91,470 older people at more than 600 meal sites across the state. An additional 50,185 older people receive home-delivered meals.

Through the Elder Abuse and Neglect Program, reports of suspected cases of abuse, neglect or exploitation of older people are investigated. Trained case workers from designated local agencies work with victims to prevent further abuse and to arrange for needed services, which can include in-home care, counseling, medical assistance, housing, legal intervention or law enforcement assistance.

The Long-Term Care Ombudsman Program works to protect the rights of those who live in a variety of long-term care facilities, including nursing homes and assisted-living facilities. The program's activities include investigating and resolving complaints made by or on behalf of residents, providing information about long-term care facility placement, and monitoring the development of laws, regulations and policies that relate to long-term care facilities.

The Senior Community Service Employment Program helps older people maintain their economic independence by working to create and promote part-time community service jobs for low-income persons who are at least age 55.

This federally funded program provides salary subsidies that encourage local employers to provide part-time work for senior citizens.

Long-Term Care

The Department on Aging administers the Community Care Program, a major initiative to prevent the unnecessary institutionalization of Illinois citizens age 60 and over. The program is designed to meet the needs of elderly people who have difficulty with household and personal care tasks but could continue to live in their own homes with appropriate assistance. Services include case management, homemaker services, money management, adult day services and, in limited areas, senior companions.

The number of persons receiving Community Care Program services has increased steadily. The average number of persons receiving services each month has grown from 3,600 in 1980 to more than 38,000 in Fiscal Year 2001.

The Community Care Program is funded through state general revenue funds as appropriated by the legislature. A portion of the cost for Medicaid-eligible clients is reimbursed to Illinois under a home and community-based services waiver for senior citizens.

A case coordination unit (a local senior center, social service agency or health department) determines an individual's eligibility, designs a care plan and makes arrangements with the contractual provider agencies for delivery of the appropriate services. These units also serve as central access points for information on additional government and other services for senior citizens. Additionally, case managers pre-screen individuals who are planning to enter a long-term care facility. If the case manager determines that community-based care is appropriate, the individual may choose to live at home and receive Community Care Program services.

Communications and Training

The Speakers Bureau, audiovisual resources, statewide training sessions and the myriad of publications available to the aging network and senior advocates have greatly increased the awareness of senior services in Illinois. Information outreach also is achieved through various public/private partnerships among business and labor, medical professionals, the religious community, educators, local government and the media.

Advisory Committees

The Illinois Council on Aging is a 31-member advisory body that reviews and reports on the department's distribution of public funds, and evaluates and reports on state programs and services for the aging. The council's powers and duties include: reviewing and commenting on department reports to the Governor and the General Assembly; preparing and submitting to the Governor, the General Assembly and the director an annual report on the level and quality of all programs, services and facilities provided to the aging by the department; reviewing and commenting on the comprehensive state plan prepared by the department; reviewing and commenting on disbursements of public funds by the department to private agencies; and consulting with the director regarding the operations of the department.

Community Services and Intergenerational Programs

To carry out its mission to serve and advocate for older Illinoisans through programs and partnerships that encourage independence, dignity and quality of life, the department funds intergenerational programs, a statewide information and referral service and a program assisting grandparents raising grandchildren. Intergenerational programs are administered by the department but operated locally by project coordinators or steering committees to meet the needs of individual communities. Training and technical assistance, recruitment tools and resources are available to assist in developing, initiating and maintaining programs.

The division also supports special functions that encourage intergenerational activities and recognize the contributions of older persons. Examples of these activities are the Ms. Illinois American Classic Woman Pageant, an annual event now in its 11th year, the Intergenerational Dialogue event and the Intergenerational Programs Development Training.

Senior HelpLine

The Senior HelpLine at 1-800-252-8966 (voice and TTY) provides information and assistance on programs and services and directs seniors age 60 and over and their caregivers to local services. Professional staff assess needs, send literature and provide written referrals for a range of services, including case management, the Long-Term Care Ombudsman program, legal services, transportation, employment and nutrition services. Senior HelpLine staff also provide elder abuse intake and accept appeals and service queries from Community Care Program clients. More than 60,000 calls per year are handled by the Senior HelpLine.

ADMINISTRATIVE PERSONNEL

Margo E. Schreiber .... *Director*
Lynda Ganzer .... *Deputy Director, Community Services*
Nancy S. Nelson .... *Deputy Director, Programs*
C. Jean Blaser .... *Executive Assistant to the Director*
Deborah Pilapil .... *Legislative Liaison*
Gale S. Thetford .... *General Counsel*
Roger Wilton .... *Manager, General Services*
Janet S. Costello .... *Manager, Communications and Training*
Cheryl A. Sugent .... *Manager, Older American Services*
Fred Kimble .... *Manager, Long-Term Care*
Steve Buecker .... *Manager, Community Services & Intergenerational Programs*

DEPARTMENT OF AGRICULTURE

Springfield: State Fairgrounds
P.O. Box 19281; 62794-9281
(217) 782-2172
TDD: (217) 524-6858

Chicago: James R. Thompson Center
100 W. Randolph, Ste. 10-700; 60601
(312) 814-6900

Fiscal Year 2002 Appropriation: $143.4 million

Joe Hampton
Director

The Department of Agriculture promotes, regulates and protects the state's agricultural industry and its products while providing a wide range of consumer services. The department also ensures that quality agricultural products and services are labeled accurately and sold fairly.

The department sponsors and supports numerous promotional events and generates marketing information for Illinois agribusinesses.

Responsibilities of the department include: inspecting meat and poultry; checking scales, gasoline pumps and greenhouses; regulating the use of pesticides; livestock waste management; implementing soil and water conservation programs; and regulating the grain, feed, seed and fertilizer industries.

Agricultural Industry Regulation

The department serves as a regulatory and service agency for grain dealers, grain warehouses, personal property warehouses, salvage warehouses and the public. Its inspectors work to protect farmers' financial investment in grain crops, at both local markets and local storage facilities, as well as their financial investment in private property.

Feed and fertilizer samples submitted by state inspectors are analyzed to confirm the products' label guarantees. Samples that fail to pass within the analytical variance are declared illegal, and stop sale orders are initiated. Pesticide samples also are secured by state inspectors and analyzed for their label guarantees. Seed samples are drawn at warehouse and dealer establishments by state inspectors, which are submitted to the seed laboratory to verify purity and germination label guarantees. Stop sale orders are issued to manufacturers whose seeds fail to meet label guarantees.

Because honeybees are responsible for 80 percent of the pollination performed by insects, the department supports programs to maintain an adequate and healthy bee population.

Under the Insect Pest and Plant Disease Act, the department is responsible for inspection of all establishments that grow plants. It also promulgates and enforces quarantines against all plant pests that are not generally distributed throughout the state, and inspects planting materials imported from foreign countries for latent diseases that may develop.

Consumer Services

By inspecting a wide range of produce and prepackaged food, the department serves Illinois consumers by assuring quality products and confirming the accuracy of labels. The department also checks all anhydrous ammonia storage locations in Illinois to ensure that equipment is in good repair and that the manager and employees are competent operators.

The department also calibrates weights and measures used for testing of commercial scales, volume measures for petroleum products, and other types of commercial meters. It also standardizes moisture meters used by state inspectors to calibrate field meters used in determining grain moisture.

Marketing

One of the department's more important goals is developing markets for Illinois agricultural products. Market service programs include the Federal-State Livestock Market News Service and the Federal-State Grain Market News Service, which provide current market information to buyers and sellers.

Trade shows and trade missions at home and abroad develop markets for raw and processed agricultural products. Export trade seminars, designed to interest new business in exports and provide technical assistance to those who require it, are conducted.

The department works closely with farm organizations and commodity groups to promote agricultural programs and marketing activities. Directories listing suppliers of Illinois food and agribusiness products are published annually. Transportation information and assistance to shippers of agricultural and food products also are provided.

The Illinois Agricultural Statistics Service, operated in conjunction with the U.S. Department of Agriculture, provides information on crop production, livestock numbers, prices and related agricultural data, to aid producers, the public, business and government in agriculture and marketing. Information for the published reports is obtained through the cooperation of farmers, livestock feeders, grain elevators and agribusiness firms by mail questionnaires, telephone contacts, personal enumeration and in-the-field observations. The estimates are based on sample surveys, using some of the most modern sampling methodology for selection of farm operators for interviews and fields for observation.

Export services to assist Illinois companies in entering and expanding international markets for food and agricultural products are provided by the department. This includes consulting with exporting firms, operating a trade lead referral system to Illinois exporters, managing participation by Illinois companies in international trade shows and missions, assisting Illinois firms with personal international business contacts, working with foreign visitors to Illinois, and publishing the *Illinois Food Guide*, the *Illinois Agribusiness Guide* and the quarterly newsletter, *Marketing Perspectives*. The department has representatives in Hong Kong, Belgium, Mexico and Canada.

Animal Industries

Livestock production is an important segment of the state's agricultural economy. The department administers many programs to ensure healthy livestock, proper regulation of meat products, and the humane care and treatment of animals. It conducts programs aimed at control or eradication of many livestock and poultry diseases, including bovine tuberculosis, cattle scabies, scrapie in sheep, pseudorabies and equine viral encephalitides. Regulatory action is taken when occurrence of a disease warrants. Regional animal disease diagnostic laboratories are located at Centralia and Galesburg. In Springfield, the State-Federal Serology Laboratory, operated in cooperation with the U.S. De-

Illinois, the second-leading state in corn production, harvested 1.7 billion bushels in 2000.

partment of Agriculture, tests blood and milk for specific disease antibodies. All these laboratories, through veterinarians, assist livestock and pet owners with problems relating to animal diseases, and provide support for various disease control and eradication programs.

The department licenses and inspects all establishments in which animals or poultry are slaughtered or meat or poultry is processed for intrastate sale. Meat and poultry inspection activities range from antemortem inspection through slaughtering and processing to the retail level. It also licenses and inspects businesses that sell, produce or serve pet and companion animals, including pet shops and dealers, kennel and cattery operators, animal control facilities and shelters. The program helps ensure that pets receive proper feeding, watering and general care in a clean environment. It also helps ensure that pet buyers receive healthy animals.

Natural Resources

Soil conservation is one of the Department of Agriculture's top priorities. The department works with state agencies to limit the irreversible conversion of rich Illinois farmland and provides technical assistance to units of local government in developing programs for farmland protection. It administers all state soil erosion programs and provides assistance to the 98 Illinois soil and water conservation districts. Soil conservation activities include coordinating a state erosion and sediment control program, providing public presentations, assisting private and public organizations and agencies in the development of soil erosion and water quality programs, overseeing agricultural enhancements through Conservation 2000, and representing the state in all matters arising from the provisions of the Soil and Water Conservation District Act.

The department also enforces the Livestock Management Facilities Act, which helps ensure that livestock waste is managed in an environmentally sound manner. The act requires owners of new or modified facilities to register and certify construction with the department. Waste lagoons must be built according to strict design standards.

Fairs and Horse Racing

Founded in 1853, the Illinois State Fair has operated both as a separate state agency and as a part of the Department of Agriculture. In September 1979, the fair again became a division of the department after having been the State Fair Agency since 1966. The state fairgrounds in Springfield encompass 366 acres with more than 100 permanent buildings. In 1986, the State of Illinois purchased the DuQuoin State Fair in Perry County located on 1,500 acres. Harness racing has been a tradition at the DuQuoin State Fair, home of the famous World Trotting Derby. The Illinois State Fair and the DuQuoin State Fair showcase Illinois agriculture and offer wholesome family entertainment.

In Illinois, county fairs are an historical tradition dating back to the 1840s. Today, there are 105 county fairs and expositions. Revenue for fairs is generated through a tax on pari-mutuel betting.

The department administers the Illinois Standardbred Breeders Fund and the Illinois Thoroughbred Breeders Fund, which encourage the breeding and racing of quality Standardbred and Thoroughbred horses in Illinois, and the establishment and preservation of subsequent agricultural and commercial benefits. It also is responsible for qualifying eligible Illinois stallions and foals, and establishing conditions and purses of the races for eligible horses at the pari-mutuel tracks, the Illinois State Fair, the DuQuoin State Fair, and the county fairs.

ADMINISTRATIVE PERSONNEL

Joe Hampton . . . . *Director*
Joan Messina . . . . *Assistant Director*
Mike Williams . . . . *Policy Advisor*
John Cross . . . . *Legislative Liaison*
Cindy Ervin . . . . *Legal Counsel*
Joe D'Alessandro . . . . *Fiscal Officer*
Lynette Jones . . . . *Chief, Office of Human Resource Management*
John Herath . . . . *Chief, Office of Public Information*
Brad Schwab . . . . *State Statistician, USDA Agricultural Statistics*
Sandra Rolando . . . . *Chief, Bureau of Marketing and Promotion*
Warren Goetsch . . . . *Chief, Division of Natural Resources*
Scott Frank . . . . *Chief, Bureau of Environmental Programs*
Steve Chard . . . . *Chief, Bureau of Land and Water Resources*
Tom Jennings . . . . *Chief, Division of Agricultural Industry Regulations*
Sid Colbrook . . . . *Chief, Bureau of Weights and Measures*
Mark Ringler . . . . *Chief, Bureau of Agricultural Products Inspection*
Julie King . . . . *Chief, Division of Food Safety and Animal Protection*
Dr. Kris Mazurczak . . . . *Chief, Bureau of Meat and Poultry Inspection*
Dr. Richard Hull . . . . *Chief, Bureau of Animal Health*
Dr. David Bromwell . . . . *Chief, Bureau of Animal Welfare*
Harold "Bud" Ford . . . . *Bureau Chief, Illinois State Fair*
Sammye Fark . . . . *Bureau Chief, DuQuoin State Fair*

DEPARTMENT OF CENTRAL MANAGEMENT SERVICES

Springfield: 715 Stratton Building; 62706
(217) 782-2141

Chicago: 100 W. Randolph
4th Floor; 60601
(312) 814-2141

Fiscal Year 2002 Appropriation: $2.6 billion

Michael S. Schwartz
Director

The Department of Central Management Services (CMS) provides a variety of centralized services for the operation of State Government. The department provides personnel services for state agencies; administers the State Employee Benefits Program; purchases goods and services for state agencies; supplies telecommunications, data processing, videoconferencing and office automation; manages state property, and disseminates information about State Government to the news media and general public. The department is comprised of about 1,381 employees. It employs volume purchasing and economies of scale to reduce costs and improve government efficiency.

Bureau of Personnel

The Bureau of Personnel develops and administers the state's Merit Employment System for the 65,000 employees under the jurisdiction of the Governor. It is responsible for serving all state agencies by overseeing production classification, compensation, employee transactions, payroll certification, recruiting, counseling and testing of applicants for more than 1,000 job classifications. The examination process has continued to be streamlined with advances made to computerized testing in Springfield and Chicago. Written examinations also are administered and counseling services provided at the Marion, Rockford and Champaign offices. The bureau assists in collective bargaining and labor relations for all state agencies. The bureau's plan for developing human resources spans a broad spectrum of professional growth and advancement opportunities for state employees, including staff development training courses and the Upward Mobility Program.

Bureau of Benefits

The Bureau of Benefits administers several employee benefit programs, including group health, dental, vision and life insurance, workers' compensation and the Deferred Compensation Plan. The bureau works with labor representatives, health care providers and insurance carriers to provide a plan of benefits for all active and retired state employees, while at the same time working to contain and control costs. The state provides employees and retirees with term life insurance, and they may purchase optional coverages. In addition, the bureau administers health benefits programs for downstate retired teachers and community college retirees. The bureau also administers the Local Government Health Plan, which is a separately-funded, self-insured option available to qualified units of local government to provide comprehensive coverage for their employees and elected officials.

The Bureau of Benefits is responsible for payment of medical and workers' compensation claims for work-related accidents of state employees. It maintains case histories, conducts investigations and confers with appropriate authorities concerning court settlements of claims against the program. Additionally, the bureau administers auto liability and insurance procurements for all property, casualty and liability expenses.

The Deferred Compensation Plan, an optional savings and retirement plan for state employees, also falls under the responsibility of the bureau. Employees can invest, tax-free, a predetermined percentage of their annual incomes in professionally managed investment funds to build a more financially secure future for themselves and their families.

Bureau of Support Services

The Bureau of Support Services provides centralized purchasing of supplies and equipment for state agencies, maintains the state's fleet of vehicles, administers the State Use Program and coordinates statewide travel programs for the Governor's Travel Control Board. As the state's central purchasing authority, the bureau establishes contracts that ensure quality products are obtained at the lowest possible prices, using a computerized procurement system that saves money, time and reduces paperwork. The bureau administers the Joint Purchasing Act, which allows local governments to take advantage of volume discounts by purchasing supplies and equipment from state contracts. As the state's fleet manager, the bureau oversees all state vehicle purchases. The state's fleet consists of some 13,500 vehicles, which are maintained through a network of 23 garage facilities and a motorpool facility in Springfield. The Governor's Travel Control Board has established discount agreements with hotels, airlines and car rental companies, and administers the state's corporate charge card program.

The Illinois State Use Program is a national leader in providing both traditional and technology-based employment opportunities for persons with disabilities. The program allows state agencies to purchase goods and services from approved rehabilitation facilities serving persons with disabilities. Agencies have realized considerable savings while receiving high-quality products and services. Through this program, new employment opportunities have been created for more than 25,000 Illinois citizens with disabilities.

Business Enterprise Program for Minorities, Females and Persons with Disabilities

The Business Enterprise for Minorities, Females and Persons with Disabilities Act helps State Government promote the economic development of businesses certified as owned and controlled by minorities, females and persons with disabilities. It does so by establishing a goal that at least 19 percent of procurement contracts let by the state go to businesses certified under the Act. Currently, there are 62 agencies and nine universities letting contracts subject to the Act.

Bureau of Communications and Computer Services

The Bureau of Communications and Computer Services provides data processing and telecommunications services to state agencies. It operates the state's central computer facility in Springfield, where it provides electronic data processing services to its users and safeguards computer operations from security threats, power outages and other operation disruptions. The bureau also reports on computer usage and capacity and makes recommendations about future needs. It assists agencies in the selection and use of computer services and office automation equipment, and oversees the state's data processing training center for state employees.

The bureau manages a secure, statewide telecommunications network, available 24 hours a day, seven days a week. The network serves more than 800 cities in all 102 Illinois counties. CMS telecommunications provides needed, on-demand bandwidth to the myriad of state and local government agencies serving the public safety, human services, employment and economic needs of Illinois residents.

The bureau also is the Internet service provider for all state agencies, boards and commissions. In association with the Illinois Century Network, the bureau provides Internet connections for Illinois schools as well. Services include establishing Internet access, installing on-site Web servers and developing Web pages. The bureau also operates a Web server that houses the State of Illinois home page.

Bureau of Property Management

The Bureau of Property Management is responsible for managing the state's real, personal and surplus property. It obtains leased office space for state agencies, evaluates proposed locations and ensures that leased space conforms to legal, physical and state standards. The bureau operates the state surplus warehouse where state agencies can relinquish items no longer needed and acquire other used items. By recycling state equipment, furniture and other items, the dollar savings for State Government is considerable. The Federal Surplus Property Program, which makes federal surplus items available to state and local government units as well as not-for-profit qualifying entities, also is administered by the bureau. Public auctions are held of state and federal surplus items. Revenue generated from the auctions and on-site sales of surplus property and vehicles totals about $1.5 million annually and is deposited in the State Surplus Revolving Fund. State real estate no longer needed is declared surplus and, under certain conditions, may be sold at auction after it has been determined that no other state agency can use the property. Revenue from state-owned land leased for farm purposes also is deposited in the fund.

The bureau also maintains state and regional office buildings throughout the state, including the James R. Thompson Center (JRTC) and the State of Illinois building, both in Chicago. Designed by renowned architect Helmut Jahn, the JRTC at 100 W. Randolph opened in 1984 with a design as innovative as the building's multi-use concept. The building occupies a full city block in the heart of the Chicago loop. There are three floors of commercial space and 14 floors of balconied, open offices that house more than 60 state agencies. The JRTC attracts more than 2.5 million visitors annually.

After extensive renovation to the two-story interior skylight and colonnaded second-floor balcony, the State of Illinois building at 160 N. LaSalle St. was reopened in 1992. A fifth-floor exterior sculpture by Illinois artisan Richard Hunt distinguishes the building from others in the city. The building accommodates a courts complex and offices for state agencies.

Bureau of Information Services

The Bureau of Information Services provides essential communication-related services. Specialists in writing, editing, photography, radio and television assist state agencies in furnishing information to the public through the news media. The bureau provides clipping services from newspapers across the state and issues news releases on behalf of state agencies. It also operates an information service for radio stations that features interviews with state newsmakers, and creates radio and television public affairs programs and public service announcements for state agencies and state officials.

The Bureau of Information Services operates a Ku-band satellite uplink system, which enables it to transmit live or taped programs to radio and television stations throughout the United States. It operates a mail and messenger service to Springfield and Chicago State Government offices, which generates millions of dollars of savings for state agencies.

ADMINISTRATIVE PERSONNEL

Michael S. Schwartz .... *Director*
Glenn Good .... *Assistant Director*
Lula Ford .... *Assistant Director*
S. Michael Bartletti .... *Associate Director*
Paul Lopes .... *Associate Director*
Tammy McClure .... *Deputy Director of Human Resources*
Judy Pardonnet .... *Administrator, Office of Public Affairs*
Gary South .... *Manager, Office of Finance and Management*
Frank Cavallaro ...... *Manager, Bureau of Communications & Computer Services*
Kathy Maple .... *Manager, Bureau of Information Services*
Diane Hurrelbrink .... *Manager, Bureau of Personnel*
Carole Fox .... *Manager, Bureau of Property Management*
Robert Kirk .... *Manager, Bureau of Support Services*
John Headrick .... *Director of Governmental Affairs*
Robert Schwarz .... *Chief Internal Auditor*
Steve Seiple .... *Chief Legal Counsel*
Sondra Phillips .... *Director, Business Enterprise Program for Minorities, Females and Persons with Disabilities*

DEPARTMENT OF CHILDREN AND FAMILY SERVICES

Springfield: 406 E. Monroe St.; 62701
(217) 785-2509

Chicago: 100 W. Randolph
6th Floor; 60601
(312) 814-6800

Fiscal Year 2002 Appropriation: $1.4 billion

Jess McDonald
Director

The Illinois Department of Children and Family Services (DCFS) is the agency that protects and cares for children who have been abused or neglected. Established in 1964, DCFS became the first cabinet-level state agency in the nation expressly dedicated to serving children and families. The goals of the department are to provide for the safety, permanency and well-being of children who have been abused or neglected. It strives to achieve these goals by protecting children who are at risk of harm, remedying family problems that place children at risk of being removed from their homes, providing children with a safe, nurturing environment when out-of-home placement is needed and, when appropriate, placing children in suitable adoptive or guardianship homes.

The department and its more than 4,100 employees are organized by divisions and offices. These include the Divisions of Child Protection, Foster Care and Permanency Services, Administrative Case Review, Support Services, Health Policy, Operations, Education and Transition Services, Quality Assurance, Training, Clinical Services and Purchase of Services Monitoring. Offices include African-American Services, Latino Services, Affirmative Action, Legal Services, External Affairs, Communications, Internal Audits, Guardian, Medical Director, Legislative Liaison, Child and Family Policy, Employee Services and the Advocacy Office for Children and Families.

Progress in Caring for Children

DCFS is committed to ensuring that Illinois children are safe, have loving, permanent living arrangements and that their emotional, physical, mental and medical needs are met through quality services. In Fiscal Year 2000, the department became fully accredited by the Council on Accreditation for Children and Family Services. Effective July 1, 2001, all private agencies also must be accredited to receive contracts to provide regular or relative foster care services.

The department has experienced a dramatic improvement in the number of adoptions. In Fiscal Year 1998, 4,293 adoptions were finalized. In Fiscal Year 1999, a record was set by the department when adoptions increased to 7,275 children. In Fiscal Year 2000, the percentage of children moved to adoptive settings increased to an all-time high of 18.4 percent of the foster care population. The dramatic increase in adoptions was recognized by the federal Department of Health and Human Services, which awarded Illinois the Excellence in Adoptions award two consecutive years.

Safety/Protective Services

In 1980, DCFS established a State Central Register in Springfield, which maintains a 24-hour statewide hotline to report suspected abuse or neglect of a child. The number is 1-800-25-ABUSE and TTY 1-800-358-5117. The hotline received 306,818 calls during Fiscal Year 2001. Of those calls, reports of alleged abuse or neglect involving 100,228 children were taken, a decrease of 3.3 percent from the previous year. A call is considered a report if the hotline worker has reasonable cause to suspect that abuse or neglect has occurred, thus warranting investigation. When a worker determines that a legitimate complaint has been made, the department's investigative staff must respond immediately if it is an emergency or within 24 hours for non-emergency reports.

All department and private agency child protection workers, child welfare workers and direct service supervisors must be trained and certified on the Child Endangerment Risk Assessment Protocol (CERAP), developed by a statewide multi-disciplinary team and the American Human Association. As a result of CERAP and other changes, the number of children taken into custody was reduced by 62.4 percent between Fiscal Years 1995 and 2001. That means that children benefit because they are safer. Likewise, the number of instances where maltreatment recurred within 60 days of an indicated report actually decreased by 55.8 percent between 1995 and 2000.

Family Maintenance/Intact Family Services

Child welfare staff work closely with families whose cases may have been confirmed but it is judged that the children can safely remain at home. Staff work with and link families to services to help them safely care for their children, prevent further abuse or neglect and avoid out-of-home placement. Intact services may include homemaker services, parenting skills, emergency cash assistance, counseling, respite day care, links to substance abuse treatment services and other supportive services.

Family Reunification and Substitute Care

Children are placed in substitute care when workers determine it is not safe for them to remain at home. Substitute care can include relative foster homes, regular foster homes or, if the child suffers mental or emotional problems and needs high-intensity treatment services, an institution or group home. At the end of Fiscal Year 2001, there were 26,438 children living in substitute care, a 16 percent decrease from the previous year. When making a placement, the department tries to keep the child in his or her home community and in an arrangement best suited to meet the child's needs.

All children removed from their homes have permanency goals, with the initial goal for most children to be returned home. Staff work with families and link them with services to help correct the problem that led to the child's removal. Services provided are similar to those that intact families receive.

The well-being of children in substitute care is a priority. Caseworkers help children deal with their abuse or neglect and adjust to their new surroundings. Children are linked to needed services and are prepared to return home when appropriate. While in substitute care, the child receives health care services through Healthworks, the department's health care system. Child welfare staff also work closely with schools to ensure the child is receiving an appropriate education. Foster families receive support from the department, including training, counseling services and day care services for the child.

Adoption/Guardianship

When it is not possible to return a child to the natural family, adoption is the preferred alternative. DCFS leads the nation in the number of adoptions completed. In Fiscal Year 1999, 7,275 children were adopted, representing a record year for both the State of Illinois and the nation. In Fiscal Year 2001, 4,176 children were moved to adoptive settings, representing 15.3 percent of the foster care population. Assistance is available to families who are considering adopting department wards with special needs, including monthly assistance payments, medical assistance for the child, and one-time cash payments for legal fees or medical expenses.

To provide a permanency alternative for children without adoption goals, the State of Illinois received a federal waiver to offer subsidized guardianship for children who have been in care for at least two years, at least one year with the same family and for whom reunification or adoption have been ruled out. Under subsidized guardianship, parental rights do not have to be terminated, and the new parents become the legal guardians until the child turns 18, or 19 if the child is still in high school. Medical assistance and subsidies are available for special needs children in guardianship, similar to adoptive children. From Fiscal Year 1997 through Fiscal Year 2001, a total of 6,274 children were moved to subsidized guardianship.

Licensing

In its mission to keep children safe, DCFS is the licensing body for child care agencies and facilities, including foster homes, institutions and group homes, child welfare agencies, adoptive and guardianship homes and day care providers. The department currently licenses 2,750 day care centers, 9,783 day care homes, 241 group day care homes, 19,623 foster homes, 226 agencies and 106 institutions.

ADMINISTRATIVE PERSONNEL

Jess McDonald .... *Director*
Denise Kane .... *Inspector General*
Martha Allen .... *Chief of Staff*
Mary Sue Morsch .... *Executive Deputy Director*
Jim Kaufmann .... *Deputy Chief of Staff, Governmental Affairs*
Debbie McCarrel-Haacke .... *Executive Assistant to the Director*
Jeanie Ortega-Piron .... *Guardian*
Cheryl Cesario .... *General Counsel*
Ed Cotton .... *Deputy Director, Child Protection*
Jane Elmore .... *Deputy Director, Foster Care & Permanency Services*
Renard Jackson .... *Deputy Director, Purchase of Service Monitoring*
Roy Miller .... *Deputy Director, Support Services*
Jerry Slomka .... *Deputy Director, Operations & Community Services*
Jo Anna Sullivan .... *Deputy Director, Health Care Services*
Marcia Williams .... *Deputy Director, Administrative Case Review*
Velma Williams .... *Deputy Director, Clinical Services*
Bernadette McCarthy .... *Deputy Director, Training*
Mike Sumski .... *Associate Director, Quality Assurance*
Luis Barrios .... *Chief, Office of Latino Services*
Al Lambert .... *Chief, Office of Affirmative Action*
Donnella Bishop-Ward .... *Chief, Office of African-American Services*
Susan Hardesty .... *Employee Relations Liaison*
Jon Gaciala .... *Internal Auditor*
Dr. Paula Jaudes .... *Medical Director*
Gloria Fitzgerald .... *Deputy Director, Education & Transition Services*

DEPARTMENT OF COMMERCE AND COMMUNITY AFFAIRS

Springfield: 620 E. Adams; 62701
(217) 782-7500
TDD: 800-785-6055

Chicago: 100 W. Randolph
Ste. 3-400; 60601
(312) 814-7179
TDD: 800-419-0667

Fiscal Year 2002 Appropriation: $2.1 billion

Pam McDonough
Director

The Department of Commerce and Community Affairs (DCCA) enhances Illinois' economic competitiveness by providing technical and financial assistance to businesses, local governments, workers and families. As the state's lead economic development agency, DCCA accentuates Illinois' position as the nation's transportation hub, manufacturing center and fourth-largest technology economy. Whether it's offering expansion incentives, technology support services, access to capital or job training and education, DCCA is committed to forging partnerships with the private sector in an effort to build upon Illinois' reputation as a center for business and industry.

The department also promotes Illinois resources and attractions through aggressive marketing of Illinois products and travel destinations.

Bureau of Business Development

The Bureau of Business Development helps existing Illinois businesses prosper while fostering the development of new businesses in the state.

The Market Development Division is the department's "sales force," providing economic development information to businesses, local governments, locally based organizations and site selection consultants. The division assists companies wishing to expand or locate in Illinois by informing them of the state's resources and providing direct representation through its network of geographically assigned area development coordinators.

The Small Business Office provides assistance to small- and medium-sized Illinois businesses and entrepreneurs. The office administers the statewide network of Small Business Development Centers, which provide consulting on a broad range of topics, including financing, marketing, exporting, government contracting, e-business and technology. The First-Stop Business Information Center of Illinois offers businesses information and assistance to guide them through the business start-up process, the permitting, licensing and regulatory processes, and refers them to other resources.

The Small Business Environmental Assistance Program helps small businesses understand their environmental requirements. The program provides assistance through a toll-free help line and informational workshops and seminars. It also provides easy-to-read fact sheets and guides, conducts research on environmental issues, provides permit assistance for Clean Air Act requirements and publishes a quarterly newsletter.

The Business Finance Division manages DCCA's business loan programs, including the Participation Loan Program, Enterprise Zone Participation Loan Program, the Minority, Women and Disabled Participation Loan Program, the

Capital Access Program, the Surety Bond Guaranty Program and the Development Corporation Technical Assistance Program.

The bureau also administers the Business Development Public Infrastructure Program, the Large Business Development Program, Enterprise Zones, the High Impact Business Program, EDGE and the Affordable Financing of Public Infrastructure Program.

Bureau of Community Development

The Bureau of Community Development works to enhance the quality of life for Illinois citizens by providing a wide range of programs designed to assist local governments with their management and infrastructure needs and create economic opportunity for low-income citizens.

The Office of Local Initiatives supplies communities with strategic planning assistance through the Competitive Communities Initiative and Main Street Program. The Community Assistance Division provides services that help communities meet their economic development, infrastructure and housing needs. The division administers numerous programs, including the Community Development Assistance Program, a federally-funded block grant program that provides assistance to communities with populations of 50,000 or less that are not located within one of the eight urban counties receiving assistance directly from the U.S. Department of Housing and Urban Development. These grants help address infrastructure needs that threaten public health and safety, provide safe, decent housing for low-income citizens, and attract economic development opportunities.

The Economic Opportunity Division administers the Low-Income Home Energy Assistance Program, the Illinois Home Weatherization Assistance Program and the Community Services Block Grant Program. The division works closely with the state's network of Community Action Agencies to help people in need pay their energy bills, make their homes more energy efficient and become more self-sufficient.

The Local Development Division combines education and training with one-on-one technical assistance to help local officials operate efficient and effective governments. Satellite video-conference training helps keep local officials informed about issues faced by local governments, including applying for grants, economic development incentive tools, tax increment financing, marketing a community, local government finance, disaster planning, downtown redevelopment, running an effective board meeting and promoting tourism.

Bureau of Tourism

The Bureau of Tourism markets Illinois as a destination for both domestic and international travelers. The bureau works closely with the state's network of Local Convention and Visitors Bureaus and Regional Tourism Development Offices, funds grant programs to help market Illinois destinations, and administers the state's innovative tourism advertising and promotion efforts.

The Local Tourism Division helps local entities promote business and leisure travel. Financial assistance is provided through the Local Tourism and Convention Bureau Grant Program, the Tourism Marketing Partnership Grant Program, the Tourism Attraction Development Grant and Loan Program and the Tourism Private Sector Grant Program. The division also operates the Heritage Tourism Grant Program, which provides start-up funding to develop tourism and attractions in 11 heritage areas across the state.

The Marketing Division's mission is to leverage the DCCA brand — "*Illinois. Right Here. Right Now.*" — to instill in consumers a sense of excitement about experiencing all that Illinois has to offer. Television, print, radio, news media and targeted public relations are used to deliver the message through a research-based, integrated marketing effort and technology. Services provided to consumers include a toll-free hotline (1-800-2CONNECT) and an interactive Web site at **www.enjoyillinois.com**, which allows visitors to book reservations. The division also operates the state's network of 15 tourist information centers, which provide assistance and hotel reservations for travelers at 13 points of entry along Illinois interstates and two locations in Chicago. Additionally, the division produces several tourism-related publications, including the *Illinois Travel Guide* and *Illinois Now!*, a quarterly publication highlighting seasonal activities and special events in every region of the state. Other publications include the *Aqui Y Ahora* brochure for Spanish-speaking travelers, and the *What's Up in Illinois* publication for African-American travelers.

Bureau of Energy and Recycling

The Bureau of Energy and Recycling provides Illinois citizens and businesses technical advice, financial assistance and research support to develop promising technologies in energy conservation, alternative energy, recycling and waste reduction.

The Energy Conservation and Alternative Energy Division conducts programs to promote energy efficient technologies, such as ethanol production and use. Staff engineers also provide technical assistance to government facilities, helping save millions of dollars through the efficient use of energy resources in state buildings. Financial assistance is provided to Illinois schools and hospitals for energy improvements, allowing less money to be spent on operations and more on services. The division also assists Illinois industries and businesses to become more competitive by reducing the costs of energy services. In addition, the division manages the Renewable Energy Resources Fund, which provides grants for alternative energy projects, such as solar photovoltaics, wind and hydropower.

The Recycling and Waste Reduction Division promotes alternative methods to manage solid waste, reducing reliance on land disposal facilities. Technical, educational and financial assistance through loans and grants is provided to local governments, institutions, businesses and industries. This assistance helps to improve the collection and handling of recycled materials, the development and expansion of industries that produce products from recycled materials, and the efficient recovery and use of used tires.

Bureau of Technology and Industrial Competitiveness

The Bureau of Technology and Industrial Competitiveness emphasizes the importance of technology, workforce development and safety to the state's economic and community development efforts. For nearly 20 years, DCCA has successfully administered various state- and federally-funded technology and training programs. The bureau allows technology, along with job training development and safety programs, to be more fully coordinated and integrated into Illinois' economic development activities.

The Technology Division coordinates programs to increase the awareness of technology to the Illinois economy. The division administers the state's Technology Challenge Grant Program, the Manufacturing Extension Program and the Digital Divide Grant Program. In partnership with the Illinois Coalition, the bureau provides funding for Illinois Technology Enterprise Centers, which provide in-depth assistance to technology-based entrepreneurs and small businesses.

The Training Division coordinates programs to improve the competitiveness of Illinois businesses by developing the skills of their workers, providing access to new technologies and modern business practices, creating a cooperative labor-management environment, and promoting family-friendly workplaces. The division administers the state's Industrial Training Program, the Labor-Management Community Relations Program, the Job Training Economic Development Program and the High Technology School-To-Work Program.

The Occupational Safety and Health Administration (OSHA) Division provides services to small businesses, including on-site hazard audits; health and safety program review and assistance; training and education; and information, safety and health management program development and assistance. Using a free consultation service funded 90 percent by OSHA and 10 percent by the State of Illinois, employers can find out about potential hazards at their work sites, improve their occupational and health management systems and even qualify for a one-year exemption from routine OSHA inspections.

Director's Office

The Director's office is the central administration point that includes the Offices of Audits, Legislative Affairs, Legal, Communications and Information, Marketing and Policy Development, Planning and Research. The office also oversees the Illinois Trade Office, the Illinois Film Office, which promotes film and television production in the state, and the Divisions of Agency Services, Coal Development and Marketing, and Fiscal Management.

ADMINISTRATIVE PERSONNEL

Pam McDonough .... *Director*
Lourdes Ortiz .... *Assistant Director*
Deborah Murphy .... *Chief Operating Officer*
Desi Harris .... *Managing Director, Marketing*
Jeff Mitchell .... *Special Assistant to the Director*
Dennis Pescitelli .... *Deputy Director, Bureau of Business Development*
Dennis Stratton .... *Acting Assistant Deputy Director, Bureau of Community Development*
Mitch Beaver .... *Deputy Director, Bureau of Energy and Recycling*
Lori Clark .... *Deputy Director, Bureau of Technology and Industrial Competitiveness*
Cathy Ritter .... *Deputy Director, Bureau of Tourism*
Ron Ver Kuilen .... *Managing Director, Illinois Film Office*
Joe Hannon .... *Managing Director, Illinois Trade Office*
Mona Martin .... *Managing Director, Policy Development, Planning and Research*
Mike Murphy .... *Chief, Coal Development and Marketing*
Dan Kahle .... *Manager, Division of Audits*
Barb Hoecker .... *Manager, Human Resources*
Brian Reardon .... *Managing Director, Communications and Information*
John Glazier .... *Manager, Legislative Affairs*
Scott Harry .... *Chief Fiscal Officer*
Michael Rosenfeld .... *Chief Legal Counsel*

DEPARTMENT OF CORRECTIONS

Springfield: 1301 Concordia Ct.
P.O. Box 19277; 62794-9277
(217) 522-2666

Chicago: 100 W. Randolph
Ste. 4-200; 60601
(312) 814-2955

Fiscal Year 2002 Appropriation: $1.4 billion

Donald N. Snyder, Jr.
Director

Fiscal Year 2000 marked the 30th anniversary of the Illinois Department of Corrections (DOC). During DOC's creation in 1970, the department combined the administration of all state prisons, juvenile centers and adult and juvenile parole services under one direction for the first time. Creation of the Training Academy followed in 1974, which set the foundation for training the best staff possible for Illinois correctional facilities.

When the department originated, Illinois had only seven adult facilities. Since then, stricter laws have resulted in increased sentencing and longer terms for inmates. Today, the department operates 27 adult and eight juvenile correctional centers as well as various work camps, boot camps and 11 work release centers. Several innovative prison systems also are being built, including two adult facilities — the Lawrence and Thomson Correctional Centers — and a juvenile facility — IYC-Kewanee — which are slated to open in late 2001. The department now is responsible for nearly 80,000 adult inmates, incarcerated juveniles and parolees.

To meet the challenge of the growing inmate population, the department continues to develop new management initiatives. A new focus has been on establishing a military-style organization at the Training Academy in Springfield to achieve a system that is more professional and team-oriented, with increased discipline and accountability.

The department recently reorganized the command structure of the prison system into five geographic districts, which divide the state into smaller, more manageable units. Changes to DOC's internal audit control process also are underway to help ensure that the department achieves its predetermined competency-based objectives. Technology continues to define the way correctional facilities are being run, with surveillance networks and biometric capabilities providing for safer and more efficient operations.

Bureau of Operations

As part of the largest reorganization since the creation of the department, four divisions under the old system merged to become the Bureau of Operations, which oversees adult, juvenile, adult transition centers and parole operations. To effectively monitor operations from reception to discharge, new designation levels offer a step-down program for inmates showing good behavior. The new levels are designed to ensure continuity of services and flexibility to appropriately address the inmate population from reception through parole. Operations such as inmate classification, program delivery, security and controlled movement will be similar at all the same-level facilities. To ensure its effectiveness, every program and service provided to offenders, beginning at reception and classification through discharge from

230

parole, are being thoroughly assessed and evaluated by the Program Services Division.

The department's new parole initiative became operational in July 2000. The goal of the program is to assign responsibility for effective supervision of each parolee to a specific agent. Supervising the state's parolees was shifted from the department to the community.

The Bureau of Operations includes the Office of the Bureau Chief, Program Services, Administrative Services, Investigations and Intelligence, Operations, and Adult and Juvenile Operations.

District #1 (Adult Operations) includes Joliet and Stateville Correctional Centers; Joliet, Jesse "Ma" Houston, West Side, Crossroads and North Lawndale Adult Transition Centers, and parole offices in the area. District #2 (Adult Operations) includes Dixon, East Moline, Hill, Sheridan, Thomson and Illinois River Correctional Centers; Peoria and Winnebago Adult Transition Centers, and parole offices in the area. District #3 (Adult Operations) includes Danville, Jacksonville, Logan, Pontiac and Western Illinois Correctional Centers; Decatur and Urbana Adult Transition Centers, and parole offices in the area. District #4 (Adult Operations) includes Centralia, Graham, Menard, Pinckneyville, Southwestern Illinois, Taylorville and Vandalia Correctional Centers; Southern Illinois Adult Transition Center, and parole offices in the area. District #5 (Adult Operations) includes Big Muddy River, Lawrence, Robinson, Tamms, Vienna and Shawnee Correctional Centers, and parole offices in the area.

The Juvenile Division includes Illinois Youth Centers in Harrisburg, St. Charles, Chicago, Murphysboro, Joliet; Pere Marquette and Valley View. Another is expected to open Kewanee in late 2001, and a center in Rushville is planned for construction.

The divisions of Program Services and Women and Family Services were created to better focus on program needs and the needs of female inmates. Program Services includes the Placement Resource Unit, School District #4278, Victim Services, Medical Services, Food Services and Mental Health Service.

Women and Family Services includes female adult facilities in Decatur, Dwight and Lincoln. A fourth female adult facility, Hopkins Park, is planned for construction. The division also includes a female juvenile facility, IYC-Warrenville, two adult transition centers, Metro and Fox Valley, and Correctional Industries.

Administrative Services includes the Office of Technology, Planning & Research, Agency Record Office, Chaplaincy Services, Volunteer Programs, Grants, Management Information Systems, Capital Programs, Transfer Coordinator and Telecommunications. Investigations and Intelligence includes sections for the central, northern and southern regions.

Investigations Internal Affairs and Intelligence

The department has established the Investigations Internal Affairs Unit (IAU) and the Central Intelligence Unit (CIU). Internal Affairs serves as a watchdog for the integrity of the department and acts as the central repository for policy complaints that cannot be handled at the institutional level and for criminal complaints. The unit participated in Operation Recovery, which was the most extensive cooperative venture involving the apprehension of felons ever undertaken by the department. The operation resulted in more than 40 felons being apprehended in a five-day period.

Since the formation of the IAU and CIU, the number of gang-related incidents within the department has dramatically declined. Gang-related assaults on both staff and inmates have become nearly nonexistent.

Corrections Employee Memorial

Efforts continue toward building a Corrections Employee Memorial Wall. The non-profit Illinois Correctional Employees Memorial Association was formed to recognize and memorialize correctional employees killed or permanently disabled in the line of duty; construct a permanent monument to record the names of fallen employees; and provide scholarships, grants and other assistance to family members of employees killed or permanently disabled in the line of duty. Groundbreaking for the memorial wall was held at Corrections' Springfield headquarters in May 2001, and dedicated in September 2001.

Office of the Director

The Office of the Director includes the Chief of Staff, Labor Relations, Inmate Issues, Payroll/Timekeeping and Claims, Personnel and Employee Services. The Policy and Recruitment Division includes the Policy and Directives Unit and the Affirmative Action Officer. The Staff Development and Training Division includes Graphic Design and Reproduction Center, Concordia Maintenance, Commander of Operations, Curriculum Design/Instructor Development and Regional Training. The Office of the Special Assistant to the Director includes the Extradition and Jail and Detention Standards Units, and the Division of Finance and Budget includes Fiscal Services and Budget Services. Other offices include Women and Family Services, Intergovernmental Relations, Legal Counsel, Performance Based Standards, Communications and Internal Auditor.

ADMINISTRATIVE PERSONNEL

Donald N. Snyder, Jr. .... *Director*
Andrew Walter .... *Chief of Staff*
George DeTella .... *Associate Director*
Nancy Miller .... *Bureau Chief*
Dwayne Clark .... *Chief, Operations*
Linda Dillon .... *Chief, Program Services*
G.A. Pecoraro .... *Chief, Administrative Services*
Mary Hodge .... *Chief, Investigations & Intelligence*
Sergio Molina .... *Chief, Communications*
Matt Overaker .... *Chief, Intergovernmental Relations*
Don Zoufal .... *Chief Legal Counsel*
Mark Krell .... *Chief Internal Auditor*
Rod Tally .... *Chief, Labor Relations*
Missy Stutler .... *Deputy Director, Women & Family Services Division*
Rodney Ahitow .... *Deputy Director, Juvenile Division*
Tony Small .... *Deputy Director, Finance & Budget Division*
Ralph Grayson .... *Deputy Director, Policy and Recruitment Division*
Lamark Carter .... *Deputy Director, Adult Division 1*
Michael O'Leary .... *Deputy Director, Adult Division 2*
Thomas Page .... *Deputy Director, Adult Division 3*
Michael Baker .... *Deputy Director, Adult Division 4*
Richard McVicar .... *Deputy Director, Adult Division 5*
Carl Flagg .... *Special Assistant to the Director*
Tony Scillia .... *Director, Staff Development & Training*

DEPARTMENT OF EMPLOYMENT SECURITY

Springfield: 400 W. Monroe St.; 62704
(217) 785-5069

Chicago: 401 S. State St.; 60605
(312) 793-5700

Fiscal Year 2002 Appropriation: $592.1 million

Gertrude W. Jordan
Director

The Illinois Department of Employment Security administers the state's unemployment insurance, employment service, job training and labor market information programs. With 2,106 employees, the department serves the public through the Illinois Employment and Training Center Network at 56 locations throughout the state.

The department collects unemployment contributions (taxes) from nearly 300,000 employers in the state, which are used solely for the payment of benefits to unemployed workers. In 2000, more than 636,000 initial claims for unemployment insurance were filed, with more than $1.1 billion in benefits being paid to eligible Illinois workers.

The Illinois Employment Service program matches job seekers with the hiring needs of the state's employers using its new Web site — Illinois Skills Match — at www.illinoisskillsmatch.com. In its first year of operation, more than 358,000 new job seekers logged on to the site, and 15,000 employers registered as users.

In Fiscal Year 2001, the department assumed responsibility of administering state job training programs funded through the federal Workforce Investment Act. Among those eligible for federally funded job training assistance are workers who have lost their jobs due to business closings or mass layoffs, economically disadvantaged adults, and youth ages 14 to 21 who have significant barriers to employment. Training services are provided under the direction of local workforce boards and designed to reflect local needs and opportunities.

The department disseminates a vast array of labor market information, including monthly reports on employment, unemployment rates and employer payroll surveys for the State of Illinois, individual counties and municipalities with populations of more than 25,000. Most information is available online at www.IlWorkInfo.com, or in print by request. In 2000, the annual average unemployment rate for Illinois was 4.4 percent. Special programs also serve Illinois veterans, women, dislocated workers, the underemployed, the economically disadvantaged and ex-offenders.

ADMINISTRATIVE PERSONNEL

Gertrude W. Jordan . . . . *Director*
Wess Butler . . . . *Inspector General*
Dennis Devlin . . . . *Deputy Director, Information Services*
John Gingrich . . . . *Budget Officer*
Shari Kertez . . . . *Public Information Officer*
Joseph Mueller . . . . *General Counsel*
Jim Nelson . . . . *State Legislative Liaison*
Roderick Nunn . . . . *Executive Deputy Director, Workforce Development*
Miles Paris . . . . *Deputy Director, Operations Support*
Robert Plowright . . . . *Special Assistant to the Director*
John Waters . . . . *Deputy Director, Finance & Administration*

233

DEPARTMENT OF FINANCIAL INSTITUTIONS

Springfield: 500 Iles Park Place
Ste. 501; 62718
(217) 782-2832

Chicago: 100 W. Randolph St.
Ste. 15-700; 60601
(312) 814-2000

Fiscal Year 2002 Appropriation: $10.2 million

The Illinois Department of Financial Institutions regulates various state-licensed financial institutions to ensure their safety and soundness, and works to protect consumers in their interactions with these entities. The department licenses, examines and regulates all state-chartered credit unions, currency exchanges, consumer installment lenders, sales finance companies, title insurance companies, money transmitters, foreign exchange offices and debt management companies. The department also administers and enforces 11 statutes in the Illinois Financial Institutions Code and its attending rules and regulations. The department licensed and regulated 3,302 financial institutions in Fiscal Year 2000.

Sarah D. Vega
Director

Credit Unions

The Credit Union Division oversees the chartering and regulation of all state-chartered credit unions. During Fiscal Year 2000, the division supervised 462 credit unions with total assets of $11.8 billion. These credit unions provided financial services to about 2.4 million Illinois residents.

As authorized by the Financial Institutions Code, the department administers the Illinois Credit Union Act, which sets forth the department's authority regarding chartering, examination responsibilities, fees, fines, cease and desist powers, suspension authority, mergers and liquidations. The Act also outlines the general authority given to state-chartered credit unions in the areas of lending, investment of funds, share accounts, interest rates, membership expansion, compensation of directors and general operations.

The division conducts statutorily-required annual examinations of all state-chartered credit unions to ensure compliance with the Act, its rules and regulations, and to assure Illinois residents a safe and sound credit union industry.

Consumer Credit

More than 1,800 businesses providing a diverse array of financial services are licensed and regulated under nine separate statutes administered by the Consumer Credit Division. All licensed institutions are regulated and examined according to the provisions of their respective statutes to ensure full compliance with Illinois laws and regulations. The division also investigates consumer complaints and works to resolve disputes between consumers and consumer credit companies.

The division enforces the following Illinois statutes: *Consumer Installment Loan Act*, which regulates businesses making direct installment loans to consumers in amounts not exceeding $25,000, and as otherwise prescribed by the Act, including payday and auto title lenders; *Sales Finance Agency Act*, which regulates entities that purchase or make loans secured by retail installment contracts, retail charge agreements, or the outstanding balances under such contracts or agreements; *Title Insurance Act*, which certifies and regulates companies that guarantee or insure titles for real estate and companies that are independent escrow agencies; *Transmitters of Money Act*, which regulates businesses that sell or issue payment instruments, transmit money and exchange foreign currency; *Debt Management Services Act*, which regulates businesses that prepare financial plans for the restructuring of consumer debt and provide assistance with debt management; *Safe Deposit Boxes, Safes and Vaults Act*, which regulates companies that provide and maintain safekeeping devices, including safe deposit boxes, safes and vaults; *Development Credit Corporation Act*, which regulates businesses that make loans to small- and medium-size companies unable to obtain financing from other sources; *Retail Installment Sales Act*, which regulates the retail installment sales of goods used primarily for personal, family or household purposes; and the *Motor Vehicle Retail Installment Sales Act*, which regulates retail installment sales of motor vehicles.

Currency Exchanges

There are more than 1,000 licensed currency exchanges in Illinois. During Fiscal Year 2000, the department's Currency Exchange Division licensed and regulated 674 community currency exchanges and 334 ambulatory currency exchanges in accordance with the provisions of the Currency Exchange Act. Compliance with the Act is determined through an examination and inspection process that emphasizes public protection and the financial soundness of currency exchanges. The division also investigates consumer complaints and works with consumers and currency exchanges to resolve disputes. In the interest of consumer protection, the department sets maximum rates that can be charged for cashing checks and selling money orders.

Currency exchanges offer a variety of services, including money orders, processing motor vehicle and title registration forms, license plate and sticker sales, payment of utility bills, Illinois LINK and Social Security disbursements, public transportation passes and credit card cash advance services. Other products and services include out-of-state money transfers, foreign currency exchange, income tax services, Secure Check, prepaid phone cards, mail box service, bail bond cards, notary public services, copies of birth, death and marriage certificates, and fax and photocopy services.

ADMINISTRATIVE PERSONNEL

Sarah D. Vega .... *Director*
Edgar I. Lopez .... *Assistant Director*
Lois Olson .... *Assistant to the Director*
Elizabeth Byrne .... *Chief Legal Counsel*
Tony Goldstein .... *Acting Chief Fiscal Officer*
George Preski .... *Chief Internal Auditor*
Mary Kendrigan .... *Chief of Communications*
Craig Cellini .... *Legislative Liaison*
Sarah Troehler .... *Program & Policy Advisor*
Deanna Bandy .... *Human Resources Administrator*
Ronald Miller .... *Manager, Information Systems*
Patrick Smith .... *Acting Supervisor, Credit Union Division*
Carl LaSusa .... *Supervisor, Consumer Credit Division*
Michael Goldman .... *Supervisor, Currency Exchange Division*

DEPARTMENT OF HUMAN RIGHTS

Springfield: 1st Floor, 101-A
222 S. College; 62704
(217) 785-5100
TDD: (217) 785-5125

Chicago: 100 W. Randolph
Ste. 10-100; 60601
(312) 814-6200
TDD: (312) 263-1579

Carlos J. Salazar
Director

Fiscal Year 2002 Appropriation: $9.8 million

The Department of Human Rights works toward promoting civil rights and abolishing discrimination in Illinois. In conformance with the Illinois Human Rights Act of 1980, the department protects and ensures individual rights in regard to employment, financial credit, public accommodations, real estate transactions and other areas of human interest.

Assuming its role as a regulatory agency, it may issue, settle and dismiss charges of unlawful discrimination — whether the charge is a violation against a race, minority, woman or person with a disability. The Charge Processing Division, the largest of the department's divisions, receives, investigates and resolves discrimination charges in employment, housing, financial credit, places of public accommodation and sexual harassment in higher education. All charges of discrimination must be supported with sufficient evidence.

More than 3,600 investigations were completed in Fiscal Year 2000. The department's legal staff negotiates all conciliations, reviews all investigation reports, and responds to all legal inquiries, including requests for reviews.

Both state institutions and public contractors are held accountable to the legalities, rules and regulations enforced by the Department of Human Rights. The Compliance Division monitors state agencies, boards, commissions, colleges, universities and public contractors to ensure equitable employment practices and compliance with their legal obligations. These institutions must abide by state affirmative action and equal employment opportunity laws.

ADMINISTRATIVE PERSONNEL

Carlos J. Salazar . . . . *Director*
Helen Jett . . . . *Deputy Director*
Jacqueline Lustig . . . .*Chief Legal Counsel*
Jeffry Drager . . . . *Manager, Charge Processing Division*
Ben Bonales . . . . *Manager, Compliance Division*
Maria Ulmer . . . . *Fiscal Officer*
Bobby Wanzo . . . . *Office Manager*
David Espinoza . . . . *Public Information Officer*
Yoon Lee, Ph.D. . . . . *Manager of Research, Planning and Development*

DEPARTMENT OF HUMAN SERVICES

Springfield: Harris Building
100 S. Grand Ave.
3rd Floor; 62762
(217) 557-1601

Chicago: 401 S. Clinton St.
7th Floor; 60607
(312) 793-1547

Fiscal Year 2002 Appropriation: $5 billion

Linda Reneé Baker
Secretary

The Department of Human Services (DHS) consolidates most of the state's human services under one umbrella, making it the largest agency in State Government with more than 20,000 employees. The department's program diversity allows clients to be connected to a wide range of human services through a single agency. DHS strives to help Illinois residents achieve self-sufficiency, independence and health to the maximum extent possible by providing integrated, family-oriented services and promoting prevention in partnership with communities through its various divisions and offices.

Mental Health and Developmental Disabilities

This division provides for the treatment, care and habilitation of persons with mental disabilities and operates developmental centers and psychiatric hospitals across Illinois. DHS funds and oversees a statewide network of community-based services and programs for persons with mental and developmental disabilities through the Offices of Developmental Disabilities, Mental Health and Clinical, Administrative and Program Support.

Community Health and Prevention

This division includes the Office of Family Health and Prevention, which coordinates the Special Supplemental Nutrition Program for Women, Infants and Children, along with other core maternal and child health programs. The office also provides comprehensive prevention services for youth, including substance abuse prevention and Teen REACH, a program of structured activities during non-school hours. The office manages juvenile delinquency prevention, diversion and intervention programs targeting youth, and domestic violence programs that meet the needs of victims and their families.

Transitional Services

The Division of Transitional Services includes the Offices of Employment and Training, Child Care and Family Services, and Financial Support Services. Some of the services provided include child care subsidies to low-income families covering 212,000 children, and helping clients make the transition from welfare to work. New skills training in a client's community also is available. The division manages transportation assistance, employment training and other support services to help clients achieve self-sufficiency. It also develops policies regarding eligibility requirements and program provisions for Temporary Assistance for Needy Families (TANF); Aid to the Aged, Blind or Disabled;

food stamps and general assistance. The Electronic Benefits Transaction system, which enables clients to access their cash and food stamp benefits, also is managed by the division.

Community Operations

This division operates through 131 DHS offices throughout Illinois, one Food Stamp Employment and Training office and five regional offices. The division is responsible for the direct delivery of a wide range of services, including Temporary Assistance for Needy Families (TANF), food stamps, Aid to the Aged, Blind or Disabled, Medicaid and KidCare. It also makes direct referrals for other services in the areas of mental health, domestic violence, substance abuse, employment and training, maternal and child health and child support. Community Operations Intake and Service Coordination personnel in each local office use a family-centered approach to identify the needs of families and individuals and determine their eligibility for benefits and other community services. Staff also help teen parents stay in school and develop good parenting skills, assist clients in establishing legal paternity for their children and connect clients with child support enforcement services.

Administering the TANF program, which replaced the state's Aid to Families with Dependent Children program in 1997, has been a principal focus of the division. TANF was developed to comply with changes in federal welfare laws designed to help people get off welfare by encouraging employment, family stability and personal responsibility. TANF requires that most clients work or participate in work-related activities and limits the length of time clients can receive benefits.

Office of Alcoholism and Substance Abuse

DHS is the lead agency for the licensing and oversight of all substance abuse treatment centers and services in Illinois. The Office of Alcoholism and Substance Abuse administers a statewide network of community-based programs, which provide intervention, treatment and aftercare to at-risk or ad-

Linda Reneé Baker, Secretary of the Department of Human Services, holds a child enrolled in the DHS-funded Rogy's Educational Center in Peoria.

238

dicted individuals and their families. The office coordinates the efforts of state programs and maximizes the effectiveness of new and existing resources. It also is responsible for education, prevention and treatment programs for pathological or compulsive gamblers.

Office of Rehabilitation Services

DHS is the state's lead agency for providing services to persons with disabilities. The mission of its Office of Rehabilitation Services is to assist persons with disabilities and their families in making informed choices in an effort to achieve full community participation through suitable employment, education and independent living opportunities. The office administers several disability-related programs that affect more than 230,000 persons with disabilities in Illinois. Programs include the federal Vocational Rehabilitation program, the state-funded Home Services program, the federally funded Disability Determination Services and three state-funded residential schools for children and youth with disabilities.

ADMINISTRATIVE PERSONNEL

Linda Reneé Baker . . . . *Secretary*
Daniel J. Miller . . . . *Assistant Secretary*
Carolyn Cochran Kopel . . . . *Associate Secretary*
Doris Davidson . . . . *Special Assistant to the Secretary*
William Holland . . . . *Special Assistant to the Secretary, Special Projects*
Reginald Marsh . . . . *Press/Communications Secretary*
Thomas R. McMahon . . . . *General Counsel*
Odell Thompson, Jr. . . . . *Inspector General*
Jim Donkin . . . . *Chief Internal Auditor*
Matt Magalis . . . . *Chief Liaison*
Audrey McCrimon . . . . *Assistant for Compliance Access & Workplace Safety*
Jose J. Lopez . . . . *Assistant for Hispanic/Latino Affairs*
Daniel G. Harris . . *Administrator, Strategic Planning & Performance Management*
Jim Nelson . . . . *Director, Community Health & Prevention*
Stephen Saunders, M.D. . . . . *Associate Director, Family Health*
Connie Brooks . . . . *Associate Director, Prevention*
Karan Maxson . . . . *Director, Transitional Services*
Randy Valenti . . . . *Associate Director, Child Care & Family Services*
Mary Ann Langston . . . . *Associate Director, Financial Support Services*
Amina Everett . . . . *Director, Community Operations*
Jim Berger . . . . *Deputy Director, Community Operations*
Richard Matassa, M.D. . . . . *Administrator, Mental Health & Developmental Disabilities Services*
Leigh Steiner . . . . *Associate Director, Mental Health*
Melissa Wright . . . . *Associate Director, Developmental Disabilities*
John Budny . . . . *Manager, Clinical Administrative & Program Support*
Melanie R. Whitter . . . . *Associate Director, Alcoholism & Substance Abuse*
Carl Suter . . . . *Associate Director, Rehabilitation Services*
Kevin Steelman . . . . *Manager, Budget*
Joe Schlouski . . . . *Manager, Business Services*
David Hanbury . . . . *Manager, Contract Administration*
Gary Anderson . . . . *Manager, Fiscal Services*
Glen Freeberg . . . . *Manager, Human Resources*
Gene Hagerman . . . . *Chief, Management Information Services*

ILLINOIS EMERGENCY MANAGEMENT AGENCY

Springfield: 110 E. Adams; 62701-1109
(217) 782-7860

Fiscal Year 2002 Appropriation: $170.6 million

Mike Chamness
Director

The Illinois Emergency Management Agency (IEMA) is responsible for the coordination, management and administration of the state's emergency management programs. IEMA functions as the State Emergency Response Commission and maintains a 24-hour Communications Center, the Emergency Operations Center and eight regional offices. The agency assists local governments with multi-hazard emergency operations plans and maintains the Illinois Emergency Operations Plan. Seventy-four employees form the administrative staff and five divisions.

Operations

The Division of Operations is comprised of five programs. Emergency Operations is responsible for coordinating the state's response to disasters and other emergencies. The Communications Maintenance and Development program manages IEMA's statewide communications system. The Exercise program coordinates disaster exercises, and the Training program provides emergency response training for first responders. Support Services handles agency-wide printing, warehousing and emergency response vehicles.

Disaster Assistance and Preparedness

The Division of Disaster Assistance and Preparedness develops, maintains and validates emergency operations plans. These plans are implemented by state and local governments when responding to and recovering from disasters. In times of disaster, the division administers disaster assistance programs to local governments, individuals and families. It also coordinates an ongoing hazard mitigation program to reduce the impact of future disasters.

Chemical Emergency Preparedness and Prevention

In its capacity as the State Emergency Response Commission, IEMA's Division of Chemical Emergency Preparedness and Prevention oversees and assists 105 Local Emergency Planning Committees. The committees are responsible for local planning for hazardous chemical emergencies, scheduling exercises of the chemical emergency plan, assessing local emergency response capabilities, and maintaining an inventory of hazardous chemicals in their areas. The division also is the repository for chemical inventory forms filed annually by about 8,000 Illinois businesses.

Regional Offices

The Division of Regional Offices facilitates the efforts of local emergency management agencies, response agencies and voluntary organizations to save lives and protect property. Eight regional coordinators interface between local and county governments and the State of Illinois' emergency management

An aerial view of Campbell's Island shows the magnitude of the spring 2001 flooding along the upper Mississippi River. The flooding resulted in 10 Illinois counties being declared presidential disaster areas.

program. During non-disaster times, the regional coordinators provide technical and conceptual assistance to local governments in program development, planning, training and exercising programs. During times of disaster, the coordinators become the affected jurisdiction's principal on-site point of contact for state assistance.

Finance

The Division of Finance administers the agency's annual appropriation, maintains accounting records and administers disaster assistance and federal funding. The division also participates in the Business Enterprise Program. Federal funds represent about 90 percent of IEMA's budget.

Central United States Earthquake Consortium

The director represents the Governor on the Board of the Central United States Earthquake Consortium, a non-profit, seven-state organization that provides multi-state planning for a major earthquake in the New Madrid Seismic Zone.

ADMINISTRATIVE PERSONNEL

Mike Chamness . . . . *Director*
Cristy Donaldson . . . . *Assistant to the Director*
Julie Gentile . . . . . *Chief Counsel/Chemical Emergency Preparedness & Prevention*
Dave Smith . . . . *Disaster Assistance & Preparedness*
Dennis Miner . . . . *Finance Division*
James H. Watts, Jr. . . . . *Operations*
Leanne Jacobs . . . . *Personnel Officer*
Tom Zimmerman . . . . *Policy Advisor*
Christine Tamminga . . . . *Regional Offices/Public Information Officer*

ILLINOIS ENVIRONMENTAL PROTECTION AGENCY

Springfield: 1024 N. Grand Ave. East; 62702
(217) 782-3397

Fiscal Year 2002 Appropriation: $1.2 billion

Renee Cipriano
Director

The Illinois Environmental Protection Agency (IEPA) fosters a cleaner and healthier environment through responsibilities granted under the state Environmental Protection Act and other state and federal laws and regulations.

With technical expertise of engineers, biologists, attorneys and other professionals, the agency is charged with enforcing anti-pollution rules and regulations and proactively promotes good environmental stewardship by both business and individuals.

IEPA monitors and issues permits for environmental quality on air, land and water and supervises the quality of public water supplies. The agency also responds to environmental emergencies and investigates and makes referrals to the Illinois Attorney General for enforcement action against those who violate the law.

The agency increasingly has been delegated primary responsibility for carrying out federal environmental laws in Illinois. IEPA encourages companies to go beyond complying with regulations and change their processes to reduce sources of pollution. The agency has formed partnerships with companies and citizen groups to voluntarily improve the environment and encourage new, cost-effective technology. IEPA is a national leader in using innovative marketing mechanisms to reduce air pollution and address the causes of smog.

IEPA has reached out to small businesses and to specific industry sectors, such as its co-sponsorship of the Great Printers program. The agency is recognized for its innovative "brownfields" voluntary cleanup program to restore abandoned, contaminated industrial and commercial sites to productive use. IEPA strives to streamline regulations and educate the public about good environmental practices. In cooperation with local agencies, it sponsors household hazardous waste collections throughout the state and used tire collection programs. The agency also encourages safe disposal of paint through a partnership with a network of paint retailers.

Among the agency's specific operational activities are: issuing permits for air, water and land to restrict emissions into the environment from industrial and commercial sources; regulating pollution control facilities and solid waste disposal sites; testing the quality of water processing procedures for operators of sewage treatment plants and public water supplies, and training operators of wastewater treatment plants. IEPA also administers grants and loans to local governments for wastewater and water facilities and certifies requests by industries for tax incentives for pollution control facilities.

The agency operates a comprehensive groundwater protection and lake monitoring program and administers a program to reimburse the owners of leaking underground storage tanks for the cost of cleaning up contamination.

As part of the state's program to meet anti-smog requirements under the federal Clean Air Act, IEPA operates a vehicle emissions testing program in

The Illinois Environmental Protection Agency sponsors several household hazardous waste collection days throughout the year at various sites in the state.

the Chicago and East St. Louis metropolitan areas. It also collects extensive data on air, land and water quality. Agency laboratories analyze more than 1 million samples each year, and the agency operates a network of more than 300 air quality monitors.

Illinois EPA is expanding efforts to make environmental information readily accessible to the public through the Internet and other resources.

ADMINISTRATIVE PERSONNEL

Renee Cipriano .... *Director*
Bernard P. Killian .... *Deputy Director*
William D. Seith .... *Deputy Director*
David Kolaz .... *Chief, Bureau of Air*
Bill Child .... *Chief, Bureau of Land*
Marcia Willhite .... *Chief, Bureau of Water*
Roger Selburg .... *Manager, Division of Public Water Supplies*
Mark Hurley .... *Legislative Liaison*
Dennis McMurray .... *Manager, Office of Public Information*
Kurt Neibergall .... *Manager, Community Relations*
Lisa Bonnett .... *Budget Officer*

ILLINOIS HISTORIC PRESERVATION AGENCY

Springfield: Old State Capitol; 62701
(217) 782-4836

Chicago: 100 W. Randolph
Ste. 4-900; 60601
(312) 814-1500

Fiscal Year 2002 Appropriation: $23.8 million

The Illinois Historic Preservation Agency collects, preserves and interprets the history of the State of Illinois. The agency is governed by a board of trustees, which establishes policy and appoints a director responsible for the agency's day-to-day activities. Members of the board are Julie Cellini, *chair*; Pamela Daniels, Carol Stein, Samuel Lilly and Ed Genson.

Susan Mogerman
Director

The Illinois State Historical Library was created by the General Assembly in 1889 to collect and publish information relating to the history of the state. Today, the Historical Library is a modern research facility holding more than 173,000 bound volumes, 82,900 microfilm reels, 4,700 broadsides, 3,000 maps, 350,000 photographs and 10.2 million manuscripts. The Historical Library's collection on the life of Abraham Lincoln is the most extensive in the country.

The Historical Library is the official repository for Illinois newspapers on microfilm. The microfilm reels are available through interlibrary loan. The collection includes rare, original copies of Illinois newspapers, among which is an issue of the first paper printed in the Illinois Territory, the *Illinois Herald* of Kaskaskia in 1814. The Historical Library is the headquarters institution in Illinois for the nationwide newspaper cataloging project funded by the National Endowment for the Humanities.

The Preservation Services Division oversees the Federal Historic Preservation Program in Illinois and identifies, protects and promotes historically important sites throughout the state. The division also reviews plans, examines specifications and inspects historic buildings undergoing rehabilitation under provisions of the Economic Recovery Tax Act, and authorizes projects applying for tax incentives available to owners of historic income-producing buildings. The Illinois Historic Sites Advisory Council reviews nominations and recommends structures in the state to include in the National Register of Historic Places.

The Public Affairs and Development Division manages the public outreach programs of the agency. The division, in coordination with the other programmatic divisions, publishes the *Journal of Illinois History*, a scholarly quarterly; *Illinois History*, a magazine written by students; *Illinois History Teacher*, a how-to magazine for junior and senior high school teachers; and *Historic Illinois*, a bimonthly newsletter designed to keep preservationists up-to-date on issues relevant to their field. The division also is responsible for agency special events and management of the Chicago office.

The Illinois Educational Services Program also is managed through the division. Each year, nearly 10,000 Illinois students and teachers participate in local, regional and state history fairs sponsored by the agency in cooperation with the Chicago Metro History Education Center. State winners go on to compete at the national level.

The David Davis Mansion State Historic Site in Bloomington was built in the 1870s for U.S. Supreme Court Justice David Davis and his wife, Sarah.

The Historic Sites Division administers all 59 of the state-owned historic sites and memorials, which are visited by about 3 million tourists annually. The time period interpreted at the historic sites ranges from A.D. 700 when the Indians settled Cahokia Mounds, to 1904, the year Frank Lloyd Wright completed what is now the Dana-Thomas House in Springfield.

The life of Abraham Lincoln is an important component of interpretation at a majority of the sites. Lincoln's New Salem, the Lincoln Tomb, the Old State Capitol and the Lincoln-Herndon Law Offices are all Springfield area sites important to Abraham Lincoln's rise to the Presidency.

ADMINISTRATIVE PERSONNEL

Susan Mogerman . . . . *Director*
Robert Coomer . . . . *Division Manager, Historic Sites*
Maynard Crossland . . . . *Division Manager, Public Affairs and Development*
Kathryn Harris . . . . *Division Manager, Illinois State Historical Library*
Robert Weichert . . . . *Division Manager, Administrative Services*
William Wheeler . . . . *Associate Director, Division Manager, Preservation Services*

ILLINOIS STATE POLICE

Springfield: 103 Armory Building
P.O. Box 19461; 62794-9461
(217) 782-7263

Fiscal Year 2002 Appropriation: $385.8 million

The Illinois State Police is a multifaceted police agency, enforcing the laws, protecting the public and providing an array of specialty services to local, state and federal agencies. The primary goal of the State Police is to ensure highway safety through enforcement, investigation, service to the public, education, patrol and technical assistance.

Sam W. Nolen
Director

Operations

The Division of Operations incorporates highway safety and criminal investigation. About 1,900 uniformed and plainclothes officers in 21 districts provide comprehensive law enforcement services. Troopers patrol the highways enforcing speed limits and traffic laws, conducting truck weight inspections and overseeing hazardous materials control. A motorcycle patrol provides rapid response to emergencies on congested urban highways. Safety education officers conduct traffic and personal safety programs for youth and community groups statewide. Specially trained canine (K-9) units and tactical response teams aid in a wide range of emergencies or investigations, such as narcotics trafficking, searches for missing persons and hostage situations. The State Police operate their own aircraft to search for missing persons, provide local agencies with prisoner extradition flights, recover fugitives, locate illicitly grown marijuana and help enforce traffic laws.

Special agents use state-of-the-art equipment and technology to investigate such crimes as homicide, sexual assault and fraud. In cooperation with federal and local police agencies, the State Police has helped crack international narcotics rings, solve mass murders and apprehend international terrorists.

Administration

The Division of Administration supports department operations through the Communications Services, Logistics and Personnel bureaus. The Communications Services Bureau is responsible for the design, operation and management of the department's voice/radio communications systems, which include 800 MHz technology and the migration to seamless statewide coverage through the STARCOM 21 project.

The Logistics Bureau oversees land acquisition, new facility construction and leasing contracts, as well as the repair and maintenance of State Police-owned facilities and coordination of departmental logistical efforts. Acquisition and management of the State Police fleet, as well as the purchase, distribution and storage of supplies and uniforms, are overseen by the bureau. Logistics staff operate a print shop for printed materials and coordinate internal distribution and delivery of mail and supplies.

The Personnel Bureau handles all employee transactions, including new hires, job description approval, transfers, promotions, departures, award designations and presentations, and employee insurance and workers compensation issues. Employee performance evaluations are managed by the bureau through the Integrated Strategic Performance program. The bureau also oversees department policies.

Forensic Services

Crime scene investigators and nine forensic science laboratories statewide provide an array of services for federal, state and local law enforcement. In addition to collecting, interpreting and packaging evidence, investigators can produce computer-generated and freehand facial composite drawings. Using a full-service photographic laboratory as well as digital imaging and illustration equipment, they can produce animated crime scene recreations, computer-assisted sketches of crime scenes and crash reconstruction diagrams.

The forensic science laboratory system in Illinois has been accredited by the American Society of Crime Laboratory Directors/Laboratory Accreditation Board for more than 19 years. Forensic scientists study evidence, including drugs, chemistry, trace chemistry, toxicology, microscopy, biology, latent prints, firearms and toolmarks, documents, footwear, tire tracks and polygraph. The Combined Offender DNA Index System compares DNA profiles from evidence with profiles from convicted offenders or other forensic cases, detecting possible suspects or associated serial crimes. The Integrated Bullet Identification System and Drugfire databases can link cartridge cases and bullets from different crime scenes as well as a bullet or cartridge to a particular weapon. These systems assist law enforcement agencies in solving crimes and preventing additional crimes from occurring in Illinois, across the country and throughout the world through links to similar databases in other states and countries.

Internal Investigation

The Division of Internal Investigation has two principal roles. First, it investigates charges of improper conduct or illegal behavior by Illinois State Police employees. Second, the division acts as the "watchdog for integrity in State Government" by conducting criminal investigations of alleged misconduct or wrongdoing by any state official or state agency employee.

Human Resource Command

The Human Resource Command is comprised of the Illinois State Police Academy and the Diversity Resource Bureau. The primary responsibility of the Command is to ensure a quality, proactive career development process for all State Police employees. The Command models leadership, innovation and effective problem solving with an overall goal to improve the quality of life for employees as they enhance public safety.

The State Police Academy provides training and education to members of the police community through basic and in-service training as well as leadership and management education. Basic training offerings include the 26-week Illinois State Police Cadet Program, in which students learn the laws, ordinance techniques and skills necessary to perform the duties of a state trooper. In-service training includes legal updates, new officer survival techniques, emergency vehicle operation, drug resistance education and issues related to domestic violence. The Academy also provides a 10-week recruit program that trains officers for local police agencies. Employees can advance their critical and creative thinking skills through management and leadership education.

The Diversity Resource Bureau works to maintain a workforce that is physically, mentally, emotionally and spiritually fit. The Employee Assistance Program, Medical Response Program, Critical Incident Stress Management and Peer Support are among services provided by the bureau. The Recruitment Unit develops and implements the department's strategy to recruit high-caliber applicants for Illinois State Police law enforcement positions.

Information and Technology Command

The Information and Technology Command is comprised of five bureaus responsible for information technology, data collection and analysis, and information sharing for the State Police. The Information Services Bureau supports the department's mainframe computer systems and a myriad of programs that orchestrate the compilation, analysis and dissemination of computerized criminal history record information. These systems promote information sharing among local, state and federal public safety agencies. The Law Enforcement Agencies Data System, or "LEADS," handles more than a half million messages each day.

The Bureau of Identification, headquartered in Joliet, serves as the state's criminal history record repository, maintaining more than 2.7 million fingerprint files. The Automated Fingerprint Identification System expedites fingerprint analysis of individuals arrested for serious crimes, prints found at crime scenes and applicants for positions of public trust.

The Firearms Services Bureau administers the Firearm Owner's Identification (FOID) and Firearms Transfer Inquiry programs in collaboration with federal programs to identify individuals prohibited from acquiring or possessing firearms or ammunition.

Research and Development captures and stores agency data on arrests, investigations and traffic events, allowing analysts to provide decision-making information to senior policy makers about how best to deploy resources. An extensive development and administration function oversees state and federal grants that fund department activities ranging from highway safety to marijuana eradication.

The Strategic Management Bureau guides the development of the agency's strategic plan, ensuring alignment with organizational goals and priorities. The bureau communicates the agency's strategic direction to all work units and assists other state agencies in implementing the Governor's Planning for Excellence program.

ADMINISTRATIVE PERSONNEL

Sam W. Nolen . . . . *Director*
Douglas W. Brown . . . . *First Deputy Director*
Jessica L. Trame . . . . *Chief of Staff*
James W. Redlich . . . . *Chief Legal Counsel*
James A. Finley III . . . . *Chief, Governmental Affairs/Legislative Liaison*
David L. Sanders . . . . *Public Information Officer*
Gail E. Pruett . . . . *Chief Fiscal Officer*
Daniel W. Kent . . . . *Deputy Director, Operations*
Timothy J. DaRosa . . . . *Deputy Director, Administration*
Alex Ferguson . . . . *Deputy Director, Information & Technology Command*
Teresa M. Kettelkamp . . . . *Deputy Director, Forensic Services*
George A.P. Murphy . . . . *Deputy Director, Internal Investigations*
Harold E. Nelson II . . . . *Deputy Director, Human Resource Command*

DEPARTMENT OF INSURANCE

Springfield: 320 W. Washington
4th Floor; 62767-0001
(217) 782-4515

Chicago: 100 W. Randolph
Ste. 15-100; 60601-3251
(312) 814-2420

Fiscal Year 2002 Appropriation: $33.6 million

The Department of Insurance regulates 1,942 insurance companies and 106,462 insurance producers licensed to do business in Illinois.

Nathaniel S. Shapo
Director

Consumer Protection

The department's consumer protection programs include investigating complaints against insurance companies and producers; examining and licensing insurance producers; licensing and regulating premium finance companies and bail bondsmen; evaluating product offerings, advertising, and rate and form filings; and examining insurance companies' market conduct.

The department also provides direct assistance to consumers through resource programs, such as Consumer Outreach, Disaster Assistance and the Senior Health Insurance Program.

Financial Regulation

The department oversees the corporate and financial activities of all licensed life, accident and health, and property/casualty insurance companies, health maintenance organizations and fraternal organizations through financial analysis and periodic financial examinations.

The department also examines the financial statements of all Illinois public employee pension funds, and regulates religious and charitable risk-pooling trusts, workers compensation pools, self-insured auto fleets, risk retention groups and captive insurance companies.

ADMINISTRATIVE PERSONNEL

Nathaniel S. Shapo . . . . *Director*
Madelynne Brown . . . . *Assistant Director*
Arnold Dutcher . . . .*Chief Deputy Director*
Lesslie Morgan . . . . *Internal Auditor*
Sinéad Rice . . . .*Legislative Liaison*
Robert Enoex . . . . *Chief Counsel*
J. Barry Becker . . . . *Deputy Director, Administrative Services Division*
Robert Heisler . . . . *Deputy Director, Consumer Market Division*
Jack Messmore . . . . *Deputy Director, Financial Corporate Regulatory Division*

249

DEPARTMENT OF LABOR

Springfield: 1 Old State Capitol Plaza
3rd Floor; 62701
(217) 782-6206
(217) 782-0596 (FAX)

Chicago: 160 N. LaSalle St.
C-1300; 60601
(312) 793-2800
(312) 793-5257 (FAX)

Marion: 2309 W. Main, 62959
(618) 993-7090

Robert M. Healey
Director

Fiscal Year 2002 Appropriation: $7.4 million

The Department of Labor promotes and protects the rights, wages, welfare, working conditions, safety and health of Illinois workers through enforcement of the state labor laws. The department also safeguards the public interest through the regulation of amusement rides, employment agencies and counselors and nurse agencies. The department also administers the Displaced Homemaker Program and reports annually on the progress of women and minorities in the workforce. Responsibility for the administration of statutes under the agency's jurisdiction is shared by the divisions of Fair Labor Standards, Conciliation & Mediation, Public Safety and Administration.

Fair Labor Standards

The Fair Labor Standards Division monitors compliance with state labor laws, including minimum wage, overtime, day labor services and child labor laws. It also settles wage claim disputes between workers and employers, and licenses private employment agencies, counselors and nurse agencies, which provide temporary staffing to health care facilities. This division also enforces the Personnel Records Review Act and Right to Privacy in Employment Act.

Conciliation and Mediation

The Conciliation and Mediation Division investigates complaints and monitors public works projects to assure that workers receive prevailing wages and that the Illinois workers hiring preference law is enforced. Upon request, Conciliation and Mediation staff assist labor and management groups in resolving grievances, negotiating contracts and conflict arbitration.

Public Safety

The Public Safety Division administers statutes and regulations enacted to protect the health and safety of the public and Illinois workers. These include health and safety inspection and education, carnival and amusement safety and toxic substance disclosure to workers. The public safety section enforces the Occupational Safety and Health Act for the public sector. The program is designed to protect the lives, health and safety of public workers by educating the employers and workers about safe working conditions. This is accomplished by providing training seminars and programs, technical assistance, consultation services and on-site inspections. The Carnival and Amusement Ride Safety section performs annual inspections of carnival and amusement rides and attractions, including ski lifts, rope tows and bungee jumps.

Administration

The Administration Division facilitates operations of the entire department, including fiscal management, procurement, personnel, public information, data processing, legislative liaison and affirmative action services. It is also responsible for the administration and coordination of the Displaced Homemaker Program, which provides 12 service centers throughout the state.

ADMINISTRATIVE PERSONNEL

Robert M. Healey .... *Director*
William A. Rolando .... *Assistant Director*
Scott Miller .... *Chief Legal Counsel*
Michael Bartolomucci .... *Fiscal Officer*
Suzanne Davis .... *Manager, Fair Labor Standards*
Al Juskenas .... *Manager, Public Employee Safety*
Carl Kimble .... *Manager, Carnival Safety*
John Freitag .... *Manager, Conciliation and Mediation*
Anita Morley .... *Legislative Liaison*

DEPARTMENT OF THE LOTTERY

Springfield: 201 E. Madison; 62702
(217) 524-5155

Chicago: 676 N. St. Clair
Ste. 2040; 60611
(312) 793-3026

Fiscal Year 2002 Appropriation: $357.3 million

The Illinois Lottery sells a variety of gaming products to raise funds for the state's Common School Fund. The state's fourth largest revenue generator, the Illinois Lottery is one of a handful of funding sources not derived from taxation. The Lottery's fund-raising ability is impressive. Annual sales of $1.5 billion and profits of more than $500 million place the Illinois Lottery squarely in line with Fortune 50 companies. Equally impressive is the Lottery's efficiency — operating expenses are among the lowest in the industry, registering just 4 percent of total sales.

Lori Spear Montana
Director

The 1980 introduction of the first computer online game — Pick 3 — marked a major milestone in Lottery history. During its first full year of operation (1981), Pick 3 sales equaled the total sales of 1978 and 1979 combined. In 1982, a second online game — Pick 4 — was added. This was followed by the 1983 introduction of LOTTO, which offers the chance to win million-dollar jackpots. In 1988, Little Lotto was introduced, a LOTTO-type game with smaller jackpots and more winners. The expanded online game menu helped propel a wave of sales increases that continued into the 1990s. The 1996 addition of the Big Game has further bolstered online sales, culminating with a $363 million jackpot in May 2000.

Growth and diversification have been equally impressive on the instant game side of the sales equation. Over the years, the Illinois Lottery has continually increased the number of scratch-off games it offers players. These increases were nominal — usually only one game per year — during the early- and mid-1980s. By the early 1990s, however, instant-game growth snowballed to more than 20 instant games per year. In Fiscal Years 1993 and 1994, instant sales ballooned by 23 and 11 percent, respectively. Instant games, which are frequently supported by special promotions and second-chance drawings, are now the Lottery's top sales product.

The lottery operates a network of more than 8,200 retailers throughout the state. Businesses from hardware stores to restaurants to neighborhood grocers are part of the extensive network. All Lottery retailers sell scratch-off instant games, and some 6,200 retailers sell both instant and online games. A Lottery license is granted only after the Illinois State Police perform a thorough background check on the applicant.

ADMINISTRATIVE PERSONNEL

Lori Spear Montana . . . . *Director*
Joan Fawell . . . . *Associate Director*
David Mizeur . . . . *Deputy Director, Finance*
Jeff Berry . . . . *Deputy Director, Operations*
Cathy Beres . . . . *Deputy Director, Marketing*
Kurt Freedlund . . . . *General Counsel*

DEPARTMENT OF MILITARY AFFAIRS

Maj. Gen. David Harris
Adjutant General

Springfield: 1301 N. MacArthur Blvd.; 62702
(217) 761-3500

Fiscal Year 2002 Appropriation: $31.9 million

The Department of Military Affairs oversees the military forces of the State of Illinois. The Illinois National Guard, consisting of the Army and Air National Guard, is designated as the military force of the state. The department is the official military link between the State of Illinois and the U.S. Department of Defense, working closely with the National Guard Bureau and the Departments of the Army and Air Force to ensure that federal resources are appropriately and effectively utilized. The Governor is Commander-in-Chief and appoints the Adjutant General to head the department. Major General David Harris was appointed as the state's Adjutant General on Aug. 1, 1999. He is the 35th appointee to the position; the first was Elias Rector, who was selected as the Adjutant General of the Illinois Territory in 1809.

The Adjutant General has the statutory responsibility to carry out policies of the Governor, issuing orders and serving as advisor to the Governor on all matters relating to the Illinois Army and Air National Guard. He is responsible for the policies and programs that provide for the organization, training, equipment and mobilization of the National Guard for state emergencies and national defense. All military property, equipment and installations of the Illinois National Guard are under his jurisdiction.

Illinois National Guard

The Army National Guard maintains 53 armories (50 state-owned, two leased and one federally owned), one state headquarters facility, two outdoor weapons ranges, three training areas and 43 vehicle storage/maintenance buildings in 47 communities throughout the state. The Air National Guard maintains large flying bases at two major civilian airports and one on an active U.S. Air Force Base. Each base supports a specific operational aircraft, including F-16C fighters, C-130E airlifters and KC-135E refuelers.

The Illinois National Guard has both a state and a federal mission. Its state mission is to respond to a call of the Governor for military support that is trained and equipped to protect life and property and to preserve peace, order and the public safety, as directed by the Governor. The National Guard also provides special programs for drug demand reduction, drug interdiction and resident and non-resident programs for at-risk youth. The Guard's federal mission is to support the active duty military forces of the Unites States when called to federal service in time of war or national emergency at the direction of the President. During federal mobilization, the role of Commander-in-Chief passes from the Governor to the President.

The Illinois Army and Air National Guard have a combined authorized strength of 13,000, which ranks Illinois among the top 10 states in the nation for Guard membership. While the majority of the organization is comprised of traditional volunteer members, 1,557 positions are funded as full-time federal positions. Additionally, the Department of Military Affairs is authorized 298 full-time state employees. Federal reimbursement helps fund many of these state positions; 118 are 100 percent federally reimbursed, and 40 are 75 percent federally reimbursed, leaving 140 positions that are state funded. Thus, the department brings in significant federal dollars to the state through personnel, equipment and training support funds. In Fiscal Year 2002, federal support of the department will exceed $212 million, compared with state funding of $31.9 million.

Headquarters Staffing

Major General David Harris .... *The Adjutant General*
Colonel (Ret) William L. Holland .... *Executive Assistant*
Doris Ippolito .... *Director, State Comptroller*
Sharon Dayton .... *Director, State Personnel*
Michelle Repaal .... *Legislative Liaison*
Colonel Jay Sheedy .... *Executive Support Officer*
Colonel John W. Newman .... *U.S. Property and Fiscal Officer*
Colonel Craig R. Heise .... *Director, Human Resources*
Colonel Mitchel Poodry .... *Inspector General*
Lieutenant Colonel Wayne S. Carlson .... *Staff Judge Advocate*
Lieutenant Colonel Laurence Andrews .... *Director, Public Affairs*
Andrea Leonard .... *Personal Assistant to TAG*

Illinois Army National Guard

Brigadier General Charles E. Fleming .... *Assistant Adjutant General-Army*
Colonel Ronald I. Botz .... *Chief of Staff*
Colonel Terry L. Downen .... *Director, Personnel*
Colonel Dennis Celletti .... *Director, Plans, Operations and Training*
Colonel Tom Nevill .... *Director, Logistics*
Colonel Gary Widner .... *Director, Facilities*
Colonel Michael Marvin .... *Director, State Aviation*
Colonel Paul Havey .... *Director, Information Management*
Lieutenant Colonel David Leckrone .... *Director, Resources Management*
Pam Athey .... *Executive Assistant to AAG-Army*

Major organizations: State Area Command, 33rd Area Support Group, 65th Troop Command Brigade, 66th Infantry Brigade.

Illinois Air National Guard

Brigadier General Frank D. Rezac .... *Assistant Adjutant General-Air*
Brigadier General R. Craig Nafzinger .... *Chief of Staff*
Colonel Jay Sheedy .... *Executive Staff Support Officer*
Timothy Leonetti .... *Executive Support Officer to AAG-Air*
Lara King .... *Executive Assistant to AAG-Air*

Major organizations: 126th Air Refueling Wing, 182nd Airlift Wing, 183rd Fighter Wing.

DEPARTMENT OF NATURAL RESOURCES

Springfield: 1 Natural Resources Way; 62702-1271
(217) 782-6302

Chicago: 100 W. Randolph
Ste. 4-300; 60601
(312) 814-2070

Fiscal Year 2002 Appropriation: $765.9 million

As steward of Illinois' natural and cultural resources, the Department of Natural Resources (DNR) has the responsibility to conserve, preserve and enhance the state's natural treasures, while meeting the outdoor recreation needs of Illinois' large and diverse population. The department also manages game and fish populations, while protecting endangered plant and animal species.

Brent Manning
Director

DNR maintains a main office in Springfield and a branch office in Chicago. It also operates regional offices in Sterling, Spring Grove, Champaign, Alton and Benton, as well as smaller district offices throughout the state.

Land Management and Education

Land Management and Education manages and maintains more than 260 state-owned or leased sites (state parks, fish and wildlife areas, forests, marinas, conservation areas and nature preserves), encompassing more than 417,000 acres, including 83,000 water acres. Management activities include resource compatible recreation for more than 43 million visitors, protection and enhancement of the sites' natural resources and interpretation of their unique heritage and natural features to visitors. Recreation opportunities include: boating, camping, fishing, hunting, picnicking, sight-seeing, swimming and trail use. The office also provides educational, safety and interpretive programs to increase public awareness of the state's natural and cultural resources.

Capital Development

Capital Development administers construction programs at department sites through the Division of Engineering and through grants to local units of government by the Division of Grant Administration. Construction projects include buildings, campgrounds and day use facilities, boat accesses and waterfowl habitat impoundments. Grants are provided for open space, bikeways, snowmobile trails, boating facilities and special projects approved by the legislature. The office also develops the department's annual capital budget request.

Law Enforcement

Law Enforcement protects Illinois' natural and recreational resources through enforcement of state laws. Conservation Police Officers (CPOs) have full statewide police authority and are trained to the highest standards for law enforcement professionals in Illinois. CPOs also serve as liaisons to civic groups, sportsmen's groups and sport shows and assist other agencies in emergency situations or rescue operations.

Mines and Minerals

Mines and Minerals is comprised of five divisions: Abandoned Mined Lands Reclamation; Blasting and Explosives; Land Reclamation; Mine Safety and Training, and Oil and Gas. The office permits mining, oil and gas operations throughout the state and enforces various acts that govern these industries. It also is charged with ensuring the health and safety of thousands of workers in the mining industry and regulates the possession, use and storage of explosives.

Resource Conservation

Resource Conservation consists of four divisions, an Operations Unit and a Federal Aid Unit. The Division of Wildlife Resources restores, maintains and enhances wildlife habitats and populations, while providing for the enjoyment and compatible use of those resources. More than 3.4 million Illinoisans spend more than $670 million observing, feeding or photographing wildlife. Annually, about 350,000 hunters and trappers spend more than 7.4 million trip-days afield in Illinois, resulting in about $627 million in the state's economy. Biologists survey and manage wildlife populations and habitats, developing statewide and site-specific management plans for both public and private lands. The division also manages 12 wildlife areas throughout the state.

The Division of Natural Heritage locates, preserves, protects and manages lands containing elements of Illinois' rich natural heritage. Field biologists work with department sites, volunteers, private landowners, local government and nongovernmental organizations to implement the division's services. They also manage and restore forests, prairies and wetlands; monitor and manage plant and animal populations, and protect, restore and manage endangered species.

The Division of Forest Resources provides forestry programs, services and activities to assist private landowners, other department divisions and various governmental agencies. The division promotes planting, protection and conservation of forests and is involved in reforestation, woodland management, fire management and forest marketing.

The Division of Fisheries protects, restores and enhances the state's fisheries and other aquatic resources, including Lake Michigan, reservoirs, impoundments and streams. Fisheries occur in Lake Michigan (976,640 acres - Illinois portion), three Corps of Engineers reservoirs (54,580 acres), more than 91,000 impoundments (263,900 acres) and more than 26,400 miles of streams (325,000 acres). There are four fish hatcheries in the state that annually stock about 69 million fish of 27 species.

Scientific Research and Analysis

Scientific Research and Analysis encourages effective stewardship of the state's natural resources and environment. It also contributes to the economic and environmental health of the state by providing scientific expertise, information and long-term perspectives needed for informed decision making. The office includes the State Geological Survey, Natural History Survey, Water Survey, Illinois Waste Management and Research Center, and the Illinois State Museum. They all perform both basic and applied research; maintain extensive collections; publish scientific reports and articles, and provide extensive information to a wide variety of agencies, businesses, communities and the general public.

Established in 1905, the Geological Survey conducts research, compiles maps and gathers data about the state's geology and mineral resources. The survey's goals are to provide information leading to the responsible development and use of the state's coal, oil and gas, groundwater, industrial minerals and other geological resources. It also provides information for policy development to protect groundwater resources, manage wastes, avoid or reduce natural hazards and plan for growth and development.

The Illinois Waste Management and Research Center, formed in 1984, develops solutions to Illinois' industrial waste problems through research and education; information collection, analysis and dissemination; and direct technical assistance to industry, agriculture and communities. The center works with industry to reduce the amount and toxicity of its waste streams, recycle and fund research of critical waste issues, and develop environmental technology.

The Illinois State Museum collects, preserves and interprets the natural history, art and anthropological resources of Illinois. Its research and educational programming advances understanding of the state's landscapes; organisms, both living and extinct, and art and cultural heritage, past and present. Its quality research programs and collections are recognized nationally and internationally.

The Natural History Survey, with early work dating to 1858, acquires, organizes and utilizes collections and data pertaining to all aspects of the biotic resources of Illinois. Staff members perform scientific inquiry concerning the diversity, life histories, growth and development, ecology, population dynamics, ecosystem properties and management of the biotic resources of Illinois.

Founded in 1895, the Water Survey serves as the state's archives of scientific information on its atmospheric and water resources. Staff members conduct research and provide information on the availability, use and quality of the state's surface and groundwater resources. The Water Survey also maintains statewide and Midwest regional data on weather, severe storms, air quality, climate change and meteorology.

Water Resources

Water Resources administers regulatory programs over construction in the floodways of rivers, lakes and streams; construction in the shore waters of Lake Michigan; construction and operation of dams; construction in public bodies of water; diversion of water from Lake Michigan, and withdrawal of water from Lake Shelbyville, Carlyle Lake and Rend Lake. The office is the lead state agency for water resources planning, navigation, floodplain management, the National Flood Insurance Program and interstate organizations on water resources. Interagency duties include the state water plan, drought response, flood emergency situation reports and the comprehensive review of Illinois water use law. The primary capital activity of the office is to reduce urban flood damage.

Public Services

Public Services is responsible for the department's marketing and merchandise programs. It also oversees still and video photo programs and agency publications, including the monthly magazine, *Outdoor Illinois*.

Realty and Environmental Planning

Realty and Environmental Planning analyzes the state's natural resources, their use and management; develops regional and comprehensive outdoor recreation and landscape planning; acquires land for public use, and designs and implements public park improvements.

Boards and Commissions

DNR has 13 boards and commissions, including the: Natural Resources Advisory Board; Illinois Nature Preserves Commission; Illinois Council on Forestry Development; Endangered Species Protection Board; State Mining Board; Miner's Examining Board; Oil and Gas Advisory Board; Board of the Illinois State Museum; Board of Natural Resources and Conservation; Illinois Waste Management and Research Center Advisory Board; Surface Mining Council; Illinois Conservation Foundation Board, and Illinois Geographic Information Council.

Office of the Director

The Director's office administers several key interdisciplinary functions, including fiscal management, legal services and internal auditing. Legislation and Constituent Services acts as a liaison to state legislators, helps enact new laws and works with the department's constituent groups. Public Affairs provides information to the media and the public, and the Equal Employment Opportunity Office implements policies for effective affirmative action programs and equal employment opportunity. The Conservation Foundation raises funds to further conservation and recreation programs.

Administration

Administration provides internal support functions through the Divisions of Administrative Support, Concessions and Lease Management, Employee Services, and Systems and Licensing. The office is responsible for central warehouse and shop functions, purchasing, telecommunications, messenger services and vehicle fleet management. It also handles general legal agreement negotiations, coordination and maintenance; general leasing; rights of way, special land use permits, and park concessions. Personnel, labor relations and data processing as well as the issuance of licenses, stamps or permits for regulated outdoor activities, such as hunting, fishing and boating, also are handled by the office.

ADMINISTRATIVE PERSONNEL

Brent Manning .... *Director*
Jim Garner .... *Deputy Director*
Jim Riemer .... *Deputy Director*
John Bandy .... *Director, Office of Fiscal Management*
Robert Lawley .... *Director, Office of Legal Counsel*
Diane Hendren .... *Director, Office of Legislation*
Carol Knowles .... *Director, Office of Public Affairs*
John Schmitt .... *Executive Director, Conservation Foundation*
Kevin Sronce .... *Director, Office of Administration*
Bruce Clark .... *Director, Office of Capital Development*
Jerry Beverlin .... *Director, Office of Land Management & Education*
Larry Closson .... *Director, Office of Law Enforcement*
Neal H. Merrifield .... *Director, Office of Mines & Minerals*
Jim Fulgenzi .... *Director, Office of Public Services*
Tom Flattery .... *Director, Office of Realty & Environmental Planning*
Kirby Cottrell .... *Director, Office of Resource Conservation*
Don Vonnahme .... *Director, Office of Water Resources*

DEPARTMENT OF NUCLEAR SAFETY

Springfield: 1035 Outer Park Dr.; 62704
(217) 785-9900

Glen Ellyn: 800 Roosevelt Rd., Bldg. C
Ste. 200; 60137
(630) 790-5300

Fiscal Year 2002 Appropriation: $31.2 million

The Illinois Department of Nuclear Safety, established in 1980, is one of only two cabinet-level state agencies in the country devoted exclusively to nuclear and radiation safety. The department monitors nuclear facilities, prepares technical emergency response plans for radiological accidents, ensures the proper operation of radiation-producing equipment, regulates radioactive materials and low-level radioactive waste, inspects shipments of radioactive cargo, and measures radioactivity in the environment to ensure that it is within safe levels.

Thomas W. Ortciger
Director

Emergency Preparedness

One of the department's most important functions is to ensure that Illinois citizens are protected from the harmful effects of ionizing radiation, which could be caused by an accident at a nuclear power reactor. If an accident were to occur, the director would be responsible for recommending to the Governor actions to protect the public.

The Office of Nuclear Facility Safety develops and maintains monitoring and analytic capabilities necessary to evaluate reactor accidents in Illinois, and implements the Illinois Boiler and Pressure Vessel Safety Act and the Illinois Nuclear Facility Safety Act. The office also develops and updates the *Illinois Plan for Radiological Accidents*, a 10-volume document detailing actions to be taken by state and local governments during an accident.

The Illinois Nuclear Facility Safety Act, as amended in August 1992, established a program that places a state resident inspector at each nuclear power plant in Illinois. The state resident inspectors, under a cooperative agreement with the U.S. Nuclear Regulatory Commission (NRC), conduct independent inspections of critical safety systems at their assigned plants and are present during plant decommissioning. In the event of an accident, the state resident inspectors would be a vital communication link between the plant and the department.

The department has a technically sophisticated, comprehensive remote monitoring system at each of the six operating and one closed nuclear power stations in Illinois. The system includes three components. First, a ring of environmental radiation monitors encircles each site at a distance of about two miles. The monitors would confirm a radiological release into the atmosphere and permit estimation of the potential impact on the public. Second, a direct data link connects each plant's on-site computer with the department's Radiological Emergency Assessment Center in Springfield. The link provides the current status on hundreds of key reactor safety systems and instruments. And third, an automated monitoring system samples the gases being discharged from the nuclear power plant and analyzes the samples automatically for the types and quantities of radioactive materials in them.

No other governmental organization in the U.S. has such a comprehensive remote monitoring system. The data received from the system is available immediately to the department's technical staff, which would enable it to make recommendations to protect nearby residents during an accident.

In 1994, the department implemented the Illinois Boiler and Pressure Vessel Safety Act at the nuclear power plant sites. A Memorandum of Understanding with the NRC was signed in May 1990, which allows the department to inspect boilers, pressure vessels and steam systems at the state's 11 commercial nuclear power reactors.

In 2000, the Office of Mitigation and Response was created, and the department's emergency planning functions were consolidated into this office. The department takes part in several simulated accidents, or "exercises," at Illinois nuclear power reactors each year to test the ability of state and local governments to respond to a serious accident. Since 1980, the department has participated in more than 670 of these exercises. The department also has special equipment and trained personnel for responding to hazards involving radioactive materials. The Radiological Assessment and Coordinated Emergency Response team (RACER) is prepared to handle virtually any radiological emergencies.

Low-Level Radioactive Waste Management

The department has responsibilities for licensing of a new low-level radioactive waste (LLRW) disposal facility in Illinois, and has developed regulations and standards for LLRW management that will assure protection of public health and safety. The new LLRW disposal facility is being developed under provisions of state law and the Central Midwest Interstate Low-Level Radioactive Waste Compact, an interstate agreement between Illinois and Kentucky to establish new LLRW disposal capacity. All generators of LLRW within the state are registered with the department and pay fees to fund the program.

Agreement State

An agreement between the State of Illinois and the NRC, transferring regulatory authority over most users of radioactive materials from the federal government to the department, became effective June 1, 1987. Illinois now administers about 1,200 radioactive material licenses, which are held by medical, industrial and academic facilities. On Nov. 1, 1990, the department assumed regulatory authority over thorium mill tailings under its Agreement State Program. Under this authority, the department oversees the cleanup of the former Kerr-McGee factory site in West Chicago.

Safe Use of Medical Radiation

DNS is responsible for regulating more than 10,400 radiation facilities in Illinois and about 28,000 radiation-producing machines. Periodic inspections of x-ray equipment are performed, and about 11,000 radiological technologists are accredited to ensure that only qualified individuals administer radiation to patients. Under the U.S. Food and Drug Administration's States as Certifiers Demonstration Project, the department administers all aspects of mammography facility certification, including inspection, assessment of fees and enforcement actions. There are more than 400 mammography facilities in Illinois.

Transportation of Radioactive Materials

The department inspects and escorts all highway and rail shipments of spent nuclear fuel in Illinois. Since 1983, more than 470 shipments have been inspected and escorted safely. The department provides training to local emergency response personnel and technical assistance to the Illinois State Police, the Illinois Commerce Commission and the Illinois Department of Transportation to ensure that all radioactive materials are transported safely.

Public Safety Measures

The department is the lead state agency for evaluating any public health problem posed by indoor radon, an odorless, colorless gas produced by the decay of naturally occurring radioactive elements in soil. Prolonged exposure to excessive levels of radon in residential dwellings and schools may increase an individual's chances of contracting lung cancer. A study by the department in 1991 indicated that a significant number of homes and schools in Illinois have radon concentrations exceeding federal voluntary standards. The department has an extensive program for providing radon information and assistance to citizens, and under the Radon Industry Licensing Act of 1997 administers a licensing program for radon measurement and mitigation contractors.

The department is certified by the U.S. Environmental Protection Agency to measure radioactivity in Illinois' drinking water supplies. More than 80 communities in Illinois have concentrations of radium, a naturally occurring radioactive element, higher than permitted by federal regulation.

Department staff and a satellite laboratory are stationed in West Chicago, former site of the contaminated Kerr-McGee factory, to assist with verification analyses of areas being cleaned up under the U.S. Environmental Protection Agency's Superfund program. The department also continues to monitor activities at the closed LLRW disposal site near Sheffield and the former site of Enrico Fermi's early nuclear reactor experiments at the Palos Park Forest Preserve.

ADMINISTRATIVE PERSONNEL

Thomas W. Ortciger . . . . *Director*
Gordon Appel . . . . *Deputy Director*
Stephen England . . . . *Chief Legal Counsel*
Patti Thompson . . . . *Director of Communications*
John Webb . . . . *Director of Legislative Affairs*
Dave Kelm . . . . *Director of Governmental Affairs*
Rich Allen . . . . *Office Manager, Environmental Safety*
John Hall . . . . *Office Manager, Mitigation and Response*
Gary Wright . . . . *Office Manager, Nuclear Facility Safety*
Paul Eastvold . . . . *Office Manager, Radiation Safety*
David Joswiak . . . . *Office Manager, Administration*

DEPARTMENT OF PROFESSIONAL REGULATION

Springfield: 320 W. Washington
3rd Floor; 62786
(217) 785-0800

Chicago: 100 W. Randolph
Ste. 9-300; 60601
(312) 814-4500

Fiscal Year 2002 Appropriation: $30.5 million

Leonard A. Sherman
Director

The Department of Professional Regulation protects the public by working to ensure quality professional services. The department is able to serve the best interests of Illinois consumers by scrutinizing applications for professional licenses and following through with enforcement of established standards of competence.

The department issues licenses to about 500,000 people in 48 professional and occupational groups. The issuance and restriction of these licenses are within the department's jurisdiction.

Licensing and Testing

Eligibility for licensure is based on the background, training and education of the applicants. Staff members maintain licensee records, test results and school approvals for future reference and use in determining questionable license renewal cases. Applications for licensure by endorsement, reciprocity or acceptance by examination are processed by two application sections within the Licensing and Testing Division: Professional Services and Health Services. Each section is staffed by department liaisons to the various professional boards and committees. This close association provides the ability to interact in the best interest of both the department and the professions.

Some professionals are asked periodically to extend their education or attend refresher courses to meet department standards. Various boards and committees within the department review applicant credentials. Responsibilities of these bodies include developing licensee criteria, hearing formal charges filed against licensees, assisting the department in administering standard examinations and making disciplinary recommendations to the director.

Following are boards and committees within the department: Advanced Practice Nursing Board; Anesthesia Review Panel; Architect Licensing Board; Barber, Cosmetology, Esthetics and Nail Technology Committee; Board of Acupuncture; Board of Athletic Trainers; Board of Dentistry; Board of Environmental Health Practitioners; Board of Interior Design Professionals; Board of Licensing for Professional Geologists; Board of Nursing; Board of Orthotics, Prosthetics and Pedorthics; Board of Perfusion; Board of Speech-Language Pathology and Audiology; Boxing and Wresting Board; Certified Shorthand Reporters Board; Clinical Psychologists Licensing and Disciplinary Board; Collection Agency Licensing and Disciplinary Board; Detection of Deception Examiner Committee; Dietetic and Nutrition Services Practice Board; Funeral Directors and Embalmers Licensing and Disciplinary Board; Home Medical Equipment and Services Board; Land Surveyors Licensing Board; Landscape Architect Registration Board; Marriage and Family Therapy Licensing and Disciplinary Board; Medical Disciplinary Board; Medical

Licensing Board; Naprapathic Examining Committee; Nursing Home Administrators Licensing and Disciplinary Board; Occupational Therapy Board; Optometric Licensing and Disciplinary Board; Physical Therapy Licensing and Disciplinary Committee; Physician Assistant Advisory Committee; Podiatric Medical Licensing Board; Private Detective, Private Alarm, Private Security and Locksmith Board; Professional Counselor Licensing and Disciplinary Board; Public Accountant Registration Committee; Respiratory Care Board; Roofing Advisory Board; Social Work Examining and Disciplinary Board; State Board of Pharmacy; State Board of Professional Engineers; Structural Engineering Board; Veterinary Licensing and Disciplinary Board, and Wholesale Drug Distributor Advisory Committee.

It is the responsibility of the Licensure Maintenance and Technical Assistance Section to oversee the maintenance of more than 1 million licensure records, including renewals, restorations, inactive requests, status checks, duplication of licenses, corrections, data changes, certifications of licensee records and verification of licensure. The section also provides all form and application requests for prospective licensees, answers inquiries from the licensees and provides information to other divisions within the department.

Statewide Enforcement

The department is legislatively mandated to administer and enforce 43 separate legislative acts that regulate the conduct of many professions and occupations in Illinois. Responsibility for the enforcement of these acts rests with the Statewide Enforcement Division. The division consists of three enforcement teams: Medical, Health-Related and General.

The disciplinary process begins when the department becomes aware of a grievance against a licensee. All complaints against licensees merit an investigation and, thus, trigger the licensee discipline process. Allegations involving violations of a licensing law or failure to abide by department rules and regulations either must be confirmed or dismissed. If the allegations are not dismissed following an investigation, a formal complaint is filed and a hearing is held before the appropriate board or committee.

Following the hearing, the board or committee delivers to the director its findings, conclusions and recommendations. Disciplinary action may include termination of a license, revocation, suspension, probation, reprimand and/or censure. The licensee also may be ordered to remain in good standing. Illinois law allows for the imposition of fines for any of the professions regulated. When ordering disciplinary action, the director often accepts the recommendation of the board or committee but is not required to do so. Following a final decision by the director, the licensee has 35 days to make an appeal in circuit court under the Illinois Administrative Review Act.

ADMINISTRATIVE PERSONNEL

Leonard A. Sherman .... *Director*
Pat Daniels .... *Deputy Director*
John Coghlan .... *Director, Statewide Enforcement*
James Covert .... *Program Executive, Licensing and Testing*
Adrienne Hersh .... *General Counsel*
Dan Bluthardt .... *Legislative Liaison*
John Hasselbring .... *Fiscal Officer*
Jeanine Hamm .... *Acting Director, Human Resources*

DEPARTMENT OF PUBLIC AID

Springfield: 201 S. Grand Ave. E.; 62763
(217) 782-3458

Chicago: 401 S. Clinton Ave.; 60607
(312) 793-4721

Fiscal Year 2002 Appropriation: $8 billion

The Illinois Department of Public Aid improves the health and self-sufficiency of Illinoisans in need by providing health coverage for low-income adults and children, and helping to ensure that children receive support from both parents. In addition to two program divisions, the department houses an independent Office of the Inspector General.

Jackie Garner
Director

Medical Programs

Each month, the Illinois Medicaid and KidCare programs provide health coverage to 1.5 million Illinoisans. Of those covered, about 920,000 are children. Since its inception in 1998, KidCare has enrolled more than 150,000 children and pregnant women. Many families whose earnings make them ineligible for Medicaid can receive children's coverage under KidCare's higher income standards. Illinois created KidCare under the federal State Children's Health Insurance Program.

Medicaid covers low-income families with children as well as low-income seniors and persons with disabilities. Both Medicaid and KidCare pay for services, including physician care, dental care, prescription drugs, hospital care, long-term care, hospice care, home health care, transportation and medical equipment. The KidCare and Medicaid programs receive both federal and state dollars and are administered under federal and state rules.

The Division of Medical Programs also operates other medical programs with only state dollars, including limited health coverage for people with chronic renal disease or hemophilia.

Child Support Enforcement

Each year, the Division of Child Support Enforcement helps more than 1 million Illinois families locate absent parents, establish paternity, obtain child support and medical support orders and collect delinquent support payments. The federally mandated Title IV-D program originally focused on families receiving cash assistance, but it now serves any family requesting help with obtaining or enforcing an order for child support.

Methods used to collect delinquent child support payments include:

- Intercepting federal and state income tax refunds or any check issued by the Comptroller of the State of Illinois;

- Referring a delinquent account to private collection agencies, and having liens placed against the non-payer's assets by the Illinois Department of Revenue;

264

- Suspending or revoking a professional, recreational or driver's license;

- Stopping issuance of a passport.

In Fiscal Year 2001, child support collections totaled $722 million, including $428 million from the department's Title IV-D child support enforcement activities. The State Disbursement Unit is a processing center for child support payments that employers withhold from the paychecks of non-custodial parents. Employers forward the payments by mail or electronic funds transfer, and the unit issues a check to the receiving family. The unit processes more than 100,000 checks weekly.

The division also conducts outreach programs to help strengthen families and help non-custodial parents recognize and meet their child support obligations.

Office of the Inspector General

The Office of the Inspector General works to assure the integrity of Illinois' human services programs. Independent in function, the office is administratively housed in the Department of Public Aid. The office investigates to prevent and detect fraud and abuse and was responsible for $38.3 million in savings and collections in Fiscal Year 2000.

ADMINISTRATIVE PERSONNEL

Jackie Garner .... *Director*
David Citron .... *Assistant Director*
Lynn Handy .... *Deputy Director*
Theron D. Aslaksen .... *Deputy Director, Administrative Operations*
Matt Powers .... *Medical Programs*
Nancy Woodward .... *Child Support Enforcement*
Ellen Feldhausen .... *Communications*
Owen Field .... *General Counsel*
Fred Backfield .... *Finance and Budget*
Bill Dart .... *Legislative Affairs*
Elvin Lay .... *Internal Audits*
Robb Miller .... *Inspector General*
Raven Knighten ....*EEO Officer*
Bill Mills .... *Strategic Planning*
Valerie Brooks .... *Program Operations and Policy*
Deneen Omer .... *Chief Information Officer*

DEPARTMENT OF PUBLIC HEALTH

Springfield: 535 W. Jefferson St.; 62761
(217) 782-4977

Chicago: 100 W. Randolph St.
Ste. 6-600; 60601
(312) 814-2608

Fiscal Year 2002 Appropriation: $322.8 million

The Department of Public Health, the state's second-oldest agency, created in 1877, promotes health through the prevention and control of disease and injury. Its nearly 200 programs strive to eliminate health hazards, regulate health care facilities and identify and control outbreaks of disease.

John R. Lumpkin, M.D.
Director

Epidemiology and Health Systems Development

To create a state health policy that assures effective, accessible and affordable health services, the Office of Epidemiology and Health Systems Development collects and evaluates information on the health needs, disease occurrence and health status of Illinois residents. This information is used to identify the need for epidemiological studies; prevention and regulatory programs; and future needs for hospitals, nursing homes and other health care facilities, services and personnel. The office manages several data collection systems, including the Adverse Pregnancy Outcome Reporting System, the Illinois State Cancer Registry, the Health and Hazardous Substances Registry, the Adult Blood Lead Registry and the Occupational Disease Registry. Other responsibilities include producing the state's annual vital statistics report and performing population estimates and health needs assessments. The office also reviews and makes recommendations to the Illinois Health Facilities Planning Board on certificate-of-need applications, and assesses the need for various health care services and facilities on a geographic basis.

Health Care Regulation

To ensure the health and safety of patients, the Office of Health Care Regulation oversees the state licensing and federal certification of Illinois' health care facilities and conducts complaint investigations. Facilities subject to review include nursing homes, assisted-living centers, hospitals, trauma centers, rural health clinics, ambulatory surgical treatment centers, pregnancy termination centers, and independent hospital and physician office laboratories. The office operates a 24-hour hotline through which people can register complaints against health care facilities. The office licenses paramedics and other emergency medical technicians, certified nurse aides and physical therapists in private practice. The office also regulates hospices, health maintenance organizations (HMOs), home health agencies, ambulances, emergency medical services helicopters and fixed wing aircraft, watercraft and off-road vehicles, and the state's poison control resource center.

266

Health Promotion

The Office of Health Promotion focuses on enhancing the quality of life of all individuals, especially children. Printed educational materials, laboratory testing, professional training, local project funding, computer services, consultations and research are used to address basic and specialized health needs. The office's program responsibilities include men's health issues; violence prevention; coordinating tobacco control and cessation efforts; screening children for genetic diseases, lead poisonings and eye and ear disorders and disease; cardiovascular disease risk reduction; identifying other potential health problems and their solutions; encouraging healthy life-styles; monitoring fluoridation of community water, and funding Alzheimer's disease research and assistance centers. The office also is responsible for educating the public about child passenger restraints; sudden infant death syndrome (SIDS) prevention, and organ transplant support services.

Health Protection

The Office of Health Protection administers programs to prevent and control disease, reduce and eliminate exposure to environmental hazards and ensure a safe, wholesome and nutritious food supply. Among its major responsibilities are efforts to reduce the spread of the HIV virus, AIDS, sexually transmitted diseases and tuberculosis; coordinate childhood immunizations; reduce the incidence of disease and injury related to environmental factors; prevent contamination of food and drugs, and provide clinical and environmental laboratory testing services. The office also is responsible for setting minimum standards for local health departments and restaurant inspections, emergency response, rabies control, non-community public water supplies, manufactured housing, generic drug information, and asbestos inspection, abatement and control. Licensing responsibilities include plumbers, water well contractors, private sewage system installers, lead inspectors and contractors, asbestos inspectors, contractors and workers, tanning parlors, public bathing beaches and pools, mobile home parks, campgrounds, youth camps, migrant labor camps and structural pest control companies and technicians.

Finance and Administration

The Office of Finance and Administration maintains the state's vital records on births, deaths, marriages, divorces, adoptions and abortions. Since birth and death records began being reported in 1916, about 30 million have been placed on file, including some delayed records dating back to the mid-1800s. Today, more than 500,000 vital records are registered annually. The office also oversees the operation of the agency's seven regional health offices. Internally, the office is responsible for a number of administrative services, including budget, data processing, financial services, training, purchasing, telecommunications, and personnel, employee services and benefits.

Women's Health

The Office of Women's Health was established in 1997 to improve the health of Illinois women and girls by initiating and coordinating awareness, education and programming throughout the state; to encourage healthier life-styles among women, and to promote equitable public policy on health issues that affect women. With funding from the U.S. Centers for Disease Control and

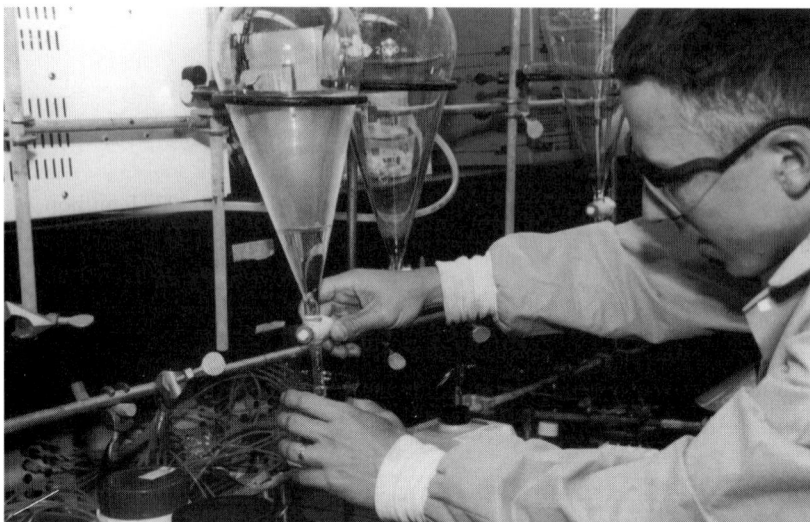

The Department of Public Health operates laboratories in Chicago, Springfield and Carbondale, which annually provide nearly 2 million clinical and environmental test results.

Prevention, the Illinois Breast and Cervical Cancer Program provides free mammograms, Pap smears and other screening and diagnostic services to eligible women in all Illinois counties. The office also awards about $2 million each year in women's health grants to local agencies to conduct women's health outreach activities and some direct services. And it administers the Penny Severns Breast and Cervical Cancer Research Fund.

The office maintains a toll-free Women's Health Helpline that allows Illinois women to obtain health information, order educational materials and be referred to services within the department and through other state agencies. The office also facilitates partnerships between the department and agencies, as well as between the department and outside consumer and professional groups. Working with the Interagency Cabinet on Women's Health, the office identifies areas where agencies can share resources and combine audiences to deliver health messages and services more efficiently.

ADMINISTRATIVE PERSONNEL

John R. Lumpkin, M.D., M.P.H. . . . . *Director*
Michelle Gentry-Wiseman . . . . *Assistant Director*
Mark Schmidt . . . . *Deputy Director, Health Promotion*
Margaret Richards . . . . *Deputy Director, Epidemiology and Health Systems Development*
Gary T. Robinson . . . . *Deputy Director, Finance and Administration*
William Bell . . . . *Deputy Director, Health Care Regulation*
Janet Stone . . . . *Acting Deputy Director, Health Protection*
Sharon Green . . . . *Deputy Director, Women's Health*
Deanna Mool . . . . *Chief Counsel*
Thomas J. Schafer . . . . *Communications*
Catherine Narup . . . . *Governmental Affairs*
Darrel L. Balmer . . . . *Internal Audits*

268

DEPARTMENT OF REVENUE

Springfield: 101 W. Jefferson St.; 62702
(217) 785-7570

Chicago: 100 W. Randolph; 60601
(312) 814-3190

Fiscal Year 2002 Appropriation: $979.5 million

Glen L. Bower
Director

The Department of Revenue collects taxes for both Illinois State Government and units of local government. The department also provides tax relief and helps seniors and disabled adults purchase prescription medication. Additionally, it has general oversight of the local property tax assessment system and equalizes the level of property tax assessment among the state's 102 counties. The department also provides administrative support to the Illinois Gaming Board, which oversees riverboat gambling in Illinois.

In Fiscal Year 2001, the Department of Revenue collected $24.9 billion in taxes, with about one quarter going to local governments. Taxes account for more than 70 percent of state general funds receipts. The department collects and allocates sales taxes imposed by home rule governments, counties, mass transit districts and the DuPage County Water Commission. It also distributes to local governments their shares of state income and sales tax collections, use taxes and personal property replacement taxes.

In support of its mission to collect the taxes needed to operate state and local governments, the Department of Revenue provides help to taxpayers, enforces the collection of taxes due to State Government and works to increase its efficiency through electronic commerce.

Availability to the Public

The department operates toll-free telephone lines manned by taxpayer service representatives to answer questions involving 73 different tax laws, fielding 912,000 calls in Fiscal Year 2001. Staff members respond to written questions and research inquiries involving specific taxpayer accounts. The department provides services in Springfield and Chicago, at 10 district offices around the state and, during the tax season, at various Internal Revenue Service offices. The department uses the Internet and an automated fax system to make tax forms available to the public.

The department is committed to giving taxpayers the opportunity to comment on changes in the way tax laws are administered. It routinely reaches out to taxpayers and tax professionals for suggestions on how to improve its operations. The department also has an open regulatory process that seeks input from affected parties before proposing new rules.

Enforcement

The department works to ensure that taxpayers pay their correct taxes and strives to collect all taxes owed. Methods of collecting delinquent tax payments include offsetting other state payments and federal income tax refunds, phone calls, wage levies and liens. In Fiscal Year 2001, the department collected $401 million in delinquent tax debt and another $34 million in overdue child support for the Department of Public Aid.

269

The department's audit staff reviews the accounts of specific taxpayers to ensure they are in compliance with state tax laws. Auditors conduct traditional field audits that involve reviewing taxpayer records, together with sophisticated computer tape matches that compare what is reported on state tax returns with other databases. The computerized matches allow auditors to cover many more taxpayers than do traditional audits.

Electronic Commerce

The Department of Revenue has successfully used technology to reduce operational costs associated with the receipt of 17 million tax returns annually. In Fiscal Year 2001, the department received 1.27 million electronically filed individual income tax returns — about 22 percent of all returns filed. The number of electronic filers has doubled in three years. On the payment side, more than $10.3 billion in collections — 42 percent of total collections — was made by electronic bank transfers. On the refund side, more than 765,000 individuals had their refunds deposited directly into their bank accounts. The department also has expanded electronic filing to businesses with the introduction of sales tax filing programs.

Circuit Breaker/Pharmaceutical Assistance

The department operates the Circuit Breaker and Pharmaceutical Assistance programs that provide low-income senior citizens and disabled adults with grants to help offset the cost of property taxes and assistance in purchasing prescription medicine. In Fiscal Year 2001, the department provided property tax relief to 245,000 households, and 145,000 individuals received prescription coverage. Those numbers will continue to grow with the expansion of income limits and medical coverage and reduced costs to participants in the program, which became effective Jan. 1, 2001.

Illinois Gaming Board

The Illinois Gaming Board, established in 1990, is a five-member board charged with licensing and regulating riverboat gambling in Illinois. Its staff includes administrative personnel and officers from the Illinois State Police and agents from the Internal Revenue Service.

The board investigates potential owners, suppliers and employees of the riverboats. As of July 1, 2001, licensed entities operated riverboats in Alton, Aurora, East St. Louis, Elgin, Joliet (two licenses), Metropolis, East Peoria and Rock Island. Since the first boat began operating in September 1991, the state has realized more than $1.68 billion in taxes, and local municipalities where the boats are docked have shared more than $596 million more in taxes.

ADMINISTRATIVE PERSONNEL

Glen L. Bower . . . . *Director*
Patricia Marriott . . . . *Assistant Director*
Mary Ann Dobucki . . . . *Associate Director*
Georgia Marsh . . . . *Associate Director*
John Roupas . . . . *Associate Director*
Thomas F. Swoik . . . . *Interim Administrator, Illinois Gaming Board*

DEPARTMENT OF TRANSPORTATION

Springfield: 2300 S. Dirksen Pky.; 62764
(217) 782-5597
TDD: (217) 524-4875

Chicago: 310 S. Michigan Ave.
Rm. 1600; 60604
(312) 793-2250
TDD: (312) 524-4875

Fiscal Year 2002 Appropriation: $8.2 billion

Kirk Brown
Secretary

The Department of Transportation (IDOT) is responsible for the planning, coordination, construction and maintenance or operation of Illinois' extensive transportation network, which encompasses airports, roads, highways and bridges, as well as public transit, rail freight and rail passenger systems. The department works with local public and private transportation agencies to ensure that the state's overall transportation network is cost-effective, safe and efficient for the people who live, work and do business in Illinois. The department's goal is to ensure that the state's transportation infrastructure can support a healthy economy.

Planning and programming are key tools to the department's efforts to provide a well-maintained, efficient and balanced transportation system. Planning provides an important framework for developing transportation improvement programs that identify specific capital projects and estimates of available funding for all modes of transportation, including air, highways, public transit and rail.

Beginning in 2000, Governor Ryan's Illinois FIRST program funded projects for road and bridge rehabilitation, public transportation operations and equipment, airport improvements and high-speed rail design work as part of a $12 billion initiative to rebuild the critical infrastructure of the state.

Aeronautics

Illinois' air transportation system, the second-largest in the United States, is comprised of 120 public use airports, including one of the world's busiest, O'Hare International in Chicago; 277 heliports for helicopters, and nine balloon ports for hot-air balloons. The department is responsible for ensuring safe and effective aviation facilities and services and assists local agencies in airport development projects that meet operations and safety standards.

The department registers more than 19,000 pilots and 6,000 planes. It is responsible for developing and promoting aviation education and safety programs for the aviation community, youth and schools, the general public and community leaders. It also provides administrative support for the Illinois Wing of the Civil Air Patrol.

The department cooperates with the Department of Public Health's Emergency Medical Services (EMS) Program by providing EMS helicopter transportation. The program was established in 1971 to enable rapid transportation of critically ill persons from local hospitals to trauma centers or other hospitals that provide specialized care. Since the program began, more than 15,000 people have been transported by IDOT/EMS flights.

Through Governor Ryan's Illinois FIRST program, the "Hillside Bottleneck" in Western Cook County was untangled following the reconstruction of three interstate highways, including the Eisenhower Expressway, over a two-year period beginning in 2000.

Highways

The department is responsible for the planning, design, construction, operation and maintenance of the 17,000-mile state highway system and for the administration of the local roads and streets program. Nine district offices perform the work related to these functions.

The highway program emphasis has been shifting over the past three decades since the interstate system in Illinois was completed. Today, more than 95 percent of the state's highway investments focus on preservation and modernization of the existing system. Less than five percent of the highway program is targeted for the construction of new highway facilities.

This approach protects past highway investments and maximizes the economic benefits of each improvement. Particularly important is keeping the state's 2,165-mile interstate highway network in good condition. In Illinois, more than half of all goods transported over highways move on the interstate network, which is the third largest in the nation and includes three transcontinental routes.

While actual construction work on projects is carried out by private contractors, department employees perform planning and engineering work to prepare projects for construction. Department employees also perform ongoing maintenance work, including pothole repairs; roadside, bridge and drainage system maintenance; snow and ice removal; mowing; installation of traffic signs and repainting road markers.

Public Transportation

The department provides technical assistance and administers state and federal funding to 46 public transit systems throughout the state. This includes the three bus and rail transit systems under the Regional Transportation

Authority in northeastern Illinois, which carry an average of more than 550 million riders each year and comprise the second-largest transit network in the nation.

Funding administered by the department provides for capital, operating and technical assistance grants. Capital grants allow transit systems statewide to purchase new buses and rail cars, build new facilities, and rehabilitate and upgrade facilities and infrastructure. The department also administers funding for capital improvements that support and enhance the operation of public transit and alleviate congestion in urban areas. The department also assists non-profit and public agencies throughout the state in the purchase of paratransit vehicles equipped to serve the elderly and persons with disabilities.

Operating assistance grants administered by the department help fund public transit systems statewide. In downstate Illinois, the grants provide the major source of funding for public transit.

Technical assistance grants are critical in addressing new service and service expansion issues, as well as providing technical assistance for evaluating major capital project design issues.

Rail Transportation

With its 7,300 route-mile network, Illinois has the second-largest rail transportation system, which is the principal mode of transport for commodities such as coal and grain. Under Governor Ryan's Illinois FIRST program, additional funding has been provided for rail freight improvements, construction and station rehabilitation and for improving the signal system, track and equipment along the Chicago-St. Louis corridor.

Funding administered by the department provides both loans and grants for operating and capital projects. Under the Rail Freight program, capital assistance is provided in the form of low-interest loans to communities, railroads and shippers to preserve and improve rail freight service in Illinois.

In addition, Amtrak provides rail passenger service across the state, including 18 state-supported trains that serve more than 15 colleges and universities in Illinois. The primary goal of the department is to increase ridership, maximize revenues and optimize the state's investment in passenger rail operations. Capital grants for rail passenger service allow for station rehabilitation, while operating funds support daily Amtrak trains.

The Chicago-St. Louis corridor was designated as a high-speed rail corridor under the federal Intermodal Surface Transportation Efficiency Act. The department completed and circulated for public response its Draft Environmental Impact Statement in June 2000, with a final report to be completed in late 2001.

Traffic Safety

The department administers highway safety programs aimed at reducing the number and severity of motor vehicle crashes, fatalities, personal injuries and property damage. Programs include public information and education, enforcement in the areas of police traffic services, emergency medical services, alcohol countermeasures, traffic records and highway operational improvements.

A statewide crash data base developed by IDOT is used to help determine highway improvements and traffic safety programs. The department is the

273

The Illinois FIRST program has allowed IDOT to turn many more proposed improvements into reality, including more than 2,250 highway and bridge rehabilitation projects in Fiscal Year 2000 and 2,644 projects in Fiscal Year 2001.

lead agency in implementing the state's safety belt use law. The department also inspects the mechanical safety of large trucks, school buses and ambulances involving approximately 475,000 vehicles in 2000. Other safety activities include regulating the transportation of hazardous materials and enforcement of the Motor Carrier Safety Regulations. Beginning July 1, 2001, the department began conducting diesel emission inspections on registered vehicles weighing more than 16,000 pounds operated in Illinois within a nine-county area. Through four major universities, the department provides motorcycle rider training programs that have trained more than 153,000 persons in safe motorcycle practices.

ADMINISTRATIVE PERSONNEL

Kirk Brown .... *Secretary*
Joseph L. Banks .... *Assistant Secretary*
Robert Newbold .... *Deputy Secretary*
Hugh VanVoorst .... *Director, Division of Aeronautics*
Edward Gower .... *Director, Office of Chief Counsel*
Randy Vereen .... *Director, Office of Finance and Administration*
Jim Slifer .... *Director, Division of Highways*
Matt Davidson .... *Director, Office of Governmental Affairs*
Linda Wheeler .... *Director, Office of Planning and Programming*
Richard Adorjan .... *Director, Office of Public Affairs*
Stephen Schindel .... *Director, Division of Public Transportation*
Roger Sweet .... *Director, Division of Traffic Safety*

274

DEPARTMENT OF VETERANS' AFFAIRS

Springfield: 833 S. Spring St.; 62794
(217) 782-6641
Toll free 1-800-437-9824

Chicago: 100 W. Randolph
Ste. 4-650; 60601
(312) 814-2460

Fiscal Year 2002 Appropriation: $81.2 million

John W. Johnston
Director

The Department of Veterans' Affairs is comprised of the central office in Springfield, the Chicago administrative office, the Veterans' Services Division, the Illinois Veterans' Homes at Quincy, Manteno, LaSalle and Anna, and the State Approving Agency.

Through the Veterans' Services Division, the department assists Illinois veterans, their dependents and their survivors in applying for and continuing their eligibility for federal, state and local entitlements. Forty-three Veterans' Services offices are located throughout the state to allow access by veterans and their family members in need of information or assistance. Information is provided on benefits and resources available to veterans, including educational benefits, pension and compensation awards, health and hospital services, financial assistance programs, insurance and other programs of interest.

The department also maintains liaison with the U.S. Department of Veterans' Affairs and other federal and state agencies that provide programs for veterans. These include educational institutions, county officials, funeral directors and employment service personnel.

Veterans' Benefits

The department administers numerous awards and state grants to assist veterans with their financial responsibilities, physical disabilities and employment opportunities. These services include grants for specially adapted housing; awards and scholarships for primary, secondary and post-secondary education at many state schools, colleges and universities for veterans' dependents; bonus payments for wartime service for Illinois veterans or their families; free hunting and fishing licenses for disabled veterans as well as free camping permits for certain disabled veterans, and payment for setting a government headstone or marker for a deceased veteran. Evaluations of curricula, apprenticeship programs and varied training courses are effected by the staff of the State Approving Agency; approval allows eligible veterans to receive G.I. Bill payments. The department also maintains an honor roll of all veterans buried in Illinois.

Illinois Veterans' Homes

The department operates four skilled nursing homes throughout the state. The Illinois Veterans' Home at Quincy has served thousands of veterans of eight wars and conflicts, as well as their spouses, by providing residential and nursing care facilities. The home consists of 52 buildings spread over 210 acres. It has barber and beauty shops, a library, social service and recreational activities, and a post office, bank, store and coffee shop for the more than 600 resident Illinois veterans and their spouses, widows and widowers. The Quincy Veterans' Home is supported with state and federal funds, resident contributions and Medicare payments. Residents are required to pay a monthly charge for their care; however, inability to pay does not preclude admission to eligible veterans.

The Illinois Veterans' Home at Manteno has been in operation since April 1986. On 122 acres, there are four nursing-care structures housing 300 veterans and two ancillary buildings with dietary, therapy, radiology, pharmacy, social, commissary, banking and other quartered services. There also is a 12-bed transitional housing unit for homeless veterans on the campus.

The Illinois Veterans' Home at LaSalle sits on 4.63 acres at the northwest corner of O'Conor Avenue in the City of LaSalle. This 120-bed nursing facility, which opened in December 1990, provides veterans with a full spectrum of nursing care services, including social services and physical, recreational and occupational therapy.

The Illinois Veterans' Home at Anna, which opened in August 1994, consists of 50 nursing care beds plus 12 residential beds. The $3.9 million single-story facility provides medical and nursing care, apartment living, dietary, occupational and physical therapy, social services and recreational activities.

ADMINISTRATIVE PERSONNEL

John W. Johnston . . . . *Director*
George Cramer . . . . *Assistant Director*
Harold "Hal" Fritz . . . . *Deputy Director*
Dee Easley . . . . *Personnel Manager*
Ronald Frillman . . . . *Administrator, Quincy Veterans' Home*
Richard Bateman . . . . *Administrator, Manteno Veterans' Home*
James Arrington . . . . *Administrator, LaSalle Veterans' Home*
John Lippert . . . . *Administrator, Anna Veterans' Home*
Paul Taplin . . . . *Manager, State Grants and Awards*
Trudy Long . . . . *Fiscal Officer*
John O'Neill . . . . *Legislative Liaison*
Larry Motley . . . . *Veterans' Homes Coordinator*
Keith Votava . . . . *Administrator, State Approving Agency*
William Moran . . . . *Supervisor, Metro Veterans' Service Division*
Chet Connaway . . . . *Supervisor, Southern Veterans' Service Division*
Donald Frye . . . . *Supervisor, Central Veterans' Service Division*
Harry Sawyer, Jr. . . . . *Supervisor, Northern Veterans' Service Division*
Richard Wood . . . . *Supervisor, Western Veterans' Service Division*

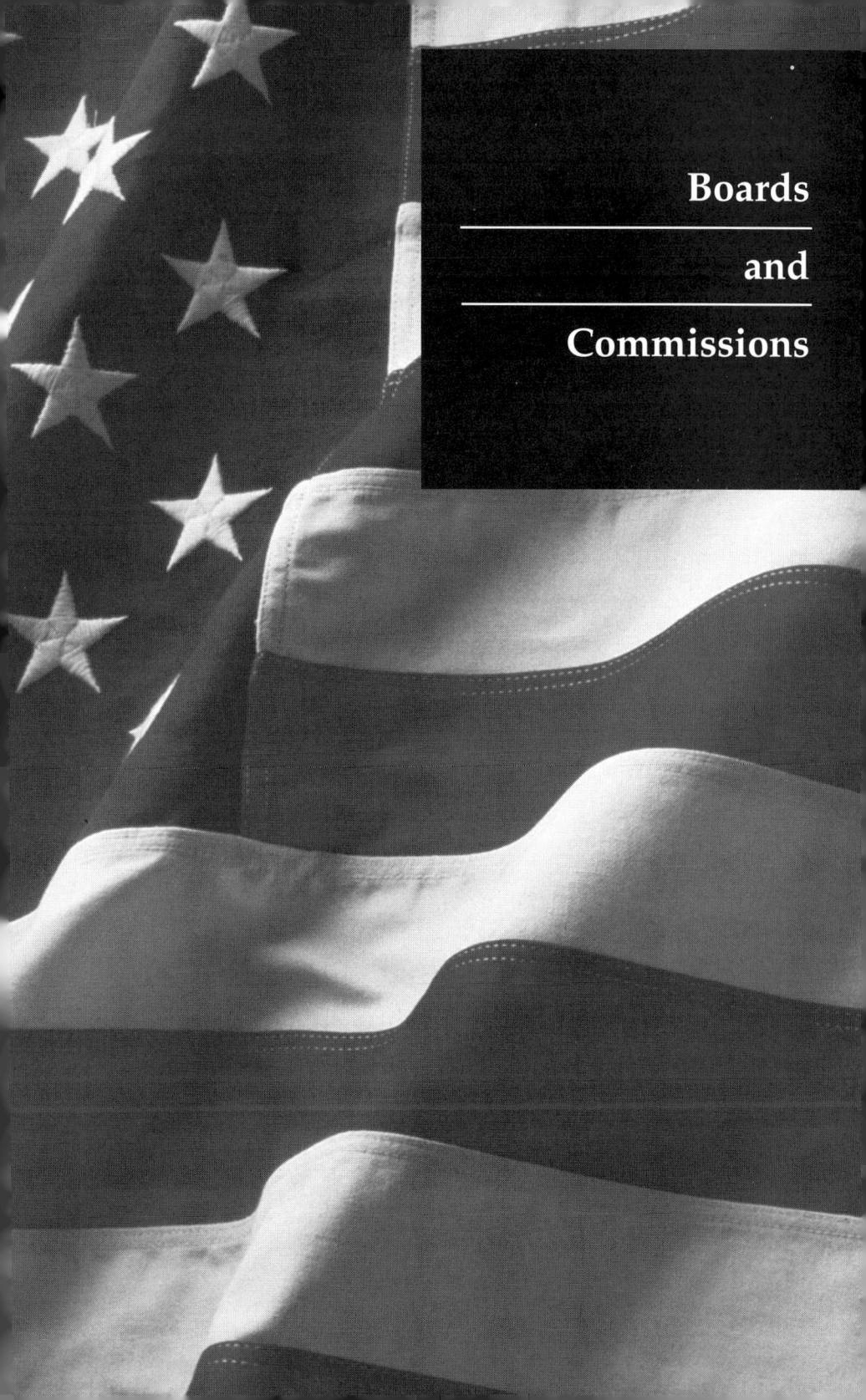

Boards
and
Commissions

BOARDS AND COMMISSIONS

ARTS COUNCIL, ILLINOIS — Shirley Madigan, *chairperson;*William Alldredge, Glenda Anstine, Ilene Antoniou, Ralph Arnold, Meta Berger, Virginia Bobins, Rosemarie Buntrock, J.P. Carney, Henry Chapman, Debra Detmers Fansler, John Flynn, Christina Gidwitz, Barbara Gold, Martin Janis, Hekmat Jha, Catheleen Kahn-Healey, Margaret Kenny, Judy Kjellander, Giacomo Leone, Averill Leviton, David Logan, Jeanne Randall Malkin, Marietta Marsh, Peggy Montes, Constance Mortell, Elaine Muchin, Roche Schulfer, Terry Scrogum, Smita Shah, Jean Shlofrock, Melanie Tomaszkiewicz, Abram Van Meter and Ed Ward, *members*; Rhoda Pierce, *executive director.*

*BANKS AND REAL ESTATE, OFFICE OF

*CAPITAL DEVELOPMENT BOARD

CIVIL SERVICE COMMISSION — George E. Richards, *chairperson*; Dan Fabrizio, John "Jack" Dorgan, Raymond Ewell, Barbara "Bobbie" Peterson, *members*; Bruce Finne, *executive director.*

*COMMERCE COMMISSION, ILLINOIS

*COMMISSION ON INTERGOVERNMENTAL COOPERATION

*COURT OF CLAIMS

CRIMINAL JUSTICE INFORMATION AUTHORITY, ILLINOIS — Peter B. Bensinger, *chairperson;* Albert Apa, Timothy Bukowski, Jane R. Buckwalter, Barbara Engel, Maureen Josh, John Millner, John Piland, State's Attorney Michael J. Waller, Attorney General Jim Ryan, Director of State Police Sam Nolen and Department of Corrections Director Donald Snyder, *members*; Robert P. Boehmer, *general counsel*; Candice Kane, *executive director.*

DEVELOPMENT FINANCE AUTHORITY, ILLINOIS — Michael Zavis, *chairperson;* George Beck, Martin R. Binder, Steven M. Cisco, Warren "Bo" Daniels, Jr., Howard Feldman, Peter Gidwitz, Howard Kaplan, John Koliopoulos, Peter O'Brien, Terrence M. O'Brien, Philip K. Rigsby, Ron Santo, Perry J. Snyderman and Ruth Vrdolyak, *members*; Patrick E. Rea, *executive director.*

DEVELOPMENTAL DISABILITIES, ILLINOIS PLANNING COUNCIL ON — Jill Garrett, *chairperson;* John Scott Aiello, Erik D. Austin, Ken Best, Diana Braun, Wanda Campbell, Susanne Carrescia, Colleen Dunigan, Rebecca Froman, Kevin Hall, Marilyn Hughes, Shawn Jeffers, Patrick Lee, John Leber, Gerald Maatman, Joseph Paul Meadours, Bill Peters, John Porter, Lester Pritchard and Brenda Yarnell, *members*; Sheila T. Romano, *executive director.*

*ECONOMIC AND FISCAL COMMISSION

ECONOMIC DEVELOPMENT BOARD, ILLINOIS — Hans Becherer, Diane Cullinan, Thomas Donovan, Donald Fites, Christopher Galvin, Sue Gin, Ross Glickman, Jack Greenberg, Merlin Karlock, John LaSage, Lynn Martin, John Miller, Mike Moran, Margarita Perez, James Reynolds, Jr., Christine Roche, Courtney Shea, Thomas Tunney, Cynthia Williams and Lucy "Jill" York, *members.*

*EDUCATION, ILLINOIS STATE BOARD OF

*ELECTIONS, STATE BOARD OF

FARM DEVELOPMENT AUTHORITY BOARD, ILLINOIS — Carolyn B. Stone, *chairperson*; Richard S. Williamson, Garry Niemeyer, Robert F. Nickel, Bernard T. Donovan, Jr., Gary E. Luth and Curtis Faber, *members.*

*FIRE MARSHAL, OFFICE OF THE ILLINOIS STATE

*See Index

GOVERNOR'S ETHICS COMMISSION — Roger H. Bickel, *chairperson;* James Donnewald, Nancy Easum, Thomas Lyons, Mark A. Novak, J. William Roberts and Philip J. Rock, *members.*

GUARDIANSHIP AND ADVOCACY COMMISSION — Susan Suter, *chairperson;* Chris DeAngelis, The Honorable Mary Flowers, The Honorable Todd Sieben, Betty Bollmeier, Michael Howie, Joseph Lassner, Ph.D., Joanne Perkins, Mary T. Reddick, Aaron M. Schmidt and Susan Tatnall, *members;* Gary E. Miller, *director.*

*HIGHER EDUCATION, ILLINOIS BOARD OF

HUMAN RIGHTS COMMISSION, ILLINOIS — Rose M. Jennings, *chairperson;* Eva Betka, Dominic DiFrisco, Marylee V. Freeman, Mary Jeanne Hallstrom, Sakhawat Hussain,Yvette Kanter, Spencer Leak, Sr., Girvena M. LeBlanc, James A. Maloof, Arabel Rosales, Daniel C. Sprehe and Isiah Thomas, *members;* Denise Brewer, *executive director.*

HUMANITIES COUNCIL, ILLINOIS — J. Paul Hunter, *chairperson;* Martha Belluschi, John Fascia, Katherine Glennon, Constance Mortell and Miriam R. Zayed, *members;* Kristina A. Valaitis, *executive director.*

*INDUSTRIAL COMMISSION, ILLINOIS

INVESTMENT, ILLINOIS STATE BOARD OF — Joseph P. Cacciatore, Peter Fasseas, John "Jack" Marco, Susan McKeever and Robert H. Newtson, *members;* Jane Paterson, *executive director.*

JUDICIAL INQUIRY BOARD — Rodney R. Gholson, Jill Landsberg, Lindsay Parkhurst, Christine Takada and William Sunderman, *members;* Kathy Twine, *executive director.*

LAW ENFORCEMENT TRAINING AND STANDARDS BOARD, ILLINOIS — Marilyn Sindles, *chairperson;* Steven R. Allendorf, *sheriff;* Jeffrey W. Doherty, *city manager;* James E. Kingston, *mayor;* Valerie L. Salmons, *city manager;* Gary J. Schira, *chief of police;* John H. Schlaf, *chief of police;* James A. Vazzi, *sheriff;* Eddie Adair, Robert J. Hogan and Ted J. Street, *members;* Thomas Jurkanin, *executive director.*

*LEGISLATIVE AUDIT COMMISSION

*LEGISLATIVE INFORMATION SYSTEM

*LEGISLATIVE REFERENCE BUREAU

*LEGISLATIVE RESEARCH UNIT

*LEGISLATIVE SPACE NEEDS COMMISSION

LIQUOR CONTROL COMMISSION, ILLINOIS — Don W. Adams , *chairperson;* Leonard L. Branson, Robert Hayes, James M. Hogan, Irving J. Koppel, Lilly Lopez and Myrna E. Pederson, *members;* Mark Bishop, *executive director.*

LOTTERY CONTROL BOARD — Hilder L. Garrison, James T. Hadley, Paul M. Tomazzoli and David A. Zaransky, *members.*

MEDICAL DISTRICT COMMISSION, ILLINOIS — Dr. Kenneth D. Schmidt, *chairperson;* William Cadigan, Abraham C. Morgan and John Partelow, *members;* Thomas E. Livingston, *executive director.*

*NATURAL RESOURCES, ADVISORY BOARD TO THE DEPARTMENT OF — Michael D. Kepple, *chairperson;* Victoria Cianciarulo, Harry C. Fitzgerald, George H. Fleischli, Arthur L. Janura, Thomas Mansfield, Constance Newport,

*See Index

279

ILLINOIS COMMERCE COMMISSION

Scott Wiseman
Executive Director

Springfield: 527 E. Capitol; 62794
(217) 785-7456

Chicago: 160 N. LaSalle St.; 60601
(312) 814-2841

More than a century ago, the first Illinois General Assembly pioneered the concept of state supervision and regulation of public utilities. In those days, grist mills, ferries, canals, toll bridges and turnpikes made up the bulk of public utilities.

The Illinois Commerce Commission, as structured today, was created by the Legislature in 1921 with passage of the Public Utilities Act. It is an independent body of five commissioners appointed to five-year terms by the Governor, with the advice and consent of the Senate. Under the law, no more than three commissioners may be of the same political party at the time of appointment. The Governor designates a chairman, and the commission employs an executive director who manages the agency's staff.

The commission has the following responsibilities:

- Assuring the citizens of Illinois safe, efficient and reliable service at reasonable prices from investor-owned public utilities.

- Enforcing registration and insurance compliance of motor carriers of property and tow trucks in Illinois.

Illinois Commerce Commission members are (left to right): Edward C. Hurley, Mary Frances Squires, Richard L. Mathias, Ruth K. Kretschmer and Terry S. Harvill.

281

- Ensuring public safety through the Grade Crossing Protection Fund and the inspection of railroads and natural gas pipelines within the state.

- Assisting in the development and implementation of local 911 emergency telephone systems throughout the state.

- Overseeing the distribution of telecommunication devices for the hearing impaired (TTY) and the dual party relay service, which allow hearing-impaired persons to communicate by telephone.

The commission also deals with broad national issues, including the financing of nuclear plant decommissioning, the impact of technological change on regulated firms, and competition in the telecommunications, electric and gas industries.

In all the issues that come before it, the commission's first concern is the convenience and needs of the people of Illinois. The commission holds hearings and conducts administrative investigations to ascertain the facts in a case.

In the absence of competition, government regulation, historically, was established to protect the consumer. Utility companies supplying the services are privately owned and must be allowed to earn enough on their investments to raise the large amounts of capital necessary to maintain service. The commission balances the needs of the utility and the cost to the individual consumer carefully.

The commission has an authorized head count of 340 employees, including a professional staff of attorneys, engineers, economists, accountants, policy analysts and consumer counselors. Staff responsibilities include analyzing and evaluating rate proposals, conducting hearings, inspecting for rail and gas safety, responding to consumer complaints, monitoring interstate and intrastate motor carriers for safety, fitness and insurance and promoting competition among utilities and other service providers as markets mature.

The commission receives its authority from the following legislation: Public Utilities Act; Illinois Commercial Transportation Law; Electric Supplier Act; Illinois Gas Pipeline Safety Act; 911 Emergency Telephone Act, and Commercial Relocation of Trespassing Vehicles Law.

STATE BOARD OF ELECTIONS

Springfield: 1020 S. Spring; 62704
(217) 782-4141

Chicago: 100 W. Randolph
Ste. 14-100; 60601
(312) 814-6440

Ronald D. Michaelson
Executive Director

The State Board of Elections has general supervision over the administration of registration and election laws throughout the state. The board's duties include receiving nominating papers and certificates of nomination, and determining the validity of petitions and the order in which names appear on the ballot. The board certifies to each county clerk the names of all candidates who have filed petitions with the board and who are to appear on the ballot. Returns from both primary and general elections are filed with the board, and a canvass is conducted before results are certified.

The board also administers the Campaign Financing Act, which covers the public's right to know certain financial information about individuals and groups involved in political campaigns. The board makes information available to the public continually as required by law, and conducts informational and educational programs that provide assistance in the interpretation of the law.

Members of the State Board of Elections are (seated): Elaine Roupas (left), *chairman*, and Wanda Rednour, *vice chairman*, and (standing, left to right): John R. Keith, David E. Murray, William M. McGuffage, Philip R. O'Connor, Albert S. Porter and Jesse Smart.

283

OFFICE OF BANKS AND REAL ESTATE

Springfield: 500 E. Monroe St.; 62701
(217) 782-3000

Chicago: 310 S. Michigan Ave.
Ste. 2130; 60604
(312) 793-3000

The Office of Banks and Real Estate was created in June 1996, when the Commissioner of Banks and Trust Companies and the Office of the Commissioner of Savings and Residential Finance merged. The agency has 301 employees with offices in Springfield and Chicago.

William A. Darr
Commissioner

The Bureau of Banks and Trust Companies supervises, regulates and examines 522 state-chartered banks with assets in excess of $115 billion, 30 foreign bank branches with assets in excess of $55 billion and 289 corporate fiduciaries with trust assets in excess of $1.8 trillion. The bureau licenses 45 foreign bank representative offices and certifies 116 foreign corporate fiduciaries. The bureau also examines and regulates data processing centers of state banks and electronic funds transfer networks and switches; registers sellers and distributors of checks and non-financial institution deployers of cash dispensing terminals, and licenses 218 pawnbrokers.

The Bureau of Real Estate Professions administers and enforces the Illinois Real Estate License Act of 2000, the Time Share Act, the Land Sales Registration Act of 1989, the Real Estate Appraiser Licensing Act and the Auction License Act. The bureau licenses more than 27,000 real estate brokers, 49,000 real estate salespeople, nearly 4,500 real estate appraisers and more than 1,500 auction licenses.

The Bureau of Residential Finance regulates and charters savings and loans and savings banks and regulates the residential mortgage banking industry. The bureau examines seven savings and loans and 50 savings banks with assets in excess of $7 billion, and licenses 1,244 mortgage brokers/bankers.

The Bureau of Administration provides internal support to the office. The Fiscal Division supports the office's financial operations, the Human Resources Division handles personnel and labor relations, and the Information Systems Division pioneers the use of new technologies while providing technical support.

ADMINISTRATIVE PERSONNEL

William A. Darr .... *Commissioner*
David S. Rodriguez .... *First Deputy Commissioner*
Patrick A. Brady .... *Deputy Commissioner*
Dan Karnatz .... *Deputy Commissioner*
Scott Clarke .... *Assistant Commissioner, Bureau of Banks and Trust Companies*
Norm Willoughby .... *Deputy Assistant Commissioner, Bureau of Real Estate Professions*
Jay Stevenson .... *Assistant Commissioner, Bureau of Residential Finance*
Robert Thompson .... *Assistant Commissioner, Bureau of Administration*
Dale Turner .... *General Counsel*
Alan Anderson .... *Legislative Liaison*
Brenda Jack .... *Executive Assistant to the Commissioner-Springfield*
Debra Niemann .... *Executive Assistant to the Commissioner-Chicago*

284

CAPITAL DEVELOPMENT BOARD

Ray Mota
Chairman

Kim Robinson
Executive Director

Springfield: 3rd Floor, Stratton Building; 62706
(217) 782-2864

Chicago: 100 W. Randolph, Ste. 14-600; 60601
(312) 814-6000

Carbondale: 150 Pleasant Hill Rd., Box 43; 62901
(618) 453-8232

Peru: 1222 Shooting Park Rd., Ste. 108; 61354
(815) 220-1360

As the construction management agency for State Government since 1972, the Capital Development Board (CDB) oversees the construction of new state facilities, such as prisons, college and university buildings, mental health hospitals and state parks. CDB also is responsible for renovation projects at 7,357 state buildings, with more than 90 million square feet of floor space.

CDB administers more than 2,000 active projects every year, with a total value of more than $3 billion. The board does not initiate projects but responds to capital improvement needs identified by other state agencies and governmental units and approved by the General Assembly and the Governor. Projects range in size and scope, from the new $143 million maximum-security prison at Thomson to construction of the $115 million Abraham Lincoln Presidential Library and Museum Complex in Springfield, to the renovation of a $75,000 salt storage facility for the Department of Transportation. CDB also works with the Board of Education to administer grants for the construction and renovation of schools. In renovating state buildings, CDB removes hazardous materials, such as asbestos and lead, replaces leaking underground storage tanks on state property and remodels buildings to accommodate persons with disabilities.

Established to better manage the state's capital improvement programs, CDB is guided by a seven-member, bipartisan board that deliberates matters of policy, approves the selection of design professionals through the 1991 Qualifications-Based Selection System and sets the direction for the agency. The executive director, selected by the board, manages the agency and its 167 employees.

Capital Development Board members are: Ray Mota, *chairman*; Dennis J. Gannon, George Fleischli, Joby H. Berman, Louis Jones and Michael N. Skoubis, *members*; and Kim Robinson, *executive director*.

ILLINOIS STATE FIRE MARSHAL

Springfield: 1035 Stevenson Dr.; 62703
(217) 785-0969

The Office of the State Fire Marshal coordinates the state's fire prevention, boiler and pressure vessel inspection and certification, firefighter training and fire investigation programs. The office has five operating divisions — Arson/Fire Investigation; Boiler and Pressure Vessel Safety; Fire Prevention; Petroleum and Chemical Safety, and Personnel Standards and Education — and two administrative divisions — Management Services, which includes data processing, fiscal and the Illinois National Fire Incident Reporting System (INFIRS), and Personnel.

Ernest E. Russell
State Fire Marshal

The State Fire Marshal investigates fires in which a fatality or great loss has occurred or for which staff assistance has been requested by local fire and law enforcement officials; inspects and certifies more than 100,000 industrial and commercial pressure vessels; inspects buildings in accordance with Illinois State statutes and Life Safety codes; promulgates rules and regulations for fireworks safety and for gasoline, volatile oils and liquefied petroleum gas safety; carries out the Underground Storage Tank Safety Program in cooperation with the Illinois EPA under state rules and regulations; administers the state mandate to protect the health, safety and welfare of the people of Illinois through the development of more professionally trained firefighters, and develops firefighter training for hazardous material incidents.

The Management Services Division processes INFIRS data; provides inspection information, billing and cash receipts data for boiler and pressure vessels; supervises word processing throughout the agency; records fire code violations for the Fire Prevention Division; computerizes claim reimbursement calculations for Personnel Standards and Education; supervises the agency's accounting, budgeting, billing, property control, facilities' management, purchasing and mail and messenger services, and collects and distributes information on all fires in Illinois as required by state law.

ADMINISTRATIVE PERSONNEL

Ernest E. Russell .... *State Fire Marshal*
Dan L. Williams .... *Deputy Director & Arson Investigation*
Jack Ahern .... *Deputy State Fire Marshal/Fire Prevention*
Sandy Hill .... *Personnel Standards and Education*
Melvin Smith .... *Petroleum and Chemical Safety*
Dave Douin .... *Manager, Boiler and Pressure Vessel Safety*
Kent Hill .... *Manager, Management Services*
John Pavlou .... *General Counsel*
Connie McCaslin .... *Human Resources*

INDUSTRIAL COMMISSION

Springfield: 701 S. Second St.; 62704
(217) 785-7087

Chicago: 100 W. Randolph St.
Ste. 8-200; 60601
(312) 814-6611

Peoria: 202 N.E. Madison Ave.
Ste. 201; 61602
(309) 671-3019

Rockford: 200 S. Wyman; 61101
(815) 987-7292

John W. Hallock, Jr.
Chairman

The Industrial Commission is the administrative court for Workers' Compensation, a no-fault system of benefits paid by employers to workers who experience job-related injuries or illnesses. When the Workers' Compensation Act first took effect in 1912, the civil courts handled the cases. In 1913, the legislature created a special administrative body, now known as the Industrial Commission, to handle the high volume of cases.

About 400,000 work-related injuries and illnesses occur annually in Illinois, costing $1.7 billion in benefits to employees. Benefits are paid for injuries or illnesses caused by an employee's work and are based on a worker's earnings. Employers pay for the benefits through insurance policies or by self-insurance. The commission evaluates employers who wish to self-insure and investigates those who fail to meet their legal requirement to cover their Workers' Compensation liabilities. Arbitration decisions may be appealed to a panel of three commissioners — one who represents the employer, one who represents the employee and one who is not identified with either. Cases may be appealed to the Circuit Court, Illinois Appellate Court and the Illinois Supreme Court.

The seven members of the Industrial Commission are appointed to four-year terms by the Governor, with consent of the Senate. The chairman serves as the chief executive officer of the commission. Members of the Industrial Commission are: John W. Hallock, Jr., *chairman*; Richard Gilgis, Jacqueline A. Kinnaman, Robert A. Madigan, Barbara A. Sherman, Diane Dickett Smart and Douglas F. Stevenson, *commissioners*.

ADMINISTRATIVE PERSONNEL

John W. Hallock, Jr. ....*Chairman*
Robert M. Harris .... *Executive Assistant to the Chairman*
Kathryn Kelley .... *Legal Counsel*
Charles Kusar .... *Fiscal Officer*
Janice Montoya.. *Manager, Operations*
Dirk May ....*Legislative Liaison*
Rebecca Loredo Paz .... *Manager, Human Resources*
Susan Piha .... *Manager, Research and Education*
Paul Rink.. *Associate Legal Counsel*
Maria Sarli-Dehlin .... *Manager, Self-Insurance*
Terry W. Spurlin .... *Manager, MIS*

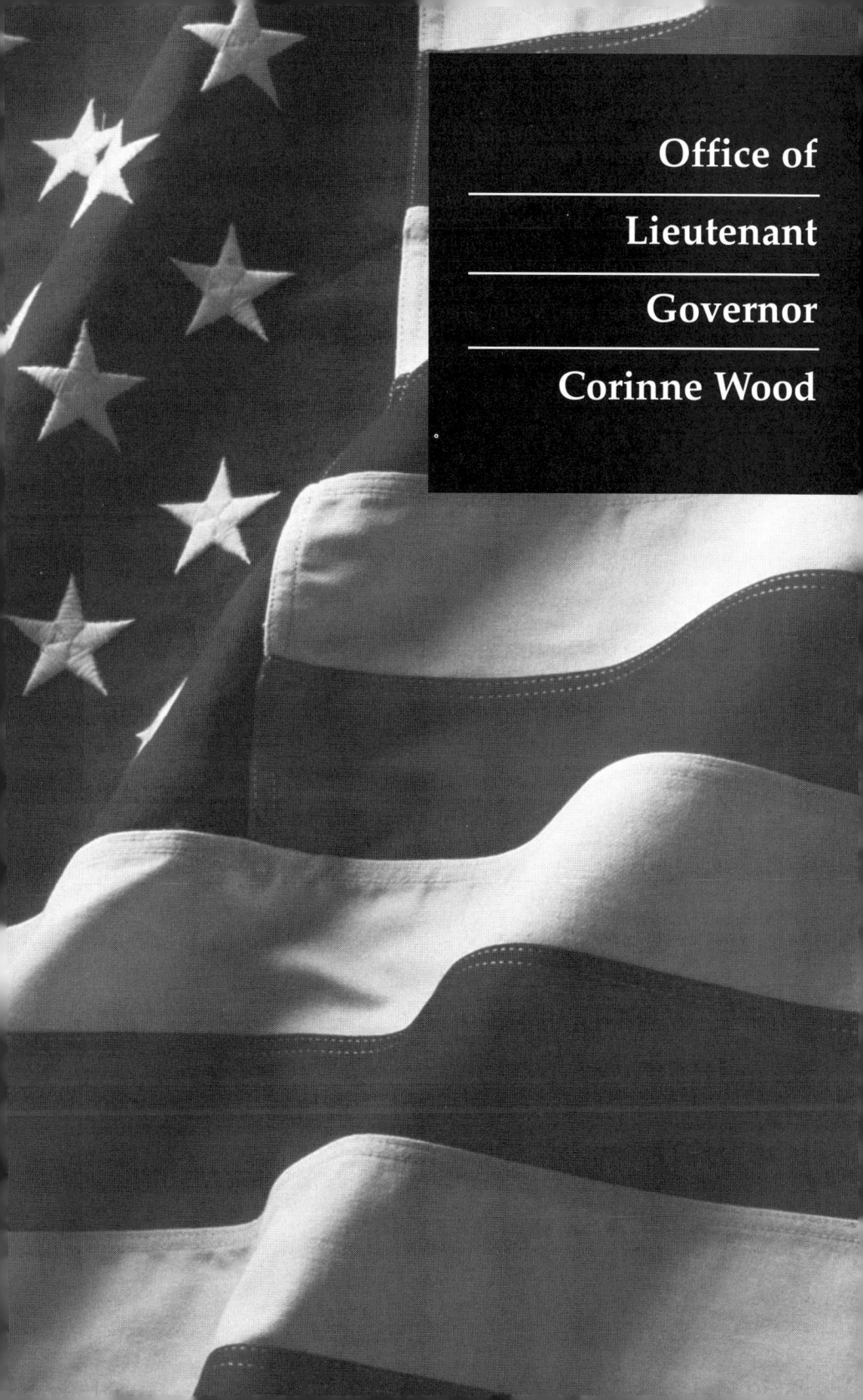

Office of

Lieutenant

Governor

Corinne Wood

OFFICE OF THE LIEUTENANT GOVERNOR

Through Lieutenant Governor Corinne Wood's leadership, the office has played a key role in several state policy areas, including women's health, rural affairs, downtown redevelopment, conservation of natural resources and children and family issues.

Women's Health Illinois

It is estimated that more than 75 percent of health care decisions are made by the female member of the household. Often, women must manage the health care needs of their children, spouse and even an elderly parent. As a breast cancer survivor, Lt. Governor Wood understands the importance of making the right health care decisions and has developed a program to provide women and families with the information they need to be healthy, safe and strong.

As chair of the Women's Health Illinois Interagency Cabinet, Lt. Governor Wood leads Women's Health Illinois, a program to better coordinate more than 60 state programs impacting women's health and the well-being of their families. To date, Wood has expanded the Illinois Breast and Cervical Cancer Screening Program to all 102 counties in the state, tripled funding for the state's Office of Women's Health, secured passage of legislation requiring insurance companies to cover clinical cancer trials, and secured passage of federal and state legislation to include treatment funding for women who are diagnosed under the Illinois Breast and Cervical Cancer Program. She also oversees the Penny Severns Breast and Cervical Cancer Research Fund, which has become the state's leading tax checkoff fund, and conducts public education campaigns on breast cancer awareness, heart health and osteoporosis.

Illinois River Coordinating Council

About 90 percent of Illinois' population lives in the 55-county Illinois River watershed. As chair of the Illinois River Coordinating Council, Lt. Governor Wood works with communities to improve water quality, enhance wildlife habitat and encourage environmentally sound recreational opportunities throughout the watershed.

As a breast cancer survivor and chair of Women's Health Illinois, Lt. Governor Corinne Wood is the state's leading spokesperson for women's health.

290

As chair of the Illinois River Coordinating Council, Lt. Governor Wood leads clean-up efforts on the Illinois River during Illinois River Sweep 2000.

The council includes citizen members, state agency representatives and ex officio representation from federal agencies. Its primary thrust is to implement the Integrated Management Plan for the Illinois River. The council works with community-based public, private and not-for-profit entities to make progress on those recommendations. It also monitors the state's progress in watershed conservation and looks for opportunities for improvement.

The council was instrumental in developing Illinois Rivers 2020, a $2.5 billion federal/state initiative to restore the Illinois River watershed. The program received a $100 million authorization from Congress for its first three years and a $5.4 million state appropriation in 2001.

Illinois Main Street Council

Established by executive order in 2000, the Illinois Main Street Council, chaired by Lt. Governor Wood, is responsible for reviewing and recommending new Main Street communities, approving and awarding the Lt. Governor's Awards of Excellence in Downtown Revitalization, and acting as a liaison and advocate for Main Street communities within State Government.

Originally created in 1993, the Illinois Main Street program works to preserve our downtown areas and enhance business opportunities in our communities. Based on a national model, the program provides training and technical assistance to participating communities through educational workshops and on-site consultation. Design services are available through a cooperative agreement with the Illinois Historic Preservation Agency. The program is closely linked with a variety of services provided by the Illinois Department of Commerce and Community Affairs, where it is housed.

Since its inception, the program has resulted in $245 million in downtown reinvestment and has expanded from nine to 55 communities. Key goals of the program are to provide new jobs and business opportunities, renew the historic appearance of downtown areas, promote downtown business and recreational opportunities and restore a strong sense of community in villages and cities across the state.

Governor's Rural Affairs Council

Lt. Governor Wood chairs the Governor's Rural Affairs Council, made up of 19 state agencies that deal with rural development efforts. Created in 1986, the council is designed to strengthen the rural economy, improve rural education and human services opportunities and support efforts of local government. The council works to better coordinate the activities of these state agencies to ensure the needs of rural Illinois are being addressed.

With the support of council members, Wood has assisted in the development of a statewide plan to support the 74 rural counties in Illinois. The plan includes better coordination of state transportation services, utilizing technology to improve access to health care, increasing job training programs and assisting rural regions in business attraction and retention efforts. Working with local leaders, the council has increased access to dental care and assisted in job training programs in Southern Illinois, increased marketing for business attraction in 24 rural counties and provided training materials and education equipment for youth in rural Illinois.

Illinois Rural Bond Bank

Chaired by Lt. Governor Wood, the Illinois Rural Bond Bank provides local governments with low-cost capital for infrastructure and other public improvement projects. It also helps local governments raise working cash and refinance existing debt.

Communities with relatively small financing needs, little or no credit history or a lack of financing expertise are effectively prohibited from issuing bonds on their own behalf in the municipal bond market. Often, there is little investor interest, the costs are burdensome and the process is too complex. Teaming up with the Rural Bond Bank helps communities overcome these obstacles and obtain capital at reduced interest rates and lower financing costs. The bank also provides communities with capital for equipment purchases through lease financing and short-term construction capital for U.S. Department of Agriculture Rural Development borrowers.

Lt. Governor Wood promotes new export markets for Illinois agricultural products in her role as chair of the Governor's Rural Affairs Council.

The municipal bond market is the primary source of capital for Rural Bond Bank programs. The bank sells its bonds in the market and lends the proceeds to participating local governments. The bank then retires its debt with the principal and interest payments it receives from local government loans. The bonds are backed by the moral obligation of the state, and the interest on the bonds is exempt from state and federal taxes, lowering overall borrowing rates. The bank also can pool a number of small financing needs into one large bond issue, providing additional savings by spreading the costs of issuance among participating local governments.

Over the past 10 years, the Illinois Rural Bond Bank has helped communities build new water systems, improve sewer systems, purchase new fire protection equipment and repair school buildings.

Governor's Commission on the Status of Women

Despite their increased presence in the American workforce, women continue to make about one-fourth less than men in comparable jobs. As honorary chair, Lt. Governor Wood works with the 23-member commission to identify and remove barriers to equality for Illinois women. The commission's focus is on improving women's economic opportunities by working with lawmakers, government agencies, the business community and other organizations.

Children and Family Leadership Subcabinet

Supporting families who are taking care of young children and our elderly is becoming the most challenging public policy issue facing Illinois. As chair of the Children and Family Leadership Subcabinet, Lt. Governor Wood convened this board to advise the administration on policies regarding children and families issues, research possible solutions to the problems these issues pose and develop administrative and legislative strategies to address these issues. The subcabinet consists of representatives from private industry, community-based human services providers, faith-based organizations, child advocates and advocates for seniors.

The subcabinet issued its first report in February 2001. The report outlined recommendations to assist in the coordination and evaluation of youth programs; to promote training, resources and assistance for the caregivers of the elderly; to assist businesses in becoming more family-friendly and responding to the needs of working parents, and to help State Government work more effectively with private sector partners.

Under Wood's leadership, legislation was passed in 2001 to create the Family-Friendly Workplace Task Force to address many of the issues facing today's working families.

Scott's Law

At the request of the brother of slain Chicago firefighter Lt. Scott Gillen and the Chicago Fire Commissioner, Lt. Governor Wood led an effort to protect emergency workers on the job. In cooperation with more than 15 state and local organizations, she worked to ensure passage of Scott's Law in 2001, which increases penalties for drivers who fail to yield to emergency vehicles or who cause accidents or injury to personnel assisting at emergency scenes.

Lieutenant Governor's Staff Members

Tom Hughes
Chief of Staff

Chris Hensley
Deputy Chief of Staff

Lori Williams
Director of Policy

Suzanne Baase
Senior Policy Executive

Jeff Fulgenzi
Executive Director
Rural Affairs

Cris Cray
Director
Legislative Affairs

ADMINISTRATIVE PERSONNEL

Jeff Fulgenzi .... *Executive Director, Rural Affairs*
Don Barber .... *Associate Director, Rural Affairs*
Susan Barfield-Roop .... *Senior Policy Advisor*
Susan Vespa-Stacey .... *Senior Advisor to the Lieutenant Governor*
Shon McCray .... *Senior Assistant to the Lieutenant Governor*
Joe Calomino .... *Director, Local Government Affairs*
Saffiya Shillo .... *Director, Ethnic Affairs*
Eric Hawkinson .... *Information & Technology*
Cris Cray .... *Director, Legislative Affairs*
Barbara Smith .... *Executive Director, Springfield Office*
Chrissy Tarpey .... *Executive Assistant to the Lieutenant Governor*
Jenny Carrell .... *Scheduling*
Leslie Barrow .... *Chief Fiscal Officer*

294

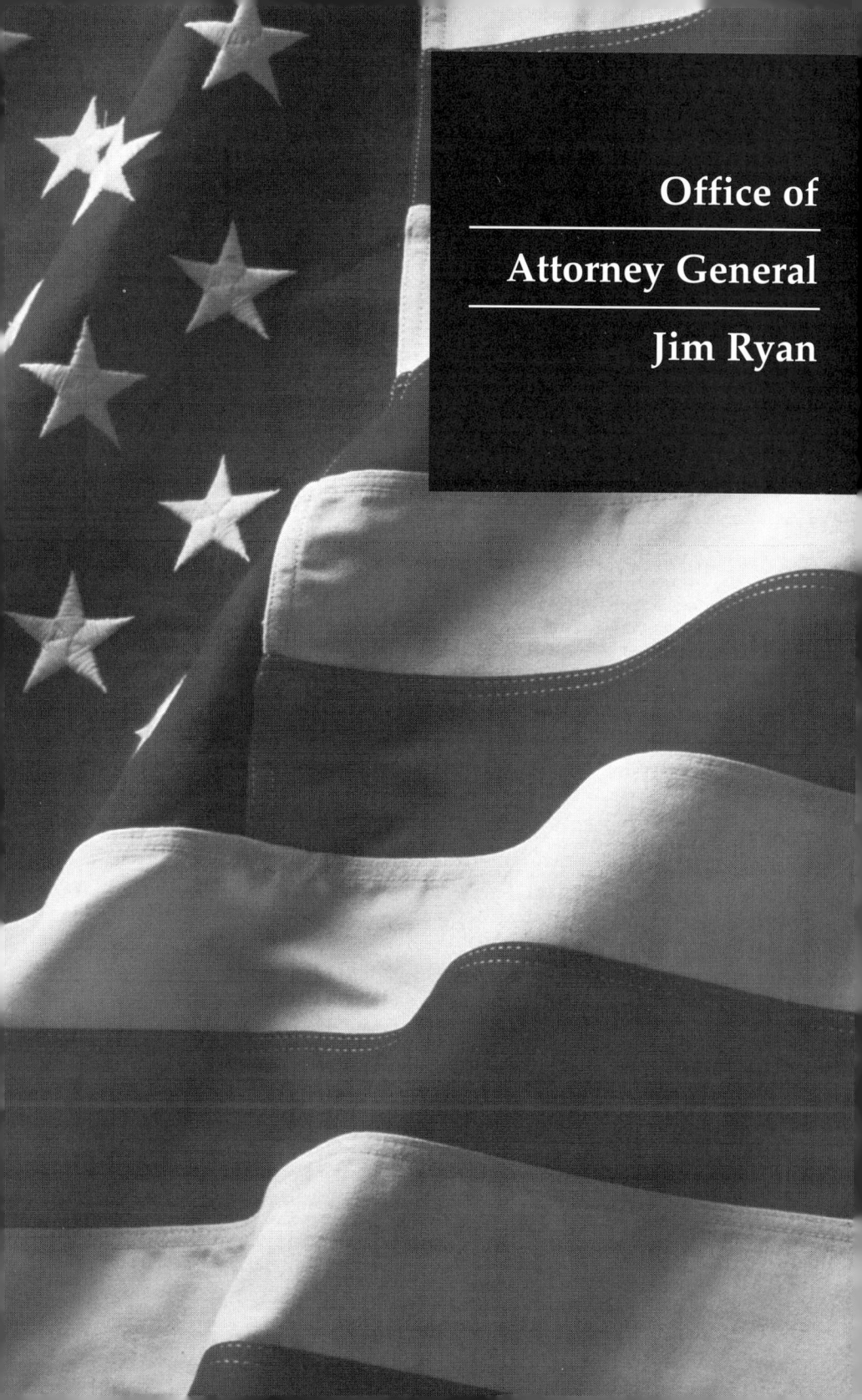

Office of

Attorney General

Jim Ryan

OFFICE OF THE ATTORNEY GENERAL

The Attorney General is the state's chief legal officer as established by the Illinois Constitution. Charged with this responsibility, the Attorney General directs a broad range of services dedicated to protecting and assisting Illinois citizens.

As Illinois' chief law enforcement official, Attorney General Jim Ryan leads the statewide fight against crime and violence. The Office of the Attorney General also assists local State's Attorneys in the prosecution of major crimes, provides legal representation to all elected state officials as well as the departments and agencies of State Government, and guards the interests of the people of Illinois.

Fighting Crime

Ryan drafted legislation to impose harsher sentences on those who commit violent crimes in Illinois. Under the state's truth-in-sentencing law, parole is eliminated for first-degree murderers, and other violent offenders must serve at least 85 percent of their sentenced terms. Additionally, Ryan marshaled bills through the Legislature that impose tougher punishment for murderers of children, increase penalties for child abuse offenders and mandate jail time for adults attempting to recruit gang members.

In an effort to put sophisticated criminal operations out of business, the Attorney General heads the Statewide Grand Jury, which indicts drug dealers and gun runners whose operations cross county lines. In 1997, legislation was passed to establish a second statewide grand jury downstate so prosecutors can go to Springfield, as well as Chicago, to battle drugs, gangs and gun runners in the courts. Later, the Chicago grand jury was moved to Kane County to bring the charging entity even closer to where most cases are brought.

Attorney General Jim Ryan announces development of a protocol for police and prosecutors to follow when dealing with friends and relatives of missing or murdered children.

Attorney General Ryan meets with students in Carbondale during a Safe To Learn hearing to solicit public input on how to make our schools safer.

Former Governor Edgar appointed Attorney General Ryan as chairman of the Governor's Commission on Gangs in 1995 to address the most serious crime threat facing the state. After 16 public hearings, the commission proposed a series of legislative recommendations and other initiatives to help combat the growing gang menace. Many of the proposals have been put into place, including new laws providing tougher penalties for gang-related crimes, offering gang witness protection from intimidation and implementing a system to track guns discovered in Illinois schools. A Gang Crime Prevention Center also was established to assist communities and law enforcement agencies mobilize against gangs.

The Attorney General convened a statewide summit on the emerging problem of "date rape drugs," and a task force produced a comprehensive report distributed to colleges, universities and law enforcement leaders giving them new tools to use in fighting these deadly drugs.

During the spring 2001 legislative session, the Illinois General Assembly enacted Attorney General Ryan's reforms of the state's Firearm Owners Identification Card (FOID) statute. The new legislation bolsters enforcement of existing laws prohibiting felons from buying or possessing firearms. It also provides greater oversight of the card application process and tightens the felony exemption. The measure was widely hailed and won widespread bipartisan support in the legislature.

Public Interest

The Attorney General won the largest public settlement ever in Illinois when the tobacco industry agreed in 1998 to pay the state $9.1 billion over 25 years. Attorney General Ryan filed suit in 1996 against the tobacco industry to stop cigarette companies from marketing to children, require the industry to tell consumers the whole truth about tobacco and reimburse Illinois taxpayers the billions of dollars paid to cover the cost of tobacco-related illnesses. The

Attorney General has strongly urged that settlement money be earmarked for anti-tobacco education programs and for programs that help children.

Helping Crime Victims

The Office of the Attorney General administers two major programs that benefit crime victims. Under the Violent Crime Victims Assistance Program, grants are distributed by the Attorney General to help relieve the devastating effects of violence to victims and their families. Money to fund the program comes from fines imposed on criminals and traffic offenders throughout the state, not tax dollars. Hundreds of public and non-profit organizations providing victim advocacy receive grants from the office.

In 2000 and 2001, Attorney General Ryan distributed more than $12 million to 258 social service and government agencies and individuals throughout the state to aid, comfort and counsel victims of violent crimes.

Additionally, the Attorney General administers the Illinois Violent Crime Victims Compensation Program. Under the program, victims of violent crimes or their families may directly receive up to $27,000 for expenses not reimbursed by other sources.

Preserving the Environment

Since taking office, Ryan has aggressively attacked the state's largest and most enduring environmental problems. He created the Environmental Crimes Bureau to prosecute criminal violations of the Environmental Protection Act, ensuring that those who intentionally and blatantly pollute Illinois' environment are held responsible for their criminal conduct.

Attorney General Ryan also has enjoined the dangerous operations of an Illinois oil refinery, battled irresponsible corporations over the disposal of toxic and radioactive wastes, and indicted numerous violators of Illinois' environmental laws. The central commitment in all such actions is that polluters, not taxpayers, pay the cost of environmental clean-up.

The Attorney General explains a program aimed at curbing smoking by teenagers.

Attorney General Ryan visits a Neighborhood Resource Center in Rockford, an initiative of the Governor's Commission on Gangs that Ryan chaired.

Protecting Consumers

The Attorney General serves as the chief consumer protection official in Illinois, handling about 28,000 complaints annually. Nearly half of the complaints involve motor vehicles and home repair fraud.

The Consumer Protection Division protects consumers and businesses victimized by fraud, deception or unfair competition. Attorney General Ryan has been vigorous in his fight against the emerging menace of telecommunications fraud. His office has instituted lawsuits against companies involved in the unauthorized switching of consumers' long-distance telephone service carriers without their prior consent. Ryan sued a major online service to force a settlement requiring it to live up to its promise of guaranteeing access to its subscribers. A 1997 law authored by the Attorney General created the Automotive Repair Act, requiring auto repair facilities and dealers to fully disclose all information on repairs and warranties.

Law Enforcement Leadership

The Office of the Attorney General lends the assistance of its experienced attorneys to local prosecutors on some of the most complex and difficult criminal trials in the state, ranging from murder trials to financial misconduct cases and drug investigations.

The Attorney General also represents the state in criminal appeals and has successfully petitioned the Illinois Supreme Court to uphold numerous death penalty sentences for some of the state's most heinous killers.

Advocacy

Advocacy on behalf of the people is one of the most important functions of the Attorney General's office. In addition to his commitment to advocacy on behalf of abused women and children, Attorney General Ryan has provided advocacy legal assistance in the implementation of the Americans With Disabilities Act and has investigated allegations of discrimination toward individuals with disabilities. The Office of the Attorney General also extends its services to Illinois veterans.

Protecting Children

Attorney General Ryan authored the Sexual Violent Persons Act, which allows authorities to keep sexually dangerous persons civilly confined once their prison terms are up if it can be determined that they remain dangerous. Already, a number of individuals judged to be threats to society remain institutionalized so they can continue receiving treatment for their disorders.

Ryan also authored a series of bills aimed at reducing school violence. The measures, providing funds to help school districts implement their own safety plans and stiffening penalties for violent acts committed on school property, emanated from a statewide summit of school and law enforcement personnel.

The Attorney General also has channeled thousands of dollars in discretionary funds to assist child advocacy centers in the state. Ryan set up the first such center when he was a county prosecutor and has supported them since as a way to more humanely treat child abuse victims.

In early 2000, Attorney General Ryan launched a campaign focusing nationwide attention on ultra-violent video games, encouraging manufacturers and retailers to uphold their own rating systems. As a result, seven major national retailers have either stopped selling ultra-violent video games or developed "carding" policies to avoid selling them to young people.

Attorney General Ryan talks with students at a Bloomington Early Intervention program, which was developed by the Governor's Commission on Gangs to work with young people at an early age before they consider joining gangs.

Attorney General's Staff Members

Richard M. Stock
Chief of Staff

Carole R. Doris
*Chief Deputy Attorney
General*

John Pearman
*Deputy Chief of Staff
Policy & Legislative
Affairs*

Ed Ludwig
*Deputy Chief of Staff
Administration*

Joel Bertocchi
Solicitor General

Roger Flahaven
*Deputy Attorney General
Civil Litigation*

John Farrell
*Deputy Attorney General
Criminal Justice*

Mardyth Pollard
*Deputy Attorney General
Springfield & Regional
Coordination*

ADMINISTRATIVE PERSONNEL

Shawn Denney .... *Senior Counsel to the Attorney General*
Keith Letsche .... *Counsel to the Attorney General*
Dan Curry .... *Press Secretary*
Deborah Ahlstrand .... *Chief, Civil Appeals Division*
William Browers .... *Chief, Criminal Appeals Division*
Daniel Callahan .... *Chief, Investigations Division*
Matthew Dunn .... *Chief, Environmental & Asbestos Litigation Division*
Patricia Kelly .... *Chief, Consumer Protection Division*
Doug Simpson .... *Chief, Criminal Enforcement Division*
Norma Medina .... *Chief, Operations & Administrative Services Division*
Kathleen Flahaven .... *Chief, Government Representation Division*
Don Sampen .... *Chief, Public Interest Division*
William Franklin .... *Chief Financial Officer*

.

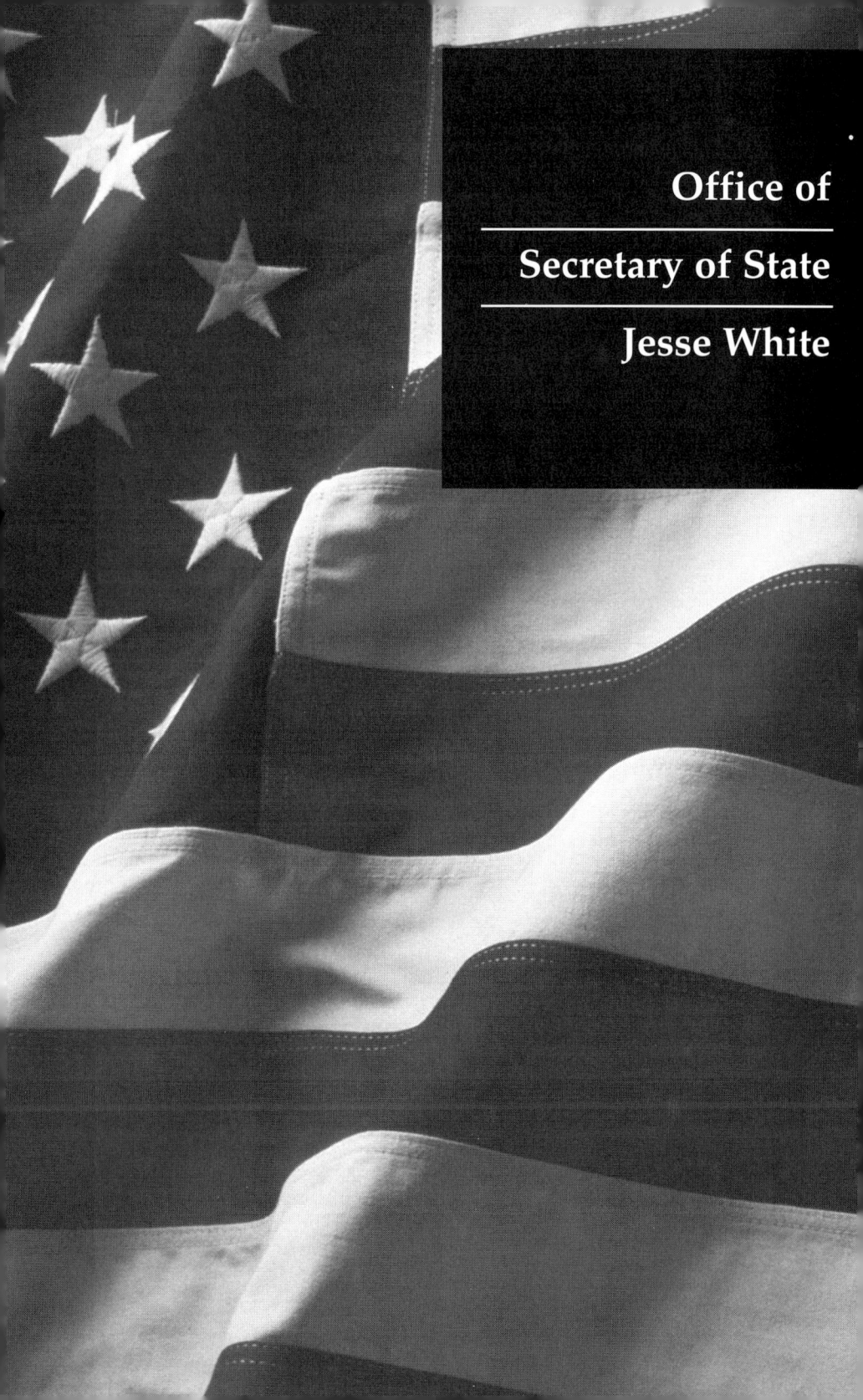

Office of

Secretary of State

Jesse White

OFFICE OF THE SECRETARY OF STATE

The second-largest constitutional office — the Office of the Secretary of State — is visited by more Illinois residents than any other in State Government. The office generates more revenue than all but two other state agencies, raising about $983 million a year for the state highway construction fund.

The Secretary of State manages one of the largest computer databases in Illinois, keeping track of more than 8.5 million drivers and 11 million vehicles, nearly 385,000 corporations and about 146,000 people and companies registered to sell securities.

The office also is an important tool for educating citizens about issues that affect their everyday lives, including anti-drunk driving, traffic safety, school bus safety, securities fraud, literacy and organ donation.

The office's functions are described in the Illinois Constitution, mainly addressing the Secretary of State's duty to maintain official state records and the state seal. However, law and tradition have assigned many additional responsibilities to the office, which has one of the largest and most diverse collections of responsibilities of any of its counterparts nationwide. These duties

Secretary of State Jesse White announced in July 2001 that more than 640,000 notices for new-design license plates had been mailed to Illinois motorists with vehicle registrations expiring in August. The announcement marked the beginning of the one-year replating cycle for the estimated 8.5 million passenger vehicles in Illinois.

are divided among 21 departments employing about 3,600 people, whose responsibilities range from maintaining the 28 buildings in the Capitol Complex to overseeing the state's network of libraries to preserving some of the state's most precious historical documents.

Still, to many Illinoisans, the Secretary of State's office is the place to go for a new driver's license or license plates, and about 60 percent of the office's annual resources are devoted to providing those two services.

Secretary of State Jesse White testifies before the Senate Judiciary Committee for his DUI legislative package during the spring 2001 legislative session. Seated with White is State Sen. Debbie Halvorson, sponsor of the legislation, which was passed and signed into law in August 2001.

The Secretary of State oversees 136 Driver Services facilities statewide, including 116 full-time facilities and 20 part-time facilities in rural Illinois.

During his second year in office, Secretary of State Jesse White successfully laid the groundwork for the most ambitious replating effort in Illinois history. As part of the intricate logistical preparations, the office introduced cutting-edge automation to the license plate order and distribution process. For the first time, license plate registration records can be updated within minutes, instead of days or months. The state's primary plate manufacturer is using digital press technology — the first in the nation — combined with electronic ordering. These two improvements will ensure that all Illinois passenger vehicles get replated within a one-year time frame that began in August 2001. The new plate design, featuring the likeness of Abraham Lincoln and larger, bolder lettering, was chosen by the people of Illinois during a statewide contest in summer 1999.

Secretary White is taking advantage of new technology to improve customer service. Beginning in July 2001, the office launched its online vehicle registration renewal option. With a renewal notice and an accepted credit card, millions of motorists are expected to renew their vehicle registrations from the comfort of their homes or businesses.

Under White's leadership, the state is cracking down on the fraudulent use of parking placards and license plates for persons with disabilities. In June 2000, he established the ACCESS Committee to review and make recommendations on improving the Secretary of State's Parking Program for Persons with Disabilities. Using the committee's recommendations as a blueprint, White pushed for and passed legislation to streamline services by creating a new section in his office to handle only disability plates and placards. The legislation also set stricter eligibility requirements and usage guidelines for obtaining special parking privileges. Three new parking placards also were designed with special features that make them more difficult to duplicate or forge.

The office's role in licensing motorists makes the Secretary of State one of Illinois' chief advocates for traffic safety. In the interest of public safety, White began his term by implementing a new program, "Highway Safety 2000." The work of his Highway Safety 2000 Advisory Panel led to 15 legislative changes in White's office — several of them related to commercial driver's licenses — that will improve safety on Illinois roads. In spring 2001, White's office installed new automated examination devices in several Driver Services facilities to help reduce cheating on exams by driver's license applicants, including those applying for a commercial driver's license.

White has taken a leadership role in addressing the problem of hard-core DUI offenders. In summer 2001, with the support of an unprecedented array of interest groups, White's DUI legislative package was passed and signed into law. The measure sets new mandatory penalties for offenders who register at more than twice the illegal blood-alcohol content (.16 or over) and those caught driving drunk with a child in the vehicle. The law also expands the use of ignition interlock devices to combat impaired driving and increases penalties for persons who habitually drive with a suspended or revoked driver's license.

Driver Services facilities are an important link in registering potential organ/tissue donors in the state. When Chicago Bears Hall of Famer Walter Payton announced his illness in early 1999 and began promoting organ donation, people signed up at a banner rate in Illinois, as well as nationally. Illinois now boasts the largest state registry in the country, and its public awareness program is cited as a model for the nation. Illinois currently has more than 5 million donors in its registry. White, whose sister is the recipient of an organ transplant, is a strong proponent of the program.

Illinois' Secretary of State also serves as State Librarian. In that capacity, White oversees the Illinois State Library in Springfield, which has a collection of more than 5 million items and serves as the primary information source for State Government officials and employees. As one of the nation's leaders in library development, the State Library administers more than $70 million in grants annually to the state's 4,000 public, academic, school and special libraries for construction, technology, materials and programming to meet the informational needs of Illinois citizens.

As State Librarian, White established a unique mentoring program for young people called "Project Next Generation." The program is the first of its kind to be administered through the public library system. Through a mix of state-of-the-art technology experiences and life skills enhancement, mentors provide junior high-age students a solid academic and social support system.

White also chairs the Illinois Literacy Council and oversees an $8.4 million literacy grant program. He has been instrumental in his work to involve the private sector in funding for literacy efforts. The Illinois Literacy Foundation and White have worked together to create greater awareness for family literacy programs. The office also implemented a summer reading program for families in honor of the late State Senator Penny Severns of Decatur.

ACCOUNTING REVENUE

Glenna White Jones
Director

The Department of Accounting Revenue receives and deposits all revenue collected by the Office of the Secretary of State into funds designated by statute. In Fiscal Year 2000, the department collected more than $1.3 billion — the third-largest source of income for the State of Illinois. Additionally, the department oversees all aspects of money management associated with revenue collections, including development of payment options and new technologies to make services more convenient and accessible to the public; providing bookkeeping and auditing services for all Secretary of State departments; processing refunds; collecting on checks returned for insufficient funds, and analyzing revenue and sales data for comprehensive office-wide program planning.

Accounting Revenue field staff conducts audits on Illinois-based interstate trucking companies registered under the International Registration Plan (IRP), more than 500 remitters who issue Temporary Registration Permits (TRPs), more than 2,500 banks and currency exchanges participating in the Secretary of State's Over-the-Counter Sticker Sales Program (OTC) and the collection of nearly 11,000 insufficient fund accounts.

Under the IRP program, about 1,800 to 2,000 new IRP registrants file annually. Audits are conducted on about 3,500 IRP registrants on a three-year cycle. More emphasis is being placed on increasing the number of audits as well as those out-of-state registrants, and timely collection of monies for all IRP audits presently being performed. Through restructuring, the department is intensifying its efforts to reduce the present level of accounts receivable by 50 percent through increased collections and timely write-offs.

The department continues to vigorously monitor TRPs against abuse or misuse. As a result of working closely with law enforcement, community groups and other Secretary of State departments, the office put into place a new TRP system, effective September 2001. The new program, which includes redesigned TRPs, will increase the accountability of issuing agents, improve efficiency in the department and reduce the fraudulent use of the permits.

The OTC program allows federal- and state-chartered banks, savings and loans, credit unions, armored carriers and any currency exchange to act as an agent of the Secretary of State in the distribution of license plate stickers.

The department's Returned Check Division continues to be a leader in the percentage of bad checks it collects. During Fiscal Year 2000, more than $2 million in insufficient checks was collected, resulting in a collection rate of nearly 70 percent.

Accounting Revenue strives to aid in the development of efficient money management systems; therefore increasing the level of services to the public and lowering processing costs to the agency while maximizing revenue for the State of Illinois.

ADMINISTRATIVE HEARINGS

The Department of Administrative Hearings conducts the majority of hearings under the jurisdiction of the Secretary of State. The department also provides legal and technical assistance to the public in the interpretation of the Illinois Vehicle Code.

The largest number of hearings are held for individuals seeking reinstatement of their driver's license after it is suspended or revoked. The primary focus of the department is on the driver whose license was sanctioned as a result of violations related to driving under the influence (DUI) of alcohol or other drugs. In these hearings, a detailed inquiry is made to determine whether DUI offenders are low risks to repeat the offense if they are granted driving privileges.

Allen Mitzenmacher
Director

Other "non-drivers" hearings involve the denial, cancellation, suspension or revocation of titles and registrations of vehicles, automobile dealerships, remittance agents, commercial driving school licenses, reciprocity/prorate audits, motor vehicle review board and Business Services cases.

Informal hearings concerning driver's license matters are held in Secretary of State facilities around the state. Informal hearing officers are authorized to handle most cases other than multiple DUI offenders and individuals challenging their revocations/suspensions on legal grounds. They also provide consultations for DUI offenders requiring a formal hearing.

Formal hearings are held in the department's offices in Springfield, Chicago, Joliet and Mount Vernon. These hearings most often involve multiple DUI offenders seeking to regain driving privileges.

Safety Responsibility hearings are conducted in regions throughout the state to determine probable fault for motorists involved in crashes. Individuals found to be culpable and who were not insured face driver's license suspensions for up to two years.

ILLINOIS STATE ARCHIVES

The State Archives maintains state records of permanent, legal, administrative or historical value dating back to 1734, with more than 76,000 cubic feet of records. Important documents that have deteriorated are restored and repaired in the restoration laboratory, which treats more than 50,000 documents each year.

Information available through the Archives ranges from material relating to the Illinois Territory, public land sales, federal and state censuses, Civil War units, banking and state finance to internal improvement and public works projects, the Illinois and Michigan Canal, transportation, education, mental health and social service agencies, labor issues, law enforcement and corrections, veterans and military affairs.

John Daly
Director

Between its in-house staff and 50 online data bases, the Archives handles more than 8.5 million reference requests annually — more than 8.46 million from attorneys, surveyors, historians, genealogists and the general public, and 40,000 from other state agencies.

The Records Management Section acts as a service agency for state and local agencies. It offers advice and provides for the economical and efficient management of records, ensures maintenance and security of those documents to be preserved, and separates records of temporary value for disposal.

The Archives provides professional and clerical support to both the State and Local Records Commissions. These commissions meet regularly to act upon applications for authority to dispose of records received from state agencies and from county or local governments, and to determine whether such records should be retained permanently or destroyed.

The Archives also works to preserve historical local government records through the Illinois Regional Archives Depository System. Working with the Local Records Commission and local officials, the Archives transfers valuable records to seven state universities designated as official regional depositories.

BUDGET AND FISCAL MANAGEMENT

Budget and Fiscal Management prepares the Secretary of State's budget for presentation to the State Legislature and provides for continuing fiscal responsibility in its execution, including processing payments made by the office.

The department prepares the office payroll and all agency financial statements and is responsible for the procurement of all goods and services through its Purchasing Division. It also serves as a fiscal research and reference center for the Office of the Secretary of State.

Carol Lampard
Director

BUSINESS SERVICES

The Department of Business Services is a centralized repository for three divisions of service to the business community — Corporations, Liability Limitation and Uniform Commercial Code (UCC).

The Corporations Division maintains the records of 322,344 corporations and 65,302 not-for-profit corporations registered to do business in Illinois. In 2000, the division incorporated 37,552 new business corporations and 5,086 not-for-profit corporations, collecting $160.8 million in revenue.

Kenneth V. Buzbee
Director

The division maintains electronic records of corporations dating back to the mid-1800s. The oldest active record is People's Gas, Light and Coke Company, incorporated on Feb. 12, 1855.

With enactment of the Revised Uniform Limited Partnership Act in 1987, centralized filing was created for limited partnerships doing business in Illinois. With more than 28,000 filings on record, the Limited Partnerships Section provides information to the public daily. Filings are accepted in both the Springfield and Chicago offices on both an expedited or routine basis.

As a result of the Limited Liability Company Act, effective in January 1994, and the Registered Limited Liability Partnership Act, effective in August 1994, the department now has more than 45,000 limited liability companies and 598 registered limited liability partnerships on file. Records of limited partnerships, limited liability companies and registered limited liability partnerships all are maintained electronically through the department's Liability Limitation Division. In 2000, the division collected more than $12.1 million in revenue.

The UCC Division administers the Uniform Commercial Code. With nearly 1.4 million secured interest filings on record, the division collected more than $3.8 million in revenue in 2000.

COMMUNICATIONS

The Communications Department coordinates the writing, design and production of printed, audio-visual and computer online materials distributed by the Secretary of State's office.

Major publications include the *Illinois Blue Book*, the *Handbook of Illinois Government*, Illinois highway maps and *Rules of the Road* booklets for automobiles, large trucks, bicycles and motorcycles. The department also creates and coordinates various materials on office programs as

Bob Yadgir
Director

well as several departmental newsletters. By statute, the department is required to print the weekly *Illinois Register*, which contains State Government's proposed and adopted rules of administrative procedures.

Through the Secretary of State's press office, the Communications Department disseminates information on office programs, policies and procedures to the news media, including about 750 newspapers and radio and television stations statewide. A newspaper column, *Traffic Safety Hints*, is distributed to nearly 200 newspapers, and feature articles about office programs are provided for special interest publications.

Communications oversees the ongoing development and maintenance of the Secretary of State's Web site at www.cyberdriveillinois.com. The department also provides photographic services to the Secretary of State's office and prepares displays for the Illinois State Fair, the DuQuoin State Fair, county fairs, the Chicago Auto Show and other events. It also houses a Traffic Safety Video Library, which offers videos free on loan to schools and civic organizations.

COURT OF CLAIMS

The Court of Claims was established as a forum of specific jurisdiction to decide the monetary claims and lawsuits against the state, with the exceptions of workers compensation claims and federal claims. Its judges are appointed by the Governor and confirmed by the Senate. Their orders serve as recommendations to the General Assembly to appropriate the payment of claims. The Office of the Attorney General represents the State of Illinois on all matters.

Ellen Schanzle-Haskins
Director & Deputy Clerk

The Secretary of State serves as the Ex Officio Clerk of the Illinois Court of Claims. The Court of Claims Department fulfills that statutory duty by maintaining case files and official records of the Court, by providing support services to the judges, commissioners and claimants, and by dispersing awards. The Court also awards compensation to victims of violent crimes and survivors of police officers, firefighters and National Guard members killed in the line of duty.

The Clerk of the Court of Claims maintains and ensures the integrity of all case files before the Court. Currently, there are more than 10,000 open claims of all types. The Clerk tracks case activity and provides periodic reports to state agencies, claimants and crime victims showing the status of open cases.

In Fiscal Year 2001, the Court awarded more than $25 million to crime victims and more than $18 million in other cases for a total of $43 million.

310

DRIVER SERVICES

Allan Woodson
Downstate Director

The Driver Services Department issues driver's licenses and ID cards at 136 Driver Services facilities statewide. In addition, five mobile units provide driver services at 20 part-time locations and special events throughout the state. The department also maintains driving records and takes administrative action against unsafe drivers. Currently, there are about 8.4 million licensed drivers and 2.6 million photo ID card holders in Illinois.

Superior customer service is Secretary of State Jesse White's primary goal. Driver Services facilities offer a wide range of services, including driver abstracts and vehicle sticker sales, voter registration and an organ donor registry.

The "Safe Driver Renewal" program allows qualified drivers to renew their licenses online, by phone or through the mail. Participants receive a sticker to affix to their driver's licenses, extending the expiration date by four years. More than 1 million drivers are eligible for this program each year.

Secretary White continues the fight against drunk driving in Illinois. His most recent successful legislative efforts, aimed at repeat offenders, set stricter mandatory penalties for drunk drivers who register at more than double the illegal BAC level of .08, as well as for those drivers who habitually drive with a suspended or revoked license. The law also expands the use of ignition interlock devices to combat impaired driving.

Gary Lazzerini
Metro Director

Secretary White's office provides on-site testing programs at commercial driver's license (CDL) driving schools and community colleges with truck driver training programs. In spring 2001, several Driver Services facilities were equipped with new automated examination machines to help reduce the risk of cheating on driver's license and CDL exams.

Driver Services oversees one of the office's largest highway safety initiatives — the establishment of a statewide database of court supervisions. This information, which yields a more complete history of a person's driving record, is made available only to courts and law enforcement authorities in an effort to identify habitual traffic offenders.

To prevent traffic injuries and deaths among Illinois' youngest drivers, Secretary White oversees the state's graduated driver licensing system, called "Graduate to Safety." Without raising the driving age, this program removes young people from our roadways who have proven to be poor drivers. Subsequently, they are placed into further training, thus affording their parents to become more involved in preparing their teenage children to drive responsibly.

Another program that protects Illinois' young people is "Safe Ride." This program changed the entire school bus licensing process, mandating fingerprinting of all new school bus driver applicants and allowing the Illinois State Police and the FBI to conduct thorough criminal background checks.

Secretary White is deeply committed to the office's organ donor program. The "Life Goes On" program provides state funding to educate the public about the critical need for organs and tissues. Driver Services facilities are an important link to registering organ/tissue donors. More than 5 million Illinoisans have joined the state organ donor registry, making it the largest in the nation.

Driver Services manages more than $1 million in federal highway safety grant funds for educational programs and other projects that improve traffic safety in Illinois. Among them is the "Kids in Safe Seats" program, launched in 2000. The program has led to the establishment of two facility-based Child Passenger Safety Seat Fitting Stations, with three more in the planning stages. The department also conducts public education presentations in the areas of pedestrian, bicycle and school bus safety, anti-drunk driving for both youth and adult audiences and a new feature, DUI Victim Testimonial Displays.

INDEX

Jacqueline Price
Director

The Index Department derives its duties directly from the Illinois Constitution. The Constitution states: "The Secretary of State shall maintain the official records of the acts of the General Assembly and such records of the Executive Branch as provided by law."

Since Illinois achieved statehood in 1818, the Index Department's duties — besides being the keeper of the Great Seal of the State — have been expanded by the Legislature to include more than 300 additional responsibilities. These duties vary greatly, from serving as the official depository for numerous state documents to the appointment of notaries public and filing census information on a biennial basis. Following each census, the department is charged with conducting a lottery to determine the length of terms of General Assembly members. The department also is responsible for convening the Illinois Electoral College following the presidential election.

The Index Department has four divisions: Administrative Code, Public Documents, Lobbyist and Notary. The Administrative Code Division maintains official copies of all administrative rules of every state agency, as required by the Illinois Administrative Procedure Act. The division is responsible for publication of the weekly *Illinois Register*, containing all proposed and adopted rules, and the annual *Illinois Administrative Code* and its quarterly updates on CD-ROM.

The Public Documents Division files statements of economic interest as required by the Illinois Governmental Ethics Act. In 2000, the department notified more than 19,000 elected and appointed officials and public employees of the need to file economic interest statements.

The Notary Division commissioned more than 186,000 Illinois notaries public and issued more than 43,000 Apostilles, Certificates of Authority for notaries and Certificates of Incumbency for county and circuit clerks.

The Lobbyist Division primarily is responsible for registration of lobbyists and maintenance of their expenditure disclosure reports filed biannually for 1,691 registered entities and 2,733 registered lobbyists.

The department maintains the official records of a large number of activities vital to the operation of the state, including appointments to oversight boards and commissions; bonds of elected state officers and appointed state officials; leases entered into by all state agencies, and deeds for state-owned property.

Major department publications include the *Origin and Evolution of Illinois Counties, Illinois Counties and Incorporated Municipalities, Illinois Governmental Ethics Act, Lobbyist Registration Act, Illinois Notary Public Handbook* and the *Administrative Code Style Manual*. The department also produces brochures on proposed amendments to the State Constitution, published in English and Spanish and mailed to all state residents.

INFORMATION TECHNOLOGY

Terry Lutes
Director

The Department of Information Technology provides information technology services within the office. The department is responsible for maintenance of the technology and communications infrastructure for all Secretary of State departments and facilities, consolidating and streamlining redundant processes and developing better ways of serving the public through technology.

The department is involved in all technology initiatives within the office, from the telephone system to the Secretary of State's Web site at www.cyberdriveillinois.com, to maintenance of computers and wireless devices. It also is the source of development and maintenance for all computer-based systems, regardless of platform, including computer generated reports and computer-based entry screens.

The Secretary of State's computer network has more than 3,300 users in 24 office buildings and 138 customer service facilities. The network centers around an IBM 390 mainframe and utilizes 234 servers for the distribution of computer applications. Another 1,600 people from other agencies have access to the Secretary of State's database. Through the law enforcement community's LEADS system, officers can access the database for driver's license and license plate information, with more than 500,000 inquiries daily.

Primarily a service department for the Secretary of State, Information Technology's public face is the e-commerce application that allows the public to access Secretary of State services from the comfort of home. With installation of state-of-the-art technology in early 2001, online vehicle registration renewals were made available in June 2001, with online Safe Driver license renewals and annual filings for corporations following.

INSPECTOR GENERAL

The Inspector General investigates allegations of wrongdoing involving personnel of the Secretary of State's office and presents reports on its findings to the Secretary. The department also conducts fiscal and compliance audits of Secretary of State operations.

The department is headquartered in Willowbrook, with offices in Springfield, Mt. Vernon and Chicago.

Jim Burns
Inspector General

INTERGOVERNMENTAL AFFAIRS

Intergovernmental Affairs provides information and services of the Secretary of State's office to elected officials and statewide associations. Working with other elected officials and their associations, the department serves as the information source, responds to inquiries and seeks feedback from other government entities. The department creates a working network and builds relationships with those entities. It also serves as an information clearinghouse for local and statewide issues involving the Secretary of State and provides a central, reliable source for serving the needs of other elected officials, their staffs and associations.

Jill Zwick
Director

313

INTERNAL AUDIT

Al DiSilvestro
Chief Auditor

The Office of Internal Audit serves the Secretary of State in a staff capacity, responsible for reviewing and testing accounting and financial activities to provide a continuing appraisal of the adequacy and effectiveness of management controls. Secretary White has charged the office with providing informed and constructive analysis and evaluation of existing and proposed procedural, operational and other non-accounting functions and duties within the scope of internal auditing.

LEGISLATIVE AFFAIRS

Dale Swinford
Director

The Legislative Affairs Department develops, coordinates and directs the Secretary of State's legislative agenda in and serves as the Secretary's official liaison to the General Assembly. The department analyzes legislation affecting the office, represents the Secretary before House and Senate committees and provides an array of constituent services for legislators.

PERSONNEL

Tina Prose
Director

The Department of Personnel administers personnel services as established by the Secretary of State's Merit Employment Code. The department is responsible for establishing positions, testing, hiring and disciplining about 4,000 employees, including 200 seasonal and intermittent workers.

Other programs under the department include insurance, workers compensation, deferred compensation, unemployment compensation, affirmative action, equal employment opportunity, the employee assistance program and labor contract negotiations.

PHYSICAL SERVICES

Cecil Turner
Director

The Physical Services Department is responsible for property management of the 28 buildings that comprise the Capitol Complex in Springfield and five buildings in the Chicago metropolitan area. General maintenance and rehabilitation is provided for more than 2.3 million square feet of office space, 25 surface parking lots with more than 3,700 individual parking spaces, and 1.5 million square feet of grounds with more than 3,600 trees and shrubs.

Rehabilitation of state-owned buildings is a major function of the department. Recent projects include renovating the Capitol/Howlett Building pedestrian tunnel, netting the north and east Capitol porticos, replacing the Capitol's west side lead-coated copper roof, adding an entrance to the west side of the Capitol and removing several dead trees. A major upgrade of the

Capitol Complex steam generation power plant is in its final phase. New state-of-the-art controls will continue to help exceed U.S. EPA emission standards and meet the heating demands of the Capitol Complex well into the 21st century.

As a result of a major accessibility project undertaken by the department, all Capitol Complex buildings are now in compliance with the Americans with Disabilities Act. The project included construction of new ramps, lifts, electronic doorways and other modifications in all 28 buildings in the complex. Future plans will enhance these modifications, making the Capitol Complex even better equipped to serve persons with disabilities.

Other recently completed projects in Springfield include replacing the lead-coated copper roof on the other three wings of the Capitol, replacing all windows in the north and south towers of the Capitol, renovating its third- and fourth-story windows, installing barrier netting on the Michael J. Howlett and Margaret Cross Norton buildings, restoring the Senate and House chamber ceilings, and renovating Room 309 and the media studio in the Capitol.

Major Chicago projects include renovating the Secretary of State's Chicago North facility, including the addition of an accessibility ramp, upgrading parking lot lighting at the Chicago North and Chicago West facilities, installing the Plate Room conveyor systems at the Chicago North, South and West facilities, installing parking lot barriers and exterior electronic signage, and replacing all entrances at the three facilities.

Other major capital improvement projects are being considered for the Illinois State Museum, Herndon Building, Stratton Building, Howlett Building, Visitors' Center, Dirksen Parkway facility and three Chicago facilities.

As custodian of the Capitol Complex and Secretary of State offices in Chicago, the department cleans the offices of 50 departments and 14 boards and commissions. Snow removal and maintenance are performed on more than 100 miles of sidewalks and parking lots. The department also provides around-the-clock security for the Capitol Complex, performs preventive and routine maintenance of all Capitol Complex buildings, maintains 215 state-owned vehicles, manages 30 leased facilities, provides warehousing for office supplies and custodian and trades materials, processes more than 14 million pieces of mail annually and keeps an inventory of 40,000 equipment items.

The department supports many special events and civic activities in Springfield, including the Illinois State Fair, Air Rendezvous and First Night. It also supports the DuQuoin State Fair, the Chicago Auto Show and the annual Secretary of State Antique Vehicle Show.

Tours of the State Capitol are given daily from 8 a.m. to 4 p.m., except on major holidays. The Visitors' Center across from the Capitol provides parking for autos and buses, as well as information and a video presentation. More than 200,000 people visit the State Capitol annually.

POLICE

Robert J. Howlett
Director

The Department of Police is a statewide law enforcement agency. Founded in 1913 as an investigative unit in the Vehicle Services Department, it is one of the oldest law enforcement agencies in Illinois. The department employs 127 sworn peace officers and 56 civilian support personnel.

The department's primary responsibility is to regulate the entire automotive industry and its major components, and to enforce all laws and administrative regulations pertaining to the Secretary of State's office. As a fully empowered law enforcement agency, the department's investigators are trained in all aspects of law enforcement and have expertise in auto theft investigations, vehicle-related consumer fraud, fraudulent identification, explosive recognition and disposal and traffic regulation enforcement. The department also provides training to other law enforcement and government agencies on provisions of the Illinois Vehicle Code and other police-related subjects.

An equally important task is providing security for the Capitol Complex. The Emergency Response Team and Special Event Team handle high-risk situations that require training in crowd control, hostage-barricaded subjects, demonstrations and dignitary protection. The Bomb Squad, staffed by highly trained bomb technicians, provides logistical support to these special units and renders statewide service to federal, state and local agencies.

The Operations Division is the department's primary uniform division. It deploys staff resources through district offices in Bellwood, Rockford, Springfield and Mt. Vernon, and satellite facilities in Joliet and East St. Louis. Plainclothes operations are part of the division, with undercover squads concentrating on covert operations to combat auto theft and fraudulent identification rings. Personnel also inspect licensed automobile and automotive parts dealers, handle consumer complaints and conduct anti-drunk driving patrols and other traffic enforcement programs.

The Department of Police continues its aggressive anti-auto theft campaign through grant programs initiated by the Motor Vehicle Theft Council. Special audit teams conduct in-depth audits of licensed automotive rebuilders, repairers, scrap processors and salvage yards. Grants also helped initiate the department's Beat Auto Theft program. The program allows Illinois motorists to voluntarily obtain and display a window decal to alert police officers that the vehicle owner has consented to have the vehicle stopped between 1 and 5 a.m.

Additional grants from federal and state transportation programs are used to operate the Anti-Drunk Driving Enforcement Program that conducts patrols throughout the state, and the Speeding and Traffic Accident Reduction Program that reduces accidents by citing speeding motorists. The Illinois Department of Transportation funds the department's Operation Straight ID program, which teaches business owners, their employees and law enforcement personnel how to identify fake state driver's licenses and ID cards.

PROGRAMS AND POLICIES

Terri Coombes
Director

The Programs and Policies staff researches and develops initiatives to fulfill the long-range objectives and goals set forth by the Secretary of State. The staff works closely with Secretary of State departments in developing innovative programs targeted toward improving overall service to the public. In addition, it works to ensure the timely implementation of new intitiatives required by the General Assembly.

Programs and Policies tracks and researches initiatives in other states relevant to the operations of the Illinois Secretary of State. When possible, the staff then works to implement programs found to be successful in other states. The department also coordinates meetings with public and private organizations to develop and maintain partnerships toward improving services to the public and reducing costs to taxpayers.

SECURITIES

The Securities Department regulates the offer and sale of securities pursuant to the Illinois Securities Law of 1953. The department registers securities offerings, broker-dealers, investment advisers and their salespersons and representatives. With the passage of three statutes in 1995, the department obtained jurisdiction over loan brokers, business brokers and those who offer and sell business opportunities.

All securities offered or sold in Illinois must be registered with the Securities Department, unless exempt by law. One of the registration options offered to entrepreneurs is the Small Company Offering Registration process. This program assists small businesses in raising capital in the equity markets, while minimizing the registration process and simultaneously providing full disclosure of risks to potential investors.

Tanya Solov
Director

In 2000, the department began implementing the newly established Investment Adviser Registration Depository. The depository permits electronic filings by investment advisers, similar to the Central Registration Depository used for broker-dealer filings. Both depositories provide for more efficient registration and enhance investor protection by allowing regulators to view the disciplinary history of registrants.

The Securities Department is an administrative agency designated as a criminal justice agency for informational gathering purposes. Enforcement investigators and attorneys investigate complaints from investors and issue subpoenas and administrative orders in cases where the law is violated. Enforcement staff also refers cases to criminal authorities and assists in the investigation and prosecution of investment fraud. Although the department cannot order perpetrators to return funds to investors, in recent years it has been successful in negotiating rescission offers on behalf of investors.

The department's audit staff conducts both routine and unannounced audits of broker-dealers and investment advisers with less than $25 million of assets under management. Audits that uncover fraud are referred to the enforcement staff, and deficiencies requiring corrective actions are noted in letters to the audited entities.

The Securities Department is active in investor education and financial literacy programs, conducting seminars for investors and providing financial literacy teaching guides to Illinois schools. It also has a page on the Secretary of State's Web site that provides information for the industry and investors as well as a KIDSINVEST program geared toward students in grades K-12.

SENIOR AND COMMUNITY SERVICES

The Senior and Community Services Department provides programs and services to seniors, veterans, persons with disabilities and community groups.

The department administers the Rules of the Road Review Course, which provides senior citizens and drivers with disabilities the knowledge needed to pass the driver's license renewal examination. The free course is offered more than 2,500 times a year at about 440 locations throughout the state. The program is the first of its kind in the nation and has helped nearly 750,000 Illinois drivers prepare for their driver's license renewal exams. The course

Mary Lou Kearns
Director

317

is taught by department employees and volunteer instructors. Review courses are offered through senior centers, service clubs, rehabilitation facilities, literacy programs, veterans organizations and labor unions.

The department has generated more than 1 million official Illinois photo ID cards to both drivers and non-drivers. The non-expiring card is free to those age 65 and over and to persons with disabilities. There is a $4 fee for others.

Discounts on automobile liability insurance premiums are available to drivers age 55 and over who successfully complete a defensive driving course approved by the office.

The Office of the Secretary of State is committed to the intent of the Americans with Disabilities Act and promotes accessibility to all of its programs and services. The department disseminates a wide variety of information and materials and conducts workshops and other outreach programs relevant to its services for persons with disabilities.

The department's veterans' outreach program advocates veterans-oriented legislation and provides career consultation services and employment referrals to veterans. Department staff members serve as liaisons between veterans organizations and promote special events commemorating historic and educational events.

The Secretary of State's Speakers Bureau, administered by the department, provides speakers for community, civic and fraternal organizations throughout the state at no charge. The department also maintains a toll-free hotline, 1-800-252-2904 (voice and TTY), to assist seniors, veterans and persons with disabilities who have problems or concerns about programs and services offered by the Office of the Secretary of State.

ILLINOIS STATE LIBRARY

Jean Wilkins
Director

The Illinois State Library serves as the principal information resource for State Government. To achieve that goal, the library has amassed a collection of more than 5 million items, with particular strengths in government, public policy, political science, education and selected fields of history. The State Library subscribes to more than 900 journals to provide the most current information on a wide range of subjects. The library also subscribes to numerous electronic databases and services that allow patrons access to thousands of resources.

To ensure both timely and in-depth access to government information, the State Library serves as Illinois' regional federal documents depository. As such, it receives 100 percent of the material distributed by the library programs service of the U.S. Government Printing Office, maintains an authoritative collection of historic and contemporary Illinois state documents, and houses more than 180,000 maps. The library also is one of only two federal patent and trademark depository libraries in the state.

In addition to its role as the library of State Government, the State Library serves Illinois citizens directly through the Illinois Library and Information Network (ILLINET), consisting of nearly 3,000 libraries statewide. ILLINET includes public, academic, school and special libraries both publicly and privately funded. The State Library supports ILLINET in a variety of ways. For example, the library's staff is available to any library in the state to advise on topics such as service to the aged, disabled and youth, collection management, automation and library administration.

318

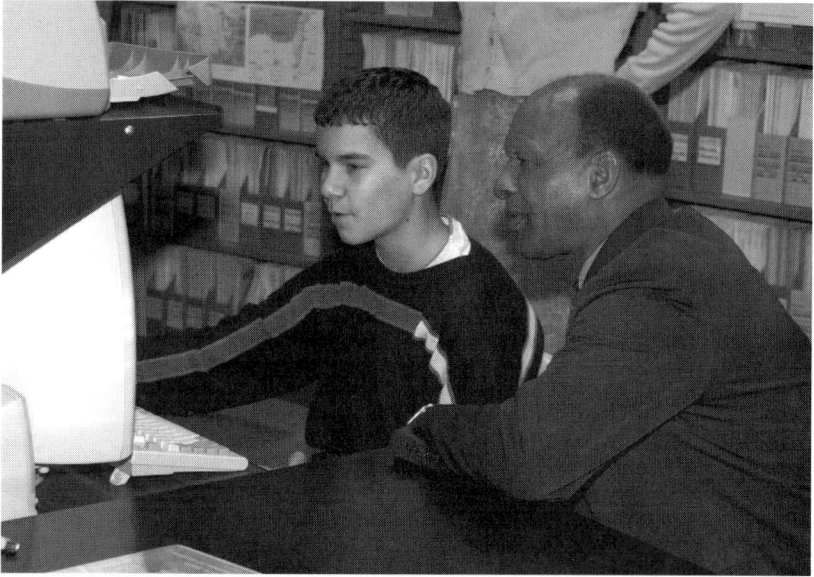

A Project Next Generation student from Effingham shows off his technology expertise to Secretary of State Jesse White during a visit to the program site in February 2001.

The State Library funds a network of 12 regional library systems that work with member libraries at the grass roots level. The library coordinates a network of 56 selective federal document depositories and 28 state document depositories to ensure that government information is available to all Illinois citizens. The library also supports a statewide delivery service for books and other materials and partially funds a statewide online union catalog of more than 7.3 million titles and 22 million holdings.

The State Library administers grants to support and expand library services to citizens as well as to build and renovate libraries. It also provides state-of-the-art continuing education opportunities for librarians, library staff and trustees, and grants are awarded annually to Illinois students studying library science.

The Secretary of State's Educate & Automate Program provides $5 million annually for enhanced technology to Illinois libraries and increased funding for family literacy programs. Libraries and literacy programs also receive nearly $19 million annually under the Secretary of State's Live & Learn Program for library construction, automation and other projects.

In May 2000, Secretary White launched his innovative mentoring program to be administered through the public library system. The first program of its kind, Project Next Generation provides state-of-the-art technology experiences and life skills training for students in sixth through ninth grades. The program began with nine pilot sites in fall 2000, and was expanded to include nine more sites in spring 2001.

"Find-It! Illinois," the State Library's new Internet portal, was implemented in October 1999, as a one-stop resource for government and library information. The site at http://finditillinois.org includes the Virtual Illinois Library, Illinois Government Information, FirstSearch database, Every Library in Illinois index and the Illinois Digital Archive.

Illinois Literacy Program

Since January 1986, the Illinois State Library's Literacy Office has administered a community literacy grant program to fund public and private adult literacy volunteer projects to improve the reading, writing, math and communication skills of Illinois adults. The first of its kind in any state, the program has served 225,551 students with the assistance of 88,983 volunteers. Libraries, education agencies and community-based organizations throughout the state receive funds to operate tutoring sites, purchase adult new reader book collections, provide professional training and integrate technology into literacy instruction. Grants also support the Adult Learning Hotline (1-800-321-9511), which links students and tutors with local literacy programs.

In 1990, the program was expanded to include workplace literacy grants for businesses to improve the basic skills of their employees with on-site instruction. In 1992, the Literacy Office initiated a family literacy program, calling upon libraries, adult education programs and agencies serving children at-risk to work together to enhance literacy levels of at-risk families. The Educate & Automate initiative, effective in January 1997, tripled state funding for family literacy and technology efforts.

In 1999, three new literacy grant programs were initiated. The New Chapters program is a partnership among local literacy programs and domestic violence facilities to provide on-site basic literacy, career and life skills training. In honor of the late State Senator Penny Severns, legislation created annual funding for summer enrichment programs for low-literate families. And the Making Work Pay program provides funding to businesses to hire and train new employees.

The Literacy Office links Illinois residents to local, state, national and international literacy resources, organizations and current events in the literacy field through the Secretary of State's Web site. It also publishes a quarterly newsletter, *Illinois Literacy*, which serves as a clearinghouse of information on community, business and family literacy efforts, and provides technical assistance to more than 250 literacy programs in Illinois.

VEHICLE SERVICES

- 3.5 million title documents issued annually
- 9.5 million vehicles registered annually
- $850 million generated from vehicle title and registration-related fees annually
- More than 3 million vanity and personalized plates issued, generating $27 million since the program's inception

Ed Michalowski
Director

The Vehicle Services Department is responsible for processing vehicle titles, registering vehicles, issuing license plates and renewal stickers, licensing vehicle dealers and maintaining vehicle records. The Secretary of State's office provides Illinois vehicle owners with the most secure title document in the nation, greatly enhancing protection from theft or fraud.

Secretary White's massive replating project began in 2001, with the state's estimated 6.5 million passenger plates expected to be replated in one year. Many of the old plates had been on vehicles for more than 17 years, making them difficult for law enforcement to read. To accommodate this aggressive time frame, the office installed state-of-the-art technology throughout the department, resulting in more efficient and effective use of manpower and providing better service to Illinois citizens. The new technology also enabled the department to offer vehicle owners online registration renewals beginning in June 2001, through the Secretary of State's Web site at www.cyberdriveillinois.com.

Since 1983, Illinois license plates have been manufactured by Macon Resources, Inc., in Decatur, a rehabilitation training facility for people with disabilities. Bringing plate production back to Illinois has resulted in a savings of millions of dollars and encouraged the development of skills of persons with disabilities.

To assist fixed-income senior citizens and motorists with disabilities in meeting the rising costs of maintaining a vehicle, the office provides reduced-fee license plate registration for various plate categories, including passenger car, B-truck, disability plates, RVs, Purple Heart and Korean War Veteran.

The Vanity and Personalized License Plate Program has issued more than 3 million sets of plates for an array of plate categories since its inception in 1979, generating more than $27 million for the Illinois Road Fund. Vanity and personalized plates are available for passenger vehicles, B-trucks, vans, motorcycles, recreational vehicles and trailers, antique vehicles and motorcycles, and plates for persons with disabilities, as well as for Environmental, Organ Donor and Prevent Violence specialty plates.

In mid-2001, the department implemented the new Temporary Registration Permit (TRP) program. Along with a new computerized tracking system, the new permits provide law enforcement a better way of identifying vehicles displaying these permits and their owners. The new TRPs are made of a weather-resistant cardboard and are displayed in the rear license plate location.

Licensing vehicle dealers to protect buyers from illicit or temporary operators is an important function of the department. Dealer licensing also regulates dealerships to prevent the sale of stolen vehicles and parts.

The department also maintains records of all vehicles registered and titled in Illinois, distributing information to law enforcement agencies, the courts and the public. Vehicle information is processed through the National Crime Information Center and the Law Enforcement Agencies Data System "Hotcheck" to determine if a vehicle has been reported stolen.

Vehicle Services administers the Mandatory Auto Insurance Program. To monitor compliance with the state's mandatory insurance law, the department mails random questionnaires to vehicle owners and verifies coverage with insurance companies. The department suspends the registrations of uninsured motorists and processes registration reinstatements.

The department provides information on the laws, policies and procedures relating to the titling and registration of vehicles, through its toll-free information line, 1-800-252-8980. The Chicago Information Line at 312-793-1010 provides information in the Chicago area.

MERIT COMMISSION

The Secretary of State's Merit Commission approves rules and actions of the Department of Personnel under the Merit Employment Code. The commission also conducts hearings on the appeals of employees regarding their position classifications and on certain disciplinary actions taken against employees. The commission then enforces compliance with its decisions.

No more than three of the five commission members can be affiliated with the same political party.

Members of the Merit Commission are Monroe L. Flinn, *chairman*; George Dunne, Sharon Roberts, Charles Summers and Michael Masterson.

Secretary of State's Staff Members

Thomas Ned Benigno
Deputy Secretary of State & Chief of Staff

Terri Coombes
Deputy Chief of Staff

Linda Piccioli
Executive Assistant to the Secretary

Lillian Jenkins
Executive Secretary

Anthony Arnieri
Executive Staff

Anthony Burnett
Executive Staff

Annette Czarobski
Executive Staff

Chester C. Czesak
Executive Staff

Jacqueline Dicianni
Executive Staff

Leo Louchios
Executive Staff

Irene Lyons
Executive Staff & Special Counsel

Bob Yadgir
Executive Staff & Director, Communications

Dave Druker
Press Secretary

Randy Nehrt
Deputy Press Secretary

Elizabeth Kaufman
Deputy Press Secretary

Bertha Doss
Assistant Press Secretary

ADMINISTRATIVE PERSONNEL

Thomas Ned Benigno .... *Deputy Secretary of State & Chief of Staff*
Jim Burns .... *Inspector General*
Terri Coombes .... *Deputy Chief of Staff & Director, Programs & Policies*
Linda Piccioli .... *Executive Assistant to the Secretary*
Lillian Jenkins .... *Executive Secretary*
Anthony Arnieri .... *Executive Staff*
Anthony Burnett .... *Executive Staff*
Annette Czarobski .... *Executive Staff*
Chester C. Czesak .... *Executive Staff*
Jacqueline Dicianni .... *Executive Staff*
Leo Louchios .... *Executive Staff*
Irene Lyons .... *Executive Staff & Special Counsel*
Bob Yadgir .... *Executive Staff & Director, Communications*
Dave Druker .... *Press Secretary*
Randy Nehrt .... *Deputy Press Secretary*
Elizabeth Kaufman .... *Deputy Press Secretary*
Bertha Doss .... *Assistant Press Secretary*
Michael Igoe .... *Special Counsel, General Counsel Office*
Donna Leonard..*Special Counsel*
Glenna White Jones .... *Director, Accounting Revenue*
Allen Mitzenmacher .... *Director, Administrative Hearings*
John Daly .... *Director, Illinois State Archives*
Carol Lampard .... *Director, Budget & Fiscal Management*
Kenneth V. Buzbee .... *Director, Business Services*
Ellen Schanzle-Haskins .... *Director & Deputy Clerk, Court of Claims*
Allan Woodson .... *Director, Driver Services*
Gary Lazzerini .... *Director, Metro Driver Services*
Jacqueline Price .... *Director, Index*
Terry Lutes .... *Director, Information Technology*
Jill Zwick .... *Director, Intergovernmental Affairs*
Al DiSilvestro .... *Chief Auditor*
Dale Swinford .... *Director, Legislative Affairs*
Tina Prose .... *Director, Personnel*
Cecil Turner .... *Director, Physical Services*
Robert J. Howlett .... *Director, Police*
Tanya Solov .... *Director, Securities*
Mary Lou Kearns .... *Director, Senior & Community Services*
Jean Wilkins .... *Director, Illinois State Library*
Cyndy Colletti .... *Manager, Literacy Office*
Ed Michalowski .... *Director, Vehicle Services*
Liz Nicholson .... *Director, Scheduling*
Sal Raymond .... *Director of Advance, Downstate*

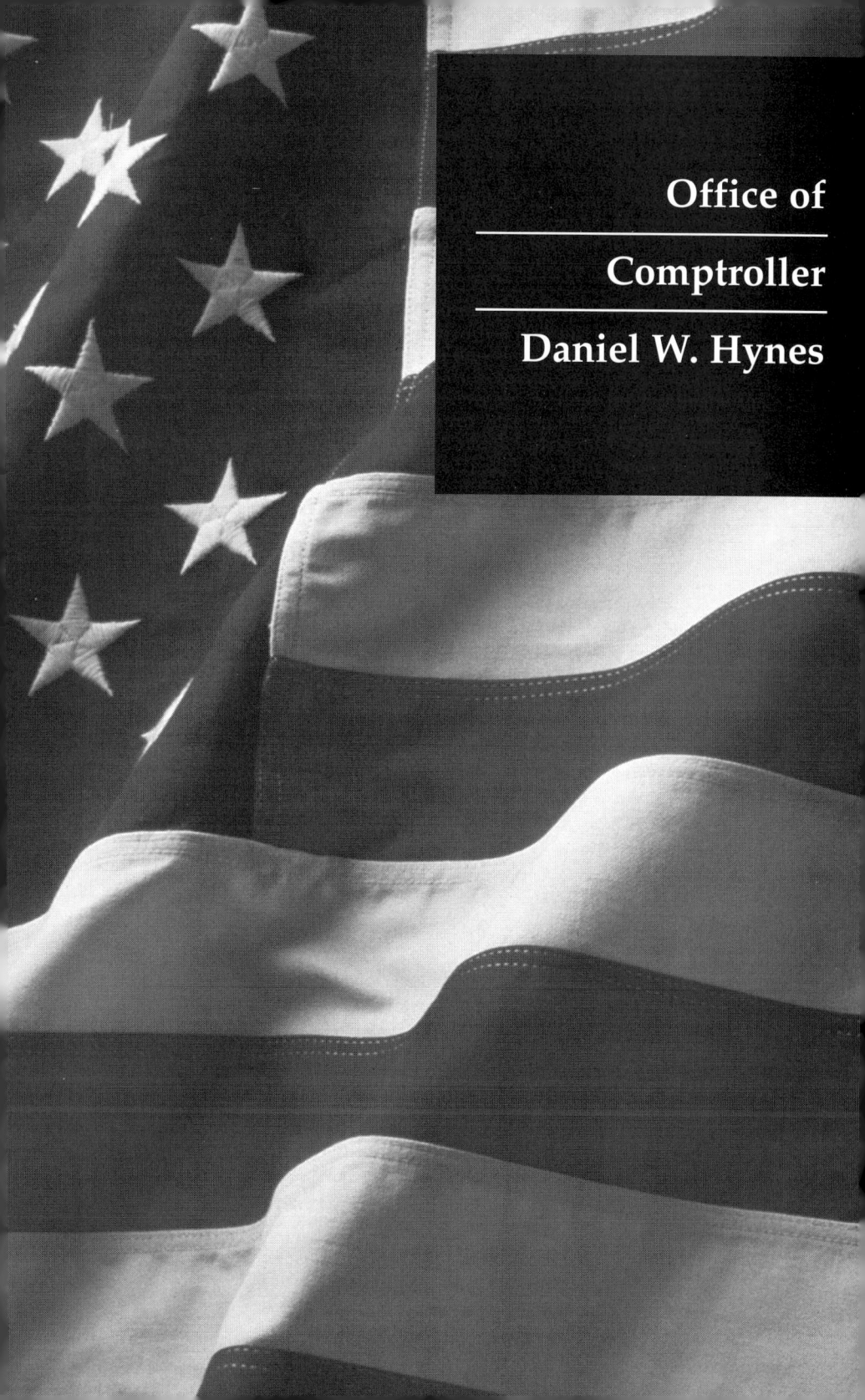

Office of

Comptroller

Daniel W. Hynes

OFFICE OF THE COMPTROLLER

Daniel W. Hynes became the sixth State Comptroller since the office was created in 1970 with the adoption of Illinois' new Constitution. Prior to 1970, the financial reporting functions of the state were the responsibility of the Auditor of Public Accounts, an office that dated back to 1812 when Illinois became a territory.

The Comptroller is the chief fiscal officer for Illinois' $53 billion budget — comparable in size to that of a Fortune 100 corporation. Additionally, the Comptroller maintains all fiscal records, serves as a member of the Debt Collection Board and is a trustee of the Illinois State Employees' Retirement System.

The central mission of the Comptroller's office is to manage the state's financial accounts by recording transactions, processing data, pre-auditing expenditures and contracts, issuing financial reports and providing leadership on the fiscal affairs of the state. The office processes more than 15 million transactions a year, through both paper processing and electronic payments. In this function, it performs a "watchdog" role to ensure that all state payments meet the requirements of the law.

A fundamental responsibility of the Comptroller's office is to provide accurate fiscal information and analyses to the Governor, the General Assembly, local government officials and the public. The Governor and members of the General Assembly must be provided with timely and accurate information so they can make the most effective decisions about the state's fiscal policy. The Comptroller's focus is on the management of funds — revenue receipts and spending. Once this is complete, simulations, impact analysis and other studies can be performed to assist the Governor and lawmakers in making better budget decisions.

Comptroller Daniel W. Hynes established the first-ever Asian-American Advisory Council and Latino Advisory Council as part of his office's effort to gain advice on fiscal concerns of diverse communities throughout the state. The Comptroller's office is a repository of fiscal information for 7,200 units of local government.

Comptroller Hynes answers a reporter's questions about the need for a "Rainy Day Fund" following his keynote address at a University of Illinois policy luncheon in Springfield. Hynes proposed a "Rainy Day Fund" in light of new pressures on the state's general revenue fund balance.

Fiscal Leadership & Financial Reporting

The Illinois Constitution empowers the Comptroller to maintain the state's central fiscal accounts. The office must also provide meaningful and timely fiscal information to help state policymakers adopt effective fiscal policies.

One measurement of the state's fiscal health is the rating issued by bond rating companies. Key components of the bond rating are cash balances and outstanding payables. The Comptroller is involved in the management of both components as well as the approval for any short-term borrowing by the state.

The office must keep current with technology advancements and continually seek new ways to improve how it serves the public. One such way the office is adapting new technologies to meet the demands of the future involves the use of "electronic commerce," which allows vendors, employees and retirees to receive payments from the Comptroller's office electronically. Vendors also can check on the status of a payment due from the state on the Comptroller's Web site at www.ioc.state.il.us.

Comptroller Hynes' commitment to putting more understandable fiscal information into the hands of taxpayers was demonstrated by his support of a law requiring the Department of Revenue to provide easy-to-understand budget summaries in the annual tax booklet mailed to millions of taxpayers each year.

The Comptroller's office is required to report periodically on the fiscal status of the state to the Constitutional Offices and the General Assembly. At the end of each year, the Comptroller's office prepares an account of the state's financial affairs called the *Comprehensive Annual Financial Report*. The report is published according to generally accepted accounting principles and standards set by the Government Accounting Standards Board.

Periodically, the Comptroller's office publishes *Fiscal Focus,* a newsletter containing updates of key state fiscal facts and in-depth articles about timely fiscal issues. The annual *Illinois Traditional Budgetary Financial Report* provides summaries of revenues, expenditures and year-end balances by fund and category. The *Tax Expenditures Report* highlights the more than $5 billion in tax breaks each year, while the *Fiscal Responsibility Report Card* provides an annual report on the financial status of the 7,200 units of local government in Illinois.

Other annual financial reports prepared by the Comptroller's office include the *Executive Summary,* the *Fee Imposition Report,* the *Detailed Annual Financial Report, Appropriations and Bonded Indebtedness* and the *Long-term Obligations Report.*

Since the adoption of the *Illinois State Collection Act* of 1986, the Office of Comptroller is required to report on receivables and establish collection procedures through its statewide accounting system. The Comptroller's *Receivables Report* provides a compilation of the state's receivables and an analysis of debt collection efforts by agencies and the Comptroller's office. As a member of the Debt Collection Board (along with the Attorney General and the Department of Central Management Services), the office continues to look for new ways to increase the return of debt owed to the state.

Statewide Accounting

As the state's chief fiscal office, the Comptroller's office records transactions and ensures proper payment and management of payables. The office processes more than 15 million transactions a year to fund necessary programs, pay state employees and issue more than 3 million state income tax refunds. During fall 2000, under the Tax Relief Rebate Program, the Comptroller's office mailed $279 million in property tax rebates to 2.26 million homeowners.

To ensure fiscal integrity, the office implements a pre-audit process prior to the payment of any invoice. The pre-audit process ensures that the state does

Comptroller Hynes monitors the SAMS (Statewide Accounting Management System) with staffer Zetta Pullen-Robinson. The Comptroller's office now issues more than 18 million payments a year, through both electronic transactions and paper processing.

Comptroller Dan Hynes, during a Statehouse news conference, announces a series of regional consumer meetings across Illinois to gather new ideas about reforming the cemetery and funeral home industries. Hynes is the first Comptroller to ever revoke a license based on lack of care and maintenance.

not exceed the appropriation given to a state agency authorized by the General Assembly and that the invoice has been properly approved for payment.

An integral part of the Statewide Accounting Management System (SAMS) is the Comptroller's linc.net, an electronic warehouse that gives taxpayers on-line access to state financial information in "real" time (i.e., as transactions occur) through the Internet. The linc.net provides immediate financial information to taxpayers and increases government accountability.

Serving Local Governments

The Comptroller's office is the repository of local government fiscal information used for financial analysis, oversight and forecasting. The office collects and analyzes Annual Financial Reports (AFRs) that state law requires the 7,200 units of local government to file. One of the newest local government resources offered by the office is the Comptroller Connect Internet Filing program, which allows local governments to file their AFRs over the Internet. Local governments with Tax Increment Financing (TIF) districts also are required to file annual reports for each TIF with the Comptroller's office.

In his first two years in office, Comptroller Hynes increased financial reporting compliance among local governments by 40 percent through more aggressive follow-up and by offering technical support to smaller units of government. As part of his fiscal outreach effort, Hynes' office offers training seminars for county treasurers. The division has a 30-member local government advisory board to provide valuable input from around the state. The office also is looking for new ways to reach out more to local governments through regional sites at state universities.

329

Cemetery & Funeral Home Industries Oversight

One of the little known responsibilities of the Comptroller's office is to audit and regulate the state's private cemetery and funeral home industries. With more than $700 million in Cemetery Care and Burial Trust Fund monies, the office audits individual accounts to make sure money invested in these trust funds is preserved and spent for the ongoing care and maintenance of cemeteries and appropriate funeral and burial services as prescribed by law.

The Comptroller held regional meetings throughout the state in 1999 to hear firsthand about the condition of local cemeteries and issues related to pre-need sales of cemetery and funeral services. The information gathered at these meetings was used to help draft comprehensive cemetery and funeral home care legislation.

The first session of the 92nd General Assembly saw overwhelming support for Comptroller Hynes' initiatives. The legislation ensures that pre-need salespeople are knowledgeable about the laws regarding the cemetery care and funeral home industries, mandates that consumers be furnished with booklets outlining their rights, and increases the Comptroller's abilities to screen, deny and revoke pre-need service licenses.

In addition to setting up a cemetery care Web page on the Comptroller's Web site, Comptroller Hynes established a hotline (1-877-203-3401) for consumer complaints and concerns about cemetery conditions and funeral home contracts.

Public Accountability

Comptroller Hynes strongly believes that State Government should be customer-oriented, provide the most efficient services possible and be accountable to the taxpayer for what it spends. As part of its Public Accountability Project, the Comptroller's office worked with the Governor's Office of Strategic Planning on a performance audit of State Government called the *Service, Efforts and Accomplishments Report.* The comprehensive report provides a first-rate indication of what types of services the state is providing and whether they are being provided efficiently and effectively. State agencies will use the report's findings to make improvements.

The four chief goals of the Public Accountability Project include making State Government results-oriented, increasing public awareness of State Government services, improving state management of resources and providing taxpayers with more effective and efficient services. By compiling a taxpayer-friendly report on how the state uses taxpayer dollars, and what results are achieved, the public will be better able to judge how State Government performs for them. The final report is available on the Comptroller's Web site at www.ioc.state.il.us.

Comptroller's Staff Members

Keith Taylor
Chief of Staff

Don Templeman
Assistant Comptroller
Operations

Ann Sundeen
Assistant Comptroller
Fiscal Policy

Laura Zaremba
Deputy Chief of Staff

Stan Brown
Director
Administrative Services

Peg Roth
Assistant Comptroller
Chicago Office

Chris Belle
Director
Budget & State Payroll

Charles Schmadeke
Chief Legal Counsel

Amalia Rioja
Deputy Legal Counsel

ADMINISTRATIVE PERSONNEL

Rick Cornell .... *Director, Policy & Planning*
Frank Bilecki .... *Director, Chicago Office*
Karen Craven .... *Press Secretary*
Gail Lobin .... *Special Assistant to the Comptroller*
Nikki Budzinski .... *Director, Scheduling*
Kevin Schoeben .... *Director, Legislative Affairs*
Steve Valasek .... *Director, State Accounting & GASB 34*
Robert Brock .... *Director, Research & Fiscal Information*
Carol Reckamp .... *Director, Local Government*
Larry Selinger .... *Director, Human Resources*
Mike Hoffman .... *Director, Public Accountability Project*
Katherine Cutler .... *Manager, Expenditure Analysis & Research*
Michelle Anderson .... *Executive Assistant, Springfield*
Camille Manderfeld .... *Executive Assistant, Chicago*

331

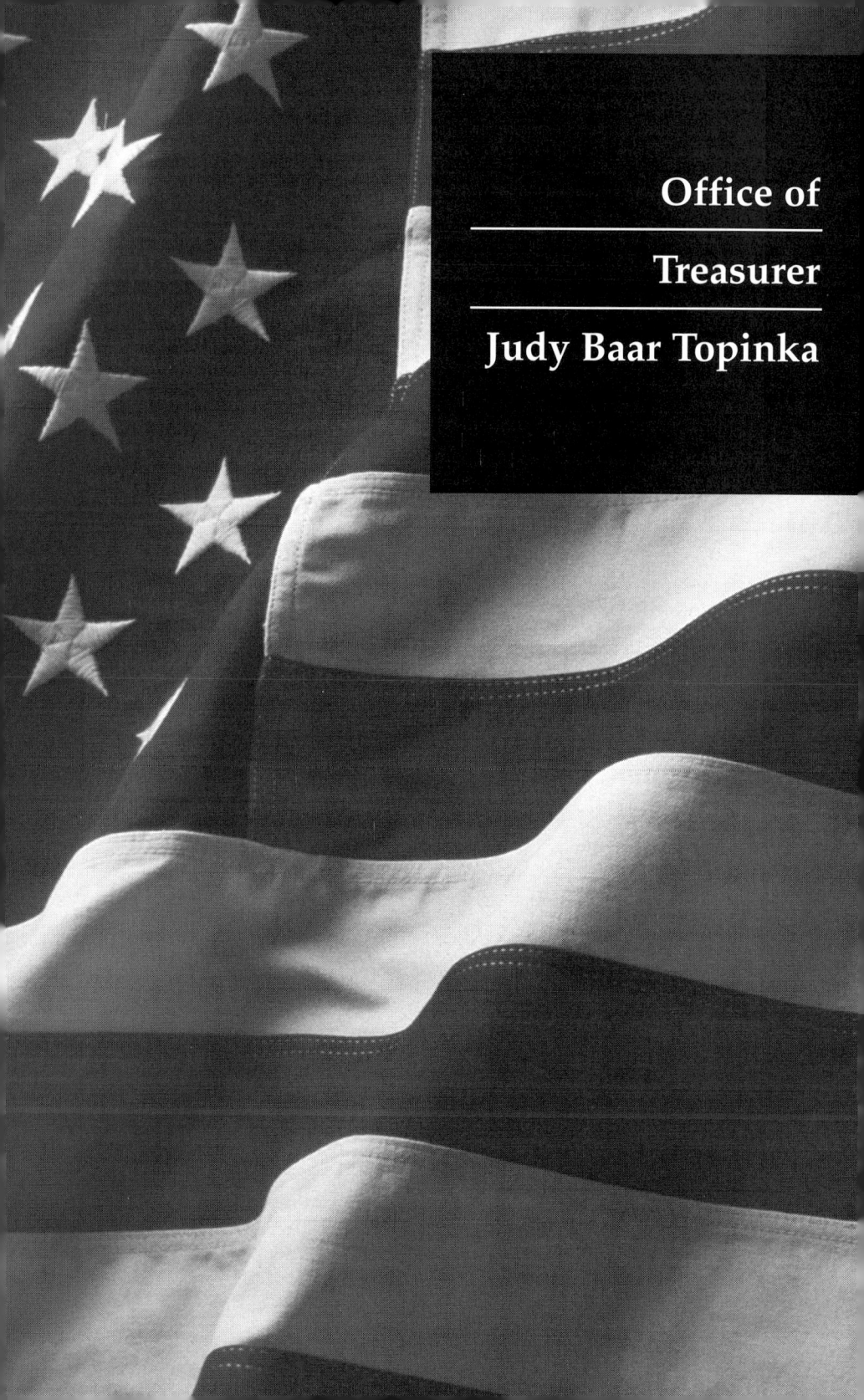

Office of

Treasurer

Judy Baar Topinka

OFFICE OF THE TREASURER

The Treasurer is the state's chief investment officer, acting as both custodian and investor of state funds. The Treasurer receives all taxes and fees collected by State Government and deposits them with financial institutions across the state. Cash balances representing more than 600 state funds are then invested in the safest financial instruments possible, consistent with the need to provide liquid funds for the payment of the state's bills while earning the highest rate of return for the taxpayers.

The Treasurer also serves as part of the state's financial management team, verifying the sufficiency of funds prior to countersigning all state warrants.

Community Development Deposit Program

Treasurer Judy Baar Topinka has the authority to deposit funds into local financial institutions at discounted rates to promote community development. She has committed more than $200 million for community development throughout Illinois, creating and retaining more than 8,000 jobs. She also has developed deposit programs that offer low interest loans to encourage safe and affordable day care, social service facilities, abuse shelters and group homes for needy children. These investments are monitored for compliance to ensure that they provide the intended benefits to the community.

State Treasurer's Economic Program (STEP) — The STEP program provides Illinois companies access to affordable capital to expand their operations and create or retain jobs in the state. For each permanent, full-time job created or retained, the Treasurer's office can deposit up to $25,000 at below-market rates into the borrower's financial institution. The institution then lends the money to the borrower at below prevailing interest rates.

Economic Recovery Loan Program — This program complements the STEP program by bringing domestic and international business to Illinois. The focus is to bring good-paying jobs with benefits to the state.

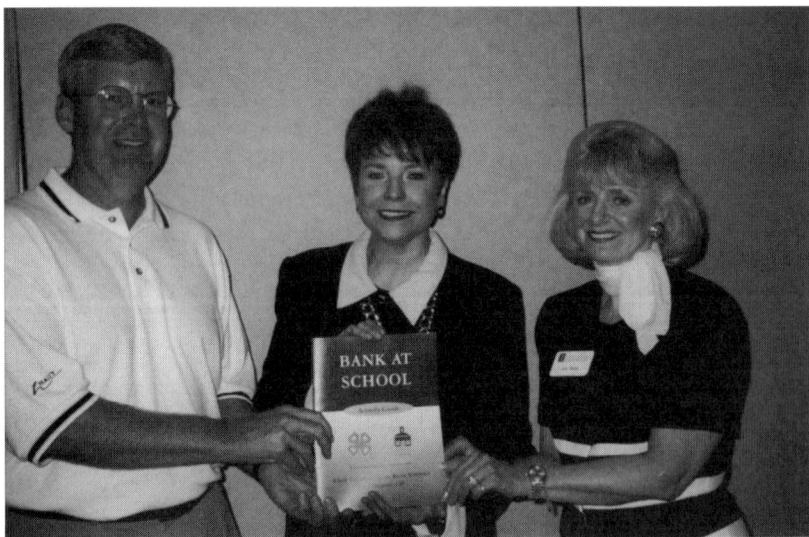

State Treasurer Judy Baar Topinka announces a new Bank at School partnership to help teach money management skills to fourth, fifth and sixth graders involved in the 4-H program.

Treasurer Topinka participates in the groundbreaking ceremony for Progressive Manufacturing Corporation's new facility in Lake Zurich, financed in part by the STEP program.

Targeted Initiative Program —Through this program, Treasurer Topinka provides Illinois community service organizations with access to affordable capital to enhance and expand their services. The program also supports organizations that help individuals find jobs, prevent the early institutionalization of the elderly, care for the disabled, cure the sick and revitalize and strengthen communities.

Day Care Initiative — Believing there is no better investment than that of our children, Treasurer Topinka created the Day Care Initiative to address the continuing need for quality day care in Illinois. The program is designed to encourage the construction and expansion of licensed day care facilities in Illinois by helping them obtain low-interest financing.

Ready Access Program — This program provides persons with disabilities affordable financing to make their homes and vehicles more accessible or to purchase assistive technology to improve their independence and productivity.

Experience Illinois Program — This program promotes tourism, historic preservation and community development projects throughout Illinois. Communities can develop or enhance tourism destinations, restore historic buildings or landmarks and rejuvenate tired public areas.

Illinois' Agriculture Loan Program — One of the largest linked-deposit programs in the nation, this program is available to farmers statewide through more than 1,000 financial institutions. Lending operational money at a rate that is attractive to both agricultural lenders and farmers helps keep the agricultural backbone of Illinois strong.

Alternative Agriculture Loan Program — Treasurer Topinka has expanded her efforts in the agricultural community by providing Illinois farmers financing if the funds are used for goods and services related to the production of alternative agricultural products, such as grapes, strawberries, hydroponically-grown food and Christmas trees.

Record Interest Earnings

The principal duty of the State Treasurer is to invest state funds. To that end, every business morning, the Treasurer's office invests billions of dollars in a variety of financial instruments. It is the Treasurer's responsibility to provide the best return and the necessary liquidity to pay the state's bills. In 1995, Treasurer Topinka published the first-ever written investment policy for the State of Illinois. The current policy has resulted in a record investment return of nearly $3 billion since Treasurer Topinka took office.

Safety and Soundness Law

This law requires all taxing bodies with responsibility for investing public funds to formulate an investment policy and make it available for inspection by the general public. The legislation was inspired by statewide hearings conducted by the Illinois Public Investor Task Force, chaired by Treasurer Topinka.

Illinois Funds

Illinois Funds is an investment pool operated by the Treasurer's office to provide local governments a way to maximize their interest income. The benefits include higher rates, complete liquidity, full collateralization of funds and electronic transfer into and out of participants' accounts. Under Treasurer Topinka's leadership, the fund is rated "AAAm" by Standard and Poor's and has $4.5 billion under management.

In June 2000, Treasurer Topinka created E-Pay exclusively for Illinois Funds participants. Through an Illinois Funds E-Pay Clearing Account, participants can extend credit and debit card payment services to constituents without the time and effort of building the system from scratch.

Financial Education

Recognizing the need to better educate citizens about financial issues, Treasurer Topinka developed a financial education curriculum that provides basic financial instructions to students of all ages. The basic foundation of this curriculum is the Bank At School program.

The Treasurer also encourages money management through initiatives, such as "Money, Banking, Credit and Students" and the Smart Money/Smart

Treasurer Topinka studies some of the unclaimed contents of safe deposit boxes on display at the Knox County Courthouse.

Women Conference. The Treasurer's office also provides financial symposiums to help local public treasurers stay informed on issues such as investment strategies, new technology and reporting requirements.

Unclaimed Property

The Division of Unclaimed Property officially became part of the Treasurer's office July 1, 1999. The division is responsible for the receipt and safekeeping of all unclaimed and abandoned property and for aggressively searching for the rightful owners. The division assumes control of more than $100 million annually. Treasurer Topinka has returned record amounts of unclaimed property to its owners during her administration of the program.

Bright Start

During the 1999 legislative session, Treasurer Topinka received statutory authority to begin a college savings program for Illinois families. Bright Start is an innovative investment program that gives parents, grandparents and friends of school-age children a smart way to save for a child's college education. Under the program, investment earnings are exempt from state and federal income taxes and, beginning Jan. 1, 2002, all contributions to a Bright Start account are excluded from a taxpayer's gross income for purposes of state tax liability. The program covers tuition, books, fees, some room and board costs and other college expenses and can be used at any college in the United States — public or private, in-state or out-of-state, graduate schools, community colleges and certain vocational schools.

Bright Start has become one of the fastest growing college savings programs in the nation. In its first 18 months of operation, more than 22,500 accounts were opened, with more than $125 million being invested.

Home Loan Collateral

One of Treasurer Topinka's newest initiatives, the Home Loan Collateral Program, is a two-pronged approach to help individuals avoid using a predatory lender to obtain a home loan. The volunteer program assists first-time home buyers, as well as those who have missed a couple of mortgage payments, by allowing them to pledge 10 percent of the value of their homes to a participating bank as security for the borrower's loan.

Capital Litigation

The Capital Litigation Trust Fund was created by state law to promote fairness in the prosecution and defense of capital crimes. Established Jan. 1, 2000, the fund is administered by the Treasurer's office to provide funds for costs associated with the prosecution and defense of capital cases in Illinois.

Medallions

Treasurer Topinka authored a bill that will allow civic and community groups to mint commemorative medallions. The program will help Illinois residents celebrate their rich heritage.

Additional Responsibilities

Treasurer Topinka serves as a member of the following boards, commissions and authorities: Community Development Finance Corporation; Judges Retirement System Board of Trustees; Municipal Retirement System; Illinois Public Investor Task Force; Rural Bond Bank; State Board of Investment; State Records Commission; Toll Highway Authority, and the Governor's Travel Control Council.

Treasurer's Staff Members

Jim Stapleton
Assistant Treasurer

Nancy Kimme
Chief of Staff

Ed Buckles
*Deputy Chief of Staff/
Chief Fiscal Officer*

John Hoffman
*Deputy Chief of Staff/
Programs*

Martin Noven
*Deputy Chief of Staff/
Law and Policy*

Crystal Caison
Inspector General

Barb Ringler
Chief Internal Auditor

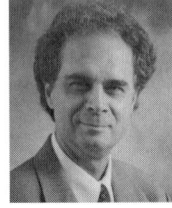

Ken Kamps
*Director
Human Resources*

Stacey Willenborg
*Director
Legislative Affairs*

ADMINISTRATIVE PERSONNEL

Carolyn Barry Frost ....*Press Secretary*
Sharon Brown ....*Director, Communications*
Rick Hackler ....*Director, Illinois Funds*
Alissa Camp ....*Director, Unclaimed Properties*
Jane Hay..*Manager, Scheduling*
Rhonda Poeschel ....*Manager, Banking*
Chad Dierking ....*Manager, Accounting*
Jim Millburg ....*Manager, Management Information Systems*
Betty Atkins ....*Manager, Estate Tax*
Jim Kramp ....*Manager, Warrant Division*
Janet Dobrinsky ....*Director, Financial Education*
Cory Jobe ....*Program Administrator, Tourism & Agriculture*
Don Gray ....*Manager, Planning & Special Events*
Chuck Hagopian ....*Director, Community Initiatives*
John Cieslik ....*Director, Economic Development*
Bartt Stevens..*Manager, Bright Start*
Gina Dellamorte ....*Executive Assistant to the Treasurer*
Rosemary Echeverry ....*Executive Assistant to the Treasurer, Scheduling*

338

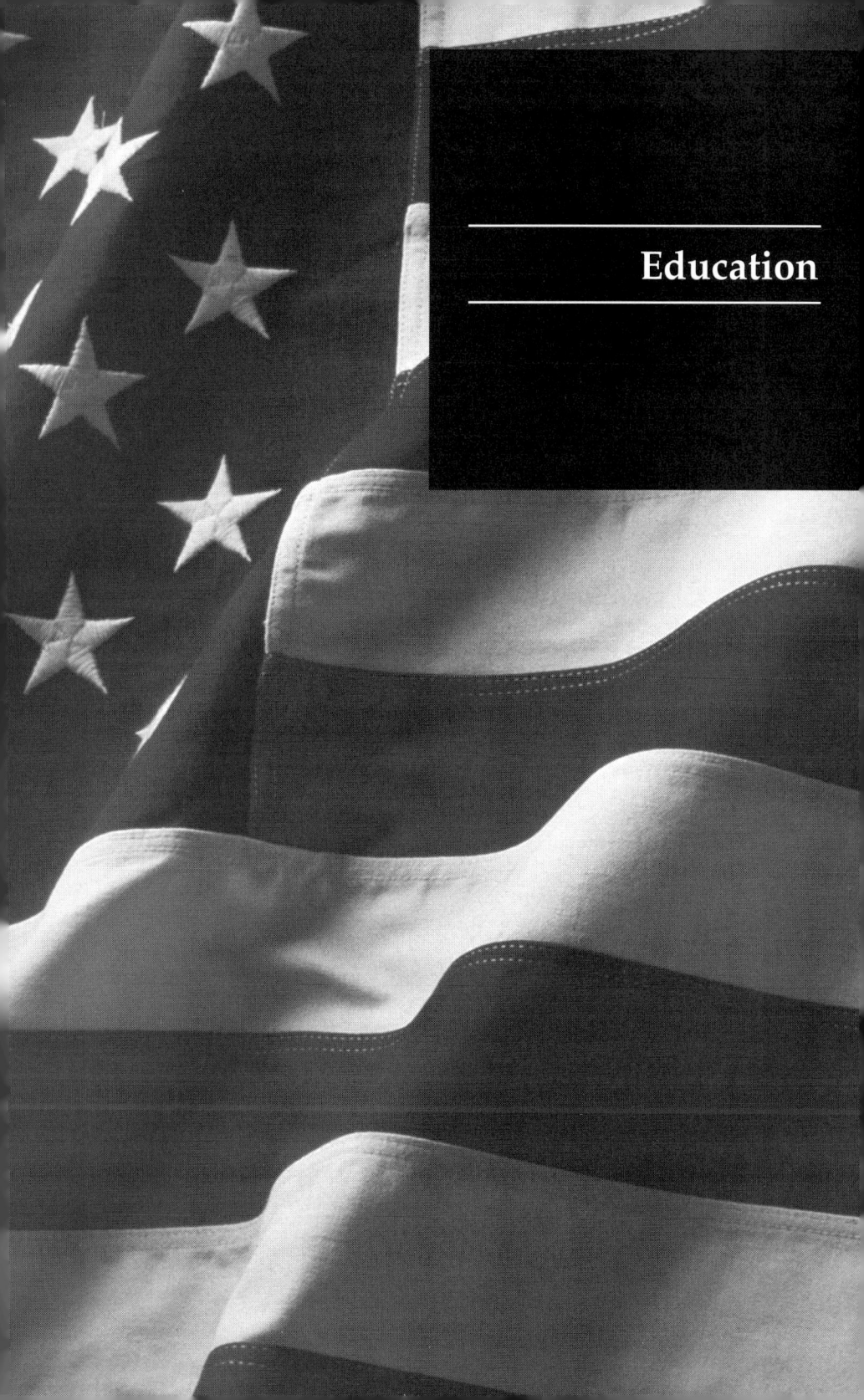

Education

ILLINOIS STATE BOARD OF EDUCATION

Glenn W. McGee
State Superintendent of
Education

The Illinois State Board of Education was created in 1975 after the 1970 Illinois Constitution directed that responsibilities for elementary and secondary education in Illinois be transferred from an elected superintendent to an appointed board of citizens.

The board sets state educational policies and guidelines for public and private schools, preschool through grade 12, and vocational education. It analyzes the aims, needs and requirements of education and recommends legislation to the General Assembly for the benefit of the more than 2 million schoolchildren in Illinois.

Newly constituted in 1997, the State Board consists of nine members who are appointed by the Governor with the consent of the Senate. Board members serve six-year terms, with State Board membership limited to two consecutive terms.

Members of the State Board of Education are: Marjorie B. Branch — *Cook County/Chicago*; Marilyn McConachie — *Cook County outside Chicago*; Connie Rogers and Vincent J. Serritella — *Collar Counties outside Cook County*; Beverly Turkal and Janet Steiner — *Downstate*, and Ronald J. Gidwitz and two vacancies — *members at large*.

The Governor appoints the State Board chairperson, and State Board members elect other officers. Current officers are Ronald J. Gidwitz, *chairman*; Marilyn McConachie, *vice chair*, and Connie Rogers, *secretary*.

The board appoints a chief executive officer as the State Superintendent of Education. On Jan. 1, 1999, Glenn W. McGee became Illinois' sixth State Superintendent to be appointed by the board. McGee is an Illinois native who has worked in Illinois schools for all but three years of his 25-year career in education. Prior to assuming his new position, he was superintendent of the Deerfield schools in north suburban Lake County. During his career, McGee has taught, coached, worked as an elementary school principal and served as school superintendent in Buffalo Grove. He was president of the Lake County superintendents' organization and has worked with legislators for numerous school improvement measures, including special education funding reform and reading grant eligibility. Born and raised in LaGrange, McGee holds a master's degree and a doctorate degree in educational administration from the University of Chicago and a bachelor's degree in political science from Dartmouth.

Commitment to Improved Teaching and Learning

The State Board of Education provides leadership for elementary and secondary education to local school districts, disburses more than $7 billion in state and federal funds each year, and administers a policy of equitable educational opportunity for all children. The State Board's headquarters are in Springfield, with a large regional office in Chicago and a smaller facility in Mt. Vernon.

Under the leadership of Superintendent McGee and Chairman Gidwitz, the State Board has adopted goals in the following areas for 2001-2002:

- High levels of achievement for all Illinois students and eliminating achievement gaps among student groups.

- Quality programs, products and services that meet the needs of school districts, Regional Offices of Education and policymakers to foster improved student learning.

- Availability and equitable distribution of educational resources, including funding.

- Joint goal-setting with state partners to improve Illinois education overall, with subsequent support from State Board and partner initiatives.

- Accountability systems that encourage continuous educational improvements and innovation, while assuring fiscal integrity and protecting student welfare.

The State Board of Education has adopted a performance management approach that includes measures and data collection related to each goal; business plans for delivering programs, products and services; and internal improvement mechanisms. Customer service measures adopted last year will continue to play a strong role in agency planning and evaluation.

Jo Crow, the 2001 Illinois Teacher of the Year, teaches 7th and 8th grade science at Metamora Grade School.

ILLINOIS EDUCATION STATISTICS
1999-2000

Number of students (public schools) 2,027,600
   Elementary 1,459,926
   Secondary 567,674
Number of certified staff 148,971*
   Elementary teachers 68,697
   Secondary teachers 31,029
   Special education teachers 21,338
Number of public school districts 895**
Number of students (non-public schools) 323,869***
   Elementary 255,688
   Secondary 68,181
Percent of students in non-public schools 14

* Represents a full-time equivalent number, including 1,676 administrators, 5,082 principals and assistant principals, 7,819 pupil personnel specialists, 4,212 supervisors and 2,582 other certificated staff. For the first time, the total also includes 1,480 pre-kindergarten teachers and 4,904 kindergarten teachers.

** Number of operating school districts excluding Department of Rehabilitation Services, Board of Regents, Board of Trustees and Illinois Mathematics and Science Academy.

*** Some schools report only total enrollment; therefore, the elementary and secondary enrollments do not equal the total non-public school enrollment.

ILLINOIS STATE BOARD OF EDUCATION LEADERSHIP

Glenn W. McGee .... *State Superintendent of Education*
Lynne Haeffele Curry .... *Chief Deputy Superintendent*
Respicio Vazquez ....*General Counsel*
Kathy Nicholson-Tosh .... *Director of Board Services*
Kim Knauer .... *Director of Communications*
Ray Schaljo .... *Director of Customer Services*
Gail Lieberman .... *Director of Federal Relations*
Tammy Rust .... *Director of Internal Audit*
Lee Patton .... *Director of Policy Development*
Peter Leonis ....*Director of State Relations*
Doris Langon .... *Director of Chicago Office*
Michael Dunn .... *Assistant Chief Deputy for Education*
Christopher Koch .... *Deputy Superintendent, Special Education*
Diana Robinson .... *Deputy Superintendent, Partnerships/Workforce Development*
Carmen Chapman Pfeiffer .... *Deputy Superintendent, Standards, Assessment &*
Accountability
Mary Jayne Broncato .... *Deputy Superintendent, School Support*
Frank Llano .... *Deputy Superintendent, Professional Preparation & Certification*
Brenda Heffner .... *Deputy Superintendent, Regional Office Support*
David Wood .... *Assistant Chief Deputy for Operations & Finance*
Gary Ey .... *Deputy Superintendent, Finance*
Christine Schmitt .... *Deputy Superintendent, Fiscal Administration*
Vivian Najim .... *Acting Deputy Superintendent, Human Resources*
Lugene Finley ....*Chief Technology Officer*

ILLINOIS BOARD OF HIGHER EDUCATION

Philip J. Rock
Chairman

Keith R. Sanders
Executive Director

The Board of Higher Education, created in 1961, is a planning and coordinating agency for all sectors of Illinois higher education. The board consists of 15 members, including 10 members appointed for six-year terms, the respective chairs of the Illinois Community College Board and the Illinois Student Assistance Commission, a member of a public university governing board, a member of a private college or university board of trustees, and a student member elected by the recognized student advisory committee to the board.

The chairman of the Board of Higher Education is Philip J. Rock, Oak Park, whose term expires in 2001. Members whose terms expire in 2003 are: Jerry D. Blakemore, Chicago; Steven H. Lesnik, Winnetka; Lourdes Monteagudo, Chicago, and Jane T. Williamson, Kenilworth. Members whose terms expire in 2005 are: Samuel K. Gove, Urbana, and Cordelia Meyer, Chicago. Members whose terms expire in 2007 are: Mark E. Barmak, Lake Bluff; Robert J. English, Aurora; James L. Kaplan, Lincolnshire, and Lucy A. Sloan, Carbondale. The student member for 2001-2002 is John Thompson, Sherman.

The representative of the Illinois Community College Board is Edward T. Duffy, Arlington Heights. The member representing the Illinois Student Assistance Commission is J. Robert Barr, Evanston. The representative of public university governing boards is Thomas R. Lamont, Springfield. Philip J. Rock is the representative of an independent college or university board of trustees. Keith R. Sanders is executive director of the Board of Higher Education.

The board's major statutory responsibilities include a continuing analysis of the aims, needs and requirements of Illinois higher education; making budget recommendations to the Governor and General Assembly for higher education operations, grants and capital improvements; approving proposals for new units of instruction, research and public service for public colleges and universities; approving operating and degree-granting authority for independent and out-of-state institutions; administering designated state and federal grant programs, and other responsibilities specified in the *Illinois Compiled Statutes*.

ILLINOIS COMMUNITY COLLEGE BOARD

Edward T. Duffy
Chairman

Joseph J. Cipfl, Ph.D.
President/CEO

The Illinois Community College Board was created by legislation enacted in 1965. The board has statutory responsibility for planning and coordinating the programs and activities of the state's 39 community college districts.

Illinois has the third-largest community college system in the nation. Each year, nearly 1 million students attend Illinois community colleges in credit and non-credit programs. About 65 percent of all students in Illinois public higher education are enrolled in community colleges.

Of the 39 public community college districts, 38 have locally-elected boards of trustees, and one (City Colleges of Chicago) has a locally-appointed board of trustees. There are 37 single-college districts with one or more extension campuses. Two districts have multiple colleges, City Colleges of Chicago and Illinois Eastern Community Colleges. All districts have local taxing authority to provide local support for district operations. Also within the system is the East St. Louis Community College Center that is administered by the Southern Illinois Collegiate Common Market, a consortium of four community colleges, and Southern Illinois University (Carbondale and Edwardsville).

The Illinois Community College Board consists of 11 members appointed by the Governor and one student member selected annually by the recognized student advisory committee. Board members are appointed at large for six-year terms. The chairman is selected by the Governor. Board members include: Edward T. Duffy, Arlington Heights, *chairman;* Joseph J. Neely, Metropolis, *vice chairman;* A. James Berkel, Peoria; Inez A. Galvan, Lombard; Laurna Godwin, Alton; Martha E. Olsson, Peoria; Gwendolyn D. (Laroche) Rogers, Chicago; Delores S. Ray, East St. Louis; Lee H. Walker, Burr Ridge; James K. Zerkle, Springfield, and the student member. The president and chief executive officer of the Illinois Community College Board is Joseph J. Cipfl, Ph.D.

UNIVERSITY OF ILLINOIS

More than 800,000 students have attended the University of Illinois since it was created as a land-grant school in 1867. Each year, about 15,000 students graduate with baccalaureate, professional and advanced degrees in a vast assortment of academic fields. Students come from every state in the nation and more than 120 foreign countries. Illinois is the home of about 90 percent of all University of Illinois students.

James J. Stukel has been president of the University since 1995. He has worked to increase visibility of the university within its home state, logging more than 150,000 miles in visits to communities downstate and in metropolitan Chicago. He also works to reconnect the university with alumni and friends across the country.

James J. Stukel
President

The University of Illinois has three campuses. The largest at Urbana-Champaign opened with three faculty members and 77 students in 1868. Enrollment now is about 37,000 students; 75 percent of which are undergraduates. The Urbana-Champaign campus, which covers 1,450 acres, is a national leader in many fields, including engineering, music, library science and computing.

The Chicago campus, which is within walking distance of the Chicago Loop, is an international leader in health research. The UIC Medical Center serves more than 480,000 patients each year, and one of every six Illinois physicians is a UIC graduate. The 300-acre campus has about 24,500 on-campus students.

In 1995, the university added its third campus when Sangamon State University became the University of Illinois at Springfield (UIS). UIS is situated on 746 acres on the southeast side of the city and enrolls nearly 4,000 students. The first-ever class of freshmen enrolled in fall 2001.

University of Illinois academic programs are broad and deep, and its faculty are among the best in their fields. The Urbana-Champaign campus offers bachelor's degrees in 150 fields of study, and there are more than 100 graduate and professional programs. The Chicago campus offers bachelor's degrees in 92 academic areas, master's degrees in 83 academic areas and doctorates in 57 specialties. Together, the two campuses educate fully three-fourths of all Ph.D. and professional students who attend Illinois public universities. The Springfield campus offers bachelor's and master's degrees in 22 areas and a doctorate in public administration.

The university is more than a collection of colleges; it reaches throughout the state with its Extension Service, a uniquely American contribution to off-campus learning. The university also established UI-Online as an electronic link to university courses on and off campus. The university has an extensive continuing education program, offering degree and non-degree courses to people who need job retraining or professional upgrading, or who simply desire to continue learning.

A view of the engineering campus, with Beckman Institute on the north side of the Urbana-Champaign campus.

Admission to the University

Admission to the University of Illinois is based on factors that best predict the applicant's future success in his or her chosen academic field. At both the Urbana-Champaign and Chicago campuses, beginning freshmen are evaluated for admission on the basis of their high school course work and a combination of class rank and score on either the SAT or ACT.

Admissions are selective. Average test scores and high school rankings of incoming students are high. Admissions decisions take into account a student's transfer credits and grades. Special admissions cannot exceed 10 percent of the previous fall term's entering freshman class, and applicants have the opportunity to bring special circumstances to the attention of the admission offices during the application process.

In fall 2001, the Springfield campus admitted its first freshman class under the Capital Scholars program. Formerly, the campus served only juniors, seniors and graduate students.

UNIVERSITY ADMINISTRATION

James J. Stukel .... *President*
Chester S. Gardner .... *Interim Vice President for Academic Affairs &*
Vice President for Economic Development & Corporate Relations
Craig S. Bazzani .... *Vice President for Administration*
Thomas R. Bearrows .... *University Counsel*
Richard M. Schoell .... *Executive Director for Governmental Relations*
Susan J. Sindelar .... *Executive Assistant to the President*
Michele M. Thompson .... *Secretary of the University*
Alexis M. Tate .... *Interim Executive Director for University Public Affairs*

UNIVERSITY OF ILLINOIS AT URBANA-CHAMPAIGN

Since its founding in 1867, the University of Illinois at Urbana-Champaign has earned a reputation of international stature. Its distinguished faculty, outstanding resources, breadth of academic programs and research disciplines, and large, diverse student body constitute an educational community ideally suited for scholarship and research.

Nancy Cantor
Chancellor

The university has a fundamental commitment to undergraduate education. More than 26,000 undergraduate students are enrolled in 10 undergraduate divisions that offer some 4,000 courses in more than 150 fields of study. Undergraduate admission is highly selective. In a recent freshman class, the average student was in the top 10 percent of his or her high school graduating class and scored in the top 10 percent of those taking the national college entrance examination.

The university enrolls some 9,000 graduate and professional students in more than 100 disciplines.

Among the university's most significant resources is its talented and highly respected faculty. More than 80 faculty members belong to the American Academy of Arts and Sciences, the National Academy of Sciences or the National Academy of Engineering. Eleven scientists have received the National Medal of Science, and more than 80 have received the National Science Foundation Young Investigator Award.

Academic resources on the campus are among the finest in the world. The University Library is the third-largest academic collection in the nation, housing more than 21 million items in the main library and in the more than 40 departmental libraries and units. Only Harvard and Yale have larger collections.

The university is home to the National Center for Supercomputing Applications, which created the NCSA Mosaic Web browser. Mosaic, released in 1993, stimulated the exponential growth of the World Wide Web and the Internet. NCSA is the leading-edge site for the National Computational Science Alliance, a partnership of more than 50 research institutions from across the country that is creating prototypes of the computational and informational infrastructure of the 21st century. The center receives support from the National Science Foundation, the State of Illinois, the University of Illinois and industrial partners.

The Beckman Institute for Advanced Science and Technology is an inter- and multi-disciplinary research institute devoted to basic research in the physical sciences and engineering, and in the life and behavioral sciences. Research at the institute focuses on three broadly defined themes: biological intelligence, human-computer intelligent interaction and molecular and electronic nanostructures. Thirteen research groups, composed of faculty and students from 34 UIUC departments, work within and across these three areas.

Integral to the university's mission is a commitment to link the campus to needs expressed across the State of Illinois. Each year, thousands of Illinois residents participate in scores of conferences, credit and non-credit courses and workshops presented on campus and statewide. Extension, technical support and education programs are available in every Illinois county and touch the lives of thousands of citizens. Faculty members as well as students are engaged in helping local communities, schools and businesses meet the challenges they face. This commitment is being advanced through Partnership Illinois, a campus initiative dedicated to sustaining partnerships with Illinois governmental and private institutions, organizations and associations across Illinois.

A major center for the arts, the campus attracts dozens of nationally and internationally renowned artists each year to its widely acclaimed Krannert Center for the Performing Arts. The Krannert Art Museum and Kinkead Pavilion is second only to the Art Institute of Chicago among Illinois public art museums in size and value of collections.

The Urbana-Champaign campus was the first major university to provide comprehensive access and programs for students with disabilities, setting a worldwide standard for accessibility. Located in east central Illinois in the twin cities of Urbana and Champaign (population 104,000), the University of Illinois at Urbana-Champaign is the state's flagship public university.

ADMINISTRATIVE OFFICERS — Urbana-Champaign

Nancy Cantor .... *Chancellor*
Richard Herman .... *Provost and Vice Chancellor for Academic Affairs*
Tony Waldrop .... *Vice Chancellor for Research*
Patricia E. Askew .... *Vice Chancellor for Student Affairs*
Charles C. Colbert .... *Vice Chancellor for Administration and Human Resources*
William M. Murphy .... *Associate Chancellor for Public Affairs*
Katharine J. Kral .... *Assistant Vice President for Business and Finance*

The Hallene Gateway Plaza, the focal point of the east entryway to the University of Illinois campus, prominently features the stone portal from the entrance to the first university-built classroom building, University Hall, completed in 1873.

UNIVERSITY OF ILLINOIS AT CHICAGO

Sylvia Manning
Chancellor

The Chicago campus is the realization of the University of Illinois' commitment to the creation of a comprehensive public university in a vital urban center. The University of Illinois at Chicago (UIC) is the largest institution of higher learning in the metropolitan area, and a significant center of international education and research.

UIC is both one of the oldest and one of the newest major research universities in Chicago: the College of Pharmacy and the College of Medicine were founded more than 125 years ago, while UIC's new campus opened in 1965. The 200-acre campus, just west of Chicago's Loop, includes 100 buildings. UIC's 25,000 students (about 65 percent undergraduate, 35 percent graduate and professional) can pursue doctorates in 55 specialties, master's degrees in 84 fields and bachelor's degrees in 91 fields. The faculty includes renowned scholars, researchers, artists, writers and health professionals.

Academic units offering undergraduate, graduate and professional degree programs include the Colleges of Applied Health Sciences; Architecture and the Arts; Business Administration; Dentistry; Education; Engineering; Graduate College; Honors College; Liberal Arts and Sciences; Medicine; Nursing; Pharmacy; the Jane Addams College of Social Work; the School of Public Health, and Urban Planning and Public Affairs.

The School of Public Health is the only graduate-level program of its kind in the state, as is the College of Pharmacy. The College of Dentistry is one of only two in Illinois. Since the 1970s, the College of Medicine programs at Peoria, Rockford and Urbana-Champaign have increased access for Illinois residents to the university's health care education and services. More doctors graduate from the university's College of Medicine than from any other United States medical school. The College of Medicine consistently ranks high nationally in the number of African-American and Latino physicians it graduates.

More than 2 million volumes are housed in the university's library and specialized collections, which include the Architecture and Art Library, Mathematics Library, Science Library and the Library of the Health Sciences, one of the largest in the nation.

UIC makes a particular effort to address its teaching, research and outreach programs to urban issues. The "Great Cities" program is a commitment to address human needs in Chicago and in metropolitan areas worldwide. It includes UIC's extensive health and health-care activities, efforts to improve K-12 education, business development and assistance, work with local governments, community, civic, business and social service organizations, and enhancement of culture and the arts. New programs that strengthen UIC's work include the Great Cities Institute, the College of Urban Planning and Public Affairs, the UIC Neighborhoods Initiative and the Center for Urban Business. These join other units that deal with urban issues, such as the Center for Educational Research and Development, the Prevention Research Center, the Center for Urban Economic Development, the Institute on Disability and Human Development, the Urban Transportation Center and the Chicago

Technology Park. A joint effort between UIC and Rush Presbyterian St. Luke's Medical Center, the park provides incubator space for high-technology ventures.

Also located on the Chicago campus is Jane Addams' Hull-House. Restored on its original site by the university, it was named a national historic landmark by the U.S. Department of the Interior when it reopened in 1967.

ADMINISTRATIVE OFFICERS — Chicago campus

Sylvia Manning .... *Chancellor*
Charlotte Tate .... *Interim Provost & Vice Chancellor for Academic Affairs*
Stanton Delaney .... *Vice Chancellor for Administration*
Barbara Henley .... *Vice Chancellor for Student Affairs*
Eric Gislason .... *Interim Vice Chancellor for Research*
Charles Rice .... *Vice Chancellor for Health Affairs*
Arthur Savage .... *Associate Chancellor*

A view of the East-Side Residence Halls at the University of Illinois at Chicago.

UNIVERSITY OF ILLINOIS AT SPRINGFIELD

The University of Illinois at Springfield (UIS) is widely respected for providing personalized, high-quality education for a public university price. UIS is known for its trademark teaching focus and excellent faculty, its proven record in business education and its historic public affairs mandate. The nearly 4,000 students who attend UIS benefit from individual attention from professors in small classes, numerous internships and assistantships and a personal campus climate.

UIS, previously known as Sangamon State University, joined the University of Illinois in 1995 as part of a statewide reorganization of public higher education, becoming the third campus of the U of I. The campus is located on 746 acres on the southeast side of Springfield, near Lake Springfield.

Richard D. Ringeisen
Chancellor

Established in 1969 as an upper-division and graduate institution serving the educational needs of juniors, seniors and graduate students, UIS has become a more comprehensive and traditional institution over the years. In fall 2001, UIS admitted its charter class of freshman students to the university's first four-year baccalaureate program. Called Capital Scholars, the highly selective program offers an innovative approach to general education through interdisciplinary courses that emphasize public affairs, leadership development and civic life. Students must have strong high school records for admittance and may choose their majors from among UIS's bachelor's degree programs. Capital Scholars live in a residence hall specifically designed to meet their living/learning needs.

UIS has a large population of nontraditional students — older students (ages 33-48) who have jobs and families and who commute to campus from within a 60-mile radius. About 500 students live on campus in apartment-style housing and townhouses. Many students transfer from community colleges and four-year colleges and universities to take advantage of UIS's range of academic and professional programs, including 20 bachelor's degree and 18 master's degree programs. Programs range from traditional disciplines such as history, psychology and biology to more career-oriented concentrations such as business administration and management information systems. Interdisciplinary programs such as environmental studies and communication also are available, as well as a doctoral program in public administration.

UIS now offers courses online, including a baccalaureate completion degree in liberal studies and master's degrees in management information systems and educational leadership. During the last three years, online enrollment has soared as students increasingly choose to study from their homes. About 25 percent of UIS faculty members teach courses online.

Located in the state's capital, UIS provides students with research and special project opportunities in State Government; numerous internships and assistantships are available with government and public service offices and on campus. Research, training and service activities are coordinated by the UIS Institute for Public Affairs, which includes the Illinois Legislative Staff

Internship Program, Graduate Public Service Internship Program, Center for Legal Studies, *Illinois Issues* magazine, WUIS/WIPA (a National Public Radio affiliate), UIS Television Office, Survey Research Office and Office of Policy and Administrative Studies.

Brookens Library at UIS has a collection of more than a half-million volumes, as well as cooperative relationships with the library of the SIU medical school, the Illinois State Library and special agency libraries within the community. Students also have electronic access to 44 other academic libraries in Illinois. Campus resources include the Public Affairs Center with its 2,000-seat performing arts auditorium and conference facilities.

ADMINISTRATIVE OFFICERS — Springfield campus

Richard D. Ringeisen .... *Chancellor*
Michael R. Cheney .... *Provost and Vice Chancellor for Academic Affairs*
John Conner .... *Vice Chancellor for Administrative Services*
Patricia Swatfager-Haney .... *Vice Chancellor for Student Affairs*
Cheryl D. Peck .... *Associate Chancellor for Public Relations*
Vickie Megginson .... *Associate Chancellor for Campus Development*
Lawrence Johnson .... *Associate Chancellor for Access and Equal Opportunity*

A view of the Health and Sciences Building at the University of Illinois at Springfield.

SOUTHERN ILLINOIS UNIVERSITY

Southern Illinois University (SIU) is a multi-campus university composed of two institutions, Southern Illinois University Carbondale (SIUC) and Southern Illinois University Edwardsville (SIUE), serving nearly 35,000 students. SIU was chartered in 1869 as Southern Illinois Normal University — a teachers college. In 1947, the name was changed to Southern Illinois University, reflecting the institution's academic expansion. The university began offering off-campus academic courses in the metropolitan East St. Louis area, which led to the development of a separate institution in Edwardsville.

James E. Walker
President

As SIU has grown and flourished, its campuses have developed programs of instruction, research and public service, which have attracted and served students, faculty and staff from the region, from every county in Illinois, every state in the nation and from more than 100 countries throughout the world. In addition to many undergraduate degree programs, SIUC and SIUE offer more than 95 academic programs leading to master's degrees and 28 leading to doctorate degrees. Professional degrees also are available through SIUE's School of Nursing in Edwardsville and School of Dental Medicine in Alton, and SIUC's School of Law in Carbondale, School of Medicine in Springfield and a campus in Nakajo, Japan.

The instruction, research and service missions of the two campuses meet the needs of the geographic areas in which they are located, but SIU also is committed to serving statewide, national and international needs. This commitment is reflected in educational activities located off the main campuses, in inter-institutional agreements for research and in training exchanges with foreign universities and worldwide student exchange programs.

Southern Illinois University is governed by a nine-member Board of Trustees. Administratively, the university is headed by the President, who reports to the Board of Trustees; the Chancellors of SIUC and SIUE report to the President.

Board of Trustees: Molly D'Esposito, Winnetka, *chair*; Gene Callahan, Springfield, *vice chair*; Harris Rowe, Jacksonville, *secretary*; John Brewster, Marion; Ed Hightower, Edwardsville; Mark L. Repking, Alton; A. D. VanMeter, Jr., Springfield, and student members Nathan Stone, Carbondale, and Jason Holzum, Edwardsville.

UNIVERSITY ADMINISTRATION

James E. Walker .... *President*
John S. Haller, Jr .... *Vice President for Academic Services*
Elaine Hyden .... *Vice President for Financial Services and Board Treasurer*
Ron Cremeens .... *Executive Director of Internal Audits*
Garrett L. Deakin .... *Executive Assistant for Government Relations*
Sharon Holmes .... *Executive Secretary to the Board*
Peter Ruger .... *General Counsel*
Scott Kaiser .... *Assistant to the President for Corporate, Community & Media Relations*

SOUTHERN ILLINOIS UNIVERSITY CARBONDALE

Walter V. Wendler
Chancellor

Southern Illinois University Carbondale (SIUC) is dedicated to the belief that university graduates should be educated to understand the world they are entering and be prepared to contribute to the health and strength of society. In recent decades, the preparation process has been augmented by the expansion of basic and applied research, much of it meaningful to the region the university serves most closely.

Today, SIUC offers 84 undergraduate majors and four associate degrees, as well as graduate and professional education, including Ph.D.s in 28 fields and medical and law degrees. More than 22,000 students from throughout the nation and the world take part in a comprehensive education program enriched by a full range of student services and numerous internship and externship opportunities. In Fiscal Year 1999, the university awarded 214 associate degrees, 4,429 bachelor's degrees, 813 master's degrees, 119 doctoral degrees and 191 professional degrees (law and medicine).

More than $121 million in grants and contracts from 792 public and private agencies (excluding financial aid awards) fueled 792 research, training and service projects at SIUC in Fiscal Year 2000. The university has taken a leading role in a number of research areas important to the economy and strength of Illinois and the nation, including clean-coal technology, reclamation and land use, materials science, aquaculture, groundwater quality, soybean research, information management, early childhood education, rehabilitation and health professions training.

In 1997, SIUC opened the Public Policy Institute, headed by former U.S. Sen. Paul Simon. The institute studies issues related to public policy and their implications for government leaders, journalists and society at large. Those issues include Social Security, campaign finance reform, environmental and health law and television violence.

SIUC faculty, staff and students tackle problems from improving brake linings to plastics recycling; endangered species monitoring to wetlands restoration; pharmaceuticals testing to computer neural network development for medical diagnostic devices; nicotine addiction to AIDS education; biomechanical studies to studies of banking efficiency and regulation.

Several campus units participate in research, education and service programs coordinated by the Coal Extraction and Utilization Research Center, established in 1974 as a focus for coal and related energy and environmental research activities in Illinois. The center, together with the Illinois Department of Commerce and Community Affairs, manages the Illinois Coal Development Park at SIUC's Carterville campus. The facility, established in 1990, houses the Illinois Clean Coal Institute, research laboratories and a well-equipped high bay for industrial process development. It also houses the country's only Dragline Productivity Program, offering worldwide, hands-on simulator training for operators of massive surface mining equipment. Coal research on campus and at the Coal Development Park focuses on finding solutions to the energy and environmental problems associated with coal use worldwide, with strong emphasis on increasing market opportunities for Illinois coal while enhancing environmental protection.

Other specialized research units at SIUC include the Center for Advanced Friction Studies, the Cooperative Wildlife Research Laboratory, the Fisheries and Illinois Aquaculture Center, the Crime Studies Center, the Center for Archaeological Investigations, the Pontikes Center for Management of Information, and the Center for Alzheimer Disease and Related Disorders at the School of Medicine in Springfield.

Additional research offices or organizations administered by SIUC include the Illinois Groundwater Consortium, the Universities Council on Water Resources and the Meyers Institute for Interdisciplinary Research in Organic and Medicinal Chemistry.

College of Agriculture faculty members received more than $1.5 million in Fiscal Year 2000 from the Illinois Council for Food and Agriculture Research. Research efforts concentrate on areas such as soybeans, with attention to sudden death syndrome, soybean cyst nematodes, biotechnology advances and germ plasma. Researchers also look for interdisciplinary approaches that will improve animal waste management, forestry, field and fruit crops, nutrition and physiology. The college is home to the Illinois Grape and Wine Resources Council.

Many years of cooperative relations with other nations have brought about 110 international linkages with educational institutions in 47 countries. American students may enroll in SIUC semester-abroad programs in Japan, summer travel/study seminars or direct exchanges in countries such as Australia, Austria, Germany, Great Britain, France or Switzerland. Nearly 1,800 students from 115 foreign countries study at SIUC in degree programs, technical training programs and intensive English studies. More than 90 Japanese students study at SIUC's off-campus program in Nakajo, Japan.

Shyrock Auditorium (left) and Altgeld Hall (right) anchor SIUC's Old Main Mall. Faner Hall runs directly behind both of these old campus landmarks.

The most comprehensive collection of the works on any American philosopher, those of John Dewey, is held at SIUC. The SIU Press and the Center for Dewey Studies are publishing the great educator's complete works. Noted for the breadth and excellence of its publications, the SIU Press has received many awards for works in history, literature and drama. Among its distinguished series are exhaustive scientific studies on Illinois plant communities and the papers of Ulysses S. Grant.

School of Law

The Southern Illinois University School of Law is a small school with a strong program, a dedicated faculty and a high faculty-to-student ratio. Graduating classes have consistently exceeded the average pass rate for the State Bar examination. SIU usually places graduates in employment within six months of graduation, about the same rate as the national average.

The School of Law's moot court teams have won several regional and national competitions.

The school operates an extensive legal clinic, providing legal assistance to elderly clients in 13 Southern Illinois counties. The school also has an active dispute resolution clinic, which concentrates on mediation and arbitration of disputes. These programs offer students practical experience with clients, as do the School of Law's internship opportunities with judges, local state's attorneys and public defenders' offices.

The law library holds about 196,000 volumes, including more than 810,000 microform units. Videotapes, audiotapes, CD-ROMs, conventional and online catalogs and computer-assisted systems (LEXIS and Westlaw) provide the tools for legal research. Law-trained librarians are an important resource for area attorneys and the university's students and faculty.

School of Medicine

The Southern Illinois University School of Medicine was established in 1970, with the primary purpose of helping the people of Central and Southern Illinois meet their health care needs. Currently, 288 students, primarily residents of Illinois, are enrolled, and as of May 2001, 1,711 physicians have graduated. The school ranks nationally in the percentage of its graduates (52 percent) who are practicing in primary care specialties, and 27 percent of its graduates have entered family practice. MEDPREP, a preparation program for educationally disadvantaged students, has helped minority students enter medical fields.

Medical students take a year of basic science courses at the Carbondale campus, where Memorial Hospital is a primary affiliate, then transfer to Springfield for the last three years of clinical study, much of which takes place at Memorial Medical Center and St. John's Hospital, also affiliated hospitals. The curriculum is competency-based and includes many active learning situations using written cases and simulated patients.

An extensive residency program annually fills 260 residency positions in dermatology, family practice, internal medicine, neurology, obstetrics and gynecology, pediatrics, psychiatry, psychiatry and medicine combined, radiology and five surgical specialties — general surgery, orthopedics, otolaryngology, plastic/reconstruction and urology. Family practice centers for training students and residents have been established in Carbondale, Decatur, Quincy and Springfield. Affiliation agreements with additional hospitals provide clinical facilities for the residency program.

The school conducts a continuing education program for physicians and allied health care professionals in the state. An extensive medical library is located in Springfield. The Practice Opportunity Program assists communities without doctors and gives students and residents a look at possible practice locations. Many tertiary medical services are available from the clinical faculty, who conduct specialized clinics in seven departments. They treated more than 80,000 patients for a total of 400,960 clinic visits projected for Fiscal Year 1999.

ADMINISTRATIVE OFFICERS — Carbondale

Walter V. Wendler .... *Chancellor*
Margaret E. Winters .... *Interim Vice Chancellor for Academic Affairs and Provost*
Larry H. Dietz ..... *Vice Chancellor for Student Affairs and Enrollment Management*
Carl Getto, M.D. .... *Dean and Provost, School of Medicine*
Glenn Poshard .... *Vice Chancellor for Administration*
Rickey N. McCurry .... *Vice Chancellor for Institutional Advancement*

SOUTHERN ILLINOIS UNIVERSITY EDWARDSVILLE

David J. Werner
Chancellor

As a comprehensive university, Southern Illinois University Edwardsville (SIUE) maintains a wide range of undergraduate, graduate and professional programs, supports research and promotes public activity directed primarily toward improvement of the schools and economic development of southwestern Illinois.

SIUE's schools and programs have received accreditation from a wide range of national associations, including the North Central Association of Colleges and Schools, the Accreditation Board for Engineering and Technology, the American Assembly of Collegiate Schools of Business, the American Chemical Society, the American Speech-Language-Hearing Association, the Council on Dental Education of the American Dental Association, the Council on Social Work Education, the National Association of Schools of Music, the National Council for Accreditation of Teacher Education, the National League for Nursing and the American Art Therapy Association. These accreditations, small class sizes, accessible faculty and the successes of SIUE students and graduates are evidence of the quality of education available at SIUE, which also is one of the most affordable four-year public universities in Illinois.

SIUE offers 42 undergraduate programs and 39 graduate and professional programs. The university encourages diversity on campus through a number of programs devoted to cultural and social sensitivity and understanding, as well as academic programs aimed at under-represented minorities.

The core of the SIUE campus sits in the middle of 2,660 wooded acres on the bluffs near the Mississippi River, halfway between the rural beauty of Southern Illinois and the attractions of St. Louis, just 20 minutes away.

SIUE thrives as a commuter and residential university, with about 2,900 students housed on campus. The university is enjoying enrollment and campus growth rivaled only by its earliest days. Since 1993, SIUE has added 11 new facilities, including three residence halls and two classroom buildings; enrollment has grown to more than 12,200 students.

In addition to its core campus, SIUE also encompasses the School of Dental Medicine in nearby Alton and the East St. Louis Center. The university's roots can be traced to these two cities, which were the homes for "residence centers" that led the way to the creation of SIUE.

The School of Dental Medicine, the only school of its kind in the area, offers students from across the state a top-notch education — as evidenced by the students' performance on national exams. Few facilities in the country provide the specialized and innovative dental instruction and patient care available in the Dental Implant Clinic, which opened in Edwardsville in 1997.

SIUE's East St. Louis Center provides community services for East St. Louis residents of all ages, from pre-schoolers to senior adults. These services include a nationally recognized Head Start program, dental and vision care, latch-key, school-day and after-school educational programs.

Approaching its 50th anniversary, SIUE has matured into a strong and distinctive source of educational opportunity, a focus for research and creative activity, and a continuing stimulus for regional growth and development.

ADMINISTRATIVE OFFICERS — Edwardsville

David J. Werner .... *Chancellor*
Sharon Hahs .... *Provost and Vice Chancellor for Academic Affairs*
Kenneth R. Neher .... *Vice Chancellor for Administration*
G. Patrick Williams .... *Vice Chancellor for Development and Public Affairs*
Narbeth Emmanuel .... *Vice Chancellor for Student Affairs*

The SIUE campus is situated among the hills and forests of southwestern Illinois, 80 miles from Springfield and 20 miles from St. Louis.

CHICAGO STATE UNIVERSITY

Dr. Elnora D. Daniel
President

Chicago State University (CSU), the oldest public university in the Chicago metropolitan area, is a fully accredited public institution located in a residential community on the south side of Chicago. It was founded in 1867 as a teacher training school with 13 students from Cook County, and its current enrollment stands at about 7,000 students from the United States and throughout the world. The President is CEO and is responsible for providing leadership and vision for the 21st century in the administration of campus initiatives and policies. The President reports to the institution's eight-member Board of Trustees, which includes seven members appointed by the Governor and one student representative elected by the CSU student body.

The university boasts an academic program that encompasses four colleges: Arts and Sciences, Business, Education and Health Sciences, and offers 36 undergraduate and 20 graduate degree-granting programs. In addition, there is a Division of Continuing Education and Nontraditional Programs, which reaches out to the community with extension courses, distance learning and not-for-credit programs. As an engaged institution working with and for the community in which it is located, Chicago State University also provides for the varied needs of the myriad of constituencies it serves within and beyond the state as well. Specifically, the university offers academically rigorous day and evening course schedules, international programming and addresses the specific needs of minorities and older, non-traditional populations.

Chicago State University has long enjoyed a reputation as the institution of choice for traditional and non-traditional populations. With leadership from its 325 faculty members, the university has an effective academic support system that helps students graduate, enter the nation's most competitive graduate and professional schools and achieve their career goals. CSU's rigorous academic programming in the arts, sciences and education features such luminaries as Illinois Poet Laureate Gwendolyn Brooks and a long-term relationship with the Chicago Public Schools System. These and all other university programs challenge students to achieve their personal pinnacles in the intellectual domain and beyond.

Chicago State University is a leader in efforts to boost minority business ownership in the City of Chicago. The university is a center of programs encouraging minorities to enter into fields in which they are currently underrepresented, such as science, mathematics and medicine. CSU has a new $51.6 million Greenhouse Science Annex that will strengthen the university's efforts in training scientists. A new $20 million student center contains conference facilities, a commons area, auditorium, cafeteria and student lounges.

The campus, which was dedicated in 1971, includes classroom buildings, the Douglas Library, the Robinson University Center, the Williams Science Center, the Cook Administration Building and the Jacoby D. Dickens Physical Education and Athletics Center, which houses three Olympic size pools and a Nautilus training room. The university has NCAA Division I men's and women's teams in multiple sporting areas, including baseball, golf, tennis, basketball, cross country and track and field.

For 132 years, CSU has served the Chicago metropolitan area. As the university enters the new millennium, it is driven by a collectively defined Strategic Plan that identifies six strategic goals designed to enhance and expand the university's academic capabilities and outreach potential. With a new president, a collectively defined Strategic Plan and its historical commitment to serve and empower, Chicago State University anticipates its most triumphant epoch in the coming years.

Board of Trustees: Dr. Niva Lubin, Chicago, *chair*; Mary Denson, Chicago; Jacoby Dickens, Olympia Fields; Peggy A. Montes, Chicago; Dr. William Malone, Chicago, and Betsy Hill, Wilmette.

A view of the Chicago State University campus.

EASTERN ILLINOIS UNIVERSITY

Eastern Illinois University (EIU), located in Charleston, is a traditional, selective, residential institution that offers a high quality education at a relatively low cost. EIU is among the nation's top 100 public universities for quality and value according to *Kiplinger's Personal Finance Magazine* and *U.S. News and World Report*. The university's high academic standing is reflected in quality undergraduate and graduate programs taught by an experienced and caring faculty. High admission standards and a flourishing Honors Program ensure an academically talented student body that benefits from small classes, strong academic advising and other student services.

Louis V. Hencken
Interim President

Student graduation and retention rates are well above state and national averages, and more than half of those who enroll choose EIU because of its academic reputation. Job placement and alumni and employer satisfaction rates also are high.

With reasonable tuition and fees, room and board rates and a cost-saving textbook rental system, EIU is an attractive alternative to more costly public and private colleges and universities.

More than half of the university's more than 10,000 students attend classes on an attractive, 320-acre campus with one of the lowest crime rates of all Illinois public universities and one of the lowest nationwide.

The university's academic programs are organized into four colleges.

Academic Organization

The College of Arts and Humanities offers undergraduate degree programs in African-American studies, art, English, foreign languages, history, journalism, music, philosophy, social science, speech communication and theater arts. Minors are available in creative writing, professional writing, public relations and women's studies.

The Lumpkin College of Business and Applied Sciences includes three schools: the School of Business, which offers majors in accounting, business administration, computer information systems and organizational studies, finance and management and marketing; the School of Family and Consumer Sciences, offering a major in family/consumer sciences, and the School of Technology, which offers majors in career and technical education and industrial technology. Minors are available in interdisciplinary business administration and military science.

The College of Education and Professional Studies offers undergraduate programs in early childhood, elementary and middle-level education; health studies; physical education; recreation administration and special education. Minors are available in adult education, health communication and safety and driver education.

The College of Sciences offers programs in biological sciences, chemistry, clinical laboratory science, communication disorders and sciences, economics, engineering, geography, geology, mathematics, mathematics and computer science, physics, political science, psychology and sociology. Minors are available in anthropology, earth science, Latin American studies and pre-law studies. Pre-professional programs are offered in pre-dentistry, pre-engineering, pre-medicine, pre-nursing, pre-optometry, pre-pharmacy, pre-physical therapy and pre-veterinary medicine. Teacher preparation and honors programs are available in many undergraduate degree majors.

The Graduate School complements the undergraduate program, both by building upon the undergraduate curriculum and by providing outstanding master's and specialist degree programs.

The School of Adult and Continuing Education offers an individualized Board of Trustees Bachelor of Arts degree program for working adults.

Enrollment and Student Activities

Eastern Illinois University has enrolled more than 10,000 students in each of the past several years. Total enrollment for fall 2000 was 10,637 — including 9,843 students on-campus and 803 off-campus students. More than 4,000 live on campus in residence halls, student apartment buildings and Greek Court.

The university offers an extensive orientation program to assist all new students in the transition to EIU's academic, social and cultural environment. The 14 student-run committees of the university board schedule activities for the student body. The Interfraternity Council, Panhellenic Council and Black Greek Council coordinate the activities of the 27 national fraternities and sororities on campus.

The theater arts and music departments offer involvement in their productions and performances to any EIU student. Broadcast activities at the Radio-TV Center (WEIU-FM and WEIU-TV) serve an 11-county area and are open to all full-time students regardless of their majors. Student publications include: *The Daily Eastern News*; *Minority Today*, a monthly newspaper; *The Vehicle*, a literary magazine; *Heartland*, a general interest magazine, and the *Warbler* yearbook.

Board of Trustees: Nate Anderson, East St. Louis; Roger Dettro, D.D.S., Mattoon; Jeffery Lezotte, Chicago; Robert Manion, Hinsdale; Betsy Mitchell, Champaign; Julie Nimmons, Litchfield, and Julie Ward, Springfield.

Eastern Illinois University's Mary Josephine Booth Library is undergoing renovations that will greatly enhance its ability to meet the information needs of the campus community for the next 20 years.

GOVERNORS STATE UNIVERSITY

Dr. Stuart Fagan
President

In fall 1971, Governors State University offered its first classes and enrolled its first students. Over the more than three decades since its founding, the university's core commitment has been to form a community of learners, a community that embraces all who join it and that challenges all to make learning live in the world around them.

GSU's mission is: 1) to offer an excellent education that meets the demands of the state for engaged, knowledgeable citizens and highly-skilled professionals, and that is accessible to those traditionally underserved by higher education; 2) to cultivate and enlarge a diverse and intellectually stimulating community of learners guided by a culture that embodies openness of communication, diversity of backgrounds, experiences and perspectives, mutual respect and cooperation, critical inquiry, constant questioning and continuing assessment, and ongoing research and scholarship; and 3) to strengthen and enhance the educational, cultural, social and economic development of the region through partnerships with governmental, business, educational, civic and other organizations.

GSU is an upper-division university offering junior and senior level courses for completion of bachelor's degrees in 21 majors and master's degrees in 25 majors. Today, its more than 9,300 students each year commute to the 760-acre campus in University Park from the Chicago metropolitan area, including Cook, DuPage, Kankakee, Kendall, Grundy and Will counties, and Lake County, Indiana. While students of all ages attend the university, the average student is in his/her mid-30s and employed full or part time outside the university. The university staff has developed special assistance programs for students returning to college, including adult re-entry programs, learning assistance, advisement and student services.

The university has a strong commitment to cultural diversity in every facet of university life. It also is nationally recognized for its innovative approaches to distance learning techniques (video courses, television instruction, Web-based and Web-assisted learning) that allow students to learn at their own pace at work or at home. Several GSU-produced, award-winning teleclasses are being distributed throughout the world by cable and educational networks.

The university's outreach efforts include several national videoconferences that link hundreds of viewers to audio/video discussions on current issues. These presentations enable GSU students to be a part of that discussion from campus. The university also is involved in workforce development and retraining projects for regional businesses through curricula specially designed by GSU faculty and staff.

The university's involvement and service to its communities enables GSU to continually improve the quality and delivery of its academic programs. GSU offers degree programs that address the rapidly changing needs of its students and employers in the region. Special emphasis is given to fields in which entry-level employment and advanced training opportunities exist within the GSU service area. The university meets the needs of its neighbors, the region and the state by offering courses, seminars and programs that take a holistic approach to education and continually connects the university to the community. Through services offered by the university's South Metropolitan Regional Leadership Center, the College of Business and Public Administration's

"CenterPoint" program, the Learning in Context Partnership in the community of Ford Heights, and the Department of Human Services' Leadership Development Institute, GSU addresses issues that impact the way people live and creates a community of lifelong learners.

In serving its diverse population, GSU utilizes a blend of the traditional and more experiential instructional modes, including internships and practical field training. These on-site opportunities serve as an additional dimension to faculty instruction and provide an important link to community service.

The university's facility, designed as six buildings under one roof, covers 400,000 square feet. The setting enables interaction among the four colleges and offers a full-service music recital hall, student media labs, television studios, state-of-the-art computer labs and recreational facilities, including an Olympic-style swimming pool. The Center for Performing Arts, a 1,200-seat theater, brings world-class entertainment to the region. Performers at the Center have included the Joffrey Ballet of Chicago, The Second City, Jim Brickman, the Hubbard Street Dance Company, the Verve Jazzfest, Paula Poundstone and national touring companies of "A Chorus Line," "A Christmas Carol," "42nd Street" and "Crazy for You."

The Governors State University campus also boasts the internationally renowned Nathan Manilow Sculpture Park, which has been described as "perhaps the finest exhibition of monumental sculpture in the country."

Academic Programs

The university is organized into four colleges — Arts and Sciences, Business and Public Administration, Education and Health Professions. Each college offers undergraduate and graduate programs. Students prepare for professions in accounting, business, government, industry, teaching, counseling, school psychology, educational administration, nursing, health administration, social work, physical and occupational therapy, addictions counseling, speech-language pathology, communications, the arts, computer science, chemistry, social sciences, political studies, biology, English, management information systems, public administration, and criminal justice.

GSU first was accredited by the North Central Association of Colleges and Secondary Schools in 1975. This accreditation was renewed in 1980, in 1990 and in 2000, for a maximum of 10 years. Individual programs at GSU have received accreditation or entitlement from the National League for Nursing, the American Medical Association's Committee on Allied Health Education and Accreditation, the Illinois State Board of Education, the Accrediting Commission on Education for Health Sciences Administration, the Association of University Programs in Health Administration, the American Speech-Language-Hearing Association, the Council for Accreditation of Counseling and Related Educational Programs, the Council on Social Work Education, the Association of Collegiate Business Schools and Programs, and the National Association of School Psychologists.

Admissions and Enrollment

To be admitted into the university, undergraduates must have earned a minimum of 60 semester hours with at least a "C" average. Graduate admission is based on an undergraduate degree earned from a regionally accredited college or university and fulfillment of specific criteria for individual majors.

NORTHEASTERN ILLINOIS UNIVERSITY

Salme H. Steinberg
President

Northeastern Illinois University (NEIU) is a comprehensive state university serving nearly 11,000 commuter students. Located on 67 acres in an attractive residential area on the northwest side of Chicago, the university offers more than 80 undergraduate and graduate majors. Dedicated to both excellence and affordability, the university serves a population diverse in age, culture and language, including many returning adult students, recent immigrants and people who are the first in their families to attend college. They represent a wide range of cultural and ethnic backgrounds and bring a variety and wealth of experiences that help enhance classroom learning. Nationally recognized as the "most diverse university in the Midwest," NEIU ranks among the top 50 universities in the U.S. for producing Hispanic and Asian graduates with baccalaureate degrees in computer science and education. NEIU is the only Illinois public university that is a federally designated Hispanic Serving Institution.

NEIU is divided into four colleges: Arts and Sciences, Business and Management, Education and the Graduate College, with three learning sites around Chicago. The Center for Inner City Studies (CICS) on Chicago's southeast side has been serving the educational needs of Chicago's inner city community for more than 30 years. The Chicago Teachers' Center (CTC), located at River West Plaza, has been an educational center for elementary and secondary schoolteachers for 20 years. El Centro de Recursos Educativos (El Centro) on the northwest side has served Chicago's adult Hispanic-American community for more than 20 years.

NEIU offers high-quality undergraduate and graduate programs to a broad spectrum of students to foster student growth and development. To this end, NEIU attaches primary importance to excellence in teaching. The university also offers students the opportunity to strengthen academic foundations or participate in rigorous independent study. Because program quality is enhanced by professional activities outside the classroom on the part of the faculty, emphasis also is given to applied research and to academic and public service. Students and faculty enjoy many opportunities to integrate field-based learning, research and service with classroom instruction. Recognizing the advantage that international experience brings in education and the workplace, the university offers short-term and traditional study abroad programs.

In the 21st century, NEIU continues to seek ways to meet the growing interest in higher education of students who want a quality educational experience that integrates technology with classroom learning but who cannot travel to the main campus. To that end, NEIU has joined in various consortia to provide distance education at off-campus locations. The Distance Education Program uses on-site professors as well as a two-way interactive video network system that allows many courses to be offered at several sites around the Chicago area simultaneously, making distance education a convenient alternative. CICS, CTC and El Centro are part of this network system as are several sites in Lake, Cook and DuPage counties.

Access to technology is another important factor in providing a quality education. Not only does the university provide its students with state-of-the-art computer labs, but it also has been increasing the number of technology-enhanced classrooms (TECs) available for instruction. TECs import a wide variety of technologies into the classroom, supplementing traditional instruction with such resources as DVD players, digital enhancements and sound recording and playback equipment. In these special classrooms, professors are able to use more creative methods of instruction by integrating technology into traditional coursework.

NEIU recognizes the importance of creating a student-centered learning environment. The university's new Fine Arts Center supports the academic programs in the departments of Art, Music and Dance, and Speech and Performing Arts. The Recital Hall, which attracts touring professionals as well as student and faculty artists, has been recognized by both performers and music critics for exceptional acoustics. Additionally, in creating the Wellness Center at the Physical Education Complex, the refurbished fitness facility features state-of-the-art equipment designed to attract regular use and encourage exercise and a healthful lifestyle. NEIU also is committed to enhancing the overall beauty of the campus through the restoration of native prairie grasses and flowers.

NEIU is an exciting and dynamic place that offers a quality education at an affordable price. Students explore new educational and professional opportunities in friendly surroundings, learn from experienced professors, and receive the attention needed to thrive and prepare for future education or a successful career in a challenging world.

WESTERN ILLINOIS UNIVERSITY

Donald S. Spencer
President

Western Illinois University's (WIU) commitment is to provide the premier undergraduate education among all public universities in Illinois and in selected disciplines far beyond Illinois' borders.

With more than 12,600 students, WIU is large enough to offer the benefits of a major university, yet small enough to provide the personal support and attention so vital to a superior education. WIU maintains a student-faculty ratio of 15 to 1 and has an average class size of 25.

Established in 1899, WIU offers 46 undergraduate and 34 graduate degree programs. Its faculty hold degrees from many of the nation's top universities and engage their students in the active process of discovery and understanding.

Currently celebrating its Centennial, WIU takes pride in its past achievements, its growth and commitment to the future. The university's facilities, programs and people make WIU one of the leading forces in preparing citizens to face the challenges of the 21st century.

The College of Arts and Sciences equips students to lead useful and productive lives within their communities. The humanities, mathematics and the natural and social sciences form the core of human knowledge. The college's degree programs lead to the specialized study required in graduate and professional schools, while simultaneously providing a liberal arts education that serves to create knowledgeable, flexible and broad-minded individuals. WIU students today are the teachers, government officials, business executives, scientists, engineers and community leaders of tomorrow.

WIU's College of Business and Technology augments its superior classroom teaching with a wide variety of lectures, symposia and discussions designed with an emphasis on the broad social responsibility of the business world. Accredited by the American Assembly of Collegiate Schools of Business, WIU produces today's professionals in accountancy, agriculture, computer science, economics, industrial education and technology, management, marketing and finance and transportation.

The College of Education and Human Services is a pioneer in meeting the humanistic and technological needs of a changing society. The college's electronic multimedia classroom was one of the first in the state to provide long-distance learning in Illinois. The breadth of the college's programs prepares professionals for education, child care, health education, physical education, law enforcement and justice administration, leisure, recreation and tourism, apparel design and merchandising, food services and lodging. In 1997, the college received a five-year Star Schools grant of $9.9 million from the U.S. Department of Education. WIU was the only institution of higher education in the country to receive Star Schools funding in three funding cycles.

The College Student Personnel program ranks among the top in the United States. WIU's ROTC program is Illinois' largest, while maintaining the highest quality, and is considered the flagship program in its three-state brigade.

The university's College of Fine Arts and Communication is the center of music, theater, communication and visual arts on campus and throughout the community. Students and faculty perform in major theater and studio shows. The annual Jazz Festival features world-renowned artists such as Arturo

Sandoval, DIVA and the Count Basie Orchestra. Summer Music Theater rounds out the year with Broadway musical productions. National Forensic Debate tournaments are held, as well as regularly scheduled student radio and television broadcasts. The art department fosters a creative environment for students to pursue the visual arts.

The university's library is an architectural and visual showplace as well as a superb learning center. It contains more than 1 million catalogued volumes, 3,300 current periodical subscriptions, 430,000 microforms and computer access to resources worldwide. There are more than 900 computers for student use on campus in 20 labs and 11 resource centers. All students have access to the Internet and the World Wide Web.

The University Honors College offers enriched learning for promising scholars in 34 areas of study. WIU honors students have received an International Ambassadorial Scholarship, research grants, Fine Arts Laureate awards and national Best Paper awards for honors theses.

Lifelong learning is recognized through the programs of the School of Extended and Continuing Education. WIU offers the opportunity for nontraditional students to earn bachelor's degrees through a variety of programs, including long-distance learning and off-campus classes. The school offers many credit and noncredit workshops for multiple professions and summer camps for adolescents. The Cross-Cultural Educational Program is a multifaceted, multipartnership educational program designed to help prospective Hispanic students gain access to institutions of higher learning. The WIU Regional Center in Moline serves Quad Cities-area residents and place-bound undergraduate students through credit and noncredit activities. The regional center provides distance learning classrooms and graduate degree programs.

Admission Policy and Accreditation

Western Illinois University admits students with ACT scores of 22 or higher (SAT-I 1010 or higher) or with ACT scores of at least 18 (SAT-I 850) if they rank in the upper 50 percent of their high school graduating class. Students not meeting these standards may be considered for alternative admission. This application should be supported by a letter of recommendation from the high school counselor and a letter of appeal from the student.

Eighty percent of WIU students are undergraduates and 20 percent are graduate students. The university's enrollment represents 89 Illinois counties, 45 states and 49 nations.

WIU is accredited through the specialist's degree level by the North Central Association of Colleges and Secondary Schools. The university's teacher certification programs are accredited by the National Council for Accreditation of Teacher Education and approved by the Illinois State Board of Education. The College of Business and Technology is accredited by the American Assembly of Collegiate Schools of Business, and many other degree programs are accredited by their respective accrediting groups.

WIU is located in Macomb and covers more than 1,050 acres. It is composed of 52 academic and service buildings, a university golf course, the Frank Horn Field Campus just south of Macomb and the Alice L. Kibbe Life Sciences Station on the Mississippi River, the only biological field station on a major American river.

Board of Trustees: Carolyn Ehlert, Moline; Lorraine Epperson, Macomb; George J. Guzzardo, Macomb; J. Michael Houston, Springfield; Dace E. Richardson, Wheaton; Zack Stamp, Springfield, and student representative Shawn Wochner, East Moline.

ILLINOIS STATE UNIVERSITY

Victor John Boschini, Jr.
President

Founded in 1857, Illinois State University (ISU) in Normal was the first public institution of higher learning in Illinois. Abraham Lincoln, as attorney for the Illinois Board of Education, drafted documents establishing the university, and Jesse Fell, great-grandfather of the late Adlai E. Stevenson II, helped found Illinois State. The institution became one of the nation's first "normal" (a title given to institutions for teachers) schools, establishing a precedent and a model for the normal school movement throughout the United States.

From its historic origins as a teacher preparation institution, ISU has become a major multipurpose university offering diversified curricula. Today, ISU is fulfilling the dream of its founders by serving the needs of the citizens and businesses of the State of Illinois with quality programs of education, research and public service. ISU is committed to continuing its three-fold mission, continually evaluating and changing its educational and service offerings to accommodate our changing society.

Illinois State University offers a wide range of programs at the bachelor's, master's and doctoral levels to its 20,504 students from 49 states and 71 countries. The Chicago area boasts the largest segment of the student body at 43 percent. Central Illinois claims the next largest group at 28 percent. About 88 percent are undergraduate students and 12 percent are graduate students. The enrollment includes full-time (86 percent) and part-time (14 percent) students, including 11 percent minority students, students with disabilities and adult learners. Among the entering students, the mean ACT score is 22.7, with 86 percent in the top half of their high school graduating class.

ISU offers a small college experience with large university opportunities. The university takes pride in its core values of individualized attention, public opportunity, active pursuit of learning, diversity and creative response to change.

Through the interaction of teaching, research and public service, the university provides abundant intellectual opportunities for a large and diverse student population in an environment that responds to student needs and interests, stresses personalized student-faculty interaction and contributes to the development of individuals who will participate responsibly in society.

The hundreds of cultural and athletic events presented annually enhance the quality of life in the Normal-Bloomington community. Public service programs sponsored by the university serve people of all ages, offering opportunities for economic development and lifelong learning.

Thirty-five academic departments offer more than 160 undergraduate programs of study through the Colleges of Business, Arts and Sciences, Fine Arts, Education, Applied Science and Technology and the Mennonite College of Nursing. The Graduate School coordinates 37 master's degrees, two specialist degrees and seven doctoral programs. The academic programs are supported by the services and collections of Milner Library, which contains more than 3 million holdings and special collections.

Board of Trustees: Jaime Flores, Chicago; Nancy Froelich, Hudson; Diane Glenn, Chicago; Jack Huggins, East Peoria; Carl Kasten, Carlinville; Stan Ommen, Bloomington, and William Sulaski, Bloomington.

NORTHERN ILLINOIS UNIVERSITY

Dr. John Peters
President

Chartered in 1895, Northern Illinois University (NIU) opened its doors in 1899 as a teacher's college with 173 students. A century later, NIU is a nationally recognized institution holding the highest Carnegie ranking of doctoral/research university-extensive, with seven degree-granting colleges, doctoral programs in the arts and sciences and education, and an enrollment of more than 23,000 students.

Northern confers 21 types of degrees in 51 undergraduate majors, 70 graduate majors and one professional (Juris Doctor) degree through 41 departments and divisions. NIU's academic offerings are provided through the Colleges of Business, Education, Engineering and Engineering Technology, Health and Human Sciences, Law, Liberal Arts and Sciences, and Visual and Performing Arts.

Other major academic units include the Graduate School, Social Science Research Institute, University Libraries, the Centers for Biochemical and Biophysical Studies, Black Studies, Governmental Studies, Latino and Latin-American Studies, Plant Molecular Biology and Southeast Asian Studies, which is ranked among the top three such centers in the United States. NIU has the world's only Center for Burma Studies and is the home of the American Farmland Trust's Center for Agriculture in the Environment, the Center for the Study of Family Violence and Sexual Assault, and the Northern Illinois Center for Accelerator and Detector Development.

Northern Illinois University's Swen Parson Hall, College of Law.

Northern's academic and student life facilities have undergone substantial expansion during the past five years, and more improvements are underway. The Center for Diversity Resources, the Latino Center, the Campus Child Care Center, the Recreation Center addition, the remodeled Stevenson Residential Complex and, currently under construction, a new 10,000-seat multipurpose convocation center and Barsema Hall, the new College of Business facility, are prominent examples of new buildings that are enhancing the overall student experience on campus. Faraday West (chemistry and physics) and the Engineering Building are state-of-the-art learning facilities rated among the best in the nation by experts in science and technology education. Barsema Hall, scheduled to open in fall 2002, will feature a first-class teaching environment and unprecedented technological capability for College of Business students and faculty.

NIU offers degree programs off-campus at state-of-the-art regional sites in Hoffman Estates, Rockford and Naperville. These outreach efforts will continue to grow along with the professional education needs of working adults in the Chicagoland area.

NIU's Board of Trustees continues to serve as a model governing board in Illinois, guiding NIU's efforts to meet the demands of higher education in the 21st century.

STATE OF ILLINOIS TOLL-FREE NUMBERS

— A —

Adoption Information	800-572-2390
AIDS Hotline	800-243-2437
Amtrak	800-872-7245
Army National Flood Insurance	800-638-6620
Arson Hotline	800-252-2947
Arts Council, Illinois	800-237-6994

— C —

Cancer Information Service	800-422-6237
Child Abuse Hotline	800-252-2873
Citizen's Assistance, Governor's Office	800-642-3112
Citizens Utility Board (CUB)	800-669-5556
Client Assistance Program (Disability Rights)	800-641-3929
Commerce and Community Affairs	
Business Information	800-252-2923
Consumer Protection, Attorney General	
Springfield	800-243-0618
Chicago	800-386-5438
Crime Victim Clearinghouse, Attorney General	800-228-3368

— D —

Dental Referral Services	800-252-2930
Disability Determination Services	800-637-8856
Drug and Alcohol Abuse	800-662-4357

— E —

Emergency Management Agency, Illinois	800-782-7860
Employment Security, Illinois	
Unemployment Insurance Tax Hotline	800-247-4984
Problem Resolution	800-247-4987
Energy Assistance and Weatherization	800-252-8643

— F —

Foster Parenting Hotline	800-624-5437

— H —

Hearing-Impaired Phone Access	
TTY users	800-526-0844
Voice users	800-526-0857
TTY distributor	800-833-0048
Human Services, Illinois	
Cash Assistance, Food Stamps, Medical Assistance,	
Child Care Assistance, Fraud or Abuse, Mental Health,	
Persons with Disabilities, Services for Women,	
Infants & Children	800-843-6154
Help Me Grow - Futures for Kids	800-323-4769

TOLL-FREE NUMBERS (Concluded)

— I —

Illinois Housing Authority 800-942-8439
Illinois State Board of Education
  Teacher Certification 800-845-8749

— L —

Legislative Information.. 800-252-6300
Lottery Information 800-252-1775

— M —

Medicare & Medicaid/Fraud or Abuse.. 800-447-8477
Missing Children — "I-Search" (Illinois) 800-843-5763
Motorcycle Safety Project 800-322-7619

— N —

Nuclear Safety, Illinois 800-346-4542
Nursing Home Information and Abuse 800-252-4343

— P —

Poacher, To Report... 800-252-0163
Poison Control (Statewide) 800-942-5969

— S —

Secretary of State's Office (General Information) 800-252-8980
  Literacy Hotline 800-321-9511
  Organ/Tissue Donor Bilingual Hotline 800-210-2106
  Securities Department... 800-628-7937
  Seniors and Community Services Hotline 800-252-2904
  State Library 800-665-5576
Senior Citizens Hotlines (Statewide)
  Aging, Senior Assistance and Elder Abuse Hotline 800-252-8966
  Attorney General, Consumer Fraud Hotline (Seniors only)
    Springfield 800-252-2518
    Chicago 800-243-5377
Sexually Transmitted Diseases 800-243-2437

— T —

Taxpayer Assistance (State) 800-732-8866
Toll-Free Directory Assistance 800-555-1212
Tourism, Illinois 800-226-6632
Transportation, Overweight Permits 800-252-8636

— U —

University Admissions Information
  Eastern Illinois University 800-252-5711
  Illinois State University 800-366-2478
  Northern Illinois University... 800-892-3050
  Southern Illinois University at Edwardsville 800-447-7483
  University of Illinois at Springfield 800-252-8533

— V —

Veterans Affairs 800-827-1000

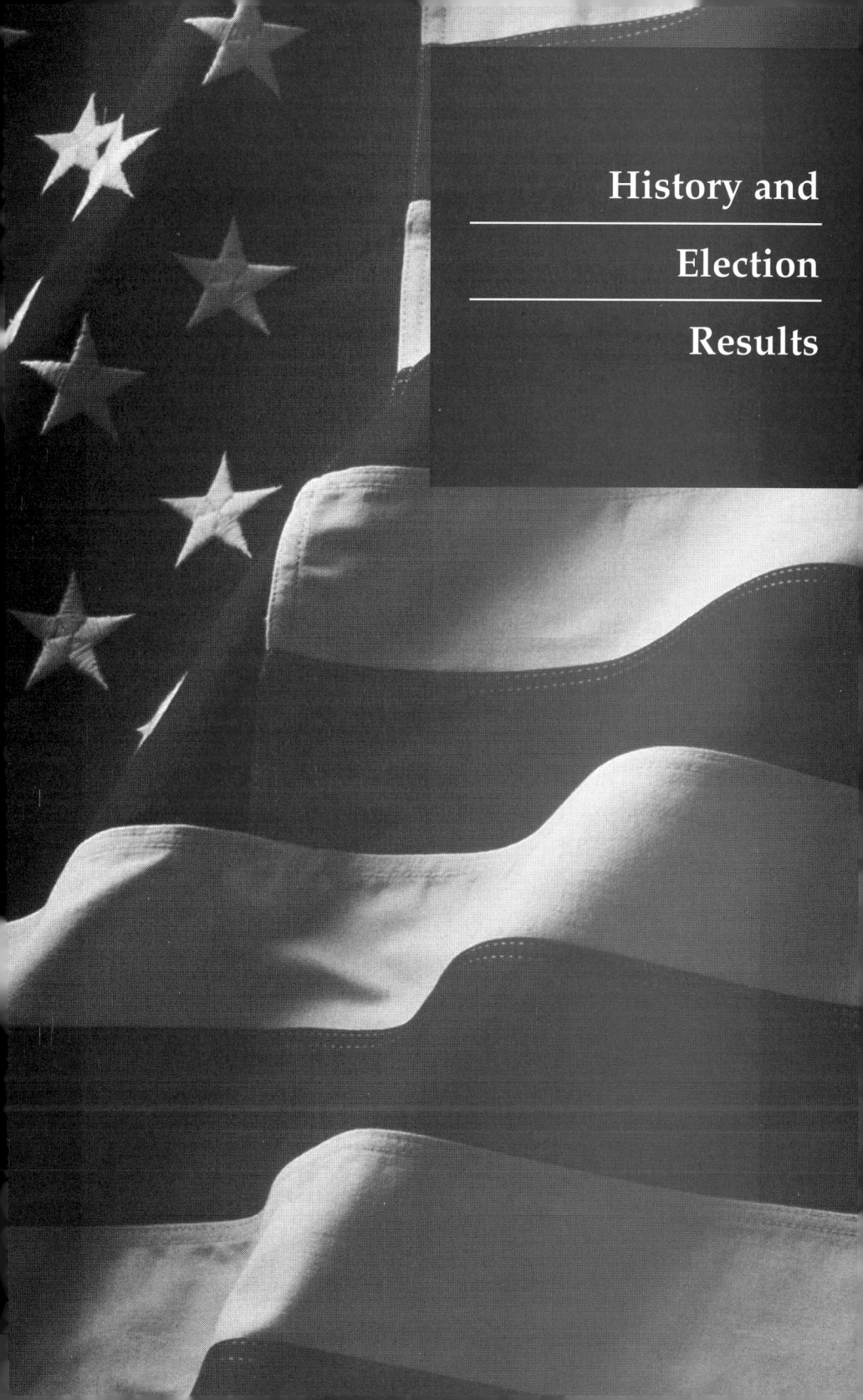

History and
Election
Results

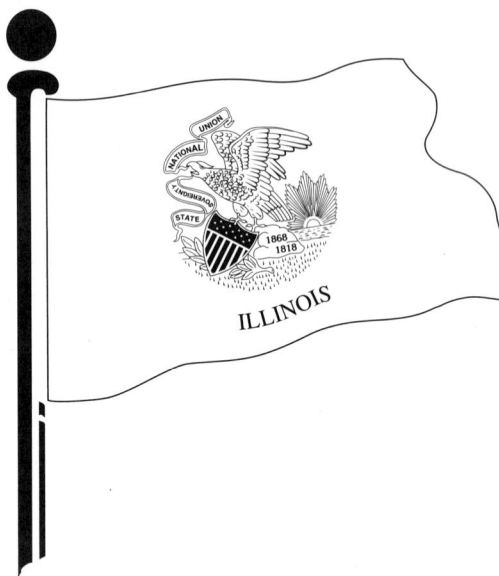

CHAIN OF TITLE

OWNERS, OCCUPANTS OR CLAIMANTS	NATURE OF CLAIM	EXTENT OF CLAIM
INDIANS:		
Illinois (Illini and others	Occupancy and use of soil.	Indefinite
Illinois tribes:		
1. Mitchigamis	Occupancy and use of soil.	1. Originally west of the Mississippi River.
2. Kaskaskias	Occupancy and use of soil.	2. Region between Lake Michigan and Lake Peoria.
3. Peorias	Occupancy and use of soil.	3. Region of Lake Peoria.
4. Cahokias	Occupancy and use of soil.	4. Region of Cahokia and the American Bottom.
5. Tamaroas	Occupancy and use of soil.	5. Region of Southeastern Illinois.
SPAIN:	Columbus' Discovery, 1492.	Western Hemisphere.
ENGLAND:	Cabot's Discovery, 1498.	Continent of America.
SPAIN:	1. De Leon's Discovery of Florida, 1513.	1. North America south of Great Lakes.
	2. De Soto's Landing on the Mississippi, 1541.	2. Region on Mississippi River and its tributaries.
	3. Menendez' Proclamation, 1565.	3. All North America.
FRANCE:	De Chastes—De Monts' Charter, 1603.	North America between 40 degrees and 46 degrees north latitude.

ENGLAND:	1.	Patent for Virginia, 1606 and 1609.	1.	North America between 34 degrees and 45 degrees north latitude.
		London Company, South Virginia.		34 degrees to 38 degrees north latitude.
		Intermediate district open to both.		Bancroft, Hist. U.S., Vol. 1, 120.
		Plymouth Company, North Virginia.		41 to 45 degrees north latitude.
	2.	Massachusetts Bay Charter, 1629.	2.	Massachusetts Bay Country to sea on west.
	3.	Connecticut Colony Rights.	3.	Connecticut River Country.
FRANCE:	1.	Canada and Indians of the west Treaty, 1671.	1.	Northwestern Lake Region.
	2.	Discovery of Illinois, etc., by Marquette et al., 1673.	2.	Illinois and the Northwest.
	3.	La Salle ceremony at the mouth of the Mississippi, 1682.	3.	Mississippi and tributaries from Gulf to New France.
	4.	Crozat patent, 1712.	4.	Same as far as the Illinois.
	5.	Company of the West, 1717.	5.	Same.
ENGLAND:	1.	Treaty of Paris, 1763.	1.	French possessions east of Mississippi River except New Orleans and islands.
	2.	Transfer of Fort Chartres. 1765.	2.	Same.
VIRGINIA:	1.	Capture by Clark, 1778.	1.	Northwest of Ohio River.
	2.	Erected into Illinois County.	2.	Same.
UNITED STATES:	1.	Cession from Virginia, 1784.	1.	Country Northwest of the Ohio River.
	2.	Cession from Massachusetts, 1785.	2.	42 degrees, 2 minutes to 43 degrees, 43 minutes, 12 seconds, north latitude, west of New York to Mississippi River.
	3.	Cession from Connecticut, 1786.	3.	41 degrees to 42 degrees, 2 minutes north latitude, west of Pennsylvania to Mississippi River.
	4.	Northwest Territory, by ordinance of 1787.	4.	Country northwest of the Ohio River.
	5.	Indiana Territory, by Act of Congress, 1800.	5.	Indiana, Illinois, etc.
	6.	Illinois Territory, by Act of Congress, 1809.	6.	Illinois, Wisconsin, etc.
	7.	Illinois Territory, Second Grade, 1812.	7.	Same.
	8.	Indian Cessions.	8.	Various tribes.
ILLINOIS:		Admitted as a State by Act of Congress, 1818.		Illinois.

From Perrin's History of Illinois

CHRONOLOGY OF ILLINOIS HISTORY

French explorers Marquette and Jolliet are depicted in a mural in the State Capitol.

20,000 B.C.E.-8,000 B.C.E. **Paleo-Indians** migrate into Illinois. They gather wild plants and hunt animals, including the giant bison, wooly mammoth and mastodon.

8,000-1,000 B.C.E. During **Archaic Period,** Illinois inhabitants cultivate plants and create specialized tools for hunting and fishing.

700-1500 Mississippian Native American culture builds large planned towns containing flat-topped temple mounds along rivers.

Near present-day Collinsville, 120 mounds are built in a city with a population of more than 20,000. **"Monks Mound"** is the largest prehistoric earthen construction in North America.

Extraction of salt from Saline County begins.

1655 **Iroquois** invade Illinois and defeat Illini. Indian wars continue sporadically for 120 years.

1673 The **"Illiniwek"** (tribe of men), a Native American confederation consisting of Cahokias, Kaskaskias, Mitchagamies, Peorias and Tamaroas, encounter French explorers who refer to the people and country as "Illinois."

Frenchmen **Jacques Marquette** and **Louis Jolliet** descend the Mississippi to the Arkansas and return to Lake Michigan by way of the Illinois River.

1680 La Salle builds **Fort Crevecoeur** on the Illinois River near present Peoria.

SEPTEMBER — Iroquois chase Illini from Illinois. Twelve hundred Tamaroas are tortured and killed.

1682 La Salle builds **Fort St. Louis** on Starved Rock.

1691-92 Tonti and La Forest build the second Fort St. Louis, better known as **Fort Pimitoui,** on Lake Peoria.

1696 Jesuit priest Francois Pinet organizes the **Mission of the Guardian Angel,** the first permanent place of worship in the pre-Chicago wilderness. It will be abandoned in 1699.

1699 Montigny and St. Cosme, priests of the Seminary of Foreign Missions, establish the **Holy Family Mission** at Cahokia.

1703 APRIL — The French Jesuits transfer their Illinois Indian mission from Des Peres (present St. Louis) southeast to a site near the mouth of the Kaskaskia River, thereby founding the town of **Kaskaskia.**

1719 **Fort de Chartres,** near present Prairie du Rocher, is established and becomes the seat of military and civil government in Illinois. It is rebuilt in 1727, 1732 and 1753.

378

1757 The French build **Fort Ascension,** later known as Fort Massac, on the Ohio River near present Metropolis.

1755-63 The **French and Indian (Seven Years') War.** The struggle between France and Great Britain for colonial supremacy in North America brings an end to French rule. With the Treaty of Paris, France cedes her North American possessions east of the Mississippi to Great Britain.

1772 The British abandon and destroy **Fort de Chartres,** leaving behind a small garrison in Kaskaskia.

1775 APRIL — The **American Revolution** begins. The British control the Illinois Territory.

1776 JULY 4 — American colonists adopt the **Declaration of Independence** in Philadelphia.

1775-1783 American **War of Independence** against Great Britain.

1778 JULY 4 — Virginian **George Rogers Clark** and about 175 men defeat the British at Kaskaskia. Illinois is organized as a county of Virginia.

1779 FEBRUARY 24 — After a 19-day, 180-mile march across Illinois, Clark defeats the British at Vincennes.

George Rogers Clark is portrayed in a mural in the State Capitol.

MAY — Kentuckian John Todd, first county lieutenant, organizes the civil and military government. About this time, **Jean Baptiste Pont du Sable** builds the first permanent settlement at what will become Chicago.

1783 The **Treaty of Paris,** ending the American War of Independence, extends the infant nation's western boundary to the Mississippi.

1784 MARCH 1 — Virginia relinquishes her claim to Illinois, paving the way for territorial organization.

1787 JULY 13 — Congress passes the **Ordinance of 1787,** providing for the organization of the Northwest Territory, of which Illinois becomes a part.

1788 **Arthur St. Clair** is appointed Governor of the Northwest Territory, which includes Illinois.

1790 St. Clair (APRIL 27) and Knox (JUNE 20) counties are organized.

1795 Randolph County is organized. AUGUST 3 — Through the **Treaty of Greenville,** the U.S. government reserves certain locations for the building of forts. Within what is present Illinois, sites were designated at Chicago, Peoria and the mouth of the Illinois River.

1800 MAY 7 — Legislation creating the **Indiana Territory,** including Illinois, is approved by Congress.

1801 JANUARY 10 — **William Henry Harrison,** Governor of the Indiana Territory, arrives at Vincennes, the territorial capital.

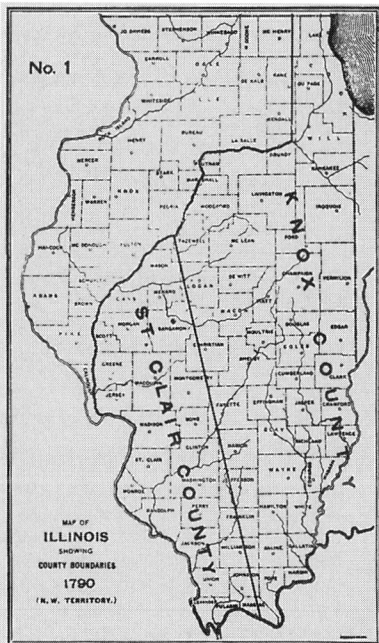

A map of St. Clair and Knox Counties in 1790.

1803   American troops build and occupy **Fort Dearborn**, on the site of Chicago. Governor Harrison concludes a treaty with the Kaskaskia Indians at Vincennes, by which their claim to all land in the Illinois Country, excepting a small area around Kaskaskia, is relinquished.

1804   MARCH 26 — Congress directs the establishment of a U.S. land office at Kaskaskia. This is the first of 10 such offices in Illinois, with the purpose of selling land to settlers.

1809   FEBRUARY 3 — The Illinois Territory, including portions of the present states of Wisconsin, Michigan and Minnesota, is created by an act of Congress. Kaskaskia, located along the Mississippi in the area known as the "American Bottom," becomes the first territorial capital.

FEBRUARY 12 — **Abraham Lincoln** is born in Kentucky.

APRIL 24 — **Ninian Edwards** of Kentucky is appointed the first Territorial Governor by President James Madison.

1810   Population: 12,262. Coal is shipped from southern Illinois to New Orleans for the first time.

1812   MAY 20 — Illinois becomes a territory of the second grade, with suffrage for all white males over 21 who pay taxes and have lived in the territory more than a year.

Shadrach Bond was inaugurated the first Governor of Illinois in 1818.

AUGUST 15 — Native Americans attack U.S. troops and civilians who are evacuating Fort Dearborn; 52 whites are killed.

1812-1814 The **War of 1812** becomes a watershed in the American battle with the British and Indians for trade and territory.

1813   **Fort Clark** is constructed on Peoria Lake. It is garrisoned by American troops and state militia during the War of 1812. In 1819, it is destroyed by Native Americans.

1814   **Matthew Duncan** brings the first printing press to Kaskaskia and there publishes Illinois' first newspaper, the *Illinois Herald*.

1816   The United States builds and garrisons Fort Armstrong (Rock Island) and Fort Edwards (Warsaw) and rebuilds Fort Dearborn (Chicago).

1818   APRIL 18 — Congress passes the **Illinois Enabling Act**, which provides for the organization of a state government, fixes the northern boundary of Illinois, and establishes a permanent school fund from a portion of the proceeds from the sale of public lands.

AUGUST 26 — The Illinois Constitutional Convention, meeting at Kaskaskia, adopts a State Constitution and selects Kaskaskia as the first state capital.

OCTOBER 6 — **Shadrach Bond**, the first Governor of the State of Illinois, is inaugurated.

DECEMBER 3 — President Monroe signs the congressional resolution making Illinois the 21st state.

1820   Population: 55,211.

DECEMBER 1 — By act of the General Assembly, **Vandalia** is declared the capital of Illinois for 20 years.

1821   FEBRUARY — The General Assembly charters a state bank at Vandalia.

1822   DECEMBER 5 — **Edward Coles** is inaugurated Governor.

1823   The rush to the Galena lead mines begins.

1824   AUGUST 6 — Illinois voters refuse to call a convention to amend the Constitution in order to legalize slavery in Illinois. After a long and bitter campaign, the anti-slavery forces led by **Governor Coles** narrowly defeat the pro-slavery element.

1825   The General Assembly levies the first tax for public schools.

Locks on the Illinois and Michigan Canal at Marseilles.

1826 DECEMBER 6 — **Ninian Edwards** is inaugurated Governor.

1827 Congress grants land to Illinois to aid in the construction of the Illinois and Michigan Canal.

The General Assembly establishes a state penitentiary at Alton.

A threatened Native American uprising comes to be known as the "**Winnebago War.**"

1829 JULY 29 — The Potawatomi, Ottawa and Chippewa Indians cede to the state more than 3,000 square miles in northern Illinois.

1830 Population: 157,445.

Abraham Lincoln, along with his family, moves to Macon County from southern Indiana.

DECEMBER 6 — **John Reynolds** takes office as Governor.

1832 APRIL — The **Black Hawk War**.

AUGUST 3 — Black Hawk is captured, and the Potawatomi and Winnebago are compelled to cede land in northern Illinois.

1833 AUGUST 12 — The newly elected **Chicago Board of Trustees** meets for the first time, marking the beginning of the legal existence of the town.

SEPTEMBER 26 — With the **Treaty of Chicago**, the Potawatomi, Ottawa and Chippewa Indians relinquish all claim to their lands in northeastern Illinois. This is the last of the Indian treaties pertaining to land in Illinois.

The **Jacksonville Female Seminary**, the first institution for the higher education of women in the state, is opened.

1834 NOVEMBER 17 — **William L.D. Ewing** is inaugurated Governor to fill out the unexpired term after Governor Reynolds' resignation.

DECEMBER 1 — **Abraham Lincoln**, now living in New Salem, takes his seat for the first time as a member of the Illinois General Assembly.

DECEMBER 3 — **Joseph Duncan** is inaugurated Governor.

1836 JULY 4 — Construction of the Illinois and Michigan Canal commences at Canalport on the Chicago River.

1837 FEBRUARY 27 — The General Assembly passes the **Internal Improvement Act**, calling for a statewide program of public works. Roads and railroads are to be built, and rivers and streams made navigable, all at state expense. This grandiose scheme will collapse under its own weight by 1841, leaving in its wake a huge state debt.

MARCH 3 — The General Assembly passes an act providing for the removal of the state capital from Vandalia to **Springfield** in 1839.

MARCH 4 — The General Assembly approves a city charter for Chicago.

Mormon leader Joseph Smith was slain by an anti-Mormon mob at the Carthage jail in 1844.

JULY 4 — The cornerstone of the first statehouse in Springfield is laid.

NOVEMBER 7 — **Elijah P. Lovejoy**, editor of the abolitionist newspaper, the *Alton Observer*, is slain by a mob in Alton.

John Deere invents the steel plow at Grand Junction.

1838   DECEMBER 7 — **Thomas Carlin** is inaugurated Governor.

1839   FEBRUARY 22 — A **State Library** is created by the General Assembly.

Mormons, driven from Missouri, found the town of Nauvoo on the Illinois side of the Mississippi River. By 1845, it will have grown to become the largest city in Illinois, with a population of at least 12,000.

Potawatomis near Chicago are the last Native Americans to leave Illinois.

1840   Population: 476,183.

1842   FEBRUARY 15 — The first train reaches Springfield over the tracks of the Northern Cross Railroad.

DECEMBER 8 — **Thomas Ford** takes office as Governor.

1844   JUNE 27 — Climaxing a growing dissension between the Mormons and their neighbors, the religion's founder, **Joseph Smith**, and his brother **Hyrum** are slain by an anti-Mormon mob at the Carthage jail in western Illinois.

1846   AUGUST 3 — **Abraham Lincoln** is elected to the U.S. House of Representatives.

DECEMBER 9 — **Augustus C. French** is inaugurated Governor.

In early spring, the Mormons leave Nauvoo on their long journey to Utah. The forced exodus ends a two-year period marked by frequent clashes among the Mormons, anti-Mormons, and the state militia in Hancock County.

1846-48   Illinois furnishes six regiments and several independent companies for the **Mexican War**.

1848   MARCH 5 — Illinois adopts its second Constitution, giving the Governor more power and making all state and county offices subject to popular elections.

APRIL 23 — The first boat passes through the Illinois and Michigan Canal. Linking Lake Michigan with the Illinois River, it will remain in operation until 1935.

1849   JANUARY 8 — **Augustus C. French** is inaugurated for a second term as Governor.

1850   Population: 851,470.

1851   The Illinois Central Railroad is chartered; it is completed in 1856.

JANUARY 28 — **Northwestern University** is chartered by the General Assembly.

In September, **Newton Bateman** organizes Illinois' first free public high school in Jacksonville.

1853   JANUARY 10 — **Joel A. Matteson** takes office as Governor.

FEBRUARY 12 — **Illinois Wesleyan University** at Bloomington is chartered.

OCTOBER 11-13 — The first **Illinois State Fair** is held at Springfield, as it is in October of the following year. Thereafter, it is held annually at different locations across the state until 1893, when it returns to Springfield permanently.

1854   MARCH 15 — **Ninian W. Edwards** is appointed first superintendent of the newly created Office of Public Instruction.

1855   FEBRUARY 15 — Legislation is approved to provide a free public school system.

1855-58   **George M. Pullman** engineers much of the raising of the street grades and buildings in Chicago by four to seven feet.

1856   MAY 29 — The first Illinois Republican State Convention is held in Bloomington.

DECEMBER 25— The **Union Stock**

Robert Root's painting of the Lincoln-Douglas Debate in Charleston.

Yards open, helping Chicago become "hog butcher for the world." The yards are closed on July 30, 1971.

1857   JANUARY 12 — **William H. Bissell** is inaugurated Governor.

FEBRUARY 18 — The first state normal university is established in what was formerly North Bloomington.

1858   AUGUST-OCTOBER — **Abraham Lincoln** and **Stephen A. Douglas** hold one debate in each of the seven Illinois congressional districts as a part of their senatorial campaigns. Douglas wins the election, but the exposure makes Lincoln a national figure.

1860   Population: 1,711,951.

MARCH 21 — Lieutenant Governor **John Wood** becomes Governor, succeeding William H. Bissell, the first Illinois Governor to die in office.

MAY 16-18 — The Republican National Convention meets in Chicago and nominates **Abraham Lincoln** for President. Lincoln's old nemesis, **Stephen A. Douglas**, is nominated by the northern wing of the Democratic Party in Baltimore.

1861   JANUARY 14 — **Richard Yates** is inaugurated Governor.

1861-65   The **Civil War** begins on APRIL 12 when Confederate forces fire on Fort Sumter. It ends four years later on April 9, with Lee's surrender at Appomattox. Though possessing considerable southern sympathy, Illinois answers every call for troops and is one of the few states to exceed its quota: 259,052 Illinoisans serve in Union forces.

1862   A **constitutional convention** meets at Springfield, but the new Constitution is not ratified by the voters.

Former slave Andrew Jackson Smith suffers a head wound while assisting Illinois Major John Warner at the Battle of Shiloh in 1862. After recovering in Clinton, IL, Smith enlists in the Union Army and serves with valor for three years. He received the Congressional Medal of Honor posthumously on Jan. 16, 2001.

1863   JUNE 10 — Governor Yates prorogues (adjourns) the Illinois General Assembly.

1864   AUGUST 29 — The Democratic National Convention, meeting in Chicago, nominates **Gen. George B. McClellan** for President.

Andrew Jackson Smith received the Congressional Medal of Honor posthumously in 2001 for bravery in action during the Civil War.

Lincoln meets with Union troops during the Civil War.

1868 MAY 20-22 — **Ulysses S. Grant** is nominated for President by the Republican National Convention in Chicago.

OCTOBER 5 — The cornerstone for the new statehouse is laid, with work being completed in 1888.

OCTOBER 26 — Authorized by the General Assembly on March 7, 1867, the redesigned state seal is used on a document for the first time.

1869 JANUARY 11 — **John M. Palmer** is inaugurated Governor.

1870 Population: 2,539,891.

AUGUST 8 — The new Illinois State Constitution goes into effect.

SEPTEMBER 5 — The first classes are held at Chicago's Saint Ignatius College. In 1909, the Jesuit-founded school will be rechartered as **Loyola University**.

Chicago experiences some 600 fires.

1871 APRIL 15 — The Illinois State Department of Agriculture is created.

OCTOBER 8-9 — The **Chicago Fire** razes an area of three and one-half square miles in the heart of the city, at the cost of 300 lives and $200 million worth of property.

1872 APRIL 15 — The first legislation for the protection of miners in Illinois is approved.

1873 JANUARY 13 — **Richard J. Oglesby** begins his second term as Governor.

JANUARY 23 — **John L. Beveridge** is inaugurated Governor when Oglesby resigns to become U.S. Senator.

1877 JANUARY 3 — The new Capitol opens unfinished.

State Rep. John W.E. Thomas takes his seat as the first African-American to serve in the General Assembly.

State Rep. John W.E. Thomas was the first African-American to serve in the General Assembly.

Destruction caused by the 1871 Chicago Fire.

1880   Population: 3,077,871.
        JUNE 2-8 — The Republican National Convention in Chicago nominates **James A. Garfield** for President.
1881   JANUARY 10 — **Shelby M. Cullom** begins his second term as Governor.
1883   FEBRUARY 6 — **John M. Hamilton** becomes Governor, succeeding **Shelby M. Cullom**, who resigns to become a U.S. Senator.
        JUNE 23 — Illinois' first compulsory school attendance law is passed by the General Assembly.
        OCTOBER 11 — The General Time Convention meets in Chicago and sets "Standard Time" for all U.S. trains starting November 18.
1884   JUNE 3-6 — The Republican National Convention, meeting in Chicago, nominates **James G. Blaine** for President and **John A. Logan** of Illinois for Vice President.
        JULY 8-11 — The Democratic National Convention meets in Chicago and nominates **Grover Cleveland** for President.
1885   JANUARY 30 — Richard J. Oglesby becomes the first man in Illinois history to be inaugurated Governor three times.
        The first skyscraper, William Le Baron Jenney's Home Insurance Building, is completed in Chicago.
1886   MAY 4 — When a detachment of police moves to break up a mass labor meeting at **Haymarket Square** in Chicago, a bomb explodes and police open fire. Seven officers are killed, and many other persons are killed and wounded. Numerous arrests are made, and four

An 1886 labor rally resulted in a riot in Chicago's Haymarket Square.

alleged anarchists are eventually hanged. In 1893, Governor Altgeld will pardon the three surviving prisoners.
1888   JUNE 19-25 — The Republican National Convention in Chicago nominates **Benjamin Harrison** for President.
1889   JANUARY 14 — **Joseph W. Fifer** is inaugurated Governor.
        MAY 25 — The General Assembly enacts legislation creating the Illinois State Historical Library.
        SEPTEMBER 18 — **Jane Addams** and her associates found one of the earliest social settlement houses in the United States, Hull House in Chicago.
1890   Population: 3,826,352.
        SEPTEMBER 10 — The University of Chicago is chartered.
1891   JUNE 19 — By act of the General Assembly, the right of suffrage in school elections is granted to women.
        Illinois adopts the principles of the Australian secret ballot.
1892   JUNE 21-23 — The Democratic National Convention in Chicago nominates **Grover Cleveland** for President and **Adlai E. Stevenson** of Illinois for Vice President.
1893   JANUARY 10 — **John P. Altgeld** is inaugurated Governor.
        MAY 1-OCTOBER 30 — The **World's Columbian Exposition**, commemorating the 400th anniversary of Columbus' discovery of America, is held in Chicago.
        JUNE 17 — The General Assembly passes the **"Sweatshop Act"** providing for the inspection of factories and the regulation of child labor.
1894   MAY-JULY — A strike of **Pullman Car Company** employees develops into a general railway strike. Before order is restored, mob violence and destruction of property necessitate the calling out of federal troops.
1896   JULY 7-11 — The Democratic National Convention in Chicago nominates Illinois native **William Jennings Bryan** for President.
1897   JANUARY 11 — **John R. Tanner** is inaugurated Governor.
1898   APRIL 25 — The United States declares **war on Spain** after the destruction of the battleship *Maine* in Havana harbor. Illinois provides more than 12,000 men for the conflict. By August, hostilities have ceased, and the peace treaty is signed in Paris on Dec. 10.
1899   APRIL 11 — The General Assembly establishes free employment offices in

A one-room school in Illinois at the beginning of the 20th century.

cities with populations of more than 50,000 and provides for the licensing of private employment agencies.

1900 Population: 4,821,550.

The flow of the Chicago River is reversed as the main channel of the **Chicago Sanitary and Ship Canal to Lockport** is opened.

1901 JANUARY 14 — **Richard Yates**, the son of Illinois' Civil War Governor, is inaugurated Governor.

1903 MAY 15 — An improved law for the regulation of child labor is passed by the General Assembly. Under the provisions of this act, Illinois is the first state to establish an eight-hour day and a 48-hour week for children.

DECEMBER 30 — A fire in Chicago's **Iroquois Theater** results in the death of 571 persons. The tragedy is followed by passage of improved safety legislation throughout the nation.

1904 JUNE 21-23 — The Republican National Convention in Chicago nominates **Theodore Roosevelt** for President.

1905 JANUARY 9 — **Charles S. Deneen** is inaugurated Governor.

MAY 11 — The General Assembly enacts a state Civil Service Code to be administered by an appointive commission.

MAY 13 — The State Board of Health is authorized to distribute diphtheria antitoxin.

1906 The **Chicago White Sox** defeat the **Chicago Cubs** to win the World Series.

1907 MAY 16 — A local option law regulating the consumption of alcoholic beverages is passed by the General Assembly.

The **Chicago Cubs** defeat the Detroit Tigers to win the World Series.

DECEMBER 24 — **De Paul University** is chartered.

The Hennepin (Illinois-Mississippi) Canal, authorized in 1890, is completed. It extends from Great Bend on the Illinois River to the Mississippi River, three miles below Rock Island.

1908 FEBRUARY 21 — The "Native Oak" becomes the official state tree, and the

More than 500 people were killed in the 1903 Iroquois Theater fire in Chicago.

Illinois was one of the first states to enact legislation to improve safety conditions for coal miners.

"Native Violet" is designated as the state flower by the General Assembly.

JUNE 16-19 — The Republican National Convention, meeting in Chicago, nominates **William Howard Taft** for President.

The new Illinois Supreme Court Building is dedicated in Springfield.

For the second consecutive year, the **Chicago Cubs** defeat the Detroit Tigers to win the World Series.

1909   JANUARY 18 — **Charles S. Deneen** begins his second term as Governor.

JUNE 15 — The General Assembly passes the "Ten-Hour Law" for women. The constitutionality of the law is upheld by the Illinois Supreme Court.

NOVEMBER 13 — A disastrous mine fire in Cherry, IL, kills 259 men.

"The Chicago Plan," the first comprehensive urban development program ever offered to an American city, is published.

1910   Population: 5,638,591.

MARCH 4 — Illinois is the first state to pass legislation providing for mine firefighting and rescue stations in coal mining centers.

MARCH 9 — After several unsuccessful attempts, the General Assembly passes a direct primary law, which is upheld by the courts.

1911   FEBRUARY 6 — **Ronald W. Reagan**,

40th President of the United States, is born in Whiteside County at Tampico.

MAY 26 — The General Assembly enacts legislation protecting workmen against occupational diseases.

JUNE 5 — By providing a fund for the care of dependent and neglected children, Illinois becomes the first state to pass "mothers' aid" legislation.

JUNE 10 — The "Starved Rock State Park Bill" becomes law. By the end of the year, **Starved Rock State Park** is transferred to state control.

JUNE 10 — The General Assembly passes the first **Workmen's Compensation Act**, providing compensation

Starved Rock State Park, located in Utica, came under state control in June 1911.

for death or injury in designated industries.

1912 JUNE 18-22 — The Republican National Convention in Chicago nominates **William Howard Taft** for President.

AUGUST 5-7 — The first National Convention of the Progressive Party meets in Chicago and nominates **Theodore Roosevelt** for President.

1913 FEBRUARY 3 — **Edward F. Dunne** is inaugurated Governor.

JUNE 26 — The General Assembly grants women the right to vote for presidential electors, making Illinois the first state east of the Mississippi to do so.

JUNE 26 — The General Assembly creates a **Legislative Reference Bureau**.

Catharine McCulloch, a "lady lawyer," drafts the Illinois Women's Suffrage Bill and fights for its passage every year from 1893 to 1913.

1915 JULY 6 — A state flag is adopted by the General Assembly. On July 1, 1970, a modified version with the word "Illinois" becomes official.

JULY 24 — The excursion steamer *Eastland* capsizes as it leaves its wharf in the Chicago River. Of some 2,000 passengers, 812 are lost.

1916 JUNE 7-10 — The Republican National Convention in Chicago nominates **Charles E. Hughes** for President.

Catharine Couger Waugh McCulloch fought for women's suffrage from 1893 to 1913.

This World War I Memorial is located on the first floor of the Michael J. Howlett Building, adjacent to the State Capitol.

1917 JANUARY 8 — **Frank O. Lowden** is inaugurated Governor.

MARCH 2 — The General Assembly passes the **Civil Administrative Code**, providing for the reorganization and consolidation of State Government.

In MAY, and again in JULY, the Illinois National Guard is sent to East St. Louis to restore order. Race rioting broke out when a stream of black laborers from the south flooded the labor market.

The **Chicago White Sox** defeat the New York Giants to win the World Series.

SEPTEMBER — The Assyrian American Association of Chicago was founded by Reverend Joel E. Warda.

1917-18 The United States enters **World War I** on the side of the allies. In Illinois, a State Council on Defense is appointed, and all state facilities are mobilized. More than 350,000 men, including the 33rd Division, composed entirely of Illinois National Guard units, are inducted into the Army and

World War I soldiers prepare to leave Springfield.

Navy. The war claims the lives of 4,266 Illinois soldiers.

1918 NOVEMBER 5 — Illinois voters approve the first bond issue ($60 million) for the construction of a statewide system of hard roads.

1919 JULY 27-AUGUST 3 — The **Illinois National Guard** is called out when serious race riots break out in Chicago.

1920 Population: 6,485,280.

JANUARY 6 — The Illinois Constitutional Convention convenes at Springfield.

JUNE 8-12 — The Republican National Convention in Chicago nominates **Warren G. Harding** for President.

NOVEMBER 6 — Construction of the Illinois Waterway is begun at Bell's Island, west of Marseilles.

1921 JANUARY 10 — **Len Small** is inaugurated Governor.

1922 JUNE 21-22 — Twenty-two miners are slain in Herrin when violence breaks out during a general coal strike.

NOVEMBER — **Lottie Holman O'Neill** becomes the first woman elected to the General Assembly. She serves for 38 years.

DECEMBER 12 — Illinois voters reject the proposal submitted by the Constitutional Convention.

1923 The State Library, State Museum, and State Historical Library move into the first section of the new **Centennial Building** in Springfield.

1924 NOVEMBER 4 — The second bond issue ($100 million) for the construction of hard roads is approved by Illinois voters.

1925 JANUARY 12 — **Len Small** begins his second term as Governor.

MARCH 4 — **Charles Gates Dawes** of Evanston becomes Vice President under **President Calvin Coolidge**.

JUNE 30 — "Illinois" is adopted as the official state song by the General Assembly.

1929 JANUARY 14 — **Louis L. Emmerson** is inaugurated Governor.

FEBRUARY 14 — **Al Capone's** gangland execution of seven men on Chicago's north side creates a public outcry for an end to the corruption caused by Prohibition.

MARCH 25 — A tax on motor fuel is authorized by the General Assembly. Money collected is to be used for the state hard road program.

JUNE 4 — The "Cardinal" is named the official state bird by the General Assembly.

OCTOBER 29 — The stock market crash signals the beginning of 12 years of the **Great Depression** across the United States.

1930 Population: 7,630,654.

MAY 12-JUNE 27 — A special session of the General Assembly passes a series of bills to relieve the financial difficulties of Chicago.

1932 JUNE 14-16 — The Republican National Convention in Chicago nominates **Herbert Hoover** for President.

June 27-July 2 — The Democratic National Convention in Chicago nominates **Franklin D. Roosevelt** for President.

Four special sessions of the General Assembly are called in an effort to relieve the economic distress of Illinois. An unemployment relief commission and an emergency relief commission are created. A state income tax is passed but is later declared unconstitutional, and money is borrowed from the Reconstruction Finance Corporation.

1933 January 9 — **Henry Horner** is inaugurated Governor.

May 27-November 13 — A Century of Progress International Exposition, celebrating the 100th anniversary of the city, is held in Chicago.

June 22 — The arrival in Chicago of a flotilla of river barges from New Orleans marks the official completion of the Illinois Waterway.

June 25 — The retailers' occupation tax of two percent is passed by the General Assembly.

July 6 — An act establishing a fair **minimum wage standard** for women and minors is passed by the General Assembly.

1934 February 19 — A 10-year-old boy starts a fire that destroys the State Arsenal and thousands of war records. It

The State Arsenal in Springfield after being destroyed by fire in 1934.

is replaced by the State Armory in 1937 and the Illinois State Archives in 1938 at a total cost of more than $1.9 million.

1935 June 29 — The Old Age Security Act, providing state aid for qualifying persons, is passed by the General Assembly.

1937 In January, oil is discovered on the Merryman farm, near Patoka in Marion County. This is the beginning of an oil boom in southern Illinois. By the end of the year, Illinois ranks 11th among the oil producing states, with about 7.5 million barrels.

January 4 — **Henry Horner** begins his second term as Governor.

June 23 — The General Assembly passes the **"Saltiel Marriage Law,"** requiring a physical examination prior

In 1939, Illinois was the fourth-ranking oil-producing state in the nation.

391

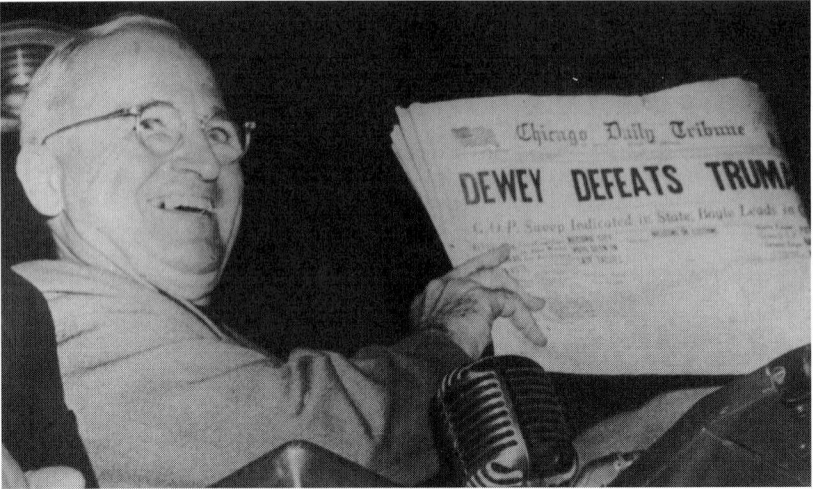

President-elect Harry S Truman holds up an infamous headline from the *Chicago Daily Tribune.*

to the issuance of a marriage license.

JUNE 30 — An act setting up a system of unemployment compensation is passed by the General Assembly.

JULY 1 — The **"Eight-Hour Law,"** limiting the hours of work for women, is passed by the General Assembly.

1939 JUNE 1 — By an act of the General Assembly, Illinois becomes the first state to establish a separate division for the prevention of delinquency.

Illinois ranks fourth among the oil-producing states, with a total output of about 94 million barrels.

1940 Population: 7,897,241.

JULY 15-18 — The Democratic National Convention meets in Chicago and nominates Franklin D. Roosevelt for a third term as President.

JULY 25 — The **Illinois Institute of Technology** in Chicago is created by the consolidation of Lewis Institute with the Armour Institute of Technology.

OCTOBER 6 — **Governor Horner** dies at Winnetka, the second Illinois Governor to die in office. He is immediately succeeded by Lieutenant Governor **John Stelle**.

1941 JANUARY 13 — **Dwight H. Green** is inaugurated Governor.

MARCH 5 — The Illinois National Guard is inducted into federal service.

It is replaced by the recently created Illinois Reserve Militia.

APRIL 17 — Governor **Dwight H. Green** signs a bill providing for a State Council of Defense.

MAY 16 — A State Department of Public Safety, consolidating divisions dealing with public safety, crime fighting and penal administration, is created by the General Assembly.

DECEMBER 18 — With the United States having declared war on Japan on Dec. 8, a special session of the General Assembly convenes to put Illinois on war footing. About 670,000 Illinois men and women serve in the armed forces during **World War II**.

1942 MARCH 3 — The mine sweeper *YMS-84*, the first Navy vessel built for World War II in Illinois, is launched in the Chicago River.

NOVEMBER 24 — In the first treason trial ever held in Illinois, sentence is passed in Chicago federal court on three German-Americans and their wives. The men are sentenced to death, the women to fine and imprisonment.

DECEMBER 2 — The world's first controlled nuclear reaction takes place under the direction of **Enrico Fermi** at the University of Chicago.

1943 JANUARY 21 — The 551-mile oil pipeline from Longview, TX, to Norris City,

IL, is completed. The line has a capacity of 300,000 barrels per day.

1944 JUNE 28 — **Thomas E. Dewey** of New York and **John W. Bricker** of Ohio are nominated for President and Vice President by the Republican National Convention meeting in Chicago.

JULY 20-21 — The Democratic National Convention meeting in Chicago nominates **Franklin Delano Roosevelt** of New York for President and **Harry S Truman** of Missouri for Vice President.

1945 JANUARY 8 — **Dwight H. Green** is inaugurated Governor for a second term.

MAY 8 — Illinois joins in the celebration of V-E Day as the unconditional surrender of Germany marks the end of the war in Europe.

AUGUST 14 — The unconditional surrender of Japan is announced by President Truman, although V-J Day is not officially observed until Sept. 2.

NOVEMBER 19 — Weekly airline service from Chicago to London is inaugurated by **American Airlines**.

1946 JULY 7 — **Mother Frances Xavier Cabrini**, who died in Chicago in 1917, is proclaimed a saint. She is the first U.S. citizen to be so honored by the Roman Catholic Church.

AUGUST 9 — The first Illinois State Fair since 1941 begins. (The state fairgrounds was leased to the War Department during the war.)

1947 MARCH 25 — A coal mine explosion at Centralia kills 111 miners.

JUNE 17 — The Legislature passes the first congressional reapportionment bill since 1901.

JULY 11 — A child labor law passed in 1945 goes into effect and calls for more effective regulation of employment of minors between ages 14 and 16.

DECEMBER 12 — The United Mine Workers, under the leadership of **John L. Lewis**, withdraw from the American Federation of Labor, following the latter organization's compliance with the **Taft-Hartley Act**.

1948 JULY 20-OCTOBER 3 — The **Railroad Fair**, commemorating 100 years of railroad progress, is held in Chicago at the site of the 1933 World's Fair.

1949 JANUARY 10 — **Adlai E. Stevenson** is inaugurated Governor.

1950 Population: 8,712,176.

MARCH 5 — **Edgar Lee Masters**, poet and author, best known for his *Spoon River Anthology*, dies at Melrose Park, PA.

MARCH 14 — **Lewis Fablinger** of Downers Grove, the last Civil War veteran in the state, dies at age 103.

MAY — **Gwendolyn Brooks** of Chicago receives the Pulitzer Prize in poetry for her poem, *Annie Allen*. She is the first African-American woman to receive this award.

JUNE 25 — North Korea invades South Korea, an action challenged by the United States as a breach of the peace. Two days later, President Truman authorizes the use of U.S. air and naval power in support of South Korea.

1951 JULY 9 — The **Illinois Civil Defense Act**, creating a State Civil Defense Agency to act with local units in the event of an atomic explosion or other wartime disaster, becomes law.

1952 JULY 7-11 — The Republican National Convention meets in Chicago and nominates **Dwight D. Eisenhower** for President and **Richard M. Nixon** for

In 1950, Illinoisan Gwendolyn Brooks became the first African-American woman to win a Pulitzer Prize.

Vice President.

JULY 19-26 — The Democratic National Convention meets in Chicago and nominates **Governor Adlai E. Stevenson** of Illinois and **John J. Sparkman** of Alabama.

NOVEMBER 4 — The Eisenhower-Nixon ticket is successful, bringing an end to 20 years of Democratic control of the White House.

1953   JANUARY 12 — **William G. Stratton** is inaugurated Governor. His appointments include Vera M. Binks, director of Registration and Education, and Joseph J. Bibb, director of Public Safety, the first woman and the first black to hold positions of this rank in Illinois.

MAY 2 — The first Baha'i Temple in the Western Hemisphere is dedicated at Wilmette.

JUNE 18 — By joint resolution, the Legislature agrees to submit a constitutional amendment for reapportioning the state's legislative districts at the General Election of 1954.

1954   FEBRUARY 15 — Ground is officially broken for a new state office building in Springfield. Later named for **Governor William G. Stratton**, it will open in December 1955.

1955   MAY 17 — Although placed on 1954 license plates, "Land of Lincoln" is now approved as the official state slogan by the General Assembly.

JUNE 16 — The first successful Reapportionment Act since 1901 creates 58 Senate districts and 59 House districts that are to be reapportioned following each decennial census.

OCTOBER 30 — **O'Hare International Airport,** west of Chicago, begins commercial operation.

1956   MARCH 3 — The Illinois Terminal System makes the last run of an interurban electric train over its St. Louis-Springfield tracks.

JULY 16 — State Auditor **Orville E. Hodge** resigns. He is later sentenced for embezzlement of public funds.

AUGUST 13-17 — The Democratic National Convention meets in Chicago and again nominates **Adlai E. Stevenson**, Governor of Illinois from 1949 to 1953, for President. Senator Estes Kefauver of Tennessee is nominated for Vice President.

Construction of the Stratton Building, west of the Capitol, began in 1954.

SEPTEMBER 22 — Governor Stratton officially opens construction on the first Illinois toll road near Rockford.

1957   JANUARY 14 — **William G. Stratton** begins his second term as Governor. Inaugurated with him is **Mrs. Earle B. Searcy**, clerk of the Supreme Court, the first woman elected to state office in Illinois.

FEBRUARY 9 — The first nuclear power generating system in the United States is activated at **Argonne National Laboratory** in DuPage County.

1958   JUNE 16-20 — A special session of the 70th General Assembly meets to consider anti-recession measures, appropriates $15 million for relief, and extends unemployment compensation benefits to 13 weeks.

DECEMBER 1 — A fire at Our Lady of the Angels School in Chicago claims the lives of 87 students and three nuns.

1959   APRIL 29 — The Governor approves a bill making Daylight Saving Time uniform throughout the state for the first time.

JULY 6 — **Queen Elizabeth and Prince Philip** visit Chicago, the city's first visit of a reigning British sovereign.

SEPTEMBER 22 — The **Chicago White Sox** win the American League pennant, their first in 40 years.

1960   Population: 10,081,158.

JUNE 25-28 — The Republican National Convention meets in Chicago and nominates **Richard M. Nixon** for President and **Henry Cabot Lodge** for Vice President.

OCTOBER 12 — The first full-scale, privately financed, nuclear power plant in the United States is dedicated at Morris.

1961 JANUARY 4 — The Illinois General Assembly convenes in regular session, with **Paul Powell**, a Democrat from Vienna, elected speaker. This marks the first time that the minority party has elected a speaker.

JANUARY 9 — **Otto Kerner** is inaugurated Governor.

JULY 2 — Illinois native and Nobel and Pulitzer Prize winning novelist **Ernest Hemingway** dies of a self-inflicted gunshot wound at his home in Ketchum, ID.

1962 Following eight years as a state lawmaker, **George W. Dunne** was elected to the Cook County Board of Commissioners. He served as chairman of the Finance Committee prior to his unprecedented 21 years as County Board President.

FEBRUARY 28 — **Carl Sandburg** is named the first Poet Laureate of Illinois.

NOVEMBER 6 — The 14th Amendment to the 1870 Constitution, establishing a unified court system, is approved.

NOVEMBER 14 — By action of the Legislature, Illinois becomes the first state to ratify the 24th Amendment to the U.S. Constitution, prohibiting the paying of a poll tax as a requisite for voting in federal elections.

1964 JANUARY 1 — The **University of Illinois** football team defeats the University of Washington in the Rose Bowl.

AUGUST — The **Gulf of Tonkin Incident** marks the beginning of the American phase of the Vietnam War, the longest war in U.S. history.

1965 JANUARY 11 — **Otto Kerner** begins his second term as Governor.

JULY 7 — By an act of the General Assembly, fluorite (calcium fluoride) is designated the official state mineral.

JULY 14 — **Adlai E. Stevenson,** former Governor and two-time Presidential candidate, dies in London, England.

1966 NOVEMBER 8 — **Charles Percy** is elected U.S. Senator from Illinois.

DECEMBER 15 — **Walter E. Disney**, a Chicago native, cartoonist and creator of Disneyland, dies at age 65.

DECEMBER 16 — The U.S. Atomic Energy Commission announces DuPage County as the site for the construction of the world's most powerful atom smasher.

Illinois is the leading export state in the nation for 1966.

1967 JANUARY 26–27 — The largest single

Carl Sandburg was named Illinois' first Poet Laureate in February 1962.

Everett M. Dirksen, who was elected to four terms in the U.S. Senate, appears with Richard Nixon at the Illinois State Fairgrounds.

snowstorm in Chicago history dumps 23 inches on the city in 29 hours.

MARCH 12 — The **Chicago Black Hawks** capture their first National Hockey League title.

JULY 22 — Noted poet and Lincoln historian **Carl Sandburg** dies at his home in North Carolina at age 89.

1968   Under the direction of Chicago Mayor **Richard J. Daley**, General Superintendent of the Forestry Department, Ned Benigno, developed a plan to eliminate the spread of Dutch Elm disease and to introduce new species of trees throughout the City of Chicago.

JANUARY 8 — **Gwendolyn Brooks** of Chicago is named the new Illinois Poet Laureate by executive order of the Governor.

MAY 19 — Governor **Otto Kerner** resigns to become judge of the U.S. Court of Appeals.

MAY 21 — Lieutenant Governor **Samuel H. Shapiro** is sworn in as Governor.

AUGUST 27–30 — The Democratic National Convention meets in Chicago amid great civil disorder and nominates **Hubert H. Humphrey** for President and **Edmund S. Muskie** for Vice President.

NOVEMBER 5 — Republican **Rich-**

ard B. Ogilvie and Democrat **Paul Simon** are elected Governor and Lieutenant Governor, respectively. Also elected is **Everett M. Dirksen,** who returns to the U.S. Senate for a fourth term.

1969   MARCH 20 — A federal grand jury indicts eight police officers and eight demonstrators on criminal charges stemming from disturbances during the Democratic National Convention of the previous summer.

JULY 1 — **Governor Ogilvie** approves a bill creating a state income tax.

SEPTEMBER 7 — **Everett M. Dirksen,** longtime Republican Senator from Illinois, dies at age 73.

OCTOBER 15 — Throughout Illinois, thousands of people give peaceful support to the nationwide war moratorium.

1970   Population: 11,113,976.

FEBRUARY 18 — The celebrated "Chicago 7" trial ends as five of the defendants are found guilty of crossing state lines to incite a riot.

MAY 20 — **Dr. Albert Crewe,** University of Chicago physicist, announces that he has accomplished the feat of seeing a single atom.

SEPTEMBER 3 — Illinois' Sixth Constitutional Convention adjourns with ceremonies at the Old State Capitol.

DECEMBER 15 — Illinois voters approve a new State Constitution while rejecting the appointment of judges,

Abraham Lincoln's home in Springfield became a national historic site in 1971.

abolition of the death penalty and lowering of the voting age to 18.

1971 JANUARY 11 — **Michael J. Bakalis** was the youngest elected Superintendent of Public Instruction and the last elected office holder to that position.

AUGUST 18 — **President Richard Nixon** visits Springfield and signs a bill making Abraham Lincoln's home a national historic site.

1972 JANUARY 1 — The **Illinois Department of Transportation** is created to oversee one of the largest state highway systems in the nation.

JUNE — Charging racial discrimination, Operation PUSH boycotts Chicago-area stores.

JULY 8 — The Neo-Nazi Party demonstrates in Berwyn, clashing with the Jewish Defense League.

OCTOBER 30 — An Illinois Central train accident in Chicago kills 45 people and injures 350. It is the worst U.S. rail crash in 14 years.

1973 JANUARY 9 — **Dan Walker** is inaugurated as Illinois' 36th Governor.

FEBRUARY 19 — **Judge Otto Kerner** is convicted on 17 counts of conspiracy, fraud, perjury, bribery and income tax evasion in connection with the purchase and sale of racetrack stock while serving as Governor.

MAY 3 — The topping of the Sears Tower, standing 1,454 feet tall, makes it the world's tallest building.

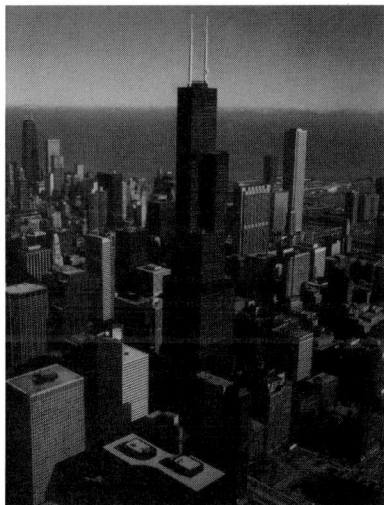

At 1,454 feet, the Sears Tower was the tallest building in the world until February 1996.

Richard J. Daley served as Mayor of Chicago for nearly a quarter of a century.

SEPTEMBER 17 — By act of the General Assembly, the "White Oak" replaces the "Native Oak" as the official state tree.

AUGUST 9 — **Governor Walker** signs a bill to create the Illinois Department on Aging.

1974 MAY 7 — **Governor Walker** declares state trooper jobs open to women.

JULY 30 — The first **Illinois lottery tickets** go on sale in Chicago. In August, the first bonanza winner of the Illinois lottery is awarded $300,000.

1975 APRIL 1 — **Richard J. Daley** is reelected to an unprecedented sixth four-year term as Mayor of Chicago.

APRIL 18 — **James B. Parsons** is named as the first African-American chief judge on the U.S. District Court in Chicago.

AUGUST 19 — The "Monarch Butterfly" is designated the official state insect by the General Assembly.

1976 JULY 4 — Illinois celebrates the nation's 200th birthday.

JULY 17 — Race riots over integration in Chicago's all-white **Marquette Park** result in injury to 33 people.

DECEMBER 20 — **Richard J. Daley**, Mayor of Chicago since 1955, dies from a heart attack at age 74.

1977 JANUARY 4 — Four elevated train cars fall to the street in Chicago, killing 12 and injuring nearly 200 people.

JANUARY 10 — **James Thompson,**

The James R. Thompson Center in Chicago.

elected for a modified two-year term, is inaugurated as Illinois' 37th Governor.

The Legislature is unable to act for six weeks as 186 roll calls are taken before a Senate President is selected.

APRIL 15 — Treasures of ancient Egyptian **King Tutankhamen** go on display at the Field Museum in Chicago before record-breaking crowds.

MAY 1 — Illinois' ban on self-service gas stations is lifted.

JUNE 21 — Governor Thompson signs a bill providing for the **death penalty** of adults convicted in any of 16 categories of murder.

1978 MARCH 4 — The *Chicago Daily News,* the city's last afternoon newspaper, ceases publication.

JULY 22 — Inmates erupt in a bloody takeover at Pontiac prison in which three guards are killed.

NOVEMBER — **Roland W. Burris** is the first African-American to be elected as a constitutional officer in Illinois. He served as State Comptroller from 1979 to 1991 and as Attorney General from 1991 to 1995.

NOVEMBER 7 — Elections of Illinois state officers are altered so they will no longer be held during presidential election years.

1979 APRIL 3 — **Jane Byrne** becomes Chicago's first female mayor.

MAY 25 — The worst air disaster in American history occurs when American Airlines flight 191 crashes on take-off in Chicago, killing 275 people.

AUGUST 21 — Governor Thompson signs a bill returning the Illinois drinking age to 21, effective in 1980.

Pope John Paul II visits Chicago and celebrates mass for nearly 1.5 million people in Grant Park.

1980 Population: 11,426,518.

MARCH 19 — Illinois Attorney General **William Scott** is convicted of federal tax fraud.

APRIL 1 — The Illinois Department of Nuclear Safety is created.

JULY 1 — The Illinois Department of Human Rights is established.

NOVEMBER 4 — Illinois voters pass the **Cutback Amendment**, reducing the number of House members by one-third.

1981 JUNE 8 — **Morton Grove** enacts a strict gun control ordinance that attracts national attention.

JUNE 10 — Reports from the 1980 census indicate that major congressional redistricting is necessary.

DECEMBER 17 — The state announces a $20 million loan to the ailing

Chrysler Corporation in Illinois.

1982 JANUARY 1 — The "White-tailed Deer" becomes the official state animal by act of the General Assembly.

MAY–JUNE — Seven women engage in a 37-day hunger strike and 17 women chain themselves to a rail in the statehouse in an effort to win approval for the federal **Equal Rights Amendment.** Despite their efforts, the amendment is defeated.

SEPTEMBER — Pain reliever capsules laced with cyanide kill seven in the Chicago area.

Governor James R. Thompson and **Lieutenant Governor George H. Ryan** narrowly defeat **Adlai E. Stevenson III** and **Grace Mary Stern,** 1,816,101 to 1,811,027, a plurality of 5,074 votes or 0.1 percent.

1983 APRIL 5 — **Harold Washington** becomes Chicago's first African-American mayor.

AUGUST — A record-breaking drought, the worst since the "dust bowl" of the 1930s, withers Illinois crops; the month is cited as the hottest on record.

NOVEMBER 1 — Rupert Murdock purchases the *Chicago Sun Times* for

$90 million in cash.

DECEMBER 2 — The Governor signs a no-fault divorce law.

1984 Construction of the new **State of Illinois Center,** with estimated costs of $118 million, nears completion in Chicago's North Loop.

JULY 1 — The Department of Alcoholism and Substance Abuse and the Department of Employment Security are created.

NOVEMBER 6 — Representative **Paul Simon** ousts incumbent Senator **Charles Percy** from his seat in the U.S. Senate.

1985 MARCH 11 — Twenty-two downstate counties are declared disaster areas by the Governor as flooding of the Illinois River wreaks havoc.

APRIL 24 — Officials announce the worst of the Illinois **salmonella epidemic** is over. A total of 10,154 cases were confirmed in Illinois and four other states, reportedly in part from contaminated dairy products.

JUNE 29 — Lebanese terrorists release 153 hostages, many from Illinois.

JULY 1 — A strict new seat belt law goes into effect in Illinois; all front seat occupants must now "buckle up."

1986 JANUARY 26 — The **Chicago Bears**

The Illinois Vietnam Veterans Memorial at Springfield's Oak Ridge Cemetery.

play in, and win, their first Super Bowl.
JUNE 13 — Chicago holds a Vietnam Veterans Parade more than 11 years after the end of the war. Some 200,000 take part in the march.

Teacher strikes in dozens of Illinois school districts idle more than 10,000 students.

NOVEMBER 17 — The Illinois Department of Public Health institutes regulations restricting smoking in its statewide offices.

1987 JANUARY 12 — A U.S. district judge rules that Springfield's commission form of government violates the federal Voting Rights Act by denying access to blacks.

Governor James Thompson takes the oath of office for a fourth term and participates in the 50th inauguration of an Illinois Governor.

APRIL 7 — **Harold Washington** becomes the first Chicago Mayor to be reelected since the late Richard Daley; he will die of a heart attack in November.

1988 JANUARY — The AIDS epidemic leads to a requirement for a marriage blood test; the act will be repealed in September 1989.

JULY 2 — Ceremonies celebrate the centennial of the **State Capitol** and mark an end to 20 years of intensive restoration work on the building.

A severe summer drought necessitates water restrictions throughout much of central Illinois.

A memorial to those Illinoisans who died in the Vietnam War is erected in Springfield's **Oak Ridge Cemetery.**

1989 APRIL — **Richard M. Daley** is elected Mayor of Chicago.

JULY — The General Assembly approves a temporary two-year increase in the state income tax, intended to aid education and local governments.

AUGUST 31 — "Big Bluestem" is made the official state prairie grass by the General Assembly.

SEPTEMBER 1 — The "Tully Monster" becomes the official state fossil.

1990 Population: 11,430,602.

FEBRUARY 7 — **Riverboat Gambling** law goes into effect. The first boat, the Alton Belle, is launched on the Mississippi River in September 1991, and 10 licenses exist by 1995.

AUGUST 17 — The "Square Dance" is designated as the official state dance by the General Assembly.

Harold Washington was the first African-American to become Mayor of Chicago.

AUGUST 22 — The U.S. begins massive military buildup in the Persian Gulf under the auspices of **Operation Desert Shield.** About 20,000 Illinois soldiers are involved in the effort.

AUGUST 28 — A tornado levels Plainfield High School and destroys an apartment complex. The tornado kills 27 people, the second-highest death toll from a storm in state history. An additional 350 people are injured.

NOVEMBER — **Dawn Clark Netsch** is the first woman to be elected to a state constitutional office in Illinois. She served as Comptroller from 1991 to 1995.

1991 JANUARY 14 — Republican **Jim Edgar** is inaugurated as Illinois' 38th Governor, succeeding **James Thompson,** who served a record 14 years.

FEBRUARY 27 — President **George Bush** announces a cease-fire in the six-week-old war against Iraq. Thirteen Illinoisans are killed in the conflict.

JUNE — The **Chicago Bulls** beat the Los Angeles Lakers to capture the NBA championship—the team's first in its 25-year history.

JULY 19 — The **Illinois General Assembly** adjourns, following a record 19-day overtime brought on by the budget impasse.

SEPTEMBER 4 — The "Bluegill" becomes the official state fish by act of the General Assembly. Illinois schoolchildren selected the "Bluegill" in 1986.

1992 APRIL — **Chicago** is declared a disaster area when a leak in an underground freight tunnel system causes more than

250 million gallons of Chicago River water to flood tunnels and basements in Chicago's business district, sending 250,000 workers home and costing at least $40 million in lost productivity.

JUNE — The **Chicago Bulls** beat the Portland Trail Blazers to win the NBA championship for the second year in a row.

NOVEMBER 3 — **Carol Moseley-Braun** becomes the first African-American woman ever elected to the U.S. Senate.

NOVEMBER 18 — The Centennial Building in Springfield's Capitol Complex is renamed in honor of the late **Michael J. Howlett**, the first Democrat to serve four consecutive terms in state office. Howlett served three terms as State Auditor and one term as Secretary of State.

George W. Dunne was the longest serving President of the Cook County Board of Commissioners (1969-90).

1993   One of the largest and costliest **floods** in U.S. history causes extensive damage in Illinois: 500,000 acres of land are flooded, causing $1.5 billion of crop and property damage.

MAY 10 — The State of Illinois Center in Chicago is renamed in honor of former Governor **James R. Thompson.**

JUNE — The **Chicago Bulls** beat the Phoenix Suns to capture the NBA championship for the third straight year.

1994   MAY 10 — **John Wayne Gacy** is executed. Gacy was convicted March 12, 1980, in Chicago of murdering 33 men.

OCTOBER 31 — An American Eagle flight to Chicago from Indiana crashes, killing 15 people from Illinois.

NOVEMBER 14 — **U.S. Senator Paul Simon** announces his plans to retire from politics after 42 years in elective office.

1995   JANUARY 25 — The Illinois Supreme Court orders the adoptive parents of "**Baby Richard**" to turn over the boy "forthwith" to his biological father in one of the most celebrated court cases in Illinois history.

MAY 26 — The Illinois General Assembly recesses early for the first time in 25 years.

JULY 12 — Navy Pier reopens with a landmark 148-foot-high Ferris Wheel. Navy Pier attracts about 5 million visitors in its first year.

OCTOBER 25 — A school bus is struck by an express commuter train in Fox River Grove, killing seven students and injuring 30.

NOVEMBER 15 — A plaque commemorating the 75th anniversary of the passage of the 19th Amendment (women's suffrage) is dedicated in the Capitol next to the statue of **Lottie Holman O'Neill** (the first woman elected to the General Assembly).

1996   AUGUST 26-29 — The Democratic National Convention meets at the United Center in Chicago and nominates **Bill Clinton** for President and **Al Gore** for Vice President for re-election.

JUNE — The **Chicago Bulls** beat the Seattle SuperSonics to win their fourth NBA championship in six years.

November — **Richard J. Durbin** (Democrat) is elected to the U.S. Senate, succeeding **Paul Simon** who retired.

NOVEMBER 14 — **Cardinal Joseph Bernardin**, archbishop of Chicago, dies at age 68.

1997   JUNE — The *Chicago Tribune* celebrates 150 years.

JUNE — The **Chicago Bulls** beat the Utah Jazz for their fifth NBA championship.

JULY 1 — The new Department of Human Services becomes the largest state agency in Illinois with 20,000 employees and a $4.3 billion budget.

401

SEPTEMBER 5 — **Sir Georg Solti**, music director laureate of the Chicago Symphony Orchestra, dies at age 84.

1998 JUNE — The **Chicago Bulls** beat the Utah Jazz in the NBA finals, giving Chicago its sixth championship of the decade.

SEPTEMBER — St. Louis Cardinal **Mark McGuire** (70 home runs) and Chicago Cub **Sammy Sosa** (66) each surpass **Roger Maris'** Major League Baseball record of 61 home runs in 1961.

1999 JANUARY 6 — Illinois Congressman **J. Dennis Hastert** (R-14th District) is elected Speaker of the U.S. House of Representatives.

JANUARY 11 — Republican **George H. Ryan** is inaugurated as Illinois' 39th Governor.

JANUARY 11— Republican **Corinne Wood** is inaugurated as the first female Lieutenant Governor of Illinois.

JANUARY 11— Democrat **Jesse White** is inaugurated as the first African-American to serve as Illinois Secretary of State.

JANUARY 11— Comptroller **Daniel W. Hynes** (Democrat) is inaugurated as the youngest Illinois constitutional officer since **William Stratton** was elected Treasurer in 1942.

FEBRUARY 23 — **Richard M. Daley** is re-elected to his fourth term as Mayor of Chicago.

OCTOBER 23-27 — **Governor Ryan** becomes the first sitting U.S. Governor to visit Cuba in more than 40 years. Joining Ryan on the historic humanitarian mission was an official delegation of more than 45 people and 40 members of the Illinois press corps.

NOVEMBER 1 — Chicago Bears' great, **Walter Payton**, who compiled a National Football League record of 16,726 rushing yards in his 13-year Hall of Fame career, dies at age 45.

2000 Population: 12,419,293.

As a result of the 2000 census, Illinois loses one of its Congressional seats. The state is reapportioned into 19 Congressional districts, down from 20 in the 1990s.

JANUARY 31 — Governor **George H. Ryan** orders a moratorium on executions in Illinois.

NOVEMBER 7 — The presidential election of 2000 is among the closest in history. Illinois' 22 electoral votes are won by Vice President Al Gore, but Texas Governor George W. Bush wins the presidency by claiming a majority of the overall electoral votes. Bush won the Electoral College vote 271 to 266 with one abstention.

DECEMBER 3 — Illinois Poet Laureate **Gwendolyn Brooks** dies.

2001 FEBRUARY 12 — A groundbreaking ceremony is held for the new **Abraham Lincoln Presidential Library & Museum** in Springfield,

Michael Jordan, who led the Chicago Bulls to three straight NBA championships in 1991, 1992 and 1993, surprised fans by announcing his retirement on Oct. 6, 1993. However, Jordan returned to the Bulls and resumed his basketball career on March 18, 1995. The Bulls subsequently won NBA championships in 1996, 1997 and 1998. He retired again on Jan. 13, 1999. On Sept. 25, 2001, Jordan announced his return to his basketball career as a member of the Washington Wizards. In response to the Sept. 11, 2001, tragedy, Jordan donated his first year's salary to relief and victim assistance efforts.

The Cinco de Mayo Parade travels down Cermak Road in Chicago.

which will serve as a national center for research and study of the life and times of Abraham Lincoln and the American Civil War.

MARCH 2 — **William G. Stratton,** Governor of Illinois from 1953 to 1961, dies.

APRIL — Flooding along the upper Mississippi River affects communities in Minnesota, Iowa, Wisconsin and Illinois. Ten counties in Illinois are declared presidential disaster areas.

MAY 5 — The **Cinco de Mayo Parade in Chicago** has been an annual event for 10 years. The celebration commemorates Mexico's defeat of the French at the Battle of Puebla on May 5, 1862, and highlights the culture and heritage of many Mexican-Americans in Illinois.

MAY 10 — CEO Phil Condit announces that **Boeing,** the world's largest aerospace company, will move its global headquarters to Chicago.

AUGUST 2 — The 92nd Illinois General Assembly designates "Drummer Silty Clay Loam" as the official state soil.

SEPTEMBER 11 — Terrorists use hijacked planes to attack buildings in New York and Washington, DC, resulting in thousands of deaths. The Illinois Capitol, government buildings and O'Hare airport are evacuated and closed down for the first time in history.

President Bush declares a "war on terrorism." Illinois National Guard members and reservists are called upon to boost security at Illinois airports and nuclear power plants.

"America United" license plates, sponsored by the Chicago and Illinois Fraternal Orders of Police and the Chicago Fire Fighters Union, were produced by the Secretary of State's office for display on vehicles Jan. 15-March 15, 2002. Proceeds from the sale of the plates benefit families of New York police officers and firefighters killed during the Sept. 11, 2001, terrorist attacks.

THE ELECTION PROCESS

Voting is one of the most valuable rights and privileges of an American citizen.

Under the provisions of the 1970 Illinois Constitution, to be a qualified voter in the State of Illinois, you must be 18 years of age or older and have lived in the state and the voting district 30 days. Voter registration is governed by state and federal laws and was most recently modified by the National Voter Registration Act of October 1993.

HOW CANDIDATES ARE NOMINATED

In Illinois, there are several ways in which the names of candidates are placed on the ballot.

The **Primary Election** is the most widely used method of nominating candidates and is a party election. This is the means by which a political party selects its candidates. The voters of each party have the opportunity to express their choice of the various candidates seeking the nomination. Each candidate using this system must be affiliated with a political party.

Any qualified citizen who desires to run for office may have his or her name placed on his or her party's primary ballot by filing a petition signed by a determined number of qualified voters of the party. The primary ballot will, as a rule, carry the names of several candidates for each office.

All judges, Circuit, Appellate and Supreme Court, must be licensed attorneys at law, as must the county State's Attorney. A Superintendent of an Educational Service Region also must meet specific requirements.

One additional requirement is placed on the candidate and the voter in a Primary Election in that both must affiliate with a particular party. The voter must declare himself or herself a member of a party to receive a ballot. Each party is listed on a separate ballot, and the voter can only request one ballot to indicate his or her choice of candidates. This is known as a Closed Primary. Even though he or she must vote on a one-party ballot at the primary, this in no way controls his or her freedom of choice in voting for candidates of all parties in the General Election.

The **Party Caucus** is another way in which a political party nominates candidates. The leaders of the party call a meeting to determine whom they desire as candidates for the various offices. According to state law, only the regularly elected party officers may call such a meeting, and it must be held at a convenient place and time, although the date is set by statute. The names of persons chosen as candidates then are sent to the proper election officials, who place them on the ballot.

The third method of nominating candidates is through **Party Conventions.** The County Central Committee of each party holds a county convention, at which time delegates to a state convention are chosen. State conventions have the power to select delegates and alternate delegates at large to the National Nominating Convention of the party.

The candidates for judges of the Circuit Courts, Appellate Courts and Supreme Court of Illinois are nominated at the Primary Election. Judges, once elected, run on a "retention" question without opposition.

State law also makes provisions for the nomination of persons seeking office who are not affiliated with any recognized party.

PRESIDENTIAL ELECTORS

The President and Vice President of the United States are not elected by the direct vote of the people. Instead, they are elected by presidential electors. Each state has the number of electors equal to the number of Senators and Representatives to which the state is entitled.

Every year in which a President and Vice President of the United States are chosen, each political party nominates its candidates for presidential electors at state conventions.

The names of the candidates for electors are not printed on the official ballot. Instead, the names of the candidates for President and Vice President are printed on the ballot as a "team." A vote for the Presidential and Vice Presidential "team" not only is a vote for the candidates but also is a vote for the entire list of that party's presidential electors.

After the votes have been canvassed, the Governor proclaims the persons elected as electors of President and Vice President.

The electors meet the first Monday after the second Wednesday in December in the Capitol at Springfield and give their votes for President and Vice President. This vote is certified by the electors to the President of the United States Senate.

The electoral votes of all the states are counted at a joint session of the Senate and House of Representatives in Washington, DC, on the sixth day of January. The result of the vote is announced by the President of the Senate, and this announcement is deemed sufficient declaration of the persons elected President and Vice President of the United States.

ILLINOIS GENERAL ELECTION
November 7, 2000
Summary of General Vote

Office, Party and Candidate	Percent of Total	Total Votes	Outside Cook County	Cook County	Counties Carried
PRESIDENT AND VICE PRESIDENT					
Al Gore (D) Joe Lieberman	54.60%	2,589,026	1,308,479	1,280,547	24
George W. Bush (R) Dick Cheney	42.58%	2,019,421	1,484,879	534,542	78
Ralph Nader (GRE) Winona LaDuke	2.19%	103,759	61,691	42,068	
Pat Buchanan (IND) Ezola Foster	0.34%	16,106	12,290	3,816	
Harry Browne (LIB) Art Olivier	0.25%	11,623	7,464	4,159	
John Hagelin (REF) Nat Goldhaber	0.04%	2,127			

VOTE FOR PRESIDENT AND VICE PRESIDENT

County	Party	Plurality	Republican Bush Cheney	Democratic Gore Lieberman	Green Nader LaDuke
Adams	R	5,134	17,331	12,197	371
Alexander	D	769	1,588	2,357	28
Bond	R	744	3,804	3,060	113
Boone	R	2,136	8,617	6,481	325
Brown	R	452	1,529	1,077	29
Bureau	R	772	8,526	7,754	363
Calhoun	D	81	1,229	1,310	42
Carroll	R	722	3,835	3,113	154
Cass	R	179	2,968	2,789	94
Champaign	D	870	34,645	35,515	3,543
Christian	R	738	7,537	6,799	269
Clark	R	1,466	4,398	2,932	126
Clay	R	1,577	3,789	2,212	78
Clinton	R	2,152	8,588	6,436	295
Coles	R	1,591	10,495	8,904	507
Cook	D	746,005	534,542	1,280,547	42,068
Crawford	R	1,641	4,974	3,333	118
Cumberland	R	1,094	2,964	1,870	72
DeKalb	R	2,341	17,139	14,798	1,032
DeWitt	R	1,098	3,968	2,870	133
Douglas	R	1,519	4,734	3,215	132
DuPage	R	48,487	201,037	152,550	8,711
Edgar	R	1,617	4,833	3,216	113
Edwards	R	1,234	2,212	978	42
Effingham	R	5,630	9,855	4,225	213
Fayette	R	1,314	5,200	3,886	122
Ford	R	1,799	3,889	2,090	116
Franklin	D	1,711	8,490	10,201	347
Fulton	D	2,004	6,936	8,940	276
Gallatin	D	287	1,591	1,878	40
Greene	R	639	3,129	2,490	93
Grundy	R	1,193	8,709	7,516	257
Hamilton	R	576	2,519	1,943	75
Hancock	R	878	5,134	4,256	161
Hardin	R	182	1,366	1,184	41
Henderson	D	322	1,708	2,030	74
Henry	D	1,025	10,896	11,921	428
Iroquois	R	4,288	8,685	4,397	229
Jackson	D	1,950	9,823	11,773	1,228
Jasper	R	1,304	3,119	1,815	50
Jefferson	R	1,677	8,362	6,685	211
Jersey	R	344	4,699	4,355	231
JoDaviess	R	719	5,304	4,585	314
Johnson	R	1,357	3,285	1,928	83
Kane	R	16,869	76,996	60,127	3,274
Kankakee	R	869	20,049	19,180	713
Kendall	R	5,244	13,688	8,444	481
Knox	D	2,660	9,912	12,572	455
Lake	R	5,930	120,988	115,058	4,843
LaSalle	D	2,079	21,276	23,355	992
Lawrence	R	772	3,594	2,822	101
Lee	R	1,958	8,069	6,111	320
Livingston	R	3,358	9,187	5,829	285
Logan	R	3,541	8,141	4,600	208
Macon	D	432	23,830	24,262	982

VOTE FOR PRESIDENT AND VICE PRESIDENT (Concluded)

County	Party	Plurality	Republican Bush Cheney	Democratic Gore Lieberman	Green Nader LaDuke
Macoupin	D	1,266	9,749	11,015	426
Madison	D	10,256	48,821	59,077	2,359
Marion	R	172	8,240	8,068	238
Marshall	R	575	3,145	2,570	134
Mason	R	219	3,411	3,192	117
Massac	R	764	3,676	2,912	83
McDonough	R	385	6,465	6,080	364
McHenry	R	21,414	62,112	40,698	2,751
McLean	R	9,072	34,008	24,936	1,546
Menard	R	1,698	3,862	2,164	135
Mercer	D	712	3,688	4,400	156
Monroe	R	1,835	7,632	5,797	262
Montgomery	D	316	6,226	6,542	191
Morgan	R	2,159	8,058	5,899	253
Moultrie	R	529	3,058	2,529	78
Ogle	R	4,652	12,325	7,673	467
Peoria	D	2,206	36,398	38,604	1,332
Perry	D	60	4,802	4,862	173
Piatt	R	1,131	4,619	3,488	217
Pike	R	1,508	4,706	3,198	115
Pope	R	419	1,346	927	31
Pulaski	D	88	1,430	1,518	31
Putnam	D	220	1,437	1,657	58
Randolph	R	333	7,127	6,794	229
Richland	R	2,227	4,718	2,491	134
Rock Island	D	12,763	25,194	37,957	1,364
Saline	R	506	5,933	5,427	181
Sangamon	R	11,960	50,374	38,414	2,001
Schuyler	R	490	2,077	1,587	72
Scott	R	504	1,458	954	31
Shelby	R	1,833	5,851	4,018	162
Stark	R	483	1,694	1,211	55
St. Clair	D	13,662	42,299	55,961	1,569
Stephenson	R	2,653	10,715	8,062	476
Tazewell	R	6,158	31,537	25,379	1,022
Union	R	415	4,397	3,982	189
Vermilion	R	377	15,783	15,406	605
Wabash	R	1,419	3,406	1,987	75
Warren	R	375	3,899	3,524	130
Washington	R	1,715	4,353	2,638	96
Wayne	R	3,138	5,347	2,209	77
White	R	1,563	4,521	2,958	113
Whiteside	D	1,634	11,252	12,886	515
Will	R	4,926	95,828	90,902	3,769
Williamson	R	1,820	14,012	12,192	476
Winnebago	R	1,835	53,816	51,981	2,637
Woodford	R	5,376	10,905	5,529	263

VOTE FOR STATE SENATORS

Dist.	Name	Party	Votes	Dist.	Name	Party	Votes
3	Margaret Smith	(D)	53,208	30	Terry Link	(D)	38,147
	Unopposed				Greg Kazarian	(R)	30,695
6	John J. Cullerton	(D)	62,381	33	Steven J. Rauschenberger	(R)	67,650
	Eric W. Solis	(R)	26,841		Unopposed		
9	Carol Ronen	(D)	53,344	36	Denny Jacobs	(D)	68,720
	Unopposed				Unopposed		
12	Robert S. Molaro	(D)	44,316	39	Dan Cronin	(R)	51,084
	Michael A. DeRoss	(R)	3,051		Unopposed		
15	William "Bill" Shaw	(D)	57,621	42	Edward Petka	(R)	66,772
	Unopposed				Phyllis Mary Nirchi	(D)	37,844
18	Patrick J. O'Malley	(R)	42,390	45	Robert A. Madigan **	(R)	73,785
	Rick Ryan	(D)	31,703		Unopposed		
20	Peter J. Roskam *	(R)	70,639	48	Laura Kent Donahue	(R)	68,160
	Unopposed				Unopposed		
21	Chris Lauzen	(R)	64,672	51	N. Duane Noland	(R)	58,796
	Stephanie Downs Hughes	(D)	35,045		Stephen F. John	(D)	24,329
24	Christine Radogno	(R)	38,104	54	William L. O'Daniel	(D)	65,644
	Mary Jane O'Shea Mannella	(D)	35,558		Unopposed		
27	Wendell E. Jones	(R)	34,626	57	James F. Clayborne, Jr.	(D)	43,387
	Sue A. Walton	(D)	33,683		Karron A. Waters	(R)	14,482
28	Dave Sullivan *	(R)	44,764	59	Larry D. Woolard *	(D)	51,052
	Phil Pritzker	(D)	29,196		Ronald M. "Ron" Ellis	(R)	35,065

LEGEND (Senate)
Party Abbreviations
R - Republican
D - Democratic

*For an unexpired two-year term

**Appointed to Industrial Commission.
Replaced by Claude "Bud" Stone (R).

VOTE FOR STATE REPRESENTATIVES

Dist.	Name	Party	Votes	Dist.	Name	Party	Votes
1	Susana Mendoza	(D)	10,054	22	Michael J. Madigan	(D)	28,351
	Unopposed				Terrence F. Goggin	(R)	5,910
2	Edward Acevedo	(D)	11,489	23	Daniel J. Burke	(D)	21,036
	Unopposed				Unopposed		
3	William "Willie" Delgado	(D)	15,178	24	Howard Kenner	(D)	17,909
	Unopposed				Unopposed		
4	Cynthia Soto	(D)	18,924	25	Barbara Flynn Currie	(D)	33,563
	Unopposed				Unopposed		
5	Lovana S. "Lou" Jones	(D)	25,671	26	Charles G. Morrow III	(D)	25,231
	Unopposed				Unopposed		
6	Shirley M. Jones	(D)	26,287	27	Monique D. Davis	(D)	40,574
	Unopposed				Unopposed		
7	Karen A. Yarbrough	(D)	31,789	28	Thomas J. Dart	(D)	35,117
	Unopposed				David D. Lee	(R)	2,576
8	Calvin L. Giles	(D)	30,638	29	David E. Miller	(D)	28,267
	Unopposed				Unopposed		
9	Arthur L. Turner	(D)	24,044	30	Harold Murphy	(D)	26,085
	Unopposed				Willie Jordan, Jr.	(R)	3,447
10	Annazette R. Collins	(D)	25,330	31	Todd H. Stroger	(D)	32,126
	Unopposed				Unopposed		
11	Judy Erwin	(D)	31,765	32	Constance A. "Connie" Howard	(D)	33,035
	Shawn M. Hanley	(R)	15,043		Unopposed		
12	Sara Feigenholtz	(D)	31,706	33	John A. Fritchey	(D)	25,643
	Robert Huntington	(R)	10,670		Unopposed		
13	Ralph C. Capparelli	(D)	30,058	34	Larry McKeon	(D)	24,080
	Unopposed				Vincent C. Lengerich	(R)	5,153
14	Michael P. McAuliffe	(R)	23,150		R. Brian Poynton	(LIB)	1,230
	Frank Coconate	(D)	14,346	35	M. Maggie Crotty	(D)	25,519
15	Joseph M. Lyons	(D)	23,534		Wendy Loftus	(R)	12,804
	Mitchell A. Kulwin	(R)	6,728	36	James D. Brosnahan	(D)	25,256
16	Louis I. Lang	(D)	22,628		Patricia Theresa Vlasis	(R)	9,781
	Unopposed			37	Kevin A. McCarthy	(D)	28,835
17	Harry Osterman	(D)	24,435		Maureen Burns Bekta	(R)	15,430
	Paul Bonilla	(R)	3,733	38	Renée Kosel	(R)	30,120
18	Julie Hamos	(D)	28,671		Darrell L. Sanders	(D)	29,989
	Unopposed			39	Vincent A. Persico	(R)	28,453
19	Robert J. Bugielski	(D)	23,027		Elizabeth Quaintance	(LIB)	10,103
	Unopposed			40	Randall M. "Randy" Hultgren	(R)	36,555
20	Richard T. Bradley	(D)	18,387		Unopposed		
	Joseph A. Hornowski	(R)	5,236	41	Mary Lou Cowlishaw	(R)	38,519
21	Mary E. Flowers	(D)	32,340		Gene Tenner	(D)	16,310
	Unopposed			42	Timothy L. Schmitz	(R)	27,315
					Bonnie Lee Kunkel	(D)	16,978

VOTE FOR STATE REPRESENTATIVES (Continued)

Dist.	Name	Party	Votes	Dist.	Name	Party	Votes
43	William A. O'Connor	(R)	17,713	64	Rosemary Kurtz	(R)	42,250
	John LaMantia	(D)	15,121		Lloyd N. Stoner	(D)	15,326
44	James B. Durkin	(R)	25,096	65	Patricia Reid Lindner	(R)	43,228
	Unopposed				Unopposed		
45	Kathleen L. "Kay" Wojcik	(R)	22,515	66	Douglas L. Hoeft	(R)	23,196
	Unopposed				Unopposed		
46	Lee A. Daniels	(R)	20,352	67	Douglas P. Scott *	(D)	24,830
	Joseph Martyniuk, Jr.	(D)	8,436		Unopposed		
47	Eileen Lyons	(R)	21,247	68	Ronald A. Wait	(R)	39,913
	Mark Ertler	(D)	15,805		Unopposed		
48	Anne Zickus	(R)	25,219	69	Dave Winters	(R)	28,632
	Daniel E. Krcmar	(D)	10,542		Daniel R. Mathews	(D)	15,115
49	Carole Pankau	(R)	20,582	70	David A. Wirsing	(R)	32,802
	Unopposed				Unopposed		
50	Thomas L. "Tom" Johnson	(R)	28,743	71	Mike Boland	(D)	33,924
	Stephen Bruesewitz	(D)	13,618		Unopposed		
51	Sidney H. Mathias	(R)	23,536	72	Joel Brunsvold	(D)	33,607
	Barbara J. Nash	(D)	13,441		Unopposed		
52	Mark H. Beaubien, Jr.	(R)	25,540	73	Jerry Mitchell	(R)	31,000
	Unopposed				Unopposed		
53	Terry R. Parke	(R)	16,379	74	I. Ronald Lawfer	(R)	26,184
	Richard B. Sass	(D)	11,114		Gerald Bork	(D)	13,613
54	Suzanne "Suzie" Bassi	(R)	30,836	75	Mary K. O'Brien	(D)	39,037
	Unopposed				Unopposed		
55	Rosemary Mulligan	(R)	17,448	76	Frank J. Mautino	(D)	27,315
	Mary Beth S. Tighe	(D)	16,119		Stephen J. Potthoff	(R)	14,703
56	Carolyn H. Krause	(R)	27,990	77	Angelo "Skip" Saviano	(R)	23,478
	Thomas Duda	(D)	12,669		Unopposed		
57	Elizabeth Coulson	(R)	24,987	78	Robert A. "Bob" Biggins	(R)	28,812
	Jody Wadhwa	(D)	17,758		Unopposed		
58	Jeffrey M. Schoenberg	(D)	34,986	79	Robert L. Ryan, Jr.	(D)	23,549
	Unopposed				Robert W. West	(R)	14,073
59	Susan Garrett	(D)	16,947	80	George Scully	(D)	25,880
	Cesilie Price	(R)	9,367		Susan W. Gowen	(R)	10,888
60	Karen May	(D)	25,982	81	Patricia R. "Patti" Bellock	(R)	25,292
	Nancy Flouret	(R)	16,297		Unopposed		
61	Andrea S. Moore	(R)	25,303	82	James H. "Jim" Meyer	(R)	23,355
	Geraldine Callan	(D)	12,369		Patrick A. Tallon	(D)	16,037
62	Timothy H. Osmond	(R)	22,779	83	Brent Hassert	(R)	43,431
	Spiro Georgeson	(D)	11,331		Phil Mullins	(D)	24,936
63	Jack D. Franks	(D)	25,013	84	Tom Cross	(R)	30,441
	Tom Salvi	(R)	23,476		Unopposed		

LEGEND (House)
Party Abbreviations
D - *Democratic*   *LIB - Libertarian*
R - *Republican*   *WI - Write - In*

* *Resigned. Replaced by Chuck Jefferson (D).*

VOTE FOR STATE REPRESENTATIVES (Concluded)

Dist.	Name	Party	Votes	Dist.	Name	Party	Votes
85	John "Phil" Novak Steve M. Barach	(D) (R)	27,138 11,071	102	Bill Mitchell Jeff Hawkins	(R) (D)	32,291 13,419
86	Jack McGuire Brad Stacy	(D) (R)	23,516 7,947	103	Richard J. "Rick" Winkel, Jr. Tod F. Satterthwaite	(R) (D)	24,232 19,213
87	Dan Rutherford Dan Elsey	(R) (D)	29,862 10,077	104	Tom Berns Charles "Chub" Conner David D. Wood, Jr.	(R) (D) (WI)	19,194 16,774 36
88	Dan Brady John A. Owen	(R) (D)	30,231 12,227	105	William B. "Bill" Black Unopposed	(R)	31,128
89	Keith P. Sommer Unopposed	(R)	39,072	106	Dale A. Righter Unopposed	(R)	30,975
90	John W. Turner * Frederick J. Tabor, Jr.	(R) (WI)	34,085 49	107	John O. Jones Ben Klebba	(R) (D)	30,206 10,422
91	Michael K. Smith Unopposed	(D)	32,454	108	Charles A. "Chuck" Hartke Unopposed	(D)	34,046
92	Ricca C. Slone Unopposed	(D)	25,695	109	Kurt M. Granberg Kristy Barton	(D) (R)	27,475 12,304
93	David R. Leitch Unopposed	(R)	38,315	110	Ron Stephens Jeffrey A. Hurst	(R) (D)	30,255 15,914
94	Donald L. Moffitt Josh Watson	(R) (D)	22,529 16,128	111	Steve Davis Unopposed	(D)	29,896
95	Richard P. "Rich" Myers Jon Mummert	(R) (D)	22,059 15,854	112	Jay C. Hoffman Virginia "Ginny" Ryan	(D) (R)	28,356 20,021
96	Art Tenhouse Unopposed	(R)	37,305	113	Thomas "Tom" Holbrook Unopposed	(D)	27,565
97	Tom Ryder Unopposed	(R)	34,424	114	Wyvetter H. Younge Unopposed	(D)	23,900
98	Gary Hannig Unopposed	(D)	32,080	115	Mike Bost Robert L. Koehn	(R) (D)	24,137 14,362
99	Raymond Poe Jerome A. Robinson	(R) (D)	36,595 12,372	116	Dan Reitz Harry Jankowski	(D) (R)	28,210 18,336
100	Gwenn Klingler Unopposed	(R)	38,313	117	Gary F. Forby Jack Woolard	(D) (R)	22,249 21,045
101	Julie A. Curry Unopposed	(D)	31,960	118	James D. "Jim" Fowler Eric E. Gregg	(D) (R)	24,383 19,373

LEGEND (House)
Party Abbreviations

D - Democratic   LIB - Libertarian
R - Republican   WI - Write - In

* Appointed Appellate Court Judge. Replaced by
Jonathan Wright (R).

State and Local

Government

Facts

JO DAVIESS
Galena

STEPHENSON
Freeport

WINNEBAGO
Rockford

BOONE
Belvidere

McHENRY
Woodstock

LAKE
Waukegan

CARROLL
Mt. Carroll

OGLE
Oregon

DE KALB
Sycamore

KANE
Geneva

COOK
Chicago

DU PAGE
Wheaton

WHITESIDE
Morrison

LEE
Dixon

KENDALL
Yorkville

WILL
Joliet

Rock Island

ROCK ISLAND

HENRY

BUREAU
Princeton

LA SALLE
Ottawa

GRUNDY
Morris

MERCER
Aledo

Cambridge

STARK

PUTNAM
Hennepin

KANKAKEE
Kankakee

KNOX
Toulon

Lacon

LIVINGSTON
Pontiac

IROQUOIS
Watseka

Oquawka

WARREN
Monmouth

Galesburg

PEORIA

MARSHALL

WOODFORD
Eureka

HENDERSON

Peoria

McLEAN

FORD
Paxton

FULTON
Lewistown

Pekin

Bloomington

VERMILION
Danville

HANCOCK
Carthage

McDONOUGH
Macomb

MASON
Havana

TAZEWELL

CHAMPAIGN

SCHUYLER
Rushville

LOGAN
Lincoln

DE WITT
Clinton

PIATT
Urbana

ADAMS
Quincy

BROWN
Mt. Sterling

MENARD
Petersburg

CASS
Virginia

MACON
Decatur

Monticello

MORGAN
Jacksonville

SANGAMON
Springfield

Tuscola

EDGAR
Paris

PIKE
Pittsfield

SCOTT
Winchester

CHRISTIAN
Taylorville

MOULTRIE
Sullivan

DOUGLAS

COLES
Charleston

GREENE

MACOUPIN
Carlinville

SHELBY
Shelbyville

CLARK
Marshall

CALHOUN

Carrollton

MONTGOMERY
Hillsboro

CUMBERLAND
Toledo

Hardin

JERSEY
Jerseyville

FAYETTE

EFFINGHAM
Effingham

JASPER
Newton

Robinson

CRAWFORD

MADISON
Edwardsville

BOND
Greenville

Vandalia

CLAY

RICHLAND
Olney

LAWRENCE
Lawrenceville

CLINTON
Carlyle

MARION
Salem

Louisville

ST CLAIR
Belleville

WAYNE
Fairfield

ED-
WARDS
Albion

WABASH
Mt.
Carmel

WASHINGTON
Nashville

JEFFERSON
Mt. Vernon

MONROE
Waterloo

RANDOLPH
Chester

PERRY
Pinckneyville

HAMILTON
McLeansboro

WHITE
Carmi

JACKSON
Murphysboro

FRANKLIN
Benton

WILLIAMSON
Marion

SALINE
Harrisburg

GALLATIN
Shawnee-
town

UNION
Jonesboro

JOHNSON
Vienna

POPE
Golconda

HARDIN
Elizabethtown

ALEXANDER

PULASKI
Mound City

MASSAC
Metropolis

Cairo

MAP OF ILLINOIS
Showing present counties
and county seats

Number of counties: 102

414

COUNTIES AND COUNTY OFFICERS

County and date established	County seat	2000 census population	Area square miles	Officers
ADAMS .... Jan. 13, 1825	Quincy	68,277	856.7	George E. Schrage III, County Clerk .... Dem. Glen F. Hultz, Circuit Clerk .... Dem. Larry D. Ehmen, Recorder .... Rep. Lisa A. Rapp, Treasurer .... Dem. Brent A. Fischer, Sheriff .... Dem. Byron S. Bier, State's Attorney .... Rep. Raymond A. Scheiter, Regional Supt. of Schools .... Rep. Gary W. Hamilton, Coroner .... Rep. Mike McLaughlin, County Board Chairman .... Rep.
ALEXANDER .... March 4, 1819	Cairo	9,590	236.4	Gloria B. Patton, County Clerk & Recorder .... Dem. Sharon McGinnis, Circuit Clerk .... Dem. Frances Lee, Treasurer .... Dem. Warren "Buddy" Mitchel, Sheriff .... Dem. Jeffrey B. Farris, State's Attorney .... Dem. Andrea Brown, Regional Supt. of Schools .... Rep. David W. Barkett, Coroner .... Dem. Andy Clarke, Chairman, Co. Commissioners .... Dem.
BOND .... Jan. 4, 1817	Greenville	17,633	380.2	Randy L. Reitz, County Clerk & Recorder .... Dem. John King, Circuit Clerk .... Rep. Wm. E. Johnson, Treasurer .... Dem. Jeff Brown, Sheriff .... Rep. Christopher Bauer, State's Attorney .... Dem. Delbert Maroon, Regional Supt. of Schools .... Dem. Alan D. Young, Coroner .... Dem. Hollie Willmann, County Board Chairman .... Dem.
BOONE .... March 4, 1837	Belvidere	41,786	281.4	Sylvia E. Schroeder, County Clerk & Recorder .... Rep. Julie M. Kleive, Circuit Clerk .... Rep. Carolynn G. Knox, Treasurer .... Rep. Duane E. Wirth, Sheriff .... Rep. Roger T. Russell, State's Attorney .... Rep. Richard Fairgrieves, Regional Supt. of Schools .... Rep. Lois J. Swenson, Coroner .... Rep. Donald Meier, County Board Chairman .... Rep.
BROWN .... Feb. 1, 1839	Mt. Sterling	6,950	305.7	Judy J. Woodworth, County Clerk & Recorder .... Dem. Doris O. Todd, Circuit Clerk .... Dem. Candace Knight, Treasurer .... Dem. Gerald "Jerry" Kempf, Sheriff .... Dem. Jerry J. Hooker, State's Attorney .... Rep. Don Kording, Regional Supt. of Schools .... Dem. Eugene Kerr, County Board Chairman .... Rep.
BUREAU .... Feb. 28, 1837	Princeton	35,503	868.6	Kamala S. Hieronymus, County Clerk & Recorder ..... Dem. Michael Miroux, Circuit Clerk .... Dem. Nina Cattani Urbanowski, Treasurer .... Rep. Greg Johnson, Sheriff .... Rep. Patrick J. Herrmann, State's Attorney .... Dem. Bruce Dennison, Regional Supt. of Schools .... Rep. Janice Wamhoff, Coroner .... Dem. John Brokaw, County Board Chairman .... Rep.
CALHOUN .... Jan. 10, 1825	Hardin	5,084	253.8	Lucille Kress, County Clerk & Recorder .... Rep. Yvonne M. Macauley, Circuit Clerk .... Dem. Curtis J. Robeen, Jr., Treasurer .... Dem. Richard C. Meyer, Sheriff & Coroner .... Dem. Charles H. Burch, State's Attorney .... Dem. Russell G. Masinelli, Regional Supt. of Schools .... Dem. Vincent Tepen, Chairman, Co. Commissioners .... Dem.
CARROLL .... Feb. 22, 1839	Mt. Carroll	16,674	444.2	Judith A. Gray, County Clerk & Recorder .... Rep. Sherri Miller, Circuit Clerk .... Rep. Norman L. Brinkmeier, Treasurer .... Rep. Rod A. Herrick, Sheriff .... Rep. Scott L Brinkmeier, State's Attorney .... Rep. John B. Lang, Regional Supt. of Schools .... Rep. Michael Jones, Coroner .... Rep. William C. Ritenour, County Board Chairman .... Rep.

COUNTIES AND COUNTY OFFICERS (Continued)

County and date established	County seat	2000 census population	Area square miles	Officers
CASS March 3, 1837	Virginia	13,695	376	Michael C. Kirchner, County Clerk & Recorder .... Dem. Evelyn Kathy Trenter, Circuit Clerk .... Rep. Micki Wilson, Treasurer .... Dem. David Osmer, Sheriff .... Dem. John Dahlem, State's Attorney .... Dem. Don Kording, Regional Supt. of Schools .... Dem. Wyatt Sager, Death Examiner .... Dem. H.O. Brownback, County Board Chairman .... Dem.
CHAMPAIGN .... Feb. 20, 1833	Urbana	179,669	997.2	Mark Shelden, County Clerk .... Rep. Linda S. Frank, Circuit Clerk .... Rep. Barb Frasca, Recorder .... Rep. Daniel J. Welch, Treasurer .... Rep. Geraldine "Gerrie" Parr, Auditor .... Dem. David J. Madigan, Sheriff .... Rep. John Piland, State's Attorney .... Rep. Martin L. Barrett, Regional Supt. of Schools .... Rep. Roger L. Swaney, Coroner .... Rep. Patricia Avery, County Board Chairman .... Dem.
CHRISTIAN .... Feb. 15, 1839	Taylorville	35,372	709.1	Terry E. Ryan, County Clerk & Recorder .... Dem. Donna Castelli, Circuit Clerk .... Dem. Colleen Hadley, Treasurer .... Dem. Robert E. Kindermann, Jr., Sheriff .... Dem. David Martin, State's Attorney .... Dem. Gregory J. Springer, Regional Supt. of Schools .... Dem. Jack Pearce, Coroner .... Rep. John Curtin, County Board Chairman .... Dem.
CLARK .... March 22, 1819	Marshall	17,008	501.5	William C. "Bill" Downey, County Clerk & Recorder .... Dem. Terri Reynolds, Circuit Clerk .... Rep. Carol Ann Cornwell, Treasurer .... Rep. Dan Crumrin, Sheriff .... Rep. David Lewis, State's Attorney .... Rep. John McNary, Regional Supt. of Schools .... Dem. C. Gregory Hosch, Coroner .... Rep. Bill Weaver, County Board Chairman .... Rep.
CLAY .... Dec. 23, 1824	Louisville	14,560	469.3	Phyllis Miller, County Clerk & Recorder .... Rep. Rita L. Porter, Circuit Clerk .... Rep. Minerva Mitchel, Treasurer .... Dem. Lee Ryker, Sheriff .... Dem. Alan Buck, State's Attorney .... Dem. Sam White, Regional Supt. of Schools .... Dem. Gary Bright, Coroner .... Rep. Tony Whitehead, County Board Chairman .... Rep.
CLINTON .... Dec. 27, 1824	Carlyle	35,535	474.3	Thomas LaCaze, County Clerk & Recorder .... Rep. Jeff Luebbers, Circuit Clerk .... Dem. Ferd W. Mueller, Jr., Treasurer .... Dem. Paul Spaur, Sheriff .... Dem. Stanley Brandmeyer, State's Attorney .... Rep. Danny Garrett, Regional Supt. of Schools .... Dem. David Moss, Coroner .... Dem. Herb Pingsterhaus, County Board Chairman .... Rep.
COLES .... Dec. 25, 1830	Charleston	53,196	508.3	Betty J. Coffrin, County Clerk & Recorder .... Rep. Vicki Kirkpatrick, Circuit Clerk .... Rep. Carolyn Kolling, Treasurer .... Rep. Ronald Scott, Sheriff .... Dem. C. Steve Ferguson, State's Attorney .... Dem. John McNary, Regional Supt. of Schools .... Dem. Mike Nichols, Coroner .... Dem. Robert Webb, County Board Chairman .... Dem.
COOK .... Jan. 15, 1831	Chicago	5,376,741	945.7	David D. Orr, County Clerk .... Dem. Dorothy Brown, Circuit Clerk .... Dem. Eugene M. Moore, Recorder .... Dem. Maria Pappas, Treasurer .... Dem. Laura H. Burman, Auditor .... Appt. Michael F. Sheahan, Sheriff .... Dem. Richard Devine, State's Attorney .... Dem. Joseph F. Kaczanowski, Regional Supt. of Schools ...... Rep. Arne Duncan, CEO, Chicago Public Schools .... Appt. Dr. Edmund D. Donoghue, Coroner .... Appt. John H. Stroger, Jr., County Board President .... Dem. Louis G. Apostol, Public Administrator .... Appt.

416

COUNTIES AND COUNTY OFFICERS (Continued)

County and date established	County seat	2000 census population	Area square miles	Officers
CRAWFORD Dec. 31, 1816	Robinson	20,452	443.6	Patricia Lycan, County Clerk & Recorder .... Rep. Denise Utterback, Circuit Clerk .... Rep. Doris Gill, Treasurer .... Rep. Tom W. Weger, Sheriff .... Dem. Mark L. Shaner, State's Attorney .... Dem. Samuel T. White, Regional Supt. of Schools .... Dem. Earl L. Deckard, Coroner .... Rep. Ron Legg, County Board Chairman .... Dem.
CUMBERLAND March 2, 1843	Toledo	11,253	346	Priscilla Schrock, County Clerk & Recorder .... Rep. Tina Talley, Circuit Clerk .... Rep. Patsy R. Evans, Treasurer .... Dem. Stephen Ozier, Sheriff .... Dem. Millard S. Everhart, State's Attorney .... Rep. John McNary, Regional Supt. of Schools .... Dem. Michael G. Barkley, Coroner .... Dem. Michael D. Walk, County Board Chairman .... Rep.
DeKALB March 4, 1837	Sycamore	88,969	634.2	Sharon L. Holmes, County Clerk & Recorder .... Rep. Maureen Josh, Circuit Clerk .... Rep. Christine J. Johnson, Treasurer .... Rep. Gary Hanson, Finance Director .... Appt. Roger A. Scott, Sheriff .... Rep. Ronald G. Matekaitis, State's Attorney .... Dem. Thomas R. Weber, Regional Supt. of Schools .... Rep. Dennis J. Miller, Coroner .... Rep. Robert W. Pritchard, County Board Chairman .... Rep.
DeWITT March 1, 1839	Clinton	16,798	397.6	Jayne Usher, County Clerk & Recorder .... Rep. Kathy Weiss, Circuit Clerk .... Rep. Christy Long, Treasurer .... Rep. Roger Massey, Sheriff .... Rep. Jerry A. Johnson, State's Attorney .... Rep. Eugene Jontry, Regional Supt. of Schools .... Rep. Alex Calvert, Coroner .... Rep. Roland G. Schumaker, County Board Chairman .... Rep.
DOUGLAS Feb. 8, 1859	Tuscola	19,922	416.9	James A. Ingram, County Clerk & Recorder .... Rep. Julie Mills, Circuit Clerk .... Rep. Bobbi Murray, Treasurer .... Rep. John R. Chambers, Sheriff .... Dem. Diane Sipich, State's Attorney .... Rep. John McNary, Regional Supt. of Schools .... Dem. Joseph Victor, Coroner .... Rep. Merle I.Greger, County Board Chairman .... Rep.
DuPAGE Feb. 9, 1839	Wheaton	904,161	334.4	Gary A. King, County Clerk .... Rep. Joel Kagann, Circuit Clerk .... Rep. J.P. "Rick" Carney, Recorder .... Rep. John Lotus Novak, Treasurer .... Rep. Jim Rasins, Auditor .... Rep. John E. Zaruba, Sheriff .... Rep. Joseph E. Birkett, State's Attorney .... Rep. Berardo J. DeSimone, Regional Supt. of Schools .... Rep. Richard R. Ballinger, Coroner .... Rep. Robert J. Schillerstrom, County Board Chairman .... Rep.
EDGAR Jan. 3, 1823	Paris	19,704	623.6	Rebecca R. Kraemer, County Clerk & Recorder .... Dem. Janis K. Nebergall, Circuit Clerk .... Rep. Linda L. Lane, Treasurer .... Dem. Karl E. Farnham, Jr., Sheriff .... Rep. Matthew L. Sullivan, State's Attorney .... Rep. John McNary, Regional Supt. of Schools .... Dem. David W. Dick, Coroner .... Rep. Dan Winans, County Board Chairman .... Rep.

COUNTIES AND COUNTY OFFICERS (Continued)

County and date established	County seat	2000 census population	Area square miles	Officers
EDWARDS .... Nov. 28, 1814	Albion	6,971	222.4	Ronald C. Mason, County Clerk & Recorder .... Dem. Patsy Taylor, Circuit Clerk .... Rep. Cindy Hocking, Treasurer .... Rep. Terry Harper, Auditor .... Rep. Rick Spyder, Sheriff .... Dem. Brian T. Shinkle, State's Attorney .... Rep. Linda L. Blackman, Regional Supt. of Schools .... Dem. Mark Curtis, Coroner .... Rep. Tom Hortin, Chairman, Co. Commissioners .... Rep.
EFFINGHAM .... Feb. 15, 1831	Effingham	34,264	478.7	Robert L. Behrman, County Clerk & Recorder .... Rep. B. Jane Schuette, Circuit Clerk .... Dem. Steven W. Dasenbrock, Treasurer .... Dem. Ronald J. Meek, Sheriff .... Dem. Edward J. Deters, State's Attorney .... Dem. Delbert Maroon, Regional Supt. of Schools .... Dem. Eric W. Althoff, Coroner .... Dem. Leon Gobczynski, County Board Chairman .... Dem.
FAYETTE .... Feb. 14, 1821	Vandalia	21,802	716.5	Isabelle B. Brandt, County Clerk & Recorder .... Rep. Marsha Wodtka, Circuit Clerk .... Dem. Rose S. Hoover, Treasurer .... Dem. Harold C. Johnson, Sheriff .... Rep. Stephen Friedel, State's Attorney .... Dem. Delbert Maroon, Regional Supt. of Schools .... Dem. Bruce Bowen, Coroner .... Rep. Larry Emerick, County Board Chairman .... Dem.
FORD .... Feb. 17, 1859	Paxton	14,241	485.9	Linda Kellerhals, County Clerk & Recorder .... Rep. Kamalen Johnson, Circuit Clerk .... Rep. Nancy L. Krumwiede, Treasurer .... Rep. William D. Kean, Sheriff .... Rep. Tony Lee, State's Attorney .... Rep. Martin L. Barrett, Regional Supt. of Schools .... Rep. Jeffrey Baine, Coroner .... Rep. J.R. Herriott, County Board Chairman .... Rep.
FRANKLIN .... Jan. 2, 1818	Benton	39,018	412.1	Dave Dobill, County Clerk & Recorder .... Dem. Donna Sevenski, Circuit Clerk .... Dem. Juva Wynn, Treasurer .... Dem. Bill Wilson, Sheriff .... Dem. William K. Richardson, State's Attorney .... Dem. Barry Kohl, Regional Supt. of Schools .... Dem. Stephen D. Leek, Coroner .... Dem. Harry Stewart, County Board Chairman .... Dem.
FULTON .... Jan. 28, 1823	Lewistown	38,250	865.7	Randal L. Rumler, County Clerk & Recorder .... Dem. Mary C. Hampton, Circuit Clerk .... Dem. Victoria J. Harper, Treasurer .... Dem. Dan Daly, Sheriff .... Dem. Edward R. Danner, State's Attorney .... Dem. Gary L. Grzanich, Regional Supt. of Schools .... Dem. Steven D. Hines, Coroner .... Dem. Bernard J. Oaks, County Board Chairman .... Dem.
GALLATIN .... Sept. 14, 1812	Shawneetown	6,445	323.7	Elizabeth A. Wargel, County Clerk & Recorder .... Dem. Mona L. Moore, Circuit Clerk .... Dem. Naomi Acord, Treasurer .... Dem. Raymond Martin, Sheriff .... Dem. Keely D. Dobbs, State's Attorney .... Dem. Linda L. Blackman, Regional Supt. of Schools .... Dem. Charles A. "Tony" Cox, Coroner .... Dem. Thomas R. "Randy" Drone, County Board Chairman Dem.
GREENE .... Jan. 20, 1821	Carrollton	14,761	543.1	Deborah Banghart, County Clerk & Recorder .... Dem. Virginia "Tunie" Brannan, Circuit Clerk .... Rep. Kirby Ballard, Treasurer .... Rep. Michael S. Fry, Sheriff .... Dem. Elliott Turpin, State's Attorney .... Dem. Russell Masinelli, Regional Supt. of Schools .... Dem. Dean Bishop, Sr., Coroner .... Dem. Eric Ivers, County Board Chairman .... Rep.

COUNTIES AND COUNTY OFFICERS (Continued)

County and date established	County seat	2000 census population	Area square miles	Officers
GRUNDY Feb. 17, 1841	Morris	37,535	420.1	Lana J. Phillips, County Clerk & Recorder .... Dem. Karen E. Slattery, Circuit Clerk .... Rep. Marcy Miller, Treasurer .... Dem. James L. Olson, Sheriff .... Dem. Lance R. Peterson, State's Attorney .... Dem. Thos. Centowski, Regional Supt. of Schools .... Rep. John W. Callahan, Coroner .... Rep. Donald C. Kaufman, County Board Chairman .... Rep.
HAMILTON .... McLeansboro ..... 8,621 Feb. 8, 1821	McLeansboro	8,621	435.2	Lovella Craddock, County Clerk & Recorder .... Rep. Bobbi Oxford, Circuit Clerk .... Rep. Linda Braden, Treasurer .... Rep. F.L. "Rick" Winemiller, Sheriff .... Dem. Wayne Morris, State's Attorney .... Dem. P.E. Cross, Regional Supt. of Schools .... Dem. Ronald Ewald, Coroner .... Dem. James H. "Jim" Deen, County Board Chairman .... Dem.
HANCOCK Jan. 13, 1825	Carthage	20,121	794.7	Kerry Asbridge, County Clerk & Recorder .... Dem. John Neally, Circuit Clerk .... Rep. Beverly Markey, Treasurer .... Dem. John Jefferson, Sheriff .... Rep. Karen Andrews, State's Attorney .... Dem. Robert Baumann, Regional Supt. of Schools .... Rep. Kendall Beals, Coroner .... Rep. Lee Ourth, County Board Chairman .... Rep.
HARDIN March 2, 1839	Elizabethtown	4,800	178.3	Mary Ellen Denton, County Clerk & Recorder .... Dem. Diana Hubbard, Circuit Clerk .... Dem. Kim Lamar, Treasurer .... Dem. Carl R. Cox, Sheriff .... Rep. Jeffery Stunson, State's Attorney .... Rep. Linda L. Blackman, Regional Supt. of Schools .... Dem. Roger Little, Coroner .... Dem. Wendell Brownfield, Chairman, Co. Commissioners . Rep.
HENDERSON Jan. 20, 1841	Oquawka	8,213	378.8	Marcella L. Cisna, County Clerk & Recorder .... Rep. Sandra Keane, Circuit Clerk .... Rep. Barbara Liston, Treasurer .... Rep. Mark K. Lumbeck, Sheriff .... Dem. David L. Vancil, Jr., State's Attorney .... Rep. Bruce Hall, Regional Supt. of Schools .... Rep. Kris Beals, Coroner .... Rep. Marion Brown, Jr., County Board Chairman .... Dem.
HENRY Jan. 13, 1825	Cambridge	51,020	823.3	Martha S. Roberts, County Clerk & Recorder .... Dem. Debra J. Doss, Circuit Clerk .... Rep. Charles Claeys, Treasurer .... Dem. Gilbert Cady, Sheriff .... Rep. Terence Patton, State's Attorney .... Rep. Bruce Dennison, Regional Supt. of Schools .... Rep. David Johnson, Coroner .... Rep. Tom Nicholson, County Board Chairman .... Dem.
IROQUOIS Feb. 26, 1833	Watseka	31,334	1,116.5	Mark R. Henrichs, County Clerk & Recorder .... Rep. Arlene Hines, Circuit Clerk .... Rep. David L. Perzee, Treasurer .... Rep. Joseph V. Mathy, Sheriff .... Dem. James Devine, State's Attorney .... Rep. Kay Pangle, Regional Supt. of Schools .... Rep. Eldon Sprau, Coroner .... Rep. Shane Cultra, County Board Chairman .... Rep.
JACKSON Jan. 10, 1816	Murphysboro	59,612	588.1	Larry W. Reinhardt, County Clerk & Recorder .... Dem. Cindy R. Svanda, Circuit Clerk .... Dem. Shirley Dillinger Booker, Treasurer .... Dem. William Kilquist, Sheriff .... Dem. Michael L. Wepsiec, State's Attorney .... Dem. Donald Brewer, Regional Supt. of Schools .... Dem. Thomas Kupferer, Coroner .... Dem. Gary Hartlieb, County Board Chairman .... Dem.

COUNTIES AND COUNTY OFFICERS (Continued)

County and date established	County seat	2000 census population	Area square miles	Officers
JASPER Feb. 15, 1831	Newton	10,117	494.4	Ray Diel, County Clerk & Recorder .... Dem. Sheryl Frederick, Circuit Clerk .... Rep. Anita P. Harris, Treasurer .... Dem. Ed Francis, Sheriff .... Dem. Kimberly Koester, State's Attorney .... Rep. Samuel T. White, Regional Supt. of Schools .... Dem. Jason Meyer, Coroner .... Rep. Franklin Geier, County Board Chairman .... Dem.
JEFFERSON March 26, 1819	Mt. Vernon	40,045	571.1	Don Rector, County Clerk & Recorder .... Dem. Gene Bolerjack, Circuit Clerk .... Rep. Debbie Elliott Marlow, Treasurer .... Rep. Roy Dean Bradford, Sheriff .... Dem. Gary Duncan, State's Attorney .... Dem. P.E. Cross, Regional Supt. of Schools .... Dem. Richard Garretson, M.D., Coroner .... Dem. Bill Armstrong, County Board Chairman .... Rep.
JERSEY Feb. 28, 1839	Jerseyville	21,668	369.2	Linda J. Crotchett, County Clerk & Recorder .... Rep. Charles E. Huebener, Circuit Clerk .... Dem. Shirley J. Armstrong, Treasurer .... Dem. Paul F. Cunningham, Sheriff .... Rep. Mary E. Kirbach, State's Attorney .... Dem. Russell G. Masinelli, Regional Supt. of Schools .... Dem. Larry J. Alexander, Coroner .... Rep. David L. Collins, County Board Chairman .... Dem.
JO DAVIESS Feb. 17, 1827	Galena	22,289	601.2	Jean Dimke, County Clerk & Recorder .... Rep. Sharon Wand, Circuit Clerk .... Rep. Carol Soat, Treasurer .... Rep. Steven R. Allendorf, Sheriff .... Rep. Glen R. Weber, State's Attorney .... Rep. John B. Lang, Regional Supt. of Schools .... Rep. Bill Miller, Coroner .... Rep. Merri Berlage, County Board Chairman .... Rep.
JOHNSON Sept. 14, 1812	Vienna	12,878	346	Robin Harper-Whitehead, County Clerk & Recorder . Rep. Neal Watkins, Circuit Clerk .... Rep. Carolyn McGill, Treasurer .... Rep. Elry Faulkner, Sheriff .... Rep. D. Brian Trambley, State's Attorney .... Rep. Andrea Brown, Regional Supt. of Schools .... Rep. Gary Hicks, Coroner .... Rep. Max Ray, Chairman, County Commissioners .... Dem.
KANE Jan. 16, 1836	Geneva	404,119	520.7	Bernadine Murphy, County Clerk .... Rep. Deborah Seyller, Circuit Clerk .... Rep. Sandy Wegman, Recorder .... Rep. David Rickert, Treasurer .... Rep. William F. Keck, Auditor .... Rep. Kenneth R. Ramsey, Sheriff .... Rep. Meg Gorecki, State's Attorney .... Rep. Clem Mejia, Regional Supt. of Schools .... Rep. Charles West, Coroner .... Rep. Michael W. McCoy, County Board Chairman .... Rep.
KANKAKEE Feb. 11, 1853	Kankakee	103,833	677.5	Bruce Clark, County Clerk .... Rep. Kathryn Thomas, Circuit Clerk .... Rep. Dennis Coy, Recorder .... Dem. Mark Frechette, Treasurer .... Dem. Steve Mc Carty, Auditor .... Dem. Tim Bukowski, Sheriff .... Rep. Ed Smith, State's Attorney .... Rep. Kay Pangle, Regional Supt. of Schools .... Rep. James Kelly, Coroner .... Rep. Karl Kruse, County Board Chairman .... Rep.
KENDALL Feb. 19, 1841	Yorkville	54,544	320.7	Paul P. Anderson, County Clerk & Recorder .... Rep. Shirley R. Lee, Circuit Clerk .... Rep. Thomas W. Holbrook, Treasurer .... Rep. Richard A. Randall, Sheriff .... Rep. Tim McCann, State's Attorney .... Rep. Tom Centowski, Regional Supt. of Schools .... Rep. Ken Toftoy, Coroner .... Rep. John Church, County Board Chairman .... Rep.

COUNTIES AND COUNTY OFFICERS (Continued)

County and date established	County seat	2000 census population	Area square miles	Officers
KNOX Jan. 13, 1825	Galesburg	55,836	716.3	Sally Blodgett, County Clerk .... Dem. Kelly Cheesman, Circuit Clerk .... Rep. Nancy McCune, Recorder .... Rep. Carolyn Griffith, Treasurer .... Rep. Jim Thompson, Sheriff .... Dem. Paul L. Mangieri, State's Attorney .... Dem. Robert O. Johnson, Regional Supt. of Schools .... Rep. John F. Watson, Coroner .... Dem. Sally Keener, County Board Chairman .... Rep.
LAKE March 1, 1839	Waukegan	644,356	447.8	Willard R. Helander, County Clerk .... Rep. Sally Deadrick Coffelt, Circuit Clerk .... Rep. Mary Ellen Vanderventer, Recorder .... Dem. Robert Skidmore, Treasurer .... Rep. Gary Del Re, Sheriff .... Rep. Michael J. Waller, State's Attorney .... Rep. Edward J. Gonwa, Regional Supt. of Schools .... Rep. Barbara E. Richardson, Coroner .... Rep. Suzi Schmidt, County Board Chairman .... Rep.
LA SALLE Jan. 15, 1831	Ottawa	111,509	1,135	Mary Jane Wilkinson, County Clerk .... Dem. Joseph M. Carey, Circuit Clerk .... Dem. Thomas E. Lyons, Recorder .... Dem. Dale J. McConville, Treasurer .... Dem. Jody L. Wilkinson, Auditor .... Dem. Thomas J. Templeton, Sheriff .... Rep. Joseph P. Hettel, State's Attorney .... Dem. William G. Novotney, Regional Supt. of Schools .... Rep. Jody Bernard, Coroner .... Dem. Joseph E. Hettel, County Board Chairman .... Dem.
LAWRENCE Jan. 16, 1821	Lawrenceville	15,452	372	Nancy J. Hoke, County Clerk & Recorder .... Rep. Peggy Frederick, Circuit Clerk .... Rep. Larry Umfleet, Treasurer .... Dem. Steve Chansler, Sheriff .... Dem. Todd Reitz, State's Attorney .... Dem. Samuel T. White, Regional Supt. of Schools .... Dem. Shannon Steffey, Coroner .... Rep. James Dunn, County Board Chairman .... Dem.
LEE Feb. 27, 1839	Dixon	36,062	725.4	Nancy Nelson, County Clerk & Recorder .... Rep. Denise A. McCaffrey, Circuit Clerk .... Dem. John F. Fritts, Treasurer .... Rep. Tim Bivins, Sheriff .... Rep. Linda Giesen, State's Attorney .... Dem. Delight H. Pitman, Regional Supt. of Schools .... Rep. Richard Schilling, Coroner .... Rep. Jim Jones, County Board Chairman .... Rep.
LIVINGSTON Feb. 27, 1837	Pontiac	39,678	1,043.8	Judith McGlasson, County Clerk & Recorder .... Rep. Judith K. Cremer, Circuit Clerk .... Rep. Sylvia L. Bashore, Treasurer .... Rep. Marvin R. Rutledge, Sheriff .... Rep. Thomas J. Brown, State's Attorney .... Rep. Eugene P. Jontry, Regional Supt. of Schools .... Rep. Michael P. Burke, Coroner .... Rep. John T. Jacobson, County Board Chairman .... Rep.
LOGAN Feb. 15, 1839	Lincoln	31,183	618.2	Sally J. Litterly, County Clerk & Recorder .... Rep. Carla Bender, Circuit Clerk .... Rep. Mary E. Bruns, Treasurer .... Rep. Gary Hetherington, Auditor .... Appt. Anthony Soloman, Sheriff .... Dem. Tim Huyett, State's Attorney .... Rep. George D. Janet, Regional Supt. of Schools .... Rep. Chuck Fricke, Coroner .... Rep. Dick Logan, County Board Chairman .... Rep.

COUNTIES AND COUNTY OFFICERS (Continued)

County and date established	County seat	2000 census population	Area square miles	Officers
MACON Jan. 19, 1829	Decatur	114,706	580.6	Stephen M. Bean, County Clerk .... Dem. Kathy A. Hott, Circuit Clerk .... Dem. Mary Eaton, Recorder .... Dem. Cathy A. Ashby, Treasurer .... Rep. David Sapp, Auditor .... Dem. Roger Walker, Sheriff .... Dem. Scott Rueter, State's Attorney .... Rep. Charles Shonkwiler, Regional Supt. of Schools .... Rep. Michael E. Day, Coroner .... Rep. John W. Snyder, County Board Chairman .... Dem.
MACOUPIN Jan. 17, 1829	Carlinville	49,019	863.7	John Saracco, County Clerk & Recorder .... Dem. Mike Mathis, Circuit Clerk .... Dem. Wilma Cox, Treasurer .... Dem. Gary Wheeler, Sheriff .... Dem. Vince Moreth, State's Attorney .... Dem. Russell G. Masinelli, Regional Supt. of Schools .... Dem. Wesley Charles Landers, Coroner .... Dem. Don "Pete" Denby, County Board Chairman .... Dem.
MADISON Sept. 14, 1812	Edwardsville	258,941	725.1	Mark Von Nida, County Clerk .... Dem. Matt Melucci, Circuit Clerk .... Dem. Daniel Donohoo, Recorder .... Dem. Fred Bathon, Treasurer .... Dem. Rick Faccin, Auditor .... Dem. Bob Churchich, Sheriff .... Dem. William R. Haine, State's Attorney .... Dem. Harry Briggs, Jr., Regional Supt. of Schools .... Dem. Stephen Nonn, Coroner .... Dem. Rudolph Papa, County Board Chairman .... Dem.
MARION Jan. 24, 1823	Salem	41,691	572.3	Cliff Neudecker, County Clerk & Recorder .... Dem. Ronda Yates, Circuit Clerk .... Dem. Patti J. Henry, Treasurer .... Dem. Gerald L. "Benji" Benjamin, Sheriff .... Dem. James W. Creason, State's Attorney .... Dem. Dan Garrett, Regional Supt. of Schools .... Dem. Tom Nicolay, Coroner .... Rep. Ralph Johnnie, County Board Chairman .... Dem.
MARSHALL Jan. 19, 1839	Lacon	13,180	386.1	Andrea J. Mahoney, County Clerk & Recorder .... Rep. Gina M. Noe, Circuit Clerk .... Rep. Nedra K. Junker, Treasurer .... Rep. Sheryl "Chip" Webster, Sheriff .... Rep. Donald D. Knuckey, State's Attorney .... Rep. Richard L. Herring, Regional Supt. of Schools .... Rep. David Lenz, Jr., Coroner .... Rep. Thomas V. Wenk, County Board Chairman .... Rep.
MASON Jan. 20, 1841	Havana	16,038	539	William R. Blessman, County Clerk & Recorder .... Dem. Brenda K. Miller, Circuit Clerk .... Dem. Carol C."Candy" Tomlin, Treasurer .... Dem. Richard E. Walker, Sheriff .... Dem. Alan D. Tucker, State's Attorney .... Dem. George D. Janet, Regional Supt. of Schools .... Rep. Jerome J. Hurley, Coroner .... Dem. Henry W. Imig, County Board Chairman .... Dem.
MASSAC Feb. 8, 1843	Metropolis	15,161	239.1	John D. "Bubba" Taylor, County Clerk and Recorder . Rep. Larry G. Grace, Circuit Clerk .... Rep. Sharon Glass, Treasurer .... Dem. Bob Griffey, Sheriff .... Dem. Joseph "Joe" Jackson, State's Attorney .... Dem. Andrea Brown, Regional Supt. of Schools .... Rep. Steven Farmer, Coroner .... Rep. Jim Modglin, Chairman, Co. Commissioners .... Rep.
McDONOUGH Jan. 25, 1826	Macomb	32,913	589.3	Florine Miller, County Clerk & Recorder .... Rep. Julia Woodrum, Circuit Clerk .... Rep. Angela G. Graves, Treasurer .... Rep. Stan Carman, Sheriff .... Rep. William Poncin, State's Attorney .... Rep. Robert Baumann, Regional Supt. of Schools .... Rep. Larry Jameson, Coroner .... Rep. Jere Greuel, County Board Chairman .... Rep.

COUNTIES AND COUNTY OFFICERS (Continued)

County and date established	County seat	2000 census population	Area square miles	Officers
McHENRY Jan. 16, 1836	Woodstock	260,077	604.1	Katherine C. Schultz, County Clerk .... Rep. Vernon W. Kays, Jr., Circuit Clerk .... Rep. Phyllis K. Walters, Recorder .... Rep. William W. LeFew, Treasurer .... Rep. Ruth Rooney, Auditor .... Rep. Keith Nygren, Sheriff .... Rep. Gary W. Pack, State's Attorney .... Rep. Donald R. Englert, Regional Supt. of Schools .... Rep. Marlene A. Lantz, Coroner .... Rep. Michael W. Tryon, County Board Chairman .... Rep.
McLEAN Dec. 25, 1830	Bloomington	150,433	1,183.6	PeggyAnn Milton, County Clerk .... Rep. Sandra Parker, Circuit Clerk .... Rep. Ruth Weber, Recorder .... Rep. James E. Boylan, Treasurer .... Rep. Jackie Dozier, Auditor .... Rep. David Owens, Sheriff .... Rep. Charles Reynard, State's Attorney .... Rep. Eugene Jontry, Regional Supt. of Schools .... Rep. Beth Carlson, Coroner .... Rep. Michael Sweeney, County Board Chairman .... Rep.
MENARD Feb. 15, 1839	Petersburg	12,486	314.3	Gene Treseler, County Clerk & Recorder .... Rep. Penny S. Hoke, Circuit Clerk .... Rep. Jacqueline Horn, Treasurer .... Rep. Larry N. Smith, Sheriff .... Rep. Ken Baumgarten, State's Attorney .... Rep. George D. Janet, Regional Supt. of Schools .... Rep. Larry Hollis, Death Investigator .... Appt. Barb Ryes, Chairman, Co. Commissioners .... Rep.
MERCER Jan. 13, 1825	Aledo	16,957	561	Thomas L. Hanson, County Clerk & Recorder .... Dem. Jeff Benson, Circuit Clerk .... Rep. Michael Bertelsen, Treasurer .... Rep. Larry E. Glancey, Sheriff .... Dem. Gregory McHugh, State's Attorney .... Dem. Bruce Hall, Regional Supt. of Schools .... Rep. Ronald McNall, Coroner .... Dem. Wallace Green, County Board Chairman .... Dem.
MONROE Jan. 6, 1816	Waterloo	27,619	388.3	Dennis M. Knobloch, County Clerk & Recorder .... Rep. Aaron Reitz, Circuit Clerk .... Dem. Merrill W. Prange, Treasurer .... Rep. Daniel J. Kelley, Sheriff .... Dem. Dennis Doyle, State's Attorney .... Dem. Faye Hughes, Regional Supt. of Schools .... Rep. Julie M. Gummersheimer, Coroner .... Rep. Robert "Bob" Rippelmeyer, Chairman, County Commissioners .... Rep.
MONTGOMERY Feb. 12, 1821	Hillsboro	30,652	703.8	Sandy Leitheiser, County Clerk & Recorder .... Rep. Mary Webb, Circuit Clerk .... Rep. Ron Jenkins, Treasurer .... Rep. Jim Vazzi, Sheriff .... Rep. Jim Roberts, State's Attorney .... Dem. Greg Springer, Regional Supt. of Schools .... Dem. Rick Broaddus, Coroner .... Dem. Mike Havera, County Board Chairman .... Dem.
MORGAN Jan. 31, 1823	Jacksonville	36,616	568.8	Barbara J. Gross, County Clerk & Recorder .... Dem. Barbara J. Baker, Circuit Clerk .... Rep. Gayla Hornbeek, Treasurer .... Rep. James Robson, Jr., Sheriff .... Rep. Charles M. Colburn, State's Attorney .... Rep. Don Kording, Regional Supt. of Schools .... Dem. Jeff Lair, Coroner .... Rep. Ken Coffman, Chairman, Co. Commissioners .... Dem.

County and date established	County seat	2000 census population	Area square miles	Officers
MOULTRIE .... Feb. 16, 1843	Sullivan	14,287	335.6	Georgia C. England, County Clerk & Recorder .... Dem. Deborah M. Preston, Circuit Clerk .... Dem. Johna L. Sims, Treasurer .... Rep. Rieck Kendall, Sheriff .... Dem. Sharon A. Buckler, State's Attorney .... Rep. John McNary, Regional Supt. of Schools .... Dem. Lynn Reed, Coroner .... Rep. Steve Mayberry, County Board Chairman .... Dem.
OGLE .... Jan. 16, 1836	Oregon	51,032	758.9	Rebecca Huntley, County Clerk & Recorder .... Rep. Martin Typer, Circuit Clerk .... Rep. John Coffman, Treasurer .... Rep. Melvin Messer, Sheriff .... Rep. Doug Floski, State's Attorney .... Rep. Delight H. Pitman, Regional Supt. of Schools .... Rep. Darrell Cash, Coroner .... Rep. Jerry P. Daws, County Board Chairman .... Rep.
PEORIA .... Jan. 13, 1825	Peoria	183,433	619.6	JoAnn Thomas, County Clerk .... Dem. Regina M. Spears, Circuit Clerk .... Dem. Bradley E. Horton, Recorder .... Rep. Edward "Tripp" O'Connor, Treasurer .... Rep. Robert S. "Steve" Sonnemaker, Auditor .... Dem. Charles R. "Chuck" Schofield, Sheriff .... Rep. Kevin W. Lyons, State's Attorney .... Dem. Gerald M. Brookhart, Regional Supt. of Schools .... Dem. Dan Heinz, Coroner .... Rep. David T. Williams, Sr., County Board Chairman .... Dem.
PERRY .... Jan. 29, 1827	Pinckneyville	23,094	441	Don Hirsch, County Clerk & Recorder .... Rep. Nick Dolce, Circuit Clerk .... Dem. Cha Hill, Treasurer .... Rep. Keith Kellerman, Sheriff .... Dem. David N. Stanton, State's Attorney .... Rep. Don Brewer, Regional Supt. of Schools .... Dem. Paul Searby, Coroner .... Rep. Danny Wildermuth, Chairman, Co. Commissioners ..... Dem.
PIATT .... Jan. 27, 1841	Monticello	16,365	440	Pat Rhoades, County Clerk & Recorder .... Rep. Gary L. Bickel, Circuit Clerk .... Dem. Clyde Foster, Treasurer .... Dem. Forrest Sawlaw, Sheriff .... Rep. Leonard Rumery, State's Attorney .... Dem. Charles Shonkwiler, Regional Supt. of Schools .... Rep. Dr. William Mundt, Death Examiner .... Appt. Robert H. Scheffer, County Board Chairman .... Rep.
PIKE .... Jan. 31, 1821	Pittsfield	17,384	830.3	Roger E. Yaeger, County Clerk & Recorder .... Dem. Ben R. Johnson, Circuit Clerk .... Dem. Jeffrey Gerard, Treasurer .... Dem. Paul Petty, Sheriff & Coroner .... Dem. Frank McCartney, State's Attorney .... Dem. Raymond A. Scheiter, Regional Supt. of Schools .... Rep. Scott Syrcle, County Board Chairman .... Rep.
POPE .... Jan. 10, 1816	Golconda	4,413	370.9	Connie S. Gibbs, County Clerk & Recorder .... Rep. Sean M. Goins, Circuit Clerk .... Dem. Kay Cate, Treasurer .... Dem. A.J. Sparks, Sheriff .... Dem. Charles L.P. "Chuck" Flynn, State's Attorney .... Rep. Linda L. Blackman, Regional Supt. of Schools .... Dem. Mark A. Aly, Coroner .... Dem. Kelly King, Chairman, Co. Commissioners .... Dem.
PULASKI .... March 3, 1843	Mound City	7,348	200.8	Tanna S. Goins, County Clerk & Recorder .... Dem. Cindy Kennedy, Circuit Clerk .... Rep. Robert L. Moore, Treasurer .... Rep. Russell Dakin, Sheriff .... Rep. Grayson Gile, State's Attorney .... Rep. Andrea Brown, Regional Supt. of Schools .... Rep. Lisa Doctorman, Coroner .... Rep. Jerry P. Thurston, Chairman, Co. Commissioners .... Rep.

County and date established	County seat	2000 census population	Area square miles	Officers
PUTNAM .... Jan. 13, 1825	Hennepin	6,086	159.8	Gudmund Jessen, Jr., County Clerk & Recorder .... Dem. Cathy J. Oliveri, Circuit Clerk .... Dem. Kevin E. Kunkel, Treasurer .... Dem. Kevin L. Doyle, Sheriff .... Dem. James A. Mack, State's Attorney .... Rep. Richard Herring, Regional Supt. of Schools .... Rep. Duane Calbow, County Board Chairman .... Dem.
RANDOLPH .... Oct. 5, 1795	Chester	33,893	578.4	William E. Rabe, County Clerk & Recorder .... Dem. Barbara L. Brown, Circuit Clerk .... Dem. Shirlie Robinson, Treasurer .... Dem. Gene Schorb, Auditor .... Appt. Benjamin R. Picou, Sheriff .... Dem. Darrell G. Williamson, State's Attorney .... Dem. Faye J. Hughes, Regional Supt. of Schools .... Rep. Neil Birchler, Coroner .... Dem. Terry Moore, Chairman, Co. Commissioners .... Dem.
RICHLAND .... Feb. 24, 1841	Olney	16,149	360.2	Michael T. Buss, County Clerk & Recorder .... Dem. Connie Kuenstler, Circuit Clerk .... Dem. Sheila Ritter, Treasurer .... Dem. Robert "Bob" Foerster, Sheriff .... Dem. L. Kaye DeSelms, State's Attorney .... Rep. Samuel T. White, Regional Supt. of Schools .... Dem. Randy Kistler, Coroner .... Rep. Sam Hearring, County Board Chairman .... Dem.
ROCK ISLAND .... Feb. 9, 1831	Rock Island	149,374	426.8	Richard "Dick" Leibovitz, County Clerk .... Dem. Lisa Bierman, Circuit Clerk .... Dem. Patricia "Pat" Veronda, Recorder .... Dem. Louise A. Kerr, Treasurer .... Dem. Diana L. Robinson, Auditor .... Dem. Michael Grchan, Sheriff .... Dem. Marshall Douglas, State's Attorney .... Dem. Joseph A. Vermeire, Regional Supt. of Schools .... Dem. Sharon A. Anderson, Coroner .... Dem. William R. Armstrong, County Board Chairman ...... Dem.
SALINE .... Feb. 25, 1847	Harrisburg	26,733	383.3	Willie McClusky, County Clerk & Recorder .... Dem. Jack T. Nolen, Circuit Clerk .... Rep. Danny Ragan, Treasurer .... Rep. Jim Dunn, Sheriff .... Rep. Rod Wolf, State's Attorney .... Dem. Linda L. Blackman, Regional Supt. of Schools .... Dem. Kenneth M. Sloan, Coroner .... Dem. Don Leibenguth, County Board Chairman .... Dem.
SANGAMON .... Jan. 30, 1821	Springfield	188,951	868.3	Joe Aiello, County Clerk .... Rep. Tony Libri, Circuit Clerk .... Rep. Mary Ann Lamm, Recorder .... Dem. Joseph V. Bonefeste, Treasurer .... Rep. Tom Cavanagh, Auditor .... Rep. Neil Williamson, Sheriff .... Rep. John Schmidt, State's Attorney .... Rep. Helen Tolan, Regional Supt. of Schools .... Rep. Susan Boone, Coroner .... Rep. A. D. (Andy) Van Meter, County Board Chairman ..... Rep.
SCHUYLER .... Jan. 13, 1825	Rushville	7,189	437.4	James P. Rebman, County Clerk & Recorder .... Dem. Elaine Boyd, Circuit Clerk .... Rep. Harold E. Smith, Treasurer .... Rep. Don L. Schieferdecker, Sheriff .... Rep. Scott J. Butler, State's Attorney .... Rep. Gary Grzanich, Regional Supt. of Schools .... Dem. Dr. Robert E. Cox, Coroner .... Appt. Brian Peak, County Board Chairman .... Rep.

County and date established	County seat	2000 census population	Area square miles	Officers
SCOTT Feb. 16, 1839	Winchester	5,537	251	Barbara J. McDade, County Clerk & Recorder .... Dem. Joni Garrett, Circuit Clerk .... Rep. Donna J. Montgomery, Treasurer .... Rep. George Lindsey, Jr., Sheriff & Coroner .... Rep. David R. Cherry, State's Attorney .... Rep. Don Kording, Regional Supt. of Schools .... Dem. Denton Coonrod, Chairman, Co. Commissioners ..... Dem.
SHELBY Jan. 23, 1827	Shelbyville	22,893	758.6	Marjorie J. Strohl, County Clerk & Recorder .... Dem. Cheryl Roley, Circuit Clerk .... Dem. Twilla Weakley, Treasurer .... Dem. Randall D. Sims, Sheriff .... Dem. Allan Lolie, Jr., State's Attorney .... Dem. John E. McNary, Regional Supt. of Schools .... Dem. Brian Green, Coroner .... Dem. Tom L. Hayes, County Board Chairman .... Dem.
STARK March 2, 1839	Toulon	6,332	287.9	Linda K. Pyell, County Clerk & Recorder .... Rep. Marian Purtscher, Circuit Clerk .... Dem. Paula J. Becket, Treasurer .... Rep. Lonny G. Dennison, Sheriff .... Rep. James D. Owens, State's Attorney .... Dem. Bruce Dennison, Regional Supt. of Schools .... Rep. Lonny G. Dennison, Medical Legal Investigator .... Rep. Roger Gray, County Board Chairman .... Rep.
ST. CLAIR April 27, 1790	Belleville	256,082	663.9	Bob Delaney, County Clerk .... Dem. C. "Barney" Metz, Circuit Clerk .... Dem. Michael Costello, Recorder .... Dem. Charles Suarez, Treasurer .... Dem. John J. Driscoll, Auditor .... Dem. Mearl J. Justus, Sheriff .... Dem. Robert Haida, State's Attorney .... Dem. Rosella Wamser, Regional Supt. of Schools .... Dem. Rick Stone, Coroner .... Dem. John Baricevic, County Board Chairman .... Dem.
STEPHENSON March 4, 1837	Freeport	48,979	564.3	Vici R. Otte, County Clerk & Recorder .... Rep. Karla Toelke, Circuit Clerk .... Rep. Andrew M. Smith, Treasurer .... Rep. David A. Snyders, Sheriff .... Rep. Michael P. Bald, State's Attorney .... Rep. John Lang, Regional Supt. of Schools .... Rep. Thomas Paul Leamon, Coroner .... Rep. Boyd L. Boyer, County Board Chairman .... Rep.
TAZEWELL Jan. 31, 1827	Pekin	128,485	648.9	Christie A. Webb, County Clerk .... Dem. Pamela Gardner, Circuit Clerk .... Dem. Robert Lutz, Recorder .... Dem. Duane A. Gray, Treasurer .... Rep. Vicki E.Grashoff, Auditor .... Dem. Robert Huston, Sheriff .... Rep. Stewart Umholtz, State's Attorney .... Rep. Thomas J. Wojtas, Regional Supt. of Schools .... Dem. Robert DuBois, Coroner .... Rep. James Unsicker, County Board Chairman .... Rep.
UNION Jan. 2, 1818	Jonesboro	18,293	416.2	Bobby Toler, Jr., County Clerk & Recorder .... Dem. Lorraine Moreland, Circuit Clerk .... Dem. Bobby G. Myers, Treasurer .... Dem. Jim Nash, Sheriff .... Dem. John Bigler, State's Attorney .... Dem. Andrea Brown, Regional Supt. of Schools .... Rep. Darryl Rendleman, Coroner .... Dem. Jim Watkins, Chairman, County Commissioners .... Dem.

COUNTIES AND COUNTY OFFICERS (Continued)

County and date established	County seat	2000 census population	Area square miles	Officers
VERMILION .... Danville .... 83,919 Jan. 18, 1826			899.1	Lynn Foster, County Clerk .... Dem. Susan Miller, Circuit Clerk .... Dem. Nancy J. Kelley, Recorder .... Rep. Sue Stine, Treasurer .... Rep. Linda S. Lucas Anstey, Auditor .... Dem. W. Patrick Hartshorn, Sheriff .... Rep. Frank Young, State's Attorney .... Rep. James E. Trask, Regional Supt. of Schools .... Rep. Margaret "Peggy" Johnson, Coroner .... Rep. Todd Lee, County Board Chairman .... Dem.
WABASH .... Mt. Carmel .... 12,937 Dec. 27, 1824			223.5	Marie L. Kolb, County Clerk & Recorder .... Rep. JoAnn Green, Circuit Clerk .... Rep. Larry L. Briggs, Treasurer .... Dem. Randy E. Grounds, Sheriff .... Dem. Terry C. Kaid, State's Attorney .... Rep. Linda L. Blackman, Regional Supt. of Schools .... Dem. Robert D. Cunningham, Coroner .... Rep. Charles K. Sanders, Chairman, Co. Commissioners . Dem.
WARREN .... Monmouth .... 18,735 Jan. 13, 1825			542.6	Janet Hammond, County Clerk & Recorder .... Rep. Jill M. Morris, Circuit Clerk .... Rep. Nancy Clayton, Treasurer .... Rep. Richard Hart, Sheriff .... Rep. Albert Algren, State's Attorney .... Rep. R. Bruce Hall, Regional Supt. of Schools .... Rep. William H. Underwood, Coroner .... Rep. William Reichow, County Board Chairman .... Rep.
WASHINGTON .... Nashville .... 15,148 Jan. 2, 1818			562.7	Thomas Ganz, County Clerk & Recorder .... Dem. Carol Heggemeier, Circuit Clerk .... Rep. William H. Windler, Treasurer .... Dem. John Foster, Sheriff .... Dem. Brian Trentman, State's Attorney .... Dem. Danny L. Garrett, Regional Supt. of Schools .... Dem. Dr. Thomas Coy, Coroner .... Rep. David Meyer, County Board Chairman .... Dem.
WAYNE .... Fairfield .... 17,151 March 26, 1819			713.9	Donna Endsley, County Clerk & Recorder .... Dem. Sharon L. Gualdoni, Circuit Clerk .... Rep. Gayla R. McKibben, Treasurer .... Dem. Jerry Joslin, Sheriff .... Dem. Kevin C. Kakac, State's Attorney .... Rep. Linda L. Blackman, Regional Supt. of Schools .... Dem. Jimmy I. Taylor, Coroner .... Dem. Harold Tubbs, County Board Chairman .... Rep.
WHITE .... Carmi .... 15,371 Dec. 9, 1815			494.9	Paula Dozier, County Clerk & Recorder .... Dem. Ellen Pettijohn, Circuit Clerk .... Dem. Denise Burnett, Treasurer .... Dem. Jerry W. O'Neal, Sheriff .... Dem. Kerry Sutton, State's Attorney .... Dem. Linda L. Blackman, Regional Supt. of Schools .... Dem. Carl McVey, Coroner .... Rep. Leland Sexton, County Board Chairman .... Dem.
WHITESIDE .... Morrison .... 60,653 Jan. 16, 1836			684.8	Dan Heusinkveld, County Clerk .... Rep. Jane Fransen, Circuit Clerk .... Rep. Dawn Young, Recorder .... Rep. Karen Mulnix, Treasurer .... Rep. John Gallagher, Jr., County Administrator .... Appt. Roger Schipper, Sheriff .... Rep. Gary Spencer, State's Attorney .... Rep. Gary J. Steinert, Regional Supt. of Schools .... Rep. Joseph P. McDonald, Coroner .... Dem. Tony Arduini, County Board Chairman .... Dem.

COUNTIES AND COUNTY OFFICERS (Concluded)

County and date established	County seat	2000 census population	Area square miles	Officers
WILL .... Joliet	Joliet	502,266	837.3	Jan Gould, County Clerk .... Rep. Pamela McGuire, Circuit Clerk .... Dem. Mary Ann Stukel, Recorder .... Dem. John J. "Jack" Weber, Treasurer .... Rep. Steven P. Weber, Auditor .... Rep. Brendan D. Ward, Sheriff .... Rep. Jeffery J. Tomczak, State's Attorney .... Rep. Richard Duran, Regional Supt. of Schools .... Rep. Patrick K. O'Neil, Coroner .... Dem. Joseph L. Mikan, Jr., Chief Executive Officer .... Rep.
WILLIAMSON .... Marion Feb. 28, 1839	Marion	61,296	424.2	Barney R. Boren, County Clerk & Recorder .... Rep. Stuart Hall, Circuit Clerk .... Dem. Bruce A. Troutman, Treasurer .... Rep. Tom Cundiff, Sheriff .... Dem. Charles Garnati, State's Attorney .... Dem. Barry Kohl, Regional Supt. of Schools .... Dem. Monte Blue, Coroner .... Dem. Rex Piper, Chairman, Co. Commissioners .... Dem.
WINNEBAGO .... Rockford Jan. 16, 1836	Rockford	278,418	513.8	John T. Schou, County Clerk .... Rep. Marc Gasparini, Circuit Clerk .... Rep. Ken Staaf, Recorder .... Rep. Susan J. Goral, Treasurer .... Dem. W. Thomas Ross, Auditor .... Dem. Richard A. Meyers, Sheriff .... Dem. Paul A. Logli, State's Attorney .... Rep. Richard L. Fairgrieves, Regional Supt. of Schools .... Rep. Elizabeth "Sue" Fiduccia, Coroner .... Rep. Kristine Cohn, County Board Chairman .... Rep.
WOODFORD .... Eureka Feb. 27, 1841	Eureka	35,469	528	Peggy S. Rapp, County Clerk & Recorder .... Rep. Linda Cook, Circuit Clerk .... Rep. Shirley Miller, Treasurer .... Rep. William L. "Bill" Myers, Sheriff .... Rep. Michael Stroh, State's Attorney .... Rep. Richard Herring, Regional Supt. of Schools .... Rep. Tim Ruestman, Coroner .... Rep. Thomas L. Janssen, County Board Chairman .... Rep.

ORIGINS OF COUNTY NAMES

Adams — President John Quincy Adams, Secretary of State under President James Monroe, U.S. Representative, leading defender of free speech.

Alexander — William M. Alexander, early settler of the district, also state representative in second and third General Assemblies.

Bond — Shadrach Bond, first Governor of the State of Illinois.

Boone — Daniel Boone, pioneer hunter, explorer and Indian fighter.

Brown — Gen. Jacob Brown, soldier in War of 1812 and later commanding general of the U.S. Army.

Bureau — Pierre de Bureo, French trader with Indians.

Calhoun — John C. Calhoun, southern statesman and U.S. Vice President under Presidents Adams and Jackson.

Carroll — Charles Carroll of Carrollton, signer of the Declaration of Independence.

Cass — Gen. Lewis Cass, presidential candidate, U.S. Senator, Secretary of War under President Jackson and Secretary of State under President Buchanan.

Champaign — A county in Ohio.

Christian — A county in Kentucky.

Clark — George Rogers Clark, soldier of the Revolution and captor of Fort Vincennes and Kaskaskia.

Clay — Henry Clay, U.S. Representative and Senator, author of the "Missouri Compromise" and three-time presidential candidate.

Clinton — DeWitt Clinton, Mayor of the City and Governor of the State of New York; promoter of the Erie Canal.

Coles — Edward Coles, second Governor of Illinois.

Cook — Daniel P. Cook, pioneer lawyer, first Attorney General of Illinois and member of Congress from 1819-27.

Crawford — William H. Crawford, prominent U.S. Senator from Georgia and candidate for President in 1824.

Cumberland — The Cumberland or National Road was a 19th-Century highway extending 800 miles from Cumberland, Maryland, to Vandalia, Illinois.

DeKalb — Johann DeKalb, German who fought in the Revolution; killed in 1780.

DeWitt — DeWitt Clinton (see Clinton).

Douglas — Stephen A. Douglas, U.S. Senator, 1847-61, debated Abraham Lincoln on slavery and ran against him for President in 1860.

DuPage — The DuPage River.

Edgar — John Edgar, pioneer merchant and politician.

Edwards — Ninian Edwards, Illinois' third Governor.

Effingham — Lord Edward Effingham, resigned his post in the British Army rather than fight the colonies in 1775.

Fayette — Marquis de La Fayette, French nobleman who served in the American Revolutionary Army commanding French troops at the battle of Yorktown.

Ford — Thomas Ford, Illinois' 8th Governor.

Franklin — Benjamin Franklin, famed statesman, U.S. ambassador to France during the Revolution.

Fulton — Robert Fulton, first successful builder of steamboats on American waters.

Gallatin — Albert Gallatin, financier and member of Congress from Pennsylvania.

Greene — Gen. Nathaniel Greene, commander in the southern colonies during the Revolution.

Grundy — Felix Grundy, U.S. Senator from Tennessee, Attorney General of the U.S.

Hamilton — Alexander Hamilton, revolutionary soldier and first Secretary of the Treasury, from 1789-95.

Hancock — John Hancock, revolutionary soldier, first signer of the Declaration of Independence.

Hardin — A county in Kentucky.

Henderson — The Henderson River.

Henry — Patrick Henry, famed orator, revolutionary soldier and Governor of Virginia.

Iroquois — An Indian tribe.

Jackson — President Andrew Jackson, known as "Old Hickory" because of his military toughness exhibited during the War of 1812; used presidential veto power to dramatically strengthen the office.

Jasper — Sgt. William Jasper, revolutionary hero at Charleston and Savannah.

Jefferson — President Thomas Jefferson, American revolutionary leader, political philosopher and author of the Declaration of Independence.

Jersey — The State of New Jersey.

Jo Daviess — Joseph Hamilton Daviess, prominent Kentucky lawyer and soldier; slain at the Battle of Tippecanoe in 1811.

Johnson — Col. Richard M. Johnson, reputed to have killed the Indian Chief Tecumseh; also U.S. Vice President, 1837-41.

Kane — Senator Elias K. Kane, first Secretary of State of Illinois.

Kankakee — An Indian tribe.

Kendall — Amos Kendall, Postmaster General under President Jackson and partner of S.B. Morse, inventor of the telegraph.

Knox — Gen. Henry Knox, revolutionary hero and President George Washington's Secretary of War.

Lake — Lake Michigan.

La Salle — Robert de La Salle, French explorer who navigated the length of the Mississippi River and claimed the Louisiana Territory for France.

Lawrence — Capt. James Lawrence, commander of the U.S.S. Chesapeake; killed in a naval battle in 1812.

Lee — Richard Henry Lee, orator and statesman of the Revolution.

Livingston — Edward Livingston, Secretary of State under President Andrew Jackson.

Logan — Dr. John Logan, pioneer physician and father of Gen. John A. Logan.

Macon — Nathaniel Macon, revolutionary soldier and later U.S. Senator.

Macoupin — An Indian name.

Madison — President James Madison, known as the father of the Constitution because he fought for a strong central government to replace the Articles of Confederation.

Marion — Gen. Francis Marion, known as the "Swamp Fox," distinguished soldier in the Carolinas during the Revolution.

Marshall — John Marshall, fourth Chief Justice of the U.S. Supreme Court. Known as the "Great Chief Justice" for developing the power of the Supreme Court and formulating constitutional law.

Mason — A county in Kentucky.

Massac — Fort Massac.

McDonough — Commodore Thomas McDonough, defeated the British on Lake Champlain in 1814.

McHenry — Gen. William McHenry, fought in the War of 1812 and the Black Hawk War; also served in several early General Assemblies.

McLean — John McLean, first representative in Congress from Illinois in 1818 and U.S. Senator from 1824-25.

Menard — Pierre Menard, first Lieutenant Governor of Illinois.

Mercer — Gen. Hugh Mercer, killed at the Battle of Princeton during the Revolution.

Monroe — President James Monroe, revolutionary soldier, diplomat; served two cabinet posts under President James Madison; known as co-negotiator of the Louisiana Purchase and author of the Monroe Doctrine.

Montgomery — Gen. Richard Montgomery, revolutionary soldier of Irish birth; killed at Quebec in 1775.

Morgan — Gen. Daniel Morgan, earned distinction during the Revolution at Quebec and Saratoga.

Moultrie — Gen. William Moultrie, successful defender of Fort Moultrie at Charleston, SC, during the Revolution.

Ogle — Lt. Joseph Ogle, member of the territorial militia.

Peoria — An Indian name.

Perry — Commodore Oliver H. Perry, won distinction in the Battle of Lake Erie in 1813.

Piatt — James A. Piatt, Sr., settled in that area in 1829.

Pike — Zebulon M. Pike, General in the War of 1812 and American explorer after whom Pikes Peak in Colorado was named.

Pope — Nathaniel Pope, first territorial Secretary of State from 1809-16.

Pulaski — Count Casimir Pulaski, Polish hero who was killed in the attack on Savannah, GA, in 1779.

Putnam — Gen. Israel Putnam, revolutionary soldier.

Randolph — Edmund Randolph, soldier of the Revolution, Secretary of State and Attorney General under President George Washington.

Richland — A county in Ohio.

Rock Island — A rock island in the Mississippi River.

Saline — Saline Creek.

Sangamon — An Indian name meaning "the land of plenty to eat."

Schuyler — Gen. Philip Schuyler, soldier in the Revolution and later U.S. Senator from New York.

Scott — A county in Kentucky.

Shelby — Isaac Shelby, soldier of the Revolution, the Indian Wars and the War of 1812, and Governor of Kentucky, 1792-96.

Stark — Gen. John Stark, revolutionary solider; won fame at Bunker Hill, Trenton, Princeton and Bennington.

St. Clair — Gen. Arthur St. Clair, Commander in Chief of the U.S. Army after the Revolution and Governor of U.S. Territory northwest of the Ohio.

Stephenson — Col. Benjamin Stephenson, Adjutant General of the Illinois Territory from 1813-14.

Tazewell — Lyttelton W. Tazewell, U.S. Senator from Virginia.

Union — The Federal Union of the American states.

Vermilion — The Vermilion River.

Wabash — An Indian name.

Warren — Gen. Joseph Warren, pioneer physician and soldier killed at Bunker Hill.

Washington — President George Washington, Commander in Chief of the Army during the American Revolution; set the standard for conducting the Office of the President.

Wayne — Gen. Anthony Wayne, famed revolutionary commander and Indian fighter.

White — Leonard White, member of the Constitutional Convention of 1818.

Whiteside — Samuel Whiteside, Representative in the first General Assembly and Brigadier General in the Black Hawk War.

Will — Conrad Will, member of the Constitutional Convention of 1818 and member of the first nine General Assemblies.

Williamson — A county in Tennessee.

Winnebago — An Indian name.

Woodford — A county in Kentucky.

STATE CENTRAL COMMITTEEMEN
DEMOCRAT

Michael Madigan, *chairman;* Iola McGowan, *first vice chairman;* Emil Jones, *executive vice chairman;* Vince Demuzio, William Marovitz, Iris Y. Martinez and Miki Pavelonis, *vice chairmen;* Shirley McCombs, *secretary.*

DISTRICT	NAME AND ADDRESS

1. Bobby Rush, 3361 S. King Dr., Chicago 60616
   Constance Howard, 8949 S. Stony Island Ave., Chicago 60617

2. Emil Jones, 11357 S. Lowe, Chicago 60628
   Carrie Austin, 507 W. 111th St., Chicago 60628

3. Michael Madigan, 6500 S. Pulaski Rd., Chicago 60629
   Helen Ozmina Barc, 4554 W. 66th St., Chicago 60629

4. Joseph Mario Moreno, 118 N. Clark, #3M, Chicago 60602
   Iris Y. Martinez, 2708 N. Mozart St., Chicago 60647

5. Jim DeLeo, 6839 W. Belmont, Chicago 60634
   Cynthia Santos, 100 E. Erie, Chicago 60610

6. James Walsh, 26 E. Grove, Lombard 60148
   Joan Brennan, 97 Shelley Court, Elk Grove Village 60007

7. Danny Davis, 3333 W. Arthington, Chicago 60624
   Iola McGowan, 5839 W. Midway Park, Chicago 60644

8. Jeffrey Kingsley, P.O. Box 616, Palatine 60078-0616
   Vacant

9. William Marovitz, 2800 N. Lake Shore Dr., #4101, Chicago 60657
   Carol Ronen, 6033 Sheridan, Apt. C, Chicago 60660

10. Wilbert Crowley, 55 W. Monroe, Ste. 500, Chicago 60603
    Lauren Beth Gash, 1345 Forest Ave., Highland 60035

11. Patrick Welch, P.O. Box 341, Peru 61354
    Linda Pasternak, 1227 Edgewood Dr., Calumet City 60409

12. Sam Flood, 25 Oak Knoll, Belleville 62223
    Barbara Brown, 1412 High St., Chester 62233

13. Kyle R. Hastings, 9125 W. 169th Pl., Orland Hills 60477
    Beth Ann May, 15358 Dan Patch Dr., Plainfield 60544

14. Steve Bowne, 607 6th St., Mendota 61342
    Mary Lou Kearns, 256 Canidae Ct., St. Charles 60174

15. Dean Barringer, 2105 Noel Dr., Champaign 61821
    Lynn Foster, 1009 Pries St., Danville 61832

16. John Nelson, 1318 E. State St., Rockford 61104
    Barb Giolitto, 807 Brae Burn Ln., Rockford 61107

17. Donald Johnston, P.O. Box 3164, Rock Island 61204-3164
    Mary Boland, 3658-1st St., East Moline 61244

18. Larry Johnson, 4100 S. Baker Ln., Bartonville 61607
    Shirley McCombs, R.R. 2, Box 45-Z, Petersburg 62675

19. Chuck Hartke, P.O. Box 1205, Effingham 62401
    Miki Pavelonis, 100 Sullivan, Box 532, Harrisburg 62946

20. Vince Demuzio, 4 Valley Ln., Carlinville 62626
    Ellen Sinclair, P.O. Box 429, Salem 62881

REPUBLICAN

Rich Williamson, *chairman;* Miki Cooper, *co-chairman;* Robert K. Kjellander, Jr., *national committeeman;* Mary Jo Arndt, *national committeewoman;* Ronald C. Smith, *secretary;* Dallas Ingemunson, *treasurer.*

DISTRICT	NAME AND ADDRESS
1.	Robert L. Dunne, 9701 S. Keeler, Oak Lawn 60453
2.	Aldo A. DeAngelis, P.O. Box 166, Olympia Fields 60461
3.	Paul A. Thomas, 5127 Ellington Ave., Western Springs 60558-2034
4.	George Preski, 3428 S. Hermitage, Chicago 60608
5.	James Battista, 6915 W. Diversey Ave., Chicago 60707
6.	Patrick J. Durante, 1044 Jamey Ln., Addison 60101
7.	Richard A. Walsh, 823 Ashland Ave., River Forest 60305
8.	Robert P. Neal, 38933 Delany Rd., Wadsworth 60083
9.	Shel Marcus, P.O. Box 368, Morton Grove 60053
10.	William E. Peterson, 3050 N. Main, Prairie View 60069

DISTRICT	NAME AND ADDRESS
11.	Barbara J. Peterson, 2124 W. Church Rd., Beecher 60401-3102
12.	Stephen P. McGlynn, 116 S. Charles, Belleville 62220
13.	Ronald C. Smith, 2S121 Ivy Ln., Lombard 60148
14.	Dallas Ingemunson, P.O. Box 578, Yorkville 60560
15.	Michael A. Stokke, R.R. 13, Box 85, Bloomington 61704
16.	Dave Syverson, P.O. Box 98, Rockford 61105
17.	Regan E. Ramsey, 595 N. County Rd. 2200, Bowen 62316
18.	MaryAlice Erickson, 6707 N. Greenmont, Peoria 61614-2411
19.	Bob Winchester, P. O. Box 208, Rosiclare 62982-0208
20.	Don W. Adams, 320 S. Fourth St., Springfield 62701

The General Assembly revised the Election Code, offering an alternative composition of each state central committee. Since Jan. 1, 1984, the state central committee of each political party may choose to: 1) elect one central committeeman from each congressional district; or 2) elect one male and one female committeeman from each congressional district. As a result, the Republican Party has opted for one central committeeman per congressional district, while the Democratic Party has chosen to elect one female and one male from each congressional district.

COUNTY CHAIRMEN IN ILLINOIS

County	Democrat	Republican
Adams	Vacant	Richard E. Northern, 209 Knollwood, Quincy 62301
Alexander	Billy Tatum, P. O. Box 60, Thebes 62990	Michael Caldwell, P.O. Box 93, Thebes 62990
Bond	Robert Bauer, 123 E. College Ave., Greenville 62246	Doug Knebel, 501 Ward, Greenville 62246
Boone	Glen Guthrie, 4082 Quail Trap Rd., Poplar Grove 61065	Robert L. Turner, 1230 Maple Ave., Belvidere 61008-5250
Brown	John Miley, 2 Ingelside Dr., Mt. Sterling 62353	Gary Pruden, P. O. Box 167, Mt. Sterling 62353-0167
Bureau	Frank Mautino, 108 W. St. Paul St., Spring Valley 61362	Barry W. Welbers, 30493 Ill. Hwy. 29, Spring Valley 61362
Calhoun	Keith Klocke, Box 96, Batchtown 62006	Rose Stumpf, R.R. 1, Box 127, Batchtown 62006
Carroll	Kurt Brunner, 505 E. Ridge St., Mt. Carroll 61053	Judy Gray, 301 N. Main, P.O. Box 152, Mt. Carroll 61053-0152
Cass	Michael Barnett, 10904 State Route 125, Beardstown 62618	John Butler, 401 W. Topeka, Ashland 62612
Champaign	Geraldine Parr, 1001 W. University, Champaign 61820	Daniel A. Baechle, 1815 Robert Dr., Champaign 61821-6030
Christian	Gordon John Mazzotti, 201 W. Main Cross, Taylorville 62568	J.C. Pearce, 924 W. Main, Taylorville 62568
Clark	Eugene Maurer, 13423 N. Fox Road, Marshall 62441	Gary Tingley, 5422 E. 480th Rd., Martinsville 62442
Clay	Gilbert D. Hale, R.R. 2, Box 211-B, Clay City 62824	William D. Tolliver, RR 3, Box 221, Louisville 62858
Clinton	Dale Haukap, 748 E. First St., Aviston 62216	Marc Hoffman, 313 Leisure Ave., New Baden 62265
Coles	Robert Crowder, 901 DeWitt, Mattoon 61938	Max E. Coffey, 739 Glenwood Dr., Charleston 61920
Cook	Thomas Lyons, 30 N. LaSalle St., Ste. 1717, Chicago 60602	Manny Hoffman, 32 W. Randolph, Ste. 1701, Chicago 60601-3405
Crawford	Bennie Stevenson, 5495 N. State Highway 1, Robinson 62454	Marcella Slater, 6501 E. 1200 Ave., Robinson 62454
Cumberland	Roy Gibson, 543 County Road 875 North, Neoga 62447	Jerry L. Sidwell, 02 Sportsman Club Rd. 1840 E, P.O. Box 795, Greenup 62428
DeKalb	Eileen Dubin, 1627 Schifly Ln., DeKalb 60115	Don Merwin, 1602 Mayflower Dr., DeKalb 60115-1724
DeWitt	Robert Coomer, 212 E. Jefferson, Clinton 61727	Jered Hooker, 29 Cypress Dr., Clinton 61727
Douglas	Mike Woods, 201 Douglas Drive, Tuscola 61953	David A. Albin, P. O. Box 200, Newman 61942-0200
DuPage	Jim Walsh, 26 E. Grove St., Lombard 60148	James "Pate" Philip, 224 S. Washington St., Wheaton 60187
Edgar	Allen N. Hornbrook, 11 Woodmere Dr., Paris 61944	Ted Lang, 13506 Ill. Hwy. 1, Paris 61944
Edwards	Jackie Knackmus, R. R. 2, West Salem 62476	Dennis Splittorff, RR 1, Albion 62806
Effingham	David Seiler, 802 E. North Ave, Effingham 62401	Bruce Kessler, 208 S. Third St., Altamont 62411
Fayette	Maurice Trexler, R.R. 3, Box 964, Vandalia 62471	Harold Baumann, 101 Woodland Hills Ct., P.O. Box 249, Vandalia 62471
Ford	Robert Mogged, P.O. Box 61, Piper City 60959	Eric Thompson, 201 E. Main, P.O. Box 88, Melvin 60952
Franklin	Jim Eaton, 2429 Eaton Rd, Thomsonville 62890	Dennis Mitchell, 109 Wilcox Ave., Zeigler 62999
Fulton	Michael Smith, 2 N. Main St., Canton 61520	Richard Bhear, 9765 E. Young Rd., London Mills 61544
Gallatin	Jim Stevens, 41 Ford Street - Box 3, New Haven 62867	John L. Morris, P.O. Box 306, Shawneetown 62984
Greene	Kerry Page, 263 S. Carrollton, White Hall 62092	Larry Ballard, R.R. 1, Box 63, Carrollton 62016
Grundy	Jeff Arnold, 826 E. Douglas St., Morris 60450	John V. Hanson, P.O. Box 825, Morris 60450
Hamilton	Gerald Prince, Rt. 5, Box 315, McLeansboro 62859	Jerry Hart, R.R. 1, Box 83-B, McLeansboro 62859
Hancock	Holly Wilde, 1123 East Main, Carthage 62321	Regan Ramsey, 595 N. County Rd. 2200, Bowen 62316
Hardin	Paul Lamar, P.O. Box 329, Elizabethtown 62931	A. D. Schutt, P. O. Box 202, Elizabethtown 62931-0202

County	Democrat	Republican
Henderson	Tina Thompson, P.O. Box 41, Oquawka 61469	Charles McChesney, P.O. Box 200, Gladstone 61437
Henry	James Reynolds, 113 Henry Dr., Orion 61273	Barbara J. McKibbon, 23939 State Rt. 82, Geneseo 61254
Iroquois	Maurice Seggebruch, P.O. Box 351, Buckley 60918	Shelby Jean Townsend, 608 E. Lincoln Ave., Watseka 60970-1815
Jackson	Shirley Booker, 400 Dillinger, Carbondale 62901	Mark Holt, 3353 Neunert Rd., Jacob 62950
Jasper	Paul Johnson, 105 N. Lafayette, Newton 62448	Jack L. Martin, 12274 E. 900th Ave., Newton 62448
Jefferson	Russell Dalby, 317 Spruce, Mt. Vernon 62864	Richard L. Stubblefield, 25 Wildwood Dr., Mt. Vernon 62864
Jersey	Gene Abbott, 1366 Jenny Ln., Jerseyville 62052	Bill Rolando, 312 Lynwood, Springfield 62703
Jo Daviess	Robert Johnson, 519 S. Bench St., P. O. Box 028, Galena 61036	Terry Miller, 117 Kelly Ln., Galena 61036
Johnson	Mike Hartline, 152 Center St., P. O. Box 21, Cypress 62923	Robert E. "Bob" Pippins, 210 Pearce, Buncombe 62912
Kane	Ken Vondrak, 1214 South St., Geneva 60134	Bill Keck, 61 Maple, P. O. Box 351, Sugar Grove 60554-0351
Kankakee	Gary Ciaccio, 1185 S. 8th St., Kankakee 60901	Bruce Clark, 1410 Sommerset Way, Bourbonnais 60914
Kendall	Martin Flowers, 68 Red Fox Run, Montgomery 60538	Dallas Ingemunson, P.O. Box 578, Yorkville 60560
Knox	Caroline Porter, 1220 Bridge Ave., Galesburg 61401	Gene Stull, 223 E. Main St., P.O. Box 116, Galesburg 61402-0116
Lake	Terry Link, 22 Edgewood, Vernon Hills 60061	John Schulien, 332 Peterson Rd., Libertyville 60048
LaSalle	Rocky Raikes, 858 Canal St., P. O. Box 416, Marseilles 61341	Robert F. Vickrey, 902 16th St., Peru 61354
Lawrence	Larry Umfleet, 618 S. Carey, Sumner 62466	Michael Neal, R.R. 3, Box 361, Lawrenceville 62439
Lee	Jerry Sheridan, 1197 State Rt. 26, Dixon 61021	Doug Farster, 1000 Woodhill Cir., Dixon 61021
Livingston	Vacant	Judith "Judy" K. Cremer, 1318 S. Mill St., Pontiac 61764
Logan	Nancy Amberg, 505 Mayfair Dr., Lincoln 62656	Ronald Sparks, 135 Heritage, Lincoln 62656
Macon	Maurice Doyle, 5205 W. Main St., Decatur 62522	Jerry Stocks, 385 Secretariat Pl., Mt. Zion 62549
Macoupin	Vince Demuzio, 4 Valley Ln., Carlinville 62626	Richard Mottershaw, 411 Hillcrest, Carlinville 62626
Madison	Mac Warfield, 22 Devon Hill Ln., Granite City 62040	Robert E. Hulme, 607 Lane St., Edwardsville 62025-1534
Marion	Jerry Sinclair, Box 429, Salem 62881	Gerald O. Cooper, 8501 Seavers Rd., Iuka 62849
Marshall	Bill Simmons, P. O. Box 104, Wenona 61377	Phil McCully, P.O. Box 97, Toluca 61369-0097
Mason	James Sarff, 3973 CR 200N, Chandlerville 62627	Mary Jane Jones, 200 E. Roosevelt Rd., Mason City 62664
Massac	Larry Douglas, 2555 Teague Hill Rd., Belknap 62908	Sam Stratemeyer, 6120 Waldo Church Rd., Metropolis 62960
McDonough	Bob Cook, 151 Holden Dr., Macomb 61455	Craig F. Pierce, P.O. Box 61, Bushnell 61422-0061
McHenry	Robert McGarry, 1107 N. Hayes St., Harvard 60033	William Lefew, 607 Hart, Harvard 60033
McLean	John Penn, R.R. 4, Box 410, Bloomington 61704	John Parrott, Jr., P. O. Box 790, Bloomington 61702
Menard	Sandra Klein, 587 Lime Drive, Petersburg 62675	Esther Fricke, R.R. 2, Box 128, Petersburg 62675
Mercer	Kathy Olson, P. O. Box 416, Alexis 61412	Robert Vickrey, P.O. Box 189, Aledo 61231
Monroe	Sandy Sauget, 103 Hartman St., Waterloo 62298	Joe Berry, 1351 Glenwood Dr., Columbia 62236
Montgomery	Steve White, 2002 School St., Hillsboro 62049	Paul Tomazzoli, 5 Tremont Terrace, Hillsboro 62049
Morgan	Bill Gross, 1 Westgate Circle, Jacksonville 62650	Richard Mitchell, 310 Country Club Rd., Jacksonville 62650
Moultrie	Richard Purdeu, 207 W. Harrison, Sullivan 61951	Gail E. Wolfe, R.R. 2, Box 178, Lovington 61937

435

COUNTY CHAIRMEN IN ILLINOIS (Concluded)

County	Democrat	Republican
Ogle	Bobbie Colbert, 700 N. 7th St., Rochelle 61068	Chris Martin, 512 N. 4th St., Oregon 61061
Peoria	Billy Halstead, 2210 W. Newport Court, Peoria 61614	Phil Morgan, 18 Lauterbach Dr., Bartonville 61607
Perry	John Rednour, Jr., 280 US Route 51, Du Quoin 62832	Don Hirsch, 8314 State Rt. 154, Tamaroa 62888
Piatt	Tim McAlpin, 419 N. Oak, Monticello 61856	James A. Reed, 689 County Farm Rd., Monticello 61856
Pike	Rick Orr, 802 W. Washington St., Box 536, Pittsfield 62363	Mike Thompson, P.O. Box 112, Pittsfield 62363
Pope	Don Rumsey, Rt. 3, Box 273C, Golconda 62938	Victor English, R.R. 1, Golconda 62938
Pulaski	Sam Johnson, 101 S. 4th, Mound City 62963	Randy George, P.O. Box 328, Mounds 62964
Putnam	Tony Rue, R. R. 1, Box 130, Granville 61326	George Wheeler, R.R. 1, Box 4, Putnam 61560
Randolph	Frederick D. Frederking, 10660 State Rt. 153, Coulterville 62237	David M. Holder, 9112 E. Springview Rd., Baldwin 62217
Richland	Randy Blackford, 605 E. LaFayette, Olney 62450	James Hough, 1981 Rt. 130 N., Olney 62450
Rock Island	John Gianulis, P.O. Box 3128, Rock Island 61201	Tom Getz, 8 Wildwood Dr., Moline 61265
Saline	Robert Wilson, 300 W. Poplar, P.O. Box 544, Harrisburg 62946	William "Bill" Roberts, 200 W. Logan, Harrisburg 62946
Sangamon	Bob Wesley, 1146 W. Lawrence Ave., Springfield 62704	Irv Smith, 412 E. Lawrence, Springfield 62703
Schuyler	Robert Maxwell, R.R. 1, Box 254A, Browning 62624	Jerry Ewing, R.R. 3, Box 183, Rushville 62681
Scott	Ed Hoover, 410 W. Cherry St., Winchester 62694	Danny Krueger, 654 Bloomfield Rd., Winchester 62694
Shelby	Ronald Koehler, 407 W. Main, Shelbyville 62565	Roger Shaw, 1101 W.S. Second St., Shelbyville 62565
St. Clair	Robert Sprague, 26 E. Washington, Belleville 62220	Stephen McGlynn, 116 S. Charles, Belleville 62220
Stark	Delia Townsend, Route 1, Toulon 61483	Charles Wilson, 113 N. Washington, Toulon 61483
Stephenson	Tom Jackson, 1660 S. Demeter Dr., Freeport 61032	David Shockey, 208 W. Stephenson, Freeport 61032
Tazewell	Shirley Houghton, 216 S. Mississippi Ave., Morton 61550	Claude U. Stone, Jr., 1109 Brentwood Rd., Morton 61550
Union	Randy Tucker, 509 N. Water, Jonesboro 62952	Darren Baggott, 200 Pecan St., Anna 62906
Vermilion	Bill Boyer, 205 Mill Street, P. O. Box 50, Indianola 61850	Steven D. Kelley, 4 E. Woodyard St., P.O. Box 440, Ridge Farm 61870
Wabash	Brenda Sawyer, 430 Cherry St., Mount Carmel 62863	Robert Keith Woods, 105 Fred Dr., Mt. Carmel 62863
Warren	Larry Enderlin, 1403 E. Second Ave., Monmouth 61462	Joseph S. Carlson, 2338 M-A-N Trail, Monmouth 61462
Washington	Tony Mayville, 1997 Hickory Creek Rd., Dubois 62831	Denny Hoffman, 454 N. Mill, Nashville 62263
Wayne	Gordon Endsley, R.R. 1, Box 145, Mt. Erie 62446	Garry Atteberry, R.R. 1, Box 23-G, Mt. Erie 62446
White	Billy Peyton, 381 County Rd., 100 East #4, Norris City 62869	Rick South, 1805 Co. Rd. 500 East, Enfield 62835
Whiteside	Lowell Jacobs, 3709 E. 17th St., Sterling 61081	Tim Zollinger, 804 Greenridge Dr., P. O. Box 400, Sterling 61801-0400
Will	Dan Vera, P.O. Box 4242, Joliet 60432	John E. "Jack" Partelow, 2476 Rio Grande Cir., Naperville 60565
Williamson	Flora Reilly, 6891 Route 37, Marion 62959	Robert L. "Dog" Connell, 711 N. Vicksburg, Marion 62959
Winnebago	Willie Bell, 2219 S. Central Ave., Rockford 61102	Mary Gaziano, 1 Court Pl., Ste. 200, Rockford 61101
Woodford	David McBride, 672 E. 4th St., El Paso 61738	James L. Booth, 704 Somerset Dr., Metamora 61548

INCORPORATED CITIES, TOWNS AND VILLAGES OF ILLINOIS*

City (c), town (t) or village (v)	County	Population	Mayor or President	Clerk
Abingdon	c Knox	3,612	Michael Brackett	B. Joanne Batson
Addieville	v Washington	267	Ron Kolweier	Kay Gaebe
Addison	v DuPage	35,914	Larry Hartwig	Lucille A. Zucchero
Adeline	v Ogle	139	Michael Dickinson	Karen Dickinson
Albany	v Whiteside	895	Rick L. Dettman	Christine Griser
Albers	v Clinton	878	Daniel Poettker	Belinda Tonnies
Albion	c Edwards	1,933	Ryan Hallam	Gary Mason
Aledo	c Mercer	3,613	C. William Stancliff	Brenda Benson
Alexis	v Mercer, Warren	863	Russell Ogilvie	Nancy Garrett
Algonquin	v McHenry	23,276	Salvatore Spella	Jerry Kautz
Alhambra	v Madison	630	Jeffrey Hurst	Linda K. Uhe
Allendale	v Wabash	528	Fred Deadmond	Melody Walker
Allenville	v Moultrie	154	Melvin Dyer	Penny Reynolds
Allerton	v Vermilion	293	John R. Cutsinger	Martian J. Shunk
Alma	v Marion	386	Michael D. Shumate II	Beth Settles
Alorton	v St. Clair	2,749	Carolyn Williams	JoAnn Reed
Alpha	v Henry	726	Marvin Watters	Edna Mahalovich
Alsey,	v Scott	246	Garld Jones	Bobbi King
Alsip	v Cook	19,725	Arnold A. Andrews	Penney M. Black
Altamont	c Effingham	2,283	Larry E. Taylor	Helen Moll
Alto Pass	v Union	388	Jerry Heidlegaugh	Crystal Gurley
Alton	c Madison	30,496	Donald E. Sandidge	Mary T. Boulds
Altona	v Knox	570	Otis A. Johnson	Jane E. Nelson
Alvin	v Vermilion	316	Jean P. Lete	Charlene H. Johnson
Amboy	c Lee	2,561	Leroy A. Stambaugh	M. Darlene Hinkle
Anchor	v McLean	175	Jolene Klintwork	Michael G. Molck
Andalusia	v Rock Island	1,050	Charles Capan	Don Manary
Andover	v Henry	594	Donald Olson	Beverly Josephson
Anna	c Union	5,136	Steve Hartline	Steve Guined
Annawan	v Henry	868	Kennard B. Franks Jr.	Betty M. Johnson-Atwell
Antioch	v Lake	8,788	Taso Maravelas	Candi L. Rowe
Apple River	v JoDaviess	379	Elmer E. Busch	George M. Lorenz
Arcola	c Douglas	2,652	Andrew A. Manna	Vickie Dill
Arenzville	v Cass	419	Don Cates	Sharon Huppe
Argenta	v Macon	921	Bradley E. Hunter	Linda Waters
Arlington	v Bureau	211	Dick Koch	Mary Stouffer
Arlington Heights	v Cook	76,031	Arlene J. Mulder	Edwina Corso
Armington	v Tazewell	368	Ray Billington	JoAnn Williams
Aroma Park	v Kankakee	821	Norman Grimsley	Julie Pasel
Arrowsmith	v McLean	298	John Fisher	Tina Plue
Arthur	v Douglas, Moultrie	2,203	David J. Conlin	Diane E. Conner
Ashkum	v Iroquois	724	Paul Heideman	Sheila A. Blasey
Ashland	v Cass	1,361	Dave Handy	Mary Ann Edwards
Ashley	c Washington	613	Len Piasecki	Imogene Daniels
Ashmore	v Coles	809	Clyde Griffith	Tami S. Ogden
Ashton	v Lee	1,142	Ray J. Forney	Dorthy S. Van Dam
Assumption	c Christian	1,261	Carolyn Puckett	Marilyn D. Ashinhurst
Astoria	t Fulton	1,193	William A. Hickle	Betty Wingerter
Athens	c Menard	1,726	Debra J. Richardson	Linda Ary
Atkinson	t Henry	1,001	Keith Noard	Carolyn J. Jiles
Atlanta	c Logan	1,649	Bill Martin	Kenneth Martin
Atwood	v Douglas, Piatt	1,290	Raymond F. Wicker	Cindy Ard
Auburn	c Sangamon	4,317	Joseph M. Powell	Gale A. Pruitt
Augusta	v Hancock	657	Robert Coleman	Mildred A. Derry
Aurora	c DuPage, Kane, Kendall, Will	142,990	David L Stover	Cheryl M. Vonhoff
Ava	c Jackson	662	Steve Grace	Julie Volkman
Aviston	v Clinton	1,231	Charles G. Rakers	Jennifer Jansen
Avon	v Fulton	915	Jon Prain	Virginia McKinley
Baldwin	v Randolph	3,627	Jeffrey S. Rowold	Wesley G. Stellhorn
Banner	v Fulton	149	Kenneth Fuller	Pam Holloway
Bannockburn	v Lake	1,429	Michael W. Grutza	Frances Picchietti
Bardolph	v McDonough	253	Sandy Smith	Deane Lambert
Barrington	Cook, Lake	10,168	Marshall S. Keagle	Carol J. Smith
Barrington Hills	v Cook, Kane, Lake, McHenry	3,915	James A. Kempe	Marla Russo
Barry	c Pike	1,368	Pat Syrcle	Donna Gordon
Bartelso	v Clinton	593	John B. Wilken	David Kreke
Bartlett,	v Cook, DuPage	36,706	Catherine J. Melchert	Linda Gallien
Bartonville	v Peoria	6,310	Marcia Markwalder	Cynthia Stafford
Basco	v Hancock	107	James D. Damron	Bonnie Earis
Batavia	c Kane	23,866	Jeffery D. Schielke	Hannah Volk
Batchtown	v Calhoun	218	Bernard Mager	Connie J. Sievers
Bath	v Mason	310	Joann Conway	Gerta Jean Griffin
Bay View Gardens	v Woodford	366	Howard Mayfield	Patti Cooper

*This listing of officials courtesy of Illinois Municipal League

City (c), town (t) or village (v)	County	Population	Mayor or President	Clerk
Baylis v	Pike 265		Lyndel R. Dark	Starla Lewis
Beach Park v	Lake 10,072		Milton C. Jensen	Laurie Cvengros
Beardstown c	Cass 5,766		Robert Walters	Brian Ruch
Beaverville v	Iroquois 391		Weldon Regnier	Doris Duensing
Beckemeyer v	Clinton 1,043		Michael Stock	Michelle Rakers
Bedford Park v	Cook 574		Ronald R. Robison	Linda J. Rackow
Beecher v	Will 2,033		Paul Lohmann	Janett Conner
Beecher City c	Effingham 493		Brett Schoenfeld	Sally Reed
Belgium v	Vermilion 466		Timothy A. Jenkins	Harriett Nelk
Belknap v	Johnson 133		John P. Wright	Pamela Harper
Belle Prairie City .... t	Hamilton 60		Cyrus Severs	Mark Karcher
Belle Rive v	Jefferson 371		William H. Neal	Doris Mallory
Belleville c	St. Clair 41,410		Mark A. Kern	Linda Fields
Bellevue v	Peoria 1,887		Ralph Wilson	Carol S. Howard
Bellflower v	McLean 408		Eston Ellis	Michelle Rumple
Bellmont v	Wabash 297		Edward Bowman	Vickie Rayborn
Bellwood v	Cook 20,535		Frank A. Pasquale	Lena Moreland
Belvidere c	Boone 20,820		Frederic C. Brereton	Shauna Arco
Bement v	Piatt 1,784		Steve Rittenhouse	Kay Lust
Benld c	Macoupin 1,541		Matt Turcol	Mary Ann Scopel
Bensenville v	Cook, DuPage 20,703		John C. Geils	Roxanne L. Mitchell
Benson v	Woodford 408		Arthur Brooks	Amy Burmood
Bentley v	Hancock 43		Larry Menschel	Robert Curtis
Benton c	Franklin 6,880		Patricia Bauer	Michael J. Malkovich
Berkeley v	Cook 5,245		Michael A. Esposito	Janice McCulloch
Berlin v	Sangamon 140		Marian Irwin	Rita Willhite
Berwyn c	Cook 54,016		Thomas G. Shaughnessy	Michael J. Woodward
Bethalto v	Madison 9,454		Steve A. Bryant	Martha Smith
Bethany v	Moultrie 1,287		John R. Felter	Shirley Underwood
Big Rock v	Kane 615		Kevin D. Hogle	Judy Hoffman
Biggsville v	Henderson 343		Janet Monville	Frank H. Jones
Bingham v	Fayette 117		Russel Cole	Deanna Fouts
Birds v	Lawrence 51		Janet Coonce	Dana M. Rich
Bishop Hill v	Henry 125		Laura Wendel	Marsha Carleson
Bismarck v	Vermilion 542		Julie I. Boersma	Lyle Milner
Blandinsville v	McDonough 777		Fred Hofmeister	Linda L. Peak
Bloomingdale v	DuPage 21,675		Robert G. Iden	Susan L. Bartucci
Bloomington c	McLean 64,808		Judy Markowitz	Tracey Covert
Blue Island c	Cook 23,463		Donald E. Peloquin	Pam Frasor
Blue Mound v	Macon 1,129		Elbert O. Bonn	Linda Zeeb
Bluffs v	Scott 748		Jackie Williams	Stacey Goetze
Bluford v	Jefferson 785		William A. Henderson ...	Sandra L. Richardson
Bolingbrook v	DuPage, Will 56,321		Roger C. Claar	Carol S. Penning
Bondville v	Champaign 455		Karl Kennicker	Susanne Martin-Sullivan
Bone Gap v	Edwards 272		Chris Kelsey	Mindy Henton
Bonfield v	Kankakee 364		Richard Cochran	Betty Wenzelman
Bonnie v	Jefferson 424		James M. Dycus	Gerald Hopson
Bourbonnais v	Kankakee 15,256		Robert Latham	Brian Simeur
Bowen v	Hancock 535		Mike Gooding	Valerie Peterson
Braceville v	Grundy 792		Mary Jane Larson	Rita Wright
Bradford v	Stark 787		Jeff Eubank	Joanne Holman
Bradley v	Kankakee 12,784		Gerald Balthzor	Mike LaGesse
Braidwood c	Will 5,203		Harvey Taylor	Sue A. Grygiel
Breese c	Clinton 4,048		Donald L. Maue	Robert J. Venhaus
Bridgeport c	Lawrence 2,168		Tom Nash	Lori Thacker
Bridgeview v	Cook 15,335		Steve M. Landek	Claudette Struzik
Brighton v	Jersey, Macoupin 2,196		Arlin Cunningham	Sharon Broyles
Brimfield v	Peoria 933		Danny J. Fishel	Holly Johnson
Broadlands v	Champaign 312		Ron Gast	Linda Ward
Broadview v	Cook 8,264		Henry Vicenik	Particia C. Williams
Broadwell v	Logan 169		Warren Bradley	Deanna Bradley
Brocton v	Edgar 322		Kim A. Brown	Tamela Hugg
Brookfield v	Cook 19,085		Bill Russ	Dan Raddatz
Brooklyn v	St. Clair 676		Dennis Miller	Ruth A. Winston
Brookport c	Massac 1,054		John L. Klaffer	Kay S. Hurst
Broughton v	Hamilton 193		Carolyn S. Pruitt	Betty J. Lasater
Browning v	Schuyler 130		Sam Parry	Linda L. Severns
Browns v	Edwards 175		Harry F. Duncan	Patricia A. Williams
Brownstown v	Fayette 705		Dennis Kilser	Sherry Meador
Brussels c	Calhoun 141		Sarah Kinder	Raymond Menke
Bryant v	Fulton 255		Max Mayberry	Kathleen S. Mayberry
Buckingham v	Kankakee 237		Raymond Cummins	Theresa McCue
Buckley v	Iroquois 593		Jerry Tobeck	J. C. Biggs
Buckner v	Franklin 479		Jessie Oyston	Jeanne Easley
Buda v	Bureau 592		Mark Graves	Shelby Mechling
Buffalo v	Sangamon 491		Ralph O. Fisher	Phyllis Quick
Buffalo Grove v	Cook, Lake 42,909		Elliott Hartstein	Janet M. Sirabian
Bull Valley v	McHenry 726		Brian Miller	Phyllis Keinz

438

INCORPORATED CITIES, TOWNS AND VILLAGES OF ILLINOIS
(Continued)

City (c), town (t) or village (v)	County	Population	Mayor or President	Clerk
Bulpitt v	Christian 206		Bea Hodson	Donald A. Denning
Buncombe v	Johnson 186		Denny Dorsey	Jeannie McCall
Bunker Hill c	Macoupin 1,801		Andrew Manar	Rhonda K. Whitworth
Burbank c	Cook 27,902		Harry J. Klein	Betty Trovato
Bureau Junction v	Bureau 368		Timothy Shipp	Karen Podabinski
Burlington v	Kane 452		Patricia Mueller	Mary Ann Wilkison
Burnham v	Cook 4,170		Donald J. Danewicz	Nancy C. Dobrowski
Burnt Prairie v	White 58		Carroll D. Dozier	Patsy Stahl
Burr Ridge v	Cook, DuPage 10,408		Jo V. Irmen	Karen Thomas
Bush v	Williamson 257		George Wilson	Penny Wilson
Bushnell c	McDonough 3,221		Jack Promisson	Jene M. Hall
Butler v	Montgomery 197		Donald Boliard	April Stewart
Byron c	Ogle 2,917		Kathryn A. Hamas	Betsy A. Faudree
Cabery v	Ford, Kankakee 263		Kenneth Peterson	Dolores Lovell
Cahokia v	St. Clair 16,391		Denita Reed	Jessie Brown
Cairo c	Alexander 3,632		James E. Wilson	Lorrie Hesselrode
Caledonia v	Boone 199		Susan Siek	Deidra Johnson
Calhoun v	Richland 222		Spencer Brock	Kathy Kirkwood
Calumet City c	Cook 39,071		Jerry P. Genova	
			...................Michelle Markiewicz Qualkinbush	
Calumet Park v	Cook 8,516		Buster B. Porch	Geraldine R. Galvin
Camargo v	Douglas 469		Jack Thompson	Shirley Howard
Cambria v	Williamson 1,330		Bill Herron	Sandra Sherry
Cambridge v	Henry 2,180		Eric Hanson	Barb Palmer
Camden v	Schuyler 97		Barry F. Wear	Donna R. Norton
Camp Point v	Adams 1,244		Richard Dieterle	Debra Lantz
Campbell Hill v	Jackson 333		Randy Rieckenberg	Donna L. Brown
Campus v	Livingston 145		Matthew Galeaz	Patti Galeaz
Canton c	Fulton 15,288		Jerry Bohler	Nancy Whites
Cantrall v	Sangamon 139		Mary Lou Markey	Dorothy Backer
Capron v	Boone 961		John Ustich	
Carbon Cliff v	Rock Island 1,689		Kenneth Williams	Karen Brown
Carbon Hill v	Grundy 392		John Jensen	Traci Pogliano
Carbondale c	Jackson 20,681		Neil Dillard	Janet M. Vaught
Carlinville c	Macoupin 5,685		Brad Demuzio	Judy Decker
Carlock v	McLean 456			Cheryl Weyeneth
Carlyle c	Clinton 3,406		Don W. Schmitz	Janine Ehlers
Carmi c	White 5,422		James T. Gaines	Don Kittinger
Carol Stream v	DuPage 40,438		Ross Ferraro	Janice Koester
Carpentersville v	Kane 30,586		Mark Boettger	Carol J. Miller
Carrier Mills v	Saline 1,886		Dave Rogers	Cynthia J. Murphy
Carrollton c	Greene 2,605		David Steneback	Denise Snyder
Carterville c	Williamson 4,616		Charles W. Mausey	Joyce A. Carney
Carthage c	Hancock 2,725		James R. Nightingale	Linda Rhoads
Cary v	McHenry 15,531		Donald M. Huffer	Barbara Hill
Casey c	Clark, Cumberland 2,942		Everett Bolin	Robin McClellan
Caseyville v	St. Clair 4,310		George E. Chance	Jack Piesbergen
Catlin v	Vermilion 2,087		Fred Rinehart	Donna M. Broderick
Cave-in-Rock v	Hardin 346		Michael Dutton	Jackie Fishbock
Cedar Point v	LaSalle 262		Robert Corrigan	Janet Gould
Cedarville v	Stephenson 719		Steve McWhirter	Cindy Lloyd
Central City v	Marion 1,371		Kenneth J. Buchanan	Sue Queen
Centralia c	Clinton, Marion 14,136		Robert Demijan	Tanya Bundy
Centreville c	St. Clair 5,951		Frankie Seaberry	Carolyn S. Edly
Cerro Gordo v	Piatt 1,436		James K. Morgan	Linda Ash
Chadwick v	Carroll 505		Joe Dane	Janice Queckboerner
Champaign c	Champaign 67,518		Gerald Schweighart	Marilyn L. Banks
Chandlerville v	Cass 704		Tim Richard	Cheryl Lane
Channahon v	Grundy, Will 7,344		Wayne M. Chesson	Eileen Clark
Chapin v	Morgan 592		Jerry Beams	Vickie Beams
Charleston c	Coles 21,039		Roscoe M. Cougill	Patsy J. Loew
Chatham v	Sangamon 8,583		Tom Gray	Pat Schad
Chatsworth .... t	Livingston 1,265		Richard H. Pearson	Sharon K. Birkenbeil
Chebanse v	Iroquois, Kankakee 1,148		Keith Tatro	Trudie Imhauser
Chenoa v	McLean 1,845		Walter Hetman	Nancy Wenger
Cherry v	Bureau 509		Robert McCook	Howard A. Raef
Cherry Valley v	Winnebago 2,191		Stephen J. Appell	Nancy L. Belt
Chester c	Randolph 5,185		Joe Eggemeyer	Nancy Eggemeyer
Chesterfield v	Macoupin 223		David Kanallakan	Linda Rhodes
Chicago c	Cook 2,896,016		Richard M. Daley	James J. Laski
Chicago Heights c	Cook 32,776		Angelo A. Ciambrone	Rachel M. Vega
Chicago Ridge v	Cook 14,127		Eugene L. Siegel	Charles Tokar
Chillicothe c	Peoria 5,996		Donald Z. White	Sharon A. Crabel
Chrisman c	Edgar 1,318		Tom Hoult	Paige Brooks
Christopher c	Franklin 2,836		Gary Paul Bartolotti	Judith M. Carter
Cicero .... t	Cook 85,616		Betty Loren-Maltese	Marylin Colpo
Cisco v	Piatt 264		Carolyn G. Fair	Charles E. Winters

City (c), town (t) or village (v)	County	Population	Mayor or President	Clerk
Cisne	v Wayne	673	Roy Atwood	Robert J. Howell
Cissna Park	v Iroquois	811	Rick A. Baier	Rhonda Sue Siebert
Claremont	v Richland	212	Tim Waxler	Sarah Hundley
Clarendon Hills	v DuPage	7,610	Robert E. Ryan	Mary A. Arnold
Clay City	v Clay	1,000	Trevor Bissey	Kimberly S. French
Clayton	v Adams	904	Jerry Newbrough	Marguerite Wilson
Clear Lake	v Sangamon	267	Richard Adams	Margaret Forsyth
Cleveland	v Henry	253	Jack Richardson	Loretta Mathias
Clifton	v Iroquois	1,317	Larry L. Behrends	Leslie Balthazor
Clinton	c DeWitt	7,485	Thomas R. Edmunds	Rozella Wickenhauser
Coal City	v Grundy	4,797	Gerald V. Pierard	Pamela M. Noffsinger
Coal Valley	v Henry, Rock Island	3,606	Stanley B. Engstrom	Deanna Burnett
Coalton	v Montgomery	307	Rick Cearlock	Kay Cook
Coatsburg	v Adams	226	Ronald Shanholtzer	Brenda Williams
Cobden	v Union	1,116	Elvis Pearson	Karen M. Winzenburger
Coffeen	c Montgomery	709	Dale Nowlan	Vivian Gile
Colchester	c McDonough	1,493	Robert L. Bice	Donna J. Wetzel
Coleta	v Whiteside	155	Sally Douglas	Michael Smith
Colfax	v McLean	989	Gordon Ehlers	Nancy Kiper
Collinsville	c Madison, St. Clair	24,707	Stan Schaeffer	Louis Jackstadt
Colona	c Henry	5,173	Danny McDaniel	Lories Graham
Colp	v Williamson	224	Richard Lyon	Viccy Helm
Columbia	c Monroe, St. Clair	7,922	Lester Schneider	Wesley J. Hoeffken
Columbus	v Adams	112	G. Brent Gilland	Bonnie Sue Reece
Compton	v Lee	347	Donald Swope	William Welch
Concord	v Morgan	176	Tom Miller	Roger E. Moss
Congerville	v Woodford	466	Steven Schrock	Glenn Ott
Cooksville	v McLean	213	Marvin Wyant	Hillary Stubblefield
Cordova	v Rock Island	633	Billie R. Churchill	Bennie J. Shaffer
Cornell	v Livingston	511	Ron Helander	Bonnie Fellers
Cortland	t DeKalb	2,066	Ben Suppeland	Cheryl Pearre
Coulterville	v Randolph	1,230	William Jarrett	Toni Douglas
Country Club Hills	c Cook	16,169	Dwight W. Welch	Deborah McIlvain
Countryside	c Cook	5,991	Carl W. LeGant	Shirley C. Herberts
Cowden	v Shelby	612	Kenneth E. Hudson	Mary Hovis
Crainville	v Williamson	992	William E. Wiggs	Evelyn Horsley
Creal Springs	v Williamson	702	Gary Hearn	Virgil Robertson
Crescent City	v Iroquois	631	James Ward	Dianne Freeman
Crest Hill	c Will	13,329	Donald L. Randich	Christine Vershay
Creston	v Ogle	543	William Heal	Joan Myroth
Crestwood	v Cook	11,251	Chester Stranczek	Nancy C. Benedetto
Crete	v Will	7,346	Michael S. Einhorn	Kathleen Wantuch
Creve Coeur	v Tazewell	5,448	Eugene Talbot	Judy Brandon
Crossville	v White	782	Tim Mitchell	Barbara Rawlinson
Crystal Lake	c McHenry	38,000	Aaron Shepley	Roger Dreher
Cuba	c Fulton	1,418	Bruce Barrick	Theresa Sheff
Cullom	v Livingston	563	Margeurite Kross	Krisi Buchenau
Cutler	v Perry	543	Gary R. Farley	Melvin H. Carrothers
Cypress	v Johnson	271	Roy West	Norma Adami
Dahlgren	v Hamilton	514	Jasper Gowin	Vivian Cross
Dakota	v Stephenson	499	William H. Lucas	Karen Wise
Dallas City	c Hancock, Henderson	1,055	Lila Gittings	Stanley K. Vorhies
Dalton City	v Moultrie	581	Debby Fortner	
Dalzell	v Bureau, LaSalle	717	Gloria Orlandi	Jyll Pozzi
Damiansville	v Clinton	368	Herman W. Jansen	Jackie Toennies
Dana	v LaSalle	171	Joseph L. Centeno	Becky Centeno
Danforth	v Iroquois	587	Arnold Hess	Gerald Reiken
Danvers	v McLean	1,183	Les Wellenreiter	Vickie L. Glenn
Danville	c Vermilion	33,904	Robert E. Jones	Janet K. Myers
Darien	c DuPage	22,860	Carmen D. Soldato	Joanne F. Coleman
Davis	v Stephenson	662	Brad Meinert	Kimberly K. Satness
Davis Junction	v Ogle	491	Marty Sheets	Sheryl Hawley
Dawson	v Sangamon	466	Robert Day	Gail Rexroad
Decatur	c Macon	81,860	Terry M. Howley	Celeste Harris
Deer Creek	v Tazewell, Woodford	605	James Hackney	Lori C. Lewis
Deer Grove	v Whiteside	48	Charles Brokaw	Janis L. Thompson
Deer Park	v Lake	3,102	Richard Karl	Sandra Smith
Deerfield	v Lake	18,420	Steven Harris	Robert D. Franz
DeKalb	c DeKalb	39,018	Greg Sparrow	Donna S. Johnson
DeLand	v Piatt	475	Art Sanders	Ed Fisher
Delavan	c Tazewell	1,825	Charles N. Denman	Penny L. Bright
DePue	v Bureau	1,842	Donald Bosnich	Janeann Vickers
Des Plaines	c Cook	58,720	Anthony Arredia	Donna McAllister
DeSoto	v Jackson	1,653	Mark Clerk	Paula Parks
Detroit	v Pike	93	Russ Sealock	Marion Phillips
DeWitt	v DeWitt	188	Cleo Newman	Florence Reynolds
Diamond	v Grundy	1,393	Elmer Rolando	Tami Zingre

INCORPORATED CITIES, TOWNS AND VILLAGES OF ILLINOIS
(Continued)

City (c), town (t) or village (v)	County	Population	Mayor or President	Clerk
Dieterich	v Effingham	591	Keith L. Lewis	Irma L. Horn
Divernon	v Sangamon	1,201	Eugene Brenning	M. Pamela Cronister
Dix	v Jefferson	494	Larry R. Mooney	Beverly Crawford
Dixmoor	v Cook	3,934	Erick Nickerson	Viviane Young
Dixon	c Lee	15,941	James G. Burke	Kathe A. Swanson
Dolton	v Cook	25,614	William Shaw	Judith J. Evans
Dongola	v Union	806	Teddy L. Earnhart	Meachelle Hoffman
Donnellson	v Bond, Montgomery	243	Charles McKinney	Suzanne Cunningham
Donovan	v Iroquois	351	Jerry McVey	Tracy Booi
Dorchester	v Macoupin	142	Charlie Knoche	Tracie Kirkwood
Dover	v Bureau	172	Daniel Fisher	Eleanor D. Fisher
Dowell	v Jackson	441	Dennis Stewart	Regina Jansen
Downers Grove	v DuPage	48,724	Brian J. Krajewski	April K. Holden
Downs	v McLean	776	Jeffrey Schwartz	Kathi Pritts
DuBois	v Washington	222	Thomas Barczewski	John Boczek
Dunfermline	v Fulton	262	Helen Williams	Teresa White
Dunlap	v Peoria	926	Richard E. Calhoun	Fraser En German
Dupo	v St. Clair	3,933	Ron Dell	Bruce Feltmeyer
DuQuoin	c Perry	6,448	John Rednour	Rex Duncan
Durand	v Winnebago	1,081	Gary Ingram	Connie Kahl
Dwight	v Grundy, Livingston	4,363	Daryl N. Holt	Mary Ann Denker
Eagarville	v Macoupin	128	Roger Heltsley	Catherine Rhodes
Earlville	c LaSalle	1,778	Robert G. Smith	Kathy J. Ness-Smith
East Alton	v Madison	6,830	Fred Bright	Lori Palmer
East Brooklyn	v Grundy	123	John B. Hakey	Brian S. Barna
East Cape Girardeau	v Alexander	437	Joe R. Aden	Marge Rendleman
East Carondelet	v St. Clair	267	Herbert Simmons	Ruth Price
East Dubuque	c JoDaviess	1,995	Geoffry Barklow	
East Dundee	v Kane	2,955	Roger Ahrens	Jane E. Theis
East Galesburg	v Knox	839	Connie Miyler	Jan Stremmel
East Gillespie	v Macoupin	234	Larry Norville	Martin Taylor
East Hazel Crest	v Cook	1,607	Thomas A. Brown	Helen M. Minnis
East Moline	c Rock Island	20,333	Jose Moreno	Arletta Holmes
East Peoria	c Tazewell	22,638	Charles F. Dobbelaire	Veona Dinkins
East St. Louis	c St. Clair	31,542	Debra Powell	Alzada Christian-Carr
Easton	v Mason	373	Jerry Lynn	Judy Miller
Eddyville	v Pope	153	Ralph Aly	Stacey King
Edgewood	v Effingham	527	Larry Joliff	Pamela Butts
Edinburg	v Christian	1,135	Todd Bailey	David Luttrell
Edwardsville	c Madison	21,491	Gary Niebur	Patty Thiede
Effingham	c Effingham	12,384	Robert Utz	Rick Goeckner
El Dara	v Pike	89	Judi Sutton	Mary Beard
El Paso	c Woodford	2,695	Ronald D. Mool	David Fever
Elburn	v Kane	2,756	James L. Willey	Susan Principata
Eldorado	c Saline	4,534	Billy Bradley	Pat Mahoney
Eldred	v Greene	211	Joseph Beiermann	Robert Camerer
Elgin	c Cook, Kane	94,487	Ed Schock	Dolonna Mecum
Elizabeth	v JoDaviess	682	Dale Roberts	Susan Eversoll
Elizabethtown	v Hardin	348	Eddie Rose	Lynda Schutt
Elk Grove Village	v Cook, DuPage	34,727	Craig B. Johnson	Ann I. Walsh
Elkhart	v Logan	443	Helen Dayle Eldredge	Gwen Rosenfeld
Elkville	v Jackson	1,001	Paul L. Martin	Vickie L. Bush
Elliott	v Ford	341	Marvin Beck	Michael E. Davis
Ellis Grove	v Randolph	381	Gary L. Conder	Linda Butler
Ellisville	v Fulton	87	Bill Van Tine	Kay Van Tine
Ellsworth	v McLean	271	Jay Smithson	Teresa Smithson
Elmhurst	c DuPage	42,762	Thomas D. Marcucci	Janet S. Edgley
Elmwood	c Peoria	1,945	Edward L. Cosby	Dotty S. Naumann
Elmwood Park	v Cook	25,405	Peter N. Silvestri	Elsie Sutter
Elsah	v Jersey	635	Marjorie Doerr	Jerilyn Lewitz
Elvaston	v Hancock	152	William H. Hempen	Mabel E. Heagy
Elwood	v Will	1,620	Robert Blum	Patricia Buchenau
Emden	v Logan	515	Ivan Rademaker	Frank Pieper
Emington	v Livingston	120	Daniel J. Delaney	Doris Fraher
Energy	v Williamson	1,175	Frank M. Jeters	Ann Wade
Enfield	v White	625	Tom Harbour	Deborah A. Stone
Equality	v Gallatin	721	Bobby Hopper	Marti Storto
Erie	v Whiteside	1,589	Marcia Smith	Noreta B. Franks
Essex	v Kankakee	554	Dave Dvorak	Kay Studley
Eureka	c Woodford	4,871	Laura Siscoe	Lynn Ruder
Evanston	c Cook	74,239	Lorraine H. Morton	Mary P. Morris
Evansville	v Randolph	724	Erwin Becker	Nancy Schilling
Evergreen Park	v Cook	20,821	James J. Sexton	Catherine Aparo
Ewing	v Franklin	310	Paul Walker	Patricia Walker
Exeter	v Scott	70	Roger Graves	Joy Graves
Fairbury	c Livingston	3,968	Robert P. Walter	Brenda E. DeFries
Fairfield	c Wayne	5,421	Mickey Borah	Tina Hutchcraft

441

INCORPORATED CITIES, TOWNS AND VILLAGES OF ILLINOIS
(Continued)

City (c), town (t) or village (v)	County	Population	Mayor or President	Clerk
Fairmont City v	St. Clair	2,436	Alex J. Bregen	Nicholas J. Prsha
Fairmount v	Vermilion	640	Bert T. Kirby	Vonda Kirby
Fairview v	Fulton	493	Douglas St. Clair	Donna Anderson
Fairview Heights c	St. Clair	15,034	Gail Mitchell	Harvey S. Noubarian
Farina v	Fayette	558	John R. Robinson	Patsy Thomas
Farmer City c	DeWitt	2,055	Delwin Kirby	Sandra Shaw
Farmersville v	Montgomery	768	Joe Tischkau	Yvonne Reim
Farmington c	Fulton	2,601	John DiMarsico	Donna DeGroot
Fayetteville v	St. Clair	384	Dallas Funk	Patsy Williams
Ferris v	Hancock	168	Charles H. Vass	Jean Twitchell
Fidelity v	Jersey	105	Elvin Buchanan	Audrey Bohannon
Fieldon v	Jersey	271	Betty Duggan	Shari Goetten
Fillmore v	Montgomery	362	Gary Marshall	Marian Kimbro
Findlay v	Shelby	723	Eugene Wooters	Patty Totten
Fisher v	Champaign	1,647	Milt Kelly	Debbie L. Estes
Fithian v	Vermilion	506	Lorin Kinney	Decemma Bensyl
Flanagan v	Livingston	1,083	Scott Knight	Paul Ingold
Flat Rock v	Crawford	415	Don Hepner	Carmen Walton
Flora c	Clay	5,086	Lewis L. Wolfe	Yvonne Guinn
Florence v	Pike	71	John Townsley	Barbara Andrews
Flossmoor v	Cook	9,301	Roger G. Molski	Pamela Hudson
Foosland v	Champaign	90	Paul M. Geurts	Mary Geurts
Ford Heights v	Cook	3,456	Saul Beck	Audrey M. Coulter
Forest City v	Mason	287	Eldon Bortell	Sheron Bortell
Forest Park v	Cook	15,688	Anthony Calderone	Joan White
Forest View v	Cook	778	Richard S. Grenvich	Frank Yurka
Forrest v	Livingston	1,225	Richard Sanders	Dawn Steidinger
Forreston v	Ogle	1,464	Douglas J. Elder	Carol R. Gagliardi
Forsyth v	Macon	2,434	Harold Gilbert	Cheryl K. Lehman
Fox Lake v	Lake	9,178	Nancy Koske	Helen Prosperi
Fox River Grove v	McHenry	4,862	Stephen J. Tasch	Donna M. Brouder
Fox River Valley Gardens v	McHenry	788	Jack R. Motley	Bobbie Klein
Frankfort v	Will	10,391	Raymond Rossi	Thomas E. Bartkus
Franklin v	Morgan	586	Darryl L. Smith	David Rawlings
Franklin Grove v	Lee	1,052	Robert E. Logan	Mary J. Rosenberg
Franklin Park v	Cook	19,434	Daniel Pritchett	Susan Szymanski
Freeburg v	St. Clair	3,872	Allen L. Watters	Mary Grau
Freeman Spur v	Franklin, Williamson	273	Jack Restivo	Theresa Hall
Freeport c	Stephenson	26,443	James Gitz	Latacia Ishmon
Fulton c	Whiteside	3,881	Howard Van Zuider	Jeanne M. Kettler
Fults v	Monroe	28	Eugene Williams	Ronald Rodenberg
Galatia v	Saline	1,013	Gary Schwartz	Henrietta Disney
Galena c	JoDaviess	3,460	Richard Auman	Jo Ann D. Turner
Galesburg c	Knox	33,706	Robert Sheehan	Anita Carlton
Galva c	Henry	2,758	Thomas E. Hartman	Teresa R. Byers
Gardner v	Grundy	1,406	Tom Wise	Barbara S. Bexson
Garrett v	Douglas	198	Jeff Ekiss	Kristine Issler
Gays v	Moultrie	259	Gene Goodwin	Monte Baker
Geneseo c	Henry	6,480	Merle LeSage	Cindy Gonzalez
Geneva c	Kane	19,515	Kevin Burns	Dennis A. Kabela
Genoa c	DeKalb	4,169	Todd A. Walker	Wendy Shaneen
Georgetown c	Vermilion	3,628	Darrell L. Acord	Cheryl Pearman
German Valley v	Stephenson	481	Richard L. Higar	Nancy Borchers
Germantown v	Clinton	1,118	Gerald Kohnen	Dawn M. Lakenburges
Germantown Hills v	Woodford	2,111	Marvin J. Johnson	Ann L. Sasso
Gibson City c	Ford	3,373	Brady T. Peters	Vickie Lorenzen
Gifford v	Champaign	815	Terrence G. Glazik	Cynthia M. Duden
Gilberts v	Kane	1,279	Michael P. Isitoro	Darlene Mueller
Gillespie c	Macoupin	3,412	Dan Fisher	Diane Goode
Gilman c	Iroquois	1,793	Lyle E. Price	Norma Curtis
Girard c	Macoupin	2,245	Bruce Pitchford	Shelly Hatalla
Gladstone v	Henderson	284	Donald Olson	Joyce Hetrick
Glasford v	Peoria	1,076	Jack Rudd	Jill Coats
Glasgow v	Scott	170	Walter Scoggins	Lori Mayes Doolin
Glen Carbon v	Madison	10,425	Ben Maliszewski	Rita J. Ranek
Glen Ellyn v	DuPage	26,999	Gregory S. Mathews	Patrica A. O'Connor
Glencoe v	Cook	8,762	James O. Webb	Ruby Herron
Glendale Heights v	DuPage	31,765	Linda Jackson	JoAnn Borysiewicz
Glenview v	Cook	41,847	Larry R. Carlson	Paul T. McCarthy
Glenwood v	Cook	9,000	Jeanne Maggio	Jan Presnak
Godfrey v	Madison	16,286	Michael J. Campion	Pamela E. Whisler
Godley v	Grundy, Will	594	Robert A. Willis	Tamara R. Branum
Golconda c	Pope	726	William Altman	Mary Lara
Golden v	Adams	629	Jean Lord	Betty Golden
Golden Gate v	Wayne	100	Robert Chapman	Margo Eyman
Golf v	Cook	451	Fred Stewart	Denise Gross
Good Hope v	McDonough	415	Loren G. Baker	Mary Lou Howe
Goodfield v	Woodford	686	K. Dean Hudson	Sheri Martin

INCORPORATED CITIES, TOWNS AND VILLAGES OF ILLINOIS
(Continued)

City (c), town (t) or village (v)	County	Population	Mayor or President	Clerk
Goreville v	Johnson	938	Larry L. Vaughn	Dana R. Black-Street
Gorham v	Jackson	256	Ralph A. Stone	Janice Hollmann
Grafton c	Jersey	609	Richard Mosby	Joe Wilson
Grand Ridge v	LaSalle	546	Shirley Gielow	Joyce A. Miller
Grand Tower c	Jackson	624	Randy Ellet	Lois E. Hanson
Grandview v	Sangamon	1,537	David Wysocki	Galie Traylor
Granite City c	Madison	31,301	Ronald L. Selph	Judy Whitaker
Grant Park c	Kankakee	1,358	Robert Schurman	Kenneth A. Heldt
Grantfork v	Madison	254	Robert Kloss	Judith Lawrence
Granville v	Putnam	1,414	Robert Borri	Kari J. Bouxsein
Grayslake v	Lake	18,506	Timothy R. Perry	Joanne W. Lawrence
Grayville c	Edwards, White	1,725	Joe W. Bisch	Linda L. Keepes
Green Oaks v	Lake	3,572	Thomas Adams	Clare Michelotti
Green Valley v	Tazewell	728	Roberta Bucher	Geraldine Shay
Greenfield c	Greene	1,179	Donald E. Chapman	Brenda Bishop
Greenup v	Cumberland	1,532	Randal L. Callahan	Nancy Sowers
Greenview v	Menard	862	Michael K. Wilson	Joseph L. Pisoni
Greenville c	Bond	6,955	Harold Palmer	Margaret Iberg
Greenwood v	McHenry	244	Evelyn E. Nash	Jamie Harrison
Gridley v	McLean	1,411	Brent Kirkton	Bonita Sherrill
Griggsville c	Pike	1,258	Gerald Wainman	Judy Bradshaw
Gulfport v	Henderson	207	Rick Meyers	Laurey Gray
Gurnee v	Lake	28,834	Doanld Rudny	Mary Jo Kollross
Hainesville v	Lake	2,129	Ted Mueller	Kathy Metzler
Hamburg v	Calhoun	126	Donna Kelly	Mary Jane Wilson
Hamel v	Madison	570	Ron Mulach	Helen F. Beshears
Hamilton c	Hancock	3,029	David Cornelius	Diann Means
Hammond v	Piatt	518	Timothy Flavin	Janet Sawyer
Hampshire v	Kane	2,900	William P. Schmidt	Linda Vasquez
Hampton v	Rock Island	1,626	Scott Newberg	Michael Toalson
Hanaford v	Franklin	55	Mary K. Mosley	Donna Bryan
Hanna City v	Peoria	1,013	Phil McAlearney	Myrna Klatt
Hanover v	JoDaviess	836	Donald Schaible	Susan Fulton
Hanover Park v	Cook, DuPage	38,278	Irwin A. Bock	Sherry L. Craig
Hardin v	Calhoun	959	William C. Horman	Vonetta M. Robeen
Harmon v	Lee	149	Jimmy J. Jackson	John R. Varga
Harrisburg c	Saline	9,860	Ron Morse	Toni Abraham
Harristown v	Macon	1,338	Michael Mathis	Penny J. Allen
Hartford v	Madison	1,545	William E. Moore	Sherry Smith
Hartsburg v	Logan	358	Tom Anderson	Doris Last
Harvard c	McHenry	7,996	Ralph J. Henning	Andy Wells
Harvel v	Christian, Montgomery	235	Gilbert Merkel	Max Neunaber
Harvey c	Cook	30,000	Nicholas E. Graves	Gwendolyn L. Davis
Harwood Heights v	Cook	8,297	Norbert A. Pabich	Dianne H. Larson
Havana c	Mason	3,577	Dale Roberts	Mary M. Howerter
Hawthorn Woods v	Lake	6,002	Keith Hunt	Phyllis Scheu
Hazel Crest v	Cook	14,816	William A. Browne	Shirley Smith
Hebron v	McHenry	1,038	Frank M. Beatty	Patricia C. Peterson
Hecker v	Monroe	475	Kelly Kimberlin	Donna Braun
Henderson v	Knox	319	Julie M. Baldwin	Barbara L. Billups
Hennepin v	Putnam	707	Kevin J. Coleman	Jennifer Petersen
Henning v	Vermilion	241	Stephen R. Vogel	Mary R. Vogel
Henry c	Marshall	2,540	Daryl Fountain	Jean Goldner
Herrick v	Shelby	524	Donald Heiman	Wanda Riley
Herrin c	Williamson	11,298	Victor M. Ritter	Marlene Simpson
Herscher v	Kankakee	1,523	William Carnahan	Amy DuMontelle
Hettick v	Macoupin	182	Monte Clevenger	Wanda Clevenger
Heyworth v	McLean	2,431	Gary A. Simpkins	Kandy Goughnour
Hickory Hills c	Cook	13,926	Roy Faddis	Joann Jackson
Hidalgo v	Jasper	123	Paul Jackson	Betty Gerhardt
Highland c	Madison	8,438	Rob Bowman	Barbara Bellm
Highland Park c	Lake	31,365	Daniel M. Pierce	David Fairman
Highwood c	Lake	4,143	John Sirotti	Jackie Schechter
Hillcrest v	Ogle	1,158	Lurton Pepper	Kathleen Anderson
Hillsboro c	Montgomery	4,359	Harold D. Whitten	David Booher
Hillsdale v	Rock Island	588	Michael Waterman	Jane Lundquist
Hillside v	Cook	8,155	Joseph T. Tamburino	Patrick F. O'Sullivan
Hillview v	Greene	179	Doyal Kuykendall	Connie Bugg
Hinckley v	DeKalb	1,994	Joseph Diedrich	Sharon Paradis
Hindsboro v	Douglas	361	Kent Douglas	Marilyn Talbott
Hinsdale v	Cook, DuPage	17,349	George L. Faulstic	Mary M. Reed
Hodgkins v	Cook	2,134	Noel B. Cummings	Claude R. Sexton
Hoffman v	Clinton	460	William A. Guile	Diana Donahoo
Hoffman Estates v	Cook	49,495	William D. McLeod	Virginia M. Hayter
Holiday Hills v	McHenry	831	Ken Anderson	Carol Stingel
Hollowayville v	Bureau	90	Anthony Ponsetti	Lisa Hoffert

443

INCORPORATED CITIES, TOWNS AND VILLAGES OF ILLINOIS
(Continued)

City (c), town (t) or village (v)		County	Population	Mayor or President	Clerk
Homer	v	Champaign	1,200	David Lucas	JoAnn Wallace
Homer Glen	v	Will	20,093	Russ Petrizzo	Christine Luttrell
Hometown	c	Cook	4,467	Donald L. Roberton	Mary Jo Hacker
Homewood	v	Cook	19,543	Richard Hofeld	Judi Rangel
Hoopeston	c	Vermilion	5,965	Chalmers Flint	
Hooppole	v	Henry	162	Gary Graham	Cynthia M. Jones
Hopedale	v	Tazewell	929	August C. Eilts	Paula J. Gregory
Hopewell	v	Marshall	396	Pete Christensen	Charlotte Fehland
Hopkins Park	v	Kankakee	711	David H. Leggett	Leroy Holiday
Hoyleton	v	Washington	520	Ronald Holle	Dale Sachtleben
Hudson	v	McLean	1,510	Douglas White	Sharon Willsie
Huey	v	Clinton	196	Mike Hohmeyer	Julie Hintz
Hull	v	Pike	474	Kirk A. Rueb	Manene V. Inman
Humboldt	t	Coles	481	Carl Fisher	Sandra Fisher
Hume	v	Edgar	382	Jean Keys	Patricia Thompson
Huntley	v	Kane, McHenry	5,730	Charles Sass	Cheryl Smielewski
Hurst	c	Williamson	805	Steven Greathouse	Sharron Powers
Hutsonville	v	Crawford	568	Wilburn B. Gray	Christina Callaway
Illiopolis	v	Sangamon	916	Allen Brickey	Beth Burris
Ina	v	Jefferson	2,455	Andy M. Hutchens	Pam Allen
Indian Creek	v	Lake	194	Tim Hill	Susan Schatsick
Indian Head Park	v	Cook	3,685	Richard F. Pellegrino	Norman L. Schnaufer
Indianola	v	Vermilion	207	Deborah Key	Lorri Taylor
Industry	v	McDonough	540	Randall Jones	Ruth L. Harrison
Inverness	v	Cook	6,749	John A. Tatooles	Patricia D.Ledvina
Iola	v	Clay	171	Thomas L. Butcher	Jana Marie Smith
Ipava	v	Fulton	506	Geraldine M. Smith	Phyllis J. Lamm
Iroquois	v	Iroquois	207	Jack Karr	Ed Armold
Irving	v	Montgomery	2,484	Harold W. Jurgena	Marilyn S. Taylor
Irvington	v	Washington	736	Mike Garrison	William Irwin
Irwin	v	Kankakee	92	Donald M. O'Connor	Kathryn Moody
Island Lake	v	Lake, McHenry	8,153	Charles R. Amrich	
Itasca	v	DuPage	8,302	Claudia Gruber	Carole Schreiber
Iuka	v	Marion	598	Janie Grimes	Linda Holsapple
Ivesdale	v	Champaign, Piatt	288	Bernard J. Alblinger	James A. Brewer
Jacksonville	c	Morgan	18,940	Ron Tendick	Susan Large
Jeffersonville	v	Wayne	366	Sally J. Dye	Irene Tucker
Jeisyville	v	Christian	128	Michael Drnjevic	Cheryl Drnjevic
Jerome	v	Sangamon	1,414	Steve Roth	Melissa Lamm Roth
Jerseyville	c	Jersey	7,984	Jerry Wittman	Yvonne Hartmann
Jewett	v	Cumberland	232	Wes Chambers	
Johnsburg	v	McHenry	5,391	Dave Dominguez	Claudett Peters
Johnsonville	v	Wayne	69	Robbe Brashear	Hilda Smith
Johnston City	c	Williamson	3,557	Vernon Kee	Jeanne Hatfield
Joliet	c	Will	106,221	Arthur Schultz	Janet Traven
Jonesboro	c	Union	1,853	Randy Tucker	Terri Bowen
Joppa	v	Massac	409	Sue Sandusky	Rayette Holland
Joy	v	Mercer	373	George Braucht	Gwen Terrill
Junction	v	Gallatin	139	Richard Evans	Becky Brugger
Junction City	v	Marion	559	N. Dallas Kinney	Nancy Nalewajka
Justice	v	Cook	12,193	Melvin D. VanAllen, Jr.	Kathleen M. Svoboda
Kampsville	v	Calhoun	302	Ted Schumann	Jerry Sue Clendenny
Kane	v	Greene	459	Maxine DeWitt	Wila Bogle
Kangley	v	LaSalle	287	Keith Dye	Tamra Alberts
Kankakee	c	Kankakee	27,491	Donald E. Green	Anjanita Andrew
Kansas	v	Edgar	842	Robert Walker	Pam Shaffer
Kappa	v	Woodford	170	Karyn Hasty	Suzanne Phelps
Karnak	v	Pulaski	619	Darryl Anderson	Raymond L. Davis
Kaskaskia	v	Randolph	9	Donovan DeRousse	Sandra Roth
Keenes	v	Wayne	99	Roy Evans	Teresa White
Keensburg	v	Wabash	252	William Kirby	Beverly J. McBride
Keithsburg	c	Mercer	714	Sharon L. Reason	Terri L. Gibson
Kell	v	Marion	231	Charles Bryant	Kay Rollinson
Kempton	v	Ford	235	Dean Tharp	Carol Drew
Kenilworth	v	Cook	2,494	L. Hamilton Kerr	T. Tolbert Chisum
Kenney	v	DeWitt	374	Mike Mathias	Jerry Shaw
Kewanee	c	Henry	12,944	James P. Burns	Sandra J. Murphy
Keyesport	v	Bond, Clinton	481	Jay Carter	Rita Griffin
Kilbourne	v	Mason	375	Wendell K. Daniel	Vivian F. Freeman
Kildeer	v	Lake	3,460	Alan Stefaniak	Pam McGinty
Kincaid	v	Christian	1,441	William T. Davis	Wanda E. Pezze
Kinderhook	v	Pike	249	Gary Wells	Susan Weir
Kingston	v	DeKalb	980	John Munro	Elsie Atkinson
Kingston Mines	v	Peoria	259	Charlette Hancock	Deanna Miller
Kinmundy	c	Marion	892	Elwyn Cheatum	Judi Slane

INCORPORATED CITIES, TOWNS AND VILLAGES OF ILLINOIS
(Continued)

City (c), town (t) or village (v)		County	Population	Mayor or President	Clerk
Kinsman	v	Grundy	109	Mark Harlow	Doreen Harlow
Kirkland	v	DeKalb	1,166	Les Bellah	Kathryn McNeal
Kirkwood	v	Warren	794	Harold D. Taylor	Donna K. Cunningham
Knoxville	c	Knox	3,183	Phil Myers	Margaret Bivens
Lacon		Marshall	1,979	Michael Hiell	Melody Weber
Ladd	v	Bureau	1,313	Paul Bazydlo	Carol A. DeSerf
LaFayette	v	Stark	227	Russell C. Schierer	Caryl J. Schierer
LaGrange	v	Cook	15,608	Timothy Hansen	Robert Milne
LaGrange Park	v	Cook	13,295	Susan Tutt	W. Kerry Brunette
LaHarpe	c	Hancock	1,385	Kenneth L. Brown	Carol Stevens
Lake Barrington	v	Lake	4,757	Dorothy H. Schofield	Linda Bilocerkowycz
Lake Bluff	v	Lake	6,056	Thomas Skinner	Peter Sexton
Lake Forest	c	Lake	20,059	Howard J. Kerr	Robert R. Kiely
Lake in the Hills	v	McHenry	23,152	Edwin M. Plaza	Cheryl Perrone-Hoff
Lake Ka-Ho	v	Macoupin	260	Joe Hinnen	Mary Smith
Lake Villa	v	Lake	5,864	Frank M. Loffredo	Alyce Brownlee
Lake Zurich	v	Lake	18,104	Jim Krischke	Gloria Palmblad
Lakemoor	v	Lake, McHenry	2,788	Robert Koehl	Lenore Lukas-Tutein
Lakewood	v	McHenry	2,337	Blair R. Picard	Sue A. Henn
LaMoille	v	Bureau	773	James Scully	Jamie Schultz
Lanark	c	Carroll	1,584	Mike Sutphen	Jackie Hawbecker
Lansing	v	Cook	28,332	Daniel Podgorski	Jean U. Eisha
LaPrairie	t	Adams	60	Gary D. Robbins	Ruth Ann Kinman
LaRose	v	Marshall	159	Flavel Streitmatter	Donna Rinehart
LaSalle	c	LaSalle	9,796	Art Washkowiak	Virginia Kochanowski
Latham	v	Logan	371	Jim Alltig	Pam Coogan
Lawrenceville	c	Lawrence	4,745	Eddie Ryan	Don Wagner
Leaf River	v	Ogle	555	Timothy Mulford	Loretta L. Rose
Lebanon	c	St. Clair	3,523	Matthew Berberich	Pamela Koshko
Lee	v	DeKalb, Lee	313	Jerry Olson	Linda Clark
Leland	v	LaSalle	970	Robert Heher	Betty Shumway
Leland Grove	c	Sangamon	1,592	John Andrew Davis	Irene Randolph
Lemont	v	Cook	13,098	John F. Piazza	Charlene M. Smollen
Lena	v	Stephenson	2,887	Richard A. Heinkel	Lynn Polhill
Lenzburg	v	St. Clair	577	Darryl Hagen	Alice Hazel
Leonore	v	LaSalle	110	Ronald Barnhart	Shawn Bernardoni
Lerna	v	Coles	322	Donald Pearcy	Cathy Allen
LeRoy	c	McLean	3,332	Bob Rice	Sue Marcum
Lewistown	c	Fulton	2,522	Barry D. Blackwell	Melodee W. Rudolph
Lexington	c	McLean	1,912	Frank J. Feigl	Andrea Neumann
Liberty	v	Adams	519	Michael Maas	Donna Egenes
Libertyville	v	Lake	20,742	Duane Laska	Sally Kowal
Lily Lake	v	Kane	825	Glenn Bork	Heather Gravlin
Lima	v	Adams	159	Roger Phillips	
Lincoln	c	Logan	15,369	Elizabeth A. Davis	Juanita Josserand
Lincolnshire	v	Lake	6,108	Barbara LaPiana	Barbara Mastandrea
Lincolnwood	v	Cook	12,359	Peter Moy	Carol Krikorian
Lindenhurst	v	Lake	12,539	Paul E. Baumunk	Marilyn E. Gregorin
Lisbon	v	Kendall	248	James D. Morris	Shelley Kroack
Lisle	v	DuPage	21,182	Joseph Broda	Timothy J. Seeden
Litchfield	c	Montgomery	6,815	John Dunkirk	Marilyn S. Hartke
Little York	v	Warren	269	Phillip Cooper	Tammy Sedam
Littleton	v	Schuyler	197	Jack Swearingen	Roger Marvel
Liverpool	v	Fulton	119	John Westenfield	Jackie Fitzjarrald
Livingston	v	Madison	825	Miles M. Dudley	Elizabeth B. Augustine
Loami	v	Sangamon	804	Richard W. Mowery	Laurie Glynn
Lockport	c	Will	15,191	Frank C. Mitchell	Andie McCarthy
Loda	v	Iroquois	419	Jon Boone	Carol Arseneau
Lomax	v	Henderson	477	Randy May	Leslie A. Roberts
Lombard	v	DuPage	42,322	William J. Mueller	Suzan Kramer
London Mills	v	Fulton, Knox	447	Alice S. Branch	Rhonda Bugos
Long Creek	v	Macon	1,364	Kevin Greenfield	Linda S. Beale
Long Grove	v	Lake	6,735	Tony Dean	Caroline D. Liebl
Long Point	v	Livingston	247	Richard Lefler	Jean C. Gray
Longview	v	Champaign	153	Ron Tatman	Tanya Walker
Loraine	v	Adams	363	Ken Gray	Loretta Emnsinger
Lostant	v	LaSalle	486	James K. Cooper	Luann Heider
Louisville	v	Clay	1,242	Charles Smith	Dian Bartlett
Loves Park	c	Winnebago	20,044	Darryl F. Lindberg	Robert J. Burden
Lovington	v	Moultrie	1,222	Steve Fleming	Debbie Renfro
Ludlow	v	Champaign	324	Brian Adams	Sandra Langley
Lyndon	v	Whiteside	575	Michael Kramer	Linda Pilgrim
Lynnville	v	Morgan	137	William Fred Moore	Nancy L. Preston
Lynwood	v	Cook	7,377	Russell R. Melby	W. Faye Berkheiser
Lyons	v	Cook	10,255	Marie M. Vachata	Edward Metz

445

INCORPORATED CITIES, TOWNS AND VILLAGES OF ILLINOIS
(Continued)

City (c), town (t) or village (v)	County	Population	Mayor or President	Clerk
Macedonia v	Franklin, Hamilton 51		Ralph D. Billington	Helen Campbell
Machesney Park v	Winnebago 20,759		Linda Vaughn	Nancy Metcalf
Mackinaw v	Tazewell 1,452		Phillip D. Thames	Lisa Craig
Macomb c	McDonough 18,558		Thomas C. Carper	Melanie Falk
Macon c	Macon 1,213		Dennis Ruot	Pam Windell
Madison c	Madison 4,545		John W. Hamm, III	Alexis Rozycke-Lux
Maeystown v	Monroe 148		Terryl Walster	Diana Lewis
Magnolia v	Putnam 279		Jeffrey Omei	Carl Johnson
Mahomet v	Champaign 4,877		Jeffrey Courson	Cheryl Sproul
Makanda v	Jackson 419		Bill Ross	Cecilia Cottingham
Malden v	Bureau 343		Robert Smith	Joanne Nichols
Malta v	DeKalb 969		Vince McCabe	Patricia Siebrasse
Manchester v	Scott 354		Dean Thady	Peggy Renner
Manhattan v	Will 3,330		James M. Doyle	Mattie Becker
Manito v	Mason 1,733		Timothy Sondag	Lee Lacey
Manlius v	Bureau 355		Jerry Neumann	Lori Roush
Mansfield v	Piatt 949		Steve Gaines	Susan King
Manteno v	Kankakee 6,414		Bernard Christenson	Robin Batka
Maple Park v	Kane 765		Mark Delaney	Claudia Tremaine
Mapleton v	Peoria 227		Ken Oedewaldt	Alice Dailey
Maquon v	Knox 318		James Donsbach	Adela M. Foster
Marengo c	McHenry 6,355		Dennis Hammortree	Barbara Bigalke
Marietta v	Fulton 150		Linda Bradford	Ramona Howard
Marine v	Madison 910		John Deppe	Paula Corradi
Marion c	Williamson 16,035		Robert L. Butler	Elizabeth J. Strobel
Marissa v	St. Clair 2,141		Steuart McClintock	Carol Smith
Mark v	Putnam 491		Kevin Troglio	Sandy Troglio
Markham c	Cook 12,620		Evans R. Miller	Cheri Coles
Maroa c	Macon 1,654		Ted L. Agee	Kathryn Shirey
Marquette Heights c	Tazewell 2,794		David Redfield	Sandra Brooks
Marseilles c	LaSalle 4,655		John C. Knudson	Jacquelyn Spencer
Marshall c	Clark 3,771		John W. Trefz	Richard C. Duzan
Martinsville c	Clark 1,225		Phillip Reeds	L. Marlene Wilhoit
Martinton v	Iroquois 375		Lynne Haste	Diana Cailteux
Maryville v	Madison 4,651		Larry Gulledge	Thelma Long
Mascoutah c	St. Clair 5,659		Gerald E. Daugherty	Kathleen M. Schuetz
Mason .... t	Effingham 396			Sue Ann Dyer
Mason City c	Mason 2,558		Lois Lee Rickard	Karla S. Daubs
Matherville v	Mercer 772		James Rankin	Kathy Matkovic
Matteson v	Cook 12,928		Mark W. Stricker	Dorothy Grisco
Mattoon c	Coles 18,291		David Carter	William D. Burrell
Maunie v	White 177		Bill Pollard	Sheila Majors
Maywood v	Cook 26,987		Ralph Conner	Ralph McNabb
Mazon v	Grundy 904		Sue Giddings	Karen Barkley
McCook v	Cook 254		Patrick Gorski	Charles Sobus
McCullom Lake v	McHenry 1,038		Ralph Rogner	Dawn Miller
McHenry c	McHenry 21,501		Pamela J. Althoff	Janice Jones
McLean v	McLean 808		Bill Bailey	Sandra Sheldon
McLeansboro c	Hamilton 2,945		Dick Deitz	Sharon S. Morrison
McNabb v	Putnam 310		John Dippel	Patricia Harrison
Mechanicsburg v	Sangamon 456		Howard Rogers	Dana Edwards
Media v	Henderson 130		Don Gipe	Edna Johnson
Medora v	Macoupin 501		Ronald Bellitto	Melissa Moran
Melrose Park v	Cook 23,171		Ronald M. Serpico	
				Mary Ann Paolantonio Salemi
Melvin v	Ford 465		Bardell Shelton	Carri Redeker
Mendon v	Adams 883		Randy Rosson	Susan Woodruff
Mendota c	LaSalle 7,272		David Boelk	Wendy Morris
Menominee v	JoDaviess 237		Francis C. Powers	Joan Lee Jackson
Meredosia v	Morgan 1,041		Mikeal Brown	Sally Wilhite
Merrionette Park v	Cook 1,999		Dennis Magee	Carol Sullivan
Metamora v	Woodford 2,700		Matthew O'Shea	Janet E. Mangold
Metcalf v	Edgar 213		John Morris	April Morris
Metropolis c	Massac 6,482		Beth Clanahan	Brenda Westbrooks
Mettawa v	Lake 367		Barry MacLean	Joan Roy
Middletown v	Logan 434		Kenneth G. Davison	Joyce A. Skelton
Midlothian v	Cook 14,315		Thomas J. Murawski	Robert McAdams
Milan v	Rock Island 5,348		Duane Dawson	Barbara Lee
Milford v	Iroquois 1,369		James Cook	Susan Ricketts
Mill Creek v	Union 76		Marion Turner	Betty McDermott
Mill Shoals v	White 235		Tim Isaacs	Ann Sarks
Milledgeville v	Carroll 1,016		Alvin H. Dettman	JoAnne Ludewig
Millington v	Kendall, LaSalle 458		Janet Blue	Lenee Kissel
Millstadt v	St. Clair 2,794		Weldon Harber	Linda Lehr
Milton v	Pike 274		Phil McEuen	Irma Jean Allen
Mineral v	Bureau 272		Glenn E. Morey	Linda Morey
Minier v	Tazewell 1,244		Neill Keneipp	Sandy Lancaster
Minonk c	Woodford 2,168		Mark Spencer	Roberta Evans

446

City (c), town (t) or village (v)	County	Population	Mayor or President	Clerk
Minooka v	Grundy, Kendall, Will	3,971	C. Richard Ellis	Mary Ray
Modesto v	Macoupin	252	Thomas M. Thompson	DeAnn Arnold
Mokena v	Will	14,583	Robert A. Chiszar	Jane McGinn
Moline c	Rock Island	43,768	Stan Leach	Yvonne Savala-Kletke
Momence c	Kankakee	3,171	James Saindon	Margaret Clifton
Monee v	Will	2,924	Timothy O'Donnell	Kathleen Buchmeier
Monmouth c	Warren	9,841	John R. Reitman	Susan S. Trevor
Montgomery v	Kane, Kendall	5,471	Marilyn Michelini	Barbara Argo
Monticello c	Piatt	5,138	Ron Ivall	Renee Fruendt
Montrose v	Effingham	257	Keith McKinney	Janet McMahon
Morris c	Grundy	11,928	Richard Kopczick	John D. Enger
Morrison c	Whiteside	4,447	Roger Drey	Jennie L. Huling
Morrisonville v	Christian	1,068	Matthew Wells	Alice Downey
Morton v	Tazewell	15,198	Donald F. Roth	Beth Sharpe
Morton Grove v	Cook	22,451	Daniel D. Scanlon	Daniel P. DiMaria
Mound City v	Pulaski	692	Samuel Johnson	Louise Calvin
Mound Station v	Brown	127	Stephen Perry	Mary F. Dobbs
Mounds c	Pulaski	1,117	Grace Richards	Debby Severs
Mount Auburn v	Christian	515	Jerry Seymour	Tammy J. Hamell
Mount Carmel c	Wabash	7,982	George W. Woodcock	Merle A. Weems
Mount Carroll c	Carroll	1,832	E. Robert Bulman	Julie A. Cuckler
Mount Clare v	Macoupin	433	Larry Bultema	Theresa LaChance
Mount Erie v	Wayne	105	Norman McKinney	Joseph Atwood
Mount Morris v	Ogle	3,013	Steven Mongan	Sandra Blake
Mount Olive c	Macoupin	2,150	Thomas Spears	Cathy Teetor
Mount Prospect v	Cook	56,265	Gerald L. Farley	Velma W. Lowe
Mount Pulaski c	Logan	1,701	William C. Glaze	Marla K. Durst
Mount Sterling c	Brown	2,070	Jim Jennings	Lois Urven
Mount Vernon c	Jefferson	16,269	Mark Terry	Jackie Sharp
Mount Zion v	Macon	4,845	Robert Flider	Tamara L. Mense
Moweaqua v	Shelby	1,923	Vennard Dowd	Mischelle Davis
Muddy v	Saline	78	Norman Edgar	Frances Bertino
Mulberry Grove v	Bond	671	Jana Willis	Kathy Lutz
Muncie v	Vermilion	155	Jerry McGlaughlin	Helen Welch
Mundelein v	Lake	30,935	Marilyn Sindles	Pamela J. Keeney
Murphysboro c	Jackson	13,295	Ron Williams	Frank Riley
Murrayville v	Morgan	644	Charles W. Irlam	Francis Fitzgerald
Naperville c	DuPage, Will	128,358	A. George Pradel	Suzanne L. Gagner
Naplate v	LaSalle	523	Gary Yanko	Florence M. Stricklin
Naples .... t	Scott	134	Rick Nelson	Jeri Nelson
Nashville c	Washington	3,147	Raymond Kolweier	Lloyd Dinkelman
Nason c	Jefferson	234	Jackie Dent	Linda Allison
Nauvoo c	Hancock	1,063	Thomas Wilson	Carol McGhghy
Nebo v	Pike	408	Kenneth Hubbard	Zoe Guthrie
Nelson v	Lee	163	David Nuttall	Susan Lewandowski
Neoga c	Cumberland	1,854	Gary A. Mercer	Patricia D. Ehrhart
Neponset v	Bureau	519	Tim Folger	Cindy Holton
New Athens v	St. Clair	1,981	Dennis Breithaupt	Nancy Ritter
New Baden v	Clinton, St. Clair	3,001	Timothy J. Hoerchler	Janet F. Kuhn
New Bedford v	Bureau	95	Lester Lathrop	Ruby Swanson
New Berlin v	Sangamon	1,030	William Pfeffer	Marsha J. Sweet
New Boston c	Mercer	632	Dennis Dixon	Cindy Marston
New Burnside v	Johnson	242	Larry W. Taylor	Judith G. Taylor
New Canton .... t	Pike	417	Bert Sapp	Yvonne Bruce
New Douglas v	Madison	369	Fred O. Kline	Patricia Rausch
New Grand Chain v	Pulaski	233	Herb Dover	Beth Dover
New Haven v	Gallatin	477	Kevin Edmonds	Betty Goforth
New Holland v	Logan	318	Jeffrey P. Mammen	Jennie L. Dean
New Lenox v	Will	17,771	Michael Smith	Marcia Englert
New Millford v	Winnebago	541	Bonnie L. Beard	Sharon K. Baumgartner
New Minden v	Washington	204	Candice Cross	Patti Hendricks
New Salem v	Pike	136	Jim Shields	Carolyn Baker
Newark v	Kendall	887	Roger Ness	Ray Eddy
Newman v	Douglas	956	Robert Sumption	Jud Pollocki
Newton c	Jasper	3,069	Ross McClane	Jean Ghast
Niantic v	Macon	738	Gene Gambrill	Faith Vaught
Niles v	Cook	30,068	Nicholas B. Blase	Kathy Harbison
Nilwood .... t	Macoupin	284	Phillip Starks	Lisa Connelly
Noble v	Richland	746	Richard Clark	Shirley Gehlhausen
Nokomis c	Montgomery	2,389	Tony Hard	Pamela Burdzilauskas
Nora v	JoDaviess	118	Gary Grenoble	Christine Grenoble
Normal .... t	McLean	45,386	Kent M. Karraker	Wendellyn Briggs
Norridge v	Cook	14,582	Earl J. Field	Judith Dunne Bernardi
Norris v	Fulton	194	Richard Myers	Sandra Pasley
Norris City v	White	1,057	Carl Whipple	James Crouch
North Aurora v	Kane	10,585	Mark Ruby	Carole Kerr
North Barrington v	Lake	2,918	Linda K. Starkey	Norma A. Behrend

INCORPORATED CITIES, TOWNS AND VILLAGES OF ILLINOIS
(Continued)

City (c), town (t) or village (v)	County	Population	Mayor or President	Clerk
North Chicago c	Lake 35,918		Bette Thomas	Catherine L. Collins
North City v	Franklin 630		Pete Moschino	Linda Gilbert
North Henderson v	Mercer 187		Ronald D. Brown	Karla Kuberski
North Pekin v	Tazewell 1,574		William A. Clutts	Judith A. Johnson
North Riverside v	Cook 6,688		Richard M. Scheck	Charmaine M. Kutt
North Utica v	LaSalle 977		Fred Esmond	Angela Brown
Northbrook v	Cook 33,435		Mark W. Damisch	Lona N. Louis
Northfield v	Cook 5,389		Donald Whiteman	Mark J. Morien
Northlake c	Cook 11,878		Jeffrey T. Sherwin	Joanne Floistad
Norwood v	Peoria 473		Robert Egbert	Carolyn L. Fascian
Oak Brook v	DuPage 8,702		Karen M. Bushy	Linda K. Gonnella
Oak Forest c	Cook 28,051		Patrick M. Gordon	Scott Burkhardt
Oak Grove v	Rock Island 1,318		Richard Nowack	Mary Zimmerman
Oak Lawn v	Cook 55,245		Ernest F. Kolb	Alice Jayne Powers
Oak Park v	Cook 52,524		Joanne E. Trapani	Sandra Sokol
Oakbrook Terrace c	DuPage 2,300		Thomas S. Mazaika	Elaine K. DeLuca
Oakdale v	Washington 213		Cecil D. Alfeldt	Frederick M. Endres
Oakford v	Menard 309		Diane McClain	Rebecca Gluk
Oakland c	Coles 996		Sharon Houchin	Grace Thompson
Oakwood v	Vermilion 1,502		Tom Cook	Janet Hill
Oakwood Hills v	McHenry 2,194		Chad Rider	Judith A. Sutliff
Oblong v	Crawford 1,580		Keith Waldrop	Ladora Boyd
Oconee v	Shelby 202		Kenneth A. Tedrick	Carol S. Hoehn
Odell v	Livingston 1,014		Ed Seal	Julie Wardschmidt
Odin v	Marion 1,122		Michael Kelly	Steven D. Holsapple
O'Fallon c	St. Clair 21,910		Gary L. Graham	Phil Goodwin
Ogden v	Champaign 743		Jack Reidner	Lori Frerichs
Oglesby c	LaSalle 3,647		Jerry Scott	Shaun West
Ohio v	Bureau 540		Charles L. Thomas	Cheryl A. Okland
Ohlman v	Montgomery 177		Dennis Aumann	Mildred I. Pieper
Okawville v	Washington 1,355		David Jasper	Wayland Jasper
Old Mill Creek v	Lake 251		Tempel Smith	Ruth White
Old Ripley v	Bond 127		Orville Mettler	Marlene Mollett
Old Shawneetown v	Gallatin 278		Walter Butch Oldham	Joel Gray
Olmsted v	Pulaski 299		Curtis Marshall	Dixie Walters
Olney c	Richland 8,631		Tom Fehrenbacher	Belinda C. Henton
Olympia Fields v	Cook 4,732		Linzey Jones	Carolyn Gibson
Omaha v	Gallatin 263		Joe Sadler	Patti Odle
Onarga v	Iroquois 1,438		Michael Tilstra	Robert G. Lyons
Oneida c	Knox 752		Larry Lawson	
Oquawka v	Henderson 1,539		Steven Lumbeck	Shirley Link
Orangeville v	Stephenson 751		Wayne Reed	Joyce Flannery
Oreana v	Macon 892		Dan Lightner	Michelle Fleming
Oregon c	Ogle 4,060		Mike Arians	Charlene Ruthe
Orient c	Franklin 296		Art Ambos	Monica Dorris
Orion v	Henry 1,713		William A. Larkins	Lori A. Sampson
Orland Hills v	Cook 6,779		Kyle Hastings	Kathy A. Chapman
Orland Park v	Cook, Will 51,077		Daniel J. McLaughlin	David P. Maher
Oswego v	Kendall 13,326		Craig Weber	Dorothy A. Strong
Ottawa c	LaSalle 18,307		Robert M. Eschbach	Elizabeth A. Taylor
Otterville .... t	Jersey 120		Charles P. Krausharr	Clifford Krausharr
Owaneco v	Christian 256		Alvin Mizeur	Gay Wilhour
Palatine v	Cook 65,479		Rita L. Mullins	Margaret R. Duer
Palestine v	Crawford 1,366		Richard A. Kent	Judith M. Winger
Palmer v	Christian 248		Cayle Davis	Norma Black
Palmyra v	Macoupin 733		C. Ralph March	Judy Bacon
Palos Heights c	Cook 11,260		Bob Straz	Marsha Fisher
Palos Hills c	Cook 17,665		Gerald R. Bennett	Rudy A. Mulderink
Palos Park v	Cook 4,689		Jean A. Moran	Annette Mucha
Pana c	Christian 5,614		Ken Mueller	Terry Klein
Panama v	Bond, Montgomery 323		Joseph McCario	Naomi McCario
Panola v	Woodford 33		Roger A. Bogner	Elizabeth A. Stine
Papineau v	Iroquois 196		Mike Johnson	Janice M. Salm
Paris c	Edgar 9,077		Dale E. Francis	Cathy Higgins
Park City c	Lake 6,637		Steve Pannell	Beverly Roehr
Park Forest v	Cook, Will 23,462		John Ostenburg	Joan Frontczak
Park Ridge c	Cook 37,775		Ronald W. Wietecha	Betty W. Henneman
Parkersburg v	Richland 234		Philip Rose	Ruth Esders
Patoka v	Marion 633		Eddie Dean	Robyn Pitts
Paw Paw v	Lee 852		Jared Nicholson	Sandy Schlorff
Pawnee v	Sangamon 2,647		Kenton D. Manning	Tom D. Bowen
Paxton c	Ford 4,525		James E. Kingston	Dawn Fessler
Payson v	Adams 1,066		Norbert Buswell	Cindy Epperson
Pearl v	Pike 187		Dee Holloway	Amy McClenning
Pearl City v	Stephenson 780		Robert Knoup	Cheryl Liebenstein
Pecatonica v	Winnebago 1,997		Robert V. Whetsel	Ginger R. Binger

INCORPORATED CITIES, TOWNS AND VILLAGES OF ILLINOIS
(Continued)

City (c), town (t) or village (v)		County	Population	Mayor or President	Clerk
Pekin	c	Peoria, Tazewell	33,857	R. David Tebben	Sue E. McMillan
Peoria	c	Peoria	112,936	David P. Ransburg	Mary L. Haynes
Peoria Heights	v	Peoria	6,635	Earl Carter	Dyrke Maricle
Peotone	v	Will	3,385	Dennis Baran	Donna L. Werner
Percy	v	Randolph	942	Loyde Hyde	Chrissy Taylor
Perry	v	Pike	437	Rex Olson	Martha Witham
Peru	c	LaSalle	9,835	Donald L. Baker	Judith A. Heuser
Pesotum	v	Champaign	521	Scott Morris	Cristina Mobley
Petersburg	c	Menard	2,299	Diane S. Kube	Beverly J. Leinberger
Phillipstown	v	White	28	Kenneth Wilson	Kim Whitley
Philo	v	Champaign	1,314	Craig Eckert	Eileen Painter
Phoenix	v	Cook	2,157	Terry Wells	Johnnie M. Lane
Pierron	v	Bond, Madison	653	Kent L. Weiss	Tammy Creasy
Pinckneyville	c	Perry	5,464	K. Kirwan Heisner	Frances I. Thomas
Pingree Grove	v	Kane	124	Vern E. Wester	Mary Carol Peschke
Piper City	v	Ford	781	Marcus Clark	Barbara Cupples
Pittsburg	v	Williamson	575	Keith Violett	Rosetta Sue Mandrell
Pittsfield	c	Pike	4,211	Larry Snyder	Cindy Kvorka
Plainfield	v	Will	13,038	Richard Rock	Susan Janik
Plainville	v	Adams	248	William Beckman	Richard Henderson
Plano	c	Kendall	5,633	William Roberts	Deanna Brown
Pleasant Hill	v	Pike	1,047	William R. Graham	Wyvetta Menke
Pleasant Plains	v	Sangamon	777	Jim Verkuilen	Cindy Sommer
Plymouth	v	Hancock	562	Shelva Schoonover	Phyllis Smith
Pocahontas	v	Bond	727	David L. Clark	Donna Swofford
Polo	c	Ogle	2,477	Jeff Van Dosten	Susan Corbitt
Pontiac	c	Livingston	11,864	G. Michael Ingles	Sharon L. Dunham
Pontoon Beach	v	Madison	5,620	Harold J. Denham	Susan Daugherty
Pontoosuc	v	Hancock	171	Robert Durand	Tammy Hagmeier
Poplar Grove	v	Boone	1,368	Roger Day	Martha Suhr
Port Byron	v	Rock Island	1,535	Don Johnson	Janet Fletcher
Posen	v	Cook	4,730	Kevin J. Whitney	Veronica Grabowski
Potomac	v	Vermilion	681	Rodney Rogers	Shelly Cessna
Prairie City	v	McDonough	461	Kenny Sharp	Gail Carley
Prairie du Rocher	v	Randolph	613	Larry Durbin	Wilma L. Candler
Prairie Grove	v	McHenry	960	Susan M. Friedman	William J. Hill
Princeton	c	Bureau	7,501	Keith L. Cain	Clyde W. Wray
Princeville	v	Peoria	1,621	Sidney Stahl	Patricia L. Duthoo
Prophetstown	c	Whiteside	2,023	Howard "Bud" Thompson	Karen Stuart
Prospect Heights	c	Cook	17,081	Edward Rotchford	Carol L. Jung
Pulaski	v	Pulaski	274	Dean L. Rogan, Sr.	Ardis Ward
Prospect Heights	c	Cook	17,081	Edward Rotchford	Carol L. Jung
Pulaski	v	Pulaski	274	Dean L. Rogan, Sr.	Ardis Ward
Quincy	c	Adams	40,366	Charles W. Scholz	Janet Hutmacher
Radom	v	Washington	395	Denise Liggett	Robert G. Frazier
Raleigh	v	Saline	330	Clifton Whitlock	Angie Stricklin
Ramsey	v	Fayette	1,056	David Hinton	Lois Hopfensperger
Rankin	v	Vermilion	617	Dana Alderson	Earline Probasco
Ransom	v	LaSalle	409	John Rzasa	Dale Johnson
Rantoul	v	Champaign	12,857	Neal Williams	Don Frye
Rapids City	v	Rock Island	953	Marj Dolan	Emilie Price
Raritan	v	Henderson	140	Gary R. Powless	James Blender
Raymond	v	Montgomery	927	Dennis Held	Judith Y. Martin
Red Bud	c	Randolph	3,422	John H. Horrell	Larry Ehlers
Reddick	v	Kankakee, Livingston	219	William T. O'Brien	Carrie L. Inczauskis
Redmon	v	Edgar	199	Joel Wood	Ruth A. Zane
Reynolds	v	Mercer, Rock Island	508	Marvin Remrey	Mark Allen
Richmond	v	McHenry	1,091	Kevin Brusek	Mary Buchert
Richton Park	v	Cook	12,533	Richard Reinbold	Mary E. Pierce
Richview	v	Washington	308	Kenneth Sodko	Rita Ebbs
Ridge Farm	v	Vermilion	912	Marvin Arnett	Carolyn Gallagher
Ridgway	v	Gallatin	928	Robert R. Rider	Lee Fillingim
Ridott	v	Stephenson	159	Harold Mathiot	Darlene J. Greenfield
Ringwood	v	McHenry	471	Richard E. Mack	Sue Kennebeck
Rio	v	Knox	240	Edward Gullstrand	Dee Litchfield
Ripley	v	Brown	103	Bob Livingston	Mary M. Winner
River Forest	v	Cook	11,635	Frank M. Paris	Patrick J. Hosty
River Grove	v	Cook	10,668	Thomas J. Tarpey	Joseph R. Compel
Riverdale	v	Cook	15,055	Zenovia Q. Evans	Joyce E. Forbes
Riverside	v	Cook	8,895	Harold J. Wiaduck	Coughlin, John F.
Riverton	v	Sangamon	3,048	Joe Rusciolelli	Connie Blissett
Riverwoods	v	Lake	3,843	William S. Kaplan	Eileen Stanger
Roanoke	v	Woodford	1,994	Keith Klein	Susan Bachman
Robbins	v	Cook	6,635	Irene H. Brodie	Palma L. James
Roberts	v	Ford	387	Richard Flessner	Viola Kumpf
Robinson	c	Crawford	6,822	Wallace W. Dean	Sandra Jared
Rochelle	c	Ogle	9,424	Robert Gingerich	Bruce W. McKinney

449

INCORPORATED CITIES, TOWNS AND VILLAGES OF ILLINOIS
(Continued)

City (c), town (t) or village (v)		County	Population	Mayor or President	Clerk
Rochester	v	Sangamon	2,893	David L. Armstrong	Lisa K. Sandidge
Rock City	v	Stephenson	313	Andy Lamm	Jonna Lamm
Rock Falls	c	Whiteside	9,580	Edward M. Mulvaney	Suzanne Dir
Rock Island	c	Rock Island	39,684	Mark W. Schwiebert	Jeanne F. Paggen
Rockbridge	v	Greene	189	Jack McManus	Shane L. Feltes
Rockdale	v	Will	1,888	Henry Berry	Thomas Fitzgerald
Rockford	c	Winnebago	150,115	Douglas P. Scott	
Rockton	v	Winnebago	5,296	Dale Adams	Janice Eaton-Modersohn
Rockwood	v	Randolph	41	Virginia Mansker	Tammy Smith
Rolling Meadows	c	Cook	24,604	Thomas F. Menzel	Patti Weicker
Romeoville	v	Will	21,153	Fred Dewald	Prudence Pukula
Roodhouse	c	Greene	2,214	Jim L. Crabtree	Brenda Young
Roscoe	v	Winnebago	6,244	Lowell Smith	Bonnie L. Miles
Rose Hill	v	Jasper	79	Adam Matson	Shirley McFarland
Roselle	v	Cook, DuPage	23,115	Gayle Smolinski	Linda J. McDermott
Rosemont	v	Cook	4,224	Donald E. Stephens	Rosalie Lennstrom
Roseville	v	Warren	1,083	F. Michael Kirby	Carla Oliver
Rosiclare	c	Hardin	1,213	Harold Cowsert	Yvonne Long
Rossville	v	Vermilion	1,217	Terry Prillaman	Chris Pearson
Round Lake	v	Lake	5,842	Bill Gentes	Jeanne Kristan
Round Lake Beach	v	Lake	25,859	Richard H. Hill	Sylvia Valadez
Round Lake Heights	v	Lake	1,347	Terrance M. Lumpkins	Deborah A. McIntyre
Round Lake Park	v	Lake	6,038	Ila M. Bauer	Linda M. Lucassen
Roxana	v	Madison	1,547	Fred L. Hubbard	Nona Austin
Royal	v	Champaign	279	Robert J. Vilven	Debra Rupert
Royal Lakes	v	Macoupin	190	London Simmons	Geraldine Jackson
Royalton	v	Franklin	1,130	Christy Brower	Toni K. Buckingham
Ruma	v	Randolph	260	Richard Dugan	Gay Lynn Kruse
Rushville	c	Schuyler	3,212	Lynn D. Smith	Rebecca D. Root
Russellville	v	Lawrence	119	Kenneth D. Hoke	Betty Schulz
Rutland	v	LaSalle	354	Charlotte R. Rupe	Debbie Dennis
Sadorus	v	Champaign	426	John Wood	Teresa Spence
Sailor Springs	v	Clay	128	Delbert Payne	Amy Britton
Saint Anne	v	Kankakee	1,212	Ronald R. Grubbs	Kenneth Blum
Saint Augustine	v	Knox	152	Tim Randall	Roger Springer
Saint Charles	c	DuPage, Kane	27,896	Susan L. Klinkhamer	Kristie A. Nephew
Saint David	v	Fulton	587	Robert D. Shaw	Rebecca Ellsworth
Saint Elmo	c	Fayette	1,456	Chris Worman	Cheryl A. Watson
Saint Francisville	c	Lawrence	759	Stanley B. Williams	Amy Theriac
Saint Jacob	v	Madison	801	Raymond Muniz	Kelley Robards
Saint Johns	v	Perry	218	Todd Woodside	Sandra McCune
Saint Joseph	v	Champaign	2,912	B. J. Hackler	Tiffany McElroy-Smetzer
Saint Libory	v	St. Clair	583	Phyllis Behrman	Lisa M. Ervie
Saint Peter	v	Fayette	386	Chris W. Miller	Beverly J. Lotz
Sainte Marie	v	Jasper	261	Bil Hartrichl	Annette M. Kirts
Salem	c	Marion	7,909	Leonard E. Ferguson	Jane Marshall
San Jose	v	Logan, Mason	696	Duane Worlow	Joy Zimmerman
Sandoval	v	Marion	1,434	Jerry Ratterman	Cora Oehmke
Sandwich	c	DeKalb, Kendall	6,509	Tom Thomas	Barbara G. Olson
Sauget	v	St. Clair	249	Paul Sauget	Betty Long Wilson
Sauk Village	v	Cook, Will	10,411	Roger G. Peckham	Elizabeth Selvey
Saunemin	v	Livingston	456	J. Michael Stoecklin	Nancy Haag
Savanna	c	Carroll	3,542	Eugene T. Flack	Walter I. Shrake
Savoy	v	Champaign	4,476	Robert C. McCleary	Marilyn I. Deal
Sawyerville	v	Macoupin	295	Phyllis Spurney	Mary Ann Vadalabene
Saybrook	v	McLean	764	Ronald E. Stauffer	Vicky Quinn
Scales Mound	v	JoDaviess	401	Kenneth Deckert	Margaret M. Townsend
Schaumburg	v	Cook	75,386	Al Larson	Penny M. Dietrich
Schiller Park	v	Cook	11,850	Anna Montana	Claudia L. Irsuto
Schram City	v	Montgomery	653	Michael Rhoades	Janet K. Stewart
Sciota	v	McDonough	58	David Baker	Don Collins
Scottville	v	Macoupin	140	Roy D. Close	Sandra VanBebber
Seaton	v	Mercer	242	David W. Staley	Vicki S. Chism
Seatonville	v	Bureau	303	Richard Piontek	Ellen Engel
Secor	v	Woodford	379	Mike LaFramboise	Angela Seggerman
Seneca	v	Grundy, LaSalle	2,053	David F. Yeck	JoAnne Huffman
Sesser	c	Franklin	2,128	Ned Mitchell	Marilyn Stacey
Shabbona	v	DeKalb	929	Patrick McCormick	Claudia Hicks
Shannon	v	Carroll	854	Jim Mantle	Denise Hammer
Shawneetown	c	Gallatin	1,410	Stevie Scates	Mary Frances Skaggs
Sheffield	v	Bureau	946	William Rosenow	Sheila Yepsen
Shelbyville	c	Shelby	4,971	William B. Shoaff	Carrie M. Jones
Sheldon	v	Iroquois	1,232	Frank E. Davenport	Teresa J. Seng
Sheridan	v	LaSalle	2,411	John S. Martin	Sandra K. Reno
Sherman	v	Sangamon	2,871	Frank Meredith	Karen J. Franklin
Sherrard	v	Mercer	694	Alfred Rissetto	Marilyn Davis
Shiloh	v	St. Clair	7,643	James A. Vernier	Brenda A. Kern

City (c), town (t) or village (v)		County	Population	Mayor or President	Clerk
Shipman	v	Macoupin	655	Michael Vieregge	Stacey Greenwalt
Shorewood	v	Will	7,686	Richard E. Chapman	Julia A. Russell
Shumway	v	Effingham	217	Henry Sutter	Derrick Helmbacher
Sibley	v	Ford	329	Camilla Lohmeyer	Helen Andreae
Sidell	v	Vermilion	626	Janet Nees	Susie Koss
Sidney	v	Champaign	1,062	Janet Brown	Janet Akers
Sigel	t	Shelby	386	Sheryl Long	Diane Mette
Silvis	c	Rock Island	7,269	Lyle E. Lohse	Barbara J. Fox
Simpson	v	Johnson	54	William Russell	Shirley Russell
Sims	v	Wayne	273	Hosa Caldwell	Pam Nadolski
Skokie	v	Cook	63,348	George Van Dusen	Marlene Williams
Sleepy Hollow	v	Kane	3,553	Stephen K. Pickett	Norine Olson
Smithboro	v	Bond	200	S. Susan Moore	Donna Sloan
Smithfield	v	Fulton	214	Glen Manuel	Deborah Hedden
Smithton	v	St. Clair	2,248	Virgil J. Becker	Deborah Boeving
Somonauk	v	DeKalb, LaSalle	1,295	James Back	Laura Winebaugh
Sorento	v	Bond	601	Brett Kunkel	Mary Beth Viccone
South Barrington	v	Cook	3,760	Frank J. Munao	Donna Wilkins Wood
South Beloit	c	Winnebago	5,397	William Frisbee	Marilyn J. Hartley
South Chicago Heights	v	Cook	3,970	David L. Owen	Melinda Villarreal
South Elgin	v	Kane	16,100	James W. Hansen	Margaret M. Gray
South Holland	v	Cook	22,147	Don A. DeGraff	Ruth DeVries
South Jacksonville	v	Morgan	3,475	Gordon D. Jumper	Linda Douglass
South Pekin	v	Tazewell	1,162	Richard Huse	Monica Carrington
South Roxana	v	Madison	1,888	Danny Wilcox	Tina Carpenter
South Wilmington	v	Grundy	621	Richard Alderson	Barbara McGurk
Southern View	v	Sangamon	1,695	Howard Martin	Martha L. Kurtz
Sparland	v	Marshall	504	Phillip E. Murphy	Tamara Deffenbaugh
Sparta	c	Randolph	4,486	Dennis L. Moody	Shirley A. Reimer
Spaulding	v	Sangamon	559	Joe H. Burge	Rosemary Barber
Spillertown	v	Williamson	220	Dale Whitehead	Sandra Stanton
Spring Bay	v	Woodford	436	John McCarty	Dianne Cotton
Spring Grove	v	McHenry	3,880	Robert M. Martens	Sandi Rusher
Spring Valley	c	Bureau	5,398	Joseph A. Taliano	Rebecca L. Hansen
Springerton	v	White	134	Danny Rose	Patty Clark
Springfield	c	Sangamon	111,454	Karen Hasara	Norma Graves
Standard	v	Putnam	256	James Reno	Angela Fay
Standard City	v	Macoupin	138	Steve Bormida	Joanne C. Stutsman
Stanford	v	McLean	670	George Brawner	Phyllis Fitch
Staunton	c	Macoupin	5,030	Michael R. Arnold	Marilyn A. Herbeck
Steeleville	v	Randolph	2,077	Michael Armstrong	Darlene Jaskowiak
Steger	v	Cook, Will	9,682	Louis Sherman	Carmen S. Recupito, Jr.
Sterling	c	Whiteside	15,451	Theo M. Aggen	Rosemary C. Coughlin
Steward	v	Lee	271	Brian Siwici	Angie Burkhart
Stewardson	v	Shelby	747	Ed Meers	Donald Tate
Stickney	v	Cook	6,148	Donald J. Tabor	Arthur E. Rawers
Stillman Valley	v	Ogle	1,048	James A. Leather	Anne Hildebrand
Stockton	v	JoDaviess	1,926	Rodney Brandt	Gayle Lingle
Stone Park	v	Cook	5,127	Benjamine Mazzulla	Maria Castrejon
Stonefort	v	Saline, Williamson	292	George Jackson	Leanett McFarland
Stonington	v	Christian	960	Frank Paulek	Lowell L. Swearingen
Stoy	v	Crawford	119	John D. Baud	Marjorie Baud
Strasburg	v	Shelby	603	James Connell	Roger Kull
Strawn	v	Livingston	104	Charles Goembel	Wendy Brucker
Streamwood	v	Cook	36,407	Billie D. Roth	Kittie L. Kopitke
Streator	c	LaSalle, Livingston	14,190	Ray Schmitt	Pamela K. Leonard
Stronghurst	v	Henderson	896	Eric Chockley	Eileen Cargill
Sublette	v	Lee	456	John Stenzel	Tina Strawn
Sugar Grove	v	Kane	3,909	P. Sean Michels	Cynthia Welsch
Sullivan	c	Moultrie	4,326	Richard M. Dunscomb	Floyd Buckalew
Summerfield	v	St. Clair	472	Lawrence Yates	Karen Wehrle
Summit	v	Cook	10,637	Joseph W. Strzelczyk	Andrew Zambrzycki
Sumner	c	Lawrence	1,022	Betty Brian	Blanche Piper
Sun River Terrace	v	Kankakee	383	Shirley Byrd	Ruth Collins
Swansea	v	St. Clair	10,579	Michael S. Buehlhorn	James V. Fields
Sycamore	c	DeKalb	12,020	John L. Swedberg	Candy Smith
Symerton	v	Will	106	Al Darr	Patricia Karr
Table Grove	v	Fulton	396	Larry Inman	Angela Danner
Tallula	v	Menard	638	Gary Espenschied	Jane King
Tamaroa	v	Perry	740	William C. Place	Judith E. Bathon
Tamms	v	Alexander	724	Carol Mitchell	Sharon Abercrombie
Tampico	v	Whiteside	772	Larry J. Specht	Linda Taets
Taylor Springs	v	Montgomery	583	Carl Hallers	Cindy Laurent
Taylorville	c	Christian	11,427	Jim Montgomery	Pam Peabody
Tennessee	v	McDonough	144	William Brewer	Sharon K. Foulk
Teutopolis	v	Effingham	1,559	Jerry Weber	Sharon Will
Thawville	v	Iroquois	258	Ray Johnson	Vicki Wilborn
Thayer	v	Sangamon	750	Brian Wood	Susan Evans

INCORPORATED CITIES, TOWNS AND VILLAGES OF ILLINOIS
(Continued)

City (c), town (t) or village (v)	County	Population	Mayor or President	Clerk
Thebes v	Alexander 478		James L. Sutton	Sheila Dodson
Third Lake v	Lake 1,355		Donna Golchert	Patricia Beggan
Thomasboro v	Champaign 1,233		Lionel Grilo	Joan E. Hall
Thompsonville v	Franklin 571		Ralph Sprague	Patricia Clark
Thomson v	Carroll 559		Merrie Jo Enloe	Arleta J. Vian
Thornton v	Cook 2,582		Jack C. Swan	Cheryl L. Bult
Tilden v	Randolph 922		Willard McBride	Verna Rickenberg
Tilton v	Vermilion 2,976		David Phillips	Connie S. Weddle
Timberlane v	Boone 234		Stephen M. Rapp	Sylvia Gorman
Time v	Pike 29		Conel Rogers	Virginia A. Claus
Tinley Park v	Cook, Will 48,401		Edward J. Zabrocki	Frank W. German
Tiskilwa v	Bureau 787		C. W. Hamilton	Kathryn Nordstrom
Toledo v	Cumberland 1,166		Larry A Stults	Joyce Lashnet
Tolono v	Champaign 2,700		Cecil A. McCormick	Barbara Humer
Toluca c	Marshall 1,339		Larry Harber	Roanna Richard
Tonica v	LaSalle 685		Roger Thompson	Hank McClenning
Topeka .... t	Mason 90		Dave Mason	Gloria Marshall
Toulon c	Stark 1,400		Alfred Hill........................	Sandy Langdon
Tovey v	Christian 516		Gayla L. Gudgel	Diane Bouvet
Towanda v	McLean 493		Richard McGuire	Donna Coit
Tower Hill v	Shelby 609		Fanny L. Urfer	Deborah I. Carroll
Tower Lakes v	Lake 1,310		Len Kuskowski	Kathleen Leitner
Tremont v	Tazewell 2,029		Michael Dunlap	Gerald B. Madsen
Trenton c	Clinton 2,610		Margaret Conley	Carol S. Metzger
Trout Valley v	McHenry 599		Steve Barrett	Suzanne Johnson
Troy c	Madison 8,524		Tom Caraker, Sr.	Tammy Mitchell
Troy Grove v	LaSalle 305		Marwood Kidd	Deborah Wujek
Tuscola c	Douglas 4,448		Daniel J. Kleiss	Elizabeth A. Leamon
Ullin v	Pulaski 779		Mike Dewitt	Renee Wright
Union v	McHenry 576		Robert Wagner	Phyllis Schauer
Union Hill v	Kankakee 66		Hugh VanVoorst	Barbara Bumpous
University Park v	Cook, Will 6,662		Thomas V. Johnson	Irma A. Berry
Urbana c	Champaign 36,395		Tod Satterthwaite	Phyllis D. Clark
Ursa v	Adams 595		Carl R. Bartlett	Steven Harms
Valier v	Franklin 662		Martin H. Buchanan	JoAnn Girten
Valley City v	Pike 14		James E. Phillips	Linda R. Kells
Valmeyer v	Monroe 608		Dennis F. Schreder	Laurie A. Brown
Vandalia c	Fayette 6,975		Ricky J. Gottman	Peggy R. Bowen
Varna v	Marshall 436		Robert Skaggs	M. Lynn Lewis
Venedy v	Washington 137		Earl Martens	Mark Martens
Venice c	Madison 2,528		Tyrone Echols	Wilbert Glasper
Vergennes v	Jackson 491		Donald H. Wisely	William C. Batteau
Vermilion v	Edgar 239		Kenneth R. Miller	Keith Laughlin
Vermont v	Fulton 792		Robert Young	Maureen Richey
Vernon v	Marion 178		Chester Burks	Gayle Tappy
Vernon Hills v	Lake 20,120		Roger Byrne	Jeanne Schwartz
Verona v	Grundy 257		Jeffrey Snyder	Jackie Snyder
Versailles v	Brown 567		James Rausch	Iona LeMaster
Victoria v	Knox 323		John Rask	Gail Hatch
Vienna c	Johnson 1,234		Paul V. Gage	Barbara Warmack
Villa Grove c	Douglas 2,553		Ronald H. Hunt	
Villa Park v	DuPage 22,075		Rae Rupp Srch	Suzanne Ellis
Viola v	Mercer 956		Kirk W. Doonan	Jody A. Nesbitt
Virden c	Macoupin, Sangamon 3,488		Donnie Neighbors	Judy Berry
Virgil v	Kane 266		Mike Sauber	Jean Hardt
Virginia c	Cass 1,728		David C. Sinclair	Sarah L. Fanning
Volo v	Lake 180		Burnell Russell	LaVerne Drake
Wadsworth v	Lake 3,083		Evelyn Hoselton	Lynn Schlosser
Waggoner v	Montgomery 245		Max Stewart	Avis Apps
Walnut v	Bureau 1,461		Don Steele	Judith A. Wilcoxen
Walnut Hill v	Marion 109		Roger E. Donoho	Melissa Donoho
Walshville v	Montgomery 89		Darlyne Sykes	Michelle Hutchins
Waltonville v	Jefferson 422		George Gifford	Betty Schmitt
Wamac c	Clinton, Marion/Wash 1,378		Larry Greene	Marian Suhl
Wapella v	DeWitt 651		Tom Brame	Jane Buraglio
Warren v	JoDaviess 1,496		Gregory A. Stake	Emily Whitman
Warrensburg v	Macon 1,289		Leland Hackl	Mary Christerson
Warrenville c	DuPage 13,363		Vivian M. Lund	Emily J. Larson
Warsaw c	Hancock 1,793		Jerry Baker	Kathy Thompson
Washburn v	Marshall, Woodford 1,147		Steve Forney	Bridget Marquez
Washington c	Tazewell 11,332		Gary W. Manier	Carol K. Moss
Washington Park v	St. Clair 5,345		Sherman Sorrell	Anthony Nesbitt
Wataga v	Knox 857		Joe Blickem	Georgia Lepisto
Waterloo c	Monroe 7,614		Emmett Rusteberg	Debra A. Augustine
Waterman v	DeKalb 1,224		Roger Bosworth	Kathy Bock
Watseka c	Iroquois 5,670		Ted Martin	Diane Tegtmeyer
Watson v	Effingham 729		Wanda Ashbaugh	Cherrie Foreman

INCORPORATED CITIES, TOWNS AND VILLAGES OF ILLINOIS
(Concluded)

City (c), town (t) or village (v)	County	Population	Mayor or President	Clerk
Wauconda v	Lake	9,448	James Eschenbauch	Mary C. Taylor
Waukegan c	Lake	87,901	Daniel T. Drew	Wayne Motley
Waverly c	Morgan	1,346	Ernest L. Cleveland	Patricia J. Whalen
Wayne v	DuPage, Kane	2,137	Eileen Phipps	Patricia Engstrom
Wayne City v	Wayne	1,089	Billy Choate	Diana Wood
Waynesville v	DeWitt	452	Michael Furman	Lana Shipley
Weldon v	DeWitt	440	Steve Followell	Nancy Pecora
Wellington v	Iroquois	264	Grover Wise	Rena Bruens
Wenona c	Marshall	1,065	James Kupec	Carol E. Volker
Wenonah v	Montgomery	44	Robert Bauman	Twila Presnell
West Brooklyn v	Lee	174	John J. Gehant, Sr.	Jodi Pattermann
West Chicago c	DuPage	23,469	Michael Fortner	Nancy M. Smith
West City v	Franklin	716	Le Roy Mumbower	Shirley N. Smith
West Dundee v	Kane	5,428	Larry A. Keller	Barbara Haines
West Frankfort c	Franklin	8,196	Jack Woolard	Cathy Dinn
West Peoria c	Peoria	4,762	James Dillon	Lori Simmons
West Point v	Hancock	195	Stacy Meeks	Tracy Winfrey
West Salem v	Edwards	1,001	Robert E. Stevens	Camilla Tyler
Westchester v	Cook	16,824	John J. Sinde	Kathryn J. Hayes-Gaudry
Western Springs v	Cook	12,493	John Kravcik	Jeanine M. Jasica
Westfield v	Clark	678	Roger Tinsman	Joyce Wilson
Westmont v	DuPage	24,554	William H. Rahn	Virginia Szymski
Westville v	Vermilion	3,175	Michael Weese	Sandra McElroy
Wheaton c	DuPage	55,416	C. James Carr	Emily M. Consolazio
Wheeler v	Jasper	119	Robert Flowers	Linda Flowers
Wheeling v	Cook, Lake	34,496	Greg Klatecki	Elaine E. Simpson
White Ash v	Williamson	268	Rick LaBotte	Vickie Davis
White City v	Macoupin	221	Pamela A. Simmons	Paula Hubert
White Hall c	Greene	2,629	Harold L. Brimm	Sue Reno
Williamsfield v	Knox	620	James Mackie	Mary Rice
Williamson v	Madison	251	Larry Benardin	Sherry Warren
Williamsville v	Sangamon	1,439	S. Lee Barnes	Delores Fowler
Willisville v	Perry	694	William J. Eyer	Janice Eyer
Willow Hill v	Jasper	250	Randy Smith	Marenna Hall
Willow Springs v	Cook	5,027	Terrance Carr	Sue M. Fredrickson
Willowbrook v	DuPage	8,967	Gary Pretzer	Patrick Spatafore
Wilmette v	Cook	27,651	Nancy M. Canafax	Michael Earl
Wilmington v	Greene	120	Robert T. Ridings	Carol J. Little
Wilmington c	Will	5,134	Tony McGann	James C. Johnston
Wilsonville v	Macoupin	604	Tony Jackson	Deno J. Filippini
Winchester c	Scott	1,650	Retha Anders	Mancel Day
Windsor c	Shelby	1,125	Eric Bennett	Linda Voris
Windsor v	Mercer	720	Michael Peterson	Claudine D. Johnson
Winfield v	DuPage	8,718	John D. Kirschbaum	Jeni Ozark
Winnebago v	Winnebago	2,958	David Hassel	Sally Jo Huggins
Winnetka v	Cook	12,419	Michael F. Duhl	Douglas G. Williams
Winslow v	Stephenson	345	John Ammon	Pat Miller
Winthrop Harbor v	Lake	6,670	Robert D. Loy	Jana J. Lee
Witt c	Montgomery	991	Ronald R. Rufus	Nancy J. Hughes
Wonder Lake v	McHenry	1,345	William Madeja	Susan Weir
Wood Dale c	DuPage	13,535	Kenneth P. Johnson	Shirley J. Siebert
Wood River c	Madison	11,296	David L. Ayres	Jan Sneed
Woodhull v	Henry	809	Lloyd Carlson	Sally Riddell
Woodland v	Iroquois	319	Evelyn Suver	Lori Duden
Woodlawn v	Jefferson	630	Steve Langa	Marcia Tinsley
Woodridge v	DuPage	30,934	William F. Murphy	Eileene Nystrom
Woodson v	Morgan	559	Mike Crowley	Nikki Hardy
Woodstock c	McHenry	20,151	Alan D. Cornue	Cindy Luckey
Worden v	Madison	905	Kenneth L. Wiesemann	Carol S. Lovsey
Worth v	Cook	11,047	Edward Guzdziol	Bonnie Price
Wyanet v	Bureau	1,028	John M. Gordon	Betty Knudsen
Wyoming c	Stark	1,424	Daniel Hardman	Judy St. John
Xenia v	Clay	407	Bryan Land	Gene Pieplow
Yale v	Jasper	97	Sanford Andrews	Jeanette Hickox
Yates City v	Knox	725	Denise Best	Pamela A. Ehens
Yorkville c	Kendall	6,189	Arthur F. Prochaska	Jackie Milschewski
Zeigler c	Franklin	1,669	Dennis Mitchell	Pamela S. Perry
Zion c	Lake	22,866	Lane Harrison	Judy L. Mackey

ILLINOIS AT A GLANCE

General Information
Population (2000) 12,419,293
Resident Births (1999) 182,027
Resident Deaths (1998) 104,070
Personal Income (1999, in millions) $377,744
Per Capita Income (1999) $31,145
Length (in miles) 379
Width (in miles) 210
Land Area (in square miles) 55,593
Highest Point (in feet; Charles Mound, Jo Daviess County) 1,235
Lowest Point (in feet; Fort Defiance Point, Alexander County) 279

Education
Public Schools (1999-2000)
    Elementary Schools 2,652
    Junior High Schools 600
    High Schools 661
    Others 377
Non-Public Schools (1999-2000)
    Elementary Schools 1,012
    High Schools 123
    Unit 155
    Special Education Schools & Others 101
Colleges and Universities (1999-2000)
    Non-Public Institutions 123
    Public University Campuses 12
    Community College Campuses 48

Natural and Manufactured Resources
Coal Mines (1999) 20
Coal production in tons (1999) .... 40.3 million
Grain production in bushels (1999)
    Corn .... 1.49 billion
    Soybeans .... 443.1 million
    Wheat .... 60.6 million
    Sorghum .... 9.2 million
Manufacturing Establishments (1998)
    Illinois Plants 17,975
    Primary Metal Industries 351
    Iron and Steel Foundries 61

Services
Banks
    State Banks (including foreign, 2000) 519
    National Banks (2000) 205
Hospitals (1999) 198
Mental Health Centers (2000) 20
Public Libraries (2000) 643
Recreational Areas (2000)
    State Parks 62
    Fish and Wildlife Sites 32
    Historic Sites and State Memorials (2001) 59
    State Forests 6
    Conservation Areas 27
Churches (2001) 15,584

Occupations/Professions
Attorneys (1999) 73,514
Physicians and Surgeons (2001) 39,062
Dentists (2000) 9,084
Registered Nurses (2000) 140,067
Farming (1998) 99,671
Agricultural Services, Forestry and Fishing (1998) 63,376

Transportation
Airports (2000) 120
Highway Miles (2000) 16,717
Railroad Miles (2000) 7,600
Interstate Carriers (2001) 13,819

454

CAPITOL COMPLEX

The **Michael J. Howlett Building** is south of the Capitol. Formerly the Centennial Building, it was erected to commemorate the 100th anniversary of Illinois' admission to the Union as the 21st state. The cornerstone of the $3 million building was laid in 1918, and the building was completed in 1923. Additions in 1928 and 1966 converted the original rectangular structure into a square building while retaining the original classic architectural design. Several departments of the Secretary of State's office are located in the building, and historic flags carried by Illinois regiments during the Civil War, the Spanish-American War and World War I are preserved carefully in display cases in Memorial Hall, just inside the building's two main entrances on the north side.

Immediately west of the Capitol is the **William G. Stratton Building.** Ground was broken for the H-shaped, 448,000-square-foot structure on Feb. 15, 1954, and it was completed some 20 months later at a cost of $11.5 million. It contains the offices of members of the State Senate and House of Representatives as well as some state agencies and departments.

Adjacent to the Margaret Cross Norton Building is the **Illinois State Museum,** designed to display the many historic, artistic and natural treasures of Illinois. The official groundbreaking ceremony was held Jan. 5, 1961, and the $2.2 million building was dedicated on Feb. 4, 1963. The museum has four large exhibit halls, two on each of the first two floors. Curatorial offices and related laboratories and shops are located on the third floor along with the staff's technical library. A replica of a Tlingit Indian totem pole welcomes visitors at the museum's entrance.

The **Attorney General's Building,** east of the Michael J. Howlett Building across Second Street, houses the offices of more than 140 attorneys and support staffers. Construction of the three-story, $2.8 million building began in 1968, and the formal dedication was held on Jan. 27, 1972. Sandblasted architectural concrete was used in the construction of the building's light gray exterior walls, and the interior features a center courtyard.

North of the Capitol is the **Armory**, which replaced the State Arsenal that burned in 1934. This building houses the offices of several divisions of the Illinois State Police. The offices surround a large auditorium with a seating capacity of 6,000, which often has been the site of inauguration ceremonies for state officials.

The **Margaret Cross Norton Building**, just west of the Michael J. Howlett Building, houses the State Archives, a department of the Secretary of State's office. Formerly the Archives Building, it was designed to protect the state's valuable historic records from the hazards of fire, theft and exposure. Construction began in 1936 with aid from the New Deal's Public Works Administration, and the building was completed in 1938 at a cost of $820,000. It is architecturally unique, having no windows on the fourth through seventh floors.

The **Illinois State Library Building** was opened to the public in 1990. The $36 million, 164,000-square-foot structure, just north of the Attorney General's Building, is the first building specifically designed and constructed to house the collections of the Illinois State Library. The building's classic architecture and sandstone walls were chosen to blend with other major buildings of the Capitol Complex.

The **Capitol Visitors' Center**, just west of the William G. Stratton Building, was opened formally on June 8, 1988. Covering two city blocks, the $3.7 million structure provides visitors with parking, information, picnic facilities, vending machines, rest rooms and a spacious, air-conditioned place to relax.

ILLINOIS STATE CAPITOL SCULPTURES

"Monuments and statues are the open books of civilization made to perpetuate the memories of those who have been true and faithful in the battle of life." — Judge Henry S. Baker, dedication of the Pierre Menard statue

The statues and monuments on the grounds of the Illinois State Capitol Building add beauty and dignity to the area while providing a glimpse of Illinois' rich history. Many of the statues immortalize famous Illinoisans, such as Abraham Lincoln, his Democrat rival Stephen Douglas and Civil War Governor Richard Yates. Other memorials pay tribute to those who have given their lives in the line of duty, including Illinois firefighters and police officers.

For a brochure on the *Illinois State Capitol Sculptures: A Walking Tour*, including a map of the Capitol Complex and locations of each sculpture, log on to the Secretary of State's Web site at **www.cyberdriveillinois.com**.

ABRAHAM LINCOLN

In 1913, the Illinois State Art Commission was authorized to secure a new statue of Abraham Lincoln for Illinois' centennial. The 10-foot, 6-inch bronze statue with its large granite base and backdrop stands prominently on the far east Capitol grounds along Second Street. The statue is engraved with Lincoln's "Farewell to Springfield" speech and cost about $50,000. It was dedicated on Oct. 5, 1918, the centennial of the first meeting of the Illinois General Assembly.
Sculptor: Andrew O'Connor, 1918

DR. MARTIN LUTHER KING, JR.

This 300-pound statue cost $25,000 and was first unveiled in the Capitol rotunda on Jan. 14, 1988. Dr. Martin Luther King, Jr. is the first non-Illinois resident to be honored with a statue. Then Secretary of State Jim Edgar said King "merits this special recognition for his contributions to Illinoisans of all colors and creeds." In May 1993, the sculpture was moved to "Freedom Corner" at Second and Capitol streets facing the Lincoln statue, and was rededicated on Sept. 18, 1993.
Sculptor: Geraldine McCullough, 1988

ILLINOIS WORKERS MEMORIAL

Paid for by donations from union members, this 3,000-pound memorial "is dedicated to the memory of the thousands of Illinois workers killed and injured on the job." The bronze sculpture of three workers on top of a polished granite base stands on the north Capitol grounds. The dedication ceremony on April 28, 1992, was organized and moderated by state and national AFL-CIO and labor officials.
Sculptor: Peter Fagan, 1992

PIERRE MENARD

The 8-foot bronze statue of Illinois' first Lieutenant Governor was the first to be placed on the Capitol lawn on May 28, 1886. A French-Canadian, Pierre Menard is depicted trading with a Native American along the Mississippi River. Charles Chouteau, the son of Menard's former business partner, donated about $10,000 for the statue and its 10-foot granite base. The statue was dedicated on Jan. 10, 1888, and moved to its current location on the northwest Capitol lawn in 1918.
Sculptor: John H. Mahoney, 1886

STEPHEN A. DOUGLAS

The "Little Giant's" statue was funded through the same 1913 appropriation as the Abraham Lincoln statue and was produced for about $25,000. Dedication of the Stephen A. Douglas statue — Lincoln's Democrat rival — took place on Oct. 5, 1918. The statue stands near the east entrance of the Capitol Building. Engraved on the base of the statue is Douglas' dying message to his children: "...to obey the laws and support the Constitution of the United States."
Sculptor: Gilbert P. Riswold, 1918

460

EVERETT McKINLEY DIRKSEN

This 11-foot bronze statue on the southeast Capitol lawn was commissioned by the Dirksen Memorial Commission and financed by the State of Illinois. Dirksen served Illinois for 34 years as a Republican Congressman and U.S. Senator. An elephant, donkey and oil can flank his figure, symbolizing his persuasive skills to get Republicans and Democrats to cooperate and enact vital legislation. The monument was dedicated on Sept. 16, 1976, six years after Dirksen's death.
Sculptor: Carl Tolpo, 1975

RICHARD YATES

"The wounded soldier's friend" is inscribed on the granite base of the statue of former Illinois Governor and Senator Richard Yates. The 8-foot bronze statue and its granite base, located on the southeast Capitol lawn, was paid for by the state. During a joint dedication ceremony for the Yates and John M. Palmer statues on Oct. 16, 1923, Yates' son, Richard, a former Governor himself, spoke about his father, whose most brilliant service was during the four tumultuous years of the Civil War.
Sculptor: Albin Polasek, 1921

JOHN M. PALMER

John M. Palmer began his political career as a Democrat but became an outspoken critic against slavery and helped create the Republican Party in 1856. After serving as a general in the Civil War and military governor of Kentucky, he was elected Republican Governor of Illinois in 1868. On March 11, 1891, on the 154th ballot, the General Assembly elected Palmer a Democrat U.S. Senator. The Palmer statue was dedicated during a joint ceremony with the Yates statue on Oct. 16, 1923.
Sculptor: Leonard Crunelle, 1923

THE COAL MINER

At the urging of Vachel Davis, a Southern Illinois coal miner, poet and artist, then State Representative Paul Powell introduced a bill to appropriate $15,000 for the creation of a monument honoring the Illinois coal miner. Davis worked with Tinley Park sculptor John Szaton to transform Davis' famous painting into a 7-foot bronze statue. The statue, which stands proudly on the northeast corner of the Capitol lawn, was dedicated on Oct. 16, 1964. A plaque identifying the sculptor and dedication date was added on Dec. 7, 1981.
Sculptor: John Szaton, 1964

ILLINOIS POLICE OFFICERS MEMORIAL

This memorial, with its life-size bronze figures of a male and a female police officer, was dedicated on Oct. 29, 1990, in memory of Illinois police officers killed in the line of duty. The 13-foot monument has a pedestal and base of red granite and was paid for with $85,000 in public donations. Each May, a ceremony is held at the memorial on the southwest Capitol lawn to honor officers recently killed in the line of duty. Their names are added to the original 643 officers engraved on the surrounding polished black granite slates.
Sculptor: Keith Knoblock, 1990

ILLINOIS FIREFIGHTER MEMORIAL

The Capitol's newest memorial was dedicated on May 13, 1999, "to the firefighters of Illinois who have given their lives in the line of duty and to those who heroically serve with courage, pride and honor." The monument consists of four bronze firefighters and a rescued child on a 14-foot stone cairn. It was built through public contributions and the sale of Firefighter Memorial license plates. A ceremony is held at the memorial near the Stratton Building each May honoring Illinois' fallen firefighters.
Sculptor: Neil Brodin, 1999

Photos by Heather Bradley, Secretary of State photographer.

UNITED STATES SENATORS FROM ILLINOIS

Name	Term of Service	Residence	Remarks
Ninian Edwards, Dem.	1818-1824	Kaskaskia	Resigned.
Jesse B. Thomas, Dem.	1818-1829	Kaskaskia	
John McLean, Dem.	1824-1825	Shawneetown	To succeed Edwards, resigned.
Elias Kent Kane, Dem.	1825-1835	Kaskaskia	To succeed McLean; died Dec. 12, 1835.
John McLean, Dem	1829-1830	Shawneetown	To succeed Thomas; died Oct. 14, 1830.
David J. Baker, Dem.	Nov. 12-Dec. 11, 1830	Kaskaskia	Appointed, to succeed McLean, deceased.
John M. Robinson, Dem.	1830-1841	Carmi	To succeed Baker.
William L.D. Ewing, Dem.	1835-1837	Vandalia	To succeed Kane, deceased.
Richard M. Young, Dem.	1837-1843	Jonesboro	To succeed Ewing.
Samuel McRoberts, Dem.	1841-1843	Waterloo	To succeed Robinson; died Mar. 22, 1843.
Sidney Breese, Dem.	1843-1849	Carlyle	To succeed Young.
James Semple, Dem.	1843-1847	Alton	Appointed, to succeed McRoberts, deceased.
Stephen A. Douglas, Dem.	1847-1861	Quincy	To succeed Semple; died June 3, 1861.
James Shields, Dem.	1849-1855	Springfield	To succeed Breese.
Lyman Trumbull, Anti-Neb. Dem	1855-1873	Belleville	To succeed Shields.
Orville H. Browning, Rep.	1861-1863	Quincy	Appointed, to succeed Douglas, deceased.
William A. Richardson, Dem.	1863-1865	Quincy	To succeed Browning.
Richard Yates, Rep.	1865-1871	Jacksonville	To succeed Richardson.
John A. Logan, Rep.	1871-1877	Chicago	To succeed Yates.
Richard J. Oglesby, Rep.	1873-1879	Decatur	To succeed Trumbull.
David Davis, Ind.	1877-1883	Bloomington	To succeed Logan.
John A. Logan, Rep.	1879-1886	Chicago	To succeed Oglesby; died Dec. 26, 1886.
Shelby M. Cullom, Rep.	1883-1913	Springfield	To succeed Davis.
Charles B. Farwell, Rep.	1887-1891	Chicago	To succeed Logan, deceased.
John M. Palmer, Dem.	1891-1897	Springfield	To succeed Farwell.
William E. Mason, Rep.	1897-1903	Chicago	To succeed Palmer.
Albert J. Hopkins, Rep.	1903-1909	Aurora	To succeed Mason.
* William Lorimer, Rep.	1909-1912	Chicago	To succeed Hopkins.
James Hamilton Lewis, Dem	1913-1919	Chicago	To succeed Cullom.
Lawrence Y. Sherman, Rep.	1913-1921	Springfield	In place of Lorimer.
Medill McCormick, Rep.	1919-1925	Chicago	To succeed Lewis.
William B. McKinley, Rep.	1921-1927	Champaign	To succeed Sherman.
Charles S. Deneen, Rep.	1925-1931	Chicago	To succeed McCormick.
† Frank L. Smith, Rep.	1927	Dwight	To succeed McKinley.
Otis F. Glenn, Rep.	1928-1933	Murphysboro	In place of Frank L. Smith.
James Hamilton Lewis, Dem.	1931-1939	Chicago	To succeed Deneen; died April 9, 1939.
William H. Dieterich, Dem.	1933-1939	Beardstown	To succeed Glenn.
Scott W. Lucas, Dem.	1939-1951	Havana	To succeed Dieterich.
James M. Slattery, Dem.	1939-1940	Chicago	Appointed, to succeed Lewis, deceased.
C. Wayland Brooks, Rep.	1940-1949	Chicago	To succeed Slattery.
Paul H. Douglas, Dem.	1949-1967	Chicago	To succeed C. Wayland Brooks.
Everett McKinley Dirksen, Rep.	1951-1969	Pekin	To succeed Scott W. Lucas; died Sept. 7, 1969.
Charles H. Percy, Rep.	1967-1985	Kenilworth	To succeed Douglas.
Ralph T. Smith, Rep.	1969-1970	Alton	Appointed, to succeed Dirksen, deceased.
Adlai E. Stevenson III, Dem.	1970-1981	Chicago	To succeed Smith; resigned as State Treasurer to be sworn in as U.S. Senator.
Alan J. Dixon, Dem.	1981-1993	Belleville	To succeed Stevenson.
Paul Simon, Dem.	1985-1997	Makanda	To succeed Percy.
Carol Moseley-Braun, Dem.	1993-1999	Chicago	To succeed Dixon.
Richard J. Durbin, Dem.	1997-2003	Springfield	To succeed Simon.
Peter G. Fitzgerald, Rep.	1999-2005	Inverness	To succeed Moseley-Braun.

*Unseated, election being declared illegal by Senate.
†Refused his seat by action of the Senate.

GOVERNORS OF ILLINOIS

Name	Date of commission or qualification	From what county	Remarks
Shadrach Bond, Dem.	Oct. 6, 1818	St. Clair	
Edward Coles, Dem.	Dec. 5, 1822	Madison	
Ninian Edwards, Dem.	Dec. 6, 1826	Madison	Territorial Governor, 1809-1818.
John Reynolds, Dem.	Dec. 6, 1830	St. Clair	Resigned Nov. 17, 1834, to become Representative in Congress; succeeded by William L.D. Ewing.
William L. D. Ewing, Dem.	Nov. 17, 1834	Fayette	Acting Lieutenant Governor; became Governor during interim between Reynolds' resignation and election to Congress and the election of Governor Joseph Duncan.
Joseph Duncan, Dem.	Dec. 3, 1834	Morgan	
Thomas Carlin, Dem.	Dec. 7, 1838	Greene	
Thomas Ford, Dem	Dec. 8, 1842	Ogle	
Augustus C. French, Dem.	Dec. 9, 1846 Jan. 8, 1849	Crawford	Re-elected under the Constitution of 1848.
Joel Aldrich Matteson, Dem.	Jan. 10, 1853	Will	
William H. Bissell, Rep.	Jan. 12, 1857	Monroe	Died March 18, 1860; succeeded by John Wood, Lieutenant Governor.
John Wood, Rep.	Mar. 21, 1860	Adams	
Richard Yates, Rep.	Jan. 14, 1861	Morgan	
Richard J. Oglesby, Rep.	Jan. 16, 1865	Macon	
John M. Palmer, Rep.	Jan. 11, 1869	Macoupin	
Richard J. Oglesby, Rep.	Jan. 13, 1873	Macon	Resigned Jan. 23, 1873, to become U.S. Senator; succeeded by John L. Beveridge, Lieutenant Governor.
John L. Beveridge, Rep.	Jan. 23, 1873	Cook	
Shelby Moore Cullom, Rep	Jan. 8, 1877 Jan. 10, 1881	Sangamon	Resigned Feb. 8, 1883, to become U.S. Senator; succeeded by John M. Hamilton, Lieutenant Governor.
John M. Hamilton, Rep.	Feb. 16, 1883	McLean	
Richard J. Oglesby, Rep.	Jan. 30, 1885	Macon	
Joseph W. Fifer, Rep.	Jan. 14, 1889	McLean	
John P. Altgeld, Dem.	Jan. 10, 1893	Cook	
John R. Tanner, Rep.	Jan. 11, 1897	Clay	
Richard Yates, Rep.	Jan. 14, 1901	Morgan	
Charles S. Deneen, Rep.	Jan. 9, 1905 Jan. 18, 1909	Cook	
Edward F. Dunne, Dem.	Feb. 3, 1913	Cook	
Frank O. Lowden, Rep.	Jan. 8, 1917	Ogle	
Len Small, Rep.	Jan. 10, 1921 Jan. 12, 1925	Kankakee	
Louis L. Emmerson, Rep.	Jan. 14, 1929	Jefferson	
Henry Horner, Dem.	Jan. 9, 1933 Jan. 4, 1937	Cook	Died Oct. 6, 1940; succeeded by John H. Stelle; Lieutenant Governor
John H. Stelle, Dem.	Oct. 6, 1940	Hamilton	
Dwight H. Green, Rep.	Jan. 13, 1941 Jan. 8, 1945	Cook	
Adlai E. Stevenson, Dem.	Jan. 10, 1949	Lake	
William G. Stratton, Rep.	Jan. 12, 1953 Jan. 14, 1957	Grundy	
Otto Kerner, Dem.	Jan. 9, 1961 Jan. 11, 1965	Cook	Resigned; succeeded by Samuel H. Shapiro, Lieutenant Governor.
Samuel H. Shapiro, Dem.	May 21, 1968	Kankakee	
Richard B. Ogilvie, Rep.	Jan. 13, 1969	Cook	
Daniel Walker, Dem.	Jan. 8, 1973	Lake	
James R. Thompson, Rep.	Jan. 10, 1977 Jan. 8, 1979 Jan. 10, 1983 Jan. 12, 1987	Cook	
Jim Edgar, Rep.	Jan. 14, 1991 Jan. 9, 1995	Coles	
George H. Ryan, Rep.	Jan. 11, 1999	Kankakee	

LIEUTENANT GOVERNORS

Under all of the state's constitutions, the Lieutenant Governor has been the first official in the line of succession to the Governor's office. The Lieutenant Governor served as chief presiding officer of the Senate until the 1970 Constitution removed that responsibility.

Name	Date of commission or qualification	From what county	Remarks
Pierre Menard, Dem..	Oct. 6, 1818	Randolph	
Adolphus F. Hubbard, Dem.	Dec. 5, 1822	Gallatin	
William Kinney, Dem.	Dec. 6, 1826	St. Clair	
Zodok Casey, Dem.	Dec. 9, 1830	Jefferson	Resigned March 1, 1833.
Wm. L.D. Ewing, Dem.	Mar. 1, 1833	Fayette	Speaker of Senate and Acting Lieutenant Governor and became Governor Nov. 17, 1834.
Alex M. Jenkins, Dem.	Dec. 5, 1834	Jackson	Resigned.
Wm. H. Davidson, Dem.	Dec. 9, 1836	White	Speaker of Senate and Acting Lieutenant Governor.
Stinson H. Anderson, Dem.	Dec. 7, 1838	Jefferson	
John Moore, Dem.	Dec. 8, 1842	McLean	
Joseph B. Wells, Dem.	Dec. 9, 1846	Rock Island	
Wm. McMurty, Dem.	Jan. 8, 1849	Knox	
Gustavus Koerner, Dem.	Jan. 10, 1853	St. Clair	
John Wood, Rep.	Jan. 12, 1857	Adams	Succeeded to Office of Governor, to succeed Bissell, deceased.
Thomas A. Marshall, Dem.	Jan. 7, 1861	Coles	President of Senate and Acting Lieutenant Governor.
Francis A. Hoffman, Rep	Jan. 14, 1861	Cook	
William Bross, Rep.	Jan. 16, 1865	Cook	
John Dougherty, Rep.	Jan. 11, 1869	Union	
John L. Beveridge, Rep.	Jan. 13, 1873	Cook	Succeeded to Office of Governor, to succeed Oglesby, elected United States Senator.
John Earley, Rep.	Jan. 23, 1873	Winnebago	President of Senate and Acting Lieutenant Governor.
Archibald A. Glenn, Dem.	Jan. 8, 1875	Brown	President of Senate and Acting Lieutenant Governor.
Andrew Shuman, Rep.	Jan. 8, 1877	Cook	
John M. Hamilton, Rep.	Jan. 10, 1881	McLean	Succeeded to Office of Governor, to succeed Cullom, elected United States Senator.
Wm. J. Campbell, Rep.	Feb. 6, 1883	Cook	President of Senate and Acting Lieutenant Governor, to succeed Hamilton.
John C. Smith, Rep.	Jan. 30, 1885	Cook	
Lyman B. Ray, Rep.	Jan. 14, 1889	Grundy	
Joseph B. Gill, Dem.	Jan. 10, 1893	Jackson	
William A. Northcott, Rep.	Jan. 11, 1897	Bond	
	Jan. 14, 1901		
Lawrence Y. Sherman, Rep.	Jan. 9, 1905	McDonough	
John G. Oglesby, Rep.	Jan. 18, 1909	Logan	
Barratt O'Hara, Dem.	Feb. 3, 1913	Cook	
John G. Oglesby, Rep.	Jan. 8, 1917	Logan	
Fred E. Sterling, Rep.	Jan. 10, 1921	Winnebago	
	Jan. 12, 1925		
	Jan. 14, 1929		
Thomas F. Donovan, Dem.	Jan. 9, 1933	Will	
John Stelle, Dem.	Jan. 4, 1937	Hamilton	Succeeded to Office of Governor, to succeed Horner, deceased.
Hugh W. Cross, Rep.	Jan. 13, 1941	Jersey	
	Jan. 8, 1945		
Sherwood Dixon, Dem.	Jan. 10, 1949	Lee	
John Wm. Chapman, Rep.	Jan. 12, 1953	Sangamon	
	Jan. 14, 1957		
Samuel H. Shapiro, Dem.	Jan. 9, 1961	Kankakee	Succeeded to Office of Governor, to succeed Kerner, resigned.
	Jan. 11, 1965		
Paul Simon, Dem.	Jan. 13, 1969	Madison	
Neil Hartigan, Dem.	Jan. 8, 1973	Cook	
Dave O'Neal, Rep.	Jan. 10, 1977	St. Clair	Resigned July 31, 1981.
	Jan. 8, 1979		
George H. Ryan, Rep.	Jan. 10, 1983	Kankakee	
	Jan. 12, 1987		
Bob Kustra, Rep.	Jan. 14, 1991	Cook	Resigned July 1, 1998.
	Jan. 9, 1995		
Corinne Wood, Rep.	Jan. 11, 1999	Lake	

ATTORNEYS GENERAL

Under the Constitution of 1818, the Attorney General was appointed by the General Assembly. The 1848 Constitution mentioned the Attorney General only as an officer ineligible to be elected as a member of the General Assembly, and in view of the meager definition the office was held in abeyance until an act creating the office was approved Feb. 27, 1867, when Governor Oglesby appointed Ingersoll. Under the 1870 Constitution the Attorney General became a constitutional officer.

Name	Date of commission or qualification	From what county	Remarks
Daniel Pope Cook, Dem.	Mar. 5, 1819	Randolph	Resigned March 15, 1819.
William Mears, Dem.	Dec. 14, 1819	St. Clair	
Samuel D. Lockwood, Dem.	Feb. 26, 1821	Madison	Resigned Dec. 28, 1822.
James Turney, Dem.	Jan. 14, 1823	Washington	Resigned Jan. 7, 1825.
	Jan. 15, 1825		
George Forquer, Dem.	Jan. 23, 1829	Monroe	Resigned Dec. 3, 1832.
James Semple, Dem.	Jan. 30, 1833	Madison	
Ninian W. Edwards, Dem.	Sept. 1, 1834	Sangamon	Resigned Feb. 7, 1835.
	Jan. 19, 1835		
Jesse B. Thomas, Jr., Dem.	Feb. 12, 1835	Madison	Resigned Jan. 8, 1836.
Walter B. Scates, Dem.	Jan. 18, 1836	Jefferson	Resigned Dec. 26, 1836.
Usher F. Linder, Dem.	Feb. 4, 1837	Coles	Resigned June 11, 1838.
George W. Olney, Dem.	June 26, 1838	Madison	Resigned Feb. 1, 1839.
Wickliffe Kitchell, Dem.	Mar. 5, 1839	Crawford	Resigned Nov. 19, 1840.
Josiah Lamborn, Dem.	Dec. 23, 1840	Morgan	
James A. McDougall, Dem.	Jan. 12, 1843	Morgan	
David B. Campbell, Dem.	Dec. 21, 1846	Sangamon	
Robert G. Ingersoll, Rep.	Feb. 28, 1867	Peoria	Appointed by Governor Oglesby.
Washington Bushnell, Dem.	Jan. 11, 1869	LaSalle	
James K. Edsall, Rep.	Jan. 13, 1873	Lee	
	Jan. 8, 1877		
James McCartney, Rep.	Jan. 10, 1881	Wayne	
George Hunt, Rep.	Jan. 30, 1885	Edgar	
	Jan. 14, 1889		
Maurice T. Maloney, Dem.	Jan. 10, 1893	LaSalle	
Edward C. Akin, Rep.	Jan. 11, 1897	Will	
Howland J. Hamlin, Rep.	Jan. 14, 1901	Shelby	
William H. Stead, Rep	Jan. 9, 1905	LaSalle	
	Jan. 18, 1909		
Patrick J. Lucy, Dem.	Feb. 3, 1913	LaSalle	
Edward J. Brundage, Rep.	Jan. 8, 1917	Cook	
	Jan. 10, 1921		
Oscar E. Carlstrom, Rep.	Jan. 12, 1925	Mercer	
	Jan. 14, 1929		
Otto Kerner, Dem.	Jan. 9, 1933	Cook	Resigned Nov. 23, 1938.
	Jan. 4, 1937		
John E. Cassidy, Dem.	Nov. 23, 1938	Peoria	Appointed by Governor Horner.
George F. Barrett, Rep.	Jan. 13, 1941	Cook	
	Jan. 8, 1945		
Ivan Elliott, Dem.	Jan. 10, 1949	White	
Latham Castle, Rep.	Jan. 12, 1953	DeKalb	Resigned.
	Jan. 14, 1957		
Grenville Beardsley, Rep.	May 9, 1959	Cook	Appointed by Governor Stratton.
William L. Guild, Rep.	June 17, 1960	DuPage	Appointed by Governor Stratton.
William G. Clark, Dem.	Jan. 9, 1961	Cook	
	Jan. 11, 1965		
William J. Scott, Rep.	Jan. 13, 1969	Cook	Resigned.
	Jan. 8, 1973		
	Jan. 10, 1977		
	Jan. 8, 1979		
Tyrone C. Fahner, Rep.	July 29, 1980	Cook	Appointed by Governor Thompson.
Neil Hartigan, Dem.	Jan. 10, 1983	Cook	
	Jan. 12, 1987		
Roland W. Burris, Dem.	Jan. 14, 1991	Cook	
Jim Ryan, Rep.	Jan. 9, 1995	DuPage	
	Jan. 11, 1999		

SECRETARIES OF STATE

Before the 1848 Constitution, the Secretary of State was appointed by the Governor rather than elected by the citizens of Illinois. Constitutionally, the Secretary is required to maintain acts of the General Assembly, specified records of the executive branch and the Great Seal of Illinois. Until 1973, responsibilities included supervising state elections. The administrative structure of the office and diverse departments have undergone frequent change in an effort to fulfill statutory obligations.

Name	Date of commission or qualification	From what county	Remarks
Elias Kent Kane, Dem.	Oct. 6, 1818	Randolph	Resigned Dec. 16, 1822.
Samuel D. Lockwood, Dem.	Dec. 18, 1822	Madison	Resigned April 2, 1823.
David Blackwell, Dem.	Apr. 2, 1823	St. Clair	Resigned Oct. 15, 1824.
Morris Birkbeck, Dem.	Oct. 15, 1824	Edwards	Resigned Jan. 15, 1825.
George Forquer, Dem.	Jan. 15, 1825	Sangamon	Resigned Dec. 31, 1828.
Alexander P. Field, Dem.	Jan. 23, 1829	Union	Removed Nov. 30, 1840.
Stephen A. Douglas, Dem.	Nov. 30, 1840	Morgan	Resigned Feb. 27, 1841.
Lyman Trumbull, Dem.	Mar. 1, 1841	St. Clair	Removed March 4, 1843.
Thompson Campbell, Dem.	Mar. 6, 1843	Jo Daviess	Resigned Dec. 23, 1846.
Horace S. Cooley,Dem.	Dec. 23, 1846 Jan. 8, 1849	Adams	Appointed by Governor French, then elected under Constitution of 1848. Died April 2, 1850.
David L. Gregg, Dem.	Apr. 2, 1850	Cook	
Alexander Starne, Dem.	Jan. 10, 1853	Pike	
Ozias M.Hatch, Rep.	Jan. 12, 1857 Jan. 14, 1861	Pike	
Sharon Tyndale, Rep.	Jan. 16, 1865	St. Clair	
Edward Rummell, Rep.	Jan. 11, 1869	Peoria	
George H. Harlow, Rep.	Jan. 13, 1873 Jan. 8, 1877	Tazewell	
Henry D. Dement, Rep.	Jan. 17, 1881 Jan. 30, 1885	Lee	
Isaac N. Pearson, Rep.	Jan. 14, 1889	McDonough	
Wm. H. Hinrichsen, Dem.	Jan. 10, 1893	Morgan	
James A. Rose, Rep.	Jan. 11, 1897 Jan. 14, 1901 Jan. 9, 1905 Jan. 18, 1909	Pope	Died May 29, 1912.
Cornelius J. Doyle, Rep.	June 3, 1912	Greene	Appointed by Governor Deneen.
Harry Woods, Dem.	Feb. 3, 1913	Cook	Died Oct. 11, 1914.
Lewis G. Stevenson, Dem.	Oct. 14, 1914	McLean	Appointed by Governor Dunne.
Louis L. Emmerson, Rep.	Jan. 8, 1917 Jan. 10, 1921 Jan. 12, 1925	Jefferson	
William J. Stratton, Rep.	Jan. 14, 1929	Lake	
Edward J. Hughes, Dem.	Jan. 9, 1933 Jan. 4, 1937 Jan. 13, 1941	Cook	Died June 28, 1944.
Richard Yates Rowe, Rep.	June 30, 1944	Morgan	Appointed by Governor Green.
Edward J. Barrett, Dem.	Jan. 8, 1945 Jan. 10, 1949	Cook	
Charles F. Carpentier, Rep.	Jan. 12, 1953 Jan. 14, 1957 Jan. 9, 1961	Rock Island	Died April 3, 1964.
William H. Chamberlain, Dem.	Apr. 3, 1964	Sangamon	Appointed by Governor Kerner.
Paul Powell, Dem.	Jan. 11, 1965 Jan. 13, 1969	Johnson	Died Oct. 10, 1970.
John W. Lewis, Rep.	Oct. 13, 1970	Clark	Appointed by Governor Ogilvie.
Michael J. Howlett, Dem.	Jan. 8, 1973	Cook	
Alan J. Dixon, Dem.	Jan. 10, 1977 Jan. 8, 1979	St. Clair	Resigned as State Treasurer Jan. 10, 1977, after elected as Secretary of State. Resigned as Secretary of State Jan. 3, 1981, after elected as U.S. Senator.
Jim Edgar, Rep.	Jan. 5, 1981 Jan. 10, 1983 Jan. 12, 1987	Coles	Appointed by Governor Thompson.
George H. Ryan, Rep.	Jan. 14, 1991 Jan. 9, 1995	Kankakee	
Jesse White, Dem.	Jan. 11, 1999	Cook	

AUDITORS OF PUBLIC ACCOUNTS

By mandate of the Illinois Constitution of 1818, the Office of the Auditor of Public Accounts assumed responsibility for auditing and recording all accounts of the state, keeping accounts of taxes that had been received or disbursed, and maintaining a fair record of the issuance of all warrants and certificates for disbursements. Initially, the Auditor of Public Accounts was appointed by the General Assembly for a four-year term; in 1833 the term was reduced to two years; and, under the 1848 Constitution, the office became a popularly elected one with elected officials serving four-year terms. The Office of the Auditor of Public Accounts was dissolved under the 1970 Constitution, and in 1973, the newly-created Comptroller became keeper of the state's fiscal accounts.

Name	Date of commission or qualification	From what county	Remarks
Elijah C. Berry, Dem.	Oct. 9, 1818 Apr. 6, 1819	Fayette	Auditor of Territorial Government since Aug. 28, 1817. Continued in office until 1831.
James T. Stapp, Dem.	Aug. 29, 1831	Fayette	
Levi Davis, Dem.	Nov. 16, 1835	Fayette	
James Shields, Dem.	Mar. 4, 1841	Randolph	
Wm. L.D. Ewing, Dem.	Mar. 26, 1843	Fayette	Died Mar. 25, 1846.
Thomas H. Campbell, Dem.	Mar. 26, 1846 Jan. 7, 1847	Randolph	Appointed, to succeed Ewing, deceased, then elected by General Assembly.
Jesse K. Dubois, Rep.	Jan. 12, 1857 Jan. 14, 1861	Lawrence	
Orlin H. Miner, Rep.	Dec. 12, 1864	Sangamon	
Charles E. Lippincott, Rep.	Jan. 11, 1869 Jan. 12, 1873	Cass	
Thomas B. Needles, Rep.	Jan. 8, 1877	Washington	
Charles P. Swigart, Rep.	Jan. 10, 1881 Jan. 30, 1885	Kankakee	
Charles W. Pavey, Rep.	Jan. 14, 1889	Jefferson	
David Gore, Dem.	Jan. 10, 1893	Macoupin	
James S. McCullough, Rep.	Jan. 11, 1897 Jan. 14, 1901 Jan. 9, 1905 Jan. 18, 1909	Champaign	
James J. Brady, Dem.	Feb. 3, 1913	Cook	
Andrew Russel, Rep.	Jan. 8, 1917 Jan. 10, 1921	Morgan	
Oscar Nelson, Rep.	Jan. 12, 1925 Jan. 14, 1929	Kane	
Edward J. Barrett, Dem.	Jan. 9, 1933 Jan. 4, 1937	Cook	
Arthur C. Lueder, Rep.	Jan. 13, 1941 Jan. 8, 1945	Cook	
Benjamin O. Cooper, Dem.	Jan. 10, 1949	St. Clair	
Orville E. Hodge, Rep.	Jan. 12, 1953	Madison	Resigned.
Lloyd Morey, Rep.	July 18, 1956	Champaign	Appointed by Governor Stratton.
Elbert Sidney Smith, Rep.	Jan. 14, 1957	Macon	
Michael J. Howlett, Dem.	Jan. 9, 1961 Jan. 11, 1965 Jan. 13, 1969	Cook	Office taken over by Comptroller January 1973.

COMPTROLLERS

Name	Date of commission or qualification	From what county	Remarks
George W. Lindberg, Rep.	Jan. 8, 1973	McHenry	Office established by 1970 Constitution.
Michael J. Bakalis, Dem.	Jan. 10, 1977	DuPage	
Roland W. Burris, Dem.	Jan. 8, 1979 Jan. 10, 1983 Jan. 12, 1987	Cook	
Dawn Clark Netsch, Dem.	Jan. 14, 1991	Cook	
Loleta Didrickson, Rep.	Jan. 9, 1995	Cook	
Daniel W. Hynes, Dem.	Jan. 11, 1999	Cook	

TREASURERS

The 1818 Illinois Constitution designated that the Treasurer be appointed biennially by a joint vote of the General Assembly. In 1848, the Treasurer was popularly elected, and a 1959 Constitutional provision changed the office term from two to four years. The Treasurer is empowered to receive proceeds of all taxes and make authorized disbursements from the state treasury.

Name	Date of commission or qualification	From what county	Remarks
John Thomas, Dem.	Oct. 9, 1818	St. Clair	Died July 1819.
R.K. McLaughlin, Dem.	Aug. 2, 1819	Fayette	
Abner Field, Dem.	Jan. 14, 1823	Union	
James Hall, Dem.	Feb. 12, 1827	Jackson	
John Dement, Dem.	Feb. 1, 1831	Franklin	Resigned Dec. 3, 1836.
Charles Gregory, Dem.	Dec. 5, 1836	Greene	
John D. Whiteside, Dem.	Mar. 4, 1837	Monroe	
Milton Carpenter, Dem.	Mar. 6, 1841	Hamilton	Died August 1848.
John Moore, Dem.	Aug. 14, 1848 Dec. 16, 1850	McLean	Appointed to succeed Carpenter.
James Miller, Rep.	Jan. 12, 1857	McLean	Resigned Sept. 3, 1859.
William Butler, Rep.	Sept. 8, 1859 Jan. 14, 1861	Sangamon	Appointed to succeed Miller.
Alexander Starne, Dem.	Jan. 13, 1863	Sangamon	
James H. Beveridge, Rep.	Jan. 9, 1865	DeKalb	
George W. Smith, Rep.	Jan. 10, 1867	Cook	
Erastus N. Bates, Rep.	Jan. 11, 1869 Jan. 9, 1871	Marion	
Edward Rutz, Rep.	Jan. 13, 1873	St. Clair	
Thomas S. Ridgeway, Rep.	Jan. 11, 1875	Gallatin	
Edward Rutz, Rep.	Jan. 8, 1877	St. Clair	
John C. Smith, Rep.	Jan. 13, 1879	JoDaviess	
Edward Rutz, Rep.	Jan. 10, 1881	Cook	
John C. Smith, Rep.	Jan. 5, 1883	JoDaviess	
Jacob Gross, Rep.	Jan. 30, 1885	Cook	
John R. Tanner, Rep.	Jan. 6, 1887	Clay	
Charles Becker, Rep.	Jan. 14, 1889	St. Clair	
Edward S. Wilson, Dem.	Jan. 12, 1891	Richland	
Rufus N. Ramsay, Dem.	Jan. 10, 1893	Clinton	Died Nov. 11, 1894.
Elijah P. Ramsay, Dem.	Nov. 14, 1894	Clinton	Appointed by Governor to succeed Ramsay.
Henry Wulff, Rep.	Jan. 14, 1895	Cook	
Henry L. Hertz, Rep.	Jan. 11, 1897	Cook	
Floyd K. Whittemore, Rep.	Jan. 11, 1899	Sangamon	
Moses O. Williamson, Rep	Jan. 14, 1901	Knox	
Fred A. Busse, Rep.	Jan. 12, 1903	Cook	
Len Small, Rep.	Jan. 9, 1905	Kankakee	
John F. Smulski, Rep.	Jan. 10, 1907	Cook	
Andrew Russel, Rep.	Jan. 18, 1909	Morgan	
Edward E. Mitchell, Rep.	Jan. 9, 1911	Jackson	
William D. Ryan, Jr., Dem.	Feb. 3, 1913	Vermilion	
Andrew Russel, Rep.	Feb. 20, 1915	Morgan	
Len Small, Rep.	Jan. 8, 1917	Kankakee	
Fred E. Sterling, Rep.	Jan. 8, 1919	Winnebago	
Edward E. Miller, Rep.	Jan. 10, 1921	St. Clair	
Oscar E. Nelson, Rep.	Jan. 4, 1923	Kane	
Omer N. Custer, Rep.	Jan. 12, 1925	Knox	
Garret DeF. Kinney, Rep.	Jan. 5, 1927	Peoria	
Omer N. Custer, Rep.	Jan. 14, 1929	Knox	
Edward J. Barrett, Dem.	Jan. 12, 1931	Cook	
John C. Martin, Dem.	Jan. 9, 1933	Marion	
John Stelle, Dem.	Jan. 14, 1935	Hamilton	
John C. Martin, Dem.	Jan. 4, 1937	Marion	
Louie E. Lewis, Dem.	Jan. 4, 1939	Franklin	
Warren Wright, Rep.	Jan. 13, 1941	Sangamon	
William G. Stratton, Rep.	Jan. 11, 1943	Grundy	
Conrad F. Becker, Rep.	Jan. 8, 1945	Randolph	
Richard Yates Rowe, Rep.	Jan. 8, 1947	Morgan	
Ora Smith, Dem.	Jan. 10, 1949	Henderson	
William G. Stratton, Rep.	Jan. 8, 1951	Grundy	
Elmer J. Hoffman, Rep.	Jan. 12, 1953	DuPage	
Warren Wright, Rep.	Jan. 10, 1955	Sangamon	
Elmer J. Hoffman, Rep.	Jan. 14, 1957	DuPage	
Joseph D. Lohman, Dem.	Jan. 12, 1959	Cook	Resigned Sept. 1, 1961.
Francis S. Lorenz, Dem.	Sept. 1, 1961	Cook	Appointed by Governor Kerner.

TREASURERS (Concluded)

Name	Date of commission or qualification	From what county	Remarks
William J. Scott, Rep.	Jan. 14, 1963	Cook	
Adlai E. Stevenson III, Dem.	Jan. 9, 1967	Cook	Resigned Nov. 17, 1970.
Charles Woodford, Dem.	Nov. 17, 1970	DuPage	Appointed by Governor Ogilvie.
Alan J. Dixon, Dem.	Jan. 11, 1971 Jan. 8, 1975	St. Clair	Resigned Jan. 10, 1977.
Donald R. Smith, Rep.	Jan. 10, 1977	DuPage	Appointed by Governor Thompson.
Jerry Cosentino, Dem.	Jan. 8, 1979	Cook	
James Donnewald, Dem.	Jan. 10, 1983	Clinton	
Jerry Cosentino, Dem.	Jan. 12, 1987	Cook	
Pat Quinn, Dem.	Jan. 14, 1991	Cook	
Judy Baar Topinka, Rep.	Jan. 9, 1995 Jan. 11, 1999	Cook	

JUSTICES OF THE SUPREME COURT

Under the Constitution of 1818, Justices of the Supreme Court were appointed by the General Assembly. Four justices were appointed in 1818, and five new seats were created in 1841. The Constitution of 1848 reduced the size of the court to three and provided for popular election of one justice from each of the state's three grand divisions. The Constitution of 1970 expanded the court to seven, its present size, while retaining popular election.

Name	Term of Service	Remarks
Joseph Philips	1818-1822	Resigned.
Thomas C. Browne	1818-1848	
William P. Foster	1818-1819	Resigned, never qualified.
John Reynolds	1818-1825	
William Wilson	1819-1848	To succeed Foster.
Thomas Reynolds	1822-1825	To succeed Philips.
Samuel D. Lockwood	1825-1848	To succeed John Reynolds; resigned.
Theophilus W. Smith	1825-1842	To succeed Thomas Reynolds; died.
Samuel H. Treat	1841-1855	Resigned.
Thomas Ford	1841-1842	Resigned.
Sidney Breese	1841-1843	Resigned.
Walter B. Scates	1841-1847	
Stephen A. Douglas	1841-1843	Resigned.
John D. Caton	1842-1843	Resigned.
James Semple	1843	To succeed Breese; resigned.
Richard M. Young	1843-1847	To succeed Smith; resigned.
John M. Robinson	1843	To succeed Caton; died.
John D. Caton	1843-1864	To succeed Robinson.
James Shields	1843-1845	To succeed Semple; resigned.
Jesse B. Thomas	1843-1845	To succeed Douglas; resigned.
Gustavus P. Koerner	1845-1848	To succeed Shields.
Norman H. Purple	1845-1848	To succeed Thomas.
William A. Denning	1847-1848	To succeed Scates.
Jesse B. Thomas	1847-1848	To succeed Young.
David M. Woodson	1848	To succeed Lockwood. No session during his term.
Lyman Trumbull	1848-1853	To succeed Browne; resigned.
Walter B. Scates	1853-1857	To succeed Trumbull.
Onias C. Skinner	1855-1858	To succeed Treat.
Sidney Breese	1857-1878	To succeed Scates; died.
Pinckney H. Walker	1858-1885	To succeed Skinner; died.
Corydon Beckwith	1864	To succeed Caton.
Charles B. Lawrence	1864-1873	To succeed Beckwith.
Anthony Thornton	1870-1873	Resigned.
John M. Scott	1870-1888	
Benjamin R. Sheldon	1870-1888	
W. K. McAllister	1870-1875	Resigned.
John Schofield	1873-1893	To succeed Thornton; died.
Alfred M. Craig	1873-1900	To succeed Lawrence.
T. Lyle Dickey	1875-1885	To succeed McAllister; died.
David J. Baker	1878-1879	To succeed Breese.
John H. Mulkey	1879-1888	To succeed Baker.
David J. Baker	1888-1897	To succeed Mulkey.
Damon G. Tunnicliff	1885	To succeed Walker.
Simeon P. Shope	1885-1894	To succeed Tunnicliff.
B. D. Magruder	1885-1906	To succeed Dickey.
Jacob W. Wilkin	1888-1907	To succeed Scott; died.
Joseph M. Bailey	1888-1897	To succeed Sheldon; resigned.
Jesse J. Philips	1893-1901	To succeed Schofield; died.
James H. Cartwright	1895-1924	To succeed Bailey.

JUSTICES OF THE SUPREME COURT (Concluded)

Name	Term of Service	Remarks
Joseph N. Carter	1894-1903	To succeed Shope.
Carroll C. Boggs	1897-1906	To succeed Baker.
John P. Hand	1900-1913	To succeed Craig; resigned.
James B. Ricks	1901-1906	To succeed Philips.
Guy C. Scott	1903-1909	To succeed J. Carter; died.
William M. Farmer	1906-1931	To succeed Ricks; resigned.
Alonzo K. Vickers	1906-1915	To succeed Boggs; died.
Orrin N. Carter	1906-1924	To succeed Magruder.
Frank K. Dunn	1907-1933	To succeed Wilkin.
George A. Cooke	1909-1919	To succeed Scott; resigned.
Charles C. Craig	1913-1918	To succeed Hand.
Albert Watson	1915	To succeed Vickers.
Warren W. Duncan	1915-1933	To succeed Watson.
Clyde E. Stone	1918-1948	To succeed Craig.
Floyd E. Thompson	1919-1928	To succeed Cooke; resigned.
Oscar E. Heard	1924-1933	To succeed Cartwright.
Frederic R. DeYoung	1924-1934	To succeed O. Carter; died.
Cyrus Dietz	1928-1929	To succeed Thompson; died.
Paul Samuell	1929-1930	To succeed Dietz.
Warren H. Orr	1930-1939	To succeed Samuell.
Norman L. Jones	1931-1940	To succeed Farmer; died.
Paul Farthing	1933-1942	To succeed Duncan.
Loft R. Herrick	1933-1937	To succeed Dunn; died.
Elwyn R. Shaw	1933-1942	To succeed Heard.
Francis S. Wilson	1935-1951	To succeed DeYoung; died.
Walter T. Gunn	1938-1951	To succeed Herrick; died.
Loren E. Murphy	1939-1948	To succeed Orr.
June C. Smith	1941-1947	Elected, to succeed Jones; died.
Charles H. Thompson	1942-1951	To succeed Farthing.
William J. Fulton	1942-1954	To succeed Shaw.
Jesse L. Simpson	1947-1951	To succeed Smith.
Joseph E. Daily	1948-1963	Elected, to succeed Stone; died.
Albert M. Crampton	1948-1953	To succeed Murphy.
Walter V. Schaefer	1951-1976	Appointed, to succeed Wilson; retired.
George W. Bristow	1951-1961	To succeed Gunn; died.
Harry B. Hershey	1951-1966	To succeed Simpson; resigned.
Ralph L. Maxwell	1951-1956	To succeed Thompson; died.
Ray I. Klingbiel	1953-1969	To succeed Crampton; retired.
Charles H. Davis	1955-1960	To succeed Fulton.
Byron O. House	1957-1969	To succeed Maxwell; retired.
Roy J. Solfisburg, Jr.	1960-1969	To succeed Davis; resigned.
Robert C. Underwood	1962-1984	To succeed Bristow; retired.
Thomas E. Kluczynski	1966-1976	To succeed Hershey; retired.
Daniel P. Ward	1966-1990	To succeed Daily; retired.
John T. Culbertson	1969-1970	Assigned, after Klingbiel resigned.
Marvin F. Burt	1969-1970	Assigned, after Solfisburg resigned.
Caswell J. Crebs	1969-1970	Assigned, after House died.
Charles H. Davis	1970-1975	To succeed Solfisburg, who resigned.
Howard C. Ryan	1970-1990	To succeed Klingbiel, who resigned.
Joseph H. Goldenhersh	1970-1987	To succeed House, who died.
Caswell J. Crebs	1975-1976	Assigned, after Davis died.
William G. Clark	1976-1992	To succeed Kluczynski, who retired.
James A. Dooley	1976-1978	To succeed Schaefer, who retired.
Thomas J. Moran	1976-1992	To succeed Davis, who died.
Thomas E. Kluczynski	1978-1980	Assigned, after Dooley died.
Seymour Simon	1980-1988	To succeed Dooley, who died.
Benjamin K. Miller	1984-2001	To succeed Underwood, who resigned.
Joseph F. Cunningham	1987-1988	Assigned, after Goldenhersh resigned.
John J. Stamos	1988-1990	Appointed, after Simon resigned.
Horace L. Calvo	1988-1991	To succeed Goldenhersh, who resigned.
Michael A. Bilandic	1990-2000	To succeed Ward, who resigned.
Charles E. Freeman	1990-	To succeed Simon, who resigned.
James D. Heiple	1990-2000	To succeed Ryan, who resigned.
Joseph F. Cunningham	1991-1992	Appointed, after Calvo died.
Mary Ann G. McMorrow	1992-	To succeed Clark, who resigned.
John L. Nickels	1992-1999	To succeed Moran, who resigned.
Moses W. Harrison II	1992-	To succeed Calvo, who died.
S. Louis Rathje	1999-2000	To succeed Nickels, who resigned.
Thomas R. Fitzgerald	2000-	To succeed Bilandic, who retired.
Robert R. Thomas	2000-	To succeed Rathje.
Thomas L. Kilbride	2000-	To succeed Heiple, who retired.
Rita B. Garman	2001-	To succeed Miller, who retired.

CLERKS OF THE SUPREME COURT

Prior to the adoption of the Constitution of 1848, the Clerk of the Supreme Court was appointed by the court. The record as to dates of appointment is somewhat obscure. James M. Duncan was appointed July 12, 1819. Ebenezer Peck appears as the successor of Duncan; Wm. B. Warren seems to have been the successor of Peck. From 1848 to 1902, one clerk was elected in each of the Three Grand Divisions. The Three Grand Divisions were consolidated into one, comprising the entire state, by the Act of 1897, which provided that but one clerk be elected in 1902 and every six years thereafter. The 1970 Constitution of the State of Illinois provided that this office become appointive in 1975.

Name	Term of Service	Remarks
Finney D. Preston	1848-1855	First Grand Division.
Wm. B. Warren	1848-1855	Second Grand Division.
Lorenzo Leland	1848-1867	Third Grand Division.
Noah Johnston	1855-1867	To succeed Preston; First Grand Division.
Wm. A. Turney	1855-1872	To succeed Warren; Second Grand Division.
Woodbury M. Taylor	1867-1872	To succeed Leland; Third Grand Division.
Robert A.D. Wilbanks	1867-1878	Elected to succeed Johnston as Clerk of the First Grand Division under the Constitution of 1848; re-elected under the Constitution of 1870, which renamed the grand divisions Southern, Central and Northern, as Clerk of the Central Grand Division.
Emanuel C. Hamberger	1872-1878	Southern Grand Division.
Cairo D. Trimble	1872-1878	Northern Grand Division.
Jacob O. Chance	1878-1890	To succeed Wilbanks; Central Grand Division.
Ethan A. Snively	1878-1896	To succeed Hamberger; Southern Grand Division.
Everell F. Dutton	1878-1884	To succeed Trimble; Northern Grand Division.
Alfred H. Taylor	1884-1896	To succeed Dutton; Northern Grand Division.
Frank W. Haville	1890-1896	To succeed Chance; Central Grand Division.
Jacob O. Chance	1896-1900	To succeed Haville; Central Grand Division; died in office.
Albert D. Caldwallader	1896-1902	To succeed Snively; Southern Grand Division.
Christopher Mamer	1896-1908	To succeed Taylor; Northern Grand Division. Elected in 1902 as first statewide clerk under the Act of 1897.
Oliver J. Page	1900-1902	To succeed Chance; Central Grand Division.
J. McCan Davis	1908-1914	To succeed Mamer.
Charles W. Vail	1914-1932	
Adam F. Bloch	1932-1940	Died in office.
Edward F. Cullinane	1940-1944	Appointed, to succeed Bloch.
Earle B. Searcy	1944-1955	Died in office.
Mrs. Earle B. Searcy	1955-1968	Appointed, to succeed Earle B. Searcy, then elected twice; died in office.
Clell Woods	1968-1969	Appointed, to succeed Mrs. Earle B. Searcy.
Justin Taft	1969-1975	

PRESIDENTS OF THE SENATE
(Since Constitution of 1870)

General Assembly	Name	Date first elected	County
32nd-34th	William J. Campbell, Rep.	Jan. 6, 1881	Cook
35th	August W. Berggren, Rep.	Jan. 5, 1887	Knox
36th	Theodore S. Chapman, Rep.	Jan. 9, 1889	Jersey
37th	Milton W. Matthews, Rep.	Jan. 7, 1891	Champaign
38th	John W. Coppinger, Dem.	Jan. 4, 1893	Madison
39th	Charles Bogardus, Rep.	Jan. 9, 1895	Ford
40th	Hendrick V. Fisher, Rep.	Jan. 6, 1897	Henry
41st	Walter Warder, Rep.	Jan. 4, 1899	Alexander
42nd	John J. Brenholt, Rep.	Jan. 9, 1901	Madison
43rd	John C. McKenzie, Rep.	Jan. 7, 1903	Jo Daviess
44th	Leon A. Townsend, Rep.	Jan. 4, 1905	Knox
44th	Orville F. Berry, Rep.		Hancock
45th	Stanton C. Pemberton, Rep.	Jan. 9, 1907	Coles
46th	Robert S. Hamilton, Rep.	Jan. 6, 1909	St. Clair
47th	Henry M. Dunlap, Rep.	Jan. 4, 1911	Champaign
48th	Walter I. Manny, Dem.	Jan. 22, 1913	Brown
49th	Stephen D. Canady, Dem.	Jan. 6, 1915	Montgomery
50th, 51st	Adam C. Cliffe, Rep.	Jan. 3, 1917	DeKalb
52nd	William S. Jewell, Rep	Jan. 5, 1921	Fulton
53rd-55th	Richard J. Barr, Rep.	Jan. 3, 1923	Will

PRESIDENTS OF THE SENATE (Concluded)

General Assembly	Name	Date first elected	County
56th	Martin R. Carlson, Rep.	Jan. 9, 1929	Rock Island
57th	Richard J. Barr, Rep.	Jan. 7, 1931	Will
58th, 59th	Richey V. Graham, Dem.	Jan. 4, 1933	Cook
60th, 61st	George M. Maypole, Dem.	Jan. 6, 1937	Cook
62nd, 63rd	Arnold P. Benson, Rep.	Jan. 8, 1941	Kane
64th, 65th	Edward E. Laughlin, Rep.	Jan. 3, 1945	Stephenson
66th, 67th	Wallace Thompson, Rep.	Jan. 10, 1949	Knox
68th	Walker Butler, Rep.	Jan. 7, 1953	Cook
69th-73rd	Arthur J. Bidwill, Rep.	Jan. 5, 1955	Cook
74th-76th	W. Russell Arrington, Rep.	Jan. 6, 1965	Cook
77th	Cecil A. Partee, Dem.	Jan. 6, 1971	Cook
78th	William C. Harris, Rep.	Jan. 10, 1973	Livingston
79th	Cecil A. Partee, Dem.	Jan. 8, 1975	Cook
80th	Thomas C. Hynes, Dem.	Feb. 16, 1977	Cook
81st-87th	Philip J. Rock, Dem.	Jan. 10, 1979	Cook
88th-92nd	James "Pate" Philip, Rep.	Jan. 13, 1993	DuPage

SPEAKERS OF THE HOUSE OF REPRESENTATIVES

General Assembly	Name	Date first elected	County
1st	[1]John Mesinger, Rep.	Oct. 5, 1818	St. Clair
2nd	John McLean, Rep.	Dec. 4, 1820	Gallatin
3rd	William M. Alexander, Rep.	Dec. 2, 1822	Alexander
4th	[2]Thomas Mathers, Rep.	Nov. 15, 1824	Randolph
4th	David Blackwell, Dem.	Jan. 2, 1826	St. Clair
5th, 6th	John McLean, Dem.	Dec. 4, 1826	Gallatin
7th	William Lee D. Ewing, Dem.	Dec. 6, 1830	Fayette
8th	Alexander M. Jenkins, Dem.	Dec. 6, 1832	Jackson
9th, 10th	James Semple, Dem.	Dec. 1, 1834	Madison
11th, 12th	William Lee D. Ewing, Dem.	Dec. 3, 1838	Fayette
13th	Samuel Hackelton, Dem.	Dec. 5, 1842	Fulton
14th	William A. Richardson, Dem.	Dec. 2, 1844	Schuyler
15th	Newton Cloud, Dem	Dec. 7, 1846	Morgan
16th	Zadok Casey, Dem.	Jan. 1, 1849	Jefferson
17th	Sidney Breese, Dem.	Jan. 6, 1851	Clinton
18th	John Reynolds, Dem.	Jan. 3, 1853	St. Clair
19th	Thomas J. Turner, Anti-Neb. Dem.	Jan. 1, 1855	Stephenson
20th	Samuel Holmes, Dem.	Jan. 5, 1857	Adams
21st	William R. Morrison, Dem.	Jan. 3, 1859	Monroe
22nd	Shelby M. Cullom, Rep.	Jan. 7, 1861	Sangamon
23rd	Samuel A. Buckmaster, Dem.	Jan. 5, 1863	Madison
24th	Allen C. Fuller, Rep.	Jan. 2, 1865	Boone
25th, 26th	Franklin Corwin, Rep.	Jan. 7, 1867	LaSalle
27th	William M. Smith, Rep.	Jan. 4, 1871	McLean
28th	Shelby M. Cullom, Rep.	Jan. 8, 1873	Sangamon
29th	[3]Elijah M. Haines, Ind.	Jan. 6, 1875	Lake
30th	James Shaw, Rep.	Jan. 3, 1877	Carroll
31st	William A. James, Rep.	Jan. 8, 1879	Lake
32nd	Horace H. Thomas, Rep.	Jan. 5, 1881	Cook
33rd	Lorin C. Collins, Jr., Rep.	Jan. 3, 1883	Cook
34th	[3]Elijah M. Haines, Ind.	Jan. 29, 1885	Lake
35th	William F. Calhoun, Rep.	Jan. 5, 1887	DeWitt
36th	[4]Asa C. Matthews, Rep.	Jan. 9, 1889	Pike
36th	[5]James H. Miller, Rep.	May 10, 1889	Stark
36th	William G. Cochran, Rep.	July 23, 1891	Moultrie
37th, 38th	Clayton E. Crafts, Dem.	Jan. 7, 1891	Cook
39th	[6]John Meyer, Rep.	Jan. 9, 1895	Cook
39th	William G. Cochran, Rep.	July 10, 1895	Moultrie
40th	Edward C. Curtis, Rep.	Jan. 6, 1897	Kankakee
41st, 42nd	Lawrence Y. Sherman, Rep.	Jan. 4, 1899	McDonough
43rd	John Henry Miller, Rep.	Jan. 7, 1903	Hamilton
44th-46th	Edward D. Shurtleff, Rep.	Jan. 4, 1905	McHenry
47th	Charles Adkins, Rep.	Jan. 4, 1911	Piatt
48th	William McKinley, Dem.	Jan. 29, 1913	Cook
49th-51st	David E. Shanahan, Rep.	Feb. 17, 1915	Cook
52nd	Gotthard A. Dahlberg, Rep.	Jan. 5, 1921	Cook
53rd	David E. Shanahan, Rep.	Jan. 3, 1923	Cook
54th, 55th	Robert Scholes, Rep.	Jan. 7, 1925	Peoria
56th, 57th	David E. Shanahan, Rep.	Jan. 9, 1929	Cook
58th	Arthur Roe, Dem.	Jan. 4, 1933	Fayette
59th	John P. Devine, Dem.	Jan. 9, 1935	Lee

General Assembly	Name	Date first elected	County
60th	Louie E. Lewis, Dem.	Jan. 6, 1937	Franklin
61st	Hugh W. Cross, Rep.	Jan. 3, 1939	Jersey
62nd, 63rd	Elmer J. Schnackenberg, Rep.	Jan. 8, 1941	Cook
64th, 65th	Hugh Green, Rep.	Jan. 3, 1945	Morgan
66th	Paul Powell, Dem.	Jan. 10, 1949	Johnson
67th-70th	Warren Wood, Rep.	Jan. 8, 1951	Will
71st, 72nd	Paul Powell, Dem.	Jan. 7, 1959	Johnson
73rd	John W. Lewis, Jr., Rep.	Jan. 9, 1963	Clark
74th	John Touhy, Dem.	Jan. 6, 1965	Cook
75th, 76th	Ralph T. Smith, Rep	Jan. 4, 1967	Madison
76th	[7]Jack E. Walker, Rep.	Oct. 14, 1969	Cook
77th, 78th	W. Robert Blair, Rep.	Jan. 6, 1971	Cook
79th-81st	William A. Redmond, Dem.	Jan. 21, 1975	DuPage
82nd	[8]George H. Ryan, Rep.	Jan. 14, 1981	Kankakee
82nd	[9]Arthur A. Telcser, Rep.	Jan. 10, 1983	Cook
83rd-88th	Michael J. Madigan, Dem	Jan. 12, 1983	Cook
89th	Lee A. Daniels, Rep.	Jan. 9, 1995	DuPage
90th-92nd	Michael J. Madigan, Dem.	Jan. 8, 1997	Cook

[1]From 1800 until about 1824, the party designation "Republican" meant the followers of Thomas Jefferson. By 1824 the party was splitting into two factions: the National Republicans, who soon came to be known as Whigs, and the Democratic Republicans, soon called Democrats. The word "Republican" did not acquire its present party meaning until 1854-1856.

[2]Resigned 1825, appointed U.S. commissioner to locate military roads.

[3]Originally a Democrat, then a Republican, Haines ran as an Independent in this and succeeding years.

[4]Resigned May 10, 1889, appointed U.S. Comptroller.

[5]Succeeded Matthews; died July 20, 1890.

[6]Died July 3, 1895.

[7]Elected to fill vacancy of Ralph T. Smith, who was appointed U.S. Senator.

[8]Resigned two days short of full term when sworn in as Lieutenant Governor.

[9]Elected by House acclamation and served remainder of session.

*SUPERINTENDENTS OF PUBLIC INSTRUCTION

Name	Date of commission or qualification	From what county	Remarks
Ninian W. Edwards, Dem.	Mar. 24, 1854	Sangamon	Appointed by Governor.
William G. Powell, Rep.	Jan. 12, 1857	Peoria	
Newton Bateman, Rep.	Aug. 1, 1859	Morgan	
	Jan. 4, 1861		
John P. Brooks, Dem.	Jan. 12, 1863	Sangamon	
Newton Bateman, Rep.	Jan. 10, 1865	Sangamon	Term extended to four years.
	Jan. 10, 1867		
	Nov. 8, 1870		
Samuel M. Etter, Dem.	Jan. 11, 1875	McLean	
James P. Slade, Rep.	Jan. 13, 1879	St. Clair	
Henry Raab, Dem.	Jan. 5, 1883	St. Clair	
Richard Edwards, Rep.	Jan. 6, 1887	Bureau	
Henry Raab, Dem.	Jan. 12, 1891	St. Clair	
Samuel Inglis, Rep.	Jan. 14, 1895	Jackson	Died Jan. 23, 1898.
Joseph H. Freeman, Rep.	June 23, 1898	Kane	Appointed, to succeed Inglis.
Alfred Bayliss, Rep.	Jan. 11, 1899	LaSalle	
	Jan. 12, 1903		
Francis G. Blair, Rep.	Jan. 10, 1907	Coles	
	Jan. 11, 1911		
	Jan. 14, 1915		
	Jan. 8, 1919		
	Jan. 4, 1923		
	Jan. 5, 1927		
	Jan. 12, 1931		
John A. Wieland, Dem.	Jan. 14, 1935	Clark	
	Jan. 4, 1939		
Vernon L. Nickell, Rep.	Jan. 11, 1943	Champaign	
	Jan. 8, 1947		
	Jan. 8, 1951		
	Jan. 10, 1955		
George T. Wilkins, Dem.	Jan. 12, 1959	Madison	
Ray Page, Rep.	Jan. 14, 1963	Sangamon	
	Jan. 9, 1967		
Michael J. Bakalis, Dem.	Jan. 11, 1971	DeKalb	

*The 1970 Constitution of the State of Illinois provided that this office become appointive in 1975.

TRUSTEES OF THE UNIVERSITY OF ILLINOIS

The university was incorporated by act of the General Assembly, Feb. 28, 1867, as the Illinois Industrial University; its name was changed by the General Assembly in 1885 to the University of Illinois. Originally there were 28 trustees appointed by the Governor, who, with the president of the university, Dr. J. M. Gregory (called regent), the Superintendent of Public Instruction and the President of the State Board of Agriculture, were members ex officio. The original 28 appointed members drew lots at the first meeting to decide the length of their terms, as provided in the law. The normal term is six years.

In 1873, the number of trustees was reduced to 11 — the Governor, President of the State Board of Agriculture and nine members appointed by the Governor for six-year terms. A number of trustees appointed to serve from March 1873 actually served only a few weeks, as the new law was effective in May 1873. In 1887, the General Assembly made membership on the board elective at a general state election and restored the Superintendent of Public Instruction as a member. The Office of President of the State Board of Agriculture was abolished by law, effective Jan. 1, 1919.

The following list gives the appointed members of the board from 1867 to March 12, 1889 (when the first elected trustees took office), followed by the names of the elected trustees to Jan. 1, 1996, when a new law once again made the positions appointive. However, based on a ruling of the Illinois Supreme Court on March 21, 1996, terms of elected trustees were allowed to expire, and future trustees are appointed by the Governor in groups of three every two years. The first three appointed trustees under this law took office in January 1997.

Name	Term of Service	Post office	Remarks
Lemuel Allen	1867-1870	Pekin	
Alexander Blackburn	1867-1877	Macomb	Out, 1869-1870.
Mason Brayman	1867-1873	Springfield	
Alexander M. Brown	1867-1879	Villa Ridge	
Edwin L. Brown	1867-1870	Chicago	
Horatio C. Burchard	1867-1870	Freeport	
John C. Burroughs	1867-1870	Chicago	
Emery Cobb	1867-1893	Kankakee	
Joseph O. Cunningham	1867-1871	Urbana	
Matthias L. Dunlap	1867-1869	Champaign	
Samuel Edwards	1867-1873	LaMoille	
Willard C. Flagg	1867-1878	Moro	Out, 1870-1875.
Orson B. Galusha	1867-1873	Morris	
Moore C. Goltra	1867-1873	Jacksonville	
John M. Gregory	1867-1873	Urbana	
David S. Hammond	1867-1869	Chicago	
George Harding	1867-1868	Paris	
Samuel S. Hayes	1867-1872	Chicago	
J.P. Hungate	1867-1868	Louisville	
John S. Johnson	1867-1872	Warsaw	
Luther W. Lawrence	1867-1873	Belvidere	
Isaac S. Mahan	1867-1872	Centralia	
Luke B. McMurray	1867-1869	Effingham	
James H. Pickrell	1867-1879	Harristown	
Burden Pullen	1867-1889	Centralia	
Thomas Quick	1867-1869	Irvington	
John W. Scroggs	1867-1872	Champaign	
Charles H. Topping	1867-1868	Makanda	
John M. Van Osdell	1867-1873	Chicago	
Clark R. Griggs	1869-1872	Champaign	
Edward Kitchell	1869	Olney	
John M. Pearson	1869-1873	Godfrey	
James P. Slade	1869-1875	Belleville	
Paul R. Wright	1869-1873	South Pass	
William B. Anderson	1870-1873	Mt. Vernon	
George S. Bowen	1870-1873	Chicago	
Josiah L. Pickard	1870-1873	Chicago	
L.L. Greenleaf	1871-1872	Chicago	
R. B. Harrington	1871-1872	Pontiac	
D. C. Wagner	1871-1873	Shannon	
Hiram Buck	1872-1873	LeRoy	
John J. Byrd	1873-1882	Cairo	
Robert Douglas	1873	Waukegan	

475

TRUSTEES OF THE UNIVERSITY OF ILLINOIS (Concluded)

PRESIDENTS AND VICE PRESIDENTS AND THE CONGRESSES COINCIDENT WITH THEIR TERMS

President	Vice President	Service	Congress
George Washington	John Adams	Apr. 30, 1789 -Mar. 3, 1797	1, 2, 3, 4.
John Adams	Thomas Jefferson	Mar. 4, 1797 -Mar. 3, 1801	5, 6.
Thomas Jefferson	Aaron Burr	Mar. 4, 1801 -Mar. 3, 1805	7, 8.
	George Clinton[1]	Mar. 4, 1805 -Mar. 3, 1809	9, 10.
James Madison		Mar. 4, 1809 -Mar. 3, 1813	11, 12.
	Elbridge Gerry[2]	Mar. 4, 1813 -Mar. 3, 1817	13, 14.
James Monroe	Daniel D. Tompkins	Mar. 4, 1817 -Mar. 3, 1825	15, 16, 17, 18.
John Quincy Adams	John C. Calhoun[3]	Mar. 4, 1825 -Mar. 3, 1829	19, 20.
Andrew Jackson		Mar. 4, 1829 -Mar. 3, 1833	21, 22.
	Martin Van Buren	Mar. 4, 1833 -Mar. 3, 1837	23, 24.
Martin Van Buren	Richard M. Johnson	Mar. 4, 1837 -Mar. 3, 1841	25, 26.
William Henry Harrison[4]	John Tyler	Mar. 4, 1841 -Apr. 4, 1841	27.
John Tyler		Apr. 6, 1841 -Mar. 3, 1845	27, 28.
James K. Polk	George M. Dallas	Mar. 4, 1845 -Mar. 3, 1849	29, 30.
Zachary Taylor[4]	Millard Fillmore	Mar. 5, 1849 -July 9, 1850	31.
Millard Fillmore		July 10, 1850 -Mar. 3, 1853	31, 32.
Franklin Pierce	William R. King[5]	Mar. 4, 1853 -Mar. 3, 1857	33, 34.
James Buchanan	John C. Breckinridge	Mar. 4, 1857 -Mar. 3, 1861	35, 36.
Abraham Lincoln[4]	Hannibal Hamlin	Mar. 4, 1861 -Mar. 3, 1865	37, 38.
	Andrew Johnson	Mar. 4, 1865 -Apr. 15, 1865	39.
Andrew Johnson		Apr. 15, 1865 -Mar. 3, 1869	39, 40.
Ulysses S. Grant	Schuyler Colfax	Mar. 4, 1869 -Mar. 3, 1873	41, 42.
	Henry Wilson[6]	Mar. 4, 1873 -Mar. 3, 1877	43, 44.
Rutherford B. Hayes	William A. Wheeler	Mar. 4, 1877 -Mar. 3, 1881	45, 46.
James A. Garfield[4]	Chester A. Arthur	Mar. 4, 1881 -Sept. 19, 1881	47.
Chester A. Arthur		Sept. 20, 1881 -Mar. 3, 1885	47, 48.
Grover Cleveland[7]	Thomas A. Hendricks[8]	Mar. 4, 1885 -Mar. 3, 1889	49, 50.
Benjamin Harrison	Levi P. Morton	Mar. 4, 1889 -Mar. 3, 1893	51, 52.
Grover Cleveland[7]	Adlai E. Stevenson	Mar. 4, 1893 -Mar. 3, 1897	53, 54.
William McKinley[4]	Garret A. Hobart[9]	Mar. 4, 1897 -Mar. 3, 1901	55, 56.
	Theodore Roosevelt	Mar. 4, 1901 -Sept. 14, 1901	57.
Theodore Roosevelt		Sept. 14, 1901 -Mar. 3, 1905	57, 58.
	Charles W. Fairbanks	Mar. 4, 1905 -Mar. 3, 1909	59, 60.
William H. Taft	James S. Sherman[10]	Mar. 4, 1909 -Mar. 3, 1913	61, 62.
Woodrow Wilson	Thomas R. Marshall	Mar. 4, 1913 -Mar. 3, 1921	63, 64, 65, 66.
Warren G. Harding[4]	Calvin Coolidge	Mar. 4, 1921 -Aug. 2, 1923	67.
Calvin Coolidge		Aug. 3, 1923 -Mar. 3, 1925	68.
	Charles Gates Dawes	Mar. 4, 1925 -Mar. 3, 1929	69, 70.
Herbert C. Hoover	Charles Curtis	Mar. 4, 1929 -Mar. 3, 1933	71, 72.
Franklin D. Roosevelt[4]	John N. Garner	Mar. 4, 1933 -Jan. 20, 1941	73, 74, 75, 76.
	Henry A. Wallace	Jan. 20, 1941 -Jan. 20, 1945	77, 78.
	Harry S. Truman	Jan. 20, 1945 -Apr. 12, 1945	79.
Harry S Truman		Apr. 12, 1945 -Jan. 20, 1949	79, 80.
	Alben W. Barkley	Jan. 20, 1949 -Jan. 20, 1953	81, 82.
Dwight D. Eisenhower	Richard M. Nixon	Jan. 20, 1953 -Jan. 20, 1961	83, 84, 85, 86.
John F. Kennedy[4]	Lyndon B. Johnson	Jan. 20, 1961 -Nov. 22, 1963	87, 88.
Lyndon B. Johnson		Nov. 22, 1963 -Jan. 20, 1965	88.
	Hubert H. Humphrey	Jan. 20, 1965 -Jan. 20, 1969	89, 90.
Richard M. Nixon	Spiro T. Agnew[11]	Jan. 20, 1969 -Oct. 10, 1973	91, 92, 93.
		Oct. 10, 1973 -Dec. 6, 1973	93.
	Gerald R. Ford[12]	Dec. 6, 1973 -Aug. 9, 1974	93.
Gerald R. Ford[13]		Aug. 9, 1974 -Dec. 19, 1974	93.
	Nelson A. Rockefeller[14]	Dec. 19, 1974 -Jan. 20, 1977	93, 94, 95.
James Earl (Jimmy) Carter	Walter F. Mondale	Jan. 20, 1977 -Jan. 20, 1981	95, 96.
Ronald W. Reagan	George Bush	Jan. 20, 1981 -Jan. 20, 1989	97, 98, 99, 100.
George Bush	J. Danforth Quayle	Jan. 20, 1989 -Jan. 20, 1993	101, 102.
Bill Clinton	Al Gore	Jan. 20, 1993 -Jan. 20, 2001	103, 104, 105, 106.
George W. Bush	Richard B. Cheney	Jan. 20, 2001 -Jan. 20, 2005	107,108.

[1] Died Apr. 20, 1812.
[2] Died Nov. 23, 1814.
[3] Resigned Dec. 28, 1832, to become U.S. Senator.
[4] Died in office.
[5] Died Apr. 18, 1853.
[6] Died Nov. 22, 1875.
[7] Terms not consecutive.
[8] Died Nov. 25, 1885.
[9] Died Nov. 21, 1899.
[10] Died Oct. 30, 1912.
[11] Resigned Oct. 10, 1973.

[12] First Vice President nominated by the President and confirmed by the Congress pursuant to the 25th amendment to the Constitution of the United States.

[13] Succeeded to the presidency upon the resignation of Richard M. Nixon on Aug. 9, 1974.

[14] Nominated to be Vice President by President Gerald R. Ford on Aug. 20, 1974; confirmed by the Senate on Dec. 10, 1974; confirmed by the House and took the oath of office on Dec. 19, 1974.

LEGISLATIVE TERMS BY ASSEMBLIES

Assembly	Date	Assembly	Date
1st	1819-1821	47th	1911-1913
2nd	1821-1823	48th	1913-1915
3rd	1823-1825	49th	1915-1917
4th	1825-1827	50th	1917-1919
5th	1827-1829	51st	1919-1921
6th	1829-1831	52nd	1921-1923
7th	1831-1833	53rd	1923-1925
8th	1833-1835	54th	1925-1927
9th	1835-1837	55th	1927-1929
10th	1837-1839	56th	1929-1931
11th	1839-1841	57th	1931-1933
12th	1841-1843	58th	1933-1935
13th	1843-1845	59th	1935-1937
14th	1845-1847	60th	1937-1939
15th	1847-1849	61st	1939-1941
16th	1849-1851	62nd	1941-1943
17th	1851-1853	63rd	1943-1945
18th	1853-1855	64th	1945-1947
19th	1855-1857	65th	1947-1949
20th	1857-1859	66th	1949-1951
21st	1859-1861	67th	1951-1953
22nd	1861-1863	68th	1953-1955
23rd	1863-1865	69th	1955-1957
24th	1865-1867	70th	1957-1959
25th	1867-1869	71st	1959-1961
26th	1869-1871	72nd	1961-1963
27th	1871-1873	73rd	1963-1965
28th	1873-1875	74th	1965-1967
29th	1875-1877	75th	1967-1969
30th	1877-1879	76th	1969-1971
31st	1879-1881	77th	1971-1973
32nd	1881-1883	78th	1973-1975
33rd	1883-1885	79th	1975-1977
34th	1885-1887	80th	1977-1979
35th	1887-1889	81st	1979-1981
36th	1889-1891	82nd	1981-1983
37th	1891-1893	83rd	1983-1985
38th	1893-1895	84th	1985-1987
39th	1895-1897	85th	1987-1989
40th	1897-1899	86th	1989-1991
41st	1899-1901	87th	1991-1993
42nd	1901-1903	88th	1993-1995
43rd	1903-1905	89th	1995-1997
44th	1905-1907	90th	1997-1999
45th	1907-1909	91st	1999-2001
46th	1909-1911	92nd	2001-2003

LEGISLATIVE ROSTER, 1818-2002

The following roster lists the members of all 92 General Assemblies that have met since Illinois became a state in 1818.

The 1st General Assembly, which met at Kaskaskia on Oct. 5, 1818, consisted of only 14 senators and 29 representatives. The current Assembly (92nd) has 59 senators and 118 representatives.

The members of the 16th General Assembly, which convened at Springfield on Jan. 1, 1849, were the first to be elected from defined districts.

The House members of the 74th Assembly (1965-66) were elected "At Large" because of the failure to reapportion.

Senators

Abt, Paul W., 49th Dist., 49th, 50th, 55th, 56th
Acton, William N., 22nd Dist., 44th, 45th
Adair, J. Leroy, 36th Dist., 56th, 57th
Adams, Augustus, 5th Dist., 19th, 20th
Adams, George E., 6th Dist., 32nd, 33rd
Adams, John H., 4th Dist., 19th; 22nd Dist., 25th
Adams, Richard F., 5th Dist., 22nd
Adams, Robley D., 44th Dist., 34th, 35th
Addams, John H., 4th Dist., 20th, 21st; 22nd Dist., 23rd, 24th, 26th
Adesko, Thaddeus V., 9th Dist., 65th, 66th
Ainsworth, Henry A., 21st Dist., 33rd, 34th
Albertsen, V. J., 26th Dist., 42nd; 30th Dist., 43rd
Alden, Roy, 48th Dist., 42nd; 44th Dist., 43rd
Alexander, Ethel Skyles, 16th Dist., 84th-87th
Alexander, Jediah, 4th Dist., 27th
Alexander, Samuel, 5th-7th
Allen, Edward R., 19th Dist., 23rd, 24th
Allen, James, 10th-12th
Allen, John, 10th
Allen, Sylvester, 37th Dist., 37th, 38th
Allen, Wm. H., 6th Dist., 27th
Allen, Willis, 14th, 15th
Allison, John Y., 15th
Ames, Alfred, 24th Dist., 16th
Anderson, Andrew J., 10th Dist., 44th, 45th
Anderson, Perry, 27th Dist., 37th, 38th
Anderson, Wm. B., 3rd Dist., 27th
Andrus, Henry, 10th Dist., 42nd, 43rd, 46th-49th
Anthony, George D., 23rd Dist., 39th, 40th
Applington, Zenas, 3rd Dist., 21st, 22nd
Archer, Wm. B., 5th-8th
Archer, William R., 38th Dist., 28th-32nd; 36th Dist., 33rd
Armstrong, George C., 48th Dist., 62nd-65th
Arnold, John W., 15th Dist., 37th, 38th
Arnold, J. D., 8th Dist., 19th, 20th
Arntzen, Bernard, 37th Dist., 29th, 30th
Arrington, W. Russell, 6th Dist., 69th; 4th Dist., 70th-74th; 1st Dist., 75th-77th
Artley, Sylvester, 3rd Dist., 31st, 32nd
Aspinwall, Homer F., 12th Dist., 38th-41st
Atwood, John A., 10th Dist., 50th, 51st
Austin, Henry W., 23rd Dist., 49th, 50th-52nd
Awerkamp, Thomas J., 36th Dist., 74th
Bacon, Charles H., 15th Dist., 35th, 36th
Bacon, George E., 31st Dist., 35th-37th
Bailey, M. B., 18th Dist., 42nd; 22nd Dist., 43rd, 46th-57th
Baker, B. Frank, 37th Dist., 45th, 46th
Baker, Charles W., 10th Dist., 56th-69th
Baker, Edward D., 12th, 13th
Baldwin, Elmer, 17th Dist., 28th
Baldwin, Percival G., 11th Dist., 49th, 50th
Ball, Lewis C., 2nd Dist., 46th, 47th
Baltz, Meade, 41st Dist., 75th-77th
Bangs, Mark, 16th Dist., 27th
Bankson, Andrew, 3rd, 4th
Barbour, James J., 6th Dist., 50th-59th
Bardill, J. G., 47th Dist., 49th-52nd
Bare, Thomas D., 36th Dist., 44th, 45th
Barker, Lewis, 1st-4th
Barkhausen, David N., 30th Dist., 83rd-89th

Barnes, Charles N., 20th Dist., 38th, 39th
Barnett, Robert F., 13th
Barr, Richard J., 41st Dist., 43rd, 44th-66th
Barry, Norman C., 21st Dist., 63rd-68th
Bartley, Jesse E., 48th Dist., 44th, 45th
Bartling, Henry C., 6th Dist., 38th, 39th
Bartulis, A. C., 49th Dist., 78th
Bash, Daniel N., 2nd Dist., 30th, 31st
Bass, George, 3rd Dist., 37th, 38th
Bassett, Mark M., 26th Dist., 36th, 37th
Baumrucker, Charles F., 7th Dist., 60th
Baxter, Delos W., 10th Dist., 40th, 41st
Beach, Enoch, 6th, 7th
Beaird, Joseph H., 3rd-5th
Beal, Edmond, 47th Dist., 47th, 48th
Becker, Leonard, 7th Dist., 81st, 82nd; 22nd Dist., 83rd
Beckman, Louis E., 20th Dist., 60th-64th
Begole, Henry C., 49th Dist., 41st, 42nd
Behrman, Carl, 18th Dist., 58th, 59th
Bell, Andrew J., 26th Dist., 32nd, 33rd, 34th, 35th
Bell, James F., 42nd Dist., 78th, 79th
Benefiel, Philip B., 48th Dist., 74th
Bennett, Albert E., 10th Dist., 70th, 71st; 14th Dist., 75th, 76th
Benson, Arnold P., 14th Dist., 58th-63rd
Benson, O. E., 39th Dist., 61st-66th
Bent, Charles, 11th Dist., 31st, 32nd
Berggren, August W., 22nd Dist., 32nd-35th
Berman, Arthur L., 11th Dist., 80th-82nd; 2nd Dist., 83rd-87th; 9th Dist., 88th-91st
Berning, Karl, 32nd Dist., 75th-82nd
Berry, Orville F., 24th Dist., 36th-38th; 28th Dist., 39th-41st; 32nd Dist., 43rd-45th
Berry, Wm., 10th Dist., 22nd; 14th Dist., 23rd
Bester, George C., 8th Dist., 21st, 22nd
Beveridge, John L., 25th Dist., 27th
Bidwill, Arthur J., 7th Dist., 61st-69th; 1st Dist., 70th-74th; 2nd Dist., 75th-77th
Billings, Charles L., 1st Dist., 45th, 46th
Bird, James, 4th, 5th, 8th
Bishop, Robert M., 8th Dist., 27th
Blackwell, Robert, 11th
Blanchard, Israel, 3rd Dist., 23rd
Bliss, Stephen, 4th, 5th
Blodgett, Henry W., 2nd Dist., 21st, 22nd
Bloom, Prescott, 46th Dist., 79th-82nd; 47th Dist., 83rd, 84th
Boal, Robert, 14th, 15th
Boehm, John J., 15th Dist., 49th-56th
Boeke, Harry C., 12th Dist., 58th, 59th
Bogardus, Charles, 18th Dist., 36th-41st
Bohrer, Florence Fifer, 26th Dist., 54th-57th
Bollinger, Albert C., 48th Dist., 40th, 41st
Bomke, Larry K., 50th Dist., 89th-92nd
Bond, Benjamin, 9th, 10th
Bonfield, Thomas P., 16th Dist., 30th, 31st
Boon, William, 2nd, 3rd
Borough, Joseph, 10th, 11th
Bostwick, Manoah, 11th
Boughner, Jackson L., 3rd Dist., 70th
Bowers, Jack E., 41st Dist., 80th-82nd
Bowles, Evelyn M., 56th Dist., 88th-92nd

480

Bowman, Wm. B., 1st Dist., 27th
Boyd, Randolph, 37th Dist., 53rd-56th
Boyd, Thomas A., 15th Dist., 25th-27th
Brady, Francis P., 1st Dist., 47th, 48th, 51st
Brady, Michael I., 11th Dist., 79th
Brands, Albert L., 48th Dist., 38th, 39th
Breidt, Herman H., 25th Dist., 45th, 46th
Brenholt, John J., 47th Dist., 41st, 42nd
Brewer, Thomas, 33rd Dist., 29th, 30th
Bridges, Frank M., 37th Dist., 33rd, 34th
Brink, F. E. W., 42nd Dist., 30th, 31st, 36th, 37th
Broderick, John, 17th Dist., 41st, 42nd; 27th Dist., 45th-52nd, 55th-61st
Brookins, Howard B., 18th Dist., 85th-87th
Brooks, Austin, 12th Dist., 21st, 22nd
Brooks, William S., 15th Dist., 28th
Brown, John, 15th
Brown, John S., 32nd Dist., 54th, 55th
Brown, Robert, 25th Dist., 29th, 30th
Brown, William, 39th Dist., 28th
Brown, William M., 6th Dist., 44th-47th
Browning, Orville H., 10th, 11th
Broyles, Paul, 46th Dist., 64th-74th; 55th Dist., 75th, 76th
Bruce, Terry L., 55th Dist., 77th; 54th Dist., 78th-82nd; 54th Dist., 83rd
Bryan, Silas L., 3rd Dist., 18th; 20th Dist., 19th, 21st
Buck, Clarence F., 32nd Dist., 50th-53rd
Buckmaster, Samuel A., 21st Dist., 21st, 22nd
Buehler, John, 5th Dist., 29th, 30th
Buford, John, 13th, 14th
Burgess, H. S., 46th Dist., 54th, 55th, 58th-61st
Burke, Beatty T., 40th Dist., 28th, 29th
Burke, Richard M., 11th Dist., 35th, 36th
Burnett, O. H., 50th Dist., 42nd-44th
Burns, George W., 36th Dist., 28th
Burt, Marvin F., 13th Dist., 68th, 69th; 56th Dist., 70th, 71st
Burton, Frank W., 38th Dist., 44th-47th
Burzynski, J. Bradley, 35th Dist., 88th-92nd
Bush, J. M., 6th Dist., 27th
Bushnell, Washington, 7th Dist., 22nd; 17th Dist., 23rd-25th
Busse, Fred A., 21st Dist., 41st, 42nd
Butler, Homer, 50th Dist., 64th, 65th, 68th, 69th
Butler, Marty, 28th Dist., 87th-90th
Butler, Michael J., 4th Dist., 42nd, 43rd
Butler, Peter, 10th, 11th
Butler, Walker, 13th Dist., 63rd-68th
Buzbee, Kenneth V., 58th Dist., 78th-83rd
Cadwell, George, 1st, 2nd, 3rd
Cain, John, 13th
Caldwell, Ben F., 39th Dist., 37th, 38th
Callon, Wm. P., 39th Dist., 31st, 32nd
Campbell, Daniel A., 19th Dist., 39th-42nd; 21st Dist., 43rd-45th
Campbell, F. C., 42nd Dist., 48th-51st
Campbell, James M., 16th Dist., 18th; 10th Dist., 19th
Campbell, James R., 46th Dist., 36th-39th
Campbell, W. J., 7th Dist., 31st-34th
Canaday, Stephen D., 38th Dist., 48th-51st
Canfield, Eugene, 14th Dist., 28th, 29th
Canfield, Robert R., 54th Dist., 70th-73rd
Cantwell, Thomas A., 4th Dist., 34th, 35th
Carey, Philip J., 19th Dist., 71st, 72nd
Carlin, Thomas, 4th-7th
Carlin, William H., 12th Dist., 19th, 20th
Carlson, Martin R., 33rd Dist., 51st-58th
Carpenter, Rollie C., 16th Dist., 69th-71st
Carpentier, Charles F., 33rd Dist., 61st-68th
Carpentier, Donald D., 53rd Dist., 73rd, 74th; 43rd Dist., 75th-77th
Carroll, Howard W., 15th Dist., 78th-82nd; 1st Dist., 83rd-87th; 8th Dist., 88th-90th
Carroll, John W., 4th Dist., 75th-77th
Carroll, Patrick J., 9th Dist., 47th-60th
Carter, Armetus, 25th Dist., 27th
Case, Selon H., 2nd Dist., 40th, 41st
Casey, John, 28th Dist., 28th, 29th
Casey, Samuel K., 3rd Dist., 26th, 27th
Casey, Thomas, 46th Dist., 28th, 29th
Casey, Zadok, 5th, 6th; 20th Dist., 22nd
Cash, Wilbur J., 26th Dist., 62nd-67th
Castle, Miles B., 13th Dist., 28th-30th
Catlin, Seth, 13th-15th
Cavarly, Alfred W., 13th-15th

Chaffee, George D., 40th Dist., 44th, 45th
Chamberlin, John M., Jr., 49th Dist., 47th, 48th
Chapman, Pleasant T., 51st Dist., 37th-42nd
Chapman, Thos. S., 37th Dist., 35th, 36th
Cheaney, Samuel L., 47th Dist., 31st, 32nd
Cheney, William H., 10th Dist., 25th
Cherry, Robert E., 31st Dist., 69th; 27th Dist., 70th-74th; 11th Dist., 75th-77th
Chew, Charles, Jr., 29th Dist., 75th-82nd; 16th Dist., 83rd, 84th
Churchill, George, 11th, 12th
Clark, Albert C., 13th Dist., 43rd-48th, 50th-54th
Clark, Horace S., 32nd Dist., 32nd, 33rd
Clark, Wm. G., 21st Dist., 69th
Clarke, Terrel E., 9th Dist., 75th-77th; 6th Dist., 78th, 79th
Clayborne, James F., Jr., 57th Dist., 89th-92nd
Cleary, Michael H., 12th Dist., 48th, 49th
Clewis, Richard S., 17th Dist., 80th
Cliffe, Adam C., 35th Dist., 49th-51st
Clifford, W. E. C., 24th Dist., 58th-61st
Cloonan, Thomas, 11th Dist., 33rd, 34th
Cloud, Newton, 14th Dist., 16th, 17th
Clough, John H., 3rd Dist., 33rd, 34th
Cochran, James S., 12th Dist., 34th, 35th
Cockle, Washington, 18th Dist., 18th
Coffey, E. C., 24th Dist., 20th, 21st
Coffey, Max E., 53rd Dist., 80th-84th
Cohrs, John B., 11th Dist., 24th, 25th
Coleman, C. F., 38th Dist., 42nd; 40th Dist., 43rd
Coleman, Peter E., 39th Dist., 49th, 50th
Collins, Dennis J., 35th Dist., 63rd-74th; 33rd Dist., 75th-77th
Collins, Earlean, 21st Dist., 80th-82nd; 9th Dist., 83rd-87th; 4th Dist., 88th-90th
Compton, William A., 32nd Dist., 48th, 49th
Condee, Leander D., 2nd Dist., 32nd, 33rd
Condy, Oliver, 15th
Connors, William J., 29th Dist., 60th-69th; 25th Dist., 70th-72nd
Conolly, John H., 31st Dist., 78th
Conrad, Will, 6th
Constable, Charles H., 14th, 15th
Conway, Joseph, 4th-8th
Cook, Burton C., 20th Dist., 18th; 7th Dist., 19th-21st
Coon, Reuben W., 8th Dist., 38th, 39th
Coppinger, John W., 41st Dist., 37th, 38th
Corder, Anderson P., 2nd Dist., 18th; 23rd Dist., 19th
Cornwell, Willett H., 31st Dist., 47th-52nd
Coulson, Robert, 52nd Dist., 73rd, 74th; 31st Dist., 75th-77th
Course, Kenneth W., 14th Dist., 77th; 17th Dist., 78th, 79th
Courtney, Thomas J., 11th Dist., 55th-57th
Cox, Thomas, 1st
Crabtree, John D., 19th Dist., 35th
Craig, Isaac B., 32nd Dist., 38th; 40th Dist., 39th
Craig, Larkin, 8th-10th
Crain, John, 14th
Crawford, Andrew, 21st Dist., 26th, 27th
Crawford, Charles H., 2nd Dist., 34th-37th; 5th Dist., 39th, 40th
Crawford, Samuel, 6th, 7th
Crawford, William F., 21st Dist., 37th, 38th
Crews, William J., 45th Dist., 28th
Crisenberry, R. G., 44th Dist., 60th-71st
Crittenden, Samuel H., 13th Dist., 25th, 26th
Cronin, A. L., 11th Dist., 69th; 15th Dist., 70th-74th
Cronin, Dan, 39th Dist., 88th-92nd
Crozier, Samuel, 2nd, 3rd
Cruikshank, Chas. E., 19th Dist., 45th, 46th
Culbertson, W. P., 38th Dist., 68th, 69th
Cullerton, John J., 4th Dist., 87th; 6th Dist., 88th-92nd
Cullom, Richard N., 12th, 13th
Cummings, Samuel P., 25th Dist., 28th
Cunningham, Geo. W., 30th Dist., 44th, 45th
Cunningham, John, 43rd Dist., 28th
Curley, Daniel F., 4th Dist., 40th, 41st
Curtis, Edward C., 20th Dist., 44th-50th
Curtis, Ira R., 8th Dist., 34th
Cuthbertson, Andrew S., 38th Dist., 52nd-57th
Cuthbertson, W. P., 38th Dist., 68th, 69th
Daggett, John F., 18th Dist., 27th
Dailey, John, 18th Dist., 46th-55th
Daley, John, 11th Dist., 86th
Daley, Richard J., 9th Dist., 61st-64th

Daley, Richard M., 23rd Dist., 78th-81st
D'Arco, John A., Jr., 20th Dist., 80th-82nd; 10th Dist., 83rd-87th
Darnell, John M., 34th Dist., 34th, 35th
Darrow, Clarence A., 36th Dist., 83rd, 84th
Dart, Thomas J., 14th Dist., 87th
Davidson, Charles A., 45th Dist., 41st, 42nd
Davidson, John A., 50th Dist., 78th-87th
Davidson, Wm. H., 8th-13th
Davidson, W. K., 36th Dist., 76th, 77th
Davis, Chester P., 30th Dist., 30th, 31st
Davis, David, 26th Dist., 68th-74th
Davis, Jacob C., 13th Dist., 14th, 15th; 17th Dist., 17th, 18th; 11th Dist., 19th
Davis, Lloyd E., 40th Dist., 68th, 69th
Davis, R. H., 36th Dist., 36th
Davis, Thomas G. C., 15th
Davis, William Y., 1st Dist., 16th
Dawson, Glenn V., 30th Dist., 82nd; 18th Dist., 83rd, 84th
Dawson, Thomas J., 6th Dist., 42nd, 43rd
Dean, George W., 35th Dist., 35th, 36th
DeAngelis, Aldo A., 10th Dist., 81st, 82nd; 40th Dist., 83rd-89th
Dearborn, Luther, 36th Dist., 30th, 31st
Deck, Jesse J., 28th Dist., 54th, 55th
Degnan, Timothy, 22nd Dist., 82nd; 11th Dist., 83rd-85th
DeLaCour, Joseph L., 25th Dist., 73rd, 74th; 12th Dist., 75th
DeLaney, Martin A., 6th Dist., 30th, 31st
DeLang, Frederick C., 5th Dist., 32nd
DeLeo, James A., 10th Dist., 88th-92nd
del Valle, Miguel, 5th Dist., 85th-87th; 2nd Dist., 88th-92nd
Dement, Henry D., 12th Dist., 30th, 31st
Demuzio, Vince, 49th Dist., 79th-92nd
Dennis, Elias S., 15th
Denny, John, 15th; 19th Dist., 16th, 17th
Denvir, John T., 19th Dist., 47th-56th
DeTolve, Anthony J., 7th Dist., 71st-74th
Detrick, John E. 4th Dist., 18th; 24th Dist., 19th
Dick, Frank J., 26th Dist., 63rd-65th
Dillard, Kirk W., 41st Dist., 88th-92nd
Dituri, Robert P., 10th Dist., 87th
Dixon, Alan J., 49th Dist., 73rd, 74th; 54th Dist., 75th, 76th
Dixon, George C., 35th Dist., 59th-62nd
Dixon, George William, 1st Dist., 43rd, 44th
Donahue, Laura Kent, 48th Dist., 82nd-92nd
Donahue, Michael, 10th Dist., 27th; 29th Dist., 28th
Donnelly, Timothy C., 38th Dist., 66th, 67th
Donnewald, James, 42nd Dist., 74th; 51st Dist., 75th-82nd
Donovan, John J., 17th Dist., 70th
Dore, John C., 24th Dist., 26th, 27th
Dougherty, Daniel, 13th Dist., 69th-74th; 30th Dist., 75th-79th
Dougherty, John, 13th-15th
Dow, Samuel K., 4th Dist., 28th, 29th
Dowd, Lawrence E., 1st Dist., 63rd-66th
Downing, B. F., 35th Dist., 46th
Downing, T. Mac, 32nd Dist., 60th-73rd
Drach, George E., 45th Dist., 67th-74th
Dresser, Nathaniel S., 38th Dist., 40th, 41st
Droste, Elmer H., 38th Dist., 62nd
Duda, Walter, 15th Dist., 75th, 76th
Dudycz, Walter W., 7th Dist., 84th-92nd
Dummer, Henry E., 17th Dist., 22nd; 12th Dist., 23rd
Duncan, James W., 23rd Dist., 33rd, 34th
Duncan, Joseph, 4th, 5th
Dunlap, Henry M., 30th Dist., 38th-42nd; 24th Dist., 43rd, 44th, 46th, 47th, 50th-57th
Dunlap, Samuel, 14th, 15th
Dunn, Ralph, 58th Dist., 84th-89th
Dunn, Thomas A., 42nd Dist., 85th-87th; 43rd Dist., 88th-90th
Duvall, R. E., 49th Dist., 51st-54th
Dwyer, Edward J., 17th Dist., 39th, 40th
Early, John, 23rd Dist., 27th; 9th Dist., 28th-30th
Eastman, Francis A., 24th Dist., 24th, 25th
Eberspacher, Edward C., 40th Dist., 72nd, 73rd
Eckhart, Bernard A., 1st Dist., 35th, 36th
Eddy, James W., 19th Dist., 27th
Edsall, James K., 20th Dist., 27th
Edwards, Cyrus, 9th, 10th
Edwards, John C., 46th Dist., 32nd, 33rd

Edwards, Ninian W., 14th, 15th
Edwards, W. Scott, 26th Dist., 40th, 41st
Egan, Robert J., 16th Dist., 77th, 79th-82nd; 7th Dist., 83rd
Emmons, Lyman W., 48th Dist., 54th, 55th
English, Revill W., 13th
Epler, James M., 12th Dist., 26th, 27th
Essington, Thurlow G., 39th Dist., 51st-54th
Etheredge, Forest D., 39th Dist., 82nd; 21st Dist., 83rd-87th
Ettelson, Samuel A., 3rd Dist., 45th-53rd
Evans, Aiken, 12th,13th
Evans, Henry A., 14th Dist., 32nd-45th
Evans, James, 7th, 8th
Ewing, Clinton L., 43rd Dist., 57th-62nd
Ewing, John, 4th, 5th
Ewing, Wm. Lee D., 8th, 9th
Farley, Bruce A., 17th Dist., 88th-90th
Farmer, Wm. M., 43rd Dist., 37th, 38th
Farnum, Frank C., 19th Dist., 43rd, 44th
Farrelly, J. K. P., 36th Dist., 42nd; 38th Dist., 43rd
Fawell, Beverly, 20th Dist., 83rd-91st
Fawell, Harris W., 41st Dist., 73rd, 74th; 40th Dist., 75th-77th; 41st Dist., 78th, 79th
Feaman, Jacob, 12th
Felts, James H., 50th Dist., 56th, 57th
Ferguson, Virgil S., 19th Dist., 37th, 38th
Fifer, Joseph W., 28th Dist., 32nd, 33rd
Finley, Morgan M., 9th Dist., 71st-74th
Finn, W. L., 42nd Dist., 56th-60th
Fisher, Hendrick V., 33rd Dist., 39th, 40th
Fithian, William, 11th-14th
Fitzgerald, Peter G., 27th Dist., 88th-90th
Fitzpatrick, P. V., 1st Dist., 39th, 40th
Flagg, Norman G., 47th Dist., 55th, 56th, 61st-64th
Flagg, Willard C., 5th Dist., 26th, 27th
Flaman, Jacob, 13th
Fletcher, Job, 9th-11th
Fletcher, John, 24th Dist., 32nd, 33rd
Ford, Milton M., 21st Dist., 31st, 32nd
Ford, Thomas E., 42nd Dist., 38th, 39th
Foreman, William S., 42nd Dist., 34th, 35th
Forman, Ferris, 14th
Forreston, James H., 40th Dist., 52nd-55th
Forst, Edward J., 15th Dist., 47th, 48th
Fort, Greenbury L., 16th Dist., 25th, 26th
Fort, Robert B., 20th Dist., 40th-43rd
Fosdick, Samuel T., 18th Dist., 30th, 31st
Fowler, H. R., 44th Dist., 42nd; 48th Dist., 43rd
Fox, Seymour, 10th Dist., 72nd, 73rd
Franklin, Noah Elmo, 26th Dist., 48th, 49th
Frantz, Henry J., 20th Dist., 30th, 31st
Fribley, John W., 40th Dist., 58th-67th
Friedland, John E., 2nd Dist., 81st, 82nd; 33rd Dist., 83rd-87th
Friedrich, Dwight P., 42nd Dist., 68th-73rd
Frisbee, Wm. J., 27th Dist., 36th
Fuller, Allen C., 23rd Dist., 25th-27th
Fuller, Charles E., 9th Dist., 31st, 32nd; 8th Dist., 36th 37th
Fuller, DuFay A., 8th Dist., 42nd, 43rd
Fuller, Samuel W., 17th Dist., 20th, 21st
Funderburk, Geo. W., 39th Dist., 41st, 42nd
Funk, Frank H., 26th Dist., 46th, 47th
Funk, Isaac, 10th Dist., 23rd, 24th
Funk, Lafayette, 28th Dist., 34th, 35th
Funkhouser, Presley, 19th Dist., 22nd
Gage, George, 2nd Dist., 19th, 20th
Galbreath, Wm. B., 32nd Dist., 34th
Galligan, Peter F., 15th Dist., 41st, 42nd
Galpin, Homer K., 2nd Dist., 44th, 45th
Garcia, Jesus G., 1st Dist., 87th-90th
Gardner, Corbus P., 27th Dist., 41st, 42nd; 39th Dist., 43rd-46th
Garmisa, Benedict, 23rd Dist., 69th
Garrity, Michael F., 13th Dist., 35th, 36th
Gaston, William, 11th, 12th
Gatewood, Wm. J., 9th-12th
Gear, Hezekiah H., 23rd Dist., 16th
Geary, John B., 5th Dist., 61st, 62nd
Geo-Karis, Adeline J., 31st Dist., 81st-92nd
Gibbs, George A., 3rd Dist., 35th, 36th
Gibbs, Worthington J., 11th, 12th
Gibson, James F., 32nd Dist., 46th, 47th
Gibson, Simeon K., 1st Dist., 27th

Giffin, D. Logan, 45th Dist., 64th-66th
Gilberson, Herbert G., 47th Dist., 53rd, 54th
Gilbert, John C., 44th Dist., 72nd-74th; 56th Dist., 75th-77th
Gilham, James, 13th
Gillespie, Joseph, 15th; 6th Dist., 16th-18th; 21st Dist., 19th, 20th
Gillham, Daniel B., 41st Dist., 33rd, 34th
Gillmeister, William F., 23rd Dist., 57th, 58th
Gitz, James, 35th Dist., 81st, 82nd
Glackin, Edward J., 17th Dist., 45th-54th
Glasford, Samuel M., 51st Dist., 29th, 30th
Glass, Bradley M. 1st Dist., 78th-80th
Glenn, Archibald A., 36th Dist., 28th, 29th
Glenn, Otis F., 44th Dist., 52nd, 53rd
Gore, David, 38th Dist., 34th, 35th
Gorman, Al F., 4th Dist., 46th-51st
Gorman, John J., 19th Dist., 67th-69th; 31st Dist., 70th
Goslin, Gregg, 57th Dist., 89th
Gottschalk, Arthur R., 8th Dist., 72nd-75th
Goudy, William C., 10th Dist., 20th, 21st
Graham, Benj., 19th Dist., 18th; 9th Dist., 19th
Graham, John A., 3rd Dist., 71st-76th; 2nd Dist., 78th-81st
Graham, Paul "Red", 34th Dist., 72nd-74th
Graham, R. V., 19th Dist., 57th-60th
Graham, Robert J., 25th Dist., 69th; 29th Dist., 70th
Grammer, John, 3rd, 4th, 7th, 8th
Granger, Flavel K., 8th Dist., 40th, 41st
Grass, Alfred H., 8th Dist., 16th, 17th
Gray, James W., 49th Dist., 67th-72nd
Gray, John H., 35th Dist., 47th, 48th
Gray, William A., 36th Dist., 52nd, 53rd
Green, David K., 4th Dist., 24th, 25th
Green, Henry, 10th Dist., 28th, 29th
Green, Herschel, 48th Dist., 70th-72nd
Green, Madge Miller, 48th Dist., 73rd
Green, Reed, 50th Dist., 38th, 39th
Green, Wm. H., 1st Dist., 23rd, 24th
Greenwood, Charles F., 17th Dist., 35th, 36th
Greer, Abner, 11th
Gregg, Hugh, 3rd Dist., 17th; 23rd Dist., 22nd, 23rd
Gridley, Ashbel, 11th Dist., 17th,18th
Grindle, William L., 50th Dist., 70th-74th
Griswold, Chas. A., 18th Dist., 36th
Groen, Egbert B., 30th Dist., 68th-74th; 48th Dist., 75th-77th
Grotberg, John E., 38th Dist., 80th-82nd; 25th Dist., 83rd
Guard, Timothy, 5th-7th
Guidice, Richard, 19th Dist., 80th
Gundlach, George, 42nd Dist., 28th, 29th
Gunning, Thomas P., 37th Dist., 57th-63rd
Haas, Joseph F., 25th Dist., 43rd, 44th
Haase, Christian, 16th Dist., 48th, 49th
Hackelton, Samuel, 10th, 11th
Hacker, John S., 9th-12th
Hadley, William F. L., 41st Dist., 35th, 36th
Haenisch, Herman J., 31st Dist., 53rd-56th
Hagle, Dios C., 44th Dist., 36th, 37th
Haines, John C., 1st Dist., 29th, 30th
Hall, Charles E., 42nd Dist., 40th, 41st
Hall, Harber H., 44th Dist., 78th-80th
Hall, Harry G., 23rd Dist., 41st, 42nd; 29th Dist., 43rd-46th
Hall, Kenneth, 54th Dist., 77th; 57th Dist., 78th-89th
Halvorson, Debbie, 40th Dist., 90th-92nd
Hamer, Thomas, 22nd Dist., 36th-38th; 26th Dist., 39th
Hamilton, Isaac M., 16th Dist., 40th, 41st
Hamilton, John M., 28th Dist., 30th, 31st
Hamilton, John R., 34th Dist., 48th-57th
Hamilton, Lloyd F., 39th Dist., 33rd, 34th
Hamilton, R. S., 49th Dist., 43rd-46th
Hamlin, John, 10th-12th
Hampton, Benjamin R., 14th Dist., 27th; 23rd Dist., 28th
Hanna, Louis H., 32nd Dist., 55th, 57th
Hanna, Robert P., 44th Dist., 30th, 31st
Hanson, Frank O., 26th Dist., 52nd, 53rd
Hanson, George M., 15th
Harding, Fred E., 35th Dist., 39th, 40th
Harding, George F., Jr., 1st Dist., 49th, 50th
Hardy, Jeduthan P., 3rd Dist., 16th, 17th
Hargrave, Willis, 1st
Harlan, Edwin, 8th Dist., 26th, 27th
Harold, Jesse F., 29th Dist., 29th, 30th
Harper, Robert M., 33rd Dist., 59th, 60th

Harris, George W., 6th Dist., 48th, 49th
Harris, John, 12th-15th
Harris, William C., 16th Dist., 72nd-74th; 37th Dist., 75th-77th; 38th Dist., 78th, 79th
Harris, William F., 28th Dist., 42nd
Harrison, George W., 11th, 12th, 14th
Hart, Fred J., 39th Dist., 67th-74th
Hasara, Karen, 50th Dist., 88th, 89th
Hatch, Robert F., 19th Dist., 73rd, 74th
Hawkinson, Carl E., 47th Dist., 85th-92nd
Hay, Daniel, 4th, 5th
Hay, Logan, 45th Dist., 45th-48th
Hearn, Campbell S., 36th Dist., 46th-48th
Heckenkamp, Jos. E., 36th Dist., 60th, 61st
Helm, Douglas W., 51st Dist., 43rd-48th
Henderson, Archer, 9th
Henderson, Thomas J., 9th Dist., 20th, 21st
Hendon, Rickey R., 5th Dist., 88th-92nd
Henry, George W., 44th Dist., 28th, 29th
Henry, John, 12th, 14th, 15th
Hensley, William F., 48th Dist., 68th, 69th
Henson, James Atlas, 28th Dist., 44th-47th
Herb, Charles A., 47th Dist., 39th
Herdman, George W., 40th Dist., 30th, 31st
Hereley, Millard B., 13th Dist., 33rd, 34th
Herlihy, Daniel, 25th Dist., 49th-52nd
Herndon, Archer G., 10th-12th
Hewitt, Frank M., 44th Dist., 50th, 51st
Hickey, Vivian V., 34th Dist., 78th-80th
Hickman, W. H., 22nd Dist., 58th-61st
Hicks, H. S., 10th Dist., 52nd-55th
Higbee, Chauncey L., 13th Dist., 21st, 22nd
Higbee, Harry, 36th Dist., 36th-38th; 34th Dist., 39th
Higgins, John J., 48th Dist., 34th, 35th
Hill, George W., 50th Dist., 34th, 35th
Hinchcliffe, John, 49th Dist., 28th
Hoard, Samuel, 13th
Hodges, Charles D., 39th Dist., 29th, 30th
Hoener, Ambrose, 48th Dist., 30th, 31st
Hoffelder, Walter P., 29th Dist., 73rd, 74th; 16th Dist., 75th, 76th
Hogan, Daniel, 51st Dist., 33rd-36th
Holcomb, T. A. E.,1st Dist., 27th
Holmberg, Joyce, 34th Dist., 83rd-87th
Holtshaw, D. W., 42nd Dist., 46th, 47th
Horsley, G. William, 49th Dist., 75th-77th
Houser, John L., 46th Dist., 44th, 45th
Houston, John, 12th, 13th
Houston, Samuel, 15th
Howard, Bushrod B., 23rd Dist., 18th
Howell, J. Will, 50th Dist., 62nd, 63rd
Howell, Vinton E., 28th Dist., 38th; 22nd Dist., 39th
Hubbard, Nicholas L., 28th Dist., 61st-63rd
Huckin, Frank J., 25th Dist., 57th, 59th-64th
Hudson, George "Ray", 41st Dist., 83rd-87th
Huebscn, Arthur A., 7th Dist., 55th-58th
Hughes, Charles H., 35th Dist., 43rd-45th
Hughes, Edward J., 21st Dist., 49th-56th
Hull, Charles E., 42nd Dist., 44th, 45th
Hull, Morton D., 5th Dist., 49th-51st
Humphrey, John, 7th Dist., 35th-46th
Hundley, William B., 34th Dist., 29th
Hunsacher, George, 5th, 6th
Hunt, Daniel P., 17th Dist., 37th, 38th; 29th Dist., 39th-42nd
Hunt, George, 31st Dist., 29th-33rd
Hunter, Andrew, Jr., 8th Dist., 24th, 25th
Hunter, David, 10th Dist., 38th, 39th
Hunter, James M., 22nd Dist., 27th
Hunter, William, 11th, 12th
Huntley, William B., 34th Dist., 28th
Hurburgh, Chas. F., 43rd Dist., 45th-48th
Hurley, Francis A., 2nd Dist., 48th, 49th
Hussman, Bernard L., 43rd Dist., 41st, 42nd
Hynes, Thomas C., 28th Dist., 77th-80th
Ihorn, Louis, 48th Dist., 32nd, 33rd
Iles, Elijah, 5th-8th
Isley, Albert E., 46th Dist., 46th, 47th
Jackson, John, 2nd Dist., 27th
Jacobs, Denny, 36th Dist., 84th-92nd
Jacobs, George P., 12th Dist., 28th, 29th
James, James A., 12th, 13th
Jamison, Alexander, 1st, 2nd
Jandus, Cyril R., 15th Dist., 43rd-46th
Jayne, William, 15th Dist., 22nd

Obama, Barack, 13th Dist., 90th-92nd
O'Brien, Daniel P., Jr., 12th Dist., 77th
O'Brien, Donald J., 4th Dist., 67th-69th; 14th Dist., 70th-73rd
O'Brien, William J., 9th Dist., 39th, 40th
O'Connell, Jerome, 20th Dist., 58th, 59th
O'Connor, Andrew J., 23rd Dist., 36th, 38th
O'Connor, James M., 29th Dist., 47th, 48th
Odam, Dempsey, 2nd Dist., 16th, 17th
O'Daniel, William L., 54th Dist., 83rd-92nd
Odell, William M., 25th Dist., 41st, 42nd
Ogden, Wm. B., 1st Dist., 22nd; 24th Dist., 23rd
Oglesby, Richard J., 16th Dist., 22nd
O'Grady, Edward P., 29th Dist., 57th, 58th
O'Kean, Mortimer, 8th Dist., 18th; 19th Dist., 19th, 21st
Oldfield, Ora, 42nd Dist., 64th, 65th
Olson, Albert J., 8th Dist., 46th-49th
O'Malley, John F., 13th Dist., 37th, 38th
O'Malley, Patrick J., 18th Dist., 88th-92nd
Omelveney, Edward, 5th Dist., 18th
O'Neill, Lottie Holman, 41st Dist., 67th-72nd
O'Rear, William, 10th, 11th
Orendorff, Green P., 20th Dist., 34th, 35th
Organ, Richard L., 46th Dist., 34th, 35th
Osborn, Hawkins S., 4th Dist., 16th, 17th
Osgood, Uri, 21st Dist., 18th; 6th Dist., 19th
Ottwein, Merrill, 53rd Dist., 76th
Owen, Thomas H., 10th
Ozinga, Frank M., 6th Dist., 70th-77th; 8th Dist., 78th-82nd
Paddock, Ray, 8th Dist., 56th-67th
Paisley, George W., 40th Dist., 38th; 39th Dist., 39th
Palmer, Alice J., 13th Dist., 87th-89th
Palmer, Almon S., 16th Dist., 28th, 29th
Palmer, Ben E., 13th Dist., 77th; 12th Dist., 78th, 79th
Palmer, John M., 13th Dist., 17th, 18th
Palmer, John N., 14th Dist., 19th
Parish, John J., 42nd Dist., 61st-67th
Parish, Wm. H., 47th Dist., 29th
Parker, Daniel, 3rd, 4th
Parker, Francis W., 5th Dist., 43rd, 44th
Parker, Milton, 3rd
Parker, Kathleen K., 29th Dist., 89th-92nd
Parker, Nathaniel, 10th, 13th, 14th; 10th Dist., 17th, 18th
Parkinson, Alfred J., 41st Dist., 31st, 32nd
Parks, G. D. A., 6th Dist., 20th, 21st
Parrish, Braxton, 9th-13th
Parrish, William H., 47th Dist., 30th
Parsons, Solomon, 15th Dist., 18th
Partee, Cecil A., 26th Dist., 75th-79th
Patterson, Azro, 17th Dist., 16th
Patterson, Joseph M., 11th Dist., 28th
Patton, William, 19th Dist., 25th, 26th
Payne, Joseph T., 46th Dist., 40th, 41st
Payne, William, 33rd Dist., 41st, 42nd
Pearson, Isaac N., 27th Dist., 35th
Pearson, John, 12th Dist., 13th
Peck, Ebenezer, 11th
Pemberton, Stanton C., 40th Dist., 40th-42nd; 34th Dist., 43rd-47th
Penick, Mark A., 36th Dist., 58th, 59th
Perrell, Charles M., 51st Dist., 28th
Pervier, Clayton C., 19th Dist., 49th-52nd
Peters, Everett R., 24th Dist., 62nd-74th; 47th Dist., 75th, 76th
Peters, Joseph, 9th Dist., 23rd, 24th
Peterson, Joseph R., 37th Dist., 70th-74th; 36th Dist., 75th
Peterson, William E., 26th Dist., 88th-92nd
Petka, Ed, 42nd Dist., 88th-92nd
Philip, James "Pate", 40th Dist., 79th-82nd; 23rd Dist., 83rd-92nd
Pickett, Thomas J., 9th Dist., 22nd; 21st Dist., 23rd
Pierce, John H., 21st Dist., 35th, 36th
Pierce, Wm. P., 18th Dist., 27th
Piercy, W. Duff, 46th Dist., 48th, 49th
Pinckney, Daniel J., 20th Dist., 25th, 26th
Piotrowski, John A., 27th Dist., 53rd, 54th
Plato, William B., 22nd Dist., 16th-18th
Plumb, Fawcett, 17th Dist., 29th, 30th
Poshard, Glenn, 59th Dist., 83rd-85th
Post, Joel S., 16th Dist., 20th, 21st
Potter, W. O., 50th Dist., 45th-47th
Powell, John M., 22nd Dist., 50th, 51st
Powers, George W., 14th, 15th
Powers, John, 17th Dist., 43rd, 44th

Pruyne, Peter, 10th
Putnam, James D., 24th Dist., 40th-42nd; 18th Dist., 43rd-45th
Radogno, Christine, 24th Dist., 90th-92nd
Raica, Robert M., 24th Dist., 85th-89th
Rainey, Edward J., 9th Dist., 43rd-46th
Rainey, Jefferson, 49th Dist., 29th, 30th
Ralston, James H., 12th, 13th
Rattan, Thomas, 9th
Rauschenberger, Steven J., 33rd Dist., 87th-92nd
Ray, Lyman B., 17th Dist., 33rd, 34th
Rea, James F., "Jim", 59th Dist., 85th-91st
Reavill, Andrew J., 45th Dist., 35th-38th
Reddick, William, 15th; 20th Dist., 16th, 17th; 17th Dist., 27th
Rees, Thomas, 45th Dist., 43rd, 44th
Regner, David J., 3rd Dist., 78th-81st
Reilly, Daniel, 3rd Dist., 24th, 25th
Reilly, John C., 10th
Reinhardt, Joseph, 23rd Dist., 35th, 36th
Rennick, Frederick W., 37th Dist., 64th-66th
Reynolds, George M., 39th Dist., 55th, 56th
Reynolds, Joseph, 1st Dist., 28th
Rhoads, Mark Q., 6th Dist., 80th-82nd
Rice, Isaac, 12th Dist., 32nd, 33rd
Richards, Daniel, 20th Dist., 23rd, 24th
Richardson, James H., 13th Dist., 27th
Richardson, William A., 11th, 12th
Richmond, John P., 16th Dist., 16th, 17th; 11th Dist., 21st, 22nd
Rickert, Joseph W., 48th Dist., 36th, 37th
Riddle, Francis H., 4th Dist., 30th, 31st
Rigney, Harlan, 35th Dist., 83rd-87th
Riley, William U., 2nd Dist., 42nd, 43rd
Rinehart, Erastus N., 33rd Dist., 31st-34th
Roberts, Adelbert H., 3rd Dist., 54th-58th
Robert, Thomas, 1st
Robertson, Hayes, 8th Dist., 70th, 71st
Robinson, James W., 27th Dist., 29th, 30th
Robinson, Michael W., 7th Dist., 29th, 30th
Rock, Philip J., 18th Dist., 77th-82nd; 8th Dist., 83rd-87th
Rodgers, James M., 24th Dist., 22nd; 4th Dist., 23rd
Roe, John B., 35th Dist., 78th-80th
Rogers, Jascon, 29th Dist., 33rd, 34th
Romano, Sam, 20th Dist., 75th-79th
Ronen, Carol, 9th Dist., 91st, 92nd
Roos, Frederick B., 7th Dist., 49th-54th
Rosander, Bertil T., 54th Dist., 74th; 34th Dist., 75th-77th
Rose, Hiram, 11th Dist., 20th
Roskam, Peter J., 20th Dist., 91st, 92nd
Ross, Henry J., 6th, 7th
Ross, William, 10th-12th
Rostenkowski, Daniel D., 27th Dist., 69th; 33rd Dist., 70th
Roti, Fred B., 1st Dist., 67th, 68th
Rotz, Lawrence, 28th Dist., 64th, 65th
Rountree, Hiram, 7th Dist., 16th, 17th
Ruger, W. H., 5th Dist., 33rd, 34th
Ruggles, James M., 12th Dist., 18th; 17th Dist., 19th
Ruggles, Spooner, 13th, 14th
Rupp, James H., 51st Dist., 80th-84th
Ryan, Frank, 2nd Dist., 62nd-69th
Ryan, Frank J., 11th Dist., 53rd, 54th
Ryan, Michael, 13th, 14th
Sadler, Frank P., 11th Dist., 51st, 52nd
Salteil, Edward P., 31st Dist., 65th-68th
Sanford, Patrick H., 22nd Dist., 28th, 29th
Sanger, Lorenzo P., 15th
Sangmeister, George E., 42nd Dist., 80th-84th
Saperstein, Esther, 10th Dist., 75th-77th; 11th Dist., 78th, 79th
Savickas, Frank D., 27th Dist., 77th-82nd; 15th Dist., 83rd-87th
Sawyer, Lewis M., 27th Dist., 39th, 40th
Schaffer, Jack, 33rd Dist., 78th-82nd; 32nd Dist., 83rd-87th
Schlagenhauf, Lillian E., 36th Dist., 68th-73rd
Schmitt, Frank P., 31st Dist., 45th, 46th
Schoeninger, William J., 12th Dist., 76th
Schofield, Bryant T., 13th Dist., 23rd, 24th
Scholl, Edward T., 16th Dist., 17th
Schuneman, Calvin W., 37th Dist., 82nd-87th
Schwartz, Albert L., 31st Dist., 64th
Scott, Albert, 43rd Dist., 68th-70th

486

Scott, William, 24th Dist., 30th, 31st
Searcy, Earle B., 45th Dist., 53rd-63rd
Secrist, Conrad, 16th Dist., 32nd, 33rd, 36th, 37th
Seibert, Peter, 47th Dist., 37th, 38th
Seiter, Henry, 47th Dist., 33rd-36th
Senator, Harvey S., 14th Dist., 27th
Sergeant, Wm. L., 11th, 12th
Serritella, Daniel A., 1st Dist., 57th-62nd
Servant, Richard B., 9th-11th
Severns, Penny, 51st Dist., 85th-90th
Shadid, George P., 46th Dist., 88th-92nd
Shapiro, David C., 37th Dist., 78th-82nd
Shaw, John W., 51st Dist., 53rd, 54th
Shaw, Raleigh M., 48th Dist., 50th, 51st, 58th, 59th
Shaw, Thomas M., 20th Dist., 32nd, 33rd
Shaw, William "Bill", 15th Dist., 88th-92nd
Shaw, Willis R., 28th Dist., 48th, 49th
Sheets, Benjamin F., 10th Dist., 36th, 37th
Sheldon, J. C., 30th Dist., 28th, 29th
Shepard, William, 6th Dist., 25th-27th; 21st Dist., 28th
Sheridan, Thomas H., 49th Dist., 37th, 38th
Short, John C., 31st Dist., 28th
Shumway, E. B., 15th Dist., 33rd, 34th
Shumway, Hiram P., 40th Dist., 36th, 37th
Shumway, John N., 41st Dist., 41st, 42nd
Shutt, William E., 39th Dist., 35th, 36th
Shutt, Wm. F., 35th Dist., 29th-32nd
Sieben, Todd, 37th Dist., 88th-92nd
Sieberns, L. C., 26th Dist., 58th-61st
Silverstein, Ira I., 8th Dist., 91st, 92nd
Simms, W. Timothy, 34th Dist., 82nd
Simon, Paul, 47th Dist., 73rd, 74th; 53rd Dist., 75th
Slocumb, Rigdon B., 12th, 13th
Sloo, Thomas, Jr., 3rd, 4th
Small, Len, 16th Dist., 42nd; 20th Dist., 43rd
Smith, Ben L., 30th Dist., 54th, 55th
Smith, Edward O., 11th Dist., 16th
Smith, Elbert S., 28th Dist., 66th-69th
Smith, Elbert S., 45th Dist., 49th, 50th
Smith, Fred J., 3rd Dist., 69th; 11th Dist., 70th-74th; 22nd Dist., 75th-80th
Smith, George, 13th, 14th
Smith, Guy, 1st
Smith, Guy L., 40th Dist., 56th, 57th
Smith, Jacob, 14th, 15th
Smith, Margaret, 12th Dist., 83rd-87th; 3rd Dist., 88th-92nd
Smith, Milton D., 31st Dist., 63rd
Smith, Nathan E., 48th Dist., 52nd, 53rd
Smith, Ora, 53rd Dist., 71st, 72nd
Smith, Orpheus W., 28th Dist., 52nd, 53rd
Smith, O. V., 45th Dist., 29th, 30th
Smith, T. V., 5th Dist., 59th, 60th
Smith, Theophilus W., 3rd, 4th
Snapp, Henry, 18th Dist., 26th, 27th
Sneed, William J., 50th Dist., 52nd-55th
Snyder, Adam W., 7th, 9th, 12th
Snyder, William C., 19th Dist., 33rd, 34th
Sokolnicki, Zygmunt A., 19th Dist., 75th, 76th
Solomon, Lewis, 7th Dist., 27th
Solomon, Moses, 4th Dist., 38th; 2nd Dist., 39th
Sommer, Roger A., 45th Dist., 78th-84th
Soper, James C., 7th Dist., 75th-80th
Sours, Hudson R., 18th Dist., 72nd-74th; 45th Dist., 75th-77th; 46th Dist., 78th
Southworth, Elizur, 34th Dist., 30th, 31st; 40th Dist., 34th, 35th
Sparks, David R., 47th Dist., 40th
Sparks, W. A., 4th Dist., 23rd
Speakman, John, 22nd Dist., 62nd
Spence, W. A., 51st Dist., 51st, 52nd
Sprague, Arthur W., 2nd Dist., 70th-74th
Sprinkle, Clarence E., 40th Dist., 70th, 71st
Stadden, William, 10th-12th
Stapp, Wyatt B., 12th, 13th
Starne, Alex, 11th Dist., 27th; 25th Dist., 28th
Starr, Harry W., 13th Dist., 55th, 56th
Steele, Charles B., 32nd Dist., 28th, 29th
Steinert, Theodore R., 25th Dist., 55th, 56th
Stephenson, Jas. W., 9th
Stephenson, Lloyd B., 33rd Dist., 35th, 36th
Stephenson, William J., 15th
Stern, Grace Mary, 39th Dist., 88th
Stewart, Thomas B., 14th Dist., 46th-49th
Stillman, Stephen, 3rd, 4th

Stone, Claude U., Jr., 45th Dist., 92nd
Strain, James, 14th Dist., 24th, 25th
Stratton, Augustus M., 43rd Dist., 35th, 36th
Streeter, Alson I., 24th Dist., 34th, 35th
Strevell, Jason W., 17th Dist., 26th, 27th
Stringer, Lawrence B., 32nd Dist., 42nd; 28th Dist., 43rd
Strode, James M., 9th
Strong, James B., 18th Dist., 28th, 29th
Strunck, James E., 29th Dist., 71st, 72nd
Stuart, John T., 12th Dist., 16th, 17th
Stuart, Thomas B., 14th Dist., 48th
Stubblefield, Geo. W., 22nd Dist., 40th-42nd; 26th Dist., 43rd-45th
Stuttle, Henry C., 38th Dist., 58th-61st
Sucher, George B., 18th Dist., 44th
Sullivan, Dave, 28th Dist., 90th-92nd
Sullivan, Patrick J., 29th Dist., 49th-52nd
Sullivan, William, 6th Dist., 40th, 41st
Summer, Edward P., 10th Dist., 34th, 35th
Sunderland, David H., 10th Dist., 32nd; 12th Dist., 33rd
Sutphin, Hugh L., 15th; 15th Dist., 16th; 13th Dist., 19th, 20th
Swanson, Arthur R., 17th Dist., 73rd, 74th; 28th Dist., 75th, 76th
Swanson, John A., 13th Dist., 49th, 50th
Sweat, Peter, 15th; 18th Dist., 17th, 18th
Sweeney, Edmund G., 12th Dist., 70th-73rd
Swift, Rodney B., 8th Dist., 50th-55th
Swinarski, Donald T., 25th Dist., 78th, 79th
Swinarski, Theodore, 14th Dist., 74th; 25th Dist., 77th
Syverson, Dave, 34th Dist., 88th-92nd
Talcott,Thomas B., 24th Dist., 17th, 18th
Talcott, Waite, 3rd Dist., 19th, 20th
Taliaferro, Benj. C., 22nd Dist., 30th, 31st
Tanner, John R., 44th Dist., 32nd, 33rd
Taylor, Edmund D., 9th
Taylor, James C., 26th Dist., 82nd
Telford, E. D., 42nd Dist., 47th, 52nd-55th
Templeton, James W., 31st Dist., 39th-42nd; 37th Dist., 43rd, 44th
Thiele, Emil, 11th Dist., 37th, 38th
Thomas, Horace H., 6th Dist., 36th, 37th
Thomas, John, 49th Dist., 31st, 32nd
Thomas, John T., 49th Dist., 63rd-66th
Thomas, Melvin, 34th Dist., 60th, 61st
Thomas, Randy, 36th Dist., 82nd
Thomas, William, 9th, 10th, 11th
Thompson, Charles H., 51st Dist., 55th-58th, 61st, 62nd
Thompson, John, 43rd Dist., 29th, 30th
Thompson, Martin B., 30th Dist., 34th, 35th
Thompson, Richard S., 2nd Dist., 28th, 29th
Thompson, Wallace, 43rd Dist., 63rd-67th
Thompson, W. W., 13th, 14th
Tichenor, William, 9th Dist., 16th
Tiffany, Albert N., 8th Dist., 43rd-45th
Tincher, John P., 9th Dist., 25th-27th
Topinka, Judy Baar, 22nd Dist., 84th-88th
Torrence, George, 18th Dist., 32nd-35th
Tossey, F. Jeff, 40th Dist., 46th-49th
Totten, Donald, 3rd Dist., 82nd
Townsend, Leon A., 35th Dist., 41st, 42nd; 43rd Dist., 43rd, 44th
Trager, Clyde C., 18th Dist., 64th-69th
Traynor, Stuart J., 40th Dist., 74th
Trotter, Donne E., 16th Dist., 87th-92nd
Tubbs, Henry, 27th Dist., 33rd, 34th
Turnbaugh, John D., 13th Dist., 50th-53rd
Turney, James, 10th, 11th
Turney, J. J. R., 2nd Dist., 26th
Tuttle, Oral P., 51st Dist., 59th, 60th
Underwood, William H., 22nd Dist., 20th-22nd; 5th Dist., 23rd, 27th
Upton, Clark W., 8th Dist., 28th, 29th
Vadalabene, Sam M., 53rd Dist., 77th; 56th Dist., 78th-88th
Vance, John W., 9th, 10th
Vanderen, Cyrus W., 15th Dist., 20th, 21st
Vandeveer, Horatio M., 7th Dist., 23rd, 24th
Vandeventer, Jacob, 13th, 14th
Vandever, William T., 34th Dist., 32nd; 40th Dist., 33rd
Van Dorsten, John P., 4th Dist., 26th, 27th
Van Hooser, Arthur, 51st Dist., 63rd-68th
Van Lent, George, 2nd Dist., 52nd-55th
Van Sellar, Henry, 31st Dist., 33rd, 34th

Representatives

Abbey, Frank E., 33rd Dist., 45th-47th, 50th-54th
Abbott Alfred N., 31st Dist., 41st, 42nd; 35th Dist., 47th, 48th
Abel, Thomas J., 29th Dist., 30th
Abend, Edward, 19th Dist., 16th
Able, Wilson, 8th-12th
Abney, Albert G., 51st Dist., 41st
Abraham, William M., 33rd Dist., 31st
Abrahams, Emanuel M., 17th Dist., 45th, 46th
Abrahams, Isaac, 3rd Dist., 32nd
Abramson, Michael, 14th Dist., 80th-82nd
Acevedo, Edward, 2nd Dist., 90th-92nd
Achinson, Oliver T., 41st Dist., 40th
Acker, John, 12th Dist., 54th-58th
Ackerman, Jay, 45th Dist., 81st, 82nd; 89th Dist., 85th-90th
Adamowski, Benjamin S., 25th Dist., 57th-61st
Adams, Augustus, 51st Dist., 17th
Adams, D. Emmons, 91st Dist., 27th
Adams, Darius, 13th
Adams, E., 14th
Adams, Harold J., 35th Dist., 80th
Adams, Joseph, 40th Dist., 37th
Adams, Van J., 44th Dist., 17th
Adams, Wright, 23rd Dist., 33rd
Adcock, William, 32nd Dist., 54th
Adduci, James J., 2nd Dist., 59th-67th, 69th
Aderton, George, 47th Dist., 42nd
Adkins, Charles, 24th Dist., 45th-47th
Aiken, Charles A., 46th Dist., 39th
Aiken, Walter S., 15th
Albright, Fountain E., 50th Dist., 29th, 30th
Aldrich, Cyrus, 14th
Aldrich, Mark, 10th Dist., 11th
Aldrich, Robert, 13th
Alertson, Ubbo J., 26th Dist., 41st
Alexander, Elias J. C., 34th Dist., 28th
Alexander, Ethel Skyles, 26th Dist., 81st, 82nd; 32nd Dist., 83rd, 84th
Alexander, Harmon, 11th; 45th Dist., 28th
Alexander, James H., 41st Dist., 47th, 48th
Alexander, Jas. P., 48th Dist., 66th
Alexander, Jediah F., 16th Dist., 25th
Alexander, John, 5th
Alexander, John C., 5th-7th
Alexander, Samuel, 2nd, 3rd
Alexander, W., 14th
Alexander, William, 1st, 3rd
Alexander, William M., 2nd, 3rd
Allen, Augustus, 46th Dist., 25th
Allen, Calvin, 11th Dist., 27th
Allen, Charles A., 31st Dist., 34th-37th; 18th Dist., 40th-42nd; 22nd Dist., 43rd-45th
Allen, Eben C., 18th Dist., 30th
Allen, Edward R., 46th Dist., 22nd
Allen, Edwin W., 23rd Dist., 31st
Allen, George B., 20th Dist., 60th, 61st
Allen, G. T., 14th Dist., 19th
Allen, Henry C., 35th Dist., 53rd-60th
Allen, Henry W., 27th Dist., 35th, 36th
Allen, James C., 10th Dist., 17th
Allen, James M., 43rd Dist., 17th
Allen, John, 5th, 6th, 11th
Allen, Robert H., 48th Dist., 40th
Allen, Sylvester, 37th Dist., 36th
Allen, W. H., 11th Dist., 31st, 32nd
Allen, William C., 51st Dist., 34th
Allen, William J., 3rd Dist., 19th
Allen, Willis, 11th
Alling, Edward H., 7th Dist., 41st
Allison, J. W., 16th Dist., 37th
Allison, J. W., 20th Dist., 45th, 46th
Allison, Robert H., 30th Dist., 59th-68th
Alpiner, B. W., 20th Dist., 51st, 52nd, 59th-64th
Alschuler, George W., 14th Dist., 46th, 47th
Alschuler, Samuel, 14th Dist., 41st
Alstat, Wayne, 58th Dist., 82nd
Alsup, John W., 47th Dist., 71st-73rd; 74th; 52nd Dist., 75th-77th; 51st Dist., 78th
Ambrosius, Conrad A., 41st Dist., 38th
Ambroz, Joseph A., 4th Dist., 44th
Ames, Alfred E., 13th

Ames, E. P., 48th Dist., 17th
Ames, Isaac, 17th Dist., 32nd
Anderson, Donald B., 45th Dist., 79th-81st
Anderson, Fred W., 36th Dist., 70th
Anderson, James A., 28th Dist., 41st
Anderson, James J., 42nd Dist., 38th
Anderson, James O., 24th Dist., 36th-38th
Anderson, Joseph E., 8th Dist., 47th
Anderson, Merle K., 33rd Dist., 73rd; 35th Dist., 75th-78th
Anderson, Raymond E., 50th Dist., 73rd; 45th Dist., 75th, 76th
Anderson, Robert S., 46th Dist., 28th
Anderson, Samuel, 14th
Anderson, Stinson H., 8th, 9th
Anderson, Thompson J., 24th Dist., 54th, 58th
Anderson, W. B., 8th Dist., 20th, 21st
Anderson, William E., 6th Dist., 47th
Anderson, Wm. G., 8th, 13th, 14th
Andrews, Dwight W., 43rd Dist., 32nd
Andrews, James H., 33rd Dist., 42nd
Andrus, Henry, 10th Dist., 40th, 41st
Andrus, Leonard, 13th
Ansley, J. M., 24th Dist., 33rd
Anthony, John H., 20th Dist., 37th
Antonovych, Boris R., 19th Dist., 80th
ApMadoc, William T., 5th Dist., 45th-47th
Archer, Wm. B., 4th, 11th, 12th; 28th Dist., 22nd
Arenz, Francis, 14th
Arms, Henry, 41st Dist., 17th
Armstrong, Charles F., 22nd Dist., 70th-74th
Armstrong, Fowler A., 49th Dist., 37th, 38th; 51st Dist., 39th
Armstrong, George W., 14th; 77th Dist., 27th; 17th Dist., 28th-30th
Armstrong, Perry A., 43rd Dist., 23rd; 13th Dist., 28th
Armstrong, Stanley C., 6th Dist., 63rd-66th
Arnell, Donald E., 10th Dist., 78th, 79th
Arnold, A. Otis, 36th Dist., 51st-55th
Arnold, Isaac N., 13th, 14th; 57th Dist., 20th
Arnold, Lawrence F., 46th Dist., 53rd, 54th, 58th, 59th
Arnold, S. P. V., 39th Dist., 41st
Arnold, Wilfred, 43rd Dist., 43rd, 44th
Arrand, Samuel W., 1st Dist., 42nd-44th
Arrigo, Victor A., 20th Dist., 75th-78th
Arrington, W. Russell, 6th Dist., 64th-68th
Arwedson, John S., 5th Dist., 29th
Ashby, James H., 45th Dist., 54th
Ashcraft, Alan E., 6th Dist., 62nd, 63rd
Ashton, Andrew, 9th Dist., 29th, 30th
Ashton, Henry M., 3rd Dist., 48th
Atkins, Jas. L., 28th Dist., 67th, 68th
Atkins, John, 7th
Atwater, Thomas, 10th
Atwood, John A., 10th Dist., 47th-49th
Austin, E. W., 51st Dist., 16th
Austin, Henry S., 15th
Austin, Henry W., 95th Dist., 27th; 23rd Dist., 43rd-45th
Austin, Robert, 39th Dist., 70th, 71st, 73rd
Auth, A. L., 27th Dist., 54th, 56th-60th, 62nd-65th
Avery, Myron K., 9th Dist., 29th
Avery, Oscar F., 20th Dist., 40th
Ayers, Wm. N., 9th Dist., 27th
Babb, Alfred S., 12th Dist., 54th, 55th, 57th
Babbitt, A. W., 14th
Babcock, Amos C., 33rd Dist., 19th
Backenstos, J. B., 14th
Backus, Charles H., 14th Dist., 42nd-45th
Bailey, Ashbel H., 30th Dist., 32nd
Bailey, D. B., 13th Dist., 29th
Bailey, Even, 15th
Bailey, George S., 47th Dist., 35th
Bailey, John S., 15th
Bailey, Joseph M., 56th Dist., 25th, 26th
Bailey, M. B., 18th Dist., 39th, 40th
Bailey, Ozias, 31st Dist., 17th
Bailey, Wm. W., 12th, 15th
Bailhache, John, 13th
Bainbridge, Allen, 11th
Bair, Porter, 44th Dist., 45th
Baird, Frank T., 25th Dist., 55th
Baird, Fred S., 9th Dist., 34th

Bairstow, Jack, 8th Dist., 68th, 69th; 31st Dist., 70th-73rd
Baker, Bert, Jr., 50th Dist., 69th; 57th Dist, 70th-73rd; 74th
Baker, Charles W., 10th Dist., 50th-53rd, 55th
Baker, Edward D., 10th, 11th
Baker, George B., 51st Dist., 48th
Baker, George S., 6th Dist., 36th
Baker, Henry S., 14th Dist., 19th
Baker, John C., 6th Dist., 29th
Baker, John H., 33rd Dist., 33rd-35th
Baker, Samuel L., 56th Dist., 21st
Balanoff, Clem, 35th Dist., 86th, 87th; 32nd Dist., 88th
Balanoff, Miriam, 30th Dist., 81st, 82nd
Baldridge, David, 8th
Baldwin, Benjamin, 23rd Dist., 22nd
Baldwin, Charles, 19th Dist., 30th, 32nd
Baldwin, Charles W., 5th Dist., 52nd
Baldwin, Daniel, 12th
Baldwin, Elmer, 43rd Dist., 20th; 44th Dist., 25th
Baldwin, Leverett S., 33rd Dist., 38th
Ball, Asel F., 10th
Ballou, Charles, 37th Dist 28th
Balthis, Bill W., 79th Dist., 87th-89th
Baltz, Meade, 37th Dist., 72nd, 73rd
Bancroft, Lincoln, 50th Dist., 50th-54th
Bandy, Wallace A., 50th Dist., 53rd-56th
Bane, M. M., 29th Dist., 20th, 21st
Barber, B. L., 45th Dist., 52nd, 53rd
Barbour, James J., 5th Dist., 62nd
Barclay, William, 11th Dist., 41st
Bardill, J. G., 47th Dist., 46th, 47th
Barger, Ralph H., 39th Dist., 83rd-86th
Barger, Simon S., 49th Dist., 34th, 35th
Barkhausen, David N., 31st Dist., 82nd
Barker, Elwood, 51st Dist., 47th-49th
Barker, William, 15th
Barkley, David W., 44th Dist., 28th
Barnes, Eugene M., 28th Dist., 77th; 29th Dist., 78th-80th
Barnes, Jane M., 8th Dist., 79th-82nd; 38th Dist., 83rd-87th
Barnes, John A., 42nd Dist., 39th, 40th
Barnes, Lizzie, 48th Dist., 61st
Barnes, P. W., 45th Dist., 42nd
Barnes, Roy R., 32nd Dist., 57th
Barnes, William H., 42nd Dist., 27th
Barnett, George, 8th, 10th
Barnett, James R., 35th Dist., 40th
Barnett, Robert F., 12th; 29th Dist., 17th
Barnsback, George, 14th
Barnsback, Julius J., 16th Dist., 24th
Barr, J. Robert, 11th Dist., 82nd
Barr, William G., 41st Dist., 75th, 76th
Barr, W. W., 12th Dist., 27th
Barrett, Amos B., 46th Dist., 29th
Barrett, Edward, 33rd Dist., 27th
Barrett, Elisha E., 19th Dist., 24th
Barrett, James W., 26th Dist., 21st
Barricklow, Joseph P., 40th Dist., 39th, 40th
Barron, Robinson, 11th Dist., 48th
Barry, Don T., 53rd Dist., 76th, 77th
Barry, Patrick T., 2nd Dist., 31st
Barry, Tobias, 37th Dist., 67th-69th; 40th Dist., 70th
Barry, Tobias, Jr., 40th Dist., 72nd, 73rd, 74th; 39th Dist., 75th-77th; 37th Dist., 78th
Bartels, Lawrence J., 21st Dist., 75th
Barthlow, E. C., 30th Dist., 30th
Bartleson, Horatio R., 27th Dist., 36th
Bartlett, S. M., 10th
Bartling, Henry C., 6th Dist., 40th
Bartoline, Leo J., 5th Dist., 73rd
Barton, Michael, 25th Dist., 37th, 38th
Bartulis, A. C., 53rd Dist., 77th, 80th; 49th Dist., 82nd
Basel, William H., 43rd Dist., 49th
Bassett, Mark M., 26th Dist., 34th
Bassi, Suzanne "Suzie", 54th Dist., 91st, 92nd
Bates, Erastus, 9th Dist., 25th
Bates, Thomas J., 37th Dist., 29th
Bauer, George J., 42nd Dist., 55th, 56th, 58th-62nd
Bauler, Harry P., 11th Dist., 73rd
Baumgarten, John, 10th Dist., 61st
Bayne, James, 10th Dist., 32nd
Baxter, Harry, 34th Dist., 54th, 55th
Beall, James, 12th
Beals, Reuben F., 21st Dist., 37th, 38th
Beattie, Mary, 59th Dist., 90th
Beatty, John J., 27th Dist., 78th-82nd

Beaubien, Mark, 52nd Dist., 89th-92nd
Beaupre, Jack R., 43rd Dist., 78th, 79th
Beck, Christopher, 23rd Dist., 44th-46th
Beck, Robert J., 8th Dist., 36th, 38th, 39th
Beckemeyer, H. J. C., 42nd Dist., 45th, 46th
Beckman, Louis E., 20th Dist., 55th, 56th, 67th-69th; 41st Dist., 70th
Beckmeyer, G. R. "Bob", 44th Dist., 69th
Becker, Frederick, 42nd Dist., 32nd
Beckwith, Daniel W., 7th
Bederman, Edwin B., 25th Dist., 56th-58th
Beede, Walter E., 3rd Dist., 44th
Beekman, Wm. T., 25th Dist., 17th
Beeler, George H., 8th
Beem, W. J., 40th Dist., 42nd
Beer, Simon B., 26th Dist., 40th
Beers, Philo, 4th
Beesley, John M., 26th Dist., 25th
Beever, W. George, 44th Dist., 51st
Beezhold, Ralph A., 6th Dist., 75th
Behrens, William H., 38th Dist., 45th, 46th
Beitler, Henry C., 21st Dist., 41st, 42nd; 31st Dist., 43rd
Belinski, C. J., 9th Dist., 41st
Bell, James M., 45th Dist., 47th, 48th
Bell, Robert F., 13th
Bell, Timothy A., 36th Dist., 81st, 82nd
Bell, Victor B., 8th Dist., 18th
Bellock, Patricia "Patti", 81st Dist., 90th-92nd
Benbow, Amos E., 47th Dist., 44th
Benedict, Kirby, 14th
Benefiel, Norman L., 50th Dist., 72nd
Bennett, Allen F., 51st Dist., 80th
Bennett, Isaac R., 27th Dist., 19th
Bennett, John, 12th
Bennett, Norman, 34th Dist., 54th
Bennett, O. Prescott, 29th Dist., 42nd
Benson, George H., 30th Dist., 29th
Benson, O. E., 39th Dist., 48th-50th, 53rd, 56th-60th
Benson, Samuel S., 56th Dist., 27th
Benson, Valentine S., 10th Dist., 24th
Bentley, E. B., 28th Dist., 52nd, 53rd
Bentley, James R., 41st Dist., 50th, 51st
Bentley, Richard, 10th, 12th
Bentley, William H., 16th Dist., 49th, 51st
Bergman, Robert L., 54th Dist., 89th, 90th
Berman, Arthur L., 10th Dist., 76th, 77th; 11th Dist., 78th, 79th
Berman, Louis G., 5th Dist., 59th-68th
Berns, Tom, 104th Dist., 91st, 92nd
Berrios, Joseph, 9th Dist., 83rd-85th
Berry, Daniel S., 12th Dist., 37th-39th
Berry, Francis J., 74th
Berry, George F., 42nd Dist., 30th
Berry, Isaac S., 14th
Berry, James M., 36th Dist., 27th
Berry, John F., 19th Dist., 52nd, 53rd
Berry, Peter C., 36th Dist , 34th
Berry, William, 3rd, 5th; 32nd Dist., 21st
Berryman, James R., 12th Dist., 40th, 41st
Best, Alan, 31st Dist., 65th-68th
Bestold, Fred, 16th Dist., 57th
Bethea, Solomon H., 19th Dist., 33rd
Bez, George, 15th Dist., 33rd, 34th
Bianco, Phillip, 25th Dist., 80th-82nd
Bibb, Robert S., 26th Dist., 30th
Bibbens, Elisha, 13th
Bicklehaupt, Peter, 48th Dist., 34th, 35th
Bielefeldt, J. S., 7th Dist., 30th
Biggert, Judy, 81st Dist., 88th-90th
Biggins, Robert A. "Bob", 78th Dist., 88th-92nd
Billhartz, Warren O., 42nd Dist., 69th; 55th Dist., 70th, 71st
Billings, Henry O., 41st Dist., 32nd, 33rd
Bines, William M., 18th Dist., 39th
Bingham, John A., 12th Dist., 56th, 58th-63rd
Bippus, Frederick J., 21st Dist., 49th-55th
Birchler, Vincent A., 58th Dist., 79th-81st
Birkinbine, John L., 1st Dist., 81st, 82nd; 57th Dist., 83rd
Bisbee, Louis H., 4th Dist., 31st
Bish, James E., 3rd Dist., 38th
Bishop, Henri B., 31st Dist., 28th
Bishop, Mahlon, 13th
Bishop, Richard, 8th Dist., 28th
Bissell, Wm. H., 12th
Bitner, Henry, 11th Dist., 32nd

490

Black, Charles F., 18th Dist., 43rd, 45th, 46th
Black, George M., 28th Dist., 41st; 36th Dist., 36th
Black, Harmon H., 50th Dist., 32nd
Black, Henry, 23rd Dist., 31st
Black, Jacob P., 53rd Dist., 23rd
Black, J. Edward, 45th Dist., 39th
Black, J. Edwin, 46th Dist., 36th, 38th
Black, James, 6th
Black, Jesse, Jr., 26th Dist., 41st
Black, Thomas G., 37th Dist., 30th; 35th Dist., 33rd
Black, William B., 105th Dist., 84th-92nd
Black, William Z., 24th Dist., 56th-58th
Blackaby, Inmon, 25th Dist., 32nd
Blackburn, Hiram P., 31st Dist., 35th
Blackford, Nathaniel, 9th
Blackman, David J., 12th; 3rd Dist., 16th
Blackwell, David, 2nd, 4th, 5th
Blackwell, George W., 1st Dist., 56th, 57th
Blackwell, Robert, 8th, 9th
Blades, Ben C., 56th Dist., 73rd; 58th Dist., 75th-77th;
  54th Dist., 78th
Blades, Franklin, 45th Dist., 20th, 22nd
Blagojevich, Rod R., 33rd Dist., 88th, 89th
Blaha, Joseph C., 19th Dist., 47th, 48th
Blair, Eugene K., 38th Dist., 36th
Blair, Wm., 13th, 14th
Blair, W. C., 46th Dist., 45th, 46th
Blair, W. Robert, 74th; 41st Dist., 75th-77th; 42nd Dist.,
  78th
Blaisdell, Elijah W., 53rd Dist., 21st
Blakely, Wm. H., 13th Dist., 17th
Blakely, Wm. H., 33rd Dist., 28th
Blakeman, Curtis, 3rd, 4th
Blakeman, Curtis [Jr.], 13th, 15th; 20th Dist., 16th
Blazer, William L., 74th
Blish, James K., 37th Dist., 43rd
Blockburger, Christian B., 8th, 9th
Blodgett, Henry W., 53rd Dist., 18th
Bloomstrand, Harold R., 25th Dist., 65th
Blood, F. G., 45th Dist., 40th
Bluthardt, Edward E., 2nd Dist., 75th-77th; 5th Dist.,
  78th-82nd
Boal, Robert, 42nd Dist., 19th, 20th
Boardman, Geo. B., 41st Dist., 48th
Boardman, H. M., 17th Dist., 33rd
Bocock, Cyrus, 19th Dist., 34th
Bogardus, Charles, 18th Dist., 34th, 35th
Bogue, George M., 2nd Dist., 29th
Boland, Mike, 71st Dist., 89th-92nd
Bolger, Thomas A., 8th Dist., 57th-67th
Bolin, Charles E., 36th Dist., 45th-47th
Boll, Jacob, 1st Dist., 43rd
Bolt, Francis M., 43rd Dist., 31st
Bolton, John M., 2nd Dist., 57th-59th
Bond, Lester L., 59th Dist., 25th, 26th
Bond, Lewis J., 40th Dist., 24th
Bond, Richard S., 15th Dist., 16th
Bone, Elisha, 13th
Bonk, Charles Stanley, 15th Dist., 68th
Bonny, Joel W., 35th Dist., 38th
Bookwalter, Walter J., 22nd Dist., 58th
Booth, Daniel, 7th Dist., 28th
Booth, Fenton W., 43rd Dist., 40th
Booth, Milton T., 37th Dist., 54th
Borchers, Webber, 52nd Dist., 76th, 77th; 51st Dist., 78th,
  79th, 81st
Borders, Grover C., 49th Dist., 56th-58th
Borough, Joseph, 2nd, 8th
Boshell, H. N., 26th Dist., 53rd
Bost, Mike, 115th Dist., 89th-92nd
Boswell, Paul P., 74th
Bothwell, Alex W., 12th Dist., 26th
Bottino, Louis F., 37th Dist., 70th, 71st
Boucek, Emil J., 6th Dist., 80th-82nd
Boul, Nicholas, 47th Dist., 37th
Boulware, Jefferson R., 18th Dist., 43rd, 45th
Boundmot, Elliott E., 31st Dist., 34th
Boutell, Henry S., 6th Dist., 34th
Bovey, Victor H., 10th Dist., 39th, 40th
Bowen, E. N., 50th Dist., 62nd
Bowen, Francis, 17th Dist., 31st
Bower, Eli, 12th Dist., 24th
Bower, Glen L., 54th Dist., 81st, 82nd
Bower, Robert A., 30th Dist., 30th
Bower, William, 44th Dist., 31st

Bowers, Henry, 36th Dist., 51st-53rd
Bowers, Jack E., 74th; 38th Dist., 75th
Bowler, Max L., 49th Dist., 62nd
Bowler, William H., 47th Dist., 36th
Bowles, William A., 25th Dist., 42nd; 41st Dist., 43rd,
  44th
Bowlin, John A., 48th Dist., 37th
Bowman, Joseph G., 11th
Bowman, Woods, 11th Dist., 80th-82nd; 4th Dist., 83rd-
  86th
Bowyer, George P., 8th, 9th
Boyakin, H.P., 14th, 15th
Boyd, George M., 6th Dist., 39th-41st
Boyd, John, 48th Dist., 30th
Boyd, Martin A., 22nd Dist., 32nd
Boyd, Randolph, 37th Dist., 48th-52nd
Boyd, Thomas H., 39th Dist., 27th
Boyden, Albert W., 25th Dist., 34th
Boydston, C. W., 23rd Dist., 29th, 30th
Boyer, Charles A., 43rd Dist., 23rd
Boyer, Oscar J., 22nd Dist., 37th
Boyer, Thomas A., 4th Dist., 48th-50th
Boyer, William H., 49th Dist., 33rd
Boyle, Hiram, 35th Dist., 18th
Boyle, James P., 4th Dist., 51st-57th; 49th Dist., 58th-61st
Boyle, John F., 4th Dist., 62nd-67th
Boyle, Ken, 53rd Dist., 77th; 49th Dist., 78th, 79th
Boyle, Marmontel, 15th
Bozeman, Virgil, 33rd Dist., 66th
Brace, Myrtle G., 41st Dist., 21st
Brachtendorf, Barney, 13th Dist., 34th
Brackenridge, Wm. H., 36th Dist., 34th
Bradbury, L. H., 39th Dist., 18th
Bradford, Glenn E., 112th Dist., 90th
Bradford, J., 13th Dist., 19th
Bradford, James M., 12th
Bradley, Bennett, Jr., 51st Dist., 79th
Bradley, Gerald A., 47th Dist., 76th, 77th; 44th Dist.,
  78th-82nd
Bradley, Richard A., 13th, 14th; 5th Dist., 16th
Bradley, Richard T., 20th Dist., 90th-92nd
Bradshaw, Andrew J., 31st Dist., 26th
Bradshaw, Ben H., 19th Dist., 35th, 36th
Bradwell, James B., 1st Dist., 28th, 29th
Brady, Francis P., 1st Dist., 44th-46th
Brady, Lorenzo D., 50th Dist., 16th
Brady, Michael I., 11th Dist., 80th, 81st
Brady, Bill, 88th Dist., 88th-91st
Brady, Dan, 88th Dist., 92nd
Bragg, Henry, 15th
Braiden, Miles J., 85th Dist., 27th
Brand, Michael, 60th Dist., 23rd
Brands, A. A., 44th Dist., 58th-66th
Brandt, John B., 13th Dist., 76th, 77th; 14th Dist., 78th-
  80th
Brandt, John N., 12th Dist., 38th
Branen, James, 29th Dist., 39th-41st; 35th Dist., 44th
Branson, Fred, 55th Dist., 72nd, 73rd
Branson, Nathaniel W., 36th Dist., 28th, 29th
Branson, R. J., 42nd Dist., 57th-68th
Bratton, Luther B., 20th Dist., 57th, 58th
Bray, Levi T., 12th Dist., 36th
Bray, M. E., 38th Dist., 55th-58th
Brayton, Hardin B., 96th Dist., 27th
Breckenridge, Preston, 26th Dist., 17th
Breeden, Lute C., 26th Dist., 39th
Breeden, Richard G., 27th Dist., 35th, 36th
Breen, P. J., 22nd Dist., 50th, 52nd, 53rd, 55th-60th
Breese, Sidney, 15th Dist., 17th
Breidt, Herman H., 25th Dist., 43rd, 44th
Brennan, Martin A., 26th Dist., 52nd, 53rd
Brennan, Thomas A., 33rd Dist., 60th
Brenne, Lynn G., 8th Dist., 77th
Brentano, Lorenzo, 61st Dist., 23rd
Breslin, Peg McDonnell, 38th Dist., 80th-82nd; 75th
  Dist., 83rd-86th
Brewer, F. A., 35th Dist., 49th-51st
Brewer, Thomas, 19th Dist., 21st
Brewer, Wm., 15th Dist., 17th
Brewster, John F., 34th Dist., 57th
Bridges, David Y., 4th Dist., 16th, 18th
Bridges, Francis M., 39th Dist., 31st
Bridges, John, 4th
Briggs, Benjamin, 8th
Briggs, Robert W., 28th Dist., 17th

Brigham, Robert M., 13th Dist., 31st
Brignadello, Frank J., 17th Dist., 39th, 40th
Brink, F. E., 42nd Dist., 33rd
Brinkley, Wm., 13th, 14th
Brinkman, William M., 1st Dist., 49th-53rd
Brinkmeier, Robert E., 35th Dist., 75th-79th
Briscoe, John W., 45th Dist., 29th
Briscoe, Polk, 43rd Dist., 39th; 34th Dist., 46th, 48th
Briscoe, William T., 32nd Dist., 27th
Bristol, Almon H., 24th Dist., 40th
Bristow, B. F., 24th Dist., 17th
Broadwell, Norman M., 26th Dist., 22nd
Broche, Arthur T., 1st Dist., 58th-62nd
Brock, Horace H., 14th Dist., 70th
Brockhouse, Warren E., 45th Dist., 59th
Brokoski, Francis A., 3rd Dist., 35th, 36th
Brookhart, Lewis, 17th Dist., 26th
Brookins, Howard B., 36th Dist., 83rd, 84th
Brooks, Benjamin W., 5th
Brooks, Miles, 22nd Dist., 41st
Brooks, W. S., 80th Dist., 27th
Brooks, Wilson, 4th Dist., 37th
Brosnahan, James D., 36th Dist., 90th-92nd
Broucek, Frank J., 74th
Brouillet, Hector A., 9th Dist., 68th, 69th; 30th Dist., 70th-73rd
Brown, Abraham M., 22nd Dist., 30th
Brown, Albert F., 12th Dist., 32nd; 10th Dist., 33rd, 34th
Brown, Alfred, 44th Dist., 34th, 35th
Brown, Benjamin B., 13th
Brown, Dauphin, 45th Dist., 16th
Brown, Edgar B., 22nd Dist., 54th
Brown, Horace A., 27th Dist., 19th
Brown, James N., 12th, 13th, 15th; 26th Dist., 18th
Brown, John, 11th, 14th
Brown, John J., 12th
Brown, John J., 43rd Dist., 35th
Brown, Julius A., 30th Dist., 36th, 37th
Brown, Michael J., 63rd Dist., 90th
Brown, Robert C., 48th Dist., 40th-42nd
Brown, Samuel W., 58th Dist., 19th
Brown, William, 24th Dist., 18th
Brown, William, 27th Dist., 27th
Brown, William, 55th Dist., 24th
Brown, Wm., 9th; 18th Dist., 24th
Brown, Wm. G., 6th, 7th
Brown, Wm. J., 28th Dist., 23rd
Brown, Wm. M., 6th Dist., 49th
Brown, Wm. R., 2nd Dist., 37th
Brown, W. V. 48th Dist., 67th, 68th
Brownback, Dell D., 40th Dist., 46th
Browne, Edgar S., 23rd Dist., 35th, 36th
Browne, Lee O'Neil, 27th Dist., 42nd; 39th Dist., 43rd-55th
Browner, M. F., 50th Dist., 57th-59th, 61st, 62nd
Browning, John T., 21st Dist., 29th, 30th
Browning, Orville H., 13th
Browning, Quincy E., 51st Dist., 34th
Broyles, Paul, 48th Dist., 63rd
Brubaker, Aaron H., 20th Dist., 35th
Bruce, George R., 23rd Dist., 49th, 50th
Bruer, Cassius, C. A., 16th Dist., 53rd-56th, 58th-66th
Brumback, Thomas B., 24th Dist., 31st
Brummer, Richard H., 54th Dist., 80th-82nd; 107th Dist., 83rd
Brummet, Don E., 54th Dist., 77th; 55th Dist., 78th-80th
Brundage, Edward J., 6th Dist., 41st, 43rd
Brunner, Francis M., 33rd Dist., 25th
Brunsvold, Joel, 71st Dist., 83rd-87th; 72nd Dist., 88th-92nd
Bryan, Charles P., 14th Dist., 37th-40th
Bryan, James C., 45th Dist., 32nd
Bryan, Nathan D., 44th Dist., 40th
Bryant, Francis E., 36th Dist., 18th
Bryant, Francis E., 30th Dist., 28th
Bryant, James B., 44th Dist., 41st, 42nd
Bryant, John H., 13th; 47th Dist., 21st
Bryant, Obed W., 49th Dist., 24th
Brydia, George S., 35th Dist., 61st-69th; 34th Dist., 70th-73rd
Buchanan, Henry B., 34th Dist., 18th
Buchanan, James N., 2nd Dist., 36th
Buchanan, Wm. T., 46th Dist., 34th
Buck, Azariah, 16th Dist., 31st
Buck, Eugene B., 32nd Dist., 32nd

Buck, Otto A., 41st Dist., 57th
Buckingham, Holly R., 50th Dist., 32nd
Buckley, Edward H., 15th
Buckley, John E., 24th Dist., 42nd
Buckley, William, 3rd Dist., 36th
Buckmaster, Nathaniel, 2nd, 9th
Buckmaster, Samuel A., 20th Dist., 17th, 18th; 16th Dist., 23rd; 41st Dist., 30th
Buckner, John C., 5th Dist., 39th
Budlong, John, 9th Dist., 30th
Buettner, Daniel, 3rd Dist., 44th, 45th
Bugielski, Robert J., 11th Dist., 85th-87th; 19th Dist., 88th-92nd
Bullard, Lucian, 19th Dist., 28th
Bullington, John J., 40th Dist., 50th
Bullock, Larry S., 22nd Dist., 81st, 82nd; 23rd Dist., 83rd, 84th
Bundy, Thomas E., 32nd Dist., 32nd
Bundy, William E., 42nd Dist., 42nd, 43rd
Bundy, Wm. H., 51st Dist., 35th
Bunn, Abraham B., 40th Dist., 25th
Burbank, W. M., 55th Dist., 20th
Burchard, Horatio C., 56th Dist., 23rd, 24th
Burditt, George M., 74th; 9th Dist., 75th-77th
Burgess, H. S., 46th Dist., 53rd, 62nd
Burgess, Thomas H., 8th Dist., 26th
Burgett, Carl S., 40th Dist., 41st, 42nd; 34th Dist., 43rd, 44th, 46th
Burgoon, Garrel, 48th Dist., 69th; 56th Dist , 70th, 72nd, 73rd; 54th Dist., 75th, 76th
Burhans, Robert L., 18th Dist., 66th-69th: 43rd Dist., 70th-73rd
Burke, B. T., 21st Dist., 17th, 20th
Burke, Daniel J., 22nd Dist., 87th; 23rd Dist., 88th-92nd
Burke, Frank C., 25th Dist., 47th
Burke, Richard E., 19th Dist., 43rd, 44th
Burke, William, 1st Dist., 37th, 38th; 17th Dist., 39th
Burklow, John D., 13th
Burks, Marion E., 7th Dist., 70th-72nd
Burley, Augustus H., 97th Dist., 27th
Burnett, Charles, 3rd Dist., 24th-26th
Burnett, John M., 14th
Burnidge, Richard C., 33rd Dist., 81st
Burns, Charles P., 10th Dist., 20th
Burns, James F., 29th Dist., 47th
Burns, James T., 20th Dist., 56th-59th
Burns, John S., 17th Dist., 48th-50th
Burns, Thomas F., 8th Dist., 46th
Burns, William E., 5th Dist., 37th
Burnside, Samuel, 25th Dist., 27th
Burnsmier, William G., 30th Dist., 63rd-68th
Burr, Albert G., 24th Dist., 22nd, 23rd
Burres, William F., 24th Dist., 48th, 49th
Burroughs, Harmon P., 48th Dist., 39th
Burt, Charles S., 10th Dist., 31st
Burt, Marvin F., 12th Dist., 64th-67th
Burton, C. W., 47th Dist., 58th
Burton, Frank W., 38th Dist., 43rd
Burzynski, J. Bradley, 76th Dist., 86th, 87th
Busell, David C., 12th Dist., 40th
Busey, John S., 40th Dist., 23rd
Busey, Mathew W., 12th, 13th
Busey, Simeon H., 30th Dist., 30th
Bush, Carroll, 36th Dist., 54th-57th
Bush, Guy, 14th Dist., 41st, 42nd; 41st Dist., 43rd-46th
Bushnell, Nehemia, 37th Dist., 28th
Busse, Carl, 45th Dist., 41st, 42nd; 48th Dist., 43rd
Busse, Fred A., 21st Dist., 39th, 40th
Busse, Robert C., 19th Dist., 40th
Bussell, David C., 12th Dist., 41st
Butler, H., 14th
Butler, Homer, 50th Dist., 63rd, 67th; 59th Dist., 71st, 72nd
Butler, John C., 5th Dist., 40th
Butler, Michael J., 4th Dist., 40th, 41st
Butler, Peter, 9th
Butler, William J., 39th Dist., 39th; 45th Dist., 49th
Butterfield, Bradley, 31st Dist., 32nd
Butterworth, Thomas, 9th Dist., 31st
Butts, Lucas I., 18th Dist., 46th-48th
Butz, Casper, 57th Dist., 21st
Butz, John E. P., 18th Dist., 41st
Buxton, T. C., 28th Dist., 49th
Byers, Harold D., 55th Dist., 79th, 80th
Byers, John H., 35th Dist., 52nd, 53rd

Byers, William M., 13th Dist., 30th, 31st
Cabeen, Thomas B., 32nd Dist., 23rd
Cadwallader, Jesse K., 47th Dist., 41st
Cahill, Peter, 26th Dist., 38th; 24th Dist., 39th, 41st
Cairns, Abraham, 3rd
Calagham, Patrick E., 4th Dist., 41st
Caldwell, A. C., 3rd Dist., 17th
Caldwell, B. F., 39th Dist., 33rd, 34th
Caldwell, Lewis A. H., 29th Dist., 75th-77th; 24th Dist., 78th-80th
Caldwell, Samuel, 67th Dist., 27th
Caldwell, Wm., 13th
Calhoun, John, 11th
Calhoun, William F., 30th Dist., 33rd-35th
Calhoun, William J., 31st Dist., 33rd
Califf, John A., 32nd Dist., 45th
Calla, Angello S., 5th Dist., 39th
Callahan, Ethelbert, 45th Dist., 29th, 37th-39th
Callahan, Joseph, 74th
Callan, Peter M., 16th Dist., 71st-73rd, 74th
Callans, James, 38th Dist., 29th
Callaway, James E., 39th Dist., 26th
Callon, William P., 39th Dist., 30th
Calvo, Horace L., 55th Dist., 76th, 77th; 56th Dist., 78th, 79th
Cameron, W. A., 26th Dist., 50th
Campbell, Albert C., 33rd Dist., 32nd, 38th
Campbell, Alexander, 2nd, 3rd; 6th Dist., 18th; 43rd, Dist., 21st
Campbell, Bruce A., 48th Dist., 44th
Campbell, Charles M., 45th Dist., 73rd; 49th Dist., 75th-77th; 53rd Dist., 78th-81st
Campbell, Daniel A., 9th Dist., 38th
Campbell, George H., 35th Dist., 21st
Campbell, James L., 95th Dist., 27th
Campbell, James R., 46th Dist., 34th, 35th
Campbell, John, 8th Dist., 25th
Campbell, John A., 6th Dist., 16th
Campbell, John B., 15th
Campbell, Joseph, 14th
Campbell, Matthew F., 16th Dist., 34th
Campbell, Thomas, 33rd Dist., 45th-49th
Canaday, John, 13th
Canaday, Stephen D., 38th Dist., 45th, 47th
Canady, John, 12th
Canady, Stephen D., 38th Dist., 44th
Canal, John B. E., 7th
Canfield, Robert R., 74th
Cannif, James F., 48th Dist., 33rd
Cannon, Stephen, 32nd Dist., 30th
Cantrill, William, 15th
Capparelli, Ralph C., 16th Dist., 77th-82nd; 13th Dist., 83rd-92nd
Capuzi, Louis F., 21st Dist., 69th; 18th Dist., 71st-73rd; 19th Dist., 75th-79th, 81st
Carey, John M., 2nd Dist., 82nd
Carey, William, 89th Dist., 27th
Carillon, Charles, 47th Dist., 43rd
Carins, Abraham, 2nd
Carle, William R., 51st Dist., 27th
Carlin, John, 37th Dist., 17th
Carlin, Stephen, E., 22nd Dist., 38th
Carlin, Thomas, 22nd Dist., 16th
Carlin, Walter E., 37th Dist., 33rd
Carlowski, Victor, 13th Dist., 35th
Carmody, Henry P., 11th Dist., 36th-38th
Carmody, William, 13th Dist., 40th-42nd
Carmon, Charles H., 16th Dist., 48th, 50th
Carpenter, George L., 35th Dist., 50th
Carpenter, Julius A., 83rd Dist., 27th; 14th Dist., 28th
Carpenter, Milton, 9th, 10th, 11th, 12th
Carpenter, Rollie C., 16th Dist., 61st-68th
Carpenter, Wm., 9th
Carr, James, 12th Dist., 35th
Carr, Joseph S., 39th Dist., 32nd
Carrico, John, 8th
Carrigan, James D., 18th Dist., 65th-69th; 43rd Dist., 70th-73rd, 74th; 76th, 77th
Carrigan, John S., 6th, 7th, 8th
Carroll, Howard W., 13th Dist., 77th
Carroll, John W., 6th Dist., 70th-73rd, 74th; 4th Dist., 79th
Carroll, Ray C., 50th Dist., 58th
Carroll, William M., 8th Dist., 57th-59th
Carson, Thomas B., 30th Dist., 37th, 38th

Carstens, Garrett, 38th Dist., 41st
Carston, John, 40th Dist., 36th
Carter, Allan J., 6th Dist., 50th
Carter, James H., 51st Dist., 31st
Carter, James Y., 3rd Dist., 60th; 21st Dist., 70th-73rd, 74th; 22nd Dist., 75th-77th
Carter, Joseph, 24th Dist., 46th-48th
Carter, Joseph N., 37th Dist., 31st, 32nd
Carter, Richard A., 19th Dist., 77th; 20th Dist., 78th
Carter, Robert S., 34th Dist., 38th
Cartwright, Peter, 6th, 8th
Caruso, Nicholas E., 21st Dist., 68th, 69th; 18th Dist., 70th-72nd
Casey, John, 34th Dist., 27th; 30th Dist., 38th
Casey, Lewis F., 15th
Casey, Newton R., 1st Dist., 25th, 26th; 51st Dist., 28th
Casey, Robert F., 35th Dist., 70th-72nd; 39th Dist., 81st
Casey, Thomas S., 18th Dist., 27th
Casey, Wright, 22nd Dist., 20th
Casey, Zadok, 3rd, 4th; 6th Dist., 16th, 17th
Cassed, John, 28th Dist., 28th
Cassell, Robert T., 45th Dist., 25th
Cassidy, John E., 74th; 43rd Dist., 75th
Castel, Chauncey H., 36th Dist., 45th
Castle, George J., 38th Dist., 34th
Castle, Howard P., 7th Dist., 51st-55th
Castle, John B., 35th Dist., 43rd, 44th
Caswell, Josiah, 15th
Catania, Susan, 22nd Dist., 78th-82nd
Catlin, Franklin S., 31st Dist., 47th, 48th
Caton, Homer, 26th Dist., 60th-69th
Cavan, Allison M., 66th Dist., 27th
Cavanaugh, James P., 13th Dist., 39th-42nd; 15th Dist., 43rd, 44th
Cavanaugh, William K., 51st Dist., 75th
Cavarly, Alfred W., 5th, 12th
Caviezel, Frank P., 25th Dist., 50th
Ceaser, Paul G., 3rd Dist., 70th-73rd
Cermak, Anton J., 9th Dist., 43rd-46th
Chaffee, George D., 33rd Dist., 32nd
Challacombe, John R., 38th Dist., 39th
Challis, Samuel H., 16th Dist., 26th
Chamberlain, J. M., Jr., 49th Dist., 42nd
Chambers, Jacob S., 22nd Dist., 28th
Chambers, William L., 29th Dist., 30th
Chandler, Charles V., 27th Dist., 37th
Chandler, Linus C., 36th Dist., 32nd
Chandler, Samuel B., 19th Dist., 16th
Chandler, William P., 49th Dist., 27th
Chapman, Eugenia S., 74th; 3rd Dist., 75th-82nd
Chapman, Joseph F., 57th Dist., 23rd
Chapman, Orville G., 37th Dist., 64th-66th, 68th, 69th
Chapman, Thos. C., 37th Dist., 34th
Chapman, Wylls H., 15th
Chapsaddle, Al A., 39th Dist., 45th
Charles, Elijah, 10th
Charles, John F., 12th
Chase, Durfee C., 2nd Dist., 35th
Chase, Horace R., 26th Dist., 31st
Chatfield, James, 16th Dist., 32nd
Chatfield, Wm. A., 45th Dist., 20th
Cheney, Flora S., 5th Dist., 56th
Cherry, Alfred N., 24th Dist., 34th
Cherry, Charles T., 17th Dist., 37th, 38th; 29th Dist., 41st, 42nd; 14th Dist., 43rd, 44th
Chessley, Hiram H., 44th Dist., 30th
Chestnutwood, Jonathan, 48th Dist., 29th
Chew, William, 33rd Dist., 29th
Childs, George B., 36th Dist., 36th
Childs, Henry C., 58th Dist., 24th-26th
Chiperfield, B. M., 43rd Dist., 43rd, 45th-47th
Choate, Clyde L., 50th Dist., 65th-69th; 58th Dist., 70th-74th; 59th Dist., 75th-80th
Choisser, Carl, 50th Dist., 53rd-57th
Choisser, W. V., 49th Dist., 34th
Chott, Quida J., 4th Dist., 36th, 37th
Chrisholm, Oliver P., 14th Dist., 32nd
Chrispy, Samuel, 34th Dist., 20th
Christensen, Ray A., 43rd Dist., 80th-82nd; 85th Dist., 83rd-85th
Christian, Frank E., 4th Dist., 42nd, 43rd
Christie, Isaac L., 23rd Dist., 29th
Christy, William H., 9th Dist., 18th
Church, Chester W., 3rd Dist., 42nd; 11th Dist., 43rd-47th
Church, L. S., 54th Dist., 20th, 21st

Dawson, Glenn V., 30th Dist., 79th-81st
Dawson, John, 7th, 9th-11th
Dawson, Joseph, 15th
Day, Frederick S., 43rd Dist., 19th
Day, Robert G., 43rd Dist., 75th-77th; 46th Dist., 78th
Day, William A., 30th Dist., 31st, 33rd
Day, Wm. S., 50th Dist., 35th
Dazey, Mitchell, 35th Dist., 36th, 38th
Deady, Thomas J., 9th Dist., 43rd
Dean, George W., 37th Dist., 39th
Dean, William C., 50th Dist., 38th
Dearborn, Jonathan, 35th Dist., 16th; 28th Dist., 19th
Dearborn, Luther M., 14th Dist., 37th-39th
Deavers, Gilbert L., 44th Dist., 78th-80th
DeBord, William H., 32nd Dist., 33rd
Decius, Hiram B., 17th Dist., 24th
Decker, Henry, 9th Dist., 35th
Dee, Marvin R., 20th Dist., 78th
Deering, Terry W., 115th Dist., 87th; 116th Dist., 88th-90th
DeForrest, LaVergne B., 35th Dist., 39th
DeGafferelly, Augustus F., 22nd Dist., 61st, 62nd
DeGrazio, Joseph N., 27th Dist., 59th, 60th
Deitz, Peter W., 54th Dist., 26th
DeJaegher, M. "Bob", 72nd Dist., 83rd-87th; 71st Dist., 88th
DeLaCour, Joseph L., 20th Dist., 65th-69th; 11th Dist., 70th-72nd
Delaney, P. H., 8th Dist., 39th
Delashmutt, Wm. G., 45th Dist., 36th
DeLeo, James A., 16th Dist., 84th-87th
Delgado, William, 3rd Dist., 91st, 92nd
Dement, Henry D., 12th Dist., 28th, 29th
Dement, John, 6th, 7th, 10th
DeMichaels, LaSalle J., 12th Dist., 72nd, 73rd; 74th; 13th Dist., 75th
Deneen, Charles S., 2nd Dist., 38th
Denham, Albert B., 46th Dist., 37th
Denio, Cyrenius B., 46th Dist., 16th, 18th; 51st Dist., 20th
Denning, Wm. A., 14th, 15th
Dennis, Andrew B., 22nd Dist., 47th
Dennis, Edward M., 8th Dist., 30th
Dennis, Elias S., 13th
Dennis, James H., 24th Dist., 25th
Dennison, Edward L., 6th Dist., 26th
Denny, John, 12th
Dent, John O., 45th Dist., 23rd
Derrickson, Richard P., 95th Dist., 27th
Derwinski, Edw. J., 24th Dist., 70th
Deskins, John, 14th
Desmond, John T., 49th Dist., 49th, 50th
Desmond, William, 8th Dist., 43rd
DeTolve, Anthony J., 17th Dist., 67th-69th
Detrick, John E., 6th Dist., 21st
Detrick, John E., 17th Dist., 17th
Deuchler, Suzanne L., 39th Dist., 82nd; 42nd Dist., 83rd-90th
Deuster, Donald E., 32nd Dist., 78th-82nd
Devereux, Thomas P., 21st Dist., 49th, 50th
Devine, Edward, 31st Dist., 42nd
Devine, John P., 35th Dist., 48th-59th
DeVuono, Peter K., 21st Dist., 68th
Dewey, John S., 41st Dist., 30th, 31st
Dewey, Mary R., 19th Dist., 28th
DeWitt, Benj., 28th Dist., 22nd
DeWitt, James, 25th Dist., 29th
DeWolf, J. H., 43rd Dist., 46th
DeWolf, James, 51st Dist., 21st
DeWolf, William F., 15th
DeWoody, Wm. D., 50th Dist., 40th
DeYoung, Frederic R., 7th Dist., 49th, 50th
Diamwood, John G., 1st, 3rd
Diarman, Jonathan, 10th
Dickeman, George H., 13th Dist., 24th; 43rd Dist., 34th
Dickenson, Andrew J., 13th
Dickman, Wm., 47th Dist., 47th, 48th
Dickson, Elbert H., 50th Dist., 40th
Didrickson, Loleta A., 37th Dist., 83rd-86th
Dietrich, William H., 30th Dist., 50th, 51st
Diggins, Orson C., 8th Dist., 32nd
Diggins, W., 54th Dist., 19th
Dill, James M., 47th Dist., 34th
Dillavou, Ora D., 24th Dist., 62nd-69th; 44th Dist., 70th
Dillinger, Ray A., 28th Dist., 61st
Dillon, Martin J., 12th Dist., 46th-48th

Dimond, Vincent J., 39th Dist., 65th
Dineen, Jerry W., 31st Dist., 40th
Dinneen, Dan, 28th Dist., 59th-64th
Dinsmore, James, 48th Dist., 25th, 26th
DiPrima, Lawrence, 18th Dist., 73rd; 74th; 18th Dist., 75th-82nd; 16th Dist., 83rd
Dixon, Alan J., 49th Dist., 67th-69th; 43rd Dist., 70th-72nd
Dixon, Arthur, 96th Dist., 27th
Dixon, Chas. G., 9th Dist., 35th
Dixon, George C., 35th Dist., 56th
Dixon, Sherwood, 19th Dist., 37th
Dixson, Eli, 27th Dist., 37th
Dockey, John, 15th Dist., 41st
Dodge, Abram R., 12th
Dodge, William B., 94th Dist., 27th
Doederlein, DeLoris, 65th Dist., 85th-87th
Dolan, Patrick, 14th Dist., 25th; 46th Dist., 28th
Dolezal, George E., 3rd Dist., 70th-73rd
Dollins, Achilles D., 10th, 12th, 13th
Dolton, Charies H., 7th Dist., 28th
Domico, Marco, 20th Dist., 80th-83rd
Donahue, Daniel D., 26th Dist., 46th, 47th, 49th, 50th
Donahue, Joseph H., 6th Dist., 57th
Donahue, William J., 38th Dist., 44th
Donaldson, Elijah H., 40th Dist., 37th
Donlan, James M., 27th Dist., 48th, 49th, 51st
Donnelly, John C., 8th Dist., 37th, 38th, 41st
Donnelly, Tim, 38th Dist., 62nd-64th
Donnewald, James H., 55th Dist., 72nd, 73rd
Donoghue, Francis D., 15th Dist., 42nd; 2nd Dist., 43rd, 45th
Donoghue, Thomas H., 25th Dist., 47th
Donohoo, Roy W., 36th Dist., 62nd-64th, 66th, 67th
Donohue, Joseph H., 6th Dist., 58th, 59th
Donovan, B. T., Jr., 51st Dist., 81st, 82nd
Donovan, John J., 24th Dist., 73rd
Doody, John T., Jr., 37th Dist., 89th
Dooley, George E., 26th Dist., 51st
Doolittle, Edwin A., 37th Dist., 36th
Dorman, William A., 5th Dist., 34th
Dornblaser, Benj., 35th Dist., 27th
Dorris, Thomas M., 2nd-5th
Dougherty, John, 8th-10th, 12th; 1st Dist., 20th
Dougherty, Michael J., 43rd Dist., 45th
Dougherty, Philander, 17th Dist., 23rd
Dougherty, Willis, 13th
Douglas, Bruce L., 11th Dist., 77th; 12th Dist., 78th
Douglas, John, 13th
Douglas, John J., 48th Dist., 38th, 39th
Douglas, Stephen A., 10th
Douglas, Warren B., 3rd Dist., 51st, 52nd, 54th, 55th, 59th
Dow, Augustus, 36th Dist., 38th
Dowling, Rezin H., 37th Dist., 29th
Downes, John P., 26th Dist., 70th-73rd; 74th; 28th Dist., 75th-77th
Downey, Frank X., 2nd Dist., 70th-73rd; 74th
Downey, J. Harold, 41st Dist., 64th-68th
Downing, James E., 28th Dist., 26th; 35th Dist., 33rd
Downing, T. Mac, 32nd Dist., 59th
Downs, John, 26th Dist., 34th
Downs, Robert K., 18th Dist., 79th
Doyle, Edward A., 18th Dist., 80th-82nd
Doyle, Eugene C., 52nd Dist., 83rd
Doyle, Howard L., 28th Dist., 57th, 58th
Doyle, John E., 4th Dist., 42nd; 11th Dist., 43rd
Doyle, Thomas A., 9th Dist., 51st-53rd
Drake, Harry W., 34th Dist., 49th-51st
Dresser, Hiram, 16th Dist., 24th; 38th Dist., 28th
Drevs, Henry L., 11th Dist., 42nd
Drew, Samuel J., 25th Dist., 41st, 42nd; 41st Dist., 43rd, 44th
Drummond, Thomas, 12th
Drury, Joseph W., 48th Dist., 38th, 41st
Dubois, Jesse K., 9th-11th, 13th
Dubois, Lincoln, 1st Dist., 29th
Dudgeon, Israel, 20th Dist., 45th-51st
Dudley, Oscar L., 2nd Dist., 39th
Duff, Brian B., 1st Dist., 77th-79th
Duffy, William M., 36th Dist., 32nd; 34th Dist., 33rd
Dugan, John F., 13th Dist., 33rd
Dukes, Eugene P., 27th Dist., 62nd
Dunbar, Alexander P., 10th, 14th
Duncan, John H., 51st Dist., 37th, 38th

Dunham, Charles, 21st Dist., 28th
Dunham, John H., 56th Dist., 20th
Dunham, William S., 32nd Dist., 39th
Dunlap, George, 7th Dist., 29th
Dunlap, M. L., 57th Dist., 19th
Dunlap, Samuel, 12th
Dunn, Charles, 8th
Dunn, John F., 51st Dist., 79th-82nd; 101st Dist., 83rd-88th
Dunn, John T., 9th Dist., 82nd
Dunn, Michael J., 5th Dist., 29th, 30th
Dunn, Ralph, 58th Dist., 78th-82nd; 115th Dist., 83rd
Dunn, Richard C., 35th Dist., 24th
Dunn, Tarlton, 10th, 11th
Dunn, William H., 20th Dist., 48th
Dunne, George W., 29th Dist., 69th; 11th Dist., 70th-72nd
Dunne, Patrick W., 26th Dist., 29th
Dunne, Robert L., 28th Dist., 78th
Dunne, Timothy, 13th Dist., 47th
Durfee, Bradfort K., 29th Dist., 31st, 32nd
Durfee, Charles, 51st Dist., 45th, 46th
Durkin, James B., 44th Dist., 88th-92nd
Durso, Michael R., 29th Dist., 53rd-57th
Duvall, E. W., 3rd Dist., 48th
Dwight, Samuel, 24th Dist., 27th
Dwyer, John, 19th Dist., 38th
Dwyer, Leo P., 5th Dist., 35th
Dwyer, Michael J., 6th Dist., 35th
Dyckes, Joseph, 33rd Dist., 20th
Dyer, Mrs. Robert C., 38th Dist., 76th, 77th; 41st Dist., 78th-81st
Dyer, Thomas, 54th Dist., 17th
Dysart, Alexander P., 12th Dist., 31st, 32nd
Dysert, Walter V., 22nd Dist., 45th
Eads, Abner, 15th; 46th Dist., 16th
Eagan, W. B., 54th Dist., 18th
Eakins, William C., 4th Dist., 39th
Easley, Wm. W., 54th Dist., 27th; 36th Dist., 28th
Easter, John D., 95th Dist., 27th
Easterday, C. F., 40th Dist., 59th, 60th
Eastman, Francis A., 61st Dist., 23rd
Eastman, Kirk M., 5th Dist., 35th
Easton, Charles L., 1st Dist., 30th
Eatherly, James E., 58th Dist., 75th
Ebbesen, Joseph B., 37th Dist., 78th-82nd; 76th Dist., 83rd
Eberspacher, Edward C., 40th Dist., 69th; 52nd Dist., 70th, 71st
Echols, Jesse, 1st
Echols, Randall B., 36th Dist., 44th
Eckley, Sherman W., 18th Dist., 55th
Eckton, Geo. F., 3rd Dist., 35th, 36th
Eddy, Henry, 2nd, 15th
Eddy, James W., 52nd Dist., 25th
Eddy, John, 28th Dist., 35th-37th
Edelstein, Jacob S., 8th Dist., 40th
Edgar, Jim, 53rd Dist., 80th, 81st
Edgecomb, Benjamin, 77th Dist., 27th
Edley, Bill, 95th Dist., 86th-88th
Edmiston, John D., 44th Dist., 38th
Edmonston, Wm. G., 8th, 10th, 11th
Edmunds, Amos, 24th Dist., 37th
Edwards, Cyrus, 8th, 12th; 14th Dist., 22nd
Edwards, James E. N., 50th Dist., 41st-43rd
Edwards, Lorenzo, 13th
Edwards, N. G., 20th Dist., 17th
Edwards, Ninian W., 10th, 11th; 26th Dist., 16th, 17th
Edwards, Thomas J., 26th Dist., 37th
Edwards, W. O., 22nd Dist., 57th-68th
Efner, Dean S., 87th Dist., 27th; 11th Dist., 28th
Egan, Dennis J., 15th Dist., 44th, 45th
Egan, Wiley M., 95th Dist., 27th
Ehradt, Charles, 5th Dist., 31st
Eignus, M. C., 20th Dist., 41st, 42nd
Eisenhart, Henry, 44th Dist., 54th, 55th
Eisenhower, Earl D., 74th
Ela, George, 15th
Elder, James, 49th Dist., 23rd
Elder, William, 4th Dist., 21st; 8th Dist., 27th
Eldredge, Charles M., 6th Dist., 40th
Eldredge, William V., 51st Dist., 31st
Elkin, Wm. F., 6th, 10th, 11th
Elliot, Henry M., 30th Dist., 43rd
Elliott, Asa, 9th, 11th
Elliott, Robert A., 32nd Dist., 48th, 49th

Elliott, Silas H., 39th Dist., 26th
Elliott, Simon, 19th Dist., 31st
Elliott, W. B., 43rd Dist., 48th
Ellis, DeGoy B., 14th Dist., 49th-51st
Ellsworth, Urbin S., 23rd Dist., 37th, 38th; 27th Dist., 39th
Elrod, Rena, 25th Dist., 54th-56th
Elrod, Richard J., 13th Dist., 76th
Elward, Paul F., 8th Dist., 70th-73rd; 74th; 10th Dist., 75th, 76th
Ely, John K., 29th Dist., 39th, 40th
Emerson, R., 14th
Emerson, William H., 22nd Dist., 33rd; 43rd Dist., 44th
Emge, Ben, 49th Dist., 60th
Emmerson, Allan, 11th, 12th
Emmerson, Charles, 32nd Dist., 17th
Emery, James, 53rd Dist., 79th
Emmett, John, 3rd
Emmons, Lyman W., 48th Dist., 52nd, 53rd
Engle, Wm., 34th Dist., 21st
English, George W., 51st Dist., 45th-47th
English, John N., 22nd Dist., 22nd, 23rd; 40th Dist., 30th-32nd
English, Revill W., 10th-12th
English, Robert B., 47th Dist., 40th
Enloe, Benj. S., 8th, 10th
Enloe, Enoch, 15th
Enoch, A. J., 47th Dist., 18th
Enoch, Abram I., 55th Dist., 25th
Enos, Pascal P., 26th Dist., 18th
Enslow, David C., 38th Dist., 36th, 37th
Epler, Cyrus, 27th Dist., 20th, 21st
Epler, David, 13th
Epler, James M., 25th Dist., 23rd, 25th
Epperson, Thomas, 15th
Epstein, Jacob W., 17th Dist., 49th-54th
Epstein, S. S., 19th Dist., 67th
Epton, Bernard F., 24th Dist., 76th-82nd
Erby, Charles E., 31st Dist., 44th-46th
Erickson, Frederick E., 21st Dist., 43rd-47th
Erickson, Samuel E., 13th Dist., 37th, 38th; 23rd Dist., 41st-44th
Erlenborn, John N., 36th Dist., 70th-73rd
Erwin, Hugh, 13th
Erwin, Judy, 11th Dist., 87th-92nd
Erwin, Lewis D., 30th Dist., 20th-22nd
Erwin, Milo, 47th Dist., 32nd
Erwin, Milo, 51st Dist., 33rd
Eskew, William L., 50th Dist., 43rd
Espy, Sidney B., 50th Dist., 46th
Essery, Jesse, 8th
Etherton, James M., 44th Dist., 46th-48th, 50th-52nd
Eubanks, Wm., 6th, 7th
Eustace, John V., 49th Dist., 20th
Euzzino, Andrew A., 17th Dist., 63rd-73rd; 74th
Evans, Albert H., 48th Dist., 37th
Evans, Atkins, 14th Dist., 17th
Evans, David, 45th Dist., 58th
Evans, Henry H., 14th Dist., 30th
Evans, William M., 42nd Dist., 30th
Everett, J. J., 15th
Evey, Edward, 33rd Dist., 16th
Ewell, Raymond W., 29th Dist., 75th-82nd
Ewing, Charles F., 13th
Ewing, C. L., 3rd Dist., 55th, 56th
Ewing, Elijah, 1st
Ewing, Henry A., 28th Dist., 31st
Ewing, John, 30th Dist., 26th
Ewing, Joseph H., 32nd Dist., 28th, 33rd
Ewing, Reuben B., 32nd Dist., 16th
Ewing, Thomas W., 38th Dist., 79th-82nd; 87th Dist., 83rd-87th
Ewing, Wm. Lee D., 7th, 10th-12th
Eyman, Abraham, 4th
Faherty, Edmund, 6th Dist., 22nd
Fahy, Michael, 16th Dist., 46th-58th
Fairbanks, John, 1st Dist., 33rd
Faires, William H., 41st Dist., 37th
Fairfield, Joseph M., 7th
Falder, Everett L., 32nd Dist., 69th
Falter, Arthur R., 41st Dist., 72nd
Fanta, Joseph F., 9th Dist., 70th, 71st; 74th
Fantin, Arline M., 29th Dist., 89th, 90th
Fargo, Henry B., 14th Dist., 48th
Farina, Joseph E., 29th Dist., 58th, 59th

Gaines, Duane, 45th Dist., 40th
Gaines, Harris B., 1st Dist., 57th-59th
Gaines, James, 47th Dist., 27th
Galbraith, Ashley T., 19th Dist., 27th
Galbreath, George, 10th
Gale, James V., 50th Dist., 23rd
Gale, W. Seldon, 34th Dist., 26th
Gallagher, A. J., 14th Dist., 18th
Gallagher, Arthur J., 28th Dist., 43rd
Gallagher, H. M., 77th Dist., 27th
Gallagher, Patrick W., 43rd Dist., 50th
Gallas, Walter Francis, 19th Dist., 53rd, 55th
Galligan, Peter E., 15th Dist., 40th
Galligan, Peter F., 17th Dist., 46th, 47th
Galloway, A. J., 96th Dist., 27th
Galloway, Wm. C., 24th Dist., 35th
Gallup, Joseph, 26th Dist., 32nd, 33rd
Galvin, A. O., 27th Dist., 56th-58th
Gardner, J. Horace, 21st Dist., 70th-73rd; 26th Dist., 75th-77th
Gardner, John J., 2nd Dist., 49th
Garesche, Ferdinand A., 47th Dist., 48th-53rd
Garland, James M., 35th Dist., 32nd
Garman, Tom M., 24th Dist., 60th-64th
Garmisa, Benedict, 74th; 17th Dist., 75th-77th; 19th Dist., 78th-82nd
Garrett, James O., 20th Dist., 37th
Garrett, Peter B., 13th
Garrett, Susan, 59th Dist., 91st, 92nd
Garriott, John C., Jr., 13th Dist., 55th, 57th
Garver, Samuel B., 30th Dist., 40th, 41st
Gas, Wm. L., 6th Dist., 17th
Gash, Lauren Beth, 60th Dist., 88th-91st
Gass, Wm. R., 13th Dist., 27th
Gassaway, Nicholas P., 32nd Dist., 41st
Gatewood, Wm. J., 7th
Gaumer, Clay F., 22nd Dist., 44th, 45th
Gaunt, Charles M., 50th Dist., 43rd, 44th
Gayle, William D., 28th Dist., 58th
Gaylord, George, 43rd Dist., 26th
Gehant, Henry F., 35th Dist., 45th
Geher, John L., 26th Dist., 37th
Gehring, Fred, 35th Dist., 29th
Geisler, Herbert, 74th; 14th Dist., 75th, 76th
Geisler, Philip M., 11th Dist., 52nd
Geo-Karis, Adeline J., 31st Dist., 78th-80th
George, Coleman C., 40th Dist., 35th
Gerrard, John, 39th Dist., 23rd
Geshkewich, Joseph H., 27th Dist., 43rd-46th
Getman, Jethro M., 1st Dist., 36th
Getty, Michael B., 10th Dist., 78th-82nd
Gibbons, Dennis E., 8th Dist., 44th, 45th
Gibbs, W. Joseph, 51st Dist., 77th; 50th Dist., 78th
Gibbs, William F., 36th Dist., 60th-66th
Giblin, William A., 74th
Gibson, John W., 6th Dist., 54th
Gibson, Milroy H., 5th Dist., 39th
Gibson, Theodore C., 44th Dist., 23rd
Giffin, D. Logan, 45th Dist., 57th
Giglio, Frank, 30th Dist., 78th-80th, 82nd; 77th Dist., 83rd-87th; 29th Dist., 88th
Giglio, Michael, 79th Dist., 90th, 91st
Gilbert, Alvin, 31st Dist., 30th
Gilbert, A. V. T., 40th Dist., 20th
Gilbert, Hiram T., 5th Dist., 47th
Gilbert Samuel S., 40th Dist., 29th
Giles, Calvin L., 8th Dist., 88th-92nd
Gilham, William, 11th
Gill, Charles F., 24th Dist., 30th
Gill, Joseph B., 50th Dist., 36th, 37th
Gill, Joseph L., 31st Dist., 55th, 56th
Gill, Michael J., 41st Dist., 38th
Gillespie, Edward W., 17th Dist., 44th
Gillespie, Frank, 26th Dist., 48th
Gillespie, Joseph, 12th
Gillespie, William W., 12th Dist., 43rd-46th
Gillham, Daniel B., 26th Dist., 27th
Gillham, Henry M., 6th
Gillmore, Wm., 33rd Dist., 29th
Gillogly, Raymond C., 34th Dist., 61st, 62nd
Gilmore, Ephraim, 15th
Gilmore, Ephraim, Jr., 48th Dist., 21st
Gilmore, Ephraim M., 19th Dist., 26th
Gilmore, William E., 24th Dist., 56th, 57th
Ginders, Guy W., 10th Dist., 51st, 52nd

Ginter, William E., 59th Dist., 23rd
Giolitto, Barbara, 68th Dist., 88th
Giorgi, E. J. "Zeke", 74th; 34th Dist., 75th-82nd; 68th Dist., 83rd-87th; 67th Dist., 88th
Gittings, Clarence R., 24th Dist., 34th, 35th
Glackin, Edward J., 17th Dist., 44th
Glade, Albert, 17th Dist., 39th-42nd; 27th Dist., 43rd-46th
Glass, Bradley M., 1st Dist., 77th
Glass, Robert W., 13th
Gleason, James F., 4th Dist., 35th, 38th
Glenn, Dave, 51st Dist., 70th-73rd
Glenn, Samuel P., 15th
Glover, James O., 15th
Gobble, Sergeant, 13th; 21st Dist., 24th
Gochenour, David, 37th Dist., 18th
Goforth, Charles Wayne, 115th Dist., 84th-86th
Golden, John R., 26th Dist., 45th
Golden, Thomas J., 45th Dist., 28th
Goldstick, Phillip C., 74th
Goodall, Samuel H., 51st Dist., 38th
Goode, Katherine Hancock, 5th Dist., 54th, 55th
Goode, Wm., 8th
Goodell, Addison, 42nd Dist., 23rd; 64th Dist., 27th
Goodnow, Charles N., 3rd Dist., 41st
Goodnow, Henry C., 43rd Dist., 34th
Goodrich, Luke H., 15th Dist., 29th, 30th
Goodspeed, Albert G., 18th Dist., 32nd-34th
Goodwin, Fred L., 36th Dist., 68th
Goodwin, Quentin J., 22nd Dist., 81st
Gordon, George H., 22nd Dist., 43rd
Gordon, John, 39th Dist., 28th, 29th
Gordon, Wm., 9th
Gorin, Jerome R., 36th Dist., 20th
Gorman, Howard J., 18th Dist., 59th-64th
Gorman, John J., 19th Dist., 61st-66th
Gorman, Joseph R., 3rd Dist., 32nd
Gorman, Thomas N., 18th Dist., 46th-51st
Gormley, William J., 9th Dist., 54th-68th
Goudy, Calvin, 20th Dist., 20th
Goudy, John C., 8th
Gouge, Jesse Wilson, 11th
Gould, Edson, 44th Dist., 36th
Gould, Kitt, 2nd Dist., 42nd
Gower, Bailey A., 18th Dist., 38th; 20th Dist., 39th
Grace, J. Russ, 22nd Dist., 44th, 46th
Graham, Abner W., 24th Dist., 34th
Graham, Dominick C., 27th Dist., 37th
Graham, Elwood, 22nd Dist., 70th-73rd; 29th Dist., 75th-77th
Graham, George P., 22nd Dist., 28th
Graham, James M., 29th Dist., 34th
Graham, James W., 45th Dist., 31st
Graham, John G., 33rd Dist., 21st, 22nd; 35th Dist., 23rd
Graham, Nicholas R., 14th Dist., 36th
Graham, Paul, 51st Dist., 71st
Graham, Resolve, 10th
Graham, Ross, 46th Dist., 30th; 44th Dist., 39th
Graham, R. V., 19th Dist., 56th
Graham, Thomas E., 8th Dist., 48th-51st
Graham, Wm. J., 33rd Dist., 49th
Grammer, John, 1st, 2nd
Granata, Peter C., 17th Dist., 58th-62nd, 64th-73rd; 20th Dist., 75th-78th
Granberg, Kurt M., 109th Dist., 85th-92nd
Grandfield, George M., 47th Dist., 70th
Granger, Flavel K., 8th Dist., 28th-31st
Grant, Charles M., 50th Dist., 45th
Grant, William A., 23rd Dist., 28th
Graver, Clem, 15th Dist., 67th, 68th
Graves, Charles S., 6th Dist., 48th
Graves, Hubbard, 13th
Gray, George B., 18th Dist., 30th, 31st
Gray, George W., 2nd Dist., 19th
Gray, James M., 41st Dist., 41st, 42nd; 28th Dist., 43rd, 44th
Gray, James W., 49th Dist., 66th
Gray, John, 34th Dist., 25th
Gray, John A., 25th Dist., 28th
Gray, John F., 52nd Dist., 16th
Gray, John H., 35th Dist., 46th
Gray, Robert A., 40th Dist., 34th, 35th
Grayhill, George R., 40th Dist., 41st
Grear, Sidney, 50th Dist., 33rd
Greason, Wm., 29th Dist., 35th

Harbeck, Clayton C., 39th Dist., 69th; 38th Dist., 70th-72nd
Hardie, H., 14th
Hardin, Everett C., 32nd Dist., 43rd, 44th
Hardin, John J., 10th, 11th, 12th
Hardin, Stephen, 15th Dist., 21st
Harding, Abner C., 42nd Dist., 16th
Harewood, Richard A., 3rd Dist., 60th; 20th Dist., 70th
Hargrave, Harry S., 38th Dist., 53rd
Harkin, Daniel V., 19th Dist., 41st
Harlan, Edwin, 17th Dist., 25th
Harlan, Moses, 11th
Harmon, Oscar F., 37th Dist., 25th
Harna, Robert P., 10th Dist., 25th
Harnsberger, Geo. L., 39th Dist., 40th
Harp, William H., 40th Dist., 47th
Harper, Joshua, 13th, 14th
Harperm, William H., 2nd Dist., 33rd, 34th
Harpole, William P., 15th
Harpstrite, Ben C., 53rd Dist., 75th-77th; 55th Dist., 78th
Harreld, James, 9th
Harrell, Jerome L., 48th Dist., 54th, 55th
Harrington, James, 14th Dist., 32nd, 33rd, 35th
Harrington, W. C., 29th Dist., 22nd
Harriot, James, 14th
Harris, David, 53rd Dist., 83rd-87th
Harris, Demas L., 49th Dist., 23rd
Harris, George H., 11th Dist., 41st
Harris, H. W., 21st Dist., 48th
Harris, Homer, 28th Dist., 64th, 65th
Harris, J. Edw., 32nd Dist., 44th, 45th
Harris, J. W., 21st Dist., 56th, 57th
Harris, John, 9th, 10th, 11th
Harris, Joseph W., 47th Dist., 22nd
Harris, Judson E., 44th Dist., 48th
Harris, Lloyd, 47th Dist., 59th, 60th, 62nd-69th; 53rd Dist., 70th-73rd; 74th; 55th Dist., 75th
Harris, Madison R., 1st Dist., 32nd
Harris, Mansel A., 43rd Dist., 32nd
Harris, Thomas W., 19th Dist., 22nd
Harris, William C., 16th Dist., 69th; 41st Dist., 70th, 71st
Harris, William L., 59th Dist., 80th, 81st
Harris, Willis A., 29th Dist., 91st
Harrison, Josiah, 38th Dist., 16th
Hart, Fred J., 39th Dist., 63rd-66th
Hart, John M., 26th Dist., 35th, 36th
Hart, John P., 14th Dist., 52nd, 53rd
Hart, Joseph, 17th Dist., 28th
Hart, Richard O., 58th Dist., 76th, 77th; 59th Dist., 78th-80th
Hart, Thomas, 15th
Hart, William, 45th Dist., 40th
Hartke, Charles A., 107th Dist., 84th-87th; 108th Dist., 88th-92nd
Hartnett, William E., 74th
Hartquist, William, 33rd Dist., 48th
Harts, David H., 27th Dist., 31st
Harvey, Curtis N., 22nd Dist., 29th
Harvey, Jabez, 15th Dist., 28th
Harvey, James C., 26th Dist., 49th
Harvey, Joseph S., 38th Dist., 29th
Harvey, Wesley B., 27th Dist., 32nd
Hasara, Karen, 100th Dist., 84th-87th
Hassert, Brent, 83rd Dist., 88th-92nd
Hastert, Dennis, 39th Dist., 82nd; 82nd Dist., 83rd, 84th
Hastings, Jay L., 22nd Dist., 38th
Hatch, Jeduthan, 13th
Hatch, Ozias M., 34th Dist., 17th
Haven, Dwight, 15th Dist., 35th
Haven, Orlando H., 50th Dist., 16th
Havill, Rene, 48th Dist., 50th, 51st
Hawes, Peter J., 53rd Dist., 27th; 27th Dist., 28th
Hawker, William S., 16th Dist., 33rd
Hawkes, James A., 30th Dist., 38th
Hawkins, Gerald, 115th Dist., 88th
Hawkins, H. H., 24th Dist., 55th
Hawkinson, Carl E., 94th Dist., 83rd, 84th
Hawkinson, Henry G., 43rd Dist., 57th, 58th
Hawks, James A., 30th Dist., 33rd
Hawley, Edgar C., 14th Dist., 36th-39th
Hay, Daniel, 7th Dist., 25th
Hay, Frank E., 10th Dist., 27th
Hay, Lowry, 46th Dist., 33rd
Hay, Milton, 35th Dist., 28th
Hayes, Edward G., 39th Dist., 59th-64th

Hayes, Edward J., 5th Dist., 38th
Hayes, Samuel C., 9th Dist., 36th, 37th
Hayes, Samuel S., 15th; 7th Dist., 16th
Hayne, Edward G., 39th Dist., 59th-64th
Haynie, Isham N., 6th Dist., 17th
Headen, Walter C., 33rd Dist., 34th, 37th
Headfeld, John W., 95th Dist., 27th
Healy, John F., 5th Dist., 52nd
Heard, James W., 10th Dist., 23rd
Hearn, Campbell S., 36th Dist., 44th, 45th
Heath, Randolph, 17th Dist., 19th
Heckenkamp, Jos. E., 36th Dist., 58th, 59th
Hefferman, R., 32nd Dist., 30th
Heffernan, J. F., 22nd Dist., 42nd; 26th Dist., 43rd
Heim, Ferdinand, 47th Dist., 34th
Heiman, H. H., 42nd Dist., 35th
Heimberger, Herman R., 49th Dist., 41st
Heinl, Frank J., 45th Dist., 44th, 45th
Heiple, Rae C., II, 46th Dist., 71st-73rd
Helminiak, Joseph F., 19th Dist., 42nd
Helwig, John H., 5th Dist., 49th
Henderson, George D., 45th Dist., 24th
Henderson, John W., 43rd Dist., 16th
Henderson, Thomas J., 41st Dist., 19th
Henderson, Wm. D., 14th
Henderson, William H., 11th, 12th
Hendery, William, 14th, 15th
Henderickson, James H., 37th Dist., 30th
Henehan, Thomas P., 31st Dist., 67th
Hennebry, Michael F., 25th Dist., 41st
Hennebry, Michael F., 41st Dist., 48th-59th
Henning, Edgar L., 17th Dist., 38th
Henry, Andrew G., 42nd Dist., 28th, 29th
Henry, John, 8th, 9th, 11th
Henry, Miles S., 49th Dist., 19th
Henry, Thomas N., 33rd, 34th
Henry, William C., 21st Dist., 81st, 82nd; 18th Dist., 83rd
Hensel, Donald N., 50th Dist., 83rd-87th
Henshaw, George, 10th
Henss, Donald A., 44th Dist., 75th-77th
Herdman, Alex B., 40th Dist., 38th
Herdman, George W., 38th Dist., 27th
Herndon, Wm. D., 14th
Herrick, O. W., 7th Dist., 35th
Herrin, Earl, 47th Dist., 54th
Herrington, James, 15th; 14th Dist., 28th-31st
Herron, J. J., 19th Dist., 29th, 30th
Herron, William G., 18th Dist., 41st
Herting, William A., 5th Dist., 28th
Herver, David, 26th Dist., 32nd
Heslit, Samuel M., 17th Dist., 30th
Hester, Robert S., 20th Dist., 33rd
Hewett, Thomas J., 50th Dist., 25th
Heyward, Thomas, 30th Dist., 18th
Hiatt, Luther L., 14th Dist., 33rd, 34th
Hickey, P. J., 3rd Dist., 30th
Hickman, William, 13th
Hickox, Warren R., 79th Dist., 27th
Hicks, H. S., 10th Dist., 49th, 50th, 51st
Hicks, Larry W., 108th Dist., 83rd-87th; 107th Dist., 88th
Hicks, Richardson S., 43rd Dist., 21st
Hicks, Stephen G., 12th, 13th, 14th
Hicks, Thomas B., 2nd Dist., 23rd
Hicks, Thomas S., 13th-15th; 4th Dist., 21st
Higbee, Chauncey L., 28th Dist., 19th
Higgins, James M., 15th
Higgins, Jesse, 48th Dist., 62nd-64th
Higgins, John J., 48th Dist., 33rd
Higgins, Richard T., 43rd Dist., 38th
Higgins, Van H., 56th Dist., 21st
Highsmith, John M., 45th Dist., 34th
Highsmith, Wm., 8th
Hildrup, Jesse, 92nd Dist., 27th; 9th Dist., 28th
Hill, Albert A., 28th Dist., 52nd, 53rd
Hill, Austin, 51st Dist., 50th
Hill, John, 26th Dist., 24th
Hill, John B., 33rd Dist., 75th, 76th
Hill, John Jerome, 35th Dist., 71st-73rd; 74th; 36th Dist., 75th-77th; 39th Dist., 78th, 79th
Hill, John W., 6th Dist., 44th, 45th
Hill, Josiah A., 40th Dist., 36th
Hill, Robert H., 29th Dist., 36th
Hill, Robert P., 50th Dist., 47th
Hill, Walter E., 46th Dist., 71st, 72nd
Hill, William, 28th Dist., 32nd

Hillboldt, J. Henry, 50th Dist., 41st
Hills, Erastus O., 45th Dist., 19th
Hilton, George C., 45th Dist., 45th-49th
Hilvers, Delbert J., 10th Dist., 64th
Hinch, Benjamin P., 4th Dist., 19th
Hinchcliffe, John, 16th Dist., 27th
Hinckley, T. Duane, 42nd Dist., 31st
Hinds, Andrew, 10th Dist., 31st
Hinds, J. T., 34th Dist., 43rd
Hinton, Alfred, 13th
Hire, George, 32nd Dist., 20th
Hirschfeld, John C., 48th Dist., 77th; 52nd Dist., 78th, 79th
Hirst, Seymour, 34th Dist., 45th
Hise, John, 49th Dist., 17th
Hise, John, 2nd Dist., 29th
Hite, Benj. R., 41st Dist., 28th
Hite, Luke H., 49th Dist., 28th
Hitt, E. B., 27th Dist., 20th, 21st
Hitt, Samuel M., 14th
Hitter, Elmer P., 39th Dist., 61st, 62nd
Hittmeier, Orval, 52nd Dist., 70th-73rd
Hoar, Ralph H., 14th Dist., 53rd-55th
Hobbs, J. R., 35th Dist., 17th
Hodge, Orville E., 47th Dist., 65th-67th
Hodges, Charles D., 22nd Dist., 17th, 18th
Hodges, John, 15th
Hoeft, Douglas L., 66th Dist., 88th-92nd
Hoff, Grover C., 28th Dist., 54th
Hoffelder, Walter P., 14th Dist., 72nd
Hoffman, Charles L., 17th Dist., 29th; 23rd Dist., 34th
Hoffman, Gene L., 37th Dist., 75th-77th; 40th Dist., 78th-86th
Hoffman George L., 12th Dist., 33rd
Hoffman, Jay C., 110th Dist., 87th; 112th Dist., 88th-92nd
Hoffman, Manny, 37th Dist., 87th
Hoffman, Ronald K., 5th Dist., 76th, 77th; 6th Dist., 78th, 79th
Hoffman, Wm. H., 36th Dist., 47th-49th
Hogan, John, 10th
Hogan, Timothy, 4th Dist., 39th
Hoge, Charles C., 14th Dist., 45th
Hogg, Harvey, 38th Dist., 22nd
Hogge, Andrew J., 43rd Dist., 30th
Hoiles, Charles, 13th Dist., 21st; 42nd Dist., 28th
Holaday, Wm. P., 22nd Dist., 46th-52nd
Holbrook, James C., 6th Dist., 19th
Holbrook, Thomas, 113th Dist., 89th-92nd
Holcomb, Hiram, 17th Dist., 35th
Holden, John G., 31st Dist., 31st, 32nd
Holderman, L. S., 20th Dist., 53rd
Holewinski, Michael S., 17th Dist., 79th, 80th
Holgate, James, 36th Dist., 23rd
Holiday, George H., 21st Dist., 19th
Hollenback, George M., 13th Dist., 28th
Hollenbeck, Wm. T., 34th Dist., 45th-48th
Hollerich, William C., 40th Dist., 71st
Hollingsworth, Morton H., 41st Dist., 64th
Hollister, George H., 9th Dist., 30th
Hollister, T. H., 12th Dist., 48th
Holloway, James D., 58th Dist., 71st-73rd; 74th; 57th Dist., 75th-77th; 58th Dist., 78th
Holloway, Robert H., 29th Dist., 78th
Hollowbush, Thomas, 24th Dist., 25th
Holmes, John, 26th Dist., 38th
Holmes, Richard, 17th Dist., 29th
Holmes, Samuel, 29th Dist., 20th
Holmes, Wm., 11th
Holmgren, Elmer N., 4th Dist., 55th
Holten, Frank, 49th Dist., 50th-69th; 54th Dist., 70th-73rd
Holtshaw, Daniel W., 43rd Dist., 38th
Holyoke, Joseph M., 34th Dist., 23rd, 24th
Homan, William, 3rd Dist., 29th
Homer, Thomas J., 91st Dist., 83rd-88th
Homeier, Christian H., 51st Dist., 76th
Honey, J. M., 45th Dist., 33rd
Hood, H. H., 40th Dist., 34th
Hood, J. M., 45th Dist., 21st
Hoover, Harold A., 2nd Dist., 70th-72nd
Hope, Edward, 29th Dist., 45th, 46th
Hopkins, Archibald W., 25th Dist., 37th, 38th; 31st Dist., 41st
Hopkins, C. C., 10th Dist., 19th
Hopkins, Joel W., 45th Dist., 26th
Hopkins, Solomon P., 2nd Dist., 28th-31st

Hopkins, William T., 43rd Dist., 24th
Hopp, Frank W., 14th Dist., 52nd
Hoppin, Bushrod E., 2nd Dist., 36th
Horn, Joseph A., 32nd Dist., 40th
Horn, Raymond O., 42nd Dist., 64th
Horner, Samuel, 13th
Horrabin, Humphrey, 29th Dist., 26th
Horsley, G. William, 45th Dist., 65th-69th; 48th Dist., 70th-73rd; 74th
Hoskinson, William W., 51st Dist., 33rd, 35th
Hosner, P. E., 7th Dist., 19th
Houcek, Frank, 19th Dist., 62nd-65th
Houde, Thomas R., 42nd Dist., 75th-77th
Houghton, Edwin W., 33rd Dist., 40th
Houlihan, Daniel, 28th Dist., 78th-80th
Houlihan, James M., 13th Dist., 78th-80th
Houlihan, John J., 74th; 41st Dist., 75th-77th
Houston, John, 11th
Howard, B. B., 46th Dist., 17th
Howard, Constance A. "Connie", 32nd Dist., 89th-92nd
Howard, John, 1st
Howard, Jonathan B., 13th
Howard, Robert, 34th Dist., 50th, 51st, 53rd
Howe, Daniel R., 45th Dist., 23rd
Howell, J. L., 44th Dist., 41st, 42nd
Howell, J. Will, 50th Dist., 61st
Hoxsey, Betty J., 38th Dist., 80th-82nd
Hrdlicka, Fred W., 23rd Dist., 54th, 55th
Hrubec, John, 4th Dist., 47th
Hruby, John O., 15th Dist., 45th-50th; 19th Dist., 57th-67th
Hubbard, Adolphus F., 1st
Hubbard, Gordon S., 8th
Hubbard, Nicholas L., 38th Dist., 59th, 60th
Hubbard, William A., 38th Dist., 48th, 49th
Hubbard, Wm. C., 30th Dist., 29th
Hubbard, William G., 30th Dist., 39th
Hubbard, William R., 43rd Dist., 29th
Hudson, George "Ray", 38th Dist., 77th; 41st Dist., 78th-82nd
Huey, Joseph, 10th, 11th
Huff, Douglas, Jr., 29th Dist., 79th-82nd; 19th Dist., 83rd-85th
Huff, Rufus, 41st Dist., 41st
Huffman, John D., 34th Dist., 39th, 40th
Huffman, Samuel, 14th, 15th
Huggins, David, 48th Dist., 42nd
Hughes, Ann, 63rd Dist., 88th-90th
Hughes, Charles H., 29th Dist., 42nd
Hughes, Charles L., 36th Dist., 75th
Hughes, John, 26th Dist., 42nd; 43rd Dist., 43rd
Hughes, John D., 9th
Huitt, John W., 23rd Dist., 20th
Huling, Truman, 16th Dist., 35th
Hull, Alden, 11th, 12th
Hull, Morton D., 5th Dist., 45th-48th
Hultgren, David R., 94th Dist., 85th-87th
Hultgren, Randall M., 40th Dist., 91st, 92nd
Hummell, Ernest, 2nd Dist., 34th
Humphrey, John, 7th Dist., 34th
Humphrey, John, 95th Dist., 27th
Humphrey, John G., 12th
Humphreys, Edward, 1st
Hundley, William B., 35th Dist., 27th
Hunsacker, James J., 13th
Hunsicker, Carl T., 41st Dist., 72nd, 73rd; 40th Dist., 75th-77th; 38th Dist., 78th
Hunt, Daniel D., 17th Dist., 35th, 36th
Hunt, Michael E., 3rd Dist., 42nd; 5th Dist., 43rd
Hunt, Roy D., 35th Dist., 48th
Hunt, Thomas, 8th, 9th, 10th
Hunter, Clifford C., 40th Dist., 64th-66th
Hunter, David, 10th Dist., 34th-37th, 42nd
Hunter, David, Jr., 10th Dist., 53rd-69th; 33rd Dist., 70th, 71st
Hunter, Edward C., 10th Dist., 60th, 62nd, 63rd, 65th, 66th
Hunter, James C., 41st Dist., 42nd
Hunter, Robert, 76th Dist., 27th
Hunter, William F., 14th Dist., 40th
Hunter, Wm., 8th, 9th
Huntley, Nathan W., 59th Dist., 24th
Hurd, Daniel J., 19th Dist., 30th
Hurd, Theodore F., 41st Dist., 22nd
Hurlbut, Stephen A., 54th Dist., 21st; 51st Dist., 25th

Hurst, Elmore W., 21st Dist., 36th; 33rd Dist., 41st
Hurst, Ronald A., 74th
Hurst, Seymour, 34th Dist., 52nd, 53rd
Huschle, R. H. 49th Dist., 57th, 58th, 63rd
Huschle, R. H. Ruddy, 49th Dist., 63rd
Huskey, Herbert V., 8th Dist., 78th, 80th-82nd
Hussman, Barney L., 43rd Dist., 40th
Huston, John, 38th Dist., 17th
Huston, John, 32nd Dist., 46th-49th
Hutchings, W. A., 1st Dist., 37th
Hutchins, Ozie, 17th Dist., 83rd
Hutchinson, Charles G., 25th Dist., 48th
Hutson, A. L., 26th Dist., 54th, 55th
Hutzler, Lewis, 25th Dist., 46th, 47th
Hyatt, Samuel S., 36th Dist., 53rd, 54th
Hyde, Henry J., 16th Dist., 75th-77th; 18th Dist., 78th
Ickes, Anna Wilmarth, 7th Dist., 55th
Igoe, Michael L., 5th Dist., 48th-51st, 53rd, 55th-57th
Ihnen, H. B., 36th Dist., 65th, 67th-69th; 49th Dist., 70th-73rd; 50th Dist., 75th
Ingalls, Charles H., 19th Dist., 34th
Ingersoll, Eben C., 4th Dist., 20th
Ingersoll, Ezekiel J., 48th Dist., 39th
Ingham, George K., 29th Dist., 31st
Inscore, Matthew J., 50th Dist., 28th, 29th
Ireland, Harrison T., 16th Dist., 44th-47th
Ireland, Robert M., 14th Dist., 36th
Irwin, Alex H., 50th Dist., 30th
Irwin, Robert, 12th Dist., 50th-53rd
Iserman, W. D., 27th Dist., 42nd-44th
Isham, Edward S., 60th Dist., 24th
Ives, Charles, 5th, 6th
Jack, Samuel S.. 29th Dist., 29th, 30th
Jackson, Aaron C., 13th
Jackson, B. M., 14th
Jackson, James S., 43rd Dist., 31st
Jackson, Jesse, 29th Dist., 82nd
Jackson, John E., 23rd Dist., 28th
Jackson, Noyes L., 8th Dist., 54th-56th
Jackson, Robert R., 3rd Dist., 48th-50th
Jackson, William, 59th Dist., 24th
Jackson, William H., 37th Dist., 56th-58th
Jackson, William M., 13th, 14th
Jacobs, Oral, 74th; 44th Dist., 76th, 77th; 36th Dist., 78th-80th
Jacobs, William D., 42nd Dist., 37th
Jacobson, John G., 25th Dist., 49th-51st, 53rd-56th
Jaffe, Aaron, 4th Dist., 77th-82nd; 56th Dist., 83rd, 84th
James, Austin, 8th Dist., 24th; 43th Dist., 28th, 32nd
James, Lawrence W., 35th Dist., 24th
James, Thomas, 4th, 5th
James, Thomas, 48th Dist., 34th
James, Wm. A., 8th Dist., 29th-31st
Janczak, Louis, 27th Dist., 69th; 19th Dist., 70th-73rd; 17th Dist., 75th-77th
Jandus, Cyril R., 13th Dist., 42nd
Janney, E. S., 14th, 15th
Jansen, Henry J., 32nd Dist., 37th
Jacquess, Isaac M., 44th Dist., 26th
Jarrot, Vital, 11th; 12th Dist., 20th-22nd
Jarves, Jule C., 49th Dist., 40th
Jasper, Thomas, 28th Dist., 26th
Jay, Nelson D., 26th Dist., 30th, 35th
Jayne, J. H., 32nd Dist., 48th
Jefferies, Azariah, 46th Dist., 27th
Jefferson, Charles E., 47th Dist., 92nd
Jenco, John M., 41st Dist., 55th
Jenison, Edward H., 74th; 53rd Dist., 78th
Jenkins, Alexander M., 7th, 8th
Jenkins, Charles J., 3rd Dist., 57th-68th
Jenney, Wellington, 24th Dist., 29th
Jennings, Israel, 6th
Jennings, Jesse G., 43rd Dist., 33rd
Jennings, Thomas C., 49th Dist., 31st
Jennings, Tyre, 34th Dist., 16th
Jessup, John S., 15th Dist., 28th
Jewell, E. G., 14th
Jewell, Henry L., 32nd Dist., 45th, 46th
Jezierney, Peter P., 9th Dist., 58th-68th
Job, Archibald, 4th
Job, Z. B., 14th Dist., 21st
Jobst, Carl J., 18th Dist., 57th
Johns, George P., 47th Dist., 73rd; 52nd Dist., 75th
Johns, Henry C., 36th Dist., 19th
Johnson, Benjamin, 11th

Johnson, Caleb C., 19th Dist., 34th, 35th, 38th; 31st Dist., 40th; 35th Dist., 43rd
Johnson, Calvin D., 49th Dist., 59th-61st
Johnson, Charles, 44th Dist., 56th
Johnson, Charles G., 19th Dist., 39th, 41st
Johnson, David W., 34th Dist., 75th, 76th
Johnson, Edwin, 34th Dist., 42nd
Johnson, Edwin H., 72nd Dist., 27th; 21st Dist., 28th
Johnson, Elbridge G., 41st Dist., 22nd
Johnson, Emil A. W., 6th Dist., 51st, 52nd, 55th, 56th
Johnson, Frank P., 37th Dist., 66th
Johnson, G. J., 26th Dist., 52nd-59th
Johnson, George W., 33rd Dist., 41st, 42nd
Johnson, Jesse R., 45th Dist., 31st
Johnson, John B., 43rd Dist., 29th
Johnson, John W., 26th Dist., 39th-42nd
Johnson, Nicholas J., 14th Dist., 45th
Johnson, Noah, 15th; 5th Dist., 25th
Johnson, Oliver C., 52nd Dist., 24th
Johnson, Richard M., 51st Dist., 38th, 39th
Johnson, Thomas L., 50th Dist., 88th-92nd
Johnson, Timothy V., 52nd Dist., 80th-82nd; 104th Dist., 83rd-91st
Johnson, Verne R., 28th Dist., 59th
Johnson, W. K., 39th Dist., 18th
Johnson, William H., 46th Dist., 33rd
Johnson, Wm. L. R., 16th Dist., 36th
Johnston, Alan R., 7th Dist., 73rd; 74th; 1st Dist., 75th, 76th
Johnston, John, 26th Dist., 37th
Jonas, Abraham, 13th
Jonas, Sigmund S., 3rd Dist., 43rd
Jones, Alba M., 16th Dist., 38th, 39th
Jones, Albert, 25th Dist., 19th
Jones, Alexander J., 3rd Dist., 39th
Jones, Alfred H., 45th Dist., 35th
Jones, Alfred M., 16th Dist., 28th, 29th
Jones, Benj. L., 51st Dist., 29th
Jones, Clarence A., 45th Dist., 50th, 51st
Jones, Daniel L., 7th Dist., 18th
Jones, Emil, Jr., 28th Dist., 78th-82nd
Jones, Frank H., 39th Dist., 37th
Jones, Gabriel, 4th, 11th
Jones, J. David, 74th; 51st Dist., 75th-77th; 50th Dist., 78th-81st
Jones, John B., 34th Dist., 31st
Jones, John G., 5th Dist., 42nd
Jones, John H., 16th Dist., 33rd
Jones, John O., 107th Dist., 89th-92nd
Jones, Joseph H., 75th Dist., 27th
Jones, J. Russell, 51st Dist., 22nd
Jones, Leslie N. 74th; 54th Dist., 76th
Jones, Lovana "Lou", 23rd Dist., 84th-87th; 5th Dist., 88th-92nd
Jones, Malden, 39th Dist., 24th, 25th
Jones, Marjorie, 50th Dist., 81st
Jones, Michael, 8th
Jones, Norman L., 37th Dist., 38th; 36th Dist., 39th
Jones, Paul F., 32nd Dist., 73rd
Jones, Richard T., 4th
Jones, Robert S., 42nd Dist., 47th, 48th
Jones, Samuel H., 39th Dist., 42nd
Jones, Samuel W., 42nd Dist., 31st
Jones, Shirley M., 19th Dist., 85th-87th; 6th Dist., 88th-92nd
Jones, Thomas, 3rd Dist., 20th
Jones, W. F., 50th Dist., 17th
Jones, Wiley E., 39th Dist., 35th, 36th
Jones, William, 6th
Jones, William A., 8th Dist., 31st
Jones, William C., 31st Dist.; 27th
Jordan, James, 7th
Joslyn, Merritt, L., 54th Dist., 24th
Joy, John B., 34th Dist., 40th
Joyce, John T., 29th Dist., 52nd
Juckett, Robert S., Sr., 4th Dist., 75th-79th
Judah, Noble B., Jr., 1st Dist., 47th
Judy, Thomas, 20th Dist., 18th
Juul, Roy, 31st Dist., 55th, 56th
Kagay, B. F., 29th Dist., 27th
Kahoun, Raymond J., 26th Dist., 73rd; 25th Dist., 75th-77th
Kain, Joseph, 25th Dist., 40th
Kaindl, A. M., 23rd Dist., 58th-60th
Kaiser, Louis, 27th Dist., 38th; 28th Dist., 39th

Kalahar, Maurice O., 26th Dist., 64th-68th
Kamp, Siets D., 20th Dist., 65th, 66th
Kane, Charles P., 26th Dist., 56th, 57th
Kane, Douglas N., 50th Dist., 79th-82nd
Kane, Edward T., 26th Dist., 64th-68th
Kane, Elias K., 4th
Kane, W. C., 51st Dist., 48th, 49th
Kann, Constantine, 3rd Dist., 28th
Kannally, William A., 35th Dist., 46th
Kaplan, Nathan J., 13th Dist., 70th-73rd
Karber, James W., 48th Dist., 65th, 66th
Karch, Charles A., 49th Dist., 44th, 47th, 48th
Karmazyn, Lillian K., 21st Dist., 76th, 77th
Karpiel, Doris C., 2nd Dist., 81st, 82nd; 49th Dist., 83rd
Kart, Samuel, 31st Dist., 67th
Kase, Spencer M., 49th Dist., 28th
Kase, Wm. G., 49th Dist., 29th
Kasper, Louis J., 17th Dist., 82nd
Kasserman, Homer, 46th Dist., 62nd
Kasserman, John, 46th Dist., 49th
Kasserman, R. J., 46th Dist., 48th
Kaszak, Nancy, 34th Dist., 88th, 89th
Katz, Harold A., 74th; 1st Dist., 75th-82nd
Kauffman, Harlan B., 10th Dist., 52nd
Kaune, Wm. G., 42nd Dist., 35th
Keane, James F., 28th Dist., 81st-87th
Keane, Thomas P., 23rd Dist., 51st-53rd, 56th, 57th
Kearney, Joseph J., 4th Dist., 30th
Keatling, Edward, 20th Dist., 16th
Keats, Roger A., 1st Dist., 80th
Keck, Fred, 49th Dist., 44th-46th, 48th
Kedzie, John H., 7th Dist., 30th
Keen, Ezra B., 44th Dist., 32nd
Keen, James, 44th Dist., 32nd
Keener, Charles F., 23rd Dist., 16th
Keeney, Albert F., 25th Dist., 45th
Keifer, Peter, 5th Dist., 22nd
Keith, John R., 50th Dist., 79th
Keller, Charles F., 54th Dist., 76th-79th
Keller, David P., 29th Dist., 36th, 37th
Keller, Nick, 8th Dist., 60th-66th
Kelley, Lawrence, 45th Dist., 38th
Kelley, Isaac M., 48th Dist., 32nd
Kelley, James C., 34th Dist., 82nd
Kelley, John M., 12th
Kellogg, Orson, 7th Dist., 22nd
Kellogg, William, 39th Dist., 16th
Kelly, Lawrence, 45th Dist., 37th
Kelly, Maurice, 57th Dist., 27th
Kelly, Michael, 49th Dist., 39th; 23rd Dist., 42nd
Kelly, Richard F., Jr., 9th Dist., 78th-82nd
Kelsey, David M., 46th Dist., 20th
Kelsey, Harold D., 8th Dist., 61st-65th
Kempiners, William L., 39th Dist., 78th-81st
Kendall, Samuel T., 13th
Kennedy, John A., 74th
Kennedy, Leland J., 47th Dist., 65th-68th; 53rd Dist.,
   73rd; 74th; 55th Dist., 75th-77th; 56th Dist., 78th
Kennedy, Michael, 31st Dist., 41st
Kennedy, Robert B., 1st Dist., 34th, 35th
Kenner, Howard A., 24th Dist., 89th-92nd
Kenney, Charles, 40th Dist., 27th
Kenney, James, 26th Dist., 35th, 36th
Kent, Germanicus, 11th
Kent, Mary Lou, 48th Dist., 78th-81st
Kent, William E., 11th Dist., 36th, 38th; 1st Dist., 39th
Kenny, William J., 2nd Dist., 37th
Kercheval, Gholson, 11th
Kerley, King, 28th Dist., 20th, 21st; 25th Dist., 24th
Kern, Jacob J., 5th Dist., 37th
Kerr, Daniel, 16th Dist., 26th
Kerr, Gordon E., 51st Dist., 67th-69th; 59th Dist., 70th
Kerr, Richard, 11th
Kerr, S. Bartlett, 51st Dist., 42nd
Kerrick, Josiah, 20th Dist., 41st, 42nd; 16th Dist., 43rd-
   47th
Kerrick, Leonidas H., 62nd Dist., 27th
Kersey, George T., 3rd Dist., 53rd, 55th, 56th
Kershaw, Boon, 46th Dist., 29th
Kessinger, Harold C., 14th Dist., 49th
Kettering, Albert J., 1st Dist., 41st, 42nd
Kewin, Bernard J., 5th Dist., 58th-60th
Keyes, Charles A., 20th Dist., 23rd; 39th Dist., 34th
Keyes, David, 39th Dist., 22nd
Keyll, Bernard L., 41st Dist., 47th

Keyser, Hiram M., 16th Dist., 35th
Kedwell, W. K., 34th Dist., 68th, 69th
Kilcourse, Lawrence, 23rd Dist., 39th, 40th
Kilens, Hubert, 4th Dist., 47th-50th
Kimbo, Earl C., 50th Dist., 56th, 57th
Kimbrough, E. R. E., 31st Dist., 33rd, 34th
Kimmel, Singleton H., 6th
Kincheloe, Charles F., 37th Dist., 39th, 40th
King, Alexander, 23rd Dist., 21st, 29th
King, Charles P., 40th Dist., 18th
King, Edward J., 43rd Dist., 45th-48th
King, George E., 42nd Dist., 25th
King, John M., 41st Dist., 67th-69th
King, Joseph W., 51st Dist., 40th
King, Lucien, 39th Dist., 30th
King, Robert A., 38th Dist., 27th
King, William E., 3rd Dist., 54th, 56th-58th
King, William H., 96th Dist., 27th; 3rd Dist., 38th
Kinman, Edward M., 38th Dist., 33rd
Kinnally, Nathan J., 23rd Dist., 70th-72nd
Kinnan, Paul, 26th Dist., 45th
Kinne, Captain E., 15th
Kinney, William C., 12th Dist., 19th
Kinniston, Jerry, 15th Dist., 31st
Kinsella, Joseph P., 23rd Dist., 47th
Kinsey, Samuel B., 28th Dist., 34th, 35th
Kinyon, Alonzo, 49th Dist., 26th
Kiolbassa, Peter, 5th Dist., 30th
Kipley, Edward L., Sr., 6th Dist., 76th, 77th
Kirby, Edward P., 38th Dist., 37th
Kirby, James H., 30th Dist., 50th
Kirby, James J., 16th Dist., 41st
Kirie, James C., 74th; 2nd Dist., 75th, 76th
Kirkland, James M., 66th Dist., 83rd-87th
Kirkpatrick, Francis, 1st
Kirkpatrick, John, 14th
Kirkpatrick, R. D., 50th Dist., 44th-48th
Kister, Wm. H., 20th Dist., 35th
Kistler, John, 47th Dist., 23rd
Kitchell, Wickliffe, 2nd, 12th
Kittleman, James M., 19th Dist., 44th-46th
Kitzmiller, James W., 36th Dist., 39th
Kleeman, Benton F., 13th Dist., 32nd, 44th, 46th-48th
Klehm, George C., 7th Dist., 30th
Klein, Carl L., 74th; 27th Dist., 75th, 76th
Klein, Wilfred J., 34th Dist., 39th
Kleine, John Henry, 74th; 32nd Dist., 75th-77th
Klemm, Dick, 33rd Dist., 82nd; 63rd Dist., 83rd-87th
Klingler, Gwenn, 100th Dist., 89th-92nd
Klosak, Henry J., 7th Dist., 75th-81st
Kluczynski, John C., 4th Dist., 58th-5th
Klupp, Gregory A., 13th Dist., 33rd
Knapp, Andrew, 34th Dist., 60th
Knapp, Colby, 27th Dist., 18th
Knapp, Joshua P., 13th Dist., 22nd
Knapp, Nathan N., 23rd Dist., 17th
Knapp, Robert M., 22nd Dist., 25th
Knauf, Henry J., 37th Dist., 59th-66th
Knickerbocker, Joshua C., 60th Dist., 26th
Knolla, Peter, 15th Dist., 43rd
Knowles, Samuel C., 54th Dist., 27th
Knuepfer, Jack T., 74th; 39th Dist., 75th
Koch, Fred J., 42nd Dist., 47th, 48th
Kociolko, John S., 7th Dist., 82nd
Koehler, Charles A., 50th Dist., 59th
Koehler, Judith, 45th Dist., 82nd; 89th Dist., 83rd, 84th
Koehler, Ray, 56th Dist., 70th, 71st
Koerner, Gustavus, 13th; 16th Dist., 27th
Kohlstedt, John, 25th Dist., 40th, 41st
Kohout, Joseph G., 15th Dist., 66th-69th
Kopf, Charles W., 15th Dist., 42nd; 2nd Dist., 43rd
Koplin, John A., 16th Dist., 30th
Kordowski, Charles H., 12th Dist., 70th, 71st
Kornowicz, Edmund, 25th Dist., 79th-82nd
Kosel, Renée, 38th Dist., 90th-92nd
Kosinski, Roman J., 16th Dist., 77th-82nd
Kosinski, Stanley R., 25th Dist., 62nd-69th
Kostka, James, 15th Dist., 58th, 59th
Kotlarz, Joseph S., Jr., 20th Dist., 88th-90th
Kouka, Fred, 15th Dist., 30th, 31st
Kowalski, Emil O., 4th Dist., 44th-46th, 51st
Kozubowski, Walter S., 23rd Dist., 78th-81st
Krape, William W., 12th Dist., 45th
Krasniewski, Frank, 15th Dist., 65th-67th
Krause, Carolyn H., 56th Dist., 88th-92nd

Krause, James G., 56th Dist., 75th-77th; 57th Dist., 78th
Kreicker, William, 6th Dist., 42nd
Kretsinger, George W., 15th
Kretzinger, Wm. H., 29th Dist., 35th, 36th
Kribs, Chas. J., 44th Dist., 53rd, 54th, 56th, 57th
Kriegsman, John C., 45th Dist., 78th
Kroh, Philip H., 50th Dist., 38th
Kroll, Geo. W., 3rd Dist., 32nd
Krone, Philip S., 20th Dist., 78th
Krska, Robert T., 23rd Dist., 81st, 82nd; 22nd Dist., 83rd-86th
Krump, Peter S., 2nd Dist., 52nd-55th
Kubik, Jack L., 43rd Dist., 84th-90th
Kucharski, Edmund F., 27th Dist., 78th-82nd
Kuechler, F. W., 46th Dist., 57th
Kuklinski, John, 27th Dist., 61st-67th
Kulas, Myron, 19th Dist., 81st, 82nd; 10th Dist., 83rd-87th
Kumler, Harry A., 39th Dist., 41st
Kunz, Stanley H., 13th Dist., 36th
Kurtz, Rosemary, 64th Dist., 92nd
Kustra, Bob, 4th Dist., 82nd
Kuykendall, Andrew, 13th, 14th
Kwasigroch, John A., 13th Dist., 37th, 38th
Lacey, Claude F., 51st Dist., 50th-52nd
Lacey, Royal R., 49th Dist., 36th
Lachner, Thomas F., 59th Dist., 89th
Lackie, John, 25th Dist., 33rd
Lacy, John, 5th
Lacy, Lyman, 26th Dist., 23rd
LaFleur, Leo D., 2nd Dist., 78th, 79th
Lager, Alois B., 42nd Dist., 50th-55th, 57th-61st
Lagerstrom, Carl A., 10th Dist., 64th
Lagow, Wilson, 10th
LaHood, Ray H., 36th Dist., 82nd
Lake, Chauncey A., 41st Dist., 23rd, 24th
Lamb, Thomas, Jr., 30th Dist., 42nd
Lamont, James, 10th Dist., 35th
LaMonte, William O., 5th Dist., 40th
Landholt, Hilmer C., 47th Dist., 72nd
Landmesser, Frank H., 25th Dist., 43rd, 45th
Landrigan, John, 14th Dist., 26th; 44th Dist., 29th
Landrum, Albert, 40th Dist., 27th
Lane, Alexander, 1st Dist., 45th, 46th
Lane, Edward E., 24th Dist., 28th
Lane, Tilman, 29th Dist., 28th
Lane, William, 10th
Lang, Louis I., 1st Dist., 85th-87th; 16th Dist., 88th-92nd
Langford, George W., 34th Dist., 34th
Langston, Matthew, 61st Dist., 27th
Langworthy, Cyrus, 13th
Lannon, James P., 16th Dist., 64th-69th
Lantz, Simon F., 16th Dist., 49th
Lantz, Walter A., 7th Dist., 41st, 45th, 46th
LaPorte, Charles W., 18th Dist., 51st, 52nd, 54th
Lapsey, George E., 5th Dist., 42nd
Larabee, James, 45th Dist., 35th
Large, James M., 32nd Dist., 40th
Larson, Richard R., 43rd Dist., 68th, 69th
Lasher, Melanchthon, 49th Dist., 16th
Laskowski, William J., 15th Dist., 44th
Latham, Robert B., 35th Dist., 24th
Lathrop, Wm., 53rd Dist., 20th
Lathrop, William H., 45th Dist., 40th
Latimer, Joseph F., 68th Dist., 27th; 22nd Dist., 30th, 31st
Lauer, John R., 44th Dist., 78th-80th
Laufer, J. Lisle, 14th Dist., 64th-69th; 35th Dist., 70th-73rd
Laughenry, Godfrey, 6th Dist., 38th
Laughlin, Edward E., 12th Dist., 59th
Laughlin, James, 33rd Dist., 37th
Laughlin, Wm., 12th
Laurino, William J., 14th Dist., 77th; 15th Dist., 78th-82nd; 2nd Dist., 83rd-87th; 15th Dist., 88th, 89th
Lauterbach, Wilbur H., 46th Dist., 75th-77th
Lavery, Harry D., 31st Dist., 69th
Lavezzi, John S., 22nd Dist., 63rd, 64th
Law, Robert D., 35th Dist., 75th
Law, William G., 1st Dist., 40th
Lawfer, I. Ronald, 74th Dist., 88th-92nd
Lawler, John S., 13th
Lawler, William J., 45th Dist., 57th-64th
Lawrence, Chas. S., 29th Dist., 34th
Lawrence, Johnson, 10th Dist., 43rd, 45th, 46th
Lawrence, Joseph F., 4th Dist., 33rd

Lawrence, Luther W., 51st Dist., 23rd
Lawrence, S. W., 54th Dist., 19th, 20th
Lawson, Iver, 61st Dist., 26th
Lay, Nelson, 46th Dist., 23rd
Layman, Charles H., 50th Dist., 31st
Leach, Selby, 51st Dist., 16th
Leach, William L., 35th Dist., 49th
Leahy, Dennis J., 1st Dist., 41st
Leaman, Lester, 46th Dist., 45th
Leary, Albert C., 10th, 12th
Leaverton, John W., 48th Dist., 43rd
Leavitt, Moses W., 60th Dist., 25th
Leavitt, Thomas N., 29th Dist., 38th; 28th Dist., 47th
Lechowicz, Thaddeus, 15th Dist., 76th, 77th; 17th Dist., 78th-82nd
Lederer, Charles, 3rd Dist., 46th
Lee, Arthur M., 48th Dist., 41st
Lee, Charles C., 40th Dist., 41st
Lee, Clyde, 46th Dist., 61st, 65th-69th; 57th Dist., 70th-73rd; 74th
Lee, John M., 11th Dist., 53rd-57th
Lee, John S., 67th Dist., 27th
Lee, Milton, 31st Dist., 36th
Lee, Noble W., 5th Dist., 62nd-69th; 23rd Dist., 70th, 71st, 73rd; 74th; 24th Dist., 75th
Lee, William L., 48th Dist., 19th
LeFlore, Robert, Jr., 15th Dist., 83rd-87th; 8th Dist., 88th
Leeper, John, 5th
Leeper, John A., 25th Dist., 30th
Lehman, Ed, 54th Dist., 73rd, 74th; 56th Dist., 75th-77th
Leib, John, 5th
Leighton, James, 14th
Leinenweber, Harry D., 42nd Dist., 78th-82nd
Leitch, David R., 93rd Dist., 84th-92nd
Leith, Daniel, 29th Dist., 27th
Lelivelt, Joseph J., 7th Dist., 68th, 69th; 5th Dist., 70th-72nd
Lemen, Moses, 6th
Lemke, LeRoy W., 25th Dist., 78th, 79th
Lemma, Wm. A., 6th Dist., 27th; 50th Dist., 28th
Lenane, Thomas J., 36th Dist., 58th-61st
Lenard, Henry M., 13th Dist., 68th, 69th; 24th Dist., 70th-73rd; 74th; 30th Dist., 75th-77th
Lense, Julius, A., 11th Dist., 37th
Leon, John F., 15th Dist., 71st-73rd; 74th; 14th Dist., 77th; 17th Dist., 78th, 79th, 81st, 82nd
LePage, Stephen T., 49th Dist., 49th
Lester, Andrew J., 39th Dist., 36th
Lester, Harvey, 12th
Levere, William C., 6th Dist., 45th
Leverenz, Ted F., 5th Dist., 79th-82nd; 51st Dist., 83rd-86th
Levin, Ellis B., 12th Dist., 80th, 82nd; 5th Dist., 83rd-87th; 12th Dist., 88th
Lewis, Albert W., 49th Dist., 38th
Lewis, F. W., 48th Dist., 54th, 57th-60th
Lewis, Henry M., 23rd Dist., 31st
Lewis, John H., 22nd Dist., 29th
Lewis, John W., 43rd Dist., 41st; 34th Dist., 56th, 57th
Lewis, John W., Jr., 34th Dist., 62nd-69th; 51st Dist., 70th, 73rd; 74th; 54th Dist., 75th
Lewis, Louie E., 50th Dist., 58th-60th
Lewis, Stephen G., 39th Dist., 28th
Lewis, William, 45th Dist., 45th, 46th
Libonati, Ronald V., 17th Dist., 57th, 58th, 62nd
Lichenberger, B. F., 12th Dist., 42nd
Lieberman, Marvin S., 74th
Lietze, Fred A., 42nd Dist., 28th
Liggett, Francis J., 37th Dist., 45th, 46th
Lincoln, Abraham, 9th-12th
Lindberg, Carl L., 5th Dist., 29th
Lindberg, George W., 32nd Dist., 75th-77th
Linden, John W., 14th Dist., 43rd, 44th
Linder, Usher, 10th, 15th; 11th Dist., 16th, 17th
Lindly, Cicero J., 47th Dist., 43rd-45th
Lindner, Patricia Reid, 65th Dist., 88th-92nd
Lindsey, John T., 41st Dist., 30th
Lindsey, William, 45th Dist., 30th
Lindstrum, A. O., 43rd Dist., 51st, 52nd
Linegar, David T., 50th Dist., 32nd-34th
Link, Lewis W., 8th, 9th
Link, M. S., 47th Dist., 45th, 46th
Linley, Isaac, 39th Dist., 17th
Linn, James Weber, 5th Dist., 61st
Lipka, William, 27th Dist., 53rd-55th

Lipschulch, Geo. U., 2nd Dist., 49th
Lish, Ira M., 16th Dist., 43rd
Little, H. G., 48th Dist., 20th
Little, Iverson M., 43rd Dist., 32nd
Little, Roger F., 24th Dist., 52nd-58th
Little, Thomas J., 15th; 39th Dist., 17th
Little, Wallace A., 51st Dist., 19th
Little, William E., 15th; 50th Dist., 16th
Littler, David T., 39th Dist., 33rd, 35th
Lloyd, F. E., 3rd Dist., 48th
Lloyd, Joseph W., 47th Dist., 24th
Lockard, James, 13th, 14th
LoDestro, Richard L., 5th Dist., 73rd
Lodge, Augustus N., 51st Dist., 33rd
Loftus, Hubert J., 40th Dist., 82nd
Logan, George R., 2nd-4th
Logan, John, 10th-12th, 15th
Logan, John A., 5th Dist., 18th, 20th
Logan, John A., 48th Dist., 46th
Logan, John A., 14th Dist., 42nd
Logan, Stephen T., 13th-15th; 26th Dist., 19th
Logan, William H., 6th Dist., 24th
Logsden, Perry, 34th Dist., 34th, 36th
Lohmann, Martin B., 30th Dist., 53rd-57th
Lollar, M. E., 34th Dist., 65th, 68th, 69th
Lomanto, Charles A., 12th Dist., 87th
Lomax, John A., 1st Dist., 28th
Londrigan, James T., 51st Dist., 76th, 77th; 50th Dist., 78th, 79th
Long, S. M., 32nd Dist., 34th
Long, Theodore K., 5th Dist., 51st
Long, William H., 15th
Loomis, James R., 47th Dist., 28th
Looney, William A., 2nd Dist., 24th
Loop, James L., 14th
Lopez, Edgar, 4th Dist., 88th-91st
Lorton, Sam S., 40th Dist., 58th-63rd, 66th
Lott, Peter, 14th
Lott, Peter S., 13th Dist., 30th
Loucks, Hiram, 13th Dist., 32nd
Louden, George, 42nd Dist., 41st, 42nd
Loughran, Francis I., 41st Dist., 69th; 13th Dist., 70th-73rd; 74th
Loukas, James P., 13th Dist., 70th-73rd; 74th
Love, Oscar, 11th
Lovejoy, Andrew J., 10th Dist., 48th
Lovejoy, Owen, 47th Dist., 19th
Lovell, Edward C., 14th Dist., 31st
Lovett, Obed E, 38th Dist., 40th
Lowenthal, S. L., 3rd Dist., 39th
Lowry, Alex K., 36th Dist., 35th
Lowry, William, 3rd
Loy, F. W., 43rd Dist., 42nd
Loy, James H., 42nd Dist., 44th
Loy, Thomas M., 13th
Lucas, Allen, 27th Dist., 32nd
Lucas, Allen T., 45th Dist., 69th; 48th Dist., 70th-73rd; 74th; 51st Dist., 75th
Lucas, Benjamin H., 1st Dist., 50th
Lucas, John, 27th Dist., 16th
Lucco, Joe E., 56th Dist., 79th, 80th
Lucius, Edward B., 11th Dist., 51st
Luckey, Hugh M., 22nd Dist., 53rd-57th, 59th, 62nd
Luddington, Lewis, 29th Dist., 32nd
Luehrs, George E., 41st Dist., 71st
Luft, Richard N., 45th Dist., 79th, 80th
Luke, Charles S., 44th Dist., 43rd-46th
Lukin, Samuel S., 15th
Lund, Arnold L., 19th Dist., 61st
Lundy, Joseph R., 11th Dist., 78th, 79th
Lurton, William S., 45th Dist., 43rd, 44th
Lusk, Edward, 24th Dist., 18th
Lyle, John H., 11th Dist., 49th, 50th
Lyman, Frank, 10th Dist., 71st-73rd; 74th; 11th Dist., 75th, 76th
Lyman, John S., 39th Dist., 37th
Lyman, Thomas M., 24th Dist., 52nd
Lyman, William, 53rd Dist., 19th
Lyman, Wm. H., 13th Dist., 36th-38th; 23rd Dist., 39th
Lynch, John F., 18th Dist., 49th, 50th
Lynch, Lee, 34th Dist., 67th
Lyon, Charles M., 46th Dist., 31st, 36th
Lyon, George R., 8th Dist., 40th-43rd
Lyon, Sidney, 5th Dist., 50th-55th
Lyon, Thomas E., 45th Dist., 46th-50th

Lyons, Eileen, 47th Dist., 89th-92nd
Lyons, James H., 10th, 11th
Lyons, Joseph M., 15th Dist., 89th-92nd
Lyons, Richard J., 8th Dist., 56th-60th
Lyons, William, 38th Dist., 67th-69th
Mabry, Robert E., 46th Dist., 44th
Macdonald, Virginia B., 3rd Dist., 78th-82nd
MacDowning (See Downing, T. Mac)
Mace, Septimus M., 48th Dist., 30th
Mack, Alonzo W., 45th Dist., 21st
Macklin, James, 3rd Dist., 25th
MacMillian, Thos. C., 4th Dist., 34th, 35th
MacNeil, John A., 46th Dist., 52nd
Macy, Roger J., 2nd Dist., 47th
Madden, Henry, 10th, 13th
Maddux, William H., 15th Dist., 18th
Madigan, Edward, 47th Dist., 75th-77th
Madigan, Michael J., 27th Dist., 77th-82nd; 30th Dist., 83rd-87th; 22nd Dist., 88th-92nd
Madison, Christian M., 23rd Dist., 48th, 49th
Madison, Jesse D., 21st Dist., 79th, 80th
Magill, Lawrence M., 33rd Dist., 43rd, 44th
Mahar, William F., 9th Dist., 78th-81st
Maher, Michael F., 21st Dist., 50th-54th
Mahoney, Bernard J., 6th Dist., 39th
Mahoney, Francis X., 74th
Mahoney, Joseph P., 5th Dist., 34th-36th
Majewski, Chester P., 14th Dist., 73rd; 74th
Malato, S. A., 17th Dist., 41st
Maley, Wm. C., 40th Dist., 22nd
Malloy, Charles F., 47th Dist., 54th-57th
Maloney, Edward D., 27th Dist., 87th
Maloney, John J., 41st Dist., 63rd
Manahan, John G., 19th Dist., 33rd
Mancin, Albert J., 2nd Dist., 56th-58th
Manley, James, 59th Dist., 27th
Manley, Uri, 9th; 12th Dist., 18th
Mann, Joseph B., 31st Dist., 32nd
Mann, Orrin L., 4th Dist., 29th
Mann, Robert, 15th
Mann, Robert E., 23rd Dist., 73rd; 74th; 24th Dist., 75th-80th
Mann, Sylvester, 52nd Dist., 23rd, 24th; 14th Dist., 28th
Manning, Howard P., 38th Dist., 60th
Manning, John P., 32nd Dist., 70th-72nd
Manning, Julius, 13th, 14th
Manny, Walter I., 30th Dist., 44th, 45th
Mansfield, Oscar, 30th Dist., 41st
Maragos, Samuel C., 30th Dist., 76th-79th
Marcy, Rodger J., 2nd Dist., 50th, 51st
Marek, Frank A., 19th Dist., 66th-69th; 3rd Dist., 70th-73rd
Margalos, William A., 19th Dist., 66th-69th; 3rd Dist., 70th-73rd
Marinaro, Gary, 51st Dist., 87th
Mariner, Charles E., 19th Dist., 52nd-56th
Markert, Louis A., 45th Dist., 76th, 77th
Markette, Sharon, 17th Dist., 83rd
Marks, Robert, 7th Dist., 72nd, 73rd
Marovitz, William A., 12th Dist., 79th-81st
Marquis, Seymour, 30th Dist., 40th
Marrett, John, 35th Dist., 16th
Marrs, William B., 10th
Marsh, Charles W., 51st Dist., 26th
Marsh, Frederick B., 12th Dist., 28th, 29th
Marshall, James, 12th, 13th
Marshall, John, 1st
Marshall, Randall E., 2nd Dist., 50th
Marshall, Samuel D., 11th
Marshall, Samuel P., 22nd Dist., 34th, 35th
Marshall, Samuel S., 15th
Marshall, Thos. A., 24th Dist., 36th
Marshall, William, 7th, 8th
Marshall, William, 43rd Dist., 18th
Marston, Lyford, 31st Dist., 31st
Martay, Erwin L., 6th Dist., 69th
Martens, Jacob, 26th Dist., 54th, 55th
Martin, Charles Edw., 10th Dist., 44th
Martin, Dudley S., 3rd Dist., 62nd
Martin, Euclid, 20th Dist., 32nd
Martin, George E., 51st Dist., 41st
Martin, Henry F., 40th Dist., 29th
Martin, Isaac M., 32nd Dist., 47th
Martin, James H., 33rd Dist., 24th
Martin, John F., 34th Dist., 45th

Martin, John S., 46th Dist., 38th
Martin, Lynn, 34th Dist., 80th
Martin, Peggy Smith, 26th Dist., 78th, 80th
Martin, Philip W., 8th
Martin, Samuel H., 7th Dist., 17th; 9th Dist., 19th
Martin, Samuel H., 46th Dist., 32nd, 36th
Martin, Samuel L., 20th Dist., 69th; 45th Dist., 70th, 71st
Martin, William, 15th
Martin, William H., 47th Dist., 55th, 56th
Martin, William L., 5th Dist., 41st
Martinez, Benjamin A. "Ben", 20th Dist., 85th-87th; 2nd Dist., 88th, 89th
Martire, Frank A., 19th Dist., 82nd
Martynowski, Stanley E., 27th Dist., 61st
Marvel, Edward, 40th Dist., 61st, 62nd
Marzuki, James E., 80th Dist., 83rd
Marzullo, Vito, 2nd Dist., 62nd-68th
Mason, Carlisle, 95th Dist., 27th
Mason, Aaron P., 14th Dist., 20th
Mason, Jos. M., 25th Dist., 48th, 49th
Mason, William E., 5th Dist., 31st
Massenberg, William, 90th Dist., 27th
Massey, Henry C., 37th Dist., 34th
Massey, Robert L., 25th Dist., 69th
Massie, Melville L., 38th Dist., 28th
Masters, S. D., 34th Dist., 19th
Mastro, Nicholas J., 17th Dist., 60th, 61st
Matejek, John M., 10th Dist., 80th
Matheny, Charles R., 2nd
Mather, Frederick H., 45th Dist., 22nd
Mather, Thomas, 2nd-4th, 6th
Mathias, Sidney H., 51st Dist., 91st, 92nd
Mathis, John P., 51st Dist., 47th, 53rd
Matijevich, John S., 31st Dist., 75th-82nd; 61st Dist., 83rd-87th
Matthews, Asa C., 38th Dist., 30th, 31st; 36th Dist., 36th
Matthews, R. N., 50th Dist., 18th
Matthews, Samuel T., 8th, 14th
Matthews, Trevovan L., 34th Dist., 33rd
Matula, Paul, 7th Dist., 80th, 81st
Maucker, Wm. C., 33rd Dist., 49th, 50th, 52nd, 53rd
Mauritzon, M. G., 11th Dist., 39th
Maus, Wm. S., 11th
Mautino, Frank J., 74th Dist., 87th; 76th Dist., 88th-92nd
Mautino, Richard A., 37th Dist., 79th-82nd; 74th Dist., 83rd-87th
Maxwell, Philip, 54th Dist., 16th, 17th
May, Karen, 60th Dist., 92nd
May, Stephen D., 3rd Dist., 37th, 38th; 1st Dist., 39th
May, Wm. L., 6th
Mayer, John P., 22nd Dist., 66th, 67th
Mayhew, William, 3rd Dist., 41st
Maho, Walter L., 20th Dist., 27th
Mays, Jeffrey D., 48th Dist., 82nd; 96th Dist., 83rd-86th
McAdams, John, 37th Dist., 32nd
McAdams, Mary C., 36th Dist., 55th
McAdams, Wm., 40th Dist., 28th
McAfee, David B., 47th Dist., 87th, 88th
McAliney, Frank R., 38th Dist., 34th
McAlpin, Baker, 50th Dist., 60th
McAuliffe, Michael P., 14th Dist., 89th-92nd
McAuliffe, Roger P., 16th Dist., 78th-82nd; 14th Dist., 83rd-89th
McAvoy, Tom, 27th Dist., 82nd
McAvoy, Walter "Babe", 11th Dist., 63rd-69th; 27th Dist., 70th-73rd, 75th-77th; 25th Dist., 78th-80th
McBride, Charles, 45th Dist., 45th
McBride, John T., 48th Dist., 31st
McBride, Wm., 13th
McBroom, Edward, 41st Dist., 73rd; 43rd Dist., 80th-82nd
McBroom, Victor, 20th Dist., 62nd-64th
McCabe, Edward J., 21st Dist., 60th-67th
McCabe, William R., 41st Dist., 48th-52nd
McCall, J. S., 42nd Dist., 21st
McCall, Peter, 25th Dist., 36th
McCandless, W. H., 32nd Dist., 22nd
McCann, Robert H., 13th Dist., 23rd
McCarthy, Frank A., 14th Dist., 51st, 53rd-59th
McCarthy, John W., 7th Dist., 50th-53rd
McCarthy, Kevin A., 37th Dist., 90th-92nd
McCarthy, Robert W., 28th Dist., 69th; 47th Dist., 70th, 71st
McCarthy, Wm. F., 15th Dist., 39th
McCartney, Robert W., 49th Dist., 33rd

McCarty, John F., 2nd Dist., 48th
McCaskrin, Geo. W., 33rd Dist., 44th
McCaskrin, Harry M., 33rd Dist., 52nd-61st
McCaskrin, Hazel A., 33rd Dist., 65th-69th
McClain, Dudley, 24th Dist., 19th
McClain, Elmo, 50th Dist., 74th; 75th-77th
McClain, Michael F., 48th Dist., 78th-82nd
McClanahan, John P., 24th Dist., 36th
McCleave, H. C., 17th Dist., 21st
McClellan, Robert H., 51st Dist., 22nd
McClenathan, C. V., 18th Dist., 42nd; 22nd Dist., 43rd
McClernand, J. A., 10th, 12th, 13th
McClintock, Harry W., 50th Dist., 65th-68th
McClintock, Samuel, 1st, 2nd, 8th
McClory, Robert, 8th Dist., 67th
McClugage, David H., 18th Dist., 52nd-58th
McClun, John E., 29th Dist., 18th; 38th Dist., 19th
McClung, Edward, 44th Dist., 34th
McClure, Frank W., 43rd Dist., 57th-59th
McClure, Samuel H., 20th Dist., 38th
McClure, Thomas R., 18th Dist., 19th
McClurken, James, 12th
McClusky, J. J., 39th Dist., 44th
McCollum, Harvey C., 42nd Dist., 46th
McConnell, A. B., 8th Dist., 68th, 69th; 32nd Dist., 70th-73rd
McConnell, Edward, 34th Dist., 39th, 42nd
McConnell, Geo. L., 2nd Dist., 46th, 47th
McConnell, Murray, 8th
McConnell, Robert, 15th
McConnell, William A., 93rd Dist., 27th
McCord, W. H., 27th Dist., 34th
McCormick, Andrew, 10th, 11th
McCormick, Mrs. Brooks, 74th
McCormick, C. L., 59th Dist., 70th-73rd; 74th; 59th Dist., 75th-78th, 82nd
McCormick, Medill, 29th Dist., 48th, 49th
McCormick, Wm. W., 28th Dist., 48th
McCourt, James P., 11th Dist., 78th-82nd
McCown, John, 8th, 10th
McCoy, Albert R., 11th Dist., 29th
McCoy, Alexander, 36th Dist., 24th
McCracken, Thomas J., Jr., 81st Dist., 83rd-87th
McCreery, Wm. T., 25th Dist., 30th, 31st; 34th Dist., 36th
McCrills, Lafayette, 22nd Dist., 19th
McCrone, George C., 35th Dist., 37th, 38th; 43rd Dist., 44th
McCrone, Thomas H., 5th Dist., 32nd
McCullough, Edw. D., 24th Dist., 41st, 42nd
McCully, W. Dean, 16th Dist., 67th-69th; 42nd Dist., 70th-73rd; 74th
McCune, Joseph L., 25th Dist., 32nd
McCurdy, N. M., 14th Dist., 18th
McCutchen, Jesse M., 11th
McCutcheon, John M., 8th Dist., 26th
McDaniel, Jonathan, 26th Dist., 19th
McDaniel, Thomas L, 41st Dist., 41st
McDavid, Horace W., 28th Dist., 50th, 51st
  McDermott, Frank, 4th Dist., 51st
McDermott, Michael H., 11th Dist., 69th; 27th Dist., 70th-73rd; 74th; 25th Dist., 75th-77th
McDevitt, Bernard, 16th Dist., 70th-73rd; 74th; 18th Dist., 75th-77th
McDonald, Edw., 38th Dist., 34th
McDonald, John, 12th-14th; 14th Dist., 16th
McDonald, John, 22nd Dist., 24th; 36th Dist., 36th
McDonald, Lawrence, 9th Dist., 32nd
McDonald, Martin M., 50th Dist., 39th
McDonald, Murray, 41st Dist., 39th
McDonald, Victor H., 34th Dist., 59th, 60th, 64th
McDonald, W. H., 33rd Dist., 28th
McDonald, W. J., 44th Dist., 62nd-68th; 58th Dist., 70th, 71st
McDonough, Daniel V., 17th Dist., 40th-42nd; 27th Dist., 43rd-45th
McDonough, John M., 21st Dist., 87th
McDonough, Lee, 8th Dist., 56th
McDowell, A. S., 35th Dist., 36th
McDowell, Reuben R., 15th
McElligott, Thomas, 11th Dist., 35th, 36th
McElvain, James N., 36th Dist., 27th
McElvain, John, 51st Dist., 53rd, 54th
McElvain, Robert J., 44th Dist., 43rd
McElwee, William, 30th Dist., 27th
McEvers, Byron, 37th Dist., 34th

McEwen, Lewis M., 84th Dist., 27th
McEwing, William, 33rd Dist., 40th
McFatridge, William, 2nd, 3rd
McFee, Thomas P., 47th Dist., 39th
McFerron, John, 3rd
McFie, John R., 48th Dist., 31st, 33rd
McGah, Joseph P., 5th Dist., 75th-77th; 6th Dist., 78th
McGahey, David, 3rd, 4th
McGahey, James D., 9th
McGalliard, William, 20th Dist., 25th
McGann, Andrew J., 29th Dist., 83rd-87th
McGaughey, Dean S., 28th Dist., 60th-62nd
McGee, J. P., 32nd Dist., 34th, 36th, 38th
McGee, Francis M., 51st Dist., 28th
McGee, William Q., 50th Dist., 40th
McGinley, James E., 4th Dist., 38th
McGinley, William, 28th Dist., 48th
McGinnis, John P., 12th
McGinnis, John T., 22nd Dist., 29th
McGinnis, Peter J., 2nd Dist., 40th
McGloon, James C., 19th Dist., 49th, 50th
McGootry, John P., 3rd Dist., 40th, 41st; 5th Dist., 44th, 45th
McGowan, Edwin A., 1st Dist., 72nd, 73rd
McGrath, Emmett, 7th Dist., 56th-58th, 60th-67th
McGrath, Joshua, 13th Dist., 29th
McGrath, Shelton P., 18th Dist., 50th
McGrew, Samuel M., 47th Dist., 78th-82nd
McGuire, Jack, 83rd Dist., 87th; 86th Dist., 88th-92nd
McGuire, John L., 20th Dist., 39th, 40th
McGuire, Sylvester W., 44th Dist., 43rd, 44th
McGuire, William J., 37th Dist., 45th-47th
McHale, James, 1st Dist., 34th
McHenry, Wilbur B., 10th Dist., 44th
McHenry, William, 1st, 4th, 5th, 9th
McIlvane, John, 8th Dist., 21st
McInerny, Michael, 2nd Dist., 37th, 38th
McIntosh, David, 18th Dist., 29th
McIntosh, John, 3rd
McIntyre, Archibald J., 43rd Dist., 24th
McKee, Samuel, 48th Dist., 29th
McKee, Thomas, 41st Dist., 18th
McKeene, John A., 34th Dist., 41st
McKenzie, John C., 12th Dist., 38th, 39th
McKeon, Larry, 34th Dist., 90th-92nd
McKinlay, Robert A., 24th Dist., 32nd
McKinlay, Robert L., 31st Dist., 30th, 31st, 35th, 38th
McKinley, M. L., 6th Dist., 43rd, 44th
McKinley, Robt. W., 11th Dist., 45th
McKinley, William, 32nd Dist., 43rd, 44th; 31st Dist., 48th
McKittrick, William, 41st Dist., 37th; 47th Dist., 41st
McKnight, Sargeant, 38th Dist., 38th
McLaughlin, Daniel, 15th Dist., 35th, 36th
McLaughlin, Hugh, 5th Dist., 28th
McLaughlin, John, 27th Dist., 39th-41st
McLaughlin, John J., 19th Dist., 45th-48th
McLaughlin, Robert K., 5th
McLean, James, 12th
McLean, John, 2nd, 5th-7th
McLean, Michael C., 15th
McLean, William, 26th Dist., 34th
McLean, William H., 7th Dist., 46th
McLendon, James A., 74th; 24th Dist., 76th, 77th; 22nd Dist., 78th-80th
McLoskey, Robert T., 32nd Dist., 68th, 69th; 50th Dist., 70th-72nd
McLoud, William C., 23rd Dist., 32nd
McMackin, Charles L., 42nd Dist., 45th, 46th, 50th-53rd
McMackin, J. E., 42nd Dist., 54th, 56th, 57th, 63rd
McMahon, Patrick J., 4th Dist., 32nd
McManaman, John J., 21st Dist., 43rd
McMaster, A. T., 45th Dist., 77th; 47th Dist., 78th-82nd; 73rd Dist., 83rd, 84th
McMaster, Daniel R., 14th Dist., 27th
McMasters, J. K., 42nd Dist., 29th
McMillan, Andrew, 13th
McMillan, James T., 38th Dist., 38th
McMillan, John N., 37th Dist., 27th
McMillan, Robert, 11th
McMurdy, Robert, 2nd Dist., 38th
McMurty, William, 10th
McNabb, John, 36th Dist., 35th
McNabb, Pickney L., 46th Dist., 41st
McNairy, Melvin, 74th
McNally, Thomas, 3rd Dist., 33rd, 34th

McNally, Thos. J., 1st Dist., 45th
McNamara, John J., 27th Dist., 83rd-87th
McNeil, Francis A., 50th Dist., 22nd
McNicholas, John J., 74th
McNichols, Frank J., 2nd Dist., 44th-48th
McNulty, M. B., 29th Dist., 43rd
McParland, Charles, 25th Dist., 47th
McPartlin, Robert F., 16th Dist., 72nd, 73rd, 74th; 18th Dist., 75th-79th
McPherran, James E., 11th Dist., 28th
McPike, Jim, 56th Dist., 80th-82nd; 112th Dist., 83rd-87th; 111th Dist., 88th
McRoberts, Jas. W., 49th Dist., 65th, 66th
McRoberts, Wm. G., 18th Dist., 43rd, 45th
McSurely, Wm. Harvey, 5th Dist., 44th
McSweeney, John R., 19th Dist., 54th-60th
McTaggart, Alex H., 40th Dist., 39th
McVicker, James J., 31st Dist., 56th-58th
McWhorter, Tyler, 11th Dist., 29th
McWilliams, James, 11th
McWilliams, Lewis S., 49th Dist., 48th
McWilliams, Robert, 34th Dist., 32nd
Meacham, John W., 39th Dist., 28th
Meaney, Patrick J., 15th Dist., 40th, 41st
Meany, Mary K., 74th; 28th Dist., 75th
Meehan, Thomas, 34th Dist., 41st
Meeker, Jonathan, 45th Dist., 27th
Meents, Richard R., 20th Dist., 49th-51st
Meeteren, Henry V., 13th Dist., 43rd
Meier, John, 19th Dist., 41st
Megredy, James S., 26th Dist., 20th
Meilbeck, Leo, 3rd Dist., 31st
Meites, Irving J., 31st Dist., 58th
Mell, Emeziah J., 32nd Dist., 39th
Menard, Edmund, 11th; 8th Dist., 23rd
Menard, Hypolite, 6th
Menard, Pierre, 12th, 13th
Mendoza, Susana, 1st Dist., 92nd
Merlo, John, 10th Dist., 73rd; 74th; 11th Dist., 75th-77th; 12th Dist., 78th, 79th
Merriam, Jonathan, 37th Dist., 26th
Merrill, Alva, 24th Dist., 39th-42nd
Merriman, Jonathan, 26th Dist., 39th, 40th
Merritt, Edward L., 39th Dist., 37th-39th; 45th Dist., 49th
Merritt, John W., 9th Dist., 23rd
Merritt, Thos. E., 9th Dist., 26th; 24th Dist., 27th; 43rd Dist., 29th, 30th, 35th, 36th
Messick, Joseph B., 47th Dist., 33rd-35th
Messinger, John, 1st
Mester, Henry H., 45th Dist., 55th, 56th
Metcalf, George B., 36th Dist., 40th
Metcalf, Western, 29th Dist., 21st
Mette, August, 11th Dist., 33rd
Metz, B. B., 14th
Metz, Geo. W., 30th Dist., 25th
Meyer, Charles F., 17th Dist., 38th
Meyer, Christian, 6th Dist., 31st
Meyer, Ernest, 36th Dist., 37th, 38th
Meyer, J. Theodore, 28th Dist., 75th-77th, 79th-82nd
Meyer, James H. "Jim", 82nd Dist., 88th-92nd
Meyer, John, 4th Dist., 35th, 36th, 38th; 15th Dist., 39th
Meyer, John P., 22nd Dist., 66th, 67th
Meyer, N. J., 18th Dist., 36th
Meyer, Roland J., 3rd Dist., 82nd
Meyers, Elias B., 14th
Meyers, Joseph L., 12th Dist., 50th-53rd
Meyers, Thomas J., 50th Dist., 54th
Michaels, Moses, 2nd
Middlecoff, John, 8th
Middlecoff, John P., 18th Dist., 28th
Middlekauf, C. W., 12th Dist., 42nd
Middlesworth, William, 18th Dist., 24th; 33rd Dist., 29th
Mieroslawski, S. D., 5th Dist., 32nd
Mieure, Wm. H. H., 45th Dist., 32nd; 46th Dist., 36th
Mikva, Abner J., 23rd Dist., 70th-73rd; 74th
Mileham, Samuel, 37th Dist., 31st; 35th Dist., 34th
Miles, Rufus W., 58th Dist., 21st; 22nd Dist., 31st
Miles, Stephen W., 8th Dist., 23rd
Miller, Allen P., 31st Dist., 42nd
Miller, Alonzo A., 49th Dist., 47th
Miller, Ambrose M., 20th Dist., 23rd, 24th
Miller, Andrew, 20th Dist., 17th
Miller, Anson S., 14th
Miller, Charles O., 25th Dist., 66th-68th; 12th Dist., 70th-73rd

Miller, D. B., 34th Dist., 43rd, 44th, 47th
Miller, David, E., 29th Dist., 92nd
Miller, Ezra E., 41st Dist., 48th
Miller, George A., 23rd Dist., 47th, 48th
Miller, George W., 3rd Dist., 39th, 40th
Miller, H. C., 52nd Dist., 18th
Miller, Harry L., 13th, 14th
Miller, Henry B., 59th Dist., 26th
Miller, Horace, 47th Dist., 17th
Miller, Isaac, 7th Dist., 24th; 4th Dist., 43rd
Miller, Jacob, 6th Dist., 36th, 37th
Miller, James G., 38th Dist., 39th
Miller, James H., 25th Dist., 34th-36th
Miller, James O., 49th Dist., 43rd
Miller, James R., 15th Dist., 26th; 16th Dist., 27th
Miller, John, 15th; 44th Dist., 24th
Miller, John D., 51st Dist., 43rd
Miller, John E., 50th Dist., 64th-69th; 58th Dist., 70th
Miller, Joseph E., 47th Dist., 38th
Miller, J. Bert, 20th Dist., 55th
Miller, J. H., 46th Dist., 42nd
Miller, Kenneth W., 34th Dist., 73rd; 39th Dist., 75th-
  77th; 37th Dist., 78th
Miller, Lewis W., 12th Dist., 24th
Miller, Michael M., 4th Dist., 29th
Miller, Otis, Jr., 54th Dist., 72nd
Miller, Otis, Sr., 49th Dist., 63rd-65th, 67th-69th; 54th
  Dist., 70th, 71st
Miller, Peter J., 15th Dist., 70th-73rd, 75th-77th
Miller, S. B., 50th Dist., 42nd
Miller, Samuel A., 20th Dist., 35th
Miller, Steve, 53rd Dist., 82nd
Miller, Theodore, 26th Dist., 27th
Miller, Thomas H., 10th Dist., 78th-80th
Miller, Walter R., 11th Dist., 54th
Miller, William, 14th
Miller, William H., 83rd Dist., 27th
Miller, William H. H., 24th Dist., 50th, 51st
Miller, Wm. T., 45th Dist., 17th
Mills, Benjamin, 8th
Mills, Henry I., 5th
Mills, Matthew, 31st Dist., 45th, 46th
Mills, Miles E., 42nd Dist., 62nd; 55th Dist., 71st-73rd;
  74th; 54th Dist., 75th
Mills, Otis S., 18th Dist., 44th
Milnor, Frank R., 38th Dist., 42nd
Milroy, R. A., 14th Dist., 50th
Miner, Edward G., 15th
Miner, Henry, 37th Dist., 37th
Minnis, Henry O., 40th Dist., 43rd, 44th
Minor, Gideon, 10th
Minshall, Wm. A., 8th, 10th, 12th
Minsky, Henry, 17th Dist., 55th, 56th
Mioduski, Adam S., 13th Dist., 61st, 62nd, 64th, 66th
Mitchell, Benj. M., 9th Dist., 38th; 19th Dist., 40th, 42nd;
  21st Dist., 43rd, 44th, 47th-49th, 51st, 53rd-55th
Mitchell, Bill, 102nd Dist., 91st, 92nd
Mitchell, Edward T., 13th
Mitchell, Jerry, 73rd Dist., 89th-92nd
Mitchell, J. Luther W., 19th Dist., 37th
Mitchell, Samuel M., 47th Dist., 28th
Mitchell, Thomas F., 28th Dist., 30th-33rd
Moberly, Kenneth E., 9th Dist., 70th, 72nd, 73rd
Mobley, Mordecai, 5th
Mock, Anthony R., 21st Dist., 31st, 32nd
Moffitt, Donald L., 94th Dist., 88th-92nd
Moffitt, William T., 44th Dist., 27th; 29th Dist., 28th
Molloy, Vincent E., 21st Dist., 78th-81st
Monaghan, James L., 5th Dist., 36th
Monohan, Gersham, 33rd Dist., 30th
Monroe, James O., 47th Dist., 64th
Monroe, John, 39th Dist., 23rd
Monroe, John B., 32nd Dist., 66th-68th
Monroe, William T., 13th Dist., 44th
Montelius, John A., 18th Dist., 42nd; 26th Dist., 43rd,
  46th, 47th
Montgomery, Geo. W., 37th Dist., 40th
Montgomery, William, 47th Dist., 43rd-45th
Mooers, Royal, 23rd Dist., 18th
Mooney, Wm., 15th Dist., 29th, 36th
Mooneyham, James P., 50th Dist., 51st, 52nd
Mooneyham, Thomas M., 47th Dist., 30th
Moore, Andrea S., 61st Dist., 88th-92nd
Moore, Charles E., 34th Dist., 52nd, 53rd
Moore, Clarence C., 42nd Dist., 34th

Moore, Daniel T., 12th
Moore, Don A., 2nd Dist., 73rd; 74th; 9th Dist., 75th-77th
Moore, Enoch, 2nd
Moore, Eugene "Gene", 7th Dist., 88th-90th
Moore, Hosea H. 44th Dist., 37th
Moore, Ira M., 37th Dist., 28th, 29th
Moore, J. H., 19th Dist., 29th
Moore, John, 10th, 11th
Moore, John Robert, 37th Dist., 47th, 49th, 53rd-55th
Moore, John W., 36th Dist., 33rd, 34th
Moore, Joseph, 10th Dist., 32nd
Moore, Nathaniel, 20th Dist., 28th, 29th
Moore, Risdon, 1st, 2nd, 3rd, 4th
Moore, Samuel E., 45th Dist., 53rd
Moore, T. C., 12th Dist., 17th
Moore, Thomas C., 41st Dist., 21st; 36th Dist., 25th
Moore, Wm., 9th, 10th
Moore, William A., 20th Dist., 38th
Moore, William A., 27th Dist., 30th
Moore, Wm. A., 56th Dist., 71st, 74th
Moore, William H., 42nd Dist., 29th
Moore, Wm. J., 14th
Moose, Henry H., 36th Dist., 28th
Moran, James, 74th
Moran, John P., 16th Dist., 44th
Moran, Thos. J., 3rd Dist., 35th
Moran, William J., 15th Dist., 42nd
Moray, Thomas P., 38th Dist., 40th
Morgan, Alexander W., 35th Dist., 20th
Morgan, D. H., 4th Dist., 24th, 26th
Morgan, Edward T., 11th
Morgan, James C., 15th Dist., 34th
Morgan, John P., 16th Dist., 43rd
Morgan, John T., 69th Dist., 27th
Morgan, John W. R., 32nd Dist., 32nd
Morgan, Lewis V., 36th Dist., 73rd, 74th; 9th Dist., 75th,
  76th
Morgan, M. A., 42nd Dist., 34th, 35th
Morgensen, Wm. J., 11th Dist., 67th, 68th; 26th Dist.,
  70th
Morley, John, 9th Dist., 41st, 42nd
Morrasy, Frank W., 37th Dist., 48th-53rd, 55th
Morray, James B., 4th Dist., 27th
Morrill, Milton M., 31st Dist., 23rd, 24th; 58th Dist., 27th
Morrille, Jacob C., 14th
Morris, Achilles, 8th
Morris, Edward H., 3rd Dist., 37th; 1st Dist., 43rd
Morris, Freeman P., 16th Dist., 34th, 36th, 38th-40th
Morris, George W., 56th Dist., 20th
Morris, Isaac N., 15th
Morris, James F., 45th Dist., 46th, 47th, 48th
Morris, John, 72nd Dist., 27th
Morris, John K., 12th Dist., 65th-69th; 34th Dist., 70th-
  73rd; 74th
Morris, Richard G., 14th; 10th Dist., 16th
Morris, Wm. S., 51st Dist., 30th, 32nd
Morris, W. T., 44th Dist., 49th
Morrison, Alexander L., 95th Dist., 27th
Morrison, Isaac L., 39th Dist., 30th, 31st; 38th Dist., 33rd
Morrison, J. L. D., 14th, 15th
Morrison, Napoleon B., 43rd Dist., 28th
Morrison, Thomas, 15th
Morrison, William E., 34th Dist., 30th
Morrison, William R., 11th Dist., 19th-21st; 15th Dist.,
  27th
Morrisy, Anthony, 25th Dist., 35th, 36th
Morrow, Charles III, 32nd Dist., 84th-87th; 26th Dist.,
  88th-92nd
Morse, Timothy M., 35th Dist., 24th, 26th; 60th Dist.,
  27th
Morland, William, 38th Dist., 32nd
Morton, Joseph, 10th, 15th
Moses, John, 38th Dist., 29th
Moses, John C., 35th Dist., 18th
Mosely, Robert, 24th Dist., 21st
Moseley, Vickie M., 99th Dist., 88th
Moseley-Braun, Carol, 24th Dist., 81st, 82nd; 25th Dist.,
  83rd-85th
Moss, John R., 46th Dist., 31st
Moss, Norman H., 46th Dist., 41st
Mouers, W. J. N., 51st Dist., 37th
Moulton, Samuel W., 33rd Dist., 18th; 19th Dist., 19th,
  20th
Mounts, William L., 38th Dist., 38th; 36th Dist., 39th
Mudd, Joseph C., 46th Dist., 79th, 80th

509

Mueller, A. F. C., 57th Dist., 20th
Mueller, Carl, 21st Dist., 42nd; 31st Dist., 50th-54th
Mueller, Jacob A., 25th Dist., 63rd-65th
Mueller, Milton M., 47th Dist., 63rd
Mugalian, Richard A., 2nd Dist., 78th-81st
Mugler, Charles A., 23rd Dist., 55th
Muir, Robert H., 7th Dist., 38th, 39th
Mulac, Rudolph, 2nd Dist., 39th
Mulcahey, Richard T., 35th Dist., 79th-82nd; 69th Dist., 83rd-87th
Mulcahy, Robert J., 9th Dist., 48th-50th
Mulheran, Thos. F., 13th Dist., 34th
Mulkey, Wm. T., 34th Dist., 29th
Mullaley, William J., 47th Dist., 64th
Mulligan, Joseph H., 21st Dist., 38th; 33rd Dist., 39th
Mulligan, Rosemary, 55th Dist., 88th-92nd
Mulvane, Jacob R., 19th Dist., 28th
Mundy, J. S., 34th Dist., 62nd, 63rd
Mundy, Mahon H., 48th Dist., 43rd, 44th
Mundy, Samuel, 6th, 7th
Munizzi, Pamela, 21st Dist, 86th, 87th
Munro, Fayette S., 8th Dist., 29th
Munsell, Leander, 12th
Murdock, Frank, 22nd Dist., 38th; 35th Dist., 39th, 40th
Mureen, E. W., 43rd Dist., 57th
Murphy, Edward J., 9th Dist., 46th, 47th
Murphy, Everett J., 48th Dist., 35th
Murphy, Harold, 30th Dist., 88th-92nd
Murphy, Hawkins O., 44th Dist., 49th
Murphy, John H., 10th, 11th
Murphy, John M., 37th Dist., 42nd
Murphy, Joseph L., 48th Dist., 38th
Murphy, Lawrence, 39th Dist., 80th-82nd
Murphy, Matthew, 4th Dist., 34th
Murphy, Maureen, 36th Dist., 88th, 89th
Murphy, Peter, 28th Dist., 50th
Murphy, Richard, 10th-13th
Murphy, Richard G., 8th, 9th, 11th, 12th; 16th Dist., 17th
Murphy, Timothy D., 4th Dist., 50th
Murphy, William, 4th Dist., 46th
Murphy, W. J., 8th Dist., 69th; 31st Dist., 70th-73rd; 31st Dist., 75th-77th; 32nd Dist., 78th
Murphy, William K., 8th Dist., 24th, 25th; 48th Dist., 32nd
Murray, Abner G., 39th Dist., 40th; 45th Dist., 43rd
Murray, George, 25th Dist., 38th; 31st Dist., 39th, 40th
Murray, George W., 37th Dist., 33rd
Murray, George W., 31st Dist., 39th
Murray, Hugh V., 42nd Dist., 40th
Murray, James Emmett, 4th Dist., 31st
Murray, Joseph F., 27th Dist., 55th
Murray, Patrick F., 23rd Dist., 45th, 46th
Musgrave, Charles H., 48th Dist., 45th
Musseter, Lemuel, 58th Dist., 27th
Myer, Nelson J., 18th Dist., 37th
Myers, D. S., Jr., 16th Dist., 52nd
Myers, George W., 22nd Dist., 46th, 48th
Myers, Joseph C., 30th Dist., 36th
Myers, Richard P., 95th Dist., 89th-92nd
Myers, Thomas J., 50th Dist., 53rd
Myers, William H., 24th Dist., 37th, 38th
Nagel, Nicholas J., 11th Dist., 43rd, 44th
Naines, Elijah M., 53rd Dist., 23rd
Nance, A. G., 36th Dist., 29th
Nance, Thomas J., 11th
Naper, Joseph, 10th, 11th; 50th Dist., 18th
Napolitano, Richard A., 23rd Dist., 69th; 19th Dist., 70th-73rd
Nardulli, Michael L., 19th Dist., 78th-80th
Narramore, W. P., 46th Dist., 18th
Nase, Adam, 57th Dist., 26th
Nash, Steven G., 11th Dist., 83rd, 84th
Nash, William, 1st
Navigato, William, 17th Dist., 45th
Naylor, Charles, 5th Dist., 46th
Neal, George A., 32nd Dist., 37th
Neal, Henry A., 32nd Dist., 30th, 31st
Neece, William H., 29th Dist., 24th; 59th Dist., 27th
Needles, Thomas B., 42nd Dist., 39th, 40th
Neef, Elmer O., 30th Dist., 50th
Neeley, Chas. G., 6th Dist., 35th
Neese, Thomas J., 25th Dist., 42nd
Neff, Clarence E., 50th Dist., 73rd, 74th; 45th Dist., 75th-77th; 47th Dist., 78th-82nd; 95th Dist., 83rd
Neff, James I., 10th Dist., 31st

Neistein, Bernard S., 16th Dist., 70th
Nellis, Charles S., 50th Dist., 35th
Nelson, A. C., 47th Dist., 29th
Nelson, Benjamin, 19th Dist., 68th, 69th
Nelson, Charles A., 29th Dist., 45th, 46th
Nelson, Diana, 6th Dist., 82nd; 44th Dist., 83rd
Nelson, Ragnar G., 13th Dist., 63rd-65th
Nelson, William E., 44th Dist., 27th
Nesbitt, Samuel G., 13th
Neville, William, 48th Dist., 28th
Nevitt, Edward H., 11th Dist., 30th
Newcomer, John R., 2nd Dist., 41st
Newport, John W., 43rd Dist., 22nd, 23rd
Newton, John G., 47th Dist., 28th
Newton, Revilo, 20th Dist., 33rd
Nicholis, Henry D., 15th Dist., 40th
Nichols, John L., 42nd Dist., 31st-33rd
Nichols, Smith, 25th Dist., 22nd
Niehaus, J. M., 26th Dist., 32nd
Niehoff, Conrad L., 3rd Dist., 29th
Niles, Nathaniel, 15th Dist., 24th
Nixon, A. H., 52nd Dist., 17th, 18th
Noble, Harrison, 38th Dist., 23rd, 24th
Noble, William, 26th Dist., 51st
Noel, Lunsford R., 8th
Nohe, Augustus W., 5th Dist., 37th, 38th; 2nd Dist., 40th, 42nd; 19th Dist., 43rd
Noland, N. Duane, 102nd Dist., 86th-90th
Noling, Lars M., 10th Dist., 38th-40th
Noonan, George G., 3rd Dist., 51st-69th; 29th Dist., 70th, 71st
Noonan, John, 17th Dist., 43rd
Noper, Ross E., 32nd Dist., 60th, 61st
Norden, Aaron, 5th Dist., 43rd, 44th
Norris, James, 13th
Norsworthy, John T., 46th Dist., 37th
North, Frank P., 34th Dist., 75th-78th
North, Levi, 73rd Dist., 27th
Norton, Asa, 4th
Norton, Hiram, 45th Dist., 21st
Norton, Jesse O., 50th Dist., 17th
Nothnagle, Charles W., 3rd Dist., 40th
Novak, Edward J., 5th Dist., 38th; 13th Dist., 39th, 40th
Novak, J. Philip, 86th Dist., 85th-87th; 85th Dist., 88th-92nd
Noveli, Frank, 17th Dist., 63rd
Nowers, Thomas, Jr., 21st Dist., 33rd, 34th
Nowicki, John M., 6th Dist., 41st, 42nd
Nowlan, James A., 37th Dist., 59th-62nd, 65th
Nowlan, James Dunlap, 39th Dist., 76th, 77th
Nowlan, John T., 37th Dist., 63rd-65th
Nowlin, David, 10th
Noyes, James E., 37th Dist, 43rd, 44th
Nulton, Jerome B., 39th Dist., 28th
Nunnally, Nelson W., 9th
Nye, Iram, 14th
Nyman, Carl O., 10th Dist., 57th
Oakwood, Jacob H., 31st Dist., 28th
Oakwood, John H., 31st Dist., 30th
Oberly, John H., 50th Dist., 28th
Obernuefemann, Leo B., 74th
Oblinger, Josephine K., 50th Dist., 81st, 82nd; 100th Dist., 83rd, 84th
O'Brien, Daniel J., 10th Dist., 77th
O'Brien, Daniel P., 13th Dist., 80th-82nd
O'Brien, George M., 41st Dist., 77th
O'Brien, James P., 19th Dist., 51st
O'Brien, Lawrence C., 29th Dist., 50th-57th
O'Brien, Leo F., 74th; 45th Dist., 75th
O'Brien, Mary K., 75th Dist., 90th-92nd
O'Brien, Thomas J., 21st Dist., 45th, 46th, 56th, 57th
O'Brien, Wm. W., 36th Dist., 23rd
Obrzut, Geoffrey S., 52nd Dist., 87th
O'Connell, Daniel, 20th Dist., 48th-50th
O'Connell, Edmund, 28th Dist., 37th, 38th
O'Connell, John, 15th Dist., 33rd
O'Connell, John T., 6th Dist., 82nd; 47th Dist., 83rd-85th
O'Connor, Ambrose, 14th, 15th
O'Connor, Cornelius V., 8th Dist., 42nd
O'Connor, Jack, 35th Dist., 89th
O'Connor, James, 1st Dist., 35th, 38th
O'Connor, William A., 43rd Dist., 90th-92nd
Odam, Dempsey, 10th, 12th
O'Daniel, William L., 54th Dist., 78th, 79th
Odell, David W., 11th Dist., 23rd, 25th

O'Donnell, James F., 22nd Dist., 39th, 40th
O'Donnell, Joseph A., 9th Dist., 36th-38th
O'Donnell, Thomas O., 14th Dist., 34th
Odum, Ernest J., 50th Dist., 50th
Ogle, Jacob, 3rd, 7th
Oglesby, John G., 28th Dist., 44th, 45th
Oglesby, John M., 14th
Oglevee, William H., 30th Dist., 36th
O'Grady, Edward P., 29th Dist., 59th-68th
O'Grady, Thomas J., 4th Dist., 52nd-57th
O'Hair, Harvey Z., 34th Dist., 55th, 56th, 58th
O'Hair, Karl R., 22nd Dist., 56th
O'Hair, Wm. S., 31st Dist., 29th
O'Halleren, Bernard J., 25th Dist., 76th, 77th
O'Hartnett, Morrison, Jr., 42nd Dist., 39th
O'Keefe, Raymond T., 25th Dist., 57th-68th
Okeson, George B., 28th Dist., 32nd
O'Laughlin, Michael, 23rd Dist., 37th, 38th
Oldenburg, Adams C., 11th Dist., 34th
Oldham, Harry, 6th Dist., 43rd
Olds, Francis A., 12th; 21st Dist., 16th
Oleson, Albert J., 23rd Dist., 39th, 40th
Oleson, Ingwell, 5th Dist., 28th
Oliver, John, 9th, 12th
Olsen, Peter B., 11th Dist., 41st, 42nd
Olson, Andrew, 9th Dist., 44th
Olson, Jonas W., 73rd Dist., 27th
Olson, Myron J., 37th Dist., 82nd; 70th Dist., 83rd-87th
Olson, Robert F., 90th Dist., 85th-88th
Olwin, Jacob C., 45th Dist., 32nd
O'Malley, John F., 23rd Dist., 41st
O'Malley, Thomas F., 5th Dist., 31st
O'Mara, Patrick, 21st Dist., 32nd, 33rd
O'Meara, James D., 9th Dist., 42nd
Omelveney, Edward, 15th
Omelveney, Samuel, 2nd
O'Neil, Andy, 45th Dist., 60th, 61st
O'Neil, Daniel, 74th
O'Neil, John, 27th Dist., 46th
O'Neil, Schaefer, 47th Dist., 57th-61st, 63rd
O'Neill, Lottie Holman, 41st Dist., 53rd-56th, 58th-66th
O'Neille, Edward J., 10th
Onion, J. S., 26th Dist., 42nd
Orendorf, William J., 22nd Dist., 34th
Orendorff, Alfred, 35th Dist., 28th
Orendorff, Green P., 27th Dist., 31st
Organ, John S., 51st Dist., 44th
Origin, B. S., 44th Dist., 40th
Ormsbee, Joseph W., 12th
O'Rorke, J. J., 7th Dist., 47th-49th
Osborn, Hawkins S., 15th; 7th Dist., 20th
Osgood, Stacey W., 7th Dist., 42nd
O'Shea, John, 11th Dist., 33rd, 34th; 9th Dist., 40th
Osmond, Timothy H., 62nd Dist., 91st, 92nd
Ostenburg, John A., 80th Dist., 88th
Osterman, Harry, 17th Dist., 91st, 92nd
Ostrom, William, 3rd Dist., 45th, 47th
O'Toole, James J., 11th Dist., 46th, 47th; 31st Dist., 53rd, 54th
O'Toole, James T., 2nd Dist., 36th
Ottman, Sylvester F., 36th Dist., 25th; 19th Dist., 31st, 32nd
Otwell, William, 2nd, 4th, 11th
Oughton, James H., Jr., 74th
Outhouse, James, 9th
Overland, Edward M., 23rd Dist., 50th-57th
Owen, James L., 15th Dist., 33rd
Owen, Thomas H., 9th, 13th
Owen, Thomas J. V., 7th
Owen, W. H., 44th Dist., 61st
Owen, Wesley M., 26th Dist., 43rd
Ownby, James P., 30th Dist., 39th
Ozella, Joe, Jr., 45th Dist., 82nd
Pace, Harvey T., 9th, 10th, 11th
Pace, James M., 32nd Dist., 49th-52nd
Pacelli, William V., 17th Dist., 54th-56th
Paddleford, James H., 21st Dist., 34th
Paddock, Daniel H., 16th Dist., 36th-38th
Padon, Henry H., 41st Dist., 36th
Page, John, 48th Dist., 16th
Page, Oliver J., 51st Dist., 41st
Paine, E. A., 42nd Dist., 18th
Painter, Oscar, 20th Dist., 38th
Paisley, George W., 34th Dist., 32nd
Palmer, I. A., 50th Dist., 60th, 61st

Palmer, John Mayo, 35th Dist., 30th
Palmer, Romie J., 6th Dist., 76th, 77th; 8th Dist., 78th, 79th
Palmer, Smith M., 27th Dist., 26th
Panayotovich, Samuel, 35th Dist., 83rd-85th
Pangle, Charles, 86th Dist., 83rd, 84th
Pankau, Carole, 49th Dist., 88th-92nd
Papierz, Stanley A., 74th
Pappas, Pete, 44th Dist., 75th-77th; 36th Dist., 78th
Parcells, Margaret R., 57th Dist., 83rd-88th
Parish, John J., 51st Dist., 51st, 52nd
Parish, John L., 4th Dist., 32nd
Parish, W. W., Jr., 20th Dist., 43rd
Parke, Terry R., 49th Dist., 84th-87th; 53rd Dist., 88th-92nd
Parker, Benjamin, 7th
Parker, Daniel S., 41st Dist., 25th
Parker, Francis W., 1st Dist., 34th
Parker, Frank L., 41st Dist., 45th, 46th
Parker, George W., 39th Dist., 26th; 16th Dist., 29th
Parker, Hilton A., 2nd Dist., 33rd, 34th
Parker, Isaac A. J., 51st Dist., 36th
Parker, Sidney, 46th Dist., 56th-58th, 60th, 61st
Parker, Thomas G., 46th Dist., 37th
Parker, Wm. R., 46th Dist., 20th
Parkhurst, John C., 43rd Dist., 71st-73rd; 74th; 75th
Parkhurst, Jonathan, 35th Dist., 37th
Parkinson, James, 12th
Parks, Sample G., 44th Dist., 44th
Parks, Samuel C., 35th Dist., 19th
Parrish, Braxton, 14th
Parrish, John L., 4th Dist., 33rd
Parrish, William H., 51st Dist., 40th
Parrott, Walter S., 40th Dist., 38th
Parsons, Solomon, 12th
Partee, Cecil A., 22nd Dist., 70th; 21st Dist., 71st-73rd; 74th
Partridge, Charles A., 8th Dist., 35th-37th
Partridge, Jasper, 44th Dist., 41st, 42nd
Patch, Benj. L., 51st Dist., 22nd
Patrick, Langdon, 21st Dist., 78th, 79th, 81st
Patrick, Samuel, 20th Dist., 34th, 35th
Pattern, William, 46th Dist., 19th, 21st
Patterson, Azro, 42nd Dist., 17th
Patterson, Harbert, 19th Dist., 17th
Patterson, Joseph M., 31st Dist., 43rd
Pattison, Douglas, 12th Dist., 43rd-45th
Pattison, George, 34th Dist., 16th
Patton, H. Dorsey, 2nd Dist., 37th
Patton, James W., 20th Dist., 24th
Patton, Thomas A., 23rd Dist., 65th, 67th
Patty, Mercy B., 44th Dist., 23rd
Paul, John, 25th Dist., 53rd
Paullen, Parvin, 10th
Paxton, J. H., 36th Dist., 52nd
Payne, C. C., 5th Dist., 26th
Payne, Eugene B., 53rd Dist., 24th, 25th
Payne, William, 21st Dist., 37th, 38th; 33rd Dist., 39th, 40th
Pearce, Francis M., 41st Dist., 30th
Pearce, Wm. W., 41st Dist., 34th
Pearson, Albert H., 32nd Dist., 73rd
Pearson, Harvey, 8th Dist., 66th-68th
Pearson, Isaac N., 27th Dist., 33rd
Pearson, John M., 41st Dist., 31st-33rd
Pearson, Robert N., 4th Dist., 32nd
Pease, Shaw, 29th Dist., 29th
Pebworth, Mrs. Robert, 74th; 6th Dist., 75th
Pechous, Robert C., 7th Dist., 80th-82nd
Peck, Ebenezer, 12th; 57th Dist., 21st
Pedersen, Bernard E., 54th Dist., 83rd-89th
Pedersen, Enoch H., 23rd Dist., 43rd, 44th
Pedersen, Julius, 9th Dist., 33rd
Peel, Francis M., 30th Dist., 35th
Peel, Kenneth J., 43rd Dist., 64th-67th
Peffer, Henry K., 33rd Dist., 23rd
Peffers, John M., 14th Dist., 54th-60th
Peffers, Maud N., 14th Dist., 61st-69th
Pelka, John A., 15th Dist., 60th, 61st
Pell, Gilbert T., 3rd, 6th
Pelt, Owen D, 26th Dist., 75th
Pelzer, Otto, 6th Dist., 28th
Pemberton, John, 27th Dist., 17th
Pendarvis, Robert E., 11th Dist., 42nd; 25th Dist., 43rd, 44th

Penfield, John, 30th Dist., 28th
Penn, Philip, 13th
Pennington, James T., 21st Dist., 22nd
Pepoon, George W., 12th Dist., 35th, 36th
Perina, Joseph, 15th Dist., 51st-55th, 57th
Perkins, Edwin C., 28th Dist., 46th, 47th, 49th-51st
Perrin, John N., 49th Dist., 32nd
Perrottet, Lewis, 47th Dist., 37th; 49th Dist., 39th, 40th
Perry, David D., 23rd Dist., 32nd
Perry, Elmer A., 37th Dist., 39th-41st
Perry, James M., 41st Dist., 26th
Perry, Jos. Sam, 41st Dist., 60th-62nd
Perry, Josephine, 5th Dist., 57th, 58th
Perry, Nathaniel M., 23rd Dist., 24th
Persico, Vincent A., 39th Dist., 87th-92nd
Persinger, Allen, 36th Dist., 17th
Pervier, Clayton C., 37th Dist., 45th-48th
Peskin, Bernard M., 6th Dist., 71st-73rd; 74th
Petefish, Glen, 30th Dist., 58th, 59th
Peters, David M., 28th Dist., 69th
Peters, Everett R., 24th Dist., 59th-61st
Peters, Herbert D., 30th Dist., 32nd
Peters, Matthew H., 16th Dist., 31st
Peters, Peter Piotrowicz, 15th Dist., 78th-82nd
Peterson, James, 24th Dist., 32nd
Peterson, James E., 28th Dist., 76th
Peterson, Joseph R., 37th Dist., 67th-69th
Peterson, William E., 60th Dist., 83rd-87th
Petit, John Frank, 14th Dist., 56th-60th
Petka, Ed, 82nd Dist., 85th-87th
Petlak, Edward J., 27th Dist., 58th-61st
Petlak, Joseph, 27th Dist., 50th-52nd
Petri, Ed. P., 49th Dist., 54th-56th
Petrie, Alexander P., 22nd Dist., 32nd
Petrie, John A., 32nd Dist., 42nd; 30th Dist., 43rd
Petrone, Robert, 21st Dist., 58th-67th
Pfeffer, Leo, 24th Dist., 68th, 69th; 44th Dist, 70th-73rd;
74th
Phelan, James W., 48th Dist., 87th; 24th Dist., 88th
Phelps, David D., 118th Dist., 84th-90th
Phelps, Simon D., 96th Dist., 27th
Phelps, William A., 5th Dist., 32nd
Phelps, Wm. E., 36th Dist., 26th
Phelps, Wm. J., 12th
Philip, James "Pate", 37th Dist., 75th-77th; 40th Dist.,
78th
Phillips, A. L., 26th Dist., 44th
Phillips, Alexander, 1st-4th, 11th, 12th; 49th Dist., 17th
Phillips, Ben, 42nd Dist., 52nd
Phillips, Burrell, 34th Dist., 30th; 40th Dist., 35th
Phillips, Charles E., 42nd Dist., 41st
Phillips, Frederick B., 47th Dist., 36th
Phillips, James G., 55th Dist., 27th
Phillips, Peter, 47th Dist., 30th
Phillips, W. B., 46th Dist., 51st-56th
Phillips, William M., 16th Dist., 18th
Phillips, W. M., 20th Dist., 29th
Piatt, John T., 21st Dist., 35th
Picker, Henry D., 41st Dist., 37th
Pickering, Wm., 13th-15th; 8th Dist., 16th, 17th
Pickrell, Andrew J., 50th Dist., 39th
Piel, Robert J., 10th Dist., 81st, 82nd; 79th Dist., 83rd-
86th
Pierce, Alonzo D., 51st Dist., 30th
Pierce, Daniel M., 74th; 32nd Dist., 75th-82nd; 58th Dist.,
83rd
Pierce, Ferne Carter, 32nd Dist., 70th-72nd
Pierce, Hiram L., 29th Dist., 35th
Pierce, Samuel C., 7th, 8th
Pierce, William, 10th Dist., 67th-69th; 33rd Dist., 70th-
73rd; 74th
Pierce, William L., 8th Dist., 52nd, 53rd
Pierce, William P., 52nd Dist., 25th
Piercy, W. Duff, 46th Dist., 47th
Pierson, James T., 15th
Pierson, Louis J., 7th Dist., 44th-47th, 49th
Pierson, Ornan, 39th Dist., 32nd
Pike, Franklin S., 41st Dist., 29th
Pike, Ivory H., 28th Dist., 34th, 36th
Pilgrim, William M., 31st Dist., 39th
Pinckney, Daniel H., 50th Dist , 19th, 20th
Pinckney, Daniel J., 50th Dist., 24th
Pinnell, Willis O., 31st Dist., 28th
Pinney, D. H., 15th Dist., 30th
Pintozzi, Anthony, 17th Dist., 57th

Piotrowski, Lillian, 9th Dist., 67th-69th; 30th Dist., 70th-
73rd
Pitlock, Joseph, 27th Dist., 47th, 48th
Pitman, J. M., 35th Dist., 17th, 18th
Pitner, Franklin R., 14th
Pixley, Osman, 23rd Dist., 27th
Placek, Joseph, 9th Dist., 50th-55th
Plater, Lewis F., 51st Dist., 29th
Plato, Wm. B., 46th Dist., 21st
Platt, John D., 57th Dist., 24th
Platt, John W., 48th Dist., 28th
Pleasants, James H., 38th Dist., 31st
Plotke, Isadore, 6th Dist., 39th
Plotke, Nathan, 6th Dist., 32nd
Plowman, Jonathan, 40th Dist., 28th
Poe, Raymond, 99th Dist., 89th-92nd
Pogue, John R., 24th Dist., 44th, 45th
Poindexter, Emmet P., 38th Dist., 39th
Polk, Ben, 36th Dist., 78th-82nd
Pollack, William E., 6th Dist., 67th-69th; 9th Dist., 70th-
73rd; 74th; 13th Dist., 75th
Pollard, O. W., 18th Dist., 35th, 36th
Pollock, James, 8th Dist., 32nd, 34th
Pollock, John, 18th Dist., 28th
Pollock, John J., 48th Dist., 37th
Pomeroy, Sterling, 25th Dist., 35th
Pool, Joseph J., 27th Dist., 41st, 42nd
Poorman, Edward F., 34th Dist., 47th, 48th
Pope, Abraham B., 15th Dist., 25th
Porter, David, 1st, 9th
Porter, Frank, 51st Dist., 55th-58th
Porter, John, 33rd Dist., 26th
Porter, John Edward, 1st Dist., 78th-80th
Posey, John F., 7th
Postel, Philip H., 49th Dist., 32nd
Potter, C. R., 49th Dist., 18th
Potter, E. S., 45th Dist., 18th
Poulton, John J., 13th Dist., 44th-46th
Pouncey, Taylorr, 26th Dist., 79th-82nd; 31st Dist., 83rd
Powell, Almet, 16th Dist., 40th
Powell, Israel A., 22nd Dist., 27th
Powell, John G., 9th Dist., 21st
Powell, Joseph, 5th Dist., 40th
Powell, Oliver P., 40th Dist., 29th
Powell, Paul, 51st Dist., 59th-69th; 59th Dist., 70th-73rd
Powell, Starkey R., 38th Dist., 30th-32nd
Powell, William S., 5th Dist., 34th
Powers, Abiiah, 12th Dist., 30th
Powers, Richard E., 50th Dist., 45th
Powers, William W., 13th Dist., 53rd-60th
Prather, Henry, 32nd Dist., 18th
Pratt, Isaac L., 27th Dist., 33rd
Pratt, J. M., 11th Dist., 31st
Pratt, John W., 13th, 14th
Preihs, Carl H., 40th Dist., 64th, 65th, 67th-69th
Prendergast, James T., 19th Dist., 49th-51st
Prendergast, Richard, 41st Dist., 47th
Prentice, Charles, 6th
Prentice, Owen, 12th
Prescott, Lyle M., 35th Dist., 63rd-65th
Preston, Bernard, 34th Dist., 37th, 38th
Preston, Finney D., 16th Dist., 19th, 20th
Preston, Lee, 11th Dist., 81st, 82nd; 3rd Dist., 83rd-87th
Prevo, Samuel, 14th, 15th
Price, Arwin E., 14th Dist., 46th
Price, James B., 29th Dist., 16th
Price, Joseph P., 38th Dist., 40th
Price, Oscar F., 68th Dist., 27th
Price, William, 8th Dist., 31st
Prickett, Abraham, 1st
Prickett, David, 5th
Prickett, William R., 41st Dist., 31st, 34th
Priestly, Joseph L., 7th
Prignano, A. J., 17th Dist., 59th
Prince, Francis, 5th, 6th
Prince, George W., 22nd Dist., 36th, 37th
Pritchard, Reuben M., 84th Dist., 27th
Propper, William F., 7th Dist., 55th, 56th
Prothrow, Wm., 49th Dist., 21st
Provart, Philip C. C., 48th Dist., 31st
Provine, Walter M., 40th Dist., 44th, 45th, 47th-49th
Prunty, William T., 44th Dist., 34th
Prusinski, Anthony C., 27th Dist., 63rd-66th
Prusinski, Bernard C., 27th Dist., 67th, 68th
Prussing, Laurel Lunt, 103rd Dist., 88th

Pugh, Coy, 10th Dist., 87th-91st
Pugh, Isaac C., 40th Dist., 24th
Pugh, John W., 36th Dist., 29th; 34th Dist., 36th
Pugh, Jonathan H., 3rd, 5th-7th
Pullen, Fred, 42nd Dist., 43rd
Pullen, Penny, 4th Dist., 80th-82nd; 55th Dist., 83rd-87th
Pulley, J. D., 3rd Dist., 21st, 22nd
Purdunn, Charles A., 45th Dist., 35th; 43rd Dist., 41st, 42nd; 34th Dist., 49th
Purnell, James E., 35th Dist., 33rd
Pursley, J. M., 23rd Dist., 19th
Pusateri, Lawrence X., 74th; 5th Dist., 75th
Putnam, James D., 18th Dist., 50th
Quanstrom, John F., 19th Dist., 40th
Querfield, William, 28th Dist., 62nd
Quick, Thomas, 18th Dist., 17th
Quinn, Arthur J., 29th Dist., 40th
Quinn, James F., 4th Dist., 34th, 36th, 37th
Quinn, Michael C., 26th Dist., 28th, 33rd
Quisenberry, Clifford, 28th Dist., 49th
Race, Joab A., 29th Dist., 28th
Radcliffe, George W., 47th Dist., 20th
Railsback, Thomas F., 39th Dist., 73rd; 74th
Raley, Eli V., 20th Dist., 30th; 25th Dist., 34th
Ralls, James M., 14th Dist., 27th
Ralston, James H., 10th
Ramey, Charles A., 40th Dist., 38th
Ramey, Thomas T., 41st Dist., 29th, 36th, 38th
Ramsey, David G., 47th Dist., 37th
Ramsey, George D., 44th Dist., 30th
Ramsey, Rufus N., 42nd Dist., 36th, 37th
Ramsey, Silas, 48th Dist., 18th
Ramstead, John, 51st Dist., 18th
Randall, S. W., 50th Dist., 17th
Randall, Ira V., 51st Dist., 24th
Randolph, James M., 38th Dist., 18th
Randolph, Paul J., 29th Dist., 64th-69th; 11th Dist., 70th-73rd; 74th; 12 Dist., 75th-77th; 13th Dist., 78th, 79th
Randolph, R. R., 51st Dist., 59th, 60th
Randolph, Wm. H., 14th, 15th
Rankin, David, 24th Dist., 28th, 29th, 33rd
Rankin, George C., 35th Dist., 41st, 42nd
Rankin, James, 49th Dist., 29th
Rankin, William A., 16th Dist., 42nd
Ranney, Joel A., 20th Dist., 30th, 31st
Rapp, John M., 46th Dist., 43rd, 44th, 47th, 48th
Raschke-Lind, Paula J., 67th Dist., 88th
Raser, Tillman, 43rd Dist., 32nd
Rasmussen, Charles S., 21st Dist., 52nd
Ratcliffe, C. R., 30th Dist., 65th, 66th, 68th, 69th; 46th Dist., 70th-73rd; 74th
Rategan, Joseph L., 21st Dist., 55th-65th
Rattan, Thomas, 3rd, 6th
Rausch, J. W., 20th Dist., 53rd
Ravlin, Needham N., 52nd Dist., 26th
Rawalt, Jonas, 10th, 11th
Rawleigh, W. T., 12th Dist., 47th
Rawlings, Isaac D., 14th
Rawlins, F. M., 1st Dist., 19th
Ray, A. W., 43rd Dist., 62nd-68th
Ray, G. A., 22nd Dist., 49th
Ray, Lyman B., 13th Dist., 28th
Ray, Robert B., 31st Dist., 33rd
Rayson, Leland, 74th; 9th Dist., 75th-79th
Rea, James F. "Jim", 59th Dist., 81st, 82nd; 117th Dist., 83rd-85th
Rea, Samuel H., 46th Dist., 41st
Reaburn, John J., 24th Dist., 30th, 31st
Read, John A., 42nd Dist., 45th
Read, John W., 11th
Rearick, Frederick, 34th Dist., 22nd
Reaugh, Ernest O., 32nd Dist., 50th, 51st
Reavill, Andrew F., 46th Dist., 30th, 31st
Reaville, Fred A., 48th Dist., 59th-61st
Reddick, William G., 10th, 11th
Redfield, Robert, 5th Dist., 41st
Redmon, Thomas, 28th Dist., 24th
Redmond, William A., 36th Dist., 71st-73rd; 74th; 37th Dist., 75th-77th; 40th Dist., 78th-82nd
Reed, Betty Lou, 32nd Dist., 79th-82nd
Reed, Charles G., 45th Dist., 26th
Reed, George, 8th Dist., 37th-39th
Reed, George W., 4th Dist., 30th
Reed, J. H., 14th
Reese, Addison, Jr., 7th Dist., 27th

Reeves, James A., 24th Dist., 53rd-55th
Regan, Frank S., 10th Dist., 41st
Regan, Robert P., 80th Dist., 84th-87th
Regner, David J., 3rd Dist., 75th-77th
Reich, Vernon W., 7th Dist., 65th, 66th
Reid, Frank R., 14th Dist., 47th
Reid, Lewis G., 29th Dist., 23rd
Reid, Thomas R., 49th Dist., 37th
Reilly, Jim, 49th Dist., 80th-82nd; 97th Dist., 83rd
Reilly, John R., 11th Dist., 44th
Reilly, Thomas F., 5th Dist., 54th
Reilly, Thomas H., 15th Dist., 35th
Reinhardt, Joseph, 75th Dist., 27th
Reinsberg, Perry F., 76th Dist., 27th
Reise, Augustus, 53rd Dist., 27th
Reitz, Dan, 116th Dist., 90th-92nd
Remann, Frederick, 15th; 43rd Dist., 30th
Remus, John P., 25th Dist., 52nd
Rennick, Frederick W., 37th Dist., 53rd-63rd
Reno, Wm. C., 25th Dist., 32nd
Rentchler, James W., 49th Dist., 49th-53rd
Retallic, Thomas A., 34th Dist., 41st
Rethmeier, Chris, 47th Dist., 49th-53rd
Reum, Walter J., 23rd Dist., 68th, 69th; 4th Dist., 70th-72nd
Revell, David, 21st Dist., 39th, 40th
Rew, Claude L., 51st Dist., 52nd, 54th-57th
Reynolds, Earl D., 10th Dist., 45th, 46th
Reynolds, James, 12th
Reynolds, John, 15th; 19th Dist., 18th
Reynolds, John, 5th, 6th
Reynolds, Joseph S., 59th Dist., 25th, 26th
Reynolds, Monroe G., 33rd Dist., 44th
Reynolds, Stephen A., 7th Dist., 35th, 36th
Reynolds, Thomas, 5th
Rhem, Sylvester O., 26th Dist., 82nd; 24th Dist., 83rd
Rhodes, Ben S., 26th Dist., 61st-69th; 42nd Dist., 70th-73rd; 74th
Rhodes, William, 15th
Rhodes, William V., 16th Dist., 40th, 41st
Riblett, Henry, 39th Dist., 19th
Riccolo, James M., 38th Dist., 80th
Rice, Charles H., 43rd Dist., 27th
Rice, Edward A., 38th Dist., 43rd
Rice, Edward Y., 15th Dist., 16th
Rice, Eugene, 32nd Dist., 35th, 36th
Rice, Isaac, 12th Dist., 28th; 11th Dist., 29th
Rice, James M., 67th Dist., 27th
Rice, Maurice P., 43rd Dist., 47th, 51st-56th
Rice, Nelson, Sr., 33rd Dist., 83rd-87th
Rice, Thomas J., 48th Dist., 36th
Rice, William C., 40th Dist., 19th, 21st
Richardson, Francis M., 33rd Dist., 32nd; 32nd Dist., 33rd, 35th
Richardson, George J., 57th Dist., 27th
Richardson, James J., 6th Dist., 16th
Richardson, John C., 40th Dist., 45th-49th, 51st-53rd
Richardson, Reuben, 16th Dist., 29th
Richardson, William A., 10th, 14th
Richardson, Wm. A., 37th Dist., 32nd
Richey, David, 17th Dist., 31st
Richmond, Bruce, 58th Dist., 79th-82nd, 116th Dist., 83rd-87th
Richmond, Henry, 20th Dist., 19th
Richmond, John P., 20th Dist., 19th
Richmond, Raymond S., 38th Dist., 61st
Richmond, Thomas, 56th Dist., 19th
Richter, Charles, 23rd Dist., 46th
Richton, Maurino R., 1st Dist., 70th, 71st
Rick, Wm. C., 5th Dist., 27th
Rickert, Joseph W., 48th Dist., 29th
Ricks, John B., 29th Dist., 25th; 40th Dist., 33rd
Ricks, Lewis, 14th Dist., 20th
Ricks, Wm. S., 14th
Ridgely, Reddick M., 39th Dist., 42nd
Ridgeway, John, 5th
Riess, Alfred D., 48th Dist., 42nd
Riggs, James M., 41st Dist., 27th
Riggs, Scott, 1st
Righter, Dale A., 106th Dist., 90th-92nd
Rigney, Harlan, 35th Dist., 78th-82nd
Rigney, Hugh M., 24th Dist., 78th-79th
Rigney, Stephenson, 12th Dist., 46th
Riley, Thomas H., 41st Dist., 45th, 46th
Rinaker, Lewis, 31st Dist., 44th

513

Rinaker, Pauline B., 38th Dist., 68th, 69th
Rinaker, Thomas, 36th Dist., 42nd; 38th Dist., 43rd
Rinehart, Walter E., 42nd Dist., 47th-49th
Rinella, James, 1st Dist., 66th-68th
Ring, Frank G., 7th Dist., 59th
Rink, Paul E., 39th Dist., 70th-73rd; 74th; 44th Dist., 75th
Rives, George W., 31st Dist., 16th; 47th Dist., 27th
Roane, Charles L., 33rd Dist., 33rd
Robb, Matthew, 15th
Robbins, Clyde W., 54th Dist., 81st, 82nd
Robbins, E. W., 14th
Robbins, Rollo R., 32nd Dist., 50th-57th, 62nd-69th; 50th Dist., 70th-72nd
Roberts, Adelbert H., 3rd Dist., 51st-53rd
Roberts, Caesar A., 62nd Dist., 27th
Roberts, Clyde A., 40th Dist., 66th, 67th
Roberts, Daniel A., 23rd Dist., 59th
Roberts, Levi, 4th
Roberts, Louis, 11th
Robeson, James, 15th
Robinson, Carl E., 45th Dist., 55th, 56th
Robinson, Charles F., 25th Dist., 30th, 31st
Robinson, David L., 50th Dist., 80th
Robinson, Francis M., 17th Dist., 32nd
Robinson, Hugh J., 30th Dist., 41st, 42nd
Robinson, James M., 15th
Robinson, Jeffry, 11th
Robinson, John R., 28th Dist., 44th-46th
Robinson, Joseph I., 18th Dist., 29th
Robinson, Nathaniel P., 33rd Dist., 30th
Robinson, Thomas T., 50th Dist., 31st
Robinson, William H., 3rd Dist., 69th; 20th Dist., 70th-73rd
Robison, Edward, 2nd
Robison, William, 38th Dist., 62nd-68th
Roche, John A., 5th Dist., 30th
Rockwell, Aldis L., 1st Dist., 32nd
Roderick, Solomon P., 19th Dist., 49th-52nd, 57th-60th
Rodman, Julius N., 24th Dist., 43rd, 44th
Rodriguez, Elba Iris, 3rd Dist., 90th
Roe, Arthur, 40th Dist., 48th-58th
Roe, Edward R., 63rd Dist., 27th
Roessler, Edward, 34th Dist., 27th
Roessler, Reuben, 18th Dist., 23rd
Rogers, A.F., 26th Dist., 27th
Rogers, Andrew L., 51st Dist., 27th
Rogers, Barrett, 28th Dist., 66th-69th; 47th Dist., 70th, 71st
Rogers, C. M., 27th Dist., 33rd, 34th
Rogers, Euclid B., 45th Dist., 53rd, 54th
Rogers, Jason, 29th Dist., 32nd
Rogers, Thomas P., 28th Dist., 28th-31st
Rogers, Wm. S., 50th Dist., 34th
Rohrback, George F., 11th Dist., 35th
Rohrer, Louis, 23rd Dist., 37th, 38th
Rollason, Wm. H., 31st Dist., 22nd
Roman, Wm. W., 11th; 12th Dist., 20th
Romano, Robert E., 1st Dist., 67th-69th
Romano, Sam, 2nd Dist., 69th; 17th Dist., 70th-73rd; 74th
Ronalds, Kenneth C., 51st Dist., 44th, 51st, 53rd
Ronan, Alfred G., 14th Dist., 81st, 82nd; 12th Dist., 83rd-87th
Ronan, Daniel J., 21st Dist., 66th, 67th
Rondeau, C. A., 51st Dist., 39th
Ronen, Carol, 17th Dist., 87th-91st
Rook, Jesse J., 11th Dist., 33rd
Roos, Frederick B., 7th Dist., 45th, 47th, 48th
Roosevelt, Wm. H., 31st Dist., 21st
Root, James P., 96th Dist., 27th
Ropa, Matt, 15th Dist., 69th; 29th Dist., 70th-73rd; 74th; 20th Dist., 75th-77th
Ropp, Gordon L., 44th Dist., 81st, 82nd; 88th Dist., 83rd-87th
Rorig, Edward H., 15th Dist., 41st
Rosander, Bertil T., 33rd Dist., 72nd, 73rd
Rose, Daniel E., 48th Dist., 44th, 45th
Rose, Thomas C., 50th Dist., 75th-77th; 49th Dist., 78th, 79th
Roskam, Peter, 40th Dist., 88th-90th
Ross, Alexander, 15th Dist., 26th
Ross, David, 23rd Dist., 36th
Ross, Henry J., 5th
Ross, John W., 36th Dist., 26th; 60th Dist., 27th
Ross, Joseph C., 27th Dist., 30th
Ross, Leonard W., 39th Dist., 72nd

Ross, Lewis W., 12th, 14th
Ross, Robert W., 38th Dist., 41st
Ross, Wm., 9th
Rostenkowski, Albert, 27th Dist., 48th, 49th, 53rd, 54th
Rostenkowski, Daniel D., 27th Dist., 68th
Rostenkowski, Joseph P., 27th Dist., 57th
Rotan, Byron J., 44th Dist., 29th
Rotello, Michael V., 67th Dist., 87th; 69th Dist., 88th
Rothschild, Isaac S., 5th Dist., 48th, 49th
Rottger, Frederick W., 36th Dist., 38th
Roundtree, James M., 42nd Dist., 33rd
Roundtree, John M., 6th Dist., 28th
Rourke, Cornelius, 36th Dist., 30th
Rowan, Stephen, 9th
Rowcliff Wm., 26th Dist., 29th
Rowe, Harris, 49th Dist., 72nd, 73rd; 74th
Rowe, Peter A., 2nd Dist., 40th
Rowe, William, 26th Dist., 48th-52nd
Rowett, Richard, 40th Dist., 30th
Rowland, Elbert, 44th Dist., 33rd
Rowland, John F., 31st Dist., 37th
Rowley, A. S., 17th Dist., 29th
Ruby, Virgil S., 30th Dist., 34th, 35th
Ruddle, John M., 15th
Ruddy, Michael A., 4th Dist., 56th-69th; 28th Dist., 70th-73rd; 74th
Rude, Albert, 44th Dist., 35th
Ruf, August, 24th Dist., 71st, 72nd
Rufiner, A. L., 34th Dist., 51st
Ruggles, James M., 34th Dist., 35th
Rumley, Edward, 16th Dist., 32nd
Runkel, Henry J., 41st Dist., 16th
Rush, F. P., 22nd Dist., 21st
Rush, Leonard, 13th Dist., 26th
Rush, W. V., 51st Dist., 54th-58th
Russell, David B., 3rd Dist., 18th
Russell, Horace, 20th Dist., 43rd, 44th
Russell, John, 4th
Russell, John C., 4th Dist., 44th, 45th
Russell, Joseph W., 26th Dist., 58th-62nd, 69th, 72nd-74th; 42nd Dist., 75th
Rutherford, Dan, 87th Dist., 88th-92nd
Rutledge, James M., 15th
Rutshaw, Arthur J., 4th Dist., 52nd-54th
Ryan, Ebenezer Z., 9th Dist., 16th
Ryan, Ed, 48th Dist., 53rd-57th
Ryan, Frank, 2nd Dist., 49th-61st
Ryan, Frank J., 11th Dist., 47th-49th, 51st, 52nd
Ryan, George H., Sr., 43rd Dist., 78th-82nd
Ryan, George, 49th Dist., 22nd, 25th
Ryan, James J., 2nd Dist., 60th-69th
Ryan, James L., 33rd Dist., 31st
Ryan, James W., 13th Dist., 49th-52nd
Ryan, John G., 13th Dist., 58th-69th; 25th Dist., 70th-73rd
Ryan, Norman H., 85th Dist., 27th
Ryan, Robert L., Jr., 79th Dist., 92nd
Ryan, Thomas J., Jr., 43rd Dist., 82nd
Ryberg, Charles J., 21st Dist., 47th
Ryder, Tom, 97th Dist., 83rd-92nd
Saal, George L., 30th Dist., 69th; 46th Dist., 70th, 73rd, 75th
Sage, John D., 21st Dist., 27th
Sakowicz, Al, 15th Dist., 70th
Salisbury, Albert, 32nd Dist., 62nd-65th
Salmans, G. W., 18th Dist., 40th
Salter, Paul D., 24th Dist., 29th
Saltiel, Edward P., 31st Dist., 59th-63rd
Saltonstall, Samuel R., 37th Dist., 24th, 26th
Saltsman, Donald L., 46th Dist., 82nd; 92nd Dist., 83rd-89th
Salvi, Al, 52nd Dist., 88th, 89th
Samford, Leonard F., 44th Dist., 63rd-65th
Sams, Thomas H., 5th Dist., 19th
Samuel, Absalom M., 37th Dist., 31st
Samuelson, Charles A., 35th Dist., 41st, 42nd; 33rd Dist., 43rd
Sanborn, David, 40th Dist., 17th
Sanders, Omer, 74th
Sandquist, Elroy C., 25th Dist., 59th-65th, 67th-69th; 13th Dist., 70th-73rd, 75th, 76th
Sandquist, Elroy C., Jr., 13th Dist., 80th-82nd
Sandro, Joseph P., 5th Dist., 71st
Sanford, Patrick H., 68th Dist., 27th
Sangmeister, George E., 42nd Dist., 78th, 79th
Sans, Thomas M., 5th Dist., 17th

514

Santiago, Miguel A., 9th Dist., 86th, 87th; 3rd Dist., 88th-90th
Santry, Edward M., 3rd Dist., 49th
Saperstein, Esther, 8th Dist., 70th-73rd; 74th
Sargent, Porter, 51st Dist., 19th
Satterthwaite, Helen F., 52nd Dist., 79th-82nd; 103rd Dist., 83rd-87th
Saum, Claude N., 20th Dist., 54th
Savage, Amos, 15th Dist., 28th
Savage, John W., 36th Dist., 31st
Saviano, Angelo "Skip", 77th Dist., 88th-92nd
Savickas, Frank D., 27th Dist., 75th, 76th
Sawyer, C. B., 20th Dist., 52nd-54th
Sawyer, John Y., 7th
Sawyer, Lewis M., 23rd Dist., 35th
Sawyer, Thomas S., 16th Dist., 28th
Sawyers, J. D., 37th Dist., 35th
Sayler, Walter, 11th Dist., 40th
Sayre, Edward, 39th Dist., 16th
Scaife, William, 17th Dist., 37th
Scanlan, William M., 39th Dist., 46th-52nd
Scanlon, John F., 4th Dist., 28th
Scarborough, George, 10th
Scarborough, Henry F., 36th Dist., 56th-65th
Scariano, Anthony, 1st Dist., 70th-73rd; 74th; 8th Dist., 75th-77th
Scarlett, Bartley, 33rd Dist., 31st
Schaefer, Charles Ed., 38th Dist., 65th-67th, 69th; 52nd Dist., 70th-73rd; 74th; 53rd Dist., 75th
Schaefer, Peter P., 24th Dist., 44th, 45th
Schaffer, Simon, 13th Dist., 39th
Schakowsky, Janice D., 4th Dist., 86th, 87th; 18th Dist., 88th-90th
Scharlau, Charles E., 9th Dist., 34th, 35th
Schaumleffel, Sam, 32nd Dist., 61st-67th
Scheel, John, 12th Dist., 21st
Schermerhorn, Charles, 45th Dist., 45th
Schisler, Gale, 46th Dist., 76th, 77th; 48th Dist., 78th-81st
Schlagenhauf, Wm., 37th Dist., 41st, 42nd; 36th Dist., 43rd
Schlessinger, J. J., 11th Dist., 34th
Schlickman, Eugene F., 74th; 3rd Dist., 75th-77th; 4th Dist., 78th-81st
Schmitz, Timothy L., 42nd Dist., 91st, 92nd
Schnackenberg, Elmer J., 13th Dist., 48th, 53rd-63rd
Schneider, Edward, 13th Dist., 65th-69th; 25th Dist., 70th-73rd
Schneider, J. Glenn, 38th Dist., 77th; 41st Dist., 78th-82nd
Schneider, John J., 33rd Dist., 35th, 36th
Schnipper, Martin, 49th Dist., 43rd
Schoenberg, Jeffrey M., 56th Dist., 87th; 58th Dist., 88th-92nd
Schoeberlein, Allen L., 35th Dist., 73rd; 36th Dist., 75th-77th; 39th Dist., 78th-81st
Schoeninger, William J., 74th; 12th Dist., 75th
Schoenwald, Frank E., 13th Dist., 35th
Schofield, John, 18th Dist., 22nd
Scholes, Robert, 18th Dist., 49th, 53rd-56th
Schraeder, Frank J., 74th
Schraeder, Fred J., 74th, 46th Dist., 78th, 79th, 81st, 82nd
Schubert, Ernest S., 11th Dist., 39th, 40th
Schubert, Henry F., 11th Dist., 46th-50th
Schuemann, Bertrand C., 33rd Dist., 63rd
Schuler, Leon M., 14th Dist., 61st-69th; 35th Dist., 70th
Schultz, Herman E., 3rd Dist., 50th
Schumacher, Charles A., 19th Dist., 44th-46th
Schuneman, Calvin W., 37th Dist., 79th-82nd
Schuwerk, Wm. M., 48th Dist., 36th
Schwab, Joseph S., 11th Dist., 39th, 40th
Schwartz, Wm., 6th Dist., 27th
Sconce, John J., 30th Dist., 16th
Scott, Alfred G., 19th Dist., 31st
Scott, Charles L., 48th Dist., 46th-48th
Scott, Clarence P., 18th Dist., 58th-60th
Scott, Doug, 67th Dist., 89th-92nd
Scott, James K., 13th, 14th
Scott, John, 12th, 14th
Scott, J. W., 42nd Dist., 70th-73rd; 74th; 47th Dist., 75th
Scott, Levi, 34th Dist., 29th
Scott, Wm., 24th Dist., 28th
Scroggs, George, 30th Dist., 31st
Scrogin, Arthur J., 22nd Dist., 40th-42nd
Scudamore, Joseph B., 44th Dist., 36th
Scully, George F., Jr., 80th Dist., 90th-92nd
Scurlock, James M., 50th Dist., 33rd

Searcy, Earle B., 45th Dist., 52nd
Searcy, James B., 36th Dist., 41st
Searle, Clinton, 33rd Dist., 55th-59th, 61st-67th
Seawell, C. H., 42nd Dist., 35th, 38th
Seckman, Guy D., 50th Dist., 70th
Secrist, Conrad, 16th Dist., 30th, 31st
Sedgwick, Daniel W., 32nd Dist., 25th
Sedgwick, Westel W., 51st Dist., 23rd
Seehorn, Eli, 29th Dist., 19th
Seehorn, James M., 15th
Seif, Frank J., Jr., 31st Dist., 49th-52nd
Seiter, Henry, 49th Dist., 31st
Selby, Charles E., 39th Dist., 39th, 40th
Sellers, William W., 37th Dist., 25th
Semple, James, 8th-10th
Semrow, Harry H., 14th Dist., 70th-72nd
Senne, Henry C., 97th Dist., 27th; 7th Dist., 28th
Sensor, Edward F., 74th
Sevcik, Joseph G., 7th Dist., 75th-80th
Sexton, Austin O., 6th Dist., 30th-33rd
Sexton, Orval, 14th; 3rd Dist., 17th
Seyster, John C., 10th Dist, 33rd
Shade, Delbert O., 38th Dist., 66th
Shade, J. Norman, 30th Dist., 69th; 46th Dist., 70th, 75th, 76th
Shallenberger, M., 41st Dist., 20th
Shanahan, David E., 9th Dist., 39th-44th; 8th Dist., 45th; 9th Dist., 46th-59th
Shannon, Pierce, L., 31st Dist., 57th
Shapiro, David C., 35th Dist., 76th, 77th
Shapiro, Samuel H., 20th Dist., 65th, 67th-69th; 41st Dist., 70th, 71st
Sharon, Joseph, 30th Dist., 23rd, 24th
Sharp, George A., 34th Dist., 32nd
Sharp, James M., 9th Dist., 22nd; 4th Dist., 25th; 46th Dist., 34th
Sharp, James W., 4th Dist., 23rd
Sharp, John F., 49th Dist., 78th-81st
Sharp, Joseph L., 13th, 14th
Sharp, Milton M., 42nd Dist., 34th
Sharp, Wanda J., 7th Dist., 91st
Sharrock, James E., 41st Dist., 39th, 40th
Shaver, Harry L., 31st Dist., 47th, 48th
Shaw, Aaron, 9th Dist., 17th; 17th Dist., 22nd
Shaw, Edward J., 27th Dist., 69th; 19th Dist., 70th-73rd; 74th; 17th Dist., 75th-77th
Shaw, George B., 35th Dist., 64th
Shaw, Gilbert J., 28th Dist., 21st
Shaw, Homer E., 24th Dist., 46th
Shaw, James, 88th Dist., 27th; 11th Dist., 28th, 30th, 31st
Shaw, J. Henry, 36th Dist., 32nd; 34th Dist., 34th
Shaw, John, 3rd
Shaw, John W., 51st Dist., 44th
Shaw, William "Bill", 34th Dist., 83rd-87th
Shay, Richard F., 17th Dist., 42nd
Shea, Gerald W., 7th Dist., 75th-79th
Shearer, Fred B., 14th Dist., 51st, 52nd
Sheehy, John R., 37th Dist., 88th
Sheen, Daniel R., 18th Dist., 44th
Sheffield, Daniel A., 12th Dist., 34th
Shelby, Jonathan, 14th Dist., 24th
Sheldon, Harvey L., 35th Dist., 44th, 45th
Sheldon, Jarius C., 50th Dist., 27th
Shellody, Stephen B., 6th, 7th
Shelton, Samuel T., 69th Dist., 27th
Shephard, Henry A., 38th Dist., 46th, 48th-51st, 53rd
Shephard, John A., 47th Dist., 40th-42nd
Shepherd, Frank W., 14th Dist., 46th-48th
Shepherdson, Wm., 51st Dist., 18th
Shepley, Oliver, 3rd
Sheplor, Henry, 32nd Dist., 34th
Sheppard, Henry M., 60th Dist., 25th
Sheridan, Henry F., 3rd Dist., 30th
Sheridan, Millard J., 16th Dist., 28th
Sheridan, Redmond F., 4th Dist., 33rd
Sherman, Elijah B., 4th Dist., 30th, 31st
Sherman, Francis C., 14th, 15th; 54th Dist., 16th
Sherman, Frank T., 2nd Dist., 28th
Sherman, Lawrence Y., 28th Dist., 40th-42nd; 32nd Dist., 43rd
Sherman, R. E., 19th Dist., 48th
Sherrill, Henry, 81st Dist., 27th
Shields, James, 10th
Shields, William, 31st Dist., 18th
Shirley, Elijah S., 44th Dist., 37th

Shirley, John, 13th
Shirley, Wm. C., 21st Dist., 21st, 25th
Shope, Simeon P., 35th Dist., 23rd
Short, Charles F., 49th Dist., 51st, 52nd
Short, Daniel, 26th Dist., 21st
Short, John C., 49th Dist., 27th
Shriner, Harvey W., 42nd Dist., 44th
Shumpert, Walter, 21st Dist., 80th, 81st
Shumway, Dorice D., 15th
Shumway, E. B., 15th Dist., 32nd
Shup, Isaac M., 45th Dist., 34th
Shurtleff, Edward D., 8th Dist., 42nd-51st
Shurtz, Max Warren, 54th Dist., 78th
Sibley, Joseph, 37th Dist., 17th, 18th
Sickles, Hiram F., 47th Dist., 26th; 34th Dist., 28th
Sidell, John, 31st Dist., 29th
Sieben, Todd, 73rd Dist., 85th-87th
Siemer, Joseph B., 42nd Dist., 65th, 68th, 69th: 55th Dist., 70th
Silva, Sonia, 1st Dist., 90th, 91st
Sim, Wm., 4th; 5th
Simkins, Ray, 43rd Dist., 59th, 60th
Simmons, Arthur E., 6th Dist., 70th-73rd; 74th; 4th Dist., 75th-77th
Simmons, Erwin H., 42nd Dist., 32nd
Simms, Hall, 11th, 13th, 15th
Simms, W. Timothy, 34th Dist., 77th-82nd
Simon, Jeanne Hurley, 7th Dist., 70th, 71st
Simon, Paul, 47th Dist., 69th; 53rd Dist., 70th-72nd
Simons, Cyrus, 1st Dist., 17th
Simonson, James W., 21st Dist., 31st, 32nd
Simpson, Charles, 24th Dist., 65th, 66th
Simpson, Jonathan, 32nd Dist., 24th
Simpson, Robert, 10th Dist., 36th
Simpson, S. Elmer, 38th Dist., 47th, 48th
Sims, Isaac, 19th Dist., 75th-77th; 21st Dist., 78th
Sims, James, 3rd
Singer, Ezra G., 40th Dist., 16th
Singer, Horace M., 59th Dist., 25th
Singleton, James W., 35th Dist., 17th, 18th; 29th Dist., 22nd
Sinnett, Thomas P., 23rd Dist., 54th-59th
Sisler, George F., 74th
Sittig, Eugene A., 6th Dist., 30th, 34th
Sizemore, Oda M., 33rd Dist., 60th
Skaggs, Charles P., 51st Dist., 42nd
Skarda, Edward, 15th Dist., 56th-63rd
Skelly, William H., Jr., 7th Dist., 29th
Skinner, Cal, Jr., 33rd Dist., 78th-81st; 64th Dist., 88th-91st
Skinner, Mark, 15th
Skinner, Onias C., 35th Dist., 16th
Skyles, Charles M., 5th Dist., 64th-69th
Slade, Charles, 2nd, 5th
Slanker, Gideon D., 44th Dist., 37th
Slape, Michael, 55th Dist., 81st, 82nd; 110th Dist., 83rd
Slater, Drennan J., 6th Dist., 64th-69th
Slater, Howard R., 74th
Slater, Kent, 95th Dist., 84th, 85th
Sloan, John, 22nd Dist., 31st
Sloan, Wesley, 2nd Dist., 16th-18th, 20th
Sloan, William G., 49th Dist., 35th, 36th
Slocumb, Rigdon B., 4th, 6th, 15th
Slone, Ricca C., 92nd Dist., 90th-92nd
Sloss, Joseph H., 14th Dist., 21st
Small, Roy, 74th
Smejkal, Edward J., 17th Dist., 43rd-53rd
Smiley, Burr S., 35th Dist., 47th
Smiley, Samuel C., 47th Dist., 36th
Smith, A. H., 49th Dist., 59th
Smith, Alonzo B., 13th Dist., 31st
Smith, Benjamin L., 14th
Smith, Ben L., 30th Dist., 51st-53rd
Smith, Calvin, 74th; 24th Dist., 75th
Smith, Charles G., 43rd Dist., 28th
Smith, Dietrich C., 27th Dist., 30th
Smith, D. W., 35th Dist., 30th, 32nd
Smith, Edward, 9th-11th
Smith, Frank G., 19th Dist., 47th
Smith, Frank J., 4th Dist., 68th, 69th; 28th Dist., 70th-73rd; 74th; 23rd Dist., 75th-77th
Smith, Fred J., 3rd Dist., 63rd-68th
Smith, George, 11th
Smith, George A., 41st Dist., 29th
Smith, George F., 49th Dist., 45th

Smith, George H., 6th Dist., 60th, 61st
Smith, George W., 38th Dist., 35th
Smith, Guy W., 13th
Smith, Harry J., 5th Dist., 70th
Smith, Henry, 14th
Smith, Henry W., 38th Dist., 56th
Smith, Irv, 50th Dist., 82nd
Smith, Isaac, 47th Dist., 29th
Smith, J. Ward, 39th Dist., 61st-68th
Smith, James A., 18th Dist., 36th-38th
Smith, James H., 1st Dist., 23rd
Smith, John W., 26th Dist., 16th
Smith, Joseph, 14th
Smith, Joseph E., 2nd Dist., 30th
Smith, Leander, 48th Dist., 23rd, 24th
Smith, Margaret, 22nd Dist., 82nd
Smith, Michael K., 91st Dist., 89th-92nd
Smith, Mortimer W., 86th Dist., 27th
Smith, Morton G., 19th Dist., 42nd
Smith, Ora, 33rd Dist., 61st-65th
Smith, Orpheus W., 28th Dist., 51st
Smith, Peter F., 15th Dist., 47th-53rd
Smith, Ralph T., 47th Dist., 69th; 53rd Dist., 70th-73rd; 74th; 55th Dist., 75th, 76th
Smith, Robert, 10th, 11th
Smith, Robert W., 48th Dist, 22nd
Smith, Samuel, 4th
Smith, Theo. D., 13th Dist., 54th
Smith, Truman W., 45th Dist., 20th
Smith, Washington S., 29th Dist., 38th
Smith, Wm., 13th
Smith, William H., 46th Dist., 42nd
Smith, William M., 38th Dist., 25th, 26th; 63rd Dist., 27th
Smith, William S., 15th
Smith, W. S., 29th Dist., 37th
Smyth, Samuel M., 44th Dist., 39th
Snedeker, Orville A., 37th Dist., 38th; 47th Dist., 39th
Snell, Truman A., 38th Dist., 50th-52nd, 54th, 55th, 57th
Snigg, John C., 35th Dist., 31st
Snite, Frank J., 2nd Dist., 48th
Snow, Herman W., 27th Dist., 28th
Snyder, Frank P., 23rd Dist., 34th
Snyder, John F., 36th Dist., 31st
Snyder, William H., 19th Dist., 17th, 18th
Snyder, William H., Jr., 47th Dist., 38th; 49th Dist., 39th
Soderstrom, Carl W., 39th Dist., 67th-69th; 38th Dist., 70th-73rd; 74th; 40th Dist., 75th-77th; 45th Dist., 78th
Soderstrom, R. G., 39th Dist., 51st, 53rd-59th
Solitt, Oliver, 3rd Dist., 45th, 46th
Soliz, Juan M., 20th Dist., 84th
Solomon, Lewis, 21st Dist., 18th
Somerville, John A., 10th
Sommer, Keith P., 89th Dist., 91st, 92nd
Sonneman, Otto C., 38th Dist., 49th-54th
Sonnenschein, Henry, 9th Dist., 56th, 57th
Soto, Cynthia, 4th Dist., 92nd
Soule, Lewis, 17th Dist., 28th
Southworth, G. S., 8th Dist., 36th
Spafford, Dwight S., 19th Dist., 34th
Spangler, Stephen A., 75th Dist., 88th, 89th
Spann, William A., 51st Dist., 32nd
Sparks, David R., 41st Dist., 36th
Sparks, G. D. A., 45th Dist., 19th
Sparks, H. D., 40th Dist., 54th-61st, 63rd
Sparks, Thomas J., 27th Dist., 38th
Sparks, Wm. A. J., 13th Dist., 20th
Speakman, John W., 22nd Dist., 60th, 61st
Spellman, Thomas L., 31st Dist., 37th, 38th
Spencer, Henry H., 51st Dist., 31st
Spencer, M. W., 44th Dist., 39th
Spicer, Elijah H., 17th Dist., 29th
Spicer, Reuben H., 13th
Spiege, Hamlin L., 5th Dist., 42nd
Spink, Solomon L., 39th Dist., 24th
Spitler, Frank, 33rd Dist., 36th
Sprague, Arthur W., 7th Dist., 61st, 62nd, 67th-69th
Springer, John, 19th Dist., 34th
Springer, John T., 27th Dist., 23rd, 24th
Springer, John W., 38th Dist., 37th
Springer, Lewis B., 7th Dist., 53rd, 54th
Springer, Norbert G., 57th Dist., 75th-77th; 58th Dist., 78th
Springer, Wm. M., 43rd Dist., 27th
Sprinkle, Clarence E., 40th Dist., 68th, 69th
Stacey, William C., 45th Dist., 24th, 25th
Stack, Thomas J., 18th Dist., 58th
Stage, Napoleon B., 24th Dist., 22nd; 39th Dist., 25th

Talbott, Elisha H., 51st Dist., 26th
Talbott, H. C., 11th Dist., 22nd
Talbott, Prescott H., 10th Dist., 37th, 38th
Tanner, H. B., 74th
Tanner, T. B., 8th Dist., 19th
Tappan, Harmon V. A., 15th
Tate, Michael J. "Mike", 51st Dist., 82nd; 102nd Dist., 83rd-86th
Taubeneck, H. E., 45th Dist., 37th
Taylor, Abner, 3rd Dist., 34th
Taylor, Daniel C., 16th Dist., 33rd
Taylor, Edmond D., 7th, 8th
Taylor, Edward S., 61st Dist., 25th, 26th
Taylor, Fred P., 35th Dist., 34th
Taylor, Horace W., 9th Dist., 31st
Taylor, Ira, 35th Dist., 37th
Taylor, James B., 3rd Dist., 30th; 5th Dist., 33rd
Taylor, James C., 26th Dist., 76th-81st; 31st Dist., 83rd
Taylor, James C., 32nd Dist., 42nd
Taylor, John B., 3rd Dist., 31st
Taylor, John H., 1st Dist., 48th
Taylor, Johnathan F., 49th Dist., 35th
Taylor, Ninian R., 43rd Dist., 27th
Taylor, Paul, 42nd Dist., 63rd-68th
Taylor, Richard F., 48th Dist., 49th
Taylor, W. H., 30th Dist., 39th
Teefey, Dan, 50th Dist., 72nd, 73rd; 74th
Teefey, Ed, 30th Dist., 61st, 62nd
Teefey, John J., 36th Dist., 36th
Teel, H. V., 30th Dist., 54th-56th, 58th-60th
Teel, James A., 28th Dist., 39th
Teigland, Donald C., 33rd Dist., 64th
Telcser, Arthur A., 11th Dist., 75th-77th; 12th Dist., 78th-82nd
Telford, Matthew, 43rd Dist., 36th
Templeman, J. W., 46th Dist., 45th
Templeman, Richard H., 29th Dist., 33rd, 34th
Tenbrook, John, 39th Dist., 23rd
Tenhouse, Art, 96th Dist., 86th-92nd
Tenney, Charles F., 30th Dist., 32nd
Tenny, Boynton, 38th Dist., 23rd
Terpening, Henry L., 28th Dist., 36th, 37th
Terrill, Henry, 32nd Dist., 46th, 47th
Terry, Thos. S., 46th Dist., 22nd
Terzich, Robert M., 27th Dist., 77th; 25th Dist., 78th-82nd; 48th Dist., 83rd-86th
Thiem, George, 74th
Thiem, Robert, 6th Dist., 29th
Thiemann, William, 7th Dist., 37th-41st
Thomas, Cheney, 11th
Thomas, Claude R., 2nd Dist., 58th-61st
Thomas, Horace H., 6th Dist., 31st, 32nd
Thomas, James D., 1st
Thomas, Jesse B., Jr., 9th
Thomas, John, 11th
Thomas, John, 15th Dist., 23rd, 24th; 49th Dist., 28th, 29th
Thomas, John E., 49th Dist., 40th
Thomas, J. W. E., 2nd Dist., 30th; 3rd Dist., 33rd, 34th
Thomas, Joseph, 50th Dist., 18th
Thomas, Richard S., 25th Dist., 16th
Thomas, Samuel, 15th
Thomas, Samuel R., 48th Dist., 51st, 52nd
Thomas, William, 15th; 24th Dist., 17th
Thomason, Arnold, 32nd Dist., 31st
Thomason, John W., 42nd Dist., 49th-51st
Thompson, Abraham C., 26th Dist., 48th
Thompson, Amos, 13th-15th; 25th Dist., 25th
Thompson, Andrew J., 39th Dist., 29th
Thompson, Bradford F., 36th Dist., 26th
Thompson, Frank G., 46th Dist., 57th
Thompson, H. C., 34th Dist., 33rd
Thompson, James, 8th Dist., 32nd
Thompson, John, 9th
Thompson, John M., 25th Dist., 39th
Thompson, John R., 48th Dist., 56th-61st
Thompson, John W., 8th Dist., 75th-77th
Thompson, R. R., 12th Dist., 47th-49th
Thompson, Robert L., 12th Dist., 76th, 77th; 13th Dist., 78th
Thompson, Samuel G., 10th
Thompson, Samuel H., 26th Dist., 33rd
Thompson, Samuel H., 36th Dist., 50th
Thompson, W. H., 1st Dist., 30th, 31st
Thompson, William P., 15th Dist., 31st

Thon, William G., 23rd Dist., 49th-68th
Thornton, Anthony, 33rd Dist., 17th
Thornton, Stephen Y., 25th Dist., 28th, 29th
Thornton, Thomas J., 44th Dist., 60th-69th
Thornton, Wm. F., 11th
Thornton, W. J., 36th Dist., 66th
Thorp, Amos C., 59th Dist., 23rd
Thorton, Hiram W., 12th
Thorton, James T., 20th Dist., 29th, 32nd; 25th Dist., 33rd
Threlkeld, Thomas, 12th
Tibbets, Nathaniel W., 37th Dist., 43rd, 44th
Tice, Frank N., 12th Dist., 30th-32nd
Tice, Homer J., 34th Dist., 37th, 38th; 30th Dist., 43rd, 47th-49th, 51st-57th
Tierney, Richard, 42nd Dist., 30th
Tilson, John, 37th Dist., 28th
Tilton, George R., 31st Dist., 36th
Tincher, John L., 39th Dist., 24th
Tindall, George M., 35th Dist., 45th
Tippitt, Thomas, 45th Dist., 39th, 41st, 42nd; 46th Dist., 43rd, 44th, 46th
Tipsword, Roland F., 52nd Dist., 75th-77th; 51st Dist., 78th-80th
Tisdel, Clark J., 7th Dist., 40th
Tompkins, Squire F., 41st Dist., 49th
Ton, Cornelius J., 13th Dist., 45th, 46th
Tontz, Jones, 41st Dist., 32nd, 34th
Topinka, Judy Baar, 7th Dist., 82nd; 43rd Dist., 83rd
Topping, Harry L., 20th Dist., 59th-68th
Torrence, Andrew A., 3rd Dist., 61st
Torrence, Caleb, 40th Dist., 40th
Totten, Donald L., 3rd Dist., 78th-81st
Touhy, John P., 27th Dist., 66th-69th; 18th Dist., 70th-73rd; 74th; 19th Dist., 75th, 76th
Tourtillott, Albert T., 35th Dist., 47th, 51st, 52nd, 54th
Townsend, Halsted S., 51st Dist., 21st; 89th Dist., 27th
Townsend, James J., 1st Dist., 37th
Towse, Watson A., 38th Dist., 36th
Tracy, Carter, 35th Dist., 31st
Trail, Daniel, 39th Dist., 20th
Trail, Xerxes F., 18th Dist., 16th
Trammell, Wesley, 47th Dist., 31st
Trandel, Joseph A. G., 27th Dist., 49th, 50th, 52nd, 53rd, 55th, 56th
Trapp, Albert H., 12th Dist., 19th
Trautmann, Wm. E., 49th Dist., 41st-44th
Travers, Claude D., 48th Dist., 64th-69th
Traylor, Daniel C., 16th Dist., 30th
Traynor, Stuart J., 52nd Dist., 72nd, 73rd
Trench, James P., 23rd Dist., 35th, 36th
Trexler, David, 45th Dist., 34th
Trimarco, Tony, 17th Dist., 47th, 48th
Trimble, A. H., 57th Dist., 27th
Trotier, Joseph, 3rd
Trotter, Donne E., 25th Dist., 85th-87th
Trotter, John, 20th Dist., 54th, 55th
Trousdale, Fletcher A., 51st Dist., 40th
Trowbridge, Irving H., 27th Dist., 40th, 41st
Trower, Thomas B., 9th
Troy, Daniel, 12th
Troyer, William H., 21st Dist., 44th-46th
True, James N., 39th Dist., 25th
Truedell, Bernard H., 12th Dist., 30th, 31st
Truitt, James M., 34th Dist., 28th
Trumbull, Lyman, 12th
Tucker, Cyrus J., 28th Dist., 47th, 48th
Tucker, James, 15th
Tuerk, Fred J., 43rd Dist., 76th, 77th; 46th Dist., 78th-82nd; 93rd Dist., 83rd-85th
Tumpach, Joseph, 74th; 38th Dist., 75th
Tunnell, Calvin, 9th, 14th
Turley, John S., 10th, 14th
Turnbaugh, John D., 12th Dist., 49th
Turnbull, Gilbert, 42nd Dist., 16th
Turner, Arthur L., 46th Dist., 82nd; 18th Dist., 83rd-87th; 9th Dist., 88th-92nd
Turner, Charles M., 16th Dist., 50th-60th
Turner, Edward W., 15th
Turner, Ernest W., 29th Dist., 53rd-56th
Turner, Forest, 10th Dist., 29th
Turner, George T., 40th Dist., 43rd
Turner, Giles H., 22nd Dist., 18th
Turner, Horace, 13th
Turner, James B., 3rd Dist., 23rd
Turner, J. M., 34th Dist., 59th-61st

Turner, James W., 7th Dist., 43rd
Turner, John W., 90th Dist., 88th-92nd
Turner, Sheadrick B., 1st Dist., 49th, 51st-55th
Turner, Thomas J., 52nd Dist., 19th; 90th Dist., 27th
Turney, Daniel, 10th, 11th, 12th
Turney, Isaiah, 27th Dist., 22nd
Turney, James, 3rd, 9th
Turney, John, 6th
Tuttle, Oral P., 51st Dist., 49th, 50th
Tyres, William J., 14th Dist., 25th
Tyler, Ira, 35th Dist., 35th, 36th
Tyler, John H., 29th Dist., 29th, 31st
Tyler, S. H., 37th Dist., 16th
Tyner, Wm., 31st Dist., 20th
Tyrell, Hiram, 10th Dist., 30th
Tyron, Charles H., 8th Dist., 33rd
Ufkes, LeRoy, 95th Dist., 85th
Underwood, David J., 51st Dist., 43rd
Underwood, John L., 38th Dist., 32nd
Underwood, Joseph B., 15th Dist., 23rd
Underwood, William H., 15th
Unland, Ernest F., 20th Dist., 34th
Upchurch, Herbert L., 50th Dist., 62nd-64th
Updegraff, J., 18th Dist., 21st
Updike, Pierson B., 40th Dist., 36th
Updyke, William, 45th Dist., 33rd
Uppendahl, John H., 41st Dist., 42nd; 24th Dist., 43rd
Upton, Edward J., 21st Dist., 58th, 59th
Utiger, Robert D., 41st Dist., 33rd
Utter, Henry, 1st, 4th, 5th
Vacco, Carmen, 17th Dist., 60th, 61st
Vadalabene, Sam M., 53rd Dist., 75th, 76th
Vance, Archie N., 22nd Dist., 51st
Vance, E. M., 32nd Dist., 29th
Vance, P. C., 13th
Van der Vries, Bernice T., 7th Dist., 59th-69th
Vandeveer, Horatio M., 13th; 20th Dist., 22nd
Vandeventer, Jacob, 9th
Vandeventer, William L., 36th Dist., 30th
VanDuser, Alfred L., 11th Dist., 50th
Van Duyne, LeRoy, 42nd Dist., 79th-82nd; 83rd Dist., 83rd-86th
Van Hooser, Arthur, 51st Dist., 62nd
Van Norman, Harry C., 2nd Dist., 53rd-55th
Van Praag, Solomon, 3rd Dist., 37th
Varley, John S., 2nd Dist., 41st
Varnell, George H., 43rd Dist., 33rd, 34th
Vasey, Richardson, 39th Dist., 31st
Vaughan, Schuyler B., 47th Dist., 55th-57th, 61st
Vaughey, Alexander, 17th Dist., 32nd, 33rd
Vaughn, Samuel, 38th Dist., 42nd
Vedder, F. P., 14th
Veile, Joseph, 49th Dist., 31st, 32nd, 35th
Venard, Algernon S., 58th Dist., 23rd
Vennum, Thomas, 64th Dist., 27th
Venor, Zenas H., 16th Dist., 16th
Verhines, W. O., 51st Dist., 65th, 66th, 68th, 69th
Vermilyea, Valentine, 44th Dist., 21st, 22nd
Vicars, William, 16th Dist., 59th-63rd
Vice, Frank, Jr., 46th Dist., 50th-52nd
Vickers, Alonzo K., 51st Dist., 35th
Vickers, James E., 8th Dist., 47th, 49th, 50th, 51st
Vincent, John A., 39th Dist., 41st
Vineyard, Philip, 13th, 14th
Vinson, Sam, 44th Dist., 80th-82nd; 90th Dist., 83rd, 84th
Vinton, George W., 21st Dist., 37th
Virden, Archibald L., 40th Dist., 28th
Virkus, Frederick A., 7th Dist., 63rd, 64th
Vitek, John M., 29th Dist., 72nd, 73rd; 74th; 23rd Dist., 79th-82nd; 21st Dist., 83rd, 84th
Vocke, Wm., 97th Dist., 27th
Volz, Albert F., 7th Dist., 50th-52nd
VonBoeckman, James, 74th; 46th Dist., 77th; 45th Dist., 78th-81st
Voris, Charles, 18th Dist., 25th
Voris, Francis, 10th
Voss, Arno, 6th Dist., 30th
Vursell, Chas. W., 42nd Dist., 49th
Waddell, R. Bruce, 33rd Dist., 76th-81st
Wagner, Jacob, 14th
Wagner, Rollo M., 36th Dist., 50th, 51st
Wait, Ronald A., 64th Dist., 83rd-87th; 68th Dist., 89th-92nd
Waite, George, 8th Dist., 35th
Waite, Horace F., 97th Dist., 27th

Wakefield, John A., 4th
Wakeman, Thaddeus B., 54th Dist., 23rd, 25th
Walker, A. W., 51st Dist., 43rd
Walker, Charles A., 21st Dist., 23rd
Walker, Claude A., 4th Dist., 70th-73rd
Walker, Frank H., 46th Dist., 67th
Walker, George, 37th Dist., 16th; 31st Dist., 19th
Walker, George P., 24th Dist., 30th
Walker, Henry F., 14th Dist., 33rd
Walker, Isaac H., 16th Dist., 22nd
Walker, Isaac P., 11th
Walker, Jack E., 1st Dist., 70th-73rd; 8th Dist., 75th, 76th
Walker, James, 10th
Walker, James R., 48th Dist., 36th
Walker, John L., 41st Dist, 57th, 58th
Walker, Leonidas, 46th Dist., 28th
Walker, M. R., 22nd Dist., 63rd-69th
Walker, Newton, 11th
Walker, Richard, 10th
Walker, Samuel, 1st, 4th
Wall, Hampton W., 40th Dist., 30th, 31st
Wall, John F., 29th Dist., 73rd; 23rd Dist., 75th-80th
Wall, Patrick J., 1st Dist., 42nd; 3rd Dist., 47th
Wallace, Hugh, 15th
Wallace, Lew, 34th Dist., 61st
Wallace, William H., 32nd Dist., 38th; 40th Dist., 39th
Wallace, William O., 40th Dist., 43rd
Walleck, Christian R., 9th Dist., 39th, 40th
Waller, Elbert, 44th Dist., 54th-58th, 61st
Waller, George B., 24th Dist., 16th
Walsh, David W., 5th Dist., 33rd
Walsh, James, 1st Dist., 36th
Walsh, Jeremiah F., 39th Dist., 59th
Walsh, John P., 3rd Dist., 44th-50th
Walsh, Richard A., 4th Dist., 73rd; 74th; 2nd Dist., 75th-77th; 5th Dist., 78th
Walsh, Robert V., 56th Dist., 73rd; 74th; 54th Dist., 80th
Walsh, T. J., 3rd Dist., 31st
Walsh, Thomas J., 75th Dist., 87th; 44th Dist., 88th
Walsh, William D., 54th Dist., 72nd, 73rd; 74th; 5th Dist., 75th-77th; 6th Dist., 78th-81st
Walters, John W., 37th Dist., 50th-52nd
Walters, Louis E., 47th Dist., 42nd
Walters, Robert J., 55th Dist., 77th; 56th Dist., 78th
Waltrip, W. Henry, 34th Dist., 66th, 67th
Walz, Edward, 27th Dist., 50th-52nd
Wanless, Fred W., 45th Dist., 51st
Ward, Harry B., 48th Dist., 40th
Ward, John, 5th Dist., 24th
Ward, Wm. M., 37th Dist., 35th
Warder, Walter, 50th Dist., 37th, 38th
Warder, William H., 50th Dist., 41st, 42nd
Wardlaw, Andrew, 15th
Warfield, William J., 7th Dist., 56th-63rd
Warman, Edward A., 74th; 4th Dist., 75th, 76th
Warner, John, 38th Dist., 24th
Warner, Wilder W., 21st Dist., 28th
Warren, Alvin, 35th Dist., 55th
Warren, George E., 40th Dist., 31st
Warren, Harland D., 38th Dist., 73rd
Warren, Henry L., 28th Dist., 25th
Warren, James P., 45th Dist., 38th
Warren, Julius M., 14th; 50th Dist., 17th
Washburn, George E., 6th Dist., 28th
Washburn, James M., 6th Dist., 23rd; 47th Dist., 30th
Washburn, James R., 42nd Dist., 75th-77th; 43rd Dist., 78th, 79th
Washington, Genoa, 22nd Dist., 75th-77th
Washington, Harold, 74th; 26th Dist., 75th-79th
Washington, Jerry, 24th Dist., 84th
Wasson, John N., 47th Dist., 29th
Watercott, Julius, 20th Dist., 34th
Waterloo, N. A., 23rd Dist., 58th
Waters, George T., 12th
Waters, Geo. W., 3rd Dist., 27th
Waters, Louis H., 32nd Dist., 19th
Wathier, Charles A., 1st Dist., 40th
Watkins, E. B., 51st Dist., 30th
Watkins, Joseph E., 7th, 10th
Watkins, Warren C., 63rd Dist., 27th
Watkins, Wm., 16th Dist., 23rd
Watson, Frank C., 55th Dist., 81st, 82nd
Watson, James A., 48th Dist., 47th-52nd
Watson, James H., 43rd Dist., 37th, 38th
Watson, Samuel H., 46th Dist., 39th

Watson, William D., 15th; 11th Dist., 18th
Watt, James H., 6th Dist., 20th
Wayland, William E., 22nd Dist., 65th
Wayman, William, 1st Dist., 28th
Weare, William W., 19th Dist., 43rd
Weatherford, Wm., 13th
Weaver, Michael L. "Mike", 106th Dist., 84th-90th
Weaver, Stanley B., 48th Dist., 76th
Weaver, Wm. H., 34th Dist., 34th
Webb, Daniel R., 46th Dist., 40th
Webb, Edwin B., 9th-12th
Webb, H. Watson, 1st Dist., 27th
Webb, Henry L., 4th, 11th
Webb, Henry W., 1st Dist., 24th
Webb, M. N., 51st Dist., 37th
Weber, Alanson P., 45th Dist., 25th
Weber, Bernard F., 7th Dist., 31st, 32nd
Weber, Charles H., 6th Dist., 53rd-56th, 59th-69th
Weber, Dwight J., 20th Dist., 28th
Weber, Joseph A., 6th Dist., 48th-50th
Weber, Wm. B., 30th Dist., 34th
Webster, Cyrus W., 8th Dist., 22nd
Webster, Ezra G., 26th Dist., 28th
Webster, Irvin D., 36th Dist., 43rd, 44th
Weckler, Frederick S., 47th Dist., 38th
Wedig, John, 41st Dist., 35th
Weedon, William W., 40th Dist., 37th
Weeks, Calvin T., 11th Dist., 55th, 56th, 60th
Weigler, George H., 41st Dist., 29th
Weinheimer, Henry, 41st Dist., 28th
Weinshenker, Samuel E., 2nd Dist., 51st, 52nd
Weir, Wm. H., 27th Dist., 34th
Weisbrod, Harry I., 19th Dist., 54th
Weiss, William F., 8th Dist., 52nd-55th
Welborn, George B., 46th Dist., 46th, 47th
Welch, Andrew, 17th Dist., 33rd, 34th
Weldon, Lawrence, 36th Dist., 22nd
Welker, Will P., 40th Dist., 62nd-65th, 67th, 68th
Weller, Jerry, 85th Dist., 86th, 87th; 75th Dist., 88th
Wellinghoff, J. L., 49th Dist., 61st-64th
Wells, Albert W., 35th Dist., 35th, 36th
Wells, James A., 33rd Dist., 50th, 51st
Wells, John W., 49th Dist., 30th
Welsh, Frank C., 34th Dist., 66th
Welsh, John H., 19th Dist., 32nd; 25th Dist., 33rd
Welsh, Raymond J., Jr., 4th Dist., 70th-73rd; 74th; 2nd Dist., 77th
Welters, Edward A., 1st Dist., 64th, 65th
Wendell, A., 9th Dist., 33rd
Wendell, George, 32nd Dist., 39th
Wendt, Kenneth R., 31st Dist., 68th, 69th; 10th Dist., 70th-72nd
Wenger, Elias, 37th Dist., 23rd
Wennlund, Larry, 84th Dist., 85th-87th; 38th Dist., 88th, 89th
Wentworth, Moses J., 1st Dist., 29th-31st
Werdell, John C., 31st Dist., 43rd-47th
Werts, Everett L., 33rd Dist., 45th, 48th, 51st
Wessels, Pennie von Bergen, 73rd Dist., 88th
West, Amos S., 12th
West, Benjamin, 15th
West, Emanuel J., 3rd
West, Owen B., 43rd Dist., 49th-54th
West, Simeon H., 28th Dist., 33rd, 34th
Westbrook, W. B., 51st Dist., 63rd-67th
Westcott, John W., 12th Dist., 23rd
Westfall, E. K., 23rd Dist., 28th, 30th
Weston, Sewell B., 19th Dist., 39th
Wetherbee, Charles A., 35th Dist., 43rd
Weyand, Melvin A., 45th Dist., 72nd
Whalen, Peter J., 25th Dist., 70th-73rd; 74th
Wheat, Alexander E., 28th Dist., 23rd
Wheat, Almeron, 13th
Wheaton, Warren L., 50th Dist., 16th
Wheelan, Henry L., 33rd Dist., 46th, 47th
Wheeler, Alanson K., 44th Dist., 19th
Wheeler, Alpheus, 10th, 12th
Wheeler, J. A., 39th Dist., 42nd; 45th Dist., 43rd
Wheeler, Jacob, 36th Dist., 30th, 31st
Wheeler, Rollin, 51st Dist., 20th
Wheelock, William W., 1st Dist., 38th
Whitaker, Charles H., 23rd Dist., 30th
Whitaker, James M., 49th Dist., 30th
Whitaker, John, 4th, 6th, 7th
Whitcomb, Lott, 13th

White, Charles A., 49th Dist., 46th
White, David C., 32nd Dist., 40th, 41st
White, Henry J., 35th Dist., 60th-64th
White, James, 14th
White, James M., 10th Dist., 65th
White, Jesse C., Jr., 13th Dist., 79th, 81st, 82nd; 8th Dist., 83rd-87th
White, John, 13th-15th
White, John H., 12th Dist., 32nd
White, John L., 22nd Dist., 39th
White, John W., 19th Dist., 35th-37th; 31st Dist., 39th
White, Joshua, 50th Dist., 21st
White, Martin, 12th
White, Samuel, 25th Dist., 36th, 37th
Whiteacre, Samuel, 1st
Whiteaker, Hall, 50th Dist., 47th
Whitehead, Edward A., 7th Dist., 36th, 37th
Whiteley, Robert, 38th Dist., 54th-57th
Whiteman, Henry M., 24th Dist., 32nd
Whiteside, James A., 3rd, 4th, 6th-8th
Whiteside, John D., 7th-9th, 14th
Whiteside, Samuel, 1st
Whiting, John E., 9th Dist., 20th
Whiting, Lorenzo D., 45th Dist., 26th
Whitney, Langley A., 39th Dist., 38th
Whitney, William M., 82nd Dist., 27th
Whittemore, Henry C., 17th Dist., 34th
Whitten, Easten, 10th, 13th
Wick, Bernard, 49th Dist., 28th
Wicker, Charles G., 2nd Dist., 28th
Wickizer, John H., 38th Dist., 20th
Widen, Raphael, 2nd, 3rd
Widmaier, Charles F., 4th Dist., 40th
Widmer, Harold W., 12th Dist., 68th, 69th; 34th Dist., 70th-72nd
Wightman, George F., 20th Dist., 31st
Wike, Scott, 24th Dist., 23rd, 24th
Wikoff, Virgil C., 52nd Dist., 80th-82nd
Wiktorski, Chester R., Jr., 15th Dist., 70th-73rd; 74th; 15th Dist., 75th
Wilbanks, John, 6th Dist., 18th
Wilbanks, Robt. A. D., 46th Dist., 32nd
Wilcox, Charles C., 14th, 15th
Wilcox, Isaac D., 1st
Wilcox, Joseph L., 35th Dist., 29th
Wilderman, Alonzo S., 49th Dist., 30th
Wiley, Samuel C., 44th Dist., 26th; 23rd Dist., 33rd, 34th
Wilk, William F., 9th Dist., 36th, 37th
Wilke, Fred, 15th Dist., 36th-38th
Wilkening, Conrad, 15th Dist., 38th
Wilkerson, James H., 13th Dist., 43rd
Wilkins, Isaac, 17th Dist., 20th
Wilkinson, Fred, 34th Dist., 35th, 37th
Wilkinson, W. S., 14th
Wilkinson, William R., 44th Dist., 30th
Will, Conrad, 2nd-5th
Willard, Nathan, 18th Dist., 20th
Willer, Anne, 6th Dist., 79th-81st
Willet, Reuben W., 17th Dist., 36th
Willet, Charles K., 35th Dist., 66th-69th; 40th Dist., 70th-73rd
Williams, Archibald, 10th, 11th
Williams, Gale, 58th Dist., 72nd, 73rd; 59th Dist., 75th-77th
Williams, Harry L., 1st Dist., 58th-60th
Williams, Henry N., 5th Dist., 23rd
Williams, Isaac, 14th, 15th
Williams, Jack B., 5th Dist., 78th-81st
Williams, John C., 6th Dist., 44th
Williams, Nathan, 87th Dist., 27th
Williams, Paul L., 24th Dist., 85th-87th
Williams, Samuel A., 44th Dist., 40th
Williams, Thomas J., 46th Dist., 30th
Williams, Thomas S., 42nd Dist., 41st
Williams, Walter W., 50th Dist., 44th
Williams, Wesley C., 24th Dist., 35th
Williams, William G., 45th Dist., 36th
Williamson, Clarence, 29th Dist., 81st
Williamson, Francis E., 24th Dist., 48th, 49th, 53rd
Williamson, Joseph, 17th Dist., 18th
Williamson, Linda, 52nd Dist., 84th-86th
Williamson, Rollin S., 97th Dist., 27th
Williamson, William, 11th, 15th
Williford, Edward L., 42nd Dist., 36th
Willis, Jonathan C., 2nd Dist., 26th

Williston, George A., 31st Dist., 52nd-54th, 62nd-65th
Willits, Thomas, 42nd Dist., 17th
Willoughby, F. A., 22nd Dist., 33rd
Wilmarth, Homer, 54th Dist., 18th
Wilson, Alexander, 50th Dist., 55th-57th
Wilson, Alonzo E., 41st Dist., 44th
Wilson, Benjamin M., 2nd Dist., 31st
Wilson, D., 46th Dist., 17th
Wilson, Elmer C., 20th Dist., 56th-58th
Wilson, Emmet F., 10th Dist., 54th, 56th
Wilson, Felix E., 28th Dist., 63rd, 64th, 66th
Wilson, Frank B., 10th Dist., 58th-60th
Wilson, Frank J., 25th Dist., 44th, 46th
Wilson, George C., 16th Dist., 29th
Wilson, George H., 36th Dist., 46th-49th
Wilson, George W., 49th Dist., 16th
Wilson, George W., 36th Dist., 68th, 69th
Wilson, H. Clay, 39th Dist., 38th
Wilson, Harry, 44th Dist., 49th-53rd
Wilson, Harry W., 45th Dist., 46th
Wilson, James B., 38th Dist., 35th
Wilson, James P., 10th Dist., 35th, 37th, 42nd, 43rd
Wilson, John A., 6th Dist., 18th; 8th Dist., 20th
Wilson, Kenneth E., 5th Dist., 69th; 21st Dist., 70th-73rd
Wilson, Lite, 53rd Dist., 16th
Wilson, R. B. M., 39th Dist., 21st
Wilson, Richard A., 32nd Dist., 29th
Wilson, Robert E., 6th Dist., 45th-49th, 51st, 52nd
Wilson, Robert J., 37th Dist., 56th, 57th, 58th
Wilson, Robert L., 10th
Wilson, Samuel F., 32nd Dist., 35th
Wilson, Thomas A., 44th Dist., 35th
Wilson, Ulysses A., 28th Dist., 39th, 40th
Wilson, Wm., 12th, 13th
Winchester, Robert C., 59th Dist., 79th-82nd; 118th Dist.,
    83rd
Windle, Thomas, 27th Dist., 29th
Winkel, Rick, 103rd Dist., 89th-92nd
Winslow, Edward M., 10th Dist., 34th
Winstanley, Thomas, 18th Dist., 18th
Winston, Claiborne, 50th Dist., 29th
Winter, George B., 16th Dist., 32nd
Winter, John F., 28th Dist., 29th, 30th
Winters, Dave, 69th Dist., 89th-92nd
Winters, J. C., 22nd Dist., 17th
Winthrop, Dempsey, 44th Dist., 47th
Wirsing, David A., 70th Dist., 88th-92nd
Wisner, Frank J., 5th Dist., 36th
Wist, Edward, 13th
Wite, Randal H., 2nd Dist., 32nd
Withers, Henry C., 23rd Dist., 25th
Witt, Franklin, 10th
Witt, George W., 36th Dist., 42nd; 38th Dist., 44th, 45th
Wittmond, Carl H., 36th Dist., 69th; 49th Dist., 70th-
    73rd; 74th
Wiwi, Philip, 33rd Dist., 37th, 38th
Wojcik, Kathleen L. "Kay", 45th Dist., 83rd-92nd
Wolbank, Edward W., 11th Dist., 73rd; 74th; 12th Dist.,
    75th, 76th
Wolf, David, 35th Dist., 18th
Wolf, Frank C., 19th Dist., 68th, 69th; 30th Dist., 70th-
    73rd; 74th; 21st Dist., 75th-77th
Wolf, Jacob John, 14th Dist., 75th-77th; 17th Dist., 78th,
    80th-82nd
Wolf, Sam W., 56th Dist., 79th, 81st, 82nd; 111th Dist.,
    83rd-87th
Wolfe, Bernard B., 74th; 15th Dist., 75th-78th
Wollard, James B., 14th
Wombacher, G. M., 49th Dist., 42nd
Wood, Benson, 33rd Dist., 28th
Wood, Charles H., 42nd Dist., 24th
Wood, Charles L., 47th Dist., 40th; 46th Dist., 48th, 49th,
    55th, 56th
Wood, Corinne G., 59th Dist., 90th
Wood, Daniel, 9th-11th
Wood, Erwin E., 5th Dist., 33rd
Wood, Hannibal P., 22nd Dist., 32nd
Wood, Henry, 13th Dist., 32nd; 17th Dist., 33rd
Wood, James H., 45th Dist., 41st
Wood, John D., 7th Dist., 21st
Wood, John T., 14th
Wood, Latham A., 26th Dist., 30th
Wood, Warren L., 41st Dist., 59th-69th; 37th Dist., 70th-
    73rd
Woodard, D. T., 48th Dist., 58th

Woodburn, Wm., 14th
Woodruff, Marion U., 45th Dist., 54th
Woods, Samuel, 39th Dist., 29th
Woodson, David M., 12th
Woodward, Robert M., 29th Dist., 57th-63rd; 74th
Woodward, Wm. H., 50th Dist., 30th
Woodworth, James H., 13th
Woodyard, Harry "Babe", 53rd Dist., 81st, 82nd; 106th
    Dist., 83rd; 105th Dist., 84th
Woolard, Larry D., 117th Dist., 85th-91st
Woolsey, C. Harry, 10th Dist., 39th
Worth, Evan, 28th Dist., 57th
Worthington, Thos., Jr., 36th Dist , 33rd
Wren, Johnston, 8th, 9th
Wren, Nicholas, 5th
Wright, Cyrus, 25th Dist., 18th
Wright, Ivan, 48th Dist., 55th
Wright, James G., 14th Dist., 30th-32nd
Wright, James L., 38th Dist., 76th
Wright, James M., 91st Dist., 27th
Wright, James S., 15th
Wright, Joel, 7th
Wright, John E., 38th Dist., 35th
Wright, Jonathan, 90th Dist., 92nd
Wright, Omar H., 9th Dist., 31st, 32nd
Wright, Randolph C., 50th Dist., 27th
Wright, William H., 26th Dist., 46th, 47th
Wright, Wm. P., 2nd Dist., 35th
Wuche, James E., 25th Dist., 20th
Wunson, Francis, 60th Dist., 26th
Wyand, J. E., 28th Dist., 42nd
Wyatt, John, 8th, 9th, 10th
Wylie, John, 37th Dist., 39th; 27th Dist., 40th
Wylie, John, 39th Dist., 52nd, 54th, 55th
Wymore, James L., 51st Dist., 28th
Wynne, Josiah R., 15th
Yacullo, James J., 2nd Dist., 68th
Yancy, Archelaus N., 40th Dist., 32nd; 38th Dist., 33rd
Yarbrough, Karen A., 7th Dist., 92nd
Yates, Richard, 13th, 14th; 24th Dist., 16th
Yeager, John H., 16th Dist., 25th
Yeargain, William T., 28th Dist., 24th
Yoacum, Reuben S., 50th Dist., 35th
York, Lewis E., 51st Dist., 45th, 46th
Yost, John, 49th Dist., 34th
Youle, John Clinton, 74th
Young, Anthony L., 17th Dist., 84th-87th
Young, C. A., 13th Dist., 49th-52nd
Young, E. M., 48th Dist., 45th
Young, John C., 32nd Dist., 41st, 42nd
Young, John D., 51st Dist., 32nd
Young, Linn H., 5th Dist., 41st
Young, Ogden B., 50th Dist., 26th
Young, Richard M., 2nd
Young, William, 15th Dist., 18th
Youngblood, Francis M., 47th Dist., 32nd
Younge, Wyvetter H., 57th Dist., 79th-82nd; 113th Dist.,
    83rd-87th; 114th Dist., 88th-92nd
Youngkin, John F., 14th
Yourell, Harry, 6th Dist., 75th-77th; 8th Dist., 78th-82nd;
    27th Dist., 83rd
Zaabel, Paul I., 2nd Dist., 44th-46th
Zabrocki, Edward J., 37th Dist., 89th
Zachacki, William M., Sr., 16th Dist., 75th, 76th
Zagone, Nicholas, 9th Dist., 71st, 73rd; 74th
Zeiger, Jacob, 30th Dist., 37th
Zeman, Edward J., 15th Dist., 64th
Zempel, Paul C., 43rd Dist., 69th
Zepp, David H., 34th Dist., 30th
Zickus, Anne, 47th Dist., 86th; 48th Dist., 88th-92nd
Zieber, John S., 14th
Ziegler, Paul A., 48th Dist., 67th-69th
Zientek, Joseph, 15th Dist., 62nd-66th
Zimmerman, Jacob, 11th
Zimmerman, Jacob, 44th Dist., 31st; 46th Dist., 38th
Zinger, Louis, 30th Dist., 44th-46th
Zink, George L., 34th Dist., 31st
Zipf, William F., 6th Dist., 46th
Zito, Greg, 5th Dist., 41st
Zlatnik, Michael F., 8th Dist., 70th-73rd; 10th Dist., 75th,
    77th
Zolla, Emil N., 23rd Dist., 48th
Zunn, Thomas, 38th Dist., 41st
Zwick, Jill, 33rd Dist., 82nd; 65th Dist., 83rd, 84th

CONSTITUTION OF 1970
History and Highlights

Illinois' sixth Constitutional Convention convened in Springfield on Dec. 8, 1969. One hundred and sixteen members — two elected from each Senatorial District — met at a nonpartisan convention to revise, alter or amend the 1870 Constitution.

After nine months of in-depth study and debate, the members presented their work-product to the people — a Constitution they considered to be workable for 25, 50 — or as in the case of the 1870 Constitution — 100 years. Features of the 1970 Constitution are highlighted below:

Bill of Rights. Preserves individual rights set out in the 1870 Constitution — freedom of speech and religion, protection against self-incrimination, etc., and guarantees freedom from discrimination on the basis of race, color, creed, national ancestry and sex in the hiring and promotion practices of an employer or in the sale or rental of property. Other provisions guarantee women the equal protection of the laws and prohibit discrimination based solely on physical or mental disabilities.

Suffrage and Elections. Lowered residency requirements, provided that registration and election laws be general and uniform and provided for a bipartisan board to supervise the administration of such laws. Reduced the majorities required for adoption of constitutional amendments and for calling a Constitutional Convention.

Legislative. Designated that the presiding officer of the Senate be elected from the membership. Vacancies in the General Assembly are filled by appointment as provided by law, and the appointee serves until the next General Election; the person appointed is to be a member of the same political party as the member elected. Alternative methods of reapportionment are outlined in the event the General Assembly fails to redistrict itself. Most importantly, the General Assembly is required to convene annually.

Executive. Authorized agency reorganization by executive order; this enabled the Governor to reassign functions or reorganize agencies directly responsible to him. In addition to the Governor's veto power over entire pieces of legislation and specific items in appropriation bills, he has the power to reduce appropriations. The Governor and Lieutenant Governor run as a team. A Comptroller replaced the Auditor of Public Accounts; the chief state school officer became appointive (see Education).

Judicial. Retained the elective method of selecting judges and provided for the reclassification of circuit judges. A Judicial Inquiry Board was created to hear complaints about the official conduct of judges. The Courts Commission hears complaints filed by the Judicial Inquiry Board.

Local Government. Instituted the concept of home rule for Illinois. Major local governments were given wide authority to exercise power and perform functions relating to their affairs.

Finance. Provided for an annual, balanced executive budget, a uniform system of accounting for local governments and an Auditor General appointed by the General Assembly.

Revenue. Provided that any income tax must be at a non-graduated rate and the rate for corporations cannot exceed the rate for individuals by a ratio greater than 8 to 5. Permitted the classification of real property for tax purposes in counties over 200,000. Abolished the personal property tax by 1979. Allowed homestead exemptions, exemptions of food, etc., from the sales tax, etc. Required a three-fifths vote of the Legislature or voter approval for general obligation borrowing; only a simple legislative majority is required for revenue bonds.

Education. Stipulated that all persons are to be educated to the limit of their capacities and gave the state primary responsibility for financing educational institutions and services. Provided for a State Board of Education. The board appoints the chief educational officer of the state in lieu of the Superintendent of Public Instruction, an elective office under the 1870 Constitution.

Constitutional Amendments

The Constitution was adopted in convention, Sept. 3, 1970; ratified by the people, Dec. 15, 1970; and became effective July 1, 1971. Since its adoption, 10 amendments have been approved and adopted. A brief explanation of the amended articles follows:

First Amendment — 1980 — Legislative Article (Cutback Amendment). Eliminated cumulative voting and reduced the size of the House of Representatives from 177 to 118 members. As of 1970, voters in multi-member legislative districts divided three votes between candidates for representative, with each district electing three representatives, no more than two of whom could be from the same party. With the 1982 effective date of the amendment, districts were divided into two single-member representative districts in which voters cast a single vote for state representative, and one legislative district from which they cast one vote for senator.

Second Amendment — 1980 — Revenue Article (Delinquent Tax Sales). In an effort to prevent abuse in scavenger sales by tax delinquent property owners, the minimum redemption from scavenger sales was reduced to 90 days for vacant non-farm real estate, improved residential real estate of seven or more units, and commercial and industrial real estate when at least five years of taxes are delinquent. After adoption of this amendment, the General Assembly established six months from the date of sale as the minimum redemption period for properties falling within these classes.

Third Amendment — 1982 — Bill of Rights Article (Bail and Habeas Corpus). Allows state criminal court judges to deny bail to persons accused of crimes carrying a possible life sentence. Prior to its passage, only persons accused of an offense punishable by death could be ineligible for bail.

Fourth Amendment (Amended Third Amendment) — 1986 — Bill of Rights Article (Bail and Habeas Corpus). Allows state criminal court judges to deny bail to persons accused of certain crimes when the court determines that the persons may pose a threat to the community.

Fifth Amendment — 1988 — Suffrage and Elections Article (Voting Qualifications). Reduced the voting age for every U.S. citizen voting in state elections from 21 years to 18 years and the permanent state residency requirement from six months to 30 days preceding any election.

Sixth Amendment (Amended Second Amendment) — 1990 — Revenue Article (Delinquent Tax Sales). Reduced the period of delinquent taxes to two years for the minimum six-month redemption period following tax sales on delinquent commercial, industrial, vacant non-farm and large multi-family residential properties only.

Seventh Amendment — 1992 — Bill of Rights Article (Crime Victim's Rights). Provides rights for crime victims, beginning with the right to be treated with fairness, dignity and respect for their privacy throughout the criminal justice process.

Eighth Amendment — 1994 — Bill of Rights Article (Rights After Indictment). Changes the rights of the accused in a criminal prosecution by replacing language giving the accused the right "to meet the witnesses face to face" with language giving the accused the right "to be confronted with the witnesses against him or her."

Ninth Amendment — 1994 — Legislative Article (Effective Dates of Laws). Previously, any bill passed after June 30 could not take effect before July 1 of the following year unless the bill passed the legislature by a three-fifths vote. This amendment changed the date when the three-fifths vote requirement takes effect from July 1 to June 1. As a result, any bill passed after May 31 will not take effect until June 1 of the following year unless the legislature passes it by a three-fifths vote.

Tenth Amendment — 1998 — Judiciary Article (Retirement — Discipline). Adds two citizens appointed by the Governor to the Illinois Courts Commission. The Commission, which includes one Supreme Court Justice, two Appellate Court Judges and two Circuit Judges, hears complaints filed against judges by the Judicial Inquiry Board.

Proposed Constitutional Convention

A Constitutional Convention proposed in 1988 would have been the first Constitutional Convention since the 1970 State Constitution went into effect. However, the proposal was defeated by Illinois citizens voting in the General Election, 2,727,144 to 900,109.

CONSTITUTION OF THE STATE OF ILLINOIS

Adopted in Convention at Springfield, September 3, 1970. Ratified
by the People, December 15, 1970. In force July 1, 1971.

PREAMBLE

We, the People of the State of Illinois — grateful to Almighty God for the
civil, political and religious liberty which He has permitted us to enjoy and
seeking His blessing upon our endeavors — in order to provide for the health,
safety and welfare of the people; maintain a representative and orderly government; eliminate poverty and inequality; assure legal, social and economic justice;
provide opportunity for the fullest development of the individual; insure domestic tranquility; provide for the common defense; and secure the blessings of
freedom and liberty to ourselves and our posterity — do ordain and establish this
Constitution for the State of Illinois.

ARTICLE I — Bill of Rights

Section 1. INHERENT AND INALIENABLE RIGHTS

All men are by nature free and independent and have certain inherent and
inalienable rights among which are life, liberty and the pursuit of happiness. To
secure these rights and the protection of property, governments are instituted
among men, deriving their just powers from the consent of the governed.

Section 2. DUE PROCESS AND EQUAL PROTECTION

No person shall be deprived of life, liberty or property without due process
of law nor be denied the equal protection of the laws.

Section 3. RELIGIOUS FREEDOM

The free exercise and enjoyment of religious profession and worship,
without discrimination, shall forever be guaranteed, and no person shall be
denied any civil or political right, privilege or capacity, on account of his religious
opinions; but the liberty of conscience hereby secured shall not be construed to
dispense with oaths or affirmations, excuse acts of licentiousness, or justify
practices inconsistent with the peace or safety of the State. No person shall be
required to attend or support any ministry or place of worship against his
consent, nor shall any preference be given by law to any religious denomination
or mode of worship.

Section 4. FREEDOM OF SPEECH

All persons may speak, write and publish freely, being responsible for the
abuse of that liberty. In trials for libel, both civil and criminal, the truth, when
published with good motives and for justifiable ends, shall be a sufficient
defense.

Section 5. RIGHT TO ASSEMBLE AND PETITION

The people have the right to assemble in a peaceable manner, to consult for
the common good, to make known their opinions to their representatives and to
apply for redress of grievances.

Section 6. SEARCHES, SEIZURES, PRIVACY AND INTERCEPTIONS

The people shall have the right to be secure in their persons, houses, papers
and other possessions against unreasonable searches, seizures, invasions of

privacy or interceptions of communications by eavesdropping devices or other means. No warrant shall issue without probable cause, supported by affidavit particularly describing the place to be searched and the persons or things to be seized.

Section 7. INDICTMENT AND PRELIMINARY HEARING

No person shall be held to answer for a criminal offense unless on indictment of a grand jury, except in cases in which the punishment is by fine or by imprisonment other than in the penitentiary, in cases of impeachment, and in cases arising in the militia when in actual service in time of war or public danger. The General Assembly by law may abolish the grand jury or further limit its use.

No person shall be held to answer for a crime punishable by death or by imprisonment in the penitentiary unless either the initial charge has been brought by indictment of a grand jury or the person has been given a prompt preliminary hearing to establish probable cause.

Section 8. RIGHTS AFTER INDICTMENT

In criminal prosecutions, the accused shall have the right to appear and defend in person and by counsel; to demand the nature and cause of the accusation and have a copy thereof; to be confronted with the witnesses against him or her and to have process to compel the attendance of witnesses in his or her behalf; and to have a speedy public trial by an impartial jury of the county in which the offense is alleged to have been committed. (As amended by the Eighth Amendment to the Constitution. Approved November 8, 1994, effective November 29, 1994.)

Section 8.1. CRIME VICTIM'S RIGHTS

(a) Crime victims, as defined by law, shall have the following rights as provided by law:

(1) The right to be treated with fairness and respect for their dignity and privacy throughout the criminal justice process.

(2) The right to notification of court proceedings.

(3) The right to communicate with the prosecution.

(4) The right to make a statement to the court at sentencing.

(5) The right to information about the conviction, sentence, imprisonment, and release of the accused.

(6) The right to timely disposition of the case following the arrest of the accused.

(7) The right to be reasonably protected from the accused throughout the criminal justice process.

(8) The right to be present at the trial and all other court proceedings on the same basis as the accused, unless the victim is to testify and the court determines that the victim's testimony would be materially affected if the victim hears other testimony at the trial.

(9) The right to have present at all court proceedings, subject to the rules of evidence, an advocate or other support person of the victim's choice.

(10) The right to restitution.

(b) The General Assembly may provide by law for the enforcement of this Section.

(c) The General Assembly may provide for an assessment against convicted defendants to pay for crime victims' rights.

(d) Nothing in this Section or in any law enacted under this Section shall be construed as creating a basis for vacating a conviction or a ground for appellate relief in any criminal case. (Section 8.1 added by the Seventh Amendment to the Constitution. Approved November 3, 1992, effective November 23, 1992.)

Section 9. BAIL AND HABEAS CORPUS

All persons shall be bailable by sufficient sureties, except for the following offenses where the proof is evident or the presumption great: capital offenses; offenses for which a sentence of life imprisonment may be imposed as a consequence of conviction; and felony offenses for which a sentence of imprisonment, without conditional and revocable release, shall be imposed by law as a consequence of conviction, when the court, after a hearing, determines that release of the offender would pose a real and present threat to the physical safety of any person. The privilege of the writ of habeas corpus shall not be suspended except in cases of rebellion or invasion when the public safety may require it.

Any costs accruing to a unit of local government as a result of the denial of bail pursuant to the 1986 Amendment to this Section shall be reimbursed by the State to the unit of local government. (As amended by the Fourth Amendment to the Constitution. Approved November 4, 1986, effective November 25, 1986.)

Section 10. SELF-INCRIMINATION AND DOUBLE JEOPARDY

No person shall be compelled in a criminal case to give evidence against himself nor be twice put in jeopardy for the same offense.

Section 11. LIMITATION OF PENALTIES AFTER CONVICTION

All penalties shall be determined both according to the seriousness of the offense and with the objective of restoring the offender to useful citizenship. No conviction shall work corruption of blood or forfeiture of estate. No person shall be transported out of the State for an offense committed within the State.

Section 12. RIGHT TO REMEDY AND JUSTICE

Every person shall find a certain remedy in the laws for all injuries and wrongs which he receives to his person, privacy, property or reputation. He shall obtain justice by law, freely, completely, and promptly.

Section 13. TRIAL BY JURY

The right of trial by jury as heretofore enjoyed shall remain inviolate.

Section 14. IMPRISONMENT FOR DEBT

No person shall be imprisoned for debt unless he refuses to deliver up his estate for the benefit of his creditors as provided by law or unless there is a strong presumption of fraud. No person shall be imprisoned for failure to pay a fine in a criminal case unless he has been afforded adequate time to make payment, in installments if necessary, and has willfully failed to make payment.

Section 15. RIGHT OF EMINENT DOMAIN

Private property shall not be taken or damaged for public use without just compensation as provided by law. Such compensation shall be determined by a jury as provided by law.

Section 16. EX POST FACTO LAWS AND IMPAIRING CONTRACTS

No ex post facto law, or law impairing the obligation of contracts or making an irrevocable grant of special privileges or immunities, shall be passed.

Section 17. NO DISCRIMINATION IN EMPLOYMENT AND THE SALE OR RENTAL OF PROPERTY

All persons shall have the right to be free from discrimination on the basis of race, color, creed, national ancestry and sex in the hiring and promotion practices of any employer or in the sale or rental of property.

These rights are enforceable without action by the General Assembly, but the General Assembly by law may establish reasonable exemptions relating to these rights and provide additional remedies for their violation.

Section 18. NO DISCRIMINATION ON THE BASIS OF SEX

The equal protection of the laws shall not be denied or abridged on account of sex by the State or its units of local government and school districts.

Section 19. NO DISCRIMINATION AGAINST THE HANDICAPPED

All persons with a physical or mental handicap shall be free from discrimination in the sale or rental of property and shall be free from discrimination unrelated to ability in the hiring and promotion practices of any employer.

Section 20. INDIVIDUAL DIGNITY

To promote individual dignity, communications that portray criminality, depravity or lack of virtue in, or that incite violence, hatred, abuse or hostility toward, a person or group of persons by reason of or by reference to religious, racial, ethnic, national or regional affiliation are condemned.

Section 21. QUARTERING OF SOLDIERS

No soldier in time of peace shall be quartered in a house without the consent of the owner; nor in time of war except as provided by law.

Section 22. RIGHT TO ARMS

Subject only to the police power, the right of the individual citizen to keep and bear arms shall not be infringed.

Section 23. FUNDAMENTAL PRINCIPLES

A frequent recurrence to the fundamental principles of civil government is necessary to preserve the blessings of liberty. These blessings cannot endure unless the people recognize their corresponding individual obligations and responsibilities.

Section 24. RIGHTS RETAINED

The enumeration in this Constitution of certain rights shall not be construed to deny or disparage others retained by the individual citizens of the State.

ARTICLE II — The Powers of the State

Section 1. SEPARATION OF POWERS

The legislative, executive and judicial branches are separate. No branch shall exercise powers properly belonging to another.

Section 2. POWERS OF GOVERNMENT

The enumeration in this Constitution of specified powers and functions shall not be construed as a limitation of powers of state government.

ARTICLE III — Suffrage and Elections

Section 1. VOTING QUALIFICATIONS

Every United States citizen who has attained the age of 18 or any other voting age required by the United States for voting in State elections and who has been a permanent resident of this State for at least 30 days next preceding any election shall have the right to vote at such election. The General Assembly by law may establish registration requirements and require permanent residence in an election district not to exceed thirty days prior to an election. The General Assembly by law may establish shorter residence requirements for voting for President and Vice-President of the United States. (As amended by the Fifth Amendment to the Constitution. Approved November 8, 1988, effective November 28, 1988.)

Section 2. VOTING DISQUALIFICATIONS
A person convicted of a felony, or otherwise under sentence in a correctional institution or jail, shall lose the right to vote, which right shall be restored not later than upon completion of his sentence.

Section 3. ELECTIONS
All elections shall be free and equal.

Section 4. ELECTION LAWS
The General Assembly by law shall define permanent residence for voting purposes, insure secrecy of voting and the integrity of the election process, and facilitate registration and voting by all qualified persons. Laws governing voter registration and conduct of elections shall be general and uniform.

Section 5. BOARD OF ELECTIONS
A State Board of Elections shall have general supervision over the administration of the registration and election laws throughout the State. The General Assembly by law shall determine the size, manner of selection and compensation of the Board. No political party shall have a majority of members of the Board.

Section 6. GENERAL ELECTION
As used in all articles of this Constitution except Article VII, "general election" means the biennial election at which members of the General Assembly are elected. Such election shall be held on the Tuesday following the first Monday of November in even-numbered years or on such other day as provided by law.

ARTICLE IV — The Legislature

Section 1. LEGISLATURE —POWER AND STRUCTURE
The legislative power is vested in a General Assembly consisting of a Senate and a House of Representatives, elected by the electors from 59 Legislative Districts and 118 Representative Districts. (As amended by the First Amendment to the Constitution. Approved November 4, 1980, effective November 26, 1980.)

Section 2. LEGISLATIVE COMPOSITION
(a) One Senator shall be elected from each Legislative District. Immediately following each decennial redistricting, the General Assembly by law shall divide the Legislative Districts as equally as possible into three groups. Senators from one group shall be elected for terms of four years, four years and two years; Senators from the second group, for terms of four years, two years and four years; and Senators from the third group, for terms of two years, four years and four years. The Legislative Districts in each group shall be distributed substantially equally over the State.

(b) Each Legislative District shall be divided into two Representative Districts. In 1982 and every two years thereafter one Representative shall be elected from each Representative District for a term of two years.

(c)   To be eligible to serve as a member of the General Assembly, a person must be a United States citizen, at least 21 years old, and for the two years preceding his election or appointment a resident of the district which he is to represent. In the general election following a redistricting, a candidate for the General Assembly may be elected from any district which contains a part of the district in which he resided at the time of the redistricting and reelected if a resident of the new district he represents for 18 months prior to reelection.

(d)   Within thirty days after a vacancy occurs, it shall be filled by appointment as provided by law. If the vacancy is in a Senatorial office with more than twenty-eight months remaining in the term, the appointed Senator shall serve until the next general election, at which time a Senator shall be elected to serve for the remainder of the term. If the vacancy is in a Representative office or in any other Senatorial office, the appointment shall be for the remainder of the term. An appointee to fill a vacancy shall be a member of the same political party as the person he succeeds.

(e)   No member of the General Assembly shall receive compensation as a public officer or employee from any other governmental entity for time during which he is in attendance as a member of the General Assembly.

No member of the General Assembly during the term for which he was elected or appointed shall be appointed to a public office which shall have been created or the compensation for which shall have been increased by the General Assembly during that term. (As amended by the First Amendment to the Constitution. Approved November 4, 1980, effective November 26, 1980.)

Section 3. LEGISLATIVE REDISTRICTING

(a)   Legislative Districts shall be compact, contiguous and substantially equal in population. Representative Districts shall be compact, contiguous, and substantially equal in population.

(b)   In the year following each Federal decennial census year, the General Assembly by law shall redistrict the Legislative Districts and the Representative Districts.

If no redistricting plan becomes effective by June 30 of that year, a Legislative Redistricting Commission shall be constituted not later than July 10. The Commission shall consist of eight members, no more than four of whom shall be members of the same political party.

The Speaker and Minority Leader of the House of Representatives shall each appoint to the Commission one Representative and one person who is not a member of the General Assembly. The President and Minority Leader of the Senate shall each appoint to the Commission one Senator and one person who is not a member of the General Assembly.

The members shall be certified to the Secretary of State by the appointing authorities. A vacancy on the Commission shall be filled within five days by the authority that made the original appointment. A Chairman and Vice Chairman shall be chosen by a majority of all members of the Commission.

Not later than August 10, the Commission shall file with the Secretary of State a redistricting plan approved by at least five members.

If the Commission fails to file an approved redistricting plan, the Supreme Court shall submit the names of two persons, not of the same political party, to the Secretary of State not later than September 1.

Not later than September 5, the Secretary of State publicly shall draw by random selection the name of one of the two persons to serve as the ninth member of the Commission.

Not later than October 5, the Commission shall file with the Secretary of State a redistricting plan approved by at least five members.

An approved redistricting plan filed with the Secretary of State shall be presumed valid, shall have the force and effect of law and shall be published promptly by the Secretary of State.

The Supreme Court shall have the original and exclusive jurisdiction over actions concerning redistricting the House and Senate, which shall be initiated in the name of the People of the State by the Attorney General. (As amended by the First Amendment to the Constitution. Approved November 4, 1980, effective November 26, 1980.)

Section 4. ELECTION

Members of the General Assembly shall be elected at the general election in even-numbered years.

Section 5. SESSIONS

(a) The General Assembly shall convene each year on the second Wednesday of January. The General Assembly shall be a continuous body during the term for which members of the House of Representatives are elected.

(b) The Governor may convene the General Assembly or the Senate alone in special session by a proclamation stating the purpose of the session; and only business encompassed by such purpose, together with any impeachments or confirmation of appointments shall be transacted. Special sessions of the General Assembly may also be convened by joint proclamation of the presiding officers of both houses, issued as provided by law.

(c) Sessions of each house of the General Assembly and meetings of committees, joint committees and legislative commissions shall be open to the public. Sessions and committee meetings of a house may be closed to the public if two-thirds of the members elected to that house determine that the public interest so requires; and meetings of joint committees and legislative commissions may be so closed if two-thirds of the members elected to each house so determine.

Section 6. ORGANIZATION

(a) A majority of the members elected to each house constitutes a quorum.

(b) On the first day of the January session of the General Assembly in odd-numbered years, the Secretary of State shall convene the House of Representatives to elect from its membership a Speaker of the House of Representatives as presiding officer, and the Governor shall convene the Senate to elect from its membership a President of the Senate as presiding officer.

(c) For purposes of powers of appointment conferred by this Constitution, the Minority Leader of either house is a member of the numerically strongest political party other than the party to which the Speaker or the President belongs, as the case may be.

(d) Each house shall determine the rules of its proceedings, judge the elections, returns and qualifications of its members and choose its officers. No member shall be expelled by either house, except by a vote of two-thirds of the members elected to that house. A member may be expelled only once for the same offense. Each house may punish by imprisonment any person, not a member, guilty of disrespect to the house by disorderly or contemptuous behavior in its presence. Imprisonment shall not extend beyond twenty-four hours at one time unless the person persists in disorderly or contemptuous behavior.

Section 7. TRANSACTION OF BUSINESS

(a) Committees of each house, joint committees of the two houses and legislative commissions shall give reasonable public notice of meetings, including a statement of subjects to be considered.

(b) Each house shall keep a journal of its proceedings and a transcript of its debates. The journal shall be published and the transcript shall be available to the public.

(c) Either house or any committee thereof as provided by law may compel by subpoena the attendance and testimony of witnesses and the production of books, records and papers.

Section 8. PASSAGE OF BILLS

(a) The enacting clause of the laws of this State shall be: "Be it enacted by the People of the State of Illinois, represented in the General Assembly."

(b) The General Assembly shall enact laws only by bill. Bills may originate in either house, but may be amended or rejected by the other.

(c) No bill shall become a law without the concurrence of a majority of the members elected to each house. Final passage of a bill shall be by record vote. In the Senate at the request of two members, and in the House at the request of five members, a record vote may be taken on any other occasion. A record vote is a vote by yeas and nays entered on the journal.

(d) A bill shall be read by title on three different days in each house. A bill and each amendment thereto shall be reproduced and placed on the desk of each member before final passage.

Bills, except bills for appropriations and for the codification, revision or rearrangement of laws, shall be confined to one subject. Appropriation bills shall be limited to the subject of appropriations. A bill expressly amending a law shall set forth completely the sections amended.

The Speaker of the House of Representatives and the President of the Senate shall sign each bill that passes both houses to certify that the procedural requirements for passage have been met.

Section 9. VETO PROCEDURE

(a) Every bill passed by the General Assembly shall be presented to the Governor within 30 calendar days after its passage. The foregoing requirement shall be judicially enforceable. If the Governor approves the bill, he shall sign it and it shall become law.

(b) If the Governor does not approve the bill, he shall veto it by returning it with his objections to the house in which it originated. Any bill not so returned by the Governor within 60 calendar days after it is presented to him shall become law. If recess or adjournment of the General Assembly prevents the return of a bill, the bill and the Governor's objections shall be filed with the Secretary of State within such 60 calendar days. The Secretary of State shall return the bill and objections to the originating house promptly upon the next meeting of the same General Assembly at which the bill can be considered.

(c) The house to which a bill is returned shall immediately enter the Governor's objections upon its journal. If within 15 calendar days after such entry that house by a record vote of three-fifths of the members elected passes the bill, it shall be delivered immediately to the second house. If within 15 calendar days after such delivery the second house by a record vote of three-fifths of the members elected passes the bill, it shall become law.

(d) The Governor may reduce or veto any item of appropriations in a bill presented to him. Portions of a bill not reduced or vetoed shall become law. An item vetoed shall be returned to the house in which it originated and may become law in the same manner as a vetoed bill. An item reduced in amount shall be returned to the house in which it originated and may be restored to its original amount in the same manner as a vetoed bill except that the required record vote shall be a majority of the members elected to each house. If a reduced item is not so restored, it shall become law in the reduced amount.

(e)   The Governor may return a bill together with specific recommendations for change to the house in which it originated. The bill shall be considered in the same manner as a vetoed bill but the specific recommendations may be accepted by a record vote of a majority of the members elected to each house. Such bill shall be presented again to the Governor and if he certifies that such acceptance conforms to his specific recommendations, the bill shall become law. If he does not so certify, he shall return it as a vetoed bill to the house in which it originated.

Section 10. EFFECTIVE DATE OF LAWS

The General Assembly shall provide by law for a uniform effective date for laws passed prior to June 1 of a calendar year. The General Assembly may provide for a different effective date in any law passed prior to June 1. A bill passed after May 31 shall not become effective prior to June 1 of the next calendar year unless the General Assembly by the vote of three-fifths of the members elected to each house provides for an earlier effective date. (As amended by the Ninth Amendment to the Constitution. Approved November 8, 1994, effective November 29, 1994.)

Section 11. COMPENSATION AND ALLOWANCES

A member shall receive a salary and allowances as provided by law, but changes in the salary of a member shall not take effect during the term for which he has been elected.

Section 12. LEGISLATIVE IMMUNITY

Except in cases of treason, felony or breach of peace, a member shall be privileged from arrest going to, during, and returning from sessions of the General Assembly. A member shall not be held to answer before any other tribunal for any speech or debate, written or oral, in either house. These immunities shall apply to committee and legislative commission proceedings.

Section 13. SPECIAL LEGISLATION

The General Assembly shall pass no special or local law when a general law is or can be made applicable. Whether a general law is or can be made applicable shall be a matter for judicial determination.

Section 14. IMPEACHMENT

The House of Representatives has the sole power to conduct legislative investigations to determine the existence of cause for impeachment and, by the vote of a majority of the members elected, to impeach Executive and Judicial officers. Impeachments shall be tried by the Senate. When sitting for that purpose, Senators shall be upon oath, or affirmation, to do justice according to law. If the Governor is tried, the Chief Justice of the Supreme Court shall preside. No person shall be convicted without the concurrence of two-thirds of the Senators elected. Judgment shall not extend beyond removal from office and disqualification to hold any public office of this State. An impeached officer, whether convicted or acquitted, shall be liable to prosecution, trial, judgment and punishment according to law.

Section 15. ADJOURNMENT

(a) When the General Assembly is in session, neither house without the consent of the other shall adjourn for more than three days or to a place other than where the two houses are sitting.

(b) If either house certifies that a disagreement exists between the houses as to the time for adjourning a session, the Governor may adjourn the General Assembly to a time not later than the first day of the next annual session.

ARTICLE V — The Executive

Section 1. OFFICERS

The Executive Branch shall include a Governor, Lieutenant Governor, Attorney General, Secretary of State, Comptroller and Treasurer elected by the electors of the State. They shall keep the public records and maintain a residence at the seat of government during their terms of office.

Section 2. TERMS

These elected officers of the Executive Branch shall hold office for four years beginning on the second Monday of January after their election and, except in the case of the Lieutenant Governor, until their successors are qualified. They shall be elected at the general election in 1978 and every four years thereafter.

Section 3. ELIGIBILITY

To be eligible to hold the office of Governor, Lieutenant Governor, Attorney General, Secretary of State, Comptroller or Treasurer, a person must be a United States citizen, at least 25 years old, and a resident of this State for the three years preceding his election.

Section 4. JOINT ELECTION

In the general election for Governor and Lieutenant Governor, one vote shall be cast jointly for the candidates nominated by the same political party or petition. The General Assembly may provide by law for the joint nomination of candidates for Governor and Lieutenant Governor.

Section 5. CANVASS — CONTESTS

The election returns for executive offices shall be sealed and transmitted to the Secretary of State, or other person or body provided by law, who shall examine and consolidate the returns. The person having the highest number of votes for an office shall be declared elected. If two or more persons have an equal and the highest number of votes for an office, they shall draw lots to determine which of them shall be declared elected. Election contests shall be decided by the courts in a manner provided by law.

Section 6. GUBERNATORIAL SUCCESSION

(a) In the event of a vacancy, the order of succession to the office of Governor or to the position of Acting Governor shall be the Lieutenant Governor, the elected Attorney General, the elected Secretary of State, and then as provided by law.

(b) If the Governor is unable to serve because of death, conviction on impeachment, failure to qualify, resignation or other disability, the office of Governor shall be filled by the officer next in line of succession for the remainder of the term or until the disability is removed.

(c)   Whenever the Governor determines that he may be seriously impeded in the exercise of his powers, he shall so notify the Secretary of State and the officer next in line of succession. The latter shall thereafter become Acting Governor with the duties and powers of Governor. When the Governor is prepared to resume office, he shall do so by notifying the Secretary of State and the Acting Governor.

(d)   The General Assembly by law shall specify by whom and by what procedures the ability of the Governor to serve or to resume office may be questioned and determined. The Supreme Court shall have original and exclusive jurisdiction to review such a law and any such determination and, in the absence of such a law, shall make the determination under such rules as it may adopt.

Section 7. VACANCIES IN OTHER ELECTIVE OFFICES

If the Attorney General, Secretary of State, Comptroller or Treasurer fails to qualify or if his office becomes vacant, the Governor shall fill the office by appointment. The appointee shall hold office until the elected officer qualifies or until a successor is elected and qualified as may be provided by law and shall not be subject to removal by the Governor. If the Lieutenant Governor fails to qualify or if his office becomes vacant, it shall remain vacant until the end of the term.

Section 8. GOVERNOR — SUPREME EXECUTIVE POWER

The Governor shall have the supreme executive power, and shall be responsible for the faithful execution of the laws.

Section 9. GOVERNOR — APPOINTING POWER

(a)   The Governor shall nominate and, by and with the advice and consent of the Senate, a majority of the members elected concurring by record vote, shall appoint all officers whose election or appointment is not otherwise provided for. Any nomination not acted upon by the Senate within 60 session days after the receipt thereof shall be deemed to have received the advice and consent of the Senate. The General Assembly shall have no power to elect or appoint officers of the Executive Branch.

(b)   If, during a recess of the Senate, there is a vacancy in an office filled by appointment by the Governor by and with the advice and consent of the Senate, the Governor shall make a temporary appointment until the next meeting of the Senate, when he shall make a nomination to fill such office.

(c)   No person rejected by the Senate for an office shall, except at the Senate's request, be nominated again for that office at the same session or be appointed to that office during a recess of that Senate.

Section 10. GOVERNOR — REMOVALS

The Governor may remove for incompetence, neglect of duty, or malfeasance in office any officer who may be appointed by the Governor.

Section 11. GOVERNOR — AGENCY REORGANIZATION

The Governor, by Executive Order, may reassign functions among or reorganize executive agencies which are directly responsible to him. If such a reassignment or reorganization would contravene a statute, the Executive Order shall be delivered to the General Assembly. If the General Assembly is in annual session and if the Executive Order is delivered on or before April 1, the General Assembly shall consider the Executive Order at that annual session. If the General Assembly is not in annual session or if the Executive Order is delivered after April 1, the General Assembly shall consider the Executive Order at its next annual session, in which case the Executive Order shall be deemed to have been delivered on the first day of that annual session. Such an Executive Order shall not become effective if, within 60 calendar days after its delivery to the General Assembly, either house disapproves the Executive Order by the record vote of a majority of the members elected. An Executive Order not so disapproved shall become effective by its terms but not less than 60 calendar days after its delivery to the General Assembly.

Section 12. GOVERNOR — PARDONS
The Governor may grant reprieves, commutations and pardons, after conviction, for all offenses on such terms as he thinks proper. The manner of applying therefore may be regulated by law.

Section 13. GOVERNOR — LEGISLATIVE MESSAGES
The Governor, at the beginning of each annual session of the General Assembly and at the close of his term of office, shall report to the General Assembly on the Condition of the State and recommend such measures as he deems desirable.

Section 14. LIEUTENANT GOVERNOR — DUTIES
The Lieutenant Governor shall perform the duties and exercise the powers in the Executive Branch that may be delegated to him by the Governor and that may be prescribed by law.

Section 15. ATTORNEY GENERAL — DUTIES
The Attorney General shall be the legal officer of the State, and shall have the duties and powers that may be prescribed by law.

Section 16. SECRETARY OF STATE —DUTIES
The Secretary of State shall maintain the official records of the acts of the General Assembly and such official records of the Executive Branch as provided by law. Such official records shall be available for inspection by the public. He shall keep the Great Seal of the State of Illinois and perform other duties that may be prescribed by law.

Section 17. COMPTROLLER — DUTIES
The Comptroller, in accordance with law, shall maintain the State's central fiscal accounts, and order payments into and out of the funds held by the Treasurer.

Section 18. TREASURER — DUTIES
The Treasurer, in accordance with law, shall be responsible for the safe-keeping and investment of monies and securities deposited with him, and for their disbursement upon order of the Comptroller.

Section 19. RECORDS — REPORTS
All officers of the Executive Branch shall keep accounts and shall make such reports as may be required by law. They shall provide the Governor with information relating to their respective offices, either in writing under oath, or otherwise, as the Governor may require.

Section 20. BOND
Civil officers of the Executive Branch may be required by law to give reasonable bond or other security for the faithful performance of their duties. If any officer is in default of such a requirement, his office shall be deemed vacant.

Section 21. COMPENSATION

Officers of the Executive Branch shall be paid salaries established by law and shall receive no other compensation for their services. Changes in the salaries of these officers elected or appointed for stated terms shall not take effect during the stated terms.

ARTICLE VI — The Judiciary

Section 1. COURTS

The judicial power is vested in a Supreme Court, an Appellate Court and Circuit Courts.

Section 2. JUDICIAL DISTRICTS

The State is divided into five Judicial Districts for the selection of Supreme and Appellate Court Judges. The First Judicial District consists of Cook County. The remainder of the State shall be divided by law into four Judicial Districts of substantially equal population, each of which shall be compact and composed of contiguous counties.

Section 3. SUPREME COURT — ORGANIZATION

The Supreme Court shall consist of seven Judges. Three shall be selected from the First Judicial District and one from each of the other Judicial Districts. Four Judges constitute a quorum and the concurrence of four is necessary for a decision. Supreme Court Judges shall select a Chief Justice from their number to serve for a term of three years.

Section 4. SUPREME COURT — JURISDICTION

(a)   The Supreme Court may exercise original jurisdiction in cases relating to revenue, mandamus, prohibition or habeas corpus and as may be necessary to the complete determination of any case on review.

(b)   Appeals from judgments of Circuit Courts imposing a sentence of death shall be directly to the Supreme Court as a matter of right. The Supreme Court shall provide by rule for direct appeal in other cases.

(c)   Appeals from the Appellate Court to the Supreme Court are a matter of right if a question under the Constitution of the United States or of this State arises for the first time in and as a result of the action of the Appellate Court, or if a division of the Appellate Court certifies that a case decided by it involves a question of such importance that the case should be decided by the Supreme Court. The Supreme Court may provide by rule for appeals from the Appellate Court in other cases.

Section 5. APPELLATE COURT — ORGANIZATION

The number of Appellate Judges to be selected from each Judicial District shall be provided by law. The Supreme Court shall prescribe by rule the number of Appellate divisions in each Judicial District. Each Appellate division shall have at least three Judges. Assignments to divisions shall be made by the Supreme Court. A majority of a division constitutes a quorum and the concurrence of a majority of the division is necessary for a decision. There shall be at least one division in each Judicial District and each division shall sit at times and places prescribed by rules of the Supreme Court.

Section 6. APPELLATE COURT — JURISDICTION

Appeals from final judgments of a Circuit Court are a matter of right to the Appellate Court in the Judicial District in which the Circuit Court is located except in cases appealable directly to the Supreme Court and except that after a trial on the merits in a criminal case, there shall be no appeal from a judgment of acquittal. The Supreme Court may provide by rule for appeals to the Appellate Court from other than final judgments of Circuit Courts. The Appellate Court may exercise original jurisdiction when necessary to the complete determination of any case on review. The Appellate Court shall have such powers of direct review of administrative action as provided by law.

Section 7. JUDICIAL CIRCUITS

(a)   The State shall be divided into Judicial Circuits consisting of one or more counties. The First Judicial District shall constitute a Judicial Circuit. The Judicial Circuits within the other Judicial Districts shall be as provided by law. Circuits composed of more than one county shall be compact and of contiguous counties. The General Assembly by law may provide for the division of a circuit for the purpose of selection of Circuit Judges and for the selection of Circuit Judges from the circuit at large.

(b)   Each Judicial Circuit shall have one Circuit Court with such number of Circuit Judges as provided by law. Unless otherwise provided by law, there shall be at least one Circuit Judge from each county. In the First Judicial District, unless otherwise provided by law, Cook County, Chicago, and the area outside Chicago shall be separate units for the selection of Circuit Judges, with at least twelve chosen at large from the area outside Chicago and at least thirty-six chosen at large from Chicago.

(c)   Circuit Judges in each circuit shall select by secret ballot a Chief Judge from their number to serve at their pleasure. Subject to the authority of the Supreme Court, the Chief Judge shall have general administrative authority over his court, including authority to provide for divisions, general or specialized, and for appropriate times and places of holding court.

Section 8. ASSOCIATE JUDGES

Each Circuit Court shall have such number of Associate Judges as provided by law. Associate Judges shall be appointed by the Circuit Judges in each circuit as the Supreme Court shall provide by rule. In the First Judicial District, unless otherwise provided by law, at least one-fourth of the Associate Judges shall be appointed from, and reside, outside Chicago. The Supreme Court shall provide by rule for matters to be assigned to Associate Judges.

Section 9. CIRCUIT COURTS — JURISDICTION

Circuit Courts shall have original jurisdiction of all justiciable matters except when the Supreme Court has original and exclusive jurisdiction relating to redistricting of the General Assembly and to the ability of the Governor to serve or resume office. Circuit Courts shall have such power to review administrative action as provided by law.

Section 10. TERMS OF OFFICE

The terms of office of Supreme and Appellate Court Judges shall be ten years; of Circuit Judges, six years; and of Associate Judges, four years.

Section 11. ELIGIBILITY FOR OFFICE

No person shall be eligible to be a Judge or Associate Judge unless he is a United States citizen, a licensed attorney-at-law of this State, and a resident of the unit which selects him. No change in the boundaries of a unit shall affect the tenure in office of a Judge or Associate Judge incumbent at the time of such change.

Section 12. ELECTION AND RETENTION

(a) Supreme, Appellate and Circuit Judges shall be nominated at primary elections or by petition. Judges shall be elected at general or judicial elections as the General Assembly shall provide by law. A person eligible for the office of Judge may cause his name to appear on the ballot as a candidate for Judge at the primary and at the general or judicial elections by submitting petitions. The General Assembly shall prescribe by law the requirements for petitions.

(b) The office of a Judge shall be vacant upon his death, resignation, retirement, removal, or upon the conclusion of his term without retention in office. Whenever an additional Appellate or Circuit Judge is authorized by law, the office shall be filled in the manner provided for filling a vacancy in that office.

(c) A vacancy occurring in the office of Supreme, Appellate or Circuit Judge shall be filled as the General Assembly may provide by law. In the absence of a law, vacancies may be filled by appointment by the Supreme Court. A person appointed to fill a vacancy 60 or more days prior to the next primary election to nominate Judges shall serve until the vacancy is filled for a term at the next general or judicial election. A person appointed to fill a vacancy less than 60 days prior to the next primary election to nominate Judges shall serve until the vacancy is filled at the second general or judicial election following such appointment.

(d) Not less than six months before the general election preceding the expiration of his term of office, a Supreme, Appellate or Circuit Judge who has been elected to that office may file in the office of the Secretary of State a declaration of candidacy to succeed himself. The Secretary of State, not less than 63 days before the election, shall certify the Judge's candidacy to the proper election officials. The names of Judges seeking retention shall be submitted to the electors, separately and without party designation, on the sole question whether each Judge shall be retained in office for another term. The retention elections shall be conducted at general elections in the appropriate Judicial District, for Supreme and Appellate Judges, and in the circuit for Circuit Judges. The affirmative vote of three-fifths of the electors voting on the question shall elect the Judge to the office for a term commencing on the first Monday in December following his election.

(e) A law reducing the number of Appellate or Circuit Judges shall be without prejudice to the right of the Judges affected to seek retention in office. A reduction shall become effective when a vacancy occurs in the affected unit.

Section 13. PROHIBITED ACTIVITIES

(a) The Supreme Court shall adopt rules of conduct for Judges and Associate Judges.

(b) Judges and Associate Judges shall devote full time to judicial duties. They shall not practice law, hold a position of profit, hold office under the United States or this State or unit of local government or school district or in a political party. Service in the State militia or armed forces of the United States for periods of time permitted by rule of the Supreme Court shall not disqualify a person from serving as a Judge or Associate Judge.

Section 14. JUDICIAL SALARIES AND EXPENSES — FEE OFFICERS ELIMINATED

Judges shall receive salaries provided by law which shall not be diminished to take effect during their terms of office. All salaries and such expenses as may be provided by law shall be paid by the State, except that Appellate, Circuit and Associate Judges shall receive such additional compensation from counties within their district or circuit as may be provided by law. There shall be no fee officers in the judicial system.

Section 15. RETIREMENT — DISCIPLINE

(a) The General Assembly may provide by law for the retirement of Judges and Associate Judges at a prescribed age. Any retired Judge or Associate Judge, with his or her consent may be assigned by the Supreme Court to judicial service for which he or she shall receive the applicable compensation in lieu of retirement benefits. A retired Associate Judge may be assigned only as an Associate Judge.

(b) A Judicial Inquiry Board is created. The Supreme Court shall select two Circuit Judges as members and the Governor shall appoint four persons who are not lawyers and three lawyers as members of the Board. No more than two of the lawyers and two of the non-lawyers appointed by the Governor shall be members of the same political party. The terms of Board members shall be four years. A vacancy on the Board shall be filled for a full term in the manner the original appointment was made. No member may serve on the Board more than eight years.

(c) The Board shall be convened permanently, with authority to conduct investigations, receive or initiate complaints concerning a Judge or Associate Judge, and file complaints with the Courts Commission. The Board shall not file a complaint unless five members believe that a reasonable basis exists (1) to charge the Judge or Associate Judge with willful misconduct in office, persistent failure to perform his duties, or other conduct that is prejudicial to the administration of justice or that brings the judicial office into disrepute, or (2) to charge that the Judge or Associate Judge is physically or mentally unable to perform his duties. All proceedings of the Board shall be confidential except the filing of a complaint with the Courts Commission. The Board shall prosecute the complaint.

(d) The Board shall adopt rules governing its procedures. It shall have subpoena power and authority to appoint and direct its staff. Members of the Board who are not Judges shall receive per diem compensation and necessary expenses; members who are Judges shall receive necessary expenses only. The General Assembly by law shall appropriate funds for the operation of the Board.

(e) An independent Courts Commission is created consisting of one Supreme Court Judge selected by that Court as a member and one as an alternate, two Appellate Court Judges selected by that Court as members and three as alternates, two Circuit Judges selected by the Supreme Court as members and three as alternates, and two citizens selected by the Governor as members and two as alternates. Members and alternates who are Appellate Court Judges must each be from a different Judicial District. Members and alternates who are Circuit Judges must each be from a different Judicial District. Members and alternates of the Commission shall not be members of the Judicial Inquiry Board. The members of the Commission shall select a chairperson to serve a two-year term.

The Commission shall be convened permanently to hear complaints filed by the Judicial Inquiry Board. The Commission shall have authority after notice and public hearing, (1) to remove from office, suspend without pay, censure or reprimand a Judge or Associate Judge for willful misconduct in Office, persistent failure to perform his or her duties, or other conduct that is prejudicial to the administration of justice or that brings the judicial office into disrepute, or (2) to suspend, with or without pay, or retire a Judge or Associate Judge who is physically or mentally unable to perform his or her duties.

(f) The concurrence of four members of the Commission shall be necessary for a decision. The decision of the Commission shall be final.

(g) The Commission shall adopt comprehensive rules to ensure that its procedures are fair and appropriate. These rules and any amendments shall be public and filed with the Secretary of State at least 30 days before becoming effective.

(h) A member of the Commission shall disqualify himself or herself, or the other members of the Commission shall disqualify a member, with respect to any proceeding in which disqualification or recusal would be required of a Judge under rules of the Supreme Court, under rules of the Commission, or by law.

If a Supreme Court Judge is the subject of a proceeding, then there shall be no Supreme Court Judge sitting as a member of the Commission with respect to that proceeding. Instead, an alternate Appellate Court Judge not from the same Judicial District as the subject Supreme Court Judge shall replace the subject Supreme Court Judge. If a member who is an Appellate Court Judge is the subject of a proceeding, then an alternate Appellate Court Judge shall replace the subject Appellate Court Judge. If an Appellate Court Judge who is not a member is the subject of a proceeding and an Appellate Court Judge from the same Judicial District is a member, then an alternate Appellate Court Judge shall replace that member. If a member who is a Circuit Judge is the subject of a proceeding, then an alternate Circuit Judge shall replace the subject Circuit Judge. If a Circuit Judge who is not a member is the subject of a proceeding and a Circuit Judge from the same Judicial District is a member, then an alternate Circuit Judge shall replace that member.

If a member of the Commission is disqualified under this Section with respect to any proceeding, that member shall be replaced by an alternate on a rotating basis in a manner provided by rule of the Commission. The alternate shall act as member of the Commission with respect to that proceeding only.

(i) The Commission shall have power to issue subpoenas.

(j) Members and alternates of the Commission who are not Judges shall receive per diem compensation and necessary expenses; members and alternates who are Judges shall receive necessary expenses only. The General Assembly shall provide by law for the expenses and compensation of the Commission. (As amended by the Tenth Amendment to the Constitution. Approved November 3, 1998, effective November 23, 1998.)

Section 16. ADMINISTRATION

General administrative and supervisory authority over all courts is vested in the Supreme Court and shall be exercised by the Chief Justice in accordance with its rules. The Supreme Court shall appoint an administrative director and staff, who shall serve at its pleasure, to assist the Chief Justice in his duties. The Supreme Court may assign a Judge temporarily to any court and an Associate Judge to serve temporarily as an Associate Judge on any Circuit Court. The Supreme Court shall provide by rule for expeditious and inexpensive appeals.

Section 17. JUDICIAL CONFERENCE

The Supreme Court shall provide by rule for an annual judicial conference to consider the work of the courts and to suggest improvements in the administration of justice and shall report thereon annually in writing to the General Assembly not later than January 31.

Section 18. CLERKS OF COURTS

(a) The Supreme Court and the Appellate Court Judges of each Judicial District, respectively, shall appoint a clerk and other non-judicial officers for their Court or District.

(b) The General Assembly shall provide by law for the election, or for the appointment by Circuit Judges, of clerks and other non-judicial officers of the Circuit Courts and for their terms of office and removal for cause.

(c) The salaries of clerks and other non-judicial officers shall be as provided by law.

Section 19. STATE'S ATTORNEYS — SELECTION, SALARY

A State's Attorney shall be elected in each county in 1972 and every fourth year thereafter for a four year term. One State's Attorney may be elected to serve two or more counties if the governing boards of such counties so provide and a majority of the electors of each county voting on the issue approve. A person shall not be eligible for the office of State's Attorney unless he is a United States citizen and a licensed attorney-at-law of this State. His salary shall be provided by law.

ARTICLE VII — Local Government

Section 1. MUNICIPALITIES AND UNITS OF LOCAL GOVERNMENT

"Municipalities" means cities, villages and incorporated towns. "Units of local government" means counties, municipalities, townships, special districts, and units, designated as units of local government by law, which exercise limited governmental powers or powers in respect to limited governmental subjects, but does not include school districts.

Section 2. COUNTY TERRITORY, BOUNDARIES AND SEATS

(a) The General Assembly shall provide by law for the formation, consolidation, merger, division, and dissolution of counties, and for the transfer of territory between counties.

(b) County boundaries shall not be changed unless approved by referendum in each county affected.

(c) County seats shall not be changed unless approved by three-fifths of those voting on the question in a county-wide referendum.

Section 3. COUNTY BOARDS

(a) A county board shall be elected in each county. The number of members of the county board shall be fixed by ordinance in each county within limitations provided by law.

(b) The General Assembly by law shall provide methods available to all counties for the election of county board members. No county, other than Cook County, may change its method of electing board members except as approved by county-wide referendum.

(c) Members of the Cook County Board shall be elected from two districts, Chicago and that part of Cook County outside Chicago, unless (1) a different method of election is approved by a majority of votes cast in each of the two districts in a county-wide referendum or (2) the Cook County Board by ordinance divides the county into single member districts from which members of the County Board resident in each district are elected. If a different method of election is adopted pursuant to option (1) the method of election may thereafter be altered only pursuant to option (2) or by county-wide referendum. A different method of election may be adopted pursuant to option (2) only once and the method of election may thereafter be altered only by county-wide referendum.

Section 4. COUNTY OFFICERS

(a) Any county may elect a chief executive officer as provided by law. He shall have those duties and powers provided by law and those provided by county ordinance.

(b) The President of the Cook County Board shall be elected from the County at large and shall be the chief executive officer of the County. If authorized by county ordinance, a person seeking election as President of the Cook County Board may also seek election as a member of the Board.

(c) Each county shall elect a sheriff, county clerk and treasurer and may elect or appoint a coroner, recorder, assessor, auditor and such other officers as provided by law or by county ordinance. Except as changed pursuant to this Section, elected county officers shall be elected for terms of four years at general elections as provided by law. Any office may be created or eliminated and the terms of office and manner of selection changed by county-wide referendum. Offices other than sheriff, county clerk and treasurer may be eliminated and the terms of office and manner of selection changed by law. Offices other than sheriff, county clerk, treasurer, coroner, recorder, assessor and auditor may be eliminated and the terms of office and manner of selection changed by county ordinance.

(d)   County officers shall have those duties, powers and functions provided by law and those provided by county ordinance. County officers shall have the duties, powers or functions derived from common law or historical precedent unless altered by law or county ordinance.

(e)   The county treasurer or the person designated to perform his functions may act as treasurer of any unit of local government and any school district in his county when requested by any such unit or school district and shall so act when required to do so by law.

Section 5. TOWNSHIPS

The General Assembly shall provide by law for the formation of townships in any county when approved by county-wide referendum. Townships may be consolidated or merged, and one or more townships may be dissolved or divided, when approved by referendum in each township affected. All townships in a county may be dissolved when approved by a referendum in the total area in which township officers are elected.

Section 6. POWERS OF HOME RULE UNITS

(a)   A County which has a chief executive officer elected by the electors of the county and any municipality which has a population of more than 25,000 are home rule units. Other municipalities may elect by referendum to become home rule units. Except as limited by this Section, a home rule unit may exercise any power and perform any function pertaining to its government and affairs including, but not limited to, the power to regulate for the protection of the public health, safety, morals and welfare; to license; to tax; and to incur debt.

(b)   A home rule unit by referendum may elect not to be a home rule unit.

(c)   If a home rule county ordinance conflicts with an ordinance of a municipality, the municipal ordinance shall prevail within its jurisdiction.

(d)   A home rule unit does not have the power (1) to incur debt payable from ad valorem property tax receipts maturing more than 40 years from the time it is incurred or (2) to define and provide for the punishment of a felony.

(e)   A home rule unit shall have only the power that the General Assembly may provide by law (1) to punish by imprisonment for more than six months or (2) to license for revenue or impose taxes upon or measured by income or earnings or upon occupations.

(f)   A home rule unit shall have the power subject to approval by referendum to adopt, alter or repeal a form of government provided by law, except that the form of government of Cook County shall be subject to the provisions of Section 3 of this Article. A home rule municipality shall have the power to provide for its officers, their manner of selection and terms of office only as approved by referendum or as otherwise authorized by law. A home rule county shall have the power to provide for its officers, their manner of selection and terms of office in the manner set forth in Section 4 of this Article.

(g)   The General Assembly by a law approved by the vote of three-fifths of the members elected to each house may deny or limit the power to tax and any other power or function of a home rule unit not exercised or performed by the

State other than a power or function specified in subsection (I) of this section.

(h) The General Assembly may provide specifically by law for the exclusive exercise by the State of any power or function of a home rule unit other than a taxing power or a power or function specified in subsection (I) of this Section.

(i) Home rule units may exercise and perform concurrently with the State any power or function of a home rule unit to the extent that the General Assembly by law does not specifically limit the concurrent exercise or specifically declare the State's exercise to be exclusive.

(j) The General Assembly may limit by law the amount of debt which home rule counties may incur and may limit by law approved by three-fifths of the members elected to each house the amount of debt, other than debt payable from ad valorem property tax receipts, which home rule municipalities may incur.

(k) The General Assembly may limit by law the amount and require referendum approval of debt to be incurred by home rule municipalities, payable from ad valorem property tax receipts, only in excess of the following percentages of the assessed value of its taxable property: (1) if its population is 500,000 or more, an aggregate of three percent; (2) if its population is more than 25,000 and less than 500,000, an aggregate of one percent; and (3) if its population is 25,000 or less, an aggregate of one-half percent. Indebtedness which is outstanding on the effective date of this Constitution or which is thereafter approved by referendum or assumed from another unit of local government shall not be included in the foregoing percentage amounts.

(l) The General Assembly may not deny or limit the power of home rule units (1) to make local improvements by special assessment and to exercise this power jointly with other counties and municipalities, and other classes of units of local government having that power on the effective date of this Constitution unless that power is subsequently denied by law to any such other units of local government or (2) to levy or impose additional taxes upon areas within their boundaries in the manner provided by law for the provision of special services to those areas and for the payment of debt incurred in order to provide those special services.

(m) Powers and functions of home rule units shall be construed liberally.

Section 7. COUNTIES AND MUNICIPALITIES OTHER THAN HOME RULE UNITS

Counties and municipalities which are not home rule units shall have only powers granted to them by law and the powers (1) to make local improvements by special assessment and to exercise this power jointly with other counties and municipalities, and other classes of units of local government having that power on the effective date of this Constitution unless that power is subsequently denied by law to any such other units of local government; (2) by referendum, to adopt, alter or repeal their forms of government provided by law; (3) in the case of municipalities, to provide by referendum for their officers, manner of selection and terms of office; (4) in the case of counties, to provide for their officers, manner of selection and terms of office as provided in Section 4 of this Article; (5) to incur debt except as limited by law and except that debt payable from ad valorem property tax receipts shall mature within 40 years from the time it is incurred; and (6) to levy or impose additional taxes upon areas within their boundaries in the manner provided by law for the provision of special services to those areas and for the payment of debt incurred in order to provide those special services.

Section 8. POWERS AND OFFICERS OF SCHOOL DISTRICTS AND UNITS OF LOCAL GOVERNMENT OTHER THAN COUNTIES AND MUNICIPALITIES

Townships, school districts, special districts and units, designated by law as units of local government, which exercise limited governmental powers or powers in respect to limited governmental subjects shall have only powers granted by law. No law shall grant the power (1) to any of the foregoing units to incur debt payable from ad valorem property tax receipts maturing more than 40 years from the time it is incurred, or (2) to make improvements by special assessments to any of the foregoing classes of units which do not have that power on the effective date of this Constitution. The General Assembly shall provide by law for the selection of officers of the foregoing units, but the officers shall not be appointed by any person in the Judicial Branch.

Section 9. SALARIES AND FEES

(a) Compensation of officers and employees and the office expenses of units of local government shall not be paid from fees collected. Fees may be collected as provided by law and by ordinance and shall be deposited upon receipt with the treasurer of the unit. Fees shall not be based upon funds disbursed or collected, nor upon the levy or extension of taxes.

(b) An increase or decrease in the salary of an elected officer of any unit of local government shall not take effect during the term for which that officer is elected.

Section 10. INTERGOVERNMENTAL COOPERATION

(a) Units of local government and school districts may contract or otherwise associate among themselves, with the State, with other states and their units of local government and school districts, and with the United States to obtain or share services and to exercise, combine, or transfer any power or function, in any manner not prohibited by law or by ordinance. Units of local government and school districts may contract and otherwise associate with individuals, associations, and corporations in any manner not prohibited by law or by ordinance. Participating units of government may use their credit, revenues, and other resources to pay costs and to service debt related to intergovernmental activities.

(b) Officers and employees of units of local government and school districts may participate in intergovernmental activities authorized by their units of government without relinquishing their offices or positions.

(c) The State shall encourage intergovernmental cooperation and use its technical and financial resources to assist intergovernmental activities.

Section 11. INITIATIVE AND REFERENDUM

(a) Proposals for actions which are authorized by this Article or by law and which require approval by referendum may be initiated and submitted to the electors by resolution of the governing board of a unit of local government or by petition of electors in the manner provided by law.

(b) Referenda required by this Article shall be held at general elections, except as otherwise provided by law. Questions submitted to referendum shall be adopted if approved by a majority of those voting on the question unless a different requirement is specified in this Article.

Section 12. IMPLEMENTATION OF GOVERNMENTAL CHANGES

The General Assembly shall provide by law for the transfer of assets, powers and functions, and for the payment of outstanding debt in connection with the formation, consolidation, merger, division, dissolution and change in the boundaries of units of local government.

ARTICLE VIII — Finance

Section 1. GENERAL PROVISIONS

(a) Public funds, property or credit shall be used only for public purposes.

(b) The State, units of local government and school districts shall incur obligations for payment or make payments from public funds only as authorized by law or ordinance.

(c) Reports and records of the obligation, receipt and use of public funds of the State, units of local government and school districts are public records available for inspection by the public according to law.

Section 2. STATE FINANCE

(a) The Governor shall prepare and submit to the General Assembly, at a time prescribed by law, a State budget for the ensuing fiscal year. The budget shall set forth the estimated balance of funds available for appropriation at the beginning of the fiscal year, the estimated receipts, and a plan for expenditures and obligations during the fiscal year of every department, authority, public corporation and quasi-public corporation of the State, every State college and university, and every other public agency created by the State, but not of units of local government or school districts. The budget shall also set forth the indebtedness and contingent liabilities of the State and such other information as may be required by law. Proposed expenditures shall not exceed funds estimated to be available for the fiscal year as shown in the budget.

(b) The General Assembly by law shall make appropriations for all expenditures of public funds by the State. Appropriations for a fiscal year shall not exceed funds estimated by the General Assembly to be available during that year.

Section 3. STATE AUDIT AND AUDITOR GENERAL

(a) The General Assembly shall provide by law for the audit of the obligation, receipt and use of public funds of the State. The General Assembly, by a vote of three-fifths of the members elected to each house, shall appoint an Auditor General and may remove him for cause by a similar vote. The Auditor General shall serve for a term of ten years. His compensation shall be established by law and shall not be diminished, but may be increased, to take effect during his term.

(b) The Auditor General shall conduct the audit of public funds of the State. He shall make additional reports and investigations as directed by the General Assembly. He shall report his findings and recommendations to the General Assembly and to the Governor.

Section 4. SYSTEMS OF ACCOUNTING, AUDITING AND REPORTING

The General Assembly by law shall provide systems of accounting, auditing and reporting of the obligation, receipt and use of public funds. These systems shall be used by all units of local government and school districts.

ARTICLE IX — Revenue

Section 1. STATE REVENUE POWER

The General Assembly has the exclusive power to raise revenue by law except as limited or otherwise provided in this Constitution. The power of taxation shall not be surrendered, suspended, or contracted away.

Section 2. NON-PROPERTY TAXES — CLASSIFICATION, EXEMPTIONS, DEDUCTIONS, ALLOWANCES AND CREDITS

In any law classifying the subjects or objects of non-property taxes or fees, the classes shall be reasonable and the subjects and objects within each class shall be taxed uniformly. Exemptions, deductions, credits, refunds and other allowances shall be reasonable.

Section 3. LIMITATIONS ON INCOME TAXATION

(a) A tax on or measured by income shall be at a non-graduated rate. At any one time there may be no more than one such tax imposed by the State for State purposes on individuals and one such tax so imposed on corporations. In any such tax imposed upon corporations the rate shall not exceed the rate imposed in individuals by more than a ratio of 8 to 5.

(b) Laws imposing taxes on or measured by income may adopt by reference provisions of the laws and regulations of the United States, as they then exist or thereafter may be changed, for the purpose of arriving at the amount of income upon which the tax is imposed.

Section 4. REAL PROPERTY TAXATION

(a) Except as otherwise provided in this Section, taxes upon real property shall be levied uniformly by valuation ascertained as the General Assembly shall provide by law.

(b) Subject to such limitations as the General Assembly may hereafter prescribe by law, counties with a population of more than 200,000 may classify or to continue to classify real property for purposes of taxation. Any such classification shall be reasonable and assessments shall be uniform within each class. The level of assessment or rate of tax of the highest class in a county shall not exceed two and one-half times the level of assessment or rate of tax of the lowest class in that county. Real property used in farming in a county shall not be assessed at a higher level of assessment than single family residential real property in that county.

(c) Any depreciation in the value of real estate occasioned by a public easement may be deducted in assessing such property.

Section 5. PERSONAL PROPERTY TAXATION

(a) The General Assembly by law may classify personal property for purposes of taxation by valuation, abolish such taxes on any or all classes and authorize the levy of taxes in lieu of the taxation of personal property by valuation.

(b) Any ad valorem personal property tax abolished on or before the effective date of this Constitution shall not be reinstated.

(c) On or before January 1, 1979, the General Assembly by law shall abolish all ad valorem personal property taxes and concurrently therewith and thereafter shall replace all revenue lost by units of local government and school districts as a result of the abolition of ad valorem personal property taxes subsequent to January 2, 1971. Such revenue shall be replaced by imposing statewide taxes, other than ad valorem taxes on real estate, solely on those classes relieved of the burden of paying ad valorem personal property taxes because of the abolition of such taxes subsequent to January 2, 1971. If any taxes imposed for such replacement purposes are taxes on or measured by income, such replacement taxes shall not be considered for purposes of the limitations of one tax and the ratio of 8 to 5 set forth in Section 3 (a) of this Article.

Section 6. EXEMPTIONS FROM PROPERTY TAXATION

The General Assembly by law may exempt from taxation only the property of the State, units of local government and school districts and property used exclusively for agricultural and horticultural societies, and for school, religious, cemetery and charitable purposes. The General Assembly by law may grant homestead exemptions or rent credits.

Section 7. OVERLAPPING TAXING DISTRICTS

The General Assembly may provide by law for fair apportionment of the burden of taxation of property situated in taxing districts that lie in more than one county.

Section 8. TAX SALES

(a)   Real property shall not be sold for the nonpayment of taxes or special assessments without judicial proceedings.

(b)   The right of redemption from all sales of real estate for the nonpayment of taxes or special assessments, except as provided in subsections (c) and (d), shall exist in favor of owners and persons interested in such real estate for not less than 2 years following such sales.

(c)   The right of redemption from the sale for nonpayment of taxes or special assessments of a parcel of real estate which: (1) is vacant non-farm real estate or (2) contains an improvement consisting of a structure or structures each of which contains 7 or more residential units or (3) is commercial or industrial property; shall exist in favor of owners and persons interested in such real estate for not less than one year following such sales.

(d)   The right of redemption from the sale for nonpayment of taxes or special assessments of a parcel real estate which: (1) is vacant non-farm real estate or (2) contains an improvement consisting of a structure or structures each of which contains 7 or more residential units or (3) is commercial or industrial property; and upon which all or a part of the general taxes for each of 2 or more years are delinquent shall exist in favor of owners and persons interested in such real estate for not less than 6 months following such sales.

(e)   Owners, occupants and parties interested shall be given reasonable notice of the sale and the date of expiration of the period of redemption as the General Assembly provides by law. (As amended by the Sixth Amendment to the Constitution. Approved November 6, 1990, effective November 26, 1990.)

Section 9. STATE DEBT

(a)   No State debt shall be incurred except as provided in this Section. For the purpose of this Section, "State debt" means bonds or other evidences of indebtedness which are secured by the full faith and credit of the State or are required to be repaid, directly or indirectly, from tax revenue and which are incurred by the State, any department, authority, public corporation or quasi-public corporation of the State, any State college or university, or any other public agency created by the State, but not by units of local government, or school districts.

(b)   State debt for specific purposes may be incurred or the payment of State or other debt guaranteed in such amounts as may be provided either in a law passed by the vote of three-fifths of the members elected to each house of the General Assembly or in a law approved by a majority of the electors voting on the question at the next general election following passage. Any law providing for the incurring or guaranteeing of debt shall set forth the specific purposes and the manner of repayment.

(c)   State debt in anticipation of revenues to be collected in a fiscal year may be incurred by law in an amount not exceeding 5% of the State's appropriations for that fiscal year. Such debt shall be retired from the revenues realized in that fiscal year.

(d)   State debt may be incurred by law in an amount not exceeding 15% of the State's appropriations for that fiscal year to meet deficits caused by emergencies of failures of revenue. Such law shall provide that the debt be repaid within one year of the date it is incurred.

(e)   State debt may be incurred by law to refund outstanding State debt if the refunding debt matures within the term of the outstanding State debt.

(f)   The State, departments, authorities, public corporations and quasi-public corporations of the State, the State colleges and universities and other public agencies created by the State, may issue bonds or other evidences of indebtedness which are not secured by the full faith and credit or tax revenue of the State nor required to be repaid, directly or indirectly, from tax revenue, for such purposes and in such amounts as may be authorized by law.

Section 10. REVENUE ARTICLE NOT LIMITED
This Article is not qualified or limited by the provisions of Article VII of this Constitution concerning the size of the majorities in the General Assembly necessary to deny or limit the power to tax granted to units of local government.

ARTICLE X — Education

Section 1. GOAL — FREE SCHOOLS
A fundamental goal of the People of the State is the educational development of all persons to the limits of their capacities.

The State shall provide for an efficient system of high quality public educational institutions and services. Education in public schools through the secondary level shall be free. There may be such other free education as the General Assembly provides by law.

The State has the primary responsibility for financing the system of public education.

**Section 2. STATE BOARD OF EDUCATION — CHIEF STATE
EDUCATIONAL OFFICER**
(a)   There is created a State Board of Education to be elected or selected on a regional basis. The number of members, their qualifications, terms of office and manner of election or selection shall be provided by law. The Board, except as limited by law, may establish goals, determine policies, provide for planning and evaluating education programs and recommend financing. The Board shall have such other duties and powers as provided by law.

(b)   The State Board of Education shall appoint a chief state educational officer.

Section 3. PUBLIC FUNDS FOR SECTARIAN PURPOSES FORBIDDEN
Neither the General Assembly nor any county, city, town, township, school district, or other public corporation, shall ever make any appropriation or pay from any public fund whatever, anything in aid of any church or sectarian purpose, or to help support or sustain any school, academy, seminary, college, university or other literary or scientific institution, controlled by any church or sectarian denomination whatever; nor shall any grant or donation of land, money, or other personal property ever be made by the State, or any such public

corporation, to any church, or for any sectarian purpose.

ARTICLE XI — Environment

Section 1. PUBLIC POLICY — LEGISLATIVE RESPONSIBILITY
The public policy of the State and the duty of each person is to provide and maintain a healthful environment for the benefit of this and future generations. The General Assembly shall provide by law for the implementation and enforcement of this public policy.

Section 2. RIGHTS OF INDIVIDUALS
Each person has the right to a healthful environment. Each person may enforce this right against any party, governmental or private, through appropriate legal proceedings subject to reasonable limitation and regulation as the General Assembly may provide by law.

ARTICLE XII — Militia

Section 1. MEMBERSHIP
The State militia consists of all able-bodied persons residing in the State except those exempted by law.

Section 2. SUBORDINATION OF MILITARY POWER
The military shall be in strict subordination to the civil power.

Section 3. ORGANIZATION, EQUIPMENT AND DISCIPLINE
The General Assembly shall provide by law for the organization, equipment and discipline of the militia in conformity with the laws governing the armed forces of the United States.

Section 4. COMMANDER-IN-CHIEF AND OFFICERS
(a) The Governor is commander-in-chief of the organized militia, except when they are in the service of the United States. He may call them out to enforce the laws, suppress insurrection or repel invasion.

(b) The Governor shall commission militia officers who shall hold their commissions for such time as may be provided by law.

Section 5. PRIVILEGE FROM ARREST
Except in cases of treason, felony or breach of peace, persons going to, returning from or on militia duty are privileged from arrest.

ARTICLE XIII — General Provisions

Section 1. DISQUALIFICATION FOR PUBLIC OFFICE
A person convicted of a felony, bribery, perjury or other infamous crime shall be ineligible to hold an office created by this Constitution. Eligibility may be restored as provided by law.

Section 2. STATEMENT OF ECONOMIC INTERESTS
All candidates for or holders of state offices and all members of a Commission or Board created by this Constitution shall file a verified statement of their economic interests, as provided by law. The General Assembly by law may impose a similar requirement upon candidates for, or holders of, offices in units of local government and school districts. Statements shall be filed annually with the Secretary of State and shall be available for inspection by the public. The General Assembly by law shall prescribe a reasonable time for filing the state-

ment. Failure to file a statement within the time prescribed shall result in ineligibility for, or forfeiture of, office. This Section shall not be construed as limiting the authority of any branch of government to establish and enforce ethical standards for that branch.

Section 3. OATH OR AFFIRMATION OF OFFICE

Each prospective holder of a State office or other State position created by this Constitution, before taking office, shall take and subscribe to the following oath or affirmation:

"I do solemnly swear (affirm) that I will support the Constitution of the United States, and the Constitution of the State of Illinois, and that I will faithfully discharge the duties of the office of.. to the best of my ability."

Section 4. SOVEREIGN IMMUNITY ABOLISHED

Except as the General Assembly may provide by law, sovereign immunity in this State is abolished.

Section 5. PENSION AND RETIREMENT RIGHTS

Membership in any pension or retirement system of the State, any unit of local government or school district, or any agency or instrumentality thereof, shall be an enforceable contractual relationship, the benefits of which shall not be diminished or impaired.

Section 6. CORPORATIONS

Corporate charters shall be granted, amended, dissolved, or extended only pursuant to general laws.

Section 7. PUBLIC TRANSPORTATION

Public transportation is an essential public purpose for which public funds may be expended. The General Assembly by law may provide for, aid, and assist public transportation, including the granting of public funds or credit to any corporation or public authority authorized to provide public transportation within the State.

Section 8. BRANCH BANKING

Branch banking shall be authorized only by law approved by three-fifths of the members voting on the question or a majority of the members elected, whichever is greater, in each house of the General Assembly.

ARTICLE XIV — Constitutional Revision

Section 1. CONSTITUTIONAL CONVENTION

(a) Whenever three-fifths of the members elected to each house of the General Assembly so direct, the question of whether a Constitutional Convention should be called shall be submitted to the electors at the general election next occurring at least six months after such legislative direction.

(b) If the question of whether a Convention should be called is not submitted during any twenty-year period, the Secretary of State shall submit such question at the general election in the twentieth year following the last submission.

(c) The vote on whether to call a Convention shall be on a separate ballot. A Convention shall be called if approved by three-fifths of those voting on the question or a majority of those voting in the election.

(d) The General Assembly, at the session following approval by the electors, by law shall provide for the Convention and for the election of two delegates from each Senatorial District; designate the time and place of the Convention's first meeting which shall be within three months after the election of delegates; fix and provide for the pay of delegates and officers; and provide for expenses necessarily incurred by the Convention.

(e)   To be eligible to be a delegate a person must meet the same eligibility requirements as a member of the General Assembly. Vacancies shall be filled as provided by law.

(f)   The Convention shall prepare such revision of or amendments to the Constitution as it deems necessary. Any proposed revision or amendments approved by a majority of the delegates elected shall be submitted to the electors in such manner as the Convention determines, at an election designated or called by the Convention occurring not less than two nor more than six months after the Convention's adjournment. Any revision or amendments proposed by the Convention shall be published with explanations, as the Convention provides, at least one month preceding the election.

(g)   The vote on the proposed revision or amendments shall be on a separate ballot. Any proposed revision or amendments shall become effective, as the Convention provides, if approved by a majority of those voting on the question.

Section 2. AMENDMENTS BY GENERAL ASSEMBLY

(a)   Amendments to this Constitution may be initiated in either house of the General Assembly. Amendments shall be read in full on three different days in each house and reproduced before the vote is taken on final passage. Amendments approved by the vote of three-fifths of the members elected to each house shall be submitted to the electors at the general election next occurring at least six months after such legislative approval, unless withdrawn by a vote of a majority of the members elected to each house.

(b)   Amendments proposed by the General Assembly shall be published with explanations, as provided by law, at least one month preceding the vote thereon by the electors. The vote on the proposed amendment or amendments shall be on a separate ballot. A proposed amendment shall become effective as the amendment provides if approved by either three-fifths of those voting on the question or a majority of those voting in the election.

(c)   The General Assembly shall not submit proposed amendments to more than three Articles of the Constitution at any one election. No amendment shall be proposed or submitted under this Section from the time a Convention is called until after the electors have voted on the revision or amendments, if any, proposed by such Convention.

Section 3. CONSTITUTIONAL INITIATIVE FOR LEGISLATIVE ARTICLE

Amendments to Article IV of this Constitution may be proposed by a petition signed by a number of electors equal in number to at least eight percent of the total votes cast for candidates for Governor in the preceding gubernatorial election. Amendments shall be limited to structural and procedural subjects contained in Article IV. A petition shall contain the text of the proposed amendment and the date of the general election at which the proposed amendment is to be submitted, shall have been signed by the petitioning electors not more than twenty-four months preceding that general election and shall be filed with the Secretary of State at least six months before that general election. The procedure for determining the validity and sufficiency of a petition shall be provided by law. If the petition is valid and sufficient, the proposed amendment shall be submitted to the electors at that general election and shall become effective if approved by either three-fifths of those voting on the amendment or a majority of those voting in the election.

Section 4. AMENDMENTS TO THE CONSTITUTION OF THE UNITED STATES

The affirmative vote of three-fifths of the members elected to each house of the General Assembly shall be required to request Congress to call a Federal Constitutional Convention, to ratify a proposed amendment to the Constitution of the United States, or to call a State Convention to ratify a proposed amendment to the Constitution of the United States. The General Assembly shall not take action on any proposed amendment to the Constitution of the United States submitted for ratification by legislatures unless a majority of the members of the General Assembly shall have been elected after the proposed amendment has been submitted for ratification. The requirements of this Section shall govern to the extent that they are not inconsistent with requirements by the United States.

TRANSITION SCHEDULE

The following Schedule Provisions shall remain part of this Constitution until their terms have been executed. Once each year the Attorney General shall review the following provisions and certify to the Secretary of State which, if any, have been executed. Any provisions so certified shall thereafter be removed from the Schedule and no longer published as part of this Constitution.

Section 1.	(Removed)
Section 2.	Prospective Operation of Bill of Rights.
Section 3.	(Removed)
Section 4.	Judicial Offices.
Section 5.	Local Government.
Section 6.	Authorized Bonds.
Section 7.	(Removed)
Section 8.	Cumulative Voting for Directors.
Section 9.	General Transition.
Section10.	(Removed)

Section 2. PROSPECTIVE OPERATION OF BILL OF RIGHTS

Any rights, procedural or substantive, created for the first time by Article I shall be prospective and not retroactive.

Section 4. JUDICIAL OFFICES

(a) On the effective date of this Constitution, Associate Judges and magistrates shall become Circuit Judges and Associate Judges, respectively, of their Circuit Courts. All laws and rules of court theretofore applicable to Associate Judges and magistrates shall remain in force and be applicable to the persons in their new offices until changed by the General Assembly or the Supreme Court, as the case may be.

(b) (Removed)

(c) (Removed)

(d) Until otherwise provided by law and except to the extent that the authority is inconsistent with Section 8 of Article VII, the Circuit Courts shall continue to exercise the non-judicial functions vested by law as of December 31, 1963, in county courts or the judges thereof.

Section 5. LOCAL GOVERNMENT

(a) The number of members of a county board in a county which, as of the effective date of this Constitution, elects three members at large may be changed only as approved by county-wide referendum. If the number of members of such a county board is changed by county-wide referendum, the provisions of Section 3(a) of Article VII relating to the number of members of a county board shall govern thereafter.

(b) In Cook County, until (1) a method of election of county board members different from the method in existence on the effective date of this Constitution is approved by a majority of votes cast both in Chicago and in the area outside Chicago in a county-wide referendum or (2) the Cook County Board by ordinance divides the county into single member districts from which members of the County Board resident in each district are elected, the number of members of the Cook County Board shall be fifteen except that the county board may increase the number if necessary to comply with apportionment requirements. If either of the foregoing changes is made, the provisions of Section 3(a) of Article VII shall apply thereafter to Cook County.

(c) Townships in existence on the effective date of this Constitution are continued until consolidated, merged, divided or dissolved in accordance with Section 5 of Article VII.

Section 6. AUTHORIZED BONDS

Nothing in Section 9 of Article IX shall be construed to limit or impair the power to issue bonds or other evidences of indebtedness authorized but unissued on the effective date of this Constitution.

Section 8. CUMULATIVE VOTING FOR DIRECTORS

Shareholders of all corporations heretofore organized under any law of this State which requires cumulative voting of shares for corporate directors shall retain their right to vote cumulatively for such directors.

Section 9. GENERAL TRANSITION

The rights and duties of all public bodies shall remain as if this Constitution had not been adopted with the exception of such changes as are contained in this Constitution. All laws, ordinances, regulations and rules of court not contrary to, or inconsistent with, the provisions of this Constitution shall remain in force, until they shall expire by their own limitation or shall be altered or repealed pursuant to this Constitution. The validity of all public and private bonds, debts and contracts, and of all suits, actions and rights of action, shall continue as if no change had taken place. All officers filling any office by election or appointment shall continue to exercise the duties thereof, until their offices shall have been abolished or their successors selected and qualified in accordance with this Constitution or laws enacted pursuant thereto.

(ATTESTATION)

Done in Convention at the Old State Capitol, in the City of Springfield, on the third day of September, in the year of our Lord one thousand nine hundred and seventy, of the Independence of the United States of America the one hundred and ninety-fifth, and of the Statehood of Illinois the one hundred and fifty-second.

AMENDMENTS

(A proposed amendment shall become effective if approved by either three-fifths of those voting on the question or a majority of those voting in the election.)

First Amendment — 1980 — Cutback Amendment. Amends Article IV, Sections 1, 2 and 3. Total vote, 4,868,623. For, 2,112,224; Against, 962,325.

Second Amendment — 1980 — Delinquent Tax Sales. Amends Article IX, Section 8. Total vote, 4,868,623. For, 1,857,985; Against, 798,422.

Third Amendment — 1982 — Bail and Habeas Corpus. Amends Article I, Section 9. Total vote, 3,856,875. For, 1,389,796; Against, 239,380.

Fourth Amendment (Amended Third Amendment) — 1986 — Bail and Habeas Corpus. Amends Article I, Section 9. Total vote, 3,322,657. For, 1,368,242; Against, 402,891.

Fifth Amendment — 1988 — Voting Qualifications. Amends Article III, Section 1. Total vote, 4,697,192. For, 2,086,744; Against, 1,162,258.

Sixth Amendment (Amended Second Amendment) — 1990 — Delinquent Tax Sales. Amends Article IX, Section 8. Total vote, 3,420,720. For, 1,004,546; Against, 385,772.

Seventh Amendment — 1992 — Crime Victim's Rights. Adds Section 8.1 to Article I. Total vote, 5,164,357. For, 2,964,592; Against, 715,602.

Eighth Amendment — 1994 — Rights After Indictment. Amends Article I, Section 8. Total vote, 3,219,122. For, 1,525,525; Against, 906,383.

Ninth Amendment — 1994 — Effective Date of Laws. Amends Article IV, Section 10. Total vote, 3,219,122. For, 1,476,615; Against, 667,585.

Tenth Amendment — 1998 — Retirement - Discipline. Amends Article VI, Section 15. Total vote, 2,084,123. For, 1,677,109; Against, 407,014.

STUDY GUIDE

Illinois students are required to pass a Constitution test before graduating from high school. Adults who have not graduated from high school and want to obtain a General Education Development (GED) certificate also must pass the exam. To assist those students, the Illinois State Board of Education has produced a Constitution Study Guide.

The Study Guide is available in English and Spanish. The cost must be pre-paid by sending a check or money order for $5.14, payable to CPC, to the Curriculum Publications Clearinghouse, Western Illinois University, Horrabin Hall 46, Macomb, IL 61455. Be sure to indicate either the English or Spanish edition. For additional information, call (800) 322-3905.

CONSTITUTION OF THE UNITED STATES

We the People of the United States, In Order to form a more perfect Union, establish Justice, insure domestic Tranquility, provide for the common defense, promote the general Welfare, and secure the Blessings of Liberty to ourselves and our Posterity, do ordain and establish this Constitution for the United States of America.

ARTICLE I

Section 1. All legislative Powers herein granted shall be vested in a Congress of the United States, which shall consist of a Senate and House of Representatives.

Section 2. The House of Representatives shall be composed of Members chosen every second Year by the People of the several States, and the Electors in each State shall have the Qualifications requisite for Electors of the most numerous Branch of the State Legislature.

No Person shall be a Representative who shall not have attained to the age of twenty five Years, and been seven Years a Citizen of the United States, and who shall not, when elected, be an Inhabitant of that State in which he shall be chosen.

(Representatives and direct Taxes shall be apportioned among the several States which may be included within this Union, according to their respective Numbers, which shall be determined by adding to the whole Number of free Persons, including those bound to Service for a Term of Years, and excluding Indians not taxed, three fifths of all other Persons.) *See 14th and 16th Amendments.* The actual Enumeration shall be made within three Years after the first Meeting of the Congress of the United States, and within every subsequent Term of ten Years, in such Manner as they shall by Law direct. The Number of Representatives shall not exceed one for every thirty Thousand, but each State shall have at Least One Representative; and until such enumeration shall be made, the State of New Hampshire shall be entitled to choose three, Massachusetts eight, Rhode-Island and Providence Plantations one, Connecticut five, New York six, New Jersey four, Pennsylvania eight, Delaware one, Maryland six, Virginia ten, North Carolina five, South Carolina five, and Georgia three.

When vacancies happen in the Representation from any State, the Executive Authority thereof shall issue Writs of Election to fill such Vacancies.

The House of Representatives shall choose their Speaker and other Officers; and shall have the sole Power of Impeachment.

Section 3. (The Senate of the United States shall be composed of two Senators from each State, chosen by the Legislature thereof, for six Years; and each Senator shall have one Vote.) *See 17th Amendment.*

Immediately after they shall be assembled in Consequence of the first Election, they shall be divided as equally as may be into three Classes. The Seats of the Senators of the first Class shall be vacated at the Expiration of the second Year, of the second Class at the Expiration of the fourth Year, and of the third Class at the Expiration of the sixth Year, so that one third may be chosen every second Year; (and if Vacancies happen by Resignation, or otherwise, during the

Recess of the Legislature of any State, the Executive thereof may make temporary Appointments until the next Meeting of the Legislature, which shall then fill such Vacancies). *See 17th Amendment.*

No Person shall be a Senator who shall not have attained to the Age of thirty Years, and been nine Years a Citizen of the United States, and who shall not, when elected, be an Inhabitant of that State for which he shall be chosen.

The Vice President of the United States shall be President of the Senate, but shall have no Vote, unless they be equally divided.

The Senate shall choose their other Officers, and also a President pro tempore, in the Absence of the Vice President, or when he shall exercise the Office of President of the United States.

The Senate shall have the sole Power to try all Impeachments. When sitting for that Purpose, they shall be on Oath or Affirmation. When the President of the United States is tried, the Chief Justice shall preside: And no Person shall be convicted without the Concurrence of two thirds of the Members present.

Judgment in Cases of Impeachment shall not extend further than to removal from Office, and disqualification to hold and enjoy any Office of honor, Trust or Profit under the United States: but the Party convicted shall nevertheless be liable and subject to Indictment, Trial, Judgment and Punishment according to Law.

Section 4. The Times, Places and Manner of holding Elections for Senators and Representatives, shall be prescribed in each State by The Legislature thereof; but the Congress may at any time by Law make or alter such Regulations, except as to the Places of choosing Senators.

(The Congress shall assemble at least once in every Year, and such Meeting shall be on the first Monday in December, unless they shall by Law appoint a different Day.) *See 20th Amendment.*

Section 5. Each House shall be the Judge of the Elections, Returns and Qualifications of its own Members, and a Majority of each shall constitute a Quorum to do Business; but a smaller Number may adjourn from day to day, and may be authorized to compel the Attendance of absent Members, in such Manner, and under such Penalties as each House may provide.

Each House may determine the Rules of its Proceedings, punish its Members for disorderly Behavior, and, with the Concurrence of two thirds, expel a Member.

Each House shall keep a Journal of its Proceedings, and from time to time publish the same, excepting such Parts as may in their Judgment require Secrecy; and the Yeas and Nays of the Members of either House on any question shall, at the Desire of one fifth of those Present, be entered on the Journal.

Neither House, during the Session of Congress, shall, without the Consent of the other, adjourn for more than three days, nor to any other Place than that in which the two Houses shall be sitting.

Section 6. The Senators and Representatives shall receive a Compensation for their Services, to be ascertained by Law, and paid out of the Treasury of the United States. They shall in all Cases, except Treason, Felony and Breach of the Peace, be privileged from Arrest during their Attendance at the Session of their respective Houses, and in going to and returning from the same; and for any Speech or Debate in either House, they shall not be questioned in any other Place.

No Senator or Representative shall, during the Time for which he was elected, be appointed to any civil Office under the Authority of the United States, which shall have been created, or the Emoluments whereof shall have been increased during such time; and no Person holding any Office under the United

States, shall be a Member of either House during his Continuance in Office.

Section 7. All Bills for raising Revenue shall originate in the House of Representatives; but the Senate may propose or concur with Amendments as on other Bills.

Every Bill which shall have passed the House of Representatives and the Senate, shall, before it becomes a Law, be presented to the President of the United States; If he approve he shall sign it, but if not he shall return it, with his Objections to that House in which it shall have originated, who shall enter the Objections at large on their Journal, and proceed to reconsider it. If after such Reconsideration two thirds of that House shall agree to pass the Bill, it shall be sent, together with the Objections, to the other House, by which it shall likewise be reconsidered, and if approved by two thirds of that House, it shall become a Law. But in all such Cases the Votes of both Houses shall be determined by Yeas and Nays, and the Names of the Persons voting for and against the Bill shall be entered on the Journal of each House respectively. If any Bill shall not be returned by the President within ten Days (Sundays excepted) after it shall have been presented to him, the Same shall be a Law, in like Manner as if he had signed it, unless the Congress by their Adjournment prevent its Return, in which Case it shall not be a Law.

Every Order, Resolution, or Vote to which the Concurrence of the Senate and House of Representatives may be necessary (except on a question of Adjournment) shall be presented to the President of the United States; and before the Same shall take Effect, shall be approved by him, or being disapproved by him, shall be repassed by two thirds of the Senate and House of Representatives, according to the Rules and Limitations prescribed in the Case of a Bill.

Section 8. The Congress shall have Power To lay and collect Taxes, Duties, Imposts and Excises, to pay the Debts and provide for the common Defense and general Welfare of the United States; but all Duties, Imposts and Excises shall be uniform throughout the United States;

To borrow Money on the credit of the United States;

To regulate Commerce with foreign Nations, and among the several States and with the Indian Tribes;

To establish an uniform Rule of Naturalization, and uniform Laws on the subject of Bankruptcies throughout the United States;

To coin Money, regulate the Value thereof, and of foreign Coin, and fix the Standard of Weights and Measures;

To provide for the Punishment of counterfeiting the Securities and current Coin of the United States;

To establish Post Offices and post Roads;

To promote the Progress of Science and useful Arts, by securing for limited Times to Authors and Inventors the exclusive Right to their respective Writings and Discoveries;

To constitute Tribunals inferior to the supreme Court;

To define and punish Piracies and Felonies committed on the high Seas, and Offenses against the Law of Nations;

To declare War, grant Letters of Marque and Reprisal, and make Rules concerning Captures on Land and Water;

To raise and support Armies, but no Appropriation of Money to that Use shall be for a longer Term than two Years;

To provide and maintain a Navy;

To make Rules for the Government and Regulation of the land and naval Forces;

To provide for calling forth the Militia to execute the Laws of the Union, suppress Insurrections and repel Invasions;

To provide for organizing, arming, and disciplining, the Militia, and for governing such Part of them as may be employed in the Service of the United States, reserving to the States respectively, the Appointment of the Officers, and the Authority of training the Militia according to the discipline prescribed by Congress;

To exercise exclusive Legislation in all Cases whatsoever, over such District (not exceeding ten Miles square) as may, by Cession of particular States, and the Acceptance of Congress, become the Seat of the Government of the United States, and to exercise like Authority over all Places purchased by the Consent of the Legislature of the State in which the Same shall be, for the Erection of Forts, Magazines, Arsenals, dock-Yards, and other needful Buildings; — And

To make all Laws which shall be necessary and proper for carrying into Execution the foregoing Powers, and all other Powers vested by this Constitution in the Government of the United States, or in any Department or Officer thereof.

Section 9. The Migration or Importation of such Persons as any of the States now existing shall think proper to admit, shall not be prohibited by the Congress prior to the Year one thousand eight hundred and eight, but a Tax or duty may be imposed on such Importation, not exceeding ten dollars for each Person.

The Privilege of the Writ of Habeas Corpus shall not be suspended, unless when in Cases of Rebellion or Invasion the public Safety may require it.

No Bill of Attainder or ex post facto Law shall be passed.

No capitation, or other direct, Tax shall be laid, unless in Proportion to the Census or Enumeration herein before directed to be taken. *See 16th Amendment.*

No Tax or Duty shall be laid on Articles exported from any State.

No Preference shall be given by any Regulation of Commerce or Revenue to the Ports of one State over those of another: nor shall Vessels bound to, or from, one State, be obliged to enter, clear, or pay Duties in another.

No Money shall be drawn from the Treasury, but in Consequence of Appropriations made by Law; and a regular Statement and Account of the Receipts and Expenditures of all public Money shall be published from time to time.

No Title of Nobility shall be granted by the United States: And no Person holding any Office of Profit or Trust under them, shall, without the Consent of the Congress, accept of any present, Emolument, Office, or Title, of any kind whatever, from any King, Prince, or foreign State.

Section 10. No State shall enter into any Treaty, Alliance, or Confederation; grant Letters of Marque and Reprisal; coin Money; emit Bills of Credit; make any Thing but gold and silver Coin a Tender in Payment of Debts; pass any Bill of Attainder, ex post facto Law, or Law impairing the Obligation of Contracts, or grant any Title of Nobility.

No State shall, without the Consent of the Congress, lay any Imposts or Duties on Imports or Exports, except what may be absolutely necessary for executing its inspection Laws: and the net Produce of all Duties and Imposts, laid by any State on Imports or Exports, shall be for the Use of the Treasury of the United States; and all such Laws shall be subject to the Revision and Control of the Congress.

No State shall, without the Consent of Congress, lay any Duty of Tonnage, keep Troops, or Ships of War in time of Peace, enter into any Agreement or Compact with another State, or with a foreign Power, or engage in War, unless actually invaded, or in such imminent Danger as will not admit of delay.

ARTICLE II

Section 1. The executive Power shall be vested in a President of the United States of America. He shall hold his Office during the Term of four Years, and together with the Vice President chosen for the same Term, be elected, as follows:

Each State shall appoint, in such Manner as the Legislature thereof, may direct, a Number of Electors, equal to the whole Number of Senators and Representatives to which the State may be entitled in the Congress: but no Senator or Representative, or Person holding an Office of Trust or Profit under the United States, shall be appointed an Elector.

(The Electors shall meet in their respective States, and vote by Ballot for two Persons, of whom one at least shall not be an Inhabitant of the same State with themselves. And they shall make a List of all the Persons voted for, and of the Number of Votes for each; which List they shall sign and certify, and transmit sealed to the Seat of the Government of the United States, directed to the President of the Senate. The President of the Senate shall, in the Presence of the Senate and House of Representatives, open all the Certificates, and the Votes shall then be counted. The Person having the greatest Number of Votes shall be the President, if such Number be a Majority of the whole Number of Electors appointed; and if there be more than one who have such Majority, and have an equal Number of Votes, then the House of Representatives shall immediately choose by Ballot one of them for President; and if no Person have a Majority, then from the five highest on the List the said House shall in like Manner choose the President. But in choosing the President, the Votes shall be taken by States, the Representation from each State having one Vote; A quorum for this Purpose shall consist of a Member or Members from two thirds of the States, and a Majority of all the States shall be necessary to a Choice. In every Case, after the Choice of the President, the Person having the greatest Number of Votes of the Electors shall be the Vice President. But if there should remain two or more who have equal Votes, the Senate shall choose from them by Ballot the Vice President.) *See 12th Amendment.*

The Congress may determine the Time of choosing the Electors, and the Day on which they shall give their Votes; which Day shall be the same throughout the United States.

No Person except a natural born Citizen, or a Citizen of the United States, at the time of the Adoption of this Constitution, shall be eligible to the Office of President; neither shall any Person be eligible to that Office who shall not have attained to the Age of thirty five Years, and been fourteen Years a Resident within the United States.

In Case of the Removal of the President from Office, or of his Death, Resignation, or Inability to discharge the Powers and Duties of the said Office, the Same shall devolve on the Vice President, and the Congress may by Law provide for the Case of Removal, Death, Resignation or Inability, both of the President and Vice President, declaring what Officer shall then act as President, and such Officer shall act accordingly, until the Disability be removed, or a President shall be elected.

The President shall, at stated Times, receive for his Services, a Compensation, which shall neither be increased nor diminished during the Period for which he shall have been elected, and he shall not receive within that Period any other Emolument from the United States, or any of them.

Before he enter on the Execution of his Office, he shall take the following Oath or Affirmation: — "I do solemnly swear (or affirm) that I will faithfully execute the Office of President of the United States, and will to the best of my Ability, preserve, protect and defend the Constitution of the United States."

Section 2. The President shall be Commander in Chief of the Army and Navy of the United States, and of the Militia of the several States, when called into the actual Service of the United States; he may require the Opinion, in writing, of the principal Officer in each of the executive Departments, upon any Subject relating to the Duties of their respective Offices, and he shall have Power to grant Reprieves and Pardons for Offenses against the United States, except in Cases of Impeachment.

He shall have Power, by and with the Advice and Consent of the Senate, to make Treaties, provided two thirds of the Senators present concur; and he shall nominate, and by and with the Advice and Consent of the Senate, shall appoint Ambassadors, other public Ministers and Consuls, Judges of the supreme Court, and all other Officers of the United States, whose Appointments are not herein otherwise provided for, and which shall be established by Law: but the Congress may by Law vest the Appointment of such inferior Officers, as they think proper, in the President alone, in the Courts of Law, or in the Heads of Departments.

The President shall have Power to fill up all Vacancies that may happen during the Recess of the Senate, by granting Commissions which shall expire at the End of their next Session.

Section 3. He shall from time to time give to the Congress Information of the State of the Union, and recommend to their Consideration such Measures as he shall judge necessary and expedient; he may, on extraordinary Occasions, convene both Houses, or either of them, and in Case of Disagreement between them, with Respect to the Time of Adjournment, he may adjourn them to such Time as he shall think proper; he shall receive Ambassadors and other public Ministers; he shall take Care that the Laws be faithfully executed, and shall Commission all the Officers of the United States.

Section 4. The President, Vice President and all civil Officers of the United States, shall be removed from Office on Impeachment for, and Conviction of, Treason, Bribery, or other high Crimes and misdemeanors.

ARTICLE III

Section 1. The judicial Power of the United States, shall be vested in one supreme Court, and in such inferior Courts as the Congress may from time to time ordain and establish. The Judges, both of the supreme and inferior Courts, shall hold their Offices during good Behavior, and shall, at stated Times, receive for their Services, a Compensation, which shall not be diminished during their Continuance in Office.

Section 2. The judicial Power shall extend to all Cases, in Law and Equity, arising under this Constitution, the Laws of the United States, and Treaties made, or which shall be made, under their Authority; — to all Cases affecting Ambassadors, other public Ministers and Consuls; — to all Cases of admiralty and maritime Jurisdiction; — to Controversies to which the United States shall be a

Party; — to Controversies between two or more States; — between a State and Citizens of another State; — between Citizens of different States; — between Citizens of the same State claiming Lands under Grants of different States, and between a State, or the Citizens thereof, and foreign States, Citizens or Subjects. *See 11th Amendment.*

In all Cases affecting Ambassadors, other public Ministers and Consuls, and those in which a State shall be Party, the supreme Court shall have original Jurisdiction. In all the other Cases before mentioned, the supreme Court shall have appellate Jurisdiction, both as to Law and Fact, with such Exceptions, and under such Regulations as the Congress shall make.

The Trial of all Crimes, except in Cases of Impeachment, shall be by Jury; and such Trial shall be held in the State where the said Crimes shall have been committed; but when not committed within any State, the Trial shall be at such Place or Places as the Congress may by Law have directed.

Section 3. Treason against the United States, shall consist only in levying War against them, or in adhering to their Enemies, giving them Aid and Comfort. No Person shall be convicted of Treason unless on the Testimony of two Witnesses to the same overt Act, or on Confession in open Court.

The Congress shall have Power to declare the Punishment of Treason, but no Attainder of Treason shall work Corruption of Blood, or Forfeiture except during the Life of the Person attainted.

ARTICLE IV

Section 1. Full Faith and Credit shall be given in each State to the public Acts, Records, and judicial Proceedings of every other State. And the Congress may by general Laws prescribe the Manner in which such Acts, Records and Proceedings shall be proved, and the Effect thereof.

Section 2. The Citizens of each State shall be entitled to all Privileges and Immunities of Citizens in the several States.

A Person charged in any State with Treason, Felony, or other Crime, who shall flee from Justice, and be found in another State, shall on Demand of the executive Authority of the State from which he fled, be delivered up, to be removed to the State having Jurisdiction of the Crime.

No Person held to Service or Labor in one State, under the Laws thereof, escaping into another, shall, in Consequence of any Law or Regulation therein, be discharged from such Service or Labor, but shall be delivered up on Claim of the Party to whom such Service or Labor may be due. *See 13th Amendment.*

Section 3. New States may be admitted by the Congress into this Union; but no new State shall be formed or erected within the Jurisdiction of any other State; nor any State be formed by the Junction of two or more States, or Parts of States, without the Consent of the Legislatures of the States concerned as well as of the Congress.

The Congress shall have Power to dispose of and make all needful Rules and Regulations respecting the Territory or other Property belonging to the United States; and nothing in this Constitution shall be so construed as to Prejudice any Claims of the United States, or of any particular State.

Section 4. The United States shall guarantee to every State in this Union a Republican Form of Government, and shall protect each of them against Invasion; and on Application of the Legislature, or of the Executive (when the Legislature cannot be convened) against domestic Violence.

562

ARTICLE V

The Congress, whenever two thirds of both Houses shall deem it necessary, shall propose Amendments to this Constitution, or on the Application of the Legislatures of two thirds of the several States, shall call a Convention for proposing Amendments, which, in either Case, shall be valid to all Intents and Purposes, as Part of this Constitution, when ratified by the Legislatures of three fourths of the several States, or by Conventions in three fourths thereof, as the one or the other Mode of Ratification may be proposed by the Congress; Provided that no Amendment which may be made prior to the Year One thousand eight hundred and eight shall in any Manner affect the first and fourth clauses in the Ninth Section of the first Article; and that no State, without its Consent, shall be deprived of its equal Suffrage in the Senate.

ARTICLE VI

All Debts contracted and Engagements entered into, before the Adoption of this Constitution, shall be as valid against the United States under this Constitution, as under the Confederation.

This Constitution, and the Laws of the United States which shall be made in Pursuance thereof; and all Treaties made, or which shall be made, under the Authority of the United States, shall be the supreme Law of the Land; and the Judges in every State shall be bound thereby, any Thing in the Constitution or Laws of any State to the Contrary notwithstanding.

The Senators and Representatives before mentioned, and the Members of the several State Legislatures, and all executive and judicial Officers, both of the United States and of the several States, shall be bound by Oath or Affirmation, to support this Constitution; but no religious Test shall ever be required as a Qualification to any Office or public Trust under the United States.

ARTICLE VII

The Ratification of the Conventions of nine States, shall be sufficient for the Establishment of this Constitution between the States so ratifying the Same. Done in Convention by the Unanimous Consent of the States present the Seventeenth Day of September in the Year of Our Lord one thousand seven hundred and Eighty seven and of the Independence of the United States of America the Twelfth. In witness whereof We have hereunto subscribed our Names,

Gº. WASHINGTON—Presidᵗ.
and deputy from Virginia

Attest WILLIAM JACKSON
Secretary

Delaware

GEO: READ
GUNNING BEDFORD JUN
JOHN DICKINSON
RICHARD BASSETT
JACO: BROOM

New Hampshire

JOHN LANGDON
NICHOLAS GILMAN

New York

ALEXANDER HAMILTON

Maryland	Connecticut

Maryland

JAMES McHENRY
DAN OF S^T THO^S JENIFER
DAN^L CARROLL

Connecticut

W^M SAM^L JOHNSON
ROGER SHERMAN

Virginia

JOHN BLAIR—
JAMES MADISON JR.

Massachusetts

NATHANIEL GORHAM
RUFUS KING

North Carolina

W^M BLOUNT
RICH^D DOBBS SPAIGHT
HU WILLIAMSON
J. RUTLEDGE

New Jersey

WIL: LIVINGSTON
DAVID BREARLEY.
W^M PATTERSON.
JONA: DAYTON

South Carolina

CHARLES COTESWORTH PINCKNEY
CHARLES PINCKNEY
PIERCE BUTLER

Pennsylvania

B FRANKLIN
THOMAS MIFFLIN
ROB^T MORRIS
GEO. CLYMER
THO^S FITZSIMONS
JARED INGERSOL
JAMES WILSON
GOUV MORRIS

Georgia

WILLIAM FEW
ABR BALDWIN

Amendment (I)

Congress shall make no law respecting an establishment of religion, or prohibiting the free exercise thereof; or abridging the freedom of speech, or of the press; or the right of the people peaceably to assemble, and to petition the Government for a redress of grievances.

Amendment (II)

A well regulated Militia, being necessary to the security of a free State, the right of the people to keep and bear Arms, shall not be infringed.

Amendment (III)

No Soldier shall, in time of peace be quartered in any house, without the consent of the Owner, nor in time of war, but in a manner to be prescribed by law.

Amendment (IV)

The right of the people to be secure in their persons, houses, papers, and effects, against unreasonable searches and seizures, shall not be violated, and no Warrants shall issue, but upon probable cause, supported by Oath or affirmation, and particularly describing the place to be searched, and the persons or things to be seized.

Amendment (V)

No person shall be held to answer for a capital, or otherwise infamous crime, unless on a presentment or indictment of a Grand Jury, except in cases arising in the land or naval forces, or in the Militia, when in actual service in time of War or public danger; nor shall any person be subject for the same offense to be twice put in jeopardy of life or limb; nor shall be compelled in any criminal case to be a witness against himself, nor be deprived of life, liberty, or property, without due process of law; nor shall private property be taken for public use, without just compensation.

Amendment (VI)

In all criminal prosecutions, the accused shall enjoy the right to a speedy and public trial, by an impartial jury of the State and district wherein the crime shall have been committed, which district shall have been previously ascertained by law, and to be informed of the nature and cause of the accusation; to be confronted with the witnesses against him; to have compulsory process for obtaining witnesses in his favor, and to have the Assistance of Counsel for his defense.

Amendment (VII)

In Suits, at common law, where the value in controversy shall exceed twenty dollars, the right of trial by jury shall be preserved, and no fact tried by a jury, shall be otherwise reexamined in any Court of the United States, than according to the rules of the common law.

Amendment (VIII)

Excessive bail shall not be required, nor excessive fines imposed, nor cruel and unusual punishments inflicted.

Amendment (IX)

The enumeration in the Constitution, of certain rights, shall not be construed to deny or disparage others retained by the people.

Amendment (X)

The powers not delegated to the United States by the Constitution, nor prohibited by it to the States, are reserved to the States respectively, or to the people.

Amendment (XI)

The Judicial power of the United States shall not be construed to extend to any suit in law or equity, commenced or prosecuted against one of the United States by Citizens of another State, or by Citizens or Subjects of any Foreign State.

Amendment (XII)

The Electors shall meet in their respective states and vote by ballot for President and Vice-President one of whom, at least, shall not be an inhabitant of the same state with themselves; they shall name in their ballots the person voted for as President, and in distinct ballots the person voted for as Vice-President, and they shall make distinct lists of all persons voted for as President, and of all persons voted for as Vice-President, and of the number of votes for each, which lists they shall sign and certify, and transmit sealed to the seat of the government of the United States, directed to the President of the Senate; — The President of the Senate shall, in the presence of the Senate and House of Representatives, open all the certificates and the votes shall then be counted; — The person having the greatest number of votes for President, shall be the President, if such number be a majority of the whole number of Electors appointed; and if no person have such majority, then from the persons having the highest numbers not exceeding three on the list of those voted for as President, the House of Representatives shall choose immediately, by ballot, the President. But in choosing the President, the votes shall be taken by states, the representation from each state having one vote; a quorum for this purpose shall consist of a member or members from two-thirds of the states, and a majority of all the states shall be necessary to a choice. And if the House of Representatives shall not choose a President whenever the right of choice shall devolve upon them, before the fourth day of March next following, then the Vice-President shall act as president, as in the case of the death or other constitutional disability of the President.— The person having the greatest number of votes as Vice-President, shall be the Vice-President, if such number be a majority of the whole number of Electors appointed, and if no person have a majority, then from the two highest numbers on the list, the Senate shall choose the Vice-President; a quorum for the purpose shall consist of two-thirds of the whole number of Senators, and a majority of the whole number shall be necessary to a choice. But no person constitutionally ineligible to the office of President shall be eligible to that of Vice-President of the United States. *See 20th Amendment.*

Amendment (XIII)

Section 1. Neither slavery nor involuntary servitude, except as a punishment for crime whereof the party shall have been duly convicted, shall exist within the United States, or any place subject to their jurisdiction.

Section 2. Congress shall have power to enforce this article by appropriate legislation.

Amendment (XIV)

Section 1. All persons born or naturalized in the United States, and subject to the jurisdiction thereof, are citizens of the United States and of the State wherein they reside. No State shall make or enforce any law which shall abridge the privileges or immunities of citizens of the United States; nor shall any State deprive any person of life, liberty, or property, without due process of law; nor deny to any person within its jurisdiction the equal protection of the laws.

Section 2. Representatives shall be apportioned among the several States according to their respective numbers, counting the whole number of persons in each State, excluding Indians not taxed. But when the right to vote at any election for the choice of electors for President and Vice-President of the United States, Representatives in Congress, the Executive and Judicial officers of a State, or the members of the Legislature thereof, is denied to any of the male inhabitants of such State, being twenty-one years of age, and citizens of the United States, or in any way abridged except for participation in rebellion, or other crime, the basis of representation therein shall be reduced in the proportion which the number of such male citizens shall bear to the whole number of male citizens twenty-one years of age in such State.

Section 3. No person shall be a Senator or Representative in Congress, or elector of President and Vice-President, or hold any office, civil or military, under the United States, or under any State, who, having previously taken an oath, as a member of Congress, or as an officer of the United States, or as a member of any State legislature, or as an executive or judicial officer of any State, to support the Constitution of the United States, shall have engaged in insurrection or rebellion against the same, or given aid or comfort to the enemies thereof. But Congress may by a vote of two-thirds of each House, remove such disability.

Section 4. The validity of the public debt of the United States, authorized by law, including debts incurred for payment of pensions and bounties for services in suppressing insurrection or rebellion, shall not be questioned. But neither the United States nor any State shall assume or pay any debt or obligation incurred in aid of insurrection or rebellion against the United States, or any claim for the loss or emancipation of any slave; but all such debts, obligations and claims shall be held illegal and void.

Section 5. The Congress shall have power to enforce, by appropriate legislation, the provisions of this article.

Amendment (XV)

Section 1. The right of citizens of the United States to vote shall not be denied or abridged by the United States or by any State on account of race, color, or previous condition of servitude.

Section 2. The Congress shall have power to enforce this article by appropriate legislation.

Amendment (XVI)

The Congress shall have power to lay and collect taxes on incomes, from whatever source derived, without apportionment among the several States, and without regard to any census or enumeration.

Amendment (XVII)

The Senate of the United States shall be composed of two Senators from each State, elected by the people thereof, for six years; and each Senator shall have one vote. The electors in each State shall have the qualifications requisite for electors of the most numerous branch of the State legislatures.

When vacancies happen in the representation of any State in the Senate, the executive authority of such State shall issue writs of election to fill such vacancies: Provided, That the legislature of any State may empower the executive thereof to make temporary appointments until the people fill the vacancies by election as the legislature may direct.

This amendment shall not be so construed as to affect the election or term of any Senator chosen before it becomes valid as part of the Constitution.

Amendment (XVIII)

Section 1. After one year from the ratification of this article the manufacture, sale, or transportation of intoxicating liquors within, the importation thereof into, or the exportation thereof from the United States and all territory subject to the jurisdiction thereof for beverage purposes is hereby prohibited.

Section 2. The Congress and the several States shall have concurrent power to enforce this article by appropriate legislation.

Section 3. This article shall be inoperative unless it shall have been ratified as an amendment to the Constitution by the legislatures of the several States, as provided in the Constitution, within seven years from the date of the submission hereof to the States by the Congress.

Repealed. See Amendment XXI, post.

Amendment (XIX)

The right of citizens of the United States to vote shall not be denied or abridged by the United States or by any State on account of sex.

Congress shall have power to enforce this article by appropriate legislation.

Amendment (XX)

Section 1. The Terms of the President and Vice President shall end at noon on the 20th day of January, and the terms of Senators and Representatives at noon on the 3rd day of January, of the years in which such terms would have ended if this article had not been ratified; and the terms of their successors shall then begin.

Section 2. The Congress shall assemble at least once in every year, and such meeting shall begin at noon on the 3rd day of January, unless they shall by law appoint a different day.

Section 3. If, at the time fixed for the beginning of the term of the President, the President elect shall have died, the Vice President elect shall become President. If a President shall not have been chosen before the time fixed for the beginning of his term, or if the President elect shall have failed to qualify, then the Vice President elect shall act as President until a President shall have qualified; and the Congress may by law provide for the case wherein neither a President elect nor a Vice President elect shall have qualified, declaring who shall then act as President, or the manner in which one who is to act shall be selected, and such person shall act accordingly until a President or Vice President shall have qualified.

Section 4. The Congress may by law provide for the case of the death of any of the persons from whom the House of Representatives may choose a President whenever the right of choice shall have devolved upon them, and for the case of the death of any of the persons from whom the Senate may choose a Vice President whenever the right of choice shall have devolved upon them.

Section 5. Sections 1 and 2 shall take effect on the 15th day of October following the ratification of this article.

Section 6. This article shall be inoperative unless it shall have been ratified as an amendment to the Constitution by the legislatures of three-fourths of the several States within seven years from the date of its submission.

Amendment (XXI)

Section 1. The eighteenth article of amendment to the Constitution of the United States is hereby repealed.

Section 2. The transportation or importation into any State, Territory, or possession of the United States for delivery or use therein of intoxicating liquors, in violation of the laws thereof, is hereby prohibited.

Section 3. This article shall be inoperative unless it shall have been ratified as an amendment to the Constitution by conventions in the several States, as provided in the Constitution, within seven years from the date of the submission hereof to the States by the Congress.

Amendment (XXII)

Section 1. No person shall be elected to the office of the President more than twice, and no person who has held the office of President, or acted as President, for more than two years of a term to which some other person was elected President shall be elected to the office of the President more than once. But this Article shall not apply to any person holding the office of President when this Article was proposed by the Congress, and shall not prevent any person who may be holding the office of President, or acting as President, during the term within which this Article becomes operative from holding the office of President or acting as President during the remainder of such term.

Section 2. This article shall be inoperative unless it shall have been ratified as an amendment to the Constitution by the legislatures of three-fourths of the several States within seven years from the date of its submission to the States by the Congress.

Amendment (XXIII)

Section 1. The District constituting the seat of Government of the United States shall appoint in such manner as the Congress may direct:

A number of electors of President and Vice President equal to the whole number of Senators and Representatives in Congress to which the District would be entitled if it were a State, but in no event more than the least populous State; they shall be in addition to those appointed by the States, but they shall be considered, for the purposes of the election of President and Vice President, to be electors appointed by a State; and they shall meet in the District and perform such duties as provided by the twelfth article of amendment.

Section 2. The Congress shall have power to enforce this article by appropriate legislation.

Amendment (XXIV)

Section 1. The right of citizens of the United States to vote in any primary or other election for President or Vice President, for electors for President or Vice President, or for Senator or Representative in Congress, shall not be denied or abridged by the United States or any State by reason of failure to pay any poll tax or other tax.

Section 2. The Congress shall have power to enforce this article by appropriate legislation.

Amendment (XXV)

Section 1. In case of the removal of the President from office or of his death or resignation, the Vice President shall become President.

Section 2. Whenever there is a vacancy in the office of the Vice President, the President shall nominate a Vice President who shall take office upon confirmation by a majority vote of both Houses of Congress.

Section 3. Whenever the President transmits to the President pro tempore of the Senate and the Speaker of the House of Representatives his written declaration that he is unable to discharge the powers and duties of his office, and until he transmits to them a written declaration to the contrary, such powers and duties shall be discharged by the Vice President as Acting President.

Section 4. Whenever the Vice President and a majority of either the principal officers of the executive departments or of such other body as Congress may by law provide, transmit to the President pro tempore of the Senate and the Speaker of the House of Representatives their written declaration that the President is unable to discharge the powers and duties of his office, the Vice President shall immediately assume the powers and duties of the office as Acting President.

Thereafter, when the President transmits to the President pro tempore of the Senate and the Speaker of the House of Representatives his written declaration that no inability exists, he shall resume the powers and duties of his office unless the Vice President and a majority of either the principal officers of the executive department or of such other body as Congress may by law provide, transmit within four days to the President pro tempore of the Senate and the Speaker of the House of Representatives their written declaration that the President is unable to discharge the powers and duties of his office. Thereupon Congress shall decide the issue, assembling within forty-eight hours for that purpose if not in session. If the Congress, within twenty-one days after receipt of the latter written declaration, or, if Congress is not in session, within twenty-one days after Congress is required to assemble, determines by two-thirds vote of both Houses that the President is unable to discharge the powers and duties of his office, the Vice President shall continue to discharge the same as Acting President; otherwise, the President shall resume the powers and duties of his office.

Amendment (XXVI)

Section 1. The right of citizens of the United States, who are eighteen years of age or older, to vote shall not be denied or abridged by the United States or by any State on account of age.

Section 2. The Congress shall have power to enforce this article by appropriate legislation.

Amendment (XXVII)

No law, varying the compensation for the services of the Senators and Representatives, shall take effect, until an election of Representatives shall have intervened.

Ratification Dates

Amendments I through X were ratified on Dec. 15, 1791, and are known as the Bill of Rights.

Amendment XI — Feb. 7, 1795   Amendment XIX — Aug. 18, 1920
Amendment XII — June 15, 1804   Amendment XX — Jan. 23, 1933
Amendment XIII — Dec. 6, 1865   Amendment XXI — Dec. 5, 1933
Amendment XIV — July 9, 1868   Amendment XXII — Feb. 27, 1951
Amendment XV — Feb. 3, 1870   Amendment XXIII — March 29, 1961
Amendment XVI — Feb. 3, 1913   Amendment XXIV — Jan. 23, 1964
Amendment XVII — April 8, 1913   Amendment XXV — Feb. 10, 1967
Amendment XVIII — Jan. 16, 1919 Amendment XXVI — July 1, 1971
  (Repealed by Amendment XXI)   Amendment XXVII — May 7, 1992

OFFICIAL STATE SYMBOLS

The Official State Symbols of the State of Illinois are designated by acts of the General Assembly.

State Tree — Oak: In 1907, Mrs. James C. Fessler of Rochelle suggested to state officials that Illinois schoolchildren vote for a State Tree and State Flower. They subsequently selected the Oak for the State Tree. Sen. Andrew J. Jackson of Rockford introduced a bill making it official in 1908. In 1973, a special poll of some 900,000 children changed the Official State Tree from the Native Oak to the White Oak, and it was signed into law that year.

State Flower — Violet: When the schoolchildren voted on the State Tree, they also selected the State Flower, which became law at the same time in 1908.

State Flag: Illinois has had two state flags. The first was adopted in 1915. More than 50 years later, Chief Petty Officer Bruce McDaniel of Waverly, then serving in Vietnam, urged that a new flag be designed to include the word "Illinois." Without his state's name on it, the identity of the Illinois flag hanging in his mess hall was often questioned.

Mrs. Sanford Hutchison of Greenfield had been lobbying for a uniform design to conform with the 1915 law.

Rep. Jack Walker of Lansing sponsored a bill to amend the original Flag Act of 1915. On Sept. 17, 1969, it was passed by the General Assembly and approved by Gov. Richard B. Ogilvie. Ogilvie then appointed a committee to develop specifications for the flag.

On July 1, 1970, "a white field carrying the word 'Illinois' and the emblem portion of the state seal" became the state's official flag.

State Bird — Cardinal: In 1928, the Macomb branch of the National Federation of Professional Women's Clubs urged that Illinois schoolchildren select a State Bird. The idea was approved by the State Superintendent of Public Instruction, and schoolchildren chose the Cardinal from five birds conspicuous in Illinois. Rep. James Foster introduced a bill that was adopted in 1929.

State Song — "Illinois": With music by Archibald Johnston and lyrics by Charles H. Chamberlin, "Illinois" served as the state's "unofficial" song for many years before the 54th General Assembly passed a bill making it "official." The bill was introduced by Sen. Florence Fifer Bohrer, the first woman to serve as an Illinois State Senator.

State Slogan — "Land of Lincoln": The slogan that appears on Illinois license plates was adopted in 1955 by the General Assembly. In that same year, the U.S. Congress passed a special act granting to the State of Illinois a copyright for exclusive use of the "Land of Lincoln" insignia.

State Mineral — Fluorite: A bill designating Fluorite the Official State Mineral was passed in 1965 by the General Assembly. Calcium Fluorite, commonly called "Fluorite," is a glass-like mineral that may be colorless or range in color from blue to violet-amethyst-purple to green and yellow. Fluorite plays an important part in the making of steel, enamels, aluminum, glass and many chemicals. Illinois is the largest producer of fluorite in the United States.

State Insect — Monarch Butterfly: In 1974, a Dennis School third-grade class in Decatur proposed the orange and black Monarch Butterfly as the State's Official Insect. Rep. Webber Borchers of Decatur introduced a bill in the General Assembly, and the schoolchildren lobbied for its passage. In 1975, the bill was passed, and the Dennis School class watched Gov. Daniel Walker sign it into law.

State Animal — White-tailed Deer: The State Animal was selected by a vote of Illinois schoolchildren in 1980. Candidates were nominated by the General Assembly and by the Illinois State Museum. The children selected the White-tailed Deer, and a bill, effective Jan. 1, 1982, was passed by the General Assembly and signed into law by Gov. James R. Thompson. The deer, native to North America, has a gray coat that turns reddish brown in summer and an eye-catching tail that is bright white on the underside.

State Fish — Bluegill: The State Fish was selected by schoolchildren in 1986. A member of the sunfish family, the colorful Bluegill reaches only about nine inches in length and weighs an average 14 ounces but has a reputation as one of the best fighting game fish.

State Prairie Grass — Big Bluestem: On Aug. 31, 1989, Gov. Thompson signed into law a bill designating the Big Bluestem as Illinois' Official Prairie Grass. The bill passed the General Assembly after the Big Bluestem was chosen in a poll of students conducted by the State Department of Conservation. The Big Bluestem, named for the bluish purple cast of its stem, is the tallest prairie grass in Illinois.

State Fossil — Tully Monster: A soft-bodied marine animal that lived 280 to 340 million years ago, the Tully Monster was designated as the State Fossil in 1989. An impression of the Tully Monster was discovered in 1955 by amateur archaeologist Francis J. Tully of Joliet. Since then, more than 100 specimens have been found in Grundy, Kankakee, Will and Fulton counties.

State Dance — Square Dance: In 1990, Gov. Thompson signed into law a bill designating the Square Dance as the American folk dance of the state. The Square Dance, first associated with the American People, has been recorded in history since 1651.

State Soil — Drummer Silty Clay Loam: On Aug. 2, 2001, Gov. George Ryan signed legislation establishing Drummer Silty Clay Loam as the Official State Soil. Students from Monticello High School's FFA and Chicago High School for Agricultural Sciences' FFA lobbied for House Bill 605 and testified at committee hearings. Illinois is known for its thick, dark prairie soils, and Drummer Silty Clay Loam is the most common. Drummer soils are found on more than 1.5 million acres in nearly half of Illinois' counties. They are some of the most productive soils in the world. Corn and soybeans are the principal crops.

The Great Seal: The first seal used in what is now Illinois was that of the Northwest Territory, first used in 1788. The Seal of the Illinois Territory followed in 1809.

The three state seals subsequently used in Illinois' history differed from the territorial seals in that the eagle held a banner in its beak with the words of the state motto, "State Sovereignty, National Union." The words "Seal of the State of Illinois" and the date "Aug. 26, 1818," the date that the first Illinois Constitution was signed in Kaskaskia, appeared between the circles.

After Illinois gained statehood in December 1818, the First General Assembly decreed on Feb. 19, 1819, that state officials should procure a permanent state seal. The seal they decided upon was a duplicate of the Great Seal of the United States. This First Great Seal of Illinois was used until 1839 when it was recut. The new version became the Second Great Seal.

Secretary of State Sharon Tyndale was responsible for creating the seal in use today. In January 1867, he told Senator Allen C. Fuller that the old seal had outlived its usefulness, and a new one was needed. He asked Fuller to sponsor a bill authorizing a new seal. But a controversy arose when the Senate discovered that Tyndale planned to use Fuller's bill to change the wording "State Sovereignty, National Union" to "National Union, State Sovereignty" in light of the Civil War.

The Senate disagreed with Tyndale and amended and passed the bill on March 7, 1867, restoring the original wording. Though Tyndale followed the General Assembly's decree that he not reverse the words of the State Motto, he changed the banner's placement on the seal so that, though "National Union" followed "State Sovereignty," it was much more prominent. Moreover, the word "Sovereignty" was upside down, further decreasing its readability.

The State Seal has been recut more than once since 1868, but Tyndale's design has remained essentially unchanged. The Secretary of State is the keeper of the Great Seal of the State of Illinois. Reproduction or use of the State Seal, or the State Flag, is permissible only in strict accordance with the provisions of Chapter 5 of the *Illinois Compiled Statutes.*

Present Great Seal of the
State of Illinois
1868-Present

Seal of the Illinois
Territory (sketch)
(Used circa 1809-1819)

First Great Seal of the
State of Illinois
(Used circa 1819-1839)

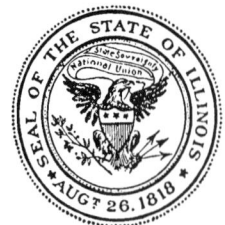

Second Great Seal of the
State of Illinois
(Used circa 1839-1868)

574

INDEX

Hay, Jane, 338
Hazelwood, Kathleen, 137
Headrick, John, 222
Healey, Robert M., 250, 251
Heckleman, David R., 141
Hedenschoug, Wayne, 141
Hedges, Sonya, 136
Heffner, Brenda, 342
Heinecke, Burnell, 145
Heise, Colonel Craig R., 254
Heisler, Robert, 249
Hencken, Louis V., 361
Hendon, Rickey R., 58, 70, bio 76, 136
Hendren, Carter, 132
Hendren, Diane, 258
Henley, Barbara, 350
Hensley, Chris, 294
Herath, John, 218
Herman, Richard, 348
Herndon, Thomas, 207
Hersh, Adrienne, 263
Hess, Frederick J., bio 203
Heupel, Dana, 146
Hightower, Ed, 353
Hildebrand, Mal, 143
Hill, Betsy, 360
Hill, Kent, 286
Hill, Sandy, 286
Hirsch, Don, 436
Historic Preservation Agency, Illinois, 244-245
Hodge, Mary, 232
Hoecker, Barb, 229
Hoeft, Douglas L., 71, bio 104, 144, 411
Hoffman, Denny, 436
Hoffman, Jay C., 71, bio 127, 412
Hoffman, John, 338
Hoffman, Manny, 434
Hoffman, Marc, 434
Hoffman, Mike, 331
Hoffman, Thomas E., 161, bio 175
Holbrook, Thomas, 71, bio 128, 143, 412
Holder, David M., 436
Holdridge, William E., 161, bio 182
Holland, Colonel William L. (Ret), 254
Holland, William G., 32, bio 33, 134
Holland, William, 239
Holmes, Sharon, 353
Holt, Mark, 435
Holzum, Jason, 353
Homer, Thomas J., 161, bio 182
Hooker, Jared, 434
Hoover, Ed, 436
Hopkins, Ed, 140
Hopkins, Terrence J., 161, 186
Hornbogen, Rebecca A., 141
Hornbrook, Allan N., 434
Hornowski, Joseph A., 410
Hornyak, Juleann, 161, bio 169

Hough, James, 436
Houghton, Shirley, 436
House Seating Charts, 68-69
House Standing Committees, 59-62
House, Carol, 137
Houston, J. Michael, 368
Hovanec, George, 208
Howard, Constance A. "Connie", 71, bio 87, 142, 410, 432
Howard, Mike, 136
Howlett, Robert J., 315, 323
Huebner, Cindy, 132
Huggins, Jack, 369
Hughes, Tom, 294
Hull, Dr. Richard, 218
Hulme, Robert E., 435
Hultgren, Randall M., 71, bio 91, 410
Human Rights, Department of, 236
Human Services, Department of, 237-239
Hunt, Bill, 140
Huntington, Robert, 410
Hurley, Edward C., 281
Hurley, Mark, 243
Hurrelbrink, Diane, 222
Hurst, Jeffrey A., 412
Husky, Betty, 137
Hutchinson, Susan F., 161, bio 180
Hyde, Henry, 36, bio 38, 44
Hyden, Elaine, 353
Hynes, Daniel W., 28, bio 29, 34, 326, 327, 328, 329, 468

I

Illinois at a Glance, 454
Illinois Chain of Title, 376-377
Illinois Court Officials, 161
Illinois Legislative Correspondents Association, 145-148
Illinois State Budget, 209-211
Illinois State Capitol Sculptures, 459-462
Illinois State Fire Marshal, 286
Illinois State Library Building, 458
Illinois State Museum, 456
Illinois State Parks and Natural Areas, 7-9
Illinois State University, 369
Incorporated Cities, Towns and Villages of Illinois, 437-453
Industrial Commission, 287
Ingemunson, Dallas, 433, 435
Insurance, Department of, 249
Intergovernmental Cooperation, Commission on, 137
Ippolito, Doris, 254

J

Jack, Brenda, 284
Jackson, Jesse L., Jr., 36, bio 37, 44
Jackson, Renard, 225
Jackson, Tom, 436

581

Schoell, Richard M., 346
Schoenberg, Jeffrey M., 71, bio 100, 136, 411
Schoenburg, Bernard, 146
Schuh, Patricia, 132
Schulien, John, 435
Schutt, A.D., 434
Schwab, Brad, 218
Schwartz, Michael S., 219, 222
Schwarz, Robert, 222
Scillia, Tony, 232
Scott, Douglas P., 411
Scott, Phyllis, 208
Scott, Roger A., 417
Scott, Ronald, 416
Scully, George F., Jr., 71, bio 111, 141, 411
Searby, Paul, 424
Secretaries of State, 467
Secretary of State
    bio, 27
    office of the, 304-323
    staff members, 322
Seggebruch, Maurice, 435
Seiler, David, 434
Seiple, Steve, 222
Seith, William D., 243
Selburg, Roger, 243
Selinger, Larry, 331
Senate President, Office of the, 52-53
Senate Seating Charts, 66-67
Senate Standing Committees, 57-58
Serati, Carrie, 137
Serati, Ray, 145, 208
Serritella, Vincent J., 340
Shadid, George P., 70, bio 117, 138
Shah, Niranjan, 366
Shapo, Nathaniel S., 249
Shaw, Andy, 148
Shaw, Roger, 436
Shaw, William "Bill", 58, 70, bio 86, 141, 142, 409
Shea, Gerald W., 477
Sheedy, Colonel Jay, 254
Sheridan, Jerry, 435
Sherman, Leonard A., 262, 263
Shillo, Saffiya, 294
Shimkus, John M., 36, bio 43, 45
Shockey, David, 436
Shull, John L., 141
Sidles, Tracey, 58
Sidwell, Jerry L., 434
Sieben, Todd, 70, bio 108, 139
Siegel, Myron, 371
Silverstein, Ira I., 70, bio 79, 141
Simmons, Bill, 435
Sims, Elgie, 132
Sims, Larry E., 144
Sinclair, Ellen, 432
Sinclair, Jerry, 435

Sindelar, Susan J., 346
Skoien, Gary, 371
Skoubis, Michael N., 285
Slater, Kent F., 161, bio 183
Slater, Marcella, 434
Slifer, Jim, 274
Sloan, Lucy A., 343
Slomka, Jerry, 225
Slone, Ricca C., 71, bio 117, 412
Small, Tony, 232
Smart, Jesse, 283
Smedstad, Alice, 208
Smith, Barbara, 294
Smith, Dave, 241
Smith, Gordon, 208
Smith, Irv, 436
Smith, Margaret, 58, 70, bio 74, 137, 139, 143, 409
Smith, Melvin, 286
Smith, Michael K., 71, bio 117, 140, 144, 412, 434
Smith, Patrick, 235
Smith, Ronald C., 433
Snyder, Donald N., Jr., 230, 232
Sodemann, Marjorie E., 477
Solis, Eric W., 409
Solov, Tanya, 317, 323
Sommer, Keith P., 71, bio 116, 412
Soto, Cynthia, 71, bio 73, 410
Souter, David H., 48
South, Gary, 222
South, Leslie E., 161, bio 174
South, Rick, 436
Southern Illinois University Carbondale, 354-357
Southern Illinois University Edwardsville, 357-358
Southern Illinois University, 353-358
Sparks, Ronald, 435
Speaker of the House, Office of the, 54-55
Speakers of the House of Representatives, 473-474
Spencer, Donald S., 367
Splittorff, Dennis, 434
Sprague, Robert, 436
Spurlin, Terry W., 287
Squires, Mary Frances, 281
Sronce, Kevin, 258
Stacy, Brad, 412
Stamp, Zack, 368
Stapleton, Jim, 338
State Capitol Building, 131
State Central Committeemen, 432-433
State of Illinois Toll-Free Numbers, 372-373
State Police, Illinois, 246-248
Steelman, Kevin, 239
Steigmann, Robert J., 161, bio 185
Steinberg, Salme H., 365

BLUE BOOK CREDITS

The 50th edition of the *Illinois Blue Book* is a publication of the office of Jesse White, Illinois Secretary of State; Thomas Benigno, Deputy Secretary of State. It was produced by the Secretary of State's Communications Department, Bob Yadgir, director; H.W. Devlin, chief deputy director; Jack Hrabak, managing editor; Gary McPeek, production manager; Leanne Dent, graphic artist; Kristie Metrow, assistant editor; Tad Kicielinski, editorial assistant; Kim Nehrt, special graphics; LaDaryl Hale, Ayesha Ferguson, Joan Thomas, Audrey Price, Michael Voges, Mary Reljic, Jim Daniels and Laurie Orris, copy editors; Heather Bradley, photographer, and Sandy Johnson, photo scanning. Special thanks to Mark Sorensen, Marietta Zarack, Russ Nagel, Tom Massey and Tim Anderson for their assistance.

Photo Credits

Bill Waldmire, Illinois Information Service, provided the photo of Jo Crow, the 2001 Illinois Teacher of the Year.

Terry Herbig, *Moline Dispatch,* provided the photo of Campbell's Island, IL, April 2001 – Flooded homes on the swollen Mississippi.

Thompson/McClellan Photographers of Champaign provided the photo of the engineering campus and Beckman Institute at the University of Illinois at Urbana-Champaign.

UIC Photo Services provided the photo of the East-Side Residence Halls at the University of Illinois at Chicago.

Curt Neitzke provided the photo of the Health and Sciences Building at the University of Illinois at Springfield.

University Photocommunications, Southern Illinois University Carbondale, provided the photo of Old Main Mall.

NIU Media Production-Imaging provided the photo of Swen Parson Hall, College of Law, at Northern Illinois University.

Andrew S. Bowman provided the photo of his grandfather, Andrew Jackson Smith, for the Chronology of Illinois History.

The Illinois State Historical Library provided the photos of John W.E. Thomas and Catharine Couger Waugh McCulloch for the Chronology of Illinois History.

La Raza newspaper provided the photo of the Cinco de Mayo Parade for the Chronology of Illinois History.

Tom Reedy of the National Soil Survey Center provided the photo of Drummer Silty Clay Loam, the Official State Soil.

Printed by authority of the State of Illinois
P.O. #3233871 – 23M – Jan. 2002

VIOLET

state flower

SQUARE DANCE

state dance

BIG BLUESTEM

state prairie grass

Illinois State Symbols

WHITE OAK

state tree

TULLY MONSTER

state fossil